D1278055

Twentieth-Century
Literary Criticism

Guide to Thomson Gale Literary Criticism Series

For criticism on	Consult these Thomson Gale series
Authors now living or who died after December 31, 1999	*CONTEMPORARY LITERARY CRITICISM (CLC)*
Authors who died between 1900 and 1999	*TWENTIETH-CENTURY LITERARY CRITICISM (TCLC)*
Authors who died between 1800 and 1899	*NINETEENTH-CENTURY LITERATURE CRITICISM (NCLC)*
Authors who died between 1400 and 1799	*LITERATURE CRITICISM FROM 1400 TO 1800 (LC)* *SHAKESPEAREAN CRITICISM (SC)*
Authors who died before 1400	*CLASSICAL AND MEDIEVAL LITERATURE CRITICISM (CMLC)*
Authors of books for children and young adults	*CHILDREN'S LITERATURE REVIEW (CLR)*
Dramatists	*DRAMA CRITICISM (DC)*
Poets	*POETRY CRITICISM (PC)*
Short story writers	*SHORT STORY CRITICISM (SSC)*
Literary topics and movements	*HARLEM RENAISSANCE: A GALE CRITICAL COMPANION (HR)* *THE BEAT GENERATION: A GALE CRITICAL COMPANION (BG)* *FEMINISM IN LITERATURE: A GALE CRITICAL COMPANION (FL)* *GOTHIC LITERATURE: A GALE CRITICAL COMPANION (GL)*
Asian American writers of the last two hundred years	*ASIAN AMERICAN LITERATURE (AAL)*
Black writers of the past two hundred years	*BLACK LITERATURE CRITICISM (BLC)* *BLACK LITERATURE CRITICISM SUPPLEMENT (BLCS)*
Hispanic writers of the late nineteenth and twentieth centuries	*HISPANIC LITERATURE CRITICISM (HLC)* *HISPANIC LITERATURE CRITICISM SUPPLEMENT (HLCS)*
Native North American writers and orators of the eighteenth, nineteenth, and twentieth centuries	*NATIVE NORTH AMERICAN LITERATURE (NNAL)*
Major authors from the Renaissance to the present	*WORLD LITERATURE CRITICISM, 1500 TO THE PRESENT (WLC)* *WORLD LITERATURE CRITICISM SUPPLEMENT (WLCS)*

ISSN 0276-8178

Volume 191

Twentieth-Century Literary Criticism

**Criticism of the
Works of Novelists, Poets, Playwrights,
Short Story Writers, and Other Creative Writers
Who Lived between 1900 and 1999,
from the First Published Critical
Appraisals to Current Evaluations**

**Thomas J. Schoenberg
Lawrence J. Trudeau
*Project Editors***

THOMSON

GALE

Detroit • New York • San Francisco • New Haven, Conn. • Waterville, Maine • London

Comsewogue Public Library
170 Terryville Road
Port Jefferson Station, NY 11776

Twentieth-Century Literary Criticism, Vol. 191

Project Editors
Thomas J. Schoenberg and Lawrence J. Trudeau

Editorial
Dana Ramel Barnes, Tom Burns, Elizabeth A. Cranston, Kathy D. Darrow, Kristen A. Dorsch, Mandi Rose Hall, Jeffrey W. Hunter, Jelena O. Krstović Michelle Lee, Catherine Shubert, Russel Whitaker

Data Capture
Frances Monroe, Gwen Tucker

Indexing Services
Laurie Andriot

Rights and Acquisitions
Jacqueline Key, Kelly Quin, Timothy Sisler

Composition and Electronic Capture
Amy Darga

Manufacturing
Cynde Bishop

Associate Product Manager
Marc Cormier

© 2008 Thomson Gale, a part of The Thomson Corporation. Thomson and Star Logo are trademarks and Gale is a registered trademark used herein under license.

For more information, contact
Thomson Gale
27500 Drake Rd.
Farmington Hills, MI 48331-3535
Or you can visit our Internet site at
http://www.gale.com

ALL RIGHTS RESERVED
No part of this work covered by the copyright herein may be reproduced or used in any form or by any means—graphic, electronic, or mechanical, including photocopying, recording, taping, Web distribution, or information storage retrieval systems—without the written permission of the publisher.

This publication is a creative work fully protected by all applicable copyright laws, as well as by misappropriation, trade secret, unfair competition, and other applicable laws. The authors and editors of this work have added value to the underlying factual material herein through one or more of the following: unique and original selection, coordination, expression, arrangement, and classification of the information.

For permission to use material from the product, submit your request via the Web at http://www.gale-edit.com/permissions, or you may download our Permissions Request form and submit your request by fax or mail to:

Permissions Department
Thomson Gale
27500 Drake Rd.
Farmington Hills, MI 48331-3535
Permissions Hotline:
248-699-8006 or 800-877-4253, ext. 8006
Fax 248-699-8074 or 800-762-4058

Since this page cannot legibly accommodate all copyright notices, the acknowledgments constitute an extension of the copyright notice.

While every effort has been made to secure permission to reprint material and to ensure the reliability of the information presented in this publication, Thomson Gale neither guarantees the accuracy of the data contained herein nor assumes any responsibility for errors, omissions or discrepancies. Thomson Gale accepts no payment for listing; and inclusion in the publication of any organization, agency, institution, publication, service, or individual does not imply endorsement of the editors or publisher. Errors brought to the attention of the publisher and verified to the satisfaction of the publisher will be corrected in future editions.

LIBRARY OF CONGRESS CATALOG CARD NUMBER 76-46132

ISBN-13: 978-0-7876-9966-6

ISBN-10: 0-7876-9966-7
ISSN 0276-8178

Printed in the United States of America
10 9 8 7 6 5 4 3 2 1

Comsewogue Public Library
170 Terryville Road
Port Jefferson Station, NY 11776

Contents

Preface vii

Acknowledgments xi

Literary Criticism Series Advisory Board xiii

Preface

Since its inception *Twentieth-Century Literary Criticism* (*TCLC*) has been purchased and used by some 10,000 school, public, and college or university libraries. *TCLC* has covered more than 1000 authors, representing over 60 nationalities and nearly 50,000 titles. No other reference source has surveyed the critical response to twentieth-century authors and literature as thoroughly as *TCLC*. In the words of one reviewer, "there is nothing comparable available." *TCLC* "is a gold mine of information—dates, pseudonyms, biographical information, and criticism from books and periodicals—which many librarians would have difficulty assembling on their own."

Scope of the Series

TCLC is designed to serve as an introduction to authors who died between 1900 and 1999 and to the most significant interpretations of these author's works. Volumes published from 1978 through 1999 included authors who died between 1900 and 1960. The great poets, novelists, short story writers, playwrights, and philosophers of the period are frequently studied in high school and college literature courses. In organizing and reprinting the vast amount of critical material written on these authors, *TCLC* helps students develop valuable insight into literary history, promotes a better understanding of the texts, and sparks ideas for papers and assignments. Each entry in *TCLC* presents a comprehensive survey on an author's career or an individual work of literature and provides the user with a multiplicity of interpretations and assessments. Such variety allows students to pursue their own interests; furthermore, it fosters an awareness that literature is dynamic and responsive to many different opinions.

Every fourth volume of *TCLC* is devoted to literary topics. These topics widen the focus of the series from the individual authors to such broader subjects as literary movements, prominent themes in twentieth-century literature, literary reaction to political and historical events, significant eras in literary history, prominent literary anniversaries, and the literatures of cultures that are often overlooked by English-speaking readers.

TCLC is designed as a companion series to Thomson Gale's *Contemporary Literary Criticism,* (*CLC*) which reprints commentary on authors who died after 1999. Because of the different time periods under consideration, there is no duplication of material between *CLC* and *TCLC*.

Organization of the Book

A *TCLC* entry consists of the following elements:

- The **Author Heading** cites the name under which the author most commonly wrote, followed by birth and death dates. Also located here are any name variations under which an author wrote, including transliterated forms for authors whose native languages use nonroman alphabets. If the author wrote consistently under a pseudonym, the pseudonym is listed in the author heading and the author's actual name is given in parenthesis on the first line of the biographical and critical information. Uncertain birth or death dates are indicated by question marks. Single-work entries are preceded by a heading that consists of the most common form of the title in English translation (if applicable) and the name of its author.

- The **Introduction** contains background information that introduces the reader to the author, work, or topic that is the subject of the entry.

- The list of **Principal Works** is ordered chronologically by date of first publication and lists the most important works by the author. The genre and publication date of each work is given. In the case of foreign authors whose works have been translated into English, the English-language version of the title follows in brackets. Unless otherwise indicated, dramas are dated by first performance, not first publication. Lists of **Representative Works** by different authors appear with topic entries.

- Reprinted **Criticism** is arranged chronologically in each entry to provide a useful perspective on changes in critical evaluation over time. The critic's name and the date of composition or publication of the critical work are given at the beginning of each piece of criticism. Unsigned criticism is preceded by the title of the source in which it originally appeared. All titles by the author featured in the text are printed in boldface type. Footnotes are reprinted at the end of each essay or excerpt. In the case of excerpted criticism, only those footnotes that pertain to the excerpted texts are included. Criticism in topic entries is arranged chronologically under a variety of subheadings to facilitate the study of different aspects of the topic.

- A complete **Bibliographical Citation** of the original essay or book precedes each piece of criticism. Source citations in the Literary Criticism Series follow University of Chicago Press style, as outlined in *The Chicago Manual of Style,* 15th ed. (Chicago: The University of Chicago Press, 2003).

- Critical essays are prefaced by brief **Annotations** explicating each piece.

- An annotated bibliography of **Further Reading** appears at the end of each entry and suggests resources for additional study. In some cases, significant essays for which the editors could not obtain reprint rights are included here. Boxed material following the further reading list provides references to other biographical and critical sources on the author in series published by Thomson Gale.

Indexes

A **Cumulative Author Index** lists all of the authors that appear in a wide variety of reference sources published by Thomson Gale, including *TCLC*. A complete list of these sources is found facing the first page of the Author Index. The index also includes birth and death dates and cross references between pseudonyms and actual names.

A **Cumulative Topic Index** lists the literary themes and topics treated in *TCLC* as well as other Literature Criticism series.

A **Cumulative Nationality Index** lists all authors featured in *TCLC* by nationality, followed by the numbers of the *TCLC* volumes in which their entries appear.

An alphabetical **Title Index** accompanies each volume of *TCLC*. Listings of titles by authors covered in the given volume are followed by the author's name and the corresponding page numbers where the titles are discussed. English translations of foreign titles and variations of titles are cross-referenced to the title under which a work was originally published. Titles of novels, dramas, nonfiction books, and poetry, short story, or essay collections are printed in italics, while individual poems, short stories, and essays are printed in roman type within quotation marks.

In response to numerous suggestions from librarians, Thomson Gale also produces a paperbound edition of the *TCLC* cumulative title index. This annual cumulation, which alphabetically lists all titles reviewed in the series, is available to all customers. Additional copies of this index are available upon request. Librarians and patrons will welcome this separate index; it saves shelf space, is easy to use, and is recyclable upon receipt of the next edition.

Citing *Twentieth-Century Literary Criticism*

When citing criticism reprinted in the Literary Criticism Series, students should provide complete bibliographic information so that the cited essay can be located in the original print or electronic source. Students who quote directly from reprinted criticism may use any accepted bibliographic format, such as University of Chicago Press style or Modern Language Association (MLA) style. Both the MLA and the University of Chicago formats are acceptable and recognized as being the current standards for citations. It is important, however, to choose one format for all citations; do not mix the two formats within a list of citations.

The examples below follow recommendations for preparing a bibliography set forth in *The Chicago Manual of Style,* 15th ed. (Chicago: The University of Chicago Press, (2003); the first example pertains to material drawn from periodicals, the second to material reprinted from books:

Morrison, Jago. "Narration and Unease in Ian McEwan's Later Fiction." *Critique* 42, no. 3 (spring 2001): 253-68. Reprinted in *Twentieth-Century Literary Criticism.* Vol. 127, edited by Janet Witalec, 212-20. Detroit: Thomson Gale, 2003.

Brossard, Nicole. "Poetic Politics." In *The Politics of Poetic Form: Poetry and Public Policy,* edited by Charles Bernstein, 73-82. New York: Roof Books, 1990. Reprinted in *Twentieth-Century Literary Criticism.* Vol. 127, edited by Janet Witalec, 3-8. Detroit: Thomson Gale, 2003.

The examples below follow recommendations for preparing a works cited list set forth in the *MLA Handbook for Writers of Research Papers,* 5th ed. (New York: The Modern Language Association of America, 1999); the first example pertains to material drawn from periodicals, the second to material reprinted from books:

Morrison, Jago. "Narration and Unease in Ian McEwan's Later Fiction." *Critique* 42.3 (spring 2001): 253-68. Reprinted in *Twentieth-Century Literary Criticism.* Ed. Janet Witalec. Vol. 127. Detroit: Thomson Gale, 2003. 212-20.

Brossard, Nicole. "Poetic Politics." *The Politics of Poetic Form: Poetry and Public Policy.* Ed. Charles Bernstein. New York: Roof Books, 1990. 73-82. Reprinted in *Twentieth-Century Literary Criticism.* Ed. Janet Witalec. Vol. 127. Detroit: Thomson Gale, 2003. 3-8.

Suggestions are Welcome

Readers who wish to suggest new features, topics, or authors to appear in future volumes, or who have other suggestions or comments are cordially invited to call, write, or fax the Associate Product Manager:

Associate Product Manager, Literary Criticism Series
Thomson Gale
27500 Drake Road
Farmington Hills, MI 48331-3535
1-800-347-4253 (GALE)
Fax: 248-699-8054

Acknowledgments

The editors wish to thank the copyright holders of the criticism included in this volume and the permissions managers of many book and magazine publishing companies for assisting us in securing reproduction rights. Following is a list of the copyright holders who have granted us permission to reproduce material in this volume of *TCLC*. Every effort has been made to trace copyright, but if omissions have been made, please let us know.

COPYRIGHTED MATERIAL IN *TCLC*, VOLUME 191, WAS REPRODUCED FROM THE FOLLOWING PERIODICALS:

boundary 2, v. 21, spring, 1994. Copyright © 1994 Duke University Press. All rights reserved. Used by permission of the publisher.—*Comparative Literature,* v. 57, winter, 2005 for "Revisiting the Circuitous Odyssey of the Baroque Picaresque Novel: Reinaldo Arenas's *El mundo alucinante,*" by Angela L. Willis. Copyright © 2005 by the University of Oregon. Reproduced by permission of the author.—*Contemporary Literature,* v. 42, fall, 2001; v. 45, winter, 2004 Copyright © 2001, 2004 by the Board of Regents of the University of Wisconsin System. Both reproduced by permission.—*Critique: Studies in Contemporary Fiction,* v. 32, spring, 1991; v. 35, spring, 1994; v. 40, summer, 1999. Copyright © 1991, 1994, 1999 by Helen Dwight Reid Educational Foundation. All reproduced with permission of the Helen Dwight Reid Educational Foundation, published by Heldref Publications, 1319 18th Street, NW, Washington, DC 20036-1802.—*Forum for Modern Language Studies,* v. 29, July, 1993 for "Carl Zuckmayer's *Des Teufels General* as a Critique of the Cult of Masculinity," by Anthony Waine. © *Forum for Modern Language Studies* 1993. Republished with permission of Oxford University Press, conveyed through Copyright Clearance Center, Inc.—*The German Quarterly,* v. 76, fall, 2003. Copyright © 2003 by the American Association of Teachers of German. Reproduced by permission.—*Hispanic Review,* v. 53, autumn, 1985. Copyright © 1985 by the Trustees of the University of Pennsylvania. Reproduced by permission.—*Journal of Evolutionary Psychology,* v. 5, March, 1984. Copyright 1984 by the Institute for Evolutionary Psychology. Reproduced by permission.—*The Journal of the Midwest Modern Language Association,* v. 28, spring, 1995 for "Grotesque Identities: Writing, Death, and the Space of the Subject (Between Michel de Montaigne and Reinaldo Arenas)," by Brad Epps. Copyright 1995 by The Midwest Modern Language Association. Reproduced by permission of the publisher and the author.—*MELUS,* v. 30, winter, 2005. Copyright MELUS: The Society for the Study of Multi-Ethnic Literature of the United States, 2005. Reproduced by permission.—*Mosaic,* v. 6, fall, 1972. Copyright © Mosaic 1972. Acknowledgment of previous publication is herewith made.—*Philological Papers,* v. 29, 1983. Reproduced by permission.—*PMLA,* v. 117, fall, 2002. Copyright © 2002 by the Modern Language Association of America. Reproduced by permission of the Modern Language Association of America.—*Prose Studies,* v. 17, April, 1994. © Frank Cass & Co. Ltd. 1994, originally published in *Anti-Apocalypse: Exercises in Genealogical Criticism,* edited by Lee Quinby, University of Minnesota Press, 1994. Reproduced by permission of Taylor & Francis, Ltd., http//:www.tandf.co.uk/journals and the author.—*The Review of Contemporary Fiction,* v. 9, fall, 1989. Copyright © 1989 *The Review of Contemporary Fiction.* Reproduced by permission.—*Studies in the Novel,* v. 36, fall, 2004. Copyright © 2004 by North Texas State University. Reproduced by permission.—*University of Dayton Review,* v. 13, winter, 1976 for "Type-Casting in Carl Zuckmayer's *The Devil's General,*" by Roy C. Cowen. Reproduced by permission of the author.

COPYRIGHTED MATERIAL IN *TCLC*, VOLUME 191, WAS REPRODUCED FROM THE FOLLOWING BOOKS:

Bauer, Arnold. From "German Legend—German Truth," in *Carl Zuckmayer.* Translated by Edith Simmons. Frederick Ungar Publishing Co., 1976. Copyright © 1976 by Frederick Ungar Publishing Co., Inc. Republished with permission of The Continuum International Publishing Company, conveyed through Copyright Clearance Center, Inc.—Biron, Rebecca E. From *Murder and Masculinity: Violent Fictions of Twentieth-Century Latin America.* Vanderbilt University Press, 2000. © 2000 Vanderbilt University Press. All rights reserved. Reproduced by permission.—Conte, Joseph M.. From *Design and Debris: A Chaotics of Postmodern American Fiction.* The University of Alabama Press, 2002. Copyright © 2002 The University of Alabama Press. All rights reserved. Reproduced by permission.—Ellis, Robert Richmond. From *They Dream Not of Angels but of Men: Homoeroticism, Gender, and Race in Latin American Autobiography.* University Press of Florida, 2002. Copyright © 2002 by Robert Richmond Ellis. All rights reserved. Reproduced with the permission of the University Press of Florida.—Girman, Chris. From *Mucho Macho: Seduction, Desire, and Homoerotic Lives of Latin Men.* Harrington Park Press, 2004. Copyright © 2004 by The Haworth Press, Inc. All rights reserved. Reproduced by permission.—

Glück, Robert. From "The Greatness of Kathy Acker," in *Lust for Life: On the Writings of Kathy Acker.* Edited by Amy Scholder, Carla Harryman, and Avital Ronell. Verso, 2006. © in the collection Verso 2006. © in the contributions, the individual contributors. All rights reserved. Reproduced by permission.—Manners, Marilyn. From "The Dissolute Feminisms of Kathy Acker," in *Future Crossings: Literature between Philosophy and Cultural Studies.* Edited by Krzysztof Ziarek and Seamus Deane. Northwestern University Press, 2000. Copyright © 2000 Northwestern University Press. All rights reserved. Reproduced by permission.—Mews, Siegfried. From "The Last Plays" in *Carl Zuckmayer.* Twayne Publishers, 1981. Copyright © 1981 by G. K. Hall & Co. Reproduced by permission of the author.—Ortíz, Ricardo L. From "Pleasure's Exile: Reinaldo Arenas's Last Writing," in *Borders, Exiles, Diasporas.* Edited by Elazar Barkan and Marie-Denise Shelton. Stanford University Press, 1998. Copyright © 1998 by the Board of Trustees of the Leland Stanford Jr. University. All rights reserved. Used with the permission of Stanford University Press, www.sup.org.—Saltzman, Arthur. From *This Mad "Instead": Governing Metaphors in Contemporary American Fiction.* University of South Carolina Press, 2000. Copyright © University of South Carolina 2000. Reproduced by permission.—Soto, Francisco. From *Reinaldo Arenas: The Pentagonía.* University Press of Florida, 1994. Copyright © 1994 by the Board of Commissioners of State Institutions of Florida. Reproduced with the permission of the University Press of Florida.—Soto, Francisco. From *Reinaldo Arenas.* Twayne Publishers, 1998. Copyright © 1998 by Twayne Publishers. All rights reserved. Reproduced by permission of Thomson Gale.—Weinstein, Sheri. From "The Lay of the Land: Piracy and the Itinerant Body in Kathy Acker's *Pussy, King of the Pirates,*" in *Devouring Institutions: The Life Work of Kathy Acker.* Edited by Michael Hardin. Hyperbole Books, 2004. Copyright © 2004 Hyperbole Books, an imprint of San Diego State University Press. All rights reserved. Reproduced by permission of the author.—Winterson, Jeanette. From an introduction to *Essential Acker: The Selected Writings of Kathy Acker.* Edited by Amy Scholder and Dennis Cooper. Grove Press, 2002. Copyright © 2002 by the Estate of Kathy Acker. All rights reserved. Used by permission of Grove/Atlantic, Inc.

Thomson Gale Literature Product Advisory Board

The members of the Thomson Gale Literature Product Advisory Board—reference librarians from public and academic library systems—represent a cross-section of our customer base and offer a variety of informed perspectives on both the presentation and content of our literature products. Advisory board members assess and define such quality issues as the relevance, currency, and usefulness of the author coverage, critical content, and literary topics included in our series; evaluate the layout, presentation, and general quality of our printed volumes; provide feedback on the criteria used for selecting authors and topics covered in our series; provide suggestions for potential enhancements to our series; identify any gaps in our coverage of authors or literary topics, recommending authors or topics for inclusion; analyze the appropriateness of our content and presentation for various user audiences, such as high school students, undergraduates, graduate students, librarians, and educators; and offer feedback on any proposed changes/enhancements to our series. We wish to thank the following advisors for their advice throughout the year.

Barbara M. Bibel
Librarian
Oakland Public Library
Oakland, California

Dr. Toby Burrows
Principal Librarian
The Scholars' Centre
University of Western Australia Library
Nedlands, Western Australia

Celia C. Daniel
Associate Reference Librarian
Howard University Libraries
Washington, D.C.

David M. Durant
Reference Librarian
Joyner Library
East Carolina University
Greenville, North Carolina

Nancy T. Guidry
Librarian
Bakersfield Community College
Bakersfield, California

Heather Martin
Arts & Humanities Librarian
University of Alabama at Birmingham, Sterne Library
Birmingham, Alabama

Susan Mikula
Librarian
Indiana Free Library
Indiana, Pennsylvania

Thomas Nixon
Humanities Reference Librarian
University of North Carolina at Chapel Hill, Davis
  Library
Chapel Hill, North Carolina

Mark Schumacher
Jackson Library
University of North Carolina at Greensboro
Greensboro, North Carolina

Gwen Scott-Miller
Assistant Director
Sno-Isle Regional Library System
Marysville, Washington

Kathy Acker
1948-1997

American novelist, short story writer, playwright, essayist, and screenwriter.

The following entry provides an overview of Acker's life and works. For additional information on her career, see *CLC*, Volumes 45 and 111.

INTRODUCTION

Kathy Acker is recognized as one of the most prominent and controversial literary figures associated with the punk movement in America during the 1970s and 1980s. She is also considered among the most significant proponents of radical feminism and the postmodern aesthetic in art and literature. Acker is best known for her avant-garde novels *Great Expectations* (1982), *Blood and Guts in High School* (1984), and *Don Quixote, Which Was a Dream* (1986), in which she bluntly treats such taboo subjects as violence, sadomasochism, incest, and sexuality and plagiarizes texts from other writers, including Charles Dickens, Marcel Proust, and Miguel de Cervantes. Although Acker's work has received a mixed response from critics because of its violent, pornographic imagery and its experimental form, many acknowledge its influence on postmodern fiction and praise it as an important contribution to feminist discourse. In 1989, Naomi Jacobs noted that "through semantic and stylistic crudeness, pastiche-appropriations of famous literary texts, and outrageous manipulations of historical and literary figures, Acker attempts simultaneously to deconstruct the tyrannical structures of official culture and to plagiarize an identity, constructing a self from salvaged fragments of those very structures she has dismantled."

BIOGRAPHICAL INFORMATION

Acker was born April 18, 1948, in New York City. She was raised by her mother, Claire, and her stepfather, Donald Weill. Her biological father, Harry Lehmann, left her mother before Acker was born. Acker studied at private schools during her early education and later attended Brandeis University and University of California, San Diego, where she earned a bachelor's degree in 1968. In 1966, she married Robert Acker, but they were later divorced. Acker spent two years as a doctoral student in classics and philosophy at the City University of New York and New York University, before she quit to pursue a career in literature. In the 1970s, while trying to get her work published in small press publications, she lived in New York and worked as a secretary, a stripper, and a performer in pornographic films. She was also deeply influenced by the visual artists that she encountered in New York during that time. Her mother, Claire, committed suicide when Acker was in her thirties.

In 1972, Acker published her first book, a mixed-genre work titled *Politics,* which was influenced by the work of Beat Generation novelist William S. Burroughs. She published her next book, *The Childlike Life of the Black Tarantula,* under the pseudonym Black Tarantula in 1973. Acker wrote and published four more novels during the 1970s, including *I Dreamt I Was a Nymphomaniac* (1974), *Florida* (1978), *Kathy Goes to Haiti* (1978), and *The Adult Life of Toulouse Lautrec by Henri Toulouse Lautrec* (1978). Her second marriage, to composer Peter Gordon, in 1976 also ended in divorce. In 1979, Acker won a Pushcart Prize for her novel *New York City in 1979.* It was during the 1980s, however, that she wrote and published her most notable work, including *Great Expectations, Blood and Guts in High School, Don Quixote,* and *Empire of the Senseless* (1988). Early in the decade, Acker left the United States and moved to London. In the mid-1980s, she began experimenting with other artistic mediums. She collaborated on an opera libretto with Peter Gordon titled *The Birth of the Poet,* which was performed at the Brooklyn Academy of Music in 1985. A film based on her screenplay *Variety* appeared that same year. In the 1990s, Acker returned to the United States and published several more novels, including *In Memoriam to Identity* (1990), *My Mother: Demonology* (1993), and *Pussy, King of the Pirates* (1996). She began teaching as an adjunct professor at San Francisco Art Institute in 1991 and also as a visiting professor at a number of universities in California and Idaho over the next few years. In 1997, Acker published a collection of essays titled *Bodies of Work* and a book of short fiction titled *Eurydice in the Underworld.* She died of breast cancer on November 30, 1997, in Tijuana, Mexico.

MAJOR WORKS

Great Expectations, Acker's first novel to attract major critical attention, blends drama, fiction, autobiography, poetry, and the epistolary form with sections of plagiarized texts taken from various sources, most notably Charles Dickens's famous nineteenth-century novel by the same name. The narrative begins with a revision of Dickens's introduction to *Great Expectations* and employs—while it deconstructs—the novel's *Bildungsroman* structure. In part one of the book, titled "I Recall My Childhood," Acker introduces multiple protagonists, including Peter, a character reminiscent of Dickens's protagonist, and an unnamed young girl, who is mourning the death of her mother. The second part of the novel, which some scholars consider autobiographical, relates the experiences of Sarah, a woman haunted by her mother's suicide. In addition to Dickens's novel, Acker borrows text from the erotic novel *The Story of O,* by Anne Desclos, and alludes to writings by Herman Melville, John Keats, and Madame de La Fayette. The novel ends with a comma instead of a period. Despite the formal disjointedness of *Great Expectations,* recurring themes of maternal suicide, sadomasochism, and gender, as well as issues of personal identity, connect the three parts and help to establish a sense of cohesion.

Violence and sexuality are also dominant themes in *Blood and Guts in High School.* The plot of the novel centers on the misadventures of ten-year-old Janey Smith, who is involved in an incestuous relationship with her father. Janey, who is infected with pelvic inflammatory disease, is ultimately rejected by her father, so she flees to New York and joins a gang. As a gang member, she participates in numerous violently sexual acts. She is then captured by a Persian slave-trader, who gives her daily instruction on how to be a prostitute. He releases her after she is diagnosed with cancer. Janey travels to Tangiers, where she wanders the desert with the French writer Jean Genet. Other well-known figures also appear in the novel, including feminist author Erica Jong and former president Jimmy Carter. Once again, Acker makes use of other texts within her novel. Her plagiaristic manipulations of Nathaniel Hawthorne's *The Scarlet Letter* are used to signify Janey's quest to discover her identity. When Janey is alone during her captivity, she begins to write a "book report" on Hawthorne's novel. Gradually, the lines between the text and Janey's own life story begin to blur, and she transforms the protagonist, Hester Prynne, into a version of herself. Many critics consider *Blood and Guts in High School* a harsh critique of patriarchal, capitalist society. In 2004, Susan E. Hawkins argued that in this novel Acker voices "one long, outrageous scream at America, its obsessive economic motor and capital-driven social values, its naïve, shallow, destructive politics."

In *Don Quixote,* Acker re-envisions the titular protagonist of Cervantes's novel as a woman. Quixote's sidekick, Sancho Panza, is also recast, as a dog named St. Simeon, and together the two characters wander through London and New York. Acker explores themes of abortion and alienation in *Don Quixote,* and she interweaves figures from events of the period, such as formerpresident Richard Nixon and Henry Kissinger. Other texts, including passages from African folktales, history books, German plays, and English novels, also infiltrate the narrative. In the novel, Acker confronts organized religion, particularly Catholicism, as well as the institution of the American family. The religious leaders that Don Quixote encounters are characterized as wild dogs, and their antipathy for her is rooted in misogyny. In a section titled "A Portrait of an American Family," a daughter returns home from urban horrors to seek refuge; she finds that family life is indeed safe but only because it is a prison to which she must submit her freedom. Like Cervantes, Acker uses the quest structure in her novel to challenge contemporary social mores. In 1999, Christopher L. Robinson described Acker's *Don Quixote* as "an effort to undermine the androcentric conventions of romance and the masculinist system of beliefs and values that give rise to and sustain those conventions in both literary and sociopolitical contexts."

CRITICAL RECEPTION

Acker's avant-garde and complex novels, which subvert traditional literary forms and challenge established methods of engaging readers, have elicited a broad range of responses from critics, both negative and positive. Whereas some scholars have praised Acker's formal skill and linked her stylistic and thematic choices to the writings of Jean Genet, Alain Robbe-Grillet, Marguerite Duras, and William S. Burroughs, particularly the latter's cut-up formal method and frank treatment of sexuality, others have argued that her methods, including her unapologetic use of plagiarized texts, are unnecessarily confusing and indecipherable. Many critics, however, maintain that Acker's technique of appropriation serves a thematic purpose in her art and results in works that are both imaginative and innovative. For example, writing in 1991, Richard Walsh pronounced that Acker had elevated plagiarism "into a formal strategy, emptied of its pejorative connotations by the blatancy of its operation." And Rod Phillips argued that "her fictions may begin with what seem to be borrowings, extensions, or plagiarisms of male works; but they move quickly beyond these original works—into new meanings and new forms that their authors could never have imagined."

Acker's focus on graphic violence and sex in her work has also generated mixed reactions from critics. In 2006, Robert Glück observed that "Acker expanded the range of what can be said about the body, and all who write about sex owe her a debt of gratitude." Similarly, Catherine Rock lauded Acker's writing for giving a "voice to the cultural underside, in order to symbolize libidinal activities and desires that have been muted or made unspeakable by normative representations." On the other hand, some commentators have asserted that the potency of the pornographic imagery in her fiction is undermined because of its frequent occurrence, and that readers eventually become numb to its shocking effects. In response to these critics, Rock concluded that "the contention aroused by her work issues from the fact that she takes up rather than averts the violent oppression wreaked upon the margins, and textualizes also the ambivalent complexities of trying to turn pain into a new, productive state." Despite such differing opinions among scholars, most regard Acker's contributions to postmodern literature as significant and influential. In 1989, Ellen G. Friedman asserted that "Acker's narratives, in their subversive appropriations of master texts, their aggressive assertions of criminal perspectives, their relentless interrogations of art, culture, government, and sexual relations, are designed to be jaws steadily devouring—often to readers' horror and certainly to their discomfort (which is part of the strategy)—the mindset, if not the mind, of Western culture."

PRINCIPAL WORKS

Persian Poems (poetry) 1972

Politics (novel) 1972

The Childlike Life of the Black Tarantula: Some Lives of Murderesses [as Black Tarantula] (novel) 1973; also published as *The Childlike Life of the Black Tarantula by the Black Tarantula*, 1975

I Dreamt I Was a Nymphomaniac: Imagining (novel) 1974

The Adult Life of Toulouse Lautrec by Henri Toulouse Lautrec (novel) 1978

Florida (novel) 1978

Kathy Goes to Haiti (novel) 1978

New York City in 1979 (novel) 1979

Great Expectations (novel) 1982

Hello, I'm Erica Jong (novel) 1982

Algeria: A Series of Invocations because Nothing Else Works (novel) 1984

Blood and Guts in High School (novel) 1984

My Death My Life by Pier Paolo Pasolini (novel) 1984

The Birth of the Poet (libretto) 1985

Lulu Unchained (play) 1985

Variety (screenplay) 1985

Don Quixote, Which Was a Dream (novel) 1986

Empire of the Senseless (novel) 1988

Literal Madness (novels) 1988

In Memoriam to Identity (novel) 1990

Portrait of an Eye (novels) 1992

My Mother: Demonology (novel) 1993

Essays (essays) 1996

Pussy, King of the Pirates (novel) 1996

Bodies of Work (essays) 1997

Eurydice in the Underworld (short stories) 1997

Requiem (play) 1997

Essential Acker: The Selected Writings of Kathy Acker (novels and short stories) 2002

CRITICISM

Ellen G. Friedman (essay date fall 1989)

SOURCE: Friedman, Ellen G. "'Now Eat Your Mind': An Introduction to the Works of Kathy Acker." *Review of Contemporary Fiction* 9, no. 3 (fall 1989): 37-49.

[*In the following essay, Friedman interprets the attitude toward the relationship between narrative description and reality in the works of Kathy Acker.*]

> GET RID OF MEANING. YOUR MIND IS A NIGHTMARE THAT HAS BEEN EATING YOU: NOW EAT YOUR MIND.
>
> —Kathy Acker, *Empire of the Senseless*

In a 1984 *Artforum* article, **"Models of Our Present,"** Kathy Acker summarizes some current models of time and knowledge in theoretical physics and applies them to personal time and personal knowing. These theories, including the principle of "local causes," quantum mechanics, and the Clauser-Freedman experiment, interrogate, according to Acker, the dominant way of knowing, the way of apprehending the world, which depends on Newtonian causal relationships. She asks, "what possible experimental model doesn't have the form, 'If I do x then x_1 happens'?" She offers two alternatives, gleaned from interpretations of quantum mechanics. The first is the Many Worlds interpretation of quantum mechanics, which implicates the observer in the phenomenon observed: "Whenever a choice is made in the universe between one possible event and another, the universe splits into different branches." That is, "If I do x, then x_1 and $-x_1$ and . . . happen" (ellipsis in original). The second, also involving the observer in the observation, is the Copenhagen interpretation of quantum mechanics, which proposes that "the model is not the reality"; "any model's utility depends on the experience of the experimenter."[1] Both interpretations assume a non-Newtonian and relativistic model of causality. Acker's interest in these "models of our present" is clearly reflected in her fictional world, which is informed by them. It is a world filled with sets of disrupted moments over which not even discontinuity rules since Acker's texts, constructed of fragments, generally have a central persona embarked on a quest, although that persona is often metamorphic and fades in and out of the narrative. Indeed, instability and unpredictability provide a liberating context for Acker's works, all of which are profoundly political. As a character in *The Childlike Life of the Black Tarantula by the Black Tarantula* asserts, "I can see anything in a set of shifting frameworks" (97).[2]

Description in such a model of the present cannot be objective; rather, it is always an interpretation. This insight helps to explain the directness of Acker's fictional method. Invoking the words of the English physicist David Bohm, Acker suggests that "Description is totally incompatible with what we want to say." In this view, the link between description and the described is tenuous, if not broken. Description is neither an approximation of, nor a substitute for, the described. Acker questions the motives in describing since description is a mode of control, a way of gaining authority over the object described. She writes, "The act of describing assumes one event can be a different event: meaning dominates or controls existence. But desire—or art—is." Description interprets; it does not replicate. She illustrates her theory by asking her reader to "examine the two statements, 'Help!' and 'I need help.'" Making the point that "The first language is a cry. The second, a description," she explains, "Only the cry, art, rather than the description or criticism, is primary. The cry is stupid; it has no mirror, it communicates" (**"Models of Our Present"** 64). In offering the emotion itself, without a description or interpretation of it, Acker attempts to bring fiction closer to unmediated experience, also thereby relinquishing authorial control over readers' reactions.

In a second *Artforum* example, Acker illustrates the direct engagement with (and often assault on) her readers that her fiction attempts by contrasting two images that she entitles "Past Time" and "Time Renewed":

Past Time

For *Women's Wear Daily* Helmut Newton photographed two women, their legs against a grand ancient city street. The women, being fashion models, are desirable and untouchable. This is that time which is separate from the observer, that time which is enclosed: time gone.

The past's over. It's an image. You can't make love to an image.

Time Renewed

Now in color: In front of an orange yellow street, female long red stockinged legs in black pumps're nudging female long blue stockinged legs in black stilt heels. Touching me. This is our time cause we're making the world. This is a description of *Honey, Tell Me . . .* , 1983, a painting by Jenny Holzer and Lady Pink.

(62)

The difference that interests Acker between these two images may be described with the distinction Roland Barthes makes between the readerly and the writerly text. "Past Time" is a readerly text: conforming to traditional codes, it is complete, closed, culturally determined. Since its function is to exhibit products, the relationship it establishes with the viewer is formal and distant. Any desire the image wells up within the viewer must be satisfied outside the frame of the image. "Time Renewed," on the other hand, is a writerly text, experimental, open, and incomplete. The viewer is involved with the image; they are in a relationship of play. The image is erotic, suggestive, inviting the viewer into its frame. It violates cultural norms and promises danger. With its disturbing signposts—e.g., strident colors, suggestive relationship of female legs—it undermines complacency, extends to the viewer the hope of risk and ultimately self creation. As a mystery, it inspires desire for itself.

II

It is important to emphasize the intellectual contexts of the work of Kathy Acker because her work does not feel quite "literary," despite her frequent adaptations (appropriations, plagiarisms and cannibalisms) of literary works from Shakespeare to Beckett.[3] Although her works are writerly, Acker eschews the rhetoric of ambiguity so valued among literary critics, particularly since the advent of modernism. Her surfaces are almost anti-literary, despite their allusiveness, deliberately assaultive and overt. She hopes to make the abstract material, physical. In *Empire of the Senseless,* she pleads, "It seemed to me that the body, the material, must matter. My body must matter to me." She makes explicit her treatment of the body as a desiring and desirable "text": "If my body mattered to me, and what else was any text: I could not choose to be celibate" (64). Her works offer many justifications of this position. Through the words of her female Don Quixote, for instance, Acker proffers one explanation of her emphasis on the body: "All the accepted forms of education in this country, rather than teaching the child to know who she is or to know, dictate to the child who she is. Thus obfuscate any act of knowledge. Since these educators train the mind rather than the body, we can start with the physical body, the place of shitting, eating, etc., to break through our opinions or false education" (*DQ [Don Quixote]* 165-66). The language of the body in Western culture is taboo, therefore not as thoroughly constructed by the cultural powers as the mind.

Thus, the body, particularly the female body, becomes the site of revolution. In this regard, Acker, perhaps more directly than many other women writers, creates the feminine texts hypothesized by Hélène Cixous in essays such as "Castration or Decapitation?"[4] Feminine writing, according to Cixous, should be rooted in the woman's experience of her body, her sexuality.[5] In *The Childlike Life of the Black Tarantula by the Black Tarantula,* Acker connects writing and sexuality in a way that Cixous would approve: "My work and my sexuality combine: here the complete sexuality occurs within, is not expressed by, the writing" (84). Such writing creates an erotic and thus, for Acker, subversive text: "Every position of desire, no matter how small, is capable of putting to question the established order of a society" (*BG* [*Blood and Guts in High School*] 125). Like Acker, Cixous feels that women must overthrow their education, the metalanguage of their culture, in order to really speak: "Stop learning in school that women are created to listen, to believe, to make no discoveries. . . . Speak of her pleasure and, God knows, she has something to say about that, so that she gets to unblock a sexuality. . . ." The return of this repressed language of female sexuality would, according to Cixous, "'de-phallocentralize' the body, relieve man of his phallus, return him to an erogenous field and a libido that isn't stupidly organized round that monument, but appears shifting, diffused, taking on all the others of oneself."[6] Through the delirium of her protagonist Abhor in *Empire of the Senseless,* Acker offers an iteration, though qualified, of Cixous's insight:

> A man's power resides in his prick. That's what they, whoever they is, say. How the fuck should I know? I ain't a man. Though I'm a good fake lieutenant, it's not good enough to have a fake dick. I don't have one. Does this mean I've got no strength? If it's true that a man's prick is his strength, what and where is my power? Since I don't have one thing, a dick, I've got nothing, so my pleasure isn't any one thing, it's just pleasure. Therefore, pleasure must be pleasurable. Well, maybe I've found out something, and maybe I haven't.
>
> (127)

For Cixous, reorganization of education to unblock female sexuality would not only expand possibilities of expression, but in revolutionizing narrative—the way we construct our world—would also transform modalities of thought. Acker, as the last sentence of the above-quoted passage suggests, is less sure of the ramifications of "de-phallocentralization," though her narratives relentlessly indict law by the phallus. Both Acker and Cixous define the obstacles in the way of such reorganization similarly. In Cixous's words, it would be "very difficult: first we have to get rid of the systems of censorship that bear down on every attempt to speak in the feminine" (50-51). These systems imply not only the metalanguage of education, but all the metalanguages that direct individual and group thought and action, values and goals in Western society.

A particular system of censorship of the kind to which Cixous refers has been vigorously applied to Acker. She is a media figure in England, where she now lives, called upon to represent the interesting or evil, but de-

finitively crazy fringe, the extreme by which the public measures its distance from the edge. Thus defined as the products of the devil or madness, or at least eccentricity, her books—as far as the public is concerned—have no authority and are thus disarmed. Applying a different system of censorship, some mainstream feminists, particularly in England, take her work seriously enough to condemn it as pornography. Since her language is often crude—not just "fuck" or "shit," but "cunt juice," for instance—and she graphically depicts sadomasochistic sexual acts, they view her work as misogynistic; the pornographic sequences typical in it, they argue (quite correctly) would not be tolerated in the work of men.

Acker's texts are, however, marked by radically feminist positions and attitudes. In the following passage, Acker slides from truism to profundity as she describes the power of language to work the ends of masculinist culture:

> Traditionally, the human world has been divided into men and women. Women're the cause of human suffering. . . . Men have tried to get rid of their suffering by altering this: first, by changing women; second, when this didn't work because women are stubborn creatures, by simply lying, by saying that women live only for men's love. An alteration of language, rather than of material, usually changes material conditions . . .
>
> (*DQ* 27)

Acker sometimes renders her sense of the patriarchal grip of culture in lashing, gutter metaphors. For instance, she has her feminist protagonist Hester Prynne declare: "The most important men in the world decide it's their duty to tear the mother away from her child. They want to keep the child so they can train the child to suck their cocks. That's what's known as education" (*BG* 94). Since she habitually casts feminist positions and attitudes in brutal language that *is* a cry, those feminist literary critics intent on smoothly executed social reform have generally not taken up the challenge of her texts. Feminist narratives such as Margaret Atwood's *The Handmaiden's Tale* and even such a feminist classic as Erica Jong's *Fear of Flying* seem mild in comparison with Acker's terroristic cultural assaults. Most readers would agree that Atwood's work is not intended to challenge certain progressive *ideals* of marriage, motherhood, and childrearing. She would simply like to see society live up to them, provided that women have equal opportunity to develop full personal and professional lives. Such a goal in the context of patriarchal cultural incarceration seems to Acker (who views cultural oppression as crushing) simply delusionary. Jong, on the other hand, does seem, as Acker suggests, rather self-congratulatory as she triumphantly describes male genitals and seems self-promoting as well in her self-consciously "daring" descriptions of sex from the "woman's point of view." Thus, she has perhaps earned the satire Acker executes in *Hello, I'm Erica Jong,* which begins "Hello, I'm Erica Jong. I'm a real novelist. I write books that talk to you about the agony of American life, how we all suffer, the growing pain that more and more of us are going to feel" and ends with "My name is Erica Jong. If there is God, God is disjunction and madness. Yours truly, Erica Jong."

In Acker's works, sadistic men victimizing slavish, masochistic women represents conventional sexual transactions in society, the underlying paradigm for normal relationships in patriarchal culture. In this scheme, de Sade is the quintessential lover. In one of her many metamorphoses, the protagonist of *The Childlike Life of the Black Tarantula by the Black Tarantula* dreams herself into Laura Lane, a murderer who will do anything for her lover: "I descend into slavery, I let a man drive his fingers into my brains and reform my brains as he wants" (30). Abhor, in *Empire of the Senseless,* exclaims, "No wonder heterosexuality a bit resembles rape" (127). Insofar as the culture constructs individual experience by interpreting experience, Acker presents women as accomplices in their own victimization. In an exchange of letters, for instance, Charlotte Brontë writes to Emily that "All rapists who come to my door are lovers" (*PP* [*My Death My Life by Pier Paolo Pasolini*] 306).

Acker frequently embodies patriarchal domination in sadistic, cowardly father figures (often adopted or step-) and embodies women's relation to the patriarchy with self-destructively dependent daughter figures. Part I of *Empire of the Senseless,* which relates a quest for a new, saving myth, is entitled "Elegy for the World of the Fathers," in which the first chapter remembers, by savaging, the world of the fathers; its title is "Rape by the Father." On the third page of *The Childlike Life of the Black Tarantula by the Black Tarantula,* the sixteen-year-old protagonist tells the reader, "When my (adopted) father suspects I've been sleeping with my future husband, he slobbers over me. Rape" (7). Fathers in Acker's work literally control with their phalluses. Acker's fathers practice rape and incest and then abandon their daughters. In these moves, they are identified with the phallogocentrism of the culture: "My father is the power. He is a fascist. To be against my father is to be anti-authoritarian sexually perverse unstable insane . . ." (*PP* 215). The daughter's weapon of revolt is irrationality and desire, the feminine language that as it writes the female body, defies the law of the father. However, in rare narrative moments, false fathers (that is, adopted or stepfathers) are contrasted with ideal (thus nonexistent) fathers. In the following passage from *My Death My Life by Pier Paolo Pasolini,* Acker depicts the father as himself a victim of thought control. The ideal father would have been the city of art, but this possibility has been killed by the stepfather, society.

To think for myself is what I want. My language is my irrationality. Watch desire carefully. Desire burns up all the old dead language morality. . . . My father willed to rape me because in that he didn't want me to think for myself because he didn't think for himself. My father isn't my real father. This is a fact. I want a man. I don't want this man this stepfather who has killed off the man I love. I have no way of getting the man I love who is my real father. My stepfather, society, is anything but the city of art.

(215-16)

A recurring and sometimes complex metaphor for patriarchal oppression in Acker's fiction is abortion: "Having an abortion was obviously just like getting fucked. If we closed our eyes and spread our legs, we'd be taken care of. They stripped us of our clothes. Grave us white sheets to cover our nakedness. Led us back to the pale green room. I love it when men take care of me" (*BG* 33). In Acker's *Don Quixote,* the abortion with which the novel opens is a precondition for surrendering the constructed self. For Acker, the woman in position on the abortion table over whom a team of doctor and nurses presides represents, in an ultimate sense, woman as constructed object. The only hope is somehow to take control, to subvert the constructed identity in order to "name" oneself: "She had to name herself. When a doctor sticks a steel catheter into you while you're lying on your back and you do exactly what he and the nurses tell you to; finally, blessedly, you let go of your mind. Letting go of your mind is dying. She needed a new life. She had to be named" (9-10).

The acquisition of a new life and a name is the quest erratically and erotically pursued in several of Acker's works, including *The Childlike Life of the Black Tarantula by the Black Tarantula, Blood and Guts in High School,* and *Don Quixote.* The means of acquisition are outside, unavailable in a culture locked in patriarchy. In order to constitute the self differently, the quester is required to find an alternative site for enunciating that self. Acker moves her protagonists toward this site through the appropriation of male texts. As the epigraph to Part II of *Don Quixote* reads: "BEING BORN INTO AND PART OF A MALE WORLD, SHE HAD NO SPEECH OF HER OWN. ALL SHE COULD DO WAS READ MALE TEXTS WHICH WEREN'T HERS" (39). These texts represent the limits of language and culture within which the female quester attempts to acquire identity. Once inside the male text, the quester, by her very posture, subverts it: "By repeating the past, I'm molding and transforming it." In *Don Quixote,* she explains the subversive effects of plagiarism through Arabs, who in incarnating an "other" of Western culture are comparable to women:

Unlike American and Western culture (generally), the Arabs (in their culture) have no (concept of) originality. That is, culture. They write new stories paint new pictures et cetera only by embellishing old stories pictures . . . They write by cutting chunks out of allready written texts and in other ways defacing traditions: changing important names into silly ones, making dirty jokes out of matters that should be of the utmost importance to us such as nuclear warfare.

(25)

Like the motives of artist Sherrie Levine, who creates nearly identical replicas of well-known art and photography, Acker's are profoundly political. With their plagiarisms, Acker and Levine propose an alternate explanation of the sources of power than the classical Marxists. With Jean Baudrillard they believe that power is held more by those who control the means of representation than by those who control the means of production. Plagiarism undermines the assumptions governing representation. That is, in plagiarizing, Acker and Levine do not deny the masterwork itself, but they do interrogate its sources in paternal authority and male desire. Levine justifies her replicas on polemical grounds: "I felt angry at being excluded. As a woman, I felt there was no room for me. There was all this representation . . . of male desire. The whole art system was geared to celebrating these objects of male desire. Where, as a woman artist, could I situate myself? What I was doing was making this explicit: how this oedipal relationship artists have with artists of the past gets repressed; and how I, as a woman, was only allowed to represent male desire."[7] By locating the search for modes of representing female desire inside male texts and art, Acker and Levine clearly delineate the constraints under which this search proceeds. However, Acker's plagiarism, while intent on subverting the notion of the master text, is often allied with the political messages of particular texts. In her appropriation of *The Scarlet Letter,* for instance, she updates its politics to show its relevance for her contemporaries.

Moreover, in Acker's texts, the subversion is always incomplete, the remolding and transformation of textual appropriation provide only limited success. She has a more pessimistic, perhaps more practical sense of humanity's cultural imprisonment than Cixous, whose theory-inspired imagination proposes that writing of the body, *l'écriture féminine,* will lead to radical cultural transformation. Acker's questers' searches for identity and a new healing myth lead to silence, death, nothingness, or reentry into the sadomasochism of patriarchal culture. As she said in an interview, "You can't get to a place, to a society, that isn't constructed according to the phallus."[8] The attempts to subvert male texts and thus male culture result in revelation rather than revolution; the path to an alternate site of enunciation blocked by the very forces this path is meant to escape.

III

Acker's constant target is the infrastructure of Western patriarchal society, the government, business, education, and legal institutions that construct identity and which the oppression of women serves to sustain. Acker is often polemical in her attack: "Civilization and culture are the rules of males' greeds" (*DQ* 69). In applying elements of *The Scarlet Letter* to contemporary society, she records the degradation of values since the nineteenth-century society that Hawthorne's narrative indicted:

> Long ago, when Hawthorne wrote *The Scarlet Letter,* he was living in a society that was more socially repressive and less materialistic than ours. He wrote about a wild woman. This woman challenged the society by fucking a guy who wasn't her husband and having his kid. The society punished her by sending her to gaol, making her wear a red "A" for adultery right on her tits, and excommunicating her.
>
> Nowadays most women fuck around 'cause fucking doesn't mean anything. All anybody cares about today is money. The woman who lives her life according to nonmaterialistic ideals is the wild antisocial monster; the more openly she does so, the more everyone hates her. . . .
>
> [A] reason Hawthorne set his story in the past (in lies) was 'cause he couldn't say directly all the wild things he wanted to say. He was living in a society to which ideas and writing still mattered. In "The Custom House," the introduction to *The Scarlet Letter,* Hawthorne makes sure he tells us the story of *The Scarlet Letter* occurred long ago and has nothing to do with anyone who's now living. After all, Hawthorne had to protect himself so he could keep writing. Right now I can speak as directly as I want 'cause no one gives a shit about writing and ideas, all anyone cares about is money. Even if one person in Boise, Idaho, gave half-a-shit, the only book Mr Idaho can get his hands on is a book the publishers, or rather the advertisers ('cause all businessmen are now advertisers) have decided will net half-a-million in movie and/or TV rights. A book that can be advertised. Define culture that way.
>
> You see, things are much better nowadays than in those old dark repressed Puritan days: anybody can say anything today; progress does occur.

(*BG* 66)

In ***Don Quixote*** Acker portrays a society so blind to its own incarceration by greed and corruption that it requires an outside perspective to sort out what is even human. In a passage in which she allies the "rational" with deadening social institutions, she proposes Godzilla as providing such perspective:

> Total destruction is rational because it comes from rational causes. Why are human beings still rational, that is, making nuclear bombs polluting inventing DNA etc.? Because they don't see the absolute degradation and poverty around their flesh because if they did, they would be in such horror they would have to throw away their minds and want to become, at any price, only part-humans. Only Godzilla who not only isn't human but also wasn't made by humans therefore is unidentifiable and incomprehendable to humans can give the human world back to humans.

(71-72)

Godzilla provides Acker with a more complex perspective than her flip presentation of it suggests. Designed by Japanese filmmakers to make big bucks with a cheap monster movie pandering to the 1950s atom bomb and cold war fears, Godzilla represents the exploitation and commercialization of those fears. It represents the degree to which taste, judgment, and critical issues are held hostage by materialism and paranoia. The fact that Godzilla, a creation of atomic waste, was constructed by the Japanese only a decade's distance from Hiroshima and Nagasaki gives more resonance to Acker's description of Godzilla's creators as "non-human" than a stab at Western bigotry. In creating Godzilla, Japanese filmmakers sacrificed the meaning of Hiroshima and Nagasaki to greed and accepted the acts of their destroyers in order to make money—for Acker, an obscenely transcendent (that is, outside the human) act of self-prostitution. Through the lens of *Godzilla,* as the cardboard Tokyo is crushed and torn by a greed-inspired terror, Acker suggests that the devaluation of the culture and humanity's fall from sanity and its own best ideals come into focus.

Populated by outlaws and outcasts, her texts provide subversive glosses on convention. "Only excreate" was Stein's advice in *Tender Buttons,* an experiment in non-traditional linguistic structures to yield what she thought of as contemporary composition—linguistic structures that are democratized, non-hierarchical, without center—and to release signifiers from signifieds. As Stein excreated traditional linguistic grammar, syntax, and modes of meaning, Acker deconstructs social grammar, syntax, and modes of meaning. She perceives Americans as having become so thoroughly roboticized by their institutions that the hope for love, for an authentic life and identity, can only be reimagined in some other space, outside of institutions, outside of society, outside the law. Acker writes, "I'm trying to destroy all laws, tell you not to follow laws, restrictions" (*BT* [*The Childlike Life of the Black Tarantula by the Black Tarantula*] 150). Pirates, murderers, Arabs, terrorists, slave traders and other Acker permutations of the extreme (sometimes a fantasy) outsider for whom society is a field for illicit and, above all, selfish harvests and who, besotted with death, theft, hypocrisy, paranoia, and ugly sex, give back a portrait of society horrifyingly consistent with their values.

Just as appropriating male texts results in subversive disclosure, crime and criminals propose sites where the bondage of self to the culture's deadening prescriptions may be demonstrated, and perhaps more important, where liberating strategies may be tested. In a section on *The Scarlet Letter* in *Blood and Guts in High School,* Acker writes, "In Hawthorne's and our materialistic society the acquisition of money is the main goal 'cause money gives the power to make change stop, to make the universe die; so everything in the materialistic

society is the opposite of what it really is. Good is bad. Crime is the only possible behaviour" (67). For women, any attempt to achieve power (equated with money) puts them outside the law: "For 2,000 years you've had the nerve to tell women who we are. We use your words; we eat your food. Every way we get money has to be a crime. We are plagiarists, liars, and criminals" (132).

IV

Like William Burroughs, who greatly influenced her, Acker has embraced the stance of cultural outlaw not only in her narratives, but has adopted it for her life. For example, when middle-class college students in the sixties were intent on "sexual revolution," she tested the meaning of this revolution by performing in 42nd Street sex shows, an experience which led to her first published work, *Politics.* Although she describes the time as "schizophrenic," living in two cultures—hippie (which she views as middle class) and Times Square—she also implies the experience gave her a window onto social hypocrisies, particularly class divisions and sexism, disguised by the free love rhetoric. In practice, Acker suggests, there were disturbing similarities between the two cultures.[9] Alienated from her family and living as an American expatriate in London, she embodies the perspective of outsider and outcast that she cultivates in her fiction. Raised on 57th Street and First Avenue in New York City, child of upper-middle-class Jewish parents, Acker, now over forty, is heavily tattooed and a bodybuilder.

The tattoo, in fact, is the central image in her most recent narrative, *Empire of the Senseless,* a work dedicated to her tattooist. A precise metaphor for her writing, the tattoo is an outlawed, magical language written directly on the body, becoming part of the body, the body turning into text, an audacious rendering of Cixous's writing the body. In a short history of the tattoo, she discusses its semiotic function, as well as its association—crucial for Acker—with criminals:

> The tattoo is primal parent to the visual arts. Beginning as abstract maps of spiritual visions, records of the "other" world, tattoos were originally icons of power and mystery designating realms beyond normal land-dwellers' experience.

> The extra-ordinary qualities of the tattoo's magic-religious origin remain constant even today, transferring to the bearer some sense of existing outside the conventions of normal society.

> In decadent phases, the tattoo became associated with the criminal—literally the outlaw—and the power of the tattoo became intertwined with the power of those who chose to live beyond the norms of society.

> (140)

As this passage on the tattoo confirms, Acker obsessively explores the territory of the taboo, claims it as the proper domain from which to launch attacks on

Western culture—an empire of the senseless. In *Empire of the Senseless,* she systematically summons every taboo she can think of—including incest, rape, terrorism, vomit, shit, menstruation, homosexuality, a very long list—rendering them in vivid, forbidding, hallucinatory prose ("I remembered the scarlet pigeon nibbling at the blood seeping out of my cunt" [48]). In an explanatory passage, Acker offers her most lucid defense of the use of taboos in her fiction:

> That part of our being (mentality, feeling, physicality) which is free of all control let's call our "unconscious." Since it's free of control, it's our only defence against institutionalized meaning, institutionalized language, control, fixation, judgement, prison.
>
> Ten years ago it seemed possible to destroy language through language: to destroy language which normalizes and controls by cutting that language. Nonsense would attack the empire-making (empirical) empire of language, the prisons of meaning.
>
> But this nonsense, since it depended on sense, simply pointed back to the normalizing institutions.
>
> What is the language of the "unconscious"? (If this ideal unconscious or freedom doesn't exist: pretend it does, use fiction, for the sake of survival, all of our survival.) Its primary language must be taboo, all that is forbidden. Thus, an attack on the institutions of prison via language would demand the use of a language or languages which aren't acceptable, which are forbidden. Language, on one level, constitutes a set of codes and social and historical agreements. Nonsense doesn't per se break down the codes; speaking precisely that which the codes forbid breaks the codes.
>
> (133-34)

In *The Newly Born Woman,* Catherine Clément argues that "every society has an imaginary zone for what it excludes," a zone located on the "fault lines" of the culture.[10] She and Cixous, her collaborator on the book, propose that "women bizarrely embody [that] group of anomalies showing the cracks in the culture" through which the silenced of culture exerts its pressure, makes itself known—the cracks through which the repressed returns.[11] In Acker's political translation and transformation of this idea, the repressed is embodied by figures and concretized as acts outside the social code—outlaws, outcasts, taboos—that threaten it. In unlikely partnership with Emily Dickinson, she says madness is divinest sense: "No to anything but madness" (*BT* 35). She sees the culture in the same position as the dying animal whose leg is caught in a trap: in order to escape, it must chew through its leg. Similarly, for a chance to transform contemporary culture from the deadly trap it is, Acker cautions you must "eat your mind," which has been so completely constructed by the phallus, so thoroughly written by society's metalanguages, that there is no room, in her terms, to truly name oneself.[12] Acker's narratives, in their subversive appropriations of master texts, their aggressive assertions of criminal perspec-

tives, their relentless interrogations of art, culture, government, and sexual relations, are designed to be jaws steadily devouring—often to readers' horror and certainly to their discomfort (which is part of the strategy)—the mindset, if not the mind, of Western culture.[13]

Notes

1. Kathy Acker, *Artforum* 22 (1984), 64. Subsequent page references to this article will be given in parentheses in the text.

2. Page references to Acker's works will be included parenthetically in the text and are taken from the following editions (also, please note the abbreviations used in this essay): *BT, The Childlike Life of the Black Tarantula by the Black Tarantula* (New York: TVRT Press, 1975); *EJ, Hello I'm Erica Jong* (New York: Contact II, 1982); *BG, Blood and Guts in High School* (New York: Grove, 1984); *DQ, Don Quixote* (New York: Grove, 1986); *KH, Kathy Goes to Haiti* and *PP, My Death My Life by Pier Paolo Pasolini,* both in *LM, Literal Madness* (New York: Grove, 1987); *ES, Empire of the Senseless* (New York: Grove, 1988).

3. In addition to the essays in this issue, see Ellen G. Friedman and Miriam Fuchs, "Contexts and Continuities: An Introduction to Women's Experimental Fiction in English" in their *Breaking the Sequence: Women's Experimental Fiction* (Princeton: Princeton Univ. Press, 1989), 39-42, and Larry McCafferey, "The Artists of Hell: Kathy Acker and 'Punk' Aesthetics," ibid., 215-30.

4. Trans. Annette Kuhn, *Signs: Journal of Women in Culture and Society* 7 (1981): 41-55.

5. By feminine writing (*l'écriture féminine*), Cixous means writing that imitates female sexuality. The signature on this writing, according to Cixous, can be either male or female.

6. Cixous, 52-53.

7. Sherrie Levine, "Art in the (Re)Making," *Art News* 85 (May 1986): 96-97.

8. See her interview with me in this issue, 17.

9. Ibid., 14.

10. *The Newly Born Woman,* trans. Betsy Wing (Minneapolis: Univ. of Minneapolis Press, 1986), 8-9.

11. Ibid., 7.

12. The title of the *New York Times Book Review* (16 October 1988, p. 9) review of *Empire of the Senseless* by R. H. W. Dillard is "Lesson No. 1: Eat Your Mind."

13. See Ellen G. Friedman, "'Utterly Other Discourse': The Anticanon of Experimental Women Writers from Dorothy Richardson to Christine Brooke-Rose" for a discussion of women's anticanonical literature to which Acker's works belong: *Modern Fiction Studies* 34 (Autumn 1988): 353-70.

Richard Walsh (essay date spring 1991)

SOURCE: Walsh, Richard. "The Quest for Love and the Writing of Female Desire in Kathy Acker's *Don Quixote*." *Critique* 32, no. 3 (spring 1991): 149-68.

[In the following essay, Walsh examines the way in which Acker's formal decisions influence the theme of sexuality and power in her novel Don Quixote.*]*

In **Don Quixote,** Kathy Acker obsessively confronts the problematic of the interface between sexuality and power, and her persistence contradicts the apparent nihilism of her findings. She also uses radical narrative methods that locate the trauma of this confrontation in the form of the text itself. This interaction of form and theme needs more careful articulation: how exactly do Acker's formal decisions in this novel impinge upon its thematic argument? To begin with, why **Don Quixote**?

At first sight, Acker's **Quixote** owes little to Cervantes' original, but her own account of its inception suggests otherwise. The abortion that sets the novel in motion has an autobiographical source, and the fusion of this material with Cervantes is a result of subjective association: "Ms. Acker picked up Cervantes' text two years ago . . . when she was looking for something to divert her attention from her own impending abortion. 'I couldn't keep my mind off the abortion so I started writing down what I was reading, but the abortion kept getting into it.'"[1] This way of reading-writing closely parallels the way in which the other texts that she plagiarizes are mutated within the novel by the preoccupations of the context into which they are imported. Such is Acker's concept of "plagiarism." She has elevated it into a formal strategy, emptied of its pejorative connotations by the blatancy of its operation. The motive is no longer to gain credit for another's work, but to access a cultural heritage too loaded with subjective significance to countenance the dissociating frame that is set up by attributed quotation. Her use of Cervantes, however, is at one remove and exploits formal and thematic characteristics more often than the words themselves.

Acker's use of material and motifs from Cervantes is even more dominated by her own purposes than with her other texts and functions as no more than a fine thread of allusions, points of anchorage in the host text.

Her Sancho Panza is not a single character but a series of largely undifferentiated dogs. The dog in Acker's work equates with Sancho Panza in that it stands in opposition to Don Quixote's madness, symbolizing deference to the imperatives of realism. But realism here is debased, dehumanized: it has become a crude self-interested materialism. The dogs in **Don Quixote** divide into the dehumanized victims of this ideology, those who accompany the knight at various stages through the novel, and the ideology's unabashed proponents—notably Richard Nixon and his entourage. Apart from the debasement of their speech into barks and woofs, their doggishness manifests itself in their universal designation by the ungendered pronoun "it." This is not a negation of the fact of sex, but of the human psychological dialectic between the sexes—the basis of love. While Nixon goes home to "copulate" irredeemably with "its bitch,"[2] the neutral pronoun in the case of the dog Villebranche who narrates "A Dog's Life" emerges as a critical flaw in its relation to Don Quixote in the section "Heterosexuality": "'My God!' Don Quixote exclaimed. 'You're not the sexual gender I thought you were! And I love you'" (127). This ambiguity is also central to the story of Villebranche and De Franville, in which a mutual confusion of sexual identities becomes the only model for heterosexuality's salvation.

Another direct borrowing from Cervantes is the motif of the Evil Enchanters, who are identified as the enemies of free sexual and emotional expression, from Ronald Reagan to the editors of the *Times Literary Supplement* to Andrea Dworkin (101-2). The theme of enchantment is prominent in the only extended episode that closely follows Cervantes' novel, the vision of paradise (184-90) that is taken from the vision of Montesumo's Cave.[3] But Acker generally does not treat of the original *Don Quixote* in such detail: her use of Cervantes is more abstract, better seen in terms of authorial stance than textual appropriation. In fact, Acker's subversive plagiarism allows her to claim allegiance with Cervantes on the basis of a shared concern with other texts (in Cervantes' case his parodic use of popular ballads and chivalric romances); "I write by using other written texts, rather than expressing 'reality' which is what most novelists do. Our reality now, which occurs so much through the media, *is* other texts. I'm playing the same game as Cervantes."[4] This analogy translates into thematic terms, because the chivalric code of courtly love that motivates the first Quixote finds an equivalent in Acker's novel as the obsessional romantic idea of love that possesses her knight. The transition from a courtly to a romantic concept of love, as well as from a male to a female knight, converts her protagonist's quest into a vehicle of Acker's inquiry into female sexuality and the social pressures that impinge upon it. Writing the novel in response to her reading of Cervantes, she became fascinated with the knight's "trying to transform a faintly intolerable social reality into what really is the grail, this totally romantic search. All sorts of feminist issues got involved—it just took off."[5]

The attributes Acker's Quixote derives from the original are mostly paradoxical. She adopts this identity with a self-conscious emphasis on its contradictions, deciding to "become a female-male or a night-knight" (10). Acker also plays with the tension between the old knight and her youthful (adolescent) ideal of love: "she had been irritated then angry with him because he was younger than her—forty-two compared to her sixty-six years" (18). But the main source of paradox is inherent in the original character himself: in both protagonists the pursuit of idealistic ends with complete disregard for pragmatic realities indicates an ambiguous combination of the lunatic and the visionary. "The First Adventure" of Acker's Quixote is a paradigmatic instance of this opposition. Setting out "to right all wrongs" she intervenes in a beating with visionary fervor: "Don Quixote cried, 'Stop that! In this world which's wrong, it's wrong to beat up people younger than yourself. I'm fighting for all of your culture'" (14). But her idealistic resolution of the situation displays a lunatic incomprehension of its realities:

> Don Quixote thought carefully. "You have to go back for your teacher, deep inside him, wants to help you and has just been mistaken how to help you. If he didn't care for you, he wouldn't want you back."
>
> The old man took the boy back to school and there flogged him even more severely. . . . The boy tried to enjoy the beating because his life couldn't be any other way.
>
> (15)

The contradictions of Acker's knight operate within a framework also appropriated from Cervantes, that of the quest. The sublime folly of this quest is established in the first paragraph and defines the whole action of the novel: "When she was finally crazy because she was about to have an abortion, she conceived of the most insane idea that any woman can think of. Which is to love" (9). But the novel does not fulfill the expectations of a singular purposeful orientation aroused by this narrative model. Acker is not concerned to produce a linear narrative because her objective is not to pursue, through her protagonists, a developing argument or sequence of events, but to articulate a perspective or state of affairs. This is a shift from a temporal to a spatial model of the novel, which redefines coherence as no more than the recognition of significant thematic relationships between disparate textual fragments. On this assumption, "Narrative isn't a problem anymore. Even if you use a discontinuous story people will make connections."[6]

The form of Acker's work in general is not predicated upon narrative, but upon tableaux; she does not offer events but positions. Speaking of more conventional realistic narratives, she complains "when I read novels now they don't seem to have anything to do with anything. I can't tell where the writers' guts are—novels should be aimed at adding to cultural discourse."[7] Nevertheless, there is a problem of momentum in the mode of writing she practices; its lack of temporal development tends to deaden the temporal activity of reading. By incorporating the narrative structure of *Don Quixote* into her novel, she seeks to avoid this propensity toward aimlessness: "I won't allow myself to be cut off from the very powerful resources of the linear story. In ***Don Quixote*** I've laid a narrative over the cutups and since Cervantes' novel is episodic the problem of sequence is solved."[8]

Acker's invocation of the quest, as a strongly end-directed but episodic form, is intended to achieve the maximum sense of narrative direction with the minimum commitment to narrative structure. The episodic narrative and the quest framework that unifies it operate in contradiction to each other in Acker's novel, because the sexual problematic she explores in its various scenarios does not progress, but is static, paralyzed. The novel does not offer a dialectical evolution: its argument is cyclical, stalemated by a series of double-binds. The proposed structure of the quest, therefore, functions only potentially, as the will to escape this cycle. The cyclical nature of the narrative episodes is affirmed in the subtitle of the section "The Last Adventure," which adds "Until This Book Will Begin Again" (175), as well as by repetition and reiteration throughout the book and by the series of false endings, last visions, and deaths of Don Quixote. The double-bind structure of the argument is given epigrammatic form in several variations: "If a woman insists she can and does love and her living isn't loveless or dead, she dies. So either a woman is dead or she dies" (33). This foregrounded circularity or failure to progress is modified by its tension with the quest narrative. The lack of evolution in the narrative has less effect on the novel's momentum than the *expectation* of development that the invoked structure generates. The subordination of a static argument to a dynamic linear structure results in an inversion that incorporates this dynamism *within* the static argument, energizing and intensifying it. The cyclical form that constrains the narrative is, therefore, not viewed from outside as repetitious and fruitless but from within as a potent condition of frustration.

The static condition of the novel is mirrored in the arrested emotional development of its incompletely differentiated characters. Don Quixote, Saint Simeon, Villebranche, Lulu, Juliette, and other unnamed female narrators all share a sensibility in which obsessive sexual and emotional need is held in a constant and necessary state of frustration. Through these characters Acker explores an emotional impasse in which the character, although denied emotional freedom by the realities of her situation, does not easily relinquish her impossible desires. As one reviewer of the novel noted, "Acker speaks from a level that is both above and below the urbanity of everyday life,"[9] in a world of fantastic desires and abject miseries that coexist but do not modify each other. This alienation from everyday life is reflected in the dominant tone of the novel, which is impassioned and naive and characterized by idealistic affirmations of the emotionally unattainable and declamations against the inevitable. The tone is not confined to the characters of the novel but encompasses the impersonal narrative voice, which exhibits a close emotional affinity with the characters it tells about and tends to further merge their sensibilities. This narrative voice appears to be partly authorial, the mouthpiece of an autobiographical id for Acker. It also has a calculated satiric function that is most apparent in its political digressions. One early example, clearly marked as an authorial aside by the heading "Insert," begins: "I think Prince should be President of the United States because all our Presidents since World War II have been stupid anyway . . ." (21). This position is defended by arguing that "Prince, unlike all our other images or fakes or Presidents, stands for values. . . . The Prince believes in feelings, fucking, and fame" (21) and is, therefore, both refreshingly amoral and (possibly) conscious.

This is the adamant naiveté of adolescence, when the confrontation between self and society is at its height, when desire and the libidinous are new and as absolute as the repressive social and political codifications that impinge upon them in every social and sexual interaction. In this way the protagonists of **Don Quixote** are caught between a will to connect and a refusal to compromise their emotional integrity. Social integration is impossible because of the antipathy of society's dominant values to emotional openness and its subordination of human to economic values: "Emerging militarily and economically unrivalled from the Second World War, America was uniquely and fully able to impose its hatred of nonmaterialism—its main ideal—on the remainder of the world" (72). Materialism is seen as the rational development of the drive for self-preservation; its sole value is the domination of natural, social, and political structures. Hence it has become "'the universal principle of a society which seeks to reduce all phenomena to this enlightenment ideal of rationalism, or subjugation of the other'" (72). The guardians of materialism are the evil enchanters, and Don Quixote's quest for love is, therefore, a struggle against them. "'As soon as we all stop being enchanted,' Don Quixote explained, 'Human love'll again be possible'" (102). The rejection of materialism by Don Quixote and the novel's other central characters alienates them from authority and places them in a state of perpetual rebellion. This estrangement from social values is extreme; Acker's characters are absolutely unreconciled, in a way that would be impossible to sustain against the forces of social reality. Their continuous hovering on the brink of emotional self-destruction is, within the context of the novel (subtitled "which was a dream"), a nightmare condition of arrested or cyclical time. This dream sense is accentuated by the repetition and variation of its narrative and the sense of entrapment generated by the novel's false development. Its function for the reader is analogous to the access to the unconscious a dream can provide, exposing lost or suppressed selves that have been obscured by the framework of assimilation to a socialized condition, the assimilation Acker's characters refuse.

The *strangeness* of the world of **Don Quixote** allows the reader to acknowledge the price of socialization. By elevating absolute loyalty to primal emotions from a presocial stage of development into a state of being, the novel defamiliarizes and exposes these emotions to the reader's self-consciousness. The access it offers to the reader's impossible lost selves is one of the novel's most considerable affective strengths. By engaging social reality in ways that reality does not allow but that are discernibly present in the mentality individuals relinquish in the process of assimilation, Acker questions the values prioritized by society. Acker's other work functions similarly. The titles of several of her books prioritize the naive, the adolescent, and the presocial: **The Childlike Life of the Black Tarantula, Blood and Guts in High School**; she invokes the Bildungsroman convention, **Great Expectations**. The centrality of this orientation to her concept of **Don Quixote** and the novels that preceded it is supported by her comments on art and on her own writing. She affirms allegiance to a sensibility unreconciled to society, emphasizing and privileging inarticulateness and a concept of art as prerational expression, as the direct articulation of inner emotions unmediated by logical or aesthetic consideration for the culture that it addresses. She wishes to resist mimesis in favor of an expressive function and seeks to subvert the concept of description by characterizing it as a belated imposition upon the reality it purports to represent: "The act of describing assumes one event can be a different event: meaning dominates or controls existence. But desire—or art—is."[10] The direct equation of desire and art identifies art as concerned with the prerational libidinous realm that is evoked in **Don Quixote.** The congruity also insists upon the asocial quality of artistic production, denying it any formative intent or aesthetic or didactic design upon its audience. Refusing art any purposeful address is not intended to deny it cultural value. In fact, the insubordinate self-presentation of art, its refusal to submit to the parameters of a ruling culture by which it is framed and homogenized, constitutes its value. Acker wants art to confront culture *unframed*, rather than already contained by self-description or self-distancing, which she sees as pre-emptive criticism:

If art's to be more than craft, more than decorations for the people in power, it's this want, this existence. . . . Examine the two statements, "Help!" and "I need help." The first language is a cry; the second, a description. Only the cry, art, rather than the description or criticism, is primary. The cry is stupid, it has no mirror; it communicates.

I want to cry.[11]

This concept of art as a cry insists that art does not offer itself as a self-sufficient reflection of the artist's engagement with reality, but as a raw artistic enactment of it, the value of which is determined by how readers or audience confront and respond to it. The definition is appropriate to both the form and the argument of ***Don Quixote*** and is supported by the literary practice of the knight herself: "'I wasn't sent to Oxford or anywhere, so what I do to write is cut crosses into the inside of my wrists. I write in fever'" (107).

Acker's novel deals directly with the expression of desire and the confrontation of limitations on its expression and fulfillment. These limitations are political, moral, and religious as well as the hazards of sexual politics. The central issue is always the confrontation between desire and control, between immediacy and restraint. In political terms, Acker's advocacy of desire translates into a pursuit of individual freedom, an anarchic response to authority. In America, Land of Freedom, this involves an exposure of those establishment myths of freedom that consolidate the power structure. Acker's view of American society is Hobbesian, her canine vision of humanity a metaphor about the materialist reduction of society, and therefore human relations, to Hobbes's state of nature: "'Doggish life depends upon unequal power relations or the struggle of power. This is the society in which we live. The life of a dog, even if the dog's dead like me, is solitary, poor, nasty, brutish, short. The condition of a dog is a condition of war, of everyone against everyone: so every dog has a right to everything, even to another dog's body. This is freedom'" (114). Acker offers a series of demystifications of America's myths of freedom. These take the form of possible answers to the question "What are the myths of the beginning of America?" (117) followed by subversively paradoxical explanations to justify the formulation:

> Answer: The desire for religious intolerance made America or Freedom. Explanation: . . . these New Worlders had left England not because they had been forbidden there to worship as they wanted to but because there they and, more important, their neighbors weren't forced to live as rigidly in religious terms as they wanted.
>
> (117-18)

From this reading of the founding myths of America emerges an equation between Puritans and politicians, Quakers and citizens, which leaves no place in the sys-

tem between political authoritarianism and pacifistic abdication from control: "Answer: Individual freedom was the choice between militarism and the refusal to partake in government" (119). Acker's protagonists defy this absence of political freedom by an alienation from the system, which is a refusal of its parameters. Don Quixote writes for and of the outcast, among whom she includes all women who refuse "the bickerings and constraints of heterosexual marriage" (202). But she insists that these women exist in a condition of deprivation, not an alternative community: "'The only characteristic freaks share is our knowledge that we don't fit in. Anywhere. It is for you, freaks my loves, I am writing and it is about you'" (202). Acker's concentration on the outcast "freaks" derives theoretical support from Julia Kristeva's concept of "abjection," which relates the formation of structures in society to the process of exclusion by which it operates and identifies a subversive potential in "defilement," embracing this exclusion as a positive value. Acker's protagonists are abjects not only in relation to the dominant social structures but also in relation to themselves, to the form of a stable ego that constitutes an established position vis-à-vis society. Lulu, in Acker's plagiarism of Wedekind's *Earth Spirit* and *Pandora's Box,* can defy Schön: "You can't change me cause there's nothing to change. I've never been" (78). For Kristeva, this quality of abjection demonstrates the constitutive function of absence in differential structures, including (particularly significant for Acker) the structure of desire: "There is nothing like the abjection of self to show that all abjection is in fact recognition of the *want* on which any being, meaning, language or desire is founded."[12] Therefore, for Acker's characters the primacy of desire guarantees their suffering and their failure. The affirmation of desire is necessarily an introduction of absence into the self. This equation of desire and suffering is encapsulated in the novel by Villebranche: "The dog explained her myth of rejection: 'I'm almost never attracted to men, physically. About once a year, I see a man whom I actually want and then . . . the usual happens: Either he walks away or, after a day or two, he walks away. For me, sexuality is rejection'" (128).

At the beginning of the novel, Don Quixote meets a young Irish Catholic who has come to London and lost her possessions while concealing her abortion from her friends and family. The confrontation with Catholicism grows into a more general antagonism between religion and the autonomy of individual desires. It culminates in Don Quixote's "Battle Against the Religious White Men" in which she proposes to lead the pack of dogs "'in a fight to death or to life against the religious white men and against all the alienation that their religious image-making or control brings to humans'" (178). This confrontation is worked out largely in the contested religious imagery of blood and virginity that punctuates the novel. Don Quixote's quest is framed by blood from her abortion to her defeat and death, as her final will to the dogs records: "'Dogs of this world. You are holding bleeding flesh between your sharp reddened teeth. I recognize this flesh because its mine'" (201). The knight suffers as a parodic female Christ-figure. Whereas the alienated wild dogs flock around her, "Probably because they smelt she was about to get her period" (177), to men ""'nuclear bomb leakage's less dangerous than ours'"" (173). The antithesis of blood is virginity, a condition of denial, presented as the universal sexual character of women: "'Women are bitches, dog. They're the cause of the troubles between men and women. Why? Because they don't give anything, they deny. Female sexuality has always been denial or virginity'" (27). This sexuality has been defined by male religion and is the cause and result of misogyny: "'Religious white men hate women because and so they make women into the image of the Virgin Mary'" (178). Affirmation of blood over virginity is, therefore, a subversion of women's socialized sexual role and a refusal of the prescriptions of religion. It also is an opening up to desire, and hence to suffering: ""'I'll whip you by breaking you down by breaking through your virginity or identity. As soon as you're no longer a virgin, you're going to leak. You'll keep on leaking so you won't be able to retain any more of their teachings. . . . I have to warn you. As soon as you start leaking, you're going to need desperately. You won't be secure ever again'"" (173).

The forces opposing the free expression of desires similarly are manifest in the repressive code of social morality and the internalizing of this code through social integration. The novel presents a Hobbesian vision of socialization, although ironically Hobbes proposes hope and good actions as the pleasures of his society. As the Angel of Death who returns to haunt Nixon, he relentlessly explains his teachings: "'What is this hope and good actions? . . . I think either by receiving thoughts or by wanting. Wanting's either thoughtless or, being taught, resembles receiving. In short, I'm a dog. My hope and actions're mechanical'" (113).

The novel also confronts the family as a mode of social integration. In "A Portrait of an American Family," the prodigal daughter returns from the horrors of New York to the safety of her family. The environment of love and security she anticipates is rapidly transformed into a nightmare of constraint: "You were perfectly right to come back here. . . . The family is the only refuge any of us has. Daddy and I've been discussing this. . . . It's normal for children to break from their parents. You wanted to wallow in the outside world. You wallowed in all the hatred and filth that is outside. . . . You've come back to prison of your own free accord. . . . From now on, you will do whatever I woof you to do and, more important, be whoever I order you. This is a safe unit" (116). The scene ends in a total annihilation

of self as the father has his daughter electrocuted while he watches on television. Against the repressions of social respectability Acker uses pornography, as a total embrace of unregulated desire; it works to confront the reader's taboos and to liberate and lay bare the sexuality of the participating characters. This exploration of sexuality is never sanitized, and includes an extended plagiarism of Sade: the tension between sexual freedom and sexual degradation is not ignored but heightened, as a means of exposing the raw nerves of sexual relations. In the episode from Sade's *Juliette,* Juliette's violent sexual education is given traumatic form by the triple and quadruple repetition of each paragraph of its progress, but the trauma leads to sexual enlightenment. When Juliette is able to articulate the contradictions of her sexuality and social identity, the repetitions cease.

The primary oppressive power relationship in the novel is that between the sexes. Don Qiuxote and her surrogates are impeded in their quest for love less by the external forces of society than by the structure of sexual relations, which denies mutuality in love because the structure is one of domination in which the controlling (male) sex defines the other as object in the mechanism of desire. Reciprocal love is frustrated by desire's objectifying function: ""'When you love us, you hate us because we have to deny you. Why? Objects can't love back'"" (28). Because this structure of sexual dominance is socially encoded, the sexuality of the oppressed sex is already negated and her desire within the social framework of sexuality is preempted. To speak the language of desire involves a subject position that the oppressed sex is denied by the grammar of that language: ""'I'm your desire's object, dog, because I can't be the subject. Because I can't be a subject: what you name 'love,' I name 'nothingness.' I won't not be: I'll perceive and I'll speak'"" (28). Acker's portrayal of women as occluded in sexual relations owes much to Luce Irigaray.[13] Irigaray's analysis of the concept of woman defined by men as an absence or void—and of the commodification of women into sexual goods—is present in all the book's sexual relations, but most concisely in Acker's insertion of Wedekind's Lulu into the plot of Shaw's *Pygmalion*. In "The Selling of Lulu," Lulu's father, Schigold, sells her to Schön: "The girl belongs to me. You got her. Don't you believe in free enterprise?" (79). When Schön, whose "social experiment" is to make Lulu into something out of nothing, finally reacts against the paternal-sexual relationship he has evolved with her, he is recoiling from the threat posed by the absence he has defined: "I hate you, hole. . . . I will not have you show me love. You are nothing, nothing. I will not have you break into my world, break me up, destroy me" (89-90).

For Acker, the central issue of feminism is the need to affirm female sexuality without accepting the social determination this sexuality implies in a male-dominated

society. To her, it is the fundamental paradox of feminist dissent: "On the left, and on the right, and in the
middle and everywhere, men have used women's sexualities and sexual needs and desires in order to control
women. . . . One result of this historical situation is
that heterosexual women find themselves in a double-
bind: If they want to fight sexism, they must deny their
own sexualities. At the same time, feminism cannot be
about the denial of any female sexuality."[14] Acker's
feminism is not a definitive condemnation of sexual relations. She always seeks to recuperate some viable
form for them and repudiates the separatist tendency in
feminism, preferring the dangerous quest for a liberated
heterosexuality. As a result, her characters are vulnerable and desperate: they have no autonomy but are almost wholly other-directed. As Cindy Patton observes,
"The voice of her women is much more ambiguous
than the idealized 'strong woman' of much feminist fiction."[15] ***Don Quixote*** includes its own parable of this
dissent from hard political commitment in order to acknowledge individual susceptibility to painful desire.
Don Quixote has three friends, the leftist, the liberal,
and the feminist:

> Don Quixote's friends dragged her toward her bed,
> which was a mattress on the floor, but just as they were
> dragging her across the floor, they saw she didn't have
> any wounds. They didn't need to care for or love her.
>
> "My wound is inside me. It is the wound of lack of
> love. . . ."
>
> Her friends, aghast at femininity, determined to burn it
> out.
>
> (16-17)

Acker's stance is not apolitical; rather, it detects in affirmative autobiographical feminist fiction a complicity
with the ground rules of contemporary political control
that she wishes to subvert:

> For some feminists the autobiographical mode is the
> form of political defiance. Well, there are many levels
> of coming out of oppression and it was important at
> one stage to say "Me," and to ask "Who am I?" But
> that strategy simply doesn't interest me. For if what
> language can mean is the first major problem of today,
> the second one is the I/other relationship. Writing which
> says all the time "here I am, and I want, I want . . ."
> presents a Hobbist universe which suits Reagan and
> Thatcher fine. Autobiography really is selfish.[16]

Acker is concerned to affirm the possibility of an I/other
relationship, to acknowledge desire at the price of emotional vulnerability. For her, sexual emancipation cannot
wait upon political emancipation. "The connecting
thread in Acker's work is her insistence on expressing
sexual desire now, even before we have created a safer
world for those desires to find their practice."[17] Early in
Don Quixote the knight affirms her need to connect; all
subsequent impediments are related to the conditions for
realizing desire, which are the reciprocal identity of
love's object and its subject and the unity of the sexual
and the emotional:

> "Why can't I just love?"
>
> "Because every verb to be realized needs its object.
> Otherwise, having nothing to see, it can't see itself or
> be. Since love is sympathy or communication, I need
> an object which is both subject and object: to love, I
> must love a soul. Can a soul exist without a body? Is
> physical separate from mental? Just as love's object is
> the appearance of love; so the physical realm is the ap-
> pearance of the godly: the mind is the body. This," she
> thought, "is why I've got a body."
>
> (10)

Because the inadequacy of conventional sexual relations to these criteria is amply demonstrated, Acker
considers a series of alternatives: the will to find a form
for sexual relations that involves no self-negation or
subjugation leads along convoluted paths of sexual inversion and experiments in sado-masochism. The strategies against the dominant sexual power relations that
the novel explores—gender confusion, sexual deviancy,
lesbianism—are all ultimately failures. Their attacks on
the power structure of sexual relations are misdirected:
they work not to rectify this structure but to avoid, ignore, or invert it.

Villebranche, resolving to have nothing to do with men,
seeks refuge in lesbianism: "'Since women when they
make love to each other're both controlling, there's no
question of control or power between them'" (127).
This is unsatisfactory because her lesbianism is not a
fulfillment of desire but an avoidance of it, because she
is not attracted to women: "'Since I didn't want to sleep
with women, sleeping with women couldn't endanger
me, didn't touch the ranting, raving unknown. A woman,
rather than being the unknown, is my mirror'" (126-
27). She turns instead to the sexually ambiguous De
Franville and bids for control of the relationship by
wooing him as a Nazi captain. This mutual gender confusion—they are referred to throughout as "she(he)"
and "he(she)" respectively—evolves into a stalemate of
erotic unattainability. In an attempt to break the dead-
lock, they reconcile themselves to being controlled by
adopting sado-masochistic roles: "'How could I eradi-
cate, not my being controlled, but my fear of being
controlled? By being controlled as much as possible'"
(134). As their educational sado-masochism reaches extremes, the sexual ambiguity is lost, and with it the balance of controlling and being controlled. The transition
is marked by a change to the unambiguous third person
pronoun:

> "Due to my increased ferocity, she(he) twists so much
> that for the first time just as my whip strokes have be-
> come hard enough to make her(him) realize that the
> pain isn't pretense that pain is only pain and eradicates
> all pretense and stupid thinking, she(he) reveals a fault
> that is absolute. She(He) had actually tricked me.

"Then, I hit him without control. I hit him because I hated him."

(139-40)

Through pain they grow from a fear of the functions of domination and submission implied by their sexuality to an acceptance of it: "'This man had no intention of taking responsibility, for he hated and feared his masculinity as much as I did. By making all this pain clear, both he and I for the first time accepted that sex'" (140). They have not changed the parameters of their sexuality, but willfully have submitted themselves to it by embracing a regime of violence and pain: "Don Quixote was disgusted that human heterosexuality had come to such an extreme end" (141).

The section "An Examination of What Kind of Schooling Women Need" plagiarizes Sade's *Juliette* to explore the emotional possibilities of a sexual world entirely outside "healthy" society: "'Living here in disease and being diseased strangely bring us closer to each other: we can now have emotions for each other. We don't care about the people who control us . . . the world of almost total death's the world of almost freedom. The closer we're living to total human death, the weaker the socio-political constraints on us'" (104). Acker excludes all of Sade's male characters to develop the sexual power play between women. First, the acknowledgment of sexual pleasure and pain forces Juliette out of her socially defined passivity or nonexistence: "'"My physical sensations scare me because they confront me with a self when I have no self: sexual touching makes these physical sensations so fierce, I'm forced to find a self when I've been trained to be nothing"'" (171). This physical enlightenment is pursued to the extremes of pain and the assertion of sexual identity to the extremes of subjugation of the other, until Juliette takes on the vestments of a man: "'Unfortunately I didn't know how to fuck Laure. Desperately I strapped a dildo around my waist. I was aghast: wearing a dildo is like wearing plastic. Is wearing plastic. I was no longer natural'" (174). She takes Laure's virginity in panic, but emotionally refuses the role she is enacting: "'I made Laure wail . . . I was more terrified by what I was doing now than I had been by my strapping on the dildo. How could I be doing this to one whom I loved? I wailed as loudly as the child'" (175). The women succeed only in recreating the abuses of male sexual dominance, albeit with painful self-awareness.

The novel does not affirm any possibility for equal sexual relations, but neither does it confirm the absence of any possibility. The attempted relations it explores all end in failure, but without extinguishing the want that motivated them. It allows a solipsistic interpretation of its failure to establish a viable form for love or the relationship of self to other:

A real vision: There's no longer nature: trees bushes, mainly: unboxed space and time. There're only rooms. Whatever you do, whether you're successful or unsuccessful, you are only in some room.

The vision is: there's no joy.

(190)

But the novel's ending is a limited refutation of this nihilistic vision. Don Quixote dreams that she accepts the impossibility of relations with men, or her "master." She turns away from the self-negation imposed upon her by her master's sexuality and equates its absolute power with the power of God, until God intervenes:

"Suddenly, I heard my master's voice. 'Shut up.

"'Where, where in hell—from Hell?—did you get your idea that I am male?'"

(206)

He proceeds to discredit his identity with absolute manhood by relating the verdict of Satan: "'"he has no respect for me because I make love to old women, spinster virgins. That he personally would rather boil over in a fourteen-year-old cunt, even if it is rape, than hide beneath his mother's skirts. He's a real man I'm a mealy-mouthed hypocrite, dishonest"'" (207). If God is inadequate by Satan's standards of manhood, the concept of male sexuality as an absolute, fixed in the transcendent order of things, is specious. The Absolute is self-discredited, of indeterminate gender, and unavailable as the rationale for a predetermined structure of sexual relations. "'"God continued condemning Him—or Herself: "So now that you know I'm imperfect, night, that you can't turn to Me: turn to yourself"'" (207). Don Quixote can no longer lay the failure of her sexuality at the door of an absolute male sexual code. The knight accepts these teachings and ascends from her dream to re-engage the world: "As I walked along beside Rocinante, I thought about God for one more minute and forgot it. I closed my eyes, head drooping, like a person drunk for so long she no longer knows she's drunk, and then, drunk, awoke to the world which lay before me'" (207). Her affirmation is qualified, suggesting no resolution, no success but the survival of the will. The cycle of defeats inflicted upon Don Quixote's quest for love leaves behind a residue of desire. This remnant, which is the continuing will to connect, to find a viable form of love, is Acker's primary value and her refutation of emotional nihilism.

Don Quixote's quest is not resolved or abandoned but reaffirmed in the last of the novel's cycles—the cycle of day and night that identifies the quest with existence itself. This cyclical form, which is essential to the novel's thematic argument, also has a structural function. Acker's use of this reiterative, episodic narrative model allows her to introduce multiple subnarratives: the continuity of the text is a function of thematic characteristics and the quest framework she takes from Cervantes: its substance has the freedom of extreme discontinuity. This discontinuity creates a plurality of textual articulations and subverts any monolithic narratorial identity. Again, the theories of Luce Irigaray are relevant: her equation of women's sexuality—and hence women's writing—with multiplicity, with the absence of a single voice: "Her sexuality, always at least double, goes even further: it is *plural.* Is this the way culture is seeking to characterize itself now? Is this the way texts write themselves/are written now? Without quite knowing what censorship they are evading?"[18] The plurality of Acker's texts is quite self-conscious; she explains in interview that her use of plagiarism is a strategy central to this process: "I've always seen writing as to do with attacking the ego, breaking down the autobiographical 'I,' playing a range of voices against each other in the text. That's a golden light I see in Dickens, that plurality of voices, and that's why, until very recently, I've worked by juxtaposing other people's texts, representing our cultural inheritance, attacking any central, moral voice. So plagiarism became a strategy of originality."[19] Plagiarism, then, is both an attack on the autobiographical "I" and a strategy of originality: not an abdication of authorial control but a textualization of it. Acker uses it throughout **Don Quixote,** but most explicitly in Part II, "Other Texts," which is her most extreme abuse of the novel's narrative framework, justified by a cursory subheading: "Being Dead, Don Quixote Could No Longer Speak. Being Born Into and Part of a Male World, She Had No Speech of Her Own. All She Could Do Was Read Male Texts Which Weren't Hers" (39). This section of the novel bases itself upon five texts: Bely's *Petersburg,* Lampedusa's *The Leopard,* an unidentified science fiction story, and Wedekind's *Earthspirit* and *Pandora's Box.* According to Tom LeClair, the point is that "Quixote has to read works by four male writers who create or unwillingly perpetuate harmful stereotypes of women," which "Ms. Acker bashes with broad parody and grotesque revision."[20] This comment mistakes the purpose of Acker's revisionary plagiarism, which is not polemical but expressive. Her plagiarism does not engage the original texts directly or coherently enough to constitute a critique of their perpetuation of "harmful stereotypes of women," which in any case is not a quality they obviously share: it is rather a process by which these texts are bent to her own thematic concerns. Although her use of plagiarism is a foregrounding of textuality over authorial identity and an insistence upon the primacy of given language over the mythic process of creative origination, it is not a denial of the authorial role per se. If it were, David Van Leer's objection to the use of plagiarism and discontinuity would be pertinent: "Fragmenting or plagiarizing the narrative voice does not 'deconstruct' the

self. It only refocuses attention where Acker least wishes it—back on the author."[21] Acker's plagiarism *does* return the reader to the plagiarizing author; it is not an attempt to hide behind other texts but to appropriate them. Her plagiarism is not a mechanical principle but a highly subjective revisionary process, in which the plagiarized text is overwhelmed by the preoccupations she imposes upon it. This state is clearly evident in her use of a poem by Catullus ("Miser Catulle, desinas ineptire . . .") that is surrounded by a highly idiosyncratic gloss and critical analysis. The Latin text itself is printed with interjections, which enact the erratic subjective process of its reading:

> Nunc iam illa non vult: tu quoque,
>   impotens can't fuck any
>   boyfriends these days, bad
>   mood no wonder I'm acting
>   badly, noli NO
> nec quae fugit sectare, nec miser
>   vive
> good advice sed obstinata mente
>   perfer, obdura.
>   vale, puella. (my awful telephone
>   call . . .)
>
>   (48)

More explicitly, her use of Lampedusa's *The Leopard* includes a direct statement of its subjective significance:

> The world is memory. I don't remember anymore because I refuse to remember anymore because all my memories hurt.
>
> *The Leopard* equals these memories. I'll remember: I won't repress I won't be a zombie, despite the pain, I will have life. This's why *The Leopard*'s romantic.
>
>   (63)

This self-assertive plagiarism, like the reading of *Don Quixote* that Acker records as the origin of her novel, implies a close association between her mode of writing and a mode of reading: reading not as the reception of text but as an interaction between an active, subjective reader and a text that is always regarded as open or undetermined. This is also the mode of reading that her work invites. In a review of **Empire of the Senseless,** Danny Karlin objected that "the shock-value of such writing is diffused by the context of its literary production; readers who buy this book have already read it." Certainly shock-value is by now a derelict literary attribute: but this is only an objection if it is assumed that Acker really intends to subject the reader to "'ultimate outrage' . . . [the] commodity being peddled by her agents and publishers. . . ."[22] The only readers she is likely to shock are those such publicity is sure to deter. Those who persevere in spite of the dust jacket are looking for, and find, something rather different: a novel that rather than reaching out to seize the reader, presents itself as an alien but potentially recognizable textual other with which the reader may interact.

Writing and reading are equated as forms of an interface between self and text. This coexistence of textuality and subjectivity is enacted in some of the novel's stylistic mannerisms, which tend to combine rigid textual formalism with extreme idiosyncracy. Acker's embedded narratives call for frequent doubling and tripling of quotation marks, which is done faithfully and reiterated with each new paragraph according to convention, even where this continues over many pages and a great diversity of material. (There are exceptions, such as the slippage of inverted commas by which Villebranche's consciousness is made to merge with that of Sade's Juliette in the section "Reading: I Dream my Schooling"). She extends this regard for the mechanics of the text to the frequent use of brackets, which are similarly doubled up when embedded and reopened without having closed when beginning a new paragraph, and to her use of the colon to indicate speech in dramatic form, which is reiterated with each new paragraph. This extension of the conventions applying to quotation marks presents itself as extreme deference to textual form, but its effect is defiantly individualistic.

Acker achieves a similar effect on a semantic level by using "or" to link equivalents rather than alternatives. This device (and its variants "which is," "that is") is ubiquitous in the novel and creates the impression of a philosophical discourse in which the argument proceeds by establishing the logical equivalence of certain central concepts. In fact, the connection between concepts that are related in this manner is rarely one of necessary equivalence, but is highly associative. Concepts are yoked not on the basis of any general logical identity but according to their previous connection in a specific, often emotionally charged context. Aside from its significant fusion of the subjective and the objective, this raising of affective association to the level of logical equivalence contributes significantly to the atmosphere of the novel. The dominant motifs, which express the themes of the impossibility of sexual relations, the negation of woman, the constriction of social and political conditions, and the perverse persistence of desire, become so inextricably intertwined that the writing has a tangible sense of imprisonment within a matrix of contradictory imperatives.

Another stylistic choice that enacts the coexistence of the personal and textual is Acker's persistent contraction of all parts of the verb *to be,* not just in speech but also in narrative report. Such a mannerism, suggesting the idiom of speech, creates a strong sense of a narrating individual, of the text as transcribed speech. But Acker extends the use so far beyond normal speech idiom as to reverse that tendency and to present instead

a defamiliarizing textual device: "'That's how males're'" (148). This negation of the idiomatic character of the device is supported by a discussion of the verb within the text, which suggests its implication in an obtrusive metaphysic. The context is the exegesis of Catullus, a meditation on separation and the tyranny of time:

> The first main verb is *is,* an *is* which isn't Platonic. This common *is* leads to the first person subjunctives, *fear* and *hinder,* as well as the *is'* subject noun, *fear.* This kind of time or the world makes human fear.
>
> Common time's other or enemy is death. *Is* is bounded by death. So the other of *is* is *be without* in the present tense.
>
> (50)

Being in time is infected with its other by the condition of being without. Being is attenuated by separation; therefore, the state of separation or lack of connection that dominates the novel is reflected in its attenuation of all forms of *to be.*

Acker's narrative disruption, then, does not destroy the sense of authorial identity but ultimately turns the reader's attention back upon it, as the orchestrator of the disruptions. This is true to some extent in the autobiographical sense, as in the abortion on which *Don Quixote* is founded. There is a core autobiographical narrative that runs through all of Acker's novels, the salient features of which are neatly summarized in *Don Quixote,* though by Villebranche rather than the impersonal narrator:

> "These are the particulars of my life: when I was a puppy, I lived among rich dogs because my family was haute bourgeoisie; I was a special mutt in dog society because I was trained to think that way. I lived on the outskirts of, in the lowest part of, society because I worked a sex show; then I believed that I deserved to be shat on, that if I didn't pull myself up by my nonexistent bootstraps out of the muck I would die, and that I had to be very tough. I was a member of a certain group—the art world—whose members, believing that they're simultaneously society's outcasts and its myths, blow up their individual psychologies into general truths. Do these three canine identities have anything to do with each other?"
>
> (112)

Even here the authorial self is presented as a plurality of selves, personae seeking rather than signifying identity. Similarly the subjectivity of her use of plagiarism means the reader's attention is returned to the author, but it is a return to the author-as-reader, someone now implicated in language rather than generating it. This is the subject of a quasi-metafictional argument in the novel—its ambivalent consideration of language as a structure of communication to which the individual must subordinate her- or himself. This ambivalence originates in the difficulties of the self-other relationship that preoccupies Acker, the conflict between woman's desire to connect and her fear of subjugating the self. The position of woman is characterized throughout as being both subjugated to language and disinherited from it. Men have attempted to exercise control, "'first, by changing women; second, when this didn't work because women are stubborn creatures, by simply lying, by saying that women live only for men's love. An alternation of language, rather than of material, usually changes material conditions . . .'" (27). An instance of this control is the power to name, an aspect of the experience of Acker's Lulu that is present in both Wedekind and, in the larger context of the power of language, in *Pygmalion*. Schön's command of language is the instrument by which Lulu is stripped of identity:

LULU:

I don't know *what* you are.

SCHÖN:

Who I am.

LULU:

Who I am.

SCHÖN:

You do not know who you are because you do not know how to speak properly.

(78)

And Schigold consolidates his mercantile rights as her father by asserting his power to name and unname:

SCHIGOLD:

. . . What's a fifty to you? What's Lulu to me?

SCHÖN:

Lulu? Is that her name?

SCHIGOLD:

Of course not. What's in a name?

(80)

Therefore the knight, as she faces her abortion at the beginning of the novel, has to name herself. Acker plays with her own name, punning upon "hack" and "hackneyed," and the instrument of abortion, the catheter: "So, she decided, 'catheter' is the glorification of 'Kathy,' By taking on such a name which, being long, is male, she would be able to become a female-male or a night-knight" (10). The quest for love is tied up with the problem of finding a position from which woman can speak. But the nonconformism of the quest denies the possibility of community upon which communication depends, as Don Quixote discovers: "'TO MYSELF: I was wrong to be right, to write, to be a knight, to try to do anything: because having a fantasy's just

living inside your own head. Being a fanatic separates you from other people. If you're like everyone else, you believe opinions or what you're told. What else is there? Oh nothingness, I have to have visions, I have to love: I have to be wrong to write'" (36). For the knight as for Lulu, the alternative to accepting the norms of society by which the community of language is established is to lapse into autism:

SCHÖN:

. . . I have nothing more to say to you because you will not be worth speaking to until you learn to be a person and to act in manners acceptable to this society.

(Lulu looks around her and no longer bothers to speak to anyone because IT ISN'T WORTH COMMUNICATING ANY MORE.)

(83)

Alienation from society is alienation from speech. For woman, this means communication is incompatible with her sexuality. At the end of the Sade episode, when Juliette's attempts at masculine mastery of Laure have ended with both women wailing in pain and fear, language and sexuality come together:

"DELBÈNE:

'Shut the fuck up. What are you: women? Do women always wail? . . . Do women take no responsibility for their own actions and therefore have no speech of their own, no real or meaningful speech?'

"'No,' I managed to reply. 'I'm coming.' Those were my words."

(175)

Juliette can have no language but the affirmation of sexuality. Whether this language can have meaning depends upon the possibility of its finding or establishing community. The knight in her madness offers two conflicting visions of the possibility of attaining a meaningful language outside the dominant discourse. The first is optimistic: "'I write words whom I don't and can't know, to you who will always be other than and alien to me. These words sit on the edges of meanings and aren't properly grammatical. For where there is no country, no community, the speaker's unsure of which language to use, how to speak, if it's possible to speak. Language is community. Dogs, I'm now inventing a community for you and me'" (191). Here community is the creation of language. Later the reverse possibility is faced: "'I wanted to find a meaning or myth or language that was mine, rather than those which try to control me; but language is communal and here is no community'" (194-95). The novel does not provide a resolution, nor does Acker believe there is one. However, she commits herself to a use of the language that defines her, which can communicate its rebellion only in its articulateness: "I write. I want to write I want my writing to be meaningless I want my writing to be stupid. But the language I use isn't what I want and make, it's what's given to me. Language is always a community. Language is what I know and is my cry."[23]

Notes

1. Lori Miller, "In the Tradition of Cervantes, Sort of," interview with Kathy Acker, *New York Times Book Review* 30 Nov. 1986: 10.

2. Kathy Acker, *Don Quixote* (London: Grafton, 1986) 109. All subsequent references in the text are to this edition.

3. Miguel de Cervantes Saavedra, *Don Quixote*, trans. J. M. Cohen (Harmondsworth: Penguin, 1950) part II, chap. xxiii.

4. Miller 10.

5. Ibid.

6. Tony Dunn, "A Radical American Abroad," interview with Kathy Acker, *Drama*, No. 160 (1986) 17.

7. Miller 10.

8. Dunn 17.

9. Ann Haverly, "In the (K)night-time," rev. of *Don Quixote, Times Literary Supplement* 23 May 1986: 554.

10. Kathy Acker, "Models of Our Present," *Artforum* Feb. 1984: 64.

11. Ibid.

12. Julia Kristeva, *Powers of Horror: An Essay on Abjection,* trans. Leon S. Roudiez (New York: Columbia UP, 1982) 5.

13. Luce Irigaray, *This Sex Which Is Not One,* trans. Catherine Porter (New York: Cornell UP, 1985).

14. Kathy Acker, introduction to *Boxcar Bertha: An Autobiography,* as told to Dr. Ben L. Reitman (New York: Amok, 1988) 10-11.

15. Cindy Patton, "Post-Punk Feminism," *Women's Review of Books,* 1, No.7 (1984): 11. Quoted in Glenn A. Harper, "The Subversive Power of Sexual Difference in the Work of Kathy Acker," *SubStance* 16, No.3 (1987) 48.

16. Dunn 17.

17. Patton 17.

18. Irigaray 18.

19. Dunn 17.

20. Tom LeClair, "The Lord of La Mancha and Her Abortion," rev. of *Don Qixote, New York Times Book Review* 30 Nov. 1986: 10.

21. David Van Leer, "Punko Panza," rev. of *Don Quixote, New Republic* 4 May 1987: 40.

22. Danny Karlin, "Antinomian Chic," rev. of *Empire of the Senseless* and "Russian Constructivism" (extract from *Don Quixote*), *London Review of Books* 2 June 1988: 10.

23. Acker, "Models of Our Present" 64.

Karen Brennan (essay date spring 1994)

SOURCE: Brennan, Karen. "The Geography of Enunciation: Hysterical Pastiche in Kathy Acker's Fiction." *boundary 2* 21, no. 2 (spring 1994): 243-68.

[*In the following essay, Brennan theorizes about the epistemological significance of location in Acker's novel* Blood and Guts in High School.]

> In [the postmodern] situation, parody finds itself without a vocation; it has lived and that strange new thing pastiche slowly comes to take its place. Pastiche is, like parody, the imitation of a particular mask, speech in a dead language: but it is the neutral practice of such mimicry, without any of parody's ulterior motives, amputated of the satiric impulse, devoid of laughter and of any conviction that alongside the abnormal tongue you have momentarily borrowed, some healthy linguistic normality still exists. Pastiche is thus blank parody, a statue with blind eye-balls.
>
> —Fredric Jameson, "Postmodernism, or, The Cultural Logic of Late Capitalism"

> Whatever word one uses to describe the breakdown of the master discourses, it is clearly a question of a breakdown in the symbolic function, an inability of words to give form to the world—a crisis in the function of techne. Whether or not one wants to attribute this "agnosis" to a precise event or historical situation, the fact remains that the war between Res (God and thing) and Verba (his son and his word) has increasingly become a violent battle among jealous gods over the power of procreation; over the space which has begun to threaten all forms of authorship (paternity). If this space is maternal—and I think it is (if only for the male body and imagination)—what can be the feminist relationship to this desperate search through the maternal body characterizing our modernity?
>
> —Alice Jardine, *Gynesis*

> Politics don't disappear but take place inside my body.
>
> —Kathy Acker

Tangier

In the final section of *Blood and Guts in High School,* Kathy Acker's world-weary protagonist, Janey, finds herself in Tangier. There she encounters the famous French avant-garde author, Jean Genet, who tells her a story:

I knew a young sailor who was working on a ship in France. The maritime court of Toulon had exiled to Tangier an ensign who had turned over to the enemy the plans of some weapon or battle strategy or boat. Treason, at its best, is that act which defies the whole populace, their pride, their morality, their leaders and slogans. The newspaper said that the ensign acted ". . . out of a taste for treason." Next to this article was the picture of a young, very handsome officer. The young sailor was taken with this picture and still carries it with him. He was so carried away that he decided to share the exile's fate. "I shall go to Tangier," he said to himself, "and perhaps I may be summoned among the traitors and become one of them."[1]

Blood and Guts in High School

Genet's tale marks Tangier as an epistemological space, a place where "treason, at its best," may flourish. Indeed, Janey's progress from Merida, Mexico, where she lived in an incestuous liaison with her father, and from New York, where the Persian slave trader taught her to become a whore in a locked room, finally brings her to this iconoclastic territory where she believes even she might flourish. Janey's perceptions about culture (it "stinks" [*BG* [*Blood and Guts in High School*], 137]), her experiences with her father (who dumped her for Sally, "a twenty-one-year-old starlet who was still refusing to fuck him" [*BG,* 7]), and with the Persian slave trader (who dumped her when he found out she had cancer [*BG,* 116]) have prepared her for Tangier, and most especially for her encounter with Genet. Dumped from the world of the father and the world of the slave trader (which is, of course, an extension of the incestuous world of the father), Janey enters a place where, in Baudrillard's words, "there is a nonreflecting surface, an immanent surface where operations unfold":[2]

> What [had been] projected psychologically and mentally, what used to be lived out on earth as metaphor, as mental and metaphorical scene, is henceforth projected in reality, without any metaphor at all, into an absolute space which is also that of simulation.[3]

Like Genet's Tangier, Acker's subheading "Tangier" exists not so much as a "metaphorical scene" but as a sign/signifier whose only reference is to the unfolding operation of other signs/signifiers. Just as Genet's Tangier refers us to a newspaper article and a print of a photograph—the story of a story, the representation of a representation—Acker's subheading functions to designate an array of simulacra, where signs proliferate and counterfeit each other. In this sense, "Tangier," further specified as "excerpts from Janey's diary while she's in Tangier" (*BG,* 117), can be understood as designating a proliferation of textual and fictional surfaces, each signifying the other and thereby confounding the mental and metaphorical operations of the reader. Thus, Janey's diary begins by referring us to other fictions, most notably, nostalgic thirties and forties films, such as *Morocco* (1930) and *Casablanca* (1942):

> This time when I run after a man who doesn't want me, I'm *really* going to run after him.
>
> I'm sitting in the Café Tangier and smoking a cigarette.
>
> (*BG,* 117)

Here, Janey fashions herself as a version of, say, Marlene Dietrich, who, as Josef von Sternberg's ill-fated chanteuse, Amy Jolly, smokes as she sings in the cafe where she first encounters Foreign Legion Lieutenant Tom Brown (Gary Cooper) (*Morocco*). At the film's disconcerting and ambivalent conclusion, Amy joins the troop of "mad women" who follow the Legion into the desert, forsaking a life of luxury with Monsieur La Bessiere (Adolph Menjou), whose love for her is unequivocal. Janey's resolve to really run after her man "this time," which announces her intention to change the script, echoes, therefore, the resolve of Amy Jolly (Dietrich) and other "suicide passenger"[4] film heroines who have titillated and dismayed us.

It is especially interesting, therefore, that the man Janey pursues is the homosexual Genet and that she pursues him not for sexual reasons but in order to find out about writings—a turn that once again locates us in Acker's text and in Janey's diary. Indeed, the problem of feminine subjectivity is a textual, as well as a sexual, one, implicated as it is in the sexual/textual dilemma that positions women as objects of discourse and desire. The realm of the text and the realm of romance are thus inextricable, as Acker's ironic (and cinematic) description of Janey's encounter with Genet makes clear:

> Genet's walking. I walk slowly towards him. He stops, about three feet in front of me, his hands in his pockets, swaying slightly and leaning forward.
>
> I know I'm looking too hard at him. I say, "You're Monsieur Genet, aren't you?"
>
> He hesitates for a minute. He notices me but doesn't want to. "Who are you?"
>
> For a second I can't speak. "I'm a writer."
>
> He holds out his right hand to me. "Enchanté."
>
> (*BG,* 118)

Such a "romantic" (and writerly) encounter is suitably placed in Tangier not only because it recalls our own romantic fictions, such as Hollywood's Tangier, but because as a city situated at the northernmost tip of Africa, on the Strait of Gilbraltar, Tangier has always been an appropriate city, a sort of text upon which various imperialisms have inscribed themselves.[5] Tangier is, in this sense, a feminine territory that has been fought over and bartered by patriarchy in the same way that those tragic film heroines (Ingrid Bergman's Ilsa and Dietrich's Amy) who have found themselves trapped in the Middle East have often functioned as objects of exchange among powerful heroes who don't really want *them*.[6]

Nonetheless, Janey's project with Genet, as I hope to make clear, is to participate in this unstable textual territory made up of signs for signs (fictions of fictions) in order to create a space for feminine subjectivity. "This time," instead of being the plot-space upon which heroic men play out their heroic scenes, Janey wants to be the subject of her desires and discourse—she wants to be a writer. The new epistemology, marked by the simulated, "depthless" (in Baudrillard's sense) space of Tangier, which, according to Genet, is a place of exiles and traitors, seems to offer her this opportunity.

Such a territory (much like Acker's own text) may also recall the topography of postmodern writing, the flat collage of fragments that Fredric Jameson has termed "pastiche" and that he distinguishes from modernist "parody" as being a "neutral practice," a practice that does not redound to the "healthy linguistic normality" of patriarchal discourse.[7] In this new dimensionless, undiscriminating space, which is quintessentially a writing space, symbolized by the figure of French avant-garde homosexual author(ity), even the distinction between Janey and Genet (male/female, homosexual/woman), already phonetically approximate, may theoretically vanish.

This disruption of androcentric values by what appears to be a feminine territorialization of desire draws the embattled Janey to Tangier (as it has presumably drawn Acker to postmodern pastiche) and ultimately to Genet, who serves as a snapshot (like the ensign) of a hopeful new order. Janey's enthusiasm for Genet echoes the enthusiasm of French feminists for the fathers of modernity—Lacan, Derrida, Deleuze, among others[8]—and the feminist hope that the new epistemological territory will offer a real liberation for women. Acker's Tangier, whose traitorous possibilities are linked with the disruptive *écriture* that characterizes postmodernism, represents a space beyond the borders of dominant discourse systems, where the feminine may at last be written. Like Hélène Cixous, Janey is thus "overjoyed one day to run into Jean Genet" and seems to share Cixous's perception that Genet is one of the few men "who [isn't] afraid of femininity."[9] Like the young sailor, Janey hopes to be "summoned among the traitors and become one of them."

Genet's story about the young sailor, however, is instructive; for though "treason, at its best, is that act which defies the whole populace," the young sailor's yearning to break from the ranks of his military calling and to join the traitorous is founded on his homoerotic desire for the "young, very handsome officer" with whose photograph he has been "carried away." We might say that the young sailor is seduced by a representation that promises liberation from certain homophobic restraints imposed not only by the Navy but also by the pride, morality, leaders, and slogans of pa-

triarchal establishment. As patriarchy is bound up with phallic, Oedipal ideals—the military being a particularly apt synecdoche for a world whose apotheosis is "the real man"—so the very nature of treasonous homosexual desire will entail, for Genet and his followers into "modernity," a desire for the reappearance of the feminine. The new homoerotic order (as opposed to the old, *wholly* phallic one) will privilege the *jouissance* of feminine ecstasy, will allow the sailor to become as woman, "taken" or "carried away."

It is this appropriation of "the feminine"—the other, the pre-Oedipal, the gap (or *seme* or trace), *physis*, and *jouissance*—and the wary conjunction between feminism and postmodernism that Jardine asks feminists to consider in her brilliant study of modernity, *Gynesis*. If master discourses of modernity have indeed broken down, they are not, Jardine seems to imply, shut down but rather birthing themselves again and, as usual, through the figure of Woman. What should concern feminists, Jardine says, "[are] the uses of women as part of a radical strategy of reading and writing—the urgently explicit and unavoidable attempts of modernity to think the unnameable (God or Woman?) before it thinks 'us'."[10]

Indeed, Janey soon discovers that Genet's desire to be a woman is incommensurate with the political reality of women. Eventually she decides that

> Genet doesn't know how to be a woman. He thinks all he has to do to be a woman is slobber. He has to do more. He has to get down on his knees and crawl mentally every minute of the day. If he wants a lover, if he doesn't want to be alone every single goddamn minute of the day and horny so bad he feels the tip of his clit stuck in a porcupine's quill, he has to perfectly read his lover's mind, silently, unobtrusively, like a corpse, and figure out at every changing second what his lover wants. He can't be a slave. Women aren't just slaves. They are whatever their men want them to be. They are made, created by men. They are nothing without men.
>
> (*BG*, 130)

In Janey's/Acker's perception, Genet and the fathers of modernity do not concern themselves with the technology of gender, to borrow Teresa de Lauretis's term, which has given rise to the oppressed roles of women in social life. Rather, Genet wants to occupy a feminine territory that will permit him to slip among positionalities and to become both sadist and masochist, subject and object of his own discourse. Genet, as Janey rightly perceives, does not realize that to assume a woman's identity, her doubleness and ecstasy, he must also assume her cultural dilemma, her powerlessness and disease. Instead, he teaches her the same old stuff. The hierarchy she must memorize is "Rich men/poor men/ Mothers/Beautiful Women/Whores/Poor female and neo-female slut-scum/Janey" (*BG*, 130-31). In the guise of a writing mentor, "he kicks [her] around and tells her to be worse than she is, to get down, there, down in the shit, and learn" (**BG,** 131). When Janey envisions her future with Genet, she sees him spitting on her and kicking her:

> The more she tries to be whatever she wants, the more he despises her. Finally she decides her black wool hood and dress aren't enough. If Genet thinks she's shit, she should be invisible. When she follows him around she hides in the walls like a shadow. She secretly washes his dirty underpants. She takes on his moodiness and his hating.
>
> (**BG,** 131)

In fact, Genet, as Janey/Acker portrays him, participates in the transferential machinery in which the very identities of women are trapped.

Hence, Janey does not know how to be other than the servile creature "lying in the dirt outside Genet's ritzy hotel and dreaming of fucking rock n' roll stars" (**BG,** 130): She cannot manage to be other than the masochistic, contemptible woman of Genet's imagination/ projection. At the end of her travels with Genet, after she has traveled in the hot garb of an Arab woman with two slits for eyeholes (**BG,** 129), after she has visited the lowest whorehouses where even a "crippled drunken lobotomy case . . . controls the whores because he is a man" (**BG,** 129), after she is thrown in jail for stealing Genet's hash and a copy of *Funeral Rites* (**BG,** 133), and after Genet leaves to see a production of one of his plays, when, mimicking the negotiation of the world's oldest profession, "[he] hands Janey some money and tells her to take care of herself," Janey dies of cancer (**BG,** 140). Compared to the masterful writer, Genet, Janey's struggle to write "[doesn't] amount to a hill of beans in this crazy world" (*Casablanca*).

Thus, in a production that literally stages the death of the subject, Acker demonstrates the very different outcomes for male and female subjects in the seemingly "neutral" space of postmodernism. Janey's masochism, even her death—her very disappearance from Acker's pages—reifies Genet's conception of her. Indeed, it is Genet's conception, in every sense of this word, that has endowed her with the ability to be "whatever men want [her] to be," finally to be "nothing"—that is to say, dead—when Genet (or the father or the slave trader) ceases to conceive of her at all.

Postmodernism, Acker implies with Jardine, does not liberate women; rather, the new epistemology ensures the survival of "the engine of transference," to borrow a phrase from Jane Gallop, the projective machinery that compels women "to perfectly read [their] lovers' mind[s], silently, unobtrusively, like corpse[s]." Genet's homosexuality, so tantalizing to Janey and to Cixous, provides him with a strategy—a writing strategy—de-signed to re-hystericize women's bodies and, finally, to put the issue of feminine subjectivity to death. The death of the author, as Acker seems to see it, is a gendered phenomenon: Janey, the female protagonist who hammers a relentless and doomed heteroglossia throughout the novel—poems, journal entries, plagiarisms, translated Persian phrases scrawled in a large girlish script, hand-drawn dream maps—cannot survive. Only Genet, her writing mentor, her apparent double (in treason, in masochism), will live to see the production of his plays.

Thus, for Acker, the lure of Tangier and of Genet, the emblem of this new epistemological territory, does not change anything for women. As a writer who has chosen to write a postmodern text, to engage in "pastiche" and all the attendant "neutrality" of such a practice, Acker's challenge is to unravel the very politics of gender that have, once again, silenced a feminine subjectivity. To be sure, Jardine suggests that, historically, it is when women find their voices that the paradigms of the world seem to shift: "Might it not be that a series of if not causal at least etiological links could be established between those periods in the West when women were most vocally polemical and [these] so-called 'epistemological breaks'?"[11] We might wonder, with Jardine, if it is a coincidence that the "epistemological break" known as postmodernism on this continent and as modernity in France should occur at a time when the woman's movement has gathered considerable force on both sides of the Atlantic, when the individual and quite clearly gendered voices of women have become most eloquent. After all, as Acker suggests through her protagonist Janey, feminist fiction writers who want to engage in postmodern writing are expected to assume the gender-neutral, deliberate, representational blindness of "the statue with blind eyeballs"—to drop the parody and engage in pastiche.

In fact, Jameson's distinction between parody and pastiche is considerably vexed in Acker's writing. For Jameson, pastiche displaces parody in the same measure as a de-centered, open-ended discourse displaces the discourse of a centered and absolutist worldview. The postmodernism Jameson describes, devoid of patriarchal ideology—that is to say, "the healthy linguistic normality" of an earlier Oedipal paradigm—makes way, as we have seen in Genet's tale of the sailor, for a new homoerotics: Here, the treasonous subject is willing to split (like an amoeba) in order to proliferate. The feminine prerogatives—doubleness and *jouissance*—are embraced, as is a kind of theoretical castration. This "gynetic" agenda, however, as Jardine has observed, is deceptive. Women are sacrificed to the abstract theory of Woman, split into body and theory-of-the-body, cut off from themselves once more, and, in this sense, re-hystericized. What Acker's writing suggests is that pastiche is hardly a neutral mode but is impelled by some utopian longing of the male soul to reclaim its place in the "center" of language.

On the other hand, the peripheral discourses of feminism have managed to constitute an if not "normal" at least "healthy" praxis that sustains the laughter and conviction of parody. I am thinking of that growing body of feminist writers—Jardine, Mary Jacobus, Jane Gallop, Teresa de Lauretis, Nancy K. Miller, Peggy Kamuf, and Luce Irigaray (to name a very few)—who have taught us to tease out the subversive subtexts of the culture and to read "differently." It is this new feminist convention of reading (which is also a writing) that Acker engages in and, as I hope to demonstrate, pushes forward. Such a reading/writing relies on both pastiche and parody—parody to subvert pastiche and pastiche to engender parody—vacillating hysterically between the two modes, as Acker does, to present a fiction of feminine subjectivity. In this sense, Acker's novels both participate in postmodernism and disrupt this already disruptive thinking.

Blood and Guts in High School (1978), her second novel, attempts to explore the issues that have troubled the feminist fiction writer's entry into this new postmodern territory: How is the feminine subject inscribed in a text whose mission is to document the loss of subjectivity? How can a postmodern fiction writer expose the ruse of postmodern fiction—its "gynesis"—its recuperation of authority at the expense of women? How is hysteria, the privileged vacillation of feminine writing, preserved without collapsing into the pastiche of postmodern writing?[12] Finally, how (and this is another way of restating all of the above) is the feminist writer of fiction to continue her project of documenting the feminine personal and the feminine unauthorized in a project that has co-opted (indeed, erased) these very elements?

Acker's discoveries are necessarily incomplete and fragmentary, and will not always sound friendly.

MERIDA

If Acker's Tangier is the debased space of capitalism and Logos—the land, as "Genet" notes in his Journal, of "TRAITORS FASCISTS WHO NEED TO CONNIVE"—then Acker's Merida, where 10-year-old Janey lives with her father, represents an older, more familiar epistemology. Like Tangier, Merida exists beyond the borders of "culture" (which Acker equates with the United States' abject brand of blood and guts and stink). But Merida, unlike Tangier, is less a flat surface of unfolding operations than a historical disjuncture, the site of an inevitable struggle. Here, "the cheapest outdoor cafes" and "expensive European-type joints for the rich" exist in close proximity to tiny Mayan villages where "beautiful thin-boned" people live (***BG***, 13). "Mexicans think money is more important than beauty; Mayans

say beauty is more important than money," one of these villagers tells the narrator (***BG***, 13), thereby reading the age-old Mexican/Mayan struggle as a matter of aesthetics and economics.

Not surprisingly, in Merida, the industry of the poor—hemp, baskets, hammocks—is exploited by the rich hemp growers, who, we are told, "possess one boulevard of rich mansions" (***BG***, 13). While the Mexicans are engaged in an intricate capitalism, however, the Mayans are nonetheless implicated in a no less sinister practice of exchange: On Sunday, in a Mayan village, Acker's narrator tells us,

> the men, normally dignified and gentle, get drunk. The man driving the big yellow truck is the head man. All the male villagers are touching his hand. They're showing him love. He will get, they say, the first newborn girl. In return, he says, he will give them a pig. All of the men's bodies are waving back and forth. The women watch.
>
> (***BG***, 13)

In Acker's view, what links between two systems, Mexican and Mayan, is defined not only by the exploitation of one group by another but also by motifs of exploitation that characterize each. At the root of capitalism, Acker suggests (contrary to Marx), is the oppression of women, the male exchange of daughters for pigs. Such a practice, which takes Lévi-Strauss's kinship discoveries to a horrific conclusion, resonates uneasily with the Mayan preference for beauty over money—and, in fact, erases the distinction between beauty and money by making them exchangeable values: Daughters, somehow, equal pigs.

The women (mothers? daughters?), on the other hand, are clearly on the peripheries of this ritualistic exchange, as silent and motionless and mysterious as the Mayan ruins that everywhere leave enormous, provocative gaps in an otherwise populated topography:

> Mayan ruins, huge temples, all the buildings are huge, scary, on high. Low low land in centre. Everything very far apart. Makes forget personal characteristics. Wind blows long grass who! whoot! Jungle, not Amazonian swamp, but thick green leafage so beautiful surrounds. Hear everything. No one knows how these massive rectangular structures were used. Now birds screech in the little rooms in the buildings, fly away; long iguanas run under rocks. Tiny bright green and red lizards run down paths past one tiny statue, on lowish ground; on a small concrete block, two funny-monkey-hideous-dog-jaguar faces and paws back-to-back. Janus? The sun?
>
> (***BG***, 13)

The ruins, like the Mayan women, are spectacles of beauty as well as silent, perhaps two-faced, spectators. In the topography of Merida, they signify, like Woman, both absence and uncanny presence, designating a female territory, other and inconjunct from the rest. As "ruin," slowly crumbling over time, the Mayan site is also a figure for the mother's cut-up body, a figure that itself resembles Acker's pastiched text, suggesting, especially in this poetic and fragmented account, not only the dreamy half-remembered semiotics of the pre-Oedipal but also the geography of a woman's body, a site that is all too often perceived by patriarchy as "memorable" fragments. In Acker's description, we proceed downward from the high promontories of the buildings, "far apart" (like, perhaps, breasts), to the low belly "in centre" (*enceinte?*) to the "thick thick green leafage" (not a swamp, Acker is careful to tell us) like the pubis. Even the noises—the "who! whoot!" of the wind, birds screeching, lizards running—are like the semiotic "la langue"[13] that characterizes the pre-Oedipal, in which indeed "personal characteristics" are forgotten, entangled as they are in the mother's body.

If the Mexicans are distinct from the Mayans because of a "thinking" that privileges money over beauty, which results in a division between rich and poor, then the Mayans are set apart from their ancestors according to pure scale—tiny versus gigantic, therefore familiar versus "scary." The idealized space of the little villages and the humble, traditional industry of the people exist strangely within and without the impersonal vast spaces of the temples and buildings, whose use-value, like that of an ancient mother, is indeterminate, and whose habitation by screeching birds and running lizards evoke, as we've seen, an eerie pre-Oedipal *unheimlich*. We might see the ruins themselves—traces of a vanished *episteme*, here and not-here—as a matrix for the encounter of Mexican and Mayan, everywhere surrounding that encounter, which is itself fraught with ambivalence and a kind of uncanniness. In this sense, the ruins represent an "unconscious" of the present civilization, a maternal "chora" that always already erupts on the landscape and gives Merida significance as both a space of social revolution and a space of poetic language, in Kristeva's sense of those terms.[14]

Indeed, these borders between the present evolving society of Merida and the ancestral Mayan ruins are like the inconclusive, unstable borders between conscious and unconscious, or between the superego and the id, or between the symbolic and the semiotic. In all these processes, as Leon S. Roudiez notes in his Introduction to *Revolution in Poetic Language,* "there is a dialectic at work [that] comprises drives and impulses on the one hand, the family and society structures on the other."[15] It is within this familial/social dialectic, represented by the allegorized topography of Merida, that Acker's Janey constitutes herself in the novel. "Never having known a mother," Acker's narrator begins, "her mother died when Janey was a year old, Janey depended on her father for everything and regarded her father as boy-

friend, brother, sister, money, amusement, and father" (*BG,* 7). Acker illustrates these opening lines with a loose, sophisticated sketch captioned "boyfriend, brother, sister, money, amusement, and father." The sketch depicts two headless male figures, dressed identically in tee shirts and jackets, naked from the waist down. These figures are jauntily posed, hands on hips, as if modeling for the drawing—one full frontal view and the other a three-quarter view. Both display large penises—one graphically erect and the other pointed down, though not quite flaccid.

Acker's pastiche—her juxtaposition of text and drawing—reiterates the topography of Merida, the historical, political dialectic that operates between Mayan (hut)/Mexican (mansion)/Ancient (ruin). The absent/present mother—that is to say, the mother whose death generates the "portrait" of the father-in-two-poses—thus connects the historical with the psychoanalytic, the outside (territory of Merida) with the inside (territory of the self). Such conflation of two incommensurate realms becomes the foundation for Acker's reading of feminine subjectivity. Just as Merida is a site for a psychoanalytic reading within a historical, political paradigm, so the constitution of the daughter is situated, for Acker, not only in "Freud's family theater" (to borrow Deleuze and Guattari's phrase) but also in (patriarchal) history and politics.

In fact, Acker's witty pastiche systematically deconstructs and parodies Freudian, Lacanian, and Kristevan constructs by making the penis—clearly the focal point(s) of Acker's illustration—stand for "everything" Janey wants. This fantasy of the father's penis, which recalls Freudian theory,[16] is therefore linked to Janey's discovery of her own castration and to the attendant penis envy that accompanies this phase of femininity.[17] At the same time, Janey's depiction of the penis-in-two-poses forces the eye (the I) to shuttle between the two, an action that parodies Lacan's notion of split subjectivity.[18] In this sense, the portrait of Janey's father may be understood as a reconstitution of her own split self—a projection that occurs at the moment of the subject's enunciation and that, for Kristeva and Lacan, is the essence of the mirror stage.[19] Here, in fact, the configurations of father and daughter are hopelessly entangled, mirroring each other's splits, castrations, and hysteria to the point at which locating a difference between them is difficult, indeed.

Acker's/Janey's "portrait," clearly rooted in Freudian and Lacanian thinking, also reenvisions psychoanalytic paradigms by hystericizing the father into a series of multifarious identities, decapitating (castrating?) him and splitting him into two poses. Such specularization of the father transforms the daughter into a pornographer and the phallic father into a sex object, a consumable product. Feminized, the father's penis reflects the daughter's confused subjectivity, a subjectivity she has, in turn, borrowed (by assuming the phallus) from hegemonic, capitalist discourse. The fantasy of the father thus becomes a *mise en abîme* of the daughter's dilemma: "Never having known a mother," Janey is trapped in a language system signified by the phallus, which, according to Acker, at least, seems to be the equivalent of the father's penis.

Indeed, Acker's *misprision* of Lacan and Freud, her deliberate conflation of the penis and the phallus,[20] takes the issue of feminine subjectivity out of the realm of psychoanalysis and into the realm of feminist politics. As "boyfriend, brother, sister, money, amusement, and father," Janey's father's penis arguably becomes, like the body of the mother, the guarantor of all needs—the phallus. Even his castration, which is symbolized by his headlessness(es), is, in the context of Janey's/Acker's drawing, a rhetorical device, a trompe l'oeil that Acker creates in order to focus elsewhere—just as, Acker seems to suggest, the fathers of modernity have employed the rhetoric of psychoanalysis, emptied of sociopolitical content, to persuade us that we are all *castratos*.[21] In fact, the penis/phallus, far from being absent in Acker's/Janey's drawing, is tantalizingly doubled. Startlingly erect or gracefully unerect, the penis/phallus of the father is never not not-there but occasionally, shall we say, unwilling. Such a misreading of the penis/phallus echoes Nancy K. Miller's perceptive observation that "only those who have it can play with not having it."[22]

Acker's pastiche suggests that it is in the interstices of such "playing around"—not unlike the sexy masquerade of drag queens—that the split (male) subject appropriates feminine otherness into male representational systems and pretends to kill off gender difference. Janey's portrait of her father in two poses, like Genet's tale of the sailor, exposes the homoeroticism of the new epistemology. Because it is both subject and object, the mirror image of Janey's split subjectivity, the father's penis/phallus appropriates femininity in its wily masquerade. The frame of Janey's drawing, which reifies the frame of Lacanian psychoanalysis, renders feminine subjectivity impossible.

It is within this stifling paradigm, nonetheless, that Acker situates Janey. Like the topography of Merida, the site of the enunciated self commingles absence and presence, ancient and modern history. The body of the mother, narratively dismantled, becomes the site of the text itself, a *corps morcelé*, Acker's pastiche, which functions (like the mysterious Mayan ruins) as a place of disruption and inscription. The mother's absence-presence, consistent with Freudian and Lacanian psychoanalysis, thus becomes the ground upon which the daughter and father (or son and father) will play out the final (Oedipal) scenes of the family drama.

Acker, however, as we've begun to see, offers a parody of psychoanalysis by giving the Oedipal scene a peculiar twist. At the moment of the daughter's enunciation (Janey's entry into Acker's novel), it is the father who is suffering from an identity crisis. As her father's best friend Bill tells Janey, "You've dominated his life since your mother died and now he hates you. He has to hate you because he has to reject you. He has to find out who he is" (*BG*, 11). Bill's psychoanalysis refigures the family roles by casting Janey as the overbearing mother and her father as the daughter/son on the threshold of the Oedipal stage. The father-daughter relationship, for Bill, is really a son-mother relationship. Bill's analysis (like Janey's drawing) perverts Freudian theory by ignoring the distinctions between the Oedipal and pre-Oedipal, between the father and the mother, and even between the son and the daughter. Indeed, as "subject supposed to know," Bill is a pervert, since he had "once fucked Janey, but his cock was too big" (*BG*, 10) (Janey is 10, remember). Bill's pedophilia thus parallels the father's incest, but his slipping (as it were) into the role of psychoanalyst makes him, Acker seems to suggest, the biggest prick of all.

Likewise, Janey's constitution in Acker's text is perversely self-reflexive. Janey tells Bill: "Right now, we're at the edge of a new era in which, for all sorts of reasons, people will have to grapple with all sorts of difficult problems, leaving us no time for the luxury of expressing ourselves artistically" (*BG*, 10). Thus, Janey/Acker announces the demise of the luxury of the artistic expression—a luxury that is inseparable from the invention of the expressive self—simultaneously problematizing her own textual inscription. Just as the daughter's portrait of the father conflates and confuses the identity of each, so Janey becomes both Acker and not-Acker in the novel, both the authorial voice and whatever undermines and confuses the presence of authority: As author/parent/daughter/lover/10-year-old/adult—hysterical designations that recall us to the father's multiple identities in Janey's drawing—the writing self, whose integrity is shattered for "all sorts of reasons," associates with the maze of "all sorts of difficult problems."

Deleuze and Guattari point out that the classical family, as perceived by Freud, preserves its unity by the way it inscribes all the instability of the world into the family system.[23] By destabilizing family identities and, especially, family roles, Acker dissolves this drama that maintains the family. Such dissolution reverberates everywhere, collapsing the distinction between inside/outside (that is, the distinction between the family and the world, public and private realms), and exposes, therefore, the fiction of family unity. In Acker's/Janey's world, the fiction of the self, as founded on Freudian premises, is contaminated on all sides, afflicted, as is Janey's/Acker's text, with the rush of discourses—historical, political, psychoanalytical, literary, punk-porn-pop—that, "heard" together (in pastiche), constitute a kind of semiotic babble. What this suggests is that the self, in such a text, is indistinguishable from the mother's cut-up body, the self is indistinguishable from the text.

Unlike the mother, however, the self is not appropriated to serve as text; rather, the writing self in Acker's novel is mixed up in the text just as the pre-Oedipal child is mixed up in the Imaginary of the mother's gaze. In the same way, the author is mixed up with her character, so that "author," like "mother," becomes just one among many options for self-expression/enunciation.

Thus, Janey becomes the multiplicitous subject who expresses her own desires for the father; and Johnny, as we've seen in Janey's drawing, becomes the feminized, specular object of his daughter's desires. Daughter and father disappear in such exchanges, making way for Janey and Johnny, who function to parody and thus to expose "the intricate buttoning of incest and politics," as Kathleen Hulley puts it, that forms the basis for Acker's critique of culture.[24] It is at this point that things becomes "too entangled" for Johnny, and he, like Genet, dumps Janey. Once again, for masculine subjectivity to remain central, feminine subjectivity must be either appropriated (for the male) or rejected. It is precisely this unsettling entanglement between male and female subjectivities that Lacan tries to sort out when he pronounces the impossibility of feminine subjectivity: "About this pleasure, woman knows nothing," he insists.[25] Luce Irigaray counters:

> The question whether, in his logic, they can articulate anything at all, whether they can be heard, is not even raised. For raising it might mean that there may be some other logic, one that upsets his own. That is, a logic that challenges mastery.[26]

Like Irigaray, Acker challenges the mastery of the male postmodern text by raising the possibility of another articulation. The site of Merida, as we've seen, conflates geography and history with psychoanalysis, entangling these separate discourses in order to expose the problematic of feminine enunciation. In a drawing captioned "Merida," for example, a curled penis protrudes from zippered pants; a woman's hands flank the penis, one finger pointing to a spot within the man's public hair. So, too, history and politics (the outside world) are embedded, like lice, in the shadow of the father's penis, parodying (by revising) not only the conventions of inside and outside but also the psychoanalytic thinking that claims to sort out hysterical entanglements by banishing feminine desire. In fact, as Teresa de Lauretis argues, such entanglements must be tolerated in order to reach a feminist understanding of the female subject: "Feminism understands the female subject as one that

. . . is not either 'in ideology' or outside ideology (e.g., in science) but rather is at once inside and outside the ideology of gender, or . . . is at once woman and women."[27] Indeed, Janey, like the Janus figure who guards the portals of the Mayan ruins, engages in a monstrous double vision that affords her both an inside and an outside view. She is both her father's conception of her and that "other" Janey: hystericized and hysterical, wandering through Acker's text and writing through, or in spite of, "the lousy material conditions" that make any articulation of her subjectivity so difficult. Predicated on the death of the mother, Janey nonetheless presides over a sort of maternal "chora," a semiotic stream of poetic discourse that prevents the dogma of postmodern theory from taking hold.

NEW YORK

We might understand Merida to be a kind of Imaginary, a mirror-stage that continuously reflects/plays back a kind of narration/image that traps the protagonist and, as we've seen, sets the stage for her difficult enunciation. Tangier, on the other hand, is Symbolic—a writing space, specifically the scene of the treasonous discourse of postmodernism. This space, despite its allegiance to alterity and polyvalent writing schemes, does nothing, as we've seen, to radically alter the terms of enunciation for female subjects. As de Lauretis puts it, "The subject [of postmodernism] is envisioned as non-gendered—gender being precisely an effect of delusion, an imaginary construct, nothing to do with the Real[,] which is to say, once again, that the subject is still (usually) white and male."[28] New York, however, which in Acker's novel exists in between these problematic territories, attempts to represent—textualize—the unpresentable. As the site of confusion, poverty, the abject, and, indeed, remainders of every sort, New York is the place of the Real.[29] It is here that Janey "chooses" to live in a slum:

> Garbage covers every inch of the streets. The few inches garbage doesn't cover reek of dog and cat piss. All of the buildings are either burnt down, half-burnt down, or falling down. None of the landlords who own the slum live in their disgusting buildings.
>
> (*BG*, 56)

New York, as the textual centerpiece between Merida and Tangier—literally occurring at the middle of the novel—is a center in perpetual dissolution: not holding, over and over again. Like Acker's text, New York is heteroglossic—the slum neighborhood contains hookers, junkies, welfare Puerto Ricans, Ukrainian and Polish families, bums, pimps, a few white artists, and a few "semi-artists" "who . . . will never make it" (*BG*, 56). Everyone is poor and either imperiled, terrified, or dangerous. It is here, nonetheless, that Janey, in the words of Acker's subheading, "becomes a woman."

If a maternal "chora"[30] is alluded to in Merida, signaled by the Mayan ruins and by Janey's own textual forays into the pre-Oedipal semiotic, it nonetheless keeps its place. The ruins, as we've seen, leave gaps in the topography. The vast empty buildings, scary unoccupied spaces, around which the Mexican-Mayan civilization struggles flourish, become, in Acker's lexicon, the absence upon which history and politics are predicated. In New York, however, the reflexive movement of the mirror is shattered. Gone are the paradigms of psychoanalysis in which history and politics are played back, and vanished is the allegorical landscape that stages the absent-present motifs of psychoanalytic thinking. The "chora" (literally a container) of the maternal has erupted, infecting, confusing, and making no sense— just as, Acker seems to suggest, life for marginal, poverty-stricken people is chaotic and senseless, and, therefore, unpresentable, indeed inarticulable:

> Most people are what they sense and if all you see day after day is a mat on a floor that belongs to the rats and four walls with tiny piles of plaster at the bottom, and all you eat is starch, and all you hear is continuous noise, you smell garbage and piss which drips through the walls continually, and all the people you know live like you, it's not horrible, it's just . . .
>
> (*BG,* 57)

Acker's narrator's failure to say just what it is, beyond "not horrible," that inhabitants of New York City slums experience is an indictment of a bourgeois discourse that claims to be able to articulate everything in the name of the father. The Real, for Acker, may be unspeakable, but it exists. Like feminine subjectivity, the "other" logic of slums and crime has been relegated to the outskirts where it may be ignored and, eventually, repressed.

Janey's "choice" (to live in a slum) is thus questionable. If the slum represents, as I'm suggesting, a marginalized territory not unlike the territory of feminine desire, then, indeed, Janey's situation there would seem not to be a matter of her choosing. As a woman struggling to resist patriarchal constructs that invite her complicity, Janey would seem to have no choice but to locate herself, along with the hookers, bums, and junkies, outside the peripheries of mainstream culture. But enunciation, for women, is, inevitably, a choice—that is to say, an inevitable choice, an oxymoron that the opposing tensions of Woman and women inhabit. Janey's "choice" and her "becoming a woman" are, in this sense, conjoined in a textual project that attempts to reveal the hysterical contradiction at the root of theories of subjectivity. "Janey becomes a woman" (the subheading of a subversive text) has a double message—it refers both to Janey's kidnapping by the thug employees of the Persian slave trader (her co-option by male enterprise) and to the intense, and often maniacal, reading and writing that constitute her as a fluid entity-voice (not really a character) in Acker's novel.

In an effort to articulate this paradoxical formulation for feminine subjectivity, de Lauretis cites an oxymoron of Paul de Man, who, in attempting to illustrate the contradictory disjuncture between grammar and rhetoric and to preserve a sense of "a double, self-contradictory coherence," comes up with the phrase "subverted support." De Lauretis's interest in de Man's figure—indeed, her appropriation of it as a figure for the contradiction inherent in feminine discourse—is linked also to her interest in (and appropriation of) Jameson's notion (in *The Political Unconscious*) of a meaningful ideological subtext that may be unveiled by a reading process. A feminist reading of a feminine subject requires "a strategy of coherence" for de Lauretis, and her conflation of de Man's figure and Jameson's interpretive model creates a feminist rhetoric for such a strategy. Fittingly or not, her model participates in the very hysterical discourse it is trying to articulate:

> What has come to mind, as I struggle to put into words something that will not fit, like the sense of a double, self-contradictory coherence, is the figure that I teased out a while ago from de Man's discussion of the relation between grammar and rhetoric: the oxymoron of a "subverted support." The relation of women to woman, as well as the female subject's relation to narrative . . . seems to me to be graspable in that contradictory, mutually subversive, and yet necessary or coexisting relationship of grammar and rhetoric.[31]

Hence, in the discontinuous and contradictory relationship between grammar (signs) and rhetoric (narrative logic), de Lauretis finds an analogy to the paradoxical and hysterical presence/absence of Woman on "the scene of Western representation"[32]—as, perhaps, "reader/writer" and "read." "Teasing" de Man, and even Jameson, she is able to locate a hermeneutic model in feminist narrative, an ideological subtext that she suggests, quoting Jameson, "draws the Real [those contradictions which are unpresentable in master narratives] into its own texture."[33] The feminist writer, therefore, is always a feminist reader, a discoverer (and appropriator) of subtexts that subvert the historical and political regime of hegemonic representation systems.

It is finally the impossibility of creating such a text (or self) in desire, however, that causes Janey's dis-ease:

> The Persian slave trader finally decided Janey was ready to hit the streets. She had demonstrated that she knew how to make impotent men hard, give blow and rim jobs, tease, figure out exactly what each man wants without asking him, make a man feel secure, desirable, and wild. Now she was beautiful. There was only one thing wrong, at least according to the Persian slave trader. At this moment he found out that she had cancer.
>
> (*BG,* 116)

Janey, who becomes for the slave trader (or father or culture) the "ideal" woman, is simultaneously hystericized (diseased) by the process. Hysteria (like the monster in the text,[34] Janus/Janey), however, is two-faced. It is both a process in which women are trapped in male configurations and a strategy for enunciation, as the following analogy will make clear: "Having cancer," Janey/Acker writes,

> is like having a baby. If you're a woman and you can't have a baby 'cause you're so starving poor or 'cause no man wants anything to do with you or 'cause you're lonely and miserable and frightened and totally insane, you might as well have cancer. You can feel your lump and you nurse, knowing it will always get bigger. It eats you and gradually, you learn, as all good mothers learn, to love yourself.

> Janey was learning to love herself. Everything was shooting out of her body like an orgasming volcano. All the pain and misery she had been feeling, crime and terror on the streets had come out. She was no longer totally impotent and passive about her lousy situation. Now she could do something about the pain in the world: she could die.

> (*BG*, 116)

Cancer, like pregnancy, is the body's inscription of the teachings/desires of the slave trader/father/culture. At the same time, it is the body's revolt against these teachings/desires, a revolt that shoots out "like an orgasming volcano"—a metaphor that links pregnancy and disease to feminine desire, to feminine subjectivity, and, not coincidentally, to the volcanic surges of Acker's own novel. In Acker's/Janey's reading of her "cancer," we witness the transformation of the hystericized body, passive and impotent, to the hysterical speaking subject, powerful and articulate. Like pregnancy (and like Janey's/Acker's text), cancer is wildness "made public."

Nonetheless, in Acker's heavily ironic view, this powerful articulation depends upon the disappearance of its author. The analogy between motherhood and terminal illness heralds a troubled return of the mother in Acker's novel—this time refigured as cancer-ridden host and thus only temporarily (albeit significantly) resurrected as a trope. In the same way, Acker seems to speculate, postmodern writers have temporarily rhetoricized the mother's pre-Oedipal prerogatives in order to insist upon the death of subjectivity. In the last analysis, it seems as if the female subject is deprived of all hope, that the erasure of this wild feminine "publication," sealed by the authorial death that is exacted by the postmodern agenda, is inevitable.

THE WORLD

The epilogue to Acker's novel is a twenty-five page series of textual illustrations entitled "The World." The pages are unnumbered—like an art catalog? a comic book?—and tell a story that begins as a retelling of Genesis stories:

> A light came into the world. Dazzling white light that makes lightness dazzling burning Happiness. Peace. The forms of the ancient arts of Egypt this is the time that wolves come out of the trees.

Here, Acker's narrative voice shifts to the cool omniscience of biblical authority, perhaps since Janey, the passionate and self-questioning voice of feminine subjectivity, has disappeared from the novel. Or has she?

We might understand this voice to be either the voice of Acker, who survives her own protagonist, or the voice of Janey from beyond the grave, or both at once. Finally, what this voice-shift seems to suggest is that Acker can and cannot be split off from her female subject and from her text that inscribes the demise of feminine subjectivity. She (and Janey) are both dead and resurrected, in this sense, in the epilogue.

These undecidable borders between the author, Acker, and her subject, Janey (which I have had to convey as Janey/Acker in my own text), reified throughout the novel as the fragile borders between Acker's enunciative territories, may also recall Paul de Man's remarks on autobiography "as de-facement." In this unstable writing, de Man points out, "two subjects [are] involved in the process of reading in which they determine each other by mutual reflexive substitution."[35] Acker's creation of Janey as fictional subject could be understood as such a fiction itself, since it veils Acker's symbolic autobiography. At the same time, Janey "as subject" makes possible an articulation of the difficulties that autobiography itself veils: "the [mutually] reflexive substitution" between two subjects—author and protagonist. Acker's concern with feminine subjectivity requires such a strategy, since (1) that concern necessarily implicates her own enunciation as feminine/feminist author, and (2) her concerns with feminist authorship are problematized by postmodernism's insistence on the death of the subject/author, as we have seen. If, as Jameson observes, the cultural logic of late capitalism is characterized by the integration of aesthetic production into commodity production,[36] then women, whose bodies have long functioned as aesthetic commodities, must necessarily speak from outside of themselves, so to speak—hysterically.

Janey's resurrection in Acker's epilogue can therefore be understood as her epitaph, or as Acker's epitaph on the death of the female subject. This resurrection of a dead voice, the arrogation of authority to a dead author, may be familiar to us as the rhetorical figure of prosopopoeia, "a fiction," as de Man explains it, "of an apostrophe to an absent, deceased or voiceless entity, which posits the possibility of the latter's reply and confers upon it the power of speech."[37] Such a figure, for de Man, is generically linked to autobiography, since it unites the living with the dead. The use of prosopopoeia has a particular relevance in Acker's feminist fiction, since the complications of feminine enunciation and the attendant death of the subject in postmodernism would seem to require a metaphorical vehicle to resolve, or at least demonstrate, the certain political and narratorial ambivalence that is left hanging darkly at the end of Acker's novel.

Acker's last word, her "fiction of the voice-from-beyond the grave,"[38] functions, therefore, to alleviate the darkness of the inevitable death of the female subject. Within this pictorial, highly pastiched space, this voice, which has been figuratively silenced, speaks eloquently. The fact that Acker entitles her "apostrophe" "The World" loosens the textual screw, expanding it outward to include all that has been excluded from the liminal territories she has explored thus far.

At the same time, Acker's parody of Genesis stories seems also to be a parody of her own use of prosopopoeia. The tongue-in-cheek assumption of an authority that is traditionally male exposes that authority as a fiction and, like prosopopoeia, as a rhetorical trick. We are told,

> A human is a being halfway between an alligator and a bird who wants to be a bird. The ancient books say there are ways humans can become something else. The most important book on human transformation is hidden with the corpse Catullus in the Saba Pacha Cemetery in Alexandria because all books were written by dead people.
>
> Shall we look for this wonderful book? Shall we stop being dead people? Shall we find our way out of all expectations?
>
> (*BG*, 147)

Indeed, this narrative "we" sets out on a journey to Catullus's grave, finds him, and persuades him to tell where the "book" is hidden. Not only does the resurrected figure of Catullus parody the prosopopoeia of Acker's narrator (and vice versa), but the quest for a text of wisdom seems to recapitulate bitterly Acker's/Janey's futile textual search for a "magical" way to transform the feminine from the appropriated figure of postmodernism to speaking subject.

Moreover, Acker's narrative "we" implicitly includes the reader in its prosopoesis, as death becomes a figure for a state of mind and even a point of view, presumably the cultural point of view that has killed Janey. Therefore, when "we" find the book, we are able to fly, which in Acker's lexicon means to be "free souls," and "we [dream up] the world in our own image" (*BG*, 143, 163, 164):

> We are dreaming of sex,
> of thieves, murderers,
> firebrands,

> of huge thighs opening
> to us like this night.
>
> (*BG*, 163)

Hence, the circularity of cultural discourse, the inexorable link of word and image, seals "our" (cultural) fates by making real transformation impossible. Stuck in the trap of power and desire, we cannot change our conceptions and so continue to conceive the same way.

Yet, the figure that reconstitutes the dead author and all of us dead readers—which is to say, participants in the death of the female subject and in our own fates—also delivers Acker's instruction in the form of a parable. The parallels between this exegetic shift and the paradigmatic shifts in the Bible are worth noting, for as the Old Testament gives way to the New, the epistemes change: Parables, for one thing, displace creation stories.[39]

This is not to say that Acker would have women become didactic purveyors of parabolic wisdom but rather that, at the end of her novel, she instructs us to change our paradigms, to imagine the world differently. Finally, it is the imagination that Acker believes will create our freedom; fictions, hysterical and female, may make possible our human transformations.

"Soon many other Janeys were born and these Janeys covered the earth" (*BG*, 165), Acker's narrator assures us at the end, an assurance that is fraught with the ambivalence and instability of feminine fiction itself.

Notes

1. Kathy Acker, *Blood and Guts in High School* (New York: Grove Press, 1978), 119; hereafter cited in my text as *BG*.

2. Jean Baudrillard, "The Ecstasy of Communication," in *The Anti-Aesthetic: Essays on Postmodern Culture,* ed. Hal Foster (Port Townsend, Wash.: Bay Press, 1983), 127.

3. Baudrillard, "The Ecstasy of Communication," 128.

4. In von Sternberg's *Morocco,* the ship's captain refers to Amy Jolly, who has bought a one-way ticket, as one of those "suicide passengers [who] never return."

5. Historically, Tangier has seen the rule of the Phoenicians, Romans, Moors, Portuguese, and was transferred to the English in 1471. Divided between French and Spanish protectorates in 1912, it became an international zone administered by France, Spain, and Britain in 1923-1924. Under the rule of Spain during World War II, it was nonetheless the site of struggle for Axis powers. It wasn't returned to the Moroccans until 1956.

6. In *Casablanca,* for example, Ilsa (Ingrid Bergman) figures as the commodity that spurs the negotiations between Rick and Victor Lazlo. Eventually, the priorities of the patriarchy win out over the romantic entanglements of "three little people."

7. For more about postmodernism as "the yet untheorized original space of some new 'world system,'" see Fredric Jameson, "Postmodernism, or, The Cultural Logic of Late Capitalism," *New Left Review* 146 (July-August 1984): 59-92.

8. See Alice Jardine, *Gynesis: Configurations of Women and Modernity* (Ithaca: Cornell University Press, 1985). Jardine also includes Sollers, Bataille, Barthes, and male American postmodern fiction writers, such as Thomas Pynchon.

9. Hélène Cixous, "The Laugh of the Medusa," in *New French Feminisms,* ed. Elaine Marks and Isabelle de Courtivron (New York: Schocken Books, 1981), 255-56.

10. Jardine, *Gynesis,* 102.

11. Jardine, *Gynesis,* 93.

12. Jameson characterizes postmodernism as also demonstrating "a shift in the dynamics of cultural pathology." Hysteria, he claims, gives way to schizophrenia, since "the alienation of the subject is displaced by the fragmentation of the subject" (see "Postmodernism," 63). I will argue that Acker retains hysterical prerogatives, especially since the postmodern agenda continues to alienate women even as (or inasmuch as) it fragments her body for its texts.

13. See Julia Kristeva, *Revolution in Poetic Language,* trans. Margaret Waller (New York: Columbia University Press, 1984).

14. See Kristeva, *Revolution in Poetic Language,* 57-61.

15. Kristeva, *Revolution in Poetic Language,* 4.

16. See Sigmund Freud, "Femininity," in *The Complete Introductory Lectures,* trans. and ed. James Strachey (New York: Basic Books, 1966). "In the Oedipal Situation the girl's father has become her love object" (583). Freud explains that young women wish for the penis from their fathers, the penis their mothers have not given them (593).

17. Freud, "Femininity," 588.

18. See "The Mirror Stage as Formative of the Function of the I as Revealed in Psychoanalytic Experience" and "The Agency of the Letter in the Unconscious," in Jacques Lacan, *Écrits: A Selection,* trans. Alan Sheridan (London: Tavistock Publications, 1977), 1-7 and 146-75, respectively.

19. See Lacan, "The Mirror Stage," 1-7. Also see Kristeva, *Revolution in Poetic Language,* 46-48, for a reiteration of Lacan's concepts of the mirror stage and its links to the thetic, or phase of enunciation.

20. In "Femininity," Freud refers to the mother's phallus (penis), which has been unavailable to the little girl (593). Lacan bases his notion of the mother's phallus on the Freudian notion and extends the idea. In Lacan, the phallus (of the mother) becomes "the privileged signifier of that mark where the share of the logos is wedded to the advent of desire" (see Jacques Lacan, "The Meaning of the Phallus," in *Feminine Sexuality,* trans. Jacqueline Rose and Juliet Mitchell (London and New York: Routledge, 1988), 82. It is crucial to Lacanian psychoanalysis that the phallus, a "veiled" signifier of desire, not be confused with the male organ, the penis. Such a confusion would problematize Lacan's theory of feminine sexuality—which is what I believe Acker is trying to do.

21. See Lacan, "The Meaning of the Phallus," in *Écrits,* 74-85, and "The Mirror Stage" for a thorough discussion of castration and split (castrated) subjectivity.

22. Nancy K. Miller, "The Text's Heroine: A Feminist Critic and Her Fictions," in *diacritics* 12 (1982): 50.

23. Gilles Deleuze and Félix Guattari, *Anti-Oedipus: Capitalism and Schizophrenia,* trans. Robert Hurley et al. (New York: Viking, 1977).

24. Kathleen Hulley, "Transgressing Genre: Kathy Acker's Intertext," in *Intertextuality and Contemporary American Fiction,* ed. Patrick O'Donnell and Robert Con Davis (Baltimore: Johns Hopkins University Press, 1989), 171. I am indebted throughout this study to Hulley's perceptive analysis of Acker's intertextuality.

25. Lacan, "God and the Jouissance of the Woman," in *Feminine Sexuality,* 145.

26. Luce Irigaray, "Cosi Fan Tutti," in *This Sex which Is not One,* trans. Catherine Porter (Ithaca: Cornell University Press, 1985), 90.

27. Teresa de Lauretis, *The Technologies of Gender* (Bloomington: Indiana University Press, 1987), 114.

28. de Lauretis, *Technologies of Gender,* 123.

29. See Jane Gallop, *Reading Lacan* (Ithaca: Cornell University Press, 1985). "The Imaginary will always block us from apprehending the real (the original text)" (67), and "there is no direct apprehension of the real, no possible liberation from

imagoes" (70). Gallop explains that for Lacan, "the symbolic and the imaginary along with the real are tied together" (70). Jameson, as recapitulated by de Lauretis, seems to be after something like this when he asserts the possibility of reweaving the Real into the texture of an interpretive text. See Fredric Jameson, *The Political Unconscious: Narrative as Socially Symbolic Act* (Ithaca: Cornell University Press, 1981), 81. De Lauretis, as I go on to summarize, relies on Jameson's perception in order to suggest a way to understand a feminine/feminist textual praxis.

30. See Kristeva, *Revolution in Poetic Language,* 26. Kristeva's use of *chora* is derived from Plato, who saw it as a receptacle. Kristeva complicates Plato's idea, asserting that the chora "as rupture and articulations (rhythms) precedes evidence, verisimilitude, spatiality, and temporality." At the same time, Kristeva says that we "move with and against the chora" and that the chora can be designated and regulated." In this sense, Kristeva keeps the notions of receptacle/container/chora as a discrete entity—just as the pre-Oedipal is distinct from the Oedipal, for example. In a certain kind of discourse (postmodernism), as I have argued through Baudrillard and Jameson, these distinctions vanish.

31. de Lauretis, *Technologies of Gender,* 115.

32. de Lauretis, *Technologies of Gender,* 113.

33. de Lauretis, *Technologies of Gender,* 111.

34. See Barbara Johnson, "My Monster/My Self," *diacritics* 12 (1982): 10, for a discussion of the monster in the text; also see Mary Jacobus, *Reading Woman: Essays in Feminist Criticism* (New York: Columbia University Press, 1986), 16-24 and 229-48, for a reading of this figure as bisexual and hysterical.

35. Paul de Man, "Autobiography as De-facement," in *MLN* [Modern Language Association] 94 (1979): 921.

36. Jameson, *Political Unconscious,* 56.

37. de Man, "Autobiography as De-facement," 926.

38. de Man, "Autobiography as De-facement," 927.

39. See Frank Kermode, *The Genesis of Secrecy: On the Interpretation of Narrative* (Cambridge: Harvard University Press, 1979) for a fuller discussion of parables, which are themselves vehicles for a duplicitous discourse. "Parable, it seems, may proclaim a truth like a herald does, and at the same time conceal a truth like an oracle. . . . [A] double function, this simultaneous process of proclamation and concealment" (47).

Rod Phillips (essay date spring 1994)

SOURCE: Phillips, Rod. "Purloined Letters: *The Scarlet Letter* in Kathy Acker's *Blood and Guts in High School.*" *Critique* 35, no. 3 (spring 1994): 173-80.

[*In the following essay, Phillips postulates the reasons why Acker chose to "plagiarize" Nathaniel Hawthorne's* The Scarlet Letter *in her novel* Blood and Guts in High School.]

In the years since critics first took notice of Kathy Acker, considerable comment has been made on her use of other writers' language and plot lines in her fiction—and rightfully so. Acker has taken literary "borrowing" to its most bizarre extreme. Large portions of her books are undisguised reworkings of earlier writers' fictions; often such passages are used verbatim with no clue as to where the borrowed material ends and Acker's own language begins. Her 1982 work, *Great Expectations,* has as the title of its first section a single word: "Plagiarism." The novel's first few lines do indeed live up to the title:

> My father's name being Pirrip, and my Christian name Philip, my infant tongue could make of both names nothing longer or more explicit than Peter.

> (*Great Expectations* 5)

In her earlier works, Acker chose to supply her readers with footnotes or authorial credits when she made use of other writers' words; but as her career progressed, she dropped this convention and has since borrowed, paraphrased, and plagiarized from the words and ideas of others with impunity. Ironically, plagiarism—the negation of another writer's trademark—has become one of the most distinctive trademarks of Acker's own fiction.

In fiction as experimental, fragmented, and disorienting as Acker's, these moments of familiar text can provide brief comfort in an otherwise very uncomfortable body of work. As critics, we are trained to look for "keys" to a text's "meaning," such as allusion, influence, and symbol. This is, no doubt, why so many of Acker's critics have made mention of the element of plagiarism in her art. As critics trained in the analysis of more traditional forms of literature, we may feel uncertain of how to approach many aspects of Acker's writing: her multigeneric style, her merging of visual art with text, and her shifting, often unreliable, narration. But we recognize Dickens when we see it (and Hawthorne, and Jong, and Genet), and we feel compelled to make use of these familiar handholds as a way of making meaning within Acker's fictions.

But, unfortunately, most critics have done little more than note that plagiarism is an element in Acker's writing; little analysis has been done of how it functions in her work. Poet and critic Ron Silliman (himself a character in Acker's novel *The Adult Life of Toulouse Lautrec*) has offered an oversimplified equation for what he calls the "persistent formula" for Acker's fiction: "plagiarism + pornography = autobiography" (165). Other critics have been almost as dismissive in their remarks on Acker's borrowings. Larry McCaffery, one of the first critics to deal seriously with Acker's work, also has put forth a rather limited view of the purpose and function of Acker's plagiarism of earlier, more well-known texts:

> Part of the point behind such strategies is to foreground textual jouissance, to insure that readers perceive that the "unity" found here is not produced by the questionable concept of an authorial ego or character "identity," but results from a confrontation with a consciousness presenting moments in its experience-in-practice.
>
> (225)

Both critics are correct—at least in part. Acker's plagiarism is, as Silliman suggests, one of the ways in which she talks about her own life. And it is also, just as McCaffery points out, a means of unsettling reader expectations about authorial identity. But there is more to Acker's extensive use of plagiarized material than either critic's explanation can afford.

Acker's 1978 work, *Blood and Guts in High School,* may offer some answers concerning the purposes, and the effects, of her plagiarism. The novel deals with a ten-year old's journey through a dark world whose most distinct features are the absence of love and the presence of sexual perversion. Janey, Acker's protagonist, is the victim of first, her father's incest and second, his rejection. Forced to live on her own in New York City, Janey enters into a life of drugs, gratuitous sex, and violence—culminating in her kidnapping and captivity at the hands of a "Persian slave trader" (61).

Like her other fictions, *Blood and Guts* contains a number of borrowings from other texts and from popular culture. The figures of Erica Jong, Jean Genet, and Jimmy Carter, among others, drift in and out of Acker's text like players in a nightmare. But the authorial presence most clearly felt in the book, except for Acker's of course, is that of Nathaniel Hawthorne. While Janey is being held captive by the Persian slave trader, she lives in total isolation, with no outside contact except for daily visits from her captor—visits in which she is "taught to be a whore." "One day she found a pencil stub and a scrap of paper in a forgotten corner of the room," Acker writes. "She began to write down her life." What follows is a lengthy section entitled "A Book Report," in which Janey writes, ostensibly at least, about Hawthorne's *The Scarlet Letter.* From the start, however, it is clear that Janey is indeed "writing down her own life" as much as she is engaging in a book report. "We all live in prison," she begins. "Most of us don't know we live in prison" (65).

The question arises: Why select Hawthorne's *Scarlet Letter* as the fictional device with which to describe Janey's life? What qualities make Hawthorne's novel, written over one and a quarter centuries earlier, suitable collage material for Acker's postmodern, punk fiction? One answer, certainly, lies in the similarity of the two protagonists. Both are female outsiders who violate societal rules. Both are victims of male oppression, and both are in some way imprisoned. Most importantly, perhaps, both are "prisoners" of their own desire to be loved.

The popularity and high regard of Hawthorne's novel may suggest a second reason for Acker's use of the book. Few books can be considered to be universally known by Americans, but *The Scarlet Letter* is certainly one of the most widely taught novels in American schools. It follows that if Acker were seeking a work to use as a source of symbol and meaning, she would select a well-known text like Hawthorne's. Beyond this instant recognition, however, Larry McCaffery suggests a more perverse reason for using the novel in Acker's work. He notes the punk penchant for "crossing images together unexpectedly." Often this is done, McCaffery writes: "by profaning, mocking, and otherwise decontextualizing sacred texts (Johnny Rotten blaring out 'God Save the Queen,' . . .) into blasphemous metatexts" (221). *The Scarlet Letter,* with its high position in the canon of American literature, is ripe for this type of approach. What, after all, could be more unexpected than a juxtaposition of Puritan and punk cultures? This may be at the root of Acker's choice of Hawthorne's "sacred text."

Early in her "book report," Acker's Janey engages in the kind of image crossing that McCaffery speaks of. By joining together thumbnail sketches of Hester Prynne's world and Janey's, Acker is able to discuss the current position of women in American society:

> Long ago, when Hawthorne wrote *The Scarlet Letter,* he was living in a society that was more socially repressive and less materialistic than ours. He wrote about a wild woman. This woman challenged the society by fucking a guy who wasn't her husband and having his kid. The society punished her by sending her to gaol, making her wear a red 'A' for adultery right on her tits, and excommunicating her.
>
> (66)

In the next paragraph, Janey abruptly shifts from her "book report" on Hester's life and times and focuses on the realities of her own:

> Nowadays most women fuck around 'cause fucking doesn't mean anything. All anybody cares about today is money. The woman who lives her life according to nonmaterialistic ideals is the wild antisocial monster: the more openly she does so, the more everyone hates her.
>
> (66)

Clearly Acker is engaging in social criticism by using the borrowed text as a touchstone for Janey's present reality. By attempting to assimilate Hawthorne's world, Janey tries to understand the forces of history that have led to what she sees as the near collapse of her society:

> The society in which I'm living is totally fucked-up. I don't know what to do. . . . If I knew how society got so fucked-up, if we all knew, maybe we'd have a way of destroying hell. I think that's what Hawthorne thought. So he set his story in the time of the first Puritans: the first people who came to the northern North American shore and created the society Hawthorne lived in, the society that created the one we live in today.
>
> (66)

But Acker's use of Hawthorne's text allows for more than just a simple critique of American society; it also gives her a device with which to discuss the powers and the limitations of literature. Locked in her cell-like room, Janey uses a series of images—Hawthorne's novel—to describe her condition, to "write down her life." Soon after, however, she finds a Persian grammar book and begins to learn to write and compose poetry in Persian. The language system of her captor, the Persian slave trader, replaces, for a time at least, the language and plot of Hawthorne's tale. Unstated, but implicit in this plot development, is the idea that we adopt—perhaps without knowing it—the language of our oppressors. Just as the slave trader's grammar book has colored and shaped Janey's thinking, so have Hawthorne and all those who have contributed to the "fucked-up culture" to which she belongs.

Janey, unlike Acker, seems quite unaware of the power that the literature of her oppressors has over her. She negates the power of the written word—claiming it to be a part of a much older time. Hawthorne, she says, "was living in a society to which ideas and writing still mattered" (66). Janey sees her position as a writer as nearly meaningless—because literature is treated as a commodity:

> Right now I can speak as directly as I want 'cause no one gives a shit about writing or ideas, all anyone cares about is money. . . . A book that can be advertised. Define culture that way.
>
> You see, things are much better nowadays than in those dark old repressed Puritan days: anybody can say anything today; progress does occur.
>
> (66)

Blind to the power that literature has had over her, Janey believes her own pen to be powerless. Unlike Hawthorne, who had to cloak "all the wild things he wanted to say" because his society valued ideas, Janey can say anything she wants because ideas no longer matter.

Janey's comments on the commodification of literature may point to another reason behind Acker's use of other writers' texts. In a time when the only ideas that count are those that "will net a half-million in movie and/or TV rights" (66), perhaps Acker's borrowings from Hawthorne and other writers is a radical denial of literature as property. McCaffery has noted that deeply ingrained in the punk aesthetic is a distrust of the "conventions which govern traditional artistic forms"—a belief that "the traditions and language of Great Art had derived from the same elitist, authoritative sensibility that had elevated profit and reason at the expense of human needs and feelings" (220). By using Hawthorne or other writers, as the basis for her own text, Acker may be rejecting the notion that art can be turned into property, and in turn may be rejecting the entire system that has tried to do so. Under such a mindset, plagiarism is not stealing because that which cannot be owned cannot be stolen. Words and ideas then, are not property but are free-floating objects that (like the title of the Poe story which I've used as the title for this essay) can be used freely by all.

For Janey, this characteristic punk distrust of literature and culture is an enigma. She faces the Catch 22 of wanting to rail against her culture but finding that she has no means to do so except those that are culturally prescribed (i.e., a book report on Hawthorne). Later, in her "Persian Poems," Janey again faces this problem. One of her poems, written in Persian and translated, reads:

> Culture stinks: books
> and great men and the
> fine arts
> beautiful women
>
> (73)

Written in the language of her captors, the poem—like the book report—is a product of the culture that Janey so violently hates.

But the possible reasons for Acker's use of Hawthorne that I've outlined so far—forum for social critique, symbol for male literary dominance, and subject for punk literary anarchy—may prove to be secondary to what I believe to be the main effect realized by the author's borrowings from *The Scarlet Letter.* Above all, I think, the sections of the novel dealing with Hawthorne allow a radical feminist reworking of the story of Hester Prynne—a kind of "taking back" of a woman's story from a male author. By removing the story of Hester Prynne and her daughter Pearl from the limits of Hawthorne's text and placing them in Janey's consciousness, Acker both modernizes and feminizes the novel.

The *Scarlet Letter* section of the book is not the only part of **Blood and Guts** in which Acker voices the desire to revise male texts along feminist lines. In the section of the novel in which Janey travels with French novelist Jean Genet, she notes a passage from Genet's autobiographical novel *Le Journal du Voleur* in which the author describes his masochistic joy at being "beaten up and hurt" by his male lovers. Janey's response is not one of recognition with her own situation as a woman who has had similar experiences; instead, it is one of disgust at his lack of understanding for the true position of women in a male-dominated culture:

> Genet doesn't know how to be a woman. He thinks all he has to do to be a woman is slobber. He has to do more. He has to get down on his knees and crawl mentally every minute of the day. If he wants a lover, if he doesn't want to be alone every single goddamn minute of the day and horny so bad he feels the tip of his clit stuck in a porcupine's quill, he has to perfectly read his lover's mind, silently, unobtrusively, like a corpse, and figure out at every changing second what his lover wants. He can't be a slave. Women aren't just slaves. They are whatever men want them to be. They are made, created by men. They are nothing without men.
>
> (130)

The passage is a telling one concerning the authenticity of texts written by men about women. Genet, although perhaps closer in his experience to what Janey sees as the position of women in society, still lacks the necessary emotional, physical, and social conditioning to portray accurately the experience of being a woman. In Janey's view, Genet has the wrong mind-set, the wrong genitals, and the wrong social status to do anything more than play-act the role of woman.

The type of feminist correction to which Janey submits Genet's text is also at the heart of her treatment of Hawthorne's novel. The story line of the book is taken back from Hawthorne and his omniscient narrator as Janey and Hester merge in Acker's text. The structure of Acker's text becomes more confused and fragmentary as Janey's isolation and illness change the form of her discourse from a standard high school book report to a hallucinatory stream of consciousness:

> Everything takes place at night.
> In the centres of nightmares and dreams,
> I know I'm being torn apart by my needs,
> I don't know how to see anymore.
>   I'm too bruised and I'm scared. At this point in
> *The Scarlet Letter* and in my life politics don't
> disappear but take place inside my body.
>
> (97)

As Janey's assimilation of Hester's character becomes complete, all punctuation that might have separated the quoted material of Hester from Janey's speech disappears. Janey seems to melt into the character of Hester Prynne, voicing openly the desires of the heroine from Hawthorne's novel. But the words she uses also fit her own situation; it is a speech that could be addressed to either Hester's Reverend Dimmesdale or Janey's absent, incestuous father:

> I want to fuck you, Dimwit. I know I don't know you very well you won't ever let me get near you. I have no idea how you feel about me. You kissed me once

with your tongue when I didn't expect it and then you broke a date. I used to have lots of fantasies about you: you'd marry me, you'd dump me, you'd fuck me. . . . Now the only image in my mind is your cock in my cunt. I can't think of anything else.

> I've been alone for a very long time. I'm locked up in a room and I can't get out. . . . I don't know how to talk to people, I especially have difficulty talking to you; and I'm ashamed and scared 'cause I want you so badly, Dimwit.
>
> (95)

Critic Linda Hutcheon has written that the type of postmodern intertextuality that we see in passages such as this is a "manifestation of both a desire to close the gap between past and present for the reader and a desire to rewrite the past in a new context" (67). The two texts—Hawthorne's and Acker's—ricochet off each other, creating, if not great art, at least a brief moment of recognition in the reader's mind concerning their connectedness. Such a text, Hutcheon writes:

> uses and abuses these intertextual echoes, inscribing their powerful allusions and then subverting that power through irony. In all, there is little of the modernist sense of a unique, symbolic, visionary "work of art"; there are only texts, already written ones.
>
> (67)

Clearly, in the section of **Blood and Guts** dealing with Hawthorne, Acker attempts, as Hutcheon says, "to rewrite the past in a new context." But in Acker's novel, such a revision of older texts does not just involve the addition of a feminist subtext or the inclusion of pornographic elements to the original work: it also involves experimentation with language that strives to break free from traditional genres (like the Romantic novel) and move toward a more meaningful form. "TEACH ME A NEW LANGUAGE, DIMWIT," Janey writes, "A LANGUAGE THAT MEANS SOMETHING TO ME" (96).

One passage that illustrates this quest for a "new language" occurs when Janey engages in a "lesson" with another voice in Acker's text. Prefaced with the line "Teach me a new language," the passage involves an exercise in repetition of simple phrases, first uttered, presumably, by a male voice (perhaps Hawthorne's Reverend Dimmesdale) and then repeated by Janey. At first, Janey repeats the lines verbatim; but as the lesson continues, she begins to alter the phrases—subtly at first, and then radically:

"The night is red."	"The night is all around me and it's black."
"The streets are deserted."	"I can't even see the streets from my room; how would I know if they're deserted?" (96)

The passage is emblematic of the entire section of the novel dealing with Hawthorne. It begins with an acceptance of the male voice (Hawthorne's text) but finally Janey begins to question and ultimately reject the syntax and logic of her teacher's voice. What began as a straightforward exercise in repetition (plagiarism) ends in a complete rejection of authority and a further blurring of "sanity and insanity":

"The children in the city are going insane."	"How can I tell the difference between sanity and insanity? You think in a locked room there's sanity and insanity?" (96)

The "new language" that Janey strives for, this departure from the traditional, male-dominated form of the novel (represented by Hawthorne and Dimmesdale), takes many forms in Janey's reworking of *The Scarlet Letter.* Often, her ramblings seem almost incoherent, as in this prose paragraph that melts suddenly into poetry:

> Sex in America is S & M. This is the glorification of
>   S & M and slavery
> and prison. In this society there was a woman who
> freedom and suddenly the black night opens up and
> fucked a lot and she got tied up with ropes and
> on upward and it doesn't stop
> beaten a lot and made to spread her legs too wide
> the night is open space that goes on and on,
> this woman got so mentally and physically hurt
> not opaque black, but a black that is extension
> she stopped fucking even though fucking is the thing
>   to do.
>
>   (99)

On its surface, the poem seems a jumble of images, without any real relation to the rest of the text. But at work here is one of the "new language" systems that Janey speaks of. By reading alternate lines of the poem, a new meaning emerges: one that has considerable relevance to the stories of both Hester and Janey:

> In this society there was a woman who
> fucked a lot and she got tied up with ropes and
> beaten a lot and made to spread her legs too wide
> this woman got so mentally and physically hurt
> she stopped fucking even though fucking is the thing
>   to do.

For Kathy Acker, the rejection and subversion of the traditional forms of discourse that have been dominated by males seem as important as the subversion of their meanings. Her fictions may begin with what seem to be borrowings, extensions, or plagiarisms of male works; but they move quickly beyond these original works—into new meanings and new forms that their authors could never have imagined. Larry McCaffery has called Acker's work "fiction to slam dance by" (228). Acker

at times also seems to downplay the complexity of her work: "Everything is surface," she writes, "that everything is me: I'm just surface: surface is surface" (Blood 97). But her work is more than just "surface," more than just simple "plagiarism," more than just punk "fiction to slam dance by." Acker's ***Blood and Guts in High School,*** with its strange and complex reworking of Hawthorne, offers a new and powerful perspective on literature and gender in postmodern America.

Works Cited

Acker, Kathy. *Blood and Guts in High School.* 1978. New York: Grove, 1989.

———. *Great Expectations.* 1982. New York: Grove, 1989.

Hutcheon, Linda. "'The Pastime of Past Time': Fiction, History, Historiographic Metafiction." *Postmodern Genres.* Ed. Marjorie Perloff. Norman: U of Oklahoma P, 1988.

McCaffery, Larry. "The Artists of Hell: Kathy Acker and 'Punk' Aesthetics." *Breaking the Sequence.* Ed. Ellen G. Friedman and Miriam Fuchs. Princeton: Princeton UP, 1989.

Nissenbaum, Stephen, preface, *The Scarlet Letter and Selected Writings,* by Nathaniel Hawthorne. New York: Modern Library, 1984. vii-lxviii.

Sciolino, Martina. "Kathy Acker and the Postmodern Subject of Feminism." *College English* 52 (1990): 437-45.

Silliman, Ron. "New Prose, New Prose Poem." *Postmodern Fiction: A Bio-Bibliographical Guide.* Ed. Larry McCaffery. New York: Greenwood, 1986.

Sam McBride (essay date summer 1999)

SOURCE: McBride, Sam. "Un-Reason and the Ex-Centric Text: Methods of Madness in Kathy Acker's *Great Expectations.*" *Critique* 40, no. 4 (summer 1999): 342-54.

[*In the following essay, McBride examines the methods Acker employs to render madness in her novel* Great Expectations.]

> *They call me CRAZY. [. . .] I just don't believe there's any possibility of me communicating to someone in this world.*
>
>   (*Great Expectations* 74)

Madness is perpetually bound up with contemporary works of art. Michel Foucault, toward the end of *Madness and Civilization,* describes contemporary texts as frequently "explod[ing] out of madness" (286), creating a dialectic in which madness and art continually, radically oppose one another. The relationship between unreason and art becomes one of competition, "a game of life and death" (287). An insurmountable gulf exists between the two because "madness is the absolute break with the work of art" (287), which tries to make sense of the world.

Shoshana Felman, reading Foucault (as well as Jacques Derrida's reading of Foucault), defines such madness in *Writing and Madness,* as an "irreducible resistance to interpretation" (254) and implies that all texts, including her own, are incapable of being completely, accurately, reliably interpreted. Texts, therefore, are inhabited by madness, which works as and against the text. All texts oppose yet are filled with madness.

The text-madness dichotomy must have a profound impact on a writer attempting to write (or write about) madness. Foucault, according to Felman, felt compelled to "search for a *new status of discourse,* a discourse which would undo both exclusion and inclusion, which would obliterate the line of demarcation and the opposition between Subject and Object, Inside and Outside, Reason and Madness" (42, italics Felman's). Such a project, Foucault realized, is inherently impossible because the notion of Madness "speaking itself" carries with it the problematic concept of "senseless words anchored by nothing in time" (qtd. in Felman 43). Foucault himself, judging by the fact that he worded his history of madness in the form of truth-statements, was apparently trying to "make sense," using words "anchored" to some communicable meaning, even to the extent of attempting to convince his reader of the "rightness" of his own interpretation of history (as events grounded "in time"). The impossibility of speaking

> I couldn't understand why anyone would read me. I honestly thought I was writing the most unreadable stuff around.
>
> ("McCaffery interview with Kathy Acker" 90)

or writing taking any form but logic is, according to (Felman's reading of) Derrida, one of the primary critiques of Foucault's project.

So any project of "writing madness" is doomed; yet Felman's observation remains that texts that "are not conscious [of] (are not *present to*) their own madness, [are . . .] the very madness they are speaking about" (252, Felman's italics). How then can a writer of texts remain simultaneously aware of both the inability

> I'm going to tell you something. The author of the work you are now reading is a scared little shit. [. . .] She doesn't believe what she believes [. . .] She doesn't know a goddamn thing [. . .] so anything she's writing is just un-knowledge.
>
> (*Great Expectations* 70-71)

to write madness and the inherent madness of his or her own text, yet still attempt to write? How can a writer, if not *speak* madness, at least somehow *paraphrase* it, *point to* it, *allow it* to emerge from the text? If Derrida is correct that "madness, being in its essence *silence,* cannot be rendered, *said* through logos" (Felman 46, Felman's italics), then can an author use some "non-logos" technique to render madness? To *render*: "to surrender or relinquish: yield; to represent in a[n . . .] artistic form; to perform an interpretation; to express in another language or form; to cause to become" (*American Heritage Dictionary*). Could a non-logos rendering of madness escape the inherent impossibility of speaking madness? How would such a rendering look and would it be "logically" perceived as communicating madness? And could such a text be approached and criticized in the same way as a more traditional text (in other words, through reason)?

> I have never yet been able to perceive how anything can be known for truth by consecutive reasoning.
>
> (*Great Expectations* 69)

Furthermore, how would such a text, attempting to render madness, relate to the madness inherent within itself?

One exploration of these questions can be found in the art (or anti-art) of Kathy Acker. Acker's ***Great Expectations,*** ostensibly a "novel" about the author's mother's suicide, purposely avoids writerly conventions that have traditionally served to make a text appear "reasonable." Even more extreme, her methods of textualizing, methods she shares with a number of experimenters in the modern and contemporary arts, appear mad compared to more traditional writing methods by not meeting the "Great Expectations" the reader has for a novel. The text combines ("throws together" would perhaps more accurately describe Acker's technique) narrative, autobiography, fiction, drama, the epistolary novel, history, criticism, and poetry. The narrator and the author both

> (Stylistically: simultaneous contrasts, extravagances, incoherences, half-formed misshapen thoughts, lousy spelling, what signifies what? What is the secret of this chaos? [. . .] Expectations that aren't satiated.)
>
> (*Great Expectations* 107)

occasionally intrude as characters in the text, or occasionally as commentators, and at other times "disappear." The text incorporates (plagiarizes) quotations from other published works, virtually at random, with little or no attempt to meld them into the flow of the book. The text incorporates un-reasonable (or extra-reasonable) paradoxes based on conceptual fission and fusion; concepts are split into opposing binaries with both sides of the opposition stated as true, while other apparently ("reason-ably") disparate ideas are fused together. Overall, the text is so purposely diverse that any effort to reduce it to a theme would appear obviously contrived (even the theme of the impossibility of reducing a text to a single theme).

These observations regarding Acker's text lead to an important question: does *Great Expectations* render madness through its eccentricity and its (to borrow Felman's pun) ex-centricity? If so, the rendering is not so much in the language Acker uses, but in the methods Acker applies to language-writing, methods that communicate or imply madness to the reader. Sentences such as "When a sentence becomes distinct, it makes no more sense or connection" (*Great Expectations* 34) Derrida asserts, "are normal by nature. They are impregnated with normality, [. . .] with meaning" [qtd. in Felman, 44]). Simultaneously, Acker's work exposes the madness of rhetoric by emphasizing its resistance to linearity, cohesion, and interpretation.

ACKER'S GENRES

"Everything is thrown into my writing."
("A Few Notes on Two of My Books" 31)

One way in which *Great Expectations* resists interpretation is through its relationship to genre. The existence of literary genres is a symptom of the desire to classify, to make order. By deciding to which category a literary text belongs, the critic gains a level of understanding, mastery, power, over the text. The tendency to classify genres extends back at least to Aristotle's division of tragedy and comedy in the *Poetics*. The tendency seems natural, readily apparent, to modern society (texts really are either tragedy, or comedy, or something else).

> I think these categories: this logic way of talking (perceiving) is wrong.
>
> (*Great Expectations* 24)

The politics driving such a tendency is based on normalization and exclusion: book A fits into category X and is therefore normal/acceptable/superior/reasonable, while book B does not quite fit into any of the pre-established categories, therefore abnormal/unacceptable/inferior/folly. Of course, not all critics agree as to which genre should encompass a given text; and if consensus is achieved for a text, its classification may be radically changed in the next generation. Furthermore, some critics may reverse the fit = normal = superior vs. not-fit = abnormal = inferior dichotomy (instead, a text that is not readily classified into a given genre will be classified as superior, while fitting into a genre becomes a sign of weakness). Nonetheless, these observations still serve to emphasize the critic's (apparently irresistible) urge to classify, the critic's need to avoid chaos and madness.

Many artists of this century have experimented with transgressing genre and classification. Aaron Copland, Leonard Bernstein, Benjamin Britten, and Mark Blitzstein have all written compositions for orchestra and narrator (a speaker, rather than a singer). Schoenberg's *sprech-stimme,* speech-singing, combined the vocal qualities of singing and talking in works such as *Pierrot Lunaire.* Bernstein's Second Symphony is a piano concerto, while his First Symphony is a song cycle. Gershwin's *Rhapsody in Blue* is both composed jazz and a free-form classical piano concerto. Robert Rauschenberg and Jim Dine transformed their paintings into vertical platforms for sculptures that extend outward from the canvas. Performance artists such as Laurie Anderson combine visual art, music, dance, narrative, poetry, and stand-up comedy into artistic events that sometimes verge toward rock concerts.

Twentieth-century writers have also experimented with genre. John Steinbeck, with *Of Mice and Men, The Moon is Down,* and *Burning Bright,* wrote novels that could be presented as plays with only the addition of performance cues. Poet-composer Charles Amirkhanian has created musical works using only voices speaking. Richard Kostelanetz has created poems that bridge the gap between poetry and music, visual art, and mathematics. The work of those writers, however, has tended not to transgress genres, but rather to successfully become two genres. Expanding the limits of the novel has become virtually standard practice, thanks to writers ranging from James Joyce to Kurt Vonnegut (with Lawrence Sterne and Herman Melville as important predecessors); those writers have purposefully meddled with form, typography, narrative conventions, and so forth; yet they maintain an overall narrative form.

In contrast, Acker's *Great Expectations* uses genres without becoming any of them. At times Acker herself speaks her story, based, she claims, on her "real" life (Friedman Interview 15). At other times, the narrator speaks first person

> The influence of [Pier Paolo] Pasolini's theories on my work is particularly important. He refused to separate genres—film, poetry, criticism. He refused to separate body and mind.
>
> (Friedman Interview 20)

accounts of "fictional" events. Occasionally either autobiography or fiction is presented as drama (the "hubby-wife" dialogue, 19-23; the "Clifford-Sara" exchange, 91-93, and the "Cynthia-Propertius-et al." sequence, 106-11 and later), as epistolary novel (the letters from Rosa, 25-30, and the "Dear mother" conclusion), or as poetry (the observations, statements, and commands of male domination, 38-42). At other times the text speaks as history (the brief excerpt from the account of the Roman empire, 104), and frequently Acker, or the narrator, or both engage in literary theory-criticism: "A narrative is an emotional moving" (58), "one text must subvert (the meaning of) another text" (15).

Acker's extreme mixture of genres keeps the reader from comfortably placing **Great Expectations** into a predefined category. The reader then is forced into confronting several options, one of which is to redefine an existing genre. Acker herself considers her works such as **Great Expectations** narratives, but her definition of that term is hardly conducive to the formation of a rethought classification:

> I was [. . .] trying to make a text that was an "environment" rather than a centralized, meaningful narrative [. . .] a kind of a "de-narrative."
>
> ("McCaffery Interview" 89)

"the reader has to go from A to Z and it's going to take a long time and that's narrative," she says (Friedman 14). Acker's definition is based on what the reader does, rather than what the author did (the form or content of the work); her definition would require a completely new classification system of literary works, starting from a radically different premise.

Another option would be to create a new genre for works such as Acker's; such a new classification would surely have to be based on a concept such as "the conglomerate" or the "mixed-genre genre," terms which, rather than expressing the genre as different from all others, expresses its inclusion of all others. Such a classification would not readily fit into the present, neatly differentiated genres.

Of course the literary critic would be tempted to classify Acker's work as experimental or even postmodern, classifications Acker suggests are applied to "hide the political radicalness of some writers. [. . .] 'Experimental,'" she asserts, "means they're not really important" (Friedman 21). Any of these methods of

> What they're doing is marginalizing the experimental and that's why I hate the word "experimental." It's another form of sticking people into the corner."
>
> (Friedman Interview 21)

> "Marginal," "experimental," and "avant-garde" are often words used to describe texts in this other tradition. Not because writing such as Burrough's or Genet's is marginal, but because our society, through the voice of its literary society, cannot bear immediacy, the truth, especially the political truth."
>
> (**"A Few Notes"** 31)

dealing with Acker's text, any of these attempts to classify and control it, reveals the inability of the classification system to fit Acker's text, and further displays the critic's urge to dominate and control. Attempting to redefine or create a genre, or marginalizing as "experimental," reveals an attempt to hide the unreasonableness of Acker's text, to mask Acker's madness. Acker's multigenres, therefore, render madness to the reader accustomed to traditional genre classifications.

ACKER'S PLAGIARISM

I was interested in [. . .] what happens when you just copy something, without any reason.

(Kathy Acker, Friedman Interview 12)

I just started finding these different texts and putting them together.

("McCaffery Interview" 88)

Another of Acker's methods, plagiarism, is madness on many levels. The college composition student who plagiarizes an essay practices folly because the student learns nothing about writing (and therefore gains no reward in the class for an investment in money and energy), just as the politician or academician who plagiarizes a portion of a speech practices folly because getting caught could jeopardize his or her career. This equation of plagiarism with madness reveals that plagiarism is firmly grounded in a social ethic. Just as important, plagiarism is grounded in the notion of private property; plagiarism is condemned (and therefore set aside as other, as unreasonable, as madness) because the plagiarist takes someone else's words or ideas, that person's private property, and claims it as her or his own.

The history of plagiarism reveals its connection with the concepts of private property and capitalism. Plagiarism of created work is not a significant issue in a society where there is no means of readily copying and selling created work. The printing press and movable type made possible the notion of plagiarism. Before the printing press medieval bards orally retold stories they had acquired from other sources. Chaucer borrowed stories from Boccaccio, without giving due credit. Even as the printing press was becoming a prominent technology, Shakespeare borrowed entire plot structures from other writers. After the printing press, when money could be made from selling writing, publishers, and later authors, began to concern themselves with owning the writing they had produced. However, for more than a century after plagiarism had become established as taboo for the written word, plagiarism remained an acceptable option for musical compositions. Bach, for example, stole from Vivaldi and Handel, and was in turn stolen from by other composers; composers from the Baroque (and earlier) periods were able to "get by" with plagiarism because a given composition was generally composed for one performance only, or for didactic purposes, not for later publication. Sanctions against plagiarism become established in the music world only as Mozart and Beethoven (or more accurately, their publishers), came to realize they

> I suspect that the ideology of creativity started when the bourgeoisie—when they rose up in all their splendor, as the history books put it—made a capitalistic marketplace for books. Today a writer earns money or

a living by selling copyright, ownership to words. We all do it, we writers, this scam, because we need to earn money, only most don't admit it's a scam. Nobody really owns nothing."

("A Few Notes," Acker's emphasis 33)

Ellen G. Friedman:

Why did you leave the United States?

Kathy Acker:

Not enough money.

(Friedman Interview 18)

could make money (small amounts) through publishing their compositions. Plagiarism is in opposition to the modern capitalistic, patriarchal social system based on ownership; plagiarism, then, appears stupid, antisocial, unreasonable, mad, to modern society, unless it takes the form of allusion, a brief quote invoking the presence of an earlier text, as in the modernist works of Eliot, Pound, and Williams.

Yet plagiarism has held a fascination for many contemporary artists, a fascination that extends significantly beyond the use of another artist's work through allusion. Lukas Foss's *Baroque Variations* (1967) takes compositions by Bach, Handel, and Domenico Scarlatti, fragments the originals, juxtaposes the fragments, and composes "holes" (silences) into the music. The third movement of Luciano Berio's *Sinfonia* (1968) is the third movement of Mahler's Symphony No. 2 played essentially in its entirety, with additional "quotations" from the music of Bach, Schoenberg, Debussy, Ravel, Strauss, Berlioz, Stravinsky, and others, even Berio's earlier compositions, layered on top of the Mahler. *Sparrows* (1978-79) by Joseph Schwantner, who won the 1979 Pulitzer Prize for Music for his *Aftertones of Infinity,* plagiarizes not so much specific compositions but rather stylistic traits associated with Renaissance and Baroque music. The composition does not allude to Renaissance forms and structures—as do many early twentieth-century compositions; it becomes a Renaissance composition. Plagiarism in modern visual art can perhaps be traced to Marcel Duchamp and Salvador Dali, who both appropriated the Mona Lisa as their own, adding only a mustache above her famous smile. More recently, Sherrie Levine has photographed duplicates of famous and not-so-famous photographs, not as forgeries but as original works themselves.

Acker claims Levine's visual plagiarism as a major influence on her own work with literary plagiarism. Acker's *Don Quixote* (1986) was an attempt "to do [. . .] a Sherrie Levine painting" (Friedman 12). Since Acker's first work with plagiarism in the early 1980s, she has refined the technique so that in *Empire of the Senseless* (1988) she claims to have incorporated "tons" of other

texts; she describes that later plagiarism as more "hidden" than in her early work (Friedman 16), including *Great Expectations.* Acker asserts her selection of particular texts is not merely random, but an attempt "to find writers who describe the particular place [she] want[s] to get to" (Friedman 17); for example, the third section of *Empire of the Senseless,* ostensibly "about how you live free in a society that isn't," incorporates portions of *Huckleberry Finn,* "one of the primary American texts about freedom" (Friedman 17). At the same time, Acker claims her motivation for plagiarizing is primarily just to do "what gives [her] the most pleasure: write" ("A Few Notes" 34).

Whatever Acker's motivation, the result is disruptive to a well-read reader within patriarchal society. Acker opens "her" novel with the opening lines of Dickens's novel by the same title; later she intermixes "her own" (autobiographical?) story with excerpts from a Victorian pornographic novel, material from a Greek history, and a line from a Keats letter. Because the "original" authors are not given "due credit" in Acker's text, the impact of a work such as *Great Expectations* on an "ordinary" reader would likely include the tendency to marginalize Acker's text as not creative, not really literature, as not within society's norms for literary works: as other. The text (and perhaps its author) would be looked at as mad: not because of what the plagiarized words said, but because the plagiarized words were actually said by someone other than Acker. Acker's method, then, produces an assessment of madness.

Acker's Paradoxes

This is not a possible situation. This identity doesn't exist.

(*Great Expectations* 44)

Another Acker idiosyncrasy is paradox. The twentieth century is not the first in which artists have shown an interest in paradox, but some modern and postmodern artists show an interest in extreme paradox. Picasso's cubist paintings display two (or more) incongruous perspectives of an object, both equally "true."

> The Cubists went further. They found the means of making the forms of all objects similar. If everything was rendered in the same terms, it became possible to paint the interactions between them. These interactions became so much more interesting than that which was being portrayed that the concepts [. . .] of reality were undermined or transferred.

(*Great Expectations* 81-82)

Leonard Bernstein's *Prelude, Fugue and Riffs* sounds improvised (like jazz), but is completely notated (which jazz is not).

Acker takes paradox to a new level. Traditionally, paradox has implied two opposing, mutually exclusive concepts that appear, after some contemplation, to be naturally, reasonably true. Acker's paradoxes are indeed opposing, mutually exclusive concepts, but they do not appear true; they are simply stated and are

> Dualisms such as good/evil are not real and only reality works.

("A Few Notes" 36)

therefore implied, or at least inferred, as true.

Acker's paradoxes can be seen as either fission or fusion. A fission paradox takes one idea, splits it into two opposite extremes and declares both parts to be true; a fusion paradox takes two differing concepts and coerces them together. The first ten pages of the novel reveal at least two dozen examples of fission and a half dozen of fusion; most of the remainder of the book, excluding some lengthier, more-or-less verbatim plagiarisms, contain similar levels of paradox.

Some of the concepts Acker splits apart include:

EXISTENCE:

"As the dream: there is and there is not."

(7)

"There is no time; there is."

(7)

"My mother thinks my father is a nobody."

(12)

IDENTITY:

"My Christian name [is] Philip [. . .] so I called myself Peter."

(5)

"The soldiers [. . .] they are cattle."

(8)

"My mother is adoration hatred."

(14)

"Any other country is beautiful as long as I don't know about it."

(14)

APPEARANCE:

"Her breasts look larger and fuller than they are."

(9)

"The flesh directly above the cunt seems paler than it has to be."

(9)

SELF-CONCEPT:

"[D]espite my present good luck my basic stability my contentedness [. . .] I have the image obsession I'm scum."

(6)

WOMAN:

"I am separating women into virgins or whores."

(6)

Acker's fissions tend to take the reader by surprise, seeming unreasonable and therefore mad. Her fusions are equally disturbing: "This TERROR is divine" (7); "Love [. . .] is forgiveness that transforms need into desire" (6). Fusions often occur on a larger scale. Humans and animals are fused when she writes of a cabby shoving his fist into a goat's face, and then a few lines later speaks of females lullabying kids at their breasts (7). Beauty and ugliness become fused when a lengthy, violent description of soldiers burning and crushing is interrupted by a passage beginning "My mother is the most beautiful woman in the world" (9). At one point the narrator's passive father is fused to a rape scene; the rape is preceded by "My father never beats my mother up. The father grabs a candle, the curly brownhaired soldier [. . .] jerks the sleepy young girl's thighs to him [. . .]" (13).

The narrator herself becomes fused with the rape in the course of a large paragraph punctuated as a single sentence; when the soldier's sweat "wakes the young girl [the rape victim] up, I walked into my parents' bedroom [. . .] my father was standing naked over the toilet [. . .] I'm shocked [. . .] the curly brownhaired lifts her on to her feet lay her down" (13). The narrator's mother becomes fused with the soldier's rape victim through unclear pronoun reference; "I love mommy. I know she's on Dex, and when she's not on Dex she's on Librium to counteract the Dex jitters so she acts more extreme than usual. A second orgasm cools her shoulders, the young girl keeps her hands joined over the curly brownhaired's ass" (15). Both fusion and fission paradoxes appear, not as the metaphysical poet's conceit but as raw, contradictory (and therefore unreasonable) statements. If "there is no time; there is" is not quite meaningful, then we are approaching Foucault's "senseless words anchored by nothing in time."

ACKER'S THEMES

I've never been sure about the need for literary criticism.

("A Few Notes" 11)

The concept of theme is one of the most powerful weapons in the critic's arsenal. With it, she or he can reduce any artistic creation into just one or two basic, supposedly central ideas. Musical and artistic compositions, both theoretically less prone to thematization because musical sound and visual representation are generally assumed to be less directly tied to meaning than are words, have regularly been forced to reveal a theme. Beethoven's Sonata No. 14 is variously about reflected moonlight or a spiritual calm after experiencing an emotional loss. Michelangelo's *David* is about man's ability to conquer his environment. Even artists classified as experimental have been thematized; Jackson Pollock's abstract expressionist drip paintings have been described as about the unconscious or the creative process, whereas Arnold Schoenberg's 12-tone compositions have been labeled about applied socialist democracy.

Discovering theme, like classifying a text into a given genre, gives literary critics power over the text, allows them to feel they have conquered the text, cracked the text's code, made the unknown (text) speak the known (theme), eliminated the text's mystery through mastery. Even the most problematic texts have shown themselves helpless against the critic who single-mindedly wrests a theme from the text. Seemingly inchoate texts such as *Tristram Shandy, The Waste Land,* and *Finnegan's Wake* have all been coerced into proclaiming a theme. That very

> Writing isn't a viable phenomenon anymore. Everything has been said.
>
> (*Great Expectations* 123)

study, for example, is intent on finding "the rendering of madness" as a more-or-less thematic element in Acker's *Great Expectations.* The enterprising critic could find a theme anywhere, even in a randomly generated list of words, as Stanley Fish has memorably illustrated.

Perhaps more important than the possibility that any text could be forced to reveal a theme is the critic's drive to do so. That theme lust hides the notion that every text should—or should be made to—reveal theme. Traditionally, critics spent their careers arguing over which theme in a given work was the right theme or, among more enlightened critics, which themes were the least unlikely. Postmodern critics, on the other hand, suggest that theme is simply the imperialist critic's attempt to colonize meaning within a text. Either way, theme is associated with reason, and the notion that a text might lack a theme seems mad. My study of Acker's text, for example, was motivated largely because I didn't understand the text, yet I wanted to understand it, to "get a handle on it," to feel as if the text were not apparent madness. I felt compelled that the text must mean something, and I have been unable seriously to entertain the notion that Acker's text might not have a theme, or that it might by unknowable.

Acker herself implies that her texts have themes. In her early books, she says, from *The Adult Life of Toulouse Lautrec by Henri Toulouse Lautrec* through *The Child-*

like *Life of the Black Tarantula by the Black Tarantula* to *I Dreamt I Was a Nymphomaniac!: Imagining,* "the major theme was identity" (Friedman 15). Her *Don Quixote* "is about appropriating male texts," whereas the middle portion of

> I wasn't interested in "saying" anything in my work. The only thing I could use my works to say is 'I don't want to say things!'
>
> ("McCaffery Interview" 90)

that novel "is very much about trying to find your voice as a woman" (Friedman 13). She further implies that the general purpose of her texts, up until *Empire of the Senseless* (1988), was "to deconstruct, to take apart perceptual habits, to reveal the frauds on which our society's living" (**"A Few Notes"** 35).

Yet her texts make thematizing exceptionally difficult. A given passage may seem to be about something, yet after immersing that passage into the vat of critical inquiry along with other passages from the text, no major theme seems to float to the surface. The text seems to say, "So you will extract theme from me? I will make it as difficult as possible for you, not by being deceptively complex, but by being simply fragmented." The text seems intent on pointing out the foolishness, the irrelevance of any such theme encountered in the text. The insistence on the folly of thematizing itself seems mad, and a reader is hard pressed to overcome that

> You too, Maecenas, one day, are going to have to realize you're not rational and then in your desperation, ignorant, you'll turn to my words.
>
> (*Great Expectations* 122)

perception of madness, even while attempting to interpret, as I attempt, the theme of the text as "thematizing is mad." In other words, the text seems to say, "looking for a theme is crazy," but its saying so seems equally crazy.

THE MADNESS OF ACKER'S METHOD

> *"Is there anything else? Is there anything else? What is it to know?"*
>
> (*Great Expectations* 23)

And so, does Acker's *Great Expectations* render madness? Does it yield madness, or represent, or interpret it? Does it cause madness to become? I have argued that the text does render madness, a madness by way of method, rather than content, method that does not meet the "Great Expectations" of the reader.

By revealing Acker's nontraditional novelistic methods, by cataloguing the genres that Acker incorporates, by explaining the reason for Acker's plagiarism or offering a reasonable explanation of the plagiarism's effects, by adapting the term paradox to Acker's technique and by classifying the text's paradoxes, by suggesting that the purpose of the text is to render madness, the text has been made sensible; it is seen with a single, overall purpose, toward which it logically and inexorably moves, by presenting arbitrary un-logic. The use of mixed genres is not a chaotic mess, but a logical method of rendering disruption, madness. The use of plagiarism is not senseless thievery, but a reasonable method of forcing the reader into unease as a result of apparent madness. The unreasonable, ridiculous paradoxes, too, have a purpose, a reason for being, as a method of revealing the unrevealable illogic, madness, of language. The theme, "all texts/interpretations are madness, including this one," has been found revealed

Language means nothing anymore.

(*Great Expectations* 29)

logically, clearly, and forcefully, just as all good themes in all good texts should be revealed. In other words, the text renders madness, because I interpret it that way, but my interpretation (a reasonable act) makes the madness void. Acker's text may have "attempted to resist interpretation," but the resistance has been rendered futile in the face of the critic's inexorable drive to create understanding; the text's strategy of presenting madness has been overcome by the critic's strategy of interpretation. By Felman's definition, then, Acker's text is perhaps not mad because it has not shown an "irreducible resistance to interpretation" (254). Proving that the text renders madness, further proves that it does not.

Madness is a reality.

(*Great Expectations* 119)

A writer makes reality.

("**A Few Notes**" 33)

And yet the average book store patron, perhaps purchasing Acker's text by accident under the assumption that it was Dickens's, may not perceive the methods I have explored here, but would surely experience them. The mixed genres would be merely a hodgepodge, the plagiarism would be craziness, the paradoxes would be

I'm aware of an audience. There has to be that element of entertainment, really, or there's limited accessibility. So I do care about my readers in that way.

(Friedman Interview 20)

stupid contradictions, all terms that imply madness. Such a reader would surely have no illusion as to whether the text has a theme. The reality of Acker's text, Mr. or Ms. Average Reader would assume, is pure madness.

Ultimately, then, the answer to the question, Does *Great Expectations* render madness? must be, "that all depends on whether or not you think the text is crazy."

I don't think I'm crazy, There's just no reality in my head.

(*Great Expectations* 65)

Works Cited

Acker, Kathy. "A Few Notes on Two of My Books." *Review of Contemporary Fiction* 9.3 (1989): 31-36.

———. *Great Expectations.* New York: Grove, 1982.

Felman, Shoshana. *Writing and Madness (Literature/ Philosophy/Psychoanalysis)*. Trans. Martha Noel Evans, Shoshana Felman, and Brian Massumi. Ithaca, NY: Cornell UP, 1985.

Foucault, Michel. *Madness and Civilization: A History of Insanity in the Age of Reason.* New York: Vintage, 1965.

Friedman, Ellen G. "A Conversation with Kathy Acker." *Review of Contemporary Fiction* 9.3 (1989): 12-22.

McCaffery, Larry. "An Interview with Kathy Acker." *Mississippi Review* 20.1-2 (1991): 83-97.

Marilyn Manners (essay date 2000)

SOURCE: Manners, Marilyn. "The Dissolute Feminisms of Kathy Acker." In *Future Crossings: Literature between Philosophy and Cultural Studies,* edited by Krzysztof Ziarek and Seamus Deane, pp. 98-119. Evanston, Ill.: Northwestern University Press, 2000.

[*In the following excerpt, Manners explicates the nature of Acker's "dissoluteness" and "debauchery" as manifested in such works as* Blood and Guts in High School, Kathy Goes to Haiti, Pussy, King of the Pirates, *and* My Mother: Demonology.]

Near the beginning of Kathy Acker's 1993 novel ***My Mother: Demonology,*** an unidentified narrator says: "Most of my life, but not all, I've been dissolute. According to nineteenth-century cliché, dissoluteness and debauchery are connected to art."[1] This introductory revelation might serve as an ironic emblem for Acker's writing: it voices self-recrimination from an indeterminate source; it qualifies an already qualified assertion ("Most . . . but not all"); its many meanings bleed out into relations among text, writer, and reader. In one direction, the statement acknowledges some readers'—including feminist readers'—adverse reactions to Acker's "dissolute" inscription of pornographic sex scenes; in another direction, it self-reflexively suggests Acker's own disdain for and brutal destruction of nineteenth-century aesthetic "clichés," particularly, although not exclusively, what she calls "bourgeois linear narrative."[2] Further, there is no guarantee that these apt words are even Acker's own: her dissolution, in many senses, extends to rampant plagiarism of other texts—ranging from formulaic porn to Artaud to Kristeva. Such "debauchery," both textual and sexual, has been part of Acker's writing from its beginnings. It need not be seen, however—as it sometimes has been—simply as a corrosive, destructive, or even deconstructive enterprise (although it has been that too); nor can this dissoluteness be attributed to derivative, superficial, or banal writing (even, or especially, when her writing is most self-consciously derivative, superficial, or banal). Rather, Acker's "dissoluteness and debauchery are connected to art" indeed. More than a simple strategy, Acker's dissolute writing is both a form of epistemology and a poetics.

Although Acker described her early work as a process of deconstruction, she spoke later about how she "started thinking about constructing rather than destructing-deconstructing-destructing"[3] in her writing. She also began to look to and incorporate classical Western myth, a revisionary practice which has itself become a traditional feature of feminist writing. Such interests on her part should not, however, have led anyone to anticipate a turn to convention, in any sense: Acker's writing—early and late, in deconstructive or constructive modes—remains as distant from probity or utopian feminist visions as from traditional linear narrative or character construction. In fact, Acker's renewed interest in myth provides an apt example of her writing's improper confusion, and profusion, of categories of all sorts. Although Acker studied as a classicist, and although she incorporates stories of Antigone and Andromeda, for instance, in her novels, her references to myth-making and her revision of Greek female figures bear little resemblance to other feminists' rewriting of classical Western mythology; instead, her reconstruction of these myths remains thoroughly dissolute. Acker's idea of myth encompasses using "non-accessible . . . [o]r not readily accessible language" (*2GZ* ["Interview" in *Varieties of Violence*] 3), such as the languages of dreaming and sex. She has explained that she's "just very interested in trying to access what goes through the mind say as you go through orgasm. And it wouldn't even make sense to say one could deconstruct that" (*2GZ* 3). Her writing, that is, traverses the troubled intersection between language and body, while eschewing visions of a pre- or extralinguistic body, or of a corporeally saturated feminine language. Yet Acker's writing has also regularly transgressed a perhaps even more well-regulated border, that between philosophical thought or theory (including feminist thought) and popular culture. When Acker deploys mythological female figures, therefore, the graffiti-covered halls they roam are not likely to be those of Pompeii. Indeed, when Acker participates in immediately recognizable feminist discourses (as opposed to her use of pornography or her emphasis on passive female characters, which have taken many much longer to "read" as

feminist), a mixture of "high" and "low" culture often characterizes her particular contribution. Whereas Cixous conceptualizes an emblematically beautiful and laughing Medusa, for instance, or Irigaray employs Antigone's narrative to illustrate women's place as guardian of the blood and as the ground which supports male subjectivity,[4] Acker's Andromeda wanders through an abbey set up for performance art, while remembering an early REM video,[5] and her Antigone rides a motorcycle and says to Creon: "I left your lousy world. Only a fool will now attempt to stop us girls" (*PKP* [*Pussy, King of the Pirates*] 182).

Further, Antigone—although she is useful for Acker as one in a long series of incestual yet Oedipal-triangle-destroying women—is merely one voice, one name in her chorus of pirate girls. Acker's Antigone is introduced as follows:

> *Hegel, or the panopticon, sees all, except for the beginning of the world. In that beginning, which is still beginning, there is a young girl.*
>
> *Her name's not important. She's been called King Pussy, Pussycat, Ostracism, O, Ange. Once she was called Antigone. . . .*
>
> (*PKP* 163; Acker's emphasis)

It would be foolish to argue, however, that Acker's mythological revisions have nothing whatsoever to do with those of Cixous or Irigaray. Her "I left your lousy world" echoes Cixous's "Not another minute to lose. Let's get out of here" in "Laugh of the Medusa";[6] and Irigaray's essay "The Eternal Irony of the Community" addresses Hegel on the subject of Antigone, noting that in Sophocles' *Antigone* "the privilege of the proper name is not yet pure."[7] Irigaray writes in the same essay that "at times the forces of the world below become hostile because they have been denied the right to live in daylight. These forces rise up and threaten to lay waste the community" ("EIC" 225); this statement could serve to summarize the first part of Acker's novel *Pussy, King of the Pirates,* in which women set fire to their brothel, inciting revolution and destroying the city and its environs (*PKP* 44). There are, furthermore, constant references in late Acker novels to both flying and fluidity—tropes certainly familiar to readers of Cixous and Irigaray.[8]

The improper intermingling so characteristic of Acker's written texts exceeds textual bounds, moreover. Acker's readers must not only learn to negotiate with the (heterogeneous, morsellated, dissolving) bodies of those texts themselves (as well as the relentlessly deglamorized bodies described within them); they have also had to confront the (text-in-process) body of the writer herself. Before her untimely death, Acker's own body could also be read as "sext," as Cixous termed it in the 1970s ("LM" 255). In Acker's words, "It's the text. It's the body, it's the real body, which is language, the text.'"[9] ["Interview"] This included Acker's own tattooed, body-building, shaved and bleached, motorcycle-riding, and labia-pierced body, that is, a body similar to those in the illustrations on the inside front and back covers of *Pussy, King of the Pirates*—a rendering which complicates even further any question of where the dissolution of bodies and texts begins and ends.

Furthermore, unless Acker's readers distance themselves and refuse to take the trip, they must consider the textual relation of their own bodies: "If there's this distance between the reader and the text, the reader's just an observer. I want the reader to come right into the text because that's the only way you can take the journey. . . . I know how to make the reader at least come along on the journey and enter into the text."[10] ["Devoured by Myths"] Although perhaps a bit optimistic here about her ability to entice all her readers "to come right into the text," Acker often spoke in similarly spatial and corporeal terms when discussing relations among writer/text/reader. Her ideal reader, therefore, is not merely affected or infected but becomes another kind of body-worker. What Acker has had to say about the parallel work of writer and tattooist might be transposed to the work of the reader as well:

> The process of tattooing for him [Acker's tattooist] is learning about someone's body, which is learning about someone. He's not going in there to re-make the body in terms of some model that's outside that body. It's the difference between listening and making. When you listen to something you're not imposing your shtick on whatever you're making. For me, it's like writing, using other texts the way I do now. . . . To learn to work a text is partly to learn to listen.
>
> ("CKA1" ["A Conversation with Kathy Acker"] 4)

Acker's characteristically dissolute feminism changed in manifestation but not in effect over the course of the last twenty years. If Acker's "pornography" and passive or victimized female characters baffled or offended some feminists, she herself found a good deal to criticize in much feminist writing of the time. Of British feminist writers, for instance, she charged that "[i]t's diary stuff and the diary doesn't go anywhere, and there's not enough work with language."[11] In contrast, Acker explained her own constantly transforming writing project at length, sometimes describing it as a series of theoretical problems (for example, of identity or of language and the body); she also rejected conventional narrative from the beginning: "I came out of the poetry world, not out of prose, so I wasn't concerned with the traditional narrative or even narrative at all. I wasn't interested in telling a story, where you make up one or two fictional characters and tell about their relation to the world."[12] As Acker became more accepted by feminist readers—and as a feminist writer—her dissolution of feminism's (often unacknowledged) borders contin-

ued unabated, although the contours of her project may have shifted to mocking Kristeva's orientalism, deflating Cixous's universalizing pretensions, or muddying Irigaray's sometimes rather pristine fluidity.

To argue for entangled complexities within more recent Acker texts is not, however, to suggest that Acker's early texts were simple, although they have nevertheless sometimes appeared so. In the case of two early Acker novels, *Kathy Goes to Haiti* (1978) and *Blood and Guts in High School* (1978; pub. 1984), relative simplicity seems in fact to have led to some of their more obvious—and in one instance, graphically blatant—aspects being strangely ignored. These texts provide, therefore, particularly useful test cases of how we might best "journey" through ("DM" ["Devoured by Myths"] 15) and "listen to" ("CKA1" 4) her dissolute textual bodies.

Blood and Guts in High School is one of the many Acker texts which some readers have found both fascinating and difficult to "listen to." This novel opens with a certain "Janey Smith" who is ten years old: "Never having known a mother, her mother had died when Janey was a year old, Janey depended on her father ["Johnny Smith"] for everything and regarded her father as boyfriend, brother, sister, money, amusement, and father."[13] The novel has three separate endings: in the first, "[s]he dies" (*BGHS* [*Blood and Guts in High School*] 140); the text of the second closes with "Shall we look for this wonderful book? Shall we stop being dead people? Shall we find our way out of all expectations?" (*BGHS* 147); and in the third, we read that "[s]oon many other Janeys were born and these Janeys covered the earth" (*BGHS* 165).

This novel's character- and narrative-mocking beginning and ending might in themselves alert a reader to the hazards of reading literally; as Karen Brennan puts it, Janey is constituted "as a fluid entity-voice (not really a character) in Acker's novel."[14] Indeed, *Blood and Guts* is an early but full-scale dismantling of both the literal and the literate: Acker undoes, through excessive repetition, both Oedipal triangulation and the unbearable banalities of heterosexual "romance" in a text that contains almost forty pages of illustrations (some embedded "narratives" in their own right), a section of Persian poems, and entire pages of "text" that un-write themselves.

. . . . .

All this, and more, has not dissuaded some readers from literal-minded sense-making (particularly regarding Janey's incestuous relationship and submissive behavior), even though the novel itself contains an emphatic warning about the dangers of representation very early on: "If the author here lends her 'culture' to the amorous subject, in exchange the amorous subject affords her the innocence of its image-repertoire, indifferent to the properties of knowledge. Indifferent to the properties of knowledge" (*BGHS* 28).[15] *Blood and Guts in High School* was in fact banned in Germany on grounds of literalism regarding both content and form, as Acker has explained:

> I kept wondering where's kindersex in the novel at first. That's between Janey and her father. They didn't get it that it was a double play. They thought it was real. They took everything absolutely literally. Janey has sex with her father, that's kindersex. Then there's S/M, which is probably the most correct thing they came up with. . . . And then there's experimentality.
>
> ("DM" 19)

More perplexing, however, are readings which do not in the least insist on the literal, and which indeed perform exquisitely complex bodywork overall, but which nonetheless make an oddly selective "journey" through *Blood and Guts in High School.* In the course of several pages of discussion on drawings included in the novel, Karen Brennan carefully analyzes two of Acker's drawings of penises ("GE" 255-60; *BGHS* 8 and 14), and Gabrielle Dane, although in less detail, also refers to Acker's penis drawings as well as to "ODE TO A GRECIAN URN" (*BGHS* 63),[16] a sketch of a headless, bound, female body. What seems surprising, however, is that neither mentions, even in passing, two proximate, full-page drawings of female genitalia, "My cunt red ugh" (*BGHS* 19) and "GIRLS WILL DO ANYTHING FOR LOVE" (*BGHS* 62)—the latter in fact a facingpage of "ODE TO A GRECIAN URN." Even more strikingly, both essays nonetheless directly discuss issues which evoke their own omissions, as they call attention to "Acker's (scandalous) feminist aesthetic" ("HFP" 251), "try[ing] to express that for which no ready words exist" ("HFP" 248), "attempts to represent—textualize—the unpresentable" ("GE" 261), and Janey's "very disappearance from Acker's pages" ("GE" 250). Such incongruous neglect brings rather sharply to mind the continued relevance of Irigaray's exposure of "the non-visible, therefore not theorizable nature of woman's sex and pleasure" (*S* 139). Perhaps, as Kathleen Hulley has noted in a different context, "CUNTS made visible are blinding" indeed.[17]

Kathy Goes to Haiti evokes additional "blind spots" in feminist and gender-attentive readings of Acker. In *Kathy Goes to Haiti,* narrative development and character construction are much more conventional than is usually the case in Acker's work: Acker's protagonist Kathy remains Kathy throughout, without the vertiginous slippage into other personae and points of view so typical of Acker's other novels; the plot is also extraordinarily straightforward—with only a few stream-of-consciousness digressions and jarring leaps in continuity. Acker has explained that she wrote *Kathy Goes to Haiti* specifically as

a parody of a porn novel. I tried to write the dumbest book I could. . . . It's a joke . . . to call it Kathy first of all. I wrote the novel really to make money—they were buying porn novels at the time. So I took the formula of the porn novel, and I made a structure, a mathematical structure. In this chapter we have psychology, and here we have this happen . . . and then I wrote it according to this structure. It was the most boring thing in the world to write. I tried to make the characters as dumb as possible, and I basically tried to make nothing happen.

("IRD" ["Interview by Rebecca Deaton"] 281-82)

Kathy is, as promised, "as dumb as possible." Her dialogue ranges from the merely inane, "Oh goody. I'm so happy,"[18] to the dangerously foolish: "If you have love in your heart and live for other people, these people will have love in their hearts. I know I'm sounding soppy, but it's what I believe" (*KGH* [*Kathy Goes to Haiti in Literal Madness*] 90).

Nonetheless, *Kathy Goes to Haiti,* whether acknowledged or even intended by Acker to be so, is not as dumb as it might look. This early novel also ruthlessly parodies conventional travel books and tourism, and Acker has in fact admitted that it is "also my version . . . of a travel journal."[19] Specifically, *Kathy Goes to Haiti* concerns white North American tourism in the Caribbean, as its opening lines suggest: "Kathy is a middleclass, though she has no money, American white girl" (*KGH* 5). *Kathy Goes to Haiti* follows its protagonist Kathy as "[o]ne summer she goes down to Haiti. She steps out of the American Airlines plane and on to the cement runway, her first example of Haitian soil" (*KGH* 5). From this ironic statement onward, Kathy serves as a parodic emblem of postcolonial relations as distilled in the tourist industry—whether she is sneaking always-inadequate food to beggar boys from a pension or serving as a sort of traveling Western-culture lending library—until, at the very end of the novel, she "turns around and walks outside into the sun. She's more dazed than before" (*KGH* 170).

Few critics—excluding Acker herself—have written on *Kathy Goes to Haiti* in any detail,[20] and for Robert Siegle, *Kathy Goes to Haiti* concerns itself primarily with gender and sexuality; Acker's depiction of the protagonist Kathy as a tourist in Haiti is therefore purely incidental, or useful only for emphasizing problems in male-female relations.[21] Siegle argues, for instance, that,

> [c]oaxed by her desires into sexual scripts that pain as well as please her, Kathy is drawn by necessity into mortal competition in order to survive emotionally. Haiti is a locale that shows an unsubtle version of the double bind that such a subject faces, its *local color* and *lush sexual undergrowth* used as the *Day-Glo accenting* to Acker's nascent reading of American culture.
>
> (*SA* 76; emphasis added)

Siegle's exoticized "Haiti" is, however, very hard to locate in Acker's *Kathy Goes to Haiti.* There, a reader is presented instead with Kathy's abysmal ignorance regarding U.S.-Haitian relations, while the (generally stable, sober, and omniscient third-person) narrator, on the other hand, periodically provides less naive information (including even a "New York 1950s cocktail lounge" called, significantly, the Imperial [*KGH* 38]). There, the most lyrical passage on the natural beauty of Haiti ends in the following manner:

> The roosters are crowing their lungs out and small goats are pissing on the sand and dry dust which covers everything and the pigs are rooting in the sand for whatever garbage the rising waves are leaving behind. . . .
>
> A group of eleven-year-old boys are sitting on a curb. Alex has two toothpicks, one long and one short, legs from rickets or polio and for the last two days has been running a fever.

(*KGH* 101)

Acker's interwoven parodies of pornography and tourism (the latter crisscrossing issues of postcoloniality and ethnography) in *Kathy Goes to Haiti* bring to mind the numerous connections drawn between pornography and ethnography by Christian Hansen, Catherine Needham, and Bill Nichols, and one of their observations seems particularly pertinent in the present context: "The body itself looms as the 'star' of pornography and ethnography."[22] Acker's "ethnography" may be as unburdened by "stars" as is her "pornography," but "the body" in Acker's writing is indeed everywhere (in endless specific permutations) and nowhere (in coherent or universalizing form) to be found.

Siegle's elision of the postcolonial politics of *Kathy Goes to Haiti* allows disregard of the numerous complications of who is "victimizing" whom in power relations there; it also ignores the novel's exposure of the universalizing pretensions of whiteness. On the other hand, Colleen Kennedy's feminist critique both of Acker's use of pornography and of Siegle's praise of Acker does not directly discuss *Kathy Goes to Haiti,* except insofar as she claims that Acker "mak[es] these [victimized] characters reflections of herself (in two books the main character is actually named Kathy)."[23] Reading Acker's "dissoluteness and debauchery" quite literally, Kennedy concludes that "pornography written by women ultimately renders them victims of it" ("SS" 175). As she conflates author and protagonist, so too does Kennedy repudiate Acker's use of parody: "Clichés cannot be distinguished from their parody. To borrow from Toril Moi's analysis of Irigaray, 'the mimicry fails because it ceases to be perceived as such; it is no longer merely a mockery of the male, but a perfect reproduction'" ("SS" 183)[24]

Whether as a positive or negative touchstone, reference to Irigaray often seems strangely appropriate in discussions of Acker. Brennan at one point cites Irigaray's criticism of Lacan on the issue of women's pleasure, but in that context as well as in the present one, Irigaray's words seem strangely to wind back around to address Acker's readers—notably in these cases her feminist readers—as well: "The question whether, in his logic, they [women] can articulate anything at all, *whether they can be heard,* is not even raised. For raising it might mean that there may be some other logic, one that upsets his own. That is, a logic that challenges mastery" (quoted in "GE" 259; emphasis added). Acker herself has also "cited" and parodied (if rather respectfully) Irigaray's writing on logic and mastery, pleasure and the sex which is not one, Lacan and whoever else isn't listening:

> A man's power resides in his prick. That's what they, whoever they is, say. How the fuck should I know? I ain't a man. Though I'm a good fake lieutenant, it's not good enough to have a fake dick. I don't have one. Does this mean I've got no strength? If it's true that a man's prick is his strength, what and where is my power? Since I don't have one thing, a dick, I've got nothing, so my pleasure isn't any one thing, it's just pleasure. Therefore, pleasure must be pleasurable. Well, maybe I've found out something, and maybe I haven't.[25]

For academic feminists in particular, Acker's dissoluteness is perhaps especially fraught with hazard. Even beyond specific cases of inattention to significant details—such as the sex about which apparently nothing can be said (Brennan and Dane), content having to do with race, tourism, and postcolonialism (Siegle), or formal questions of representation (Kennedy)—academic feminists must especially concern themselves with fastidious focus and discipline. However "interdisciplinary" our interests or fields of study, we are not generally at liberty to pursue "a logic that challenges mastery," either in theory or practice. Yet, although Acker's wanton excesses and academic feminist discipline may indeed be ill paired, her dissoluteness provides more than vicarious thrills or voyeuristic peeks at an alternate episteme or fictional universe or "lifestyle." Her writing—with its deadpan, but insistent, inscription and parody of pornography and female victimization; its unraveling of assumptions about originality, a woman's voice, and "the" body; its dismantling of the universality of whiteness; and its admixture of theory and popular culture—might in many ways be seen as an extended interrogation of Anglo-American feminism, and certainly of any notion of a homogenous "feminism."

I want to look particularly now at the beginnings and endings of two late Acker novels, *Pussy, King of the Pirates* (1996) and *My Mother: Demonology* (1993). In these books she works on constructing, rather than deconstructing, as formerly, novels in which myths of witches and mothers and daughters, pirates and lesbian lovers take shape. Specifically, I would like to think about the dissolute form of these beginnings and endings, to examine how Acker constructed the friable borders of her textual bodies, writings which are called novels only for the sake of convenience.

Part I of *My Mother: Demonology* is preceded by an epigraph:

> My mother began to love at the same moment in her life that she began to search for who she was. This was the moment she met my father. Since my mother felt that she had to be alone in order to find out who she was and might be, she kept abandoning and returning to love.
>
> My mother spoke:
>
> (*MMD* [*My Mother: Demonology*] 3)

Because of this introductory colon, the "I" speaker of the statement referred to earlier—"Most of my life, but not all, I've been dissolute"—seems likely to be "my mother," which leaves the speaker of the epigraph nonetheless unidentified. At any rate, the narration begins with the words: "I'm in love with red. I dream in red." For this narrator, red represents, among other things, "the color of wildness and of what is as yet unknown" (*MMD* 10). (And if we were reading the novel itself, we would be reading within its bright red covers.) I, "my mother"—if "I" is indeed she—has a mother of her own, moreover, a "great lady" (*MMD* 9) who "commands" her daughter to the point of imprisoning her (*MMD* 10) and who has a quite different relation to redness: "Mother just hates everyone who isn't of our blood. She uses the word *blood*. She hates everyone and everything that she can't control; everything gay, lively, everything that's growing, productive. Humanness throws her into a panic; when she panics, she does her best to hurt me" (*MMD* 11). Ellen Friedman has said that

> *My Mother: Demonology* turns at the end suddenly quasi-mystical. Its last line has the narrator seeing "a reflection of [her] face before the creation of the world." Despite the fact that the narrator sees this reflection in a roll of toilet paper, the statement is the closest Acker has come to a discourse of inclusion, to a statement of individual identity in the world. Yet this hesitant, self-mocking affirmation is only a resting place at the end of a text whose tone is better summed up in its epigraph.[26]

The epigraph to which Friedman refers, however, is not the one I just cited, the epigraph ending in the words "My mother spoke:" (an epigraph which falls between the second title page of the book and the title of Part I). She refers instead to the epigraph which precedes both a title page and the table of contents but which comes after the book's first title page and its dedication ("to Uma"). Acker is nothing if not playful, yet the first epigraph of this novel takes up a different subject from the second and is playful only painfully:

> After Hatuey, a fifteenth-century Indian insurrectionist, had been fixed to the stake, his Spanish captors extended him the choice of converting to Christianity and ascending to Heaven or going unrepentantly to Hell. Gathering that his executioners expected to go to Heaven, Hatuey chose the other.
>
> (*MMD*, n.p.)

Among *My Mother: Demonology*'s false, repetitive, duplicitous beginnings, among its multiple titles and citations and sections, among Hatuey and Spanish executioners, among nameless daughters and mothers and the color red, the narrator says, a few pages in, "I told myself story after story. Every story is real. One story always leads to another story" (*MMD* 11). The first story of this novel, unless we take its dedication, or its title, to be the first story, is that of Hatuey.

Ellen Friedman does not say why she believes that this first epigraph "sums up" the "tone" of *My Mother: Demonology*; one can only suppose that she refers to the biting political irony of much of the novel. Nor does Friedman suggest what the relation between the novel's first and second epigraphs might be. Yet thinking the relation between these two epigraphs can be quite helpful when one encounters, for example, a section of the novel called "About Chinese Women" (*MMD* 80-81), a segment that plagiarizes Kristeva's book of the same name. Acker repeats one sentence of Kristeva's text almost exactly: "when a woman doesn't believe in God, she, like everyone else, validates her existence by believing in man" (*MMD* 80).

Half a page later, Acker revises a second statement. Kristeva's original (in English translation) reads as follows:

> Otherwise, I would have had to write the dizziness which, before China or without China, seizes that which is fed up with language, and attempts to escape through it: the abyss of fiction. However, that's not what I felt called upon to do here, where an imaginary 'we' is trying above all to understand what, in the various modes of production, has to do 'with women'—and not only to experience the general impossibility of this plural. Thus, a writing once more deferred . . .[27]

Acker abruptly rewrites this passage as: "I write in the dizziness that seizes that which is fed up with language and attempts to escape through it: the abyss named *fiction*. For I can only be concerned with the imaginary when I discuss reality or women" (*MMD* 80; emphasis in original).

The most obvious point to be drawn here is that Acker shifts Kristeva's elaborate and anxious concern over standing at the edge of the "abyss of fiction" into a plunge into that abyss. But also, in between the two Kristeva plagiarisms I have cited, Acker adds:

Since they were all Chinese, I couldn't communicate with any of them.

There were times when I thought, I shouldn't be here.

(*MMD* 80)

It is difficult not to hear in this statement echoes of Jamaica Kincaid's indictment of colonialism and slavery, tourism and racism in her work *A Small Place*: "There must have been some good people among you, but they stayed home. And that is the point. That is why they are good. They stayed home."[28] Many might also be reminded of Spivak's critique of Kristeva (in "French Feminism in an International Frame") in which she not only skewers Kristeva's reading of Chinese women as nameless masses or Kristeva's refusal to examine her own positionality, but also charges her with a sloppy reading of the figure of Electra.[29] This brings us, rather dizzily, back to Acker herself, since most of her texts contain some version of an incestuous Electra figure. But Acker does not stop playing with Kristeva there. She also takes Kristeva's Chinese women, described as "full-blown, even buxom . . . always with oval contours" and parodically deflates Kristeva's lyrical and exoticizing image: Acker's Chinese women become fat maids wielding meat cleavers who regard the narrator "the way one gazes at an object that is so other it can't be human" (*MMD* 81).

The end of *My Mother: Demonology* harks back both to this segment and to the beginnings of the novel: "my face before the creation of the world" is not simply reflected in a roll of toilet paper but in a "roll of white toilet paper [which] was covered with specks of black hairs" (*MMD* 268). It would be disingenuous to ignore two closing references to color in this novel so saturated with color from cover to cover. "Black" and "white," while not strictly referential here, serve at least a doubled purpose: racial politics permeate this text from its first epigraph regarding Hatuey's choice of hell over continued proximity to the Spanish, and that epigraph plays off against references to sexuality, desire, and identity in the second epigraph ("My mother . . ."), references which are transformed at the end of the novel to anonymous public hairs. But whereas the issues raised by the epigraph concerning "[m]y mother" are carefully analyzed in readings of Acker's work, the issues raised in the Hatuey epigraph are too often neglected—as are any possible relations between the two.[30] Despite this neglect, however, the intersection of the politics of race and colonialism, on the one hand, with the politics of sexuality and gender, on the other, has been an important element in Acker's work at least since her 1978 novel *Kathy Goes to Haiti* (which is equal parts scurrilous parody of porn and scathing parody of white tourism in the Caribbean).

Acker's novel *Pussy, King of the Pirates* also ends with an overt reference to black and white: "Ange and I grabbed all the money we could and got into the rowboat that was hidden by the two, the white and the black, stones" (*PKP* 276). *Pussy, King of the Pirates,* like *My Mother: Demonology,* has more than one beginning; in this case, the first, a preface, opens with the death of the father (*PKP* 3), while the second, the first chapter, opens with the death of the white world (*PKP* 28). In the sequence leading up to the novel's end, the pirate girls begin to fight each other, and "[w]ater mixed with air and earth. . . . It looked as if the end of the world was the same as its beginning" (*PKP* 240). A bit later:

> Water was all over the place, had already flooded the world,
> there was no more ground.
>   This was the realm of continual ecstasy.
>   Now everything was wet, dripping with it. Dank and rot-
> ten. This world was never going to stop. . . . They [the pirate
> girls] were still very dirty and exceedingly smelly.
>
> (*PKP* 251)

Yet, for all the references to "the world of mud" (*PKP* 241), the cave in which the pirate treasure is finally found is "a large, airy place, with a little spring and a pool of clear water" (*PKP* 275). This idyllic cave echoes Ange's mother's box—from whence both Ange and the treasure map came. Here, in the cave, conflict ends, and we would seem to find an atypically utopian ending to this novel—except that things are not in fact so clearcut. Ange and O, after all, grab all the money they can in a novel, as well as a corpus, which consistently rails against acquisition. There also remains ambiguously indeterminate pirates' blood, associated both with the realm of death and with the realm of female sexuality. Further, the treasure map which comes from Ange's mother's box contains a segment referring to James Baldwin's writing, which shows "what it's like to be a black man in our society" (*PKP* 260). Nor does the novel end when the narrative ends; rather, there follows "A Prayer for All Sailors," which itself ends with the line, "For your lips have been stained by blood" (*PKP* 277). The "Prayer" is then followed by a map of pirate island ("pas sang rouge"); this map comes with instructions, among them an invocation to dive into perfectly blue water so that you will look like the pirates, that is to say—though these instructions fail to mention it—filthy and slimy and bloody.

The doublings of these novels' beginnings and endings cannot simply be read as yet another hall of mirrors, however dirty or distorted. Indeed, we are far from the realm of mirrors altogether: mirrors with their frozen, reflecting surfaces and their replication of the Same (see Irigaray, especially *Speculum*). Acker's late novels are instead texts of accretion which confound both beginnings and endings, while nonetheless constructing what she calls "mythical magic" ("CKA1" 2) among all their elements: intra-, inter-, and extratextual, even, if you like, extraterrestrial: "Antigone decided to celebrate this day . . . by changing her name to Angelique, who used to be some whore, because she told us, she was currently talking to an angel" (*PKP* 273). Acker, like Irigaray, has written extensively through and of tropes of the elements: earth, air, fire, and especially water—water with its amniotic fluidity, its relation to the flow of blood and of language. Yet both also became interested in such unexpected figures and strategies as angels and the possibility, if not the promise, of happy endings. In Irigaray's terms, "A sexual or carnal ethics would require that both angel and body be found together. This is a world that must be constructed or reconstructed."[31] One must remember that these angels and other possibilities in no way imply a transcendent escape from the material, the fleshy, or the messy—and that in the realms of either sex or politics, or even messier yet, in both at once.

Given Acker's increasing popularity with academics, her recent greater, and warmer, reception among feminists, and her nearly cult status in some quarters (such as the World Wide Web or cyberpunk), it can be quite bracing to encounter the hackles she still raises in others, particularly in more mainstream popular media, where, for example, a character from *My Mother: Demonology* has been dubbed "full of anger and shallow references to academic feminist philosophers."[32] Indeed, snide implications that Acker is nothing more than a slightly talented literary poseur may bring to mind something like the treatment often served up to Courtney Love (of the band Hole, and, if this identification is still necessary, widow of Kurt Cobain):

> To read the novel [*Pussy, King of the Pirates*] . . . is to be constantly reminded that Acker's self-consciously postmodern soup would be much more effective in other media—as a video game, a graphic novel or cartoon, a multimedia CD. . . . Acker invokes many literary touchstones . . . but you find yourself thinking that this pushing of the novelistic envelope has been done better, and more originally, by others.[33]

The clichéd notion of "pushing the envelope" is virtually synonymous with Madonna, of course, and Acker herself "self-consciously" smashed the icon of "originality" for years: "I now wonder where the idea or the ideology of creativity started. Shakespeare and company certainly stole from, copied each other's writings. Before them, the Greeks didn't bother making up any new stories. . . . Nobody *really* owns nothing."[34] These critics describe fairly accurately Acker's particular recipe for "postmodern soup" (self-conscious, angry, plagiaristic, and so forth); indeed, it is precisely her dissolute project itself which garners disapproval. It would

not be entirely inappropriate, however, to take a clue from readings that characterize Acker as "shallow," unoriginal, or "postmodern," if only because they force recognition of the enormous distance so often still maintained (whether or not articulated) between high and low culture, theory and cultural production, originality and mimicry, the serious and the playful.

If there are links (and many think there are) between Acker's writing and Irigaray on fluidity and multiplicity and mimicry or Cixous on "writing the body" and theories of the maternal and feminist hysteria, I would argue that Acker's writing takes full part in that feminist theoretical process—rather than that Acker is merely influenced by, or heir to, a certain theoretical discourse operating in another realm or, more likely, another level. That is to say that feminist genealogies do not develop in strictly linear fashion but rather undulate and intermingle, so that sometimes Cixous, for instance, seems to make more sense, though not for more mastery, when read back through Acker—or for that matter, through Courtney Love. In the same vein, Acker's work serves as an impressive reminder that there exists no stable hierarchy ranging from theory (down) to literature and (finally) popular culture. To put this somewhat differently, it seems more productive, and accurate, to consider Acker not simply an appropriate target for the "application" of Cixous's theory but rather to consider Acker as an active contributor to theoretical discourse, including feminist thought. I can, in fact, only second Acker on this general point because she suggested it herself often enough—if somewhat less directly and more humbly—although she also underscored the differences between her writing and theory as such: "I don't talk through theory, I talk through fictional process. There's a different sort of language" ("CKA1" 2).

Acker has not, of course, been the only one engaged both in a theoretical feminist process and at the same time in the production of a more "popular culture." If Courtney Love's shifting personae sometimes sound like sisters to Acker's Janey Smith ("I tell you everything / And I hope that you won't tell on me . . . Peegirl gets the belt / It only makes me cry . . . I've got a blister from / Touching everything I see"), Love also renders Cixous's maternal metaphor in a wide range of shades of "white ink" ("LM" 251) that undo "the" universalized maternal (much as Acker dismantles "the" universalized female body): "Your milk is so sick / Your milk has a dick / Your milk has a dye . . . Your milk is so mean / Your milk turns to mine / Your milk turns to cream."[35]

When Acker performs what Friedman calls "an audacious rendering of Cixous's writing the body,"[36] she similarly takes it elsewhere quite graphically:

> Everytime I talk to one of you, I feel like I'm taking layers of my own epidermis, which are layers of still

freshly bloody scar tissue, black brown and red, and tearing each one of them off so more and more of my blood shoots into your face. This is what writing is to me a woman.

(ES [Empire of the Senseless] 210)

These lines are spoken by a character named Abhor, said to be (on the first page of the text and by the other major character/narrator of *Empire of the Senseless,* Thivai) "my partner, part robot, and part black." Abhor's parody of "writing the body" is layered over a parody of Thivai's/Tom Sawyer's irritatingly ludicrous "rescue" of Abhor/Jim, inscribing, alongside references to tattooing, a racial positionality markedly absent in Cixous. "Black brown and red" function at least doubly in this passage: they underscore the missing specificity of "the" body-which-is-written, problematizing the universalized "body"; they also mark a body which is both painful writing and painfully written upon, and that in a text "dedicated to my tattooist" (Acker has said, "That's what tattooing is for me, it's myth" ["DM" 21]). Gender, furthermore, blurs messily as Acker plagiarizes her own pornography with a reverse money shot: "my blood shoots into your face."

Kathy Acker wrote theory in a dissolute mode characterized by a tattooed pirate's brew of autobiography, textual "appropriation," poetry, parody, pornography, essayistic prose, nonlinear fiction, (feminist, poststructuralist, postmodern, and posthuman) theoretical statements, political proclamations, punk grrl "lyricism," and myth. She was also a very good listener. That Acker would have taken up and deployed the stereotypical model of the "good woman" as "good listener" underscores once again her connections with other feminist theorists, and Irigaray's use of mimicry might come first to mind here:

> One must assume the feminine role deliberately. Which means already to convert a form of subordination into an affirmation, and thus to begin to thwart it. . . . To play with mimesis is thus, for a woman, to try to recover the place of her exploitation by discourse, without allowing herself to be simply reduced to it. It means to resubmit herself . . . to 'ideas,' in particular to ideas about herself, that are elaborated in/by a masculine logic, but so as to make 'visible,' by an effect of playful repetition, what was supposed to remain invisible: the cover-up of a possible operation of the feminine in language. It also means 'to unveil' the fact that, if women are such good mimics, it is because they are not simply resorbed in this function. *They also remain elsewhere.* . . .[37]

Acker was one of the many women recently engaged in highly improper projects of mimicking, mocking, and otherwise disrupting ("these Janeys covered the earth," according to Acker). Although her writing and overall cultural production are otherwise quite different, Trinh T. Minh-ha's description of reactions to her own theory, for example, has a good deal to say to Acker's writing, including the issue of mimicry as the excessive repetition of the same old thing:

> The mixing of different modes of writing; the mutual challenge of theoretical and poetical, discursive and 'non-discursive' languages; *the strategic use of stereotyped expressions in exposing stereotypical thinking*; all these attempts at introducing a break into the fixed norms of the Master's confident prevailing discourses are easily misread, dismissed, or obscured in the name of 'good writing,' of 'theory,' or of 'scholarly work.'[38]

In the hands of a writer such as Trinh, "theory" is itself broken up, startled out of its delusions of coherence and mastery. Her writing provides, therefore, one of the many answers to Irigaray's question, *"Isn't the phallic tantamount to the seriousness of meaning?"* (*TS* 163; Irigaray's emphasis). If we listen carefully enough, we will hear Acker also answer: "The dead cock was no longer leading us, 'cause we were back at the edge of the water" (*PKP* 275).

Notes

1. Kathy Acker, *My Mother: Demonology* (New York: Pantheon, 1993), 8. Hereafter cited as *MMD.*

2. Kathy Acker, "A Conversation with Kathy Acker," interview by Benjamin Bratton, *Speed* (http://www.arts.ucsb.edu:80/~speedPast/1.1/acker.html): 1-5, esp. 5. Hereafter cited as "CKA1."

3. Kathy Acker, interview in *Varieties of Violence,* a special issue of *2gz* (formerly *Girls Review*), 1, no. 1 (Spring 1995): 3. Hereafter cited as *2GZ.*

4. Luce Irigaray, *Speculum of the Other Woman,* trans. Gillian C. Gill (Ithaca: Cornell University Press, 1985), 214-26. Hereafter cited as *S.*

5. Kathy Acker, *Pussy, King of the Pirates* (New York: Grove, 1996), 185. Hereafter cited as *PKP.*

6. Hélène Cixous, "The Laugh of the Medusa," trans. Keith Cohen and Paula Cohen, in *New French Feminisms: An Anthology,* ed. Elaine Marks and Isabelle de Courtivron (New York: Schocken, 1981), 255. Hereafter cited as "LM."

7. Luce Irigaray, "The Eternal Irony of the Community," in *Speculum of the Other Woman,* 214-26. Hereafter cited as "EIC."

8. There is a growing body of critical writing which closely links Acker's writing to that of Irigaray, Kristeva, and especially Cixous: hysterical feminine writing and writing the (female) body, for example, have both been discussed, in passing and at length, in relation to Acker's work (Martina Sciolino, Ellen G. Friedman, Gabrielle Dane, Karen Brennan).

9. Kathy Acker, interview by Rebecca Deaton, *Textual Practice* 6, no. 2 (Summer 1992): 280. Hereafter cited as "IRD."

10. Kathy Acker and Sylvere Lotringer, "Devoured by Myths," in *Hannibal Lecter, My Father* (New York: Semiotext[e], 1991), 15. Hereafter cited as "DM."

11. Ellen G. Friedman, "'Now Eat Your Mind': An Introduction to the Works of Kathy Acker," *Review of Contemporary Fiction* 9, no. 2 (Summer 1989): 37-49.

12. Kathy Acker, interview by Lisa Palac, *On Our Backs* (May/June 1991): 19.

13. Kathy Acker, *Blood and Guts in High School* (New York: Grove Weidenfeld, 1978; first published London: Pan Books, 1984), 7. Hereafter cited as *BGHS.*

14. Karen Brennan, "The Geography of Enunciation: Hysterical Pastiche in Kathy Acker's Fiction," *boundary 2* 21, no. 2 (1994): 263. Hereafter cited as "GE."

15. The original text copied here is Roland Barthes, *A Lover's Discourse: Fragments,* trans. Richard Howard (New York: Hill and Wang, 1978), 9. Acker changes the masculine pronouns and repeats the final phrase.

16. Gabrielle Dane, "Hysteria as Feminist Protest: Dora, Cixous, Acker," *Women's Studies* 23 (1994): 249-50. Hereafter cited as "HFP."

17. Kathleen Hulley, "Transgressing Genre: Kathy Acker's Intertext," in *Intertextuality and Contemporary American Fiction,* ed. Patrick O'Donnell and Robert Con Davis (Baltimore: Johns Hopkins University Press, 1989), 182.

18. Kathy Acker, *Kathy Goes to Haiti in Literal Madness* (New York: Grove, 1988; first published by Rumor Publications in 1978), 7. Hereafter cited as *KGH.*

19. Cited on the Kathy Acker, *Kathy Goes to Haiti* homepage as from the introduction to Acker's *Young Lust* (http://euro.net/mark-space/ bkKathyGoesToHaiti.html).

20. One exception is Terry Engebretsen, "Primitivism and Postmodernism in Kathy Acker's *Kathy Goes to Haiti,*" *Studies in the Humanities* 21, no. 2 (December 1994): 105-19. While usefully discussing the representation and subversion of primitivism in the novel, Engebretsen also insists that "[f]inally . . . the novel is interested in the psychology of Kathy's relationship with Roger—a relationship conditioned by her primitivist assumptions—rather than in historical and political analysis of the situation in Haiti" (118 n. 4).

21. Robert Siegle, *Suburban Ambush: Downtown Writing and the Fiction of Insurgency* (Baltimore: Johns Hopkins University Press, 1989), 72-76. Hereafter cited as *SA.*

22. Christian Hansen, Catherine Needham, and Bill Nichols, "Pornography, Ethnography, and the Discourse of Power," in Bill Nichols, *Representing Reality: Issues and Concepts in Documentary* (Bloomington: Indiana University Press, 1991), 220.

23. Colleen Kennedy, "Simulating Sex and Imagining Mothers," *American Literary History* 4, no. 1 (Spring 1992): 176. Hereafter cited as "SS."

24. Toril Moi, *Sexual/Textual Politics: Feminist Literary Theory* (London: Methuen, 1985), 142.

25. Kathy Acker, *Empire of the Senseless* (New York: Grove, 1988), 127. Hereafter cited as *ES.*

26. Ellen G. Friedman, review of *My Mother: Demonology* by Kathy Acker, *Review of Contemporary Fiction* 14, no. 1 (Spring 1994): 213-14.

27. Julia Kristeva, *About Chinese Women,* trans. Anita Barrows (New York: Marion Boyars, 1977), 160.

28. Jamaica Kincaid, *A Small Place* (New York: Plume, 1988), 35.

29. Gayatri Chakravorty Spivak, "French Feminism in an International Frame," in *Other Worlds: Essays in Cultural Politics* (New York: Routledge, 1988), 139-40.

30. An exception is C. Jodey Castricano's "If a Building Is a Sentence, So Is a Body: Kathy Acker and the Postcolonial Gothic," in *American Gothic: New Interventions in a National Narrative,* ed. Robert K. Martin and Eric Savoy (Iowa City: University of Iowa Press, 1998). Castricano's essay, which appeared after my own essay was completed, carefully examines *Empire of the Senseless* in light of both postcolonial theory and feminism.

31. Luce Irigaray, *An Ethics of Sexual Difference,* trans. Carolyn Burke and Gillian C. Gill (Ithaca: Cornell University Press, 1993), 17.

32. Kate Wilson, review of *My Mother: Demonology* by Kathy Acker, *Entertainment Weekly* (1 October 1993): 50.

33. Chris Goodrich, review of *Pussy, King of the Pirates* by Kathy Acker, *Los Angeles Times Book Review* (24 March 1996): 10.

34. Kathy Acker, "A Few Notes on Two of My Books," *Review of Contemporary Fiction* 9, no. 2 (Summer 1989): 33.

35. Courtney Love and Hole, "Softer, Softest," on *Live Through This* (BMI, 1994).

36. Friedman, review of *My Mother: Demonology*, 213-14.

37. Luce Irigaray, *This Sex Which Is Not One*, trans. Catherine Porter (Ithaca: Cornell University Press, 1985), 76. Hereafter cited as *TS*.

38. Trinh T. Minh-ha and Judith Mayne, "From a Hybrid Place," in *Framer Framed* (New York: Routledge, 1992), 138; emphasis added.

Bibliography

Acker, Kathy. *Blood and Guts in High School*. New York: Grove Weidenfeld, 1978 (first published London: Pan Books, 1984).

———. *Empire of the Senseless*. New York: Grove, 1988.

———. "A Few Notes on Two of My Books." *Review of Contemporary Fiction* 9, no. 2 (Summer 1989): 31-36.

———. Interview. In *Varieties of Violence*, special issue of *2gz* (formerly *Two Girls Review*) 1, no. 1 (Spring 1995; http://www.2gz.com/acker.html): 1-12.

———. Interview by Rebecca Deaton. *Textual Practice* 6, no. 2 (Summer 1992): 271-82.

———. Interview by Lisa Palac. *On Our Backs* (May/June 1991): 19.

———. *Kathy Goes to Haiti in Literal Madness*. New York: Grove, 1988 (first published by Rumor Publications in 1978).

———. *My Mother: Demonology*. New York: Pantheon, 1993.

———. *Pussy, King of the Pirates*. New York: Grove, 1996.

———. "A Conversation with Kathy Acker." Interview by Benjamin Bratton. *Speed* (http://www.arts.ucsb.edu:80/~speedPast/1.1/acker.html): 1-5.

———. "Devoured by Myths." With Sylvere Lotringer. In *Hannibal Lecter, My Father*. New York: Semiotext(e), 1991.

Barthes, Roland, *A Lover's Discourse: Fragments*. Trans. Richard Howard. New York: Hill and Wang, 1978.

Brennan, Karen, "The Geography of Enunciation: Hysterical Pastiche in Kathy Acker's Fiction." *boundary 2* 21, no. 22 (1994): 243-68.

Castricano, C. Jodey. "If a Building Is a Sentence, So Is a Body: Kathy Acker and the Postcolonial Gothic." In *American Gothic: New Interventions in a National Narrative*. Ed. Robert K. Martin and Eric Savoy. Iowa City: University of Iowa Press, 1998.

Cixous, Hélène. "The Laugh of the Medusa." Trans. Keith Cohen and Paula Cohen. In *New French Feminisms: An Anthology*. Ed. Elaine Marks and Isabelle de Courtivron. New York: Schocken, 1981. 245-64.

Dane, Gabrielle. "Hysteria as Feminist Protest: Dora, Cixous, Acker." *Women's Studies* 23 (1994): 231-56.

Engebretsen, Terry. "Primitivism and Postmodernism in Kathy Acker's *Kathy Goes to Haiti*." *Studies in the Humanities* 21, no. 2 (December 1994): 105-19.

Friedman, Ellen G. "'Now Eat Your Mind': An Introduction to the Works of Kathy Acker." *Review of Contemporary Fiction* 9, no. 2 (Summer 1989): 37-49.

———. Review of *My Mother: Demonology* by Kathy Acker. *Review of Contemporary Fiction* 14, no. 1 (Spring 1994): 213-14.

Goodrich, Chris. Review of *Pussy, King of the Pirates* by Kathy Acker. *Los Angeles Times Book Review* (24 March 1996): 10.

Hansen, Christian, Catherine Needham, and Bill Nichols. "Pornography, Ethnography, and the Discourse of Power." In Bill Nichols, *Representing Reality: Issues and Concepts in Documentary*. Bloomington: Indiana University Press, 1991. 201-28.

Hulley, Kathleen. "Transgressing Genre: Kathy Acker's Intertext." In *Intertextuality and Contemporary American Fiction*. Ed. Patrick O'Donnell and Robert Con Davis. Baltimore: Johns Hopkins University Press, 1989. 171-90.

Irigaray, Luce. *An Ethics of Sexual Difference*. Trans. Carolyn Burke and Gillian C. Gill. Ithaca: Cornell University Press, 1993.

———. *Speculum of the Other Woman*. Trans. Gillian C. Gill. Ithaca: Cornell University Press, 1985.

———. *This Sex Which Is Not One*. Trans. Catherine Porter. Ithaca: Cornell University Press, 1985.

Kennedy, Colleen. "Simulating Sex and Imagining Mothers." *American Literary History* 4, no. 1 (Spring 1992): 165-85.

Kincaid, Jamaica. *A Small Place*. New York: Plume, 1988.

Kristeva, Julia. *About Chinese Women*. Trans. Anita Barrows. New York: Marion Boyars, 1977.

Love, Courtney, and Hole. "Softer, Softest." On *Live Through This*. BMI [Broadcast Music, Inc.], 1994.

Moi, Toril. *Sexual/Textual Politics: Feminist Literary Theory*. London: Methuen, 1985.

Sciolino, Martina. "Kathy Acker and the Postmodern Subject of Feminism." *College English* 52, no. 4 (April 1990): 437-45.

Siegle, Robert. *Suburban Ambush: Downtown Writing and the Fiction of Insurgency.* Baltimore: Johns Hopkins University Press, 1989.

Spivak, Gayatri Chakravorty. "French Feminism in an International Frame." In *Other Worlds: Essays in Cultural Politics.* New York: Routledge, 1988. 134-53.

Trinh T. Minh-ha and Judith Mayne. "From a Hybrid Place." In Trinh T. Minh-ha, *Framer Framed.* New York: Routledge, 1992. 137-48.

Wilson, Kate. Review of *My Mother: Demonology* by Kathy Acker. *Entertainment Weekly* (1 October 1993): 50.

Arthur Saltzman (essay date 2000)

SOURCE: Saltzman, Arthur. "Kathy Acker's Guerrilla Mnemonics." In *This Mad "Instead": Governing Metaphors in Contemporary American Fiction,* pp. 110-28. Columbia: University of South Carolina Press, 2000.

[*In the following essay, Saltzman explores the effect and purpose of Acker's plagiarization of canonical texts in her novels* Great Expectations *and* Don Quixote, *asserting that "if plagiarism is the key to Acker's method, it is plagiarism in which there is as much mutilation of forms as there is assimilation."*]

The uniqueness of their treatments of metaphor aside, most of the works addressed in *This Mad Instead* imply a shared set of assumptions about the virtues of enameled expression. By these lights, successful writing for the novelist and for the critic alike is a matter of getting oneself elegantly in and out of trouble. Turning to Kathy Acker's fictions introduces a tonic or a toxin into the mix, depending on one's taste. Acker's brazen appropriations of precursor texts are not subtle, formal, or thematic negotiations but hostile takeovers. Acker does not pick pockets but robs graves; to steal a title from Jean Genet, one of her clearest influences, each of her texts is a thief's journal.[1]

But her method has little to do with stealth and embezzlement. On the contrary, Acker does not try to heal the breaches her burglaries create. Rupture is the order of the day, and instead of smooth transition we find in-your-face, flagrant indigestion. If lyrical intricacy and syntactic grace serve as humanistic affirmations, Acker's fractures and dissonances disdain reconciliations of any sort. Scorning the genteel, navigable measures of things poetically put, she deals in harangues and blasphemies, hysterics and snarls. Her demographic range takes us from lofted bohemian hieratics and Witwoulds to the seething, leprous denizens of drug dens and snuff shows. She takes human relationships immediately and

exclusively down to lurid, devouring antagonisms between alienated characters who anguish openly and fuck in clusters.

In Acker's world, men are the regime, predatory and self-absorbed; women who exhibit any of the conventional feminine protocols—self-denial, provision, modesty, all the etiquettes of endearment and receptivity—grow carapaces or get consumed. A similar male-female division may govern the politics of plagiarism as well. Whereas the male writer conducts his smuggling within a tradition hospitable to—indeed, prominently featuring—his experience, the female writer, who generally finds herself outside those validating confines, typically employs and revises precedent texts "either to point up the biases they encode or to make them into narratives that women can more comfortably inhabit" (Walker 3). So there are thieves, and then there are thieves: the male plagiarist as insider trader versus the female plagiarist as pariah. The latter sends forth an infidel text to spy upon the amenities of its ancestors. A writer like Kathy Acker cases the canon in order to ransack its locked premises.[2] Adrienne Rich makes much the same point in "When We Dead Awaken: Writing as Re-Vision": studying the literature of the past is not a strategy of emulation but a means of discovering how to "break its hold" (35). In this way, Acker's writings absorb the language and the legacy of prior texts but refuse them priority over her constructions.

Plundering the classics is also a way for the female writer to achieve penetration, as her texts crawl on top of his, seducing the books they host via the female-superior position. Refusing marginalization, Acker's fictions operate close to the front lines, where they finally infiltrate. Naomi Jacobs describes the technique as being part of a war on discrimination: "This undifferentiated use of figures from history, literature and contemporary literary circles merges all realms of language in which meanings reside, and thus destroys meanings by destroying the contexts which focus them. Brought into forced conjunction, these irreconcilable contexts split open and spill their constituent parts into a formless intertext" (51). With the myth of originality deposed for catering to the (chiefly male) bastion of canonical literature, proprietorship is up for grabs. Accordingly, Raymond Federman, for whom plagiarism is really "playgiarism," strikes this blow against reactionary conceptions of authority by boasting about a destabilizing mimesis: "I shall not reveal my sources because these sources are now lost in my own discourse, and, moreover, because there are no sacred sources for thinking and writing" (566). The result is a rowdy, intertextual nexus of quote-soaked hybrids—in Acker, the literary equivalent of group sex. Be honest, *Great Expectations* urges, "How can purity be a story?" (80). The whore text is a vortex; allusions are panderings; Acker's passages are passed around like the featured girl in Victorian porn. "It'd be good to get you out of my body cause then I'd be strong that is single. I don't want to and why should I?" (*Great Expectations* 118). Like William Gass's *Willie Masters' Lonesome Wife,* Acker's novels are flirtatious, practiced, ingenious mistresses.[3] But whereas Gass's book is struck with sallow attendants and bemoans the absence of something impressive to enter the body of the text, Acker's novels spread for the famous.

That Acker is so brazen about her adaptations not only intensifies our awareness of the several norms—codes of behavior, narrative structure, and literary canonization—under indictment; it serves to undermine the anticipated effect of plagiarism. Thus, for example, in *Great Expectations,* instead of leaching prestige from Dickens, Proust, Keats, Colette, and others, Acker dissolves it in a context in which they are essentially additional narrative grafts, graced with no more intrinsic legitimacy or honor than the dreams, shards of dialogue, political disputations, or pornographic tableaus with which they share quarters. She is allusive and antiliterary—crude, lewd, vile, furious—at the same time. Hence, the title promise of *Great Expectations* is tempered by the debt to its predecessor and savaged by an unprecedented horrific context of war crimes, sexual violence, and surreal fantasy:

> I want: every part changes (the meaning of) every other part so there's no absolute/heroic/dictatorial/S & M meaning/part the soldier's onyx-dusted fingers touch her face orgasm makes him shoot saliva over the baby's buttery skull his formerly-erect now-softening sex rests on the shawl becomes its violet scarlet color, the trucks swallow up the RIMA soldiers, rainy winds shove the tarpaulins against their neck, they adjust their clothes, the shadows grow, their eyes gleam more and more their fingers brush their belt buckles, the wethaired-from-sweating-during-capture-at-the-edge-of-the-coals goats crouch like the rags sticking out of the cunts, a tongueless canvas-covered teenager pisses into the quart of blue enamel he's holding in his half-mutilated hand, the truck driver returns kisses the blue cross tattooed on his forehead, the teenager brings down his palm wrist where alcohol-filled veins are sticking out. These caterpillars of trucks grind down the stones the winds hurled over the train tracks, the soldiers sleep their sex rolling over their hips drips they are cattle, their truck-driver spits black a wasp sting swells up the skin under his left eye black grapes load down his pocket, an old man's white hair under-the-white-hair red burned face jumps up above the sheet metal, the driver's black saliva dries on his chin the driver's studded heel crushes as he pulls hair out the back of this head on to the sheet metal, some stones blow up

> (*Great Expectations* 8-9)

Molly Bloom stoned in Soho, Emma Bovary literally torn between crazed lovers—the novel is a montage of violent yokings, or yoked violences, whose metamorphic progression infects Rauschenberg with Baudelaire.

Torment is a kind of integrity here, so if plagiarism is the key to Acker's method, it is plagiarism in which there is as much mutilation of forms at work as there is assimilation. We face an escalation of Pound's dictum "Make it new" in Acker's lab, where innovation is a matter of making a new "it."

So we have the book, Dickinson's ideal frigate to take us worlds away, stocked with acids. History, childhood experience, fantasy, literary allusion—all are equivalent ingredients of trawled memory, and they are provided outside of any moral or logical hierarchy. Instead, the standard of inclusion and organization (or better, in view of the antiregimental nature of her novels, juxtaposition) is intuitive, a startling response to what John Barth has called "felt ultimacies" ("Literature of Exhaustion" 67).

Most of Acker's novels exploit other literature to some extent. I have chosen to concentrate primarily on *Great Expectations* and *Don Quixote,* in part because their titles are obviously thrown gauntlets, and in part because they are overtly and consistently attentive to the seductive incarceration of images. Each novel demystifies the mechanics of the rational, with its invidious syntactical linkages and imaginative thrall, glamorless and chill; each features a persona who, disillusioned by depraved circumstances, means to dispense with the deceptions of consecutive reasoning and figurative refinement.

Under these conditions, then, the narrators, or narrative guises, of Acker's *Great Expectations* are orphans in more ways than Dickens had ever intended his questing Pip to be, for they are sexually and linguistically, not just socioeconomically, disfranchised. (Because "everyone is one kind of orphan or another" by virtue of all manner of letdowns and abandonments, we are told in *Don Quixote,* "None of us is anyone else's kind" [157].) In fact, the very convention of a dominating protagonist, much less a redoubtable quester, recalls commitments to authoritarian (and, historically, male) control that "anticanonical" women writers repudiate (Friedman, "'Utterly Other Discourse'" 361).[4] *Great Expectations* is a novel-long crisis of positionality, as Acker shifts in and out of the roles of witness, debater, and puppeteer. "Character," as such, always hides a plural; there is no innocent "I." An "opera of fluids," to borrow a phrase from Hélène Cixous, the novel conceives of character not as a consolidated code or mannerly digit but as a "trans-subjective effervescence," a bursting chorus of multiples "on the run" (Cixous 384-90).[5] By this definition, donning inverted quotes like epaulets of promotion, "character" embodies the free play of the signifier made notorious by deconstructionist criticism. Character contains multitudes and restrains none of the population.

Acker agrees: being compacted into a singular, modulated "I" means the death of the writer ("interview with Sirius" ["Kathy Acker"] 19, 21). "I'll say it again: without I's, the I is nothing," warns Acker's Don Quixote, echoing "every book" Acker has written (*Don Quixote* 101). Unprobed, untouched, the Self deteriorates in seclusion from Others, especially as they are embodied as other selves: "For, being untouched, I can do (be) anything(one) and so, am nothing," explains a troubled dog in *Don Quixote,* complaining like an untended tenor bereft of a vehicle to take him out of himself (161).

But reanointments of the narrator in *Great Expectations* do little to alter the bare spectrum of options available to her. "The flickering subject dreams the cultural fiction that she can live outside the discourse she mimics. But as the subject disappears before our eyes, Acker drops her audience abruptly into an abyss where the polyvalent dependences of meaning slide ceaselessly, one against the other" (Hulley 174). Like meager insurgent colonies, Rosa, Natalie, Sarah, Kathy, and O (abducted from the pornographic classic *The Story of O*) seem destined to choose between victimization and co-optation by male power politics, the latter unerringly directed toward what Louise Glück terms "the low, humiliating / premise of union—" ("Mock Orange," lines 10-11).

To circumvent the stifling orthodoxies of men, one must undermine their linguistic tendencies. For Acker, they are manifested as virile, chiseled images; regardless of their employment as whispered endearments, art criticism, sadistic assaults, or sexual provocations, they thwart female desire.[6] Acker's reaction is consistent, and consistently blunt: "And the only thing guys have to learn is that there's nothing wrong with dicks and cocks but don't think you've got the only cocks in the world" (quoted "interview with Sirius" 23). The credo "You have to keep up this image to survive" suggests, and overtly grants advantage to, a phallic version of endurance and potency; the role to which the "whore" is relegated in this economy, of course, is "to make this image harder" (*Great Expectations* 48, 49). As Marge Piercy relates in "You Ask Why Sometimes I Say Stop,"

> If you turn over the old refuse
> of sexual slang, the worn buttons
> of language, you find men
> talk of spending and women
> of dying.

(lines 11-15)

Acker also chafes against a double standard so prevalent that one feels neurotic about noting its daily presence. "'Don't worry about seeing:' my new husband said, 'I'll do the looking'" (**"The Language of the Body"** n.p.).

Therefore, images in *Great Expectations* are treated as obstacles instead of as viable transports. "Terence told me that despite my present good luck my basic stability my contentedness with myself alongside these images, I have the image obsession I'm scum," says Peter (6), a homosexual artist who cannot progress until he outgrows the endorsement of images (here, those provided by an absolutist reading of Tarot cards). Stability and contentedness, however enticing, could cause this Pirrip/Pip/Peter to languish and abort the quest. Only when Peter embarks upon his series of (chiefly female) incarnations can he conduct his yearnings and, if not mature into a hero, reorient as an eternal initiate. In keeping with this hypothesis, the opening pages of the novel include literary allusion, quotation, drugs, dream, childhood memory, and Tarot—all brute investitures in surrogacies designed to defy congealing. This lesson is emphasized by the mother, who not only advises against all-but-momentary stays—"Now that you know what this experience is, you have to leave" (10)—but also introduces the novel's standards of unassimilatability and protean forms: "My mother is adoration hatred play. My mother is the world. My mother is my baby. My mother is exactly who she wants to be. . . . I don't have any idea what my mother's like" (14). What cannot be pointed at, fixed, or phrased cannot be fastened to a bankrupt metaphysics: "You are moving. You never stay still. You never stay. You never 'are.' How can I say 'you,' when you are always other? How can I speak to you? You remain in flux, never congealing or solidifying. What will make that current flow into words? . . . These rivers flow into no single, definitive sea. . . . All this remains strange to anyone claiming to stand on solid ground" (Irigaray 214-15).

So much for the poised reenactment of autobiography, its measured, segmented narrative line. As Acker sees it, autobiography is the story of the story, not of its prime inhabitant; writing does not commemorate identity, it manufactures it ("interview with Perilli" 31). To be sure, *Great Expectations* refuses to "capitulate" to consistent meaning, much less to the idols of character, plot, or appointed setting. Experience recovered is experience re-covered: "the inextricability of relation-textures the organic (not meaning) recovered" (*Great Expectations* 15). If Acker's novels strike us as splenetic action paintings, it is partly due to the author's conviction that sense (often presented as a construct of male hegemony) is a betrayal of sensation (the female elixir of liberation).[7] Anwar Sadat makes a cameo appearance in the novel primarily to confirm this aspect of Armageddon, as he comments on the war that will end the reigning significations: "There's no way to prepare for horror. Language like everything else will bear no relations to anything else. . . . Culture has been chattering and chattering but to no purpose. When a sentence becomes distinct, it makes no more sense or connection" (34).[8]

For Clifford Still, a New York painter to whom Peter attaches himself after his metamorphosis into "Sarah," language is basically upholstered silence, intractable and self-absorbed as the male membership of the novel. He wishes to be Clifford *Still,* to employ aesthetic materials that, like compliant women, do not exert their own demands or move on him. No wonder he feels terrorized: "A language that I speak and can't dominate, a language that strives fails and falls silent can't be manipulated, language is always beyond me, me me me. Language is silence. Once there was no truth; now I can't speak" (96).

Again, language cannot be dependably about "me" if the self perpetually subdivides or if "language is always beyond me." As a result, despite this author's reputation as a maker of manifestos, Acker's so-called masterpoets "will be informed of nothing" (71), which is either to disclaim within the text what may lie beyond the rather ghastly valley of its saying—the poet nothing affirmeth, however loudly she rails—or to promise that Acker herself, through her manipulation of stolen articles, will let them in on nothing. So volatile a compound as an Acker novel "cannot be upheld as a thesis" (Irigaray 79); nor do Acker's political inserts in this novel and later in *Don Quixote,* which tilts at the din of inequity that is the American history of repression, intolerance, and viciousness, especially the sorceries of the Nixon and Reagan administrations (revealing the "blood hidden under the clean white male weaponry" [*Don Quixote* 125]) fully transcend this context of negation. In short, *Great Expectations* is a chaos of thresholds, raveling, reveling in unendingness; but its language crests over the void.

One result of these re-visions is to reconceive reality as a function of desire—desire that does not "thingify" into an image, that standard of male satiety (99). We are told in *Great Expectations* that a "perfect image" is closed (49), much as a pure text is undefiled by reference (the charge of promiscuity) or strict interpretation (the charge of sadism). "The act of describing," Acker writes, "assumes one event can be a different event: meaning dominates or controls existence. But desire—or art—is" (quoted in Friedman, "'Now Eat Your Mind'" 38). On the contrary, therefore, Acker touts the novel that prizes vulnerability and unrelenting sensation over the appeals of secure understanding and the monarchy of the finished image. To ensure that one's "line of flight" is not "captured and normalized" by regime apparatus: that is woman's wish because it is woman's nature, as well as the artist's prerogative (Dix 58).[9] For all of the ghoulishness delineated in Acker's fiction, the greatest sin is stanched desire, the cheat of mediation and what ceases. Hélène Cixous speaks of "the surplus reality produced by the indomitable desire in the text" (383). From this formula we get the Ego as unlimited citizenry resisting parentheses, the hypersexual transit citizenry resisting parentheses, the hypersexual transit of the female quester, and the multiple orgasm of language baring its devices.

Acker's overheated prose refutes the composure of "beautiful" writing, which implies a domestication of desire. When its ultratolerance is expressed in terms of the fate of female characters, her style can become an invitation to ravishment or rape. ("Female sexuality has always been denial or virginity," observes *Don Quixote* [27], due largely to the linguistic and material conditions that constitute a woman's legacy.) Understood more broadly, however, it can be taken as a plea for polymorphous perversity as sexual reality and fictional technique alike: "Women's sexuality isn't goal-oriented, is all-over. . . . [S]ex isn't a thing to them, it's all over undefined, every movement motion to them is a sexual oh. . . . Women hate things the most" (*Great Expectations* 49-50). And among those pernicious "things" is the end-directed quest, which in *Don Quixote* is a "proposed structure" that "functions only potentially, as the will to escape this cycle" of paralyzed scenarios (Walsh 139).[10]

For Acker, images are *things*—arrested acts, fatalities of experience. "The past's over. It's an image. You can't make love to an image" (Acker, **"Models of Our Present"** 62). Because such reductions of force come from steering one's writing into a closed account, she must turn desire into an art that diminishes neither desire's nor the artist's vitality (Acker, *Literal Madness* 221). Finished or totalized desire is a contradiction in terms. "To write is to submit to not-knowing, and to begin is to figure an originary absence with which the writer may identify, the very figure of self-abnegation" (Sciolino 66). The feeling that a novel like *Great Expectations* does not so much conclude as desist largely derives from this priority.

"Watch desire carefully," Acker advises in *My Death My Life by Pier Paolo Pasolini.* "Desire burns up all the old dead language morality" (*Literal Madness* 215). But a paradox survives the immolation: the language itself betrays the trace of the regime she would undermine. Don Quixote's poem to an audience of dogs concludes lamely as she realizes that she cannot conceive outside of controlling language and that, in any case, poetry requires a sympathetic community nowhere in evidence (194-95).[11] Reconstituting the self with contaminated components, like banking on priapic attentions to redeem female erotics or on plagiarism to author innovative fictions, may be objectionable by definition. At best, as Ellen G. Friedman explains, "The attempts to subvert male texts and thus male culture result in revelation rather than revolution; the path to an alternative site of enunciation is blocked by the very forces this path is meant to escape" ("'Now Eat Your Mind'" 44). Furthermore, as Acker herself explains, her manner of plagiarism is perhaps better understood as possession—hers by the precedent author, that is ("interview with Stone" 54). The consolation is that such an interpretation has the virtue of avoiding the sort of psychic imperialism (a copy of the devalued patriarchal model) implied by stealing another's words for one's own advantage.

Yet to what degree is even the revelation Friedman proposes as an alternative to revolution, willfully objectionable and prodigal though that revelation may be, compromised by its having negotiated within this context?[12] This remains a critical problem for Acker. "[M]erely by evoking these absent texts, she allows their ideologies to loom visibly through contemporary obscenities." Defacements are inescapably inscriptions. "Naturally . . . 'dirty' words, too, are thick with connotation, for as 'graffiti' they inevitably provoke those class and canonic distinctions they would defy" (Hulley 178). The most repellent rhetoric is still shadowed by the conditions that incited it; it is still dogged by etymological debts, and "the sense of imprisonment within a matrix of contradictory imperatives is tangible in the writing" (Walsh 156). The captivity is summarized in *Don Quixote* when Baudrillard is chased down a blind semiotic alley: "'[He] says our language is meaningless, for meaning—any signs—are the makings of the ruling class.' 'But he's still using meaningful signs to say this'" (55). A scorched-earth stylistic program gives onto scenes of corrosion, perversion, and purgation in Acker's novels, but the anxiety of stultifying influences—repressive institutions, social codes, and sublimated desires—perseveres. "Ten years ago it seemed possible to destroy language through language which normalizes and controls by cutting that language. Nonsense would attack the empire-making (empirical) empire of language, the prisons of meaning. But this nonsense, since it depended on sense, simply pointed back to the normalizing institutions" (*Empire of the Senseless* 133). In a way, all of the thrashing about Acker's novels do may rattle the fixities some, but the proposed "all-over" movement of narrative meant to parallel the polymorphous/metamorphic perversity of the protagonist can never be fully accomplished except in principle: "There is just moving and there are different ways of moving. Or: there is moving all over at the same time and there is moving linearly. If everything is moving-all-over-the-place-no-time, anything is everything. If this is so, how can I differentiate. How can there be stories?" (*Great Expectations* 58). All these shifts and contortions may cause us to question the authority of arrow-to-target certainties in the world or between words; nevertheless, tangles like "moving-all-over-the-place-no-time," "anything is everything," or, for that matter, "hair under-the-white-hair red" are as likely impasses as exits. "Real moving, then, is that which endures. How can that be?" (59). The flares and spatters out of which Acker ignites revelations she can

trust are triggered by her willingness to let events and characters play out, but, as we must stop to analyze, understanding also refutes moving (60).

To contend with this dilemma in *Great Expectations,* Acker decides to mine the text at the level of the image complex, where the concrete and the abstract are linked. Her models are often as not taken from the visual arts, as we see in this testimony to the Cubists, whose genius lies in their trump of process over product. The way it is rendered here echoes Walter Sickert's motion sickness in *The Women of Whitechapel:* "If everything was rendered in the same terms, it became possible to paint the interactions between them. These interactions became so much more interesting than that which was being portrayed that the concepts of portraiture and therefore of reality were undermined or transferred" (81-82). We might think of an Acker novel as a sort of "punk carnivelesque." Many readers have commented on Acker's adaptation of William Burroughs's "cut-up method," whereby the chaos of process is made apparent and integral to fictional form. For Acker, "cut-up" also recalls the physical bodies of characters, sliced, branded, and shorn—Kathleen Hulley offers the memorable term *morselated* to refer to her scarified presences (187)—in addition to her depictions of tattoos, piercings, diseases, and hermaphrodites. Furthermore, it relates to her use of spliced lexicons and mixed dictions to counteract dogma. By foregrounding the lapse between related terms—by mapping the gaps in sexual, generic, and linguistic conjunctions, in other words—Acker wishes to exploit her reputation as literary outlaw, as "bad writer."

She sets herself an extraordinary task, one made all the more complex by the situation of the female characters (or narrative proxies) in *Great Expectations.* As numerous feminist critics have outlined, only a disjunctive poetics can sustain female figures laboring in the shadow of the conceptual dominant, which is variously characterized as iconic, monolithic, and phallocentric. Typically, the female is defined as a prop, worshiper, contender for, or pretender to that preordained eminence; she is the goal to be attained or a distraction from the true path. Among the guises adopted in *Great Expectations,* O (moonlighting from the pornographic classic *The Story of O*) is quintessential in this regard: as her name implies, she is the universal donor, itinerant cipher, vaginal target, speculative portal, hapless access.[13] With the self an "endless hole" (*Don Quixote* 158)—a stuck cunt, sewer, wound, or drain through which viscera, irritants, ejaculations, and longings flow—personality is more readily identifiable as a site of clash than of saving conjunction. In the orgy of decentered, decertified identities in *Great Expectations*— "She tells him she wants to become another, as if at this point it's even a question of a decision, though it always is" (45)—this grounded zero seeks a coup of personal inscription that nevertheless abjures the power politics of male sovereignty.

But what other alternative to the cycle of rough employment and random erasure (a cycle that sadomasochism exacerbates instead of shatters in *Great Expectations*) is available? "Impenetrable is stupid," we are assured, but it is formidable and dangerous, too—traits that a regularly assaulted O might well envy (95). We may recall the comment made by the hero's mother in *Don Quixote* during her temporary withdrawal home: "You've come back to the prison of your own free accord" (116). Intended as a reminder that this retreat was of her own choosing and that she cannot hold her parents responsible, the statement also provides a phrase—"the prison of your own free accord"— that suggests that even a valiant hero's will is never entirely free of suspicious motives or models.

Naomi Jacobs encapsulates the predicament in this way: "Complete lack of definition is nothingness; but it is also perfect potentiality, complete freedom to redefine, to experiment, to live in what Cixous has called 'permanent escapade.' The Acker protagonist, then, embarks upon an anxious search for balance between the isolate nothingness of noidentity and the death of fixed identity" (52). Actually the challenge is even subtler than Jacobs suggests here. For example, "perfect potentiality," which Acker articulates through the logic of "If everything is living, it's not a name but moving" (*Great Expectations* 63), does help ensure that, to again use Acker's vocabulary, she does not sacrifice her "holes" to male "endings"—"not desiring beyond desire to be an image" (99). However, differentiating between the riot of the inchoate and the limbo of the unformed is a matter of considerable faith, to say the least. The dilemma is neatly approximated by Luce Irigaray's title *This Sex Which Is Not One*: whether the emphasis is on "not," in which case we have a complaint of negation, or on "one," in which case we have an affirmation of unchecked multiplicity.

Despite their several proclamations of freedom, all of Acker's females seem to be hooked on one sort of junk or another. Catatonia, not blazing, infinitely directed vision, is the common prayer of the abused. If literate elegance is a false lead, a full pardon from words tempts them with psychic relief. Furthermore, achieving a "balance" of any sort, even one so deliberately precarious and steadied by the integrity of refusal as the one Jacobs describes, may also be seen as a stay against profusion, that fundamental scuttling of "anatomical destiny" (Irigaray 71). Nor does "permanent escapade"— Luce Irigaray's phrase "disruptive excess" dovetails effectively with Cixous's (78)—even temporarily escape from the prison house—or better, given Acker's predilections, the bordello—of language.

So Acker's demolition of sexual and linguistic orthodoxies really seems to be more on the order of a finesse. Its hallmarks are didactic testimonies: preferring a Life of Sensation over a Life of Thoughts (69); asserting a self loosely composed of desires, dreams, and visions, all of which slip the boundaries of the male-supervised evident (76); honoring dissatisfaction, chaos, questioning; and bombing grammatical networks— "Stylistically: simultaneous contrasts, extravagancies, incoherences, half-formed misshapen thoughts, lousy spelling, what signifies what?" (107). We may be entering upon that domain of experience Barbara Freeman calls the "feminine sublime," which, by confronting an otherness that is "excessive and unrepresentable," resists the "masculinist" bias toward neutralization and mastery (2, 4). It is the ecstasy of insubsumability; the purest rapture displaces all ideological, conceptual, or linguistic residences.

Acker announces early in *Great Expectations* that she seeks to intimate texture, not to target meaning (15). Paralleling this is the paradox that allover sexuality, with its technical complement of multiple (sometimes playful, sometimes anonymous) reference, is presumably aligned with a repudiation of finished concepts and images, a creed which, surprisingly, sounds more on the order of textual celibacy. Once again, Acker relies on the prerogatives of the ongoing *process* of desire— desire unmitigated by specific direction, achieved vantage, or ultimate gratification—to evade logical constraints.

Seen in this manner, desire becomes incentive, experience, and scourge at the same time: "Desire drives everything away: the sky, each building, the enjoyment of a cup of cappuccino. Desire makes the whole body-mind turn on itself and hate itself. Desire is Master and Lord" (*Great Expectations* 70). To prevent processes from becoming things, Acker conducts her experiments behind the arras of mischief; artists love what runs away from them better than the convictions they can reach and embrace (81). So as not to fall prey to subduction by terminal images (so as not to desire "beyond desire"), Acker is addicted to means. The search for the Grail *is* the Grail. Instead of concepts, Acker focuses on the interactive synapses between them; instead of images, she approves of obsession, randomness, dreaming (82, 126).[14] As she writes in *Don Quixote,* "What you call *history* and *culture* is the denial of our flowing blood" (198).

There may be an insatiability at the core of desire that appears to invalidate any but the most elliptical, obliquely plotted narratives. Desire may require a system to harbor and transmit it, but it is "always on the move," an "unending process of displacements and substitutions," whereby literary structures are relegated to stages upon which "radical psychic mobility" may be demonstrated, even though it may involve "brutally dehumanizing activities." Kathy Acker may have found a champion in the critic Leo Bersani, from whom the above quotations are taken (quoted in Clayton 72-78). Whereas Bersani is concerned with the psychology of the reading process, with its deferrals and subjugations, Acker imports his interest in how one might break the tendency of "Narrative and mimesis . . . to pin desire down" in terms of identity, politics, and sexual behavior to speed the deunification of fiction itself.[15] "I'm sort of coming all the time," we learn in *Don Quixote* (55), in which unchecked momentum keeps the quest pure and provocative. Desire, in other words, is the force that keeps sexual arousals from being consummated, formal turbulences from being quelled, and narrative "middles" from being synthesized. "If you want to understand an event, always increase its (your perceptive) complexity" (*Great Expectations* 79). By extension, if you want to keep from being fettered by sexual roles or architected, pinnacled imagery, do not sell out your freedom of association at any price.

By transferring—admittedly, some would see it as demoting—the role of figurative language from the establishment of meaning to the discovery of "affective resonance" (Cable 9), the writer not only resists the impressment of her texts into the service of ruling ideology (the "phallocracy," if you will),[16] she also contributes to "a psychic tensional process of response to disparates that involves subverting, suspending, sacrificing, or even destroying the ordinary direct reference of language in order to assert a greater truth that conventional reference would deny" (Cable 16). Irigaray relates this unstructured, uncensored alternative to several healthy trends for the "psychic economy." Chiefly, it "impugns the privilege granted to metaphor (a quasi solid) over metonymy (which is more closely allied to fluids)"; it revives and validates unconscious energies against "the subjection, still in force, of that subject to a symbolization that grants *precedence to solids*" (110; author's italics).[17] Meanwhile, the vulnerable female protagonist devises a vision in which metaphorical consolidations cannot hold: "No thing in this world or room had anything to do with any other thing. Each thing by itself was beautiful. Each thing had no meaning other than itself, or meant nothing. The room was existing surfaces, as TV" (*Don Quixote* 190). "The only condition freaks share is our knowledge that we don't fit in. Anywhere" (202). The axiom pertains to stray dogs, wandering knights, and dis-figured language. Apparitions are uncontainable; the mad, the autistic, or the obstinately unique resist the common grids. For this reason, Don Quixote's hallucinations and tortured allegories, such as the story of "The Raven and the Lambkins" (151-53), are questionably illuminating analogs. Don Quixote claims to be "imaginatively saving the world" (154), but is it in spite of getting things wrong or by virtue of it?

The next step may be to configure psychic and stylistic insurrections as demonstrations of an ethical program, or, in this case, an antiprogrammatic ethic. Julia Kristeva provides a possible definition for this reformulation: "Ethics used to be a coercive, customary manner of ensuring the cohesiveness of a particular group through the repetition of a code—a more or less accepted apologue. Now, however, the issue of ethics crops up wherever a code (mores, social contract) must be shattered in order to give way to the free play of negativity, need, desire, pleasure, and jouissance, before being put together again, although temporarily and with full knowledge of what is involved" ("The Ethics of Linguistics" 23). We immediately recognize terms compatible with Acker's own slogans. The problem is to access instead of counter "upheaval, dissolution, and transformation." "Situating our discourse near such boundaries might enable us to endow it with a current ethical impact" (Kristeva, "Ethics of Linguistics" 25).[18] From Don Quixote's perspective, deliberate transgressions of grammar, meaning, and eloquence are the foundation of poetry—the madness of unique, inexpressible, hence unconfiscatable, insight (*Don Quixote* 191). Pushing the body in the text and the body of the text beyond "the limit of their figures," in the phrase of Gilles Deleuze and Felix Guattari, ambushes the forces of domination by exasperating recuperative arrangements. Somatic and semantic violations are thereby proposed as purification rites (quoted in Redding 284). Complementing this reasoning is Gabrielle Dane's reference to "hysteria" as extendible beyond the level of psychological debility to that of feminist protest through a rhetorical style that "eschews the bonds of conventional discourse, lacking closure, spending language lavishly, delving into the underworld of the psyche to explore phantasy and desire. . . . Such writing has the potential to become a political aesthetic, since distancing itself from logical linguistic practice, yet able to be 'heard,' the very presence of hysterical rhetoric as an alternative yet audible voice disrupts the unicity of phallocentric discourse" (241).

It is the currency of conventional definitions of "ethical impact" that Acker interrogates in *Don Quixote,* a self-proclaimed search for love that repudiates all courtly fixtures, including the romance of sacrifice, the purity of the Grail, and the grand figurative inheritances of language in which the knight, quest, and character are conventionally clad. From the outset, when a *female* Don Quixote undergoes an abortion, we know that "this's no world for idealism" because the contemporary stakes are too severe, and contemporary Evil Enchanters too formidable, to afford high-flown aesthetics. Under the conditions set in *Don Quixote,* desire is distinguished from desire *for.* Knight and Grail are "completely hole-ly" (13), a pun and oxymoron through whose satirical transformations armorial splendor is reduced to the paper dress she wears on the operating table (she herself is "perforated"), travels give way to randomness, and the most inspired dubbings do not take hold.

Since morality and culture are partners in a royal, repressive masquerade (21)—since, for that matter, thanks to a bizarre Ovidian calamity, everyone from Richard Nixon to Sancho Panza is a dog, basely instinctive and low to the ground—Don Quixote seeks desire unmitigated by objectification and domination, which are the auspices of a rulership that "loveless" barely begins to describe. In order to skirt the social determinations seemingly built into relationships, Acker's hero embarks on a quest for love that is not aimed at a beloved but toward an expansion of atmosphere. ("I won't not be: I'll perceive and I'll speak," she proclaims to her canine cohort [28].) Bitchy, recalcitrant, sexually voracious, her Don Quixote finds that all contacts scald and, as her parade of Panzas indicate, never adhere. This is desire as pure verb, asking no object to vindicate it (10).

"My sexuality is wanting not to exist," the dog declaims (149), and in doing so recollects the evacuated "I" of *Great Expectations* considered above. When under Acker's canine dispensation men are relegated to slobbering sexual engines and women to bitches, little better can be expected. The point is made during the revival of a Sadean nightmare in which degradation causes recoil, then erasure: "My physical sensations scare me because they confront me with a self when I have no self. . . . I'm forced to find a self when I've been trained to be nothing" (171). Sex may be glamorized in some novels as a metaphor for love, trust, reverence, even valor; more likely in Acker it heralds abuse, fraud, murder, or an essential solitude.

In regard to Don Quixote herself, therefore, she must achieve the ambiguous shift from nonidentity to "an identity that always fails" so that she might love beyond the barrier of connection—hence, the announcement that she is "aphasic" works to ensure that the willful itinerant will not be moored (16, 18). This is not a matter of achieving presence so much as one of positing presences: "a plurality of selves, personae seeking rather than signifying identity" (Walsh 157). Or perhaps this regendered hero represents Acker's literal effort to realize the "androgynous mind" exalted by Coleridge, which, in the words of Virginia Woolf, "is resonant and porous; . . . transmits emotion without impediment" (102). What may appear to be a Journey to the End of the Knight—Acker herself seldom refrains from "wholly/holy/holely," "hack/hackneyed/hack-kneed," "knight/night," "Kathy/catheter" verbal snideness—is really a means of exchanging exploitation (in the form of terminations, abortions, and deaths) for exploits (cast as "stalemate[s] of erotic unattainability").[19]

A commitment to "possessionless love" (***Don Quixote*** 24) is likewise intended to undo the corruptive model of the traditional male romance. The male-female polarities in ***Don Quixote*** tend to repeat those found in ***Great Expectations***: while the male is associated with unification, order, unilateral statement, dualistic reductions, and terminals, the female is allied with magic, vision, collectivity (or anarchy), and open-endedness. We recall Virginia Woolf's depiction in *A Room of One's Own* of the obdurate "I" of a man's writing: "[T]his 'I' was a most respectable 'I'; honest and logical; as hard as a nut, and polished for centuries by good teaching and good feeding. . . . But—here I turned a page or two, looking for something or other—the worst of it is that in the shadow of the letter 'I' all is shapeless as mist. Is that a tree? No, it is a woman" (103-4). That "I," dispatched from the court of Rationality, is a general of a looming regiment of letters from which the woman writer must unsentence herself. Similarly for Acker, male reason

> is the court of judgement of calculation, the instrument of domination, and the means for the greatest exploitation of nature. As in De Sade's novels, the mode of reason adjusts the world for the ends of self-preservation and recognizes no function other than the preparation of the object from mere sensory material in order to make it that material of subjugation. Instrumental or ossified reason takes two forms: technological reason developed for purposes of dominating nature and social reason directed at the means of domination aimed at exercising social and political power.
>
> (***Don Quixote*** 72)

On the contrary, female "re-vision" renders life, literature, and human interaction a ferment and a shambles. To make use of Barbara Claire Freeman's categories, "Unlike the masculinist sublime that seeks to master, appropriate, or colonize the other, I propose that the politics of the feminine sublime involves taking up a position of respect in response to an incalculable otherness. A politics of the feminine sublime would ally receptivity and constant attention to that which makes meaning infinitely open and ungovernable" (11). Just as Acker's dismantled "I" (or "dis-mentaled," if one will allow, in light of the priorities she rejects) demands uneclipsed, proliferating agency, "[a]ll being is timelessly wild and pathless, its own knight, free" (28).

As I have argued, we are faced with the paradox of a polemically charged novel whose knight-errant, instead of being Cervantes's unwitting victim of misprision, confesses her benightedness all of the time, in the service of "romanticism of no possible belief" (42). Consider the following syllogistic impasse: "Inasmuch as nothing human is eternal but death, and death is the one thing about which human beings can't know anything, humans know nothing. They have to fail. To do and be the one thing they don't know" (35). The quester is a refugee from totalitarian understandings, a vagrant among vague surmises. While it may seem perverse to refer to modesty during an examination of Acker's fiction, in regard to achieved certitude, as squired by immaculate imagery (the coin of the patriarchal realm), Acker turns out to be modest indeed. Among detractors, Acker's fiction seeks a cheap pose of difference because conventional dimensionality eludes her. Exposing scavenged texts to shock treatment, so this argument runs, is the practice of a technician who cannot adequately handle her tools. In fact, for all her rancor, her obsessive detailing of topical indecencies, and her recruitment of other literature to her personal and political preoccupations, she is not so much polemical as "expressive" (Walsh 153-54). "I have no ideas," we are told in *Don Quixote,* by way of transition between two representative, lengthy broadsides (105).

In place of an art predicated on ideas, Acker pans excellence and opts instead for the art of the "cry." Ironically, perhaps, in view of so sordid a set of motifs as those ulcerating in novels like *Great Expectations* and *Don Quixote,* excess, escapade, and abundance express optimistic potential at optimum frequency, at which extreme the cry shrills and nothing comes to order. Primary, inarticulate, "stupid," yet poignantly alive, Acker's cry exposes "this want, this existence" that exceeds the deftness of craft and decorous figurative cunning (Acker, **"Models of Our Present"** 64). Forays of love and libel persist beyond the usual fusions of precedent and successor texts, self and community, male and female, quester and objective, and tenor and vehicle.

Notes

1. In "The Geography of Enunciation," Karen Brennan expands on parallels and deceptive divisions between the "new homoerotic orders" devised by Acker (specifically in *Blood and Guts in High School*) and Genet (244-52).

2. The protagonist of Gail Godwin's *Odd Woman* also reads compulsively to find answers and, like Acker, learns that she must avoid absorption by "already-written stories" if she is to locate an identity undefiled by preconception (quoted in Greene 8). She fits the mold of Blanche H. Gelfant's "hungry women," defiantly avid for books, voracious "for knowledge, for power, for possession of her self" (223).

3. See in this regard Rosa's metafictional epistolary complaints in *Great Expectations* (25-30).

4. Friedman's straw man critic is F. R. Leavis, whose "Great Tradition" only allows access to women's fiction when it can be perceived as conforming to its strictures.

   In this context, the "moral seriousness" demanded by Leavis is "revealed as a code, rationalizing patriarchal dominance. The operation of this code is

evident in the particular vocabulary of his judgments, including key terms such as 'morality,' 'reverence,' 'civilization,' terms driven by imperatives defined and maintained by a strict system of patriarchal constraints" ("'Utterly Other Discourse'" 354). While Acker is not specifically covered in this essay by Friedman, her unruliness would clearly exempt her from consideration by an F. R. Leavis; as she puts it in *Empire of the Senseless,* "Literature is that which denounces and slashes apart the repressing machine at the level of the signified" (12). Friedman might say that Acker's experimental integrity is a justification for her unmanageability.

5. Cixous is interested, in "The Character of 'Character,'" in bringing the subject "back to its divisibility," as befits the Ego outside of its usual compression into "character." The following comment is inspired by Hoffman's tales, but it suits Acker's novel admirably: "No preperson is ever held back in his precipitation into the other who speaks to him in his name or who makes him reverberate with the convulsive airs of his libido" (390). Or as Luce Irigaray puts it, "'She' is indefinitely other in herself" (28).

6. See for example the passage in *Don Quixote* in which the androgynous hero imagines a closed, forbidding circuit among "the image," "a man's suit," untouchability, imperviousness, and being "totally elegant" (56). Cixous's concept of "vatic bisexuality" also seems relevant to Acker's gender editing (quoted in Moi 108-9).

7. Another Acker title, *Empire of the Senseless,* neatly expresses this coup.

8. It is useful in this instance to bring in someone like Sven Birkerts for counterpoint. Birkerts celebrates our experience of "deep durational time" as it is traditionally guaranteed by the novel, which "through language, through the complex decelerating system of syntax, pushes us against the momentum of distraction" (10). By contrast, Acker's novels are positively permeable affairs, keen for sensation. They do not combat "the momentum of distraction"; they welcome it.

9. Douglas Shields Dix prefaces this comment by depicting the paradox of a collective radical movement, in that collectivity makes the rebel force ripe for co-optation by the existing order (56-57). (If Love is Don Quixote's goal, it must be a sleepless, unconsolidated love.) Thus the female must resist her tendency toward collectivization in order to sustain her polymorphic power and her threat of uncompromising emotion.

10. As Walsh goes on to explain the deliberate failure of progress in the novel, "The combination of the argument's thematic stasis with its dynamic linear

structure results in the incorporation of this dynamism *within* stasis, producing an argument in dynamic equilibrium. The cyclical form that constrains the narrative is therefore not viewed from outside, as repetitious and fruitless, but from within, as a potent condition of frustration" (140).

11. As "dehumanized victims" of the ideology of "a crude self-interested materialism," it is to be expected that the dogs would prove to be less than attentive to poetry (Walsh 136).

12. Arthur F. Redding wonders more or less the same thing, as he maintains that any emancipation effected by Acker's outrageous poetics is "illusory and provisional at best" (283-84). See also the discussion in Toril Moi's *Sexual/Textual Politics* of how deconstructive texts confess their parasitism, whereby subversion retains the taint of the assaulted "host" (139-43).

13. Luce Irigaray's commentary on woman's "consignment to passivity" further glosses this "O": "While her body finds itself thus eroticized, and called to a double movement of exhibition and of chaste retreat in order to stimulate the drives of the 'subject,' her sexual organ represents *the horror of nothing to see*. A defect in the systematics of representation and desire. A 'hole' in its scoptophilic lens" (26; author's italics).

14. There may be a critical price to pay for assigning the quality of "betweenness" to woman: the subordination of her presence to the status of "interval" or "copulative link." See Irigaray 108-9.

15. In his chapter "Theories of Desire," Jay Clayton pits Bersani against Peter Brooks, who underscores the social benefits of sublimation toward the creation of "an enduring civilization," the very defining constructions of which Bersani's version of desire may be directed to overturn (78). As for Bersani's reference to the possible involvement of "brutally dehumanizing activities," Clayton obligingly samples a number of contemporary novels in which sadistic sex is prominently considered (64)—a bang gang Acker's books could readily consort with.

16. The dubious values of the "phallocracy" are listed by Irigaray as "property, production, order, form, unity, visibility . . . and erection" (86). By refusing to subscribe to these values, a writer like Acker presumes a female presence under another model of truth and/in discourse.

17. In his discussion of Peter Brooks's *Reading for the Plot: Design and Intention in Narrative* (1984), Clayton highlights Brooks's consideration of metonymy and metaphor, which are here, too, seen as an "organizing principle of narrative middles" and as "the figure that governs totalizing interpretations at the end of story," respectively (66). It should be noted that Brooks treats these as stages in the reading process, in which deferrals are necessary but temporary. Meanwhile, Acker's interest seems rather a matter of sustaining the dynamism of desire for its own liberating (and indefinite) sake.

18. Also relevant to Acker is the phrase "enunciation's motility," which Kristeva employs in "The Novel as Polylogue" (175). See also Fredric Jameson's contrast between Modernist parody and postmodern pastiche, the latter which does not restore the paradigm of "normal healthy discourse" (cited Brennan 247). By way of contrast to Kristeva's idea, see Arthur F. Redding's analysis of masochism in Acker's writings, in particular the contention that "Even a victim is entrenched within a discursive figuration that allows only limited semantic flexibility" (284).

19. Richard Walsh coins this last phrase and proceeds to list instances of these stalemates in the novel (146-51).

Works Cited

Acker, Kathy. *Don Quixote*. New York: Grove, 1986.

———. *Empire of the Senseless*. New York: Grove, 1988.

———. *Great Expectations*. New York: Grove, 1982.

———. "Kathy Acker: An Interview." By Paul Perilli. *Poets & Writers* 21.2 (March/April 1993): 28-33.

———. "Kathy Acker: From Mascot to Doyenne of the Avant-Garde." Interview with Judy Stone. *Publishers Weekly* (11 December 1995): 53-54.

———. "Kathy Acker: Where Does She Get Off?" Interview with R. U. Sirius, *io* 2 (1994): 18-23.

———. "The Language of the Body." *CTHEORY* (1992): Internet. 21 February 1996.

———. *Literal Madness: Kathy Goes to Haiti; My Death My Life by Pier Paolo Pasolini; Florida*. New York: Grove, 1988.

———. "Models of Our Present." *Artforum* (February 1984): 62-65.

Barth, John. "The Literature of Exhaustion." In *The Friday Book: Essays and Other Non-fiction*, 62-76. New York: G. P. Putnam's Sons, 1984.

Birkerts, Sven. "Second Thoughts." *Review of Contemporary Fiction* 16 (1): 7-12.

Brennan, Karen. "The Geography of Enunciation: Hysterical Pastiche in Kathy Acker's Fiction." *Boundary 2* 21.2 (1994): 243-68.

Cable, Lana. *Carnal Rhetoric: Milton's Iconoclasm and the Poetics of Desire*. Durham and London: Duke University Press, 1995.

Cixous, Hélène. "The Character of 'Character.'" *New Literary History* 5 (1974): 383-402.

Clayton, Jay. *The Pleasures of Babel: Contemporary American Literature and Theory*. New York: Oxford University Press, 1993.

Dane, Gabrielle. "Hysteria as Feminist Protest." *Women's Studies* 23 (1994): 231-56.

Dix, Douglas Shields. "Kathy Acker's *Don Quixote*: Nomad Writing." *Review of Contemporary Fiction* 9.3 (1989): 56-62.

Federman, Raymond. "Imagination as Plagiarism [an unfinished paper]." *New Literary History* 7 (1976): 563-78.

Freeman, Barbara Claire. *The Feminine Sublime: Gender and Excess in Women's Fiction*. Berkeley: University of California Press, 1995.

Friedman, Ellen G. "'Now Eat Your Mind': An Introduction to the Works of Kathy Acker." *Review of Contemporary Fiction* 9.3 (1989): 37-49.

————. "'Utterly Other Discourse': The Anticanon of Experimental Women Writers from Dorothy Richardson to Christine Brooke-Rose." *Modern Fiction Studies* 34.3 (1988): 353-70.

Gass, William. *Willie Masters' Lonesome Wife*. Tri-Quarterly Supplement 2. Evanston, Ill.: Northwestern University Press, 1968.

Gelfant, Blanche H. *Women Writing in America: Voices in Collage*. Hanover, N.H.: University Press of New England, 1984.

Glück, Louise. "Mock Orange." *The First Four Books of Poems: Firstborn, The House on Marshland, Descending Figure, The Triumph of Achilles,* 155. Hopewell, N.J.: Ecco, 1995.

Greene, Gayle. *Changing the Story: Feminist Fiction and the Tradition*. Bloomington: Indiana University Press, 1991.

Hulley, Kathleen. "Transgressing Genre: Kathy Acker's Intertext." In *Intertextuality and Contemporary American Fiction,* ed. Patrick O'Donnell and Robert Con Davis, 171-90. Baltimore and London: Johns Hopkins University Press, 1989.

Irigaray, Luce. *This Sex Which Is Not One*. Trans. Catherine Porter. With Carolyn Burke. Ithaca, N.Y.: Cornell University Press, 1985.

Jacobs, Naomi. "Kathy Acker and the Plagiarized Self." *Review of Contemporary Fiction* 9.3 (1989): 50-55.

Kristeva, Julia. "The Ethics of Linguistics." In *Desire in Language: A Semiotic Approach to Literature and Art,* ed. Leon S. Roudiez. Trans. Thomas Gora, Alice Jardine, and Leon S. Roudiez, 23-35. New York: Columbia University Press, 1980.

————. "The Novel as Polylogue." In *Desire in Language: A Semiotic Approach to Literature and Art,* ed. Leon S. Roudiez. Trans. Thomas Gora, Alice Jardine, and Leon S. Roudiez, 159-209. New York: Columbia University Press, 1980..

Moi, Toril. *Sexual/Textual Politics: Feminist Literary Theory*. New Accents. Gen. ed. Terence Hawkes. London and New York: Methuen, 1985.

Piercy, Marge. "You Ask Why Sometimes I Say Stop." In *Contemporary American Poetry,* ed. A. Poulin Jr. 6th ed. 458-59. Boston: Houghton Mifflin, 1996.

Redding, Arthur F. "Bruises, Roses: Masochism and the Writing of Kathy Acker." *Contemporary Literature* 35.2 (1994): 281-304.

Rich, Adrienne. "When We Dead Awaken: Writing as Re-Vision." In *On Lies, Secrets, and Silence: Selected Prose 1966-1978,* 33-49. New York: Norton, 1979.

Sciolino, Martina. "Confessions of a Kleptoparasite." *Review of Contemporary Fiction* 9.3 (1989): 63-67.

Walker, Nancy A. *Feminist Alternatives: Irony and Fantasy in the Contemporary Novel by Women*. Jackson and London: University Press of Mississippi, 1990.

Walsh, Richard. *Novel Arguments: Reading Innovative American Fiction*. Cambridge Studies in American Literature and Culture 91. New York: Cambridge University Press, 1995.

West, Paul. *The Women of Whitechapel and Jack the Ripper*. New York: Random, 1991.

Woolf, Virginia. *A Room of One's Own*. New York and Burlingame: Harcourt, Brace & World, 1957.

Kathryn Hume (essay date fall 2001)

SOURCE: Hume, Kathryn. "Voice in Kathy Acker's Fiction." *Contemporary Literature* 42, no. 3 (fall 2001): 485-513.

[*In the following essay, Hume argues that, contrary to critical opinion, a recurring voice links all of Acker's writings, and that this voice "sheds light on her concept of the individual."*]

A voice reverberates through Kathy Acker's novels—their most obvious characteristic, I assumed, until I read the criticism they have generated, as well as her interviews and obituaries. Acker denies having any voice at all and explains her so-called plagiarisms as a solution to that problem.[1] Other texts gave her a starting point for speaking without her first having to dominate her material. Indeed, she came to affirm her lack of voice as ideologically desirable. Our cultural demands for originality and creativity, she decided, derive from capitalist and phallic values (**"Few Notes"** [**"A Few Notes on Two of My Books"**] 10). Or, as she makes her point (elliptically and ungrammatically), "The writer took a certain amount of language, verbal material, forced that language to stop radiating in multiple, even unnumerable directions, to radiate in only one direction so there could be his meaning"; "Want to play. . . . If had to force language to be uni-directional, I'd be helping my own prison to be constructed" (**"Humility"** 116). Because Acker's stance gratifies a variety of feminist and poststructuralist predilections, most work done on Acker assumes no voice or the many voices of her decentered protagonists who change gender or identity at the drop of a hat.

My talking about a recurring voice may seem like a misguided attempt to foist a modernist reading on Acker.[2] The impulse grows out of reading all her fiction, and reading each work from beginning to end—a perverse act. Acker "didn't expect anyone to read any of her books all the way through from beginning to end."[3] If scores of voices speak out in a dozen novels, and every fourth one or so has the same tone and talks of similar material, then a coherent and recurrent, if not constant, voice emerges. A reader can focus on the disruptive, centrifugal effect of the many, the effect we are conditioned by current theory to notice in postmodern texts. However, the many voices, because they are one-offs, do not achieve much memorability, while what I call the voice gradually coheres out of the background babble. Reading two Acker novels may call attention to a pair of similar characters, and little meaning attaches to that. Reading all the novels, though, makes this persona seem much more prominent, and it stays in the mind when the postmodern pastiche characters based on Heathcliff, Pip, and Jane Eyre have become indistinct or are themselves taken over and made to sound like that voice.

I am asking how this voice functions in Acker's fiction, and what it can tell us about the tensions in her work. Deconstructive readings of modernists and the premodernist canon usefully disclose the contradictions and suppressions that created tensions in those works, and similar skepticism toward a postmodern author's declarations seems equally warranted. Acker labors to disrupt and fragment plot, character, and idea, but the violence of that impulse attests to a prior system of order still very much operational. What type of order, other than patriarchal, is she trying to disrupt? What notion of character, other than bourgeois, is she decentering, and what ideas does she attack? The last has been explored by the critics who look at her exaltation of irrationality and madness, and her focus on body as a means of opening mind-forged manacles.[4] Some of the narratives and plots she attacks have been illuminated by the critics who study her appropriation of particular canonical texts.[5] Acker's use of voice sheds light on her concept of the individual.

I am defining voice as a combination of verbal flavor, attitude, and subject matter designed to display the attitude and encourage it in readers. Voice in this sense resembles the orchestration and the preferred tonalities that let one identify a couple of measures of Tchaikovsky from the Russian intervals, or Dvořák from the tonalities preferred in Czech folk melodies, that let one differentiate between Brahms and Wagner through their different handling of horns. The voice in Acker's fiction is similarly individual to her, and paying attention to it helps us uncover her assumptions about character and understand what she is reacting against. Susan Sniader Lanser's definition of voice as the element that claims authority to speak is somewhat different from mine, though Lanser's articulation of "communal voice" bears some resemblance to Acker's letting the voice shift among her characters, such that many speak in the same tonalities and collectively come to be a community of the freakish, the dispossessed, those who do not fit in. In *My Mother: Demonology, a Novel,* for instance, the first speaker, a typical Acker persona, a wild child with a dominating mother, gibbers about fear, ecstasy, sexual experience; the letters between mother and father use the same tones; so does Beatrice; so does the father talking about his art; even the Farsi lessons, like the Persian poems in *Blood and Guts in High School,* use simple primer sentences and most unprim vocabulary. In *In Memoriam to Identity,* the voice of Rimbaud and the voice telling a Japanese tale exhibit the same basic tone and concerns.

I shall differentiate this recurring voice that I consider a major element in Acker's fiction from the one that Acker rightly denies having. The reiterated one is, for a start, a fictional creation, not to be carelessly conflated with a personal authorial voice, although the repeated elements suggest that it represents something important to the author. We know it is not her social self: as friends of hers were wont to comment, this raging, anguished, sexually voracious voice was not the witty, friendly Kathy Acker they knew at parties, the woman who claims not to have been into free love and to have gone long periods of time without sex.[6] It could be a character that she constructs for badgering readers, a version of herself she hates, someone she wishes she were, a fantasized being whose experiences justify rejecting her family, or something else altogether. The persona's relationship to the author is not determinable, and I shall treat the persona as a narrative convenience that Acker used for raising issues of interest to her.

Scenarios involving the ongoing voice compress Acker's fictive world into an agon between forces of control and her minimally differentiated personae, who resist being shaped, modified, and limited. In this, Acker shares with Thomas Pynchon, William S. Burroughs, and other contemporary artists a paranoid vision in which the individual is threatened by many forms of control.[7] The voice in her fiction is so recognizable and so rabidly determined to resist all manipulation from outside that it troubles many assumptions about postmodern decentering. The irreducibility, consistency, and repeated appearance of the voice suggest that Acker might usefully be studied as a postmodern romantic. Acker has been classified in many fashions: postmodernist, punk, feminist, gothicist, hysteric, and pornographer.[8] Her romantic elements, I suggest, come out in this voice, with its passionate defense of a remarkably stable core against the demands of society. Listening to this voice lets us register the contradicting dynamics that underlie her work as a clash between poststructuralist and more romantic values.

The Voice We Hear

Materials that help form the individual qualities of an author's voice differ from writer to writer. Great precision in choice of words and mellifluous syllables are not among Acker's qualities. She relies heavily on run-on sentences, sentence fragments, and informal abbreviations. The varied range of subjects in her narrative subunits at first supports the sense of there being no unified center of consciousness. A single novel, *Empire of the Senseless,* features scenes based on texts by William Gibson, Jean Genet, Sigmund Freud, the Marquis de Sade, Mark Twain, probably Juan Goytisolo, and possibly others I do not recognize. In addition, we find echoes of the Haitian revolution, voodoo, pirates, biker gangs, and adolescent love in Paris. Other novels include dream maps, Japanese stories and Japanese-style pictures, tantric pictures, Egyptian *Ba*-souls, creation myths, play scenes, Latin verse, pornography, Persian grammar-book phrases, and echoes of authors from Chaucer to cyberpunk. They seem random and chaotic, drawn from many areas of interest, and in their way they seem an orthodox postmodern manifestation of fragmentation.

In almost all of Acker's novels, however, we find a repeated situation that brings forth the characteristic tone of protest and anguish: a world that is hostile to the focal figures and tries to dominate them. The same emotional dynamic governs the relationship between protagonist and surrounds in virtually all Acker's narrative sequences. Someone or something tries to control the focal figure, and that figure usually resists, or sometimes becomes complicit with the controller through desire for love.

We see this control or dominance dynamic if we look at *Great Expectations.* Short though that novel is, such situations of dominance occur with regard to Peter (his mother's effects on him, that mother being the one frequently described by the Kathy-personae), a "Hubbie" and "Wife" dialogue in which they tear at each other's nerves; letters expressing self-abasement by "Rosa" (whose status as a writer and lover of Sylvére [*sic*] aligns her with Acker), masochistic sequences based on *The Story of O,* a masochistic sequence based on de Sade's *Justine,* Sarah's sequences with a mother who is functionally the same as Peter's mother; Sarah, sick, being bullied by Clifford, and Cynthia letting down all barriers to Propertius, who then scorns and avoids her. Even though Propertius is the one who dominates Cynthia in some sequences, he is himself similarly threatened and disdained by Maecenas.

This dominance dynamic with its attendant plangency of protest and resistance does not simply exemplify the need in fiction for opposing forces to generate action. Acker does not use plots, so generating conventional narrative action is not the point of this dynamic. The less powerful figure keeps feeling controlled, or fights being controlled, or gives in to the dominator or dominatrix. While love occasionally offers her characters fleeting happiness, it often proves compromised by complicity with this controlling force, and the only thoroughgoing happiness comes from achieving freedom from the pressures exerted by other people and institutions. In *Don Quixote,* the controllers are intrusive and powerful: doctors, assassins, priests, editors of *TLS,* Ronald Reagan, Nixon, landlords, the U.S. government, and teachers in a girls' school devoted to sadism, to name but some. Much the same could be said of any of the other books.

Besides this positioning of the vocal viewpoint as underdog with regard to an active, manipulative power, the other element of Acker's voice that stands out is a long-sustained lyric scream. This aspect of the voice produces forceful emotions, such as outrage on behalf of others, fear, horror, and disgust, emotions appropriate to particularly intimate and brutal attempts at oppression and coercion. Sometimes the scream is expressed by characters, sometimes more diffused through the narrative voice as it describes horrors. Janey and her projection Hester provide it in *Blood and Guts.* In *Don Quixote,* we hear it in the female knight and then in the person named Peter whom she addresses, and in the scenario in which Peter is "you" and he is paired with Juliet of *Romeo and Juliet.* That voice also adds tonalities to the Lulu/Eliza Doolittle character, and to the Jane Eyre pastiche.

The voice experiences and comments on oppression at the family, social, and national level. The family represents the most personal form of Acker's hostile world scenario. Many of the personae have a family background that forms a variation on a narcissistic mother who kills herself and a stepfather who makes a pass at or actually rapes the daughter and whose heart attack is commented upon in the hospital corridor by family members (*Great Expectations, My Death My Life by Pier Paolo Pasolini, Empire* [*of the Senseless*]*, In Memoriam* [*to Identity*]*, My Mother*). Further displacements from this scenario show up as incest stories (*Blood and Guts* [*in High School*]*,* where patriarchal incest becomes the archetypal image for men controlling women) and the incestuous creation myths in *Pussy, King of the Pirates.* The focal figure suffers from the family's oppressive demands that she conform, and she may find herself being sent to boarding school as punishment, or being strapped to a chair to watch executions and be executed herself (*Don Quixote*). Scenes of family oppression are what apparently drew Acker to reformulate *Romeo and Juliet* and *Hamlet* in *Pasolini* [*My Death My Life by Pier Paolo Pasolini*]. Such scenes generate the fantasias based on *Jane Eyre* and *Wuthering Heights* found in *I Dreamt I Was a Nymphomaniac: Imagining, Pasolini, My Mother,* and *Pussy.* Worst is the parental threat to lock the undutiful daughter away in an institution or lobotomize her (*The Childlike Life of the Black Tarantula by the Black Tarantula, My Mother*).

When the family is not the site of coercion, then society takes over through its class, gender, and money structure. The first chapter of *Tarantula* provides the fictional autobiographies of three murderesses, women who have nothing but looks and brains with which to make their way in the man's world of economic power and class. If class or wealth do not supply the primary power to control poor underlings in society, then institutions do, particularly jails and schools. *Nymphomaniac* shows us Folsom Prison; "Humility" and *Pasolini,* the legal world. Numerous novels display the world of school. *Blood and Guts* proclaims education to be the process whereby children are taught to suck the cocks of authorities. *In Memoriam* shows Rimbaud attending acting school, so-called because children are taught to act like someone other than their true selves. In *My Mother,* the Jewish girl is sent to a Wasp school to be made more Waspish.

At the highest level, the forces of control manifest themselves in governments, agencies, and world leaders. Acker's personae write letters of protest to them or engage them in fantasias of sex and perversity. Anwar Sadat, Richard Nixon, Jimmy Carter, and George Bush all come in for extended comment, and the treatments of Carter and Nixon in *Blood and Guts* and *Don Quixote* are replete with grotesque sexual and anal images that mingle all nauseating bodily exudations. Nixon gloats over raping America, and Bush wants to lobotomize artists. *Nymphomaniac* and *The Adult Life of Toulouse Lautrec by Henri Toulouse Lautrec* figure the Rockefellers as part of the conspiratorial secret society of bankers that rules the world. In *Empire,* the CIA is shown torturing and lobotomizing people.

When the focal persona of some control-routine is not lamenting unrequited love for a mother or lover, that persona laments a bootless desire for a friendly world where he or she would be accepted as is. In *Lautrec,* a waitress longs to go to San Francisco; to her it represents "a possibility of living in a world to which she's not always alien" (208). At the end of *Don Quixote,* an authorial persona speaks to the audience, saying, "Even freaks need homes, countries, language, communication. The only characteristic freaks share is our knowledge that we don't fit in. Anywhere. . . . We who are freaks have only friendship" (202).[9] *Empire* ends with an expression of this utopian strain: "And then I thought that, one day, maybe, there'd be a human society in a world which is beautiful, a society which wasn't just disgust" (227). The only "fitting in" permitted by Acker's worlds, however, is that brought about by mental mutilation, the forcible changing of behavior and thought patterns. Their obtrusive interest in evil and pain are one characteristic that makes society's watchdogs so eager to control Acker personae. The personae seeming different to other members of society brings out the mob instinct to make such personae "the same" or destroy them as unacceptable.

Naturally, if the focal figure is being forcefully pressured to change, painful emotions will intrude into other activities and concerns. Often in Acker's world, a lover's impulse to control spoils the relationship. In *Lautrec,* for instance, we find a myth called "The Creation of the World." In this myth, a little cat is hopelessly in love with a selfish baboon.[10] She brings him all the food in the world, but when he demands control over everyone, she runs and hides. He manages to eat all the animals in the world. When no more animals remain, the skinny, starving little cat comes out and the baboon finally falls in love with her, but she is too weak and hungry to love anyone. In this case, she loves, but recognizes the evil of the dictatorial impulse and resists collaborating with it. In *In Memoriam,* however, Rimbaud comes to love the man who controls him:

> A man stuck his hand up the kid's ass, repeatedly making and unclosing a fist. . . . Then the man pushed his arm up until he was holding the heart. The heart felt like a bird. Holding on to the heart, he threw the kid to the ground, kicked him in the side until the kid knew that he was nothing, had no mother.
>
> Unable to bear or stop these tortures, R moved into the imaginary. . . . "I need what you're doing to me because it's only pain and being controlled which're going to cut through my autism. Because it's pain you give me I love you."
>
> (5)[11]

Unlike the little cat, he is not attached enough to his core to resist being co-opted.

Fear is another emotion provoked by attempts to impose control. Acker's affinity for *Jane Eyre* shows in her reworking of the red room scene where young Jane is terrorized by her unsympathetic kin. The strongest expressions of fear involve a parental threat. One variation appears in *Tarantula*: "I'm forced to enter the worst of my childhood nightmares, the world of lobotomy: the person or people I depend on will stick their fingers into my brain, take away my brain, my driving willpower, I'll have nothing left, I won't be able to manage for myself" (53).[12] In *My Mother,* the persona overhears her parents murmuring, "She's evil. . . . She should be institutionalized, or put away" (86). The subsequent references to red carpet invoke the *Jane Eyre* sequences by shorthand, even as other passing references to lobotomy remind us of this fundamental fear of being committed against her will to some institution where lobotomy is a real possibility.

The narrator need not be the victim to invite readers to feel horror at accounts of brutal control. The Puritans of the Massachusetts Bay Colony punished two young men who preached Quakerism: "Twice a week the boys got whipped. They were whipped fifteen times the first time. Each time thereafter the lash number increased by three" (*Don Quixote* 118). Slaveholders in the Caribbean, we are told, punished slaves by forcing them to eat dumb cane, and we learn what its splinters do to their throats (*Empire* 74). Folsom Prison has a terrifying armament of coercive powers (*Nymphomaniac* 176-84). A narrative voice describes the history of a man whom the Folsom authorities would not release from segregation confinement unless he submitted to the "Maximum Psychiatric Diagnostic Unit." There, helpless, he might be forced to undergo electric or insulin shock, induced fevers, sodium Pentothal, Anectine (a death-simulating drug), or antitestosterone injections among other "treatments." Such attempts to force people to conform to the demands of others provide Acker with both an ongoing subject and a continuous trigger for distressed emotions. Both contribute substantially to the voice through horrifying subject matter. The voice's concern with such torments is part of what characterizes it so strongly.

The one emotion outside the variations on protest, whether lamenting or more dryly accusatory, is ecstasy at achieving freedom. Freedom is defined against oppressive familial and social expectations and is experienced when narrators violate those social norms because they wish to. In *Nymphomaniac,* the female who wears male drag loves Peter, a man who dresses like a woman. While they dance, the narrator sees people flinging off clothes and "transcending every possible barrier," and as various violent fantasies of murderers develop, she says, "I see ecstasy everywhere, and I want to be there totally insane" (116). For Acker, insanity involves discarding reason, that tool of orderly re-

pression. In a gender-bending sequence in *Don Quixote,* Villebranche and De Franville shift genders back and forth, and, temporarily, the control impulse even intensifies love in a sadomasochistic relationship. In *Pasolini,* we learn that "All the thoughts society's taught me're judgemental, usually involving or causing self-dislike, imprisoning, and stopping me. When I just let what is be what is and stop judging, I'm always happy" (250). In *Empire,* the persona says,

> I knew that pleasure gathers only in freedom. For I was soaring through the sky, my huge white and grey wings stretched out to the horizontal limits of my vision. . . . Everything burst. Carolled. There is only glory. Because I know there are angels and visions, there is freedom.
>
> (12-13)

She imagines the whole city suddenly liberated from torture, boredom, and fear and able to experiment. Such moments of relaxation into freedom are very important to Acker's impact. Without them, the explosive tensions would be so bleakly unremitting that most readers might withdraw sympathy to protect their own sensibilities. Acker makes us rejoice when some character can find a crack in the walls and slip through into freedom as sailor, pirate, biker, or gender bender. When that soul can expand and happiness well up, we are bound the more tightly to her outlook. Greg Lewis Peters suggests that Acker engages in a specifically female version of the sublime when she celebrates such sudden expansions horizontally beyond fixed barriers. Douglas Shields Dix and Rob Latham link this horizontal breakthrough to Gilles Deleuze and Felix Guattari's nomad and schizophrenic breaking of boundaries. Various narrative voices frequently call for violence to break down oppressive systems of belief and social control, and that violence should be loosed inwardly as well as outwardly. Only thus can freedom be seized.

Acker's narrative routines show individuals living in a hostile world and passionately in need of returned love and acceptance. What they mostly find instead are demands that they conform to patterns totally alien to their personalities. Acker's few intimations of ecstasy do not suggest a state of mind or way of life compatible with any current social system. With "NOW EAT YOUR MIND" (*Empire* 38), Acker clamors for a radical revolution that starts by our destroying our rationality. The dynamic of the relationship between persona and surrounds occurs repeatedly as a subtext throughout her fictions. This subtext supplies only one component of voice, but the voice speaking out of these situations is driven by desires for sex, love, and friendship, is constantly threatened with victimization, and does start to articulate a path that anger may follow toward revolutionary fervor.

THE VOICE SHE DOES NOT HAVE

Acker is especially sensitive to any issue involving control, seeing most forms of control as wrong, consensual sadomasochism being a possible exception. Not surprisingly, then, she rejects the sort of poetic lawgiver's voice valued by the Black Mountain poets. Given Acker's forcefulness, however, we might wonder how well she manages not to hand down the rules. What are the gaps in her awareness? Where does her desire to change things override her sensitivity to the inner nature of others? If one speaks out as forcefully as she does, how can one avoid imposing one's ideas on others?

Expressions of passion illustrate one of Acker's methods. In a *Scarlet Letter* fantasia found in **Blood and Guts,** Hester cries out her feeling for "Dimwit":

> I want to write myself between your lips and between your thighs. How can I get in touch with you? You don't answer your door and you don't answer your phone. I think you're a creep.
>
> I want to fuck you, Dimwit. I know I don't know you very well you won't ever let me get near you. I have no idea what you feel about me. You kissed me once with your tongue when I didn't expect it and then you broke a date. I used to have lots of fantasies about you: you'd marry me, you'd dump me, you'd fuck me, you were going again with your former girlfriend, you'd save me from blindness. You'd. Verb. Me. Now the only image in my mind is your cock in my cunt. I can't think of anything else.
>
> (95)

This statement goes on for pages, but note that it is delivered in the absence of the beloved object. Dimwit is not being directly pressured by this rhapsodic, tormented effusion, the voice expressing itself through Hester Prynne. Furthermore, Hester, in her masochistic lack of self, imagines him free to make love to any other woman, as long as she can be near him sometimes. Control over him is not something she tries for.

To a great extent, Acker even avoids dictating to the readers what they should feel upon reading her many extreme passages. Consider the passage quoted above of Rimbaud's response to being fist-fucked. The pain itself is distanced through affectless, third-person description. When the narrative shifts to first person, the speaker is numbly analytic, speaking from some space far beyond pain, saying that the controlled pain will break through his autism, and for that, the speaker loves the tormentor. That exhausted, drained, desperate love is abstract, a result for readers to contemplate and possibly to feel threatened by, since most readers do not like to think that they would fall in love with a sadistic tormentor. Acker gives us the chance to feel strongly if we wish by describing horrible acts but does not lushly express the emotions accompanying them in order to provoke our empathy.

A few times, Acker uses affectless presentation to create a childish persona. Such a voice is, by all our conventions regarding childhood's estate, emphatically not in control of what is happening. This artful naïveté lets her present her material in a fashion that sounds uncritical. *Tarantula* supplies an example of this:

> My mother tells me why I was born: she had a pain in her stomach, it was during the war, she went to some quack doctor (she had just married this guy because it was the war and she loved his parents); the doctor tells her she should get pregnant to cure the pain. Since she's married, she gets pregnant, but the pain stays. She won't get an abortion because she's too scared. She runs to the toilet because she thinks she has to shit; I come out. The next day she has appendicitis.
>
> (63)

This is not truly childish; "quack" carries adult judgment, and knowledge of abortion and marriage psychology are adult concerns. However, the short sentences run together, the simple vocabulary, and the refusal to supply grammatical subordination or causal explanation let it evoke the childish incomprehension and pain felt by the resultant daughter, and perhaps by the immature, ignorant mother as well. The rhetorical avoidance of subordination, cause, and reason (all developed at a somewhat later stage than that of the young child) help her avoid dominating us through her description.

Acker comes closest to violating her own rules when she approaches a political subject. She uses dry factuality to build statistical arguments, and her statistics are evidently meant to be unarguable: "Thus in 1973, according to the Federal Reserve, nine New York City banks, six of which belonged to the Rockefeller-Morgan group, accounted for more than 26% of all commercial and industrial lending by banks in the US" (**Lautrec** 279). She lists the percentage of various key industries owned by these banks. Such forms of affectless reportage give her rhetoric a ring of informed reliability but also establish its intransigence. Acker does not usually concern herself with the possible validity to any vision but her own when she comes to what she sees as political oppression. However, she does not call directly for any action. We must make up our own minds on what we want to do.

Such a statistical approach is rare for Acker. In part, she avoids ruling her audience by avoiding obvious logic and reason, though one can never avoid them entirely. Instead, she prefers lyric outbursts of feeling. Those do not bind us as strongly because our culture leaves us freer to reject emotion than it does reason. "Reason is always in the service of the political and economic masters" (**Empire** 12). "Reason is the court of judgement of calculation, the instrument of domination, and the means for the greatest exploitation of nature" (**Don Quixote** 72). "What the fuck is *reason* in this life, a life of disease and sex show?" (*In Memoriam* 133). Her alternative to reason and statistics is a lyric attack on the results of capitalism, where she comments on life for those who are not part of the owning class. Their world is "creepy disgusting horrible nauseous shit-filled exacerbating revolting, humans not revolting, green smelling of dead rats which were decaying and, in endless decay, covered in, like a royal blanket of flowers, purple herpes pustules which had rivetted and cracked into fissures either to the body's blood or to the earth's blood, pale green and pale pink liquid minerals in the bottoms of one-thousand-feet diameter strip mines in Arizona" (*Empire* 73).

For all that her tone is powerful, Acker rarely indulges in tear-jerking vocabulary, and any bodice ripper would develop erotics with more coherent detail and at a more stimulating pace. She makes the point herself: "You never know what might turn some people on, but mostly I can't see how people would get aroused by the sex I'm describing in my books. Certainly titillation isn't what I've been after except maybe in a few early ones like *Tarantula* and *Toulouse*" ("Interview" 94-95). Likewise, when dealing with fear and pain rather than desire, cheap horror fiction works far more directly. Acker prefers to describe a terrifying situation in relatively flat language and invites readers who are sympathetic to feel the outrage. A reader can, of course, resist. I have had students who were rendered furious by *Don Quixote* and felt the focal figure's complaining and misery to be completely unjustified. Readers of phlegmatic temperament and middle-class values are likely to find a good deal of the tonal anguish unnecessary; to them it represents a defect in the outlook of Acker or of her personae, rather than a true defect in the world. Like the parental figures in these novels, such students do not respond to the needs of those who are fundamentally different from others in their society. They have never felt the pains of being at odds with their culture.

The central core found in all Acker's personae *is* threatened, however, and the emblematic experience of that threat is lobotomy.[13] By defending that self against any such surgical intervention, she makes her terror of being forcibly tamed rather similar to male fears of castration.[14] This panic resonates dissonantly and contributes a reiterated sense of fear to the voice's tonal inflections of desire, pain, and frustration.

PAIN, POLITICS, AND THE CORE SELF

To determine politics, one needs first to determine how an author views the nature of the world and human life. Are people basically decent if given a decent upbringing, or does one assume human selfishness and even malevolence, whether from flawed oedipal development or original sin? Should we expect life to be pleasant

overall—as most middle-class people can—or is life dangerous and full of travails, and is pain the chief experience? In *The Dean's December,* Saul Bellow calls this expectation of pain as a constant the archaic picture of life, and the archaic attitude is not just a thing of the past. People do not think much about happiness if they must sift through garbage or sell their bodies in order to survive, and temporary cessation of pain is happiness enough. Acker's concept of pain in life links directly to her politics, and from this bond springs a major contradiction at the heart of her fiction. Acker defines the very fabric of creation as disgusting and implies that pain is the nature of the universe. Nevertheless, illogically, she protests pain as unjust and unfair and assumes that we are somehow owed decent living conditions. The absence of those conditions directs her thoughts toward revolution. Here her investment in the individual and that being's core desires for decent living conditions prevents her from accepting the logic of her own political metaphors. She refuses to accept suffering as humanity's basic experience, even though that is manifestly what follows from her image of the nature of the world.

Creation myths constitute a form of fantasy that almost inevitably defines how one understands the nature of one's world, and Acker narrates creation several times. *Empire* contains one such creation:

> The beginning of any person must be the beginning of the world. . . . The cats were so thin they looked like knives. Predatory knives ran down the streets. Just like in Detroit. No human could walk on the streets without blood covering her limbs. . . . Rock became sky. . . . The first light which was air sat on the sea. It appeared to be weird. Or a haze which resembled human nausea. . . . The day after the beginning of this disgusting world, the rock formed a cave.
>
> (7-8)

How could anyone expect a pleasant, fair, welcoming life to emerge in this world? A similarly threatening creation emerges in *My Mother,* during a Heathcliff and Cathy fantasia. Cathy scrambles through a dream house until she finds "complete horror in this world: darkness and decay. Flesh is rotting frogs. . . . This is real creation, the beginning of the world, evil is always born in a cloud of pink smoke emanating from pink incense" (141).

Pussy gives us two related creation myths. In the first, "Incest begins this world. Incest begins the beginning of this world: A father's fucking his daughter. Night's fucking with morning. Night's black; morning, red. There's nothing else" (68). Later, a mythological boy, who plays with skulls and has snakes dreaming inside his own skull, is passionately desired by a girl (whom the narrator says is like herself). The girl tries becoming his slave to entice him to bed her, but he hates procreation because his father, "the horniest father in the world, though there wasn't yet a world," was having sexual relations with the boy's sister. Within the economy of this myth, father, son, and daughter exist as categories, although mother does not, and we are told "there wasn't yet any procreation so there was no difference between father and son" (100). Such metaphysically tangled incest may be common in myths where the number of actors is limited, but it does set the tone for Acker's world.

The fabric of creation is nauseating. The earliest agents are driven by insatiable desires and relish hurting each other. When Acker expands this picture of origins into a representation of society, she emphasizes the oedipal patterns of power within families and the state.[15] Even as the father demands subordination and fucks his daughter, so the state demands conformity and subordination, people being expected to adapt themselves to the needs of a capitalist economy and women to the needs of men. *Empire* makes this mode of thinking explicit, and Acker has commented in interviews about how she killed off all manifestations of the father she could think of in that novel and tried then to imagine a nonoedipal society. She did not advance very far in picturing a society without phallic order. Within her anarchic vision of Paris, the strong still prey upon the weak, and prior possessors of power still retain some. The CIA is present, potent, and lobotomizing unsuspecting victims and murdering rebel leaders. Acker does not comment on why she was so unsuccessful in imagining a nonoedipal society, but one possibility is that the voice she relies on so heavily is unsuited to that material. Skill at protest does not readily translate into utopian rhapsody, any more than leaders of a revolution necessarily turn into good heads of state. That voice's key note is protest, and its function is oppositional, not analytic and not laudatory.

Acker's politics seem to point toward anarchy as the desired form of government, but her hostility to reason cripples her ability to imagine an anarchy of the sort described by Pyotr Kropotkin, Mikhail Bakunin, and others.[16] They, after all, built on an Enlightenment concept of reason. For Acker, though, reason makes us susceptible to coercive orderliness. Reason tells us to modify ourselves to fit in with others. Rather than exalt reason, she feels we must escape its clutches. She claims that her writing prior to *Empire* was all unplanned, because "I never wanted to touch anything that was rational, because I felt that would intrude on whatever was going on" ("Path" ["The Path of Abjection"] 26). Near the end of her *Don Quixote,* the protagonist remarks, "The Spain of the Spanish Republic of 1931 is my dream or model." However, she describes the anarchist leaders of that movement as "abstemious wanderers, proud to possess little. . . . They were motivated by that inner certainty which by its very being denies human leadership and any hierarchy except for that of gentleness and kindness" (204-5). Like the Knight's other dreams, this seems unreal, and unable to serve as a solid model for mass implementation in the real world. For positive pictures of anarchy as a peaceful and productive way of living, we can look to Ursula K. Le Guin's *The Dispossessed* and *Always Coming Home,* but Le Guin believes that people can be reasonable and can govern their emotions and that this is desirable. For Acker, those notions are unthinkable. Her anarchies are those of chaos or something close to that—life as a pirate or biker outlaw, where the strongest common bond is that of being an outsider banned from mainstream society.

When Acker does imagine a positive move toward freedom, she couches it in terms that look like torture. In a pornographic fantasy of schoolgirls (also called dogs) down in a crypt, the girls learn that "All the accepted forms of education in this country, rather than teaching the child to know who she is or to know, dictate to the child who she is" (*Don Quixote* 165-66). Juliette is exposed to many forms of violation and stimulus and is told that she doesn't know which she likes or dislikes because society has labeled some bad. She is forced through repetition to reach more authentic judgments on what her body really does like. The sequence includes sadistic and masochistic experiences, and Don Quixote concludes that she wishes she had gone to this dog school rather than to the boarding school she did attend.

In other words, although Acker's personae are angry at unnecessary pain, they sometimes see the point to pain undertaken to achieve a breakthrough in consciousness or understanding of self. Such pain might be unnecessary if society did not warp our self-comprehension, but if we take the damaged self as a given, then we may find pain the tool that can open us up to freedom and greater authenticity. In *Kathy Goes to Haiti,* Kathy is strongly drawn to the description of a voodoo practitioner who "stuck these long needles into his skin, all over his body" (66). Kathy's interlocutor finds this nauseating, but Kathy speculates eagerly that he may be elevating himself to a new consciousness. Since she mentions sticking razor blades into her wrists (86), and other personae also claim this habit (see, for example, *Empire* 9-10), the protagonist is evidently questing for insight into her own behavior and possible spiritual gain. In an interview with Andrea Juno, Acker says, "A woman who does a cutting on herself and lets herself bleed a little is hardly as unhealthy as a man who beats up his own wife. . . . Someone who deliberately puts a few cigarette burns on their body is so much more healthy—well, at least they're trying to deal with [the violent feelings]" ("Kathy Acker" 185).

Philosophically, a lot of contradictory sentiments adhere to pain in Acker's narratives.[17] Acker "tries out" attitudes that represent other cultural answers to pain, since each would demand a different politics of response. In the graphics section at the end of **Blood and Guts** entitled "The World," the narrative voice says, "So we create this world in our own image." The context for this statement is saturated with tantric images out of Hindu and Buddhist traditions, and within that context, she seems to be trying out the Eastern belief that the world is illusion and we have control over how it appears to us and how we respond to it. Were the Acker persona willing to give up desire, the appearance and feel of her world would change. That, however, is something she is evidently not willing to do; the final text is a poem that ends, "All I want is a taste of your lips" (165), and desire is central to the construction of the voice.[18] Similarly, in **Great Expectations** (67) the narrative voice runs through a list of such philosophical statements about pain: "The world is paradise. Pain doesn't exist. Pain comes from askew human perceptions. A person's happy who doesn't give attention to her own desires but always thinks of others. . . . Every event is totally separate from every other event. If there are an infinite number of non-relating events, where's the relation that enables pain?" In **Haiti** [**Kathy Goes to Haiti**], Kathy remarks, "Emotions are like thoughts. They come and go. They're not me" (87). Acker is aware of other philosophical answers to her problems. The values adhering to the core voice, however, prevent her from considering them for herself. She does not wish to change the core values for any reason.

Could Acker accept any of these explanations of suffering, she and her narrators could solve many of their problems. Nunlike renunciation of desire would totally change the anguish level of the voice of this fiction. Students who have rejected the books certainly think that much of the pain derives from "askew human perceptions" and that the implied author would be well advised to work on normalizing her perceptions. If her various personae could see emotions, like ideas, as separate from self, they might be able to cultivate happier outlooks. Acker ultimately resists all these solutions, though. Her sense of an unaltered, authentic core is too precious to give up.

This core persona, represented by this voice that she does have (whether acknowledged or not), is central to Acker's trajectories of thought. That core has suffered from the efforts by parents, schools, lovers, and government to alter it to fit more conventional and convenient templates. When Acker focal figures fall in love, the lovers usually prove incompatible at the core level, a fact found after a few days at most. Those core selves and values are thus responsible for much unhappiness in her fiction. However, though logic might suggest that more happiness would result from an altered core self, Acker's unhappy personae violently resist all of society's attempts to modify individual behavior and

thought. They prefer what they see as an authentic self to one taught (or brainwashed) to embrace normalcy. In her world, you may be damned by having an individual core, but you will be equally damned if you permit it to be modified in any fashion.

ACKER AS POSTMODERN ROMANTIC

The Acker celebrated by most critics is dazzlingly postmodern. Her literary strategies all function to escape or deny old-fashioned concepts of the liberal self. She "plagiarizes" and, in doing so, deconstructs individual ownership of famous texts. She writes fictional autobiographies. She destabilizes gender. She fragments her narratives and decenters her posthumanist characters.

The protesting voice that emerges in all the novels, however, problematizes and modifies this postmodernism. The values espoused by the voice are humanist insofar as it defends the individual self and sees human life in this world as its only concern. Acker seems to have been ruefully aware of this departure from poststructuralist norms: Wollen quotes her as saying, "If you scratch hard, you find I'm a humanist in some weird way. Well, humanist, you know what I mean!" (11). The voice also seems liberal/radical in considering much suffering unnecessary and unjust. That sense of injustice clashes oddly with Acker's images of creation as putrid and agonizing. Her metaphoric universe gives us no reason to expect justice, but that does not prevent the voice from demanding it and feeling aggrieved at the lack of such fairness. The voice's elements suggest a literary heritage that is not just the line of experimental underground writers Acker cites—de Sade, Baudelaire, Céline, Lautréamont, Artaud, Burroughs, Bataille, and Genet. They clearly influence her narrative forms, her total attack on all social patterns, and the darkest elements of her subject matter. The narrative voice, though, bears traces of another heritage—the Romantics. Of course the *poète maudit* tradition also has ties to Romanticism, and so do gothicism and punk.[19] All of them are movements of rebellion against a bourgeois culture, and so they naturally have much in common. My point is not to construct a new line of descent, but to identify a set of values embraced by the voice.

The authentic self is what matters to the Romantics, and society is negligible or actually harmful, as Rousseau argued, and others like Emerson partly agreed. Howard Mumford Jones identifies four cardinal types of Romantic individualism: the revolutionary, the sufferer, the rebel, and the liberated woman (243). All of these are present in or manifest themselves in Acker's personae. Those personae also value heightened passions over emotional pragmatism, stability, and practicality, as did many Romantics. Steven Bruhm argues that thinking about pain (and not just suffering it) was an important part of Romantic self-construction (xvii).[20]

Whereas English Romantics looked for a "higher" truth and transcendence, Acker's focal figures look for a kind of "lower" bedrock truth, not in aesthetics but in the body and physical pain, and some of them hope for some kind of breakthrough in consciousness through pain. As she puts this to McCaffery, "It's in the body finally which [*sic*] we can't be touched by all our skepticism and ambiguous systems of belief. The body is the only place where any basis for real values exists anymore" ("Interview" 93). The body is where one can look to undo the damage done by society in its obfuscation of one's true feelings. Anne K. Mellor points out that female Romantics identified the family as an important site and concerned themselves with the relationship between family and state; so do Acker protagonists. Romantics often valued the wound, the violation or injury to body or soul that enables art to crystallize in the soul. So do Acker's personae, and like the Romantics, the Acker voices value madness over bourgeois sanity.[21]

While some of these qualities are also found in the other rebellious art movements, Acker's concern with justice and decency for the self who can feel hurt seems a more Romantic concern than it does gothic, punk, or surreal. McCaffery has argued that her aesthetic is a punk aesthetic because it "emphasizes power, obscenity, passion, incoherence, delirium, pure sensation at the expense of refinement, order, logic, beauty" (220). She and the punks exalt the unclean or taboo side of the sacred. However, punk is also a venue for "thuggery, misogyny, racism, homophobia" and a "yearning for final solutions to questions it barely asked" (Marcus 80). Punk evinces a great deal of self-hate, and Acker expresses that too, but she fights against it, tries to overcome it, attacks the society that induced that hatred. She wants that self to be at ease with itself and, preferably, happy. In this, she seems to go in a direction that is more Romantic than gothic or punk.

Acker's postmodern concerns naturally take her in directions that differ from those of the original Romantics. They too were anticapitalist but turned back in history for solutions; Acker rejects their rural idylls, accepts the cityscape, and is concerned to find a viable future.[22] They strove for beauty; she seems to find beauty an outrage to the pain in the world and embraces ugliness as a more appropriate mode for her expressions (a punk attitude). She avoids beauty in prose, preferring fragments, rough rhythms, ungrammaticality, irregular punctuation, repetitions, and casual imprecision in words. Richard Walsh describes her sensibility as "unreconciled to society, emphasizing and privileging inarticulateness and a concept of art as prerational expression, as the direct articulation of inner emotions unmediated by logical or aesthetic consideration" (154). Even that privileging inarticulateness, though, points to a core self apart from the rational self that can produce art and expression, one that she does not even think should be guided or modified by the more social and rational part of one's being.

Not everyone would agree, but to my way of thinking, Acker's narrative voice and her fragmented narrative forms are at odds with one another. Intellectually, Acker seems to wish to escape core existence through decenteredness, denial of any authority, rejection of any voice that lays down the laws, and ecstasy at any breakthrough into uncharted freedom. These postmodern aspects of her work function centrifugally and provide the dazzling display that has intrigued most of her readers.[23] However, her desire to flee the center is so strong because that center is so very powerful. Emotionally, her personae reflect that core and protect its integrity with every ounce of power they have. Centripetally, they pull every experience in and recompose it in the idiom of the narrative voice. That voice projects itself through lyric lamentation, cries, the vocabularies of sex, pain, and oppression. Its values are traditional and humanist, and include fair treatment, decent living conditions, the inner self's authenticity, and its right not to conform to social norms. This is the voice that some postmodern critical perspectives filter out. One experiences that voice, though, when reading her works, however perverse it may be by her own reckoning to read them straight through. The repetitions that accumulate to become that voice are the result of the reading experience. Acker identifies with Eurydice, especially when facing death from cancer, but as a writer she is also Orpheus—not Orpheus creator of divine harmony, but Orpheus dismembered by a maenad mother. Only after Orpheus is fragmented does his oracular voice emerge; so with Acker, the highly obtrusive fragmentation ultimately yields a voice that articulates the pain of "freaks" and calls for revolution.

Notes

1. See Acker's interview with Larry McCaffery ("Path" 27), where she describes her frustration over Robert Creeley's assertion that a poet could only become a real writer after finding his voice. Acker studied the Black Mountain poets with David Antin (Wollen 3) and would have learned, among other things, the Creeley-Olson emphasis on "the individual and his works," and "the 'natural' authority of some men over others (and almost all men over almost all women)" (Foster 8). Acker retells the Creeley anecdote in both interviews with McCaffery, and in her essay "A Few Notes on Two of My Books" (9).

2. This persona is not unrecognized by critics—after all, it is sometimes even named Kathy—but it has not been much considered as an aspect of all Acker's work, as opposed to being seen as an unhappy voice in any one novel. Glenn A. Harper

talks about a core narrative. Martina Sciolino recognizes a core in the voice that describes being abused as a girl by her family ("Confessions"; "Mutilating").

3. Peter Wollen (1) makes this point; it is also cited and used by Claire MacDonald (109); see also Acker's interview with Ellen G. Friedman, "Conversation" (19), for a similar comment.

4. For commentary on Acker's attack on rationality, see Dix; Friedman, "Now Eat"; Harper; McCaffery; and Walsh. For discussions of her use of the body, see Brennan; Friedman, "Now Eat"; Punday; and Redding.

5. For particularly good analyses of her novels and those they are appropriating, see De Zwaan, McHale (chapter 5), and Siegle on *Empire of the Senseless*; Robinson on *Don Quixote*; and Sciolino, "Mutilating," on *Great Expectations*.

6. In Peter Guttridge's obituary, Acker is quoted as having said that except for her mother's suicide, all seeming autobiographical references are fictional. That may or may not be true, of course, but puts in question the personal applications of stepfatherly sexual abuse, threats of lobotomy, and other harrowing material that creates the impression of being personal. Her denial of promiscuity appears in "Devoured by Myths" (2) and her times of celibacy in "Lust" (*Eurydice* 54). Her friend Sylvère Lotringer asserts, "Well, I know for a fact that you're totally different from what you write" ("Devoured by Myths" 20). Charles Shaar Murray notes that people expected an "underground sex queen" but discovered "a soft-voiced woman, five foot two, with big wide eyes; an endearing, knock-kneed walk; a ready smile; exquisite manners, and the ability to converse with just about anybody on just about any topic" (6). However, Murray also admires "the blazing courage that was all the more awe-inspiring to those who knew the depths of terror from which she had to climb each day."

7. See Hume, "Ishmael Reed," for analysis of another such "control artist." Analyses of literary paranoia in contemporary literature are performed by Patrick O'Donnell and Timothy Melley. Control is a major focus for Acker. She discusses it in the interview "Path of Abjection" (34). It surfaces in *My Death My Life by Pier Paolo Pasolini* (233, 301), *Don Quixote* (146), *Empire* (51), *In Memoriam* (141), *My Mother* (105), and *Pussy, King of the Pirates* (12, 21).

8. Acker's postmodernism attracts Leslie Dick and Kathleen Hulley. Larry McCaffery opens the window on punk. Feminists who interrogate Acker include Diane Elam, Gina Hausknecht, and Sciolino ("Kathy Acker"). Her gothicism is discussed by C. Jodey Castricano. Hysteria and nostalgia occupy Terry Brown. Pornography is the issue for Colleen Kennedy and Nicola Pitchford, who are also relevant on feminist issues.

9. Acker cultivates this concept of herself as freakish or wild and upholds her authentic self, no matter what the world may think, much as Jean-Jacques Rousseau does at the beginning of his *Confessions*: "I am not made like any of the ones I have seen; I dare to believe that I am not made like any that exist. If I am worth no more, at least I am different" (5). Similarly, Ralph Waldo Emerson upheld what felt authentic about himself in "Self-Reliance": "Nothing is at last sacred but the integrity of your own mind. . . . No law can be sacred to me but that of my nature. Good and bad are but names very readily transferable to that or this; the only right is what is after my constitution; the only wrong what is against it" (178-79).

10. Acker's choice of little cat for female love seems tied in her mind to the behavior of a cat in heat: "When she gets drunk, she lies next to anyone: an elephant, a rat, a stick, even a human. She rubs and rolls and pounces and roars and shuffles and whimpers and prowls. She then smells all the smells in the world" (*Lautrec* 226). In *Empire*, Thivai reports, "Meow. That used to be what my cunt said when she was healthy" (177), referring to Abhor, but also to her sexual flesh as a furry animal and, indeed, a pussy.

11. Rimbaud seeks a life of visionary poetry and homosexual passion with Verlaine. When frustrated of this object, he seeks control and appropriately turns into Jason Compson in a Faulkner pastiche.

12. Oddly, Acker uses this same image for an ecstatic experience, when after a Zen retreat, talking to the Zen master, she felt "like he just put his hand into my mind—literally!" While she raves about how high she was afterward, she quickly revolted against such pleasure and called the master to ask "I'm too high—how do I come down?" and on his advice got drunk ("Kathy Acker" [Juno] 184).

13. Limited acknowledgment by Acker of a core appears in an interview with McCaffery, where Acker says, "I know there are some feminists who think you can choose your sexuality. . . . But I don't agree at all. That's one of the rare theoretical opinions I have" ("Interview" 95). Sciolino is recognizing a core value when she notes, "Every Acker protagonist, however multiplied, is driven by a desire that is often indistinguishable from mourning, or rather, melancholy, 'mourning without work to do'" ("Confessions" 64). Acker gives us a convincing "primal scene" in which the specific fear

of lobotomy might take root, a parental conversation overheard by a child. She uses the term literally and metaphorically in *Tarantula, Pasolini, Empire, In Memoriam, My Mother, Eurydice, Blood and Guts,* and "Humility." Schools lobotomize children so they will fit a lobotomized society (*In Memoriam*). A murderess in *Tarantula* notes that she could murder with impunity if she were an American soldier, and she worries that if she were incarcerated for murder, she might be lobotomized by the authorities. Janey in *Blood and Guts* considers fitting into ordinary society a kind of lobotomy and shows what she means in the "Lousy Mindless Salesgirl" routine. President Bush wants to carry out that operation on artists in *My Mother.* Capitol taunts Rimbaud (in his Jason Compson manifestation): "Rape me. Lobotomize me into a good little doll" (*In Memoriam* 185). Having a poetic voice, Acker claims in "Humility," would lobotomize and imprison her. Lobotomy is her central symbol of violence, the ultimate fear.

14. Carol Siegel points out that Acker emphasizes "the horror of a masochism which is forced into those who resist the deadening of emotion that Acker believes a phallocentric, materialistic society demands" (9).

15. Rob Latham and Douglas Shields Dix do most with this construction of Acker in terms of Deleuze and Guattari's oedipal capitalism. Acker talks to Rebecca Deaton on rethinking the Freudian father-daughter relationship as it has bearing on power and will in general ("Kathy Acker").

16. Black Mountain poet Charles Olson may shed a bit of light on Acker's project in *Empire.* Olson's *The Special View of History* seems to consider anarchy appropriate for life in the city-state, but to him chaos is "nothing more than multiplicity" (51), and since he takes a rather Nietzschean view of human will, he probably imagines himself as someone strong enough to weather chaos. Edward Halsey Foster calls Olson's *Special View of History* his "fullest attempt to justify a return to what he had once called 'the primordial & phallic energies & methodologies'" (65). What Acker portrays suggests that chaos might permit the smashing of some oedipal bonds but would not prevent phallic patterns of conquest.

17. And indeed in the thinking of others as well. Elaine Scarry describes the experience of pain as reinstating a Cartesian opposition between body and mind, even in a world that has rejected Descartes's dualism. Steven Bruhm modifies that to say that pain, "as it attacks our bodies, reinstates *in our perception of it* a dualism" (9-10). Acker tries very hard to make no distinction between bodily and mental pain and metaphorically melds them when she says, "my emotional limbs stuck out as if they were broken and unfixable" (*Great Expectations* 58). In Acker's case, pain is one more force that prevents escape from a core self, since pain to that body cannot be eluded.

18. For a detailed analysis of "The World," see Hume, "Books of the Dead."

19. Renato Poggioli (47) makes the argument (via Herbert Read) that Romanticism is a system of values to which one can return; one need not derive historically from it. Greil Marcus argues, "The question of ancestry in culture is spurious. Every new manifestation in culture rewrites the past, changes old maudits into new heroes, old heroes into those who should never have been born" (21).

20. Much of what Bruhm says about gothic fixation with pain would apply to the gothic side of Acker's imagination (see Castricano).

21. Glenn A. Harper (47) discusses this preference in regard to *Blood and Guts.*

22. Ellen G. Friedman argues that such searching for an unimagined future is central to female modernist and postmodernist writing ("Missing Contents"). Peter Bürger and Charles Russell see trying to create an art of the future as a sign of the avant-garde but would probably differ on the degree to which Acker is trying to imagine the future (avant-garde) or simply reflecting the present (postmodernism).

23. Diane Elam brings together romance as a form of excess, postmodernism as a form of excess, and feminism as an excess beyond the masculine standard and applies them to Acker and Derrida, stressing the "persistent disruption of the identity of the speaking subject" (158).

Works Cited

Acker, Kathy. *The Adult Life of Toulouse Lautrec by Henri Toulouse Lautrec.* 1975. *Portrait of an Eye* 185-311.

———. *Blood and Guts in High School. Blood and Guts in High School Plus Two.* London: Pan, 1984. 3-166.

———. *The Childlike Life of the Black Tarantula by the Black Tarantula.* 1973. *Portrait of an Eye* 1-90.

———. "A Conversation with Kathy Acker." Interview with Ellen G. Friedman. *Review of Contemporary Fiction* 9.3 (1989): 12-22.

———. "Devoured by Myths (Interview)." With Sylvère Lotringer. *Hannibal Lecter, My Father.* Ed. Sylvère Lotringer. Semiotext(e) Native Agents Ser. New York: Semiotext(e), 1991. 1-24.

———. *Don Quixote: Which Was a Dream.* New York: Grove, 1986.

———. *Empire of the Senseless.* 1988. New York: Evergreen, 1989.

———. *Eurydice in the Underworld.* London: Arcadia, 1997.

———. "A Few Notes on Two of My Books." *Bodies of Work: Essays.* London: Serpent's Tail, 1997. 6-13.

———. *Great Expectations.* 1982. New York: Evergreen, 1989.

———. "Humility." *The Seven Cardinal Virtues.* Ed. Alison Fell. London: Serpent's Tail, 1990. 112-31.

———. *I Dreamt I Was a Nymphomaniac: Imagining.* 1974, 1980. *Portrait of an Eye* 91-184.

———. *In Memoriam to Identity.* 1990. New York: Pantheon, 1992.

———. "An Interview with Kathy Acker." With Larry McCaffery. *Mississippi Review* 20.1-2 (1991): 83-97.

———. "Kathy Acker." Interview with Andrea Juno. *Angry Women: Re/Search #13.* Ed. Andrea Juno and V. Vale. San Francisco: Re/Search, 1991. 177-85.

———. "Kathy Acker Interviewed by Rebecca Deaton." *Textual Practice* 6 (1992): 271-82.

———. *Kathy Goes to Haiti.* 1978. *Literal Madness* 1-170.

———. *Literal Madness: Three Novels.* New York: Evergreen, 1988.

———. "Lust." 1981. *Eurydice* 53-76.

———. *My Death My Life by Pier Paolo Pasolini.* 1984. *Literal Madness* 171-394.

———. *My Mother: Demonology, a Novel.* 1993. New York: Grove, 1994.

———. "The Path of Abjection: An Interview with Kathy Acker." With Larry McCaffery. *Some Other Frequency: Interviews with Innovative American Authors.* By Larry McCaffery. Philadelphia: U of Pennsylvania P, 1996. 14-35.

———. *Portrait of an Eye: Three Novels.* New York: Pantheon, 1992.

———. *Pussy, King of the Pirates.* New York: Grove, 1996.

Brennan, Karen. "The Geography of Enunciation: Hysterical Pastiche in Kathy Acker's Fiction." *boundary 2* 21 (1994): 243-68.

Brown, Terry. "Longing to Long: Kathy Acker and the Politics of Pain." *LIT: Literature Interpretation Theory* 2 (1991): 167-77.

Bruhm, Steven. *Gothic Bodies: The Politics of Pain in Romantic Fiction.* Philadelphia: U of Pennsylvania P, 1994.

Bürger, Peter. *Theory of the Avant-Garde.* 1974. Trans. Michael Shaw. Theory and History of Literature 4. Minneapolis: U of Minnesota P, 1984.

Castricano, C. Jodey. "If a Building Is a Sentence, So Is a Body: Kathy Acker and the Postcolonial Gothic." *American Gothic: New Interventions in a National Narrative.* Ed. Robert K. Martin and Eric Savoy. Iowa City: U of Iowa P, 1998. 202-14.

De Zwaan, Victoria. "Rethinking the Slipstream: Kathy Acker Reads *Neuromancer.*" *Science-Fiction Studies* #73, 24 (1997): 459-70.

Dick, Leslie. "Feminism, Writing, Postmodernism." *From My Guy to Sci-Fi: Genre and Women's Writing in the Postmodern World.* Ed. Helen Carr. London: Pandora, 1989. 204-14.

Dix, Douglas Shields. "Kathy Acker's *Don Quixote*: Nomad Writing." *Review of Contemporary Fiction* 9.3 (1989): 56-62.

Elam, Diane. *Romancing the Postmodern.* New York: Routledge, 1992.

Emerson, Ralph Waldo. "Self-Reliance." *Selected Essays.* Ed. Larzer Ziff. New York: Penguin, 1982. 175-204.

Foster, Edward Halsey. *Understanding the Black Mountain Poets.* Columbia: U of South Carolina P, 1995.

Friedman, Ellen G. "'Now Eat Your Mind': An Introduction to the Works of Kathy Acker." *Review of Contemporary Fiction* 9.3 (1989): 37-49.

———. "Where Are the Missing Contents? (Post)Modernism, Gender, and the Canon." *PMLA* 108 (1993): 240-52.

Guttridge, Peter. "Kathy Acker" [obituary]. *Independent* [London] 2 Dec. 1997: 22.

Harper, Glenn A. "The Subversive Power of Sexual Difference in the Work of Kathy Acker." *Sub-Stance* 54 (1987): 44-56.

Hausknecht, Gina. "Self-Possession, Dolls, Beatlemania, Loss: Telling the Girl's Own Story." *The Girl: Constructions of the Girl in Contemporary Fiction by Women.* Ed. Ruth O. Saxton. New York: St. Martin's, 1998. 21-42.

Hulley, Kathleen. "Transgressing Genre: Kathy Acker's Intertext." *Intertextuality and Contemporary American Fiction.* Ed. Patrick O'Donnell and Robert Con Davis. Baltimore, MD: Johns Hopkins UP, 1989. 171-90.

Hume, Kathryn. "Books of the Dead: Postmortem Politics in Novels by Mailer, Burroughs, Acker, and Pynchon." *Modern Philology* 97 (2000): 417-44.

————. "Ishmael Reed and the Problematics of Control." *PMLA* 108 (1993): 506-18.

Jacobs, Naomi. "Kathy Acker and the Plagiarized Self." *Review of Contemporary Fiction* 9.3 (1989): 50-55.

Jones, Howard Mumford. *Revolution and Romanticism.* Cambridge, MA: Belknap-Harvard UP, 1974.

Kennedy, Colleen. "Simulating Sex and Imagining Mothers." *American Literary History* 4 (1992): 165-85.

Lanser, Susan Sniader. *Fictions of Authority: Women Writers and Narrative Voice.* Ithaca, NY: Cornell UP, 1992.

Latham, Rob. "Collage as Critique and Invention in the Fiction of William S. Burroughs and Kathy Acker." *Journal of the Fantastic in the Arts* 5.3 (1993): 46-57.

Le Guin, Ursula K. *Always Coming Home.* 1985. New York: Bantam, 1986.

————. *The Dispossessed.* 1974. New York: Avon, 1975.

MacDonald, Claire. "Requiem for the Self: Kathy Acker's Final Work." *Woman and Performance: A Journal of Feminist Theory* #19, 10.1-2 (1999): 105-16.

McCaffery, Larry. "The Artists of Hell: Kathy Acker and 'Punk' Aesthetics." *Breaking the Sequence: Women's Experimental Fiction.* Ed. Ellen G. Friedman and Miriam Fuchs. Princeton: Princeton UP, 1989. 215-30.

McHale, Brian. *Constructing Postmodernism.* New York: Routledge, 1992.

Marcus, Greil. *Lipstick Traces: A Secret History of the Twentieth Century.* 1989. Cambridge, MA: Harvard UP, 1990.

Melley, Timothy. *Empire of Conspiracy: The Culture of Paranoia in Postwar America.* Ithaca, NY: Cornell UP, 2000.

Mellor, Anne K. *Romanticism and Gender.* New York: Routledge, 1993.

Murray, Charles Shaar. "The Last Love of Kathy Acker." *Observer* [London] 7 Dec. 1997: 1, 6.

O'Donnell, Patrick. *Latent Destinies: Cultural Paranoia and Contemporary U.S. Narrative.* Durham, NC: Duke UP, 2000.

Olson, Charles. *The Special View of History.* 1956. Ed. Ann Charters. Berkeley, CA: Oyez, 1970.

Peters, Greg Lewis. "Dominance and Subversion: The Horizontal Sublime and Erotic Empowerment in the Works of Kathy Acker." *State of the Fantastic: Studies in the Theory and Practice of Fantastic Literature and Film.* Ed. Nicholas Ruddick. Westport, CT: Greenwood, 1992. 149-56.

Pitchford, Nicola. "Reading Feminism's Pornography Conflict: Implications for Postmodernist Reading Strategies." *Sex Positives? The Cultural Politics of Dissident Sexualities.* Ed. Thomas Foster, Carol Siegel, and Ellen E. Berry. New York: New York UP, 1997. 3-38.

Poggioli, Renato. *The Theory of the Avant-Garde.* 1962. Trans. Gerald Fitzgerald. Cambridge, MA: Belknap-Harvard UP, 1968.

Punday, Daniel. "Theories of Materiality and Location: Moving Through Kathy Acker's *Empire of the Senseless.*" *Genders OnLine Journal* 27 (1998): 1-25. <http://www.genders.org/g27/g27_theories.html>

Redding, Arthur F. "Bruises, Roses: Masochism and the Writing of Kathy Acker." *Contemporary Literature* 35 (1994): 281-304.

Robinson, Christopher L. "In the Silence of the Knight: Kathy Acker's *Don Quixote* as a Work of Disenchantment." *Yearbook of Comparative and General Literature* 47 (1999): 109-23.

Rousseau, Jean-Jacques. *The Confessions and Correspondence, Including the Letters to Malesherbes. The Collected Writings of Rousseau.* Vol. 5. Ed. Christopher Kelly, Roger D. Masters, and Peter G. Stillman. Trans. Christopher Kelly. Hanover, NH: UP of New England, 1995.

Russell, Charles. *Poets, Prophets, and Revolutionaries: The Literary Avant-garde from Rimbaud through Postmodernism.* 1985. New York: Oxford UP, 1987.

Scarry, Elaine. *The Body in Pain: The Making and Unmaking of the World.* 1985. New York: Oxford UP, 1987.

Sciolino, Martina. "Confessions of a Kleptoparasite." *Review of Contemporary Fiction* 9.3 (1989): 63-67.

————. "Kathy Acker and the Postmodern Subject of Feminism." *College English* 52 (1990): 437-45.

————. "The 'Mutilating Body' and the Decomposing Text: Recovery in Kathy Acker's *Great Expectations.*" *Textual Bodies: Changing Boundaries of Literary Representation.* Ed. Lori Hope Lefkovitz. Albany: State U of New York P, 1997. 245-66.

Siegel, Carol. "Postmodern Women Novelists Review Victorian Male Masochism." *Genders* 11 (1991): 1-16.

Siegle, Robert. "A Sailor's Life in the Empire of the Senseless." *Review of Contemporary Fiction* 9.3 (1989): 71-77.

Walsh, Richard. "The Quest for Love and the Writing of Female Desire in Kathy Acker's *Don Quixote.*" *Critique* 32 (1991): 149-68.

Wollen, Peter. "'Don't Be Afraid to Copy It Out': Peter Wollen Writes about Kathy Acker." *London Review of Books* 5 Feb. 1998. <http://www.lrb.co.uk/v20n03/woll2003.html>

Joseph M. Conte (essay date 2002)

SOURCE: Conte, Joseph M. "Discipline and Anarchy: Disrupted Codes in Kathy Acker's *Empire of the Senseless*." In *Design and Debris: A Chaotics of Postmodern American Fiction*, pp. 54-74. Tuscaloosa: University of Alabama Press, 2002.

[*In the following essay, Conte maintains that Acker's methodology in her novel* Empire of the Senseless *envisions "the collapse of the patriarchal order into a state of liberating and enabling anarchy as a function of the book's structure."*]

> I like a look of Agony,
> Because I know it's true—
>
> —Emily Dickinson, Poem #241

> Discipline organizes an analytical space.
>
> —Michel Foucault, *Discipline and Punish*

> Good authors, too, who once knew better words,
> Now only use four-letter words
>   Writing prose.
>   Anything Goes.
>
> —Cole Porter, *Anything Goes*

A double-edged dagger, hilt up, on which is impaled a whorled and leafy rose. The rose, a heart, bleeds droplets. Around the blade and point are intertwined banners that read "Discipline and Anarchy." This hand-drawn figure appears at the close of Kathy Acker's ***Empire of the Senseless*** (1988), a book which she dedicates to her tattooist. Although this tattoo design is inscribed on the back of the book, the pain of its needle and the poison of its ink are felt throughout the novel. Acker drives the sword of pain through the rose of pleasure; she binds the cords of discipline and unties the knot that restrains anarchy. The iconography suggests that the competing principles of discipline and anarchy, intentionality and impulse, control and freedom are inextricably linked in the novel. The Pandora of postmodernism releases a flurry of evil and disease into a culture ready to receive it. Acker's writing is anarchistic to the core: she plunders the cultural storehouse of Western literature, liberating the classics through plagiarism; she violates every known taboo, revels in obscenity, smashes genre rules, and commits violence on her characters that would make the Marquis de Sade blanch. But like Sade, she displays a penchant for discipline as control as well as punishment. Anarchism runs its course without resistance, entropically feeding on the fuel of stale and repressive social order until that fuel is exhausted. And discipline carried to any restrictive extreme will at last inspire revolt.

With the pain of her own writing in mind, Emily Dickinson declared that "The Attar from the Rose . . . is the gift of Screws" (Poem #675; *Final Harvest* 171). The belle of Amherst was no stranger to agony and violence in her work; literary form can only be painfully "expressed." The writing of ***Empire of the Senseless*** more vigorously courts anarchy. The reader may well be appalled by the mayhem encountered on any page. But the text finally deports itself in a disciplined fashion. Acker claims in an interview with Ellen G. Friedman that "it was the structure [of ***Empire*** [***Empire of the Senseless***]] that really interested me—the three-part structure" ("Conversation" ["A Conversation with Kathy Acker"] 17).[1] The question nags as to why a text so engrossed with disorderly behavior would be preeminently interesting to its author for its structure. Acker the plagiarist might want to lift a line from that most patriarchal poet of suburban Connecticut, Wallace Stevens: "This is form gulping after formlessness" (*Collected Poems* 411). She envisions her novel as a triptych with a rather deliberate progression of effects: the deconstruction of the patriarchal order in "Elegy for the World of the Fathers," the liberation that follows from an end to repression and inhibition in "Alone," and the formation of a new society on the very ground of transgression in "Pirate Night." Acker provides the structure's rationale as follows:

> The first part is an elegy for the world of patriarchy. I wanted to take the patriarchy and kill the father on every level. And I did that partially by finding out what was taboo and rendering it in words. The second part of the book concerns what society would look like if it weren't defined by oedipal considerations and the taboos were no longer taboo. I went through every taboo, or tried to, to see what society would be like without these taboos. . . . The last section, "Pirate Night," is about wanting to get to a society that is taboo, but realizing it's impossible.
>
> ("Conversation" 17)

I want to discuss these three effects and the turbulence that accompanies each in turn. But Acker's statement reveals something important about her methodology as an artist.[2] As the princess of violation and disruption, Acker can be expected to disregard the traditional rules of fiction. But an aimless thrashing of the novel form does not follow. Instead she claims adherence to the method of conceptual artists such as David Antin and William Burroughs. In an interview with Sylvère Lotringer, Acker argues that "Form is determined not by arbitrary rules, but by intention." Her emphasis has been "on conceptualism, on intentionality" ("Devoured" ["Devoured by Myths"] 3). On the one hand Acker rejects the plotting of conventional fiction writing and the proceduralism of some other avant-garde novelists as overly constrictive. On the other hand she finds reliance on impulse and intuition alone to be inadequate to her task. She writes "by process" (4), but finds the form of the novel in conceptualism. In this way the event of the novel as a whole can be orderly even though its many actions may be chaotic. Acker's methodology thus weds impulse and intention. She envisions the collapse of the patriarchal order into a state of liberating and enabling anarchy as a function of the book's structure. Her methodology is directly supportive of the concept of *Empire of the Senseless,* which is not unlimited anarchy but the intrinsic relation between discipline and anarchy, as the banner on the tattoo declares.

THE DECLINE OF ORDER: SADOMASOCHISM

In "Elegy for the World of the Fathers" Acker contemplates the utter corruption of the patriarchal order, attacking monotheism, capitalism, the phallic power bestowed by Freud in the Oedipal myth, marriage as a "collective crime" (*Empire* 7), and the relegation of the sexual body to a commodity. Acker's female protagonist, Abhor, is described as "part robot, and part black" (3). The character's name and her cybernetic-minority status (derived from William Gibson's *Neuromancer* [1984])[3] suggest the contempt, the abhorrence that patriarchal society has traditionally bestowed upon women, half-breeds, and the disenfranchised poor. Acker deliberately neglects to develop her character's status as robot or black, which suggests that these are political identities—"sub-human" designations—against which Abhor must struggle as an individual. The initial chapters purport to provide the protagonist's genealogy and early years, a gesture toward the *bildungsroman* which Acker quickly deconstructs. Part I of the novel is preceded by a tattoo drawing of a skull and rose branch bearing the legend "My Family Fortune." Abhor's paternal grandmother is a German-Jewish refugee fleeing Nazi persecution and the father-führer; upon her deliverance in Paris, she is immediately forced into child-prostitution. For Acker, who documents her performances in Times Square sex-shows during the 1970s, any sex within the patriarchal system becomes equated with money. Or, as literally stated by Abhor, "Sex was joined to money" (9).

Acker wastes no time exploring the primal taboos of incest in the first chapter, "Rape by the Father." Abhor is already a victim of patriarchal moralism: "I knew I was evil cause I was fucking" (11). Her teenage sexual activity inspires Daddy's transgression. Her appeal (by telephone) to her mother hardly delays father's actions because the female lacks the authority to enforce a taboo within the patriarchal order. Abhor's reaction to her violation is typically complex: "Part of me wanted him and part of me wanted to kill him" (12). Western culture has of course punished women for both responses— admitting desire for the father, and patricide. Acker explores the divergent and yet related responses of submission (desire) and revolt (hatred). In trying to enforce taboo the patriarchy has declared "Neither. Nor." Abhor's release from that order is her willingness to

contemplate both the unthinkable desire for her father and the resentment for his unspeakable violation of her. She sees her oppression and her freedom in the same figure.

Daddy's transgression of the moral code may not have been salutary for Abhor, but it makes an important contribution to her concept of social order:

> Daddy left me no possibility of easiness. He forced me to live among nerves sharper than razor blades, to have no certainties. There was only roaming. My nerves hurt more and more. I despised those people, like my mother, who accepted easiness—morality, social rules. Daddy taught me to live in pain, to know there's nothing else. I trusted him for this complexity.
>
> (10)

The moral code enforces an absolute distinction between "right" and "wrong." It rewards conformity with "easiness," an illusory sense of self-satisfaction. The world, approached from comfortably within these "social rules," is simple. But for Abhor the simplicity of the moral code and those who adhere to it are despicable. Rather than endure the restrictions and submit to the governance of the patriarchy, she prefers to dwell in uncertainties and in pain. Abhor recognizes that to defy the dominant order is to invite discomfort, insecurity, and conflict. But no matter how much the dominant order rewards conformity, that in itself does not give it sole purchase of the truth in reality. The dominant order always seeks to suppress conflicting systems, ambiguity, and any form of disorderly conduct.[4] Ironically, Abhor finds in the amoral figure of her father the impetus to defy the oversimplification of the world, embrace pain, and seek out complexity. Just as her grandmother, charged with prostitution, realizes that "the Vice-Squad swore whatever the Vice-Squad swears in order to maintain the scheme of things. Which might or might not exist" (5), so Abhor realizes that the patriarchy has imposed a falsely simplified order to maintain its power. Her father's transgression introduces her to a complexity in the world which is both more painful and more truthful.

Consistency in the narrative style of a novel orients the reader to the social order that the fiction describes. The sophistication and urbanity of the Jamesian narrator constantly reminds the reader of the Anglo-European aristocracy through which he moves. The folkloric and dialect quality of Samuel Clemens's *Adventures of Huckleberry Finn* locate the reader within a mid-American community and an unpretentious, populist milieu. Low-life confidence men and swindlers such as the king and the duke appropriate and mangle elevated discourse to comical effect: "I say orgies, not because it's the common term, because it ain't—obsequies bein' the common term—but because orgies is the right term.

Obsequies ain't used in England no more, now—it's gone out. We say orgies now, in England. Orgies is better, because it means the thing you're after, more exact. It's a word that's made up out'n the Greek *orgo,* outside, open, abroad; and the Hebrew *jeesum,* to plant, cover up; hence in*ter.* So, you see, funeral orgies is an open er public funeral" (134). Acker disturbs the confidence with which the reader ascertains the social order from narrative discourse. Such transgression of the boundaries between high and low art forms is a recognized tenet of postmodernism. Acker's Abhor is supposedly illiterate because "being black, she was uneducated" (*Empire* 201). She generally speaks in the patois of the urban teenager. But her language and intellectual engagement just as often smack of the political theorist or the psychoanalyst. Acker herself has been a student of the urban punk movement, left-wing political theory, and post-Freudian analysis, but the turbulent mixing of these discourses does violence upon the readerly conventions of fiction. The first-person narration in which Abhor accounts for her father's amoral upbringing provides a good example of such cross-coded discourse:

> [H]e had no morals, for any morality presumes a society. Since my grandmother loved him, she saw no reason to teach him anything or that he should learn anything.
>
> This substitution of *primitivism* which must be *anarchic* (in its non-political sense) for *morality* gave my father his charm. His charm blinded not only his parents but even every old farty schoolteacher to both his complete lack of social awareness and of education. Politics, for my father, was, always, a hole.
>
> (8)

Abhor's defense of her father's primitivism (which she supposedly shares) and her attack on the educatory system of "old farty schoolteachers" that enforces both a moral code and social order is nevertheless couched in the abstract terminology and the structure of argument that suggests a higher standard of education. Acker charges that education is chiefly a measure of the individual's training in obedience to the dominant culture. In the same gesture she defeats the readerly conventions that have trained us to expect a consistent narrative style and characters that remain locked within the referents of a single social class.

The scumbling of levels of discourse in the novel reflects Acker's anarchistic methodology, undermining the reader's presuppositions of dominant-intellectual and subordinate-proletarian cultural positions. Acker combines the use of essay-like titles for several subsections of the novel, such as "3. Beyond The Extinction of Human Life" (31), with crude and frankly obscene passages: "'If you finance her fucking for money,' said my father whose IQ was 166, 'I'll let her do it.' My father knew his mother-in-law was the cheapest thing on earth,

even cheaper than himself" (16). Her characters are just as likely to be pimps as economics professors and she challenges the social order that distinguishes too finely between the two. Intensive, poetic, and gratuitous obscenity, "almost as beautiful as a strand of my grandmother's cunt hair" (4), can be followed without pause by the high abstractions of literary theory:

> The German Romantics had to destroy the same bastions as we do. Logocentrism and idealism, theology, all supports of the repressive society. Property's pillars. Reason which always homogenizes and reduces, represses and unifies phenomena or actuality into what can be perceived and so controlled. The subjects, us, are now stable and socializable. Reason is always in the service of the political and economic masters. It is here that literature strikes, at this base, where the concepts and actings of order impose themselves.
>
> (12)

This passage, no doubt plundered from her reading, appropriates theory in defense of Acker's radical poetics. Like the German Romantics or the anarchist who assassinated President William McKinley at the Pan-American Exhibition in Buffalo, NY in 1901, Acker intends to shock (through obscenity) and upbraid (in theory) the bourgeoisie. For Acker, the purpose of literature is indeed to assault the authority figures of an imposed order. The conjunction of obscenity and literary theory so that one is no less capable of affective impact than the other, and the very introduction of a passage of commentary in the midst of an uneducated character's discourse, work to deconstruct (or fuck up) the reader's well-trained expectations for novelistic discourse.

But why stop there? Acker commends Sylvère Lotringer for introducing her to the "French philosophes" Gilles Deleuze and Michel Foucault: "I didn't really understand why I refused to use linear narrative; why my sexual genders kept changing; why basically I am the most disoriented novelist that ever existed." Their theory places "this whole language at my disposal. . . . I know exactly what they're talking about. And I could go farther" ("Devoured" 10). In addition to the conflicting modes of discourse in *Empire of the Senseless,* Acker's disorientation as a novelist compels the reader to abandon other orderly conventions of reception. The many irruptions in causality in the novel defeat the reader's understanding of why one event proceeds from another. This apparent disorder collides with the vestiges of argumentative structure and the hectoring tone of the narration that propels the reader through the three sections of the novel. A temporal uncertainty ensues from the setting of the novel in a future-imperfect world (after the sack of Paris by the Algerians), yet with many references to the institutions and insults of the Reagan Eighties.

One section of "Elegy for the World of the Fathers" carries the academic subtitle "1. A Degenerating Language" (53). Acker's novel attempts a daring break from the prison-house of patriarchal language, shattering signs and conventions as she goes. At times she makes her text unreadable, "a sign of nothing" (53). She interpolates text in Persian, an invasion of the Western literary tradition by an Eastern literature which few are capable of reading except in translation. The Persian text, which is read from right to left, literally disrupts the flow of her text in English from left to right. Although the Persian text is "unknowable" for most readers, it still signifies the arbitrariness of literary conventions. Logocentrism is indeed supportive of a repressive society.

Acker views the degeneration of language, the collapse of the rules that guide and restrain the writer, as a largely positive effect of the death of the patriarchy. As a literary terrorist, she does her part in eroding standard English constructions and promoting slang expressions. The conditions of language, sexuality, and anarchy—the word, the body, and the body politic—are directly related: freedom in one sphere is an expression of freedom in the others; repression in one is signatory to repression in the others. This relation has a disturbing effect on daddy:

> Here language was degraded. As daddy plumbed and plummetted [*sic*] away from the institute of marriage more and more downward deeply into the demimonde of public fake sex, his speech turned from the usual neutral and acceptable journalese most normal humans use as a stylus mediocris into . . . His language went through an indoctrination of nothingness, for sexuality had no more value in his world, until his language no longer had sense. Lack of meaning appeared as linguistic degradation.

(17; Acker's ellipsis)

Daddy's "stylus mediocris" remains in force so long as he is bound to the moral strictures and social institutions that restrict his personal freedom. Such "neutral and acceptable journalese" is a commodity of exchange sanctioned and controlled by the social order, permitting little if any individual expression. Personal expression becomes equated with deviance because the sense-value isn't immediately transmittable. The degradation of daddy's language and sexuality is expressed in terms of a pirated text riddled with lacunae: "This is what daddy said to me while he was fucking me: 'Tradicional estilo de p . . . argentino. Q . . . es e. mas j . . . de t . . . los e . . . dentro d. . . .' He had become a Puerto Rican" (17; all but the final set of ellipses are Acker's). The unreadable Spanish text ironically codifies the qualities of traditional style in Latin America. Acker's anarchism acknowledges a lapse into "nothingness," the absence of rules and the disappearance of conventional values. Daddy's transgression of the taboo against incest consigns him to a subordinate and oppressed racial identity and to unintelligibility. But for

Acker linguistic degradation is also linguistic freedom. Language confined to the transmission of codified values has no appeal. Language liberated from conventional meaning entertains at least the possibility of individual expression amidst disorder.

In order to understand the oedipal society, Acker devotes her attention to the Sadean obsession with dominance and punishment in the first part of *Empire of the Senseless.* As with her incestuous desires, Abhor experiences a strange attraction to the forces of control and obedience: "I saw a torturer. He was spending most of his time sticking electrodes on the genitals of men who protested against the government. He was paid to do what he was told to do because he had a job. I saw I wanted to be beaten up. I didn't understand" (51). A beating would confirm Abhor's sense of marginality in the oedipal world; pain insures her identity as renegade "other." But her confusion only reflects the role of sadism within patriarchal culture. Sade was imprisoned or confined to asylums for 27 years, punished for what society called the deviance of his devotion to sexual violence and physical discipline. His pleasure was his deviance, the violation of socially adjudicated rules and inhibitions. Michel Foucault points out that "in Sade, sex is without any norm or intrinsic rule that might be formulated from its own nature; but it is subject to the unrestricted law of a power which itself knows no other law but its own. . . . [T]his exercise carries it to a point where it is no longer anything but a unique and naked sovereignty: an unlimited right of all-powerful monstrosity" (*History* 149). For Sade the denial of inhibiting regulation leads to despotism. Abhor recognizes that the perennial devotees of sadistic punishment are those regimes most concerned with enforcing conformity to phallocentrism. The torturer operates within an economy of instruction; one is paid to do what one is told. Sadism is both attractive for its deviance and repulsive as a weapon beloved by right-wing dictatorships. Acker makes that connection explicit in her comments on *Empire*: she turned to "the Marquis de Sade because he shed so much light on our Western sexual politics that his name is still synonymous with an activity more appropriately named 'Reaganism.' Something of that sort" (**"A Few Notes"** [**"A Few Notes on Two of My Books"**] 35). Sadomasochism, which derives sexual pleasure from simultaneously inflicting pain and enduring punishment, informs Abhor's reaction: "This isn't enough. Nothing is enough, only nothing. I want to get to what I don't know which is discipline. In other words I want to be mad, not senseless, but angry beyond memories and reason. I want to be mad" (51). Abhor's quest for anarchy, which she cannot know within the patriarchal system, leads her in the track of discipline. Although a half-robot, Abhor wishes to depart from the empire of the senseless where her behavior is automatized—performed unconsciously—in order to emerge among the "mad," in revolt against reason.[5]

In the revolution that closes Part I of the novel, Algerians led by a one-armed proletarian guerrilla named Mackandal wrest Paris from the control of François Mitterrand, the bourgeoisie, and the French government.[6] "Paris was in chaos. Thousands of Algerians were walking freely. Ragged. Dirty. Sticks. Dolls. Voodoo" (67). Acker considers the only remaining source of resistance to Western capitalism and its homogenized culture to be the Muslim world. "I thought, for Westerners today, for us, the other is now Muslim. In my book, when the Algerians take over Paris, I have a society not defined by the oedipal taboo" (**"A Few Notes"** 35). The principal methods by which the French middle class retain their exploitative control of the African labor force are the media and disease. The Algerians chant "With this cry—MASTER—reap your profits in us, out of us. With this cry, by means of your press, press and oppress us" (70). The inescapable saturation of the media controls the minds of the masses, disciplining them to their social responsibilities and enslaving them to materialist needs. But in Acker's near-future world, disease controls the proletarian body: the Algerians protest, "No longer will you work in our muscles and our nerves creating herpes and AIDS, by doing so controlling all union, one and forever: being indivisible and narcissistic to the point of fascism, you have now closed down shop" (71). Sexually transmitted diseases become a device of the moralist middle class in suppression of the proletariat. Their "union" is corrupted, their bodies are stigmatized. Pervasive STDs are an intrinsic form of punishment that holds the Algerians in check. Mackandal's response is a terrorist campaign that involves the poisoning of the Parisian middle class using readily available herbs: "Poison entered the apartments of the bourgeoisie. There is a way to stop guns and bombs. There's no way to stop poison which runs like water. The whites had industrialized polluted the city for purposes of their economic profit to such an extent that even clean water was scarce. They had to have servants just to get them water and these servants, taught by Mackandal, put poison in the water" (77). As the bourgeoisie sought to discipline the proletariat through the transmission and stigmatization of a naturally occurring disease, the revolution of the dispossessed is fostered by the introduction of a natural toxin. The terrorism succeeds by striking at the weaknesses created by the bourgeoisie's exploitation of their human and natural resources. Disease as discipline confronts its twin in poison as anarchic revolt.

THE DOMINION OF ANARCHY: BREAKING THE CODE

The second part of the novel, "Alone," explores the possibility of society in which phallocentric domination "on the political, economic, social, and personal levels" has collapsed (**"A Few Notes"** 35). The section is preceded by a tattoo-drawing of a storm-buffeted schooner with sails furled, pitching through the roiling waves. The legend below reads "The Deep" (88). Acker's figure for individual freedom from social restraint is the pirate. "Sailors leave anarchy in their drunken wakes" (113). But the turbulence that follows in the wake of these (now frequently female) pirates can be as creative as it is destructive. In a chapter titled "The Beginning of Criminality/The Beginning of Morning," Acker advances an aesthetic and political theory of creative disruption. Criminality as a violation of the established law is regarded as destructive; but criminality in an environment of instability has the capacity for genesis—the beginning of morning. During the dark centuries of European colonization and enslavement of Africa, the Algerian coast became a stronghold of pirates. The oppressive rule and the claim to human property by Europeans fosters "criminal" transgression of property law. In the Algerian revolution (1954-1962), those Muslims who fought the war for independence to dislodge the French from Africa turned criminal revolt into nation-building. Abhor proposes that "All good sailors espouse and live in the material simplicity which denies the poverty of the heart. Reagan's heart is empty. A sailor is a human who has traded poverty for the riches of imaginative reality" (114). Acker's pirates are also equated with artists whose creative powers enable them to transcend materiality. "Such an act constitutes destruction of society thus is criminal. Criminal, continuously fleeing, homeless, despising property, unstable like the weather, the sailor will wreck any earthbound life" (114). The artist, the sailor, and the revolutionary challenge the Western illusion of material permanence and ownership. Their production of the new arises only out of the destruction of the old: "Though the sailor longs for a home, her or his real love is change. Stability in change, change in stability occurs only imaginarily. No roses grow on sailors' graves" (114). Acker proposes a generative instability.

Acker challenges the literalist who perceives order only in stable forms and unchanging institutions. These literalists are invariably shocked when confronted by the sudden obsolescence of a familiar order because they have denied the process of change. They cannot understand that *an* order is always impermanent, and as a limiting and limited case, not to be taken as *the* order of things. It emerges from a vast array of possible orders—as much by accident as by action. Like a wave it eventually dissipates, possibly supplanted by another formation. One proponent of "stability in change" is the male pirate, Thivai. While searching for a whore, he declares, "If there is any variability to reality—functions which cannot be both exactly and simultaneously measured—reality must simultaneously be ordered and chaotic or simultaneously knowable and unknowable by humans" (102-103). Just as the "beginning of criminality" (or the violation of an apparent order) can also be the "beginning of morning" (or the creation of a new system), so the presence of variability in reality signifies the simultaneity of order and chaos. It takes a pirate mind to appreciate that order and chaos, the measurable and the unmeasurable, are not exclusive to one another in experience but co-present, the one emanating from the other in continuous change and exchange.

Acker's pirates question whether "the demand for an adequate mode of expression is senseless" (113). The pursuit of an adequate means of expression leads to conventional discourse, its methods and rules governed by the empire. The unique expression of the self is imprisoned, rendered senseless to the individual in being made accessible to and consumable by the many. Acker challenges the function of adequate language through the tattoo as writing and the flagrant disregard for convention and decorum in a taboo language. For Acker, "writing the body" represents a profoundly ambiguous system of signification and is thus less susceptible to commodification and devaluation by the empire.[7] The arrival of Abhor and her newly acquired friend, Agone (a male Cuban sailor) at a tattoo parlor allows for a short disquisition on the etymology and cultural history of the art form:

> Cruel Romans had used tattoos to mark and identify mercenaries, slaves, criminals, and heretics.
>
> For the first time, the sailor felt he had sailed home.
>
> Among the early Christians, tattoos, stigmata indicating exile, which at first had been forced on their flesh, finally actually served to enforce their group solidarity. The Christians began voluntarily to acquire these indications of tribal identity. Tattooing continued to have ambiguous social value; today a tattoo is considered both a defamatory brand and a symbol of a tribe or of a dream.
>
> (130)

The tattoo can be both an artistic expression and an identification mark. It is an embellishment of the body through design, and an ineradicable injection of poison ink under the skin. The Romans used the tattoo on the early Christians, and the Nazis on European Jews, to identify and control the heretic and pariah. The sailor welcomes this identifying mark of difference. He celebrates his outcast status. That writing which facilitated the control and purging of the undesirable becomes an expression of group identity. The double value of "defamatory brand" and "symbol of a tribe," purging and bonding through identification of difference and sameness, a painfully forced marking and a defiant self-expression makes the tattoo an ideal signifying system for Acker. In searching for a myth in *Empire of the Senseless,* Acker says that the "most positive thing in the book is the tattoo. It concerns taking over, doing your own sign-making. In England . . . the tattoo is very much a sign of a certain class and certain people, a part of society that sees itself as outcast, and shows it.

For me tattooing is very profound. The meeting of body and, well, the spirit—it's a *real* kind of art, it's on the skin" ("Conversation" 17-18). The Algerians, pirates, and sexual pariahs in the novel seize control by taking as their own the very means by which the empire has suppressed them. The tattoo is a figure for Acker's art: a non-linear writing that foils the plot-driven causality of traditional fiction; an all-over writing that entwines its subjects rather than pursues its conclusion; a writing of the body (either female or male) expressive of sexuality and the visceral as opposed to the rational, concentrated mind. The tattoo-drawings that appear in the novel—at the start of each section, and at the conclusion—are more than illustrations: they are expressions of the artist's control of her medium, signs of her revolutionary discourse.

The disquisition on tattoos in the novel concludes with the declaration, "In Tahitian, writing is 'ta-tau'; the Tahitians write directly on human flesh" (130). On the equation of writing and tattooing Acker says, "I'm fascinated with the relationship between language and body. . . . I'm interested in the material aspect of the tattoo. . . . Erotic texts at their best—I don't mean pornographic, which is something else—are very close to the body; they're following desire. That's not always true of the writer, whereas it's always true that the tattooist has to follow the body. That's the medium of tattoo" ("Conversation" 18). Acker's novels follow desire, and they seek a "language of the unconscious." Intervening in the action as the tattooer approaches Agone with a knife, Acker calmly describes the crisis in language: "That part of our being (mentality, feeling, physicality) which is free of all control let's call our 'unconscious.' Since it's free of control, it's our only defence against institutionalized meaning, institutionalized language, control, fixation, judgement, prison" (133-34). Acker wishes to emulate the freedom of the unconscious in her writing, to pursue desire without arresting it, to wrest language from its civilizing discipline and reinvest it with an anarchic impulse.

Acker reflects on her efforts to free language from institutional control: "Ten years ago its seemed possible to destroy language through language: to destroy language which normalizes and controls by cutting that language. Nonsense would attack the empire-making (empirical) empire of language, the prisons of meaning" (134). The cut-up texts of William Burroughs, for instance, employ aleatory operations to defeat the writer's culturally infused determinations and thus oppose the empire's senseless blague with nonsense. To some degree Acker's plagiarism as an excision of classic texts participates in this conceptualism. "But this nonsense," she recognizes, "since it depended on sense, simply pointed back to the normalizing institutions." The binary opposition imperils avant-garde writing as simply the negation of conventional discourse, defined by its opposition to the institutional code without actually eliminating those codes. Acker prefers instead to attack the codes themselves through speech that is not unintelligible but forbidden, to speak the unspeakable:

> What is the language of the "unconscious"? (If this ideal unconscious or freedom doesn't exist: pretend that it does, use fiction, for the sake of survival, all of our survival.) Its primary language must be taboo, all that is forbidden. Thus, an attack on the institutions of prison via language would demand the use of a language or languages which aren't acceptable, which are forbidden. Language, on one level, constitutes a set of codes and social and historical agreements. Nonsense doesn't per se break down the codes; speaking precisely that which the codes forbid breaks the codes.
>
> (134)[8]

The prison houses and asylums are suffused with the shouts and screams of their inmates. The system has no need to suppress the nonsensical protests of the damned and convicted. But these institutions forbid the subversive communication that passes secretly from cell to cell—plotting the demise of the guardians of civilization and the downfall of the wardens of culture. Punishment is the silencing and the isolation of the lawbreaker. Acker smashes codes and disrupts societal agreements through the insinuations and assaults of proscribed speech. Her achievement lies not in opposing the linguistic code with meaningless cipher but in forcing the repeal of prohibitions through relentless violation—the code must then be revised to permit what it previously denied.

Plagiarism is the fundamental taboo of the literary world, and Acker has paid a price for violating its ethic. If Hannibal Lecter is her father, she has cannibalized the bloated corpse of patriarchal fiction. In her conversation with Lotringer, she recounts:

> A collection of my earliest work was published in England, and in the section about TOULOUSE LAUTREC there's four pages which I took out of a Harold Robbins novel, a best-selling book called *The Pirate* that had been published some years before. There is a scene there where a rich white woman walks into a disco and picks up a black boy and has sex with him. I changed it to be about Jacqueline Onassis and I entitled the piece **"I Want to Be Raped Every Night. Story of a Rich Woman."** I think the joke's quite obvious, but the journalist called my publisher and then she called Harold Robbins' publisher, and their response was that, my God, we've got a plagiarist in our midst. So they made a deal that my book would be immediately withdrawn from publication and that I would sign a public apology to Harold Robbins for what I had done.
>
> ("Devoured" 12)

Acker had no intention of deceiving her readers in the appropriation of Robbins' novel. She's "always talked about [plagiarism] as a literary theory and as a literary method" ("Devoured" 13). Even so, she has *pirated* Robbins's *The Pirate,* seizing its precious cargo and redirecting it for her own purposes. "Hijacking a copyright, no wonder they got upset," says Lotringer, "Terrorism in literature" ("Devoured" 13). To deceive a reader by appropriating a work as one's own would only reinforce the taboo against plagiarism and strengthen the capital investment in copyright.[9] Changing the intentionality of Robbins's "soft core porn" by intensifying the sexuality of the language, Acker breaks the code—of a patriarchal fondling of women's bodies, of protection of literary property—by speaking precisely that which the code forbids.

Another literary code that Acker flagrantly violates is that of genre. She upsets the literary hierarchy of genres that designates the linguistic difficulty of poetry or the subtle aestheticism of the *künstlerroman* as elite modes and the world-making of science fiction, the action-adventure novel, and the sexual arousal of pornography as populist modes. Her method in this postmodern leveling of high and low cultural signifiers is the mixing of familiar characteristics of these genres when the literary code would normally demand their separation. Leslie Dick points out that genres acquire their power through the formulaic assertion of rules: "a specific genre can be an 'enabling device,' a formal structure that allows and controls and prevents meaning, a syntax" (208). Acker frequently invokes the syntax of genres only to thrust the pelvis of a taboo language at them. The pirates' quest ends in pornographic satisfaction, as the obscene reality of buccaneering confronts *Treasure Island*: "the pirate who had just been fucked bent over the child tightly bound in ropes, already raped. His hands reached for her breasts. While sperm which resembled mutilated oysters dropped out of his asshole, he touched the breasts" (*Empire* 21). The figurative language only further confounds genre rules. In response to the rigidity of literary genres, the artist can (according to Leslie Dick) "isolate and extract forms from the institution, without getting involved in the institution" (209). Acker's piracy certainly extracts cultural booty from high and low genres, but her aesthetic of the taboo demands a frontal assault on the institution; or as Dick concludes, "it's more like scavenging, ripping the genre off. It's making use of some of the elements of the genre, while discarding the implicit values of the genre as institution. It's destructive, and disrespectful of the genre, which it treats like an abandoned car" (209). As an example, Acker introduces the character of Sinbad the Sailor among her rogues in the second part of *Empire.* Although lifted from the oriental tale, he describes his family history in the code of science fiction: "My father, I remembered, came from Alpha-Centauri. His head, the case with most Centaurians, had been green and flea—or dried-drool—shaped. Unlike him, my mother, a moon-child, was just a good-for-nothing. She was beautiful by night-time or lightless standards. Like the moon which hides behind the sun, mommy kept her brains hidden" (154). This passage takes advantage of the science-fiction genre's capacity for invention—any combination is possible in a new world—but still attacks the present code of gender inequity which relegates female intelligence to pale reflection of the dominant bull-Centaur. Sinbad reflects that he is thus a product of "cross-racial union. Multi-racial marriages usually lead to disaster" (154). In crossing the codes of genres, Acker challenges the institutional enforcement of racial and literary homogeneity. Her multi-generic fiction is one method by which the institutional code of language is broken.

HER RULES: RE-INVENTING THE CODE

In the third part of **Empire of the Senseless,** "Pirate Night," Acker's renegades are questing after a "society that is taboo," that is established on the very ground of transgressive acts. This section begins by plagiarizing *Huckleberry Finn,* which Acker describes as "one of the main texts about freedom in American culture" ("**A Few Notes**" 36). Thivai and his gay friend Mark (Huck and Tom) go to elaborate lengths to liberate the imprisoned Abhor (Jim), who is part black and referred to as a "runaway nigger" (**Empire** 212). In Acker's transformation, Abhor's enslavement is not to racism but to sexism; after much effort to spring her from prison, Abhor walks out of the jailhouse unmolested and determined to form a motorcycle gang. Male assistance in breaking the chains of sexism is worse than ineffectual; on the other hand, breaking out of the restraints of the old order won't suffice to establish a new society. Abhor forms a motorcycle gang "because motorcycle gangs don't let women ride bikes" (212). Rather than protest her exclusion from a male-dominated activity or attempt to dissolve the institution for its discrimination, she acts on her own to establish a social order based on that tabooed behavior. In one of many ruptures of causality and probability in the novel, Abhor—lacking the cash for a new or used bike—simply "finds" the motorcycle, gasoline, and oil that she needs: "I turned around, walked into the woods, and found a Honda which was only a year old, prerevolutionary, and in perfect shape except for one cracked mirror" (211). Abhor's unlikely discovery occurs outside of the capitalist economy of labor, wages, and the purchase of commodities; and it also violates the fictional economy of motivation that demands a reason for the motorcycle's presence when and where it's desired. Launched into a taboo society, the forbidden is not only permissible but unquestioned.

Abhor's motorcycle adventures represent the struggles involved in the creation of a taboo society. Never having been allowed to ride a motorcycle, Abhor becomes frustrated as she attempts to engage the motorcycle's clutch properly: "I got angry at the clutch and called him or her a shitsucker. This showed that both men and women do evil. But this knowledge and understanding didn't help me deal with my clutch" (213). Acker toys with the politically correct injunction against sexist language, in particular those instances when the speaker adopts the masculine pronoun to refer to someone whose sex cannot be identified. As a recently published handbook for writers advises, "If you want to avoid sexist language in your writing, follow the guidelines in Chart 99. Also, you can avoid sexism by avoiding demeaning, outdated stereotypes, such as *women are bad drivers* or *men are bad cooks*" (Troika 400). Abhor hopes to shatter the stereotype that a woman is incapable of riding a motorcycle. But the clutch—which obviously has no gender as an inanimate object—frustrates her efforts. Both genders are capable of becoming angry and resorting to profanity. Following the non-discriminatory principle of non-sexist language, Acker (through the persona of Abhor) admits that her taboo society needn't be theorized as a feminist utopia in which violence and evil have been completely expunged. The world of "Pirate Night" puts the brakes on such feminist fantasias as Abhor concerns herself with the challenges of vehicular realpolitik. Abhor learns that "a clutch controls power; to get more power, you have to control power. That was good" (213). Only recently freed from patriarchal captivity, Abhor learns to master power on her own, for her own purposes. She refuses to identify evil with a single class of oppressor, nor does she deny the continued need for discipline and control.

Abhor's male accomplices are skeptical, however, of her ability to ride because she doesn't know the "rules of road behaviour. They're found in a book called *The Highway Code*" (213). Her demonstration of individual capacity and self-governance runs afoul of this instance of "prerevolutionary" regulation and restriction of freedom. Abhor declares, "I had never heard of any rules so I didn't know that there were any, so I went back into the woods where I found a wet copy of *The Highway Code*. This was an English book, dated 1986. I had the CODE so now I could drive" (213). In *Elements of Semiology* Roland Barthes points out that the Highway Code is one of the most intractable of semiological systems: "by reason of its very purpose, which is the immediate and unambiguous understanding of a small number of signs, the Highway Code cannot tolerate any neutralization" (84). Neutralization refers to "the phenomenon whereby a relevant opposition loses its relevance, that is, ceases to be significant" (83). Thus the opposition of red and green as signifiers and their signified behavior must be maintained. The Highway Code is irreproachable. Or as Barthes suggests, it "must be immediately and unambiguously legible if it is to prevent accidents" (80). Barthes describes the Highway Code as one of the most rigid and limiting of semiological systems because, unlike the fashion system or literature, it forbids polysemy. It is a distinctly masculine, authoritarian system that regulates by establishing arbitrary but inflexible conventions. Abhor learns to ride by feel and intuition; the masculine code is a deterrent to her feminine experience.[10] She observes, "Its first rule for bikers said that a biker should keep his (I had to substitute *her* here, but I didn't think that changed its sense) bike in good condition. Since this bike wasn't mine, I could keep her in any condition. Since this is only commonsense and commonsense is in my head, I tore out this section of *The Highway Code* and tossed it into a ditch" (213). The masculine Code's presumptions of appropriate gender behavior, its discriminatory language, and its property fetishes don't deter Abhor from being a freethinker or acting on empirical observation. Nevertheless, her fitful attempts to follow the Code rather than discard it entirely lead her to vehicular chaos. The restrictions of the Code in a postrevolutionary era provoke anarchic behavior.

No theme is more prevalent in issues of *Outlaw Biker* magazine than the libertarian beckonings of the open road. And yet Abhor halts at the intersection between transgressive-taboo behavior that acknowledges the Code in its violation of it and a fully invested, self-determined behavior that invents its own customs. In order to disrupt the male Code of the Motorcycle Gang that forbids the woman driver, Abhor must first be initiated into the Rules of the Road. She pays literal attention to

> Rule 55.
>
> c) Watch your speed; you may be going faster than you think.

She assumes that she "was driving correctly by staring down at the speedometer" (218). Following the rules, when the rules don't mediate female experience, has its dangerous consequences; the result is a rear-end collision with a truck. Following the code prevents following the road. As the injured truck driver approaches menacingly, Abhor realizes that one paradigm of behavior has been destroyed by the revolution though no other has yet taken its place: "I was confused about what was happening because there were no more rules. Perhaps I was on the crossroads of Voodoo" (218). The remnants of patriarchal order and its unambiguous Code are thus incompetent in the world of orderly disorder into which Abhor has rushed and from which a new Code has yet to be created. The monologic, hermeneutically forbidding Highway Code has given way to the terrible beauty of a free polysemy. Abhor has entered the domain of crossed signals and Voodoo intersections: "One road was that the old man was trying to give me an important message. The other road was that the old man was trying to kill me" (218-19). Rather than the neutralization of opposing signals, Abhor encounters the ambiguously legible, potentially fatal, crossing of the blinking yellow light.

In denouncing the impositions of patriarchal order, Abhor (most probably speaking for Acker) issues the po-

litically charged pronouncement that "the problem with following rules is that, if you follow rules, you don't follow yourself. Therefore, rules prevent, dement, and even kill the people who follow them. To ride a dangerous machine, or an animal or human, by following rules, is suicidal. Disobeying rules is the same as following rules cause it's necessary to listen to your own heart" (219).[11] Acker endorses an essential principle of anarchism, that the impulse to personal freedom more frequently leads to salutary and creative behavior, whereas authoritarian strictures imposed on individuals more frequently lead to violent and destructive behavior. In their essay on the discourse of the Paris Commune of 1871, Donald Bruce and Terry Butler point out that anarchy has been historically "synonymous with the notion of chaos understood to mean 'utter confusion, the absence of all order, disorder.'" In the Paris Commune, however, and in the postrevolutionary Algerian-controlled Paris of Acker's *Empire*, the "actual political notion . . . should rightly be understood as the *radical decentralization of authority*: in other words a type of *order within disorder*" (231, their emphasis). Abhor's repudiation of externally imposed authority in favor of listening to the heart implies a commitment to spontaneity, self-discipline, and self-organization. "From now on *The Highway Code* no longer mattered. I was making up the rules" (*Empire* 222). The anarchy of Acker's postrevolutionary Paris conforms most closely to the definition of chaos that provides for an intrinsically originating creative dimension, that is, as an "*order [which] arises out of chaotic systems.*"[12] Drawing here on the propositions of Ilya Prigogine and Isabelle Stengers in *Order Out of Chaos*, Bruce and Butler argue that in a community in which self-organization and spontaneity are emphasized, "an explanation of chaos envisages (physical and social) systems which are capable of renewing themselves. Instead of falling victim to the inescapable entropic diffusion of all energy concentrations in the physical and social universes (as postulated in the second law of thermodynamics), this notion of chaos proposes a theory of renewal by which complexity arises out of simpler physical and social systems as a response to surrounding conditions" (235-36). In the chaotic social system of "Pirate Night," Acker theorizes a generative anarchism that initially hastens the collapse of repressive systems characterized by a simple homogeneous order, and in the erosion of closed-system boundaries, has the negentropic capacity to invigorate the newly opened environment. Abhor's declaration that "I was making up the rules" represents the possibility of self-organization and renewed complexity in an anarchic, heterogeneous society. Acker's confidence in the creative capacity of anarchy invokes a comparison with the poet Arthur Rimbaud,[13] whose call for a "'dérèglement de tous les sens' constitutes a chaotic subversion of order the aim of which is to let *emerge* a spontaneous and as-yet-unknown order"

(Bruce and Butler 236, their emphasis). Abhor's world suggests as well a "twofold vibration" (to borrow the title of Raymond Federman's novel) comprised of sadism and masochism, the instigation of anarchism and the declaration of self-governance, spontaneity and organization. She reflects, "I'm the piercer and the pierced. Then I thought about all that had happened to me, my life, and all that was going to happen to me, the future: chance and my endurance. Discipline creates endurance" (224). A new order emerges from the subversion of the old; anarchy and discipline are closely entwined. Anarchy permits the irruption of chance that may destroy life, but discipline fosters the endurance that sustains life.

Abhor's creativity takes the form of rewriting the authoritarian *Code* as a book called *The Arabian Steeds* because "My heart said these words. Whatever my heart now said was absolutely true" (219). Purportedly illiterate, Abhor draws pictographic images over the familiar diamond-shaped warnings signs of the *Code* that are reproduced in the novel, icons of a Western industrialized, petroleum-dependent, contaminated, asphalt-topped, inflammable society. Abhor converts, deciphers, and performs a hermeneutical transformation of the warning signs of an industrialized world in collapse into the vitalism, free will, and Bedouin-nomadic values of North African cavaliers: the motorcycle becomes Arabian steed; the partitioned and industrialized city of Paris becomes open desert; cold metal becomes hot sand; and masculine becomes feminine. Thus, for example, the icon for "corrosive" (a property of acids that causes the gradual destruction of metals, and so inimical to an industrialized society) is translated as "Let anger be anger: neither self-hatred nor self-infliction. Let the anger of the Arabian steeds be changed through that beauty which is blood into beauty" (221). In Acker's conception of the post-revolutionary nomadic social order anger isn't neutralized—as the chemist treats an acid with a base—but transformed in a salutary, sublimated manner. The corrosive aspect of anger, as a warning sign of the entropic breakdown in the steel sinews of industrialized Western culture, becomes a proclamation against a psychological and emotional breakdown in the individual through self-hatred. Anger is transformed, not neutralized in this post-patriarchal society from self-infliction to self-definition. Abhor's adoption of the nomadic creed expresses the release or de-institutionalization of the individual from the metallic cocoon of Western culture. Here Acker appears to draw upon concepts of "deterritorialization" and "smooth space" in the work of Gilles Deleuze and Félix Guattari, especially in their discussion of the nomad: "The nomads are there, on the land, wherever there forms a smooth space that gnaws, and tends to grow, in all directions. The nomads inhabit these places; they remain in them, and they themselves make them grow, for it has been established that the nomads make the desert

no less than they are made by it. They are vectors of deterritorialization. They add desert to desert, steppe to steppe, by a series of local operations whose orientation and direction endlessly vary. . . . The variability, the polyvocality of directions is an essential feature of smooth spaces of the rhizome type" (382). The free range, self-definition, and polyvocality of nomadic life express Abhor's liberation from and transformation of the fixities, entropophobia, and hortatory univocality of Western society.[14]

With something of the air of a cartomancer turning over the last card at a reading, Abhor declares, "I drew a final picture which summed up all the other pictures" (*Empire*, 221). This picture appears in the text as the tattoo design of the rose-piercing sword, around which is the legend proclaiming *Discipline and Anarchy*. The enlacing banner does in fact summarize the interdependent domains of Acker's novel: sexuality and language; political identity and individualism; sadism and masochism; order and disorder; striated and smooth space; literary and subliterary genres; masculinity and femininity. Acker's tattoo of the piercer and the pierced entwined slashes at the designation of one component or subject position as the dominant and the other as the subordinate. She refuses to replace the crumbling patriarchal order in an oppositional hierarchy with a feminist-utopian world that merely reverses the polarity of values. Acker finds that even in the domain of anarchy—in nomadic space, after the disruption of the state apparatus, where women ride motorcycles—there must be discipline present. Just as Abhor attains her feminine identity through the realization of her anger, and in the chaos of the postrevolutionary state a self-governing system reveals itself, so discipline and anarchy are recognized as interdependent functions. Discipline without anarchy is repressive; discipline in anarchy promotes endurance. Anarchy without discipline is destructive; anarchy in discipline promotes creativity. Spontaneity *and* organization. Beauty *and* violence. A rose and a sword.

Notes

1. In an interview with Larry McCaffery, Acker attributes her introduction to the theories of Gilles Deleuze, Félix Guattari, and Michel Foucault, by Sylvère Lotringer, as providing her with "a greater degree of control and precision about what I was doing. By the time of *Empire of the Senseless* I could even *plan* things! Whereas before I never even wanted to touch anything that was rational, because I felt that would intrude on whatever was going on ("Path of Abjection" 26). As a result, *Empire* is one of the first novels in Acker's *oeuvre* of non-narrative fiction to show evidence of plotting or consistent characterization.

2. Discussing *Empire* with McCaffery, Acker agrees that she sought a more "constructive" approach to

the problems of the patriarchy, to produce "a myth that people could live by." Here she reiterates her three-part plan for the novel, in both deliberate and affirmative terms: "What was involved in the writing itself was a dialectic between trying to get to another society and realizing you can't. So in the first part of the book I basically took the world of patriarchy and then killed the father on every level I could imagine. Part of this involved my attempt to find a way to talk about taboo—those basic transgressions patriarchy is responsible for but tries to cover over and deny. In the second part of the book I tried to imagine a society where you didn't have any of these taboos because it wasn't defined by Oedipal considerations. But even though I wanted to get to that world, I couldn't get there. . . . And so in the last section, there's only the sense of, 'Well, what the fuck do we do now?' That section is the synthesis of what you have in the first two parts of the dialectical movement: the wanting to get to that society of taboo and freedom from the central phallus, but realizing this is impossible. Finally *Empire* isn't just about getting to another society (which is a literal impossibility) but about searching for some kind of myth to replace the phallic myth" ("Path of Abjection" 31-32).

3. Brian McHale carefully examines Acker's appropriation and rewriting of material from Gibson's *Neuromancer* as a form of blank parody distinct to postmodernism in "POSTcyberMODERNpunk-ISM" (*Constructing Postmodernism* 225-42). McHale's essay is included with modification in McCaffery, ed., *Storming the Reality Studio* (308-23).

4. In his discussion of the "antihegemonic" tendencies of Acker's fiction, "Expectations of Difference: Kathy Acker's Regime of the Senseless," Joseph Natoli pursues a similar line of argument regarding her refusal of clarity, cogency, and orderly behavior. Acker creates "an empire of the senseless only because her constructions are wary of sense and its empire, only because sense is reward for following an order already established to communicate sense. A formation of her own signs, a putting an ending to her own following of that arrangement of signs she is already producing *within* as well as already produced *by,* and a devising in a way that the reader begins to construct and not to follow, a creation of desire so as to uncode desire—this is Acker's empire of the senseless" (*Mots d'Ordre* 140-41).

5. Arthur F. Redding offers a more thorough evaluation of the interplay of sadomasochism and disgust in "Bruises, Roses: Masochism and the Writing of Kathy Acker."

6. For a further disquisition on the Algerian revolution by Acker, see her *Algeria: A Series of Invocations Because Nothing Else Works* (1984). The historical source for Acker's Mackandal can be found in C. L. R. James, *The Black Jacobins.* James identifies Mackandal as a maroon, or runaway slave, from Guinea who organizes a slave revolt in Haiti between 1751 and 1758. A one-armed chieftain, Mackandal leads raids on the French colonists. James observes that an "uninstructed mass, feeling its way to revolution, usually begins by terrorism, and Mackandal aimed at delivering his people by means of poison. . . . He arranged that on a particular day the water of every house in the capital of the province was to be poisoned, and the general attack made on the whites while they were in the convulsions and anguish of death" (20-21). Mackandal's (eventually failed) slave revolt serves as model for the fall of Paris to the Algerians in Acker's *Empire.* In Haitian Voodoo (also alluded to in Acker's text), Mackandal is a loa, or supernatural being invoked by impassioned worshippers, who is manifest as a giant mosquito (Mackandal was captured and burned at the stake, and his followers believed he had metamorphosed into that plaguing insect). In keeping with Acker's characterization, he represents the spirit of revolution on Haiti, he abhors any form of slavery, and he punishes slave traders in a variety of terrible ways. "Agouné" is a loa manifest as the Sea-Master. In *Empire of the Senseless,* Agone (Abhor's partner) is a Cuban-born sailor (119). Acker's further adventures in Haitian voodoo appear in the first work collected in *Literal Madness, Kathy Goes to Haiti* (1988).

7. Greg Lewis Peters asserts in "Dominance and Subversion in Kathy Acker" that "Acker takes [Hélène] Cixous's concept of 'writing the body' very seriously indeed. Her texts are attempts to make the abstract physical through ('through' meaning literally in one side and out the other) the body, giving a visceral form to the feminine writing hypothesized by Cixous and Luce Irigaray" (150). Likewise, Ellen G. Friedman in "'Now Eat Your Mind': An Introduction to the Works of Kathy Acker" argues that for Acker "the body, particularly the female body, becomes the site of revolution. In this regard, Acker, perhaps more directly than many other women writers, creates the feminine texts hypothesized by Hélène Cixous" (39). The tattoo thus becomes the central figure equating the body with the text.

8. This rather Foucauldian passage may be an instance of Acker's infamous "plagiarism." As she remarks in her interview with Friedman, "I did use a number of other texts to write [*Empire*], though the plagiarism is much more covered, hid-

den. Almost all the book is taken from other texts" ("Conversation" 16). Michel Foucault, of course, has had much to say about language and the prison. One passage from "The Discourse on Language" seems directly relevant to Acker's concern with taboo: "In a society such as our own we all know the rules of *exclusion*. The most obvious and familiar of these concerns what is *prohibited*. We know perfectly well that we are not free to say just anything, that we cannot simply speak of anything, when we like or where we like; not just anyone, finally, may speak of just anything. We have three types of prohibition, covering objects, ritual with its surrounding circumstances, the privileged or exclusive right to speak of a particular subject; these prohibitions interrelate, reinforce and complement each other, forming a complex web, continually subject to modification. I will note simply that the areas where this web is most tightly woven today, where the danger spots are most numerous, are those dealing with politics and sexuality. It is as though discussion, far from being a transparent, neutral element, allowing us to disarm sexuality and to pacify politics, were one of those privileged areas in which they exercised some of their more awesome powers. In appearance, speech may well be of little account, but the prohibitions surrounding it soon reveal its links with desire and power" (*Archaeology of Knowledge* 216).

9. In "Writing, Identity, and Copyright in the Net Age," Acker suggests that in the "free zone" of the Internet, "*copyright* as we now define it will become a thing of the past" (*Bodies of Work* 101). Recent copyright infringement cases pitting the music industry against Napster and MP3.com suggest that this conflict is far from resolution. But Acker is certainly astute when she suggests that the "work isn't the property, it's the copyright" ("Devoured" 12); it's not the material, it's the code of law that defines the work in capitalism. For further discussion of plagiarism in Acker, see Naomi Jacobs, "Kathy Acker and the Plagiarized Self," and Arthur Saltzman, "Kathy Acker's Guerilla Mnemonics."

10. Peters observes in "Dominance and Subversion," "In *Empire*, Abhor . . . is imprisoned linguistically and sexually as well as literally. She is eventually freed from literal prison to form her own, one-cyborg motorcycle gang. In this world without patriarchy and taboo, she creates chaos by attempting to drive on the highway according to the rules of the Highway Code, computing stopping distances and measuring speed while other vehicles crash all around her. She is metaphorically learning the codes of a language that has no semantics to accommodate her. Just as Acker ex-plodes patriarchal language by reinventing/plagiarizing its sacred texts, so Abhor's actions reveal the fundamental uselessness of any male code to express a specifically female experience. That both Acker and Abhor reject the spirit of the codes while working within the letter of them is one more form of capitulation, but a reasoned capitulation that is subversive in intent" (154-55).

11. One wonders just what it means to ride a human by the rules. What equipment would be called for? What injuries might result?

12. For the emergence of order in systems far from equilibrium, see Prigogine and Stengers, *Order Out of Chaos*.

13. As an indication that Acker is enamored with the figure of Rimbaud, she includes a fictionalized biography of the symbolist poet, "Rimbaud," as the first section of *In Memoriam to Identity* (1990).

14. For an interesting application of the principle of the nomad and smooth space in Deleuze and Guattari to Acker's earlier novel, *Don Quixote* (1986), see Douglas Shields Dix, "Kathy Acker's *Don Quixote*: Nomad Writing."

Works Cited

Acker, Kathy. *Algeria: A Series of Invocations Because Nothing Else Works*. London: Aloes Books, 1984.

———. *Bodies of Work: Essays by Kathy Acker*. London and New York: Serpent's Tail, 1997.

———. "A Conversation with Kathy Acker." With Ellen G. Friedman. *Review of Contemporary Fiction* 9.3 (1989): 12-22.

———. "Devoured by Myths: An Interview with Sylvère Lotringer." Acker, *Hannibal Lecter* 1-24.

———. *Empire of the Senseless*. New York: Grove, 1988.

———. "A Few Notes on Two of My Books." *Review of Contemporary Fiction* 9.3 (1989): 31-36.

———. *In Memoriam to Identity*. New York: Grove, 1990.

———. *Literal Madness: Kathy Goes to Haiti; My Death My Life By Pier Paolo Pasolini; Florida*. New York: Grove, 1988.

———. "The Path of Abjection: An Interview with Kathy Acker." With Larry McCaffery. Larry McCaffery, ed. *Some Other Frequency: Interviews with Innovative American Authors*. Philadelphia: University of Pennsylvania Press, 1996. 14-35.

Barthes, Roland. *Elements of Semiology*. Trans. Annette Lavers and Colin Smith. New York: Hill and Wang, 1968.

Bruce, Donald, and Terry Butler. "Towards the Discourse of the Commune: Characteristic Phenomena in Jules Vallès's *Jacques Vingtras*." *Texte* 13-14 (1993): 219-49.

Clemens, Samuel Langhorne. *Adventures of Huckleberry Finn*. Ed. Sculley Bradley, Richmond Croom Beatty, and E. Hudson Long. New York: Norton, 1962.

Deleuze, Gilles, and Félix Guattari. *A Thousand Plateaus: Capitalism and Schizophrenia*. Trans. Brian Massumi. Minneapolis and London: University of Minnesota Press, 1987.

Dick, Leslie. "Feminism, Writing, Postmodernism." *From My Guy to Sci-Fi: Genre and Women's Writing in the Postmodern World*. Ed. Helen Carr. London: Pandora Press, 1989. 204-14.

Dickinson, Emily. *Final Harvest: Emily Dickinson's Poems*. Ed. Thomas H. Johnson. Boston: Little, Brown, 1961.

Dix, Douglas Shields. "Kathy Acker's *Don Quixote*: Nomad Writing." *Review of Contemporary Fiction* 9.3 (1989): 56-62.

Federman, Raymond. *The Twofold Vibration*. Bloomington: Indiana University Press, 1982.

Foucault, Michel. *The Archaeology of Knowledge and the Discourse on Language*. Trans. A. M. Sheridan Smith. New York: Pantheon, 1972.

——. *Discipline and Punish: The Birth of the Prison*. Trans. Alan Sheridan. New York: Vintage, 1979.

——. *The History of Sexuality*. Volume I: An Introduction. Trans. Robert Hurley. New York: Random House, 1978.

Friedman, Ellen G. "'Now Eat Your Mind': An Introduction to the Works of Kathy Acker." *Review of Contemporary Fiction* 9.3 (1989): 37-49.

Gibson, William. *Neuromancer*. New York: Ace, 1984.

Jacobs, Naomi. "Kathy Acker and the Plagiarized Self." *Review of Contemporary Fiction* 9.3 (1989): 50-55.

James, C. L. R. *The Black Jacobins: Toussaint L'Ouverture and the San Domingo Revolution*. 2nd ed., rev. New York: Vintage, 1963

McCaffery, Larry. ed. *Storming the Reality Studio: A Casebook of Cyberpunk and Postmodern Science Fiction*. Durham, NC and London: Duke University Press, 1991.

McHale, Brian. *Constructing Postmodernism*. New York and London: Routledge, 1992.

Natoli, Joseph. *Mots d'Ordre: Disorder in Literary Worlds*. Albany: State University of New York Press, 1992.

Peters, Greg Lewis. "Dominance and Subversion in Kathy Acker." *State of the Fantastic: Studies in the Theory and Practice of Fantastic Literature and Film*. Ed. Nicholas Ruddick. Westport, CT: Greenwood Press, 1990. 149-56.

Prigogine, Ilya, and Isabelle Stengers. *Order Out of Chaos: Man's New Dialogue with Nature*. New York: Bantam, 1984.

Redding, Arthur F. "Bruises, Roses: Masochism and the Writing of Kathy Acker." *Contemporary Literature* 35 (1994): 281-304.

Saltzman, Arthur M. "Kathy Acker's Guerrilla Mnemonics." *This Mad "Instead": Governing Metaphors in Contemporary American Fiction*. Columbia: University of South Carolina Press, 2000. 110-28.

Stevens, Wallace. *The Collected Poems of Wallace Stevens*. 1954. New York: Knopf, 1982.

Troika, Lynn Quitman. *Simon and Schuster Handbook for Writers*. 4th ed. Upper Saddle River, NJ: Prentice Hall, 1996.

Jeanette Winterson (essay date 2002)

SOURCE: Winterson, Jeanette. Introduction to *Essential Acker: The Selected Writings of Kathy Acker*, edited by Amy Scholder and Dennis Cooper, pp. vii-x. New York: Grove Press, 2002.

[*In the following essay, Winterson briefly outlines Acker's aesthetics as a writer, asserting that "Acker took the garbage, the waste, the revolt, the sickness and made it into a knightly tool—that is, something shining and bright, piercing and free, to cut life loose from its manacles."*]

There are three things to say about Acker:

> 1) She was ahead of her time.
>
> 2) Her fiction is closer to the European literary tradition of Borges and Calvino, than it is to the Anglo-American narrative drive of Salinger or Roth or Amis.
>
> 3) She was a woman—therefore she was locked out of tradition and time.

I know it is usual to talk about Acker in relation to Burroughs and Ginsberg, but while Kathy was a true New Yorker, her sensibility and her sense of exile were European. Her family on her mother's side was German, and Acker lived in Germany and France, as well as in England, for significant periods of her life.

Acker positioned herself on the outside—on the side of exile—not only out of disaffection with the United States but also because her cultural and literary interests were wider than any single tradition could offer. Acker the wild girl was Acker the well-educated and voracious reader. I have seen her in her piercings and leopardskin, suddenly put on her reading glasses and look exactly like perfect casting for *The Prime of Miss Jean Brodie.*

In the 1970s Acker began a series of experiments with form and language, many of which included herself as a character. I have noticed that when women include themselves as a character in their own work, the work is read as autobiography.

When men do it—say Milan Kundera or Paul Auster—it is read as metafiction.

Women can only write from their own experience. Men are imaginative. Women write testimony and confessional. Men write the big picture . . .—or so we're told.

Acker hated all that. She believed that a writer could be a vibrant amalgam of confession and imagination. She worked on the difficult boundary of formal experiment and naked desire.

A book she loved was De Quincey's *Confessions of an English Opium Eater.* She felt, and she was right, that the English literary tradition changed radically around 1830, as the Romantic movement dissolved into the nineteenth-century obsession with realism.

Acker was seeking something freer, but not less disciplined.

Acker was one of the most disciplined writers I have met—not only in her habits, but in her defense of form as the necessary buffer against chaos. Those who criticize her writing as a kind of bathetic splurge don't know how to read it.

She often chose a literary or legendary figure, like Don Quixote or Pasolini or Toulouse-Lautrec, as a basic shape for her inquiries, both subjective and formal. She merged her identity with these characters, creating an autonomous being who could speak personally and also without any personal agenda. She roamed these beings through time.

Do not underestimate how radical this was when Acker started doing it. Nowadays it has become a commonplace of fiction to merge the past and the present and to use real and imaginary figures in the same narrative.

Acker was doing this in the 1970s, along with Calvino and Angela Carter, but this was pioneer work of the kind that had hardly been attempted since Virginia Woolf's *Orlando* in 1928.

Acker was not alone, but she was one of the few, and she was one of the few I was able to look to in the 1980s, when I wanted to put myself into my work in *Oranges Are Not the Only Fruit,* and, later, to use invented worlds, outside of the confines of realism.

Now, everything you read that is not a novel in the realist tradition is some ghastly creative writing school attempt at colliding history, geography, and time, or a dull memoir where the author slips themselves in as a character. Dear Reader, it was not always so . . .

Acker saw herself as dispossessed—from her homeland, because of its politics, and from literature, because she was a woman. Harold Bloom's seminal *The Anxiety of Influence* is fine if you are the son overthrowing the father, but what if you are the daughter? Many of the daughters in Acker fiction end up fucking their fathers. Some castrate him later because they have no other hope of freedom, no other means of revenge.

Acker took revenge on a male literary tradition by raiding it mercilessly; her so-called plagiarism is a way of appropriating what is otherwise denied. As a woman, she can't inherit. As a pirate, she can take all the treasure for herself.

Acker was never a woman writer, but she was a writer who was a woman. Her vulnerability as a woman in a man's world set her to use her body as text. She would be a writer—fuck 'em—but she would write from the place denied, despised, and desired by men. She would not deny her own body, indeed she treated it like a fetish item, adorning, tattooing, and piercing it, feeling directly the power of the image—the image of femaleness used and abused by men for centuries.

Her female characters are both dispossessed and abused, but they are strong too, and full of hope that is not disgust. Acker may be the true mother of Brat Pack writers like Bret Easton Ellis, but there is no disgust in her work. Vomit, shit, urine, cocks, cunts, assholes, blood, the body are intimately described, and not in the language of cloudy romance. Yet there is no disgust. Disgust is reserved for the hypocrites, the morons, the authority figures, the moneymen, the politicians. Transgression is never disgust—it is a way of surviving.

"'I want love—the love I can only dream about or read in books. I'll make the world into love.' This was the way Don Quixote transformed sickness into a knightly tool."

Acker believed that desire is the only honest part of us, and she believed that art is authentic desire. She never expected that art itself could transform the world, but she knew art could awaken in us the authentic desire buried under the meaninglessness of modern life. The responsibility to act on that desire is up to us.

* * *

Acker took the garbage, the waste, the revolt, the sickness and made it into a knightly tool—that is, something shining and bright, piercing and free, to cut life loose from its manacles.

She was edging fiction forward, just as she was trying to jab humanity into a little bit of consciousness. She was a moral writer—she had high ideals and a cause.

At the end of *Empire of the Senseless,* her character Abhor says:

"And then I thought that, one day, maybe, there'd be a human society in a world which is beautiful, a society which wasn't just disgust."

Susan E. Hawkins (essay date winter 2004)

SOURCE: Hawkins, Susan E. "All in the Family: Kathy Acker's *Blood and Guts in High School.*" *Contemporary Literature* 45, no. 4 (winter 2004): 637-58.

[*In the following essay, Hawkins offers a political reading of Acker's* Blood and Guts in High School, *asserting that the novel critiques two stories—"the oedipal and the imperial"—and that it makes explicit the "dialectical relationship between sexuality and the forces of capital."*]

> [T]he idea that art has nothing to do with politics is a wonderful construction in order to mask the deep political significance that art has—to uphold the empire in terms of its representation as well as its actual structure.
>
> Kathy Acker, "A Conversation with Kathy Acker"

During her career, Kathy Acker produced fiction that is aesthetically outrageous, unrepentantly political, and singularly offensive. Larry McCaffery, who interviewed her several times, aptly evaluates her career this way: "Kathy Acker . . . produced a major body of experimental, shocking, and highly disturbing . . . work" (14). Such descriptors highlight Acker's typical fictional scenarios. Beginning with her first book, *Politics* (self-published in 1972), and proceeding to her last, *Pussy, King of the Pirates* (1996), Acker's texts insistently return to scenes of sadistic violence, rape, incest, masochistic pain, and sexual abjection of every sort. Her penchant for plagiarism, parody, pastiche, and other antirealist techniques has marked her work from the beginning as radically postmodern. No other contempo-

rary writer so determinedly eschewed "originality" by stealing from such an amazing array of both canonical and noncanonical writers: Dickens, Hawthorne, Keats, Faulkner, T. S. Eliot, the Brontës, Sade, Bataille, Rimbaud, and so on. She appropriates portions of journals and letters by real people; fiction by her contemporaries, for example William Gibson's *Neuromancer* in *Empire of the Senseless* (1988); political theory, primarily that of Gilles Deleuze and Félix Guattari; Harold Robbins; pornography. Any text is fair game. Textual piracy becomes an act, albeit small, of feminist guerrilla warfare, for Acker's method always serves political purposes.

Acker very much saw herself as part of "the other tradition" within American writing, a counterpractice visible in the works of Henry Miller, Jack Kerouac and the Beats, William Burroughs, the Black Mountain poets—writers dismissed as "experimental" rather than considered in "the tradition of political writing as opposed to propaganda" (**"A Few Notes"** [**"A Few Notes on Two of My Books"**] 31). Propaganda denotes for Acker the bourgeois world view which privileges realism in art and celebrates the universal "I," whereas political writing means the "political truth," the way things work in America ("Interview" ["An Interview with Kathy Acker"] 29). As a woman who wrote from inside her skin and her mind, Acker's contribution to this "other tradition" involves her acute awareness that the metaphor of the body politic begins as gendered experience, as actual and material.

Blood and Guts in High School (1978) occupies a pivotal position structurally and politically in terms of Acker's trajectory as a writer. Formally it marks the beginning of her serious use of plagiarism—in actuality a self-conscious appropriation of others' texts—as a technical device, "with the Genet stuff" ("Devoured" ["Devoured by Myths"] 10). The novels after that, ***Great Expectations*** (1982) and ***Don Quixote*** (1986), obviously signal this textual pre-occupation by rewriting two classics of Western literature. While she forsook such blatant deconstructions of the literary fathers as "simplistic" thereafter ("Devoured" 13), Acker continued to "us[e] language the way a painter would use paint. I use other texts—that's how I write" ("Kathy Acker" ["Kathy Acker Interviewed by Rebecca Deaton"] 279). Although she frequently dismissed the word "shocking" when applied to her work, Acker did admit to one interviewer that she "was really out to shock" with ***Blood and Guts in High School*** ("Kathy Acker" 276). And the novel retains its power due, in part, to the sheer material excess of Acker's rage, her version of a postmodern inferno, out of which no one breaks except spasmodically, through dreams, drugs, incessant fucking, criminality. But these manifested forms of resistance and escape serve as vehicles for the abiding tenor of politics throughout Acker's fiction. Her political analysis, always informed by a national and international critique of late capital, utilizes the distortions of family structure as a micromodel for the discursive and actual asymmetries within this larger political frame. Capital's deformative failures and violent disarticulations reveal themselves within the family, just as family structure models the inequities and oppressions of capital. In Acker's fiction, the father's power—like the lover's, or the capitalist's, or any president's since Nixon—derives from, and reinforces, his place within significant discursive and material regimes: the economic, the psychoanalytic, the literary, the mimetic, and so on. Women, most often those in the default position, are more subject to, and subjects of, this power.

READING ACKER'S READERS

In perceiving women's subjectification in terms of multiple economies, Acker rather presciently dramatizes theoretical considerations that have become commonplace but certainly were not in the late seventies. Since 1989, the critical discourse surrounding Acker's fiction has highlighted a number of these considerations by focusing on the radicality of her sexual politics; on her obsessive return to women's sexuality and the disruptive capacity of desire; on her repeated representation of sexualized woman as monster, as abject and criminal. This bodily extremity gets read in two fairly distinct ways, but the consequence is the same. Acker's politics end up largely restricted either to a consideration of the means through which feminine subjectivity struggles for an articulation that resists, at some points, patriarchal control, or to a consideration of the ways in which, through self-conscious and perverse participation in masochism, S/M, fetishism, etcetera, the subject seeks alternative positions in relationship to power.

For the most part, feminist critics, and Acker claimed them as her best readers, displace the violence and inherent pain of Acker's desiring protagonists onto a liberatory rhetoric that argues in favor of renegotiating or reformulating or resisting, if only momentarily, patriarchal constructions of "feminine subjectivity." In such readings, Acker's textual appropriations allow her to create, in Naomi Jacobs's terms, a "pseudonymous," "plagiarized" identity (54, 51) as she steals from, but simultaneously dismantles, the tradition and privilege of the textual fathers. This perpetual textual demolition, along with Acker's insistence on bits of her own autobiography, turn her into what Martina Sciolino calls an "autoplagiarist" as she discursively enacts a feminine identity in constant negotiation; "identity is contingent—interrelational and contextual" (443). Importantly for Karen Brennan, Acker's "fiction of feminine subjectivity" does not simply collapse into "the pastiche of [masculinist] postmodern writing" because her strategy of shuttling between parody and pastiche, "vacillating hysterically between the two modes," evades that col-

lapse (252).[1] For such critics, Acker's vehicle—blatantly desiring sexuality—affirms the possibility of a feminine subject capable of resisting patriarchal power, however temporarily, through various discursive practices. Given Acker's postmodern assumption that any stable identity is illusory, her protagonists typically move among a variety of linguistic and gendered subject positions.

For the other group of critics, almost without exception male, Acker's vehicle remains a foregrounded sexuality, and, again, desire is read as potentially liberating. However, in highlighting the issues of sexual violence, sadistic brutality, and self-inflicted pain, such critics' vocabulary shifts almost inevitably into a register of erotic pleasure; pain becomes the means to liberation. For David Brande, "Acker's cartography of masochistic sexuality" constitutes, at some level, an "erotic practice" that in its "assault on subjectivity, identity, and the oppressive hierarchies of gender" works to undermine normative "individuality" in favor of "new (or at least newly conceptualized) modes of escape from state power" (192-93). In such readings, violence to the body and physical pain become "the vehicle . . . by which desire is liberated from the familial prison of the Oedipal triangle" and "loosed onto the streets" (194). For Arthur F. Redding, Acker explores the "creative potential" of masochistic tendencies (283). Her protagonists, through their masochistic pain, engage in a "double effort to evade as well as to claim and reformulate the pain that has hitherto been felt merely to be the[ir] insipid destiny" (284).[2] To speak of "the careful and sympathetic application of pain" (Brande 208), of "the transformation of bodily violation into an object of beauty" (Redding 285), of the pornographic as a "total embrace of unregulated desire" (Walsh 157) displaces, in my view, the consequences of phallic control—violence to the female body—onto the object of that control; in that displacement, suffering transforms into pleasure. The unending sexual desperation of Acker's desiring-machine protagonists becomes the source of their freedom, however short-lived. Such interpretations reveal their own gendered assumptions about the trajectory of oedipal desire, positing yet again the male subject's universalized position vis-à-vis oedipal conflict, a position Acker critiques at every turn. Further, and far more important, such readings occlude, and thus refuse, the fundamental interconnections between heterosexual violence and its intimate construction within and through patriarchy.[3]

Blood and Guts in High School dramatizes just this sort of violence in the many sexual episodes involving Janey, the novel's protagonist. Conveyed through the narrator's overdetermined voice—flat, crudely descriptive, hyper—such violence inevitably erupts, for it cannot be separated from the explicit dialectical relationship between sexuality and the forces of capital:

"Having any sex in the world is having to have sex with capitalism" (135). The sexualization of capital, the imbrication of capital within hetero sex, has profound effects, and yet the effects remain largely hidden, for this dialectic is either denied outright or elided through discourses that seek to rationalize it.

Two discourses, two stories in particular, motivate Acker's political critique in **Blood and Guts**: the oedipal and the imperial. The classic oedipal story, which says nothing about money and everything about male desire, functions as a formative discourse within Western culture. In foregrounding male desire, the oedipal script discursively and materially normalizes patriarchy and the consequent sexual control of women. Janey's subjectification, her construction as a gendered human subject, is largely dictated by, and continually reinscribes, classic Freudian discourse. At a much larger level, the imperial story reveals Acker's most prescient political insight—her recognition of America's Other as specifically Middle Eastern and the ways in which this "othering machine" rationalizes America's corporate policies abroad. Acker's inclusion of appropriated and rhetorical figures—the Capitalists, Presidents, Egyptian rebels, Genet and *The Screens*—arises out of her sympathetic response to particular peoples in their fight against America's imperial domination. Acker perceives not only that the imperial story is underwritten through the Oriental imaginary, but that it represents a far more global instance of the conflation between sexuality and capital. Fundamentally, both stories enable and rationalize the mechanisms of patriarchal power. "You can't get to a place, to a society, that isn't constructed according to the phallus," she commented in 1989 ("Conversation" 17). In 1978, however, Acker's feminist sympathies produce a reading of Arab women's lives that is at some level ambivalent if not problematic. Nonetheless, Acker's depiction of America's Other, however fraught with contradiction, remains critical to a political reading of the novel.

High School from Hell, or America's Playground

Acker's textual demolition in **Blood and Guts in High School** of classic bildungsroman narrative elements and expectations structurally highlights such a political reading. The novel's title, a self-reflexive joke about "novels of education" signals, in part, a parodic bildungsroman, appropriately underscored by the text's three-part division: "Inside high school," "Outside high school," and "A Journey to the end of the night," an obvious echo of Céline's novel *Journey to the End of Night*. Indeed, this is the high school from hell in which teachers act as "top cops" who "replace living dangerous creatings with dead ideas and teach these ideas as the history and meaning of the world" (68). High school, in short, figures as a trope for America's psyche, its "cul-

ture" as well as its national policy; top cops morph into presidents and imperial capitalists intent on maximizing profits wherever possible. Inside or outside high school, America's citizens are, as we shall see, screwed from the get-go.

Given a generic, grade-school-reader name, Janey Smith, our "heroine," suffers a ridiculously short life span, from age ten to fourteen. True in its twisted way to the genre, Janey's story is definitely episodic. "Inside" begins in Merida, Mexico, with the subtitle "Parents stink" (7). Rejected by her father, Johnny, because he wants to "spend all his time with Sally, a twenty-one-year-old starlet who was still refusing to fuck him," Janey returns to New York sick with pelvic inflammatory disease (7). Alone in nightmare high, Janey fucks all the time, quickly becomes a punk gangbanger and member of the Scorpions, does drugs, steals, has two abortions, drops out. Outside high school, she's kidnapped by a white slave ring and held prisoner by the Persian slave trader Mr. Linker, who teaches her "to be a whore" (65). While a captive she writes an extensive "book report" on *The Scarlet Letter*, works on her Persian, breaks down, gets cancer. Of no use and rejected by Linker, she goes to Tangier, where she meets Genet. They trek through the North African desert. Janey gets thrown in jail in Egypt, is rejected by Genet, and dies. She has an after-death experience.

So much for the plot. The irreality of Janey's life coincides with increasingly larger segments of textual breakdown, marked by instantaneous shifts in generic, compositional, and narrative points of view; interpolations of various texts, including those of Vallejo, Mallarmé, Hawthorne, and Genet; segments of dramatic dialogue; excerpts from Janey's diary; Janey's letters; and so on.[4] The textual portions are, in turn, interspersed with graphics, for example line drawings of male and female genitalia; a few pages of childlike treasure maps called "A Map of my Dreams"; a childishly handwritten section entitled "The Persian Poems"; and the final section of the novel, which pictorially explores an Ackerian combination of *The Egyptian Book of the Dead*; Hindu deities, particularly Shiva and Kali; and Catullus's tomb.

Textual breakdown, bodily breakdown, characterological breakdown complement one another to some extent. They also amplify Acker's discursive use of Janey's deteriorating physical condition as a trope for resistance against the fathers, even if such resistance occurs through default. These versions of breakdown underscore Janey's inability to escape the family romance, consistently figured in Acker's fiction as the incestuous family, or the father's desire, which ceaselessly dictates her own. Thus the father/stepfather/lover appears in slightly different guises—as rapist, abuser, bully, sexual predator, object of desire—but these are all avatars of the incestuous father. In *Blood and Guts,* it's Mr. Linker, the Reverend Dimwit, President Carter, and the Capitalists, among others, who replicate and multiply the violent, off-hand fucking and rejection with which Johnny initiates Janey. Her "education" concerning men and sex (love never enters the picture) works recursively rather than progressively, and rejection compulsively returns as the primary signifier of Janey's experience. Experience, then, functions neither as sequence nor as mirror but as repetition and disjunction. Janey's need for Johnny—"I have an unlimited need of him" (20)—repeats itself in all of her manifestations. As Hester/Janey she begs the Reverend Dimwit, sometimes angrily but often pathetically, "Help. Help me. Help me. Love me" (95). With Linker she ends up as dependent kidnap victim: "I want you. I need you. I want to marry you" (116). In Alexandria, blind and in jail, Janey *"used to fantasize that when she went blind, a wonderful man would come along, take pity on her, and rescue her. Now she knows that nothing like that is going to happen"* (134). Janey's emotional-rescue scenarios remain fairly constant throughout the text; if anything, their desperate tone intensifies as her physical state deteriorates. Doomed to reproduce her primal desire for Johnny within every heterosexual relationship she encounters, Janey cannot escape this deformed asymmetry. Desire for the father recursively rules her life: "How can I be happy if a man doesn't fuck and love me?" (93)

This is her formative and fundamental lesson, the one she cannot escape and the reason parents stink. *Blood and Guts in High School* begins this way: "Never having known a mother, her mother had died when Janey was a year old, Janey depended on her father for everything and regarded her father as boyfriend, brother, sister, money, amusement, and father" (7). Johnny provides Janey with *everything*. Most importantly, he is her boyfriend and, in paltry last place, her father. As an only child, she exists outside sibling relationships, and her relation to the parental consists of a one-way sexual, and monetary, connection with Johnny. Acker here imbricates the paternal family with money, a conflation between the economies of capital and of the sexual that repeats again and again throughout the text: "Robot love. Mechanical love. Money cause. Money cause" (98). The mechanisms of sexual and economic oppression operate as quotidian entities. By literalizing the incest taboo and inextricably linking it with the power of capital, Acker demystifies one of the most pervasive and influential structures within Western culture—the oedipal formation of desire—and reveals the process of subjectification as transparent and literal; there is no classic unconscious here.

Janey, as an incest victim, blames herself for her father's indifference and thus can't handle Johnny's romantic interest in the starlet. Conversely, Johnny's attachment to Janey and his need to free himself of it sound absurdly like the emotional struggles disenchanted spouses experience in their attempts to leave a marriage made unhappy through their own midlife crises. As Johnny whines, "You've completely dominated my life, Janey, for the last nine years and I no longer know who's you and who's me" (12). When Janey calls from New York to "see if she could return home," if Johnny "ever want[s] to live with [her] again," he chides her for nagging: "[L]ighten up. Things just got too entangled. Everything between us is still too entangled for me to be with you" (25). Again, as a classic incest victim, Janey rationalizes Johnny's outright desertion in the only terms she understands: "Daddy no longer loved me. That was it. I was desperate to find the love he had taken away from me" (31).

Acker's indictment of classic psychoanalytic discourse, its reproduction and reinforcement of phallic power, is complicated by the apparent absence of the maternal space. Classic Freud presumes the cultural position, hence psychic reality, of the maternal, whether or not an actual subject occupies that place. In Acker's version, Janey's desire for Johnny apparently bypasses the usual circuit of originary desire for the mother, oedipal rivalry *for* the father, and the necessary, final sexual identification with/as woman/subject. For Janey there is no emergence from the classic oedipal phase; she is perpetually trapped within it. One of Janey's many conflicts, never resolved, is that between her pre-oedipal, presymbolic voice—the enunciated breakdown of the text—and her oedipal, phallus-obsessed voice, which repeats desire again and again for the father.

Despite her constant attempts at revolt, at life as a criminal and possible terrorist, Janey cannot get beyond this *need*. As it was with Johnny, so it is with minor hoods, rock and roll singers, and presidents. The outcome is always the same. When she recounts her affair with President Carter to Genet, she says, "I didn't want to fall in love with him because I didn't want to put something in my life, but he was screwing me so GOOD and beating me up that I knew I was going to fall in love with him" (122-23). Of course he rejects her.

No matter their social position, fathers rule; they desire, they decide, they control. The oedipal story's conflation of capital and sexuality guarantees one level of Western women's oppression. But this same conflation is at the heart of Western capital's rationalization of its global holdings and imperial control. We make the world safe for democracy and freedom through the control of bodies and their labor, most importantly women's bodies. Acker's novel dramatizes the multiple ways in which the Oriental imaginary, in justifying the necessity for imperial domination, disavows the very oppression fundamental to its success. *Blood and Guts,* in its political emphasis on the Arab world, proves to be uncannily repetitive as well as predictive about the consequences of American ignorance in relationship to this part of the world.

In the seventies America discovered the Middle East, yet again, for the first time. The civil war in Lebanon, the Palestine Liberation Movement, the Shah's increasingly authoritarian rule of Iran, but most particularly the oil embargo of 1973 began the process whereby the peoples of Middle Eastern countries became real to Americans. The Iranian occupation of the American embassy brought it all back home in 1979, but already within the American psyche "those" people had begun to act independently, to take control of their natural resources and their political lives. Suddenly "their" existence affected America's existence in a fundamental way.

IMAGINING THE WORST, OR ORIENTAL LANGUAGE LESSONS

Blood and Guts in High School presents Acker's critique of America's relationship with the Middle East, in particular with Iran, Egypt, and North Africa. One of the theoretical effects, then, of the novel is a partial deconstruction, *avant la lettre,* of Orientalism, that discursive formation which makes possible America's continued political and cultural domination of many Arab peoples. Since the publication of Edward Said's *Orientalism,* postcolonial theory has established a persuasive framework for understanding the dialectical relationship between cultural production and the politics of empire.[5]

While such a relationship was not particularly clear in 1978, Acker's text begins to analyze what might be called the Oriental imaginary, that largely unconscious (until quite recently) register within Anglo-American and European culture which motivates, in part, the West's strategic and historic rationalization for (neo)colonial domination. As we are now aware, this imaginary has constructed wholly contradictory images and desires. At the discursive level, the "Orient" figures extraordinary libidinal excess as well as raw terror, desire's double bind. While Ella Shohat and Anne McClintock work in different terrain, the former in Hollywood cinema and the latter in Victorian culture, both have contributed enormously to our understanding of the key place gender occupies within imperial discourse. The Oriental imaginary classically finds expression through an array of representational tropes focusing on the body—male and female—and most often a naked or semi-naked body. But as Shohat and McClintock make painfully clear, it's women's bodies that prove most desired and most in need of surveillance and/or containment through assimilation, incorporation, or obliteration. This sort of verbal/visual "policing" appears within and through what Shohat terms "Tropes of Empire." Most useful for my purposes are those figures and situations in **Blood and Guts** that evoke seemingly endless variations on the harem fantasy, including the white slave ring, the brothel, the veiled body. Janey narratively and compulsively reiterates her position as sexualized female body, subject to illness, physical violence, captivity, and early death.

Janey's "Persian Poems" appear in the midst of her rewrite of *The Scarlet Letter* and visually present a childishly handwritten sequence of lists that amounts to beginning Persian language lessons, sort of. The title strikingly suggests a famous French satire of the early Enlightenment, Montesquieu's *Persian Letters.* The epistolary heroes, the "foreigners" Usbek and Rica, function as the lens through which Montesquieu focuses his ridicule and critique of French culture. Usbek, in constant communication with his harem back home, exchanges much of this news with his traveling companion Rica. And constant trouble brews at home, the letters revealing a seraglio soap opera of wives, eunuchs, and slaves caught up in petty jealousies and continual sexual intrigue, just the sort of fantastic Oriental world Montesquieu's audience would find most satisfying: impossibly ignorant, pagan in its beliefs and customs, but utterly desirable.

As part of Linker's white slave ring, Janey's Persian poems are written from inside the harem, so to speak, and the writer is not some mysterious, exoticised figure of unimaginable, erotic, and always willing pleasure but as "sex slave." Since her sexuality constitutes her means of production as well as product, the Persian she practices, while a real language, contains lists of idiomatic expressions pertaining to genitalia, body parts, dirty words, verb paradigms (sex again), inflectional endings (genitalia again), and so on. Her captor, Mr. Linker, is a product of the Shah's Westernized, police-state regime. "Born on the Iranian streets," and "having been a beggar's child," he "saw how society worked" (64). Oppression, rather than powering the motor for change, for revolution, produces an economic epidemic which both motivates and rewards Linker's quest for "health," his metaphor for capital and culture. Had he remained poor, "he might have turned this glimmering of intelligence on himself and become a saint," but he escapes, as the narrator facetiously puts it, "Allah be praised, at age seven" (64). Having successfully internalized the position of the oppressor, he now teaches his hoodlums the paramount importance of the Athenian state. "All of our culture comes from ancient Greece," he informs them as he reiterates the Greek ideal: "A healthy body in a healthy mind" (61). Historically distorted, this fully Americanized Iranian, having amputated all connections with his actual culture, now rationalizes his own empire-building.

In the midst of this lecture, Acker places two drawings that shockingly interrupt Linker's tendentious assertions. Placed below the line "GIRLS WILL DO ANYTHING

FOR LOVE" is a briefly sketched "beaver shot," spread thighs and wide open labia and clitoris. On the opposite page, Acker places a barely detailed female body, headless, hanging in space, arms raised, wrists and ankles bound. That she is headless places her in a category with colonial populations—too often pure body, no mouth, no mind. At the same time, such a female prisoner evokes the passive harem inmate whose body represents a tabula rasa upon which Western white men may write their most perverse sexual fantasies. Below this classic porno bondage image are the words "ODE TO A GRECIAN URN." In a heartbeat, one of Western literature's great cultural documents gets sliced to pieces. Those famous, frozen figures, the pursued maidens and amorous young men in their moment of pastoral, perpetual beauty, which signify for Keats an ultimate truth about art and time, become, for Acker, one figure. She accomplishes her own "alienation effect" here. The image of the bound woman, one of empire's key tropes, recalls what is missing from classical Greek discourse and Romantic idealism; her body functions metonymically for all those real, material bodies, countless slaves and colonial populations that made possible the culture that Linker fondly tells his audience "separates us from the beasts" and "is our highest form of life" (64). Thus Acker's pictorial deconstruction also reasserts the Marxist perception that "There is no document of civilization which is not at the same time a document of barbarism" (Benjamin 256). As the speaker for Western multinational capital, that is, culture, Linker figures as Acker's Baudrillardian version of Matthew Arnold, "a real image, a fake" (64). Culture equals capital, capital equals culture: their power is equivalent. What produces capital is the sexual use of women's bodies.

Thrown out of Linker's harem because of cancer—she has neither use nor exchange value as a sex worker—Janey's disease marks her, just as criminality does, as materially useless but also resistant to the empire's values. Disease also figures her evolving exile; it propels her to Tangier and her appointment with Genet. Acker turns Montesquieu inside out by reversing her traveler's trajectory into the heart, so to speak, of the already textualized and highly ironized East. Here in the novel's penultimate section, Acker freely appropriates sections of Genet's play *The Screens* (completed in 1961 and staged in Paris in 1966). This play represents, in part, Genet's attack on French colonial rule in Algeria and its suppression of the Algerian independence movement.[6] Aside from the political content, much of the play's appeal for Acker (and she admired Genet's work) appears in its style—antimimetic, fragmentary, parodic, outrageous—as well as its apparent refusal to romanticize *anything,* least of all the colonized. Genet's radical politics concerning the Arab world and Western imperialism coincide with Acker's. However, her own artistic strategies finally reveal that as a European white male,

Genet cannot escape the oedipal and imperial stories that enable phallic power, and for Acker such recognition is critical.

Genet's protagonist, Said, is a loser thief and the poorest man in his village. According to the abysmal logic of the play, he marries the ugliest woman in the village, Leila, who appears throughout wearing a black hood with three holes. Simultaneously pursued by the colonial authorities and the local rebels, which he refuses to join and ultimately betrays, Said depicts that ultimate denial of stable identity, including political affiliation, and bourgeois morality which Genet proposes as the truly revolutionary spirit. Episodic, surreal, scatological, and disconnected, the play consistently deconstructs any number of binaries: colonizer/colonized; European/Arab; sense/nonsense.

In Acker's "terrible plagiarism" (137), Janey morphs into Leila and, as she does in the original, wears a black hood with two holes for her eyes because her ugliness is so great that no one, least of all Genet, who takes the part of Said, can bear to look at her. Instead of Said as the figure of revolt, Acker's Janey becomes the suspect one, thrown into jail and then out, a possible terrorist. Acker recasts the revolutionary setting as Egyptian, and the rulers become, instead of Genet's shifting catalogue of Europeans, American capitalists. The Capitalists—Mr. Fuckface, Mr. Blowjob, and Mr. Knockwurst—dismiss the rebels: "They're all Janeys. They're all perverts, transsexuals, criminals, and women" (136). Janey's criminality, sexualized and trivialized, blinds the Capitalists. While they obsess over her, Egyptians are setting fire to the trees. America's imperial position in Egypt—a "forest" that the Capitalists can't see—exists because "We own all the weapons in the world and all the scientists who design the weapons," and "we own the language" (135, 136). If only momentarily, Acker suggests that selective, covert action may unsettle capital's blind monumentality.

Despised, cursed, beaten, Genet's Leila speaks out of her "ugliness, earned hour by hour . . . minute by minute . . . second by second" (108). How she has "earned ugliness" remains unclear, but her black hood functions as an overdetermined sign of that ugliness. And while all of the characters wear such exaggerated costumes, Leila is the only veiled female. This singularity also marks her disappearance from the action, for while Said tells the assembled crowd in the final scene that Leila "died raging" (190), she never reappears, as do the other significant characters.

Genet's insistence on Leila's ugliness seemingly counters the classic Orientalist harem fantasy, the veiled woman; far from mysterious and exotic, Leila has nothing to interest anyone. Genet's assumption, however, that beauty equals desirability, wrenches the reader back to the classic image. In positing the obverse, it constructs a kind of "exploded Orientalism."[7] By inserting Janey into Leila's role, Acker reveals such assumptions as well as Genet's uncritical scripting of gender within an ostensibly revolutionary politics. Although Acker calls Genet's sexual politics into question in a number of ways, one of the first and most effective examples occurs through her realistic description of an Arab woman's actual dress, the dress Genet makes Janey put on: "A dress about twelve feet in length thrown over the head, belted around the waist, then pulled upward at the belt, so three skirts fall from the belt to the ground. Two eyeholes permit the woman to see" (129). The careful description, the complexity and totality of the dress speak to, yet again, a material reality. Such clothing is worn in public, depending on the country, and is thus a daily, practical matter, not one of beauty or ugliness.[8] Genet uses Leila's hood metaphorically, but Acker's text reminds us that such metaphors cannot be separated from a material source. Acker makes this point most dramatically when, in Egypt, Janey and Genet visit an Alexandrian brothel. Of the shifting screen settings in the play, the most repeated is the whorehouse, and the dialogue among the whores, as well as the exchanges between them and their customers, fills a good deal of stage time. Sexual jokes, insults, commentary on their customers' prowess or lack thereof provide numerous comic interludes. For Acker, the brothel constitutes a space utterly emblematic of the conflation between sexuality and capital. Mr. Linker taught Janey to be a whore, and what she sees here are the "lowest," sex *workers*: "For them there is no class struggle, no movements of the left, and no right-wing terror because all the men are fascists. All the men own all the money. A man is a walking mass of gold" (129). In *The Screens* Genet fails to consider the link between Leila, purchased for a bargain price by Said, the whores, purchased constantly, and the local population, purchased by European rulers. For Acker, this connection is fundamental.

Acker's response to the brothel metaphor also critiques a romanticized version of Genet, whose work glorifies criminality and makes use of settings such as the whorehouse and the prison as sites of resistance to bourgeois ideology. As canonized by Jean-Paul Sartre, Genet—orphan, thief, prisoner, artist—represents the privileged outlaw hero, his sexual and physical objection the means through which he achieved a transformation, an existential purity. If Janey thought she was going to find greater sympathy or kinder treatment from Genet because he too has suffered, she discovers otherwise. When Genet commands her to "get down . . . in the shit" (131) because she still has pretensions, she literally does so: lying in the dirt outside his apartment, following him everywhere, washing his dirty underpants, sharing "gaol" together. As she did with Johnny, Linker, the Reverend Dimwit, President Carter, and others, she objects herself. Her admiration for Genet only intensi-

fies her self-loathing and her need, as ever, for validation from the father. Locked as she is within the oedipal script, she's incapable of generating that value for herself. Certainly her object state does nothing to impress Genet. No matter how much he may have suffered because of his criminal status, his homosexuality, his social and political marginalization, Genet cannot recognize his own position within patriarchy: "He thinks all he has to do to be a woman is slobber. He has to do more. He has to . . . crawl mentally every minute of the day: . . . [H]e has to perfectly read his lover's mind, silently, unobtrusively, like a corpse. . . . Women aren't just slaves. They are whatever their men want them to be" (130). As an artist, Genet may "speak for" a number of constituencies, but he can never speak for women, no matter their race or class.

That Acker should perceive phallic power as monolithic and all pervasive, everywhere and always already the same, places her historically and culturally within a late seventies, radical feminism. Such a position has of course been critiqued for its essentialism and for its failure to distinguish the many cultural and racial differences between Western white women and women in the developing world. One could argue that Janey's view of Alexandrian women indicates Acker's historically limited perception of certain Arab women as *more* oppressed than Western women. Certainly Acker came to see this early, deconstructive approach as simplistic precisely because the narrative logic depends on opposition. She believed that she could resist power directly and thereby change the status quo. In ***Blood and Guts*** that means discursively fighting sense—instrumental reason, phallic logic, the fathers—with its opposite, with textual demolition. Thus Acker's creation of Janey/Leila, despite the character's twice-removed fictional identity, cannot help but obscure the issue of Arab women's agency. Acker's historical limitation, however, did not dilute the novel's most powerful point in 1978: women must function within a phallic economy that may be codified through different discursive systems, but the consequence is the same, female oppression. Obviously Acker arrived at a quite different view of Muslim culture later. In 1989 she wrote, "as more and more of the known world goes Coca-Cola and McDonalds, only the Muslim world resists" (**"A Few Notes"** 35).

As phallic logic, speaking through the incestuous father, abandoned her at the beginning, so too, at the end of her "earthly" life, she is abandoned by the authorial father. Genet pays her, leaves her in Luxor, and hurries away "to see a production of one of his plays" (140), after which Janey dies.[9] Her final lesson is a version and repetition of the many failed relationships that have constituted her discursive life. Even in death her experience does not escape the power of the father; only this time it's a search for "the most important book on human transformation" (147), hidden in Catullus's tomb, a book which provides no help. The novel ends with a dream, just whose we don't know, and the doves cooing over Janey's grave in Luxor: "Soon many other Janeys were born and these Janeys covered the earth" (165). The vision here suggests a weird dream of resurrection, of many Janeys spontaneously generating. While this wild replication of obnoxious, mouthy, teenage rebels might suggest a momentary escape, multiple Janeys can "exist" only as Janey has, as both a construction and consequence of the oedipal plot. Just as Janey's physical deterioration, bodily illness, and death mark her resistance, as well as her subjection, to the law of the fathers, so too are the metastasizing Janeys so doomed. Implicated within scripts over which they have little control, Acker's Janeys will endlessly desire the abusive father, and the fathers will endlessly desire their victim daughters, ad infinitum.

Acker offers no solutions or alternatives in **Blood and Guts.** What she does do with this novel is voice one long, outrageous scream at America, its obsessive economic motor and capital-driven social values, its naive, shallow, destructive politics. As this kind of political writer, she is merciless and unrelenting, and although her tactics mellowed over the years, she remained committed to a view of art as politically significant and necessary work. A few years before her death, Acker reaffirmed this position by asserting that the artist has an obligation to "make clear the reasons" she writes as she does and "must make those reasons which are also and always political positions, present" ("Speech" 4). If anything, Acker's critique of American culture and her political insights resonate even more eerily in the post-9/11 era; the consequences of corporate colonialism haunt us every day. And in a déjà vu all over again, the American Capitalists are now divvying up postwar Iraq. As readers of her work have pointed out, Acker's fiction arises from, and structurally manifests, a fundamentally anarchic impulse. In this she speaks as a radical individualist who is also a citizen, a kind of perverse, postmodern, very cranky Thoreau.

Notes

1. The word "hysteria" gets used frequently in discussions of Acker's work. Brennan, in fact, terms hysteria the "privileged vacillation of feminine writing" (252), while for Terry Brown, Janey, Acker's protagonist in *Blood and Guts,* is the hysterical subject. It is Janey's "hysterical desire," in traditional Freudian-Lacanian terms, that motivates the narrative (169). Kathleen Hulley focuses her analysis on Acker's structural, syntactic, and generic "disjunctive practices" (172) as a means of negotiating textual subjectivity.

2. The greatest difficulty with Redding's reading is that he reduces masochism into *one* kind of psychic field, inaugurated by the fetish, which in his interpretation is always about pain (classic Freud). His argument ultimately depends on a clearly Freudian, and thus limited, essentialism. And yet he seeks to deploy a language of Deleuzean psychic free play, multiple libidinal economies, and so forth when he states, "The suffering of the masochist . . . belongs to no one" (284). Just where the pain goes—whose body, whose suffering are we talking about?—points to the problematic confusion at the heart of his argument. Redding's own text reveals a desire both to refuse agency and its consequences and to locate material and real sources for such pain: "While pain certainly emerges from political and bodily inequity—be it patriarchal colonization of the unconscious, at one extreme of injustice, or the contractual relationship a masochist establishes with his 'top' at the other—it does not remain there" (284). Elsewhere he states, "Clearly masochism emerges from the dominant sexual order and represents a colonization of the feminine imagination" (300-301). Thus when Redding equates a male masochist who, within the confines of consensual and mutual S/M, contractually agrees to be dominated with an apparently unchanging "feminine imagination" oppressively colonized by the patriarchy, his comparative terms will not hold; they are utterly different in kind. Where is the "political and bodily inequity" in a mutually agreed upon sexual, and theatrical, display? How is this related to the systemic sexual violence suffered by women within postmodern patriarchy? Certainly Redding's text suggests some fascinating questions, the answers to which could lead to a more convincing argument: how might the male masochist be related to a "colonized unconscious"? Is he somehow more subject to the "feminine imagination" than other men, or are all human subjects subject to it?

3. As one of the few pessimistic, feminist readers of Acker's fiction, Ellen G. Friedman cannot evade the "sadomasochistic sexual acts" that define heterosexuality everywhere in Acker's work. For Friedman, such representations figure Acker's "radically feminist positions" (40).

4. Acker's language, especially in this book, most often fits the description she herself so abhorred— "experimental"—and exhibits close affinities with the early Julia Kristeva's definition of poetic language, revolutionary language. Poetic language disrupts through its very heterogeneity—shifting, fragmentary, often elliptical, and disjunctive. Hence "nonsense" or "'musical' . . . effects . . . destroy not only accepted beliefs and significations, but, in radical experiments, syntax itself" (*Desire* 133). This irruption within discourse Kristeva identifies as the semiotic "disposition," a reactivation of the presymbolic phase of psychic

development associated with the maternal. The maternal functions as a "rhythmic space" (*Revolution* 26); thus poetic writing signifies the pulsive rhythms of the body and the unknowable tracings of the unconscious that characterize the imaginary register. Karen Brennan reads the opening Merida section of the novel as a kind of Imaginary, New York as the Real, Tangier as the Symbolic—an ingenious reading but one which, despite her attempts to the contrary, suggests a far too linear Lacan. The imaginary breaks out *all over* this text, not simply in the first section.

5. This article assumes certain premises, terms, and tropes that would not be possible without the extraordinary intellectual and theoretical work done in the field of postcolonial studies, including Homi K. Bhabha's *The Location of Culture,* Anne McClintock's *Imperial Leather,* Edward W. Said's *Orientalism* and *Culture and Imperialism,* and Gayatri Spivak's *In Other Worlds.* Particularly in relationship to feminist, postcolonial film studies, see Ella Shohat's "Gender and the Culture of Empire: Toward a Feminist Ethnography of the Cinema." For an enlarged and revised version of this article, see Shohat and Stam, *Unthinking Eurocentrism,* particularly chapter 4, "Tropes of Empire."

6. For a sample of interpretive readings, see Said, "On Jean Genet's Late Works"; Sohlich; and Watts.

7. I take this phrase from Edward Said ("On Jean Genet's Late Works" 235). The veil continues to function within Orientalist discourse as a dominant figure for the Arab world in general and Islamic fundamentalism in particular. The American "victory" in Afghanistan was repeatedly represented as a liberation for Afghani women from the burka. The modern history of the veil as a discursive and political trope within Arab cultures is extremely complicated and inextricably linked to (neo)colonial domination. Leila Ahmed, in *Women and Gender in Islam,* analyzes the ways in which the veil, in early twentieth-century Egyptian politics, served as an organizing signifier for both "progressive" and nationalist narratives. In the former, Western-style modernity demands rejection of the veil because it represents all that is backward and inferior about Islamic society; in the latter, anticolonial nationalism demands retention of the veil because it represents the validity and dignity of Islamic, non-Western tradition. As Ahmed notes, the "resistance narrative thus reversed—but thereby also accepted—the terms set in the first place by the colonizers" (164). See, in particular, chapter 4.

8. For Fatima Mernissi, Moroccan feminist and sociologist, the daily reality of the veil entails, in part, its function within a system of sexual, spatial boundaries. Her now-classic study *Beyond the Veil* constitutes an attempt to "grasp sex as it materializes, as it melts into and with space and freezes it in an architecture" (xv). For Mernissi, the Islamic tradition is characterized through its use of space as a means of sexual control. Thus the veil represents one of the most obvious material and symbolic markers of this control of social, sexual spaces, male and female: "The veil is an expression of the invisibility of women on the street, a male space *par excellence*" (97).

9. For Acker's use of ancient sources in the final section of the novel, see Hume.

Works Cited

Acker, Kathy. *Blood and Guts in High School.* New York: Grove, 1978.

———. "A Conversation with Kathy Acker." Ellen G. Friedman. *Review of Contemporary Fiction* 9.3 (1989): 12-22.

———. "Devoured by Myths." Interview. Conducted by Sylvère Lotringer. *Hannibal Lecter, My Father.* Ed. Sylvère Lotringer. New York: Semiotext(e), 1991. 1-24.

———. "A Few Notes on Two of my Books." *Review of Contemporary Fiction* 9.3 (1989): 31-36.

———. "An Interview with Kathy Acker." Conducted by Paul Perilli. *Poets & Writers Magazine* Mar.-Apr. 1993: 28-33.

———. "Kathy Acker Interviewed by Rebecca Deaton." *Textual Practice* 6 (1992): 271-82.

———. Speech. The Artist in Society Conference. Chicago, Oct. 1994. <http://acker.thehub.com.au/ackademy/speech.htm>.

Ahmed, Leila. *Women and Gender in Islam: Historical Roots of a Modern Debate.* New Haven, CT: Yale UP, 1992.

Benjamin, Walter. "Theses on the Philosophy of History." *Illuminations.* Ed. Hannah Arendt. Trans. Harry Zohn. New York: Schocken, 1986. 253-64.

Bhabha, Homi K. *The Location of Culture.* London: Routledge, 1994.

Brande, David. "Making Yourself a Body without Organs: The Cartography of Pain in Kathy Acker's *Don Quixote.*" *Genre* 24 (1991): 191-209.

Brennan, Karen. "The Geography of Enunciation: Hysterical Pastiche in Kathy Acker's Fiction." *Boundary 2* 21 (1994): 243-68.

Brown, Terry. "Longing to Long: Kathy Acker and the Politics of Pain." *LIT* 2 (1991): 167-77.

Friedman, Ellen G. "'Now Eat Your Mind': An Introduction to the Works of Kathy Acker." *Review of Contemporary Fiction* 9.3 (1989): 37-49.

Genet, Jean. *The Screens*. Trans. Bernard Frechtman. New York: Grove, 1962.

Hulley, Kathleen. "Transgressing Genre: Kathy Acker's Intertext." *Intertextuality and Contemporary American Fiction*. Ed. Patrick O'Donnell and Robert Con Davis. Baltimore, MD: Johns Hopkins UP, 1989. 171-190.

Hume, Kathryn. "Books of the Dead: Postmortem Politics in Novels by Mailer, Burroughs, Acker, and Pynchon." *Modern Philology* 97 (2000): 417-44.

Jacobs, Naomi. "Kathy Acker and the Plagiarized Self." *Review of Contemporary Fiction* 9.3 (1989): 50-55.

Kristeva, Julia. *Desire in Language: A Semiotic Approach to Literature and Art*. Ed. Leon S. Roudiez. Trans. Leon S. Roudiez, Thomas Gora, and Alice Jardine. New York: Columbia UP, 1980.

———. *Revolution in Poetic Language*. Trans. Margaret Waller. New York: Columbia UP, 1984.

McCaffery, Larry. "The Artists of Hell: Kathy Acker and 'Punk' Aesthetics." *Breaking the Sequence: Women's Experimental Fiction*. Ed. Ellen G. Friedman and Miriam Fuchs. Princeton, NJ: Princeton UP, 1989. 215-30.

McClintock, Anne. *Imperial Leather: Race, Gender, and Sexuality in the Colonial Contest*. New York: Routledge, 1995.

Mernissi, Fatima. *Beyond the Veil: Male-Female Dynamics in Modern Muslim Society*. Rev. ed. Bloomington: Indiana UP, 1987.

Redding, Arthur F. "Bruises, Roses: Masochism and the Writing of Kathy Acker." *Contemporary Literature* 35 (1994): 281-304.

Said, Edward W. *Culture and Imperialism*. New York: Vintage, 1994.

———. "On Jean Genet's Late Works." *Imperialism and Theatre: Essays on World Theatre, Drama and Performance*. Ed. J. Ellen Gainor. New York: Routledge, 1995. 230-42.

———. *Orientalism*. New York: Vintage, 1978.

Sciolino, Martina. "Kathy Acker and the Postmodern Subject of Feminism." *College English* 52 (1990): 437-45.

Shohat, Ella. "Gender and Culture of Empire: Toward a Feminist Ethnography of the Cinema." *Film and Theory: An Anthology*. Ed. Robert Stam and Toby Miller. Oxford: Blackwell, 2000. 669-96.

Shohat, Ella, and Robert Stam. *Unthinking Eurocentrism: Multiculturalism and the Media*. New York: Routledge, 1994.

Sohlich, W. F. "Genet's *The Blacks* and *The Screens*: Dialectic of Refusal and Revolutionary Consciousness." *Comparative Drama* 10 (1976): 216-34.

Spivak, Gayatri Chakravorty. *In Other Worlds: Essays in Cultural Politics*. New York: Routledge, 1988.

Walsh, Richard. "The Quest for Love and the Writing of Female Desire in Kathy Acker's *Don Quixote*." *Critique* 32 (1991): 149-68.

Watts, Richard. "The Poetics of Disintegration: Colonial Authority in Jean Genet's *Les Paravents*." *Authorship, Authority/Auteur, Autorite*. Ed. Vincent Desroches and Geoffrey Turnovsky. New York: Columbia UP, 1995. 107-12.

Christina Milletti (essay date fall 2004)

SOURCE: Milletti, Christina. "Violent Acts, Volatile Words: Kathy Acker's Terrorist Aesthetic." *Studies in the Novel* 36, no. 3 (fall 2004): 352-73.

[*In the following essay, Milletti examines the connections between language, sex, and power in Acker's fiction, focusing, in particular, on the effect her "'terrorist' aesthetics have on the discursive systems of power she regularly targets in her work.*"]

A day is a blank sheet of paper. Bound up over a year, these sheets make a book which bears the title The Past and contains no lessons for the future.

—Cedric von Halacz, explosive terrorist in a psychological test[1]

Only process matters.

—Acker, **"Critical Languages"** (83)

"THE GREATEST WORK OF ART"

The title of this article immediately puts into proximity terms that generated international scandal for musician Karlheinz Stockhausen when he referred to the events of 9/11 as "the greatest work of art." The moral outrage that suffused Western media from Stockhausen's analogue of catastrophic destruction with aesthetic innovation-a relation at the heart of this inquiry—at once signals and yields insight into the dimensions of a new sociocultural paradigm that has arisen since the World Trade Center attacks: what Baudrillard in effect describes as a culture of terrorism. It also provides a useful lens through which critical questions about intersections of language and power—specifically how Western hegemony is shaped and disseminated by normative narratives—can be reframed in a post 9/11 context. Indeed, while the dispute about Stockhausen's statement continues to remain centered on questions of representation (i.e., what was said vs. what was meant), little consideration has been given to *why* an aesthetic evaluation of a terrorist act catapulted a musician into the political limelight. *Why* and *how* did Stockhausen's statement create such an impact? What does the public's reaction to his choice of language reveal about normative interpretive models and the discursive operations that are at work to corral them into shape?

Kathy Acker is no stranger to the stakes raised by these questions and the potent reaction that can be provoked by the intersection of art and violence. Her transgressive fictions—***Blood and Guts in High School, My Mother: Demonology, Empire of the Senseless*** and ***Pussy, King of the Pirates*** (to name just a few)—in fact often deploy terrorist characters, themes, and what I will argue is a terrorist prose style, in order to exacerbate and exploit just this relation. Indeed, where the furor over Stockhausen implicates anecdotally the power by which normative discourses constrain subjectivity, Acker's project is specifically designed to examine (and undermine) the formidable processes that are at work maintaining discursive integrity. Why her project deploys terrorism as an essential mode of critique, however, requires specific attention to, as Judith Butler might say, how "we do things *with* language . . . produce effects *with* language, and . . . do things *to* language," because "*language is the thing that we do*" (8, my italics). In this regard, Acker's interest appears to lie in how language promotes as well as prevents access to power—how language is "done" to marginalized subjects—and how shifts in power occur at all.

"When I use words, any words," Acker writes, "I am always taking part in the constructing of the political, economic, and moral community in which my discourse is taking place. All aspects of language—denotation, sound, style, syntax, grammar, etc-are politically, economically, and morally coded. . . . The only possible chance for change, for mobility, for political, economic, and moral flow lies in the tactics of guerilla warfare, in the use of fiction, of language" (**"Postmodernism"** 4-5). Acker's "guerilla" or "terrorist" use of fictional language takes on multiple forms throughout her prolific body of writing. Her renowned use of plagiarism, for instance, attacks fundamental precepts in the tradition of the humanities: specifically the authority, if not the originality, of the artist. As Sylvere Lotringer notes in an interview with Acker regarding her use of Harold Robbins' *The Pirate* (and the uproar that ensued), "Hijacking a copyright, no wonder they got upset. . . . Terrorism in literature" ("Devoured by Myths" 13). Yet it is Acker's use of explicit, often violent, sexual content to "break," as she claims, "the rational mind" that has perhaps caused the greatest shockwaves within the system of literary discourse (*Algeria* 117). How she makes the connection between language, sex, and power in her fictions—above all, to what effect—is at the core of this inquiry. My aim in the following pages is, there-

fore, to suss out the conditions under which her linguistic strategies arise, the focal points around which her fiction strategically centers, and, where possible, what effects Acker's "terrorist" aesthetics have on the discursive systems of power she regularly targets in her work, particularly in a post 9/11 context.

Not so long ago, Acker's deployment of terrorism would have been a less difficult or at least, rhetorically speaking, a less thorny project to scrutinize. In 1987, for instance, Peter Widdowson felt comfortable remarking that he wanted "to recuperate the notion of 'terrorism' as a position from which to challenge—with a positive skepticism—every facet and feature of our culture: to see how far that culture is contaminated and deployed to coerce and exploit us, and how far it can be redirected against the monstrous regimen which incorporates and implicates us 'for our own good'" (4). For Widdowson, a terrorist "stance" once offered the possibility of evaluating Western, capitalist hegemony. Given the current political climate, however—the ongoing "war" on "terror" that has erupted into the "with us or against us" mentality now fostered by the Bush administration—terrorism has become an increasingly rigidified conceptual paradigm designating specific cultural and political praxes: non-Western, non-Christian, non-democratic, etc. We have moved, in other words, severely but without complexity from one rhetorical stance to another without interrogating how a discourse of terrorism has been fostered and disseminated—and to what hegemonic ends. So, while Craig Dworkin considers whether we must feel shame at the lurid rhetorical language often used to describe the "frisson" between the language of "radical politics and radical poetics" fostered by authors such as Kathy Acker, or under what conditions we might once again feel excitement "at the bitter promise of a poetry as dangerous as a pistol shot, or a bombing," it is his final question—might it be possible to "understand poetry, once again or for the first time, as that mode of terrorism in which the victims are merely, and ruthlessly, words?"—that reveals the teleological complexity of the post 9/11 landscape for transgressive projects that endeavor to challenge dominant hegemony (Dworkin 2,4). How can we begin to evaluate Acker's work if the very terms she uses to question structures of power are no longer "morally" scrutable?

The aim of this project, therefore, is specifically to account for and evaluate Acker's discourse of terrorism, the political stakes she sets forth in her fiction, and the nature of terror in which she founded her work several years before the events of 9/11 brought the "war on terrorism" to the forefront of American consciousness. At what varying modulations—and to what apparent ends—does Acker cultivate these intersections of political and literary violence? What "lessons" might they offer her readers now about the interaction of power and language? Above all, how does her evident preoccupation with sex and gender fit into the matrix of these concerns: what relations does she draw between power, language, and sexuality in order to elaborate a theory of normativity?

It is of no doubt that the political stakes of Acker's fictions cannot be separated from her *techne*. She has written often enough on the subject, both directly and indirectly, to circumvent questions of intention about this chiasmus in her work. We might therefore begin investigating the discourse of terrorism that has evolved in her writing by returning to the epigraph of this article in which the "blank page" of The Past signals an impossibly indeterminate, even hopeless, future for terrorist, Cedric von Halacz. Acker's terrorist characters, Abhor and Thivai, in **Empire of the Senseless** often embrace a similar despair. Yet it is never lost on the reader that, whatever future they do possess, it is *in* and *as* writing: that a subject's future is determined by marks on the page. For the terrorist, that mark is a bomb. For Acker, by contrast, that bomb is a fictional language which creates—not simply spurs—subjects to action. If it is through such textual acts that Acker hopes one day to figure a "society," as she writes in the final line of **Empire,** "which isn't just disgust," then probing why she enacts her poetics through a terrorist model may offer insight into the culture of power from which the so-called "apolitical" postmodern novel arises (18).

John Collins observes an environment in which ". . . the obvious and important question now being asked by critically minded citizens (What exactly is 'terrorism?') needs to be modified to take into account the process through which the concept of 'terrorism' [is] *made understandable. . . .*" (158). Given this, Acker's project offers an opportunity to not only examine how language is used to represent terror, but also create it in the minds of the public. It is this process—the interrelation of power, language, and identity—that initiates this study of her transgressive textual acts.

> [Terrorism] is the other fellow's crimes, not our own comparable or worse ones.
>
> —Noam Chomsky (qtd. in Collins 163)

WHAT IS TERRORISM? OR, ENDURING FREEDOM

The meaning of terrorism has a long history of debate. The League of Nations first attempted to pass an acceptable definition for all member states in 1937. It is worthy of note, and it may shed light on Acker's subsequent interest in terrorist themes, that, since then, the League (now the United Nations) has been unable to do so. Even shortly after 9/11 during a "Debate on Measures to Eliminate International Terrorism" at the UN, when one might think a definition of terrorism would become self-evident, the dispute continued. While Sir

Peter Greenstock (the UK representative to the UN), for instance, easily resorted to a first world tautology— "Terrorism is terrorism. . . . What looks, smells, and kills like terrorism is terrorism"—Hasmy Agam (Malaysia's representative) offered a circumspect, if loaded, statement condemning "terrorism in all its forms and manifestations"—a remark evidently meant to indict individual and state terrorism, along with the violent, unacknowledged effects of first world imperialism within the global landscape (Collins 168, 167). In other words, while the events of September 11 at first appeared to uniformly clarify the meaning of terrorism on a global scale (to render at once obsolete the adage "one man's terrorist is another man's freedom fighter"), terrorism remains even now a volatile term—perhaps more so in light of subsequent political developments by Western powers (the passing of the Patriot Act in the U.S., for instance, and the rejection of UN policy during the "coalition-led" war in Iraq). "Terrorism," it has become patently clear, is a term used equally to protect as well as to disenfranchise.

I therefore propose that "terrorism" offers Acker a conceptual space immersed in both socio-political and linguistic turmoil that enables her to investigate the relationship between language and power with respect to subject formation—what Jonathan Culler describes as "the attitude which determines contemporary literature . . . a fascination with the power of words to create thought" (258-59). Indeed, for Acker, terrorism is never a stable term. By contrast, its very indeterminacy—its dependence on questions of agency, on who uses the term against whom—appears to be a source from which she draws a sustainable body of critique. For instance, in **Blood and Guts in High School,** she links sexuality with a terrorism that has neither motive, nor tactical organization. "Terrorism," she writes, "is letting rise up all that rises up like a cock or a flower. . . . Terrorism is straightforward. . . . As far as big goals go, it has no goals. . . . Terrorists believe in nothing and everything; serious terrorists every time they kidnap someone don't believe they're changing anything" (124). Elsewhere in an interview, however, terrorism appears to have specific, strategic goals (here kidnapping):

> As far as I know, "terrorists" are people who use chance methods to hurt people in a society in order to get the rest of that society to realize a particular political situation. I'm not sure you do that with books. I've never taken someone by chance and hurt them, or killed them, in a way that would wake a society up. What I did in **Blood and Guts in High School** was to attack a certain relation between a political situation and literature. It seemed to me that in high culture there were certain presuppositions behind high culture and these were political presuppositions that had a lot to do with class structure. What I was interested in was attacking the

very close relations between a fairly rigid class and
structure and high literature. I don't think that's terroristic. That is, I wasn't kidnapping someone by chance.

(Dodge, par. 12)

These are not, I should note, the only considerations of
terrorism Acker reveals in her work; loose definitions
appear regularly, if to less extreme ends of the spectrum
presented here. In fact, over her body of work, it becomes evident that terrorism or the terrorist act itself
offers Acker a turbulent nexus, a volatile lens, through
which she can investigate how discursive networks
shape and transform the identities of marginalized subjects. In this regard, she identifies a literary genealogy
of writers who similarly position themselves against
prevailing discursive systems. "Both Baudelaire and
Rimbaud posited themselves as writers against a society
of power," she remarks, for instance, in her 1994 speech
at the Artist in Society Conference (during which she
reflected at length on the censorship of her work). "They
saw themselves, writers, as dandies, friends of whores,
slackers, as anything but powerful."[2] Seen in this light,
the idea of terrorism offers Acker a similarly abject position with regard to Western hegemony—an identity
that is "anything but powerful" through which she can
foment a challenge to, and become an unsettling force
within, a system of power that positions marginalized
figures (the feminine, the queer, the poor, and the non-
western) outside dominant narratives.

While Acker spends a great deal of time in her fictions
exploring how language sustains systems of power on
the behalf of "dandies" and "whores"—which is to say,
of those without power—the agency of the "Other" itself is admittedly treated with little complexity in her
fiction. Gendered, racial, ethnic, and global Others are
unconditionally grouped together, though the systems of
power that marginalize them no doubt vary in both kind
and degree. Similarly, there is an apparent equivalence
in Acker's work between Middle Eastern figures and
terrorists, a tie which, it should not need to be noted, is
entirely specious, but which certainly represents a first
world chauvinism that has arisen, more clearly than
ever, in the post-9/11 environment: so-called "turban
sightings," for instance, are still regularly reported to
police. Though there is certainly room for an expanded
critique of subjectivity in Acker's fiction, I would argue
that it is exactly these prejudicial generalizations themselves that have evidently captured Acker's interest: to
the Western gaze, Acker suggests, *all* Arabs are in fact
terrorists (much the same way, for instance, homosexuality is often made equivalent to AIDS, or blackness to
criminality), and it is on this lack of distinction, this
powerful bias, that her fiction fundamentally capitalizes.
One might say that in the figure of the Arab/terrorist—
through the idea of terrorism—Acker discovers a
uniquely "fictional" pose: one through which she can
offer a rich critique of normative, *equally fictionalized*
conditions that continue to constrain subjectivity.

Her project, in this regard, gains clarity over time. In
Blood and Guts in High School, for instance, Acker
initiates her first use of a Persian "primer" in her novels
(such primers continue to appear in ***Empire of the
Senseless, My Mother: Demonology,*** and ***Pussy, King
of the Pirates***), relating its use to her feminine protagonist's inability to use a patriarchal/dominant language
(English). Yet the use of Persian also takes on a further
and equally significant imperative in Acker's project as
her political motives become more explicit: representations of Middle Eastern figures evidently present for her
a locus of abjection within the framework of late capitalism. Indeed, in ***Blood*** (1978), the duplicitous use of
first world power is viewed through the backdrop of
Iranian oppression and the Carter presidency. In her
short piece ***Algeria*** (1984), Acker introduces and critiques a relation between French colonialism, first world
hegemony, and political resistance. Two years later in
Don Quixote (1986), she addresses the growing mo-
nopoly of multi-national corporations within the global
landscape, and presents the Arab position with respect
to Western power in its growing negative bias: "The
Arab leaders are liars; lying is part of the Arab culture
in the same way that truth telling and honest speech're
American" (25). Not two years after that, terrorism becomes a central theme in ***Empire of the Senseless***
(1988) in which protagonists, Abhor and Thivai, are
themselves terrorists resisting an institution of power
disseminated by the media and governed by money, so
that "Empire" refers equally to systems of representation *and* the Western hegemony that governs them. Indeed, Thivai's initial remark, "Money is a kind of citizenship. Americans are world citizens," comes to
fruition later in the novel when he makes precisely this
link: "What is language[?] . . . Does language control
like money?" (38, 164). Meanwhile, chapter titles in
Empire such as "Let the Algerians take over Paris" and
"On Becoming Algerian" refer back to prior texts, as
well as prefigure those to come in her ongoing consideration of the possibility of socio-political opposition
for marginalized Others. As Acker's female "Don Quixote" notes, America is not the land of freedom it proposes to be: "The USA government is run out of
fear. . . . One plus one equals zero. There's no way I
can directly fight America because there's no way I can
fight the landlord" (***DQ*** [***Don Quixote***] 103, 105). In
this light, Acker's texts might be seen as an ongoing
campaign of resistance in which language itself is a
fundamental weapon of choice. Indeed, she might as
well be defining her own project when, as she remarks
in her essay on the Marquis de Sade, he "write(s) in order to lead the reader into a labyrinth from which the
reader cannot emerge without destroying the world"
("The Words to Say It" 66). In ***Empire,*** however, Acker
puts it another way: "GET RID OF MEANING. YOUR
MIND IS A NIGHTMARE THAT HAS BEEN EAT-
ING YOU. NOW EAT YOUR MIND" (38).

AT RISK

Since Kathy Acker's death from breast cancer in 1997, critical studies of her work have continued to examine the multiple modalities of transgression invested within her poetics. To admirers of her controversial project, the sustained interest in her fiction is promising—particularly since the field of literary criticism can be historically characterized by its tendency to marginalize experimental writing, particularly experimental writing by women. Even as the more provocative elements of Acker's poetics are recuperated, however, its most "troubling" aspects—not only the tensions she investigates within normative systems with particular regard for sex and gender, but also the risks she takes to defy them—still require deft negotiation. I refer less to the lawsuits and censorship hearings that have frequently accompanied her publications (in Germany, Canada, England, and New Zealand to name a few[3]) than to Acker's intense examination of normative social codes which, even now, her novels continue to scandalize and to put at risk by virtue of her unique prose style: a "performative" prose that, as I will argue, is uniquely designed to arouse readers (to action), as well as highlight itself as a discourse imbricated within and by power. If, as Judith Butler suggests, gender and sex are not essential qualities, but instead represent regulatory practices that give subjects cultural coherence, then Acker's novels might be said to trespass—to muck it up—within the interpretive space from which subjects elicit and perform their identities. The resulting fictions enable a unique discursive interaction that, as Jonathan Culler writes, "violates the implicit contract between author and reader that forms the basis of the novel as a genre" (*Surfiction* 262). The nature of that "violation" is not simply Acker's deployment of violent sexual content, but her unprecedented performative outreach—a terrorist prose style through which, as she notes in ***Don Quixote,*** "sexual desire [can] tear down the fabric of society" (137).

> "I shall establish in a few lines how Maldoror was good during his early years, when he lived happily. There, that's done."
>
> —Lautreamont (1)

> "All stories or narratives," the dog barked, "being stories of revolt, are revolt."
>
> —*Don Quixote* (146)

HOW THE TERRORIST TEXT PERFORMS, OR
'STUPID' WRITING

In her essay, **"Models of Our Present,"** Acker explains her own writing method while simultaneously calling for new writing "models," which are more responsive to contemporary theories of language. As such, she applies the linear logic of the scientific model, "If I do x, then x1 happens," to her own writing in order to reveal the failure of critiques that evaluate contemporary fiction against the empirical causality represented by this formula (63). She writes: "Today the common complaint against 'avant-garde' work is a complaint against discontinuity. Yet the model of time has progressed beyond simultaneous continuity and discontinuity to a picture of *simultaneous presence and absence*" (63, my emphases). In other words, since physicists have discarded traditional models that maintain that time progresses linearly, and now embrace concepts that discuss time in terms of simultaneous, multiple realities, writing likewise need not subscribe to traditional linear styles. Fiction instead must begin to consider how "presence and absence" can be rendered through writing. Just as physics has reevaluated the linear model, she suggests, so fiction must begin to examine its own base model: language.

Acker then goes on to claim that, in its present form, fictional language fails to convey "meaning" since "the act of describing assumes one event can be a different event. . . . Understanding in terms of describing won't work. For instance, the stronger sexual desire is, the stupider it makes the desirer" (64). Here, Acker at first appears to take on a patently poststructuralist pose. Yet, where Derridean logic might suggest that signification in language is often fortuitous, Acker's insertion of desire into the mix instead leads her to conclude that, not only are traditional methods of communication layered by a patriarchal law that fundamentally obstructs the feminine subject, but, at the level of syntax, a clutter of semantics, grammar, diction etc. further functions to dilute the potent (desirous) meaning of any user. Intensity, in effect, is dulled by the opaque screen of language. Acker's response is to design a direct and provocative writing style based on the language of the "desirer": it must be basic, she proposes, sheared of all but the essential "cry" within expression in order to directly target her readers. "Examine the two statements, "Help!" and "I need help!" The first language is a cry; the second, a description. Only the cry . . . is primary. *The cry is stupid; it has no mirror; it communicates*" (64; my emphasis). Here, Acker provides the foundation for her terrorist poetics—what might be called a "visceral" language through which she hopes her "cry" will be heard and form a direct connection with the reader. In this sense, Acker's project appears to be patterned after Antonin Artaud's "theater of cruelty," in which he attempts to write a theater without mimesis, a drama that *is* life, as opposed to its representation. Like Artaud—a writer from whom, Acker admits, she draws her own literary genealogy—Acker manifests an atmosphere that aggressively interacts with her readers (audience) in order to affect them violently, engulf them in a "crossfire," as Artaud writes, so that they can't "leave the theater 'intact' morally or emotionally" (Sontag 248, xxxiv). Acker's direct—what she calls "stupid"—writing is similarly designed to have an impact on her readers, because as she remarks, "There are no longer any safe places in our world. . . . [T]he writer who chooses to write in ways that do not support the status quo can no longer rest in elitism but . . . must make clear the reasons for writing as she or he does, must make those reasons which are also and always political positions present."[4] The ethical situation of the contemporary writer, Acker seems to insist, demands an unprecedented engagement with the reader. Acker's message is clear: if language is inflected with systems of power, then readers must begin to recognize their culpability within the discourses they embody or reject, and become equally accountable in the endeavor to resist those structures of power that marginalize the Other. Acker's prose is therefore specifically designed to shock readers into an awareness of the normative systems they embody.

As a terrorist aesthetic, the fundamental gesture of "stupid" writing is to create contact, to form a direct connection between writer and reader. In this regard, Acker's work takes on the performative quality of the speech act—using language to collapse distinctions between representation and act, between what is said and what is done. For instance, as J. L. Austin remarks in *How To Do Things With Words,* the baptizing of a child, the pronouncement of judicial sentence, the launching of a ship, are all performatives: in other words, the statements—"I baptize" or "I marry" spoken by a priest—are accomplished the moment they are named. It is this relation between word and effect that pervades Acker's essays. To this end, her manifesto appears in *Empire of the Senseless*:

> That part of our being (mentality, feeling, physicality) which is free of control, let's call it our "unconscious." Since it's free of control, it's our only defense against institutionalized meaning, institutionalized language, control, fixation, judgement, prison. . . . What is the language of the unconscious? . . . *Its primary language must be taboo, all that is forbidden.* Thus, an attack on the institutions of prison [language] via language would demand the use of a language or languages that aren't acceptable, which are forbidden. Language, on one level, constitutes a set of codes and social and historical agreements. *Nonsense doesn't per se break down the codes; speaking precisely that which the codes forbid breaks down the codes.*
>
> (133-34, my emphases)

Acker's texts are often characteristically direct as possible, in order to foreground what "the codes forbid"— "taboos" she reintegrates into a system based on an apparent structure of prohibition. In this regard, Acker appears to adopt Foucault's hypothesis in *The History of Sexuality*: that sexual interdiction in fact serves as a means of incitement, dissemination, and proliferation of heterogeneous sexualities (12). As Foucault remarks: "What is peculiar to modern societies . . . is not that

they consigned sex to a shadow existence, but that they dedicated themselves to speaking of it *ad infinitum,* while exploiting it as *the* secret" (35). Foucault's aim throughout his *History,* therefore, is to attend to the discursive deployment of sex in order to examine in what ways, and to what effects, sexuality has become aligned with the production and propagation of power. Acker takes this model and, by transgressing specific codes within the sex/gender system—by 'stupidly' exposing them—underscores how they control her readers' perceptions. As such, Acker is as equally interested in marginal as in dominant sexual behaviors in her fiction, equally attentive to rape, incest, and heterosexuality.[5] Yet, while the conflation of heterogeneous behaviors might seem suspicious, Acker's project in no way denies the distinctions between a multiplicity of sexual orientations and behaviors. By contrast, her work appears to identify the heterogeneity of sexual praxes she embraces as both similar and singular: each is governed, she suggests, by the normative codes of the sex/gender system that both constitute and constrain their subjects. It is the codes themselves that are her target— the social order that controls normative constructions of identity.

Acker identifies and introduces these "forbidden" constraints by deploying several strategies in her fictions— most characteristically, in her efforts to defer lyricism in order to "speak precisely" scenes of incest and rape. For instance, from the very outset of ***Blood and Guts in High School,*** the reader learns that Janey, the protagonist, regards her father as her boyfriend, and that to keep him from leaving her, she "fucks him even though it hurts like hell 'cause of her Pelvic Inflammatory Disease'"—a revelation that presents an initial and powerful shock to normative sexual mores on the first page (10). Of course, Acker's transgressive prose is the cornerstone of her style. Such passages are commonplace in her work—the content merely changes. For instance, in the three excerpts below, one can identify the similar rhetoric of shock Acker promotes with regard to rape, anal sex, and suicide.

Empire of the Senseless

Fatty dove in, ground and pounded his cock up into the so tight it was almost impenetrable asshole. He pound and ground until the brat started wiggling; then thrust hard. Thrust fast. Living backbone. Jewel at top of hole. The asshole opened involuntarily. The kid screeched like nerves.

(21)

Don Quixote

I stick my right hand's third finger into Eddie's asshole. It easily enters. He bucks and looks at me with surprise and openness unusual for him. Openness makes me open. My finger is reaching up and toward his cock. That opening. As his thighs're reaching up for me.

Sometimes I coldly turn him over, spread the asscheeks, stick my tongue into his asshole. I don't mind doing this though I usually mind doing this on men.

(56)

My Mother: Demonology

Francesca's body hung from a long Tampax string attached to the bathroom ceiling, all the way down to the luxurious tiled vestibule below. Her blood streamed out of every part of her and made all of the apartment smell like bleeding cunt. A jagged piece of glass had cut her hymen, or identity, into two parts.

(47)

Elsewhere, "conventions" like sex and gender lose their apparent rigidity through her linguistic play, so that in many of her novels, the anatomical status of her characters remains unclear. In *Empire of the Senseless,* for example, even though Acker identifies which of the two narrators (Abhor [female] or Thivai [male]) is speaking at the beginning of each chapter, their gender is subverted by the "neutered" writing of each section, designed specifically, it would seem, so that the narrators' voices cannot be distinguished from one another. In fact, the only way to determine the identity of the narrator (without returning to the first page of the chapter) is by the narrator's references to his/her genitalia. In this way, Acker highlights her sentiments regarding gender. It is, she suggests, strictly performative: the only distinction between males and females, one might surmise, is biology. Yet biology becomes at best a temporary placeholder before Acker attacks it too, reconstructing the body with mechanical parts—"transparent casts" and "derms" and "transdermal units." Indeed, when Acker describes the narrator Abhor, the reader discovers that she is not quite human, she is not quite woman. Abhor is a cyborg. Or as Acker writes, "A construct."

A transparent cast ran from her knee to a few millimetres below her crotch, the skin mottled by blue and purple and green patches which looked like bruises but weren't. Black spots on the nails, finger, and toe, shaded into gold. Eight derms, each a different colour size and form, ran in a neat line down her right wrist and down the vein of the right upper thigh. A transdermal unit, separated from her body, connected to the input trodes under the cast by means of thin red leads.

(33-34)

In Acker's fiction, biology is revealed as nothing less than a material ploy. The sexed body does not exist in a pure state of "impossible impermeability," but rather depends upon a series of reiterations—revealed in the insistent "girling" of "girls" throughout their formative years, as Judith Butler suggests—to make sex *appear* to be fixed (*GT* 134). In **"Seeing Gender,"** Acker poses the problem this way: "When I was a child, the only thing I wanted was to be a pirate. Because I wasn't a

stupid child, I knew that I couldn't" (158). It doesn't take long before she concludes why: "because I was a girl" (159). For Acker, the issue of sex and gender therefore returns to questions about the production of subjects and the social codes that limit identity in order to make subjects viable within the "Empire" of Western culture—a matrix of concerns that is also at the heart of Acker's use of plagiarism, of multiple "other" voices within her "own" fictions. As Acker notes, "If I had to force language to be uni-directional, I'd be helping my own prison to be constructed" (**"Humility"** 116). Her prison, of course, is one of normative representation, so Acker resists representing "herself"—incarcerating herself in language as it were—by borrowing the words of other writers, thereby distressing the rigidity of her own "authorial" subject position and, effectively, encouraging her readers to evaluate the strategies they rely on in order to interpolate subjects as females, heterosexuals, cyborgs, pirates—or "authors"—as well.

Signification itself is therefore a core issue to Acker's project, and throughout her fiction, she pays close attention to how language works, reveals inflections of power (*DQ* 37). For instance, sentences like, "Since a broom's sweeping hisandorher bald pate, heandorshe is a which," or "He whom I love is my eyes and heart and I'm sick when I'm not with him, but he doesn't love me; he's my I's; I see by my I's; he's my sun. My son lets me see and be. Thus he's my and the ," are clearly examining the relation of language to the formation of gender identity (*DQ* 75, 101). Yet, Acker is not simply exploiting puns to form sentences with multiple possible meanings. In contrast to James Joyce's work, which celebrates an infinite web of language and meanings, Acker tends to exacerbate fictional language, present it as a faulty tool that, because of its figural structure, lacks an essential clarity. Indeed, for her, narratives seem to be designed so poorly for communicative purposes that understanding itself is a fraud, ineffably deadlocked within language itself. "Stupid" writing, by contrast, is designed to collapse and then bypass this language logjam she identifies. By writing sentences based on a simple, visceral prose, her efforts appear focused on shearing linguistic clutter to an emotional core that affects/affronts her readers. As a result, Acker's work can be identified by two distinct syntactic styles she tends to exploit: the "direct" writing through which she strives to introduce abject constructs to her readers, and elaborately rendered sentences that highlight the ability of language to complicate meaning and confound the emotional directness that her work strives to achieve. One might argue that Acker's writing oscillates between these styles, creating another that encapsulates her terrorist aesthetic as the volatile movement between them.

Through these tactics—deployed in recombinant forms throughout her multiple novels—Acker creates opportunities to challenge systems of power with apparently exo-systemic constructs. In contrast to writing that similarly invokes topics of a sexual nature, but that simultaneously obfuscates them in prose, she makes sexuality viscerally negotiable so that she can confront her reader's conventions directly. By paring "propriety"—a learned social skill—from her writing, Acker enables an explicit discussion of the sexual spectrum that is unique to her work. Compare the following passages about incest/pedophilia, for instance, which appear in Nabokov's *Lolita* and Acker's **Empire of the Senseless.**

Nabokov:

My life was handled by little Lo in an energetic, matter of fact manner as if it were an insensate gadget unconnected with me. While eager to impress me with the world of tough kids, she was not quite prepared for certain discrepancies between a kid's life and mine. Pride alone prevented her from giving up. . . .

(132)

Acker:

"Abhor," daddy explained, "I'm the only man who'll ever take care of you properly."

His hands were reaching for my breasts while tears were coming out of his eyes.

"Why don't you do it with mommy, daddy?"

"We're too old. We don't do it anymore."

His right hand was rubbing my breast.

"I'm going to phone mommy."

Over the phone, I told her that her husband was trying to do something to me. I didn't use the word "fuck."

She said, "Let me speak to him."

"Daddy, mommy wants to speak to you."

I don't remember if his hand left my nipple, I don't know what they said to each other.

After he put the receiver down on the table, he put his cock up to me. There was no more blood than in a period.

(11-12)

Acker lifts the veils Nabakov employs to clothe the "forbidden," the elaborate prose that makes *Lolita* "a book written in a difficult style, filled on every page with literary allusions, linguistic experiment and fits of idiosyncrasy" (Pritchett 312). This is in no way a criticism of Nabokov's work. Rather, given Nabokov's extreme expressionism and cunning linguistic gamesmanship, he arguably suggests that language itself is a violence, that the word governs a power to both confound and enrich—a poetics that by nature reconsiders conventions of how meaning *works.* Certainly, *Lolita* shocked the public when it was initially released in 1955.[6] Without a doubt, however, the temperament of the times has changed. In an era marked by a media

gluttony indulgent of explicit "sex and violence" that, for the most part, affirms the dominant system's codes, Nabokov's text disturbs only the closest readers, couched as it is in the "startling beauty" and "the exquisite shape" of his prose (Toynbee 312; Levin 313). By contrast, Acker suggests that in order to disturb a contemporary audience, she must be candid in her sexual descriptions, embrace brusquely-textured writing in order to shake her readers up and, so, disrupt their conventions. Quite simply, only "stupidity" can get through: only terror can create shock in an audience numbed to the normative status quo to which its subjects have become accustomed.

Lolita, however, does spur an important issue regarding textual terrorism. Quite simply, Nabokov's novel demonstrates that terrorist texts are dependent upon the color of the times; what shocks readers today may not shock them tomorrow. Certainly, Acker's own texts become less startling the further the reader advances through novel after novel based on a similar and remarkable, yet eventually familiar, premise. The question must be raised then: How long can Acker's writing function in a disruptive manner upon the same reader and upon the same society? How long before the reader becomes resistant, even numb, to the issues Acker raises, to her novels' so-called "shock effect?" In short, how long before the terrorist text becomes "inefficient?"

I propose, however, that reader resistance is not in fact a flaw of the terrorist text. On the contrary, the moment Acker's texts do become familiar, one might say, trite for her readers, the moment the audience fails to recoil from the "forbidden," Acker's texts have, quite arguably, *succeeded* in their aim: they have desensitized her readers, thereby disrupting—albeit in a limited way— the normative order. Acker, after all, is not a sexual lobbyist. And the cumulative numbing effect of her texts upon her readers is arguably a necessary phase of her poetics.

By many contemporary accounts, however, critics and reviewers agree that Acker's writing does continue to shock and disturb,[7] balanced as it is between what is forbidden and what is permitted, taking advantage of a system that has become dependent upon a prohibitive structure, and which therefore cannot easily reconcile homosexuality, bisexuality, pedophilia, heterosexuality, rape, incest (and so on). It is perhaps of no surprise that Acker's novels, therefore, continue to produce extreme reactions in her readers at the individual, educational, and even the legal level. The explicit sex and violence of **Blood and Guts in High School,** for instance, gave rise to a successful petition in 1986 that banned its distribution in Germany. Karin Haderhold, a critic cited in that petition, notes in particular Acker's deployment of language as a provocative means of reader engagement: "Language is first of all a method of verbal communication, at any given time in daily life, but it also can be alienated and lifted to a level where it works as communication in the sense of emotional contact. This kind of literature utilizes texts and functions as a distorting mirror" (**"Immoral"** 145). The petition's reproach here is not at all off target, which is arguably one of the many reasons that Acker later published it in her collection *Hannibal Lecter, My Father.*[8] Acker's fictions do in fact attempt to reach out directly to her readers, to make them accountable for their complicity within the sex/gender system—their own performance of social codes—and the discursive baggage that shapes them and by which they shape others (See, for instance, *Empire of the Senseless* 5). Moreover, Acker does not let up. She persistently maintains her explicit writing—a terrorist aesthetic of excess that shocks boundaries, pushes the limits of what is "acceptable" and "unacceptable." The result, often enough, is nothing more than a readerly wince. Yet, while this may not seem like much—a mere tick in response to an outrage of prose—Acker's project suggests that, for readers who embody a discursive matrix of social mores, a wince is in fact *nothing less* than proof that the sociocultural matrix is always active and in play—it is not rigid, and if it is learned, it can also be changed.

> . . . You can't isolate yourself from the world. . . . [Consider] . . . the separatist feminists. You form your own group. In the end you pull things that way a little, but it can't work successfully. [It's not] a viable model of true separation. . . . In the same way you try to imagine a society that wasn't constructed according to the myth of the central phallus. It's just not possible when you live in this world.
>
> —Acker (in Friedman 17)

THEORIZING TERRORISM

Acker's fictions may at first resemble militant feminist literature, such as Monique Wittig's and Ti-Grace Atkinson's respective novels *Les Guerilleres* and *The Amazon Odyssey,* which generate images of warfare in their texts. Wittig's *Les Guerilleres* portrays the "longest most murderous war . . . ever known," the one between men and women, the struggle, "against texts, against meaning, which is to write violence" (127, 143). Atkinson's project is just as combative. She writes in *The Amazon Odyssey*: "The 'battle of the sexes' is commonplace, both over time and distance. But . . . a 'battle' implies some balance of powers, whereas when one side suffers all the losses . . . that is called a *massacre*. As women begin massing together, they take the first step from *being* massacred to *engaging in* battle . . ." (49). Although Acker, Wittig, and Atkinson may all be termed militant because of their confrontation of discursive power structures, Acker's project differs from theirs since it is not based in a concern for the feminine subject *per se*. For Acker, by contrast, the feminine subject is, as Butler puts it, "neither a stable or abiding term" (*GT* 1). Instead, Acker redirects her investigation into how the feminine, the queer—the Other in short—is represented in language. While a range of feminist concerns is certainly evident throughout Acker's work, what specifically the feminine subject represents remains a site of opacity in her fiction into which she regularly inserts pirates, terrorists, cyborgs—even Don Quixote *herself*—as substitutes. Whereas Wittig and Atkinson, in other words, might agree on what they mean by "woman" (via biology for instance), Acker consistently circumvents this question by examining *how* the idea of the feminine has become a discursive norm (one she clearly hopes to undermine) that functions to constrain the subject position of woman. Acker's attention, in other words, is focused less on representing the feminine through writing, than on investigating through the language of fiction what constitutes the Other *as such*.

Moreover, unlike the writing of Wittig and Atkinson, Acker's poetics resist a comparison to the binary terms of warfare against which terrorism is, by nature, opposed. As distinct from conventional forms of combat represented by fighting units with discrete missions working toward the same goal, terrorism's most apparent intention is to destroy the sense of safety and order on which societies fundamentally rely. As Charles Townshend notes, for instance, ". . . the essential distinction between war and terrorism lies in their operational logic: war is ultimately coercive, terrorism is impressive. War is physical, terrorism is mental" (15). In fact, the most explicit message of terrorism is not its political agenda. Rather, the terrorist act functions beyond the deaths of its victims (to return to Karen Haderhold's critique) as "emotional contact" upon the survivors: as a *reminder* and an *insertion* that discursive subjects can, in fact, be compromised by that which is abject to them. By contrast, Wittig and Atkinson admittedly fight in terms of "warfare." They have enemies to usurp, and battles to win, alternative power relations to install. The implicit objective of their war is to *reconstruct* a new system, replace structures of patriarchal power, with those founded in feminine, polyvocal forms. To this end, Wittig herself compares avant-garde fiction to a well known war-time strategy—the Trojan horse—in her essay by that name. "Any work with a new form operates as a war machine," she writes, "because its design and its goal is to pulverize the old forms and formal conventions" (45).

Acker's poetics, however, reveal pessimism about such a strategy (indeed throughout *Don Quixote,* the predicted "failure" of "revolution" is a common refrain). Whereas both Wittig and Atkinson attempt through their fiction to destroy the "law of the father," Acker suggests that they in fact promote a new law, new ways in which women can be conceived within a system of dominance and marginalization—that to "fix" the system is merely to invest it with new systems of meaning and interpretation in which subjects are hierarchically inscribed; more, that erecting a new system immediately corrupts the validity of the old system's destruction. "Ten years ago it seemed possible to destroy language through language," Acker writes, "to destroy language which normalizes and controls by cutting that language. Nonsense would attack the empire-making (empirical) empire of language, the prisons of meaning. *But this nonsense, since it depended on sense, simply pointed back to the normalizing institutions*" (*EOS* [*Empire of the Senseless*] 134, my emphases). The question of "revolution" for the feminine, Acker suggests, begs a further complexity.

In his essay, "The Subject and Power," Foucault remarks that power is an experience "rooted deep in the social nexus, not reconstituted 'above' society as a supplementary system whose radical effacement we once could perhaps dream of" (429). If, in fact, norms were localized supplemental to society, they could be expunged from it without changing the system itself, above all, without altering the "new" parameters invested within it. Because power structures are imbricated throughout the discursive matrix, however, it is impossible to discuss, predict, or even imagine such changes. As Foucault remarks, "A society without power relations can only be an abstraction" (429).

Indeed, Acker's work takes up this question: what *can be* reconstructed in the wake of a system's destruction? Her terrorist poetics—as distinct from those of "warfare"—arise in response: literary terrorism, she suggests, does not attempt to "pulverize" the sex/gender system but, instead, attacks its processes, creates uncertainty, in normative systems of power. The key, she seems to suggest, is not altering means of representation, but the matter of language itself. If, as in *Don Quixote*, she notes, "an alteration of language rather than of material usually changes material conditions," then Acker's challenge is not to reinvoke the paradigm of dominance and marginalization that she continues to identify within the basic tenets of most feminist theories—not, in other words, to work toward the destruction of "normalizing institutions." Rather, the force of her poetics prevents such institutions from working in a manner to which the culture has become *accustomed* in language. The issue, as Luce Irigaray writes in "The Power of Discourse," "is not one of elaborating a new theory of which woman be the subject or the object, but of *jamming the theoretical machinery itself, of suspending its pretension to the production of a truth and of a meaning that are excessively univocal*" (78, my emphases). In other words, since an alternative discourse cannot be enacted, cannot even be imagined, because what is "feminine" has been (mis)represented within discursive systems of power, the only plausible response is to jam the institutional "machinery" and so prevent the continued pretension to a consensus that

fixes sexuality as primarily heterosexual, and the feminine as subordinate. Acker's terrorist poetics are designed specifically for this task: not only do they disrupt the system's gears, jam its institutional organs, but, above all, they refuse to install "replacement" parts which might erect a new system from the scrap of the old. In this regard, it might be said that Acker reconceives "revolution" to mean "revelation"—an enhanced awareness of the function and proliferation of discourses among their subjects: an opening up (or dehiscence) of the system to itself by a writing that highlights its own boundaries. Her poetics thereby enable a state of perpetual dismantling: a jamming that is not the cease of motion, but ceaseless oscillation; a chaos that is neither destructive nor constructive, but that always reveals the limits that keep the masculine and the feminine, the homo and the hetero, the first and third worlds, apart.

Texts, of course, are not bombs (though some bombs are surely texts). Still, Acker's mode of literary terrorism does in fact reveal a promising model that causes discontinuous rifts within the apparent continuity of the sex/gender system. In much the same way that terrorism attacks notions of safety, Acker's fictions "disarm" social codes to a level where they co-exist in an amoralistic state with what has been made "forbidden" to them, thus disrupting a discourse that has based itself upon a structure of exclusion.

> There's a curious knot that binds novelists and terrorists. In the West we become famous effigies as our books lose the power to shape and to influence . . . Years ago I used to think it was possible for a novelist to alter the inner life of the culture. Now bomb-makers and gunmen have taken that territory. They make raids on human consciousness. What writers used to do before we were all incorporated.
>
> —Don DeLillo, *Mao II* (41)

TERRORISM INC.

Acker is skeptical at times, however, about the promise of the "terrorist" text. Her irony is self-evident, for instance, in the novel in which she promotes a call for change most directly: not *Great Expectations,* but *Don Quixote.* Elsewhere, in *Empire of the Senseless,* her narrator reflects pessimistically that "terrorists being aware of the huge extent to which the media now divorce the act of terrorism from the original sociopolitical intent [are] not so much nihilists as fetishists" (35). Similarly, one might examine the role industry has played in the publication of Acker's work by commodifying her literary terrorism. One look at the binding in which Grove Press has packaged most of her novels illustrates the relish with which the marketplace has embraced her project. The glossy covers, embossed in neon, glare from bookshelves; photographs of Acker embellish their front panels. Though the packaging was likely designed to be as aggressive as the novels' content, the book jackets clearly work to the publisher's advantage. As Acker writes elsewhere in *Empire*:

> "Any revolution, right-wing left-wing nihilist, it doesn't matter a damn, is good for business. Because the success of every business depends on the creation of new markets."
>
> He drummed his left finger into the table. "Do you know what human death really means? It means disruption."
>
> Drum. Drum. "Disruption is good, necessary for business. Especially comic books."
>
> (182)

Capitalism, Acker is acutely aware, can profit even off that which attempts to destroy it.

I would argue, however, that the process of commodification does not in fact remark on the (im)potency of literary terrorism. Although the very act of selling (and purchasing) Acker's texts smacks of systemic approval, and may therefore seem to undermine her efforts to disrupt its mechanisms, there is no denying that her writing, upon first reading, is still shocking. Both feminist and non-feminist readers and critics alike have been outraged by Acker's writing. In fact, her book jackets promote her novels' "horrifying" qualities, characterize her work as "violent, searing, angry.'"[9] This permits an interesting insight into the processes of commodification, and the relation of the terrorist text to systems of power. In contrast to Acker's implication that industry may prevent her "cries" from reaching the reader, the commodification that publication renders is not an absolute barrier. The process of commodification, after all, is not entirely external to the reader: much as the market commodifies objects, so does the individual, if to a less influential degree. And since published texts can shock readers just as unpublished texts can, what deserves highlighting is not the condition of agency, but the *process* itself. In short, just as the individual reader/commodifier reads Acker's novels (published or unpublished) and is shocked, then desensitized, to her work, so the market *as such* has changed as well. The process of commodification can be understood, then, as complicitous with acts of terrorism upon its marketplace. Just as Acker's writing eventually desensitizes her readers, the market's receptive attitude toward her poetics demonstrates that it has likewise altered to permit the exchange of apparently taboo subjects.

The final question, then, that current critics of Acker's project must ask is contextual in nature: can Acker's terrorist aesthetic engender the same effect on readers in a post-9/11 environment? Can terrorism, in short, still be deployed "merely" as a means of figuration? Has the concept of terror sufficiently changed since the World Trade Center's collapse that Acker's project will automatically be rejected by a public radically disinterested in the connections between language, power, and violence with respect to Western hegemony?

As Acker seems acutely aware, the idea of terrorism, not only the act of terrorism itself, is volatile in nature. And, indeed, since 9/11, terrorism—always a troubling site of inquiry—has become more difficult to position exclusively in terms of questions of power. As Baudrillard argues, The World Trade Center's destruction not only took lives, it also "eclipsed all of our interpretive models": it altered the terms of power themselves. "There is no longer a boundary that can hem terrorism in," he writes. "It is at the heart of the very culture it's fighting with, and the visible fracture (and the hatred) that pits the exploited and underdeveloped nations of the world against the West masks the dominant system's internal fractures. It is as if every means of domination secreted its own antidote" (14). Baudrillard, in other words, implicates terrorism *within* (not Other to) a situation of power. This relationship undoubtedly causes (and should cause) great discomfort: if nothing else, Karlheinz Stockhausen's remark (to return to the introduction of this paper) reveals the powerful quality of distress generated on a global scale by the events of 9/11. Yet Judith Butler's lament that serious inquiry into the "grounds and causes of the current global conflict is considered impermissible" suggests that Acker's radical project—rather than becoming less apt in a post-9/11 context—has in fact arguably become more relevant than ever. As Butler continues, "The cry that 'there is no excuse for September 11th' has become a means by which to stifle any serious public discussion of how US foreign policy has helped to create a world in which such acts of terror are possible" (1). Rather than dismissing Acker's project, then, for its patent use of linguistic terror as a means of creating emotional shock and disruption, it might be more strategic to look to her novels for their extended reflection on power and subjectivity that, without in any way exonerating the events of 9/11, provides a framework for understanding the oppressive governance of systems of representation on the subjects they impact.

Notes

1. Epigraph to Gregor von Rezzori's *Oedipus in Stalingrad.*

2. See the full text of Acker's speech for the Artist in Society Conference (Chicago, 1994) at http://www.class.uidaho.edu/english/Fugue/acker.html

3. It was also banned in South Africa. See Rick Lyman's *New York Times* obituary of Acker (December 3, 1997) and Ruben Reyes interview of Acker in *LOG Illustrated.*

4. See http://www.class.uidaho.edu/english/Fugue/acker.html Oct. 1994. Next-to-last par.

5. I make no distinction here between sexualities and what might be called "criminal behaviors" such as, for example, rape and incest, because Acker herself makes no distinction between them.

6. Although *Lolita* was officially banned only in New Zealand, Nabokov was unable to find a publisher for it with the exception of Olympia Press in Paris (a publisher of sexual materials, ranging from pornography to the work of Georges Bataille) due to legal concerns resulting from the novel's sexual content. It was not until 1958, in fact, that *Lolita* was printed by an American publisher.

7. Reviews and articles are often characterized by remarks such as: "Kathy Acker's *Don Quixote* is a literary trash compactor, collapsing with hammer thumps and electronic whine the fictional containers—the genres, stories and characters—from which we take nourishment and, Ms. Acker says, sup poison" (LeClair, 10); "*Empire of the Senseless* is a difficult and upsetting novel, one that insults and may even injure its readers" (Dillard 9).

8. Another reason might be the petition's notably humorless catalog of the book's stylistic attributes that function to highlight the "normalizing institutions" that Acker's project critiques: ". . . Some paragraphs are printed six times each, each with differing subsequent dialogues," the petition points out for instance. "On page 32, two sentences with identical wording are printed consecutively. On page 35 there is an insert by the author. . . . On pages 36 and 37 the author comments her own dialogues. In another text the main character describes herself as a 'Lousy mindless salesgirl.' On page 55 some sentences end with the word 'SPLIT.' . . . Some text are shown in the form of stanzas. In some poems you find sentences contrary to the grammatic rules." And so on (144, "Immoral" sic).

9. From book review excerpts printed on the front covers of Acker's Pantheon Press editions of *Literal Madness* and *In Memoriam to Identity*, by C. Carr of the *Village Voice* and Tom Clark of the *LA Times Book Review* respectively.

Works Cited

Acker, Kathy. "Algeria." *Hannibal Lecter, My Father.* New York: Semiotext(e), 1991. 114-41.

———. *Blood and Guts in High School.* New York: Grove Press, 1978.

———. "Critical Languages." *Bodies at Work.* London: Serpent's Tail, 1997. 81-92.

———. "Devoured by Myths: An Interview with Sylvere Lotringer." *Hannibal Lecter, My Father.* New York: Semiotext(e), 1991. 1-24.

———. *Don Quixote.* New York: Grove, 1986.

———. *Empire of the Senseless.* New York: Grove, 1988.

———. "A Few Notes on Two of My Books." *Review of Contemporary Fiction* 9.3 (1989): 31-36.

———. "Humility." *The Seven Cardinal Virtues.* Ed. Alison Fell. London: Serpent's Tail, 1990. 112-31.

———. "I lost my soul in San Francisco: an interview/journal entry starring Kathy Acker, Portland, and *Pussy.*" Int. Trevor Dodge. http://acker.thehub.com.au/portland.html

———. "Immoral (document)." *Hannibal Lecter, My Father.* New York: Semiotext(e), 1991. 142-48.

———. "Models of Our Present." *Artforum* 22 (Feb. 1984): 62-65.

———. "On Violence." *Review of Contemporary Fiction* 9.3 (1989): 23-31.

———. "Postmodernism." *Bodies at Work.* London: Serpent's Tail, 1997. 4-5.

———. "Seeing Gender." *Bodies at Work.* London: Serpent's Tail, 1997. 158-68.

———. Speech for the Artist and Society Conference: Chicago, October 1994. http://www.class.uidaho.edu/english/Fugue/acker.html

———. "The Words to Say It," *Bodies at Work.* London: Serpent's Tail, 1997. 66-80.

Atkinson, Ti-Grace. *The Amazon Odyssey.* New York: Links Books, 1974.

Austin. J. L. *How To Do Things With Words.* Oxford: Oxford UP, 1962.

Baudrillard, Jean. *The Spirit of Terrorism and Requiem for the Twin Towers.* Trans. Christ Turner. New York: Verso Books, 2002.

Butler, Judith. *Bodies That Matter.* New York: Routledge, 1993.

———. "Explanation and Exoneration, or What We Can Hear." *Social Text* 20.3 (2002): 177-88.

———. *Gender Trouble.* New York: Routledge, 1990.

Califia, Pat and Janine Fuller, eds. *Forbidden Passages: Writings Banned in Canada.* Pittsburgh: Cleis, 1995.

Collins, John. "Terrorism." *Collateral Language.* Eds. John Collins and Ross Glover. New York: New York UP, 2003. 155-73.

Culler, Jonathon. "Towards a Theory of Non-Genre Literature." *Surfiction.* Ed. Raymond Federman. Chicago: Swallow, 1975. 255-62.

DeLillo, Don. *Mao II.* New York: Penguin Books, 1991.

Dillard, R. H. W. "Lesson No. 1: Eat Your Mind." *New York Times Book Review* (October 16, 1988): 9+.

Dodge, Trevor. "I Lost My Soul in San Francisco: An Interview/Journal Entry Starring Kathy Acker, Portland, and *Pussy*" (1996). http://acker.thehub.com.au/portland.html

Dworkin, Craig. "Trotsky's Hammer." *American Letters & Commentary* 14 (2002): 1-5.

Foucault, Michel. *The History of Sexuality: An Introduction.* New York: Vintage, 1990.

———. "The Subject and Power." *Art After Modernism: Rethinking Representation.* Ed. Brian Wallis. Boston: David R. Godine, 1984.

Friedman, Ellen. "A Conversation with Kathy Acker." *Review of Contemporary Fiction* 9.3 (1989): 12-22.

Hulley, Kathleen. "Transgressing Genre: Kathy Acker's Intertexts." *Intertextuality and American Fiction.* Eds. Patrick O'Donnell and Robert Con Davis. Baltimore: The Johns Hopkins UP, 1989.

Irigaray, Luce. "The Power of Discourse." *This Sex Which is Not One.* Trans. Catherine Porter. Ithaca: Cornell UP, 1985. 68-80.

Lautreamont, Comte de. *Maldoror.* Trans. Alexis Lykiard. Cambridge: Exact Change P, 1993.

LeClair, Tom. "The Lord of La Mancha and Her Abortion." *New York Times Book Review* (November 30, 1986): 10.

Levin, Bernard. "Appendix." *Lolita.* London: Weidenfeld and Nicolson Publishers.

Lyman, Rick. "Kathy Acker, 53, Novelist, Performance Artist." *New York Times* (December 3, 1997): 20.

Madden, David. "An Interview with Paul West." *The Review of Contemporary Fiction* 11 (1991): 154-76.

Nabokov, Vladimir. *Lolita.* London: Weidenfeld and Nicolson Publishers, 1959.

Pritchett, V.S. "Appendix." In *Lolita.* London: Weidenfeld and Nicolson Publishers, 1959.

Reyes, Rubin. "Candle in the Wind: Kathy Acker Interviewed by Rubin Reyes." *LOG Illustrated* 3 (Summer 1998). http://www.physicsroom.org.nz/log/archive/3/acker/

Sontag, Susan, ed. *Antonin Artaud: Selected Writings.* Berkeley: U of California P, 1988.

Stockhausen, Karlheinz. "The greatest work of art." http://www.stockhausen.org/message_from_karlheinz.html

Townshend, Charles. *Terrorism: A Very Short Introduction.* Oxford: Oxford UP, 2002.

Toynbee, Philip. "Appendix." *Lolita.* London: Weidenfeld and Nicolson Publishers, 1959.

von Rezzori, Gregor. *Oedipus in Stalingrad.* Trans. H. F. Broch de Rothermann and Gregor von Rezzori. New York: Farrar, Straus and Giroux, 1994.

Widdowson, Peter. "Terrorism and Literary Studies." *Textual Practice* 2 (Spring 1988): 1-21.

Wittig, Monique. *Les Guerilleres.* Trans. David Le Vay. Boston: Beacon Press, 1985.

Sheri Weinstein (essay date 2004)

SOURCE: Weinstein, Sheri. "The Lay of the Land: Piracy and the Itinerant Body in Kathy Acker's *Pussy, King of the Pirates.*" In *Devouring Institutions: The Life Work of Kathy Acker,* edited by Michael Hardin, pp. 111-33. San Diego, Calif.: Hyperbole Books, 2004.

[*In the following essay, Weinstein interprets* Pussy, King of the Pirates *as Acker's critique of the patriarchal and masculinist enterprise of conquest, which includes domination of both land and the female body.*]

> *Free of her former embraces, free for the moment from my desire for sex, I awoke. Awoke, went down to the bottom of the world. Where girls become pirates. In the light of the mourning of the world.*
>
> ***Pussy, King of the Pirates***

> *As soon as she was at her destination, she no longer knew where she was . . .*
>
> ***Pussy, King of the Pirates***

Kathy Acker's fiction has consistently fascinated and frustrated critical imaginations. The literary critic finds herself strongly compelled by what is happening in the text, intrigued by the dizzying array of language through which Acker communicates. At the same time, that critic finds her usually suitable interpretative skills thwarted by the text and may end up feeling complicit with the very struggle for ideological domination that Acker's novels scrutinize and assail. Put bluntly, Acker's work dares us to look straight at it while diminishing our abilities to articulate, with anything more than postmodern finesse, what exactly it is that we are seeing.

Perhaps we can start approaching the "how" and "why" components of such a statement at the very place where Acker's novels usually start: the body. In a 1996 interview with Larry McCaffrey, Acker explains her investment in the Marquis de Sade: "[he] wasn't really interested in sadism per se but in how the political realities of rationalism deny the body" (20). Acker, like Sade, is indeed insistent that we confront not only abstract "bodies" (i.e., bodies of knowledge), but also tangible, actual bodies. Acker's version of the material body—the body which houses sex and language and performs their complicated acts—is indeed replete with Sade's influence: for both writers, the body is the foundation for our confrontation of the "political realities" of gender and sexuality. As Acker also tells McCaffrey, "there's an undeniable materiality [about the body] which isn't up for grabs. . . . The body is the only place where any basis for real values exist anymore" (21).

These "real values" are found in Acker's female bodies and are positioned against a larger, collective body of oppression. In *Empire of the Senseless,* Acker has said, she attempted to imagine "the world of patriarchy" and then to "kill the father on every level" (McCaffrey, 31). She wanted a new way for her heroine Abhor to traverse social, political, and sexual constraints. The characters in *Pussy, King of the Pirates,* Acker's final novel, go well beyond attacking the patriarchy. They come to *embody* it, acting as both its victims and victimizers, its subjects and objects, using their bodies in ways that redefine the very violence done to them. In a novel filled with literal women and symbolic men, Acker's characters are insistent travelers, itinerants, and pirates.

This essay investigates the topos and topography of both the bodies of *Pussy*'s female characters as well as the places and spaces in which these bodies exist. O and Ange are the novel's main characters and, except for brief sections whereby King Pussy "speaks," its narrators and their itinerancy are ceaseless. Wandering itself becomes a route. They project themselves onto the landscapes of Europe, the Americas, Asia, and finally, they travel not horizontally across the globe, but vertically, descending into the "land of the pirates."

The apparent teleological goal of O and Ange's journey is the buried treasure located on the map that has been bequeathed to them by Ange's dead mother. However, as I will argue, the larger orientation and direction of their quest is to figure out how and why women indeed "search" at all and what they might find in an "underworld" in which women are pirates. This, and not the itinerary and trajectory of the buried treasure, is the search to which we are encouraged to pay the closest attention.

As a concept and a genre, piracy operates through theft and appropriation. Put another way, the trope of piracy is about claiming a right to something and someone that is not inherently yours and behaving as if it were indeed yours; it is about the very irrelevance of "permission" when it comes to both creative and physical possession. Piracy and appropriation allow Acker's text to dramatize the interdependence of bodies (whether they be textual or sexual, figurative or literal). Through

the search for buried treasure as well as the sexual experiences and psychological revelations that occur along the way, *Pussy* dramatizes the very problematic of seizure—what it means both to take and to possess persons, bodies, and "treasures."

The female pirates in this novel are, as we might expect from any pirates, anarchic. Yet their anarchy is not lawless; they do follow a system of law, but it is a law of their own. However marginalized and subversive the pirates appear against the masculine, dominant culture from which they have rebelled, piracy is an attempt to work within that dominant culture. Specifically, it is a discourse of lawlessness and freedom that positions itself against normative discourses of identity and community, which for Acker are also patriarchal, normalizing discourses. In this way, *Pussy* takes its place among all of Acker's novels wherein there is no way to be wholly outside patriarchy, but only to be against patriarchy from within its borders. Put bluntly, the pirates cannot assume their nomadic, appropriative position without hegemony preexisting and to a degree compromising their rebellion. According to my argument, then, piracy is about assuming the status of an identity that has previously not been available for the taking; it is not about the acquisitive theft and annihilation of that identity, but about the appropriative capture and reassignment of it within the "regime."

Through piracy, Acker endeavors to solve, or at least to confront, the problem that "[y]ou can't get to a place, to a society, that isn't constructed according to the phallus" (Friedman 17). Like tattooing, piracy signifies "not just outcasts—outcasts could be bums—but people who are beginning to take their own sign-making into their own hands" (Friedman 17-18). In order to find the "buried treasure," O and Ange must destroy or at least revise masculinist histories and territories. This is not to say that Acker believes in the romantic possibility of a society in which anyone has absolute autonomy and self-determination. Rather, it means that Acker wants to install and inscribe women into what, as far as *Pussy* is concerned, has long been a male quest and journey. The following exchange makes this clear:

> "We can't stay here," O said. "We need to do more than be whores and masturbate."
>
> "I agree."
>
> "Let's go to Europe."
>
> "No way. I don't want to go to Europe. Europe's dead."
>
> "We'll just go back to Europe to steal."
>
> "Okay."
>
> (56)

What happens, then, when "woman" as a body and "women" as a cultural nomenclature "steal" the patriarchy? Do they find a new way to exist as literal bodies within patriarchy's rule, or do they find themselves still assigned symbolic roles of "woman," unable to literalize their identities even as they appropriate the pirating power to do so? O and Ange's itinerancy points to a mobility that is beyond the actual transportation of their bodies. As their literal bodies move from the whorehouse in which they meet one another to the women-only world of Pussy and her pirates, so do the symbolic conceptions of women's gender and sexuality translate into new figurations. These characters are aware that the feminine identities in which they have found themselves living are constructed by an authority other than their own. What is at stake is whether or not their *knowledge* that "girl" and "women" are in reality "the names of nothing" and can indeed liberate them from the autocracy of metaphor and install them within an insistently literal, autonomous status.

Even further, is piracy adequate to this task? For as much as the female pirates are their own rulers and subjects, they are, as I have noted, still behaving responsively to the values of the land from which they have fled. Given that they are continuously aware that they, as women, occupy multivalent positions as cultural currency in a misogynist economy, even "a name such as *pirate*" seems inadequately metaphorical. The metaphor of the pirate "isn't good enough," writes Acker. "I want to *see* my body" (**Bodies** [**Bodies of Work**] 162).

The search for buried treasure, then, is a search for the body itself, fully realized and self-defined. Acker's attempt in this novel is to recuperate the female body through a vision of its literalization. This literal body is problematic in itself, because it remains caught between the two central paradigms of the novel, piracy and itinerancy, which are discrepant. More specifically, the nature of piracy is one of the theft of real objects from their rightful owners and the manipulation of authority to one's own desired ends; pirates look to acquire and to own. But the nature of itinerancy as a form of exploration is one that looks to appropriate, to "borrow," and resists the literalization of found objects such as women's bodies, preferring figurative versions of embodiment in which, as I will argue, women stand *for* the land and its spoils. As a result of this split between the "actual" nature of piracy and the "virtual" values of imperialism, O, Ange, and the pirates discover that, on the one hand, their bodily identities and desires are quite real but, on the other hand, their essences, origins, and cores are mythical and even unreachable. As they discover their bodies, they also discover that, as O puts it, "My center just shivered" (59).

In an essay on postmodernism and travel, Karen R. Lawrence remarks that women's travel narratives frequently "present both narratives of and narratives as journey severed from origin and *telos*" (207). Certainly, the alinear form of Acker's prose and plot problematizes authorial privilege and treats narrative itself as a spatial journey. Her characters similarly do not travel in progressive ways. As Ange replies to O, who is worried about her precarious "center," "This is what travel is. . . . The only way you can wake up, O, is by going down there" (59). The trajectory of travel indeed posits a "center" to the self, but this self cannot be accessed through lateral movement across space. If it can be accessed at all, this will occur through a gradual and vertical descent into the "down there" of the feminine self and the female body.

Later, following signs to London that read "You'll never get there," O and Ange continue to descend "[l]ower, closer to the imaginary center of the earth" (141). The pirating women of **Pussy** are on an Orpheus-like journey, searching perpetually for the descent that will save them from the anguish, loss, and dissolution at the center of their beings. With interiority that they indeed know exists but nonetheless have trouble gaining access to, O and Ange value not the internalization of conflict but the topographical enactment of it. This move is quintessentially Ackerian and somewhat paradoxical: they use their bodies in order to move across the land in order to *find* their bodies. To "*get out is to remember*"—to flee the father, to learn what the female body in fact is and to put it back together (181).

The fact that they can "never get there" points not to the delusional nature of their journey but to the fact the feminine subject cannot ultimately be demystified by others. Orpheus lost Eurydice not because he had the arrogance to think that he could look back at her but because "he was ignorant; he never knew who she was, just like we don't know who Eurydice was" (256). At the very least, Ange knows the limits to her knowledge here, the things that she in fact *cannot* know. The narrative of Orpheus, however, is a narrative of the descent into art and desire in which the organizing, and foolhardy, myth is one of omniscience. Ange points out that unlike herself, Orpheus does not realize that the hubris of thinking you know what you cannot know—and that you own what you do not own—is the most dangerous of all acts of the self. Alternately, O and Ange embark on an alternate quest with full knowledge, perhaps even too *much* knowledge, of what it is that they lack.

The novel is divided into three sections. In the first, "O and Ange," O and Ange are prostitutes who meet in and together escape from an Alexandrian whorehouse, whereupon they receive the map of buried treasure. The second section, "Pirate Girls," recounts the childhood and sexual history of "King Pussy;" with its emphasis on female biography and the violence of familial life, this section has the most resonance with Acker's oeuvre. The novel's final section, entitled "In the Days of the Pirates," merges the worlds of O, Ange, and the pirates. O and Ange commission a group of pirate girls, of which Pussy is king, to sail to treasure island in search of the buried treasure; it is a journey full of ineffectual maps and sororicide, loosely alluding to Robert Louis Stevenson's *Treasure Island* (1883).

Acker's 1995 essay **"Seeing Gender"** anticipates *Pussy* in many ways and inserts piracy into a traditionally Ackerian trope of parents who thwart the physical and psychological development of their offspring. Acker writes, "When I was a child, the only thing I wanted was to be a pirate. Because I wasn't a stupid child, I knew that I couldn't. . . . I concluded that I wasn't a pirate because my mother wouldn't allow me to be one. I argued; as if she's a map, she's the key to my buried treasure" (158-59). Acker's pirates, women who roam and steal, are signs not of a hyper-realized subjectivity, but of one that recognizes its own limited agency, its own blindness: "I do not see, for there is no *I* to see. This is what the pirates know. There is only seeing and, in order to go to see, one must be a pirate" (159).

If "seeing" calls into question the agency of the "seer," then we may ask, *how* does one see with an annihilated or nonexistent subjectivity, and where exactly does one "go to see" in such a way? Pussy, O, and Ange cannot move "backward," for "home" is a fictional construct which is either violent or unlocatable. Thus, they move downward; they descend into a spatial search for the obscure origins of their identities, the "buried treasure" of the underworld that is both their sexual bodies and their social lives. Their bodies thus function not only as their means of travel, but also as the actual sites of travel—they travel with, in, and through the body. We might even say that O and Ange are politically regulated spaces that want to investigate yet protect their own permeability as such spaces. As public bodies unable to accept social convention and all that it demands of them, the pirates, O, and Ange yearn for a stable center, an epistemological "home" whose borders they determine and whose story they write. They cannot see this home, this buried treasure, but refuse nonetheless to accept that it does not exist. Indeed, until the end of their journey, which I will subsequently discuss, O and Ange are unable to accept that there may in fact be no such thing as an actual home and a "real" buried treasure, that both are mutually mythical constructs.

In *Pussy,* Acker theorizes the performing, mobile body as if it is "not a 'being,' but a variable boundary" (Butler, *Gender Trouble* 139). This "boundary" is never neutral, but always gendered, and is forbidden the sign of the universal (/male). Because she always travels *as a woman,* the "borders" of the female body vary according not only to where she is but, even more importantly, according to who has *access* to her. In part, this itinerant female body becomes hyper-visible when it travels in *Pussy*: put simply, a person's increased mo-

bility augments her visibility. This is not necessarily to indicate what feminist scholarship has long deemed the phenomenon of women insistently watching themselves being watched, the male gaze turned inward and violent, although that concept is certainly relevant to Acker's work.[1] That is to say, even more compelling in Acker than the problem of being seen in a patriarchal scopic regime is that in fact women also *see*. They are trapped in a world that is not of their making, yet they envision a future whereby they will access the buried treasure and thereby travel back in time to a place of origin that is not the "masochistic reign" of the (whore)house (19).

The pirates, dissatisfied with what they have seen as well as how they have been seen in their homeland/domestic nation of England, have no alternative but to believe in a futuristic form of sight, a visionary and alternate future. When the pirate Bad Dog embarks on a search for her mother, her friends warn her "Don't go in there" but "she defied her bad friends because her visionary eye was seeing this map" (191). The map points out to Bad Dog neither where she is nor where she will be but what she will eventually *see*; X marks the spot, for example, of a "store which *will be seen*" (191). The future is thus not a temporal vision but a spatial one—it imagines not what will happen in time but what will happen in spaces/places; indeed, as O and Ange roam, they begin to possess a surveillant, panoptical vision that has never before been theirs: "Seeing is becoming broader, higher, and lower" (178). They may be seen more than when they were immobilized in the whorehouse, but they can also see more now that they are itinerant women.

As they see increasingly further and are seen in new ways by other women instead of men, the map gets more and more unwieldy and the world becomes larger and larger. The opportunities for where they can go, and therefore for what they can see and who they can be, are potentially limitless. For example, O's immediate environment is never satisfactory and is always unreadable, perpetually secondary to where her next move through but away from the patriarchy might take her: "I had been searching for my father. . . . I stood on the edge of a new world" (23). While O speaks constantly of travel, asking "how can I do this? Begin," she yearns, "being a whore," to discover "the origin of whoredom," family and history. Yet it is in fact not where her body is, but what her body *does* when it "sees" new lands which provides for O the liberatory praxis of travel (27). It is important to note that "what her body does" in its itinerancy is not to acquire land and its spoils but to acquire sexuality and to act as a sexual being. Travel implicates the body of the traveler, demands that the traveler reckon with both the place and the body that she inhabits. As O travels, she finds bodily spaces, or identities, that are much more than just cartographic places. This is no big surprise: O and Ange are fleeing because they no longer want to live in a whorehouse, but they do not flee their sexuality. Instead, their sexuality is itself a means of journeying to new places and is a site of exploration. O says, "By fucking each other, Pussycat and I traveled to the edge of a territory that was unknown and, perhaps, unknowable. Into territories whose existences I had never experienced before Pussycat touched me . . ." (138).

Without this desire for and annexation of the female body, O and Ange seem to realize, they cannot "find" anything else, such as the buried treasure. For instance, when O is dissatisfied with her sexual performance with Pussy, she has a dream in which she implores Circe to cure her "dead" desire (145). O feels she can go no further while lacking such desire; the satiation/destination is not important, but the desire to embark on sexual "adventures" and to "recognize" women's bodies is a crucial component of O's quest. Circe is unsympathetic to O's plight and tells O that she cannot be cured. When O throws herself at Circe and "kiss[es] her until [she] could kiss no more," Circe murmurs, "Maybe you've got your genders mixed up" (146).

O is indeed "mixed up," but not because she thinks she is a man. Rather, O and Pussy do not accept in their sexual and itinerant exploits that because they are *women,* they are supposed to *be desired,* not to desire. They assume a sexual prerogative, working with their bodies as particularly female bodies but at the same time, appropriating a "long tradition of male travel as an erotics of ravishment" *of* the female body (McClintock, 22). But how, specifically, does annexing the physical territory of women's bodies alongside annexing the land actually pose a resistance to the historical masculine pursuit of land and power through the sexual conquest of women? How are O, Ange, and Pussy not merely "passing" as men and behaving with equal impunity?

Perhaps what makes this a feminist critique of masculine sexuality and power and not merely a reinscription of imperialism and patriarchy is that these pirates are actual women and the bodies they interact with are acknowledged as such. There are ramifications to their sexual actions that have to do with their bodies in and of themselves and not only the territories and privilege to which their bodies provide access. Even further, O and Ange do not disappear after the sexual act as did the anonymous "johns" of their prostitution or as do the women of imperial conquest. Instead, they remain in one another's lives, insisting that they be reckoned with. Acker is revising a male travel narrative tradition and a generic cultural fantasy that says, *while land is quite real, women are not*; women may signify a literality, but this is exactly the point. As signifiers, as signposts on road maps, women are fantasized as symbolic obstacles to be overcome and discarded.

Here is O and Ange's dilemma as explorers of the underworld: they want to possess women's bodies as part of a "new" territory and land, but not to turn women's bodies into the land and into mere territory as masculine, imperial tradition would have it. In desiring such, they immediately and inherently position themselves against male traditions of exploration and annexation in which the female body is either something symbolic or something only to be ravished. Consider the case of Christopher Columbus's record of his third voyage through the Caribbean, in search of India. Columbus writes home,

> I have been led to hold this concerning the world, and I find that it is not found as they describe it, but that it is the shape of a pear which is everywhere very round except where the stalk is, for there it is very prominent, or that it is like a very round ball, and on one part of it is placed something like a woman's nipple, and that this part, where this protuberance is found, is the highest and nearest to the sky, and it is beneath the equinoctial line an in this Ocean sea at the end of the West. I call that "the end of the East," where end all the land and islands.
>
> (30)

Anne McClintock's *Imperial Leather,* a landmark study of the polyvalent, multifaceted relationships between gender, race, and imperialism, provides additional insights into the significance of a travel narrative like Columbus's. McClintock writes,

> Columbus' image feminizes the earth as a cosmic breast, in relation to which the epic male hero is a tiny, lost infant, yearning for the Edenic nipple. The image of the earth-breast here is redolent not with the male bravura of the explorer, invested with his conquering mission, but with an uneasy sense of male anxiety, infantilization and longing for the female body. At the same time, the female body is figured as marking the boundary of the cosmos and the limits of the known world, enclosing the ragged men, with their dreams of pepper and pearls, in her indefinite, oceanic body.
>
> (22)

O and Ange accept none of this. For these female pirates, the land is not like a woman's breast; instead, the breast is like a land. As I will discuss subsequently, changing the ways in which women travel means also transforming the very definition of "woman" in the world that they inhabit and explore. As they contest the symbolic assignations given to women's bodies in the name of imperial conquest, O and Ange find themselves still working within the realm of metaphor, but capable of inverting that metaphor. Bodies do not take a backseat position to lands; rather, bodies *are* lands. When O *must* acknowledge a difference between the topography of the body and the topography of place, the land is not female, but *male.* She says, "As yet I didn't understand that I was in the city's heart," and that this heart belongs to a tyrannical male body (77). "This city was patriarchal, that which allows the existence of none but itself" (83).

Thus, *Pussy*'s heroines may travel to claim the "treasure" of distant lands, but their imperialism is not based on the metaphor of women as prey and refuses to assign women a primarily symbolic status. Instead, their imperialism is based upon a refusal to "see" and exist in places that will not recognize their freedom to roam psychically, physically, and especially sexually. O and Ange thereby avoid the metaphorical equations of women with conquered land, and if men participate in the equation at all, they exist as symbolic and figurative values and as vehicles for the enactment of female desire.

We might even say that this very insistently dynamic energy of the historically symbolic and metaphorical female body is what saves the traveling women from participating in the "wrong" kind of exploitation of bodies of land and women. In other words, the pirates in this novel are anything but safe from one another's treachery, let alone safe from the threat of male treachery. However, they are not feminized versions of male, conquest anxiety, and they are not fantasized as anything other than what they are: greedy, avaricious bodies. As is typical throughout her oeuvre, Acker is keenly aware of literary and political history, and her usual manipulation of traditionally male texts for her own ends is especially noteworthy here as Acker revises the masculinist canons of both literature and imperialism.

On the one hand, O oftentimes *refuses* to see because, first, she does not like what she sees ("[t]o see equaled to *accept*") and second, she realizes that knowledge is about more than a vision of conquest (to "*find out*" is not "simply to *see*") (85, 84). On the other hand, she panics when she realizes that *being seen* makes her vulnerable and "open to every fucking stranger, to anyone who just wanted to enter for any reason at all" (90). O realizes that if there are "no curtains over the windows, so everybody could see everything" in the house where she lives with her mother (91), then her only alternative is to become a moving target.

As Acker notes in her essay, **"Red Wings: Concerning Richard Prince's 'Spiritual America,'"** "The father of the United States of America is a cowboy. . . . We who live under the sign of myth know that the cowboy is that lonely male individual who, against all odds including Indians, braved all in order not to get rich quick, nor to survive, but to keep on traveling" (*Bodies,* 53). Acker understands what McClintock calls the "pornotropics" of the European imagination, the tradition of male desires projected onto myths of far-away and treasure-filled lands. She investigates the acquisitive and appropriative imagination whereby the conquests of

travel function as "a fantastic magic lantern of the mind onto which Europe project[s] its forbidden sexual desires and fears" (McClintock 22).

In *Pussy,* women who want adventure, who do not want to be bourgeois, who can find no satisfying way to live, travel; it is not a pre-existent freedom which enables them to roam but is rather the only freedom *from* the tyranny of stasis and the status quo that they can find. In her essay on American hobo Boxcar Bertha, Acker points out that Bertha, who once worked as a whore, "had noted that women hoboes considered their own bodies their working capital" (*Bodies,* 129). Just as capital must travel in order to retain its value, so must women.

As a matter of fact, pirates are the ultimate figures of circulation. They are confined by neither geography nor law but participate in an endlessly mobile economy of survival, which is perhaps circulation in its purest form. Of course, pirates do not in their behavior and identities escape a complicity with the imperial project, however indirect this complicity might be. But it is important to realize that the pirates do not want territory per se. They may want to occupy and determine what happens within various territories, but this is so that they may reap its spoils, its treasures, and thereby cultivate the liquid assets that will be exchangeable in the market and not confine them to singularity and fixity.

Boxcar Bertha, O, Ange, and the pirates realize that the body, or "capital," which does not retain its status as a particularly *dynamic* currency becomes dangerously susceptible to devaluation. Even further, women who do not stay on the move and do not find a way to use *themselves* are in danger of becoming static symbols, defined and used by others.[2] If women's values are their bodies, then they must keep those bodies valu*able* by using them constantly. Their exchange and circulation may transform their literal bodies into symbolic values, but such "circulatory abstraction" can be a welcome liberation from the historical theorization of women's circulation as dangerous and the subsequent confinement of the female body to a mythical, domestic sphere at supposed remove from the marketplace. These women are not hoarded as treasure, but instead keep themselves nomadic by insisting on a definition of capital as circulatory and fluid. This prompts the question: is there a way for women to recoup some notion of a feminine subjectivity within an exchange economy, or is the material body "lost" to a figurative and symbolic status when it has exchange value?

Acker's implicit response to this question is, typical for Acker, yes and no. That is to say, on the one hand, Acker revises the notion that women occupy a domestic, familial space at remove from the marketplace, and that women's value is based not on their productive participation within a market economy, but instead on their reproductive removal from the public realm. Thus, "using" their bodies for these itinerant and pirate women also means gaining the ability to determine how, when, and for what purpose the body is deployed. On the other hand, though, keeping the body in motion threatens the mobile woman with the reduced status of mere capital, and responds to the salient and perhaps unsolvable problem that the novel first presents us with: there is no "true" home for a woman. She may search for it, but must realize at the same time that in order to do so, she must refuse to stay in any one place. As Acker writes in her Boxcar Bertha essay, there is "[n]owhere to run. Nowhere to hide, but, like Marguerite Duras's Lol Stein, in the lack of self. Or, like Boxcar, keep on travelin,' Girl" (**Bodies** 130).

Why, though, *is* travel a mode of survival? "This parking lot is a graveyard," says O. "The only thing that remains in the world is my motorbike," a bike which she can barely see (110). The parking lot signifies a deadly, arrested mobility. It poses a danger not only because its potential is untapped, but also because the parking lot is, like the woman who does not abandon "home," a form of absolute visibility. As that which can be seen but cannot itself see, the parking lot/immobile woman is vulnerable to epistemological and particularly sexual surveillance and seizure. Travel, then, becomes a destruction of the parking lot, an *un*settling of the land and ideologies which circumscribe femininity.

In part, women in this novel can and must travel so readily because, as Acker points out about Boxcar Bertha, if a woman has any true location, then it is in her body, and she must learn to reassign that body to an identity which she both desires and controls. The precedent for travel as a form of prostitution against which O and Ange must position themselves is clear. O says, "I had come to China the way I usually came: I had been following a guy," and the sexual pun on "came" is compelling. **Pussy** demonstrates that when women travel with and for men, and when they have sexual relationships with men instead of other women, their own desires are secondary.

However, even when they abandon the whorehouse, O and Ange do not attempt to dismantle entirely the conceptual apparatus of prostitution. Instead, they learn how to manipulate its ideologies so that it represents and serves them, not vice versa. O and Ange choose to determine, not to eliminate, forms of penetration. Put simply, O and Ange refuse what Pussy, in her pre-piracy days, found she could not refuse: "Since Pussy was a nice girl, she offered him her apartment, or hole, as a refuge" (72).

If men hide in women, though, where do women hide? They hide, paradoxically, in their own visibility, and they take refuge in their perpetual motion, which con-

structs a dynamic visibility that allows a woman never to be "found." The female traveler in **Pussy** is no "virgin territory." A woman's body, her "place," is one of insistent entrances and exits, a literal and symbolic whorehouse. In fact, **Pussy** insists that whorehouses are not the most detrimental aspect of the social order. For one, they can offer the ideal compromise between circulation (the business of sexuality, the exchange of women, the interchangeablity of men, and so on) and fixity (the whorehouse is a single location, an immobile place). Furthermore, refusing hypocrisy and duplicity, the whorehouse is what it claims to be, unlike the maternal home which O discusses earlier, which is replete with curtainless windows that expose and threaten the self and fathers and mothers who are anything but benevolent. Brothels "do not have windows that lead to what lies outside." This means that women can hide in them. They are "refuges to all the shipwrecked of the world"; "every revolution starts" in a church or brothel, says O (31).

At first thought, this devilification of the whorehouse may not seem an adequate response to its inherent misogyny; however, for Acker, female piracy is "as utopian as I can get at the moment" (Garrett 17-18). Piracy is undoubtedly not a perfect solution to the fact that the trajectories taken and activities undertaken by women's bodies are (over)determined by masculinist versions of women's "place." What does it mean, for instance, that on the one hand, piracy is supposedly an anti-legislative, anti-bureaucratic, and lawless pursuit, inscribed within but nonetheless opposing the dominant culture and that, on the other hand, these pirates indeed have a king among them? It means that the pirates have not found a way to escape the hierarchies of the land and the masteries of the state; the "most" utopian they can get "at the moment" is to assign the role of king to a woman and proceed from that revision. A society with a king is not properly anarchic; a society with a female king, though, does contest the very premise of absolute and localized power for which a king stands. As O tells Pussy, "You're the king, but you're not the king of anything. Even of girls as greedy, as ravenous, as dreamy as you" (188).

It comes as no surprise, given that there is in fact a king, that there are clearly delineated rules of piracy. Likewise, it is no surprise that these rules connote not a monarchy but a more democratic collective that in fact does not place Pussy on a more powerful plane than the other pirates. On the one hand, then, the very existence of these rules marks the failure of the pirates to imagine a truly alternate world; instead, the rules grant the pirates access to the very ideologies of authority to which they are opposed. But on the other hand, the rules base themselves around liberating revisions of ideological, gendered, and juridical codes. Rule One, "Regarding Purpose," reads, "To find that place out of which we come"; they search not in a series of progressions, but in a regressive pattern, overlooking the "rule" of the father in an effort to locate their true, bodily origins: the mythical mother. For that matter, a pirate is "half-human, half-beast," which we may read also as half-self, half-Other—the epitome of the essentially divided subject.

The "purpose of pirating" is theft; this theft has little to do with actual objects or with what, even in an abstract sense, the pirates can "take" from those who oppose them. Rather, the theft has everything to do with removing the gendered boundaries and cultural barriers between women and other women as well as between women and the state/male authority—the very barriers that have made them resort to piracy in the first place, as the sole explanation of theft reads: "[p]irates are destroyers of all obstacles." Lastly, an appropriate pun: "Nothing and no one's straight" in the caves where pirates live free of external authority (204-6).

Thus, these pirates not only rewrite masculine imperialism, as I have argued in my discussion of Columbus's discovery of the "breast," but also they appropriate and revise, or pirate, the gendered norms to which they have been assigned. The tradition to which they respond is one in which "[t]he feminizing of the land represents a ritualistic moment in imperial discourse, as male intruders ward off fears of narcissistic disorder by reinscribing, as natural, an excess of gender hierarchy" (McClintock 24). In search of a feminine but not feminized land, in search of the buried treasure "in caves at the centers of labyrinths" of the female body and identity, the pirates destroy all correlations between biological sex and cultural gender and refuse all heteronormative assignations.

Pussy and her kingdom of pirates in fact belong to a historical tradition of subversive, lawless, female pirates who embrace transvestitism and in the process even come to embody a sort of hermaphroditism—that is, to occupy the status of both masculine privilege and feminine resistance.[3] Early in the eighteenth century, during the heyday of Anglo-American piracy, Irish born Mary Read and British born Ann Bonney became especially notorious for their piracy. The majority of our knowledge of Read and Bonney's exploits derives from the two volume *A General History of the Pyrates* (1726), a text written by Daniel Defoe under the pseudonym "Captain Charles Johnson."[4] Much like Acker's pirates, Read and Bonney "were fleeing not only their sex-role stereotypes and the law, but the development of British imperialism itself" (Gooch i). Physically strong, fending off rapists, carrying pistols and machetes, Read and Bonney were ready for war. Carrying as well an "antinomian disdain for state authority," the women took extramarital lovers and arranged their own divorces, calling for the popular custom of a "wife sale," *when* it so suited them (Rediker, "Liberty" 13-14).

On board ship, Read initially cross-dressed as a man, but she was "outed" when Bonney fell in love with her, making the ship captain so incensed with jealousy over his supposed rival that Read had to confess that she was actually a woman in order to save her life. Later, the women successfully wielded their bodies as weapons against the law when England brought Bonney and Read to court. A female witness against them, Dorothy Thomas, testified that she could easily pick out the cross-dressed women among the male pirates due to the "largeness of their Breasts," forging yet another Columbus-esque metonymic equation between women's breasts and their entire bodies. However, Read and Bonney received a respite from execution, the fate to which the male pirates succumbed, because they claimed to be pregnant (out of circulation) ("Liberty" 7). (The court called them "hell-hounds," making the name of Acker's pirate "Bad Dog" resonate even more strongly.)

According to Marcus Rediker, "these two bold women pirates were not entirely unusual cases. Women had long gone to sea, and in many capacities—as passengers, servants, wives, prostitutes . . ." ("When Women" 104). Indeed, even beyond their literal roles, women were far from absent at sea, historically occupying an iconic status through the female names given to ships and through the wooden, female figures bound to ships' prows. What makes the case of Read and Bonney extraordinary is their insistently aggressive status in a male environment which has attempted to render them tangential. *Pussy* goes even further than this history, construing an entire world in which power is a journey, the world of piracy, as an *entirely* female world.

This women-only world is far from perfect; bellicose and conniving, these pirates do not forge a society of peace and trust, do not build some sort of idealized, feminist alternative to a masculine project of patriarchy. As O narrates, "The viciousness of girls cannot be imagined" (266). However, what the pirate women do is to learn how to use a system that can be violent, duplicitous, and tyrannical for their own gains, a knowledge to which they have not heretofore had access. When Silver says, "Let's kill 'em," another pirate replies, "I can't kill girls." Silver's subsequent response is emblematic of this world in which women must learn to survive, both physically and psychologically, at all costs: "You haven't *yet*. But they've got the map" (225, emphasis added). Their quest, we might say, is not only for the buried treasure, but for a map written by women and an itinerary followed by women. When Ange reminds O that her "dead mother" gave them the map, O responds, "Don't get sentimental. . . . That map might have come from your mother's body, but it's dead men's talk. Pirate tales. Men who cut off women's fingers so they could do worse" (233).

But what does a world of pirates look like when dead men can't "talk?" It looks like a world where women "live in silver and gold and do whatever they wanted to and spit on the world if they could be bothered" (245). What, really, are O and Ange questing *for*? Why do they so want this "buried treasure?" They are looking for a way to acquire, as is typical for the quest genre, and to do so while thwarting their own victimization and without victimizing others. When they arrive at Pirate Island, Ange whispers, "I don't want to own . . . much less be a landlord. . . . I wanna go back and be a sailor" (214). Ownership, of course, entails all that is institutional and proprietary, such as heterosexuality, monogamy, matrimony. Conversely, "[t]his decrease of the separation between private and public property, finally, this disappearance, was directly related to a movement away from, and then to the passing away of the memory of, patriarchy" (40).

To maintain their "revisioned patriarchy" whereby they appropriate but at the same time refuse ownership, the pirates need O and Ange, the escapees from the whorehouse of the "other world," as much as O and Ange need the pirates to help them find the treasure in and of the underworld. Silver begs O, "Take me with you on your search for buried treasure." Ange, more innocent and fearful than O, finally asks for the meaning of their direction: what, exactly, is "down" anyway? O recounts, "I told her to fuck off" (217). O's aggression results from the fact that none of these women, whether they are travelers or pirates, knows what "down" really is. The journey denigrates and even destroys the typical and expected routes for women, leaving in its wake an urgent but perpetually blind spot as to what this new "treasure down below" in fact will be.

Ironically, maps are no help in this respect. The maps throughout the novel are antithetical to the tradition of treasure maps in colonial and imperialist narratives. That is, *Pussy* refuses to give to maps any objective authority, refuting that "the knowledge constituted by the map both preceded and legitimized the conquest of territory." The map is not "a technology of knowledge that professes to capture the truth about a place in pure, scientific form" (McClintock 27). It does not align representation with authority, does not function as a "technology of possession" (McClintock 28).

Instead, maps are important to *Pussy* precisely because they are unreliable forms of representation. They seem to lead one toward a treasure, but in fact, this treasure is a moving target, and the path to it is marked by unreliable signs and indecipherable representations. Maps in this novel signify not a single reality, but multiple realities. Much like bodies, maps can stand for things that they are not themselves. They need deciphering, interpreting, and what seem to be keys often in fact get a person absolutely nowhere. Both maps and bodies are a

form of plagiarism: that is to say, both appropriate names and identities for their own uses as they chart their various courses. The goal in this novel is to make the map and the body lead Acker's heroines not forward in a progressively decipherable telos, but backward, to a previously unreadable sovereignty that they never in fact knew they had.

"Keys" to the maps Acker draws throughout the text neither outline intractable characteristics of the land nor provide legible answers and access to the questions of where, indeed, a traveler is. Rather than provide a ledger to the land, the keys decipher bodily and sexual relationship between women. They work against causality; the movement of the body is spatial, and its sexuality is creative, but not procreative. At one point, Ange begins to incestuously "feel her mother up." When O asks Ange "why she was doing what she was doing," Ange answers, "There's the key, O." O is confused: "The key?" "The key to the box that contains treasure. We're going to search for buried treasure, aren't we?" (62-63).

This key to what we have long realized is a feminine and feminized treasure in this novel, then, is not only a key to the body/territory represented in the map. From Ange's comment, we can see that the key is also the female body itself—or, that the act of possessing the (symbolic and literal) mother's body instead of the father's body is the key which will unlock the "treasure" that is women. O calls the brothel "*the male regime . . . the territory named women's bodies*" (8). They abandon the brothel at the novel's inception because O and Ange yearn to cultivate a female body under a female regime and because they want to find a female body that is more than nominal, more than "the name of nothing."

Lost in Pirate World and endangered by pirates who want to seize the treasure promised by Ange's mother's map, O removes the tattered map from her pocket. She finds nothing pictorial, but instead only words labeled, "James Baldwin's novel." On the "map" are levels of descent, not lateral directions but hierarchical ones. On the top are "colors like I've never seen / deepest, darkest reds / no black." On the next level is "a prison because it's a room of the heart," and the "stream" running through this level is the "blood stream." At the bottom, beneath a cell door, the maps tells us, "THIS IS THE PRESENCE OF THE HEART—I know this now" (260). The map is a translation of the human body, with angry eyes, a head that "sees red"; through the "torso" of the map, there is a heart, but the "real" heart is further down, in the body's lower extremities—the woman's genitals, we could say, or her legs, which assure her mobility and therefore her survival.

Ultimately, O becomes disillusioned with the pirate girls because they have not learned, really, how to be female pirates, but are instead, in keeping with the very tradition of piracy which O wants to rewrite, both male and female, or "half-beast, half-human": "For the first time, I was seeing the pirate girls in their true colors. Black and red" (265). There is no core, untainted and intact, to these women: the center for which O and Ange have been searching is absent. The female pirates wear "their insides on their outsides, blood smeared all over the surfaces. When opened, the heart's blood turns black" (265). Their attempt to navigate the underworld has left the pirates ravaged and therefore of no avail to O and Ange; the pirates have not withstood the "tension between the thrilling possibilities of the unknown and the weight of the familiar, between a desire for escape and a sense that one can never be outside a binding cultural network" (Lawrence, 19).

O realizes that in a world where women "steal" the patriarchy, the first lesson is that there is no such thing as "woman," that not all women are alike and that "girls must accept girls who aren't like them" (264). When, within the forest, O, Ange, and the pirates think that they have found the spot on the map wherein the treasure lies, they actually find nothing but a dead, male pirate with a postmortem erection. O comments that this "goes to show that a dead pirate is better than nothing at all" (273). Through the sexually signifying but dead body of the only male that they have encountered on their travels, O and Ange realize the fictions of male power, realize that in fact, "Cocks weren't treasure, but pointed to treasure" (274).

Here, Acker manipulates canonical ideas of travel narratives and even of a more general literary history. Firstly, this passage about the erect penis occurs very near the novel's conclusion, "pointing" to closure but not fulfilling it. The "cock" which "pointed to treasure" thus offers a critique of the masculine sense of an ending. The story does not "end" when ejaculation happens and, in fact, ejaculation does not happen at all. Secondly, that the male pirate is dead makes him, instead of a woman, part of the landscape; it is ultimately the male pirate who is the "lay of the land."[5] The subversion is clear: a male pirate is supposed to explore and conquer territory, not function as the loot and casualty of such exploration.

Even further, that the pirate's penis is erect even in death and that it is not itself a treasure but *points to treasure* prompts us to consider the treasure to which the erect penis points—the vagina. In this case, the vagina is liberated from the penetration that an erect penis might demand because the pirate, while signifying in ways typical for a (hetero)sexual male, cannot act. Thus, not only is the treasure the woman's sexual body, but the "cock" also points to "treasure" of this realization: male virility is in fact a form of impotence. The women's ultimate discovery of a male pirate lying dead and

with an ineffectual sex organ, poised for action but unable to act, both ratifies and ensures the all-female society. As O narrates, "And so we left the pirate girls to do what pirate girls do" (274).

What, though, does it mean to write a feminist novel in which a world of women abandon the "whorehouse" of their lives in a quest for the buried treasure of femininity and find nothing but a dead pirate with an erect penis? Does this ultimate discovery of a treasure that, in reality, does nothing but refer to the *idea* of treasure mark a failed or a successful quest? Perhaps it marks neither. That is to say, what itinerant and pirate women need to understand according to Acker is that the accessibility of treasure is itself a male fiction and that the acquisitive quest is problematic in itself. Ultimately, O implies as much when she tells Ange her version of the myth of Pandora:

> When the man, because he couldn't resist beauty, opened up Pandora's cunt, her evil excretions, her excrescence, smelled up the world. So badly that all those who could smell those smells—that is, men—wanted to die, and would have if they couldn't get rid of that which lies within women. That's where treasure is.
>
> (275)

Treasure, then, lies also in the realization that men refuse the autonomous physicality of women's bodies in favor of myths that control them, silence them, and blame them for the plagues of the world. If they want to remain pirates, the women must resist closure, must refuse to "find" the treasure that will not only curtail their quest for anarchic freedom, but also will remove them from the realm of women and reinsert them into male narratives and paradigms. "I'd rather go a-pirating," says Silver. "If me and my girls take all this treasure, the reign of girl piracy will stop, and I wouldn't have that happen" (276). Silver must forego the treasure to which the dead, erect penis points; she must leave the cave with the other pirates as O gazes after them with awe and comprehension (276). Silver must ignore the demystification which has made the map credible and the treasure material and continue seeking the other, ineffable treasure of a piracy that is thoroughly female and open-ended. By rejecting the literalizaton of the treasure, Silver perpetuates the figurative status of piracy and treasure-hunting, although the process of doing so does not necessarily entail deliteralization of the female pirate's body.

It is helpful to recall here that Acker's female characters embark on quests throughout her novels, from *Don Quixote* to *Empire of the Senseless* to *Pussy*. Throughout these quests, and in *Pussy* to the most dramatic degree, Acker's heroines know that "fetishized, vilified, and codified by a system of male-defined conventions and standards, the would-be hero who remains faithful to inauthentic images of female selfhood is led ever deeper into self-denial, passivity, and inertia" (Heller, 12). O and Ange reject these "inauthentic images of female selfhood" in favor of a female subjectivity that is perpetually under construction. We might say that they forego the path that leads them endlessly outside themselves and into explorations of the land for an "internal" quest that allows the female subject to remain decentered and amorphous. This means that O and Ange ultimately choose to live a life in which their "center" does indeed "shiver," in which there is no name of "woman," but only women, and in which "the 'I' neither precedes nor follows the process" of gendering, but instead "emerges only within and as the matrix of gender relations themselves" (Butler, *Bodies that Matter,* 7). They do not want to do away with their gendered bodies or even with gender itself, but, as Judith Butler so accurately puts it, "to interrogate what the theoretical move that established foundation authorizes, and what precisely it excludes or forecloses" ("Contingent Foundations," 7).

In her introduction to *The Feminization of the Quest-Romance,* Dana Heller argues that typically, woman is either excluded from the journey plot of exile and adventure, her very exclusion helping to define masculinity (think of Penelope's body functioning as "home" on Odysseus's journey), or else she is the territory of the foreign (think of the "savage," betrothed woman in Joseph Conrad's *Heart of Darkness*). *Pussy*'s resistance to such male paradigms for sex and topography—the characters' attempts to determine what they do with their bodies and where they take their bodies—does not necessarily mean that they are not subject to persons more powerful and forces greater than themselves. It does, however, mean that whatever system that they are inscribed within, they have had a hand in "writing."

The novel's conclusion encourages us to see a gray area between the alternatives of being inside and outside a system, between being either incorporated or marginalized, a whore or a pirate. To exist in that gray area, the pirate girls insist on a perpetual quest, a path without resolution. Certainly, when O and Ange turn away from the buried treasure, back to the "whorehouse" from which they came, their quest does not resist closure as does the pirates'. At the same time, though, O and Ange have successfully refused to be mere symbols on an imperialist road map that they did not write, have refused to have either a purely literal body or a purely metaphorical one, and have wound up somewhere in between the two. The implication that O and Ange are now returning to the virtual if not literal "whorehouse" of the Western city from which they came is not paramount. What is paramount is that unlike the dead, male pirate, and even unlike the female community of pirates from which they depart, O and Ange are not and will never again be the "lay of the land."

Notes

1. I am thinking here especially of John Berger's seminal *Ways of Seeing* (1973) and Laura Mulvey's groundbreaking contribution to feminist and visual studies, "Visual Pleasure and Narrative Cinema" (1975), both of which continue to influence feminist theory in implicit and explicit ways.

2. It is interesting to recall at this juncture that a main character in Acker's *In Memoriam to Identity* (New York: Grove, 1990) is named "Capitol" and fights these very problems of occupation and possession, unable to find the route to self-possession and self-definition for which O and Ange search.

3. As a matter of fact, "female warrior ballads" enjoyed huge popularity in the eighteenth century. The transvestite heroine, which Diane Dugaw calls "the female soldier bold," was a common, romantic idealization of intrepid women, directed at and apparently appealing most strongly to the British working class. See Dugaw's "Female Soldiers Bold: Transvestite Heroines and the Markers of Gender and Class," *Iron Men, Wooden Women: Gender and Seafaring in the Atlantic World, 1700-1920,* ed. Margaret S. Creighton and Lisa Norling (Baltimore: Johns Hopkins UP, 1996), 37.

   Although I have neither the space nor the ideal medium here to discuss the role of music in this novel, it should be noted that it indeed plays a large part in Acker's revision of women's history and piracy. There are "songs" scattered throughout the novel but even more importantly, our knowledge of historical working class ballads of lawbreaking, sexual, and aggressive women illuminates Acker's work on the musical companion to *Pussy,* on which she collaborated with the Mekons (1996). The liner notes to the compact disk read in part, "Recorded onboard Her Majesty's Frig-it The Lion of Leeds, July 1795." On the recording, Acker reads and chants sections of *Pussy,* while one can hear in the background the band's somber, dramatic accompaniment, in the spirit of a dirge.

4. There is still debate among historians as to whether or not Defoe was indeed the author of this text. My sources for the claim that Defoe is the definitive author are Marcus Rediker's "When Women Pirates Sailed the Sea," *Wilson Quarterly* 17.4 (1993) and his "Liberty Beneath the Jolly Roger," *Iron Men, Wooden Women: Gender and Seafaring in the Atlantic World,* 1700-1920, eds. Margaret S. Creighton and Lisa Norling (Baltimore: Johns Hopkins UP, 1996).

5. I take this phrase from McClintock's *Imperial Leather,* wherein chapter one is entitled, "The Lay of the Land: Genealogies of Imperialism." Al-

though I, too, refer to the colonial project through the use of this pun, my context is less interested in the figure of "woman" as the "boundary markers of empire" (McClintock, 24) so much as it is in the figuration of "woman" as a particularly sexualized embodiment of literal lands.

References

Acker, Kathy. *Bodies of Work*. New York: Serpent's Tail, 1997.

———. *Pussy, King of the Pirates*. New York: Grove, 1996.

Butler, Judith. *Gender Trouble: Feminism and the Subversion of Identity*. New York: Routledge, 1990.

———. *Bodies that Matter: On the Discursive Limits of "Sex."* New York: Routledge, 1993.

———. "Contingent Foundations: Feminism and the Question of 'Postmodernism.'" 3-21. *Feminists Theorize the Political*. Ed. Joan W. Scott. New York: Routledge, 1992.

Columbus, Christopher. *The Four Voyages of Columbus*. (1847). Trans. Cecil Jane. New York: Dover, 1988.

Friedman, Ellen G. "A Conversation with Kathy Acker." *Review of Contemporary Fiction* 9.3 (1989): 12-22.

Garrett, Shawn-Marie. Interview. "Treasure out of Treasure." *Theater* 26.1-2 (1983): 170-173.

Gooch, Steve. *The Women Pirates Ann Bonney and Mary Read*. London: Pluto, 1978.

Heller, Dana. *The Feminization of Quest-Romance*. Austin: University of Texas Press, 1990.

Lawrence, Karen R. Penelope *Voyages: Women and Travel in the British Literary Tradition*. Ithaca, NY: Cornell University Press, 1994.

McCaffrey, Larry. "The Path of Abjection: An Interview with Kathy Acker." 14-35. *Some Other Frequency*. Ed. Larry McCaffery. Philadelphia: University of Pennsylvania Press, 1996.

McClintock, Anne. *Imperial Leather: Race, Gender and Sexuality in the Colonial Contest*. New York: Routledge, 1995.

Rediker, Marcus. "Liberty Beneath the Jolly Roger." 1-33. *Iron Men, Wooden Women: Gender and Seafaring in the Atlantic World, 1700-1920*. Eds. Margaret S. Creighton and Lisa Norling. Baltimore, MD: Johns Hopkins University Press, 1996.

———. "When Women Pirates Sailed the Seas." *Wilson Quarterly* 17.4 (1993): 102-109.

Primary

Fiction

Don Quixote, Which Was a Dream. New York: Grove, 1986.

"Empire of the Senseless." *Bomb* 19 (1987): 58-63. (*Empire*).

Empire of the Senseless. New York: Grove, 1988.

In Memoriam to Identity. New York: Grove, 1990.

Pussy, King of the Pirates. New York: Grove, 1996.

Essays

"Red Wings: Concerning Richard Prince's 'Spiritual America.'" *Parkett* 34 (1992): 108-16.

"Seeing Gender." *Critical Quarterly* 37.4 (1995): 78-86.

Bodies of Work: Essays. London: Serpent's Tail, 1997.

Music and Discography

Rock collaboration

with Mekons: *Pussy, King of the Pirates*. Lyrics and narration by Mekons and Kathy Acker. Chicago: Quarterstick Records, 1996.

Interviews

Friedman, Ellen G. "A Conversation with Kathy Acker." *Review of Contemporary Fiction* 9.3 (1989): 12-22.

Garrett, Shawn-Marie. "Treasure out of Treasure." *Theater* 26.1-2 (1983): 170-3.

McCaffery, Larry. "The Path of Abjection: An Interview with Kathy Acker." 14-35. *Some Other Frequency: Interviews with Innovative American Authors*. Ed. Larry McCaffery. Philadelphia: University of Pennsylvania Press, 1996.

Robert Glück (essay date 2006)

SOURCE: Glück, Robert. "The Greatness of Kathy Acker." In *Lust for Life: On the Writings of Kathy Acker*, edited by Amy Scholder, Carla Harryman, and Avital Ronell, pp. 45-57. London: Verso, 2006.

[*In the following essay, Glück discusses the effect Acker's work has on the reader, saying that she "pitches the reader into a welter of contradictions that do not resolve themselves," and that her aesthetic "is founded on double binds whose brilliance captivates me as I struggle against them."*]

Jesus saw some little ones nursing—He said to his disciples, "What these little ones who are nursing resemble is those who enter the kingdom." They said to him, "So shall we enter the kingdom by being little ones?" Jesus said to them, "When you make the two one and make the inside like the outside and the outside like the inside and the above like the below, and that you might make the male and the female be one and the same, so that the male might not be male nor the female be female, when you make eyes in the place of an eye and a hand in place of a hand and a foot in place of a foot, an image in place of an image—then you will enter the kingdom."

                              The Gospel According to Thomas

I read *I Dreamt I Was a Nymphomaniac,* I think, before I met Kathy Acker or even heard of her. I was snacking on the stock of the poetry bookstore that I co-directed. I could see the book was provocative and experimental, and the sex kept me alert. The second chapter contains a passage that begins, "Last night I dreamt I was standing on a low rise of grassy ground," and continues to describe a dream that involves family, the art world, and sex. Then the next paragraph begins, "Last night I dreamt I was standing on a low rise of grassy ground . . ."[1] I began the second passage with a sense of having been there before, like a dream. Then a dawning sense of wrongness, then certainty of wrongness and a search for an explanation. A printer's error seemed the probable cause. Lord knows, the small-press books in my store contained zillions of mistakes.

I read the second passage more carefully than the first, because if there were any differences between them, I would have the relief of seeing the author making variations, but there were no differences. That made me suffer. Since the second passage duplicated the first, my arousal and emotions were taken from me, and I wanted to hold on to them. "If I don't fuck someone soon, know someone wants me, I'll have to ride my horse for three days again: do something wilder. I can't stop myself. I get another drink. My sister who's also drunk asks me to dance . . . she kisses me . . . I ask her and she says she'd like to fuck me." The dream contains many of Acker's themes, always close at hand in any case: suicide, sex, incest, family money, romance, loneliness, the inhumanity of "this society."

Why were my feelings taken from me by this repetition? Because I no longer knew Acker's reason for telling me the dream. Like any reader, I depend on knowing the author's intention to stabilize my reading, because I use her belief to underwrite the intensities that are generated and modulated inside me. Instead, Acker dispatched these emotions while I was more or less stuck with them. It is a strange loneliness to be abandoned, emotions disowned, choking on the equipment of narrative projection. Acker destabilized my reading by a strange doubling in which I saw how artificial the emotions were—or were made to be—even as I fell into them. They became an example of emotion, quoted emotion, and the effect of her quote marks was to slide me back and forth between embrace and distance. I am describing an aesthetic effect: I was left stranded with story as the writer leaped into the cold heaven of formal abstraction.

Many of Acker's strategies keep the reader off-balance. That's why it's rather difficult to write about her work, because the best reading is an uncertain reading. I want to offer my confusion as an ideal. Rather than drawing conclusions, developing identifications or thematic connections, that is, making judgments that lead to knowledge, Acker creates a reader who is lost in strangeness. She pitches the reader into a welter of contradictions that do not resolve themselves, but replace each other continuously: a text that hates itself but wants me to love it, sex that dissolves and amalgamates, a disempowered self that tops its heated bottom-act with cold manipulations, a confession that is therapeutic without the possibility of health. Her aesthetic is founded on double binds whose brilliance captivates me as I struggle against them.

The dream passage was repeated a third and a fourth time, and I understood how coldly and elegantly the second passage turned the dream into collaged text. By the fourth repeat I was skimming—I had been turned out of the story and saw it as a block of text. Acker's location had gone from the "I" of the dreamer to the manipulator of text. My own location as reader also changed, I was deprived of one kind of identification in favor of another. When Acker applies pressure to modes of narrating, she compels me to stand with her as the writer of her book, perhaps just living with her through a chunk of time: the theme jumps from, say, incest to the materiality of print and the notion that texts themselves can be "represented." I feel a kind of joy as I attain that grander perspective. But that position is continually undermined by the story being told.

Acker says in 1989, in the useful interview that Sylvère Lotringer conducted, "The I became a dead issue because I realized that you make the I and what makes the I are texts."[2] ["Devoured by Myths"] When I lost my purchase as a reader, I felt anguish exactly because I was deprived of one identity-making machine of identification and recognition. I gained my footing on a form of identification that was perhaps more seductive, a second narrative about Acker manipulating text and disrupting identity. To treat a hot subject in a cold way is the kind of revenge that Flaubert took. Acker's second narrative acts as a critical frame where I discover how to read the work: the particular ways in which a marauding narrative continually shifts the ground of authority, subverting faith in the "suspension of disbelief" or guided daydream that describes most fiction. Acker blasts that arrangement wide open by locating the writing in her own life and in the life of the reader and then calling for the reader's disbelief. I read these and other narratives all at once and I am a tag team running from one to another. If identity equals a florescence of narratives, or the materiality of language, I must give up the sense of myself as a coherent narrative, and no matter how sophisticated my reading becomes, that is always a struggle. Hence my suffering.

If we see identity as the ongoing formation of a subject through the subject's ongoing negotiation with power, in Acker's work that negotiation is profoundly lost, because identity itself is a tyranny from above that descends *like a wolf on the fold,* as debased as the society that gives and withholds value. The self/text is at heart a political system, as nasty as the society it is part of. Identity and even subjectivity are prisons, the most intimate expressions of a domination that is almost total. "I feel I feel I feel I have no language, any emotion to me is a prison."[3] [*Great Expectations*] Struggle equals gestures that fuck with identity.

The heroines of Acker's novels want sex. Arousal may be a drug—"I've gotten hooked on sex"[4] [*Hello, I'm Erica Jong*]—but it is also a blissful jailbreak from the confines of the self. It is pleasure happening, not the self. Still, to get sex, a person must appear to be something recognizable—say, a gendered being with "appropriate" emotions. It is a double bind that Acker rejects with a grievance enacted by her narrators and characters. Acker declines to accept the terms of our confinement. She even rejects gender, the form the body takes to get "needs met," and she declines to commit to one or any. "I want to be a baby more than have sex. I would rather go GOOGOO."[5] That is, I want the freedom to have no ego boundaries. If texts and selves are prisons, would it be too fanciful to find a kind of freedom in the non-space between texts, in the silence and emptiness between juxtapositions? Some of us experience this kind of freedom as anguish, but we prisoners might also experience other kinds of freedom as anguish.

Acker takes revenge on power by displaying what it has done; she speaks truth to power by going where the power differential is greatest, to a community of whores, adolescent girls, artists and bums, the outcast and disregarded. The power imbalance itself causes a reversal that confers authority, not to identity—these characters are merely quick sketches—but to the realities of oppression, loss, and degradation. If hegemony defines itself by what it tries to exclude, then the excluded merely need to describe themselves in order to describe hegemony.

In the program where I teach, a student wrote about sex with toddlers and violence with guns. He was unrelenting. When the class he attended closed down, he was sent to work with me. Extra-literary questions swarmed his writing: he worked the nightshift at the sheriffs' office, and he brought his gun to class for show-and-tell. He was in his sixties, so no youthful hi-jinx there. Had he acted—was he going to act—on his imaginings?

Was I supposed to regard his writing as abnormal psychology rather than fiction? If so, even a fake confession was part of a true case history. He was a skillful and even funny writer. I found myself laughing—was that complicity? Was the humor intentional? I could picture the front page of *The Chronicle*: Teacher gives A+ to Killer Rapist Paedophile. Intention itself was blown wide open, so his text was in a sense illegible.

I feel again that I was in the position of Acker's ideal reader, just as I had been in the bookstore encountering Acker's work for the first time. By best reader, I mean that I was implicating myself in ways I couldn't foresee. The considerable power I enjoy—that of a professor judging a student's work—was turned upside down because it was myself I had to judge, along with the workings of the very power that kept me safe from the text, and safe generally. If I had read my student's work in a book published by Grove Press, or published by anyone, the scandal might have been contained by the form of its publication, and I would have neutralized the danger rightly or wrongly by placing it in a tradition of transgressive literature. In order to make scandal felt continually, Acker finds ways to overflow the bounds of the literary by combining the knowledge she gives us of her life with aggression, humor, unfairness, and shifts in diction and context. "I asked him if he had gotten a letter from Mother . . . 'Were you expecting the dead to tell you what it's like so you can have a new place to spread your cunt lips?'"[6] [*In Memoriam to Identity*] Cultural tenets are demolished because I can't contain this damage in the box of literature.

Kathy blabs, but not necessarily the truth. Early on, she mixed real and fake autobiography according to set formulas, as she explains in the interview with Lotringer.[7] [*Hannibal Lecter*] She manipulates my urge to build a reality behind an I. I want to believe that her story occurs in the world I inhabit: I'm hooked into her outrageous desires—they must be *real.* But Acker denies me the means to draw a conclusion, a conclusion she is not committed to herself. If this is a performance in writing, what is at stake? Belief in the fact or fiction of events is no longer a pressing issue, because the risk of performing takes its place—if I am not sure of how naked she has made herself, I can still react to the spectacle of "how far will she go." And my risk as a spectator becomes the risk of complicity, that the confessional machinery will somehow get backloaded onto me, that it is my confession in the end. It is my confession because I stage it in my psyche, because it calls a community into being that I am part of, because I already know the story so it is already mine, and because Acker has thoroughly confused belief, doubt, and emptiness.

Acker makes a nether region because she structures extra-literary relationships into her writing, which complicates the kind of judgments most readers never need to make. Finally, judgment itself is worn down and falls away in favor of a kind of astonishment. In this sense, you could say Acker creates extra-literary conflict that does not build character either on the page or in the world, as most fiction intends to do, but instead destroys character.

Acker expanded the range of what can be said about the body, and all who write about sex owe her a debt of gratitude. There's no precedent for her patient records of pleasure, coldly observed. "If I concentrate on the air my lungs draw into themselves, I can feel the nerves around my breasts move and shift in complex patterns."[8] [*The Childlike Life of the Black Tarantula*] She records consciousness as it moves through the phantasmagoria of daydream and the reality of the body as a first place: "This lasts forever: time interceded, I can feel his cock expand."[9] [*Rip-off Red, Girl Detective*]

How true the confession and how proximate the complicity that create arousal! Following the lead of Georges Bataille, Acker says that sex destroys limits: "I matter when someone touches me, when I touch someone; the touch matters; so in this way I no longer exist, nor do the men."[10] [*The Childlike Life*] But there is a contradiction here, because sex is often the place in Acker's writing that recognizable time and space begin. Sometimes Acker borrows from porn—high-class porn by Alexander Trocchi, for example—which has its own time frame of tension and release, and its own characters. But often she is simply looking at sex for a long time. So sex stabilizes the self/text as much as sex destabilizes it. Arousal occurs on a register in which continuity is reinstated. Sex operates as a kind of weather, it takes the place of representation's bric-a-brac. It puts the world in place: here's the "effect of the real." "The hair curling above the cunt, between the thighs, around the outer lips, in the red crack of the ass touches the thick pink outer lips touches the tiny red inner lips inside the outer lips touches the red berry at one end of the inner lips whose inside grows if its grazed lightly enough touches the muscles and nerves spiraling as a canal away from the red inner lips."[11] [*The Adult Life of Toulouse Lautrec*] Acker draws in the reins of all her other preoccupations in favor of close observation.

To present myself as a reader of Acker's sex writing, I include my own extra-literary commitment, both to the body in the form of my arousal and to the community of sexual experimentation that is supported by such writing. Acker's voice describing sex is most often her "real voice"—as she described it—a voice which becomes more present in her later books.

I want to take this sex-equals-stability another step. That we have bodies, and a relation to these bodies, and a lack of relation to these bodies, is politics for Acker. Flesh is what has value. Kathy and I used to trade nuggets of physical experience. Talking on the phone, one of us would say something like, "She can't have an orgasm unless a third person is watching," and the other would pounce on it. We were on the look out for an irreducible language, an irreducible chunk of experience to put together with other irreducible chunks to make a language where feeling, event, and words come together. "I need to fuck guys who fuck really slowly, for a long time, so it just comes over me. I tremble and tremble and tremble."[12] A language that can't exist, in which the most ephemeral is the most enduring. A magical language whose words fasten onto their readers' bodies in a kind of onomatopoetic fury. Sex is a bit like a magic spell, like sympathetic magic: an erection on the page can cause an erection "in the world." Using these nuggets has the same pleasure as correcting the error of generalization, since each one stands for a whole sexuality, a species of one.

Acker's ambition for literature was to site it in a queasy place where autobiography and fiction, politics and myth become indistinguishable. She brings language to its limits, to the body and emotions—where risk of nakedness derives from and supports a community. "Culture's the way by which a community attempts to bring its past up out of senselessness and to find in dream and imagination possibilities for action."[13] ["**On Art and Artists**"]

Certainly she stands with Juan Goytisolo and Thomas Bernhard in the pitch of her hatred for her country, for "this society." Against the loneliness of her experience, Acker posits the ongoing conversation of a group of whores that defines community, a gathering of outcasts that evolves into a band of pirates in her final book. They're already present in her first work, *Politics,* about her life as a dancer in a strip joint. These gatherings are composed of women, artists, and freaks who review their relationships with men and power on the eternal stage of night and empire, whether it's a New York City jail or imperial Rome. This community draws an equal sign between freeing our ability to love and the destruction of the state. Included in that community is Acker's reader; as she says, "When I use language, I am given meaning and I give meaning back to the community."[14]

In 1975 Acker wrote about "A possibility of living in a world to which she's not always alien. San Francisco!"[15] [*The Adult Life of Toulouse Lautrec* Acker's move from city to city—New York, San Francisco, London—was the story of hope and disappointment. The demand she placed on the local communities to support her in an unalienated fashion was more interesting for being unreasonable and unfair. Kathy was always on the look out for forms of collectivity—art scenes, music scenes, the tattoo or biker "communities"—that tie the fate of the individual to the fate of the group. In her essay,

"Critical Languages," she says: "May we write, not in order to judge, but for and in (I quote Georges Bataille), 'The community of those who do not have a community.'"[16] ["**Critical Languages (1990)**"] That is, generating text means generating identity. I would like to add, generating identity means generating community. If the idea of community began so heterogeneously, I wonder if the reductionist pitfalls could be avoided.

Acker included her communities in her writing by using real names, by speaking to them directly, and by speaking for them. "Friendship is always a political act, for it unites citizens into a polis, a (political) community."[17] ["**Writing, Identity, and Copyright in the Net Age**"] She loved gossip, the glue of any community, and there was never a greater sob-sister. She does not dress up romantic suffering with pretty language. Love, when it's done right, only makes things worse: "It's sick to love someone beyond rationality, beyond a return (I love you you love me). Real love is sick. I could love death."[18] [*My Mother*] And, "I knew I belonged to the community of artists or freaks not because the anger in me was unbearable but because my overpowering wish to give myself away wasn't socially acceptable."[19] [*Don Quixote*]

Kathy was the best girlfriend, because with her you could really complain. "I am lonely out of my mind. I am miserable out of my mind . . . I've got to fuck. Don't you understand don't you have needs as much as I have needs DON'T YOU HAVE TO GET LAID?"[20] ["**New York City in 1979**"] Romantic distress was a default position for human communication, and if the truest language is the unique particulars of desire spoken by the community of cock and cunt, then the lack of such communication (which means no agency, rejection, emotional harm, and poverty) makes a communal language of failure. When I was *badly loved,* no romantic bruise was too tiny to examine, no repeat of that examination was too obsessive. Kathy and I gave each other plenty of advice, the blind leading the blind. Bits of these endless conversations worked their way into each other's writing—here are two tiny passages.

This is from *Great Expectations,* 1982: Three whores are talking in ancient Rome. Kathy is the whore Cynthia, I am the whore Barbarella and Denise Kastan is Danielle.

BARBARELLA:

I'm both the wife and husband. Even though none of us is getting anything right now, except Danielle who's getting everything, our desires are totally volatile.

DANIELLE:

I can't be a wife. I can be a hostess. If I've got lots of money.

BARBARELLA:

One-night stands don't amuse me anymore.

CYNTHIA:

I think if you really worship sex, you don't fuck around. Danielle fucks around more than any of us, and she's the one who doesn't care about sex.

BARBARELLA:

Most men don't like sex. They like being powerful and when you have good sex you lose all power.

CYNTHIA:

I need sex to stay alive.[21]

[*Great Expectations*]

This is from my book *Margery Kempe* from 1994:

It's two a.m. his time; I'm in bed in San Francisco. My life occurs on the heavy satin of his skin yet he won't let me be the cause of stimulation. I give him an ultimatum: Let's live together or break up. He thinks it over a few months: he has the self-confidence to reject me. I write a blistering letter and show it to my friend Kathy. She says, "Bob, you must delete the anger and beg."[22]

[*Great Expectations*]

"One text subverts another" is the consecrated phrase. Appropriation can express a cynicism where nothing obtains ("My writing is all shit," as Kathy once affirmed in P.J.'s, a seafood restaurant in San Francisco), and the process itself can be pitched like a bomb at the custodians of identity. In her hands it's a malleable practice—in her later work Acker uses appropriation to conduct us into a state of wonder. ("I'm basically a New Age writer," Kathy said some years later at the same table.)

Great Expectations begins with episodes of family life alternating with chunks of Acker's translations of Pierre Guyotat's *Eden Eden Eden,* a novel-length sentence fragment on sex and atrocity. Soon the sections infect each other and we see the link between need and violence—that family life and war (in 1982 Guyotat's Algeria looked like our Vietnam) have their common denominator. "*Reality* is just the underlying fantasy, a fantasy that reveals need."[23] [*Blood and Guts in High School*] Need means need for love on every register. Reality is need in a simpler way than we might be comfortable acknowledging: Acker may be subverting text with text but need has a different economy: one text equals all texts and one need equals all needs. One need is not an allegory of all needs; it is all needs.

Another way to describe this economy of need is to say that appropriation is a way to look at the distance between feeling and event. One of Acker's basic tenets is that the world is against feeling. She projects her life into events that are already known, like porn or detective genre or canonical works like *Don Quixote* and *Great Expectations.* The already-known is a public stage on which to reclaim emotion. It's a theme in *Don Quixote*—how to love while ferociously transvaluing emotion and continuously redefining world and self. In works like *Don Quixote* and *Pussy, King of the Pirates,* appropriation grants Acker's own story a second fate with its own inevitabilities, its own organization of experience. You could say this fate is a fate in words with its own freedoms and resistances. The appropriated text acts as the unforeseen since—once begun—Kathy's life must somehow fit into the story.

The rereading that *is* appropriation turns Acker into a reader as well as a writer. "The more I write my own novels, the more it seems to me that to write is to read."[24] ["The Words to Say It"] Acker jumps the barrier and becomes a reader—displaying that projection of self into the text that shapes—however briefly—a reader's being. That projection of herself is presented as a kind of spectacle to myself the reader, part of my own act of self-projecting. In reading, I am pitched between the true version of the appropriated work, its theft, the facts of Acker's life, and the truth of her psychic life (the "case history" of extremity that writers since de Quincey have been reporting).

I have come to think of the trajectory of Acker's writing as going from daydream to night dream. In the first place Acker took her cue from early seventies conceptual art, banishing creativity and asserting procedural elements of writing by setting up arbitrary guidelines to set fiction outside intention: in *Kathy Goes to Haiti,* she used predetermined amounts of real and fake autobiography. She wrote so many pages per day, brute production, which she called task work. At one point she said she wrote with the TV on, and bits of histrionic soap-opera dialogue sometimes filtered through. I'll bet boredom induced daydream. Her early work, taken as a whole, can be characterized by daydream, that is, dream riffs of clear motive, immediate longings, revenge fantasies, and wish-fulfillment.

Acker used dreams in many ways—the dream maps in *Blood and Guts* for example. There is a therapeutic aspect to the repetition of the family drama, the litany of obsessions, the report of endless suffering and desire. Writing may provide the same occasion for self-revelation that therapy does—we take for granted that it's good for people to speak candidly in these "confidential" situations. But it is a therapy in which good health is impossible because the dream is turned outward—deprived of interiority, stripped of coherent subjectivity—and it is our culture itself that is sick. The endless recycling of societal messages and oppressions enlarges the sense of impossibility, except perhaps faith

in the power of storytelling itself. A therapy minus interior life, anti-expressive, and so turned outward.

In *My Death My Life by Pier Paolo Pasolini* Acker wrote, "I can wonder whatever I want. I simply see. Each detail is a mystery a wonder."[25] Acker was searching for a way to escape from duality and rational thought. In *Empire of the Senseless* she dreamt the plot forward. Acker would make a move in writing, like dreaming a plot forward, then see that she was doing it and make a commitment to the strategy, as Carla Harryman observed at the Lust for Life symposium at New York University in 2002. After *Empire of the Senseless* was finished, she said she was glad to sleep through a night again, since she had been waking herself up for months to write down her dreams. The dreams are recognizable—Kathy moving through a dream space where motive seems emphatic for her and for the reader, though located beyond the grasp of both. Dualities are cancelled in favor of an immediate consciousness of the interrelation and interdependence of things. Acker was using her unconscious like a public commons, the location of image-making that belongs to a community.

I'd like to place Acker's later work with Baudelaire's "Correspondences" and Rimbaud's *Illuminations,* works intended to change the world directly through the reality of the imagination. "If writing cannot and writing must change things, I thought to myself, logically of course, writing *will* change things magically."[26] ["**A Few Notes on Two of my Books**"] Acker's interest in magic can be seen as the grandest attempt to integrate the extra-literary into writing. Magic, in the largest sense, allows me to link my own experience, desires, and biological self to a grand order. It connects the ephemeral to the largest reality. Acker uses the emphatic but obscure motives of dreams to indicate this unknown organization of the world. Maybe she is rejecting the idea that anything is secret, so her dreams belong to the reader as well as the writer, and the goal of self-knowledge is turned outward as well. My interior life may be a cultural glue, something organizing me from the outside, something to live up to, like the idea of fidelity in the Middle Ages.

Acker founds her aesthetics on distant poles. On the one hand she champions feeling itself, and on the other she is a cold writer working from formulas that generate text.

Her continual shifts in scale stretch meaning out of shape, as she packs together extreme statements of far-flung lyricism. Belief itself is "bent out of shape," an exciting disorganization that isolates each sentence in an immensity. Acker can inhabit both sides of a cliché. A sentence like "I'm sick of this society" can seem at once post-punk self-mockery, ugly writing shedding the trappings of literature, the stupid voice of an adolescent girl who can't be controlled, an "example of language," and a *cri de cœur.* I must continually renew my trust in the process of reading while my assumptions are demolished. I attain a place of innocence, my affirmation and trust must take place in the present—past affirmations don't matter, past betrayals of that trust must be surmounted. The writing itself gains majesty as, finally, the truth of the world seems to be balanced against each sentence.

Kathy Acker had the highest ambitions: to reorient literature in a true relation to the present and to crack that moment wide open. In the end, my reading goes from unreadable to unbearable, because Acker intends that I bear the knowledge of chance, which is the acceptance of constant change. That acceptance is also the knowledge of death, the knowledge of my body which exists (whether I know it or not) in the pure intensity of arousal and dread.

Notes

1. Kathy Acker, *I Dreamt I Was a Nymphomaniac: Imagining,* in *Portrait of an Eye: Three Novels* (New York, Grove Press, 1998), pp. 101-102.

2. "Devoured by Myths" (interview), in *Hannibal Lecter, My Father* (New York, Semiotext(e), 1991), p. 11.

3. *Great Expectations* (San Francisco, Re/Search, 1982), p. 24.

4. *Hello, I'm Erica Jong* in *Essential Acker* (New York, Grove Press, 2002), p. 149.

5. Ibid., p. 148.

6. *In Memoriam to Identity* (New York, Grove Weidenfeld, 1990), p. 165.

7. *Hannibal Lecter,* "Interview," p. 7.

8. *The Childlike Life of the Black Tarantula,* in *Portrait of an Eye,* pp. 59-60.

9. *Rip-off Red, Girl Detective* (New York, Grove Press, 2002), p. 11.

10. *The Childlike Life,* in *Portrait of an Eye,* p. 53.

11. *The Adult Life of Toulouse Lautrec,* in *Portrait of an Eye,* p. 53.

12. Ibid., pp. 202-203.

13. "On Art and Artists," *Bodies of Work,* (London, Serpent's Tail, 1997), p. 4.

14. Ibid., 4.

15. *The Adult Life of Toulouse Lautrec,* in *Portrait of an Eye,* p. 208.

16. "Critical Languages (1990)" in *Bodies of Work,* p. 92.

17. "Writing, Identity, and Copyright in the Net Age," in *Bodies of Work,* p. 104.

18. *My Mother: Demonology* (New York, Pantheon Books, 1993), p. 15.

19. *Don Quixote,* in *Essential Acker,* p. 212.

20. "New York City in 1979," in *Essential Acker,* p. 139.

21. *Great Expectations,* p. 110.

22. Robert Glück, *Margery Kempe* (New York/London, Serpent's Tail, 1994), p. 134.

23. *Blood and Guts in High School,* in *Essential Acker,* p. 115.

24. "The Words to Say It," in *Bodies of Work,* p. 66.

25. *My Death My Life by Pier Paolo Pasolini,* in *Essential Acker,* p. 195.

26. "A Few Notes on Two of my Books," in *Bodies of Work,* p. 8.

FURTHER READING

Criticism

Bomberger, Ann. "The Efficacy of Shock for Feminist Politics: Kathy Acker's *Blood and Guts in High School* and Donald Bartheleme's *Snow White.*" In *Gender Reconstructions: Pornography and Perversions in Literature and Culture,* edited by Cindy L. Carlson, Robert L. Mazzola, and Susan M. Bernardo, pp. 189-204. Aldershot, England: Ashgate, 2002.

Explores "the political efficacy of shock for feminism" by studying Acker's *Blood and Guts in High School.*

Brande, David. "Making Yourself a Body Without Organs: The Cartography of Pain in Kathy Acker's *Don Quixote.*" *Genre* 24, no. 2 (summer 1991): 191-209.

Explores Acker's use of "masochistic sexuality" in *Don Quixote.*

Clune, Michael. "Blood Money: Sovereignty and Exchange in Kathy Acker." *Contemporary Literature* 45, no. 3 (fall 2004): 486-515.

Discusses the "creation myth for piracy" and a radical view of free market economics that emerged in Acker's late fiction.

Cooley, Nicole. "Painful Bodies: Kathy Acker's Last Texts." In *We Who Love to Be Astonished: Experimental Women's Writing and Performance Poetics,* edited by Laura Hinton and Cynthia Hogue, pp. 193-202. Tuscaloosa: The University of Alabama Press, 2002.

Offers readings of two of Acker's last texts, claiming that when read together the two works "reveal Acker's autobiographical poetics."

Deaton, Rebecca and Kathy Acker. "Kathy Acker Interviewed by Rebecca Deaton." *Textual Practice* 6, no. 2 (summer 1992): 271-82.
Interview with Acker in which she discusses a number of different topics, including her move from London to San Francisco, the relation of postmodernism to feminism, and the writing of her novel *Great Expectations.*

Dix, Douglas Shields. "Kathy Acker's *Don Quixote*: Nomad Writing." *The Review of Contemporary Fiction* 9, no. 3 (fall 1989): 56-62.
Relates the theories of individual transformation proposed by the French theorists Gilles Deleuze and Félix Guattari to Acker's fiction.

Friedman, Ellen G. and Kathy Acker. "Conversation with Kathy Acker." *The Review of Contemporary Fiction* 9, no. 3 (fall 1989): 12-22.
Often-cited interview in which Acker discusses a number of her novels and her aesthetics as a writer.

Hardin, Michael, ed. *Devouring Institutions: The Life Work of Kathy Acker,* San Diego, Calif.: Hyperbole Books, 2004, 271 p.
Collection of thirteen essays by various critics on Acker's writings, including a primary and secondary bibliography compiled by the editor.

Hughey, Lynn. "Cyperpunk Pilgrimages: Kathy Acker Inside/Outside of the Sublime." *Mosaic* 36, no. 4 (December 2003): 121-37.
Compares works of contemporary pilgrimage from such cyperpunk writers as Kathy Acker to the narrative, mystical testimonies of such medieval women pilgrims as Margery Kempe.

Jacobs, Naomi. "Kathy Acker and the Plagiarized Self." *The Review of Contemporary Fiction* 9, no. 3 (fall 1989): 50-5.
Argues that Acker's writings demonstrate "the complex relationships of the historical figure to postmodern concepts of text, of identity, and of the authorial self."

McCaffery, Larry. "The Artists of Hell: Kathy Acker and 'Punk' Aesthetics." In *Breaking the Sequence: Women's Experimental Fiction,* edited by Ellen G. Friedman and Miriam Fuchs, pp. 215-30. Princeton, N.J.: Princeton University Press, 1989.
Discusses Acker's relation to the "punk" aesthetic in music that evolved in the mid-1970s.

McCaffery, Larry and Kathy Acker. "The Path of Abjection: An Interview with Kathy Acker." In *Some Other Frequency: Interviews with Innovative American Authors,* pp. 14-35. Philadelphia: University of Pennsylvania Press, 1996.

Interview with Acker in which the author discusses her literary aesthetics, French feminist theory, the history of the novel, and other issues.

Peters, Greg Lewis. "Dominance and Subversion: The Horizontal Sublime and Erotic Empowerment in the Works of Kathy Acker." In *State of the Fantastic: Studies in the Theory and Practice of Fantastic Literature and Film,* edited by Nicholas Ruddick, pp. 149-56. Westport, Conn.: Greenwood Press, 1992.
Explores the central concept of dominance and submission in Acker's "fictional world."

Pitchford, Nicola. "Kathy Acker's Unreasonable Texts." In *Tactical Readings: Feminist Postmodernism in the Novels of Kathy Acker and Angela Carter,* pp. 59-104. Lewisburg, Pa.: Bucknell University Press, 2002.
Explicates three of Acker's novels from the 1980s to demonstrate "how the tension between post-structuralist and oppositional approaches plays out in Acker's attack on . . . the logic of rationalism and its accompanying economic activity, rationalization."

Redding, Arthur F. "Bruises, Roses: Masochism and the Writing of Kathy Acker." *Contemporary Literature* 35, no. 2 (summer 1994): 281-304.
Investigates "the creative potential of masochism along with questions raised by the painful and fetishistic" in Acker's writings.

Robinson, Christopher L. "In the Silence of the Knight: Kathy Acker's *Don Quixote* as a Work of Disenchantment." *Yearbook of Comparative and General Literature* 47 (1999): 109-23.
Analyzes the manner in which Acker adapts the theme of "disenchantment" present in Cervantes's *Don Quixote* in her novel by the same name.

Rock, Catherine. "Poetics of the Periphery: Literary Experimentalism in Kathy Acker's *In Memoriam to Identity*." *Literature Interpretation Theory* 12, no. 2 (2001): 205-33.
Focuses on the writing strategies Acker uses in her novel *In Memoriam to Identity,* claiming that the narrative "constructs an alternate, transgressive poetics of the margins in order to give voice to the cultural underside."

Scholder, Amy, Carla Harryman, and Avital Ronell, eds. *Lust for Life: On the Writings of Kathy Acker,* London: Verso, 2006, 120 p.
Collection of eight essays by various critics on Acker inspired by a symposium on the author at New York University in 2002.

Sciolino, Martina. "Kathy Acker and the Postmodern Subject of Feminism." *College English* 52, no. 4 (April 1990): 437-45
Maintains that Acker employs the technique of "plagiarism/autoplagiarism" to create an authentic view of female experience in a culture and language constituted of various patriarchal myths. .

————. "The 'Mutilating Body' and the Decomposing Text: Recovery in Kathy Acker's *Great Expectations*." In *Textual Bodies: Changing Boundaries of Literary Representation*, edited by Lori Hope Lefkovitz, pp. 245-66. Albany: State University of New York Press, 1997.

Demonstrates the ways in which Acker uses plagiarized texts, pornography, the "slave/master" and sado-masochist dialectic, and other forms of "intertextuality" in her novel *Great Expectations*.

Siegle, Robert. "On the Subject of Walter Abish and Kathy Acker." *Literature and Psychology* 33, no. 3-4 (1987): 38-57.

Examines Walter Abish's *In the Future Present* and Acker's *The Adult Life of Toulouse Lautrec by Henri Toulouse Lautrec* to demonstrate how both writers reconstruct the subjective "I" and the relation of narrative and identity in their fiction.

Yuknavitch, Lidia. "War, Sexuality, and Narrative." In *Allegories of Violence: Tracing the Writing of War in Late Twentieth-Century Fiction*, pp. 75-95. New York: Routledge, 2001.

Contends that *Empire of the Senseless* investigates "a set of questions about identity tied to sexuality and war by figuring them through the terms colonization and decolonization."

Additional coverage of Acker's life and career is contained in the following sources published by Thomson Gale: *American Writers Supplement*, Vol. 12; *Contemporary Authors*, Vols. 117, 122, 162; *Contemporary Authors New Revision Series*, Vol. 55; *Contemporary Literary Criticism*, Vols. 45, 111; *Contemporary Novelists*, Eds. 5, 6; *Literature Resource Center*; and *Modern American Literature*, Ed. 5.

Reinaldo Arenas
1943-1990

Cuban novelist, short story and novella writer, poet, playwright, and autobiographer.

The following entry provides an overview of Arenas's life and works. For additional information on his career, see *CLC,* Volume 41.

INTRODUCTION

Arenas is considered a significant voice in Latin-American literature of the twentieth century and is one of the most widely read and internationally acclaimed authors of Cuba's post-revolutionary generation. He is best known for his formally innovative novels, which blend elements of fantasy, philosophy, history, and autobiography, and explore the psychological effects of social oppression on the individual. Arenas was marginalized for openly opposing Fidel Castro's regime in his writings, and he was persecuted for his forthright discussions of homosexuality and depictions of homoerotic desire. Rafael Ocasio has observed that "Arenas was a brilliant writer who, despite his humble peasant background, became one of the most celebrated Latin American writers of the latter part of the twentieth century. Early on, he made himself into a gay activist with a clear understanding of his sexual and sociopolitical role in Cuba's most important moment in world history. His novels stand out as the rather exceptional production of an autodidact with minimal literary training." Ocasio has concluded that, despite his many accomplishments, Arenas "still awaits recognition for his extraordinary contributions to the political and literary scenes of Cuba, of Latin America, and of the Latino United States."

BIOGRAPHICAL INFORMATION

Arenas was born in Cuba on July 16, 1943, near the town of Holguín. Abandoned by his father when he was two months old, he was raised by his mother and lived with several members of his extended family, including his maternal grandparents, in an impoverished, rural environment. Under his mother's instruction, he learned to read and write. At the age of fifteen Arenas joined rebel forces that were fighting against the army of dictator Fulgencio Batista. In 1959, after the success of the revolution, he received a scholarship from the new government to study agricultural accounting. After com-

pleting his degree, he began working at a poultry farm near Manzanillo, in the southernmost part of Cuba's Oriente province. In 1962 he began a training program for economic planners at the Universidad de la Habana but quickly lost interest in this field of study.

Arenas became a staff member at the Biblioteca Nacional in 1963 and began writing short stories and his first novel, *Celestino antes del alba* (*Singing from the Well*). The novel won an honorable mention at the Concurso Nacional de Novela Cirilo Villaverde in 1965 and was received favorably by Cuban critics, including novelist Alejo Carpentier. The book encountered resistance from Cuba's revolutionary government, however, and it took two years before it was published. Thereafter, Arenas's work was unofficially censored. Arenas was forced to smuggle his second novel, *El mundo alucinante* (*Hallucinations: Being an Account of the Life and Adventures of Friar Servando Teresa de Mier*), out of the country for publication. The book was first published in 1969 in France, where it was well-received by both French and Spanish critics. His third novel, *Le palais des très blanches mouffettes* (*The Palace of the White Skunks*), was also smuggled out of Cuba for publication in France in 1975

In 1970 Arenas was arrested and forced to work at a sugarcane plantation, along with other writers who also had published outside of Cuba, a practice that was considered counterrevolutionary by the political authorities. While working on the plantation, Arenas composed the long poem *El central* (*El Central: A Cuban Sugar Mill*). He secretly delivered the manuscript to Spain, where it was eventually published in 1981. During the late 1960s and early 1970s, Arenas wrote several versions of a novel titled *Otra vez el mar* (*Farewell to the Sea*). The first version was lost in Havana and the second version was confiscated in 1971 by the state police. The third version was eventually published in 1982, after it was smuggled out of the country.

In 1973 Arenas was arrested and accused of immoral practices and counterrevolutionary behavior. While released on bail, he escaped and hid out from authorities for four months. But he was arrested again in 1974 and imprisoned. Ironically, Arenas was jailed at El Morro Castle, the same prison that held fugitive Friar Servando, the real-life model for the protagonist of his novel *Hallucinations*. Arenas was finally released in 1976 but was forbidden to write. He worked various odd jobs to survive until he emigrated to the United States in 1980, along with approximately 140,000 other Cubans in the mass exodus known as the Mariel boat lift. Arenas arrived in Miami and eventually moved to New York City, where he continued writing.

He published the novella *Arturo, la estrella más brillante* in 1984; an experimental play, *Persecución,* in 1986; and the novel *La loma del ángel* (*Graveyard of the Angels*) in 1987. He also published *El Portero* (*The Doorman*) in 1987 and *El asalto* (*The Assault*) in 1990. Battling complications from AIDS, with which he was diagnosed in 1987, Arenas committed suicide on December 7, 1990. In a letter published in the Miami Spanish-language newspaper, *Diario las Américas,* Arenas stated that his decision to take his own life was a political act, symbolizing a struggle for freedom and hope, rather than a defeat. His last novel, *El color del verano* (1991; *The Color of Summer; or, The New Garden of Earthly Delights*), and his highly acclaimed autobiography, *Antes que anochezca* (1992; *Before Night Falls*), were published posthumously.

MAJOR WORKS

Hallucinations: Being an Account of the Life and Adventures of Friar Servando Teresa de Mier is the fictionalized biography of an early nineteenth-century monk who was persecuted for opposing Spanish colonization in Mexico. The quest for freedom is the central theme of the novel, which was inspired by the friar's memoirs. The book chronicles the monk's childhood, his various imprisonments and escapes, and finally his disillusionment with Mexico's fight for independence. Arenas elaborates on the historical account through the use of formal innovations, presenting multiple versions of the opening chapters and allowing voices to shift in order to produce a chorus-like effect. He also incorporates fantasy and surrealistic imagery into the novel, which serve to counter the cruelty of the Spanish colonizers and suggest that the only way to achieve liberation is through language itself. Many critics consider *Hallucinations* a neo-baroque picaresque novel, as its language is closer to that of the Golden Age of Spanish literature than to that of rural Cuba. The narrative is also informed by Arenas's sexual preferences and includes instances of homoerotic imagery.

During his lifetime, Arenas worked to complete a project that he referred to as the *Pentagonía*, or "five agonies." The *Pentagonía* consists of five novels, which are connected thematically by their explorations of oppression and the struggle for freedom. In the first novel of the series, *Singing from the Well*, the protagonist/narrator is an unnamed, mentally impaired boy who experiences fantastic visions that contrast starkly with his impoverished surroundings, the pre-revolutionary Cuban countryside. He is persecuted by his grandparents for not conforming to their ideals, and he experiences liberation and consolation only through his alter ego, a poet named Celestino. The second novel, *The Palace of the White Skunks,* deals with the exploits of the ironically named protagonist Fortunato, an adolescent living in poverty with his family in a small town in rural Cuba. His sexual awakening places him at odds with the moral restrictions of society, and he eventually flees to the mountains to join rebel forces and dies fighting in the revolution. The longing for freedom on a personal and political level is the focus of the third book in the *Pentagonía, Farewell to the Sea.* The first section of the novel is comprised of an interior monologue by the wife of Hector, a homosexual poet. In this section, the wife laments both the state of affairs in post-revolutionary Cuba and her own inadequate marriage. The second part of the novel is a long poem by Hector, in which he explores his own homosexual longings and his thoughts about Castro's regime. As in *The Palace of the White Skunks,* death is characterized as an escape from oppression, and the novel ends with Hector's suicide. In *The Color of Summer,* the fourth novel of the series, Arenas continues to explore the opposing forces of homosexual desire and the oppression of government and society. The final novel, *The Assault,* presents a futuristic vision of an oppressive society, in which the rights of the individual are sacrificed for the benefit of the government. Arenas described the *Pentagonía* as both a writer's autobiography and a metaphor for Cuban history.

Arenas candidly examines his life experiences in *Before Night Falls.* He began recording his life in 1970, when he was forced to work on a sugar plantation in Cuba. He viewed writing as a means of preserving human integrity in the face of humiliating and dehumanizing circumstances. Much of the book, which chronicles events from his childhood to his final weeks of life in New York, alternates between ruminations on homosexuality and Castro's regime in Cuba. Arenas also discusses his feelings and thoughts about AIDS, after he is diagnosed with the disease, and ponders its origin. He argues that "AIDS is a perfect illness because it is so alien to human nature and has as its function to destroy life in the most cruel and systematic way. Never before has such a formidable calamity affected mankind. Such diabolic perfection makes one ponder the possibility that human beings may have had a hand in its creation." Like many of Arenas's earlier writings, *Before Night Falls* is primarily concerned with the stifling social pressures that hamper individual expression and self-realization. Arenas does not limit his criticism to Castro's Cuba, however, but speaks out against the fundamental hypocrisy of society in general, including his new home of America.

CRITICAL RECEPTION

Many critics, both Latin American and Anglo-American, consider Arenas the only writer of international stature to come out of Cuba since the revolution in 1959. Yet despite his growing reputation in America and Europe, Arenas remains a censored and controversial figure within his native country. Though copies of most of his publications circulate illegally in Cuba, only *Singing from the Well* has been officially published by the government, and Arenas is still regarded as a counterrevolutionary and sexual outlaw. From the beginning of his literary career, Arenas distained the aesthetics of Cuban revolutionary realism, opting instead for a more personal style, one that blends fantasy, illusion, reality, history, and philosophical ideas. Rather than remain silent, he antagonized Cuban authorities with his open portrayal of gay sexual life and, more significantly, gay desire in his writings.

Arenas's literary reputation has increased steadily since his death in 1990. Today, many commentators commend his writings for their piercing explorations of human emotion, their powerful and imaginative prose, and their skillful use of autobiographical detail to confront universal themes, such as exile, social oppression, erotic desire, and the relation of illusion and reality. Arenas's willingness to depict homoeroticism in an overt and unglorified manner, though troubling for some readers, has also won praise from a number of critics. Rafael Ocasio has hailed Arenas as "a forerunner in Latin American literature of the mid-sixties, when treatment of homosexuality remained a taboo subject in most Latin American countries," adding that "even today, Arenas's ample homoerotic testimony stands out among only a handful of Latin American writers willing to provoke debate on gay issues in autobiographical material."

PRINCIPAL WORKS

Celestino antes del alba [*Singing from the Well*] (novel) 1967; revised as *Cantando en el pozo,* 1982

El mundo alucinante [*Hallucinations: Being an Account of the Life and Adventures of Friar Servando Teresa de Mier*] (novel) 1969

Con los ojos cerrados (short stories) 1972; revised as *Termina el desfile,* 1981

Le palais des très blanches mouffettes [*The Palace of the White Skunks*] (novel) 1975

La vieja Rosa [*Old Rosa*] (novella) 1980

El central [*El Central: A Cuban Sugar Mill*] (poetry) 1981

Otra vez el mar [*Farewell to the Sea*] (novel) 1982

Arturo, la estrella más brillante (novella) 1984

Necesidad de libertad (essays) 1986

Persecución (play) 1986

La loma del ángel [*Graveyard of the Angels*] (novel) 1987

El portero [*The Doorman*] (novel) 1987

Voluntad de vivir manifestándose (poetry) 1989

El asalto [*The Assault*] (novel) 1990

Leprosorio: Trilogía poética (poetry) 1990

Viaje a La Habana (novella) 1990

El color del verano [*The Color of Summer; or, The New Garden of Earthly Delights*] (novel) 1991

Antes que anochezca [*Before Night Falls*] (autobiography) 1992

Mona and Other Tales (short stories) 2001

*These five novels are collectively referred to as the *Pentagonía.*

†This work includes the poetry collections *El central, Morir en junio y con la lengua afuera,* and *Leprosorio.*

CRITICISM

Kessel Schwartz (essay date March 1984)

SOURCE: Schwartz, Kessel. "Homosexuality and the Fiction of Reinaldo Arenas." *Journal of Evolutionary Psychology* 5, no. 1-2 (March 1984): 12-20.

[*In the following essay, Schwartz provides a psychoanalytical reading of Arenas's work, stating that his narratives display his "homoerotic inclination" and reveal "his anxiety and need for love and acceptance, which, unfortunately, neither society nor his family ever gave him."*]

Reinaldo Arenas, one of the best-known contemporary Latin American novelists, makes no attempt to obfuscate his homoerotic inclination, one of the realities of his unhappy life experiences in Cuba. He creates fantasies or hallucinatory situations where life and death occupy the same plane: in *Celestino antes del alba* (1967) a lonely, neurotic child invents another version of himself; in *El mundo alucinante* (1969) a real-life *rara avis,* Fray Servando Teresa de Mier, a Mexican priest and patriot, becomes a hallucinated and hallucinating friar; in *El palacio de las blanquisimas mofetas* (1980) and *Termina el desfile* (1981) desolation, despair, and madness serve as the background for a variety of implausible incidents in yet another universe of magic realism. These works, whatever the exterior creative accomplishments, reveal Arenas's need to sublimate certain narcissistic wishes and unconscious motivations through a relevant imagery.

In his fiction we encounter a variety of sexual perversions, guilt complexes, phobias, inhibitions, infantile regressions, phallic glorifications, homoerotic fantasies, and incestuous fixations, accompanied by a concomitant denigration and fear of women. Karl Abraham has shown that we often indulge in waking dreams in which we transfer ourselves into an artificial situation and form the world in accordance with our wishes.[1] This seems to be exactly what Arenas does with his creations of imagined doubles and companions.

Incest, one aspect of the homosexual and passive feminine fantasies found in his work, takes many forms. In *El palacio de las blanquisimas mofetas,* Fortunato, Onerica's fatherless son, watches his mother with her own father, Polo. Fortunato's hate (displaced onto the father by proxy) grows, and he decides to kill his grandfather. But at that moment, when Fortunato turned around he saw Polo's "enormous sex organ balancing itself between two entangled swellings . . ." Frightened by the implicit phallic aggression, he watches the immense figure go to his mother: "And now he saw the thick instrument reaching her, knocking her down, transfixing her. And she without protesting, almost laughing, supported the aggression, while he kept on watching without being able to do anything." In this remembrance of the primal scene he feels "a violent and inappeasable desire to possess his mother, just as in his imagination he was possessing her there . . ." And as he runs toward mother something gigantic, blue, hairy interposes itself, a fly which, not to be denied, attacks the tip of his nose. Fortunato, ambivalently, thinks of the relationship in terms of damnation and salvation.[2]

Throughout the novel Fortunato dreams of his mother: "His mother caressed him, but the fly, stubborn, blue, and impertinent, persisted in attacking his nose" (*PBM* [*El palacio de las blanquisimas Mofetas*], p. 113). These repeated fantasies are accompanied by a sense of loss, frustration, and fear. John Flugel points out that dreams in childhood of being chased by some wild and dangerous animal almost invariably represent the father.[3] Karl Abraham has shown that in a number of such cases, involving anxiety about a threatening or devouring animal, a fly or the equivalent is involved.[4] Flugel also notes that the repression of the original love of the parent of the opposite sex may lead to an extension of the love taboo to all persons of that sex and "heterosexual affection being now barred, to the displacement of sexual desire into the homosexual direction."[5] Moreover, the feeling of inadequacy at the thought of the genital in relationship to one's mother, and the ensuing wounded self-image, shame, and guilt, says Ernest Jones, "may declare itself in actual homosexuality."[6] In Arenas's short story, **"El hijo y la madre"** the boy tries to touch his dream mother. She turns into a gigantic bird and takes him to her breast, a dream which the boy

relates to another one in which a doorknob he attempted to grasp diminished in size and disappeared. At that moment his mother grows into an even more gigantic bird. His association is that she was "diminishing him, harrassing him, eliminating him."[7]

Most of Arenas's scenes, instead of subtly shaded connotations, involve rather graphic descriptions of what appear to be common fantasies related to an inability to love women, who represent mother. In *La vieja Rosa* Arthur, smothered by mother love, seeks in homoeroticism the satisfaction he cannot find in any heterosexual relationship, forbidden because all women symbolize mother (*TED* [*Termina el desfile*], p. 68). Fortunato discovers the solitary pleasure of multiple masturbations with mother as his mental sex object (*PBM,* p. 48), but feeling monstrous and sinful, can later achieve an erection only by evoking a fellow soldier (*PBM,* p. 292). The glorification and narcissistic love of one's own genitalia may be one path to homosexuality. Also, one who has introjected mother, through that incorporation, reacts to male objects in the way she would.[8]

Fortunato constantly identifies with his aunts, Adolfina and Digna: "Many times I had been Adolfina, and I had suffered like her or perhaps wanted even more to be embraced, penetrated, beheaded, asphixiated, destroyed by love of someone. Many times I had been called Celia" (*PBM,* p. 262). Sometimes Fortunato shifts back and forth between male and female roles: "Sometimes I stop being Adolfina; I become Fortunato again . . . I am then Dina . . . I am now Adolfina" (*PBM,* p. 228). A feminized Adolfina, in a narcissistic female role, he desires to be loved and to force others into love through his personal allurement. Throughout this novel similar transformations occur: "transformed into an old maid, he burst into the street in search of a man" (*PBM,* p. 117). These women, then, are passive entities through which Arenas projects his sexual anxieties which he modifies so that they become acceptable images. In *El mundo alucinante* Fray Servando encounters Orlando, "a rare woman, sexually ambivalent . . . through her sex, indeed, she exhibited her difference. And so she came toward me, laughing and pointing at me with Her Immense Definitive Classification, which was swinging from right to left, up and down, growing at each passing moment."[9]

Arenas employs a kind of sexual aggression to reinforce his own uncertain masculinity with a corresponding need to degrade his women characters. Adolfina, the sister-aunt, becomes a debased object, and Fortunato associates his mother Onerica with a whore (*PBM,* pp. 34-35). Thus, even mother herself in much of Arena's fiction is degraded, but more often a displacement from the mother (a sister, aunt, or some other woman) serves as a "cognate with the debased mother representation while the mother herself retains her purity."[10] In *Celestino antes del alba,* we find the good and loving mother contrasted with the aggressive, phallic, castrating one.

Where women in general are concerned, Arenas portrays them almost invariably as negative archetypes, downgrading them as restrictive "woman who ties down and makes demands" (**PBM,** p. 52); as worthless, "four females he (and he beat himself on his testicles) had brought into this hellish world" (**PBM,** pp. 55-57); and as objects to be beaten, "Moisés gave her such a blow on the chest that she almost fell to the ground" (**PBM,** p. 82). Part of the debasement of women involves their role as sex objects and their submission to men. In *El mundo alucinante* a naked woman runs toward a group of men "who instantly perforate her" (**EMA** [*El mundo alucinante*], p. 210). Though women are plentiful, sailors cruelly attack a young girl, enjoying her body and insulting her over and over: "they threw themselves on one, almost a child, and waited turns to enjoy her body, insulting her again and again" (**EMA,** pp. 50-51).

Arenas repeats, in his self-justification, that women really like and even demand phallic attention. Lady Hamilton needs three men at one time to satisfy her sexual fires, and the protagonist jumps into the water, preferring to be fish food rather than "serve two capricious women" (**EMA,** pp. 153ff). A group of naked women attack Fray Servando and undress him, but he resists. Servando's guide, on the other hand, possesses one woman after another, pointing out their self-destructive urges, finishing as "one who has fulfilled a painful duty . . . they are now satisfied and will not need me for a while" (**EMA,** pp. 84-87). Madame de Staël refuses to accept the priest's negation of her lustful needs (**EMA,** p. 128). Even the naked queen tells him: "But undress, man. Let's see if you really are . . . And thus, after feeling me up without result, the woman went off, laughing herself silly" (**EMA,** p. 99). Meanwhile, sexually satiated, Madame Recamier smiled "like a satisfied mare" (**EMA,** p. 125).

Similar scenes are endlessly repeated in all of Arenas's works. In *El palacio de las blanquisimas mofetas* the women are dying to have intercourse with a man, and Adolfina rushes out to "look for one who, although it might be for just a few minutes, would justify her whole existence" (**PBM,** p. 34). In **"A la sombra de la mata de almendras"** the women signal their readiness to the males. An enormous man violates one from behind without her crying out. As the author-protagonist exclaims in wonder: "They rape her on a full bus, and she doesn't even protest" (**TED,** p. 79). In *La vieja Rosa* the heroine falls asleep each night with "the image of that phallus, erect, swaying in the twilight." Later she stretches her hand out and "was in ecstasy, her hand touching that marvelous region, and had the noises of

the night subsided for a moment, she could have listened to the growing agitation of her blood" (**TED,** pp. 36-38). In *El central* the onlookers admire the adolescent who "fondles his testicles" in contrast to "a woman, a desperate hole which supurates, which cringes, which agitates asking for it with shouts . . ."[11]

To satisfy his belief in his own phallic power, the male protagonist in each case accepts the myth of female phallic worship (with a concomitant castration anxiety about the *vagina dentata*), a screen for his own real or imagined phallic deficiencies. Hypermanliness, together with a glorification of phallic puissance, have been standard components for a number of years in the contemporary Spanish American novel.[12]

In *El mundo alucinante,* where the author relates the size of the male organ to the pleasure given the woman, a priest, Terencio, possesses a truly monumental structure over which the noble ladies fight: "the father, completely naked and sweating, with his penis stiffer than a rock and pointing like a yardstick, passing among those ladies kneeling in a circle, and without stopping reciting his prayers in Latin . . . They looked at him in ecstasy and at each moment their faces reflected their anxiety and lust . . . while his organ acquired incredible proportions . . . And the ladies, desperate and with their hands clasped, kneeled at the priest's feet. And then the priest took that excessively developed part and with two hands began to introduce it with effort into the mouth of each kneeling lady . . . who in an attitude of complete adoration and idolatry kissed it, joyfully swallowing its entire length, which the priest withdrew at once in order to continue to satisfy . . . the ladies who grew desperate for the arrival of their own turn" (**EMA,** p. 74). This scene, aside from the blasphemy of the sacrament of the Eucharist, shows clearly the phallic worship, a common denominator among Arenas's women characters.

In evoking the Indian brought to Spain by Columbus, Arenas comments specifically: "beautiful the piece of the antipode which, cylindrical and shining, hangs there." And the queen, thanking the Admiral for his gift of multicolored parrots, looked "at that hanging proportion, so shining. And those muscles" (**EC** [*El central*], p. 13). Wherever seen, the phallus is something to admire and to be jealous of: "that prominent muscle which grew erect, brilliant, between the legs of the man" (*La vieja Rosa, TED,* p. 34). It has been said that women, keepers of the hearth, were anatomically incapable of extinguishing fire as a man does—by urination. And in those ancient primitive times, given the phallic shapes of the flame, the fire keepers experienced erotic feelings as if in a homosexual contest.[13]

Similarly, the phallus is glorified and is omnipresent in Arenas's novels to the dismay of the women who feel their phallic deficiency. He uses phallic equivalents throughout in explicit and implicit sexual situations, a quince stick, umbrellas, brooms, bottles, fish, rats, a hat, and trees in *El mundo alucinante;* lizards, rats, and trees in *Celestino antes del alba;* birds (a popular name for the phallus in several languages) and trees in *El palacio de las blanquisimas mofetas;* and rats (on which the author seems to have a fixation) and trees in his collection of short stories, *Termina el desfile.*

Although Priapean glorification is one of the leitmotifs of Arenas's works, the accompanying fears of castration seem even more abundantly present in relationship to threats from both the father and the mother figure. Arenas shares Ernesto Sábato's belief that during intercourse the woman, by retaining the semen, becomes a full person but the man, through his loss, suffers "separation, splitting, disorientation."[14] The protagonists dread the female genital and the phallic female, who by incorporating the penis makes it one with herself, especially if she bites off the male organ, a favorite part for incorporation. We see here the influence of an early genital stage of development involved in the acquisition of a female role, though castration anxiety may also represent a post-phallic restructuring of libidinal components. In any event, according to Otto Fenichel, if the passive feminine fantasy of the fear of castration is strong it may override and repress erotic interest in the opposite sex, leaving homosexual objects as the only safe ones.[15]

Arenas displays an infinite variety of these fantasies. In *Celestino antes del alba* a spider is the castrating female;[16] buzzards constantly threaten the boy (*CA* [*Celestino antes del alba*], p. 110); and the mother repeatedly attacks him with a club, penetrating him with it on several occasions (*CA*, pp. 26-28; 78). The mother in *La vieja Rosa* is a destroyer. Finding her son in a homosexual relationship, she attempts to shoot him with a gun which explodes in her hands as she thinks of "that region of the body where man shows his virility . . . that cursed region . . ." (*TED*, pp. 72-73). In *El mundo alucinante* the Indians come to render homage to an idol "Our Mother," a place where the priests extract hearts. In *El central,* the jealous wife, at the moment of her husband's ejaculation, grabs his organ to see the amount of semen ejected. The husband lets himself be handled. When she discovers his infidelity she approaches him with a large knife, and he, as usual, unbuttons his fly; but instead of castrating him she commits suicide by plunging the knife into her own abdomen (*EC*, pp. 71-73).

Fray Servando throughout *El mundo alucinante* is wrapped in chains and imprisoned in jails, narrow tunnels, or other enclosed spaces from which he escapes or is expelled. Fog, twilight, shadow are associated with his incarcerations, and his flights take place in darkness,

his hallucinatory reality.[17] In one episode, Fray Servando meets Borunda in a cave filled with bats which fly in and out of his mouth. Borunda was like a great moving barrel: "he opened his mouth wider and put my entire head therein . . ." (*EMA,* pp. 32-33). In "Bestial entre las flores" the protagonist "turns into a plant which the grandmother ('mother and grandmother were terribly similar') pulls out by the roots and swallows whole" (*TED,* pp. 120-23; 142). The latent womb fantasies and accompanying castration fears seem quite obvious.[18]

In *Celestino antes del alba,* the grandfather threatens the boy constantly with his axe, and cuts down the trees (which the boy relates to himself) where Celestino produced his writing (semen), [*CA,* p. 20], promoting a later fantasy of putting out his grandfather's (father's) eyes.[19] Throughout, destroying trees is equated with the loss of an erection. In *El palacio de las blanquisimas mofetas* the protagonists poetically evoke trees and tree trunks as their totemic projections, trees constantly uprooted and threatened: "What damage can that poor little tree have done them? But the fact is that only knowing that I loved it was enough for those cursed folk to want to pull it out by the roots" (*PBM,* p. 66).

To wish to be eaten or possessed by menacing animals may also represent a death fantasy which is equally equated with castration. According to Ernest Jones, dread of death clinically involves repressed death wishes against loved objects: "Themes of death and castration . . . are extremely closely associated and . . . anxiety concerning indefinite survival of the personality constantly expresses the fear of a punitive impotence."[20] Flugel, as previously stated, points out that childhood dreams involving threats by animals almost invariably represent the father. These animal agressions abound to an obsessive degree in Arenas's work where a variety of animals (elephants, crabs, lizards, snakes) attack and bite.[21] In *El mundo alucinante,* Fray Servando suffers phallic attacks by rats, which with birds and fish are the most common aggressors in Arenas's works. In one incident the rats eat his hat, and he has to beat them off with sticks (p. 56).[22] In another episode, he sees a priest-rat who "had an erection so large that it seemed he had a third leg" (pp. 63-64). His fears of being raped are somewhat relieved when he realizes it is only a man with an umbrella. Fray Servando, who himself becomes a fish, also is attacked by fish and sharks: "ready to devour whatever presented itself to them" (p. 53). In *Celestino antes del alba* fish "squeeze the protagonist's neck and tear out his tongue" (p. 200), which allows him to fall into a deep sleep.[23] In **"Los heridos"** a band of lecherous buzzards attempts to devour Reinaldo (*TED,* p. 97), and in *Celestino antes del alba* the boy kills a bird that is putting holes in his trees (p. 135) and defends himself from some buzzards (p. 200).

Of course Arenas, through his protagonist Fortunato, suffers direct attacks against his gentialia, as he is tortured in jail and violated by "men expert in raping men" (**PBM,** p. 236). Arenas also describes a number of explicit homosexual situations. In **La vieja Rosa** "the two boys almost naked were kissing each other in the center of the room. Then they fell, like one single body, on the bed" (**TED,** p. 68). The hallucinated Fray Servando, constantly protesting his sexual purity and abstinence, has direct homosexual encounters with Borunda, Father Terencio, Orlando, and the poet Heredia as well as a peripheral one, as a child, with his professor who "wanted to put the lighted quince stick in my mouth to shut me up . . ." Servando escapes by running off among the tree trunks and yelling for his mother (**EMA,** p. 12).

Arenas is a survivor, perpetually struggling for freedom, a concept associated with his writing and his homosexuality and involving fluctuation between passivity and rebellion against the anonymous forces which constantly circumscribe him. In one sense his work, a transparent metaphor for contemporary Cuba, shows how he associates his homosexuality with a thrust for political, social, and sexual liberty, much as Fray Servando is willing to sacrifice all for the cause of independence. Fortunato, ambitious to be a writer, utilizes words to "open fabulous enclosures . . . transport him . . . He was a monster, an artist, a God" (**PBM,** pp. 161-62). Celestino writes on trees, which, as we have seen, his grandfather attempts to cut down with his axe. Writing, words, and ambition to write may indeed be a urethral character trait and may be equated with orgasm and the Oedipus complex.[24] In truth, both the Cuba of his childhood and of Castro left a bad taste in Arenas's mouth, and some of his hallucinatory scenes seem to represent his ambivalence about putting into words the anxieties and fears already alluded to. Thus, Fray Servando, attacked by hungry, biting, castrating rats, uses their gleaming eyes as the light by which he is able to write (**EMA,** p. 54).

In conclusion it may be said that Arenas creates a series of almost mythical, illusory worlds, but his magic realism and metaphoric visions include, in some form, his exterior world of Cuba together with disguised relationships between symbol and meaning at unconscious levels, a process through which the Cuban author reveals his anxiety and need for love and acceptance, which, unfortunately, neither society nor his family ever gave him.

Notes

1. Karl Abraham: *Dreams and Myths: A Study in Race Psychology,* tr. William A. White (New York: Journal of Nervous and Mental Diseases Publishing Comp., 1919), p. 4.

2. Reinaldo Arenas: *El palacio de las blanquisimas mofetas* (Caracas: Monte Avila, Editores, 1980), pp. 49-50. Further citations in the text are hereafter recorded as *PBM*.

3. John Flugel: *The Psychoanalytic Study of the Family* (London: The Hogarth Press, 1972), pp. 139-40.

4. *Selected Papers of Karl Abraham,* tr. Douglas Bryan and Alix Strachew (New York: Basic Books, 1968), pp. 288ff.

5. John Flugel: op. cit., p. 53.

6. Ernest Jones: *Hamlet and Oedipus* (New York: Doubleday, 1954), p. 89.

7. Reinaldo Arenas: *Termina el desfile* (Barcelona: Seix Barral, 1981), p. 11.

8. Karl Abraham: *On Character and Libido Development* (New York: W. W. Norton and Co., 1966), pp. 87-88.

9. Reinaldo Arenas: *El mundo alucinante* (Buenos Aires: Editorial Tiempo Contemporáneo), p. 162. Further references to this edition are hereafter cited as *EMA*.

10. See Bertram D. Lewin: "Phobic Symptoms and Dream Interpretation," *Selected Writings of Bertram D. Lewin,* ed. Jacob A. Arlow (New York: *The Psychanalytic Quarterly,* 1973), pp. 208ff., for a further clarification of this point.

11. Reinaldo Arenas: *El central* (Barcelona: Seix Barral, 1981), pp. 24-25. Further citations are listed as *EC*.

12. For a discussion of this point and phallic size in José Lezema Lima's *Paradiso* (1966), Gabriel Garcia Márquez's *Cien anos de soledad* (1967), and Carlos Fuentes's *Cambio de piel* (1967), and in other novels, see Kessel Schwartz, "Sexism in the Spanish American Novel (1965-75)", *The Pacific Quarterly* (October, 1980), 522-29

13. See Henri F. Ellenberger: *The Discovery of the Unconscious* (New York: Basic Books, 1970), p. 529.

14. Ernesto Sábato: *Obras, Ensayos* (Buenos Aires: Losada, 1970), p. 326.

15. Otto Fenichel: *The Psychoanalytic Theory of Neurosis* (New York: W. W. Norton, 1945), pp. 328-41.

16. Reinaldo Arenas: *Celestino antes del alba* (Caracas: Monte Avila, Editores, 1980), pp. 77-78. Further citations in the text are referred to as *CA*.

17. Karl Abraham: *Selected Papers,* p. 203, relates darkness and womb fantasies, and as a symbol of the mother it may mean both birth and death.

18. See Lewin: "The Body as Phallus," *Selected Writings,* pp. 28-47; *The Psychoanalysis of Elation* (New York: W. W. Norton & Co., 1950), pp. 107-108; and "The Theory of Oral Erotism," *Selected Writings,* pp. 130-33.

19. Karl Abraham: *Selected Papers,* p. 180, notes that impaling a body or putting out an eye signifies castration of the genital. As previously noted, the mother constantly impales the boy on her club.

20. Ernest Jones: "The Psychology of Religion," *Psychoanalysis Today,* ed. Sandor Lorand (New York: International University Press, 1944), pp. 315-25.

21. For examples of these attacks see, "El reino Alipio" (*TED,* pp. 102-03), where the trampling and goring by cows are directly associated with a pool of semen; *Celestino antes del alba,* where lizards of varying sizes "bite him," p.220; and *El mundo alucinante,* where the protagonist is attacked by a crab, pp. 44-45.

22. Sigmund Freud: "A Connection Between a Symbol and a Symptom" *The Standard Edition of the Complete Psychological Works of Freud* (London: The Hogarth Press, 1956-66), I, p. 242 and XIV, p. 339, equates the hat with the genital, usually the male organ.

23. Melanie Klein equates fish attacks with an assault on the father's organ; see, *The Psychoanalysis of the Child* (London: The Hogarth Press, 1949), p. 211; Carl Jung, on the other hand, though accepting them as a libido symbol, states that they are not always phallic; see, *Psychology of the Unconscious* (New York: Dodd, Mead, and Co., 1944), p. 223.

24. See Lewin: "The Body as Phallus," pp. 28-47.

Jorge Olivares (essay date autumn 1985)

SOURCE: Olivares, Jorge. "Carnival and the Novel: Reinaldo Arenas' *El palacio de las blanquísimas mofetas.*" *Hispanic Review* 53, no. 4 (autumn 1985): 467-76.

[*In the following essay, Olivares explores the carnivalesque form and content of Arenas's novel* The Palace of the White Skunks.]

The first thing that disconcerts the reader of Reinaldo Arenas' third novel is its title, **El palacio de las blanquísimas mofetas,** for one does not associate skunks with novels and much less with palaces.[1] The placement of the noun "mofetas" at the very end flaunts a semantic incongruence that travesties the expected alignment of relevance among the words in the title. The components of the title seem to be out of control; there is a discontinuity of the chain of signifiers, for part A (the

palace) and part B (the skunks) are not semantically related. The adjective "blanquísimas" also contributes to the reader's uneasiness, not only for its hyperbolic denotation, but also because of the oxymoronic quality of the combination "blanquísimas mofetas." Although skunks can have a white stripe or white spots, a completely white skunk is nonexistent; thus, Arenas' "palacio" is inhabited by unreal beings, and, as a result of this takeover of the palace by the "blanquísimas mofetas," simultaneous upward and downward movements are suggested: as owners of the palace, the skunks have moved up in life, both literally (palaces are usually found on high places and skunks in subterranean caves) and figuratively (they have gained in stature, since they have replaced the aristocracy one would expect to find in such a place). At the same time, the high-sounding associations connected with the word "palacio" are defeated or downgraded when the identity of its inhabitants is revealed. This vertical trajectory, which occurs on biological, social, and topographical levels, is accompanied by an equally interesting horizontal trajectory. There is a descending backward movement as one goes from the palace at the head of the title (palaces are associated with the upper body, usually the heart and the mind)[2] to the skunks at the end, for they are animals that bring to mind the lower body, since they are mostly known for the unpleasant smell of the liquid that their anal glands produce and eject as a defense mechanism in the face of danger. Thus, Arenas' title can be said to trace a symbolic body, with its upper receiving end and its corresponding discharging orifice.

Because of its many suggestive connotations, **El palacio de las blanquísimas mofetas** is, then, more than a title on the cover of a novel. In its intermingling of hyperbole, oxymoron, and fantasy, the title reveals a ludic spirit that can be assimilated to the carnival topos of the *mundus inversus.* As Julia Kristeva has pointed out, carnivalesque structure is antirationalist and its discourse "breaks through the laws of a language censored by grammar and semantics."[3] But as Kristeva herself, Mikhail Bakhtin, and others have lucidly argued, carnival in literature entails more than linguistic anarchy. Mapping the carnival world of Rabelais, Bakhtin writes: "We find here a characteristic logic, the peculiar logic of the 'inside out' (à l'envers), of the 'turnabout,' of a continual shifting from top to bottom, from front to rear, of numerous parodies and travesties, humiliations, profanations, comic crownings, and uncrownings."[4] A systematic inversion on a number of levels, carnival discourse is, in sum, a violation of established norms on both the plane of expression and the plane of content.[5] As we shall see, the carnival spirit of Arenas' title is passed on to the novel: the trenchant smell of the skunks penetrates the text.

I should like to begin my analysis at the end—with the "Índice" that closes the text, and which I reproduce below:

Although the "Índice" at first seems to be a traditional table of contents of a tripartite novel, a closer analysis reveals its festive departure from the norm. "Primera Parte" consists of a relatively short section entitled "Prólogo y epílogo." Just as experience has shown us that skunks and palaces do not go together, literary tradition has established that prologues and epilogues, although parts of the same textual body, are to be found at opposite ends of the text. Arenas, however, persists in creating paradoxical monstrosities: the syntactic union of "prólogo" and "epílogo" with the copulative conjunction "y" produces an antithetical division heading that cannot help but startle the reader. More importantly, this coupling effects a temporal transgression that eliminates all sense of chronology: the beginning and the end are one and the same. Hence causality/linearity has been replaced by simultaneity. "Segunda Parte" has six sections: the first bears the title "Hablan las criaturas de queja" and the other five are called "agonías." By using such peculiar terms as "queja" and "agonías" to name these sections, Arenas insists on departing from traditional nomenclature, and these words suggest as well a carnivalesque litany of complaints that is graphically shown with the repetitive enumeration of the parts, since every chapter reiterates the term "agonía": "primera agonía," "segunda agonía," "tercera agonía," "cuarta agonía," "quinta agonía." With the presence of a "sexta agonía" in "Tercera Parte," a continuity is only deceptively suggested because the reader is once again thrown off balance with the other section, a "función," which will turn out to be a phantasmagoric theatrical representation whose performers are the characters of the novel reenacting their own lives and obsessions. The line of demarcation between illusion and reality, art and life, actors and spectators, novel and theater is erased. Thus, with the insertion of a play within the novel, Arenas pledges once more his allegiance to the liberating aesthetics of carnival. Itself a kind of collage, a compilation of incongruous elements, the "Índice" duplicates the linguistic playfulness of the title. But there is more. The "Índice" does not fulfill its traditional purpose, that is, to "indicate" the contents of the novel, for it does not mention some divisions in the text. It excludes three brief essays, one at the end of each part, which discuss the characteristics of the fly. Although thematically these short sections are not related to the plot of the novel, their omission from the "Índice" can be interpreted as one more festive deviation from established literary norms. But perhaps it is also possible to clear this messy table of contents by venturing that Arenas chooses to expound on the fly because this insect is easily associated with the carnival spirit. It is a prolific animal that is at home in sewers and around putrid flesh, and—as we are told—"conoce el secreto de las levitaciones y camina de *patas para arriba* aferrada al cielorraso" (p. 396; my italics). This bit of zoological information, placed strategically at the end of the novel, names the carnival logic that produced the text, especially when we recall that the name in Spanish for the topos of inversion is *mundo patas arriba,* words used in the quoted passage.

Just as the flies were not allowed on the table (of contents), the palace and the skunks were kept out of the novel.[6] But if there is no palace, there is a humble house in Holguín, a small city in the Oriente province of Cuba. And if there are no skunks, there are some quite eccentric characters: the protagonist, Fortunato, an adolescent who tries, unsuccessfully, to join Castro's revolutionary forces to escape from the "bestias," as he calls his family; Fortunato's unwed mother now working as a maid in New York; Onérica, whose letters no one reads; Celia, a crazy aunt, who only thinks about her daughter Esther, who poisoned herself at thirteen; another aunt, Digna, who cannot forget the husband who abandoned her and left her with two mischievous children—Tico and Anisia—who spend their days playing cruel games and telling each other riddles; still another aunt, Adolfina, who burns herself to death after her last futile attempt to lose her virginity during a nocturnal quest for men; and, finally, the two grandparents: Jacinta, who blasphemes and prays with equal ease, and whose verbal outbursts contrast with the self-inflicted silence of her husband Polo, a Spanish immigrant whose dreams of fortune were gradually shattered.

This short summation shows us another way in which *El palacio de las blanquísimas mofetas* exhibits a carnival logic; it does so in the form of a family saga that lacks the authoritative presence of its founding member—the patriarchal figure. Tico, Anisia, and Esther have been abandoned by their respective fathers; Fortunato is illegitimate; and Polo, the only father in the house, loses control over his progeny. Polo's passive role is responsible for the dissolution of the dynastic hierarchy; as the king or any other figure of authority during carnival, Polo lets himself be uncrowned by his subjects (his wife, daughters, and grandchildren). The house, as a result, becomes a carnival stage where fantastic occurrences, unruliness, profanations, eccentricity, incestuous drives, and insistence on physiological impulses and needs (such as Jacinta's compulsive defecation and Adolfina's lubricity) are the standard of behavior.

With the disintegration of the family unit crumbles what Patricia Tobin has called the "genealogical imperative," the equation in the family saga between the narrative line and the dynastic line.[7] In *El palacio de las blanquísimas mofetas,* paternal and narrative authority is replaced by familial and textual anarchy: there is no father to enforce obedience and there is equally no central authorial voice to beget a coherent, continuous text. The plot does not unfold as a controlled succession of events, but as a fragmented and temporally disjointed recording of voices, mostly the "quejas" of the characters. There is a basic narrator who surfaces sporadically, but who does not orient the reader. Because of its lack of a privileged authorial presence, Arenas' novel promotes a struggle between itself and the reader to make the text intelligible.

However, the frequent fantastic or irrational occurrences are not an obstacle for grasping the intelligibility of the narrative because the reader submits to a suspension of disbelief as soon as he reads the first few lines:

> La muerte está ahí en el patio, jugando con el aro de una bicicleta. En un tiempo esa bicicleta fue mía. En un tiempo eso que ahora no es más que un aro sin llanta fue una bicicleta nueva.
>
> Y yo me paseaba en ella por toda la calle de la loma colorada.
>
> Y yo me despetroncaba en la bicicleta.
>
> (p. 9)

Although this is an "unreal" occurrence, the reader can apprehend what is happening: Death, personified, is playing with a bicycle wheel. But who is this person whose bike's wheel is now Death's toy? In other words, who speaks? When does this person speak? Where does this person speak from? After reading all of Part One, these questions remain unanswered and others are raised. The following excerpt is also from this section of the novel, when Fortunato describes the behavior of some of his relatives:

> Con ocho patas, un diente de oro y un narigón en el rabo. El viejo se ha quedado dormido. La vieja se aburre de rezar y se acuesta. No acertaste, no acertaste: pensaba en una jicotea con ocho patas, un diente de oro, un narigón en el rabo y una estaca clavada en mitad del carapacho. Qué barbaridad, es que tú piensas cada cosa. A ver, ahora te toca adivinar a ti. Adolfina entra en el baño y tranca la puerta. En el baño está la

botella de alcohol. Adolfina, que no se olvida de nada, lleva los fósforos bajo las tetas. Yo ya no sé qué hacer con mi vida. Yo sí que ya no sé qué hacer con mi vida. Querido hijo, son mis deseos al recibo de esta carta te encuentres bien. Adolfina se quita la ropa y se mete en la bañadera. Adolfina se mira en el espejo y grita. Y no grita. Y grita. Qué se puede esperar de una familia de isleños. Qué se puede esperar de quien vive entre bestias. Nada, nada se puede esperar. Todo, todo se puede esperar. Adolfina empieza a bailar desnuda en la bañadera. Qué ves. Qué ves. Veo a una araña ahogándose dentro de una bañadera seca. No seas bobo, dime la verdad, ¿qué ves? Veo a una bruja jugando con una araña dentro de la bañadera. Guanajo, siempre me estás diciendo mentiras. Salgo hoy más temprano que nunca para el jial. Misael desnudo debajo de una mata de jía, me espera.

Misael desnudo.

Misael desnudo.

Misael desnudo.

Dios mío. Hijo de la Gran Puta. Dios mío. Dios. No creo en ti, pero me burlo de ti. Si existes, por qué no te acercas. Acércate, cabrón, para partirte la cara de una sola trompada.

(pp. 11-12)

With the privilege of hindsight, the reader is able to discern that onto Fortunato's narration of the goings-on of his family are grafted riddles of his cousins Tico and Anisia, Adolfina's grumblings as she prepares her suicide, excerpts from a letter Onérica has written to her son, Onérica's recollection of her seduction by Misael, and Jacinta's blasphemies. The narrative fabric of this fragment is representative of the totality of *El palacio de las blanquísimas mofetas,* for nominal elisions, the juxtaposition of incidents temporally and spatially unrelated to produce a sense of simultaneity, shifts in perspective, and polyphony are the narrative strategies that prevail throughout the novel.

Arenas wants to give a comprehensive picture of what it was like to be a poor family in Holguín in the 1950's, but he refrains from allowing his basic narrator to inform the reader overtly from the beginning about the characters or even to situate the action of the novel within its natural temporal flow and historical context. However, the text does provide clues that allow the reader to orient himself. When the reader, for example, encounters early on in the novel the verb "alzarse" (a term that acquired special significance in the Cuban slang of the middle and late 1950's), he immediately understands that Fortunato's desire is to join Castro's revolution. Thus, as the reader approaches *El palacio de las blanquísimas mofetas,* he is gradually given information—partial information at times—that provides him with the needed competence to apprehend, by reflexive reference, the totality of the text. Indeed, by the book's end, the characters and their destinies are clearly identified, but the chronological sequence of events is not totally delineated due to the temporal dislocations of the story line and the absence of precise temporal references. Spatial logic is favored over temporal logic; hence the use of the spatializing technique of fragmentation, resulting in a paratactic plot in which events are juxtaposed without explicit connections being drawn.

I shall illustrate this technique with what I consider the novel's two most memorable episodes for their carnivalesque mixture of humor and pathos: one is Fortunato's departure to Velasco and his return to Holguín a few days later to steal a rifle from a soldier and thus be able to join the ranks of the revolution; the other is Adolfina's night in the town and her virginal return home. Most of the "quinta agonía" consists of the pendular narration of these characters' respective quests; and, although aware that Fortunato left home some days before Adolfina's special evening, the reader is deceived by this narrative strategy and senses a feeling of simultaneity. Moreover, emphasis is placed on the rain that falls on both Fortunato and Adolfina, a fact that insinuates that the adolescent returns to Holguín the same evening that his aunt is searching for male companionship. Also, for more apparent chronological precision, a soldier's passing reference to the weather forecast (p. 334) when Adolfina attempts to strike up a conversation brings to the reader's mind a newspaper clipping of December 14, 1958 (grafted on the text just a few pages before) which predicts rain the next day (p. 321). These oblique references to the simultaneity of the two quests (i.e., that both occur on December 15, 1958) seem to be reaffirmed a few pages later when Fortunato, as he is tortured by the soldiers who apprehended him during his attempt to steal the rifle, reminds himself that it is the middle of December (p. 393). But there is a temporal contradiction in that same scene, for he also says that it is mid 1958 (p. 384), hence May, June or July, but definitely not December.

Two related explanations can be offered for this contradictory usage of temporal references: 1) Arenas demonstrates once more that *El palacio de las blanquísimas mofetas* can be placed within the festive spirit of carnival with its all-embracing freedom; and 2) he resorts to this temporal play to suspend time. Arenas is, as it were, telling the reader that time is unimportant, that existence should be viewed as an "eternal present":[8] simultaneity dethrones succession or, as Bakhtin would say, carnival time replaces historical time.[9] Taking the cue from Adolfina, who, as she peruses a family photo album, fancies the abolition of time (p. 249), on can view Arenas' novel as an equally atemporal album with its anecdotally arranged pictures. In other words, as a "spatial novel,"[10] *El palacio de las blanquísimas mofetas* is structured on the principle of achrony, for a "chronological order yields to a morphological order."[11]

Repetition enhances the sense of spatiality and atemporality achieved by fragmentation. Events are narrated more than once—either by the same character or someone else—to reaffirm a conviction, to provide a contradictory version, to explain the impact of an event on different individuals, or to underscore a character's obsession. Arenas has produced, then, a text redundant because of its anaphoric structure; by utilizing anaphora, a rhetorical device that etymologically means "carrying back," as a stylistic and a structural feature of the text, Arenas is suspending time rhetorically. *El palacio de las blanquísimas mofetas* can be characterized as a static, spatial novel. This insistence on creating an atemporal space where simultaneity is the norm conforms with the agonistic situation of the characters. Life for them is a hell (allusions to hell abound in the text), a hell from which there is no escape. Suffering is eternal, and Arenas manages to capture this sense of eternal suffering with the *jeu sérieux*[12] of carnival discourse.

If the title provided us with an opening into the novel, it will also show us a way out. So far I have discussed, somewhat metaphorically, the "spatial" form of *El palacio de las blanquísimas mofetas.* But spatiality in this novel is suggested in another way: in its typography. The appearance and arrangement of the written word are the product of an architecturally oriented artist, of a writer who exploits the many possibilities of the blank page. With letters of different size and type, Arenas continuously breaks typographical conventions. He bifurcates the text into two adjacent columns; he inserts— usually to the left of the page—fragments of the story line, newspaper clippings, movie advertisements, beauty tips taken from popular magazines; he indents some narrative units more than others; he underscores word-play with geometric design. As a result, *El palacio de las blanquísimas mofetas* should not merely be read, but seen, for it is a visual text, a shaped text; it is—in short—a textual palace populated by contradictory beings who are the protagonists of eccentric actions, populated by unreal beings, nonexistent but *present:* white skunks. Thus, in spite of its apparent nonsensicalness, the title fits the novel just right: in Arenas' carnival world, the Jamesian house of fiction has become a palace of skunks.

Notes

1. Reinaldo Arenas, *El palacio de las blanquísimas mofetas* (Caracas, 1980). References to the novel will be made parenthetically within the text. Before the publication of its original Spanish version, Arenas' novel appeared first in French (1975) and in German (1977). *Celestino antes del alba* (1967; titled *Cantando en el pozo* in the definitive version of 1982), *El palacio de las blanquísimas mofetas* (1980) and *Otra vez el mar* (1982) constitute part of a projected "pentagonía." See Jorge

Olivares and Nivia Montenegro, "Conversación con Reinaldo Arenas," *Taller Literario,* 1, No. 2 (1980), 53-67.

2. J. E. Cirlot, *A Dictionary of Symbols,* trans. Jack Sage (London, 1962), p. 236.

3. Julia Kristeva, "Word, Dialogue, and Novel," in *Desire in Language,* ed. Leon S. Roudiez, trans. Thomas Gora, Alice Jardine, and Leon S. Roudiez (New York, 1980), p. 65.

4. Mikhail Bakhtin, *Rabelais and His World,* trans. Hélène Iswolsky (Cambridge, MA, 1968), p. 11.

5. Other studies on carnival that I have found useful include: Barbara Babcock-Abrahams, "The Novel and the Carnival World: An Essay in Memory of Joe Doherty," *MLN,* 89 (1974), 911-37; Bakhtin, *Problems of Dostoevsky's Poetics,* trans. R. W. Rotsel (Ann Arbor, MI, 1973), pp. 83-149; Laurent Jenny, "Le Discours du carnaval," *Lit,* 16 (1974), 19-36; Kristeva, *El texto de la novela,* trans. Jordi Llovet (Barcelona, 1974), pp. 227-48; Emmanuel Le Roy Ladurie, *Carnival in Romans,* trans. Mary Feeney (New York, 1979).

6. Within the novel there is only one reference to the title. The dead Esther, alluding to her family, says to Fortunato: "Nos elevamos y nos elevamos, hasta que creemos estar elevados, y caemos, como siempre, en el Palacio de las Blanquísimas Mofetas, donde todos, alineados en el gran salón y provistos de largas garrotas, nos están aguardando. Caemos, en fin, en los brazos de las bestias, que, como nos consideran irrecuperables, ya casi nos empiezan a tomar cariño" (pp. 257-58). In the interview cited in note 1, Arenas says of the title: "Bueno, eso es completamente irónico, agresivo y burlesco. Porque no hay palacio y porque no hay mofetas blanquísimas" (p. 64).

7. Patricia Drechsel Tobin, *Time and the Novel. The Genealogical Imperative* (Princeton, 1978).

8. I borrow this phrase from Jean Ricardou, "Composition Discomposed," *CritI,* 3 (1976), 86.

9. Bakhtin, *Problems,* p. 147 *et passim.*

10. For the concept of "spatiality" in literature I have consulted: Joseph Frank, "Spatial Form in the Modern Novel," *Critiques and Essays on Modern Fiction 1920-1951,* ed. John W. Aldridge (New York, 1952), pp. 43-66; Joseph Frank, "Spatial Form: An Answer to Critics," *CritI,* 4 (1977), 231-52; Eric S. Rabkin, "Spatial Form and Plot," *CritI,* 4 (1977), 253-70; William Holtz, "Spatial Form in Modern Literature: A Reconsideration," *CritI,* 4 (1977), 271-85; Frank Kermode, "A Reply to Joseph Frank," *CritI,* 4 (1978), 579-88.

11. Ricardou, "Composition . . . ," p. 86.

12. Babcock-Abrahams, "The novel . . . ," p. 920.

Kate Mehuron (essay date April 1994)

SOURCE: Mehuron, Kate. "Queer Territories in the Americas: Reinaldo Arenas' Prose." *Prose Studies* 17, no. 1 (April 1994): 39-63.

[*In the following essay, Mehuron examines how the "homosexual prose" in Arenas's autobiography,* Before Night Falls, *functions to critique both Fidel Castro's "homophobic political regime" and U.S. urban gay culture.*]

> In Argentina [Friar Servando] was sold to a circus manager, who then took him off to Buenos Aires and exhibited him as a victim of the Inquisition. At the end of the last century this same mummy was shown in Belgium, at one of the grander circuses there. In fact his remains never knew the repose they deserved.
>
> Reinaldo Arenas, *Hallucinations*[1]

In *Hallucinations,* we learn that despite the mountains of historical material which Reinaldo Arenas collected about the Friar's life, he has discovered that he and the Friar are the same person. Arenas makes this comment to the novel's narrator, Fray Servando, in the preface to his picaresque and parodic Cuban novel. He tells the Friar that although the Friar's memoirs appear as "fundamental parts" of *Hallucinations,* yet his memoirs no longer belong to him. They are "like all great and grotesque things the property of time, whose brutal passage will shortly make you two hundred years old."[2]

Arenas' memoir, *Before Night Falls* (*BNF*)[3] is also the property of time; a mummy which will not know repose for as long as it is sold and exhibited in the circuses of our literary marketplace. He began his memoir in Cuba and completed it in New York City shortly before he chose to die rather than to undergo more AIDS-related complications in 1990. His tragicomedic novel *The Doorman,* written in 1987 after Arenas' escape from Cuba in the 1980 Mariel emigration and during his exile in New York City, parodies the fetishized character of human (non)relations in urban North America and the prosaic, dispiriting *ethos* of the Cuban exile community in the United States.[4] As do most tragicomedies, his novel's derision masks yet displays Arenas' ambivalent grief occasioned by his irreparable, exilic separation from the Island.

Both Arenas' novel *The Doorman* and his memoir *Before Night Falls* are written in the United States subsequent to his emigration from Cuba. His work explores his own negotiation of liberty in the context of Cuban homophobia and political censorship, Cuban emigré anti-Castro movements in the US and North American leftist and gay liberation discourses. In this essay I will focus on Arenas' memoir *Before Night Falls* in order to underscore how Arenas' homosexual prose functions as a form of counter-memory to depict specific deployments of sexuality in the Americas by these political constituencies.[5] Arenas critiques Castro's homophobic political regime, neo-conservative anti-Castro emigré movements in the US, the consumerist *ethos* of North American urban gay culture, and the North American left's political myopia toward institutionalized homophobia. His critique is a provocation to US multicultural discourses to take account of the complex and often conflicting imbrications of queer nationalities, queer literary contributions, and queer political alliances in the Americas.[6]

Arenas' contribution to the queer literary imaginary in the Americas is enormous, and I can only briefly summarize the key elements of his fiction that will be appropriated by multicultural efforts to represent this imaginary. *Hallucinations* for example, exuberantly desacralizes the politically exploited, mythic links between Cuba's Roman Catholic Spanish colonial legacy and the heterosexist asceticism of the Castro regime. In *Hallucinations* as well as in his earlier novels *Singing From the Well* and *The Palace of the White Skunks,* the trope of cannibalism is ironically wielded to transvalue the North American and European imperialist connotations of barbarity and civilization.[7] His novels *Farewell to the Sea* and *The Palace of the White Skunks* offer exquisite explorations of the subjective and political topographies of compulsory heterosexuality.[8] These are topographies of the sexual self as it is truncated, manipulated, and punished by the militarist, authoritarian moral codes of the Castro regime and by the Cuban indigenous norms of *machismo* masculinity.[9] Both novels explore women's and queers' banned subjectivities. The results are politicized fictional representations of excessive, affective thresholds that have been prohibited from life and fiction by the regime's masculinist and heterosexist codes of familialism. The novels' comic irreverence toward the monologic landmarks of colonial monumental history and their incisive parodies effecting a heteroglossic sexual *ethos,* are types of literary levity which are only episodically revived in Arenas' memoir.[10] Without conceding to right-wing US propaganda, both Arenas' memoir *Before Night Falls* and his tragicomic novel *The Doorman* castigates the Stalinist character of Castro's revolutionary regime and the political myopia and crass opportunism of North American left and liberal appropriations of the regime's revolutionary propaganda. The memoir's more somber use of the trope of cannibalism performs a political critique of both the colonizing militarist discourse of the Cuban revolution, as well as of North American and European ideological consumption and idealization of the revolution.

THE NARRATED LIFE IN *BEFORE NIGHT FALLS*

Arenas represents his life through picaresque contours, resembling his fiction. He writes in his memoir that he joined the rebels without ideological intent, out of hunger and restlessness. A peasant and a rebel recruited into the Castroist military regime at the age of 16, Arenas manages to produce a literary corpus by a combination of good luck and intellectual acumen. The luck that instigates the series leading up to Arenas' friendship with the gay Cuban writers Lezama Lima and Virgilio Pinera is legendary.[11] It begins with his grandmother, who determinedly taught him to read.

His grandmother's guidance, the first in a long line of beneficent "witches" memorialized in *Before Night Falls,* is augmented by the gifted gradeschool teacher who holds weekend literary salons for the children and, later, the storytelling prize won with his short story **"The Empty Shoes"** at the National Library during the Castro regime. This success is magnified by the fortuitous transfer arranged for him by the Paris-educated lesbian founder and Director of the National Library in Havana, Maria Teresa Freyre de Andrade. Arenas' labor is transformed from an accountancy at the National Institute for Agrarian Reform, to his clerkship at the National Library, during which time he wrote *Singing from the Well, Hallucinations,* and *The Palace of the White Skunks* (1963-70). He meets the French painter Jorge Comacho and his wife Margarita at an artists' exhibition. For the duration of his persecution in Cuba, they send French acquaintances on tour to Cuba who smuggle his manuscripts and letters out of Cuba and into the hands of French publishers. In this way *Farewell to the Sea* (1982), rewritten three times as a result of its destruction by Cuban State Security, finally escapes the island and is also published abroad.

The Cuban state's propagandist and militarist manipulation of sexuality is crucial to understanding Arenas' queer literary challenge, found both in *Before Night Falls* and in his novels. In **"The Closest Attention: Gays in Cuba,"** written for the *New York Native* shortly after his emigration to the US, Arenas explains this manipulation by listing the five most repressive laws in Cuba which result in "forcing the Cuban gay into prison, towards sucide or insanity, or into attempting a desperate escape." All of the laws are vaguely worded prohibitions on social characteristics of individuals which are deemed to be pathological; Arenas explains that the laws are used to criminalize those who fail to conform to the heterosexual familialism of the regime.[12] In his literary work, Arenas substitutes for Castro's repressive moralism a carnivalized peasant aesthetic of political scepticism and a voracious pansexuality which fuses hunger and sexual craving and extends this eroticism toward the whole of nature (*BNF* 118, 18-19).

The carnivalesque, as Bakhtin has shown, is a comic literary strategy by which to subvert the tyrannical effects of hierarchical social stratification on subjectivities and bodies.[13] Arenas' fiction and his memoir carnivalize the state's heterosexist and *macho* militarization of male bodies. Queer desire was represented as grotesque by Castro's declaration of the "socially pathological nature" of homosexuality at the 1971 First Congress of Education and Culture, and queer bodies are purged as filth from Castro's familialist body politic. By his literary use of the carnivalesque, Arenas transvalues the state's conflation of the monstrous with the queer. Through the ubiquity of images of pansexual voracity in his writing, Arenas rewrites the queer grotesque as "beauty," while demonstrating the monstrosity of the state's political doctrines and repressive reforms. He writes,

> A sense of beauty is always dangerous and antagonistic to any dictatorship because it implies a realm extending beyond the limits that a dictatorship can impose on human beings. Beauty is a territory that escapes the control of the political police. Being independent and outside of their domain, beauty is so irritating to dictators that they attempt to destroy it whichever way they can. Under a dictatorship, beauty is always a dissident force, because a dictatorship is itself unaesthetic, grotesque; to a dictator and his agents, the attempt to create beauty is an escapist or reactionary act.
>
> (*BNF* 87)

The opening passages of his memoir and all of his early fiction work to deterritorialize the queer body: a disengagement from the dictatorship's imposed aesthetic that criminalizes and expunges certain bodies. Beauty, or the transvaluated queer grotesque, is invented by Arenas' fluid literary boundaries between gendered subjectivities, between childhood and adult forms of consciousness, and the fusion of hunger and sexual voracity.

In *Before Night Falls,* Arenas deploys the carnivalesque to reinscribe a lyric pansexuality that resists the coercive deformations of masculinity wrought by the militarist, homophobic regime and by his *machismo* culture. However, it is more difficult for Arenas to preserve his novels' transformative levity in the face of the imprisonment, torture, and censorship which he literally endured. His fiction, also written during the life narrated in his memoir, provides the dialogical backdrop necessary for him to maintain his liberatory vision which the regime's punitive mechanisms would destroy.

In 1973, Arenas is arrested after hiding for several weeks from State Security in the bushes and ravines of Havana's Lenin Park. His arrest occurs after the Cuban Writers and Artists Union (UNEAC) report him to Castro's State Security as a "homosexual counterrevolutionary." He is imprisoned in El Morro, a medieval fortress at the Port of Havana which the Castro regime's State Security apparatus had converted into a prison; he undergoes torture and interrogation, finally signing a confession that admits he is a "counterrevolutionary." In his confession, he expresses regret at his ideological weakness shown in his published writings; admits that he detests his homosexuality; and admits that the Revolution had been extraordinarily fair to him. (*BNF* 204-5) Arenas describes the ethical humiliation, experienced when he "confessed" and was released from the same Cuban prison in which Fray Servando was detained,

> Needless to say, this only proves my cowardice, my weakness, the certainty that I am not the stuff of which heroes are made, and that fear, in my case, had won over moral principles. But I was comforted by the fact that in the communique I had written in Lenin Park to the International Red Cross, the UN, UNESCO, and many other organizations that never published it, I stated that my accusations against the regime of Fidel Castro were absolutely true to fact, even if at some point I denied them.
>
> (*BNF* 204)

The humiliating spectacle represented by Arenas of his coerced confession demonstrates the methods of terror by which the Cuban Revolution's propaganda trials twisted the anti-Castro accusations of Cuban indigenous intellectuals. In the context of terrorist distortions of testimony, writers who dare to defy the regime's official revolutionary discourse are heretics divested of the pure trappings of heroism. In Arenas' case, those trappings were attenuated by the contradiction of his communique's defiant accusations against the regime's censorship that were sent abroad before his arrest, and his "confession" extracted during interrogations while he was imprisoned. Despite the futility of heroism, Arenas exhorts other writers to take on a publicly heretical role in defiance of the monolithic rhetoric and Stalinist methods of confessions exacted by the regime. His suspicion toward and condemnation of Cuban literary critic Roberto Fernandez Retamar is motivated by this concern. Arenas calls Retamar a "sinister figure" in the Padilla trial, along with the regime's other official spokespersons of Cuban literary culture (*BNF* 146-7).

CULTURAL CANNIBALISM AS THE LATIN AMERICAN IMAGINARY

Arenas' counter-memories open up a queer-affirmative genealogy of the cannibal in Cuban literature. This is a genealogy that is historically intertwined with Afro-Carribean and Latin American literature in general. Arenas' prose contributes to the multicultural, transnational queer cultural movement which Cuban art critic Coco Fusco has called "an alliance based on a shared interest in cultural democracy."[14] His work furthers the literary debates about the de-colonization of the Latin American imaginary led by Cuban intellectuals such as Roberto Fernandez Retamar and Latin American scholars such as Emir Rodriguez Monegal.

In his memoir, Arenas notes the irony of having written an early novel about a heretical monk's imprisonment in the same fortress where he suffered detention, "Once [in prison] I decided that in the future I would be more careful about what I wrote, because I seemed destined to live through whatever I had written" (*BNF* 198). Emir Rodriguez Monegal comments on these passages from Arenas' *Hallucinations,* "It is possible that some of Friar Servando's misfortunes in his fight for freedom had uncomfortable implications from the standpoint of the Cuban government," and that since the publication of his second novel, "Arenas has become a nonperson in Cuba," who "has been conducting a private war—for the right of a novelist to follow where his creative inspiration leads him, for the freedom to write, one of Latin America's most contested rights."[15] With equal admiration, Arenas writes about Monegal, "[H]e was a great reader, and possessed the magical ability to instill the love of beauty in his students. He was the only Spanish-American professor in the United States who inspired a school of critical thought" (*BNF* 306).

Perhaps Arenas' praise is due partially to his knowledge of Monegal's earlier encomnium to him, yet the associations between the "love of beauty" throughout his memoir with his queer-affirmative resistance to authoritarian political discourses in general suggests more affinities than this. In his 1977 essay, "The Metamorphoses of Caliban," Monegal presents a brief overview of the centrality of Caliban in the European and Latin American literary imaginary, and a scathing criticism of Fernandez Retamar's approach to these matters in his 1971 essay, "Caliban: Notes Toward a Discussion of Culture in Our America."[16] Monegal places Retamar within a continuist framework of French political readings of *The Tempest* which serve, up through the twentieth century, French conservative and socialist political programs. Much of his criticism hinges on what he asserts to be Retamar's failure to critique a dichotomy that is implicit in nineteenth and twentieth century literary debates: the polarity between North American calibanesque capitalist, imperialist greed, and Latin American arielesque post-colonialist, yet Eurocentric utopias. Monegal accuses Retamar of glibly appropriating the French socialist identification with Caliban, for Latin American revolutionary consciousness. He castigates Retamar for what he takes to be Retamar's implicit racist and elitist assumptions that are also uncritically derived from Eurocentric sources.

Monegal proposes a "fresh insight" to move Latin American literary discourses beyond this polarity. He points literary theorists' attention toward the Brazilian poet and novelist Oswald de Andrade, whose "Manifesto Antropofago" (1928) parodically draws on Freud's theory of cannibalism as transformative assimilation in *Totem and Taboo,* and Nietzsche's figurative playfulness accompanying his transvaluation of values. According to Monegal, Andrade presents an iconoclastic and "truly" revolutionary vision of cultural cannibalism that can include erotic emancipation along with social and political change.[17] Monegal promises the "comic spirit" of Latin American culture to be as defiant toward Eurocentric values and categories as toward North American hegemonic values and economic systems. Noting that Andrade's manifesto came out in the same year as Bakhtin's book on Dostoevsky, Monegal urges that readers follow Andrade in envisioning the cannibal as a source of a Latin American carnivalesque that can yield social, political, and intellectual transformation. He credits the Cuban writer Severo Sarduy as the first to introduce Bakhtin's theories into Hispanic letters in 1972, and asks, "Yes, the question is still: Are we going to assume a Latin American identity just by aping the French intellectuals, or are we going to behave like the cannibals (cultural cannibals) we really are?"[18]

Monegal's note on Sarduy suggests that Sarduy's prose accomplishes more than a mere assimilation to French post-structuralist stylistics. He invites us to read Sarduy's queer post-structuralist experimentalism in terms of an intercultural exchange between French post-structuralist experimentation and Latin American indigenous literatures.[19] Although Monegal has not explicitly called for a queer aesthetic in the Americas, he helps prepare the way. The decolonizing cultural cannibalism which he promotes is synchronic with North American liberal gay critiques of homophobic, imperialist constructions of the cannibal as the alien "other" which is primitive, effeminate, and sodomic. In this regard, North American literary critic John Bergmann illustrates how "the closet" signifies through nineteenth and twentieth century literary representations of cannibalism; representations which substitute the masculinist aggressivity of the cannibal for the socially intolerable category of the queer. He argues that North American gay writers are beginning to transform "a representation that had been used to oppress them into one that in large measure is self-affirming."[20]

The Caliban debate has also been rewritten from the multicultural and feminist activist position of Miranda, such as that offered by Cuban art critic Coco Fusco in "El Diario de Miranda." She explains that Latin American leftist traditions are suspicious of the North American intercultural dynamic with Latin America; this is a suspicion based on "deeply ingrained universalist rhetoric and patriarchal and authoritarian tendencies," and an "old-school brand of Marxism" with "some kind of *machista* and Catholic resistance against taking radicalism into the privacy of the bedroom."[21] She argues that the intercultural appropriations of transnational feminist, gay and lesbian, Black and Chicano, AIDS, and multicultural activisms have dispensed with outworn nationalist paradigms in their shared interest and advocacy of cultural democracy. Liberal North American gay theory is compatible with Fusco's multicultural emphasis, for it sustains a critique of the social construction of North American white masculinity that is intertwined with hegemonic imperialist and homophobic subjectivities.

It is unlikely that Monegal intends these particular liberal critiques, which are strongly influenced by North American feminism, in his call for the "cultural cannibalism" of intercultural exchange between French poststructuralist transgendered literary play and Latin American prose. His primary concern is to formulate ways in which literature can resist the orthodoxies imposed by socialist or liberal political appropriations of its literary substance. However, Monegal's genealogical intervention strongly implies that "sexual emancipation" in a Latin American context ought to critique the Latin American cultural symbolics and institutionalization of compulsory heterosexuality, with the effect of legitimating queer sexualities. For him, the idol to be desacralized in the Latin American context are those "stiff, self-conscious and finally inauthentic one[s] produced by these black-painted Spanish American followers of Europe."[22] In other words, apologists for the sexual and intellectual repressiveness of the Castro regime such as Roberto Fernandez Retamar reinscribe retrogressive conservative values stretching back to Roman Catholic and Spanish colonialist domination, yet mask their oppressiveness by socialist revolutionary rhetoric and Eurocentric-elitist scholarly appropriations of the Caliban debate.[23]

Queer cultural cannibalism in the Americas is thus not a unitary referent but is fragmented by these political differences; in Arenas' case by his queer status as a "nonperson" within Castro's regime and his carnivalesque, indigenous peasant aesthetic. This aesthetic is occasionally at odds with the idealized, abstract versions of sexual egalitarianism which Arenas thought to permeate North American gay urban culture. His aesthetic is wielded against what he takes to be the prescriptive conformism that subtends all utopian representations of sexual pleasure and political well-being. He is emphatically critical of the curtailed liberties, social hypocrisies and betrayals that were the effect of the Cuban regime's deployment of the sexual code of *machismo,* as well as of the misogyny of the code itself. But he celebrates the queer sexual adventurism associated with this code in Cuban culture and reserves his criticisms for the intrusiveness of Cuban governmentality and its familialist deployment of sexual lives.

Arenas' carnivalesque peasant aesthetic sustains a neither/nor ideological stance with respect to North American leftist and liberal norms, and to European socialist and post-structuralist stances. His carnivalesque performs the work of cultural memory, retrieving much that has been effaced by authoritarian deployments of power through terror. His peasant aesthetic dramatizes

the raw hunger for food, the ferocious orality of need and freedom exercised by the basic irreverence of erotic conquest and poetic license. The experiential materials of this aesthetic, compounded by life under the dictatorships of Batista and Castro include the sterilization of the earth by one-crop economic policies; perpetual, gnawing hunger; dehumanized labor without end or reward by militarist labor recruitment policies; the absence (censorship) of literature; the death of private space by housing shortages and neighborhood surveillance mechanisms; the virtual shrinkage of future possibilities by imprisonment and torture in the Cuban State Security systems; and compulsory militarist masculinity exacted by the Castroist revolutionary legal and moral codes.

These are the material signifiers marking Arenas' prose with the social sign of the peasant and the anarchist. He uses tropes of celebratory homoerotic feasts to promote an aesthetic of survival and enjoyment: where there is material disenfranchisement there is commodity indifference and free imagination, where there is political doctrine there is political anarchism, where there are deliriums of erotic, poetic, and oral craving, there is sex and writing.

SEXUAL TERRITORIES

Arenas' homoerotic carnivalesque uses cannibalist representations to deterritorialize the militarized *machismo* body, and to desacralize various colonial and postcolonial cultural ideals concerning sexuality. During his clerkship at the National Library, a number of significant events etch a new gendered and sexual cartography of Cuba and bespeak the ethical relevance of Arenas' literary interventions.

Shortly after the United States' CIA-orchestrated assault on Playa Giron (Bay of Pigs, 1961), Castro announced the communist objectives of the new revolutionary government, organized the Integrated Revolutionary Organizations (ORI) that deployed Cuban youth in labor assignments, and the neighborhood Committees for the Defense of the Revolution (CDR) that deployed surveillance on "counterrevolutionary" Cubans up to the present. Censorship and unilateral control of the Cuban Press was imposed. The Federation of Cuban Women (FMC) was established and directed by Raul Castro's wife, Vilma Espin de Castro.[24] The Cuban literacy campaign began, as did socialist reforms of the domestic informal sector and of prostitution. Both campaigns continue to be promoted by feminist supporters as crucial to Cuban women's interests in the Revolution.[25] Castro openly castigated the "counterrevolutionary" character of homosexuals in his regime and to the North American press, rejecting any compatibility of homosexuality with revolutionary militancy.[26] Within the Cuban literary establishment, Castro disparaged as *maricones* ("effeminates") those writers who did not fight in the Revolution. When asked about the right of expression in Cuba, Castro's slogan was "Inside the revolution, everything, outside, nothing."[27]

Arenas writes about those times,

> In those days I endured all the prejudices typical of a macho society fired up by the Revolution. In that school, overflowing with virile militancy, there seemed to be no place for homosexuality, which, even then, was severely punished by expulsion and even jail. Nevertheless, homosexuality did occur among these young men . . . It was a sinister expulsion because it also included a dossier that would follow each person for the rest of his life and would bar him from admission to any other state school, and the state had started to control everything . . . I realized that being a "faggot" in Cuba was one of the worst disasters that could happen to anyone.
>
> (***BNF*** 48)

While the regime was codifying its homophobic moral codes and instituting domestic reforms on behalf of women, it also quashed dissent by specific constituencies of women. Historians document that in 1963 one of the last public protests in revolutionary Cuba before the Mariel emigration is quashed. The march was a peaceful protest by black housewives in Cardenas, accompanied by the slogans "Fidel, we want food" and "Down with communism," while banging on pots and pans. On Raul Castro's orders, General Osvaldo Dorticos arrived with Soviet T-31 tanks and mobilized a counterdemonstration with local trade unions, arresting and jailing many of the women while denouncing them as "worms," "rabble," and "imperialist agents."[28]

The new gendered and sexual cartography etched by these events is a territorialization of Cuba's body politic; one that used the rhetoric of anti-US imperialism and deployed the tactics of Stalinist terror. Castro's militarist revolutionary discourse *did* function as a decolonizing discourse (as does Che Guevara's less ideologically freighted prose), firing the imaginations of North American leftists, feminists, and European socialist thinkers. On the other hand, that authoritarian deployment concealed for those constituencies the oppression of Castro's moral codes. Until Castro's public support of Prague Spring, and the internationally famed Heberto Padilla Trial, these foreign constituencies did not fully acknowledge that the Castroist regime had imported Stalinist criminal codes toward homosexuality and political dissidence, agricultural policies, press censorship, and the organization of a State Security System analogous to the KGB.[29]

Stalinist legal and political codes between homosexuality, bourgeois decadence and counterrevolutionary typologies were solidified in Cuban State policy from 1965 to 1967, with the establishment and operation of UMAP camps (Military Units for the Aid of Production). They were closed at the end of the sugar harvest in 1967, after international protest and denunciation by the French press, and after inducting thousands of male homosexuals into forced labor in the sugar mills. Arenas writes that during this time UNEAC urged him away from gay writers such as Virgilio Pinera, and many of the library staff became Castro apologists and CDR informers. Rumors spread about the Library Director's sexual morality, insinuating that the Library was a "center of ideological corruption"; it was taken over by Sidrou Ramos, the Captain of Police. Books suspected of "ideological diversionism" began to disappear from the shelves; UNEAC was fraught with ideological differences over sexuality, religion, and communism, as it deliberated the merits of authors to whom prizes are to be awarded (***BNF*** 74-6).

In the midst of these early warning signals of the imported Stalinist character, doctrine and methods of the Castro regime, Arenas remarks on the State's use of carnivals and sexual vulgarity to mobilize mobs that would chant revolutionary, anti-Yankee slogans. The carnivals, once simply an indigenous expression of Cuban eroticism and religious irreverence, under the Castro regime distracted the Cuban population from the economic degeneration, failed harvests, botched and coercive agricultural policies that tyrannized their lives. The State merged them with the cruel theatrical spectacles of revolutionary trials, in which mobs chanted "To the execution wall!" in the name of justice and freedom (***BNF*** 58-9, 133).

Arenas' memoir is committed to telling the tale of another sexual cartography mapped by his own literary synaesthesia. His is a sensual voracity in writing that celebrates with readers the sexual feasts indulged amidst dangerous ideological repression. In this alternative story, writers are the rebels as well as the most profound traitors. Arenas portrays the inhabitants of the whole island as engaged in a counter-hegemonic sexual feast that defied the compulsory heterosexuality of the revolutionary moral codes. After Prague Spring, literary salons in Cuba became a security risk, and writers who held them at their homes were branded as "counterrevolutionaries." More and more Cuban citizens, in compliance with the neighborhood CDR, became informers on "counterrevolutionaries" or spoke in salutary terms toward the regime in exchange for such privileges as serving as Cuban civil servants in desirable posts abroad.

In 1970, Arenas was inducted into labor at the Manuel Sanguily Sugar Mill, where he writes the short story, **"El Central: A Sugar Mill."** Here, as everywhere, military authority is signified by men's overt exhibition of male genitalia to subordinates. At the sugar mill, one of the lieutenants asks Arenas to teach him French. "Classes started when the lieutenant said 'Let's study French,' and grabbing his testicles, he would place them on the table I used for teaching" (*BNF* 130). The authoritarian gesture signified power in the barracks, in the prisons, wherever authority must be repetitively re-inscribed for its reinforcement. Everywhere, the militarization of Cuba created the "new man" through the exaltation of revolutionary masculinity. In contrast to such displays, Arenas tells that,

> Many of the young men who marched in Revolutionary Square applauding Fidel Castro, and many of the soldiers who marched, rifle in hand and with martial expressions, came to our rooms after the parades to cuddle up naked, and show their real selves, sometimes revealing a tenderness and true enjoyment such as I have not been able to find again anywhere else in the world. . . . Sexual pleasure between two men was a conspiracy, something that happened in the shadow or in plain daylight, but always forbidden. . . . The adventure in itself, even if fulfillment did not come with the desired body, was already a pleasure, a mystery, a surprise.
>
> (*BNF* 105-6)

The sexual possibilities, dangerous as they are, proliferate and are represented by Arenas as a festival of the senses: feasting in the parks, the seashores, the rooms of friends. In this way he narrates the titillating conspiracy of pleasure as a transgendered strategy of deterritorialization that undermines the rigid heterosexist prescriptions of revolutionary nationalist discourse. Such scenes also refute hegemonic representations of homosexuality as the expunged "other" supplementing militarist *machismo*.

Arenas multiplies his own political taxonomies of homosexuality, attempting to dispel his culture's rigid categorization of the "queer" as the effeminate (*maricone*), or as the anal-receptive partner in sex between men. His multiple taxonomies also take literary revenge on writers turned informers, and on those public figures who are corrupted by political favors into praising the Revolution. His taxonomies are *not* those deployed by the regime's militarist use of biopower, rather, they turn the table on such deployments by openly staging the repressiveness of the regime's disciplinary techniques of sexual classification. For example, Arenas describes the "dog collar gay" who is boisterously, constantly arrested at the baths or beaches; "all the police had to do was hook him by the collar and take him to one of the forced labor camps" (*BNF* 77) His mentor Virgilio Pinera is a dog collar gay, imprisoned once at El Morro, "always treated with suspicion and constantly censored and persecuted. As a collar gay he was a really genuine person and willing to pay the price of being genuine" (*BNF* 79-82). There is the "common gay" who "never takes great risks, and sips tea with his friends" (*BNF* 78); the "closet gay" who is married and has children,

no one knows, and they are often the ones to censure other gays; finally the "royal gay, a species unique to communist countries." The fellow who holds an important public office through close contact with the Maximum Leader, can afford to lead an openly scandalous life, travel freely, and "cover himself with jewels and clothes" (*BNF* 78).

Arenas documents more frightful types of sexual behaviors in prison, and uses his taxonomies to show how sexual categorization was deployed in the prison as a mechanism to inflict torture. In 1973, he was arrested after UNEAC reported him as a "homosexual counter-revolutionary"; under the law, anyone's accusation of a sexual crime purportedly committed by another, was enough to be incriminated and to be prosecuted. While in prison, he describes the "levels of hell" organized by types of sexual offenders and types of sexual violence. As in his fiction, he portrays the violence of sexual cannibalism in the prison: this is sexuality transmogrified into violent feeding frenzies among the prisoners under conditions of deprivation and subjugation. Arenas writes,

> I refused to make love with any prisoner, even though some, in spite of hunger and mistreatment, were quite desirable. There was no beauty in the act, it would have been a degradation. It was also very dangerous: those criminals, after mounting a prisoner, felt they owned him and his few possessions. In jail, sexual intercourse because something sordid, an act of submission and subjugation, of blackmail and violence, even of murder in many instances.
>
> (*BNF* 179)

Like Fray Servando's sexual fastidiousness in *Hallucinations,* Arenas eschews taking pleasure within the degraded context of subjugation.[30] His prison experiences solidified his "peasant's scepticism" toward any political appropriation of sexuality as an all-encompassing symbol of a particular ideological formation, whether of the left or right. His memoir subsequently exposes the violence toward queer bodies that is inflicted by the nationalist and transnational symbolics of power exercised with and over bodies and genders.

Arenas' skeptical rejection of North American gay politics is influenced by these graphic events. Gay relationships in post-Stonewall North America struck Arenas as "tedious and unrewarding" despite the gains of gay American identity politics. He objected to another kind of "sinister social reality" which he found in North America, in which the erotic life of many is too often dictated by implicit normalizing codes within a greedy consumerist *ethos* (*BNF* 106). This view, expressed in Arenas' memoir, is resonant with certain humorous passages in *Hallucinations* and with *The Doorman*'s parody of the Oscars, a North American gay couple in New York City whose main goals in life include emulating Hollywood and trying to forget their rural backgrounds.[31] In such passages, Arenas may err by his stereotypes and by his fallacy of misplaced scale, for he seems to conflate the consumerist *ethos* of affluent gay lifestyles with the Cuban regime's punitive moral codes.[32] Although his parody oversimplifies (as do all parodies) the North American social phenomenon of gay sexual exchange, it cannot make light of the Cuban situation. Thus the extreme differences in ethical and political gravity between these scenes are acknowledged by the different rhetorical styles which he chooses to portray North American and Cuban homosexual behaviors. Additionally, what strikes Arenas as "sinister" is less the stereotypical behaviors which he notices, and more the discursive manipulation and exploitation of pluralist "free expression" in North America.

Cuban Art critic Coco Fusco explains that for many Cuban emigré artists,

> radicalism could be measured in terms of one's distance from official policy, [and they] tend to look upon the identity politics of the New Left with skepticism. . . . Multiculturalism more often than not spells manipulation of art for political ends to them.[33]

Although Fusco is characterizing what she takes to be an anachronistic political response by Cuban emigré artists, Arenas' and other emigrés' suspicions are less anachronistic if understood within a wider historical and political context. This context includes the vying interests of North American New Right, left and liberal political discourses, in which "homosexuality" continues to be a category that is deployed by all of these constituencies toward contradictory social agendas. In the following section, I examine some of the conflicts and collusions between political discourses that serve as the dialogical backdrop of Arenas' memoir.

DIALOGUES BETWEEN THE AMERICAS

Today, the queer body politic of Cuba is dismembered through analysis and subjected to distinct processes of ideological consumption in North America. The arrival of Arenas' counter-memories into the North American political landscape, especially those which are *about* North America, can signify to queer theorists the need for a more expansive political contextualization of sexuality in the Americas. Such a contextualization calls for analyses of state criminal activities practiced by the CIA's financial backing and training of Cuban emigré terrorism, as well as social criticism of the manipulation of liberal gay emancipatory discourses by neoconservative anti-Castro constituencies. By his memoir, Arenas offers the resource of effaced cultural memories and of an intercultural cannibalism that can engage in rewriting the queer body politic of the Americas. Such a reconfiguration should account for the ways that Arenas' literary contribution has been intercepted and stultified by the intricate collusions between the State Security systems of both Cuba and the United States.

His arrival in the United States with the 1980 Mariel emigration forces his confrontation with North American (in) appropriations of the Cuban queer body politic. He writes,

> I now discovered a variety of creature unknown in Cuba: the Communist Deluxe. I remember that at a Harvard University banquet a German professor said to me, "In a way I can understand that you may have suffered in Cuba, but I am a great admirer of Fidel Castro and I am very happy with what he has done in Cuba."
>
> While saying this, the man had a huge, full plate of food in front of him, and I told him: "I think it's fine for you to admire Fidel Castro, but in that case, you should not continue eating that food on your plate; no one in Cuba can eat food like that, with the exception of Cuban officials." I took his plate and threw it against the wall.
>
> My encounters with this festive and fascist left stirred a good amount of controversy.
>
> (***BNF*** 288-9)

The gravity of his testimony is repeated as farce in ***The Doorman,*** where the academic Communist Deluxe is parodied by the fictional character of Professor Cassandra Levinson, who has recently published a communist novel dramatizing the exploitation of bears; she adopts (entraps) a bear to satisfy the needs of her (precious) political empathy.[34]

In ***Before Night Falls,*** Arenas criticizes the professional opportunism of North American intellectuals, who appear to him to posture themselves as progressive in their support for Fidel Castro, yet with the international criticism of the super-Stalinization gaining currency, they are "changing their tune for political or financial expediency" (***BNF*** 300). Allen Young, in *Gays Under the Cuban Revolution,* his 1981 memoir about his own leftist activism during this time, confirms Arenas' view of the North American leftist ambivalence toward the plight of homosexuals under the Castro regime. He argues that the particular brand of homophobia that was codified in Cuba is a direct result of the old-line Cuban Communists' absorption of the ideology and codes of the Moscow-based Third International.[35]

Young relates that, as an American leftist, he did not publicly criticize Cuban homophobia until 1971, when the Cuban Congress on Education and Culture issued its antigay declaration and thus humiliated the gay American activists in the Venceremos Brigade who convened with this Congress.[36] In his chapter "The Silence of the Left," Young produces an incisive criticism of North American liberal and left media portrayals of this period in Cuban history, most of which failed to critique the Cuban Security System, the censorship of expression and political assembly, and the deployment of legal codes against homosexuals on behalf of statist familialism and compulsory heterosexuality. Young connects this myopia to a post-World War II tradition of leftist homophobia, "In its heart, the left could not and would not see homosexuals as victims of persecution—precisely the issue we are faced with in the case of Cuba."[37]

Young conjectures that the idealization of Cuban militarism by North American intellectuals may have "assuaged liberal guilt" over the collusion of US imperialist policies in Cuba and the privileged yet contradictory position intellectuals occupy as members of a "movement elite" that can maintain close ties with the island while criticizing US policies on the mainland. In his "Point/Counterpoint," Young addresses the accusation that his criticism of American leftist homophobia in this debate is synonymous with an alliance of the "militaristic, imperialistic elements in the CIA and other government agencies, not to mention big business," that colluded to overturn Castro in order to establish a right-wing dictatorship in Cuba. Against the notion that gay liberationist critiques of Cuba are a form of "cultural imperialism," he argues that "centralized male-dominated governments ultimately have more in common with their ruling counterparts elsewhere than with dissidents and critics," and urges the end of all such authoritarian regimes.[38]

Even long-time socialist feminists such as Margaret Randall, who have consistently ignored the homophobia of the Castro regime while struggling to educate the Americas about the progressive gains of women in revolutionary domestic and health reforms, are now questioning the patriarchal and heterosexist structure of the government and its institutions. Arenas himself refrained from bitterness at the double-standard in Cuban public policy and criminal law toward Cuban women and homosexuals; he also refrained from engaging polemically the North American socialist-feminist constituencies who, like Randall, have until recently denied the regime's homophobic persecutions.[39]

He does express his demoralization by the Cuban exile community in Miami, with its lack of interest in or support for exiled writers such as Lydia Cabrera (**BNF** 289-91). The alchemy of transplanted Cuban *machismo* with American commodity fetishism is dispiriting, "In Miami the obsession with making things work and being practical, with making lots of money, sometimes out of the fear of starving, has replaced a sense of life and, above all, of pleasure, adventure, and irreverence (**BNF** 292). He describes the "official" Castro gays, appointed by the Cuban Ministry of the Interior to travel worldwide to testify to the improved condition of homosexuals on the island (**BNF** 298-300). These propaganda battles in the United States and abroad, and the pervasive sense of threat from the subversive presence

of the Cuban State Security agents within the United States itself are additionally dispiriting (**BNF** 301, 304-5, 314). Arenas writes,

> [I]n exile we have no country to represent us; we live as if by special permission, always in danger of being rejected. Instead of having a country, we have an anti-country: Fidel Castro's bureaucracy is always ready to undertake all kinds of intrigues and chicanery to destroy us intellectually and, if possible, physically.
>
> (**BNF** 301)

The invisible narrator of *The Doorman* is this collective, somewhat sinister apparatus, which monologically could be characterized as the Cuban exile community, but which Arenas' ficton and testimony fragments by evocatively opening the doors to the complex affiliations of segments of that community with the North American intellectual left, the North American business community, the undercover anti-Castro and pro-Castro terrorist organizations, and with leftist and socialist constituencies abroad.

North American media representations of US trade embargos as "enlightened" tactics to "force" human rights concessions from foreign governments conceal the contradictory political deployments of the CIA, a national security mechanism established by the same US government in 1947, specifically in response to the rebel movements during the Cuban Batista regime. The genealogical effort by the political theorists Lourdes Arguelles and B. Ruby Rich to retrieve and to document this less visible topography of terror—a topography that undergirds the post-World War Americas encompassing the United States, Cuba, the Caribbean and Latin America—is crucial in this respect. In their two-part essay, "Homosexuality, Homophobia, and Revolution: Notes Toward an Understanding of the Cuban Lesbian and Gay Male Experience," they explore the social stratifications within the pre-Castro gay culture, showing the formative effects by US economic hegemony in the island on these patterns of social stratification. The queer body politic that spans the Americas, their account implies, is actively dismembered and manipulated by collusions between the CIA, organized crime, and Cuban emigré right-wing, anti-Castroist terrorist organizations. The history of CIA involvement in anti-Castroist terrorist activities in Cuba is well-documented and epitomized by the Bay of Pigs attempted coup.

The complications of queer intercultural exchange in the Americas are underscored by Arguelles' and Rich's brief references to Arenas' activism in the United States. Their comments, which I do not regard as entirely fair toward Arenas, *do* illustrate the convoluted discursive situation toward which Arenas himself was suspicious. They describe international lobbying groups such as the Committee of Intellectuals for the Freedom of Cuba, in which Arenas played a role at the committee's third annual congress in 1982. The congress, "modeled on Eastern European dissident intellectuals this country," coordinated a panel in which Arenas spoke, along with the homophobic Cuban novelist Guillermo Cabrera Infante. What also offends Arguelles and Rich was the preceding panel which featured the staffs of Senator Jesse Helms and John East and the newly formed House Committee on Intelligence, as well as other people with right-wing associations.[40] In their remarks, Rich and Arguelles imply not only that these political manipulations are deplorable, but that there can be no genuine dissident anti-Castro gay emigre culture in the United States. They comment that "the presence of Arenas at this congress marked the beginning of an unprecedented manipulation of the gay issue by those engaged in the US-financed war against the Cuban revolution."[41]

These observations, although extremely important for the analysis of the US mechanisms of terror that manipulate political sentiment, are too harsh upon Arenas' motives and they too rapidly foreclose the possibility of a genuinely dissident gay emigré culture in the United States. The substance of Arenas' memoir and his fiction leave little doubt that, although his words were politically distorted in that particular forum, he intended to address the plight of his peers, and politically stigmatized homosexualities as well. The otherwise astute analysis of Arguelles and Rich demonstrate the strategic differentiations between Cuban emigre dissident constituencies; differentiations that are vitally useful to multicultural activists.

Arguelles' work in particular is valuable for multicultural activists concerned to critique the undemocratic, covert processes that supplement and undermine the abstract rights discourses of North American leftist and liberal constituencies. She examines the US government's media manipulation of progressive American liberal constituencies to favor the Mariel emigrations and of the US Immigration Service to suspend its laws in order to receive the influx of Cuban homosexual emigrants—all to spur anti-Castro sentiment in America.[42] The blatant cynicism of these political maneuvers are highlighted by Senator Jesse Helms' participation with Arenas in such events as the Committee's third annual congress described above. Thus, while Cuban revolutionary rhetoric twists the symbolic organs of the queer body into the monstrously reductive linkage between homosexuality and "counter-revolutionary" bourgeois decadence, our notoriously homophobic public figures such as Senator Jesse Helms, with the help of the US media, promulgates the monstrous linkages between socialist reform and homophobic persecution. Arguelles examines the dual alliances of the CIA and conservative members in the US government with liberal gay anti-Castro interests. She examines the Cuban emigré right's alignment with American homophobic initiatives such as the Anita Bryant campaign, and with right-wing Cuban emigré gay-baiting in efforts to discredit progressive organizations such as the 1978 *Dialogo* and subsequent Antonio Maceo Brigade.[43]

In light of these connections, Arguelles and Rich argue unconvincingly that the Cuban UMAP period has, through the cultural productions by the survivors of Arenas' generation, acquired an excessive significance as the dystopic representative of gay experience in the Cuban revolution. I suggest that these events, rather than having accrued excessive significance, continue to be downplayed in North America as a direct result of the mystifications that Arguelles and Rich excavate, as well as by the political insularity and the abstract ideals of North American feminist and queer egalitarian discourses of liberation. The work of contextualizing the deployments of sexuality in the Americas thus remains crucial, and the Cuban history of homophobic persecution must be incorporated into an understanding of similar deployments in the present. Arenas asserts that,

> Moreover, all the rulers of the world, that reactionary class always in power, and the powerful within any system, must feel grateful to AIDS because a good part of the marginal population, whose only aspiration is to live and who therefore oppose all dogma and political hypocrisy, will be wiped out.

> (*BNF* xvii)

AIDS activism in the Americas and movements for cultural democracy in general, call for a genealogically informed cultural cannibalism that can smuggle defiant heresies, expose the scandal of hunger, and invent carnivals of queer cultural memory.[44]

Notes

1. Reinaldo Arenas, *Hallucinations: Being an Account of the Life and Adventures of Friar Servando Teresa de Mier,* trans. Gordon Brotherston (New York: Harper & Row, 1971), 287.

2. Ibid., 7.

3. Reinaldo Arenas, *Before Night Falls: A Memoir,* trans. Dolores M. Koch (New York: Viking Penguin 1993). Hereafter "*BNF.*"

4. Reinaldo Arenas, *The Doorman,* trans. Dolores Koch (New York: Grove Press, 1991).

5. For my use of the term "counter-memory," I rely on Michel Foucault's understanding of it as the effective use of history to dissipate unitary formations of power/knowledge. The effective use of history strives to discover the heterogeneous forces concealed by administrative and governmental processes of subjugation, which produce the "truths" of the self in the present. See Michel Foucault, "Nietzsche, Genealogy, History," *Language, Counter-Memory, Practice,* ed. Donald Bouchard

(Ithaca, NY: Cornell University Press, 1977), 161-2 and "Two Lectures," *Power/Knowledge: Selected Interviews and Other Writings 1972-1977,* ed. Colin Gordon, trans. Colin Gordon *et al.* (New York: Pantheon, 1980), 97.

6. For my sense of the term "queer," I rely on the analytic distinction between sex and gender, recently drawn by theorists such as Gayle Rubin and Eve Sedgwick, and the political difference between sex- and gender-hierarchies explored by queer theory. Queer theory is an emergent theoretical discourse that takes sexuality as a basic category in cross-disciplinary, multicultural research as well as in political practice. By "queer-affirmative" I mean the intellectual attitude that promotes nonheterosexual practices of sexuality and takes such practices as valuable topics for serious theoretical exploration. Adrienne Rich's concept of "compulsory heterosexuality" continues to function as a primary category for the queer-theoretical analysis of the power relations that construct the social significance of nonheterosexual practices of sexuality. For these formulations by Rubin, Sedgwick, Rich and others, see *The Lesbian and Gay Studies Reader,* ed. Henry Abelove, Michele Aina Barale and David M. Halperin (New York: Routledge, 1993).

7. Reinaldo Arenas, *Singing From the Well,* trans. Andrew Hurley (New York: Penguin, 1987; Reinaldo Arenas, *The Palace of the White Skunks,* trans. Andrew Hurley (New York: Penguin, 1990).

8. Reinaldo Arenas, *Farewell to the Sea,* trans. Andrew Hurley (New York: Penguin, 1986).

9. For studies of Latin American *machismo* and the social codifications of male homosexuality as effeminate (non)males who play the passive role in sexual analreceptivity, see Tomas Almaguer, "Chicano Men: A Cartography of Homosexual Identity and Behavior," and Ana Maria Alonso and Maria Teresa Koreck, "Silences: 'Hispanics,' AIDS, and Sexual Practices," *The Lesbian and Gay Studies Reader,* 255-73, 110-26. For a helpful discussion of the gendered character traits that are prescribed by the Cuban *machismo* cultures, see Geoffrey E. Fox, "Honor and Shame," *Working-Class Emigres from Cuba* (Palo Alto, CA: R & E Research Associates, Inc., 1979), 75-88.

10. "Heteroglossia" is M.M. Bakhtin's term for the pluralistic and stratified social context of both primary and secondary utterances. See Mikhail Mikhailovich Bakhtin, *The Dialogic Imagination,* ed. Michael Holquist, trans. Caryl Emerson and Michael Holquist (Austin, TX: University of Texas Press, 1986), 291-92.

11. For a helpful chronological overview of the literary production of Lezama Lima, Virgilio Pinera,

and Reinaldo Arenas, see Seymour Menton, *Prose Fiction of the Cuban Revolution* (Austin, TX: University of Texas Press, 1975).

12. Reinaldo Arenas, "The Closest Attention: Gays in Cuba," *New York Native* (10-23 Oct. 1983): 35.

13. For Bakhtin's account of the construction of the "grotesque" by the carnivalesque and its challenge to social stratification and to the monolithic tendencies of official discourses, see M.M. Bakhtin, *Rabelais and His World,* trans. Helene Iswoldy (Bloomington, IN: Indiana University Press, 1984). For a more distilled version of these ideas, see M.M. Bakhtin, "From the Prehistory of Novelistic Discourse," and "Forms of Time and of the Chronotope in the Novel," *The Dialogic Imagination,* 51-83, 146-258. My remarks on the political uses of "the family" as a statist tool of war which configures certain bodies as impure or filth is indebted to Nancy Armstrong, "Fatal Abstraction: The Death and Sinister Afterlife of the American Family," *Body Politics: Disease, Desire, and the Family,* ed. Michael Ryan and Avery Gordon (Boulder, CO: Westview Press, 1994), 18-31.

14. Coco Fusco, "El Diario de Miranda/Miranda's Diary," *The Subversive Imagination: Artists, Society, and Social Responsibility,* ed. Carol Becker (New York: Routledge, 1994), 109.

15. Emir Rodriguez Monegal, "Reinaldo Arenas," *The Borzoi Anthology of Latin American Literature, Volume II: The Twentieth Century,* ed. Emir Rodriguez Monegal (New York: Alfred A. Knopf, Inc., 1977) 977-8.

16. Emir Rodriguez Monegal, "The Metamorphoses of Caliban," *Diacritics* (Sept. 1977): 78-83. Roberto Fernandez Retamar, "Caliban: Notes Toward a Discussion of Culture in Our America," *Caliban and Other Essays,* trans. Edward Baker (Minneapolis, MN: University of Minnesota Press, 1989), 3-45. See Retamar's rejoinder to Retamar in his essay "Caliban Revisited" in this volume. I learned of Monegal's essay in Tom Hayes, "Cannibalizing the Humanist Subject," *Genealogy and Literature,* ed. Lee Quinby (Minneapolis, MN: University of Minnesota Press, 1995, forthcoming).

17. Other literary critics suggest that the Brazilian carnivalesque predates Andrade, and is signaled by the Brazilian writer Machado de Assis, *As Memorias Postumas de Bras Cubas* (1880). For a full argument defending an authentic Brazilian carnivalesque literary tradition that is exploratory in transvaluing latin norms of *machismo* and enacting transgendered literary play, see Judith A. Payne and Earle E. Fitz, *Ambiguity and Gender in*

the New Novel of Brazil and Spanish America: A Comparative Assessment (Iowa City, IA: University of Iowa Press, 1993). Although containing many useful historical references and clarifying the intercultural influences between Brazilian and French post-structuralist feminist thought, this account remains rigidly heterosexist and in my view overly indebted to Jungian psychologistic categories for its effort to celebrate the erotic carnivalesque. It thus falls short of the emancipatory critical vision sought in this essay.

18. Monegal, "The Metamorphoses of Caliban," 82. Monegal cites the following reference as Sarduy's introduction of Bakhtin to Latin American letters: Severo Sarduy, "El barroco y el neobarroco," *America Latin en su literatura,* ed. Cesar Fernandez Moreno (Mexico: UNESCO and Siglo XXI, 1972).

19. In *The Doorman,* Arenas parodies both himself, Sarduy, and other Cuban writers in the voice of his fictive narrator, the collective Cuban emigrant community. That community, his parody suggests, would never trust a real writer with its story of Juan, the emigrant doorman: "And as for Reinaldo Arenas, his declared and blatant homosexuality would contaminate every aspect. . . . On the other hand, if we had settled on Sarduy, the whole affair would have become a glittering neo-baroque bauble and nobody would understand a word . . ." *The Doorman,* 114. For a review of Sarduy's newly translated works in the United States, see Lawrence Chua, "Magical Eroticism, Severo Sarduy, Man of a Thousand Faces," Voice Literary Supplement, *The Village Voice* (May 1994): 27.

20. John Bergmann, "Cannibals and Queers: Man-Eating," *Gaiety Transfigured* (Madison, WI: The University of Wisconsin Press, 1991), 162.

21. Fusco, "El Diario de Miranda," 108.

22. Monegal, "The Metamorphoses of Caliban," 82.

23. Monegal writes of Oswald Andrade, "By defending cannibalism and dating some of his texts from the day the Brazilian cannibals ate their first bishop (an effective if rash way of assimilating his religious virtues), by introducing the fruitful notion of the carnival as a key to the transformation of society, Oswald de Andrade hit on the right note." Monegal, "The Metamorphoses of Caliban," 82. For a deconstructive analysis of the origin of Eurocentric conflations between Caribbean people, especially those indigenous to Cuba, and "cannibals," see Peter Hulme, "Caribs and Arawaks," *Colonial Encounters: Europe and the Native Carribean, 1492-1797* (New York: Methuen, 1986), 45-88.

24. See the Director's formal address on the "woman question" and report of the gains achieved by the FMC in Vilma Espin de Castro, *Cuban Women Confront the Future,* ed. Deborah Shnookal (Melbourne, Victoria, Australia: Ocean Press, 1991).

25. For a description of these reforms, see Carmen Diana Deer, "Rural Women and Agrarian Reform in Peru, Chile, and Cuba," and Isabel Larguia and John Dumoulin, "Women's Equality and the Cuban Revolution," *Women and Change in Latin America,* ed. June Nash and Helen Safa (South Hadley, MA: Bergin & Garvey Publishers, Inc., 1986), 189-207, 345-67.

26. North American journalist Lee Lockwood's transcription of Lockwood's interview with Castro in 1965 is excerpted from his book *Castro's Cuba; Cuba's Fidel* (Vintage 1969), in Allen Young, *Gays Under the Cuban Revolution* (San Francisco, CA: Grey Fox Press, 1981), 7-8.

27. Robert E. Quirk, *Fidel Castro* (New York: W. W. Norton & Company), 384-5. For an historical account of the successive Spanish and United States imperialist enterprises in Cuba, see Jaime Suchlicki, *Cuba: From Columbus to Castro* (New York: Charles Scribner's Sons, 1974).

28. Quirk, *Fidel Castro,* 410-12.

29. Latin American historian Robert Quirk claims that Padilla had undergone terrorist interrogations similar to those described by Koestler's novel about Stalinism, *Darkness at Noon.* The notoriety of the latter had succeeded in opening a much-needed public debate in the 1940s about the inhumane and sinister aspects of Stalinist public policies, among French socialist intellectuals such as Jean Paul Sartre and Merleau-Ponty, who had argued on behalf of a humanist Marxism in their efforts to give philosophical support to the ideological hegemony of the French Communist Party in French political life. Quirk argues that Padilla's public confession was only a superficial retraction. He claims that Padilla delivered a purposefully hyperbolic speech so that the audience could easily read between the lines for Padilla's intended satire of the whole proceeding. Quirk concedes that Padilla achieved at best a "pyrrhic victory" for which he paid a heavy price, becoming entirely discredited by the dissident intellectual community in Cuba and abroad, and participating in the direct public humiliation of his colleagues as well. However, the text of his confession was distributed in New York City by the Cuban mission to the United Nations, and *Le Monde* published an open letter to Castro that was signed by at least thirty leading intellectuals including Sartre and

Gabriel Marquez, expressing *for the first time* their opposition to these events and their misgivings about the Cuban regime. See Quirk, "Poets and Prisoners, *Fidel Castro,* 651-80.

30. Fray Servando undergoes severe temptation when confronted with the debaucheries of the Spanish priests, "your first impulse was to run towards them and lose yourself, naked, among them. But you are astute and intransigent with yourself, a tyrant towards your most highly prized feelings. That is why you ran away: for know that the evil is not in the moment you wanted to enjoy, but in the servitude which derives from that moment. . . ." Arenas, *Hallucinations,* 34.

31. Servando is entertained in the Spanish royal gardens by visions of the Three Lands of Love, each of which idealizes certain types of sexuality as the utopian site of future happiness. One of these was "something like Sodom, but not quite that because here everything seemed to be well regulated and there wasn't the least sign of anarchy." A closer look reveals same-sex serial monogamy, a practice which to Servando appeared to be a sort of boredom which "ended in melancholy, a sort of gentle sadness." Arenas, *Hallucinations,* 112-13. See Arenas' parody of the two Oscars in *The Doorman,* 69-75.

32. The concept of the fallacy of misplaced scale is used by Gayle Rubin to describe the evaluative error by which sexual acts are burdened with an "excess of significance." Arenas may be taken to burden North American gay relationships with an excess of significance as well. Gayle Rubin, "Thinking Sex," *The Lesbian and Gay Studies Reader,* 11.

33. Fusco, "El Diario de Miranda," 109.

34. Arenas, *The Doorman,* 35.

35. Young documents the exchange of letters between Allen Ginsberg, who had visited Cuba in 1965 and Manuel Ballagas, a Cuban poet who wrote Ginsberg many descriptions of the ordeals experienced by Cuban writers, including Reinaldo Arenas, Lezama Lima, and Virgilio Pinera. In one of these letters, Ballegas comments about Arenas, "The fact is that he was publishing outside Cuba books not necessarily against the revolution—and he was gay. He made a spectacular run away from a court, went underground and his (WANTED!) was all over the country at every police station . . ." Allen Young, *Gays Under the Cuban Revolution,* 30.

36. For excerpts from the Declaration, see Young, *Gays Under the Cuban Revolution.,* 32-3.

37. Ibid., 86-7.

38. Ibid., 90-91.

39. Today, socialist-feminist Margaret Randall, although cataloging the impressive gains in professional, educational, and *de jure* status for Cuban women under the Revolution, takes a retrospective look at the Cuban Women's Federation (FMC) and claims that a feminist discourse never adequately developed *"from the unique experience of women ourselves."* In her recent reflections on socialist-feminist appropriations of the Cuban revolution and unlike her earlier writings, she now acknowledges from the position of her newly-discovered lesbian perspective, that the heterosexism of these reforms is "an impediment of grave dimensions." See Margaret Randall, *Gathering Rage: The Failure of 20th Century Revolutions to Develop a Feminist Agenda* (New York: Monthly Review Press, 1992), 132-3. For her earlier analysis of the Revolution, see Margaret Randall, *Women in Cuba: Twenty Years Later* (New York: Smyrna Press, 1981). For a description of the symbolic and political importance of the FMC for Latin American women's movements generally, see Ofelia Schutte, "Cultural Identity, Liberation, and Feminist Theory," *Cultural Identity and Social Liberation in Latin American Thought* (Albany, NY: State University of New York Press, 1993), 223-25.

40. B. Ruby Rich and Lourdes Arguelles, "Homosexuality, Homophobia, and Revolution: Notes toward an Understanding of the Cuban Lesbian and Gay Male Experience, Part II," *Signs: Journal of Women in Culture and Society* 11:1 (1985): 131. Part I of this report is their evaluation of pre-Castro homophobia and homosexual practices in Cuba. See Lourdes Arguelles and B. Ruby Rich, "Homosexuality, Homophobia, and Revolution: Notes Toward an Understanding of the Cuban Lesbian and Gay Experience," *Hidden from History: Reclaiming the Gay and Lesbian Past,* ed. Martha Vicinus, George Chauncey, Martin B. Duberman (New York: Meridian, 1989), 441-45.

41. Arguelles and Rich, "Homosexuality," 132.

42. Lourdes Arguelles, "The US National Security State: The CIA and Cuban Emigre Terrorism," *Race and Class* 23:4 (1982): 287-304.

43. Ibid., 126-7.

44. Lourdes and Rich argue that North American gay tourist practices are part of US imperialist practices in the Caribbean. They want to rectify what they take to be the skewed perspective of Arenas and other critics of the Cuban regime's homophobia. They find that this perspective ignores the exploitative practices of North American gay sexual

consumerism and the pre-Revolutionary involvement of indigenous Cuban gay people with this consumerism. The Cuban regime's current practice of mandatory quarantine for HIV infected Cubans should be incorporated in this debate to waylay what threatens to become a stale polemic of accusation toward all participants in the North American and Cuban post-Revolutionary conflict. See Karen Wald, "AIDS in Cuba: A Dream or Nightmare?" *Z Magazine* (Dec. 1990: 104-9. The practices of North American gay sex tourism has also become the focus of epidemiological and ethnographic work that seeks to explain global sex tourism as a causal, social co-factor in the spread of HIV infection. These studies are particularly relevant for Caribbean countries that, unlike Cuba, have not withstood the tendency toward economic dependency on tourism. For a thorough discussion, see Paul Farmer, "The United States and the People with History," *AIDS and Accusation: Haiti and the Geography of Blame* (Berkeley: University of California Press, 1992), 177-90.

Francisco Soto (essay date 1994)

SOURCE: Soto, Francisco. "The Pentagonía: Giving Voice to the Voiceless." In *Reinaldo Arenas: The Pentagonía*, pp. 36-48. Gainesville: University Press of Florida, 1994.

[*In the following essay, Soto demonstrates how Arenas's five-book sequence,* The Pentagonía, *can be interpreted within the general principles of the* novella-testimonio, *or documentary novel form, popularized and sanctioned by the Castro government in the years after the Cuban Revolution.*]

ARENAS IN CUBA

During the late 1960s and the early part of 1970, before falling into disfavor with the revolutionary regime, Reinaldo Arenas contributed articles to *La Gaceta de Cuba* and *Unión,* two periodicals published by UNEAC. In 1968 he published a review in *Unión* of Antonio Benítez Rojo's collection of short stories *Tute de Reyes* (1967). He wrote:

> Un libro al que se le haya otorgado algún premio literario debe leerse siempre con recelo. Las lecturas de casi todas las obras premiadas nos han creado el prejuicio, muy justificado, de que dichas obras son, generalmente, panfletos de escaso valor literario o libros insignificantes y simplistas, sin puntos misteriosos u oscuros; sin atrevidas innovaciones que los jurados, en un plazo siempre limitado, no podrían descubrir ni detenerse a discutirlas. Con la mayoría de las obras premiadas en Cuba (y en cualquier sitio) se podría escribir otra *Historia universal de la infamia* más ex-

tensa, desde luego, que la ya comenzada por el gran poeta argentino Jorge Luis Borges. Obras como *Cualquiercosario, Maestra voluntaria, Gente de playa Girón, Los hombres de a caballo* y otros *horrores,* son testimonio desgraciadamente irrebatibles de que *el premio* muchas veces no es el premio.

("Benítez entra en el juego," pp. 146-47)

A book that has been awarded a literary prize should always be read with suspicion. Our readings of almost all the works that have been awarded prizes have prejudiced us, and very justifiably so, since these works are, generally speaking, propaganda of little literary worth, insignificant and simplistic books, without mysterious or dark moments; books without daring innovations that juries, always with a limited amount of time, could not discover or stop to discuss. With the majority of works that have been awarded prizes in Cuba (and in any place) one could very well write another, yet more extensive, *Universal History of Infamy* than the one already started by the great Argentine poet Jorge Luis Borges. Books like *Cualquiercosario, Maestra voluntaria, Gente de playa Girón, Los hombres de a caballo* and other *horrors,* unfortunately give indisputable testimony that *the prize* many times is not the prize.

The texts mentioned above all won prizes in the annual Casa de las Américas literary competition. Arenas's suggestion that one could well write another *Universal History of Infamy*—the title of Jorge Luis Borges's bizarre 1935 collection of fictionalized histories of unsavory individuals—makes clear his contempt for these winning texts. The short story collection *Cualquiercosario* by Jorge Onetti, the son of the celebrated Uruguayan writer Juan Carlos Onetti, won the short story prize in 1965. Daura Olema García's *Maestra voluntaria* won for best novel in 1962, while *Gente de playa Girón* by Raúl González de Cascorro was judged best short story collection in that same year. The Argentine David Viñas, an ardent Marxist, won the prize for best novel in 1967 for his *Los hombres de a caballo*. Although these are not, strictly speaking, documentary novels, they nonetheless reflect a revolutionary conceptual perspective and strive to inculcate in their readers a revolutionary consciousness.[1] It is clear that Arenas was well aware of the type of literary expression that enjoyed governmental sanction in Cuba. Ironically, he underscores that the awarding of prizes to mediocre and simplistic (propagandistic) works only attests to the (revolutionary) politics behind literary production in Cuba. The review was published at a time when criticism was still tolerated by the Revolution, and Arenas goes on sarcastically to express his amazement that a prize was awarded to Antonio Benítez Rojo's book by Casa de las Américas—"El libro no solamente merece el premio, sino que asombra que se le haya otorgado" (p. 147) (The book not only deserves the prize, but it is amazing that it received it)—for this is a complex and varied book of imagination and fantasy that erases traditional boundaries, a book intended for a sophisticated reader willing to tackle the challenges it presents. Arenas continues:

> Es además un libro variado donde sorprenden tanto los aciertos como los defectos, y donde la verdadera unidad—la médula del libro—lo forman, más que las anécdotas que se cuentan y el contenido de las mismas, el propio estilo del autor, el mundo que él inventa o recrea; su imaginación. Libro a veces fantástico y por lo tanto verdaderamente realista . . .
>
> (p. 147)

Moreover, it is a diverse book where the finer points, as well as its defects, are surprising, and where the true unity—the essence of the book—is shaped by the author's style, the world he invents or recreates, by his imagination, more than by any anecdote or theme he narrates. A book that is at times fantastic and, therefore, truly realistic . . .

In essence, what Arenas has done in this review (and we should keep in mind that at the time this review was written *Celestino antes del alba* had just appeared and was the target of unfavorable criticism for its lack of documentary realism) is to describe and defend his own aesthetic position: the literary text as a limitless space where the writer's imagination and fantasy are free to soar. With *Celestino antes del alba*—published when Arenas was only twenty-two years old—it was already clear that he had no intentions of writing a closed, linear text that presented a coherent, objective representation of empirical reality. In the novels that were to follow Arenas would become progressively more daring in his compositional experimentation and subversion of authoritarian and reductionist attitudes toward literature and life. It was this refusal to establish a clear revolutionary consciousness in his writings that forced the Revolution finally to censor and designate Arenas's texts as counterrevolutionary.

The strong government support given to documentary literature in Cuba is evident in the large print runs for certain first-edition novels: *Maestra voluntaria* (10,000 copies), *La guerrilla Tupamara* (20,000), *Biografía de un cimarrón* (20,000), *La batalla de Jigüe* (20,000), and *Canción de Rachel* (25,000). If one compares these figures to the 2,000 copies issued of the first edition of Arenas's *Celestino antes del alba* (1967) and the 4,000 copies for the first edition of Lezama Lima's *Paradiso* (1966) the discrepancy is apparent. It was obviously a question of what type of literature the Cuban state chose to support, since the new editorial houses could easily have published a greater number of copies. As Pamela María Smorkaloff writes in *Literatura y edición de libros:* "De 1962 a 1966, la nueva organización del sistema editorial posibilita el perfeccionamiento de lo aprendido en la etapa anterior con respecto al quehacer

editorial. . . . Las novelas tienen ahora tiradas más armónicas, de quince a veinte mil ejemplares" (From 1962 to 1966, the new organization of the editorial system brings about the consolidation of what was learned in the previous stage with respect to editorial work. . . . Novels now begin to be published more consistently in editions of fifteen to twenty thousand copies).[2] This revolutionary support for and monitoring of what was considered acceptable literature—that is, literature that reflected revolutionary reality and projected the revolutionary message in an attempt to help build social consciousness—was the literary atmosphere in which Arenas found himself writing until his escape from Cuba in 1980 through the Mariel boatlift.

THE PENTAGONÍA: TESTIGO-TESTAR-TESTAMENTO

While living in Cuba Reinaldo Arenas published only *Celestino antes del alba* and a few short stories. After his fall from favor with the revolutionary government, his books were no longer published on the island.[3] As a result, he secretly began to send his manuscripts abroad, many of which were printed in pirated editions. When he arrived in the United States in 1980, Arenas saw the need for definitive editions of his works. Thus, in 1982 an authorized edition of *Celestino antes del alba,* retitled *Cantando en el pozo,* appeared.[4] In the preliminary note to this revised edition, Arenas mentions for the first time a projected *pentagonía* (pentagony) about Cuban society that would consist of *Celestino antes del alba* (*Cantando en el pozo*), *El palacio de las blanquísimas mofetas, Otra vez el mar, El color del verano,* and *El asalto.* Well aware of the emphasis laid on the documentary-testimonial function of the artistic media in Cuba, Arenas appears intentionally to play off the words *testigo* (witness) and *testimonio* (testimony) in the preliminary note to this new edition:

> En todo este ciclo furioso, monumental y único, narrado por un autor-*testigo,* aunque el protagonista perece en cada obra, vuelve a renacer en la siguiente con distinto nombre pero con igual objetivo y rebeldía: cantar el horror y la vida de la gente. Permanece así en medio de una época convulsionada y terrible, como tabla de salvación y esperanza, la intransigencia del hombre—creador, poeta, rebelde—contra todos los postulados represivos que intentan fulminarlo. Aunque el poeta perezca, *el testimonio* de la escritura que deja es *testimonio* de su triunfo ante la represión y el crimen. Triunfo que ennoblece y a la vez es patrimonio del género humano (emphasis added).

In all this feverish cycle, monumental and unique, narrated by an author-*witness,* although the protagonist perishes in each work, he is reborn in the following ones with a different name, but with the same rebellion and objective: to sing of the horror and the life of the people. In this way he endures in a turbulent and terrible era, like a life raft of hope, the intransigence of man—creator, poet, rebel—against all the axiomatic truths that would censure him. Although the poet might perish, the *testimony* of writing he leaves behind is a *testimony* of his triumph in the face of repression and legal persecution. His triumph ennobles him and is at the same time patrimony of the human condition (emphasis added).

With this statement, Arenas proposes that although *Celestino antes del alba, El palacio de las blanquísimas mofetas, Otra vez el mar, El color del verano,* and *El asalto* are works of fiction, they nonetheless are valid testimonies of human dignity in the face of oppression. The testimonial or documentary structure of these texts is clearly outlined by Arenas's words: "un autor-testigo" (a writer-witness) who testifies to "el horror y la vida de la gente" (the horror and life of the people) by leaving a valuable "testimonio" (testimony) of his triumph over "la represión" (repression).[5] Arenas positions the pentalogy within the general textual structure of *testigo-testar-testamento.* Each of the five works features a witness (the child-narrator/Celestino; Fortunato; Héctor; the trinity that unites Gabriel, Reinaldo, and the Tétrica Mofeta; the nameless narrator of the final novel) with an urgent need to give testimony about his particular world. Their worlds range from the child-narrator/Celestino's rural existence of deprivation and violence; to Fortunato's frustration, extreme poverty, and tortured family existence; Héctor's personal and sexual angst; the struggle of Gabriel/Reinaldo/the Tétrica Mofeta to survive within a homosexual subculture while being persecuted by a homophobic and hostile military regime; and the nameless narrator's impressions of a tyrannical and abominable future society in which individual rights are sacrificed for the good of the state. Moreover, each witness (with the exception of the nameless protagonist of *El asalto,* who inhabits a world where citizens have virtually forgotten how to speak and are only allowed to recite the party's official dialogues) attempts to leave a written document of these events: the incessant writing of Celestino on tree trunks and Fortunato on stolen reams of paper, Héctor's anguished cantos, Gabriel/Reinaldo/the Tétrica Mofeta's determination to write and rewrite his lost novel, *El color del verano.* The testimony in each novel progressively struggles to articulate, expanding from presignification (Celestino's scribbling on trees) to signification (Héctor's cantos and Gabriel/Reinaldo/the Tétrica Mofeta's anecdotes and stories of survival). In addition, each witness dies in order to be reborn to new realities that affirm the power of the poetic spirit over repression and destruction. The only novel in which the protagonist does not die is *El asalto.* Ironically, the final novel of the pentalogy leaves the reader with a glimmer of hope. The decrepit tyrant el Reprimerísimo Reprimero (the Represident) is destroyed, and the protagonist, who has suffered countless persecutions throughout the five-book cycle, can finally stretch out on the beach and rest.

The characters-witnesses of the five novels clearly and honestly intone the persecution and anguish they experience. Indeed, the aesthetic distance of fiction in no way diminishes the authenticity of these voices, whose marginal perspectives are precisely those that the documentary novel was designed to give voice to. Not all marginal informers, however, have enjoyed the same recognition in Cuban revolutionary society; those individuals who value the imaginative over the historical or who do not represent the ideal *hombre nuevo* (new man) of the Revolution have not been given a voice within the state for they represent a threat to the established order. Cuban documentary writers give voice to witnesses who provide information about their personal lives, but nevertheless do so to emphasize how in the past certain members of society (for example, blacks, women, immigrants) were left out and alienated. These are *la gente sin historia* (people without a history) whom the writers of documentary novels wish to incorporate into the new revolutionary society. Arenas's characters-witnesses—dissidents, "extravagants," dreamers, free-thinkers, homosexuals—are also people without a history. They represent those individuals not welcomed into the new revolutionary regime, for they fail to contribute, in the government's eyes, to the political and sociohistorical legitimacy of a revolutionary consciousness.[6] It is precisely these marginal voices, these social outcasts, these victims of totalitarian utopianism, these so-called people without a history whom Arenas allows to speak and welcomes into his novels.

These texts never propose a narrow or specific historical definition; they never give an oversimplified historical explanation for a character's existential dilemmas, nor do they try to rewrite history from an official point of view in the attempt to help build a revolutionary consciousness. Nonetheless, historical realities are not ignored, as each novel is embedded in a specific sociohistorical context: *Celestino antes del alba,* the prerevolutionary years; *El palacio de las blanquísimas mofetas,* the last years of the Batista regime; *Otra vez el mar,* the first decade of the Revolution; *El color del verano,* the 1960s and 1970s in Cuba; *El asalto,* an imaginary future Cuban society that the writer allows himself to invent and examine. In 1983 Arenas stated: "En todo país, y especialmente en los países totalitarios, hay una historia oficial que es la que generalmente se publica, pero la historia real, la que se padece, solamente pueden contarla sus víctimas. . . . [A] mí me interesa más la historia contada por sus intérpretes que por los historiadores"[7] (In every country, and especially in totalitarian countries, there exists an official history, which is generally what gets published, but the real history that people suffer through can only be told by its victims. . . . I prefer history told by its interpreters rather than by the historians).

In the above statement the word *intérpretes* (interpreters) could well be replaced by the word *testigos* (witnesses). While historians claim to record and faithfully reconstruct the "facts" and "truth" of the past, interpreters (witnesses) of history provide their own versions and personal accounts of events often forgotten and overlooked by historiography. Arenas makes known his distrust of history's legitimating discourse of power, for it is subject to the changing ideological constructions of whatever group finds itself in control. Still, he does support the documentary novel's basic principle of giving voice to the voiceless, those who have been forgotten by history. Arenas proclaims his affinity with the victims of totalitarian oppression who are banished to the lower levels of the social pyramid simply because they fail to legitimate the ideology of the group in power.

El color del verano: The End of a Cycle

In his autobiography, Arenas informs us that although *El color del verano* is the fourth novel of the *pentagonía,* it was in fact the last novel he wrote (*Antes que anochezca,* pp. 12-13). He also tells of his determination, despite his precarious health, to complete the novel. In this respect *El color del verano* is a significant text, for with it Arenas was finally able to bring to a close a cycle of novels he began writing three decades earlier. In the prologue to *El color del verano,* which playfully appears halfway through the text (pp. 246-50) and purposely erases the lines between fiction and metafiction, the documentary nature of this fourth novel of the quintet is underscored:

> De alguna forma esta obra pretende reflejar, sin zalamerías ni altisonantes principios, la vida entre picaresca y desgarrada de gran parte de la juventud cubana, sus deseos de ser jóvenes, de existir como tales. Predomina aquí la visión subterránea de un mundo homosexual que seguramente nunca aparecerá en ningún periódico del mundo y mucho menos en Cuba. Esta novela está intrínsicamente arraigada a una de las épocas más vitales de mi vida y de la mayoría de los que fuimos jóvenes durante las décadas del sesenta y del setenta. *El color del verano* es un mundo que si no lo escribo se perderá fragmentado en la memoria de los que lo conocieron.
>
> (p. 249)

To a certain extent this work pretends to reflect, without flattery or high-sounding principles, the life of a great portion of Cuban youths—somewhere between the picaresque and dissolute—their desires to be young and to exist as such. The underground vision of a homosexual world, which surely will never appear anywhere in newspapers, and much less in Cuba, predominates here in these pages. This novel is intrinsically tied to one of the most vital eras of my life and that of a great majority of us who were young during the sixties and seventies. If I don't write about it, *El color del verano* is a world that will be lost and fragmented in the memory of those who knew and lived it.

Who writes this prologue? The willfully ambiguous but provocative answer lies in the fact that both Reinaldo Arenas (the flesh-and-blood writer) and Gabriel/Reinaldo/the Tétrica Mofeta (the fictitious writer) are the writers of a novel entitled *El color del verano*. This *mise-en-abyme* undermines the authority of traditional authorship that is central to the documentary novel; the writer-narrator-investigator presumes to control the work and convey precisely what he or she wishes. Yet, more important, in keeping with the general organizing principle of the genre, the writer(s) of the prologue to *El color del verano* carefully underscore(s) the importance of recording this particular era in Cuban history that would be lost forever if not preserved in writing.

The prologue also reveals how the novel, originally conceived and started in Cuba, fell victim to revolutionary censorship on the island. The distinctions between reality and fiction are blurred, instead of being carefully kept separate as in the documentary novel. The Tétrica Mofeta, Arenas's fictitious alter ego, is forever rewriting his novel because it has been either confiscated, stolen, lost, or destroyed (for example, see pages 66, 108-9, 122, 202, 441); while Arenas, the extra-literary writer, recounts how he had to memorize certain chapters of *El color del verano*—for example, "El hueco de Clara" ("Clara's Hole")—and the thirty tongue twisters in order to guarantee the survival of these portions of the manuscript.[8]

The prologue also underscores both the personal importance of the *pentagonía* in the writer's life and the societal significance of metaphorically representing twentieth-century Cuban history. Still, the writer confesses his contradictory feelings of grief and tenderness over what he refers to as the malady of Cuban history:

> Siento una desolación sin término, una pena inalcanzable por todo ese mal y hasta una furiosa ternura ante mi pasado y mi presente. Esa desolación y ese amor de alguna forma me han conminado a escribir esta pentagonía que además de ser la historia de mi furia y de mi amor es una metáfora de mi país.
>
> (pp. 248-49)

I feel an interminable anguish, an unreachable pain as a result of all that wrong. Yet, I also feel a raging tenderness for my past and present life. In some way, that anguish and that love have driven me to write this pentagony, which in addition to being the story of my fury and my love is also a metaphor for my country.

The driving force behind the writer's desire to write this cycle of novels is revealed as a complicated combination of love and pain, a fusion of conflicting emotions that requires a metaphorical (literary) language to articulate and suggest. While the documentary novel is presented as a tightly woven network of determined significations, a set of so-called real affirmations in which reference is guaranteed by the correspondence of language to some objective reality existing before being called forth in language, the novels of the *pentagonía* make no attempt to establish such a correspondence. Arenas's texts do not presume to be anything but what they are, pure fiction. And as fiction, they delight in the deployment of a poetic and metaphorical language that alludes, suggests, and evokes, touching the reader and drawing him or her into a dazzling and provocative literary space of multiple possibilities.

Toward the end of the prologue, the reader is given a summary of each novel of the cycle and the role each text plays in the total *pentagonía*. In effect, the preliminary note to **Cantando en el pozo** (1982) is here rewritten with minor but significant additions. The fact that the note reappears only underscores its importance, especially in this, the last novel Arenas wrote. It is clear that for Arenas the *pentagonía* was a living and vital testimony of his "desolación y amor" (anguish and love) for his country. It is important to reproduce the following paragraph in its entirety to better appreciate the changes from the statement in **Cantando en el pozo**. I have highlighted in the text the most significant passages added to the 1990 note:

> En todas estas novelas, el personaje central es un autor testigo que perece (*en las primeras cuatro obras*) y vuelve a renacer en las siguientes con diferente nombre pero con la misma airada rebeldía: cantar o contar el horror y la vida de la gente, *incluyendo la suya*. Permanece así, en medio de una época conmocionada y terrible (*que en estas novelas abarca más de cien años*), como tabla de salvación o de esperanza, la intransigencia del hombre—creador, poeta, rebelde—ante todos los postulados represivos que intentan fulminarlo, *incluyendo el espanto que él mismo pueda exhalar*. Aunque el poeta perezca, el testimonio de la escritura que deja, es testimonio de su triunfo ante la represión, la violencia y el crimen. Triunfo que ennoblece y a la vez es patrimonio del género humano *que además, de una u otra forma (ahora lo vemos otra vez) proseguirá su guerra contra la barbarie muchas veces disfrazada de humanismo.*
>
> (**El color del verano,** p. 250)

In all these novels, the main character is an author-witness who perishes (*in the first four works*) and is reborn in the following ones with a different name, but with the same angry rebelliousness: to sing or tell of the horror and the life of the people, *including his own.* In this way, he endures in the middle of a turbulent and terrible era (*which in these novels spans one hundred years*) like a life raft of hope, the intransigence of man—creator, poet, rebel—before all the axiomatic truths that would censure him, *including the horror that he himself is capable of emitting.* Although the poet might perish, the testimony of writing he leaves behind is a testimony of his triumph in the face of repression, violence, and legal persecution. His triumph ennobles him and is at the same time patrimony of the human condition *that in one way or another (today we see it again) continues its war against barbarity, often disguised as humanism.*

I would like to comment briefly on three of the additions in the revised note. The first is the insistence that the witness should provide a personal account of his experiences, not solely for the purpose of representing a specific group, like in the Cuban documentary novel, but also as an independent and authentic act of individual expression ("to sing or tell of the horror and the life of the people, including his own"). The responsibility of each character for creating his own "horror" is underscored by the phrase "including the horror that he himself is capable of emitting." This added revelation is significant in that it puts aside blaming a particular political group or government for the characters' vicissitudes while placing responsibility on the protagonist-witness, who in the final analysis is responsible for creating his own reality, be it a world of imaginative fantasies or an anguished hell. This final point is evident, for example, in **El asalto,** a novel in which the nameless protagonist, who in the previous four novels of the quintet emerges as a likeable character, is represented as an iniquitous and selfish individual who ultimately is responsible for the anguished hell he has created.

Secondly, the idea that barbarity (that is, exploitation, oppression, totalitarianism, intolerance, and so forth) can disguise itself as humanism comments on the sinister ambiguities, the devious and insidious nature of barbarity that can resurface and assert itself under different forms and guises. An example is a government's decision to round up so-called deviants and lock them up (as was the case in Cuba's infamous UMAP camps), at the same time presenting itself to the world as the champion of the underdogs and the downtrodden.[9] In 1984 Arenas dedicated an entire novel to this period in Cuban revolutionary history, **Arturo, la estrella más brillante.** First published in Barcelona in 1984, it is a fictitious account of one man's experiences in one of the many UMAP work camps that existed in Cuba in the late 1960s. In it the desire to document the conditions of the camps is focused from a literary perspective. It is interesting to note, however, that Arenas's text, presented as pure fiction, was born out of a desire to remember his friend Nelson Rodríguez Leyva, whose unpublished book of stories about his own experiences in an UMAP camp was confiscated and destroyed by the Cuban authorities. Far from being political propaganda, **Arturo, la estrella más brillante** is simply a defense of the individual right to dream, to rise above the oppression that threatens existence. In **El color del verano** Arenas ironically recalls the UMAP camps in a passage in which the dictator Fifo first denounces his minister of education and later has him killed for referring to these camps as "concentration camps for homosexuals" when in fact, according to Fifo, they are only "rehabilitation camps": "Nosotros lo que hacemos es educar o reducar, jamás concentramos a nadie a la fuerza. Esos jóvenes están ahí voluntariamente porque quieren reducarse" (p. 147) (What we do is educate or reeducate, we never concentrate anyone by force. Those youths are there voluntarily because they want to be reeducated).

Finally, the observation that all of the novels of the pentalogy represent "a turbulent and terrible era (which in these novels spans one hundred years) like a life raft of hope" can be read as a parodic allusion to Gabriel García Márquez's novel *Cien años de soledad,* the story of the founding of Macondo by the Buendía family and of the town's progressive decay and final apocalyptic destruction over the course of a century. Many critics have seen García Márquez's fictional world of Macondo specifically as a history of Colombia and by extension a microcosm of Latin American history from colonialism to the present. Here Arenas suggests that the *pentagonía* likewise provides for the reader a history of twentieth-century Cuban society, and by extension a microcosm of Latin American totalitarianism, be it from the political right or left.[10]

One final aspect of *El color del verano* is relevant to our discussion of the Cuban documentary novel. Early in the novel (pp. 64-68), in a chapter entitled "Del bugarrón" ("About the Bugger"), the reader is introduced to a character identified simply as *el viejo bugarrón* (the old bugger). This old bugger, disillusioned by the fact that he considers himself to be one of the last of a disappearing breed on the island, decides to visit his grandfather, "un anciano de más de 130 años llamado Esteban Montejo" (p. 66) (an old man of more than 130 years called Esteban Montejo).[11] Believing his grandfather to also be a true bugger—and by definition a true bugger does not allow himself to be passive and is repelled by effeminate homosexuals and their extravagant behavior—he is disillusioned to find Montejo dressed in women's clothing and getting ready for the carnival. The appearance of Miguel Barnet's famous protagonist (recall ex-slave Esteban Montejo from Barnet's *Biografía de un cimarrón*) dressed in women's clothing—and Barnet himself is also fictionalized and ridiculed in the text as *Miguel Barniz*, "un pájaro de la peor catadura" (p. 360) (a faggot of the worst kind)—is a parodic undermining not only of Hispanic patriarchal machismo but also of the seriousness and prominence of Barnet and his famous protagonist within the canon of Cuban revolutionary letters.[12] Significantly, the old bugger of *El color del verano* and Barnet's Esteban Montejo are both survivor-witnesses. As we recall, Barnet, a student at the Institute of Ethnography and Folklore of the Academy of Sciences, had discovered Montejo in the early 1960s and immediately began to record the stories of this unusual survivor of Cuba's past. The old man served the purpose of documenting, for the first time, Cuban history from a black man's point of view. Likewise, but on a more literarily subversive level, the old bugger of *El color del verano,* "el bugarrón número uno de la Isla de Cuba, . . . el único que se templó a Mella, a Grau San Martín y a Batista (todos

ellos notables bugarrones), y después ay, a Fifo" (p. 64) (the number one bugger in Cuba, . . . the only one that fucked Mella, Grau San Martín and Batista [all prominent buggers themselves], and later alas!, Fifo), is also a survivor who has witnessed Cuba's governmental blunders and political mismanagement from the right (Fulgencio Batista) and the left (Julio Antonio Mella, Ramón Grau San Martín, and Fifo/Fidel Castro). Arenas's old bugger is indeed a witness who gives "testimony" of the ineffectiveness of Cuban politics of the twentieth century, of the political polarization that has divided the Cuban people and failed to produce a fair and just system of government.

As we shall see in part 2 of this book, to enter the fictive universe of the novels of the *pentagonía* is to enter a precarious space that asserts its freedom from the rigid and banal set of narrative responses of orthodox Cuban socialist realism to which the documentary novel remains faithful. Arenas's novels belong to contemporary postmodern literature's unmasking of the inherent naïveté in the realistic novel's claim to veracity; to the belief that the literary text can indeed be a guarantor of fixed meaning, a repository of irrefutable truth. *Celestino antes del alba, El palacio de las blanquísimas mofetas, Otra vez el mar, El color del verano,* and *El asalto* are self-conscious texts that present a plurality of voices that dismantle all hierarchical discourses. The *pentagonía* shatters all expected generic boundaries and limitations in an attempt to provide the reader with a literary space of multiple possibilities. For Arenas, writing as a literary creative act was a necessity, a liberating act of self-expression, an emotional act of fury in which he challenged, undermined, and subverted all types of ideological dogmatism, all forms of absolute truths. This liberating energy, which takes on its own singular meaning and particular artistic goal in each text in the writer's oeuvre, is the single most salient feature of Arenas's writing.

In *The Art of the Novel* Czechoslovakian writer Milan Kundera suggests that perhaps all writers write a kind of single theme in their first work and variations thereafter. I believe that this observation is valid in speaking of Arenas's work. If one carefully examines his entire literary production, one finds an argumentative center that persistently resurfaces: a staunch defense of our imaginative capabilities and our right of self-expression in a world beset by barbarity, intolerance, and persecution.

Notes

1. David Viñas's *Los hombres de a caballo,* for example, relates the activities of an Argentine army unit sent to Peru to stop a guerrilla revolt. Viñas's portrayal of corruption and brutality in the Argentine army, supported and influenced by the imperialistic United States, is anything but subtle. "El chulo regresa" (The Return of the Pimp), a short story from the collection *Gente de playa Girón* by

Raúl González de Cascorro, one of Cuba's most outspoken supporters of the documentary novel, was published in the January-February issue of *Casa de las Américas* (2, no. 10, 1962) and is indicative of the type of literature that was actively supported by the Revolution. In this story a pimp, with no redeeming values whatsoever, returns to fight as a soldier in one of the battalions of the Bay of Pigs invasion. The story ends with the protagonist violently drowning a fellow black soldier whom he describes as "a repulsive monster." Eventually the pimp also drowns after his boat is destroyed by the Cuban Air Force. Finally, the stories of *Cualquiercosario* by Jorge Onetti all use a common, functional language to reject bourgeois values and support the social world of the proletariat.

2. *Literatura y edición de libros,* p. 146. In her book Smorkaloff provides a study of the post-revolutionary Cuban literary enterprise. She attempts to review the new social functions of the writer, reader, and the literary publishing industry that began with the triumph of the 1959 Revolution. For this purpose she investigates the extraliterary factors (for example, publishing infrastructure, mechanical aspects of production, literary workshops, and competitions that were created to foster further writing) that were and still are responsible for the increased production of (state-supported) literature on the island.

3. For a summarized account of the author's fall from grace with the Cuban revolutionary government, see Enrico Mario Santí, "Entrevista con Reinaldo Arenas." This interview was conducted shortly after Arenas left Cuba in 1980. For a more detailed account of Arenas's problems in Cuba, see the author's autobiography, *Antes que anochezca.*

4. In the interview that appears in the appendix of this book (p. 141), Arenas states that he had preferred the original title *Celestino antes del alba* for the 1982 edition. However, since the original had been published in Cuba there was the theoretical possibility of copyright infringement.

5. Whether Arenas's use of the words *testigo* (witness) and *testimonio* (testimony) specifically refers to the generic structure of the documentary novel or to the broader question of moral witness is not important. It has been shown how the cultural policy makers of the Revolution actively promoted a documentary-testimonial realism to assist in the deployment of a new revolutionary consciousness. Arenas was indeed aware of this and was also quite aware, as I demonstrated earlier, of Miguel Barnet's work and the strong support it received by the revolutionary regime. Hence, my thesis that Arenas drew material from, and built off, the Cuban documentary novel tradi-

tion in order to articulate his own particular concerns should not be controversial.

6. At the First National Congress on Education and Culture in 1971 it was stated that in Cuba "the cultural media cannot serve as a medium for the proliferation of false intellectuals who try to convert snobbishness, extravagance, homosexuality, and other social aberrations into expressions of revolutionary art, and who are far removed from the masses and from the spirit of our Revolution" (Tzvi Medin, *Cuba: The Shaping of Revolutionary Consciousness,* p. 23).

7. Monica Morley and Enrico Mario Santí, "Reinaldo Arenas y su mundo alucinante: una entrevista," p. 118.

8. In fact, it was the manuscript of *Otra vez el mar* that was confiscated and destroyed twice by the Cuban security police while Arenas was in Cuba. The author recounts his protracted struggles to rewrite and hide the manuscript of this novel in his autobiography, *Antes que anochezca.*

9. In 1980, the same year he escaped from Cuba during the Mariel exodus, Arenas granted the *Nouvel Observateur* an interview (later translated into English in *Encounter,* January 1982) in which he spoke out against the hostility of the Cuban revolutionary regime toward subversive individuals, uncommitted writers, and homosexuals. In this interview, Arenas maintained that while he lived in Cuba, the expression of any form of difference or opposition was considered counterrevolutionary, for it went against the archetype of the disciplined revolutionary.

As early as 1965 forced labor camps under the name of UMAP (an acronym for Unidades Militares de Ayuda a la Producción or Military Units for Aid to Production) were constructed in the province of Camagüey for the purpose of correcting so-called antisocial and deviant behaviors that, according to the government, threatened the creation of a true revolutionary consciousness. This period of repression has been documented by Néstor Almendros and Orlando Jiménez-Leal in their 1984 film *Conducta impropia* (Improper Conduct). *Conducta impropia* is made up of individual testimonies that document the atrocities committed by the Cuban revolutionary government against homosexuals. In the film Arenas himself recounts his experiences with homosexual discrimination while living in Cuba. During the height of the homosexual purges, Arenas states that any individual who was identified as homosexual or "extravagant" was carted off to a UMAP camp for not adapting to the revolutionary model. Allen Young's account of homophobia in Cuba (*Gays under the Cuban Revolution,* 1981) supports Arenas's accusations of the regime's intolerance toward any manifestation of "extravagant" behavior. Allen Young writes: "The people carted off to UMAP camps included youths who showed 'too much' concern with their personal appearance (long hair, colorful clothing, etc.); they were said to be victims of *la enfermedad* (the disease) or of 'cultural imperialism'" (p. 22).

10. In 1968 Arenas delivered a supportive paper on García Márquez's *Cien años de soledad* at the University of Havana entitled "*Cien años de soledad* en la ciudad de los espejismos." The paper was later published in Peter Earle's collection of essays titled *Gabriel García Márquez,* pp. 51-58. Over the years García Márquez has been an active and highly visible political supporter of Fidel Castro. Since his arrival in the United States in 1980, Arenas was extremely critical of García Márquez for his support of Castro and made his views repeatedly known in articles hostile to the Colombian Nobel laureate. See, for example, "Gabriel García Márquez, ¿esbirro o es burro?" (pp. 66-69) and "Gabriel García Márquez, C. de M." (p. 245) in *Necesidad de libertad.*

11. Arenas appears to have done his math correctly when he makes Esteban Montejo "un anciano de más de 130 años" (an old man of more than 130 years). In *Biografía de un cimarrón,* published in 1966, Montejo is presented as being 104 years old. Thus, if Montejo lived to 1999, the story time of *El color del verano,* he would indeed be around 133 years old.

12. In Cuban slang a person who hides behind a mask or does not reveal his or her true self is accused of having a *barniz* (literally, "varnish." An English equivalent might be "veneer"). Throughout *Antes que anochezca* Arenas refers to Barnet as *Miguel Barniz.* The editorial house that published the autobiography (Barcelona: Tusquets Editores) decided to use the name *Miguel Barniz* in order to avoid legal problems with Barnet, who is depicted in a very negative light in the autobiography.

Bibliography

WORKS BY REINALDO ARENAS

BOOKS

Where published English-language translations exist, their titles are given in brackets. See "English Translations" below.

Celestino antes del alba [*Singing from the Well*]. Havana: Ediciones Unión, 1967. Quotations in this volume are taken from the 1982 edition (see *Cantando en el pozo,* below).

Cantando en el pozo [*Singing from the Well*]. Barcelona: Editorial Argos Vergara, 1982.

El palacio de las blanquísimas mofetas [*The Palace of the White Skunks*]. Barcelona: Editorial Argos Vergara, 1982.

Otra vez el mar [*Farewell to the Sea*]. Barcelona: Editorial Argos Vergara, 1982.

Arturo, la estrella más brillante ["The Brightest Star" in *Old Rose: A Novel in Two Stories*]. Barcelona: Montesinos, 1984.

Necesidad de libertad (*Mariel: testimonios de un intelectual disidente*). México: Kosmos-Editorial, 1986.

El asalto. Miami: Ediciones Universal, 1991.

El color del verano. Miami: Ediciones Universal, 1991.

Antes que anochezca (*Autobiografía*) [*Before Night Falls*]. Barcelona: Tusquets Editores, 1992.

STORIES, ESSAYS, REVIEWS, AND OTHER LITERARY FRAGMENTS PUBLISHED IN CUBA

"La punta del arcoiris," "Soledad," and "La puerta del sol." *Unión* 4, no. 1 (1965): 113-19.

"Con los ojos cerrados." *Unión* 5, no. 4 (1966): 12-15.

"El encadenamiento del fraile." *La Gaceta de Cuba* 5, no. 53 (1966): 6.

"Celestino y yo." *Unión* 6, no. 3 (1967): 117-20.

"El hijo y la madre." *Unión* 6, no. 4 (1967): 222-26.

"Benítez entra en el juego." Review of *Tute de reyes. Unión* 7, no. 2 (1968): 146-52.

"Carta a la revista *Mundo Nuevo*." *La Gaceta de Cuba* 6, no. 66 (1968): 16.

"Magia y persecución en José Martí." *La Gaceta de Cuba* 6, no. 66 (1968): 13-16.

"Bajo el signo de enero." Review of *Viento de enero. La Gaceta de Cuba* 7, no. 67 (1968): 20.

"A la sombra de la mata de almendras." *La Gaceta de Cuba* 7, no. 69 (1969): 5-7.

"Tres mujeres y el amor." Review of *Tres mujeres. La Gaceta de Cuba* 7, no. 71 (1969): 26-28.

"Con los ojos abiertos." Review of *Abrir y cerrar los ojos. La Gaceta de Cuba* 8, no. 81 (1970): 10-11.

"Mariana entre los hombres." Review of *Mariana. La Gaceta de Cuba* 8, no. 86 (1970): 28-29.

"Tres sobre la mosca." *La Gaceta de Cuba* 8, no. 87 (1970): 9.

"El reino de la imagen." *La Gaceta de Cuba* 8, no. 88 (1970): 23-26.

"Granados en la casa del sol." Review of *El viento en la casa sol. La Gaceta de Cuba* 8, no. 88 (1970): 30.

"El palacio de las blanquísimas mofetas." *Unión* 9, no. 4 (1970): 37-45.

SELECTED INTERVIEWS

With Enrico Mario Santí. "Entrevista con Reinaldo Arenas." *Vuelta* 47 (1980): 18-25.

With Franz Olivier-Giesbert. "Pourquoi j'ai fui Fidel Castro." *Le Nouvel Observateur* no. 880 (September 19-25, 1981): 64-68. Later reprinted as "Dangerous Manuscripts: A Conversation with Reinaldo Arenas." *Encounter* 58, no. 1 (January 1982): 60-67.

With Mónica Morley and Enrico Mario Santí. "Reinaldo Arenas y su mundo alucinante: una entrevista." *Hispania* 66 (March 1983): 114-18.

ENGLISH TRANSLATIONS

Farewell to the Sea (translation of *Otra vez el mar*). Trans. Andrew Hurley. New York: Viking Penguin, 1986.

Singing from the Well (translation of *Celestino antes del alba/Cantando en el pozo*). Trans. Andrew Hurley. New York: Viking Penguin, 1987.

Old Rose. A Novel in Two Stories (translation of *La Vieja Rosa* ["Old Rosa"] and *Arturo, la estrella más brillante* ["The Brightest Star"]). Trans. Andrew Hurley and Ann Tashi Slater. New York: Grove Press, 1989.

GENERAL BIBLIOGRAPHY

Barnet, Miguel. *Biografía de un cimarrón*. Madrid: Ediciones Alfaguara, 1966. Translated as *The Autobiography of a Runaway Slave*. Trans. Jocasta Innes. London: The Bodley Head, 1968.

———. "La novela testimonio: socio-literatura." In the appendix to *Canción de Rachel*. Barcelona: Editorial Estela, 1969. Translated as *Rachel's Song*. Trans. W. Nick Hill. Willimantic, Conn.: Curbstone Press, 1991.

———. "Testimonio y comunicación: una vía hacia la identidad." *Unión*, no. 4 (1980): 131-43.

Benítez Rojo, Antonio. *Tute de reyes*. Havana: Casa de las Américas, 1967.

Borges, Jorge Luis. *Obras completas*. Buenos Aires: Emecé Editores, 1974.

Earle, Peter. *Gabriel García Márquez*. Madrid: Taurus, 1981.

García Márquez, Gabriel. *Cien años de soledad*. Buenos Aires: Sudamericana, 1967. Translated as *One Hundred Years of Solitude*. Trans. Gregory Rabassa. New York: Avon Books, 1970.

Lezama Lima, José. *Paradiso*. Edited by Eloísa Lezama Lima. Madrid: Ediciones Cátedras, 1980. Translated as *Paradiso* by Gregory Rabassa. Austin: University of Texas Press, 1974.

Medin, Tzvi. *Cuba: The Shaping of Revolutionary Consciousness*. Boulder: Lynne Rienner Publishers, 1990.

Olema García, Daura. *Maestra voluntaria*. Havana: Casa de las Américas, 1962.

Onetti, Jorge. *Cualquiercosario*. Montevideo: Arca, 1967.

Smorkaloff, Pamela María. *Literatura y edición de libros*. Havana: Editorial Letras Cubanas, 1987.

Viñas, David. *Los hombres de a caballo*. Mexico City: Siglo XXI, 1981.

Young, Allen. *Gays under the Cuban Revolution*. San Francisco: Grey Fox Press, 1981.

A NOTE ON TRANSLATIONS

I have used both the original Spanish texts and the published English translations of the works of Reinaldo Arenas throughout this book. In the case of *El asalto*, I have quoted from Andrew Hurley's unpublished translation. For *El color del verano*, not yet translated, and in certain cases where my analysis required a more literal reading, I have done the translation myself. Unless otherwise noted, all other translations are mine. All titles are given in their original language in the text; English versions appear in the bibliography at the end of the book.

Brad Epps (essay date spring 1995)

SOURCE: Epps, Brad. "Grotesque Identities: Writing, Death, and the Space of the Subject (Between Michel de Montaigne and Reinaldo Arenas)." *Journal of the Midwest Modern Language Association* 28, no. 1 (spring 1995): 38-55.

[*In the following essay, Epps discusses Arenas's use of the grotesque, and the accompanying images of "death, burial, emptiness, creativity, excess, and exuberance," in his novella* Arturo, la estrella más brillante.]

> I find his link with reality, then, just in the tone of the picture wrought round him.
>
> > Henry James, Preface to *The Aspern Papers*
>
> se complace en el suplemento, en la demasía y la pérdida parcial de su objeto.
>
> > Severo Sarduy, "El barroco y el neobarroco"
>
> nous ne faisons que nous entregloser
>
> > Montaigne, "De l'expérience"

Writing does not always go down and come to reading straight. At times it deviates from the norm, gets out of line, runs on and breaks off. At times it ignores the order of the page, the neat progression of syntax, the proper place of predicates, subjects, copula. Writing, at times, is overwritten, excessive, and mannered, bent and baroque, neo-baroque. Full of fancy and flourish, it seems outlandish and bizarre; as humor it falls flat; as seriousness it goes wrong and turns funny. It tends then to be read, or rewritten, as something else, as something not quite right, not quite writing. When over the top, it seems less writing than scrawling, scratching, scribbling. It falls short (of communication, comprehension, meaning) because it goes too far; it is not enough because it is just too much.

This inversion, where excess is deficit and lack, bears on the body as well. For if the word may be made flesh, given body, the body may be overrun by words, overwritten. The body, styled excessive and extravagant, is then somehow less a body than a caricature of the body, a corporeal aberration, a monstrosity, a grotesque. Staying with the grotesque, I want to consider how writing on the body, no less than the body of writing, can loop, by virtue of extravagance and excess, into cryptic signs of subjectivity and death, into beauty and fitful negation. I will be working towards the work of Reinaldo Arenas, or rather towards a place in his work where the grotesque, jolly though it can be, is invoked as the design of a self whose life is shadowed by death and whose presence is exceeded (preceded and superseded) by an absence, a lack. But first, so as to circle my subject more subtly, more sinuously, more *eccentrically,* I want to turn to a place in the work of a writer ostensibly far removed and linger there: the opening of an essay on friendship, or love, by Michel de Montaigne.

Montaigne's "De l'amitié" and its companion collection of twenty-nine sonnets by his late friend Étienne de La Boétie occupy the center of the first volume of Montaigne's *Essais,* numbers twenty-eight and twenty-nine out of fifty-seven, to be exact. This placement is hardly accidental, not only because Montaigne returns to the essays over the course of many years, supplementing, altering, and refining them, but because Montaigne opens "De l'amitié" itself with a reference to the placement of a painting, or portrait, in the middle, the most beautiful spot, of a wall:

> Considerant la conduite de la besongne d'un peintre que j'ay, il m'a pris envie de l'ensuivre. Il choisit le plus bel endroit et milieu de chaque paroy, pour y loger un tableau élabouré de toute sa suffisance; et, le vuide tout au tour, il le remplit de crotesques, qui sont peintures fantasques, n'ayant grâce qu'en la varieté et estrangeté. Que sont-ce icy aussi, à la verité, que crotesques et corps monstrueux, rappiecez de divers membres, sans certaine figure, n'ayants ordre, suite ny proportion que fortuite?

(197-98)

As I was considering the way a painter I employ went about his work, I had a mind to imitate him. He chooses the best spot, the middle of each wall, to put a picture labored over with all his skill, and the empty space all around it he fills with grotesques, which are fantastic paintings whose only charm lies in their variety and strangeness. And what are these things of mine, in truth,

but grotesques and monstrous bodies, pieced together of divers members, without definite shape, having no order, sequence, or proportion other than accidental?

(135)

This passage, placed in the middle of a volume of essays by a man who has been both celebrated and disparaged as the creator of literary self-portraiture, suggests that the center of artistic (self)-creation occupies a void or abyss.[1] Creation in the abyss is worth keeping in mind, for when Montaigne subsequently eliminates the twenty-nine sonnets from the twenty-ninth essay, he leaves what Jean Starobinski describes as "a hole in the middle of his work, a hole whose dimensions would give a precise measure of his own *inadequacy*" (232, emphasis original). That Montaigne's "own inadequacy" is not merely measured but achieved at the expense of his dead friend, of an other possibly even more "inadequate," reveals the dimensions of this "hole in the middle of his work" to be ethical and political as well as ontological and poetical. More precisely, it reveals the (in)adequacy of the self to be a function of the (in)adequacy of the other: one emptiness represented, filled in, written over, with another.

At the center of a book, then, we find a proliferating, creative emptiness: the death of a friend, the curious elimination of his work, and the depiction, in words, of a blank space. Starobinski rightly notes the baroque penchant for the "ultimate illusion" of the play within a play (3), a space within a space; and surely there is something similar at play in this series of empty centers. The *mise en abîme* that ensues spirals from theater to theory to the subject of speculation—what has been described as the speculator speculated, the observer observed—and recalls what R. A. Sayce describes as "an infinite regress."[2] For Sayce, such speculative spiraling corresponds to something close to mannerism, with its "reaction against the optimism of the early Renaissance, doubling of the personality, skepticism, narcissism, oblique and labyrinthine forms, paradox, [and] word play" (324). Yet it corresponds perhaps even more closely, as Sayce maintains, to the baroque, at least insofar as the baroque is understood in terms of "open form" and "infinite expandability" (435). Starobinski, though less inclined to pursue the relations between mannerist and baroque modalities, also suggests an affinity between Montaigne and the baroque, not just in terms of *mise en abîme,* but also in terms of disenchantment *(desengaño),* movement, and a "[s]keptical refusal . . . expressed metaphorically in the act of standing aloof, abstaining" (6). As Starobinski sees it, "secession from the world thus figures as an inaugural act" (6) for Montaigne, an act that is persistently undercut, opened, and expanded, by a skeptical, speculative interest in the world. It is just this tension between abstention and interest that is, as we shall see later on, troublingly replayed by Arenas, but so is the inaugural potential of secession.[3]

Secession and poetic inauguration entail an emptiness (a clearing or removing) that bears further speculation. I have called the emptiness that we observe at the center of Montaigne's volume prolific because it spurs a wild, exuberant, excessive productivity that *seems* to eschew order, sequence, and proportion. Like so much else in Montaigne's work, emptiness is not adequate or sufficient to itself, but requires, as the very measure of its inadequacy and insufficiency, as the very measure of its emptiness, a proliferation of signs and images, including, at times even primarily, signs and images of emptiness itself. Montaigne's empty space is, after all, the space most beautifully suited to portraiture, to the placement of a skillfully wrought picture ("un tableau élaboré de toute sa suffisance"). Or rather, Montaigne's empty space is what *surrounds* the "elaborate" picture, what encircles the product or proof of another artist's "skill and sufficiencie."[4] This is, properly speaking, the space of the grotesque, of grotesques, a space whose emptiness, promptly filled in, is not original but ancillary, not central but peripheral, even parasitic.

Likening his writing to painting, his words to grotesques, Montaigne does not just assume a position of modesty, false or not, he also assumes a position of eccentricity and marginality.[5] Starobinski reads Montaigne as writing (about) his writing as "marginal filler" (232), a reading borne out by the fact that Montaigne, even as he refers to himself, typically frames his essays around the writing of others. What arises is a self-portraiture beside itself, or better yet, a self-portraiture which consists of an elaborate circumlocution, or en-framing, of the words and images of others: La Boétie, of course, but also Horace, Catullus, Ariosto, Cicero, Terence, and so on.[6] Arenas, I might interject, invokes, though only to obliterate, the writing of Marxist-Leninism and Social Realism and effects, in the process, a strangeness (or estrangement) that Montaigne associates with the grotesque. The intertwining of strangeness and (self)-portraiture has some significant (self)-referential turns. For if the grotesque is strange, even monstrous, it is in part because it styles the self as twisted round and shot through with otherness.

This is an important point, for to depict and describe one's self is to risk a narcissistic self-absorption in which the other is denied, a risk, as I have intimated, which Arenas openly confronts. Montaigne also confronts it; so much so that M. A. Screech states that Montaigne's "originality" lies in part in the "oddness" or "strangeness" of his endeavor, the apparent willingness to flirt with condemnation by turning in on himself and settling others, along with their perceptions, lessons, and pronouncements, as naught.[7] Montaigne, quite clearly, and Arenas, less clearly, do not set others at naught: not just because they do not want to (as if we, or they, could know with complete clarity what they want), but because their writing courts a "strangeness"

through comparisons, analogies, trans-lations, and an extensive flowering of rhetoric.[8] It is the very "strangeness" of this writing, its eccentricity and marginality, its resistance to proportion, propriety, and order, in a word, its grotesqueness, that keeps the self from simply staying put: "élabouré de toute sa suffisance."

The grotesque as style, script, and sign of the self: such is the meaning I wish here to mine. Although it is now largely understood thematically, the grotesque surfaces, or resurfaces, as a formal property. It resurfaces quite literally, for the grotesque derives from the intricate ornamental designs discovered between the late fifteenth and early sixteenth centuries in the antique ruins of Italy. Etymologically, the word comes from *grotta*, meaning "cave" (or "grotto") and, by extension, the once buried walls and rooms of the ruins. *Grotta* itself comes from the Latin *crypta* (*grupta* in Vulgar Latin), meaning "vault" or "crypt," from the Greek *krupte, kruptos,* meaning "hidden," from the verb *kruptein,* "to hide." Montaigne's "crotesque" is further related to the French "crot(t)e" and "croute." The latter means "crust" and "scab," and has also come to refer to a bad painting. The former, "crotte," means "dung" or "mud." Thus, together, they imply waste and hardness. This last connection does not go unnoticed, for Sarduy describes the baroque as a "nódulo geológico," a geological node, and hence as a mineral-like protuberance, swelling, or emergence, a knot of and in signification.

The grotesque does in fact recall the excrescences of a cave, the superfluous, if subterranean, surgings of the natural world. At the same time it is tied to artifice and adornment or, even more, to a counterfeiting and outrageous reworking of nature (in Littré's definition, "qui outre et contrefait la nature d'une manière bizarre"). Raphael, Pinturicchio, and Signorelli are some of the artists who imitate the antique grotesques (as Montaigne claims to imitate, in writing, his grotesque painter), bringing them to the Vatican and setting the stage for the symbolic solidification of the grotesque into the bizarre, extraordinary, burlesque, ridiculous, and extravagant.[9] By the time Bakhtin employs the grotesque as a sign of low, comic, carnivalesque bodies, its thematization seems quite set, perhaps in part because its formal qualities (graphic, plastic, and ornamental) have again been partially interred.[10]

The grotesque is, I want to insist, a way of drawing and writing the self and (or as) others. It involves not just *what* is drawn or written, but *how* and even *where*. It is thus as much, if not much more, of the signifier than the signified. While it may be metaphorically tied to carnival, it is styled, as Wolfgang Kayser notes, in and as book illustrations, lettering, painted surfaces, tools, jewelry, architecture, and scrollwork (22). This "secret storehouse of invention" (171), to use Walter Benjamin's phrase, gives rise to a sort of convoluted formalism, where irregular shapes and wild arabesques at once reveal and conceal, engrave and encrypt, something that pushes at the established order of the natural and the human. Both Kayser and Benjamin, the latter relying on the work of Karl Borinski, intimate that the thing revealed and concealed in the grotesque is not just human and natural diversity, not just effusiveness and laughter, but death. This is the sinister, turbulent, and agonizingly fearful dimension that Kayser finds alongside the silly, funny, and coarsely humorous; this is, as convention has it, the troubling side of all that is the odd, strange, funny, and queer.

Benjamin, through Borinski, goes even further, holding the grotesque as a significant form of ruin and burial, holding death, that is, as the insoluble secret of the secret storehouse of baroque invention.[11] Montaigne seems to bear this out, for his grotesque scripting is, as we have seen, a testament to his lost friend, a thing of death. But Montaigne's scripting is also, lest we forget, a thing of friendship, a thing of love. It is that by which he engages himself, his living and mortal self, with an otherness which exceeds him and which he lacks. The dilemma of excess and lack is exacerbated by the fact that, as Marcel Tetel observes, "posterity remembers [Montaigne's] own essay, the monument to this friendship, and not La Boétie himself" (68). The more Montaigne writes, the more he dedicates himself to his friend in writing, the more he writes over him, crossing out La Boétie as he preserves him. This writing of erasuree is, in certain respects, the most graphic legacy of the grotesque: an art that is styled, over-styled, in loss, absence, and death; a form that is full, over-full, with emptiness.

In different fashions, emptiness founds and surrounds the work of the painter, La Boétie, Montaigne, and his readers. For Donald Frame, "the reader takes the place of the dead friend" (v), while for Marcel Tetel, Montaigne's "ultimate friends are his *Essays*" (68). Reading, writing, friendship, and love intersect and collide because the positions which they imply appear to have been left—in the death that might well have closed them—open, empty. Emptiness is thus a condition and effect of position, of portrait and frame, center and margin, figuration proper and improper.[12] But emptiness itself can only be *figured* through a sort of filling, spectral as well as material, by which emptiness is, as it were, emptied of itself. This paradox, smacking perhaps too nicely of deconstruction, is here nonetheless crucial to the depiction and inscription of the self. Figuring emptiness, emptying it in and as figuration, is how Montaigne generates grotesques and, furthermore, how he signals that identity, be it his or his friend's, is neither simply full nor empty of meaning, validity, or truth.

Identity, that is, is not a fullness against an emptiness of non-identity, nor can it be shed, surrendered, or emptied: mystically, magically, willfully, *absolutely*. It can

be lost, but only to or from an other; it cannot, at any rate, be lost utterly *to* its self, ab-solved (even schizophrenia entails the persistence, however shattered, of a principle of identity). This too has, I believe, ethical and political ramifications, particularly where identity has been theorized, theatricalized, and specularized as something not just problematic (which it is), but *absolutely* illusory and false, vile and dangerous, as something, in common parlance, "wrong" or "bad." This is not to say that identity is "right" and "good," but rather that it is "itself" a question, or questioning, and that it *takes place,* questionably, within a *language* of ethics, politics, and aesthetics. In fact, for all their differences, Montaigne and Arenas posit identity as a question of writing, a minute and involute marking, tracing, or shading, which resists clarity, finality, and stability, even, if not especially, when it seeks them.[13]

I have so far set my sights on Montaigne, making only brief and casual reference to Reinaldo Arenas, the writer whose work I have designated, from the beginning of my essay, as the end of my essay. I have also, for the most part, highlighted the graphics of the grotesque, striving to keep its thematics impossibly in the background. But if form and content, graph and theme, are entangled, it is in a way because the grotesque is entanglement itself. The ornamental flourish of figures neither fish nor flow, the reticular profusion of cryptic signs and images, is the most visible stuff of the grotesque, but so too are death, burial, emptiness, creativity, excess, and exuberance: an entire thematics of mortality and vitality that heightens, and is heightened by, the significance of form.

This grotesque entanglement of mortality and vitality, like that of form and content, extends to Arenas, who writes (about) writing as a matter of life and death. It extends to him, but in no wise neatly. Four hundred years separate Montaigne and Arenas, as do language, position, sexuality, and so many other things, including emotional tone. However skeptical he may be, Montaigne never attains, for instance, the anger and anguish that characterize much of Arenas's work and life, both of which are marked by poverty, imprisonment, homelessness, exile, AIDS, and suicide. It may therefore seem strange that I piece together such divers members as Montaigne and Arenas, but that too, we will remember, is of the grotesque. There is of course more. Kayser may well be right to declare that "[t]he art of our own day has a greater affinity to the grotesque than that of any other epoch" (11), if only because the grotesque signifies, now more than ever, "the dissolution of reality and the participation in a different kind of existence" (22), "a world which breaks apart and remains inaccessible" (31).

Dissolution, difference, and breakage are, to be sure, signs of a peculiarly contemporary sort; for although they are operant in Montaigne, they are there countered by highly resistant kernels of classical and religious authority. In Arenas, however, dissolution and difference do not so much spell the end of authority or reality as their ever more fervent reproduction and dissemination: authority may seek the all too real dissolution of those it depicts as its others. Arenas sees authoritative reality and real authority—a hard kernel in symbolization, as Žižek might put it—as motivating real and symbolic death, and yet at the same time as motivating a productive resistance. In this sense, the grotesque signifies not only a world which breaks apart and remains inaccessible, but one which is riven with productivity. Or to put it a bit differently: "I" write, grotesquely both for and against "my" dissolution.

Arenas's concern with the dissolution of reality, authority, and personal identity is inscribed in aesthetic as well as political terms. A champion of artistic freedom, he is adamantly, and at times contradictorily, opposed to totalitarianism and tyranny, which for him are embodied until the very end of his life by Fidel Castro. Montaigne is similarly opposed, as is, it seems, La Boétie. In fact, Montaigne's grotesques do not attest merely to the author's (in)adequacy in the absence of his friend; rather, they are also an attempt to defend the anti-tyrannical *spirit* of La Boétie's *La Servitude volontaire* (*Voluntary Servitude*). This work, written in Montaigne's words "à l'honneur de la liberté contre les tyrans" ("in honor of liberty against tyrants") is one of the few that Montaigne can recover from among La Boétie's mortal relics, "recouvrer de ses reliques" (198, 135). The history of this piece of writing exceeds the scope of the present essay (it has to do with the religious civil wars of Protestants and Catholics), but signals an intermingling of politics, death, and friendship, or love, which I find in Arenas as well.

About death, as a stylized effect of the grotesque, I have here written much; about politics, I have here written less; but about friendship, or love, I have written, here, least of all. The thematics of love, or friendship, may not seem easily suited to the figures of the grotesque, but the fit, nonetheless, is there. For Montaigne, the effort to piece together, without strict order, sequence, or proportion, an homage to his dead friend, to rescue his friend's relics from oblivion by retracing them in a different script, is one of profound personal commitment. But it is not, for all that, an effort without peril. I am thinking not only of the peril of distorting the truth, or altering the reality and authority, or othering the identity, of La Boétie, but of waxing effusive, all too effusive, about friendship itself. According to Marcel Tetel, "what [Montaigne] calls friendship we would refer to as love, and love, especially conjugal love, becomes in his eyes what we would accept as friendship" (68.)[14] Tetel's observations, concerned with anachronistic confusion, are adumbrated by Montaigne's own. For in this central essay on friendship, politics,

and death, the absence and emptiness that spurs a profusion of grotesques plays another way. The lack of friendship, the friend's lack, spurs an excess of friendship, the friend's excess: and this excess, spurred by lack, is love. This, rather anxiously, Montaigne seems to know. Friendship, of such intensity and between men, is haunted after all by the "vice" of the Greeks: "cet'autre licence Grecque . . . justement abhorrée par nos mœurs" ("that other, licentious Greek love . . . justly abhorred by our morality") (202, 138). These grotesque writings open, among so many other things, onto the love that dare not speak its name.

Montaigne dedicates a significant portion of his essay on friendship to what we would accept, to continue Tetel's phrase, as homosexuality. He does so, not surprisingly, to distance his own feelings for La Boétie from feelings more carnal, and yet, as he expands on the structure and customs of male love, he necessarily acknowledges its complexity and cultural importance. If it is debatable, because psychological, to speak of Montaigne's ambivalence and anxiety, it is less so to point out that Montaigne recognizes that the Greek licence has been celebrated as "sacred and divine" by poets and philosophers and that it has been "abhorred" by violent tyrants and cowardly crowds: "la nomment ils sacrée et divine. Et n'est, à leur compte, que la violence des tyrans et lascheté des peuples qui luy soit adversaire" ("they call it sacred and divine. And by their reckoning, only the violence of tyrants and the cowardice of the common people are hostile to it") (203, 139). Entangled in Montaigne's essay, close to its center, is the politics of love or friendship ("un amour se terminant en amitié" ("a love ending in friendship") (203, 139). It is a politics where tyranny and freedom, opposition and acceptance, even life and death are intertwined in a writing styled amid excess and lack, in a writing grotesque.

This is the politics of love or friendship—a politics, and ethics, problematically entangled, as we shall see, in aesthetics—that I have been evoking in the name of Reinaldo Arenas, a writer who engages (in) homosexual love as critical to his own writing.[15] It goes without saying that he is, in this, quite different from Montaigne, and yet, amid this difference, he shows a curious affinity with him through the intertwining of friendship, or love, and the grotesque. For while the grotesque interplay of lack and excess may be written in a number of corporeally and culturally specific manners, it appears especially relevant to homosexuality. Too masculine or too feminine, too little masculine or too little feminine: such are some of the pronouncements that gay men and lesbians negotiate. Others include the sense of the subversive, sinister, and unnatural, or the burlesque, lowly comic, and wildly exuberant, of the strange, odd, and queer. Some of these senses have been vindicated to the point that they designate entire theories, most notably "Queer Theory" with its intricately self-styled ways of envisioning the sexual self. Still others, such as narcissism and the fixation on death, present more intractable problems, but ones which, despite homophobic assertions to the contrary, are not unique to homosexuality.[16] The sense of "queerness" which I am drawing in and out of the grotesque—as Geoffrey Galt Harpham remarks, "the word itself betrays and irreducible queerness" (3)—is itself accidental and highly problematic. And yet, these two qualities actually reinforce the sense that the grotesque is accidental at its most intentional and problematic at its most sure. Together, these senses operate thematically, but they encompass, among their themes, questions of style, script, and signification: the how and where of writing.

For Arenas, writing often appears to be of will and of necessity an overwriting, a scribbling of, for, and yet against something grotesque. In *Arturo, la estrella más brillante* (*The Brightest Star,* 1984), Arenas, or rather his protagonist Arturo, focuses on the act of writing itself.[17] Stealing time to write in the state-run camp to which he has been confined for "improper conduct," that is to say, for homosexuality, Arturo attests to what is at stake politically in certain "styles" of friendship and love. Imprisonment, forced labor, and other modes of involuntary servitude are here the occasion for a paradoxically prolific creativity. But lest this creativity seem nice and easy, lest it seem optional or incidental, Arenas presents Arturo's coming to writing as absolutely vital, vital because bound up in death: "decidió que para salvarse tenía que comenzar a escribir inmediatamente" ("he decided that to save himself he had to start writing, *now*") (42, 71). With his very salvation, as he sees it, hanging in the balance, Arturo pursues a writing at once furtive and furious:

> había que darse prisa, había que seguir, rápido, y, tomando precauciones—se hacían registros, se prohibía llevar diarios, cosas de maricones, decían los tenientes como justificación oficial, irrebatible y reglamentariamente se violaba toda la correspondencia—, las libretas, las contratapas, los respaldos, los márgenes y forros de los manuales de marxismo leninismo y de economía robados de la Sección Política fueron garrapateados furtivamente, rápidamente, cuando nadie vigilaba, bajo la sábana, de pie en el excusado, en la misma cola para el desayuno, hasta los márgenes de los grotescos carteles políticos instalados en las paredes y murales para el uso interno del campamento sufrieron la invasión de aquella letra microscópica y casi indescifrable en tarea interrumpida incesantemente a la vez que constante, ahora, ahora, no ahora, ahora."

> (44)

> Hurry, hurry, keep on, keep on, fast—of course taking precautions, because there were searches, you couldn't keep diaries, "pansy-ass bullshit," said the lieutenants as official justification for going inexorably, unstoppably, and legally through everyone's correspondence—so taking at least minimal precautions, he scribbled in the notebooks, and on the inside covers, along the spines, in the margins and blank pages of Marxist-Leninist manuals and economic books stolen from the Political Section, he furtively, quickly filled them with his tiny scrawl, and when nobody was looking, under the sheets or standing in the stall in the toilet, in line for breakfast sometimes, he even filled the margins of grotesque political posters pasted up on the walls, even announcements *For Internal Camp Circulation* suffered that almost microscopic crablike invasion of virtually indecipherable letters and signs.

> (72-73)

Urgently, Arturo writes: anywhere, everywhere, possible. He is as an intricate *scriptor,* a tireless scribbler, filling the margins of a sociopolitical document with the signs and scratches of his identity. In so doing, he complicates the ostensibly straight and simple messages of manuals and political posters, charges them with something cryptic and involved, adorns them with something close to obliteration. As with a sixteenth-century grotesque, the grotesque posters on the prison walls are subjected to a grotesque reworking of their own, to a proliferation of fanciful marks, twists and turns, queer little letters. Against that grotesque, centered and straight in its authority, this other grotesque, marginal, deviant and devious, spirals across the pages, across the bindings, with its own secret, special authority.

Arturo's authority, perhaps Arenas's authority, is profoundly embattled. Slapdash, paranoiac, erratic, it *takes place,* quite literally, in, or rather on, the printed material of others, others whose authority is here that of the state. Private material such as diaries is branded as queer ("cosa de maricones") and hence as the work of an identity identified as anti-social and self-absorbed. Queerness appears to permeate this intimate, self-concerned scripting, but is as much an effect of the state as of the isolated self, imposed from without and assumed, albeit differently, from within.[18] The self is entangled in otherness, as I have said above, and yet so too is otherness. For if the otherness of the state is grotesque in its straight and centered authority, there is another otherness: the otherness of the friend, or lover, that generates, and is generated in, grotesques where fantasy, inventiveness, and freedom, or some semblance thereof, flourish. As with Montaigne, the friend is here absent, prolifically. For Arturo, he is a young man, idealized and sensualized, who comes to him at times in writing, and for whom Arturo struggles to construct a realm of ideal sensuality where he may dwell. For *Arturo* [*Arturo, la estrella más brillante*], he is Nelson Rodríguez Leyva, a homosexual counterrevolutionary who died in an attempted hijacking and to whom Arenas dedicates his work. A double absence, then, in and out of the text, an emptiness made both possible and impossible by a proliferation of signs: these are here the stakes of the self and (its) writing.

Arturo's writing is in many respects a rewriting of Arenas's own difficulties with writing under Castro. Indeed,

Arenas's work is repeatedly lost, sequestered, and destroyed; much of it, towards the end of his life, is rewritten from memory, hurriedly brought into print, and posthumously published. Autobiographically inflected, his works, not unlike Montaigne's, are attempts, or essays, at self-inscription, self-portraiture.[19] Autobiography, as the writing of the life of the self, appears to be a vital necessity, but only insofar as it involves the reading and rewriting of the death of another, including, of course, the otherness and anticipated death of the self (once again, as in Montaigne, the observer observed, the self-before-death). So involute is this process of reading and writing that the principle of identity, of clarity, integrity, and sufficiency, does not quite hold. Little wonder that autobiography, in its various manifestations, twisting in truth and falsity, history and discourse, often appears grotesque.[20]

Often, but not always: for while Montaigne openly compares his writing to grotesques, Arturo, or Arenas, just as openly *opposes* his writing to what he takes to be the grotesque writing of the state. This distinction is understandable, in part because the movement from "grotesques" to "the grotesque," from Montaigne's day to Arenas's, entails an occultation of the scriptural and the decorative and a hypostatization of content. What Bakhtin celebrates as the very substance of the grotesque (the low, burlesque, earthy, "realist" body), Arturo rejects. And yet, in rejecting this grotesque, he repeats it. For in taking grotesque administrative and military documents as the space for something lavish, in filling the margins and all but obliterating the center with uncommonly rich signifiers (*"jacintos, qurquesas, ónix, ópalos, calcedonias, jades . . . un aterido lo-fo-ro-ro, ¿lofororo?, ¡qué coño es esto!, qué cantidad de sandeces y boberías, qué verborrea, qué palabras tan raras"* [*"jacinths, turquoise, onyx, opals, chalcedony, agate, jade . . . a half-frozen pter-o-dac-tyl*—Pterodactyl! What the fuck is that! Have you ever heard such nonsense, such gobbledygook, can you believe this gibberish! I never saw such words"]) (76, 94), in describing his writing as prolific, furtive, peripheral, and parasitic, Arturo presents himself, unwittingly or not, as the author of grotesques.[21]

But he repeats the grotesque on another level as well, mercilessly describing his fellow prisoners as shrill, vulgar, weak, and unbearably campy queens. "They" ("Ellos") are characterized by "sus infinitas conversaciones inútiles, . . . sus gestos excesivamente afeminados, artificiales, grotescos" ("their endless, stupid conversations, . . . [by] their exaggerated, effeminate, affected, artificial, false, gross, grotesque gesturings and posturings") (12, 51). "They" are submissive, absurd, and disgraceful, "corrompiéndolo todo, hasta la auténtica furia del que padece el terror" ("cheapening and corrupting everything, even the authentic rage of the man who suffers terror") (12, 51). The fate of authentic-

ity, rage, suffering, and terror are crucial for Arturo's, if not Arenas's, conception of individual freedom and creativity, a conception which clashes not only with the collectivity of communism but with the solidarity of gay identity as well. In fact, Arturo's celebration of individuality is such that unity and cohesion of any form appear perilously restrictive. It is along these lines that I have said that Montaigne's act of wordly secession and poetic inauguration is *troublingly* replayed by Arenas's Arturo. Arturo may "abs-tain" and stand aloof, but hardly in the same way as Montaigne.

Aloof abstention of a particularly derisive sort is in Arenas's text the price of Arturo's "grotesques." If Montaigne's grotesques evince what many critics consider an ambivalent contact with mannerism and the baroque, Arturo's or Arenas's "grotesques" indicate an equally ambivalent relation with the neo-baroque (and social realism). In fact, while Arenas is certainly less flamboyantly cryptic than, say, Lezama Lima, he scatters recondite, sonorous words throughout his text—not just *lofororo*, but also *hastial, albarrana, canecillo, curaña, ustorio, hematita, lampadario, triforio, cocuyo*—and defers closure by refusing paragraphs and periods (except one, at the very end). *Arturo* consists of one intricate sentence, turning and returning on itself, running to and from historical reality and literary invention, to and from pain and pleasure, suffering and release. It replays, on a different plane, the grotesque intricacy of Arturo's writing, the proliferation of signs in and out of emptiness, absence, and death. According to Sarduy, such "empty" proliferation is, among other things, characteristic of the neo-baroque: "[l]a proliferación, recorrido previsto, órbita de similitudes abreviadas, exige, para hacer adivinable lo que oblitera, para rozar con su perífrasis el significante excluido, expulsado, y dibujar la ausencia que señala, esa traslación, ese recorrido alrededor de lo que falta y cuya falta lo constituye" (172). The movement around a constitutive (motivating) lack, the proliferation of signifiers brushing, sketching, intimating an excluded, expelled, absent signifier, is for Sarduy the movement of the neo-baroque. It is a movement in and of artifice and erotism, a lush expenditure of useless, sensually sterile, signs, a revolution against propriety, a subversion of order, sequence, and proportion.[22]

For us today, Sarduy's description may seem dated, testifying to a time, as Arenas's narrator writes of Arturo, "cuando aún pensaba que un grupo de signos, que la cadencia de unas imágenes adecuadamente descritas, que las palabras, podrían salvarlo" ("when he was still convinced that a cluster of signs, a cadence of images perfectly described—*words*—might save him") (9, 49). Inasmuch as this statement comes to the very opening of *Arturo,* salvation in or through words is never really viable, nor is the dream of rewriting the world as beautiful, loving, and just (a dream reiterated throughout most of the text). But still, the dream is there. What is also there, so to speak, is an impression of queerness, explicitly in Arenas's narrative and implicitly in Sarduy's essay (of Montaigne's essay, I have already written). For is not the continuous movement in artifice and erotism; the sense of unproductive sensuality, strange subversion, and improper revolution; the putatively narcissistic focus on decay and death; the ornate form and degraded content of the grotesque; is not this all already troped as homosexual? Is not this all already written in, on, and around "a body which is not one," a gay body—a body, a mind, an identity, a community—denied legitimacy because too much *and* too little, excessive *and* empty?

The rhetorical nature of these questions is only partial: the answers are—dare I say, must be—negative as well as affirmative. I have said that the relation between the queer and the grotesque is accidental and problematic: accidental insofar as it is arguably an "unintended" effect of prior critical discourse, and problematic insofar as it reiterates certain well-established stereotypes. On this latter score, Arenas himself is far from docile, for in his posthumously published autobiography as well as in his autobiographically inflected narratives (his "autofictions" as Philippe Sollers might put it), the queer is closely bound to the grotesque, not of stylish (self)-creation, but of freakishness and deformity, passive mimicry and ugly absurdity. Montaigne's anxiety that his friendship with La Boétie might be read as love, sexual love, that it might be collapsed into the Greek licence, is here again troublingly replayed in Arturo's, if not Arenas's, anxiety that his openly sexual love for the beautiful young man of his dreams might be collapsed into some sort of modern Gay licence. This is a bit queer, because Arturo, no less than Arenas, is forthrightly, even defiantly, homosexual. This queerness may be explained (away) as internalized homophobia, as a *restrictive* politics of friendship and love, but it may also be styled as something else, something aesthetic as well as ethical and political. This queerness may be styled, that is, as an ethico-political query into beauty.

Queerness may be styled, though not judged or justified, as an accident and a problem of beauty, perhaps because beauty is itself, in Arturo's conflicted world, what is most extravagant, most excessive, most strangely and surprisingly *grotesque;* perhaps because beauty, to be truly beautiful, must be lost, remembered, and rewritten: again and again, twist upon turn, note upon note. Exceeding utility and socially cohesive productivity, beauty exceeds, and yet falls forever short of, what matters, not just to the state but to any community, any communication, whatsoever. Beauty is for Arturo, if not for Arenas, the sign that exceeds signs.[23] And part of this (in)significant excess, perhaps the accursedly fatal part, is that it dismisses the excess and extravagance of others (in Arturo's case, other homosexuals, other Cubans, other historical subjects) by focusing, extravagantly and excessively, on the Other (in Arturo's case, the ideal lover, the beauteous Complement).[24] What Arturo, unlike Montaigne, does not seem to accept is that the excess and extravagance, openness and inadequacy, of others are grotesques (not just grotesque) and that these grotesques—beautiful *and* ugly, exquisite *and* monstrous, friendly, loving, *and* hateful—are his as well.

Identity may be nothing, in other words, but a cryptic entangling of grotesques.

Notes

1. Harpham's reading of Montaigne's final essay, "De l'experience," is suggestive: "Montaigne's sympathy to pied beauty does not compromise the center, but strengthens it, for it admits everything as a possible center, and admits that the true center is beyond our grasp" (76).

2. "Theater" (*theatron*) and "Theory" (*theoria*) are both from the Greek *theasthai,* meaning "to observe or watch." *Theoros* means "spectator."

3. If Montaigne stands, as Sayce puts it, on the borders of the baroque, Arenas stands on the borders of the neo-baroque, whose center, if indeed it has one, appears to be occupied by Josi Lezama Lima.

4. This last quote, "skill and sufficiencie," is from the third edition of the first English translation of Montaigne's *Essays,* by John Florio in 1632.

5. Auerbach, for one, refers to Montaigne's "reticent, ironical, and slightly self-satisfied modesty" (252).

6. As Ormiston and Schrift put it, Montaigne authors "a *commentary* that turns away from itself, toward a different text, *and* that turns in on itself (2).

7. As Screech notes, "Aesop had condemned self-love (*philautia*) as the prime source of human error," and an extensive secular and religious tradition concurred. Accordingly, "[t]o write about yourself without overwhelming cause was to stand condemned by towering and august authority, both ancient and modern." Such authority holds, if less pervasively, even today, as is evident in Screech's rather anxious assertion that "there was nothing narcissistic about [Montaigne's] study of himself" (7).

8. Montaigne is not an obscure writer, comparatively speaking. But his "strangeness" is explicitly enunciated in an analogy to painting, to another artistic medium. Arenas's strangeness is implicitly enunciated as an opposition to Marxist-Leninism and Social Realism, to what is presented as an inartistic, or even anti-artistic, medium. The difference

in enunciation is related, in turn, to a different relation to others: Montaigne abstains to encompass, while Arenas, or his narrator/character, abstains to exclude. Needless to say, the difference in their personal positions (one writing largely at home, the other in and out of prison, on the sly, on the run, in exile) should not be forgotten.

9. Burlesque comedy is associated with the grotesque, despite Littré's assertion that "le sujet ni le dessin des grotesques n'ont rien de bouffon." Of course, Littré also defines "grotesque" as "[f]igures qui font rire en outrant la nature." Grotesques are also known as "dreams of painters (*sogni dei pittori*)" (22). Luca Signorelli's grotesques are found in the Cathedral of Orvieto (1499-1504).

10. "Fundamental to the corporeal, collective nature of carnival laughter is," as Stallybrass and White remark, "what Bakhtin terms 'grotesque realism'" (8). As is well known, Bakhtin takes Rabelais as the bearer of the grotesque in writing. With respect to the question of form, Geoffrey Harpham goes so far as to say that the grotesque, "[a]s an adjective . . . has no descriptive value; its sole function is to represent a condition of overcrowding or contradiction in the place where the modifier should be. This place can never be occupied by any other single adjective but only by a number of adjectives *not normally found together.* The grotesque is concept without form" (3, emphasis mine). Harpham suggests that "overcrowding" and "contradiction" are not descriptive (which they are) and that form is simple, singular, and self-identical (which it is not). The form of the grotesque is, as I see it, the overcrowding and contradiction of signs and images, the excess, or lack, of simplicity, singularity, and self-identity, the resistance to what is normally found together, to the norms and normativity of form itself. Of course, inasmuch as the grotesque does not quite fit into the norms of form, that its form is a questioning of form, Harpham's point is well-taken.

11. Benjamin quotes Borinski who refers first to Ludovico da Feltre's grotesques and then to Pliny's passage on the balcony paintings of Serapion as having served "in literature as the personification of the subterranean-fantastic, the occult-spectral. For even at that time the enigmatically mysterious character of the effect of the grotesque seems to have been associated with its subterraneanly mysterious origin in buried ruins and catacombs. The word is not derived from grotta in the literal sense, but from the 'burial'—in the sense of concealment—which the cave or grotto expresses" (Borinski's *Die Antike,* quoted in Benjamin, 171). Kayser effects a similar citational run, referring to Vasari referring to Vitruvius's resistance, in *De architectura,* to the "monstrous forms" of the "new ornamental style" in the age of Augustus.

12. As Starobinski notes, "[e]mptiness in fact turns out, paradoxically, to be quite fecund, in that it somehow gives rise to a whole 'fantastic' growth of shapes and figures that fill it and give it life" (232). It also, as I have been arguing, gives it a sense of death.

13. This tension underlies Starobinski's study: "The *movement* that I shall try to describe is nothing other than the effort of a man who, starting from a concept of identity based on the principles of constancy, stability, and self-consistency (a goal that turns out to be impossible to achieve), begins to develop a new concept of identity without abandoning the original one, but nonetheless altering its content and meaning" (14).

14. Montaigne's own distinctions seem clearer than Tetel implies: "In friendship it is a general and universal warmth, moderate and even, besides, a constant and settled warmth, all gentleness and smoothness, with nothing bitter and stinging about it. What is more, in love there is nothing but a frantic desire for what flees from us" (201, 137).

15. In his novel *El portero,* Arenas refers to his "self-confessed homosexualism, delirious and reproachable" (97, my translation).

16. Michael Warner challenges the tendency, in both psychoanalytic and popular discourse, to characterize homosexuality as narcissistic and declares that "modern heterosexuality needs a discourse about homosexuality as a displacement of its own narcissistic sources" (206). With respect to homosexuality and death, see Leo Bersani, for whom the connection is not just acknowledged, but made hyperbolic.

17. The text may be read as an intense monologic staging of the movements of the (un)conscious subject. Its often daunting formal qualities reveal and conceal a relatively simple plot: Arturo, a young homosexual Cuban writer (or would-be writer) is imprisoned for "improper conduct" and forced to work in a governmentally organized labor camp. His world is suffused with suffering and he is excruciatingly lonely. His loneliness is, however, an effect of a rough resistance, for he is in fact *surrounded* by people.

18. In *Before Night Falls,* Arenas claims that "the sexual revolution in Cuba actually came about as a result of the existing sexual repression. Perhaps as a protest against the regime, homosexuality began to flourish with ever-increasing defiance" (107).

19. As Auerbach notes, "the title *Essais* . . . might fittingly though not very gracefully be rendered as 'Tests upon One's Self' or 'Self-Try-Outs'" (256).

20. Juan Goytisolo, playing with the borders between life and art, history and discourse, posits a "grotesque autobiography" in terms which reiterate, expand, and complicate the grotesque self-portraiture of Montaigne and the (anti)-grotesque self-inscription of Arenas. See *Paisajes después de la batalla* (*Landscapes After the Battle*) (224).

21. For Harpham, "this is the final paradox: really to understand the grotesque is to cease to regard it as grotesque" (76). If Arenas continues to use the "grotesque" as a sign of state power, he replays it, however quietly, in his own terms. In his posthumously published autobiography, *Antes que anochezca* (*Before Night Falls*), he writes: "A sense of beauty is always dangerous and antagonistic to any dictatorship because it implies a realm extending beyond the limits that a dictatorship can impose on human beings. Beauty is a territory that escapes the control of the political police. Being independent and outside of their domain, beauty is so irritating to dictators that they attempt to destroy it whichever way they can. Under a dictatorship, beauty is always a dissident force, because a dictatorship is itself unaesthetic, grotesque; to a dictator and his agents, the attempt to create beauty is an escapist or reactionary act (87). Arenas's brightest blindness may well have to do with the subjectivity of beauty, with the fact that even the state does not dispense with some conception of beauty. Then again, Arenas sees beauty as what both exceeds and lacks the transparency and straight linearity of a social-realist aesthetic, as what irritates power and flirts with destruction. Beauty, for him as for André Breton, must be convulsive or it is not to be at all. It is with this convulsion in mind that many of Arenas's texts, most notably the last volume in his *"pentogonía," El asalto* (*The Assault*), must be read. Far from being simply beautiful, *The Assault* is a work of extraordinary grotesqueness—here in the more common sense of ugly distortion and violent deformation—where beauty is retained only in a sort of ghostly, ghastly, negation.

22. The grotesque is repeatedly associated with movement. For Kayser, the grotesque "[negates] the law of statics" (21); for Bakhtin, "[t]he grotesque image reflects a phenomenon in transformation, an as yet unfinished metamorphosis, of death and birth, growth and becoming" (24); for Harpham, "[t]he perception of the grotesque is never a fixed or stable thing, but always a process, a progression" (14).

23. If the ethical and the aesthetic have long been intertwined, there seems to be nonetheless a certain amount of difference between them. Given the function of rage and disgust in Arenas's later work, the aesthetic does seem to exceed the ethical. Lacan writes in *The Ethics of Psychoanalysis* of "the true barrier that arrests the subject before the unnameable field of radical desire," the "field of absolute destruction" (256). For Lacan, this field of absolute destruction is, "properly speaking, the aesthetic phenomenon," the dazzling flash of the beautiful, "the splendor of the true" (256): "It is evidently because the true is not a pretty sight to see that the beautiful is, if not its splendor, at least its covering." What Lacan suggests is not just that beauty does not occupy the same field as goodness, but that as far as moral experience is concerned the beautiful is closer to evil than the good: "plus près du mal que le bien." If the good is the first line of defense, "the first safety net," the beautiful is the second one: "It stops us, but it also indicates in what direction ("dans quel sens") the field of destruction is found" (256: translations mine).

24. In this, I turn to Bakhtin, for whom the grotesque is a collective, not isolated, effect. I would add, however, that an instance of isolation is necessary to an appreciation of a collective; Montaigne's grotesque self-portrait is at the same time a portrait of others, not only there and then, but here and now; and Arturo's withdrawal in the midst of others underscores, albeit negatively, the significance of others. Kayser makes a similar point when he points out that the grotesque is related negatively to "our" world, that it is ascribed a truth value in inversion and negation (31).

Works Cited

Arenas, Reinaldo. *Arturo, la estrella más brillante.* Barcelona: Montesinos, 1984. *The Brightest Star.* In *Old Rosa: A Novel in Two Stories.* Trans. Andrew Hurley. New York: Grove Press, 1989.

———. *Antes que anochezca.* Barcelona: Editorial Tusquets, 1992. *Before Night Falls.* Trans. Dolores M. Koch. New York: Penguin Books, 1993.

———. *El asalto.* Miami: Ediciones Universal, 1991. *The Assault.* Trans. Andrew Hurley. New York: Viking Penguin, 1994.

———. *El portero.* Miami: Ediciones Universal, 1990. *The Doorman.* Trans. Dolores M. Koch. New York: Grove Wiedenfeld, 1991.

Auerbach, Erich. *Mimesis: The Representation of Reality in Western Literature.* Trans. Willard Trask. New York: Doubleday Anchor Books, 1957.

Bakhtin, Mikhail. *Rabelais and His World.* Trans. Hélène Iswolsky. Bloomington: Indiana UP, 1984.

Benjamin, Walter. *The Origin of German Tragic Drama.* Trans. John Osborne. London: Verso, 1985.

Bersani, Leo. "Is the Rectum a Grave?" *October* 43 (1987): 197-222.

Goytisolo, Juan. *Paisajes después de la batalla.* Madrid: Espasa-Calpe, 1990 ed. *Landscapes After the Battle.* Trans. Helen Lane. New York: Seaver Books, 1987.

Kayser, Wolfgang. *The Grotesque in Art and Literature.* Trans. Ulrich Weisstein. Bloomington: Indiana UP, 1963.

Harpham, Geoffrey Galt. *On the Grotesque: Strategies of Contradiction in Art and Literature.* Princeton: Princeton UP, 1982.

Lacan, Jacques. *Le Séminaire VII: l'Ethique de la psychanalyse.* Paris: Seuil, 1986. Translated by Dennis Porter as *The Ethics of Psychoanalysis.* New York: W. W. Norton & Company, 1992.

Montaigne, Michel de. *Essais.* Paris: Garnier, 1958 ed. 3 vols. *The Complete Essays of Montaigne.* Trans. Donald Frame. Stanford: Stanford UP, 1957-58. *The Essays of Michael Lord of Montaigne.* Trans. John Florio. London: Grant Richards, 1908 (from the 1632 edition).

Ormiston, Gayle L. and Alan D. Schrift, eds. *The Hermeneutic Tradition: From Ast to Ricoeur.* Albany: State University of New York P, 1990.

Sarduy, Severo. "El barroco y el neobarroco." In *América Latina en su literatura.* Ed. César Fernández Moreno. Mexico: Siglo XXI Editores, 1972. 167-84.

Sayce, R. A. *The Essays of Montaigne: A Critical Exploration.* Chicago: Northwestern UP, 1972.

Screech, M. A. *Montaigne and Melancholy.* London: Penguin, 1983.

Stallybrass, Peter & Allon White. *The Politics and Poetics of Transgression.* Ithaca: Cornell UP, 1986.

Starobinski, Jean. *Montaigne en mouvement.* Paris: Gallimard, 1982. *Montaigne in Motion.* Trans. Arthur Goldhammer. Chicago: U of Chicago P, 1985.

Tetel, Marcel. *Montaigne.* New York: Twayne, 1974.

Warner, Michael. "Homo-Narcissism; or, Heterosexuality." In *Engendering Men: The Question of Male Feminist Criticism.* Eds. Boone & Cadden. New York: Routledge, 1990: 190-206.

Zižek, Slavoj. *The Sublime Object of Ideology.* London: Verso, 1989.

Ricardo L. Ortíz (essay date 1998)

SOURCE: Ortíz, Ricardo L. "Pleasure's Exile: Reinaldo Arenas's Last Writing." In *Borders, Exiles, Diasporas,* edited by Elazar Barkan and Marie-Denise Shelton, pp. 92-111. Stanford, Calif.: Stanford University Press, 1998.

[*In the following essay, Ortíz places Arenas's last works—those he wrote while living in exile in the U.S.—in a "special period," a "moment of historical and cultural suspension" between the end of the Cold War and Fidel Castro's continuing domination of Cuban politics.*]

> In one of my first statements after leaving Cuba I had declared that "the difference between the communist and capitalist systems is that, although both give you a kick in the ass, in the communist system you have to applaud, while in the capitalist system you can scream. And I came here to scream."
>
> —Reinaldo Arenas, *Before Night Falls*

Outside prevailing constructions of nationality organized around the native and the immigrant, there is the exile. To the extent that Cuban-American and Cuban-exile writing of the last generation can be said to have fashioned a voice for itself in the larger contexts of mainstream and immigrant-American literature, it has retained in its own internalized dialectic a profoundly embedded tendency toward self-marginalization and self-alienation. This is nowhere more apparent than in the work produced by Reinaldo Arenas in the decade he spent in exile in the United States between his expulsion from Cuba in the Mariel boatlift and his suicide when he was in the last stages of AIDS. Arenas's work, more than that of any other Cuban writer in America, defines the role of a literary production caught in this "special period," this moment of historical and cultural suspension between the "end" of the Cold War in most of the world and the tenacious grip of Fidel Castro's vestigial Marxism on Cuba's, and Cuban America's, political present.

Particularly in his autobiography, **Antes que anochezca** (translated as **Before Night Falls**), and his less successful "first" American novel, **The Doorman,** Arenas's writing grapples with the simultaneous transition from one cultural and economic environment to another, from one prevailing conception of production and consumption, of labor and pleasure, to its arguably radical opposite. This essay charts this transition, with special attention to that most difficult space of intersection between constructions of simultaneously sexual and political subjects, which marks in the space of the Cuban-exile imagination an aporetic point in its negotiation of especially male Cuban identity as at once masculine, virile, and rigidly anti-Marxist with the stark reality of Arenas's heroic, defiant, and fluid effeminacy.

There is always a temptation to read a culture whose prevailing mythologies have so profound an oedipal cast primarily through Freudian and post-Freudian psychoanalytic categories.[1] That approach is unavoidable here as well; the essay focuses on more "material" effects of Arenas's encounter with the doubled, split history of his people(s) but also analyzes the symbolic construction of Cuban political reality as a function of a quasi-oedipal struggle between the hysterically, murderously hated Fidel, *el hombre, él,* and *Cuba bella, la patria,* the feminine-gendered fatherland to whom Cuban exiles consecrate their deepest loyalty and their most profound fidelity. This is, however, one approach among others in my analysis of Arenas's explicitly literary interrogation of the political stakes involved in the emergence of a definitive literary voice for the Cuban/exile nation(s). Put another way, I hope that asking the question of textual pleasure, as a function of both masculine and feminine, normative and queer sexual/textual praxes, in both semiotic and other terms, will lead us back to more direct political questions of what kind of labor (and by whom) produces politically efficacious forms of pleasure (and for whom).

THE DOORMAN, THE EXILE, AND THRESHOLD EXPERIENCES

Arenas completed **The Doorman** as he was falling ill but before his diagnosis, and in this sense the novel stands as Arenas's last major work of fiction before his imagination takes on the intense purgatorial pitch, the queerly undead tonality of his writing under the unequivocal sentence of death. Ironically, however, **The Doorman** shares with the later chapters of the autobiography, which were written well after the diagnosis and well into the progress of his illness, Arenas's hyperbolic vision of freedom, a vision that never lost its appreciation for both abandon and abundance. In general, Arenas's excesses have always seemed to me closer to Jonathan Swift's than to Gabriel García Márquez's.[2] He "screams," and laughs, from a position whose complexity, even impossibility, requires the kind of textual self-immolation one finds in Swift at his most perverse. The figure of Juan, the doorman, recalls the figure of the exiled writer for which Swift has traditionally served as a chief paradigm. Stationed at/on a threshold or border, Juan ministers to travelers, ferrying them from one point to another in a journey in which he plays an exclusively instrumental role. The travelers in this case, however, are only symbolically migratory; they are the New York apartment dwellers living in Juan's building, making their routine, daily journeys between work and home, between the public world and the private fantasy-spaces of their respective cubicles. They are therefore symbolically island dwellers, ensconced in their isolated cells but daily called to the mainland of collective experience; they recall the army of solipsistic projectors in Swift's Academy of Lagado on (perhaps not coincidentally) Gulliver's floating island of Laputa.

To this extent the door functions symbolically as a conduit or channel, connoting in at least the Cuban imagination *el charco,* the watery passage or "puddle" between Cuba and Florida; and in Spanish *la puerta* will always echo *el puerto,* the port, the space of both hopeful departure and safe arrival at the beginning and end of the journey. The doorman is in turn defined according (we might say *reduced*) to the object with/on which he labors, at the same time that that object has only the most tenuous relationship to objecthood. The door is also the eye, the paradigmatic "door" of perception; and thus to have one's protagonist work as a doorman also allows him to work as the paradigmatic subject in a narrative structure, to stand for the subject who works on/processes objects, and others, through its Kantian categories. The door is thus both the doorman's thing and a no-thing, his *objet* in Lacanian terms, at once solid and empty, an obstruction and a space of passage. As such it *is* text, if it is possible to say this; perhaps it is more apt to say the door performs textuality, or, more simply, *texts,* transitively and not. In either or both cases a symbol of promiscuity to be sure, the door allegorizes the promiscuity of the sign, of any symbol, that is, in the hands of a fertile artistic imagination.

Like a doorman keeping vigilant watch on a threshold, in the constant state of having threshold experiences, Arenas writes both in and out of the experience of exile. His name suggests that even symbolically, as well as in more literal ways, he was cursed (implicitly by his mother, who named him) with having to anchor his experience to a shifting surface of sand, between the border-space of the shore, between earth and sea, but also in the arena, the *arenal,* the centralized, localized space of spectacle and performance. It is (t)here that Reinaldo enjoys his uneasy, precarious rein; it is (t)here that "she" is most *la reina,* the queen, of both the arena and the shore. This play with the unmappable space of the border or threshold extends to the anachronistic structure and frame of the two texts of concern here.

Later in this essay I will analyze the last chapters of the autobiography, where Arenas inscribes the dissolution of his last years in the dissolution of reason and sense, a surrender to the forces beyond order which had always governed his life. These include madness, witchcraft, and dreams, words that serve as titles to some of the later chapters. The embodiment of madness is his lifelong friend Lázaro Gómez, who also served as the inspiration for the title character of **The Doorman.** Lázaro served as the sole witness to Arenas's own past, and his occasional bouts with mental instability and his limited education reinforced the quality of childlike innocence necessary to establish a link with childhood itself.[3] Arenas's brotherly tenderness toward his friend recalls the love of the young narrator of **Celestino antes del alba,** Arenas's first novel, for his visionary, poetic cousin. And in the later novel, Juan the doorman, described as "a young man who was dying of grief," suffers from the doubled disenchantment of having been forced to leave his own childhood behind in immigrating to the United States and in having to confront a culture profoundly alienated from its own innocence, its own authentic past or history.[4]

The "million" narrators of **The Doorman,** the Cuban exile community speaking, stereotypically perhaps, with one voice, sum up Juan's predicament thus:

> Ten years ago Juan had fled his native Cuba in a boat, and settled in the United States. He was seventeen then, and his entire past life had been left behind: humiliations and warm beaches, fierce enemies and loving friends whom the very persecutions had made even more special. Left behind was slavery, but the complicity of night as well, and cities made to the measure of his restlessness; unbounded horror, but also a human quality, a state of mind, a sense of brotherhood in the face of terror—all things that, just like his own way of being, were alien here.[5]

While the choice of an (ironically) univocal communal voice raises its own aesthetic and philosophical questions of subjectivity and the force of ideological groupthink, in Arenas's hands these questions are always directed back toward the individual and the limits of the collective to "make something" of him. This is clear, for example, in the limited sympathy with which the narrative treats its subject:

> But we, too (and there are a million of us), left all that behind; and yet we are not dying of grief . . . so hopelessly as this young man. . . . He arrived in the United States an unskilled laborer, like most of us, just one more person escaping from Cuba. He needed to learn, just as we did, the value of things, the high price one must pay for a stable life: a well-paying job, an apartment, a car, vacations, and finally one's own house, preferably near the ocean.[6]

The narrative chorus's summation of Juan as "just one more" of the million they comprise must, I think, be read doubly; the assessment absorbs him into the sum at the same time that it singles him out, makes of him the remnant or remaining one "more" in excess of that comfortable, completed sum. More than an exemplary narrative of immigrant success through hard work and the acquisition of real property, Arenas's impersonation of this community and the ironic take on its values suggested in this passage also undermines the distinction it would place on its own accounting of "value," "price," and "cost." He leaves open the question of whether the inventory of acquisitions signifies either the material comforts of "a stable life" or the "high [spiritual] price" one must pay for that life.

What Remains: The Ghost, the Decadent, and the Death of Desire

Like the alienated, ascetic Juan, never far from his threshold, Arenas occupied a perplexed position in the various "economies" into which he found himself inserted. Both in communist Cuba and late capitalist North America, Arenas, *as a gay man especially,* found himself in excess, existing as the remnant of a corrupt past constructed in the former case as a holdover of bourgeois, in the latter as a holdover of aristocratic decadence. In his study **Gays Under the Cuban Revolution,** Allen Young makes the oft-observed point that Cuban communism simply borrowed from Soviet policy the conviction that homosexuality (and the decadent sensibility it nurtured) was "the product of the decadence of bourgeois society and fascist corruption" in order to uphold a policy of homosexual persecution that for equally cynical reasons the homophobic Batista government did not pursue as comprehensively.[7] The figure of decadent sensibility plays a similarly vestigial role in the classical bourgeois imagination.

Such a figure does make an appearance on **The Doorman**'s stage, but in curiously redoubled form: while Juan himself remains sexually ambiguous, Arenas saves much of his critical commentary on urban gay America for this treatment of the one gay couple in Juan's building, the "Oscar Timeses."[8] They have changed their individual names for the one name that they share and in their years together have come "to resemble each other so closely, both in body and in temperament, that they really appear to be the same person." They are, in fact, distinguished only numerically, going as "Oscar Times One and Oscar Times Two." In this and other respects, they inhabit the extremes of assimilationism and conformity in **The Doorman.** Their homo-sexuality, their erotic orientation toward the same, literally reinforces this, and the fact that one of the Oscars hails from Cuba and the other is a Scottish-American who ironically has taken his assimilationist cues from his lover casts an even more complex irony over the situation. Arenas's attack on North American gay conformity is scathing and organized chiefly around an obsessive pursuit of pleasure which, in its narcissism and material luxuriance, seemed to the philosophically eroticist Arenas as particularly alienated and debased.[9] As he remarks of their frequently failed sex hunts in Manhattan, the Oscars would often "out of boredom, frustration, habit, or just as a last resort . . . end up sleeping together, but at the moment of reaching climax, instead of pleasure they experienced the frustration of possessing or being possessed by repulsive mirror images of themselves."[10]

This refusal to identify with the already overly identificatory structure of gay male society in the United States exacerbated Arenas's general state of exile; he discovered his chief refuge, understandably enough, in his writing, which for him was always intimately linked with his sexual dispositions. In the autobiography, Arenas makes this connection clear. In Cuban Miami especially, he observes, artists and in particular writers were considered with an odd suspicion: "The sad fact," Arenas tells us, "is that Cuban exiles were not so interested in literature; a writer was looked upon as a strange, abnormal figure."[11] It is impossible not to hear in the Spanish term *anormal* its conventional concomitant, *maricón,* or faggot. What strikes the conventional *machista* Cuban sensibility as culturally suspect immediately also strikes it as sexually suspect. Miami culture seemed to Arenas a distillation of some of the worst features of the Cuban character, especially its sexual politics: "The typical Cuban machismo has attained alarming proportions in Miami. I did not want to stay too long in that place, which was like a caricature of Cuba, the worst of Cuba."[12] It is not surprising, therefore, that Arenas's investments in his writing and in his sexuality so strongly paralleled each other. Cuba, both at home and in exile, treated its writers as badly as it treated its queers; indeed, it seemed not to distinguish one from the other.[13] Eloquently, emphatically, Arenas responds to this imposed disappearance with his own form of transgression through ostentation and excess: he wrote, and fucked, prolifically, promiscuously, with an abandon that looked to him like freedom.

It is, I think, plausible to characterize the limited aesthetic success of *The Doorman* as a symptom of what Arenas seemed to feel was the suffocatingly commodity-obsessed pursuit of happiness (that is, maximization of pleasure) among all culturally and economically assimilated "Americans," Cuban or not, queer or not. As I have already noted, each of the hyper-insulated apartment dwellers in *The Doorman*'s habitrail universe constructs a "private idaho" for him or herself, each an extension of some idiosyncratic pathology fostered and buttressed by some elaborately commodified fetish system of both possessions and beliefs. Anyone familiar with Arenas's preexile work will recognize in *The Doorman* the allegorized struggle of a literary imagination to break free of the ponderous clutter of simulacra (both material and conceptual), to reaccess the less alienated, mediated relationship with "nature" or "reality" which characterizes that earlier fiction.

ECO-CRITURE

That the narrative of *The Doorman* should also include a culmination in the reaccessing of the infinite (here in the exemplary guise of the sea) also belies the logic of "getting there" via the finite, the particular, the material. Juan's ultimate success in realizing his vision of liberation comes through a rejection of the social, of the human, and the reinvention of language in a discourse with animals, with a renaturalized, reconstituted nature. Arenas's investment in the power of the natural is one

of the signature elements of all his work. The biographical sources of this relationship are documented in the early chapters of *Before Night Falls.* In his review of the translation, Roberto Echevarría sums up this relationship nicely: "To say that Arenas grew up close to nature," Echevarría observes, "may sound like a cliché, but in this case the phrase could not be more literal. Among his favorite childhood pastimes were eating dirt, from which he got a big belly full of worms, having sex with various animals and playing with mud in the falling rain."[14] That even his reviewers should take recourse to clichés and literality to naturalize the language with which they describe Arenas's intense familiarity with the natural speaks to the force of this bond. All Arenas's writings contains a radical naturalism that, I argue, earns that writing the curious status of an *eco-criture.*

Juan discovers a method of communicating with the tame, domesticated pets of his tenants and with them plots a strategy of liberation that ultimately reintegrates him, and them, into a "past" even more distant than that of lost childhood or cultural history. In this sense he is a combination of Doctor Doolittle, Gulliver among the Houyhnhnms, and Noah effecting a new creation, a new nature out of the ruins of that murdered by decadent, materialist culture. This culminating vision in *The Doorman* is suggestively apocalyptic in scope; Juan heads with the animals on a transcontinental and eventually global procession, swelling the ranks of his natural army with all imaginable creatures and inanimate objects. Arenas leaves Juan at the conclusion of *The Doorman* on a significant threshold; as they reach "the equator," the "thunderous stampede" of animals "is deafening."[15]

Ironically, *The Doorman* should conclude with the silence into which the deafening roar of nature's rebellion relegates us, but it does not. The last words of the text are given to two competing sets of exiles: one the million narrators, who threaten to use the imminent catastrophe in revenge for their suffering, and the other the doorman himself, whose vision of nature at play, liberated from all structure, from all order except for the promiscuous symbolism of the door, necessarily, perhaps tragically, excludes the very figure of the doorman, whose fate it is to wait, in permanent exile, for no fate at all:

> At the end there would be a door for the dove to enter into her land of dreams. . . . A huge door of green branches and creeping vines in perpetual bloom would await the parrot, the squirrel, the cat and the orangutan, so they could play forever. . . . Yes, doors of sunshine, doors of water, doors of earth, doors of flowering vines, doors of ice . . . tiny doors or immeasurable ones, deeper than the air, more luminous than the sky, would be awaiting the animals to take them to a place where nobody could spy on them through telescopes,

or send undercover agents after us. . . . And through these doors everyone, finally, will eagerly rush in.

That is, all except me, the doorman, who on the outside will watch them disappear forever.

The informing wish of Arenas's text returns us to the doorlike space of the metaphor, of language as (trans)figuration, where the writer, the exile, the excluded attendant upon doors awaits, at once witnessing and enacting the rite of liberation for others.

The last chapters of the autobiography extend the apocalypticism of *The Doorman* even further into super-, one might say hyper-, naturalism. Lázaro's madness, which became the type for Juan's in the novel, quickly translates into increasingly poetic and powerful images driven by an eroticized feminine principle. Madness and queerness are semantically linked by the correct Spanish usage, and the idiomatic Spanish deviation, of the term "locura"; Arenas had had occasion in the Cuban sections of the autobiography to inventory the four classes of "locas," of queens he had known in Havana. In the New York section, he turns his attention to the relationship between that other archetype of deviant femininity, the witch, and the erotic principle organizing his life. "The world," Arenas insists, "is really full of witches" of various types, whose "reino" or reign extends beyond fantasy to reality. Arenas's world is indeed saturated by witchcraft; he not only includes most of the prominent women in his life in this category but also his mother, in whose hyperbolic symbolism the list culminates: "the noble witch, the suffering witch, the witch full of longing and sadness, the most beloved witch in the world: my mother . . . with her broom, always sweeping as if nothing mattered but the symbolic meaning of the act."[16] Arenas writes with the same appreciation of the purely symbolic value of the act; the witch extends even beyond the figure of the mother to contain the gender-transcendent figure of the queen, *la loca* ("Sometimes witches would assume a half-masculine form, which would make them even more sinister") and though he never explicitly identifies himself as such, the momentum of the passage leads us compellingly to Arenas himself, writing as his mother sweeps, the pen replacing the broom as the material locus of a labor whose production is symbolic, magical, but for that reason no less material.

BEFORE NIGHT FALLS: AIDS AND THE POSSIBILITY OF A PRO-LIFE SUICIDE

The autobiography would be incomplete without the suicide note (literally Arenas's "last" writing) to which it inexorably leads, but most of it was written not only well before his death but before the completion of his fictional work. It is preceded by an introduction entitled "El fin," which also came "last" in the chronology of its composition, a text that most directly addresses the issue of the disease that finally destroyed him. "Last words" thus come first, and last, in Arenas's recounting of his life. Time and history work different shifts in both the life and the fiction; in the former Arenas marks the transformation of his literary output by the day of his diagnosis. All his subsequent work operates in the odd, protracted time-space, the chronotope, one might say, of the anticipation of the end; this is most pointedly suggested in the title of the autobiography. It is here, in this inverted, paradoxical space, that we can return as well to the question raised by Arenas's attempt, at the end of his life, in the intimate threshold of his own fatal moment, to understand AIDS, not metaphorically but literally. AIDS stood for Arenas emphatically *outside* the register of the natural, as an unnaturally systematic, all-too-humanly perfect death machine whose only plausible source or origin was for him the closet space of state secrecy, of public conspiracy, of obscene activity perpetrated openly by silent "majorities."

Susan Sontag observes in *AIDS and Its Metaphors* the rarity with which "political metaphors" are used "to talk about the body"; "likening the body to a society, liberal or not," Sontag goes on to explain, "is less common than comparisons to other complex, integrated systems, such as a machine or an economic system."[17] Arenas not only provides one such extended comparison in the introduction to the autobiography, he also employs it in the manner which, as Sontag observes later in her essay, reflects AIDS's readily available capacity to "serve as an ideal projection for First World political paranoia," especially in the way it can stand not only as "the quintessential invader from the Third World," but more so as "any mythological menace."[18] Arenas's own feelings about AIDS, as expressed in the autobiography, suggest something of this paranoia and of the mythological extremes to which it can be carried. At the same time, they remind us of the already mythological cast of the imaginative, ideological, and cultural work done on AIDS by First-World reactionary liberalism.

To quote Arenas:

> The actual nature of AIDS seems to be a state secret . . . as a disease it is different from all others. Diseases are natural phenomena, and everything natural is imperfect and can somehow be fought and overcome. But AIDS is a perfect illness because it is so alien to human nature and has as its function to destroy life in the most cruel and systematic way. Never before has such a formidable calamity affected mankind. Such diabolic perfection makes one ponder the possibility that human beings may have had a hand in its creation.[19]

The suggestion that somehow AIDS began as an orchestrated political conspiracy against marginalized communities is certainly not exclusive to Arenas, but in his hands it takes on a particular eloquence, especially given the context of the triple exile into which AIDS throws him.

Sontag herself observes near the end of *AIDS and Its Metaphors* the connection between late-capitalist hyper-consumerism and a prevailing construction of pleasure which at least superficially informs some of the sexual and cultural practices of the gay male communities of urban America discussed earlier. "One set of messages of the society we live in," Sontag argues, "is: Consume. Grow. Amuse yourselves. The working of this economic system," she continues, "which has bestowed these unprecedented liberties, most cherished in the form of physical mobility and material prosperity, depends on encouraging people to defy limits. Appetite is *supposed* to be immoderate. The ideology of capitalism makes us all connoisseurs of liberty—of the infinite expansion of possibility. . . . Hardly an invention of the male homosexual subculture, recreational, risk-free sexuality is an inevitable reinvention of the culture of capitalism."[20] For Arenas, on the other hand, "liberty" predicated on either side of the term "connoisseurship," as either a function of the accumulation or collection of goods or of the hyper-refinement of taste, was perhaps descriptive of a "free," but always of a closed, economy on some level of circulation, but it failed to guarantee pleasure as the effect of a necessarily *open* economy. What "liberty" a closed liberal economy could promise its agents rang of liberal dogmatism to Arenas, to which he would persistently oppose the promise of a liberation from all dogmatism.

This attitude is most clearly reflected in several passages critical of totalitarian dogmatism in communist Cuba. These passages, in effect constituting brief asides within the course of his narrating the events of his life in Cuba, resonate through his subsequent experiences in exile. "All dictatorships," he observes, "are sexually repressive and anti-life. All affirmations of life are diametrically opposed to dogmatic regimes";[21] the simultaneously oppressive and repressive practices of a system as orthodoxly homophobic as Castro's translate fairly directly into the practices of all systems of power predicated on exclusion and closure. As Arenas goes on to observe about AIDS in the context of global politics, "All the rulers of the world, that reactionary class always in power, and the powerful within any system, must feel grateful to AIDS because a good part of the marginal population, whose only aspiration is to live and therefore oppose all dogma and political hypocrisy, will be wiped out."[22] All system, therefore, all dogma, takes on in Arenas's thought the function of *thanatos,* manifests the death drive even as it promises its "free" but limited menu of pleasures to the world. All such economies operate under the principle of scarcity, regardless of the wealth they generate; all such economies restrict, repress, and exclude practices and pleasures based on the antiprinciple, the unthinkable idea of life as limitlessness, as pure abundance.

Arenas thus recognizes the profound distinction between a choking totalitarianism (the aggressive intellectual impulse toward totalities) and the infinite, abundant playfulness of language (the fluid, oceanic fullness of life). His condemnation of all repressive power as life-destroying receives particularly eloquent expression in the nearly symmetrical treatment his text gives to the opposed repressions of the Right and the Left. Arenas observes, for example, the manner in which all tyranny murders laughter in his analysis of the Castro regime's most tragic effect on the once-vital Cuban character:

> One of the most nefarious characteristics of tyrannies is that they take everything too seriously and destroy all sense of humor. Historically, Cubans have found escape from reality through satire and mockery, but with the coming of Fidel Castro the sense of humor gradually disappeared until it became illegal. With it the Cuban people lost one of its few means of survival; by taking away their laughter, the Revolution took away from them their deepest sense of the nature of things. Yes, dictatorships are prudish, pompous, and utterly dreary.[23]

Arenas's own profound, proto-Bakhtinian sense of the philosophical dimensions of laughter, its ability to inform our sense of "things," extends equally to his critical evaluation of the more subtle, but similarly life-killing, thing-obsessed materialism of Miami Cubans. "In Miami," he observes, "the obsession with making things work and being practical, with making lots of money, sometimes out of the fear of starving, has replaced a sense of life and, above all, of pleasure, adventure, and irreverence."[24] This disillusionment with the bourgeoisie did not prevent Arenas from feeling an equally strong alienation from the liberal intellectual Left, especially in the academies of North America.[25]

No Conclusions: Pleasure, Politics, and the Art of the Impossible

Arenas's simultaneous and reciprocal condemnation of both conventional Left and Right positions positions him more strategically than ambivalently in the space of politically driven literary and critical discourses, posing against each an alternative critique more accurately representative of his own politics. Judging from her article on Cuban politics and art institutions, "Aesthetics and Foreign Policy," Laura Kipnis would argue against Arenas's collapsing of all restrictive cultural regimes. "If culture is seen as central to social reproduction," Kipnis posits, "it seems to follow that . . . in a society that reproduces itself, in the first instance, politically, as Cuba, artists are subjected to the terrors and rigors of current political policies," and thus "in Cuba, where art institutions are by definition political and politicized, the political meanings of works emerge unmediated, with more genuine potential to be subversive to reproduction."[26]

Later in the article Kipnis turns to a much earlier essay on Cuban culture by Susan Sontag.[27] Kipnis's response to what she feels is Sontag's overaestheticized judgment of the failures of Cuban culture might transfer fairly directly into a response to Arenas's similar views. Kipnis dismisses Sontag's claim for a "triumph of 'erotics' over 'hermeneutics,'" arguing that it merely fulfills "the desire for the self: certainty of a subjectivity outside history, a desire for the immediacy of the unmediated relation, not only to the work of art, but to all the rest of political and social life, as well."[28] Implicit in Kipnis's critique of Sontag is a critique of what she terms the subject of the Enlightenment, particularly "the eighteenth-century aesthetic subject"[29] whose intolerance of any critical dialectic had already been marked by Theodor Adorno and Max Horkheimer.[30] The idea that Sontag's or Arenas's eroticist critical strategies present little more than the retrenchment of the one-note aesthetic subject of the Enlightenment seems dangerously reductive to me, certainly restricted to the limited space of an outdated, and never fully efficacious, ideological polarity.

It is precisely the fate of art subversive to the revolution that Arenas's autobiography charts and his preexile work underwent. Whereas Kipnis concludes that in a cultural environment as radically politicized as Cuba's, "the concept of counter-revolutionary culture . . . does have a reality . . . whereas the possibility of a truly political art or a counterhegemonic art is to a large degree absorbed by art markets and institutions here," Arenas would counter that Cuba's cultural bureaucracy only ironically ensured the political power (especially of art subversive of the revolution) not by absorbing it, that is, at once co-opting it and fostering its life, but by repressing it, indirectly expelling it out of the domestic sphere of cultural exchange. Arenas was an artist in exile long before his physical expulsion from Cuba. As the history of the composition of his masterwork, the novel *Otra vez el mar*,[31] makes clear, the ideology that cultivates the political construction of all art also guarantees the disappearance, via confiscation and destruction, of art construed as politically dangerous, unless it is secreted out of the country like contraband. What "genuine potential to be subversive to reproduction" such art might be said to have, at least in theory, in a system where "the political meanings of works emerge unmediated," seems then profoundly compromised by the system's own paranoid perception of precisely that subversive potential.

A more viable analysis of the political function of art and of the concomitant experience of a subversive, irreverent, laughing pleasure can be found in the work of Slavoj Žižek. Žižek's work seems to me to offer the most opportune articulation of this impossible experience of pleasure; in a section of *Enjoy Your Symptom!: Lacan in Hollywood and Out* entitled "The Subject of Enlightenment,"[32] Žižek explains the persistence of the monstrous in bourgeois cultural artifacts by declaring,

"You cannot have both meaning and enjoyment." The monstrous, as one embodiment of the limit of meaning or sense, stands then as empty, plastic, promiscuous form, the "objective correlative" for Žižek of "the pure 'subject of the Enlightenment,'" which can no longer be "contained" or "bound" by "the texture of symbolic tradition" and therefore "is a monster which gives body to the surplus that escapes the vicious circle of the mirror relationship." Žižek likens it to both the monstrous and the phantasmatic: "The Phantom" in the Opera or out, "embodies the excess aristocracy has to renounce in order to become integrated into bourgeois society." As such, it is "a kind of 'fossil' created by the Enlightenment itself as a distorted index of its inherent antagonism: what was," Žižek goes on to explain, "a sovereign expenditure, a glitter of those in power, an inherent moment of their symbolic status . . . falls out from the social space whose contours are defined by utilitarian ideology, and is perceived as decadent debauchery epitomized in the bourgeois myth of a corrupted demonic aristocrat."[33] This association is rendered more profoundly ironic by the knowledge that Arenas himself was of the poorest social background, his entry into "decadent," cosmopolitan culture coming at the hands of the very revolution that would consequently persecute him for having taken to it so readily.

In *For They Know Not What They Do* Žižek provides the theoretical basis for the cultural analysis he presents in *Enjoy Your Symptom!* In this earlier text Žižek tries to locate the excessive place of Lacanian jouissance or Barthean bliss in the political imagination, in the political dimensions of the construction of a "subject of Enlightenment." "Where one doesn't (want to) know," Žižek argues, "in the blanks of one's symbolic universe, one enjoys . . . enjoyment [thereby being] the 'surplus' that comes from our knowledge that our pleasure involves the thrill of entering a forbidden domain— that is to say, that our pleasure involves a certain displeasure"; this inverted construction of the subject's pleasure occasions an extended train of deconstructive moves. Totalitarian social order, Žižek argues, reexternalizes, "outs" one might say, the superego; it occupies, as "the discourse of Stalinist bureaucracy" did, a position that, because it stands for "neutral, 'objective' knowledge . . . a knowledge not subjectivized by means of the intervention . . . of some Master Signifier—is in itself mischievous, enjoying the subject's failure to live up to impossible demands, impregnated by obscenity—in short: superegotistical."

Thinking of a discourse that, like Castro's, totalizes the possible by declaring that "the Revolution" defines its practical and conceptual limits ("Within the Revolution, everything; outside the Revolution, nothing"), one can appreciate the fate of the subject confronted with this looming epipsychical image; it inflicts on itself what Žižek calls a "self-torture provoked by the obscene superegotistical 'law of conscience.'" It is precisely this "superegotistical imposition of enjoyment which threatens to overflow our daily life" by thinking *for* the subject and giving the subject no choice but to obey the injunction, "*Carpe diem,* enjoy the day, consume the surplus-enjoyment procured by your daily suffering," an injunction that in turn becomes for Žižek "the condensed formula of 'totalitarianism.'" Žižek's theory thus casts in high relief Arenas's more immediate observations, quoted above, about the "chaste," "antivital" character of all "dogmatic regimes," which force-feed the masses "the surplus-enjoyment procured by [their] daily suffering" in precisely the inverted, ironic form of a boredom that saturates everything imaginable.

It is against the murderous boredom of repressive, totalizing systems that Arenas laughs and screams.[34] From the metaphor of the doorman and his door to the witch and her broom, from the metaphoric values that cluster opportunistically around the images of the madman, *la loca,* and the queen, we have to conclude that the limitless expanse of Arenas's imaginative geography is also always and only the "one" fluid space (more nomadic than monadic) of the metaphor, of the gesture of translation, of all metamorphosis in process. This place remains, however, unmappable; it remains the no-place, the aporetic point where all opposition dissolves into mere difference. Aporia does not, however, necessarily translate into atopia or utopia; what position metaphor and transformational narrative may be said to occupy in the cultural imagination of a nation as self-alienated and dispersed as Cuba may be more difficult to map than to situate. It may stand, for example, for the gaps that currently exist geographically, politically, and culturally between Cubas, and Cubans, and continue to widen and proliferate, especially as this "special period" in Cuban history becomes further attenuated. It may just as well stand for the transitional and translational hyphen upon which, as Gustavo Pérez-Firmat has observed, Cuban-Americans may be said most fully to live their own conflicted, individual, and collective cultural dualities.[35]

Although the narrative of Arenas's life begins with a chapter entitled "Las piedras," the stones, in which he recalls his earliest memories, at two, of eating the dirt off the ground of his grandparents' farm, in his final chapter, "Los sueños," or dreams, he will say that his earliest memory is of a dream in which he is about to be devoured by "an enormous mouth" (*una boca incommensurable* in Spanish).[36] The consuming incommensurability of these two competing origins, of these two "first," original memories, articulates the general indeterminacy of Arenas's life as textualized, of his text as he lived it, but they also speak to competing histories his people have embraced as the incommensurate, originating narratives of his nation. Even at the point of his death, Arenas seems to have known that the darkness

into which he was peering was that of the familiar "confusion" between life and what is not life which had always both cursed and blessed both him and his compatriots. Arenas concludes his suicide note, his "last" writing and the last piece of the text which we call his autobiography, in the temporal mode of an impossible "already." Having laid responsibility for his death at the feet of Fidel Castro and having encouraged Cubans both in and out of exile to continue their struggles for liberty, Arenas casts his suicide in terms of an impossible optimism, in a future certainty only a liberating understanding of the nonrelation of life to death can provide. "Cuba will be free; I already am."[37]

Notes

1. See Echevarría, "Outcast of the Island." In this review of Koch's English translation of *Antes que anochezca,* Echevarría observes in Arenas's temperament a clinging to transcendent innocence, "a sense of liberation attached" especially to "lovemaking that seems pre-Freudian in its candor." In general, what I term "excess" in Arenas is utopian idealism for Echevarría: "It is as if on some deep level Arenas had innocently believed in Castro's rhetoric . . . and could only measure imperfect human performance against absolute [and therefore impossible] standards of purity." Arenas is therefore for Echevarría "a true son of the revolution and of Castro," and his ultimate disillusionment with and alienation from the law attached to the name of this father translates into a more than familiar dramatic paradigm: *Before Night Falls* is for Echevarría "a narrative linking poignantly the personal and the political levels of [the] family romance, told from the point of view of the abandoned son."

2. This comparison to Swift is anything but incidental. It marks a curious genealogy in the work of political theorists, who, like Edward Said in *The World, the Text and the Critic* (Cambridge, Mass.: Harvard University Press, 1983) and Roberto Fernández Retamar in *Caliban,* trans. Edward Baker (Minneapolis: University of Minnesota Press, 1989) have observed in Swift's thoroughgoing political satires a paradigm for an ironic politics of impossibility. There are undeniable Swiftian elements in much of Arenas's apocalyptic political fiction; in addition to the references in *The Doorman* to *Gulliver's Travels,* one can find in the cannibalistic references in *The Assault,* elements of the genocidal vision of a totalizing rationalism which Swift developed between Part Four of the *Travels* and "A Modest Proposal."

3. Arenas says of his friendship with Lázaro: "In exile Lázaro has been my only link to my past, the only witness to my past life in Cuba; with him I

always had the feeling of being able to return to that irretrievable world" (*Before Night Falls*, p. 308).

4. This is precisely Arenas's take on New York as the exemplum of North American culture. In the chapter of the autobiography entitled "Eviction," Arenas discusses his disillusionment with New York at length. Although at first New York had seemed to him the fulfillment of Havana's promise of cultural and communal richness, that idea of social value was quickly replaced by one bled of its spirituality. Because in the United States "everything revolves around money," even its great cities are rendered soulless. "New York," Arenas argues, "has no tradition, no history. The city is in constant flux, constant construction . . . a huge, soulless factory with no place for the pedestrian to rest, no place where one can simply be without dishing out dollars for a breath of air" (*Before Night Falls*, pp. 293-94, 310).

5. See Arenas, *The Doorman*, p. 3.

6. Ibid., pp. 3-4.

7. Young's text is more readily available even in the United States in its Spanish translation, which is what I use here. Young argues that an emergent homosexual subculture existed in pre-Castro Havana, which fed very directly and very profitably into the larger sexual economy of the pleasure industry for which the Cuban capital especially was justifiably famous. See Young, *Los gays bajo la revolución Cubana*, esp. pp. 29-33. See also Leiner, *Sexual Politics in Cuba*. Leiner, chiefly an education specialist with a deep regard for socialist Cuba's social policy successes, attempts to address the seemingly regressive treatment of people with HIV and AIDS in Cuba by supplying a cultural and political history of Cuban sexual attitudes. Leiner is far kinder than Young to the Castro government's treatment of homosexuals, especially in the last two decades. His book is curious reading alongside Arenas's personal testimony and Young's more distanced study of the same topic.

8. See Arenas, *The Doorman*, p. 8, and all of Chapter 14, which is devoted to the Oscars, whose names are derived from the Cuban Oscar's desire to obscure his ethnicity. Born Ramón García, the character renames himself after "what he considered to be the supreme icons of his new country: the Hollywood Oscar and *The New York Times*" (ibid., p. 69).

9. This distaste partly explains why the gay male community in New York gets precious little direct mention in any of Arenas's work. This latter "cul-

ture of desire," as Frank Browning has named it, posed in a marked way for Arenas the equally problematic materialism of the liberal West, which he condemns with a vigor equal to that with which he condemns the bankrupt materialism of Marxist-Leninist-Stalinist Cuba. While Browning's text includes a fairly conventional discussion of Cuban culture's attitudes toward homosexuality (see *The Culture of Desire* [New York: Crown, 1993], pp. 142-48), it serves the larger purpose of my own discussion in its analysis of the assimilationist tendencies characteristic of much of the mainstream commercializing of especially gay male urban culture.

10. Arenas, *The Doorman*, p. 71.

11. Arenas, *Before Night Falls*, p. 290. For Arenas, the philistine attitude of bourgeois exiles toward writers was no more forgivable than the active repression of the communists. No Cuban writer, Arenas finally admits, could escape "the tragic fate Cuban writers have suffered throughout our history; on our island we have been condemned to silence, to ostracism, censorship and prison; in exile, despised and forsaken by our fellow exiles" (ibid., p. 291).

12. Ibid., p. 292.

13. Arenas's descriptions of his alienation from Miami's bourgeois Cuban culture often draws on the figure of the ghost or phantasm: "In exile," he writes, "one is nothing but a ghost, a shadow of someone who never achieves full reality" (ibid., p. 293). Like the exiled individual, the entire exile community, especially in Miami, seemed to Arenas little more than a pathetic, ghastly echo or remnant of an irrecuperably lost Cuba; Cuban Miami was for Arenas "like the ghost of our Island, a barren [*arenosa*, or sandy] and pestiferous peninsula, trying to become, for a million exiles, the dream of a tropical island: aerial, bathed by the ocean waters and the tropical breeze" (ibid., p. 292). It is worth nothing how the language in this passage submerges in its semantic resources the whole psychological drama of Arenas's own life. It is the embodiment of the phallic wish to detach itself from a solid but infected body (the infection here also identified with the barren sand [*arenal/ Arenas*] of the mainland), and to float/bathe once again in the fluid body of the ocean.

14. Echevarría, "Outcast of the Island," p. 32.

15. Arenas, *The Doorman*, p. 188.

16. Arenas, *Before Night Falls*, p. 296.

17. Susan Sontag, *AIDS and Its Metaphors* (New York: Farrar, Straus, & Giroux, 1989), pp. 6-7.

18. Sontag, *AIDS and Its Metaphors,* p. 62.

19. Arenas, *Before Night Falls,* pp. xvi-xvii.

20. Sontag, *AIDS and Its Metaphors,* pp. 76-77.

21. Arenas, *Before Night Falls,* p. 93.

22. Ibid., p. xvii.

23. Ibid., p. 239.

24. Ibid., p. 292.

25. In scattered passages recounting his time in exile, Arenas makes dismissive mention of "this festive and fascist left," which, he observes, had no better understanding of the complexity of the political experience of Cubans both in and out of the homeland than the most rabidly anti-Castro Cuban rightists. Both sides, in enlisting selectively the elements of his story that could serve their respective political needs, reduced him to a curiosity, a free-floating symbolic presence, a promiscuous political fetish-object, invited to cast its aura at events and functions. "I was surrounded," Arenas tells us, "by gossip and difficulties, and by an endless succession of cocktail parties, soirées, and invitations. It was like being on display, a strange creature that had to be invited before it lost its luster or until a new personality arrived to displace it" (ibid.).

26. See Kipnis, "Aesthetics and Foreign Policy," pp. 207-18. The quoted passage is on p. 215.

27. See Sontag, "Some Thoughts on the Right Way (for Us) to Love the Cuban Revolution."

28. Kipnis, "Aesthetics and Foreign Policy," pp. 216-17.

29. Ibid., p. 212.

30. See Theodor W. Adorno and Max Horkheimer, *The Dialectic of Enlightenment,* trans. John Cumming (New York: Continuum, 1991).

31. *Otra vez el mar* is available in a fine English translation by Andrew Hurley, *Farewell to the Sea: A Novel of Cuba* (New York: Penguin Books, 1986). The last page of the text is devoted to a record of its complex underground existence: "First version disappeared, Havana, 1969 / Second version confiscated, Havana, 1971 / The present version smuggled out of Havana, 1974 / and published in Barcelona, 1982" (p. 413). Arenas also makes frequent reference to the history of this text in *Before Night Falls.*

32. See Slavoj Žižek, *Enjoy Your Symptom!: Lacan in Hollywood and Out* (New York: Routledge, 1992), pp. 131-36. This discussion applies to filmic discourse theories developed in Žižek's earlier work,

For They Know Not What They Do: Enjoyment as a Political Factor (London: Verso, 1991), esp. pp. 2 and 236-41.

33. See Žižek, *Enjoy Your Symptom!,* pp. 131-32.

34. Arenas's scream should also be heard, I think, as an echo of that Adamic, "barbaric yawp" of Walt Whitman's, the pure noise of an original, still-originating New World poetics; it also echoes the guttural "no" of Retamar (and thus, retroactively, Martí's) insurgent, antitraditional *Calibán.* Since it also marks Arenas as that most stereotyped of subversive homosexuals, the flaming, effeminate "screaming" queen, reading Arenas's work as Adamic certainly puts a subversively sexualized spin on Retamar's and even Whitman's butch constructions of the "new" man.

35. Gustavo Pérez-Firmat, *Life on the Hyphen: The Cuban-American Way* (Austin: University of Texas Press, 1994).

36. Arenas, *Before Night Falls,* p. 311, and *Antes que anochezca,* p. 335.

37. See Arenas, *Before Night Falls,* p. 317, and *Antes que anochezca,* p. 343.

Bibliography

Arenas, Reinaldo. *Antes que anochezca.* Barcelona: Tusquets Editores, 1992.

———. *The Assault.* Trans. Andrew Hurley. New York: Viking, 1994.

———. *Before Night Falls.* Trans. Dolores M. Koch. New York: Viking, 1993.

———. *The Doorman.* Trans. Dolores M. Koch. New York: Grove Weidenfeld, 1991.

———. *Farewell to the Sea: A Novel of Cuba.* Trans. Andrew Hurley. New York: Penguin, 1986.

Arguelles, Lourdes, and B. Ruby Rich. "Homosexuality, Homophobia, and Revolution: Notes Toward an Understanding of the Cuban Lesbian and Gay Male Experience, Part I." *Signs: Journal of Women in Culture and Society* 9 (1984): 686.

Echevarría, Roberto González. "Outcast of the Island." *New York Times Book Review,* Oct. 24, 1993, pp. 1, 32-33.

Foster, David William. *Gay and Lesbian Themes in Latin American Writing.* Austin: University of Texas Press, 1991.

Kipnis, Laura. "Aesthetics and Foreign Policy." In Kipnis, *Ecstasy Unlimited: On Sex, Capital, Gender, and Aesthetics,* pp. 207-18. Minneapolis: University of Minnesota Press, 1993.

Leiner, Marvin. *Sexual Politics in Cuba: Machismo, Homosexuality, and AIDS.* Boulder: Westview Press, 1994.

Pérez-Firmat, Gustavo. *The Cuban Condition: Translation and Identity in Modern Cuban Literature.* Cambridge: Cambridge University Press, 1990.

————. *Life on the Hyphen: The Cuban-American Way.* Austin: University of Texas Press, 1994.

Retamar, Roberto Fernández. *Caliban and Other Essays.* Minneapolis: University of Minnesota Press, 1991.

Rozencvaig, Perla. *Reinaldo Arenas: Narrativa de trangresión.* Oaxaca, Mexico: Editorial Oasis, 1986.

————. "Reinaldo Arenas's Last Interview." Trans. Alfred MacAdam, Jr. *Review* 44 (Jan.-June 1991): 78-83.

Sontag, Susan. "Some Thoughts on the Right Way (for Us) to Love the Cuban Revolution." *Ramparts,* Apr. 1969, pp. 6-19.

Soto, Francisco. "*El Portero:* Una alucinante fábula moderna." *Revista de Literatura Hispánica* 32-33 (Fall 1990-Spring 1991): 106-17.

————. *Reinaldo Arenas: La pentagonía.* Gainesville: University of Florida Press, 1994.

Young, Allen. *Los gays bajo la revolución cubana.* Trans. Máximo Ellis. Madrid: Editorial Playor, 1984.

Francisco Soto (essay date 1998)

SOURCE: Soto, Francisco. "Arenas's Poetry: Politics and Sexuality." In *Reinaldo Arenas,* pp. 124-51. New York: Twayne Publishers, 1998.

[*In the following essay, Soto analyzes Arenas's poetic trilogy,* Leprosorio, *which he describes as the author's "most political text."*]

In December of 1987 I conducted an interview with Arenas in his New York City apartment. For the last question of the interview, I asked him to specifically comment on the poetic resonance and lyricism that exists in much of his prose writing. It was my estimation at the time, and still is, that the distinction between poetry and prose in much of Arenas's so-called prose texts is very difficult to discern. Arenas answered in the following manner:

> I believe that a writer should have a knowledge of poetry and from there get all the rest. Poetry is the source of everything. I read poetry. That is why I've always admired Borges, who is a great poet. Borges never abandoned poetry. Even when he wrote his last books of prose he always wrote poetry. One should never forget poetry or underestimate its power. Neither should

one limit poetry to a genre, rather it should be a literary necessity. When a text requires a more poetic tone a writer should use one; if it isn't required then he or she should not use it. But a writer should always keep poetry in mind; if not, the text becomes journalistic, very arid. One of my aspirations is that after I'm dead some reader will remember me for the rhythm of some of my sentences. I'm obviously very optimistic. I can't help it.

(Soto, 154)

Apart from Arenas's clear adoption of poetic tones and nuances into his prose writings, what he calls the rhythm of some of his sentences, the Cuban writer also composed a series of poetic texts, in the strict generic definition, during his lifetime. Perhaps his most accomplished endeavor in this field is the long poem *El central.*[1] This lengthy poetic composition, a lyrical and narrative hybrid written in prose and free verse, was Arenas's first published book of poetry in Spanish as well as one of his earliest translated English texts: *El Central: A Cuban Sugar Mill.*[2] Anthony Kerrigan's highly competent translation from the Spanish *El central* indeed supports the Mexican Nobel Laureate Octavio Paz's contention that poetry, because of its universality, can be translated—contrary to the admonition of many opposing theorists. Paz has written:

> The greatest pessimism about the feasibility of translation has been concentrated on poetry, a remarkable posture since many of the best poems in every Western language are translations. . . . Some years ago the critic and linguist Georges Mounin wrote a book about translation. He pointed out that it is generally, albeit reluctantly, conceded that . . . poetry is a fabric of connotations and, consequently, untranslatable. I must confess that I find this idea offensive, not only because it conflicts with my personal conviction that poetry is universal, but also because it is based on an erroneous conception of what translation is.[3]

If one expects a translation to be a literal equivalent of the original, then surely one would agree with Georges Mounin's position that proposes the untranslatability of poetry. On the other hand, if one sees a translation as a creative transformation of ideas and sensibilities from one language to another, an ongoing approximation, never quite finished, then Paz's words appear more accurate. Anthony Kerrigan's *El Central: A Cuban Sugar Mill* attests to the universality of Arenas's poetry regardless of the language in which it is delivered.

EL CENTRAL: A CUBAN SUGAR MILL

Like **Singing from the Well** and **The Palace of the White Skunks,** which after they were written became part of a larger project (the *pentagonía,* both a writer's autobiography and a metaphor of Cuban history), **El central,** subsequent to its composition, became the first section of a poetic trilogy that presents the Cuban experience from the time of conquest to and including the

Castro regime. The trilogy, titled *Leprosorio,* or *Leper Colony,* was published in its entirety in 1990.[4] (In the notes to the last poem of the trilogy [*Leprosorio,* 131], Arenas admits that the linguistically correct word, according to the Royal Academy for the Spanish Language, is in fact "Leprosería" and not "Leprosorio." In Spanish, the suffix "ería" is commonly used to denote a shop or store in which a specific product is sold; for example, "carnicería" is a store in which "carne," or meat, is sold; "heladería" is a shop in which "helado," or ice cream, is sold. With this logic in mind, Arenas notes that "Leprosería" would suggest to the average Spanish-speaker a store or shop in which "leprosos" or lepers are sold. Arenas's humorous and irreverent response is just another indication of his undermining of hegemonic and dogmatic institutions; in this case, the Royal Academy for the Spanish Language.)

Leprosorio is composed of: *El central* (*El Central: A Cuban Sugar Mill*), originally written by Arenas in the Cuban Sugar Mill Manuel Sanguily in the province of Pinar del Río and dated May, 1970; *Morir en junio y con la lengua afuera* (*To Die in June, Gasping for Air*), Havana, November, 1970; and *Leprosorio* (*Leper Colony*), Havana, 1974-1976, the title of which is also used for the entire collection. In the Betania edition of *Leprosorio* each composition is subtitled as well: *El central,* "**Fundación**" ("**Foundation**"); *Morir en junio y con la lengua afuera,* "**Ciudad**" ("**City**"); *Leprosorio,* "**Exodo**" ("**Exodus**").

Leprosorio is Arenas's most political text. In it the poetic voice does not hold back its anger and rage as it lashes out at the injustices and cruelties that have been committed in Cuba since the island was first settled by Spaniards more than 500 years ago. The horrors of the sugarcane fields of colonial Cuba, which turned the island into a prison first for Indians and then for African slaves, are compared to the atrocities committed by the Castro regime that likewise have turned the "111,111 square kilometers" of island surface into a "cárcel, cárcel, cárcel" (*Leprosorio,* 106) (prison, prison, prison). The leper colony, infested with outbreaks of epidemic virulent diseases, which are specifically enumerated throughout the last poem of the trilogy, serves as a tragically grotesque metaphor for what Cuba has become after successive periods of colonization, military dictatorships, and socialist occupation. *Leprosorio* falls within the tradition of that rare combination and balance of politically and poetically committed verse that very few poets can achieve. In Latin America the most noteworthy examples would be the Peruvian César Vallejo (1892-1938)—*Poemas humanos* (1939) (*Human Poems*)—and the Chilean Nobel Laureate Pablo Neruda (1904-1973)—*Tercera residencia* (1947) (*Third Residence*)—whose socio-politically committed poetry is recognized both for its aesthetics and its message of social justice. However, unlike Vallejo and Neruda, whose socio-political poetry defended Marxism and socialism as viable options for Latin America, *Leprosorio* indicts the Cuban socialist state for having defrauded—through censorship and repression, all in the name of the common good—the individual in his or her search for happiness. Moreover, in *Leprosorio* Arenas gives voice to a homosexual discourse that does not appear in the works of either Vallejo or Neruda. (Although Vallejo explores what we might call brotherly love, Neruda is better known for his heterosexual compositions of love; the most renowned being *Veinte poemas de amor y una canción desesperada* [1924; *Twenty Love Poems and a Song of Despair*]. Neruda and his love poetry were discussed in the Academy Award-winning Italian film *Il Postino.*) Arenas's *Leprosorio* technically and stylistically has more in common with the antipoems of the 1940s and 1950s of Chilean poet Nicanor Parra (b. 1914), who worked in the overwhelming shadow of fellow countryman Pablo Neruda. The Cuban poet's lyricism fits well within Parra's anguished vision of humankind. Although Parra himself was a left-wing writer, his anarchistic rebellion against society as well as his blatantly obscene remarks, satirical irreverence, and outrageous assertions into the poetic composition surely paved the way for Arenas's own rebellious poetic vision.

The first poem of Arenas's trilogy, *El Central: A Cuban Sugar Mill,* subtitled "**Foundation,**" commences with the following dedication: "For my dear friend R. who made me a present of 87 sheets of blank paper." In the notes that appear at the end of the poem, Arenas identifies "R" as Reinaldo García-Ramos, a close friend who placed himself in jeopardy by smuggling in the blank pages to the writer, who was sent to the Manuel Sanguily Sugar Mill in Pinar del Río province to cut sugarcane. Various forms of "voluntary" work have been required of all Cuban citizens since the triumph of the revolution in 1959. In 1970, the year *El central* was composed, this voluntary work was significantly increased in order to achieve the goal set by Fidel Castro of attaining a record 10-million-ton sugarcane harvest that year. (The failure of this massive endeavor contributed much to Cuba's protectionist attitude and subsequent turn to the Soviet Union for economic assistance.) In a chapter of *Before Night Falls,* titled "The Sugar Mill" (*BNF* [*Before Night Falls*], 128-34), Arenas testifies of the horrific conditions that the so-called voluntary workers were forced to endure. At one point he states:

> To be sent to one of those places was like entering the last circle of hell. . . . I came to understand why the Indians had preferred suicide to working there as slaves; I understood why so many black men had killed themselves by suffocation. Now I was the Indian, I was the black slave, and I was not alone. I was one among hundreds of recruits. . . . The vision of all that en

slaved youth inspired my long poem *El central.* I wrote
the poem right there; I could not remain a silent witness to such horror.

(**BNF,** 129)

Arenas's words attest to the testimonial or documentary
function of *El central,* in which the poet becomes a
channel of expression through which Indians, black
slaves, and young adolescent recruits are allowed to
testify of the repeated abuses and humiliations suffered
under the Cuban sugarcane industry. Throughout the
poem the voices of these slave hands are shuffled back
and forth, thus fusing and confusing different eras of
the Cuban experience and ultimately negating the reductionist notion of historical progress. *El Central: A
Cuban Sugar Mill* presents Cuban history as a constant
terror, a reiteration of abusive authoritarian systems under different names but with the same objective: to enslave and exploit, even when it is carried out under the
name of the "common good."

In *The Repeating Island: The Caribbean and the Postmodern Perspective,* [trans. James E. Maraniss (Durham
and London: Duke University Press, 1992)] Antonio
Benítez-Rojo proposes that the Plantation, "capitalized
to indicate not just the presence of plantations but also
the type of society that results from their use and abuse"
(Benítez-Rojo, 9), is the most important historical phenomenon in the Caribbean basin. According to Benítez-
Rojo, the Plantation has been responsible for producing:
"imperialism, wars, colonial blocs, rebellions, repressions, sugar islands, runaway slave settlements, air and
naval bases, revolutions of all sorts, and even a "free
associated state" [that is, Puerto Rico] next to an unfree
socialist state [Cuba]" (Benítez-Rojo, 9). Later in his
study, Benítez-Rojo briefly mentions Arenas's *El central* as an example of a discourse of resistance to sugar,
but, unfortunately, does not provide a closer examination of the text.

It is clear that Arenas was aware of the historical tragedies produced by Cuba's sugar industry. In the first
section of *El Central: A Cuban Sugar Mill,* tellingly
titled "Slave-Hands" (these words will become a leitmotiv throughout this first poem of the trilogy), the poetic voice chronicles successive stages of slave conditions on the island for Indians, black slaves, and so-
called voluntary recruits of the Castro regime, all used
as cheap fuel in the foundation of the Plantation machine that sucked in, according to Benítez-Rojo's figures, "no fewer than ten million African slaves and
thousands of coolies (from India, China, and Malaysia)"
(Benítez-Rojo, 9).[5] To these figures one must also add
the untold numbers of adolescent recruits in revolutionary Cuba who, like the Indians and black slaves before
them, have had no other choice but to participate in
such grandiose projects as, for instance, the failed 1970
10-million-ton sugarcane harvest. In this first section of

the poem, in addition to articulating the exploitation of
slave hands in the Cuban sugarcane fields, a homosexual discourse is introduced through the figures of the
Spanish Monarch Fernando of Aragon and Karl Marx,
both portrayed as repressed homosexuals:

> Beautiful is the figure of the
> naked
> Indian.
> Beautiful is a body without down. Beautiful the
> antipode's
> piece
> which hangs like a shining cylinder. Old (divine)
> Isabella,
>
> . . . . .
>
> . . . kept her gaze,
> imperturbable, riveted on the hanging piece so beauti-
>   fully
> shining.
>
> . . . . .
>
> Did Isabella's Fernando look? Did that great fairy
>   look? Did that grandson of a Jew, that piece of con-
>   vert cuckold look?

(***Sugar Mill*** [*El Central: A Cuban Sugar Mill*], 10-11)

> Behind all these public displays, behind all this
> marching around, the hymns, the unfurling of flags,
>   the
> speeches, behind every
> official ceremony,
> lurks the intent of stimulating and raising your work
> coefficient and
> intensifying your exploitation.
> It was Karl Marx who told me so, bursting into a
>   laugh as
> he wheeled
> gracefully and set off at a trot behind the militarized
> [asses] of the children who brought
> up the rear guard.[6]

(***Sugar Mill,*** 12-13)

The "outing," or accusations that certain individuals are
homosexual, should not be interpreted in Arenas's writing as an indication of self-loathing, as some critics
have proposed, but rather as a defiant stance against
Cuban homophobic hypermasculinity.[7] Arenas belittles
the panic of heterosexual masculinity, which, as a result
of its patriarchal and phallocentric logic, relegates the
homosexual to an inferior position in society.[8] Therefore, it is quite irrelevant if indeed either Fernando of
Aragon or Karl Marx had homosexual inclinations or
desires, but rather that both men utilized their respective positions of authority to create and reinforce respective homophobic ideological systems. Fernando of
Aragon, through his ardent defense of Catholicism and
the establishment of the Inquisition, furthered the intolerance of the Church toward any expressions of sexual
and gender differences. Karl Marx, for his part, proposed a totalizing theory of political economy based on

a distribution of wealth achieved by social ownership that produced a cult of production that ultimately favored procreation and, thus, was antagonistic toward homosexuality. As Michel Foucault posits in his writings, Marxism has not altered preexisting power-knowledge mechanisms, but, ironically, has replaced one class of exploiters for another. With specific regard to Marxism, Allen Young argues in his book *Gays Under the Cuban Revolution* [San Franciso: Grey Fox Press, 1981] that the Cuban revolution's homophobic positions can indeed be traced to the antihomosexual bias of the international Communist movement:

> I believe that the total elimination of homosexuality, as projected by the Cuban authorities, had an ideological basis which was derived not from within the Cuban political experience or the Cuban culture, as has often been alleged, but from the external tradition of European Marxism.
>
> (Young, 14-15)

Although in section 1 of *El Central: A Cuban Sugar Mill* the poetic voice is unidentified, the first half of section 2, titled "The Good Consciences," utilizes the voice of the famous Dominican friar Bartolomé de las Casas (1484-1566), who championed the cause of the indigenous people of the Americas through his writings and actions. Known as the "apóstol de los indios" or apostle of the indigenous, Bartolomé de las Casas is an extremely controversial figure in Latin America given his support for black slavery as a way of sparing the natives of the Americas from ultimate extermination. In fact Bartolomé de las Casas repented this racist position later in life, but section 2 of *El Central: A Cuban Sugar Mill* nonetheless underscores the Dominican friar's twisted logic. The irony of substituting one form of injustice for another is captured in the very title of this section, "The Good Consciences." At one point in section 2 we hear Bartolomé de las Casas addressing an imaginary letter to the Catholic Spanish Monarchs:

> I dare propose to Your Most Serene Majesties . . . that since this slavish system is in accord with your needs to develop these lands, this system be applied to people more suitable for these tasks in this land made for dancing and diving. The Ethiopians of Africa are stronger, and they are black, as Your Highnesses know, and by reason of their strength and the blackness of their skin and the hard kinkiness of their hair, they are in better condition to carry out the regal plans of Your Majesties. The Africans would better be able to endure these violent travails. Besides, they are ugly.
>
> (*Sugar Mill,* 19)

Bartolomé de las Casas's "good conscience" drove him to propose black slavery as a solution to spare the natives of the Americas. Utilizing the same perverted logic, the second half of "The Good Consciences" presents the voice of the leaders of the new revolutionary regime. These leaders, again in the name of social jus-

tice and the good of the Cuban revolution, exploit young adolescent recruits who, precisely because of their youth, that is, their lack of commitment to any ideology except the ideology of self, can easily be manipulated to perform the physical tasks that others would never be able to tolerate. Hence, the decree is made:

> . . . I resolve:

> That all adolescents be called up, sought out, chased, and finally enlisted, and that they be sent off to farms, sugar mills and any other productive centers where they are needed.
>
> (*Sugar Mill,* 22)

What is resolved is the enslavement of adolescents needed to work the Cuban sugarcane fields. To achieve this end, the "Law of Obligatory Military Service" is promulgated so that all adolescents more than 15 years of age are ordered to provide mandatory service to the government. The section "The Good Consciences" ends with a series of stanzas that unite commentaries on the habits of the natives of early colonial Cuba with the habits of the new socialist regime. The following stanza is noteworthy because of its homosexual allusion:

> The Florida Indians were great sodomites and openly maintained male brothels where as many as a thousand gathered at nightfall. Last night, here, there was a "sweep" at Coppelia.
>
> (*Sugar Mill,* 24)

Coppelia, a popular ice cream parlor in Havana, was a well-known homosexual cruising area. In 1961 the revolution's Operation Three P's, a round-up of pederasts, prostitutes, and pimps all with the aim of eradicating these so-called capitalistic ills, raided Coppelia in what has humorously yet sadly been called "la cacería de locas" (faggot hunting). In *El Central: A Cuban Sugar Mill* the Cuban revolution's persecution of homosexuals is compared to the persecutions suffered in the past by Indians and black slaves.

Sections 3 ("A Tropical Hunt"), 4 ("Vicissitudes en Route"), and 5 ("The Night of the Negroes") all evoke the early black slave trade in Cuba as well as the current enslavement of young recruits by the revolutionary government. In the face of so many injustices and atrocities the poetic voice feels impotent to speak out: "I know that all these words are merely useless artifices to delay inevitable decapitation" (*Sugar Mill,* 43). What can be articulated in the face of such repeated horrors?: "no word at all, no matter how fine or noble, will lend more authenticity to your poem than the cry of 'On your feet, you bastards!' at the edge of every dawn" (*Sugar Mill,* 44). How can the poem express the hypocrisy of having to applaud a system that enslaves?: "But one must / applaud, / bend one's back and applaud / raise one's head and applaud. / One must cut all the sugarcane and never stop / applauding" (***Sugar Mill,*** 55). In addition to denouncing the atrocities and oppression of Cuba's sugarcane industry throughout the ages, ***El Central: A Cuban Sugar Mill*** also turns critically on itself to question the poem's own value and effectiveness. In this way the poem, like history, cannot be idealized as a space of ultimate truth. A repository of repeated frustrations, the poem becomes a mere echo, faint words that desperately attempt to articulate the abuses that have occurred and continue to occur in Cuba while all the while conscious of its own impotence, its limited and fragmented vision:

> no grand phraseology will do, nor complicated philo-
> sophical
> speculations, nor hermetic poetry. In the face of terror
> there is the
> simplicity of epic verse: simply *to tell*.)
>   One must tell.
>   One must tell.
> A place where nothing can be told is a place where
> the most must be told.
>   One must tell.
>   Everything must be told.

>   (***Sugar Mill,*** 56)

Section 6 of the poem, entitled "Human Relations," narrates three short tales of corruption involving sexuality, power, and death. Reminiscent of, yet far more brutal than, the stories of *El conde Lucanor o el libro de Patronio* (Count Lucanor or the Book of Patronius) of Don Juan Manuel (1282-1349?), a foundational text in the Spanish literary tradition, the three tales in this section attest to the selfishness and hypocrisies of human relations, a common theme in many of Arenas's texts. Yet, unlike *El conde Lucanor,* there are no clear-cut moral lessons to be learned here.

The first story is that of Mr. Reeves, referred to as the Patriarch, who sets up a breeding farm in which he personally fathers hundreds of children with black women only to sell them to wealthy Brazilians. This story highlights the greed, ambition, and lack of human compassion that certain individuals are capable of. The second story is longer than the first but it too demonstrates the extent to which one person will go to control or enslave another. The nameless handsome blond man of this story, also a slave trader, becomes the sexual obsession of his wife who, jealous to the point of madness, will do anything to assure herself of her husband's fidelity. This story acquires a hyperbolic tone, typical in much of Arenas's fiction, as is evident from the following passage:

> Her fits of jealousy could not be allayed. Every after-
> noon she had the slave-girls paraded before her and she
> palpated their bellies. If one of them had an inch in

> girth, she had her beheaded at nightfall. She also kept
> rigorous records of their periods of menstruation: if one
> of them was a day late, she had a dagger driven through
> her belly.

>   (***Sugar Mill,*** 64)

Yet even after all her careful vigilance, one day the jealous wife discovers her husband with a blinded slave girl. After savagely killing the girl, the wife pickles her flesh and serves it to her husband who, after being told what he has eaten, shows no reaction to his wife. Desperate, in a final attempt to achieve the control she feels she must have, the wife plans to murder her husband. Yet at the very last moment, unable to actually commit the act, she turns the knife and kills herself. Unlike the tales of *El conde Lucanor,* which end with a rhymed couplet giving the moral of the story, the tale of the blond man does not have such a clear moral message. Rather, what is evoked is the nastiness of "human relations," the ironic title of the section, in which individuals either enslave others, both physically and emotionally, or are themselves enslaved by others.

The last tale of section 6 is that of Lieutenant Benito, an exemplary young military leader. With 300 recruits under his command, Lieutenant Benito begins to feel a physical homosexual attraction for a young sanitary corpsman, but as a result of his machismo, his anxious hypermasculinity, he refuses to acknowledge such a taboo desire. One night at a barrack party the lieutenant notices the young corpsman paying special attention to a distinguished visitor, "a young man with loose gestures and a playful smile." (***Sugar Mill,*** 67) Obviously jealous, although unable to give a name to his feelings, the lieutenant proceeds to order the sanitary corpsman to perform a number of meaningless duties to hinder his contact with the visitor. The story ends in the following manner:

> The corpsman completed the task as fast as a phantom
> and returned to his post beside the distinguished visitor.
> Benito now ordered his man to stop serving and go to
> bed. The corpsman acted as if he had not heard the or-
> der. Benito repeated it. The corpsman announced that
> he was not tired and did not obey the order. Lieutenant
> Benito took out his revolver and sent five bullets into
> his orderly's head. . . . At the court martial, the case
> was treated as one of gross insubordination. Lieutenant
> Benito was absolved.

>   (***Sugar Mill,*** 68; the ellipsis points appear in the
>   original)

Lieutenant Benito's repressed homoerotic desire leads him to commit a brutal act of murder, which ultimately is absolved by a military judicial panel that, likewise, is unwilling to entertain the existence of homosexual desire among so-called real masculine men. The poem's utilization of ellipsis points after Lieutenant Benito fires his five bullets visually indicates the silence that cloaks homoerotic desire in the military, in which homosexuality is seen as subversive to a nation's strength. As stated in the introduction and again in chapter 1, immediately after its triumph, the Cuban revolution institutionalized a systematic harassment and incarceration of homosexuals all in the name of cleaning up the capitalist ills on the island. Male-male relations, and to a lesser degree female-female relations, were seen as undermining the strength and ultimate survival of the revolution. The very notion of homosexuality offended the heroic sensibilities of the revolutionary leaders as is evident in the following declaration published in 1965 in the newspaper *Revolución:* "No homosexual represents the revolution, which is a matter for men, of fists and not feathers, of courage and not trembling, of certainty and not intrigue, of creative valor and not of sweet surprises."[9] Behind this simplistic binary opposition, which argues that heterosexual men are courageous while homosexual men are frightened cowards, a clear homophobic panic is evident. There has been no place within the Cuban army, which has fought hard and long for its national liberation, for males who do not reflect the ultra-virile values of Cuban machismo.

Sections 7, 8, and 9 (respectively titled "Uniquely, of One," "A Small Pretext for a Monotonous Discharge," and "The Monotonous Discharge"), although very short passages, begin to articulate the ire and fury of the poetic voice, who now begins to challenge the persecutions, high-sounding discourses, and obligatory and useless labor that befalls the young adolescent recruits on the island. History, that is, so-called official facts and figures that are manipulated by those in power to push forward particular agendas, is challenged by the poetic voice. History is presented as "a closed space" (*Sugar Mill,* 81) that only speaks to "what is now useless" (*Sugar Mill,* 81). Arenas is suggesting that historical facts or figures are incapable of capturing the vitality of the human experience because, by definition, they oversimplify and draw conclusions that dismiss the individual dimension of personal experience. Furthermore, historical discourses are deceptive in their attempts to present visions of totality.

The beginning lines of section 10 ("Finale 'Grandiose'") make it apparent that the poetic voice is now that of a homosexual interned in a sugarcane plantation, perhaps an UMAP camp:

> O what a pessimistic queen this writer is, the up-to-date bourgeois will say (at ease in a wicker chair destined to keel over), himself won over by the optimistic wall-writing and slogans of the Marxist who know that without the holy faith of a certain they would not be able to gobble up the earth before it explodes.
>
> (*Sugar Mill,* 85)

The idea that foreigners, living comfortably, sitting in their wicker chairs far away from the island, have assisted the revolution through their support is sarcastically derided. This theme is prevalent throughout *El Central: A Cuban Sugar Mill, Morir en junio y con la lengua afuera,* and *Leprosorio.* In all three poems the Cuban problem is seen as partially caused by individuals outside the island who both knowingly and unknowingly contribute to perpetuating the enslavement of the Cuban people. In section 1 of *El Central: A Cuban Sugar Mill,* for example, these individuals are the figures of the Spanish Monarchs but also those of bourgeois foreigners who consume the sugar produced by enslaved Cubans: "Slave-hands / have methodically constructed / this tiny square of sugar which you, notable / foreign consumer, so smartly dressed / in the open-air café / drop to the bottom of the modern / receptacle" (*Sugar Mill,* 12). In *Morir en junio y con la lengua afuera* [*Leprosorio*] (pp. 91-93), the poetic voice pokes fun at so-called progressive tourists who come to Castro's Cuba to enjoy themselves while ignoring the abuses that are committed against Cuban citizens who, unlike the tourists, cannot leave the island. Finally, in *Leprosorio* (pp. 15-116), after testifying of repeated horrors committed against the recruits, the poetic voice confronts with obvious irony the incredulous reader outside the island who refuses to believe what is going on: "no se inquiete: Usted no tiene porqué creerme" (*Leprosorio,* 116) (don't get upset: you have no reason to believe me).

In section 10 of *El Central: A Cuban Sugar Mill* the poetic voice serves as a witness to the abuses both of the past and of the present. Three stanzas, each commencing with the words "I see," blur the lines of official history to unite the plight of indigenous people, blacks, and armies of young recruits all presented as "enslaved and hungry." This "I see" is reminiscent of the recurrent use of the archaic predicate statement "yo vide" ("yo vi" = I saw) in Miguel Barnet's famous documentary novel, *Biografía de un cimarrón* (1966), in which Esteban Montejo revises (rewrites) history by presenting the black man's active participation in the struggle for Cuban independence.[10] Whereas in Barnet's text the direct voice of the witness, Esteban Montejo, is presented in the past tense, the "I see" of *El Central: A Cuban Sugar Mill* utilizes an epic present tense that encompasses 500 years of enslavement.

The last section of the poem ("The Introduction of the Symbol of the Faith") presents the poetic voice's incessant search for the fatherland despite the fact that "beyond death lies death" and "that there are no doors or exits from fright"—this last verse reminds the reader of Arenas's novel *The Doorman,* in which the main character searches for his own door to happiness. The voice of the poetic narrator is joined to a collective "we" who while searching for "the so-much desired land" are cognizant of the fact that it does not exist. The poem demythologizes any idealistic notion that literature can transcend human experience and find specific solutions.

Still, the poem ends with the lines: "We continue to search for you [fatherland] / we continue / we continue" (*Sugar Mill,* 91).

El Central: A Cuban Sugar Mill challenges and undermines both past and present systems of power in Cuba that have attempted to establish themselves as absolute authority, as discourses of the highest truth, by enslaving individual expression. The poem's undermining of authoritative rules should not, however, be considered as pure anarchy. Rather, the poem's subversion is creative and directed toward affirmative and positive action, as is apparent in the final verse "we continue to search." This search for an ideal space in which the individual can feel free and safe is presented not just in this poem but in Arenas's entire oeuvre.

MORIR EN JUNIO Y CON LA LENGUA AFUERA

Morir en junio y con la lengua afuera (**To Die in June, Gasping for Air**) was written six months after **El central.**[11] It, like **El central,** is a poem of denunciation in which the poetic voice is marked by the immediacy of giving testimony of the constant threat and menace surrounding him. Dated November, 1970, the poem is not divided into sections or segments like **El central,** nor is it as long. Subtitled **Ciudad,** or City, **Morir en junio y con la lengua afuera** once again casts the poetic voice in the role of critical observer, this time, riding in a Havana bus en route to the countryside, looking out the window at the world hoping to find some kind of distraction from the mediocrity and enslavement of city life, a life driven by "grandes teorías de metas y consumos" (**Morir en junio,** 75) (great theories of goals and consumption) in which everyone appears to be emotionally dead: "Todos estamos muertos" (**Morir en junio** 76) (We are all dead). The city is presented as a loud and obnoxious space filled with informers and volunteer teachers all blindly driven by the ideology of the revolutionary regime. It is in response to this excessive exemplary moral and physical loudness that the poet is driven to write:

> Por la noche los perros interfieren el *ta, ta, ta* de las
> musas divinas, ya en extinción.
> Por el día, un desafío de ollas, de cascos que se agi-
> tan,
> de latas, de piafantes maestras voluntarias,
> de esbirros disfrazados de bañistas,
> de bocinas con altoparlantes
> me impelen a tomar el artefacto.
>
> (**Morir en junio,** 76-77)

> During the evening the dogs interfere with the tap,
> tap,
> tap of the divine muses, already in extinction.
> During the day, a challenge of pots and pans, of
> agitating hard hats, of cans, of stamping voluntary
> teachers, of informers dressed as ocean bathers,

> of horns with loudspeakers
> drive me to take the artifact.
>
> (my translation)

In addition to the deafening noises of the city, the poetic voice presents the fanatical figures of volunteer teachers and informers who uphold and ardently defend the revolutionary party line. The mentioning of "maestras voluntarias," or volunteer teachers, is a direct allusion to a well-known Cuban documentary novel. The documentary-testimonial vein in Cuban revolutionary literature can in fact be traced back to 1962 and the publication of Daura Olema García's *Maestra voluntaria,* a work that won the Casa de las Américas' novelistic prize that same year. *Maestra voluntaria* relates, in documentary fashion, the experiences of a volunteer teacher during the revolution's early campaign to eliminate illiteracy on the island. In this book, which resembles a journalistic account of the literacy campaign more than a work of fiction, the protagonist converts to communism as a result of her training and subsequent dedication to the teaching of Cuba's illiterates. This novel clearly illustrates the type of literature that contributed to the shaping of a revolutionary consciousness and that was actively supported by the revolution's cultural policy makers. *Maestra voluntaria* has no grey areas but rather presents the experiences of the revolution as overly simplistic: either one ardently defends the revolution or one is considered a traitor, that is, a counterrevolutionary.

In **Morir en junio y con la lengua afuera** the adolescent youths are once again presented as living in an inferno ("Una juventud que se corrompe inútil y rápida" (**Morir en junio,** 75) (youths who are uselessly and quickly corrupted) in which there is no hope whatsoever of divine intervention: "Oh, dios, / estás postergado y silencioso, / estás muerto y vejado" (**Morir en junio,** 75) (Oh, god, you disregard us and are silent, you are dead and annoyed). Carefully watching is "el gran amo" or great master, an Orwellian tropical Big Brother, constantly vigilant and always in complete control: "El gran amo está aquí; el amo vigila. / El gran amo dispondrá cuánto debes vivir, / para qué sirves, cuál es tu fin" (**Morir en junio,** 87) (the great master is here; the master is vigilant. / The great master will decide how long you should live, / what is your use, what is your purpose).

Near the end of the poem, the poetic voice identifies itself with Perceval, one of the more famous heroes in Arthurian legend.

> Fue en Isla de Pinos
>   (hoy "Isla de la Juventud").
> Llovía y Percival lloraba sentado
> en un arado de
> tres esteras.
>
>   . . . . .

Realmente tu historia y la mía son las mismas.
Tú en Munsalwashe,
dudando por piedad de Dios mismo.
Yo en Catalina de Güines revisando el marxismo.
Tú "admitido en la tabla Redonda."
Yo obligatoriamente concurriendo a la Asamblea.

(*Morir en junio,* 88-89)

It was on the Isle of Pines
    (Today called "Isle of Youth").
It was raining and Perceval was crying
as he sat on three grass mats
on the plowed ground.
       . . . . .

Truly your story and mine are the same.
You in Munsalvaesche,
doubting God for pity's sake.
I in Catalina de Güines reviewing marxism.
You "admitted to the Round Table."
I attending the obligatory Assembly.

(my translation)

The poetic voice goes on to present other valiant and heroic feats of the legendary Perceval that are compared to the meaningless and inane tasks that the poetic voice, representing Cuban youths on the island, is forced to perform. The poetic voice transports the intrepid knight of the Round Table to his cramped cell on the Isle of Pine, where the valiant Perceval is forced to perform endless "voluntary" manual labor and as a consequence becomes "acatarrado y hambriento" (*Morir en junio,* 89) (sick and hungry). Like the poetic voice, Perceval ironically becomes a "típica figura del hombre nuevo" (*Morir en junio,* 89) (typical figure of the new man).

The Arthurian legends have been a rich source of inspiration for writers throughout the ages. The Bretons passed the Arthurian lore on to the French. The first French writer of Arthurian romance was Chrétien de Troyes, a poet who lived in the latter half of the twelfth century and who was responsible for first inventing the name Perceval, previously known in Welsh sources as Peredur, and casting him as the hero of his romance *Perceval,* also known as *Le conte de graal* (The Story of the Grail). According to Chrétien de Troyes, Perceval was raised in the woods by his overprotective mother who wanted him to know nothing of knighthood. Yet after seeing some knights in the woods near his home, Perceval becomes determined to go to Arthur's court and become a knight of the Round Table. Recently, Arthurian scholars have begun to identify half-hidden homoerotic themes in many of the Arthurian texts.[12] Many of the special friendships and comradeship of knights described in these texts, while not being explicitly homoerotic, nonetheless do suggest a homosocial context. The clearly demarcated distinction between male bonding and homoeroticism that is quite prevalent today in fact did not exist prior to the eighteenth century, as Bruce Smith argues in *Homosexual Desire in Shakespeare's England.*[13] Thus, for example, male bonding (passionate friendship) and male homosexuality (homoerotic passion) were "aspects of the same psychological and social phenomenon" (Mieszkowski, 43). Among the many feats that the legendary Perceval performs and that are enumerated in *Morir en junio y con la lengua afuera,* a homosocial allusion is made when Perceval is presented "del brazo de Tristán" (*Morir en junio,* 90) (arm-in-arm with Tristan [a contemporary of King Arthur and a Knight of the Round Table]).

At the end of *Morir en junio y con la lengua afuera,* Arenas includes a rather lengthy footnote in which he presents information concerning Perceval, a character he describes as "sencillo de espíritu y puro de corazón" (*Morir en junio,* 98) (of natural spirit and pure heart). Out of all the information concerning this legendary character, Arenas focuses on two specific aspects. The first is Perceval's mother's isolation of her son in the woods to protect him from danger. Arenas reads this act as one of control and manipulation, which the son must escape in order to be free. (The idea of escaping from the mother in order to be free is a common motivation of many of Arenas's characters; they find themselves emotionally haunted by this dictatorial and tyrannical figure who at times is also presented as loving and caring.)[14] The second point that Arenas latches onto is Perceval's search, the search for his dead father, the search for the Grail, in sum, a search for some type of meaning in his life. Hence, breaking away from the overbearing mother is united to the idea of being able to search for meaning in one's life:

La madre nos orienta hacia el terror.
La madre se transforma en "virgen casta," la madre se
disfraza de ofendida.
La madre se disuelve entre los surcos para
ser ya
el hueco que enfanga nuestras manos.
    —La madre estimulando los espantos.
Sí, nuestras historias son exactas. Sólo resta
levantar el mosquitero y abrazarte.

(*Morir en junio,* 91)

Mother directs us to the terror.
Mother transforms herself into a "chaste virgin,"
  mother
disguises herself as the offended one.
Mother dissolves herself between the furrows in order
to be
the hole that covers our hands with mud.
    —Mother prompting fears.
Yes, our histories are the same. What is only left is
to lift the mosquito net and embrace you.

(my translation)

The camaraderie that binds Perceval and the poetic voice is not one based on lionheartedly battling dragons and spirited enemies, but one in which the repressive figure of the mother is confronted. Arenas's story **"Adiós a mamá" ("Goodbye Mother")**[15] is particularly noteworthy in the treatment of this theme. In the story the death of the mother incites extravagant and delirious conduct on the part of the male protagonist's four sisters, whose fanaticism in not wanting to bury their mother's decomposing body leads them to commit suicide as a sign of solidarity with the deceased. The story ends when the protagonist, unconvinced of his slaughtered sisters' demented loyalty, rather than joining them in death, escapes to the sea declaring "I'm a traitor. A confirmed traitor. And happy" (**"Goodbye Mother,"** 66).

Through his *burla,* or mocking attacks, the poetic voice of ***Morir en junio y con la lengua afuera*** creates a temporary safe space from which he challenges and keeps at bay those forces intent on destroying him. Unlike the fabled Perceval, whose mighty sword defended him from his attackers, the poetic voice only has his *lengua* (tongue), a word anaphorically repeated in a series of verses at the end of the poem (*Morir en junio,* 95-96). The Spanish title ***Morir en junio y con la lengua afuera,*** literally "To die in June and with one's tongue hanging out," implies not just the idea of gasping for air as a result of being beaten down by a system that brutally punishes disobedience but also the metonymical idea of tongue as speech that refuses to be silenced. Regardless of the many times he is beaten down, both physically and emotionally, the poetic voice continues to speak, to cry out.

LEPROSORIO

Leprosorio (***Leper Colony***), subtitled **"Exodus,"** was written over a period of two years, 1974-1976.[16] In this last poem of the trilogy the poetic voice is desperately searching to escape from what has become an unbearable existence. Cuba is presented as an island-prison of "111,111 square kilometers" (a leitmotiv throughout the poem) infested with virulent germs, bacteria, and diseases. Reminiscent of Pablo Neruda's famous "The United Fruit Co.,"[17] in which the Chilean poet includes the names of such notorious Latin American dictators as Rafael Trujillo of the Dominican Republic, Tiburcio Carías Andino of Honduras, and Jorge Ubico of Guatemala, in ***Leprosorio,*** interspersed within stanzas that enumerate the names of pathological degenerative diseases are found the names of Cuban dictators:

> Endocarditis Lenta
> Weyler Valeriano Dictador
> Cefalea Avanzada
> Machado Gerardo Dictador

> Neuritis Periférica
> Batista Fulgencio Dictador
> Gangrena Orgánica
> Castro Fidel Dictador . . .

>   (*Leprosorio,* 114)

> Slow Endocarditis
> Weyler Valeriano Dictator
> Progressive Migraines
> Machado Gerardo Dictator
> Peripheral Neuritis
> Batista Fulgencio Dictator
> Organic Gangrene
> Castro Fidel Dictator . . .

>   (my translation)

This stanza first mentions the Spanish General Valeriano Weyler who was appointed to oversee the Spanish war effort in Cuba. Weyler, who arrived in Cuba in 1896 and was accompanied by some 50,000 Spanish troops, quickly and ferociously persecuted and imprisoned both Cubans and Spaniards who sympathized with Cuba's struggle for independence. The next three names, Machado, Batista, and Castro, represent the three longest periods of twentieth-century Cuban history in which one man has forcefully ruled with unquestionable power. Each of the three names has been altered by first mentioning the last name, the customary way in which Cubans refer to these individuals, followed by their first name, and finally ending with their unofficial yet recognized title of "dictator." Later in the poem each Cuban dictator—with the exception of Weyler who was Spanish by birth—is singled out in a stanza of his own in which one verse prominently displays the dictator's name. Let me cite the last example, that of Fidel Castro:

> Elefantiasis Compulsiva.
> Tularemia Virus.
> Sífilis Galopante.
> Cólera Morbo.
> Castro Comandante.
> Náusea y Diarrea . . .

>   (*Leprosorio,* 119)

> Compulsive Elephantiasis.
> Viral Tularemia.
> Galloping Syphilis.
> Morbid Cholera.
> Commanding Castro.
> Nausea and Diarrhea . . .

>   (my translation)

Despite the moral and spiritual disease on the island, the poetic voice vows to keep fighting, to not be defeated: "No podrán conmigo. No van a destruirme. Ya verán. Ya ven como los reto. Y al retarlos los burlo, los traiciono y derroto" (***Leprosorio,*** 129) (They can't stop me. They can't destroy me. They'll see. They'll see how I'll challenge them. And challenging them I mock them, I betray and defeat them). In such an infested environment "partir" (to leave) or "correr" (to run) (*Leprosorio,* 129) becomes the only alternative. The last stanza of *Leprosorio* ends by stating:

> Correr
> entre el tiroteo y el azote del cielo,
> burlando, traicionando, dejando atrás
> la intransferible configuración de nuestros 111,111
>   kilómetros
> cuadrados
> (cifra del ejército, naturalmente)
> de leprosorio.
>
>   (*Leprosorio,* 129-30)

> Running
> in between the shooting and the heavenly scourge,
> outmaneuvering, betraying, leaving behind
> the untransferable configuration of our 111,111
>   kilometers
> squared
> (naturally, a military number)
> leper colony.
>
>   (my translation)

The only way to survive such monstrous conditions is to escape, to flee. *Leprosorio* was composed from 1974 to 1976, years that coincide precisely with Arenas's own imprisonment and anxious struggles to leave Cuba.

Voluntad de vivir manifestándose

In 1989 the editorial house Betania (Spain) published a collection of short poems by Arenas under the title *Voluntad de vivir manifestándose* (*The Will to Live Manifesting Itself*).[18] This collection, whose poems date from as early as 1969 to as late as 1989, is marked by the same intensity, fury, and seduction that characterize all of the writer's work. As a whole, *Voluntad de vivir manifestándose* is a poetic manifestation of the repression, persecution, loneliness, and general desperation that marked Arenas's life, a life scarred by Batista's tyranny, Castro's repressive regime, the United States's capitalist economy, and, finally, the AIDS epidemic. In the prologue to the collection Arenas writes:

> He contemplado el infierno, la única porción de realidad que me ha tocado vivir, con ojos familiares; no sin satisfacción lo he vivido y cantado . . . Sólo me arrepiento de lo que no he hecho. Hasta última hora la ecuanimidad y el ritmo.
>
>   (*Voluntad,* 7)

> With familiar eyes, I have contemplated hell, the only portion of reality that I have lived; not without satisfaction have I lived and sang of it . . . My only regret is what I have not done. To the last second, equanimity and rhythm.
>
>   (my translation)

The last line, "Hasta última hora la ecuanimidad y el ritmo" (To the last second, equanimity and rhythm), is identical to one of the last sentences in *Farewell to the Sea.* As Arenas explained to me during our conversation in 1987, equanimity is necessary for the poem to be created. Equanimity is imperative because "without it there is nothing, not even madness, that can be told or narrated. Up to the end, up to the last second, Hector can not lose his sense of rhythm or equanimity, without which he would lose his sense of creation" (Soto, 150). Even after having endured repeated tragedies, Arenas was well aware that without equanimity, the composure to withstand the disasters of life, the poem had no chance of being articulated.

Voluntad de vivir manifestándose is divided into four sections, titled: "Esa sinfonía que milagrosamente escuchas" ("That Symphony Which You Miraculously Hear"), "Sonetos desde el infierno" ("Sonnets from Hell"), "Mi amante el mar" ("My Lover the Sea"), and "El otoño me regala una hoja" ("Autumn Presents Me with a Leaf").

The nine poems of the first section ("That Symphony Which You Miraculously Hear") were all written between 1969 and 1975 while Arenas still lived in Cuba. These poems articulate a profound sense of existential anguish as a result of a political system that prohibits the poet from expressing himself freely. The constant vigilance ("Carlos Marx / no tuvo nunca sin saberlo una grabadora / estratégicamente colocada en su sitio más íntimo" [*Voluntad,* 16] [Karl Marx / never had without knowing it a tape recorder / strategically situated in his most intimate spot]) as well as the enslavement of the revolutionary system ("Un millón de niños condenados bajo la excusa de 'La Escuela al campo' a ser no niños, sino esclavos agrarios" [*Voluntad,* 21] [A million children condemned with the excuse of School Camp to not be children but agrarian slaves]) are presented as being responsible for the poet's spiritual death. In the last poem of this first section, **"Voluntad de vivir manifestándose" ("The Will to Live Manifesting Itself")**, also used for the title of the collection, the poet, dead and buried, cries out:

> Me han sepultado.
> Han danzado sobre mí.
> Han apisonado bien el suelo.
> Se han ido, se han ido dejándome bien muerto y enterrado.
> Este es mi momento.
>
>   (*Voluntad,* 24)

> They have buried me.
> They have danced over me.
> They have tamped the earth well.-

They have left, they have left me dead and well buried.
This is my moment.

(my translation)

This moment of spiritual death was precisely the reality
Arenas was forced to endure after falling out of favor
with the revolutionary establishment for his unorthodox
writings and so-called improper conduct. Still, the poet
recognizes that it is precisely at this moment, when the
malevolent forces believe that they have destroyed and
silenced him, that he, like the phoenix, would rise up
and rebel against the oppression.

The second section of the collection ("Sonnets from
Hell") is made up of 37 sonnets, all written between
1969 and 1980. In these sonnets, or antisonnets—although the formal aspects of the sonnet are respected
the themes are far from traditional—death becomes an
obsessive concern. For example, in the sonnet **"También tenemos el Ministerio de la Muerte" ("We Also
Have the Minister of Death")** we read:

Hay muchas formas de aplicar la muerte.
Tenemos la muerte por muerte sin muerte.
También, la muerte y luego la másmuerte.
Y la muerte que es muerte y sobremuerte.

(*Voluntad,* 46)

There are many ways of applying death.
We have death by death without death.
Also, death and later moredeath.
And death that is death and afterdeath.

(my translation)

Since Arenas's first novel, *Singing from the Well*
(1967), the imaginative capability of the individual has
been presented in his texts as something essential and
vital that separates human beings from other beasts. In
the sonnet **"Todo lo que pudo ser, aunque haya sido"
("All That Could Have Been, Although It Was")** the
possibilities of dreaming, that marvelous gift of the
imagination, superior to any so-called objective reality,
is underscored. In the end, it is the individual's unbridled fantasy that saves him or her from the repeated
persecutions of life.

Todo lo que pudo ser, aunque haya sido,
jamás ha sido como fue soñado.
El dios de la miseria se ha encargado
de darle a la realidad otro sentido.

Otro sentido, nunca presentido,
cubre hasta el deseo realizado;
de modo que el placer aun disfrutado
jamás podrá igualar al inventado.

(*Voluntad,* 34)

All that could have been, although it was,
was never as one dreamed it.

The god of misery has made sure
of giving reality another meaning.

Another meaning, never predicted,
covers even fulfilled desire;
in such a way that enjoyed pleasure
will never equal invented pleasure.

(my translation)

Four sonnets in this section articulate clear homoerotic
themes (pp. 40, 56, 58, 61). Of particular interest is the
sonnet titled **"De modo que Cervantes era manco"**
("And So Cervantes Was Maimed"), in which an
overview of the Western canon's most recognized homosexual artists is presented. The poetic voice first
mentions some of the physical handicaps and emotional
peculiarities of Western tradition's most celebrated artists (i.e., Cervantes, Beethoven, Luis de Góngora, and
so forth) before proceeding to "out" homosexual artists
throughout the ages.

De modo que Cervantes era manco;
sordo, Beethoven; Villon ladrón;
Góngora de tan loco andaba en zanco.
¿Y Proust? Desde luego, maricón.

Negrero, sí, fue Don Nicolás Tanco,
y Virginia se suprimió de un zambullón,
Lautrémont murió aterido en algún banco.
Ay de mí, también Shakespeare era maricón.

También Leonardo y Federico García,
Whitman, Miguel Angel y Petronio,
Gide, Genet y Visconti, las fatales.

Esta es, señores, la breve biografía
(¡vaya, olvidé mencionar a San Antonio!)
de quienes son del arte sólidos puntales.

(*Voluntad,* 40)

And so Cervantes was maimed;
Beethoven deaf; Villon, a thief;
Góngora was so crazy he used stilts,
And Proust? a faggot, of course.

Don Nicolás Tanco, a slave trader, oh yes,
and Virginia eliminated herself with one dive,
Lautrémont died from some cold bench,
Oh dear, Shakespeare was also a faggot.

So were Leonardo and Federico García,
Whitman, Michelangelo and Petronius,
Gide, Genet and Visconti, those fatal queens.

This is, ladies and gentlemen, the brief biography
(Wait a minute, I almost forgot Saint Anthony)
of art's most established artists.

(my translation)

Arenas lampoons the homophobic reader who perhaps
would like to make the equation that homosexuality is a
handicap or an emotional peculiarity. The sonnet ridi-

cules, through irony, those homophobic readers who would be "surprised" to learn that many of Western tradition's most distinguished and established artists (the "sólidos puntales") were indeed "maricones." Here the term "maricón," or faggot, which Arenas uses throughout his writing with underlying affection, is purposefully deployed with the pejorative connotation it holds when used by homophobic individuals intent on ridiculing and demeaning homosexual preferences. The sonnet is dated Havana, 1971. Hence, while Arenas was still cautiously veiling homosexual themes in his prose works of the period (for example, in such texts as *The Palace of the White Skunks* and the stories of *Con los ojos cerrados* [*With My Eyes Closed*]), he was, in his poetry, directly confronting the theme of homosexuality, probably because the intensely personal tone of lyrical poetry is often written with no intention of publication.

The third section of *Voluntad de vivir manifestándose* consists of only one poem, titled **"Mi amante el mar"** (**"My Lover the Sea"**), dated 1973. This prose poem, the longest single composition in the collection, utilizes chaotic enumeration to present the disillusionment of the Cuban people, who have been reduced to simply surviving in a hostile environment. The repetition of the words "Yo veo" (I see) serve as a leitmotiv that characterizes the degeneration and degradation that the poet witnesses all around him. In order to free himself from the paltriness of life, the poet addresses himself to his lover, the sea. Arenas purposefully uses the masculine definite article "el" instead of the feminine definite article "la," the more traditional poetic choice, to denote the sea ("mar").

> Mi amante el mar me devolverá el niño que fui
> bajo la arboleda y el sol
> o con un susurro mecerá mis huesos.
> Mi amante el mar prolongará mi búsqueda y mi furia,
> mi canto, . . .
>
> (*Voluntad,* 79)

> My lover the sea will bring back the child I was
> under the grove and the sun
> or with a murmur he will rock my bones to sleep.
> My lover the sea will prolong my search and my fury,
> my song, . . .
>
> (my translation)

At the end of the poem, the male speaker unites with the lover, that is, he commits suicide by drowning himself. Suicide, a constant in Arenas's texts, often is the only escape for characters forced to live in an environment marked by cruelty, ignorance, and constant persecution.

The last section of the collection ("El otoño me regala una hoja") ("Autumn Presents Me with a Leaf") contains 16 poems, all written in the United States. Now

free from the fear of recrimination, the poetic voice allows itself to speak freely. In this section, the poem **"Si te llamaras Nelson"** (**"If You Were Called Nelson"**), previously discussed in chapter 3, appears. Still, the most moving poem of the entire section is the last, titled **"Autoepitafio"** (**"Self-Epitaph"**) and dated 1989, one year prior to Arenas's death. This poem, more than a morbid self-indulgence, is a celebration of the rebellious spirit that characterizes all of Arenas's work. The poem once again presents the indomitable spirit of the writer who refuses to surrender himself to mediocrity, an instinct that has served him as solace from "la prisión, el ostracismo, el exilio, [y] las múltiples ofensas típicas de la vileza humana" (*Voluntad,* 110) (prison, ostracism, exile, and the numerous typical offenses of human vileness). "Autoepitafio" ends with the poetic voice, speaking in the third person, recounting the poet's instructions of what to do with his body after death. These lines summarize, rather effectively, Arenas's indomitable spirit:

> Ordenó que sus cenizas fueran lanzadas al mar
> donde habrán de fluir constantemente.
> No ha perdido la costumbre de soñar:
> espera que en sus aguas se zambulla algún adolescente.
>
> (*Voluntad,* 110)

> He arranged for his ashes to be scattered into the sea
> where they would flow forever.
> Not having given up his habit of dreaming,
> he awaits a young man to dive into his waters.
>
> (my translation)

Notes

1. Reinaldo Arenas, *El central* (Barcelona: Editorial Seix Barral, 1981); hereafter cited in text as *El central.*

2. Reinaldo Arenas, *El Central: A Cuban Sugar Mill,* trans. Anthony Kerrigan (New York: Avon Books, 1984); hereafter cited in text as *Sugar Mill.*

3. Octavio Paz, "Translation: Literature and Letters," trans. Irene del Corral, in *Theories of Translation,* ed. Rainer Schulte and John Biguenet (Chicago: University of Chicago Press, 1992), 155.

4. Reinaldo Arenas, *Leprosorio* (Madrid: Editorial Betania, 1990); the poems contained herein are hereafter cited in text as *Morir en junio* and *Leprosorio.*

5. In his novel *La loma del ángel* (*Graveyard of the Angels;* trans. Alfred MacAdam [New York: Avon Books, 1987])—a parodic rewriting of Cirilio Villaverde's solemn nineteenth-century Cuban novel *Cecilia Valdés*—Arenas literally exploits the idea and image of the black slave being sucked into

the Plantation machine. In chapter 24 of the novel, titled "The Steam Engine," the impact of technology and its effects on black slaves in early nineteenth-century Cuban sugar production is sarcastically ridiculed when an English manufactured steam engine is acquired by don Cándido with the hope of grinding sugarcane more quickly and thus rendering obsolete the old grinding machines powered by horses, mules, and sometimes slaves. However, because it is a new machine, no one knows exactly how to work it. Thus, when the engine becomes clogged, a black slave is sent into the engine to unblock the machine. While the slave is inside the machine, the pressure finally builds to such a point that the machine explodes, hurling the slave through the air by the force of the compressed steam. Arenas's narrative now takes on a hyperbolic and satirical tone as other black slaves frantically throw themselves into the engine with the hope of fleeing from the plantation. Afraid of losing all his slaves, don Cándido yells out: "Stop that machine or all my slaves will disappear! I should have known you can't do business with the English! That's no steam engine, it's an English trick to send the blacks back to Africa!" (*Graveyard,* 81)

6. I have slightly modified Anthony Kerrigan's translation to account for the sexual innuendo of the Spanish original, which reads: "Esto me lo dijo Karl Marx, haciendo un gracioso giro, soltando una carcajada y marchándose apresurado tras los fondillos de los niños-militares que integraban la retaguardia" (*El central,* 14). The Spanish word "fondillos," literally the "seat or bottom of trousers," in the Cuban vernacular is synonymous to "rear end" or "ass."

7. Both Manuel Pereira in "Reinaldo antes del alba" (*Quimera* 111 [1992]: 54-58) and Miguel Riera in "El mundo es alucinante" (*Quimera* 111 [1992]: 58-59) see Arenas's accusations that certain individuals are homosexual as an indication of self-loathing.

8. I use the term "panic" as proposed by Eve Kosofsky Sedgwick in her studies *Between Men: English Literature and Male Homosexual Desire* (New York: Columbia University Press, 1985) and *Epistemology of the Closet* (Berkeley: University of California Press, 1990).

9. Samuel Feijoó, "Revolución y vicios" [Revolution and Vices], *El Mundo,* 15 April 1965, 5. As quoted in Lois M. Smith and Alfred Padula, *Sex and Revolution: Women in Socialist Cuba* (New York: Oxford University Press, 1966), 172-73.

10. For a more detailed study of the Cuban documentary novel and Arenas's subversive response to

this genre promoted and actively supported by the revolutionary cultural policy makers, see my book *Reinaldo Arenas: The Pentagonía.*

11. All translations of *Morir en junio y con la lengua afuera* are mine. Page numbers refer to the Spanish edition of *Leprosorio.*

12. See, for example, Gretchen Mieszkowski, "The Prose *Lancelot*'s Galehot, Malroy's Lavain, and the Queering of Late Medieval Literature," *Arthuriana* 5, no. 1 (1995): 21-51; hereafter cited in text. Mieszkowski studies two late-medieval Arthurian works: the Prose *Lancelot* (thirteenth-century Old French romance written by an anonymous writer) and Malory's fifteenth-century portrayal of Lavain in the story of Elaine le Blanke, the Fair Maid of Astolat. The critic discusses and convincingly argues for second levels of homoerotic meanings in these texts. Although Mieszkowski does not specifically treat the character of Perceval, other Arthurian scholars have mentioned homosocial connotations in the Perceval stories in their Internet discussions (see http://www.mun.ca./lists/arthurnet). In one example, a critic cites the German Wolfram von Eschenback's Parzival (a thirteenth-century text based on Chrétien's romance) in which, in one episode, Parzival's (Perceval's) "erect lance" is presented as a challenge to the other knights.

13. Bruce Smith, *Homosexual Desire in Shakespeare's England: A Cultural Poetics* (Chicago: University of Chicago Press, 1991).

14. During our conversation in 1987, I asked Arenas to comment on the fact that in many of his texts the mother figure is presented as tyrannizing and oppressing the son, who she wishes to destroy. He answered: "It's a dual relationship. There's this type of relationship in all my novels. It's not completely a tyrannical relationship. The mother is destructive, but at the same time she is affectionate. She can destroy, but also love. It's a relationship of power and control that she has with her son. She dominates him, but also cares for him; she destroys him, but also loves him. To a certain extent I see in this the tradition of the Cuban mother, a tradition that is the result of our Spanish heritage. The son loves his mother but also realizes that he must get away from her. I believe that Cuban mothers have had a negative and positive influence on our writers. For example, Lezama Lima publishes *Paradiso* after his mother's death. Perhaps he wouldn't have dared to publish that novel beforehand, which, among other things, pays homage to his mother. We don't dare reveal our true selves to our mothers, much less if we're homosexual. Mothers see that as absolutely taboo, completely immoral and prohibited; at least the major-

ity of mothers see it that way. That love/hate, rejection and rapprochement of the mother is a contradictory relationship, but very real. In *El asalto* at the same time the protagonist destroys his mother he does it by possessing her. Therefore, there isn't total hate, but rather obsession and passion." See Soto, 143-44.

15. The story, which appears in the collection that bears the same title, *Adiós a mamá* (Miami: Ediciones Universal, 1996), has been translated by Jo Labanyi as "Goodbye Mother" and published in *The Faber Book of Contemporary Latin American Short Stories,* ed. Nick Caistor (London: Faber and Faber, 1989), 53-66; hereafter cited in text as "Goodbye Mother."

16. All translations of *Leprosorio* are my own. In 1987 Andrew Hurley, responsible for translating a number of Arenas's novels, translated and published the first five pages of *Leprosorio.* See "Leprosorio, Leprosarium, The Leper Colony," *The World and I* (July 1987): 242-47.

17. Pablo Neruda, *Canto general* (México: Talleres Gráficos, 1950). Translated and edited by Ben Belitt in *Pablo Neruda, Five Decades: Poems 1925-1970* (New York: Grove Press, 1974).

18. All translations of the poems from *Voluntad de vivir manifestándose* are my own.

Selected Bibliography

PRIMARY WORKS

SPANISH EDITIONS

Novels

Celestino antes del alba. La Habana: Ediciones Unión, 1967.

Cantando en el pozo. Barcelona: Editorial Argos Vergara, 1982.

El palacio de las blanquísimas mofetas. Barcelona: Editorial Argos Vergara, 1982.

La loma del ángel. Málaga: Dador/ediciones, 1987.

El portero. Málaga: Dador/ediciones, 1989.

El asalto. Miami: Ediciones Universal, 1991.

Short Story Collections

Con los ojos cerrados. Montevideo: Editorial Arca, 1972.

Adiós a mamá. Barcelona: Ediciones Altera, 1995.

Poetry

El central. Barcelona: Seix Barral, 1981.

Voluntad de vivir manifestándose. Madrid: Editorial Betania, 1989.

Leprosorio (Trilogía poética). Madrid: Editorial Betania, 1990.

Other

Antes que anochezca. Barcelona: Tusquets Editores, 1992.

ENGLISH TRANSLATIONS

Novels

Graveyard of the Angels (translation of *La loma del ángel*). Trans. Alfred MacAdam. New York: Avon Books, 1987.

Singing from the Well (translation of *Celestino antes del alba/Cantando en el pozo*). Trans. Andrew Hurley. New York: Viking Penguin, 1987.

The Palace of the White Skunks (translation of *El palacio de las blanquísimas mofetas*). Trans. Andrew Hurley. New York: Viking Penguin, 1990.

The Doorman (translation of *El portero*). Trans. Dolores M. Koch. New York: Grove Press, 1991.

The Assault (translation of *El asalto*). Trans. Andrew Hurley. New York: Viking Penguin, 1994.

Short Stories

"Goodbye Mother" (translation of "Adiós a mamá"). Trans. Jo Labanyi. In *The Faber Book of Contemporary Latin American Short Stories,* ed. Nick Caistor, 53-66. London: Faber and Faber, 1989.

Poetry

El Central: A Cuban Sugar Mill (translation of *El central*). Trans. Anthony Kerrigan. New York: Avon Books, 1984.

"Leprosorio, Leprosarium, The Leper Colony" (partial translation of "Leprosorio"). Trans. Andrew Hurley. *The World and I* (July 1987): 242-47.

Other

Before Night Falls (translation of *Antes que anochezca*). Trans. Dolores M. Koch. New York: Viking Penguin, 1993.

SECONDARY WORKS

BOOKS

Soto, Francisco. *Conversación con Reinaldo Arenas.* Madrid: Editorial Betania, 1990. General introductory essay provides an overview of Arenas's work. The interview is especially useful in presenting the genesis of the novels of the *pentagonía.*

————. *Reinaldo Arenas: The Pentagonía.* Gainesville: University Press of Florida, 1994. First major book-length study in English of the *pentagonía*. The five novels are studied within the historical context of the Cuban documentary novel tradition.

Rebecca E. Biron (essay date 2000)

SOURCE: Biron, Rebecca E. "Revolutionary Matricide, Patricide, Suicide: Reinaldo Arenas's *El asalto.*" In *Murder and Masculinity: Violent Fictions of Twentieth-Century Latin America,* pp. 120-42. Nashville, Tenn.: Vanderbilt University Press, 2000.

[*In the following essay, Biron emphasizes the connection of two types of violence in Arenas's novel* The Assault: *that against the repressive police state and that against the mother-figure, who "encapsulates" for the protagonist "the negative formation of masculine identity."*]

> Cuba será libre. Yo ya lo soy.
> [Cuba will be free. I already am.]
>
>   Reinaldo Arenas, suicide note

> Matricide is our vital necessity,
> the *sine-qua-non* condition of our individuation.
>
>   Julia Kristeva, *Black Sun:*
>   *Depression and Melancholia*

Cuban exile Reinaldo Arenas's posthumously published novel *El asalto* (1991a, *The Assault*) celebrates rape and murder in its paradoxical critique of the violence of Fidel Castro's military dictatorship. With a relatively simple plot rendered in relentlessly hateful and vulgar language, the first-person narration turns a prism through which the protagonist's desires become a series of allegorical hallucinations. His perspective is the fragmented result of the state's imposition of restrictive definitions of masculinity, citizenship, and revolution. In its final scenes *El asalto* crystallizes frustration, limitation, and barriers to the self-assertion of the individual into one striking figure: the male dictator, "El Reprimerísimo Reprimero" (which Andrew Hurley [Arenas 1994] translates into English as the "Represident"), who is also the narrator's own female, nameless mother. The narrator sexually assaults that dual male and female figure, and then kills him/her before the amassed citizenry of a dystopian, futuristic society. This single act of aggression, at once incestuous and public, kills the protagonist's own domineering mother and the state's dictatorial "father."

With that conclusion, Arenas takes literally the figurative equation of citizens and sons. *El asalto* treats violent, national revolution as if it were *the same thing* as violence against the mother to whom one owes one's very existence. Therefore, although ostensibly concerned with the liberation of the individual—specifically, the artist—from political oppression and the enforced conformity of Cuba's socialist project, this novel calls on readers to consider connections and tensions between two kinds of violence. First, it exposes in extraordinarily graphic terms the violence inherent in a cultural imperative for men to eschew identification with their mothers. Second, it advocates violence as a means to oppose illegitimate locations of political power. By displaying extreme violence perpetrated against citizens in an absurdly repressive police state, the novel critiques the effects of that repression on the protagonist's sense of masculinity. It suggests that monstrous acts of violence become the only available expression of masculine subjectivity in an abusive, dehumanizing political context. Ironically, though, Arenas writes a protagonist whose thorough indoctrination into the perverse logic of state-imposed self-repression leads him to attack the supreme leader *only because* the protagonist hallucinates that the leader is his own hated mother. With *El asalto,* Arenas explodes the values of revered motherhood and respect for authority. He portrays the rape and murder of the mother as the quintessential liberating gesture for a dehumanized island, for his protagonist, and for himself as author.

In an interview with Francisco Soto (1994, 137-54), Arenas explains his view of the connection between mature masculinity and independence from mothers. He associates mothers with political oppression, especially the oppression of gay men:

> F.S. In many of your texts mothers tyrannize or oppress their sons, they want to destroy them.
>
> R.A. It's a dual relationship. There's this type of relationship in all my novels. It's not completely a tyrannical relationship. The mother is destructive, but at the same time she is affectionate. She can destroy but also love. It's a relationship of power and control that she has with her son. She dominates him, but also cares for him; she destroys him, but also loves him. To a certain extent I see in this the tradition of the Cuban mother, a tradition that is the result of our Spanish heritage. The son loves his mother but also realizes that *he must get away from her. . . .* We don't dare *reveal our true selves* to our mothers, much less if we're homosexual. Mothers see that as absolutely taboo, completely immoral and prohibited; at least the majority of mothers see it that way. That love/hate, rejection and rapprochement of the mother is a contradictory relationship, but very real. *In* **El Asalto** *at the same time the protagonist destroys his mother he does it by possessing her. Therefore, there isn't total hate, but rather obsession and passion.* (143-44, emphasis added)

The author's comments on mothers and sons both illuminate and obscure the major issues at play in a reading of *El asalto* as a political allegory and a fantasy of omnipotence. Arenas posits a true self for the son, which he must hide from the mother in order to avoid her critical and controlling gaze. This notion of loving and yet needing to escape from the mother encapsulates the negative formation of masculine identity. The son's fantasy of independence blinds him to the fact that her gaze produces his individuality as reaction. Unaware of this even more profound dependence on her, the son guards his illusion of autonomous identity as if it were life itself. Yet its demand for absolute separation prevents his love *for* the mother, frustrating his desire for union with the other. That the identity he calls "true" must be hidden associates guilt and privacy with the very construct of self that he most wants others, and especially his mother, to recognize.

On the other hand, as *El asalto's* protagonist demonstrates, the son's "obsession and passion" regarding the mother lead him to rape and murder—the ultimate expressions of possessive knowledge (to know her in a sexual sense) and absolute control (over her very life). He inflicts *on* her precisely the invasion and abuse he expects to receive *from* her. By conflating this psychoanalytic representation of the phallic mother with a political caricature of the male dictator, this novel offers a complex commentary on tyranny. It appears as a relationship between the tyrant and the people predicated on unresolved vacillation between extremes of love and hate, identity and difference. *El asalto* processes that relationship through the portrayal of the mutually threatening intimacy of mothers and homosexual sons.

El asalto is the last installment in a five-part work which Arenas had planned for years.[1] He called it his *pentagonía*, a pentalogy of agonies, and the author himself suggests that it should be read as an extended autobiography whose fantastic elements express influences primarily of Borges, Kafka, and Lezama Lima. Its five novels relate the gay writer's conflicted relationship to the Cuban state as they follow the growth of the author-identified narrators. They trace the stages of boyhood, adolescence, and manhood, and they contextualize that initiation in the stages of Cuban history from the Batista regime through the Revolution and its betrayal.

Celestino antes del alba (1967), published in 1982 as *Cantando en el pozo,* treats the perceptions of an imaginative child-narrator in the poverty-stricken, prerevolutionary Cuban countryside. He invents an alter ego, his cousin Celestino, who escapes from family violence and misunderstanding through obsessive writing and poetic sensibilities. *El palacio de las blanquísimas mofetas* (1982b) coincides with the Batista era, highlighting the frustrated efforts of the adolescent Fortunato to understand and express his family's experiences. A cacophony of voices fills the text, each character fighting to find an audience for her/his personal tale of tragedy and hopelessness. *Otra vez el mar*

(1982a) combines two monologues set in the period of institutionalized revolution. Hector and his wife (whose monologue, we learn in the end, was invented by Hector) express political and personal idealism, alienation, and self-doubt as they dream, hallucinate, and remember during a drive home to Havana. They are returning from a brief vacation, during which Hector flirted with having a homosexual encounter with a boy on the beach although his wife yearns for communication with her husband. *El color del verano* (1991b) is set in 1999, during the Cuban dictator's celebration of forty years in power (which he claims to be fifty years because that number attracts more publicity). This novel features a shared first-person narrative voice, in which Gabriel/Reinaldo/the Tétrica Mofeta write "the anecdotes, letters, tongue-twisters, stories, and so forth, that make up the novel and in turn give voice to Cuba's excluded and marginal homosexual subculture of the 1960s and 1970s" (Soto 1994, 69).

In each of the first four novels of the pentagonía, Cuban history circumscribes the writing subject. Although Arenas typically divides into different characters the alienated aspects of his *port-parole,* all of these texts deal with socioeconomic isolation of the gay male writer. They chart the changing dynamic of relative freedoms, from boyhood with *Celestino*'s child-narrator/Celestino, to adolescence with *El palacio*'s Fortunato and his family, to young adulthood with *Otra vez el mar*'s Hector, and to the gay culture of *El color del verano.* The central theme continues to be the frustrated drive to express individuality, or the true self, in prerevolutionary poverty and rural isolation, postrevolutionary conformist self-discipline, and contestatory sexual subculture. In every case, the main characters write as a form of escape and empowerment; they also always end up dead, only to reappear under a new name in the next novel.

The last installment in the series, *El asalto* projects a much more drastic reduction of individual freedoms into an unspecified future, imagining the extremes to which Castrista policies might lead. The narrative voice in this text maintains much more coherence of identity that any of the others, which split themselves off into different characters, and in this last novel of the *pentagonía*, the narrator-protagonist does not die. He kills in order to live, suggesting victory over the other characters' suffering throughout the series. However, in *El asalto* the narrator is more hostile, vindictive, and determined than the protagonists of the other novels. Dedicated to nothing other than hunting down his mother, he never considers himself a writer as they do. Soto argues that "[t]he nameless narrator of *El Asalto* is the only protagonist in the quintet that does not write, for in this futuristic world the individual, perceived only as a work dog that fuels the materialistic production of the state, has forgotten how to communicate, how to use language critically . . ."(120). This description is not entirely accurate, since *El Asalto*'s narrator does write as a form of self-identification in his control over others. He works in the surveillance forces for the state, and obsessively records his own identification number on walls, cages, and documents in order to receive recognition for his repressive zeal in arresting those who dare to break the law. Still, it is important to note that the only protagonist-narrator of the *pentagonía* who survives his own story is the one who does not pretend to be an artist, the one who assaults readers with his profanity and cruelty, and the one who finally strikes back against his mother physically rather than merely figuratively.

Accepting Arenas's own claim that the *pentagonía* constitutes a single tale concerning various creative responses to social marginalization, Soto (1994, 41) assesses *El asalto*'s contribution: "Ironically, the final novel of the pentalogy leaves the reader with a glimmer of hope. The decrepit tyrant el Reprimerísimo Reprimero . . . is destroyed, and the protagonist, who has suffered countless persecutions throughout the five-book cycle can finally stretch out on the beach and rest." This "glimmer of hope" confuses the liberation of the artist with the survival of his characters; it also confuses the liberation of an oppressed nation with the rape and murder of a woman. If we compare the first and last scenes of the pentagonía, we can begin to discern the complex relationship among gender identities, sexuality, and totalitarian power to which Arenas seems to have dedicated all of his writing. With this series of texts in particular, Arenas explores the most complicated, perverse, hopeful, and cruel elements in the production of the masculine subject who seeks personal and creative autonomy. His notion of personal and political revolution demands reconsideration of the violence of mothers and men, the transgression of genders and genres, and finally the legitimation of authority and authorship.

All of Arenas's novels feature the mother as one of the principal themes. The first scene of *Celestino antes del alba* narrates a young boy's confusion, terror, and guilt when he sees his mother run to throw herself into the well. The boy rushes to try to pull her out, but when he looks down into the well, he sees only his own reflection in the calm water. This fantasy involves multiple elements in Arenas's characteristic depiction of mother figures from the sons' viewpoints. The mother never dies in the realist plane of the novel, and her threat to commit suicide, at first horrifying for the son, comes to function as an unfulfilled promise to him. She teases him with the possibility of her death; yet by refusing to die, she creates his desire for the dreaded closure of the game. Her self-absorption, tendency toward despair, desire to be saved by the son, and indifference to his need

for her presence betray him. Her threats of suicide expose his love/need for her while demonstrating no reciprocal love/need for him.

The most haunting feature in the mother-son relationship as it appears in all of Arenas's narratives is the mutual reflection. The mother mirrors the son back to himself as in the scene at the well in *Celestino,* when the son first associates his own image with the mother's threat to kill herself. He feels guilty for not finding and saving her, yet the victim he sees when he gazes into the water is himself. Ever after that, whenever the mothers appear to bear an excessive physical similarity to the male protagonists in the *pentagonía,* the sons are repulsed by the association between their own faces and feminine characteristics. This strong negative reaction corresponds to theories of masculinity as a reaction-formation in which the male child achieves masculine identity through repudiation of associations with the mother. At a more fundamental level of identity-formation for the male child, however, perfect correspondence between the mother and the son's self-image signifies symbiosis, the deeply desired yet vigorously denied wish for absolute union. Individuated selfhood requires suppression of that wish, and so the overwhelming desire for symbiosis with the mother, fulfillment of which would lead to erasure of self, causes a severe counter-reaction. As this mirror-mother threatens to absorb the son into her own image, he feels compelled to kill her so that he might live as a separate and identifiable being. The strength of the son's desire to return to an imagined, prenatal, absolute unity with the mother prior to his entry into socialization actually fuels his reactive behavior and fantasies *against* her. Ironically, the degree to which he acts out those fantasies measures his "success" in the social, because he conforms to misogynist logic and seems to defend masculinity against women's maternal power.

Arenas wrote *El asalto* in exile, and it was published almost a year after his suicide. The novel intricately combines those elements of political disenfranchisement and psychological crisis that apparently informed its author's final decision to carry out the same threat with which the mother opens *Celestino.* Offering multiple images of revolution as integral to the performance of masculine subjectivity for the narrator-protagonist, *El asalto* frames the political within the personal, ultimately rendering the two spheres indistinguishable. While structured like a grotesque-realist thriller which denounces dictatorship, the novel includes such a proliferation of fantastic, condensed, and displaced images that it also begs to be read as a dream text. My reading traces out the multiple layers of the novel, first analyzing its references to a variety of narrative forms, its use of highly charged vocabulary, and its modes of characterization. Then I focus on the convergence of these elements in the final scene to argue that, when understood as both political allegory and masculinist fantasy *at the same time,* this novel becomes a rich source for a psychoanalytic understanding of revolution, counterrevolution, and the violence they engender.

Most critics treat *El asalto* as an experiment in genre under the rubric of anti-totalitarianism. They read it against the norms of Cuban documentary fiction, as a parody of a thriller, or as a Kafkaesque critique of bureaucracy (Soto 1994). It is a thriller as Todorov (1977) defines the genre (versus the whodunit brand of detective fiction): the narration of events coincides with their occurrence in chronological fashion, and suspense, or excited expectation about what will happen next, maintains readers' interest. "Indeed it is around these constants that the thriller is constituted: violence, generally sordid crimes, the amorality of the characters" (48).

El asalto also cites elements of epic, picaresque, and twentieth-century futuristic narrative, or science fiction. The fifty-two chapters are very short, distinct episodes in the protagonist's search to find and kill his mother. Each chapter title consists of a quotation from the Western literary canon, especially from texts reflecting major social upheaval or geographical discovery, and functions as an epigraph to the section. However, the citations do not directly refer to the chapters' content. Rather, they suggest loose associations among vague intertextual memories of conquests, exiles, illusions, and landscapes. Readers are left to ponder the implications of the juxtapositions. For instance, the title of chapter 2 is a quote from Cervantes, "De lo que le avino a Don Quijote con una bella cazadora" [Of what occurred to Don Quixote with a beautiful huntress], yet the chapter offers no plot advancement at all; it consists of a satirical description of the *Polifamiliar* [Multi-Family], a communal living arrangement designed to save space and facilitate supervision of citizens in Arenas's imagined totalitarian state. As Soto (1994) has pointed out, such descriptions of modes of social control echo dystopian novels such as Huxley's *Brave New World* or Orwell's *Nineteen Eighty-Four*. *El asalto* is more a combination of those futuristic texts with the allegorical *Animal Farm* and with Cervantine parody of courtly love, however. The narrator's accounts of such phenomena as the *polifamiliar,* with its ridiculous distribution of space, or the *guaguas,* which are comic postmotorization versions of buses, bitingly mock the Cuban government's rhetoric of social planning and organization, along with its denial of a disintegrating infrastructure in the 1980s:

> Es obligatorio vivir en el Polifamiliar. . . . Allí tenía mi lugar exacto, como todo el mundo. Como yo soy solo me toca un metro y pico de suelo, es decir la extensión de mi cuerpo y el ancho del mismo con los brazos recogidos. Otros tienen más espacio, pues tienen

mujer o hijos. Por la nonoche, cuando se reparten los espacios, hay siempre quien ocupa un poco de espacio más que el que le toca. Si se dan cuenta se le reduce su espacio a la mitad del que le toca, de manera que entonces tiene que dormir de lado. . . . Una familia quedó tan reducida que dormían todos sobre un viejo, el abuelo, quien a su vez tenía que dormir de costado. . . .

(9)

[The law states that "All citizens are required to live in the Multi-Family. . . ." Like everyone else, I was issued my own place there. Since it was just me and no one else, I was allotted a little over one square yard of floor space, which was the length of my body by the width of my body with my arms at my sides. Other people were assigned more space, because they had a wife or children. At not-night, when the spaces were assigned, there was always someone that tried to take more space than they were issued. If Multi-Family headquarters found out, the space would be cut down to one-half the original issue, so the person would have to sleep on their side. . . . One family lost so much space that they all had to sleep stacked on top of an old man, the grandfather, who in turn had to sleep on his side. . . .]

(3)[2]

Enseguida me incorporo a la fila y hago la guagua, mis codos se ensartan al siguiente y así sucesivamente, cuando sumamos setenta y cinco, el encargado del transporte grita completo, suelta un fustazo, y la guagua, nosotros enganchados en fila india por los codos, partimos veloces. Marchamos.

(17)

[Then I immediately get into line to make a bus; I hook my elbows into the next person's, and the next person hooks his into the next person's, and so on, and when there are seventy-five of us, the man in charge of transport yells *Full up!* Cracks his whip once, and the bus, which is all of us hooked into an Indian file by our elbows, takes off. We march.]

(11)

In spite of this satiric element of the novel, with its comic exaggeration of Cuba's failed social engineering, *El asalto* depicts multiple forms of serious assault on the people: psychological, physical, political, and systemic. The consistent cruelty of the narrator and government bureaucrats takes the wind out of readers' already uneasy laughter. The undefined future of Castro's state is imagined as a hellish place where human beings have been reduced to the status of rats and pigs, where any spontaneous speech—even whispering—is detected by the "contrasusurrador" forces [the counterwhisperers] and punishable by death. Citizens betray fellow citizens in order to curry government favor, and acts of ferocious violence fill the text.

Language in *El asalto* marks the cause-and-effect relationship between state tyranny and individual violent obsession. Whereas the government hypocritically (and again, hyperbolically) couches everything in the most positive terms in order to disguise its exploitation of citizens as workers, the narrator blindly projects his self-hatred onto all others. In each case, the level of exaggeration reaches ludicrous proportions and lends a dreamlike air to the novelistic world. As Soto (1994, 115) notes, Arenas's ironic inclusion of neologisms to refer to enforced productivity, satisfaction, and good humor in postrevolutionary Cuban society destroys any semblance of legitimate authority the totalitarian government might wield:

> La idea de nonoche (al igual que todas las ideas) es del Reprimerísimo. "Cómo—y aún recuerdo también este discurso—concebir que en nuestra sociedad exista la noche. No, no podemos admitirlo, la aboliremos." Y creó la nonoche, en la cual, y más aún durante el día, debemos mantener el trabajo y el optimismo. Aboliremos pues del idioma, de la memoria y de la realidad todos los conceptos decadentes y contravitales que el pasado reaccionario nos ha legado. Optimicemos el idioma así como la vida.
>
> (39)

> [The idea of the not-night (like all authentically brilliant ideas) was the Supreme Represident's. I can recall the speech introducing the concept as though it were yesterday: *How,* the Represident scolded, *can one imagine night existing in our society? No—we cannot accept that. We therefore abolish night.* And on that day he created the not-night, all during which, and even more so during the glorious day, we are exhorted to keep up our work and maintain our optimism. *We abolish from the language, from our memory, and from the world . . . all those decadent and anti-vital concepts that we have inherited from the reactionary past. We shall optimize the language as we have optimized life itself.*]
>
> (37)

Other terms such as *nonoche* [not-night] appear throughout the novel as part of the depiction of a society's loss of realism, creative thought, and human expressiveness. Citizen-workers respect the *noreposo* [not-rest] and the *nodescanso* [not-break]. They learn to avoid the nobancos del noparque [not-benches of the not-park] and strive at all times to be productive and loyal subjects of the Represident. By the end of the novel, the level of repression reaches such depths that citizens must parrot only officially approved scripts (102).

The narrator, believing himself an exception to the rules, maintains a degree of critical distance from the processes of thought and language control. However, as the story tension mounts, his diatribes become increasingly repetitive and predictable, just as his frustration level rises. Even he begins to lose vocabulary, lashing out at the readers:

> La corneta, la lata o cuero o silbato o pito, o váyase usted a la porra retumba, o suena o clama o llama, o váyase a la mierda. De modo que el traqueteo de las bestias que ansiosas y encorvadas trabajaban, cesa.
>
> (45)

> [The cornet, or tin can, or horn, or whistle, or conch shell, or whatever the hell it is—what do I care, anyway—echoes, or sounds, or cries out, or calls, or shit, you get the picture. At the sound, there is a sudden and complete cessation of the terrible racket that the beasts have been making as they feverishly worked.]
>
> (44)

This continual reference to other people as *bestias* [beasts] with *garfas* [claws], whose bodies reek with what the narrator finds to be a nauseating stench of sweat, urine, and sex, places him in the position of mindful (if cruel and distorting) observer of their inhumanity. He relies on an exaggerated mind/body split to differentiate himself from all others. While they suffer, bleed, twitch, ooze, copulate, scream, and cry, the narrator imagines himself to be a dry, silent, self-contained observer; all distanced eyes and thought, he replicates the panoptical logic of totalitarian power. Everyone whom the narrator describes receives the same deprecating treatment, but he aims the strongest and most explicit language at his mother:

> Las orejas de mi madre son largas, ásperas y anchas como las de un murciélago gigante, ratón, perro o elefante o qué coño de bicho, siempre alerta; sus ojos redondos, giratorios y saltones, como de rata o sapo, o qué carajo. Su nariz es como un pico de pájaro furioso, su hocico, su trompa, es alargada y a la vez redonda, con mucho de perro o de boa o de quién carajo podrá decirlo.
>
> (41)

> [My mother's ears are large, rough-skinned, and stick out from the side of her head as far as a giant bat's, or a rat's, or a dog's, or an elephant's, or any other fucking animal's you can think of, and they are always pricked up. Her eyes are round, revolving bug-eyes, like a rat's or a frog's, or whatever the fuck other kind of disgusting, nervous, twitching little animal you can think of. Her nose is like the beak of some furious bird; her snout, or trunk, is very, very long, but round at the same time. It reminds you of a dog's or a boa constrictor's, or—but let someone else try to describe the fucking thing, it makes me sick to think about it.]
>
> (39)

The novel opens with the narrator's attack against his mother in a chapter called "Vista de Mariel"; the act of looking, and the location from which one looks, establish from the beginning their battle to the death over subjectivity. For Sartre, people look in order to wield power over others, as in his example of peeping through the lock of a closed door; this voyeur, however, dreads being caught by another's spying look. When he raises his eyes from the peephole to exchange a look with the one who sees him seeing, both participants become subject and object of one visual moment. They share in the guilt of spying, even though the one who had looked through the closed door disallows that the original object of his observation looks back at him. Those who share a reciprocal look acknowledge the chain of sub-jectivity that uneven ocular exchanges confer. They rec-ognize that there will always be an other to see them, to relegate them to object status (being seen) in the same look that registers their guiltily positive subject status (they are spies who wish to avoid being seen).

In *El asalto,* the first moment of mutual recognition be-tween mother and adult son occurs at the Mariel port, famous for the exodus of Cuban dissidents and political prisoners in 1980, and the same port from which Are-nas himself left the island that year (Santí 1980). The novel opens with a conflation of *vista* [view] and *mirada* [look], shifting "Vista del Mariel" away from a look out to sea. It turns the view back to the land, and to a sur-reptitious act. The narrator sees his mother from be-hind; she is stealing wood. When she turns around it is not to return his look, but in fear of being caught by the authorities:

> La última vez que vi a mi madre . . . estaba así, de es-paldas, agachada. . . . No perdí tiempo y me le abal-ancé para matarla. La cabrona, parece que me miraba con el ojo del culo, pues antes de que yo pudiese reven-tarla se volvió asustada, no por mí, sino por las leyes del Reprimero y sus agentes, que si la cogen lleván-dose las sobras del aserrío Patrio, la ajustician. Es decir, la matan.
>
> (7)

> [The last time I saw my mother, . . . she was standing with her back to me, bent double. . . . This was my chance; I knew I could not waste a second. I ran straight for her, and I would have killed her, too, but the old bitch must have an eye where her asshole ought to be, because before I could get to her and knock her down and kill her, the old woman whirled around to meet me. She was terrified—oh, but not because of me. She was afraid of the represidential laws and the agents that enforce them, that's what she was afraid of. Because if she had been caught stealing scraps from the National Sawmill, she would have been arrested and tried and sentenced. Which means she would have been killed.]
>
> (1)

This uneven exchange of looks establishes from the first paragraph the dynamic of hunter and hunted that the narrator-protagonist will play out. He thinks he is the privileged observing subject, the one who under-stands government vigilance of citizens and does not fear it. He watches the people, who in turn watch out for the repressive forces of surveillance. From that po-sition, he attacks the weak beasts, precisely because their servitude disgusts him. In attacking his mother in particular, however, he sees that she never sees him, never acknowledges him as a relevant object of her de-sire or gaze. He feels that she observes him from "el ojo del culo," combining an infantile notion of anal om-nipotence (representing for himself the earliest sense of power over his own body) with one of anal birth

(representing the omnipotence with which the mother grants life to the baby). In desiring to be noticed, but despising his dependency on the look of a person he cannot respect, the son projects that look onto what is for him the foulest of his mother's body parts. She sees him from the denigrated site of production, the asshole that produces only waste.

We immediately find this vision, however, to belong solely to the narrator. When he admits that the mother never saw him at all but rather sensed the presence of the government agents, he belatedly and indirectly ex-plains his rage. His own mother looks to the military apparatus, not at her son. No maternal gaze confers ob-jectivity, subjectivity, or guilt onto him, and his resent-ment over that sense of invisibility devolves into his identification with the forces to which his mother turns her attention—the forces that threaten them all with death if they ever exceed their subjectedness to become human subjects of their own emotions and actions. Para-doxically, the narrator seeks recognition from his mother by becoming that which prevented her from looking at him in the first place. In other words, he becomes, or takes the place of, the cause of his own annihilation as subject. Although the narrator vehemently denies any desire to be seen in or by his mother, he is convinced that only by killing her can he be free of her control. The strength of his denial confirms that he seeks to kill exactly that which he wants too strongly. He must kill the object of his desire—his mother's capacity to see him—first by asserting that he does not desire it, and then by making it unavailable to be desired.

At the level of consciousness, the narrator's greatest fear is that he is becoming exactly like his mother *physi-cally.* He hallucinates his own metamorphosis into the object of his obsession, occupying through physical re-semblance the site from which he both wishes and fears to be seen:

> Naturalmente, siempre he odiado a mi madre. Es decir, desde que la conozco. Al principio mi odio hacia ese animal era por rachas. Después se quedó fijo. Un día me miré en un espejo y vi que me daba un aire a ella. . . . Volví a mirarme, y al poco tiempo, al remir-arme, vi que aún me parecía más a la maldita. En-tonces, ya mi odio no fue fijo, sino creciente. Más adelante me seguí mirando. Hasta comprender, cada vez más claramente, que me iba pareciendo cada vez más a ella, que mis ojos, mi nariz, mis patas y mi jeta iban siendo cada vez más los de ella. Que iba yo de-jando de ser yo para ser ella.
>
> (14)

> [I've always hated my mother, of course. As long as I've known her, that is. At first my hatred for the cow came in fits and starts. Then it was always there. One day I saw myself in a mirror and I noticed that there was something about me that reminded me of her. . . . I looked at myself again, and I had the same sensation,

and then not long after that, when I examined myself a fourth time, I could clearly see that I was coming to look more and more like the damned woman. And after that, my hatred was no longer just *there* anymore—it began to grow. It was then that I began looking at myself all the time, and at last I could see, more clearly every day, that everything about me was beginning to look just like her—my eyes, my ears, my paws, and my snout were becoming virtually *hers.* I was slowly but surely changing away from myself and changing into her.]

(8)

This fantasy of transformation is both a personal pathology and a negative reflection of the identification process necessary to maintain group cohesion under dictatorship. The narrator is aware of his resemblance to the mother, but remains unconscious that he condenses an image of the political dictator into that mirror image of himself (as his mother). Extreme love and hate permeate his self-contemplation, leading to murderous and objectifying (illegal, illegitimate) fantasies of omnipotence (the very form that legality takes under totalitarianism). He identifies with irreconcilable sites of power: with his own through narcissistic defensiveness, with his mother's through conscious hatred born of resentment, and with the represident's through unconscious hatred and admiration.

Brad Epps (1995) analyzes the relationship between identity, sexuality, and the iconic political leader (Castro) for the gay subject in Arenas's work, citing Žižek's attempt to account for group formation in modern totalitarianism. Žižek (1989, 105) analyzes the subject's relation to the Freudian ego ideal (*Ichideal*), the source of moral conscience and self-censorship, as "identification with the very place *from where* we are being observed, *from where* we look at ourselves so that we appear to ourselves likeable, worthy of love." In *El asalto,* however, the narrator confers that power onto his mother, and by identifying with the place from where he is observed, he appears to himself unlikable and unworthy of love. The most negative image he can reflect is the frightful ugliness he finds in that location of the gaze. His conviction that he must kill his mother in order to escape taking her place, then, has a certain psychological validity. Her death would disrupt that perverse identification, and he would be free, he thinks, of the imposition of her face between himself and his mirror.

The protagonist cannot locate his mother, though, unless he convinces the counterwhispering forces that he is a zealous patriot. He argues that he needs special clearance to enter restricted areas in order to further the state's project of controlling all individual desires and eliminating all unauthorized activities. He willingly enforces the very repression he despises in order to gain access to all the social sectors where he thinks he might

find his mother. Unaware of his unconscious association of her with the state, he assumes that he will find her in the periphery, either in the secondary work camps outside of the "represidential capital" or in the prisons. He privileges his own tendencies toward rebellion in taking for granted that his mother would be shunned or marginalized by the hegemonic center. The narrator voluntarily begins to resemble the dictator more and more *in behavior* in order to avoid physical resemblance to his mother. In attempting to oppose his own ostensibly law-abiding identity to the overtly criminal one he imagines for his mother, he shifts his allegiance to the "group ideal as embodied in the [political] leader" (Freud 1921, 79).

The psychological, emotional, and ethical web of *El asalto* is caught on three poles: the mother's threatened usurpation of the son's identity, the narrator's obsessive attention to phallic imagery, and his progress toward identification with the Reprimerísimo reprimero (coded male) as he moves up through levels of bureaucracy in the futuristic totalitarian state. This state organizes citizens into work and prison (rehabilitation) cells, and the protagonist gains access to all of them in order to search for his mother. As a pleasure only apparently secondary to his obsessive search, he enjoys torturing those accused of whispering. That sadism thinly veils the character's own masochism, since he himself is a whisperer who exploits the laws to his own ends. Therefore, his active punishment of others is a secret system of reflected desire to be caught himself and rendered passive.

The protagonist sends memos to the central government office to propose ever more invasive, reactionary, and absurd prohibitions. For example, in a particularly cutting display of homophobic hysteria, he institutes a law against glancing at the crotch of any government officials (who are all male in the novel), then orders all of his subordinates to stuff their pants and wear bizarre decorations which call attention to their genitals, ostensibly to make recognizing perverted citizens more efficient. Of course, this prohibition very efficiently produces exactly that behavior which it condemns and quickly becomes more and more exaggerated. The narrator relishes executing people for any sign at all of desire, but especially of desire directed at the male body, whether by men, women, or children. He rails against the government-approved procreative sex as a disgusting, loud, messy, filthy act, but his most extreme reaction against any evidence of desire in relation to the penis is to strangle to death one woman for having tried to seduce him. The denial and repression attain such depths that he associates glances, gestures, or even the slightest indication of any communicative capacity at all with perverse, phallic desire; the narrator punishes everyone who dares express illegitimate subjectivity, which is to say, everyone who evidences any trace of humanity. Only workers who imitate blind drones escape execution.

The novel's violence increases in intensity, horror, and rhythm just as in a thriller. In the final scenes, the narrator mounts a platform during a huge public celebration for the anniversary of the revolution. He is to receive a commendation from the Reprimerísimo himself for outstanding service to the state. He climbs to the top of the stairs, scanning the amassed citizenry, as always, for signs of his mother. Furious because he has exhausted all methods of searching for her on the island, he finds everyone, especially the dictator, to be hideous and revolting. The narrator places himself in the position of the subject who surveys all, even the seat of absolute power, with contempt; he will accept recognition from the state for his services, but he guards the secret that his work has always been only self-interested. The dictator turns to face him, and there she is, in the center of the capital, raised high on the platform for all to see, disguised as the dictator all along:

> Allí, en la parte delantera de la plataforma está él, la ventruda, peluda, gigantesca figura, de espaldas a mí, como una tortuga erguida en su carapacho, extasiado ante su mar de esclavos. . . . Entonces, . . . el culo gigantesco gira, el vientre prominente se dirije hacia mí, enfrentándome todo su fofo andamiaje, sosteniendo entre sus garfas la lata centelleante que ha de incrustarme. . . . [A]lzo la vista hasta su jeta. Y entonces la veo, la veo, la veo a ella. Es ella, ese rostro que está ante mí es el odiado y espantoso rostro de mi madre. Y ése es también el rostro del Reprimerísimo. Los dos son una misma persona. Con razón me había sido tan difícil encontrarla. Mi sorpresa, mi furiosa alegría es tal que demoro unos segundos en recuperarme.

(137)

> [And there, on the precipice of that high plateau, he stands—that big-bellied, hairy, gigantic figure—with his back to me, like some turtle in its shell standing erect and in ecstasy before a sea of slaves. . . . And then, the huge backside turns, the protruding belly swings around toward me, and I am facing that enormous doughlike mound of flesh that holds in its claws the sparkling medal which is to be bestowed upon me. . . . I raise my eyes to his face. And I see it, see that snout, see her snout—I see her. That face before me is the hated and horrible face of my mother. And it is also the face of the Represident. They are the same person. *That* is why it has been so hard to find her, I think, in fury. My surprise, my enraged joy, is so great that it takes me a second or two to recover.]

(142)

By this point in the novel, the narrator's anxious quest for recognition has been reduced to pure rage through frustration. The mother looks straight at him, and he attacks her with his suddenly enormous erect penis, imag-

ined as grossly out of proportion to the rest of his body. Wielding it as a huge weapon, he knocks layers of disguise, armor, and weaponry off of the assaulted figure until his mother stands naked before him:

> Y ahora la veo, está ahí, con sus millones de manchas y arrugas; la inmensa vaca encuera, con sus enormes nalgas y tetas descomunales, con su figura de sapo deforme, con su pelo cenizo y su hueco hediondo. . . . Entonces, la gran vaca, desnuda y deforme, blanca y hedionda, se juega su última carta de perra astuta, y cruzando por sobre sus inmensas tetas sus garfas desgarradas, me mira llorando y dice: hijo.

(138-40)

> [And now I see her—she is there before me, covered with blotches and wrinkles. She is naked. Her huge buttocks and breasts, her body like some monstrous toad's, her ash-gray hair and her stinking hole are exposed for all to see. . . . And then the great cow, naked and horrible, white and stinking, plays her last card; the sly bitch, crossing her ragged claws over her monstrous breasts, looks at me with tears in her eyes and she says *Son*.]

(144)

The narrator explicitly attributes the subsequent rape to his mother's having appealed to him as *son:*

> Todo el escarnio, la vejación, el miedo, la frustración el chantaje y la burla y la condena que contiene esa palabra llega hasta mí abofeteándome, humillándome. Mi erección se vuelve descomunal, y avanzo con mi falo proyectándose hacia su objetivo, hacia el hueco hediondo, y la clavo.

(140)

> [All the derision, all the harassment, all the fear and frustration and blackmail and mockery and contempt that that word contains—it slaps me in the face, and I am stung. My erection swells to enormous proportions, and I begin to step toward her, my phallus aimed dead for its mark, that fetid stinking hole. And I thrust.]

(144-45)

Being called *son* is the greatest insult, the most abject humiliation, for this character whose sole mission is to rid himself of traces of any origin beyond his own control. He penetrates her, and the mother/dictator howls, exploding into a shower of "tornillos, arandelas, latas, gasolina, semen, mierda y chorros de aceite" (140) [screws, washers, cans, gasoline, semen, shit, and streams of oil]. This dream-scene in which the penis performs as weapon harks back to *Otra vez el mar's* Rabelaisian fantasy of the Trojan War fought with penises rather than swords. In *El asalto,* a similar battle to the death for individual and collective identity turns the male warrior's penis simultaneously on the state and on the mother; they are both sources of his sense of inadequacy *as a man.* The mother in *El asalto* is completely annihilated, and when her remains—all that is left of the repressive machine—fall onto the platform, the assembled crowd erupts in riot, destroying everything in sight. This scene equates rape to murder, and murder of the mother to collective liberation. The fantasy gives birth to a new revolutionary hero.

If the narrator hates his mother because of his denied desire for union with her, *El asalto* treats violent, eroticized revolution with a similar ambivalence. Though revolution is unambiguously condemned throughout the text as the cause of social horror in the repression which follows the dictator's coming to power, another revolution returns in the end as the source of new freedom. Even though he acknowledges the novel's unresolved relation to revolution as renewal, Soto (1994) tends to accept all transgression as the same; in a nation under illegitimate, totalitarian rule, any transgression constitutes a form of liberty: "Clearly, the copulation with the mother, a societal taboo, can be read as a transcoding or displacement of the narrator's reaffirmation of his own (homo)sexuality" (102). One need not equate male homosexuality, and its inherent transgression of heterosexist norms, with incest, however, and certainly not with rape. Although Soto is right to point out that the final scene of the novel looses the narrator's sexual aggression, he misses the complex implications of the difference between gender and sexuality in this final assault.

In "Proper Conduct: Reinaldo Arenas, Fidel Castro, and the Politics of Homosexuality," Epps (1995) brilliantly analyzes Arenas, the man and the author, in crisis over the play between desire for and identification with the powerful other. He traces the conflicting scripts through which Arenas tries to write his singularity in the face of a political regime intent on reading male homosexuality as a crime against both the state and masculinity itself. Arenas also writes in resistance to overdetermined scripts for gay aesthetics and political positions, which makes his work improper in Epps's view. It strains at the limits of directly oppositional contestation, often "reiterating . . . without ironic subversion, some of the most troubling stereotypes of women and gay men. It disturbs, in short, the properties and proprieties of virtually all comers" (246).

While male homosexuality is a central focus of much work on Arenas's prose, relatively few literary critics focus on gender itself or male-female relations in the *pentagonía*.[3] Epps's essay, although principally dealing with Castro's shadow over all of Arenas's work, successfully distinguishes between those issues. It focuses particularly on Arenas's bold exploration of desires that not only represent anti-totalitarianism, but that also trouble those who reject sexism on ethical grounds. Epps argues that in the context of Cuba's revolutionary ideology, masculinity must be coded heterosexual, stoic, military, and submissive only to Castro himself, who paradoxically must represent collective will through his extraordinary singularity and his iconic encoding of hy-

permasculinity (taking female lovers without marrying them, wearing military garb, displaying the proverbial cigar, and so on). Arenas as author and as gay Cuban exile exists in opposition to empty socialist rhetoric and militaristic coercion as well as the version of masculinity that Castro exudes. However, Arenas's oeuvre and authorial persona depend on that very opposition for their singularity. "Castro is thus the phantasmatic coauthor of Arenas's writing, the authority who by striving to disauthorize Arenas ultimately only authorizes him all the more. This, at any rate, is what Arenas makes of Castro" (Epps 1995, 246). "The Cuban leader is for Arenas what Butler calls a 'defining negativity,'a terrible touchstone by which the subject, though abjected and repudiated is, and by which the writer writes" (267, quoting Butler 1993, 190).

Epps (1995, 271) charts representations of homosexual desire in a variety of Arenas's texts to show the complexity of his opposition to Castro's heterosexist machismo, arguing that their relationship (from Arenas's point of view) is as productive as it is destructive, as full of attraction as of direct rejection: "For Arenas, himself no stranger to the poetic potential of paradox, the predicament of homosexual desire lies in the desire for a man, a real man, a man who is not also and at the same time a homosexual. If the real object of male homosexual desire is a man who is the opposite of the male homosexual, then the paradigmatic object of desire could well be, for Arenas, Fidel Castro himself." Epps's reading, attentive to the particularities of discourse on homosexual identities versus homosexual practices in Cuba,[4] finds that the rape of the mother in *El asalto* functions like an attack against homosexuality itself. Unlike Soto, Epps sees the episode not in transgression of the taboo against homosexuality, but rather in violation of Arenas's own homosexual desires. If the narrator of the novel has abandoned all semblance of political integrity in order to find his mother at all costs, "[h]omosexual desire is likewise abandoned; in fact, it is, along with the Mother, what the narrator-protagonist most mercilessly assaults . . . [But] even though both (apparent or assumed) homosexuals and the Mother are singled out for assault, that does not mean that Arenas is simply assaulting what he truly values, what he truly loves" (282). In other words, this is not a case of inversion, in which a direct reversal of terms might reveal to us the true motivations behind the protagonist's violence.

The confusion of the protagonist's assumed homosexuality with his more fundamental sense of gender as masculinity that repudiates femininity keeps both Epps and Soto focused on the mother as representative of *either* exaggerated phallic power (the essential dictator) *or* the "passive" homosexual's surrender of power. I want to argue that, while Epps has shown that the final rebellion in *El asalto* is not reducible to any simple opposition, neither is it reducible to the issue of Arenas's (or his character's) homosexuality. The death of the mother founds a masculine subjectivity that gives birth to itself in order to be experienced in all its "desperate beauty" (Epps 1995, 283). The misogynist ending vexes our appreciation of the protagonist's revolutionary toppling of the dictator. We applaud his new freedom and his inspiring example for the masses, and yet the production of this autonomous, self-born subject requires the violation and elimination of the mother. The rape must validate phallic power, and the murder must remove evidence of the male aggressor's ontological dependence on an Other. The horror of this scene's violence and irrationality, though, resists full reader identification with the protagonist's goals.

Just as the protagonist commits multiple assaults in this novel, he also presents multiple (re)births for himself. He first appears as a lone hunter, denying from the beginning that his mother has made any positive contribution to his existence. By opening the text with his hatred for her, he establishes the primacy of his own emotional reality over any biological relation to his mother. In fact, it is she, or the image we have of her, who is born of his disdainful look. His second textual birth is as a successful agent of the state. He produces and reproduces ever more restrictive laws, justifying his own passionate infiltration of every corner of the nation by enacting the principle of total surveillance upon which totalitarianism is based. The protagonist intentionally makes himself over into an image of phallically obsessed state power. The third moment of self-generation occurs with the overthrow of the dictator.

As we saw earlier, the protagonist makes himself a hero for the collective by hunting the mother, abusing the powerless on his way to the top, and finally sexually dominating both of the figures he had perceived to hold power over him. His annihilation of the mother represents a masculinist repudiation not only of her female body, but also of her procreative power. She has always been the barrier between the protagonist and his illusion of a true self that would escape her influence. The same holds for the male Reprimerísimo. He must be destroyed in order for the whisperers to revolt. The vestiges of communication and creativity spontaneously erupt in violence and noise as the id is freed in the protagonist's assault on his mother. Birth into liberty, then, must be motivated by violent masculine desire, not by nurturing maternal desire. This masculine desire, however, must express itself as unfettered sexuality, whether homo- or heterosexual, in order to be legitimate according to the dream-logic of *El asalto.* It must resist the productive, ordered, passionless discipline enforced by the illegitimate, hypermacho Reprimerísimo.

Amidst the rioting of the crowds after the murder, the protagonist walks away unnoticed. He peacefully removes himself from the tumult:

Y cansado, abriéndome paso en medio del estruendo sin que nadie se percate de mí (tan entusiasmados están ellos en gritar *al fin acabamos con el asesino reprimero, al fin la bestia cayó*) puedo llegar hasta el extremo de la ciudad. Camino hasta la arena. Y me tiendo.

(141)

[Weary, I make my way unnoticed trough the noise and the riot (the crowd in a frenzy of destruction, like children, crying *The Represident is dead, the beast at last is dead!*), and I come to the wall of the city. I walk down to the shore. And I lie down in the sand.]

(145)

If we accept Arenas's own claims that the *pentagonía* is fantastic autobiography, we must note that the final resting place of the protagonist, after all the travails from *Celestino* to *El asalto,* is the same word as the author's name. He walks toward "la arena" [the sand], announcing that the entire textual and historical journey leads to his patronymic.

Andrew Bush (1988, 393) has established that Arenas's short story **"El hijo y la madre"** (1967), published seven months after the UNEAC edition of **Celestino antes del alba,** effects the burial of his matronym. Before that story, all of his publications were signed "Reinaldo Arenas Fuentes." Bush's cryptonymic reading finds that **"El hijo y la madre,"** a story of a son's enclosure and reduction to silence in the maternal home, exemplifies Lacanian forclusion, "a rejection of reality so radical as to be anterior to the advent of symbolization: the riddled text is one which, having failed to learn the *nom du père,* will not be led out of the mirror stage" (375). *El asalto,* the author's final work in the pentalogy, revels in the mirror stage, the conclusion literally staging its continued effects in the protagonist's phantasmic relation to power. Reasserting the patronymic in the last line of his novel as affirmation of independent subjectivity introduces the father's invasion (here, associated with the reprimero's national nom du père) into the suffocating relationship with the mother. The real author, Reinaldo Arenas, dies in suicide with this invasion. The protagonist who survives him, after successfully committing parricide, rests on the sand of the author's unstable, intangible, and yet forcefully narrated identity-in-difference, with and against both parental figures.

Masculinity for the narrator of *El asalto* is attainable only through the simultaneous overthrow of two types of power. The island dictator's illegitimate power over the people in general competes for primacy with the mother's physical and psychological power over the protagonist in particular. He is a hero for others insofar as he assaults illegitimacy, and he is a phallocentric, homophobic, misogynist monster insofar as he attacks the mother. This culmination of suffering in the *pentagonía* constitutes strong evidence that the dream of individual freedom is the same dream as that of masculinity itself, when understood as self-produced, self-contained, carefully managed identity in ambiguous, mirrored relations of desire and rejection. The last scenes of the novel celebrate the violent achievement of male individuation and resist readers' desires to privilege either the psychoanalytic or the political implications of the mother/dictator's demise. This text depicts horrific and personalized violence as a requirement for successful revolution. The narrator-protagonist believes that his own psychological, emotional, and creative freedom depends on his ability to overcome his mother's power over him. The story is carefully designed to keep her ever present in the protagonist's imagination, and yet always just out of reach in the real.

The protagonist pursues political autonomy first through duplicity. He appears to obey and even add to the tyrannical government's absurd rules of social discipline at the same time that he despises the system, which, according to the novel's hyperbolic descriptions, reduces the citizenry to animal dumbness. By the end of the novel, however, that role as double agent coalesces into the moment when the protagonist is to be rewarded for his service to the dictator by finally meeting him face to face. Such direct access to power in the person of the dictator precipitates the protagonist's murderous impulse. Killing the dictator initiates revolution against what Arenas imagines to be the most extreme results of the betrayed socialist revolution in Castro's Cuba. More importantly for the protagonist, however, it resolves the split produced in the citizens of any totalitarian system. Forced to speak, work, and even rest according to government dictates, individuals strive to conform while inwardly seething. The stress of such internal conflict produces exaggerated forms of sadomasochism, or schizophrenic self-discipline. Not surprisingly, the protagonist's personal pathology results from the political system under which he must display those elements in himself that he hates, and hide those that he most values. Necessary political revolution is paradoxically perverted and made possible by sexual attack. The protagonist overthrows the dictator's system of regimentation by raping his own mother, onto whom he had projected the power to silence individual creativity on the part of citizens/sons.

El asalto stands out among contemporary Latin American narratives on masculinity for its disturbing presentation of the protagonist's liberation. By combining the threats to his autonomy (understanding autonomy here in the two senses of independent selfhood and freedom from political coercion) into the single image of the male dictator who is also the narrator's mother, this novel explores the dynamics of Lacanian forclusion (the son's mirror reflects back to him the mother's face) as well as the violence inherent in male differentiation from the mother. This stunningly graphic text displays a fundamental contradiction in liberal notions of political liberty and self-determination which unconsciously base themselves on the ideal of autonomous masculine subjectivity while consciously touting nonviolence. The text displays the contours of a primary aggression generated by a presymbolic split within the self. It also engages in a political project of presenting totalitarianism as a groundless complex of adult neuroses. Finally, it seems to defend literary authorship as a greater freedom than life itself.

Although this combination appears to achieve resolution through the assertion of the writer's patronymic in the last lines of the novel, the fact that Arenas's assault on coercive government policies both requires and is the rape of the mother distinguishes this text for its refusal to deny contradictory desires. The rape/murder ultimately affirms a pre-oedipal narrative structure: conflation of father/mother into one figure with whom the son identifies and yet whom he kills through sexual assault. The only available freedom for subjects caught in the logic of reactionary masculinity (for the protagonist, for the author Arenas, or for Cuba) is that double form of suicide[5] effected through killing the objects/subjects with which one identifies. According to the tensions at play in *El asalto,* no matter how much this type of freedom is lauded as subversive or creative, its requirement of radical individuality is self-destructive for those who seek it in the real.

Juxtaposing his protagonist's terrible success to the author's suicide demonstrates the inseparability of individual psychology, group psychology, and political power relations in the constitution of masculinities. *El asalto* depicts successful masculinity as a goal (whether conceived as a psychological formation, a social role, or a discursive subject position) which is impossible to achieve without killing (in the real or figuratively) all figures with whom one might identify. For Arenas, its triumph is destructive, lonely, fraught with ethical contradictions, and yet also the essential enabling factor in free artistic production. The novel's aesthetic power bursts forth in its ethical ambivalence over the two most problematic terms in the construction of masculinity: the mother and the law. Arenas boldly attacks them both at once, directly confronting, and yet ironically celebrating, the principle of violent revolution necessary to the category of masculinity itself.

Notes

1. Soto 1994 traces the series's subversive relationship to the Cuban documentary novel. Soto focuses on narrative voice, chronology, documentation, and the destabilization of literary forms in each of the five novels to offer a comparative and evolutionary reading of the texts Arenas intentionally grouped together.

2. Unless otherwise noted in the text, all English versions are from Andrew Hurley's translation (Arenas 1994).

3. Kessel Schwartz (1990) and Andrew Bush (1988) are notable exceptions.

4. Epps cites Ian Lumsden (1991) and Roger Lancaster (1992) in his explication of the importance, in designating the male homosexual in Latin American contexts, placed on performance, appearance, and adopting the so-called passive sexual position. These signs outweigh the fact of having sex with another man; many men—"the active, insertive, masculine-acting *bugarrón*"—are "not necessarily labeled . . . homosexual" (Epps 1995, 232).

5. By committing suicide in 1990, Reinaldo Arenas sealed his position as political and artistic martyr to the struggle for individual freedoms in Castro's postrevolutionary Cuba. Suffering from the physical ravages of advanced AIDS, the writer penned a public declaration of independence before he killed himself. The open letter confirmed Arenas's own notion of the import of his fantastic, baroque narrative style for a country controlled by an ideology of conformity, imposed "normalcy," and censorship: "Mi mensaje no es un mensaje de derrota, sino de lucha y esperanza." [My message is not a message of failure, but rather one of struggle and hope.] The letter is reprinted in the 1991 Ediciones Universal edition of *El Asalto* (Arenas 1991a, 152). For notes on suicide as personal assertion of political autonomy, especially among postrevolutionary Cubans, see Cabrera Infante 1983a and 1983b.

Bibliography

Arenas, Reinaldo. 1967. *Celestino antes del alba*. Havana: Ediciones Unión.

———. 1967. El hijo y la madre. *Unión* 6.4:222-26.

———. 1982a. *Otra vez el mar*. Barcelona: Editorial Argos Vergara.

———. 1982b. *El palacio de las blanquísimas mofetas*. Barcelona: Editorial Argos Vergara.

———. 1991a. *El Asalto*. Miami: Ediciones Universal.

———. 1991b. *El color del verano*. Miami: Ediciones Universal.

———. 1994. *The assault*. Translated by Andrew Hurley. New York: Viking.

Bush, Andrew. 1988. The riddled text: Borges and Arenas. *Modern Language Notes* 103.2:374-97.

Butler, Judith. 1993. *Bodies that matter: On the discursive limits of "sex."* New York: Routledge.

Epps, Brad. 1995. Proper conduct: Reinaldo Arenas, Fidel Castro, and the politics of homosexuality. *Journal of the History of Sexuality* 6.2:231-83.

Freud, Sigmund. 1921. Group psychology and the analysis of the ego. *Standard Edition* 18:67-143.

Lancaster, Roger N. 1992. *Life is hard: Machismo, danger, and the intimacy of power in Nicaragua*. Berkeley: University of California Press.

Schwartz, Kessel. 1990. Maternidad e incesto: Fantasías en la narrativa de Reinaldo Arenas. *Reinaldo Arenas: Alucinaciones, fantasías y realidad*. Edited by Hernández-Miyares and Perla Rozencvaig. Glenview, Ill.: Scott, Foresman and Company.

Soto, Francisco. 1994. *Reinaldo Arenas: The Pentagonía*. Gainesville: University Press of Florida.

Todorov, Tzvetan. 1977. *The poetics of prose*. Translated by Richard Howard. Ithaca: Cornell University Press.

Žižek, Slavoj. 1989. *The sublime object of ideology*. London: Verso.

Jorge Olivares (essay date fall 2002)

SOURCE: Olivares, Jorge. "A Twice-Told Tail: Reinaldo Arenas's 'El Cometa Halley.'" *PMLA* 117, no. 5 (fall 2002): 1188-1206.

[*In the following essay, Olivares investigates Arenas's appropriation of the four female characters in Federico García Lorca's play* The House of Bernarda Alba *in his short story "El Cometa Halley."*]

> ¡Cómo gozarías de vernos a mí y a mis hijas camino del lupanar!
>
> Wouldn't you be thrilled to see me and my daughters on our way to the whorehouse!
>
> —Federico García Lorca, *La casa de Bernarda Alba*

I begin at the beginning—with the opening paragraph of Reinaldo Arenas's short story **"El Cometa Halley"**:

> Aquella madrugada de verano de 1891 (sí, de 1891) en que Pepe el Romano huye con la virginidad de Adela, mas no con su cuerpo, todo parece haber terminado de una manera sumamente trágica para las cinco hijas de Bernarda Alba: Adela, la amante de Pepe, colgando de la viga de su cuarto de soltera, Angustias con sus cuarenta años de castidad intactos, y el resto de las hermanas, Magdalena, Amelia y Martirio, también condenadas a la soltería y al claustro.
>
> (83)

> Very late one night in the summer of 1891 (that's right, 1891), when Pepe el Romano runs away with Adela's virginity, leaving her behind, everything seems to have

come to a most tragic end for Bernarda Alba's five daughters: Adela, Pepe's lover, hangs from a noose fastened to the ceiling of her maiden room; Angustias keeps intact her forty years of chastity; and the rest of the sisters, Magdalena, Amelia, and Martirio, are also condemned to spinsterhood or the convent.

("Halley's Comet" 74)[1]

This recapitulation of the ending of Federico García Lorca's *La casa de Bernarda Alba* is followed by the startling disclosure that things did not really happen that way. As we shall see, the Cuban's provocative revelation sets in motion what Gérard Genette would term a "corrective continuation" of the Spanish play (175, 192-95). Giving a humorous twist to García Lorca's tragic ending, Arenas's revised and expanded version of the history of the Alba women begins by describing how the four older sisters disobey their mother, take Adela down, and slap her back to life. This defiant act culminates in the women's escape to Cuba.

After this opening account of the daughters' transatlantic emancipation from their tyrannical mother, the narrator fast-forwards almost two decades to tell us about their participation in the frenzy generated by the return of Halley's comet in 1910.[2] Although convinced, like most people, that the world is going to end when Earth passes through the comet's poisonous tail, the sisters do not join others in prayer for the salvation of their souls. Instead, incited by the sexually liberated Adela, who comes from Havana to die with her older sisters, the Alba women participate in a communal orgy on the streets of Cárdenas, the provincial city to which the four older siblings had moved. To everyone's surprise, the comet comes and goes, leaving the world, but not the sisters, intact. Commemorating their transformation and flaunting their liberation, Angustias, Magdalena, Amelia, and Martirio—in a joint effort with Adela—turn their house into a popular whorehouse, aptly naming it El Cometa Halley. And as the narrator not unexpectedly tells us in the last line of the story, parodying the ending of García Lorca's play, "ninguna de ellas murió virgen" 'none of them died a virgin' (107; 82).

This summation makes clear that the return of Halley's comet expands the Alba sisters' horizon of experiences: sex and its pleasures, which had been barred from the maternal house in Spain, are freely welcomed into the sororal house of sexual pleasure. Insofar as Arenas's tale is a tail of sorts, a textual extension appended to the Spanish play, the comet's tail can be regarded as an emblem of Arenas's prolongation of the history of García Lorca's women. In the first part of this essay, I dovetail Arenas's and García Lorca's tales in an attempt to unpack the Alba sisters' liberating voyage to Havana, a voyage that concludes, like Ismael's in Arenas's novel ***Viaje a La Habana Voyage to Havana***, with the joyful—and, in this case, humorous—release of the char-

acters' repressed sexual desires.[3] In the second part, I enlarge on the reading of **"El Cometa Halley"** by situating the story in the mother-son dynamic that figures prominently in Arenas's life and oeuvre.

THE FIERY RETURN OF THE ALBA SISTERS

In the last scene of *La casa de Bernarda Alba,* on discovering Adela's hanging body, the servant La Poncia puts her hands around her neck and laments, "¡Nunca tengamos ese fin!" 'May we never have that ending!' (199). Bernarda immediately commands everyone not to cry and, referring to Adela, declares: "Ella, la hija menor de Bernarda Alba, ha muerto virgen. ¿Me habéis oído? ¡Silencio, silencio he dicho! ¡Silencio!' 'She, the youngest daughter of Bernarda Alba, died a virgin. Did you hear me? Quiet, quiet, I said. Quiet!' (199; *House* 172). With these famous last words, the controlled and controlling Bernarda, in the female sphere of the home, attempts to assert maternal control over her daughters by proclaiming multiple expressive orifices closed. Gaping bodies, as represented by the women's clamoring mouths and Adela's penetrated vagina, have no place in Bernarda's hermetic house. Silence, finality, closure: that is what Bernarda wants but not what she gets—or so claims Arenas. According to the Cuban's narrative, García Lorca did not complete his story, leaving it "trunca y confusa" 'unfinished and unclear' (**"Cometa"** 83; **"Halley's Comet"** 74), because he was killed by Adela's lover, after whom García Lorca had gone in hot pursuit while the events in the Alba household were still unfolding. Although García Lorca is unsuccessful in his quest to be possessed by Pepe, he is successful in having his textual body possessed by Arenas, who gladly fills its gaps, thus fulfilling La Poncia's wish for a different ending.

That the servant enables Arenas's appropriation of García Lorca's text is revealed in the story's epigraph, which is taken from *La casa de Bernarda Alba:* "Nadie puede conocer su fin" 'No one knows how one's life will end' (**"Cometa"** 83). Repeating La Poncia's warning to Bernarda about the uncertain future of the Alba women, Arenas has García Lorca obliquely authorize the continuation of the play. Beginning with a paratextual commentary about the unpredictability of endings, **"El Cometa Halley"** proceeds to narrate the death of the original author (García Lorca) and set the stage for the birth of his reader, our author (Arenas). By collapsing the distinction between life and fiction, the Cuban's textual performance dramatizes negotiations among author, text, and reader. Placing García Lorca in the same fictive space as his literary creations, Arenas not only has the author die at the hands of one of his characters but also calls attention to the need for an active reader to resume the writing of García Lorca's text by filling in the gaps left by the dead author. An allegory of reading, Arenas's writing of **"El Cometa Halley"** offers a potential ending to García Lorca's indeterminate text.

But there is more to Arenas's playful story. Deposing a canonical dramatic work, Arenas foregrounds the Alba daughters' ascent to power as they dislodge their domestically empowered mother. In other words, performing a dethronement at the level of discourse and at the level of the story, **"El Cometa Halley"** imaginatively displaces a tightly rule-governed play to tell, in a less restrictive literary genre, the story of the displacement of Bernarda's maternal authority. Through its emphasis on hyperbolic liberation and reversal, **"El Cometa Halley"** embraces a festive spirit that can be assimilated to the excessive, hybrid, topsy-turvy world of carnival. Adela's hanging body marks the end of García Lorca's play and the beginning of Arenas's story. In *La casa de Bernarda Alba,* Adela's suspended state is seen as a tragic death, as a finality; in **"El Cometa Halley,"** it is humorously seen for what it literally is: a suspension— not a termination of life but a transitory condition that leads to the animation of the lifeless Adela and the transformation of her resuscitating sisters into unlikely subversives. Besides initiating the Alba women's rebellion against Bernarda, this playfully bizarre opening scene, in which the slapping, screaming, and reproaching older sisters lower Adela's body, also sets in motion—and is emblematic of—the story's carnival logic and spirit: the systematic lowering of all that is held high.[4]

Refusing to live any longer under "la égida de aquella vieja terrible" 'the fearsome old woman's iron hand' and coming together in their desire to bring about "la caída de Bernarda Alba" 'Bernarda Alba's fall from power' (**"Cometa"** 84; **"Halley's Comet"** 74-75), the five sisters disregard their mother's threats, jump out the window, escape through the stables, cross the Sierra Morena, and end up in the port city of Cádiz, where they book passage on a ship to Havana.[5] The Alba women's liberation traces a topographical trajectory, literal and metaphoric, that conforms to the story's carnivalesque thrust. If geographically the sisters' escape from their mother country follows a downward movement in Andalusia (from Córdoba through Seville to Cádiz), a corresponding vertical and horizontal displacement is suggested in their escape from their mother's house. Once Adela has been brought down, the sisters move away from the door, which is guarded by their mother, and let themselves out through a rear window that leads to the stables, through which they have to pass to evacuate Bernarda's property. Taking into account the traditional association between the house and the human body and considering that the daughters' exit from their mother's house entails a descending backward movement, one can argue that the women's escape represents a voiding of the body. This symbolic economy, which allows us to see the Alba sisters' evacuation in physiological terms, can be read in the context of Mary Douglas's discussion of filth as "matter out of place" (40). Extricating their bodies from Bernarda's control by discharging themselves outside her house, the Alba sisters deliberately take themselves out of the ordered place in which family and culture had situated them. As a result, they become the embodiment not only of what Natalie Zemon Davis calls "female disorderliness—the female out of her place" (129) but also of symbolic impurity. More precisely, no longer in their mother's house, no longer in their place, the sisters are transformed into figurative excremental matter. Their self-expelled bodies and their movement toward and through the scatological spaces of Bernarda's stables mark the women's transgressiveness, their disrespectful departure from—and the degradation of—Bernarda's immaculate house. This initial scene in Spain introduces, then, a process of carnivalesque inversion, debasement, and defilement that will culminate two decades later in the sisters' own "stable," the house of prostitution that they will make famous in Cárdenas.

If by going to Cuba in 1891 the five Alba women distance themselves from their mother, achieving a geographic separation that allows them to seek sexual pleasure, the four older ones, who repeatedly fail to attract men in their first few months in Cuba, soon succumb once again to the emotional and ideological hold that Bernarda has over them. Their transitory liberation comes to an end when they have to confront Adela's parturition, since Pepe has left their youngest sister with child. Adela's uninhibited sexuality, which is visually marked first by pregnancy and subsequently by a child whose paternity is claimed by twenty-five men of different races, offers a public spectacle of desires that her sisters now disavow. The older sisters' reaction to Adela, which grows out of fascination and aversion, follows the logic of abjection.[6] They expel the unruly sister out of their lives in an attempt to reestablish boundaries; in other words, they aim to restore order in the Alba household by closing themselves to the threat of the abject other. To this differentiating end, they kidnap their nephew (who is christened José de Alba), move away from Havana, and settle in Cárdenas in an impenetrable and conventlike house, where Adela's name is never mentioned and where her son is spoken of as the nephew whom they brought home after his mother's death in childbirth. Angustias, Magdalena, Amelia, and Martirio, by abjecting their youngest sister, come to embody their mother's authority, reincorporating into the text the temporarily suspended oppressive maternal order. Known in Cárdenas as "las monjas españolas" 'the Spanish nuns' (88; 76), the four older Alba women devote their lives to the church and to the care of their nephew. Living in a house with "cortinas oscuras" 'dark curtains' (87; 76) and always dressed in black, the four sisters "se prometieron dejar de ser mujer" 'promised themselves to stop being women' (87), thus containing their sexuality. At the same time, they control the sexuality of their nephew, who is also always dressed in black and who is allowed to leave the house only to peddle the artificial flowers and knitted goods made by his aunts.

The Alba house in Cárdenas becomes an asexual space policed by ever-vigilant maternal eyes. The sisters not only re-create the house of Bernarda Alba but also subject their nephew to the same life of repression that their mother forced on them. They live in abnegation for two decades until the day when Halley's comet and Adela return. On that day, the youngest of the five Alba sisters suddenly returns from the dead, resurrected, as it were, just as she had been when her sisters slapped her back to life. Adela's return, paralleling the comet's, constitutes an imminent danger to the older sisters' lives; specifically, she threatens their sexually repressed existence. But unlike the comet, which does not cause the anticipated "conflagración universal" 'universal conflagration' (93; 78), Adela brings her sisters' world to an end with a metaphoric conflagration of sexual desire.

If at first Angustias, Magdalena, Amelia, and Martirio refuse to respond to Adela's loud and persistent knocking when she appears at their house, they eventually open the door. What they see is as menacing to them as the comet: Adela has arrived dressed in a magnificent evening gown, accessorized with a mantilla, white gloves, suede boots, and a fan of peacock feathers. The sisters' reaction is not difficult to guess: they step back in horror as Adela theatrically enters the house, "contoneándose a la vez que le hacía una señal al cochero para que bajase el equipaje, un monumental baúl con excelentes vinos, copas de Baccarat, un gramófono y un óleo que era una reproducción ampliada del retrato de Pepe el Romano" 'swaying her hips and gesturing to the coachman to bring down her luggage, a monumental trunk full of excellent wines, Baccarat glasses, a gramophone, and an oil painting that was an enlarged portrait of Pepe el Romano' (96; 79).

Dressed in colorful attire that her mother forbade, attire that makes her stand out—like the comet—in the darkness of the evening, the transgressive Adela frightens her sisters and not only because of her appearance (in the sense of both her unexpected visit and her extravagant dress). In her "monumental baúl" 'monumental trunk' she carries emblems of forbidden desires that for years have been kept locked in the older women's psyches. Adela's narrative portrait, which is strategically placed in the middle of the story and which is rendered visually by Adela's appearing in the frame of her sisters' front door, significantly ends with the mention of another portrait—Pepe el Romano's. A portrait within a portrait, Pepe's "enorme" 'enormous' likeness is not only sexually allusive (104; 81), because of its magnitude and its insertion in (the portrait of) Adela and her trunk, but textually emblematic as well. The *reproduc-*

ción ampliada of Pepe's portrait remands the reader to the narrative in which it is inscribed. For Arenas's story, having been written in intertextual dialogue with—and as an augmentation of—*La casa de Bernarda Alba,* is, like its pictorial metonym, a provocative *reproducción ampliada* of an existing text. Throughout Arenas's story, Pepe and the cosmic tail (and tale) are linked, as the body in the portrait is figuratively constructed as a mirroring image of the distinctive attribute of the story's heavenly body. Like Halley's comet, Pepe has returned after a long absence and commands a "tail" that the Alba women find terrifying and irresistible. Thus, in an amplified tale, with Pepe's amplified portrait as the sisters'—and the text's—guiding light, Bernarda's daughters amplify their minds and bodies.

García Lorca critics have pointed out that, although Pepe sets the action of *La casa de Bernarda Alba* in motion, he never appears onstage (Gabriele 388; Urrea 51). He is present only allusively through the women's discourse and through a picture of him that the jealous Martirio steals from Angustias in the second act, claiming later to have done so as a "broma" 'joke' (166, 169, 182; 150, 152, 160). It is in the context of the search for Pepe's missing picture that La Poncia warns Bernarda that "aquí pasa una cosa muy grande" 'something big is going on here' (*Casa* 169). Perhaps inspired by this scene in García Lorca's play and particularly by La Poncia's reaction, Arenas literally writes into his parody—his *broma*—"una cosa muy grande," Pepe's enormous portrait, in the presence of which other big things happen. Once inside the house, Adela executes her first act of possession in her sisters' inviolate space by hanging Pepe's portrait on one of the walls of their living room. In full view, the "espléndido lienzo" 'splendid canvas' immediately and simultaneously captivates Angustias, Magdalena, Amelia, and Martirio: "Ante la vista de aquella imagen las hermanas Alba quedaron súbitamente transformadas" 'At the sight of his image the Alba sisters were suddenly transformed' (**"Cometa"** 98; **"Halley's Comet"** 79). The women's once-impenetrable house and bodies succumb to a relentless and promiscuous sexuality. For Adela, convinced that the world is about to end, turns the Alba house into a carnival stage with its full range of liberating potential: the doors are flung open and a constellation of transgressive desires let in.

The devout Alba women initially heed the admonition of the local priest, who warns them that God, angered by humanity's impiety and excess, is behind the comet's imminent destruction of the world. But in a carnivalesque shift from the spiritual to the material, Adela preaches to her sisters a religion of the flesh. Although agreeing with the priest that the comet is a "castigo" 'punishment' (102; 81), an inebriated Adela offers an alternative and subversive explanation:

Pero no por lo que hemos hecho, sino por lo que hemos dejado de hacer. [. . .] Aún hay tiempo, no de sal-
var nuestras vidas, pero sí de ganarnos el cielo. ¿Y
cómo se gana el cielo? [. . .] ¿Con odio o con amor?
¿Con abstinencia o con placer? ¿Con sinceridad o con
hipocresía? [. . .] ¡Nos quedan dos horas! [. . .] En-
tremos en la casa y que nuestros últimos minutos sean
de verdadera comunión amorosa.

Not for what we did, but for what we did not do. [. . .]
We still have time, not to save our lives but to gain admission to heaven. And how does one get to heaven?
[. . .] With hate or with love? Through abstinence or
through pleasure? With sincerity or with hypocrisy?
[. . .] We only have two hours left! [. . .] Let's go inside the house and pass our last minutes in loving communion.

During her blasphemous speech, a carnivalesque inversion of the priest's sermon, Adela is helped from falling
by José, who "ya se había transfigurado en la viva es-
tampa de Pepe el Romano" 'had been transformed into
the sheer image of Pepe el Romano' (102; 81). The
painting, already an object of the transgressive female
gaze, now comes to life in the person of the son, whom
Adela passionately kisses on the mouth, a prelude to
their orgiastic sexual encounter. She then puts on a
record of "Fumando espero," further stimulating the
women's sexual appetite with the seductive lyrics of the
phallically suggestive *cuplé*. Literally intoxicated with
Adela's wine and figuratively with her words, music,
and example, the Alba women make love under Pepe's
enlarged portrait. Crossing various normative boundaries, the women's revelry with the young José and
Adela's black coachman ignites same-sex, cross-sex,
cross-class, cross-race, cross-generational, orgiastic, and
incestuous desires. Like Angel Facio in his 1972 staging of *La casa de Bernarda Alba* (Facio 15), Arenas
makes explicit, for instance, the implicit lesbianism of
García Lorca's Adela and Martirio; and he alludes at
the end of the story to a threesome formed by these two
sisters and José. By allowing his characters to express
their repressed heterosexual and homosexual desires,
Arenas not only outs García Lorca's play but also opens
up the story in multiple ways. In moving the action
from Spain to Cuba, Arenas simultaneously shifts the
center of gravity from mother-daughter and sister-sister
relationships to sister-sister and mother-son relationships. While I would not want to minimize the importance of the homoerotic sisterly dynamic in the text, it
is worth reflecting in more detail, as I do later in this
essay, on the new element that Arenas adds to the story
of the Alba women. With the resurrection of Adela and
the addition of her son to the original cast of *La casa
de Bernarda Alba*, Arenas privileges these two characters and directs the reader's attention to their incestuous
desires. It should not surprise us that in an earlier draft
of **"El Cometa Halley"** the mother-son incest motif is
even more highlighted—as, for example, in a passage
in which Adela urges her sisters to take their orgy out-

side and the narrator reveals that, while talking, she is
being "poseída apasionadamente por su hijo" 'passionately possessed by her son.'[7]

Outside the Alba house, the sisters, José, and the coachman expand their promiscuous intermingling by merging with an unruly crowd of farm laborers—while
Pepe's portrait still presides over their indiscriminate
lovemaking. Just minutes before the comet positions itself at the center of the celestial vault, Adela and Martirio retrieve Pepe's image from the house, take it out-
doors, and place it looking up toward the sky as if
mirroring the heavenly bodies above. If Pepe and the
comet are spatially associated in this scene, they are literally and discursively connected in the next. At the
level of plot they share the same fate: both ultimately
fade with hardly any public notice. And the paragraph
in which this narrative detail is revealed is tellingly
symmetrical, as it begins with the comet's disappearance and ends with the disappearance of the portrait:

Y lo ocupó [el centro del cielo]. Y siguió su trayecto-
ria. Y desapareció por el horizonte. Y amaneció. Y al
mediodía, cuando las hermanas Alba despertaron, se
sorprendieron, no por estar en el infierno o en el
paraíso, sino en medio de la calle mayor de Cárdenas
completamente desnudas y abrazadas a varios campesinos, a un cochero y a José de Alba, cuya juventud, in-
mune a tantos combates, emergía una vez más por entre los cuerpos sudorosos. Lo único que había
desaparecido era el retrato de Pepe el Romano, pero
nadie le echó de menos.

(105-06)

And so it did [occupy the central position in the skies].
And then it continued on its trajectory. And it disappeared over the horizon. And the sun rose. And by
noon, when the Alba sisters woke up, they were amazed
to see themselves, not in hell or in paradise but in the
middle of the main street in Cárdenas. Totally in the
buff, the sisters were still embracing several farm laborers, a coachman, and José de Alba, whose youthful-
ness, despite his many sexual encounters, emerged once
more from the sweaty bodies. The only thing that had
disappeared in the confusion was the portrait of Pepe el
Romano, though nobody had noticed.

(82)[8]

Like the comet, Pepe's portrait disappears by morning.
Moreover, also like the comet, which leaves behind a
trace in the name of the sisters' brothel, the portrait
leaves a trace—or tail: young José's erection looming
large over the naked and sweaty bodies of the liberated
Alba women.

The Alba sisters' transformation is brought home in a
revealing act of naming in the last scene of the story.
As the women, exhausted from a night of promiscuous
sex, enter their house, a triumphant Adela removes from
the front door the old sign, "VILLALBA FLORES Y TEJIDOS"
'VILLALBA FLOWERS AND HANDMADE KNITS,' and that after-

noon she replaces it with another, "EL COMETA HALLEY" 'HALLEY'S COMET' (106; 82). In a playfully perverse intertextual inspiration, Arenas has his characters turn their house into a whorehouse, making Bernarda's worst fears—as expressed to La Poncia and encapsulated in my epigraph—come to pass: "¡Cómo gozarías de vernos a mí y a mis hijas camino del lupanar!" 'Wouldn't you be thrilled to see me and my daughters on our way to the whorehouse!' (García Lorca, *Casa* 170). Having put a new face on their house and on themselves, the daughters yield to, while subverting, the spirit of their mother's command to achieve "buena fachada y armonía familiar" 'proper appearances and family harmony' (*Casa* 182; *House* 160).[9] Ironically, they fulfill their mother's wish, for Bernarda insists that one must always live by these words.

As in carnival, whose participants violate what are normally accepted as "impenetrable hierarchical barriers" (Bakhtin, *Problems* 123), Arenas's characters engage in incestuous, interracial, cross-generational, and class-crossing heteroerotic and homoerotic sex. True to the transgressive logic of carnival, **"El Cometa Halley"** places the enjoyment of diverse forms of sexualities above normative repressions and prohibitions, a celebration of the flesh made possible by the return of the sexually indocile Adela. The youngest sister's visit to Cárdenas connects the comet's elongated tail to Pepe's amplified portrait; in their textual dissemination and in line with Arenas's male-centered worldview, the comet's tail and Pepe's enormous portrait come to represent the male element that ultimately penetrates—and carnivalistically liberates—the Alba sisters and their repressed universe.

Arenas's work reveals little awareness of many issues raised by feminist scholars, among them the complexities of prostitution. Whether prostitution is an uncomplicated source of sexual pleasure and an empowering profession, as Arenas has it, or a quintessential symbol of patriarchal exploitation, or a dangerous occupation that nonetheless gives women agency, in **"El Cometa Halley,"** as in Arenas's imaginary more generally, patriarchal structures are reaffirmed rather than dismantled.[10] In important respects, the power achieved by the Alba sisters in their sexual liberation is illusory, for they are portrayed as becoming "mujeres" 'women' (87) only in the presence of phallic symbols (the comet, the portait) and only when they surrender to penetrative sex with men. By opening the brothel, the naming of which participates in the story's network of phallic resonances, the sisters defy maternal control and assert female sexual desires, but they do so by perpetuating male power. This should not be surprising, since the characters' sentimental journey echoes their author's. In Arenas's fantasy of sexual freedom, the ultimate desire is to submit, as the Alba women do, to a man. To further explore the complicated sexual politics of **"El Cometa Halley,"** I now turn to an analysis of the text in the context of familial patterns in Arenas's life and writings.

A SON'S FANTASY

Having viewed the comet's tail in Arenas's tale, I would now like to contemplate the tale behind the writing of "El Cometa Halley." What may account for Arenas's continuation of *La casa de Bernarda Alba,* particularly his linking of the lives of the Alba women with the 1910 return of the comet? Written in January 1986, Arenas's story had as its most immediate inspiration the upcoming visit of Halley's comet, which was to make its closest outbound approach to Earth on 11 April of that year (Calder 146). In addition, Arenas may have been prompted to revisit García Lorca's play because 1986 marked the fiftieth anniversary of its writing and of the tragic death of its author, who was murdered in 1936 by the Fascists two months after completing the work (Gibson 438, 446-70). Arenas's decision to dislocate Bernarda's daughters to a sexualized Cuba may have originated in a tropical episode in García Lorca's biography, the threemonth visit to the island in 1930 that introduced the Spaniard to a larger world of sexual alternatives (Walsh 273). More specifically, on this Caribbean island, a locale that García Lorca called "paradise" (Gibson 285), conveniently far away from his mother, the author of *La casa de Bernarda Alba* came to openly embrace his homosexuality. Like their original creator, who was unable to resist Cuban male bodies and who insisted that he spent the happiest days of his life in Cuba (Gibson 301), the Alba sisters, also at a safe distance from their mother, find sexual fulfillment and unqualified happiness on the irresistibly phallic island of Cuba.

Arenas's readers would not consider **"El Cometa Halley"** particularly remarkable, given the author's penchant for intertextuality, which is evident, for instance, in his novels *El mundo alucinante* and *La Loma del Angel.* But one can ask why, other than to pay homage to a writer he admires, Arenas decides to write a parodic continuation of the story of Bernarda Alba and her daughters. Repressive motherhood and repressed sexuality, central themes of *La casa de Bernarda Alba,* undoubtedly attracted the Cuban author to the Spanish play. Arenas appropriates these themes, which are central in his oeuvre, and rewrites them from the nostalgic and painful perspective of exile.

After years of ostracism and a period of imprisonment in his native Cuba because of his political views and sexual practices, Arenas leaves the island for the United States in 1980 in the confusion of the Mariel boatlift. Like many an exile, Arenas does not find home—or ever feel at home—once away. In an essay on José Martí, in whose life as an exile Arenas sees his own life mirrored, he observes, "Estando aquí fuera del sitio amado y odiado, fuera de la prisión, de donde tuvimos que salir huyendo para poder seguir siendo seres humanos, seres libres, no somos completamente libres, porque estando aquí, en el destierro, estamos aún allá en alma e imagen" 'Being here, away from the place we love and hate, away from prison, from which we had to flee to be able to continue existing as human beings, as free people, we are not completely free. Because, although we are here, in exile, we are nonetheless there in soul and image' ("Martí" 57). In *Antes que anochezca* (*Before Night Falls*), his autobiography, Arenas explains that soon after leaving Cuba he becomes disillusioned with the United States, a country ruled by money. Alienated from the Cuban American community because of its materialism, anti-intellectualism, and machismo, he is also dissatisfied with the ghettoization of North American gay culture. As a result, Arenas finds refuge from the adversities of exile by imaginatively journeying back, through what Benigno Sánchez-Eppler calls "narrative self-repatriation" (158), to an otherwise unattainable Cuba.

In **"El Cometa Halley,"** Arenas vicariously writes himself back to Cuba when he returns García Lorca, in the guise of the Alba women, to the tropical island that the Spanish writer visited—and fell in love with—in 1930. Returning to Cuba with—and as—Bernarda's daughters suits Arenas's literary erotics in part because this allows him to imagine being *templado* 'fucked' by "hombres de verdad" 'real men' (*Antes que anochezca* 133), a possibility that Arenas associates with Cuba rather than the United States:

> [A]l llegar al exilio, he visto que las relaciones sexuales pueden ser tediosas e insatisfechas. Existe como una especie de categoría o división en el mundo homosexual; la loca se reúne con la loca y todo el mundo hace de todo. [. . .] ¿Cómo puede haber satisfacción así? Si, precisamente, lo que uno busca es su contrario. La belleza de las relaciones de entonces era que [. . .] encontrábamos a aquel hombre [. . .] que quería, desesperadamente, templarnos. [. . .] Aquí no es así o es difícil que sea así; todo se ha regularizado de tal modo que han creado grupos y sociedades donde es muy difícil para un homosexual encontrar un hombre; es decir, el verdadero objeto de su deseo.

(*Antes que anochezca* 132)

Later, in exile, I found that sexual relations can be tedious and unrewarding. There are categories or divisions in the homosexual world. The queer gets together with the queer and everybody does everything. [. . .] How can that bring any satisfaction? What we are really looking for is our opposite. The beauty of our relationships then was that we [. . .] would find that man [. . .] who wanted desperately to fuck us. [. . .] Either conditions here are different, or it is just difficult to duplicate what we had there. Everything here is so regu-

lated that groups and societies have been created in which it is very difficult for a homosexual to find a man, that is, the real object of his desire.

(*Before Night* 106-07)

Longing for the gender-differentiated sex of his Cuban years, Arenas metaphorically transports himself back to his homeland, to a place where, like García Lorca, he spent his happiest and most sexually fulfilling days. Like García Lorca in *La casa de Bernarda Alba,* then, Arenas invites us to read his work through the lens of a "transvestite poetics," by which the reader views the heterosexual female characters as homosexual men to lay bare the text's metaphoric displacement of male homosexual desire.[11]

Having repeatedly insisted on the autobiographical dimension of his writing, Arenas would not disagree, I think, with this reading of **"El Cometa Halley."**[12] Indeed, Arenas is in his text but in ways more subtle than I have suggested so far. Although it is possible to read all the Alba women and their quest for men as an allegorical representation of the woman-identified Arenas, I find the figure of Adela most intriguing. Why does Arenas bring Adela back to life, transforming her from a rebellious daughter in *La casa de Bernarda Alba* to a sexually empowering and licentious sister and mother in **"El Cometa Halley"**? Why does Arenas have Adela save the day by sexually emancipating not only her older sisters but also her son? Why, more to the point, does Arenas juxtapose Bernarda and Adela in their roles as mothers, one despotic and sexually repressive and the other liberating and sexually permissive? To answer these questions, I take a short detour through other texts by Arenas.

In 1981, five years before writing **"El Cometa Halley,"** Arenas told Antonio Prieto Taboada that "en todo lo que yo he escrito hay una serie de constantes. Una de las más importantes es la madre. La madre es de gran importancia para mí" 'in everything I have written there is a series of constants. One of the most important is the mother. The mother is of great importance to me' (Arenas, **"Esa capacidad"** [**"Esa capacidad para soñar"**] 685). Among Arenas's maternally themed works, one finds the meaningfully titled *Adiós a mamá* *Good-bye, Mother,* a posthumous short-story collection that includes, among others, **"El Cometa Halley"** and the eponymous story. Having lost the original 1973 version, Arenas rewrites **"Adiós a mamá"** in exile in 1980, six months after he leaves Cuba. The story centers on a Bernarda-like mother who totally controls her five children—four women and one man (the youngest of the five).[13] Beginning with the announcement of the mother's death, the narrative goes on to focus on her grotesque wake. Incapable of parting with their mother, the four daughters refuse to bury her and compulsively tend to her decomposing, stinking, vermin-infested body.

Continuing to be ruled by their rotten mother, Ofelia, Otilia, Odilia, and Onelia completely submit to her by committing suicide; they stab themselves with their mother's kitchen knife and then throw themselves into "el inmenso charco pululante que es [. . .] mamá" 'the sprawling, teeming morass that is [. . .] mother' (65; "Goodbye" 58). But what about the fifth sibling, the nameless male narrator? Having been the only child who argued for the mother's burial, a position that led his sisters to call him a traitor, the narrator, after two unsuccessful attempts at killing himself, decides not to join his mother and sisters. Instead, he flees the house and rushes to the ocean, where he plunges into the waves, proudly saying to himself, "Soy un traidor. Decididamente soy un traidor. Feliz" 'I'm a traitor. A confirmed traitor. And happy' (79; 66).

Given its mother-focused plot, in which the youngest of five siblings rebels against a powerful matriarch, **"Adiós a mamá"** invites the reader to speculate about the filiation between this story and *La casa de Bernarda Alba*. Although Arenas may also have been inspired by the matriarchal household in which he lived, where his grandmother ruled over her daughters, it may not be a coincidence that **"Adiós a mamá"** is placed immediately before **"El Cometa Halley"** in the short-story collection. The textual contiguity of the two stories suggests a common Lorquian intertext.[14] One can speculate further that **"El Cometa Halley"** continues not only *La casa de Bernarda Alba* but also **"Adiós a mamá"** and not just because one follows the other in the collection. As Arenas explains in a self-conscious letter by the "Tétrica Mofeta" 'Skunk in a Funk' (his alter ego) in *El color del verano (The Color of Summer)*, "Mis libros conforman una sola y vasta unidad, donde los personajes mueren, resucitan, aparecen, desaparecen, viajan en el tiempo, burlándose de todo y padeciéndolo todo" 'My books constitute a single enormous whole in which the characters die, are reborn, appear, disappear, and travel through time—always mocking, always suffering' (358; 315). In a manner typical of Arenas, **"El Cometa Halley"** takes up where **"Adiós a mamá"** leaves off. The carnivalesque story of the rebellious child in **"Adiós a mamá,"** which ends as the son throws himself into the sea to escape from an unbearable matriarchy, continues with the carnivalesque story of Arenas's Alba sisters, which features the women's experiences after a transatlantic voyage. Thus, García Lorca's Adela in *La casa de Bernarda Alba* metamorphoses into the figure of a son, the narrator in **"Adiós a mamá,"** who in turn metamorphoses back into Adela in **"El Cometa Halley."** At the same time, although **"Adiós a mamá"** opens with the matriarch's death, the figure of the mother neither dies nor disappears in **"El Cometa Halley."** Instead, while Bernarda is left behind in Spain, the four older Alba sisters assume in Cuba, vis-à-vis their nephew, the role of the controlling mother. Eventually, however, Adela undermines their authority, bringing their stifling matriarchy to an end, and as a result a new mother—radically different—emerges, one who is an advocate for liberated pleasures and desires.

Arenas's Adela deviates, then, from the customary authoritarian mother that populates the Cuban's works—a menacing figure that finds its most extreme representation in *El asalto (The Assault)*, a novel Arenas wrote in 1974, a year after writing the first draft of **"Adiós a mamá."**[15] Both narratives, not coincidentally, thematize the son's fears of—and reactions to—the impending threat of merging with the mother, physically and psychically. In the story, when facing "el gran momento [de] unir[se] a mamá" 'the big moment [to] join mother' (**"Adiós"** 76; **"Goodbye"** 64), the son resists and escapes; in the novel, fearing that he will become like his mother, the son commits matricide. But, conceived, written, and published in exile a dozen years later, **"El Cometa Halley"** ends uncharacteristically: the son does not suffer from "matrophobia" (Rich 235) and feel compelled to flee from the smothering figure. Instead, son and mother happily "come together" in a tale that celebrates mother-son incest.

The emergence of the new mother (Adela) seems odd in the context of the familial constellation prevalent in Arenas's works, one marked by the commanding presence of the authoritarian mother and the "absence" of the father. In an attempt to understand Adela's role, I want to address, first, the issue of the father. I place *absence* in quotation marks because that absence is only apparent. Although it is true that Arenas saw his father only once, at age five, the author does not evict the paternal figure from his literary universe, as some critics have maintained he does. On the contrary, the figure of the father plays a prominent, albeit oblique, role in Arenas's life and oeuvre. The cornerstone of *Antes que anochezca,* Arenas's autobiography, is its first chapter, which briefly but movingly narrates Arenas's only encounter with his father. Suggestively titled **"Las piedras,"** a reference to the stones that Arenas's mother throws at a handsome young man when he attempts to bond with her simultaneously confused and excited child, this memorable first chapter sets in motion the oedipal dynamics of the text.[16] This oedipal telemachy, although more veiled, figures importantly in *El asalto,* to which I will turn presently.

In his interview with Prieto Taboada, Arenas addresses the role of the mother in Cuban culture:

> En el mundo en que yo me desenvolví la madre tenía un sentido patriarcal. El padre era el aventurero que podía sencillamente engendrarte y desaparecer (como sucedió en el caso mío), pero la mujer era siempre la constante: la que te vigilaba, la que te mecía, te criaba, te condenaba, te criticaba, te exaltaba . . . En fin, la que te iba a conceder el perdón o la condena. Y eso es evidente en lo que yo he escrito. Yo creo que incluso

hay un *sentido edípico* en la relación entre la madre y yo, y aun entre el pueblo cubano en general y la madre. La madre se convierte en última instancia en el poder absoluto. Entre las formas que han tenido las dictaduras en Cuba, el dictador asume hasta cierto punto la categoría de madre del pueblo. Hay entonces una especie de chantaje sentimental: una autoridad casi materna. Eso lo podemos ver también actualmente: cómo la dictadura se convierte en un poder materno que nos administra, nos dirige, nos organiza, nos dice cómo tenemos que peinarnos, cómo tenemos que vestirnos, cómo tenemos que hablar, lo que debemos hacer, lo que no debemos hacer.

(Arenas, **"Esa capacidad"** 685; my emphasis)

In the world in which I lived, the mother had a patriarchal role. The father was an adventurer who would simply conceive you and disappear (as happened in my case), but the mother was always a constant: the one who kept watch over you, rocked you, nursed you, punished you, criticized you, praised you . . . In sum, the one who would forgive you or condemn you. And that is evident in what I have written. I also believe that there is an *oedipal character* to the relationship between my mother and me, and even between Cubans in general and their mothers. The mother embodies, in the end, absolute power. In the various forms that dictatorships have had in Cuba, the dictator partly takes on the role of mother of the people. There is, as a result, a kind of sentimental blackmail: an authority almost maternal. That is what we see at present: how the dictatorship becomes a maternal power that manages us, guides us, organizes us, tells us how we must comb our hair, how we must dress, how we must speak, what we must do, what we must not do.

Although one must not consider as universal the psychoanalytic postulates regarding sexual identity formation, Diana Fuss reminds us that psychoanalysis "constitutes a powerful cultural narrative that continues to shape, in both regulative and disruptive ways, representations of sexual identity" (13). Arenas is a case in point. He not only interprets his family romance in a Freudian context but also uses a psychoanalytic model to offer an oedipal interpretation of the political situation of the Cuban people. Despite Arenas's claim about his mother's centrality in his life and works, it is important not to lose sight of the fact that the (absent) paternal figure enjoys an equally remarkable presence, albeit allusive and elusive, in his oeuvre. Moreover, one could also argue that for Arenas the losses—or absences—of father and fatherland are equally poignant, since *padre* and *patria* share an emotional space in his life and writings. His exile from his fatherland and his father's absence leave a void that Arenas fills through writing. Having been denied the love of a father, Arenas redirects his filial love toward his fatherland. And in the same way that his mother—in the eyes of the innocent child—comes between him and his father, an equally repressive figure, Fidel Castro, comes between Arenas and his fatherland. Thus, for Arenas, it proves difficult if not impossible to distinguish between Castro and the castrating mother.[17]

This conflation of the mother and Castro literally takes place in *El asalto,* where the two figures who represent absolute power share the same body. In this novel, the last volume of Arenas's *pentagonía* 'pentagony' (an "agony" in five novels, in which the Cuban author narrates a secret history of Cuba), the nameless protagonist embarks on a homicidal search for his mother.[18] In the last scene, coming face to face with the president, Reprimerísimo, in a public square, the protagonist realizes that his mother and Reprimerísimo (an obvious double of Castro) are one and the same. As the son confronts his mother, his member swells to enormous proportions, and in a fury he sexually assaults her. After an arduous struggle, the aroused son penetrates his mother with the gigantic penis, killing her instantly: "Ella al ser traspasada emite un alarido prolongado y se derrumba al mismo tiempo que yo siento el triunfo, el goce furioso de desparramarme en su interior. Ella, soltando un aullido, estalla lanzando tornillos, arandelas, latas, gasolina, semen, mierda y chorros de aceite" 'As she is pierced, she gives a long, horrible shriek, and then she collapses. I sense my triumph—I come, and I feel the furious pleasure of discharging myself inside her. Howling, she explodes in a blast of screws, washers, tin cans, gasoline, semen, shit, and spurts of motor oil' (140; 145).[19] Next, as the elated citizens advance toward Reprimerísimo's agents, eventually taking over the square and destroying everything in sight, the protagonist, unseen by anyone, walks away from the crowd in the direction of the seashore. *El asalto* comes to a close with two brief sentences: "Camino hasta la arena. Y me tiendo" 'I walk down to the sand. And I lie down' (*Asalto* 141). Giving his body to the *arena* of his fatherland, the protagonist-son (a double of the author) symbolically becomes one with Arenas, the father. The narrator has reached a safe place, a place where he regains the essence of his being, that of a son—of his absent father and his beloved Cuba. And this is told, suggestively, in the final words, "me tiendo" 'I lie down,' which coupled together produce the present participle *metiendo* 'inserting,' a phonic verbal play that participates in the passage's sexual subtext.[20]

If one keeps in mind Arenas's admiration for the *Iliad,* a text prominent in his memoirs, one can also read the final scene of *El asalto* as an evocation of a scene in book 23 of the Homeric poem in which the mournful Achilleus, having lain down on the beach away from his men, reunites with the deceased Patroklus, whose ghost appears to him in a dream. That Patroklus, whose death leads Achilleus to grieve inconsolably, has been considered a paternal figure vis-à-vis the Homeric hero (for being older, for having been named Achilleus's mentor, and for having *pateres* in his name) permits the association between the beach scenes in Homer and Arenas. And if one subscribes to the view that Achilleus and Patroklus have a sexual relationship, as some scholars have claimed, the Homeric connection is even more germane to my reading, since the two men's intimate lives help to advance the father-son incest motif in the final scene of Arenas's novel.[21]

Finally, this intertextual reading of the closing scene of *El asalto* is authorized by **Arturo, la estrella más brillante** (*Arturo, the Brightest Star*), a novel that Arenas wrote in 1971, three years before writing *El asalto.* The happy ending of the last novel of Arenas's *pentagonía* culminates not only the five-novel cycle but also, in keeping with Arenas's fondness for textual echoes and continuities, the creative process that Arturo initiated in the novel that bears his name. Referring to the fantastic castle that, while serving time in one of Castro's labor camps, he is constructing in his imagination for himself and the male lover for whom he is searching, Arturo explains, somewhat enigmatically, that "aún faltaban maravillas: arenas, orquídeas, oquedades y Patroclos" 'there were still so many marvels to be made: sands, orchids, hollows, and Patrocluses' (81; *Brightest Star* 97). But Arturo, we are told, is murdered by a troop of soldiers led by his mother before completing his sand castle. Despite Arturo's death, his dream does not go unrealized, for like the nameless male protagonist of "**Adiós a mamá**," who reappears in "**El Cometa Halley**" in the guise of Adela, Arturo reappears in *El asalto* in the guise of this novel's nameless male protagonist, who in the end fulfills his desire to be with the man he loves. In the final scene, on the beach, the protagonist of *El asalto* finds himself in a happy place, a place where *arenas* (Arenas) and Patroklus appear and come together, joining the protagonist, not in a castle as Arturo had planned, but in an echo chamber of evocative intertextualities.

The last scene of *El asalto* also resonates with the incestuous plot of Arenas's *Viaje a La Habana.* In this novel, an exiled father, persuaded by his son's mother in Cuba, returns to the island after a fifteen-year absence to reunite (sexually, as it turns out) with the son he left behind. Although metaphoric in *El asalto* and literal in *Viaje a La Habana,* the sexual reunion of father and son brings both narratives to a felicitous conclusion. But if in *El asalto* this connection is made possible only by the absence—the elimination—of the mother, in *Viaje a La Habana* it depends on her presence, since without the mother's active role father and son would not come together after years of separation. A year before completing *Viaje a La Habana,* Arenas wrote "**El Cometa Halley**," in which a mother also reunites father and son. As the reader will recall, in Arenas's continuation of *La casa de Bernarda Alba,* a pregnant woman who was abandoned by her lover has a son, from whom she is separated at birth. When she meets her son eighteen years later, the mother shows him a picture of his father and introduces the young man to a life of promiscuous sex. Because of his mother's entrance into his life, the son simultaneously becomes aware of his mother's, his father's, and his own identities and desires. Although one can see in this story a subtle reworking of the father-son theme present in various texts by Arenas, two things remain enigmatic. Why, as in *Viaje a La Habana,* is the mother in "**El Cometa Halley**" the broker of the meeting between father and son, deviating from reality, as represented in *Antes que anochezca,* in which the mother makes every attempt to thwart their union? And why, unlike her counterpart in *Viaje a La Habana,* does the mother play a central role in "**El Cometa Halley**," emerging as its protagonist?

That "**El Cometa Halley**" and *Viaje a La Habana* were written entirely in exile may explain the portrayal in these texts of a maternal figure different from the one that Arenas had depicted earlier in his career. Completed within one year of each other and at a time when Arenas begins to suspect and then confirms that he has contracted HIV, these two fictional narratives are his way of honoring his mother, whom he suspects he will never see again.[22] Instead of a forbidding and authoritative figure, from whom the son constantly has felt the need to flee, she is now cast in the role of an understanding mother in *Viaje a La Habana* and a sexually liberated and liberating mother in "**El Cometa Halley**." Unlike the repressed and repressive mother protagonists in fictional texts originally conceived in Cuba, Adela is a hedonist who literally bonds with her son through music, alcohol, and sex. In fact, she seduces him and leads him into a life of eroticism. Because of this and because José, despite his age, is characterized as sexually inexperienced, as an innocent child who undergoes his sexual awakening when his sexually aggressive mother enters his life, "**El Cometa Halley**" can be interpreted, more specifically, as a preoedipal fantasy. As in the preoedipal stage, the maternal figure introduces the child to sexual pleasure. No longer chaste, repressive, and frustrated, this new mother in Arenas's fantasy aggressively seeks and finds erotic fulfillment not just in others but also in her son. As in the dyad of infantile life, the son enters a world of blissful plenitude, in which he and his mother come together in a totalizing erotic communion.[23]

Although in *Antes que anochezca* Arenas describes his mother as an asexual woman who "siempre fue fiel a la infidelidad de mi padre" 'was always faithful to my father's infidelity' and who, much to her son's dismay, "eligió la castidad" 'chose chastity' (19; *Before Night* 3), he recalls an episode from his childhood when he experienced his mother's sexual desires on his body:

> Una de mis tías tenía el privilegio de poder escuchar alguna novela radial; a la vez que la iba escuchando se la iba contando a sus hermanas. Yo recuerdo que, sentado en las rodillas de mi madre, mi tía contaba las escenas eróticas que escuchaba; las piernas de mi madre se estremecían y yo, sobre ella, recibía aquellos reflejos

eróticos, que mi madre, joven y seguramente ansiosa de tener una relación sexual, me transmitía.

(52-53)

One of my aunts had the privilege of being allowed to listen to a soap opera; while she listened, she would pass the story on to her sisters. Sitting on my mother's lap, I remember my aunt describing the erotic scenes she heard. My mother's legs quivered and I felt the sexual tension that my mother, young and anxious to make love, transmitted to me.

(30-31)[24]

Childhood recollections such as this support reading **"El Cometa Halley"** as a text that fictionalizes its author's preoedipal remembrances of things past. In the last narrative that Arenas writes in which the maternal figure occupies center stage, he pays homage to his preoedipal mother. And he does this, not surprisingly, as he also pays homage to his (absent) father. Physically absent but symbolically present through his enlarged and commanding portrait, Pepe brings to mind the other dominating image in Arenas's life and works: that of the handsome and young *guajiro* in the Cuban countryside who is forever remembered by his jilted lover and abandoned son. I would insist, however, that **"El Cometa Halley"** is primarily a tribute to preoedipal mother love, an allegorical reenactment of the crucial bonding phase between mother and child that the father's oedipal interference has not yet begun to disrupt.

GOOD-BYE, MOTHER?

In a letter of 29 August 1989 to Jorge and Margarita Camacho, Arenas writes about his mother, Oneida Fuentes, who was in the United States on a twenty-day permit from Cuba. Although the dutiful son traveled from New York to Miami to be with her, there was not, as Arenas laments to the Camachos, "mucha comunicación de NINGÚN TIPO" 'much communication of ANY SORT.' For instance, he did not say a word to her about his precarious health. And perhaps more disheartening for Arenas was his mother's lack of appreciation for his writing. One day, as he was diligently working on *El color del verano,* she asked him whether he would get a real job some day, since—as her hurt and bitter son explains—"para ella trabajar es picar piedra en una cantera" 'for her to work is to smash rocks in a chain gang.' Partly attributing their complicated relationship to his illegitimate birth and accepting once and for all that his mother "está a mil leguas de [su] vida" 'is far away from [his] life,' Arenas comes to a sad but irrevocable determination when he writes to his friends, "En fin, *adiós a mamá*" 'In sum, *good-bye, mother*' (Letter). This is one more good-bye in a series of farewells that began years ago in Cuba when, at a young age, Arenas realized that he could not live with his mother. As he states in *Antes que anochezca:*

Toda mi vida fue una constante huida de mi madre; del campo a Holguín, de Holguín a La Habana; luego, queriendo huir de La Habana al extranjero. [. . . Y]o sólo podía abandonar a mi madre o convertirme en ella misma; es decir, un pobre ser resignado con la frustración y sin instinto de rebeldía y, sobre todo, tendría que ahogar mis deseos fundamentales.

(221)

My whole life had been a constant running away from my mother: from the country to Holguín, from Holguín to Havana; then, trying to run away from Havana to another country. [. . .] I had to leave my mother or become like her—that is, a poor, resigned creature full of frustrations with no urge for rebellion. Above all, I would have to smother my own being's innermost desires.

(*Before Night* 197)

When Arenas writes and underlines *adiós a mamá* in his letter to the Camachos, he not only graphically underscores the emotional import of a phrase that for him reverberates with past and present painful experiences of separation but also deliberately calls attention to the autobiographical dimension of his writing. Like the eponymous story of *Adiós a mamá,* **"El Cometa Halley"** is also an *adiós a mamá:* the five Alba sisters say good-bye to their tyrannical mother, whom they leave behind in Spain.

But there is more to this good-bye in the Cuban's version of the story of Bernarda Alba and her daughters, and it has to do with the chronological deviation of Arenas's text from its intertext. **"El Cometa Halley"** begins, as we are insistently told, in 1891, and reaches its climax in 1910. An allegory of Spain on the eve of the civil war (Smith 20), *La casa de Bernarda Alba* seemingly unfolds in 1936. Why, then, does Arenas depart from García Lorca's chronology? To answer this question, I briefly turn to critical elements in Cuba's history and Arenas's biography.

Having been shaped by his harrowing experiences in revolutionary Cuba, the exiled Arenas, although inspired by the 1986 appearance of the comet, rejects setting the Alba sisters' story of sexual emancipation, a story with which he identifies, in Castro's repressive post-1959 era. Instead, Arenas antedates the events and has his narrative culminate in 1910, which not only is when Halley's comet made its previous visit but also happens to be during the promising formative period of the young Cuban republic (founded in 1902). Though not blind to the social and economic inequalities and political corruption that plagued the early years of the republic, Arenas chooses to have his liberating story occur at this propitious moment in his country's history. The place that the 1910 comet holds in the Cuban cultural imaginary may also have contributed to Arenas's preference for 1910 instead of 1986. The curious coincidence that the comet was closest to Earth on 20 May (Giralt and Gutiérrez Lanza), eight years to the day after the founding of the republic, seized the Cuban imagination. Some Cubans claimed, for instance, that the comet's tail resembled the shape of their island. The "deslumbrante fenómeno" 'dazzling phenomenon' of the comet's tail indelibly marked the collective memory of a generation of Cubans, as Graciela Pogolotti has explained (123), and symbolized a country that was poised to embrace a dazzling future. Writing **"El Cometa Halley,"** Arenas affirms—in the tradition of intellectuals like Renée Méndez Capote, Marcelo Pogolotti, and Loló de la Torriente before him—the comet's penetration in the Cuban imaginary.

If Cuba's history and cultural imaginary guide Arenas's manipulation of the chronology, so does the author's family history. The Cuban's corrective continuation of the Spanish play can be read as a fanciful corrective of his primal and traumatic scene of maternal separation, about which his mother wrote to him in a letter of 3 March 1986: "Ahora recordé que hizo en febrero 24 años que te fuiste para La Habana separados desde entonces cada día más. Qué daño habremos hecho para sufrir así sólo Dios lo sabe" 'I just remembered that you left for Havana 24 years ago in February. We have been separated since then more each day. What we have done to suffer so much only God knows' (Fuentes). Oneida Fuentes's letter alludes to the fact that Arenas was eighteen when he left her—and the city of Holguín—in 1962 to begin a new life in the capital.[25] This bit of family history is pivotal for an understanding of **"El Cometa Halley."**

The story's first sentence states and immediately repeats in parentheses that the tragedy Pepe brings on the Alba household takes place in 1891. By designating 1891 the year that Pepe deflowers Adela, leaving her pregnant, Arenas makes their bastard son eighteen when Halley's comet and his mother return in 1910—a narrative detail that allows us to see Reinaldo in José. For in addition to a striking parallel between the real and fictional parental couples (in both cases, a handsome man abandons a young woman after impregnating her), there is an equally striking parallel between the two sons, who are the same age when their relationships with their mothers take crucial but inverted turns. Oneida's son is eighteen when he leaves his mother; Adela's son is eighteen when he reunites with his mother. It may not be possible to do more than speculate, but the autobiographical reading that I am suggesting may be an additional tale lurking behind Arenas's comet. In a humorous but powerful short story, Arenas recasts Adela as a sexually aggressive preoedipal mother and adds a son to the original cast of characters of *La casa de Bernarda Alba,* all in an attempt to imagine an alternative family constellation. Unlike Arenas's mother in real life and Bernarda in García Lorca's play, who are suffering

and controlling, the mother in **"El Cometa Halley"** is wild and liberating. Arenas fantasizes a mother who, understanding one's needs to satisfy one's *deseos fundamentales,* opens new worlds for her son. As Arenas alters García Lorca's story, he simultaneously alters and allegorically rewrites his own personal story to imagine what it would have been like if, on that day long ago when he was eighteen, he had not been forced to say *adiós a mamá.*

Notes

1. Written in Miami Beach in 1986, "El Cometa Halley" was first published in a Venezuelan magazine, *Exceso,* in 1989 and was subsequently included in *Final de un cuento,* a posthumous miscellany of essays and stories, and in *Adiós a mamá,* a posthumous collection of stories. I quote from the latter. For the English translation, I rely primarily on Koch's version ("Halley's Comet"), making slight emendations where noted. Where no source is indicated, translations of this work and others are mine.

2. First identified in 1682 by Edmond Halley, the comet returns to Earth every seventy-six years. Capturing the human imagination, it has been associated with the overthrow of despotic rulers and the end of terrestrial life. The 1910 comet in particular produced mass hysteria. Curiously, despite the belief that it would bring the end of the world, many people welcomed it with outrageous "comet parties," of which the Alba sisters' orgy in Arenas's "El Cometa Halley" is an imaginative re-creation. The phallic connotations of the comet's tail were common in the popular imagination of 1910. For example, a Cuban *guaracha* of that year, about a jealous wife who cuts off her unfaithful husband's penis, includes the following lyrics: "No te apures, Enriqueta / que el mundo ya no termina / porque ayer la Mallorquina / le cortó el rabo al cometa" 'Enriqueta, don't you fret / the world is not going to end / because yesterday the Mallorquina / cut the tail off the comet' (qtd. in Fernández Soneira). On Halley's comet, see Calder; Etter and Schneider; Genuth 156-77; and Gropman.

3. On *Viaje a La Habana,* see Olivares.

4. On carnivalesque "casting-down," see Bakhtin, *Rabelais* 19, 21, 370; Morson and Emerson 443; and Stallybrass and White 9, 23, 183. In my use of the carnivalesque as an analytic category, I mainly follow Stallybrass and White. Distancing themselves from those who see carnival in the strict Bakhtinian sense as a licensed—hence, ineffectual—revolt, Stallybrass and White place it in broader categories of symbolic inversion and transgression, which allow us to see carnival as a site of struggle that may lead to change.

5. If in *La casa de Bernarda Alba* there are only two ways of escaping—namely, insanity or suicide (Ozimek-Maier 84)—"El Cometa Halley" explores a third way: escape by way of the sea. Arenas, whose passion for the ocean is well known, may have been inspired by La Poncia, who says, "A mí me gustaría cruzar el mar y dejar esta casa de guerra" 'I wish I could go across the sea away from this battleground of a house' (García Lorca 189; 164).

6. According to Kristeva, "It is [. . .] not lack of cleanliness or health that causes abjection but what disturbs identity, system, order. What does not respect borders, positions, rules" (4).

7. The typescript of this draft is part of the Reinaldo Arenas Papers (box 14, folder 5, Literary Papers and Mss. Div., Dept. of Rare Books and Spec. Collections, Princeton Univ. Lib., Princeton).

8. I have made slight revisions to Koch's translation.

9. The translation into English does not fully render the etymology of *fachada;* the Spanish noun, like *façade,* can refer to the visible face of a building and to the deceptive or illusory appearance of something or someone.

10. See Rosen for a balanced historical view of prostitution.

11. On transvestite poetics, see Savran 115-20. Although one may find "transvestite criticism" problematic, as Sedgwick does (233-34), I submit that Arenas may have been aware of this common approach to García Lorca. On women as homosexual men in García Lorca, see Binding 212-16 and Urrea. Not surprisingly, in *El color del verano* (212), Arenas connects a gay character in his novel with García Lorca's Adela.

12. To cite one example: "I'm basically interested in two things in the narrative world. One is the exploration of my personal life, my experiences, my sufferings, my own tragedies. The other is the historical world" (Arenas, "Conversation" 145).

13. "Adiós a mamá" was first published in *Novísimos narradores hispanoamericanos en marcha, 1964-1980,* a 1981 anthology edited by Angel Rama. I quote from Arenas's collection.

14. The striking parallel between the author's household, which is fictionalized in his novels, and the Alba household has not escaped critics. See, e.g., Wood 21. In *Adiós a mamá,* Arenas seems to arrange the stories thematically, not chronologically.

15. Written in Havana in 1974 and revised in New York in 1988, *El asalto* was published posthumously in 1991.

16. On the role of the father in *Antes que anochezca,* see Olivares.

17. On Castro's evocative surname, see Epps 262-63.

18. On the *pentagonía,* see Soto. On *El asalto* in particular, see Biron 120-42, Epps 275-82, and Molinero. Arenas has spoken of "an entire gallery of mothers" in *Otra vez el mar* (the third novel of the *pentagonía*); among them one finds, in canto 2, "the dictator mother" ("Conversation" 144). In *Arturo, la estrella más brillante,* the figure of the mother is also associated with Castro's repressive government. As this novel concludes, the mother, dressed in military gear, leads the troop of soldiers who kill the protagonist, one of thousands of homosexuals sent to labor camps because of their sexual preferences.

19. I have made slight revisions to Hurley's translation.

20. I am grateful to my student Nicole LaBrecque for this observation.

21. On Achilleus and Patroklus, see Halperin 75-87 and Sergent 250-58. On Arenas and the *Iliad,* see Arenas ("Elogio") and Olivares.

22. Arenas worked on both texts simultaneously. He began writing *Viaje a La Habana* in 1983 and finished it in 1987. He wrote "El Cometa Halley" entirely in 1986. I am not suggesting that Arenas altogether stops depicting the mother as an oppressive figure. She appears in *Antes que anochezca* and *El color del verano,* the last works he wrote before his death.

23. On the preoedipal mother, see Sprengnether. Insightfully challenging the mother's "spectral" presence in Freud's treatment of the child's sexual development, Sprengnether underscores the profound importance of maternal power during the two-person phase in infantile life. Unlike Freud, who generally limits the mother's position to object of her son's libidinal urges, Sprengnether argues for the mother's central position as a sexually desiring and aggressive subject. I should note here that portraying José as a child is congruent with Arenas's view of himself as a child. See, e.g., his poem "Viejo niño" 'Old Child' and his interview in the documentary *Havana* (Arenas, Interview).

24. I have made slight revisions to Koch's translation.

25. Arenas was born on 16 July 1943 and left for Havana in February 1962, when he was five months shy of his nineteenth birthday.

Works Cited

Arenas, Reinaldo. "Adiós a mamá." *Adiós a mamá: De La Habana a Nueva York.* Barcelona: Altera, 1995. 53-79.

―――. *Antes que anochezca.* Barcelona: Tusquets, 1992.

―――. *Arturo, la estrella más brillante.* Barcelona: Montesinos, 1984.

―――. *El asalto.* Miami: Universal, 1991.

―――. *The Assault.* Trans. Andrew Hurley. New York: Viking, 1994.

―――. *Before Night Falls.* Trans. Dolores M. Koch. New York: Viking, 1993.

―――. *The Brightest Star. Old Rosa: A Novel in Two Stories.* Trans. Andrew Hurley. New York: Grove, 1989. 45-104.

―――. *El color del verano.* Barcelona: Tusquets, 1999.

―――. *The Color of Summer.* Trans. Andrew Hurley. New York: Viking, 2000.

―――. "El Cometa Halley." *Adiós a mamá: De La Habana a Nueva York.* Barcelona: Altera, 1995. 81-107.

―――. "Conversation with Reinaldo Arenas." Soto 137-54.

―――. "Elogio de las furias." *Necesidad de libertad.* México: Kosmos, 1986. 253-55.

―――. "Esa capacidad para soñar: Entrevista con Reinaldo Arenas." By Antonio Prieto Taboada. *Revista interamericana de bibliografía/Review of Inter-American Bibliography* 44 (1994): 683-97.

―――. "Goodbye Mother." Trans. Jo Labanyi. *The Faber Book of Contemporary Latin American Short Stories.* Ed. Nick Caistor. London: Faber, 1989. 53-66.

―――. "Halley's Comet." Trans. Dolores M. Koch. *Hopscotch* 2.1 (2000): 74-82.

―――. Interview. *Havana.* Dir. Jana Bokova. BBC, 1990.

―――. Letter to Jorge and Margarita Camacho. 29 Aug. 1989. Box 23, folder 7. Reinaldo Arenas Papers. Literary Papers and Mss. Div., Dept. of Rare Books and Spec. Collections, Princeton U Lib., Princeton.

―――. "Martí ante el bosque encantado." *Necesidad de libertad.* México: Kosmos, 1986. 56-61.

―――. *Viaje a La Habana. Viaje a La Habana: Novela en tres viajes.* Madrid: Mondadori, 1990. 109-81.

―――. "Viejo niño." *Voluntad de vivir manifestándose.* Madrid: Betania, 1989. 96-97.

Bakhtin, Mikhail. *Problems of Dostoevsky's Poetics.* Trans. Caryl Emerson. Minneapolis: U of Minnesota P, 1984.

―――. *Rabelais and His World.* Trans. Hélène Iswolsky. Cambridge: MIT P, 1968.

Binding, Paul. *García Lorca o la imaginación gay.* Barcelona: Laertes, 1987.

Biron, Rebecca E. *Murder and Masculinity: Violent Fictions of Twentieth-Century Latin America.* Nashville: Vanderbilt UP, 2000.

Calder, Nigel. *The Comet Is Coming! The Feverish Legacy of Mr. Halley.* New York: Viking, 1981.

Davis, Natalie Zemon. "Women on Top." *Society and Culture in Early Modern France.* Stanford: Stanford UP, 1975. 124-51.

Douglas, Mary. *Purity and Danger: An Analysis of the Concepts of Pollution and Taboo.* London: Routledge, 1966.

Epps, Brad. "Proper Conduct: Reinaldo Arenas, Fidel Castro, and the Politics of Homosexuality." *Journal of the History of Sexuality* 6 (1995): 231-83.

Etter, Roberta, and Stuart Schneider. *Halley's Comet: Memories of 1910.* New York: Abbeville, 1985.

Facio, Angel. "Estreno de *La casa de Bernarda Alba* en España. Entrevista con Angel Facio." By M. Pérez Coterillo. *Primer Acto* 152 (1973): 13-16.

Fernández Soneira, Teresa. "La proximidad de Halley trae recuerdos." *El nuevo herald* 17 Feb. 1986: 11.

Fuentes, Oneida. Letter to Reinaldo Arenas. 3 Mar. 1986. Box 24, folder 8. Reinaldo Arenas Papers. Literary Papers and Mss. Div., Dept. of Rare Books and Spec. Collections, Princeton U Lib., Princeton.

Fuss, Diana. *Identification Papers.* New York: Routledge, 1995.

Gabriele, John P. "Mapping the Boundaries of Gender: Men, Women and Space in *La casa de Bernarda Alba.*" *Hispanic Journal* 15 (1994): 381-92.

García Lorca, Federico. *La casa de Bernarda Alba.* Ed. Allen Josephs and Juan Caballero. Madrid: Cátedra, 1988.

―――. *The House of Bernarda Alba. Four Major Plays.* Trans. John Edmunds. New York: Oxford UP, 1999. 117-72.

Genette, Gérard. *Palimpsests: Literature in the Second Degree.* Trans. Channa Newman and Claude Doubinsky. Lincoln: U of Nebraska P, 1997.

Genuth, Sara Schechner. *Comets, Popular Culture, and the Birth of Modern Cosmology.* Princeton: Princeton UP, 1997.

Gibson, Ian. *Federico García Lorca: A Life.* New York: Pantheon, 1989.

Giralt, P., and M. Gutiérrez Lanza. "El cometa." *El diario de la marina* 21 May 1910: 2.

Gropman, Donald. *Comet Fever: A Popular History of Halley's Comet*. New York: Simon, 1985.

Halperin, David M. *"One Hundred Years of Homosexuality" and Other Essays on Greek Love*. New York: Routledge, 1990.

Kristeva, Julia. *Powers of Horror: An Essay on Abjection*. Trans. Leon S. Roudiez. New York: Columbia UP, 1982.

Molinero, Rita. "De asaltos, furias y falos: En donde Arenas descubre 'otro' de los mundos posibles." *Apuntes Posmodernos/Postmodern Notes* 6.1 (1995): 66-75.

Morson, Gary Saul, and Caryl Emerson. *Mikhail Bakhtin: Creation of a Prosaics*. Stanford: Stanford UP, 1990.

Olivares, Jorge. "¿Por qué llora Reinaldo Arenas?" *MLN* 115 (2000): 268-98.

Ozimek-Maier, Janis. "Power Plays in *La casa de Bernarda Alba*." *Things Done with Words: Speech Acts in Hispanic Drama*. Ed. Elias L. Rivers. Newark: Juan de la Cuesta, 1986. 73-84.

Pogolotti, Graciela. "Loló, la república, el cometa." *Mujeres latinoamericanas del siglo XX. Historia y cultura*. Ed. Luisa Campuzano. Vol. 1. La Habana: Casa de las Américas, 1998. 123-29.

Rich, Adrienne. *Of Woman Born: Motherhood as Experience and Institution*. New York: Norton, 1976.

Rosen, Ruth. *The Lost Sisterhood: Prostitution in America, 1900-1918*. Baltimore: Johns Hopkins UP, 1982.

Sánchez-Eppler, Benigno. "Reinaldo Arenas, Re-writer Revenant, and the Re-patriation of Cuban Homoerotic Desire." *Queer Diasporas*. Ed. Cindy Patton and Sánchez-Eppler. Durham: Duke UP, 2000. 154-82.

Savran, David. *Communists, Cowboys, and Queers: The Politics of Masculinity in the Work of Arthur Miller and Tennessee Williams*. Minneapolis: U of Minnesota P, 1992.

Sedgwick, Eve Kosofsky. *Epistemology of the Closet*. Berkeley: U of California P, 1990.

Sergent, Bernard. *Homosexuality in Greek Myth*. Trans. Arthur Goldhammer. Boston: Beacon, 1986.

Smith, Paul Julian. *Vision Machines: Cinema, Literature, and Sexuality in Spain and Cuba, 1983-1993*. New York: Verso, 1996.

Soto, Francisco. *Reinaldo Arenas: The Pentagonía*. Gainesville: UP of Florida, 1994.

Sprengnether, Madelon. *The Spectral Mother: Freud, Feminism, and Psychoanalysis*. Ithaca: Cornell UP, 1990.

Stallybrass, Peter, and Allon White. *The Politics and Poetics of Transgression*. Ithaca: Cornell UP, 1986.

Urrea, Beatriz. "Silencio, amor y muerte: El homosexual y la mujer en la obra de García Lorca." *Bulletin of Hispanic Studies* 74 (1997): 37-58.

Walsh, John K. "A Logic in Lorca's *Ode to Walt Whitman*." *¿Entiendes? Queer Readings, Hispanic Writings*. Ed. Emilie L. Bergmann and Paul Julian Smith. Durham: Duke UP, 1995. 257-78.

Wood, Michael. "No Sorrow Left Unturned." *New York Review of Books* 7 Mar. 1991: 21-23.

Robert Richmond Ellis (essay date 2002)

SOURCE: Ellis, Robert Richmond. "Reinaldo Arenas: From Forced Labor to AIDS." In *They Dream Not of Angels but of Men: Homoeroticism, Gender, and Race in Latin American Autobiography,* pp. 124-49. Gainesville: University Press of Florida, 2002.

[*In the following essay, Ellis explores Arenas's treatment of historical events "through the dynamics of homoeroticism" and the economic exploitation of gay men in the novella* Arturo, la estrella más brillante *and his autobiography,* Before Night Falls.]

The postmodern conception of the queer might seem particularly well suited to an elucidation of Latin American representations of male-male sex. Within the culture of machismo, male sexuality is performative, and the gender of the male body, susceptible to a process of both masculinization and feminization, is ultimately irreducible to the contingent meanings of male anatomy. Yet in spite of his own performance of male femininity, Reinaldo Arenas highlights not only the performative dimension of male-male sex but also the concrete social and material environment in which it operates. For this reason postmodernist queer theory, with its emphasis on parody and ludic spontaneity as effective subversions of dominant constructions of sexuality and gender, is at best only partially compatible with his writing. Indeed, Arenas writes more as a "postcolonial" than a postmodernist, though he occupies multiple vantage points as a gay male with AIDS who was born a peasant in postindependence Cuba, became a renowned dissident writer during the early decades of the Revolution, and died in exile in the United States. As Diana Brydon remarks in her analysis of postmodernist and postcolonial discourses, each interrogates the fixedness of identity, and by extension the "truth," but for her postcolonial writers are far more interested than postmodernists in "the effects of historical happenings: the effects of invasion, of military occupation, of food blockades, of revolution" (142)—in short, the very exigencies of the social milieu of a writer like Arenas.

In his fictional and autobiographical texts Arenas clearly reflects on "historical happenings" of tremendous consequence for Latin America and the world. But by reading these events through the dynamics of homoeroticism he also makes visible the economic and labor exploitation of gay and feminine-appearing men.[1] Like numerous gay Cuban men of his generation, Arenas was subjected to internment in a forced-labor camp, an experience illustrated most poignantly in *Arturo, la estrella más brillante*[2] and subsequently in his autobiography, *Antes que anochezca* [*Before Night Falls*]. In *Arturo, la estrella más brillante* Arenas depicts the overdetermining conditions of the gay male of the Cuban Revolution. In *Antes que anochezca* he aims precisely to transcend these conditions. In fact the most salient feature of Arenas's life-writing is his almost Promethean effort to write as a gay man in the face of state-sponsored, antigay terror, and eventually under the onus of AIDS.

The gay male is integral to Cuban revolutionary discourse, since it is in opposition to him, as the designated incarnation of bourgeois degeneracy, that the identity of the socialist "new man" ("el hombre nuevo") is forged. This opposition replicates bourgeois identity-formation at the beginning of the early-modern period, when aristocratic consumption and sloth were equated with male femininity, and the supposedly masculine virtues of bourgeois productivity and industriousness were asserted. In both the bourgeois and socialist orders male femininity is used as a vehicle through which the rising social class is "engendered" and empowered. But whereas in the bourgeois context of nineteenth-century capitalism a figure such as the homosexual dandy indirectly reaffirmed the dominant models of labor through his own perceived parasitism, the gay male in revolutionary Cuba becomes an exploited worker whose very status betrays the inherent contradictions of the regime.

The characteristics of the "new man" have been most fully elucidated by Ernesto "Che" Guevara in his landmark essay "El socialismo y el hombre en Cuba" ["Notes on Man and Socialism"].[3] For Che, the "new man" possesses moral fortitude and intellectual curiosity and loves work as an end in itself. But more important, he is willing to subsume his individual identity within the larger social collective. This "surrender," as Brad Epps puts it, "is understood in terms of empowerment (I surrender the I to be stronger in and as the We)" (234). The converse of the "new man's" empowering self-effacement is the sexual "surrender" of the homosexual to another man, which "is understood in terms of disempowerment, degradation, and abjection" (234). In this scenario male-male sex comes to symbolize the old order of dominance and subordination, and though the "passive" homosexual is oppressed, he is also, because of his acquiescent desire, an accomplice of oppression. Yet as Arenas contends in his autobiogra-

phy, the sexual relationship of the *activo* and the *pasivo* is not de facto one of dominance and subordination even if it is inevitably represented as such within the public culture of masculinity and femininity. And as the tale of Arturo makes excruciatingly clear, the ostensible sublimation of homoeroticism within the homosocial community of "new men" in fact fails to transcend the dynamics of dominance and subordination, since the "new man" not only enslaves the recalcitrant homosexual but ceaselessly effeminizes him through his own unbridled sexual violence. The "new man's" old machismo is therefore, as Epps so aptly observes, "the thing that at once impels and obstructs the revolution" (261).

The position of the gay male vis-à-vis the Revolution was crystallized by Castro in his 1965 interview with the journalist Lee Lockwood.

LOCKWOOD:

> Is it your position that if one is a homosexual, one cannot be a Revolutionary?

CASTRO:

> Nothing prevents a homosexual from professing revolutionary ideology and, consequently, exhibiting a correct political position. In this case he should not be considered politically negative. And yet we would never come to believe that a homosexual could embody the conditions and requirements of conduct that would enable us to consider him a true Revolutionary, a true Communist militant. A deviation of that nature clashes with the concept we have of what a militant Communist must be.
>
> (124)

In this passage, as in much of the Cuban revolutionary discourse of sexuality, lesbianism is invisible, as if despite the considerable advancements of women within Cuban society female sexuality could be conceived of solely through the mediation of masculine desire. Castro maintains that "homosexuals should not be allowed in positions where they are able to exert influence upon young people," for if communism is ever to be fully achieved, Cuban youth must be inculcated "with the spirit of discipline, of struggle, [and] of work" (124)— that is, with the virtues the "new man" is deemed to possess but that the gay male, as his logical contrary, necessarily lacks.

In a 1990 interview with the Nicaraguan revolutionary Tomás Borge, Castro seemingly softens his stance, claiming, for instance, that he does not regard homosexuality as a type of degeneracy. He instead blames any mistreatment of homosexuals under the regime on the Spanish legacy of machismo and affirms that he himself "jamás [ha] sido partidario, ni [ha] promovido, ni [ha] apoyado políticas contra los homosexuales"

(Borge 215) ["[has] never been in favor of, nor promoted, nor supported any policy against homosexuals" (trans. Lumsden, *Machos* 98)]. Yet when asked if a homosexual might become a member of the Communist Party, he avoids directly answering the question: "Te digo que ha habido bastantes prejuicios en torno a todo eso, es la verdad, es la realidad, no lo voy a negar; pero había prejuicios de otro tipo contra los cuales nosotros más bien centramos la lucha" (215) ["I would say to you that there has been quite a lot of prejudice with respect to that, that is the truth, I will not deny it; but there were other types of prejudices against which we chose to focus our struggles" (98)]. According to this response, the terrible abuse of gay men (through the period of the UMAP, the Mariel exodus, and the AIDS catastrophe)[4] somehow occurred in spite of the official policies of the regime. Moreover, the words of Castro do nothing to dislodge the image of the gay male as alien to the Revolution. He is not only excluded from the Party but in the end is not even named. He thus remains, as Epps would have it, an "in-Fidel" (268), whose marginalized sexuality prevents his incorporation within the Revolution, but also impedes his co-option by the forces of the counterrevolutionary right.[5]

THE CAGED BIRD

In the Cuba portrayed in *Arturo, la estrella más brillante,* male-male sex is positioned explicitly within relations of labor. In this context gay men, or *locas* (an identity conferred solely on the feminine-appearing *pasivo*), not only occupy the lowest rung in the hierarchy of power but are relegated to the UMAP and made to work as virtual slaves. The UMAP are characterized by scarcity (of adequate food, water, medicine, and shelter) and are riven by violence. During the day, the *locas* harvest sugarcane and thereby produce the principal commodity on which the national economy is founded. At night, they are encouraged to cultivate stereotypically feminine behaviors and submit to the sexual demands of the hypermasculine soldier-guards. Male-male sex is hence a means of dominating and atomizing a group of unpaid workers and ultimately functions as an instrument of labor exploitation. Contrary to official propaganda, the early regime seeks neither to suppress male-male sex (the homoeroticism of the soldiers is never even ostensibly challenged) nor to extirpate gay males from its midst (only when Arturo escapes and then resists arrest is he killed). Instead, it makes the *locas* work—even if this often means working them to death.

Arenas dedicates *Arturo, la estrella más brillante* to his friend Nelson Rodríguez Leyva, who suffered imprisonment in the UMAP. As Arenas explains in a note at the end of the text, Rodríguez Leyva wrote a narrative based on his camp experiences that was expunged by the authorities after his death in a failed attempt to hijack a Cuban National Airlines plane to Florida. The testimony of the fictional Arturo is also destroyed as a result of an endeavor to flee a forced-labor camp. For this reason, *Arturo, la estrella más brillante* can be read as the re-creation of the missing Rodríguez Leyva text and the enunciation of a silenced gay voice. Indeed, it stands as a kind of *testimonio,* of an individual and of an entire generation of gay Cuban men whose lives coincided with Arenas's.

Unlike the "new man," the gay Arturo regards his life in individualistic terms, and though he envisions an ideal gay lover, he feels no solidarity with his fellow gay inmates, whom he rejects as vehemently as his oppressors. His initial reaction to his plight is anger. This anger masks his ever-deepening anguish over the endemic violence of human relations as well as a growing awareness of mortality and his own imminent death. Yet Arturo's personal and existential concerns remain within the framework of the social, and as Roberto Echavarren Welker indicates, Arenas in fact employs certain elements of Cuban socialistrealism precisely in order to attack the antigay stance of the Castro regime on its own terms (121).

Despite his efforts to assert his individuality and achieve independence, Arturo is continually thwarted by the other. The initial manifestation of the other, "ellos" [them], are the *locas* with whom he is imprisoned. Arturo despises the *locas,* accusing them of unremitting artificiality and railing against them for "rebajándolo todo, corrompiéndolo todo," and in the end "reduciendo la dimensión de la tragedia, de la eterna tragedia del sometimiento, de su eterna desgracia, a la simple estridencia de un barullo" (12) ["pulling everything down to their own level, . . . corrupting everything, [and in the end] whittling the tragedy down to size, the eternal tragedy of submission, of their own eternal disgrace and misfortune, . . . shrinking it to the simple stridency of bedlam" (*Old Rosa* 51)]. For Arturo, the role of the *loca* is tantamount to slavery. He nevertheless decides that if he is to endure in the camp and eventually escape, he must appear like the *locas* while cultivating an inner superiority. He is therefore trapped in a dualistic vision that pits the individual against the world, believing that only his life has value because he alone is conscious of the magnitude of his plight.

The further manifestations of the other are "los otros" [the others], the guards within the prison, and "los demás" [the rest], those on the outside with whom Arturo has virtually no contact. "Los otros" are epitomized by a solitary soldier who watches Arturo chop sugarcane: "el soldado, impasible, sobrio, seguro, superior, allí plantado al parecer para la eternidad, sin dejar de observar y de vigilar, de vigilarlo a él, a Arturo, se rascaba lentamente los cojones" (16-17) ["the soldier stood impassive, sober, self-assured, superior, planted there stiff and straight, to all appearances for all eternity, and eternally watching, always watching, keeping his eyes fixed on him, on Arturo, and slowly scratching his balls" (54)]. Here, the gaze is specifically conflated with a gesture of masculinity. Its most immediate and most profound effect is the enslavement of praxis, and through it Arturo the *loca* becomes Arturo the chopper of sugarcane:

> seguía repitiendo, como inconsciente, instintivamente, como para nadie, como sin ninguna intención o finalidad, el ineludible ademán, y los pies [de Arturo] en el torbellino, crujiendo, y el sol reverberando sobre la plantación, y el golpe seco de su guámpara, de todas las guámparas, abriendo, cortando, mientras el sudor rodaba por el cuerpo.
>
> (17)

> [[he] kept on, kept on, as though unconsciously, as though instinctively, as though for no one, really, as though with no real reason or intention, kept on scratching his balls, making that inescapable, undeniable gesture, and Arturo's feet in a whirlwind, crunching, the sun overhead beating down, making the canefield shimmer, the dry harsh chop of his blade, all the blades, all across the field, chopping, chopping, as the sweat poured down his body.
>
> (55)

In a sense Arturo appears in this scene as masculine, brandishing the phallic blade and conquering and destroying the canefield. But his action is executed in obeyance to the masculine gesture of the soldier—even if this gesture is itself determined by social and economic forces beyond the soldier's own understanding. The upshot is that masculinity functions not to passivize the other but to control the other's labor. Femininity, in contrast, becomes synonymous with alienated labor itself.

Though Arturo has been imprisoned for being gay, he and his fellow inmates are pressured to maintain and actually develop their identities as *locas.* They typically engage in "fiestas prohibidas y perseguidas por los soldados que participaban en las mismas como entusiastas espectadores" (19) ["forbidden parties (which were in fact always discovered by the soldiers, who participated in them as the most enthusiastic spectators)" (56)]. Afterwards, Arturo is solicited by the soldier who watches him work. The two go into the canefields, where Arturo "se dedicaba minuciosamente a provocarle el placer, . . . aún cuando sentía la violencia y el goce de aquel cuerpo desahogándose en su cuerpo" (19-20) ["would painstakingly dedicate himself to producing pleasure," even when feeling "the violence and the delight of that body spending itself on his body" (56)]. In this moment the gaze of the soldier is reconfigured as an act of physical penetration on the very site of Arturo's forced labor, and the production of sugar for the regime gives way to the production of the macho's pleasure. As in the case of Manzano nearly a century and a half earlier, homoerotic violence is thus a fundamental means through which the laborer is embodied as such.

Arturo produces not only the macho's sexual pleasure but an alternate reality of dreams, and gradually he begins to conjure forth an ideal lover to replace the soldier who, "con un resoplido" (21) ["with . . . a grunt" (57)], abandons him in the field. He is haunted, however, by his memory of a hostile and threatening male world. He recalls his discovery of the dynamics of male-male sexuality in a public library, where he was once spotted by "un grupo de maricas jóvenes, siempre como en actitud de alerta, que en cuanto lo vieron quisieron captarlo" (24) ["a group of young gay men, always on the alert, and the moment they caught sight of him they wanted to capture him" (59)]. From the perspective of Arturo, sexual relations between males, both inside and outside of prison, are characterized by an inherently violent subject/object dichotomy, and any recognition of his homoerotic desire would be an act of submission to the aggression of the other. As a gay youth, he felt continually reduced to the status of an object—either through sex or through the moral opprobrium of society as a whole. Eventually, he identifies the source of his suffering as his mother, who prior to his incarceration attempted to kill him when she found him in bed with another man.[6] Whereas the soldier is the agent of physical violation, Arturo regards his mother and femininity in general as a culprit (rather than victim) of patriarchy. Indeed, as Carmelo Esterrich rightly notes: "el pájaro areniano es . . . homofóbico y misógino" (189) [Arenas's queer is . . . homophobic and misogynist].

Although Arturo at first spends his few free moments participating in the revelries of the *locas,* he quickly starts writing, initially not to escape but to record for posterity the abuses of the camp: "él se iba a rebelar, dando testimonios de todo el horror, comunicándole a alguien, a muchos, al mundo, o aunque fuese a una sola persona que aún conservara incorruptible su capacidad de pensar, la realidad" (43) ["he was going to rebel, he was going to testify to the horror, tell someone, lots of people, tell the world, or tell even just one person, as long as there was one person who still had an uncorrupted, incorruptible capacity to think, he would leave this reality with that one person" (72)]. His work takes on an urgency, and he begins to fill every scrap of paper he can possibly find. Unable to keep a diary—in his world, life-writing is viewed as a remnant of bourgeois individualism and branded "cosas de maricones" (44) ["pansy-ass bullshit" (72)]—he is obliged to place his mark within the official spaces of the regime, such as the margins and blank pages of Marxist-Leninist manuals and textbooks and on political posters. His writing is cramped and at first glance indecipherable, but it progressively permeates the entire camp. Yet strangely enough no one seems to see it, as if it were stillborn, or forever disappearing like a mirage on the background of more powerful discourses.

Arturo's death is prefigured through the drowning of a young *loca* named Celeste, whose bloated face comes to haunt him in his reveries and obstructs his plans for escape. Not only is his flight checked from within, but the material things of his milieu, "agresivas, fijas, intolerables, pero reales" (61) ["aggressive, fixed, unyielding, unbearable, but *real*" (83)], lead him to the realization that escape is impossible. It is then, in the midst of his despair, that he hears someone singing outside his cell, and when he looks through the window he catches sight of a beautiful youth directing an invisible orchestra. This music is the counterpoint to a concert he heard on the evening of his arrest, and the angelic body of the youth is the transposition in the imaginary of the menacing figure of the soldier. The scene thus marks the beginning of the final effort of Arturo to transcend his imprisonment and save himself from death.

To effect the return of the divine apparition, Arturo must imagine a setting worthy of receiving him: an ideal realm for an ideal inhabitant. He blames himself for being unable to hold him, and decides that nothing short of a sumptuous palace will suffice to entice him back. As on so many previous occasions, reality throws obstacles in his path, preventing the realization of the *locus amenus*. He pleads with God for assistance but concludes that God no longer exists and that he himself must become the God of creation. Finally, in a supreme moment of rebellion, he throws down his machete and begins running through the canefields. This decisive act threatens to crack open and topple the structure of his world, and the authorities immediately set about closing the fissure. They ransack his meager belongings and discover that unbeknown to them he has indeed been writing all along: "mira lo que escribe, contrarrevolución, contrarrevolución descarada" (76) ["look at this, look what he's written here—counterrevolution, open, bald-faced, brass-balled, faggot counterrevolution" (93)]. They then stumble upon words they have never read and whose meaning dumbfounds them: "*un aterido lo-fo-ro-ro, ¿lofororo?, ¡qué coño es esto!, qué cantidad de sandeces y boberías, qué verborrea, qué palabras tan raras . . . efectivamente, dice [el teniente], ahora sí que lo hemos agarrado con la gorda*" (76-77) ["*a half-frozen pter-o-dac-tyl*—'Pterodactyl! What the fuck is that! Have you ever heard such nonsense, such gobbledygook, can you believe this gibberish! I never saw such words . . . so it's true,' he (the lieutenant) says, 'we've hit the jackpot'" (94)].

Though the writing of Arturo attacks the regime of which he is a victim, the lieutenant refuses to consider him an enemy because of the femininity he has been made to incarnate: "para él, en el fondo, sólo existe un enemigo, el que tiene un arma y combate, los demás, piensa, son sólo maricones, como éste, y no tumban a ningún gobierno" (77) ["as far as he's concerned, there's basically just one enemy, a man with a gun who wants to fight, and everybody else, he thinks, the rest of 'em, he thinks, are just faggots like this guy, they're not going to overthrow any government" (94)]. An enemy is therefore potentially an equal, someone capable of dominating someone else, but a *loca,* because of the particular sexual identity conferred on him, is always at the bottom of the pecking order: "los humillados por todos, los que ya no podían humillar a nadie porque allí terminaba la escala de las humillaciones" (55) ["those who were humiliated by Everyone and could humiliate no one because the scale of humiliations stopped there" (79)]. It is to keep intact this "orden rigurosamente preconcebido, legalizado, [y] respetado" (55) ["strictly preconceived and preordained, legalized, and—like it or not—respected hierarchy" (79)] that the lieutenant and his men set out to capture Arturo. The masculine heterosexual (the "new man" who suddenly looks not so new, after all) is thereby affirmed only insofar as he posits the feminine homosexual as his negative contrary and effectively oppresses him. In the context of **Arturo, la estrella más brillante,** however, the project of the former is itself subsumed within the economic demands of the nation. Arturo must be caught and recast as a *loca*. But more important than that, he must return to the canefields and work.

Arturo flees into the forest surrounding the camp. As he runs, he imagines a palace-setting for the angelic youth. In narrativizing this ideal world he is filled with the "delirio de la construcción" (81) ["delirium of creation" (97)] and the power to break with that "figura tenebrosa, encorvada, pobre, asustada y esclavizada que había sido él" (81) ["stooped, poor, scared, tired, enslaved figure which he had been" (97)]. As he proceeds, he hears the sound of running feet and noises, but he does not, or chooses not, to identify them with his pursuers. Eventually, they begin to take form before his eyes as a troop of angels, but "empapados de sudor, agitados y rabiosos, [porque] habían corrido por más de cuatro horas buscando a aquel maricón desertor" (89-90) ["angry and dripping with sweat, for they had been running for more than four hours, trying to catch that faggot deserter" (102)]. All of a sudden the figure leading the procession becomes his mother, Rosa. Then the divine youth appears among the soldiers with rifle in hand, shouting "maricón" [faggot] and ordering him to surrender. Arturo, however, lunges toward the horizon, stumbling over the startled *lofororo* of his creation, until he is at last shot down and killed.

Not only is Arturo's past (his childhood with his mother and adulthood with other men) inescapable; the means of salvation, the divine youth, and indeed all his fantasies and dreams are but the internalization of his social milieu. He thinks that after drawing the ideal other into himself he will transcend the world. Yet he is undermined from within. To the extent that he does create an imaginary world, he merely serves as the accomplice to the designs of his oppressors. His rebellion thus short-circuits. His world (both real and imaginary) is a minefield and everything in his path a booby trap.

Yet this is not all. The *lofororo* remains, as Arturo himself understood, half-frozen and in a daze. The *lofororo,* or *lofóforo,* is not a pterodactyl, as the English translation of the text indicates, but a genus of pheasant originating in southern Asia and characterized by a large and colorful crest. As such, it points to the transformation of the degraded *loca,* or *pájaro* [bird] (a further slang designation for the gay male), into a new and splendid creature. It does not take wing, but neither does it disappear. It simply watches and waits. What is significant is that the soldiers are unable to see the *lofororo* or understand its name when written. For this reason, something eludes the overarching hegemony, if only in potential.

In the end, nevertheless, the Arenas text posits Cuba as a closed and fixed geographical, economic, and sexual space that cannot, at least at his moment in history, be either reordered or transcended. Arturo imagines a certain dignity, but when all is said and done dignity is granted from without, not from within. He is constituted as the expendable other and enslaved. What is more, his homoerotic desire, expressed through his fantasy of the ideal youth, is incapable of articulating itself independently of the dynamics of domination and subordination implicit in the ostensibly egalitarian ideology of the "new man." Any positive gay reciprocity is therefore an impossibility: Arturo dies, and his fellow queerbirds remain encaged with their wings tied.

LIFE BEFORE NIGHTFALL

In *Arturo, la estrella más brillante,* which was published shortly after Arenas's arrival in the United States, the active/passive dichotomy of male-male sex is rigorously enforced through the brutal dictates of prison terror. In *Antes que anochezca,* in contrast, Arenas reveals an ambivalent attitude toward male-male sex that undoubtedly results from his Cuban American, cross-cultural experience. *Antes que anochezca* was published in 1992, two years after Arenas ended a protracted battle against AIDS by committing suicide. (Julian Schnabel subsequently directed a film version, titled ***Before Night Falls.***) In this text Arenas gives an eyewitness account of the historic upheavals of the Castro Revolution, the Mariel exodus, and the Cuban diaspora, focusing largely on his sexuality while reflecting on the general question of sexual identity both in the context of the island and the United States. He further writes as a person with AIDS, adding his voice not only to the corpus of gay Latin American writing but to the international community of AIDS writers.[7]

In *Antes que anochezca* Arenas ceases to engage in the textual experimentation of much of his earlier writing and assumes a more conventional autobiographical discourse that presupposes both the autonomy of the self and the referentiality of language. In his rush to finish "before night falls," he thus remains impervious to the deconstruction of autobiography undertaken by theoreticians of the genre usually far removed from either the AIDS ward or the forced-labor camps of his youth. *Antes que anochezca* is in fact characterized by an explicitness that some reviewers have found offensive.[8] In it, Arenas responds to the mandate of his friend and mentor, José Lezama Lima, whose words affirm his own belief in the power of language to transcend the contingent: "Recuerda que la única salvación que tenemos es por la palabra; escribe" (254) ["Remember that our only salvation lies in words: Write!" (230)].[9]

The AIDS testimony of *Antes que anochezca,* which is limited solely to the prologue and epilogue, frames Arenas's life as a writer, political dissenter, and gay male. In the introductory pages he indicates that he first undertook the composition of his autobiography while hiding from police in a Havana park, writing hurriedly before the sun set and darkness fell. This event is detailed in the middle of his life-history in a moment of extreme desperation (he has fled arrest and is soon to be reapprehended and incarcerated), and is recast at the beginning and at the end of his life in the context of AIDS: "Ahora la noche avanzaba de nuevo en forma más inminente. Era la noche de la muerte. Ahora sí que tenía que terminar mi autobiografía antes de que anocheciera" (11) ["Now darkness was approaching again, only more insidiously. It was the dark night of death. I really had to finish my memoirs before nightfall" (xii)]. As a person with AIDS, Arenas documents the scandalous treatment of the uninsured within the American medical system as well as his own hospital experience and the various stages of his illness—Pneumocystis carinii pneumonia, Kaposi's sarcoma, phlebitis, and toxoplasmosis. Upon returning home after his first hospital confinement he discovers that someone has left rat poison on his night table for him to use to kill himself. At this point, however, he is determined to live. He stands before a photograph of the deceased poet Virgilio Piñera, the Cuban writer he most esteems and whose friendship he most values, and pleads for a reprieve of three years to complete his work. His wish is seemingly miraculously granted, but because he is too ill to write, he is obliged to record his autobiography on cassettes which a friend later transcribes. Like Nandino's, his "life" is thus an oral endeavor.

In reflecting on his illness, Arenas abandons the seemingly rigid social determinism of *Arturo, la estrella más brillante.* In so doing he establishes a nature/culture dichotomy that pits homoeroticism, as a natural force of resistance, against the oppressive constructs of society, among which he includes AIDS. Nature, he believes, is subversive, but also fragile and vulnerable. AIDS, in contrast, is so powerful that he cannot help but wonder if it were artificially generated in a maleficent scheme of human destruction. Through AIDS, Arenas establishes solidarity with a wide range of marginal peoples. Moreover, he makes the person with AIDS the prototypical human, inherently life-affirming and resistant to a deadening, unnatural ideology (be it the heterosexism of the Castro regime or the criminal negligence of the American free-market system), but mortally threatened by an affliction that in the final analysis works merely to maintain the privilege of the powerful.

Within the AIDS frame of *Antes que anochezca* Arenas narrates his life chronologically, starting with his childhood in rural Cuba in the early 1940s. As a youngster he felt integrated within his natural milieu but alienated from his family and in particular his mother, who saw him as a constant reminder of her failed relationship with his father and of her status as an "abandoned woman" obliged to return to the home of her parents. Not only did she remain distant and aloof, refusing Arenas the warmth and tenderness he desired, but he sees her influence on his sexual development as decidedly negative. This becomes apparent in his recollection of his first sexual encounter with his cousin Orlando. Motivated by childish curiosity, the two boys are led to what Arenas calls a "penetración recíproca" (29) ["mutual penetration" (11)]. At the same time Arenas is filled with tremendous guilt. He writes: "yo pensaba en mi madre, en todo aquello que ella durante tantos años jamás había hecho con un hombre y yo hacía allí mismo, en la arboleda, al alcance de su voz que ya me llamaba para comer" (29) ["I was thinking of my mother, and of all the things that during all those years she never did with a man, which I was doing right there in the bushes within earshot of her voice, already calling me for dinner" (12)]. To a certain degree his guilt results from the shame and responsibility he has been made to feel for his mother's abandonment. But it is also, despite his emphasis on the naturalness of sex, the socially constructed guilt of the gay male within heterosexual society. What Arenas hears is precisely the voice of the heterosexual other, extending beyond the house to the garden and woods, penetrating the natural world of his childhood sexuality, and literally catching him in a discourse whose meaning he does not yet fully understand but which will be clarified to him within a few short years.

Arenas's transition from childhood to adolescence occurs when his grandfather sells their farm and moves the family to the provincial town of Holguín. In Holguín, Arenas discovers the institutionalization of

sexuality. Whereas in the countryside sex is ubiquitous, in the urban setting it is segregated in certain spaces, chief of which is the house of prostitution. Arenas is attracted to a young friend, Carlos, who takes him to the local brothel and pairs him off with a prostitute named Lolín: "Recuerdo que lo hicimos a la luz de un quinqué y recordé a mi madre en el campo; yo estaba nervioso y no se me paraba, pero Lolín se las arregló de tal modo que, finalmente, me erotizé. ¿O fui yo el que me las arreglé pensando en el rostro de Carlos, que me esperaba afuera?" (59) ["We did it by the light of a kerosene lamp, and I remembered my mother in the country. I was nervous and could not get an erection, but Lolín was so adept that she finally got me aroused. Or rather, was it my thinking of Carlos's face while he waited for me outside?" (36)]. This episode stands in sharp contrast to the spontaneous encounter with Orlando. Here, Arenas experiences the alienation of his homoerotic desire in heterosexual intercourse. In the process sex becomes an act of performance for the heterosexual other, appearing first in the memory of his mother and eventually in the face of Carlos himself. Carlos in fact functions as the object of Arenas's desire as well as an internalized heterosexual gaze under whose surveillance his desire is appropriated and reconstituted.

In contrast to the supposed pansexuality of the country, gay and straight sexualities are explicitly differentiated in the city. Already cognizant of his homoerotic desire, Arenas attempts to conceal it by feigning an attraction for the girls in his school. Yet he is stopped short in his tracks when another student turns to him in class one day and utters the following: "Mira, Reinaldo, tú eres pájaro. ¿Tú sabes lo que es un pájaro? Es un hombre al que le gustan los otros hombres. Pájaro; eso es lo que tú eres" (61) ["Look, Reinaldo, you are a faggot. Do you know what a faggot is? It's a man who likes other men. A faggot, that's what you are" (38)]. Ultimately, then, it is the heterosexual who identifies and articulates the meaning of homosexuality. The upshot is that though in Arenas's world homoerotic desire might appear natural, its significance is socially constructed.

In his first job Arenas works on a farm as an agricultural accountant, returning on weekends to his family's home in Holguín. Once while on the bus he meets a young man named Raúl. Raúl becomes his first lover, often taking him to a gay bar in Holguín (which was soon to disappear along with the rest on the island) and to a hotel. The young Arenas falls in love with Raúl, but the latter sees him merely as a diversion and ends their relationship. In retrospect Arenas views this outcome as inevitable, and although at the time he wants a permanent lover, he comes to believe that lasting relationships between gay men are impossible: "[No] creo que pueda ser posible, por lo menos en el mundo homosexual. El mundo homosexual no es monogámico; casi por naturaleza, por instinto, se tiende a la dispersión, a los amores múltiples, a la promiscuidad muchas veces" (90) ["I do not think this is possible, at least not in the gay world. The gay world is not monogamous. Almost by nature, by instinct, the tendency is to spread out to multiple relationships, quite often to promiscuity" (64-65)]. Arenas invokes nature in an effort to support this interpretation of gay relationships. Yet it is difficult within the context of his youthful sexuality to distinguish between the over-determinism of nature and that of culture. Monogamy is of course socially constructed, but in Cuban society as elsewhere institutionalized heterosexism hampers the realization of monogamous, long-term gay relationships, dispersing not only homoerotic desire but any social or political solidarity between gays and lesbians. His use of the word "promiscuity," moreover, inscribes a heterosexist bias; and when he relates it to homosexual nature, he inadvertently reaffirms the culture that alienates him. His comments thus reveal the danger of naturalizing homosexuality and attempting to justify it in terms originally intended to condemn it.

REFLECTIONS ON SEXUALITY

At this point in the text, after discovering the "meaning" of his sexuality, Arenas assesses what he considers to be the various types of gay males in Cuban society. He identifies four categories: the "loca de argolla" ["dog collar gay"], the "loca común" ["common gay"], the "loca tapada" ["closet gay"], and the "loca regia" ["royal gay"]. The "loca de argolla" is openly gay and is arrested for having sex in public. His shackle symbolizes his sexuality as identified and interpreted within society: "El sistema lo había provisto, según yo veía, de una argolla que llevaba permanentemente al cuello; la policía le tiraba una especie de garfio y era conducido así a los campos de trabajo forzado" (103) ["As I saw it, the system had provided him with a permanent 'collar' around his neck. All the police had to do was hook him by the collar and take him to one of the forced-labor camps" (77)]. In contrast, the "loca común" expresses his sexuality among his friends but remains sexually identifiable solely within the private sphere. The "loca tapada," on the other hand, is closeted and often antigay. Unlike the previous three, the "loca regia" occupies a privileged position within the regime and manages to live conspicuously without compromising his status. Arenas describes the "loca regia" as a unique phenomenon of communist societies, although one can find examples of his capitalist counterpart in such figures as Roy Cohn and J. Edgar Hoover. The social condition of the Cuban gay-male is therefore determined by two factors: the degree to which his sexuality is made public, and his political status within the public sphere.

Arenas conceives of gay-male sexuality within a rigorous masculine/feminine binary opposition. In describing the "loca común," he writes: "Las relaciones de estas locas comunes, generalmente, son con otras locas y nunca llegan a conocer a un *hombre verdadero*" (103; emphasis added) ["Common gays generally have relations with other gays and never get to know a *real man*" (78; emphasis added)]. Here, the "real man" is the one who penetrates either a man or a woman. Despite the antipathy toward *locas* expressed in **Arturo, la estrella más brillante,** Arenas views himself not as a "real man" but as inherently feminine, and for this reason capable of sexual satisfaction solely with his masculine contrary. After arriving in the United States he encounters a gay community of presumed sexual equals that strikes him as both strange and monotonous.

> al llegar al exilio, he visto que las relaciones sexuales pueden ser tediosas e insatisfechas. . . . [L]a loca se reúne con la loca y todo el mundo hace de todo. . . . ¿Cómo puede haber satisfacción así? Si, precisamente, lo que uno busca es su contrario. . . . Aquí . . . es muy difícil para un homosexual encontrar un hombre; es decir, el verdadero objeto de su deseo.
>
> (132)

> [in exile, I found that sexual relations can be tedious and unrewarding. . . . The queer gets together with the queer and everybody does everything. . . . How can that bring any satisfaction? What we are really looking for is our opposite. . . . [H]ere . . . it is very difficult for a homosexual to find a man, that is, the real object of his desire.]
>
> (106-7)[10]

Arenas attempts to define the supposedly "real men" with whom he had sexual relations in Cuba, but a difficulty arises when he applies both Cuban and Anglo-American sexual designations to male sexuality on the island: "No sé cómo llamar a aquellos jóvenes cubanos de entonces; no sé si bugarrones o bisexuales" (132) ["I do not know what to call the young Cuban men of those days, whether homosexuals who played the male role or bisexuals" (107)]. This uncertainty is a function of Arenas's exile. Though he is unable to accept the Anglo-American model of sexual identity as his own, he gradually comes to doubt the universality of Latino-Cuban sexual categories.

According to Arenas, the Anglo-American gay-male community is unified not along an axis of masculinity and femininity but as a collectivity of inherently feminine men (*locas* rather than "real men") standing in opposition to the dominant heterosexual society. In Cuba, however, the *locas* interact with "real men" and are at least ostensibly less marginalized than their North American counterparts. Arenas believes that though something has been lost through the formation of the Anglo-American gay community, something has also been gained: namely, gay militancy.[11] But he chooses to retain his Latino-Cuban conception of sexuality and ultimately disparages the Anglo-American model: "el mundo homosexual actual es algo siniestro y desolado; porque casi nunca se encuentra lo deseado" (133) ["the homosexual world is now something sinister and desolate; we almost never get what we most desire" (108)]. For Epps, this amounts to a nostalgia for oppositionality (270). Indeed, Epps goes so far as to conclude that in the case of Arenas "the logic of opposition [*is*] the logic of desire itself" (271).

Whereas in the prison setting of *Arturo, la estrella más brillante* the active/passive roles are violently hierarchized, Arenas in fact regards freely chosen sexual relations between men as an act of solidarity and rebellion against the machismo of the Cuban political regime: "El placer realizado entre dos hombres era una especie de conspiración" (131) ["Sexual pleasure between two men was a conspiracy" (105)]. He further asserts that male-male sexual activity increased after the triumph of Castro:

> Casi todos aquellos jóvenes que desfilaban ante la Plaza de la Revolución aplaudiendo a Fidel Castro, casi todos aquellos soldados que, rifle en mano, marchaban con aquellas caras marciales, después de los desfiles, iban a acurrucarse en nuestros cuartos y, allí, desnudos, mostraban su autenticidad y a veces una ternura y una manera de gozar que me ha sido difícil encontrar en cualquier otro lugar del mundo.
>
> (131)

> [Many of the young men who marched in Revolutionary Square applauding Fidel Castro, and many of the soldiers who marched, rifle in hand and with martial expressions, came to our rooms after the parades to cuddle up naked, and show their real selves, sometimes revealing a tenderness and true enjoyment such as I have not been able to find again anywhere else in the world.]
>
> (105)

In this passage Arenas establishes reciprocity not only with the "passive" male (the referent of the possessive adjective "nuestros" ["our"]) but also with the "active" participant who reveals (in consensual sex, at any rate) an extraordinary tenderness. This tenderness functions to deflate machismo, which for Arenas is the linchpin of power. It is for this reason that homoeroticism might be seen as a threat to any regime of masculinist terror, whether of the left (the Cuba of Arenas) or the right (the Argentina of Puig as evinced in *El beso de la mujer araña*).

WRITING IN A DARK NIGHT

Arenas's autobiography, imbued with a sense of loss and desolation resulting from exile and impending death, alternates between reflections on gay sexuality and the Castro regime. Arenas contends that Cuban society becomes increasingly Stalinized in the wake of the Soviet invasion of Czechoslovakia and that as a

consequence numerous dissenters are conscripted to work in the canefields as part of a government effort to boost sugar production. In 1970 he himself is sent to a plantation in the western province of Pinar del Río. When he arrives, he identifies with the former Indians and African slaves who, as he writes, often preferred suicide to a prolonged and agonizing death toiling in the canefields: "Ahora yo era el indio, yo era el negro esclavo; pero no era yo solo; lo eran aquellos cientos de reclutas que estaban a mi lado" (154) ["Now I was the Indian, I was the black slave, and I was not alone. I was one among hundreds of recruits" (129)]. It is in the prison atmosphere of the sugar plantation that Arenas actually commences his own work as a life-writer. Although he does not undertake the actual autobiographical project until his arrest several years later, he begins at this time to keep a diary during his few free moments. In so doing he aims to maintain his own integrity under dehumanizing conditions and, like Arturo, to record the experiences of his fellow "slaves" by exposing their plight to the world.

After a failed harvest, Arenas is allowed to return to Havana, where he witnesses what for him and the other young writers of his generation is the culminating event in the entire process of Cuban Stalinization: the "Padilla Affair." One of Cuba's leading writers and intellectuals, Heberto Padilla, is forced to undergo "rehabilitation" by publicly recanting his supposedly counterrevolutionary views and denouncing many of his fellow writers. For Arenas this is the beginning of the "dark night" of Cuban intellectual life. It also marks the nadir of Cuban gays who, he argues, are persecuted with even greater fervor than before: "cada escritor, cada artista, cada dramaturgo homosexual, recibía un telegrama en el que se le decía que no reunía los parámetros políticos y morales para desempeñar el cargo que ocupaba y, por tanto, era dejado sin empleo o se le ofertaba otro en un campo de trabajos forzados" (164) ["every gay writer, every gay artist, every gay dramatist, received a telegram telling him that his behavior did not fall within the political and moral parameters necessary for his job, and that he was therefore either terminated or offered another job in the forced-labor camps" (138)].[12]

Arenas is eventually arrested, ostensibly for committing illegal sexual acts but in fact on account of his denunciation of the government through writings smuggled out of the country by friends and published abroad. After undertaking a dramatic escape from the police,[13] he is reapprehended and sent to El Morro prison, one of the worst on the island, where, with the exception of a small contingent of political prisoners, the majority of inmates are hardened criminals. The prisoners are isolated within impenetrable, dungeonlike walls and denied contact with the natural world surrounding them. What is more, though they inhabit a common space, they are completely atomized. Having internalized the institutional violence of which they are all victims, they relate to each other solely through the dynamics of domination and subordination. The primary idiom of this negative reciprocity is sex, which Arenas avoids at all cost. Arenas believes that outside of prison, sex can be experienced in a truly private space and in the process become an act of resistance against oppression. But in prison, sex is reconstituted according to the dictates of a brutal and dehumanizing system which it ultimately supports.

Arenas is falsely identified as a murderer and rapist rather than a political prisoner or simply a writer, and for this reason he is assigned to a section for common criminals.[14] He quickly becomes aware of his luck in not being relegated to the sections for gays, the worst in the entire prison. Men who are perceived as gay and/or effeminate are treated more ruthlessly than straight inmates and are subject to the harshest conditions, though they too have been indoctrinated into the regime of violence. When young straight prisoners are raped, for example, they often falsely identify themselves as gay in order to be separated from their tormentors and placed in the sections for gays. But the latter resent them and frequently perpetrate even greater acts of violence against them. The gay men attack not only the hapless young rape victims but each other as well, using sticks covered with razor blades. The guards do nothing to stop these fights, and indeed encourage them.

In spite of their cruelty (and his own effort to disassociate himself from them), Arenas discerns in the gay prisoners a certain authenticity and daring that results from their position at the bottom of the prison hierarchy. On the days they are permitted to walk in the sun, they typically don flamboyant outfits made from scraps of material and rags. Yet the guards often retaliate by denying them these few precious moments in the sun when they can look at the sea and the city and, more important, kill their body lice. According to Arenas the guards in fact vent their greatest rage and violence against the gay inmates.

Arenas is subsequently transferred for questioning to the Villa Marista, the site of government interrogations and, as he testifies, torture. After a three-month detention he agrees to sign a general confession in which he admits being both a homosexual and counterrevolutionary. In essence he repudiates everything he has ever written and rejects his whole past. The effects of the confession are catastrophic:

> eso solamente prueba mi cobardía; mi debilidad, la certeza de que no tengo madera de héroe y de que el miedo, en mi caso, está por encima de mis principios morales. . . . Antes de la confesión yo tenía una gran compañía; mi orgullo. Después de la confesión no tenía nada ya; había perdido mi dignidad y mi rebeldía.
>
> (229, 231)

> [this only proves my cowardice, my weakness, the certainty that I am not the stuff of which heroes are made, and that fear, in my case, had won over moral principles. . . . Before my confession I had a great companion, my pride. After the confession I had nothing; I had lost my dignity and my rebellious spirit.]
>
> (204, 207)

In its thrust such a confession is diametrically opposed to traditional autobiography to the extent that it is a lie inflicted upon the writing subject by the demands of an alien other rather than the truth as elucidated by the former. For this reason the entire autobiographical project of **Antes que anochezca** can be read as a renunciation of the forced confession in the Villa Marista and by extension of the life imposed on Arenas from without. Yet the moment of confession lingers on in his memory as a double defeat: not only is he robbed, at least temporarily, of his identity as a gay, dissident writer, but he is made to feel responsible for the loss. In the process the dual acts of sex and writing are coopted by the regime, and henceforth he is expected to live either as a celibate or heterosexual and to write in support of the official politics of the government.[15]

After his release from prison Arenas is ostracized from mainstream intellectual and cultural circles and made to suffer the internal exile of a pariah until he at last flees the island in the Mariel boat lift of 1980. Through an ironic twist of fate it is as a gay male that he achieves his freedom. Up to this point the state has not only sponsored a systematic persecution of gay men but through the labor camps has actually enslaved them.[16] Now the government decides to expel gay men from Cuban society altogether. One day near the door to his room Arenas discovers a sign with the words: "QUE SE VAYAN LOS HOMOSEXUALES, QUE SE VAYA LA ESCORIA" (301) ["HOMOSEXUALS, GET OUT; SCUM OF THE EARTH, GET OUT" (280)]. Arenas capitalizes on this antigay sentiment and petitions to emigrate. But to acquire an exit visa he must identify himself specifically as a "passive" homosexual. Whereas the *activo* is a "real man" and as such capable of being included within the body politic of socialist "new men," the *pasivo* is determined to possess an immutable essence of femininity that places him beyond social redemption. With both bitterness and humor Arenas notes that the officials in charge of his case are completely unaware of his international reputation as a dissident writer, and that as a result of their ignorance of literature, coupled with the fact that little of his work has been published in Cuba, he in the end leaves the country "como una loca más" (302) ["as just another queer" (282)].

DREAMING IN THE AGE OF AIDS

The exhilaration experienced by Arenas during his first years in New York[17] is gradually overshadowed by the grim reality of disease, and he comes to interpret the deaths of his friends Emir Rodríguez Monegal to cancer and Jorge Ronet to AIDS as a prelude to his own demise. One night the glass of water next to his bed mysteriously explodes, and after learning of his AIDS diagnosis, he reads this as the beginning of the end of his extraordinary luck at surviving disease, physical assault, prison, and hunger. During his illness he has two strange dreams that crystallize his vision of the gay male in heterosexual society. In one he is able to fly: "soñé una vez que podía volar, privilegio imposible para un ser humano, aun cuando a los homosexuales nos digan pájaros. Pero yo estaba ahora en Cuba y volaba sobre los palmares; era fácil, sólo había que pensar que uno podía volar" (337) ["I once dreamed I could fly, a privilege not granted to humans, even though we gays are called *pájaros* [birds]. But I was in Cuba, flying over the palm trees; it was easy, you only had to believe you could do it" (313)].[18] This is a dream of freedom and the illusion of many persecuted life-writers: that one might, through an act of volition, escape oppression and become the author of one's own life. It is followed by a nightmare of radical determinism.

> Estaba en un inmenso urinario lleno de excrementos y tenía que dormir allí. En aquel lugar había centenares de pájaros raros que se movían con gran dificultad. Aquel lugar se poblaba cada vez más por aquellos horribles pájaros, que iban cerrando la posibilidad de escapatoria; todo el horizonte quedaba sellado por aquellos pájaros que tenían algo de metálicos y hacían un ruido sordo, como de alarmas. De pronto, descubría que todos ellos habían logrado meterse en mi cabeza y que mi cerebro se agigantaba para darles albergue; mientras ellos iban albergándose en mi cabeza, yo envejecía.
>
> (337)

> [I was in a very large bathroom full of excrement and had to sleep there. Surrounding me were hundreds of rare birds that moved about with great difficulty. More and more of those awful birds kept coming, gradually closing all possibility of escape; the entire horizon was full of birds; they had something metallic about them, and made a dull noise; they sounded like buzzing alarms. Suddenly I realized that all those birds had managed to get into my head, and that my brain was swelling to accommodate them. As they entered my head, I grew old.]
>
> (313)

These dreams differ from the emancipatory fantasy of Manzano, since in the first Arenas flies alone, whereas in the second his flight is obstructed by a bevy of fellow "queer-birds," who sabotage his quest for freedom by literally filling his head with their noise and then themselves. This noise, which they have come to incarnate in the flesh, is but an echo of the ideology of machismo. Its "truth" is that the feminine gay-male is not only the negative contrary of the "real man" (whether of the new socialist variety or simply the old *chingón* of Paz), but ultimately nothingness. Like Arturo, Arenas

is undone in this dream by his own ineluctable identity ("Mira, Reinaldo, tú eres pájaro"), and as a result slowly annihilated. The upshot is that male homosexuality = femininity = death.

For Arenas, the gay condition thus seems paradoxically both free and enslaved. Although this contradiction is left unresolved, the dream of freedom occurs first and, in keeping with the logic of Arenas's life-history, takes precedence over the second. It is the given, like the natural world of his early childhood in rural Cuba. Freedom is subsequently apprehended by the discourse of the other (the voice of the mother, the pronouncement of the classmate, the ideology of the regime, the sign on the door, the noise of the birds), and locked in a cage (the home, the school, the sugar plantation, the prison, communist Cuba, the New York AIDS ward, the public toilet). And yet, despite an ever-increasing assault, freedom for Arenas is never thoroughly conquered.

Though Arenas might imagine sex between men as an act of conspiracy, he in reality establishes little solidarity with gay or feminine-identified men, and at the end of the autobiography he stands in solitary opposition to what for him is the quintessence of heterosexual masculinity and the embodiment of the "new man," Castro. In his suicide note, which functions as the epilogue to *Antes que anochezca,* he identifies Castro as the source of his suffering and blames him explicitly for his disease and impending death, for had Castro not created the intolerable conditions that led to his exile, he would never have contracted AIDS. Of course, had Arenas stayed in Cuba he might still have been infected, and even in spite of Castro he would have experienced the inner exile of the gay-male within straight society. Yet regardless of the seemingly intractable oppositionality of his autobiographical persona, he envisions an eventual emancipation, and in the moment prior to death actually declares himself free: "Cuba será libre. Yo ya lo soy" (343) ["Cuba will be free. I already am" (317)].

This final statement is significant, for strictly speaking it is not suicide that liberates him but an action undertaken prior to the deed. From his perspective, freedom is achieved precisely through the writing of the autobiography, and upon completion, as he concludes his work, he finds himself whole at last after his long exile. Through his autobiography Arenas believes that he has reappropriated his life and that it is literally his to "take." Ultimately, he affirms the preeminence of the self over the other, of consciousness over the text, and of freedom over determinism. In the context of AIDS, these choices function to endow him with the metaphysical proportions of the hero of the absurd.

Notes

1. There is, of course, a tendency in mainstream North American media to represent lesbians and

gay men as economically privileged. In part this results from observations of the lives of a small coterie of highly visible gay men, but it is also symptomatic of a more general effort of the right to downplay the economic significance of the gay-rights movement. As Nicola Field writes, "most lesbians and gays are obviously not high earners and yet the corporate identity being pushed is one of well-heeled individuals with taste and money" (348). And as the authors of an article by the Los Angeles Research Group explain: "Economically, it is our experience that many open gays are forced to work in the lowest paying, non-unionized small manufacturing shops where the boss is not much concerned with whom a person sleeps with [*sic*], but who uses a worker's status as added leverage for increased exploitation" (351).

2. Beginning in the mid-1960s, gay Cuban men were sent to the UMAP (Unidades Militares de Ayuda a la Producción) [Military Units to Aid Production]. These forced-labor camps were denounced in the film *Conducta impropia* [*Improper Conduct*], of Néstor Almendros and Orlando Jiménez Leal. At the time of its release and for years afterwards, the Cuban government and leftist critics attacked the film as an effort merely to discredit the Revolution. As Henk van den Boogaard and Kathelijne van Kammen (two observers sympathetic to the gay-rights movement) point out: "Its producers left Cuba a considerable time ago, do not report on recent developments, and certainly did not have the intention to draw a well-shaded picture of Cuba" (94). They suggest that the Cuban government's stance toward gays has significantly improved, although during the late 1980s and early 1990s gay Cuban men and others who were HIV-positive or suffering from AIDS were quarantined and separated from the general population. Sonja de Vries's 1995 documentary *Gay Cuba* attempts to show a more positive image of lesbian and gay life in contemporary Cuba. See Smith for a discussion of *Conducta impropia* and for a comparison of the autobiographies of Néstor Almendros and Arenas.

3. Marvin Leiner points out that the concept of the Cuban "new man" has its origin in the humanistic ideal propounded by Marx in the "Economic and Philosophical Manuscripts" of 1844 (Leiner 19 n. 37).

4. For comprehensive analyses of the history of gay sexuality and AIDS in revolutionary Cuba, see the studies of Epps, Leiner, Lumsden (*Machos*), and Young.

5. In two controversial essays Lourdes Argüelles and B. Ruby Rich argue that the anti-Castro right has manipulated the Cuban "gay issue" in an effort to equate socialism and homophobia and thereby discredit the Revolution in the eyes of North American gays and liberals. They furthermore go so far as to insinuate that Arenas colluded in this scheme and allowed himself to become a pawn of social and political forces that are inherently homophobic (*Signs* 132). Yet although Arenas anathematizes (and as Epps shows, actually even fetishizes the figure of Castro), his "deviant" sexuality remains subversive within capitalist as well as socialist societies insofar as both are historically grounded in similar notions of masculinity.

6. This episode is fully recounted in the Arenas text *La vieja Rosa*.

7. See *Poesída* of Carlos A. Rodríguez Matos not only for a comprehensive analysis and presentation of Latino AIDS poetry but also for the most complete bibliography of both Spanish- and English-language AIDS writing (poetry, narrative, theater, autobiography, and testimony), dance, cinema, video, music, photography, and literary and cultural criticism. For further AIDS autobiographies, see the annotated bibliography of Brooks and Murphy. For a thorough overview of *Antes que anochezca,* see Soto 1-32. For a particularly insightful analysis of the homoerotic dynamics of the Arenas autobiography, see also Bejel ("Arenas's *Antes que anochezca*").

8. Miguel Riera and Manuel Pereira not only accuse Arenas of flaunting his sexuality but of indulging in mudslinging and spiteful gossip (even in the context of imprisonment, forced labor, and AIDS) and of ignoring the accepted conventions of autobiographical discourse by mixing fact with fiction. They are particularly troubled by what they perceive to be the exaggerated number of lovers that Arenas claims to have had. Stephen Clark sharply critiques these early reviewers. Kate Mehuron, in contrast, affirms the carnivalesque mood of Arenas's autobiographical writing, which "celebrates with readers the sexual feasts indulged amidst dangerous ideological repression" (50).

9. Life-writer Paul Monette received an even more truculent directive from his AIDS-afflicted lover: "Rub their faces in it, Paulie. Nobody told us anything. You tell them" (144).

10. Of course, not all gay *marielitos* were as dismayed as Arenas by the dynamics of the North American gay-male community. After his arrival in Los Angeles, Antonio L. Cónchez writes the following to his brother: "todos los gay si los vieras en los gay bar, en las calles, ¡qué machos! . . . sólo se sabe si es activo o pasivo por el lugar donde se ponen las llaves o el pañuelo, a la derecha pasivo y a la izquierda activo y cuando la gente quiere se los

cambia cuando desean" (47) ["If you could only see how macho the gay men are in the bars and in the streets! The only way you can tell if they are active or passive in bed is where they put their keys or handkerchief. On the right is passive and on the left is active, and when they want to, they change them according to their desires" (22)]. In contrast to Arenas, Cónchez seems to perceive in sexual reversibility not a loss of "real" masculinity but a freedom from compulsory femininity.

11. As Roger N. Lancaster puts it, if homosexual identity requires the mediation of the nonhomosexual (that is, the macho) in order to be constituted as such, then a self-sustaining sexual community of gay men is never really possible (243).

12. Of course, not all gay *marielitos* were as dismayed as Arenas by the dynamics of the North American gay-male community. After his arrival in Los Angeles, Antonio L. Cónchez writes the following to his brother: "todos los gay si los vieras en los gay bar, en las calles, ¡qué machos! . . . sólo se sabe si es activo o pasivo por el lugar donde se ponen las llaves o el pañuelo, a la derecha pasivo y a la izquierda activo y cuando la gente quiere se los cambia cuando desean" (47) ["If you could only see how macho the gay men are in the bars and in the streets! The only way you can tell if they are active or passive in bed is where they put their keys or handkerchief. On the right is passive and on the left is active, and when they want to, they change them according to their desires" (22)]. In contrast to Arenas, Cónchez seems to perceive in sexual reversibility not a loss of "real" masculinity but a freedom from compulsory femininity.

13. Arenas actually attempts to escape from the island in a tire. He of course fails, and subsequently tries to flee through the American base at Guantánamo Bay. But he is unable to reach the base because the waters surrounding it are infested with caimans.

14. Arenas contends that by not placing him among political prisoners the authorities could, if they so chose, liquidate him with impunity, since those on the outside would assume that he had been murdered by fellow inmates.

15. Although the authorities force Arenas to renounce his gay past, they in fact view homosexuality as a fixed identity, and after his confession continue to terrorize him on account of it. Their goal is thus not to "reform" him but to take control of his sexuality and use it as a weapon of domination and a means of silencing him as a subversive writer.

16. The UMAP actually existed only from 1965 to 1967 and were disbanded as a result of interna-tional pressure on the government. But gay men continued to be sent to hard labor in the canefields, as Arenas's own 1970 experience reveals.

17. See Ríos Avila for a discussion of Arenas's New York experience.

18. Arenas might fancy himself a bird, but he is obliged to recognize that the air in which he flies "tampoco es nuestro" [is not even ours] (*El color del verano* [The color of summer] 390).

Bibliography

Arenas, Reinaldo. *Antes que anochezca: Autobiografía.* Barcelona: Tusquets, 1992.

———. *Arturo, la estrella más brillante.* Barcelona: Montesinos, 1984.

———. *Before Night Falls: A Memoir.* Trans. Dolores M. Koch. New York: Viking, 1993.

———. *El color del verano.* Miami: Universal, 1991.

———. *La vieja Rosa.* Caracas: Cruz del Sur, 1980.

———. *Old Rosa: A Novel in Two Stories* ("Old Rosa" and "The Brightest Star"). Trans. Ann Tashi Slater and Andrew Hurley. New York: Grove, 1989.

Argüelles, Lourdes, and B. Ruby Rich. "Homosexuality, Homophobia, and Revolution: Notes toward an Understanding of the Cuban Lesbian and Gay Male Experience." In *Hidden from History: Reclaiming the Gay and Lesbian Past,* ed. Martin Bauml Duberman, Martha Vicinus, and George Chauncey, Jr., 441-55. New York: New American Library, 1989.

———. "Homosexuality, Homophobia, and Revolution: Notes toward an Understanding of the Cuban Lesbian and Gay Male Experience, Part II." *Signs: Journal of Women in Culture and Society* 11.1 (1985): 120-36.

Bejel, Emilio. "Arenas's *Antes que anochezca:* Autobiography of a Gay Cuban Dissident." In *Reading and Writing the Ambiente: Queer Sexualities in Latino, Latin American, and Spanish Culture,* ed. Susana Chávez-Silverman and Librada Hernández, 299-315. Madison: University of Wisconsin Press, 2000.

Borge, Tomás. *Un grano de maíz: Conversación con Fidel Castro.* Mexico City: Fondo de Cultura Económica, 1992.

Brooks, Franklin, and Timothy F. Murphy. "Annotated Bibliography of AIDS Literature, 1982-91." In *Writing AIDS: Gay Literature, Language, and Analysis,* ed. Timothy F. Murphy and Suzanne Poirier, 321-39. New York: Columbia University Press, 1993.

Brydon, Diana. "The White Inuit Speaks: Contamination as Literary Strategy." In *The Post-Colonial Studies Reader,* ed. Bill Ashcroft, Gareth Griffiths, and Helen Tiffin, 136-42. New York: Routledge, 1995.

Clark, Stephen. "*Antes que anochezca:* Las paradojas de la autorrepresentación." *Revista del Ateneo Puertorriqueño* 5.13-15 (1995): 209-25.

Cónchez, Antonio L. *A Gay Cuban in Exile: Memoires and Letters of a Refugee.* Trans. Michael A. Lombardi. Los Angeles: Urania Manuscripts, 1983.

Echeverría, Esteban. *El matadero.* 1871. Barcelona: Norma, 1990.

Epps, Brad. "Proper Conduct: Reinaldo Arenas, Fidel Castro, and the Politics of Homosexuality." *Journal of the History of Sexuality* 6.2 (1995): 231-83.

Esterrich, Carmelo. "Locas, pájaros y demás mariconadas: El ciudadano sexual en Reinaldo Arenas." *Confluencia: Revista Hispánica de Cultura y Literatura* 13.1 (1997): 178-93.

Field, Nicola. "From *Over the Rainbow: Money, Class and Homophobia.*" In *The Material Queer: A LesBiGay Cultural Studies Reader,* ed. Donald Morton, 345-48. Boulder, Colo.: Westview, 1996.

Guevara, Ernesto "Che." "El socialismo y el hombre en Cuba." In *Obras, 1957-1967,* 2:367-84. Havana: Casa de las Américas, 1970.

———. "Notes on Man and Socialism in Cuba." In *Che Guevara Speaks: Selected Speeches and Writings,* ed. George Lavan, 121-38. New York: Merit, 1967.

Lancaster, Roger N. *Life Is Hard: Machismo, Danger, and the Intimacy of Power in Nicaragua.* Berkeley: University of California Press, 1992.

Leiner, Marvin. *Sexual Politics in Cuba: Machismo, Homosexuality, and AIDS.* Boulder, Colo.: Westview, 1994.

Lockwood, Lee. *Castro's Cuba, Cuba's Fidel: An American Journalist's Inside Look at Today's Cuba—in Text and Picture.* New York: Macmillan, 1967.

Los Angeles Research Group. "Material Oppression." In *The Material Queer: A LesBiGay Cultural Studies Reader,* ed. Donald Morton, 349-51. Boulder, Colo.: Westview, 1996.

Lumsden, Ian. *Machos, Maricones, and Gays: Cuba and Homosexuality.* Philadelphia: Temple University Press, 1996.

Marx, Karl. "Economic and Philosophical Manuscripts." Trans. T. B. Bottomore. In *Marx's Concept of Man,* by Erich Fromm, 90-196. New York: Frederick Ungar, 1961.

Mehuron, Kate. "Queer Territories in the Americas: Reinaldo Arenas' Prose." *Prose Studies: History, Theory, Criticism* 17.1 (1994): 39-63.

Monette, Paul. *Becoming a Man: Half a Life Story.* New York: Harcourt, 1992.

Padilla, Heberto. *La mala memoria.* Barcelona: Plaza y Janés, 1989.

———. *Self-Portrait of the Other.* Trans. Alexander Coleman. New York: Farrar, 1990.

Pereira, Manuel. "Reinaldo antes del alba." *Quimera* 111 (1992): 54-58.

Puig, Manuel. *El beso de la mujer araña.* Barcelona: Seix Barral, 1976.

———. *Kiss of the Spider Woman.* Trans. Thomas Colchie. New York: Vintage, 1980.

Riera, Miguel. "El mundo es alucinante." *Quimera* 111 (1992): 58-59.

Ríos Avila, Rubén. "Caribbean Dislocations: Arenas and Ramos Otero in New York." In *Hispanisms and Homosexualities,* ed. Sylvia Molloy and Robert McKee Irwin, 101-19. Durham, N.C.: Duke University Press, 1998.

Rodríguez Matos, Carlos A., ed. *Poesída: Antología de poesía del SIDA escrita en los Estados Unidos, Hispanoamérica, y España—An Anthology of AIDS Poetry from the United States, Latin America, and Spain.* New York: Ollantay, 1995.

Smith, Paul Julian. "Cuban Homosexualities: On the Beach with Néstor Almendros and Reinaldo Arenas." In *Hispanisms and Homosexualities,* ed. Sylvia Molloy and Robert McKee Irwin, 248-68. Durham, N.C.: Duke University Press, 1998.

Soto, Francisco. *Reinaldo Arenas.* New York: Twayne, 1998.

Van den Boogaard, Henk, and Kathelijne van Kammen. "We Cannot Jump over Our Own Shadow." In *Coming Out: An Anthology of International Gay and Lesbian Writings,* ed. Stephan Likosky, 82-101. New York: Pantheon, 1992.

Young, Allen. *Gays under the Cuban Revolution.* San Francisco: Grey Fox, 1981.

Chris Girman (essay date 2004)

SOURCE: Girman, Chris. "Historical Representations of Same-Sex Desire in Esteban Echeverría's 'El Matadero' and Reinaldo Arenas's 'Comienza el Desfile.'" In *Mucho Macho: Seduction, Desire, and Homoerotic Lives of Latin Men,* pp. 237-91. New York: Harrington Park Press, 2004.

[*In the following excerpt, Girman discusses the relationship of homoeroticism and "the construction of national identity" in Arenas's short story "Comienza el Desfile."*]

INTRODUCTION

The representation of same-sex eroticism within homophobic societies is filled with ambiguity. To represent something that "dare not speak its name" requires an emphasis on multiple, fluid, often coded voices, sometimes silent, which emerge in specific spaces at specific times, or historical moments, and that provide subjective accounts of supposedly hegemonic structures of power. If these structures of power have a sharply articulated homophobic dimension, the more likely it is that homosexuality plays a role in the construction of individual identity within the larger compulsory heterosexual discourse (Sanchez-Eppler, 1994, p. 2). The heterosexual discourse itself is a product of historical contingency, and its representation depends on the writer's ability to transform space and time into a coherent [re-]production of a specific historical period. However, representation is exactly that, *re*presentation, and writers are free to create their own disjunctions and disclosures.

This book has thus far relied on various sources to represent Latin American and Hispanic masculinity and [homo]sexuality, including ethnographic studies, sociological commentary, my own reflexive personal narratives, and, finally, the words of Latin men. This chapter aims to examine yet another masculine hegemony, but this time through the eyes of fiction. The chapter examines two short stories, Esteban Echeverría's "El Matadero" [The Slaughterhouse] and Reinaldo Arenas's **"Comienza el Desfile"** [**"The Beginning of the Parade"**], which highlight male eroticism as important components within a discourse of national identity. Both stories conceptualize same-sex desire within specific historical moments and demonstrate how male [homo-]sexuality emerges and represents itself not in contrast to the dominant discourse, but within that discourse itself. . . .

MESSY, HOMOEROTIC TEXTS

Both "El Matadero" and **"Comienza el Desfile"** rely on usages of time and space that defy traditional conceptions of space as feminine and time as masculine (Bondi, 1990). In contrast, Echeverría and Arenas highlight the movement of bodies in public spaces as a way of deconstructing binary distinctions between male/female, public/private, and young/old, among others, which traditionally sustain hegemonic power dynamics. Both men describe carnival-like atmospheres of chaotic merging and reemerging—parades, processions, and caravans—taking place during the Argentine Civil War and the Cuban revolution, respectively. By privileging space over time, both writers encourage greater sensitivity to differences and inconsistencies in local discourse (Bondi, 1990). They are grounded in material reality, which enables them to focus on experience. This focus on experience leads them inevitably to the male body, where [homo]sexual inclinations become embodied realities. By focusing on parade-like scenarios of mass movement, the authors demonstrate, first, that all reality is material, and, second, that realities are also composed of "competing and free-floating images." This notion of "free-floating images" has the potential for collapsing gender categories yet is still capable of maintaining a metanarrative of partial perspectives (Bondi, 1990). In many ways, both Echeverría and Arenas have already created the "messy texts" so desired by Calvin Thomas in his quest to reinsert the masculine body into male public consciousness.

Both works can be read as homoerotic texts. Both demonstrate the importance of the sex/gender system in the construction of national identity. Likewise, because the texts were written over a century apart, a dual analysis suggests that male eroticism can, and must, be represented differently depending on the historical circumstance. While Echeverría explicitly engages men's bodies in his depiction of male sodomy, Arenas depicts the *inability* of certain male bodies to join with others. The specific conditions of the Cuban revolution made this impossible. However, this is not to assert that [homo-]sexual relations had more prominence in the Argentine Civil War than during the Cuban Revolution. Further, a *carnivalesque*[1] reading of both stories allows us to examine men's desire by focusing on how men associate with other men in particularly violent, emotionally charged settings. These settings not only provide the backdrop for same-sex desire to reveal itself, but may even be responsible for the desire itself. Finally, both stories meet Thomas's challenge of writing the body as a way of destabilizing the "masculine corporeal misrelation" that depends on the invisibility of the male body to sustain itself (Thomas, 1996, p. 2). Echeverría and Arenas highlight the male body—particularly its abjections in the form of blood, shit, urine, and tears—as a way of revealing the inconsistent "clean and proper" body that hegemonic masculinity supposedly represents. In contrast, the bodies depicted in "El Matadero" and **"Comienza el Desfile"** are anything but "clean and proper," and therefore expose masculinity and heteronormative sexuality to be somewhat artificial and impossible to sustain.

. . . . .

LA BUSQUEDA DEL HUERFANO: DISENCHANTMENT AND [HOMO]EROTICISM IN ARENAS'S "COMIENZA EL DESFILE"

INTRODUCTION

Reinaldo Arenas's well-known collection of short stories **Con los Ojos Cerrados** [**With Closed Eyes**] (1972) begins with the critically neglected **"Comienza el Desfile."** Written sometime around 1965, the story depicts the excitement of the *pueblo* upon encountering the rebel soldiers of the Cuban revolution. The protagonist is a fourteen-year-old boy who struggles to find a way to participate in the revolutionary "parade" against the wishes of his repressive mother and grandmother. Unlike Arenas's later works, including *Viaje a la Habana* [*Trip to Havana*] and the recently acclaimed *Antes que Anochezca* [*Before Night Falls*], the stories contained in *Con los Ojos Cerrados* reflect a more cautious containment of [homo]erotic subject matter. Because the stories were written while Arenas moved in and out of jail, always in danger of being incarcerated once again, the collection shows a different side of Arenas than the much-publicized, sexually explicit, committed anti-Castro exiled writer of his later years.

Instead, **"Comienza el Desfile"** shows a writer struggling to portray the ambiguities of the Castro revolution within the minds of traditional campesinos, who experience the revolution not as an economic or social upheaval, but as an *erotic* journey beyond the rural sexual malaise that characterizes their lives. Unlike Arenas's other works, the protagonist in **"Comienza el Desfile"** does not engage in sexual relations with anyone. Nor does the work detail the sexual exploits of any other character. Instead, Arenas offers subtle, sensual clues of how the body of his protagonist—in combination with other bodies—becomes implicated in the Cuban revolution. By eventually denying the protagonist a role in the revolution, Arenas depicts the process of repression that partly defines the revolution. The protagonist is left, in the end, staring at his own naked body, aware that his desires and participation have no place in the revolution. But the repression of his [homo]sexual desires, at least in part, reveals the extent to which the new Cuban [*el nuevo Cubano*] is defined by the repression of homoerotic impulses in which "nadie parecia . . . porque todos eran" [no one seemed to be . . . because they all were]. Sanchez-Eppler (1994) makes it clear that heterosexuality, and by extension the Cuban revolution itself, is partly defined by what it leaves out:

In Arenas's representation of the ruling ideology, homosexuality emerges as categorically ever present, at the very least as a definitive danger, and at the very most, as a base—low and fundamental—proclivity which all processes of socialization must repress. With this reversal, heterosexuality appears as reactively constructed—derived, secondary, epiphenomenal—and as naturalized compulsorily rather than as essential, natural, or even freely chosen. The imperative to repress—politically and otherwise—is subverted by the denunciation of an exemplary national identity produced by that repression, and the alignment of heterosexuality with ruling definitions of national identity is effectively put into question. With this strategy, even if a Cuban gay territory still remains unavailable, Arenas has at least managed to displace homosexuality from the realm of an always occluded, always denied, always ir-

relevant practice, and to instill it as one of the elements most solidly repressed in the making of lo revolucionario, and by extension, lo cubano.

(p. 9)

Arenas thus successfully shifts homoeroticism from a *hidden* practice to a *repressed* practice, and in the process he explores the ways in which Cuban rural society in the late 1950s and early 1960s allowed [homo]sexuality to pierce the hegemonic masculine arrangement; further, "Comienza el Desfile" shows how the revolution enhanced and/or denied [homo]sexual and [homo]erotic desires.

Un Gran Escándolo

Critic Abilio Estévez (1994) claims that Arenas left a body of work "which we cannot disregard if we wish to understand this terrible Island [Cuba] at all" (p. 86). Understanding the island implies creating a space in which the island becomes known, reveals itself, not just in a Bautista versus Castro dialectic, or even that of men against women, or rural opposed to urban, but in a mutually constitutive dialogue of subject and object, here and there, then and now. From the beginning of **"Comienza el Desfile,"** Arenas demonstrates his intention of mixing up voices and movements, putting object and subject in perpetual flux, mixing men with women, people with animals, bodily matter with earthly substance:

Detrás—pero casi junto a mí—viene Rigo, silbando y haciendo rechinar sus botas. Y después, las hijas de los Pupos, con los muchachos de la mano, hablando, cacareando, muertas de risa, llamando a Rigo para decirle no sé qué cosa. . . . Que escándalo. Y el polvo del camino, levantándose, cubriendonos . . . , formando una nube que nos envuelve y casi me impide verte. [Behind, but next to me, comes Rigo, whistling and squeaking his boots. And after the Pupos daughters, with boys on their arms, talking, laughing, calling Rigo to tell him whatever. And further behind comes the Estradas, and Rafael Rodríguez, and the sons of Bartolo Angulo and of Panchita, and Wilfredo the cross-eyed. Then the grandkids of Cándido Parronda. And further behind the sons of Caridad, and those of Tano. And then Arturo, the son of La Vieja Rosa. And the people from La Loma, and from La Perrera, and from Guayacán. And behind them come the streetwalkers, the fat ladies, the rebel guys, and neighborhood kids. And further still some people on horses, even bikes and a truck. And Nino Ochoa, on crutches. And another truck that overtakes us at the Majagual. And we move to the other side of the street. The truck was full of people that waved their sombreros and took out a flag. What a scandal. And the dust from the road, raising up, covering us, falling again like crawling smoke, and falling on the skin of the horses (that have come near us already, that are in front of us), lifting up again, forming a cloud that wraps around us and makes it impossible to see.][2]

(Arenas, 1972, p. 9)

This initial juxtaposition of people and substances continues throughout the text. It reflects Arenas's belief that desire is formed through the search for opposites, as he many times asserted in later works. He is in a perpetual search for the Other, which can only be fulfilled at the level of the senses (Estévez, 1994, p. 865). "Comienza el Desfile" acts as a "shout that removes us from the torpor of 'there' and 'here'" (1994, p. 867). There is only this place, the *desfile,* in which men and women fight against the repressive regime and then return in triumph to the capital. It is a place of ambiguity and confusion, surrounded by "la gran polvareda que sube y baja" [the great dust that rises and falls] (Arenas, 1972, p. 16), as well as "Banderas y banderas. Delante y detrás. Arriba y abajo" [Flags and flags. In front and behind. Above and below] (1972, p. 18). It is above all "un gran escándolo" [great scandal] (1972, p. 17), as Arenas describes the *desfile* several times, but *un escándolo* that offers potential fulfillment for the fourteen-year-old protagonist, as he is exposed to a world of possible abjection.

The world depicted in **"Comienza el Desfile"** is a world of abjection and possible violence. Thomas (1996, p. 14) claims abjection is the fear of polluting objects that traverse the body's boundaries. These include both fluids that *emanate from* the body and those from the environment that *engulf* the body. Thomas (1996, p. 15) insists that the fear of abject things, or exfluence, comes from an original fear of the archaic mother engulfing the boy. Coming to terms with abjection and exfluence, according to Thomas, is a way of acknowledging the masculine body. Acknowledging this body exposes the limits, strains, and anxieties of heteronormative masculinity; therefore, by putting exfluence in full view, Arenas is creating a space where a liminal body, the *abject* body, threatens dissolution of hegemonic masculinity. He depicts a *desfile* full of abject substances, including *polvo* [dust], *sudor* [sweat], *agua* [water], *mujeres* [women], *lágrimas* [tears], *olores* [smells], and *sangre* [blood]:

Polvo

La polvareda que se alza, que asciende, que nos envuelve, que nos cae de pronto como un gran mosquitero. [The dust that falls on us, that rises, that surrounds us, that quickly falls on us like a mosquito net.]

(Arenas, 1972, p. 10)

y por encima de todo, la gran polvareda que sube y baja, se apaga y alza de nuevo como un estallido, envolviendonos [and on top of everything the great smoke that falls and rises, that dies out and returns with a crash, surrounding us]

(p. 15)

Y tú a mi lado, la escopeta al hombro, el uniforme empapado cubierto por el polvo, hablas. [And you by my side, shotgun on your shoulder, your sweaty uniform covered in dust, speak.]

(p. 18)

Sudor

Y tú, con el uniforme, sudando, tan orgulloso; alzando la escopeta. [And you, with the uniform, sweating, so proud; holding the shotgun.]

(p. 11)

Tú, con el uniforme que de mojado se te pega a las nalgas. [You, your uniform that sticks to your ass because of the moisture.]

(p. 12)

Los dos vamos empapados. [We go together soaking.]

(p. 13)

[L]os dos sudorosos. [The two of us sweating.]

(p. 13)

Tu brazo húmedo roza con el mío ya empapado. [Your humid arm on my soaking arm.]

(p. 17)

Agua

Veo, sí; veo que entras en el río. No lo cruzas por el pedregal. Las botas que rechinan se zambullen en el agua revuelta. Yo, detrás, casi a tu lado, también hundo mis pies. El agua nos refresca. Quizá ya no estamos tan sofocados. [I see, yes; I see that you enter by the river. You can't cross there. The squeaky boots plunge in the moving water. Me, behind, almost at your side, also sink my feet. The water refreshes them. Perhaps we are not suffocating so much.]

(p. 12)

Comienza el tercer cruce del río. Los caballos en el agua, encabritándose. Uno se echa en la corriente. Gran escándalo de mujeres. [The third crossing of the river begins. The horses bucking in the water. One falls in the current. There is a grand scandal of women.]

(p. 13)

Lágrimas

Sigue llorando mientras me abraza. [She continues crying while she hugs me.]

(p. 18)

Bañada en lágrimas sigue hablando [la negra]. [Bathed in tears, the black one continues speaking.]

(p. 21)

Las mujeres quizá griten, quizá lloren de alegría. [The women perhaps scream, perhaps cry from happiness.]

(p. 12)

Y aunque no sé por qué, también empiezo a llorar. [And although I don't know why, I began to cry.]

(p. 18)

Olores

Nobrando los diferentes olores de tu cuerpo. [Noting the different smells of your body.]

(p. 11)

Y otra vez me habla de los olores. "Pero, qué baño," me dice. "Qué baño cuando llegue por fin a casa." [And again I speak of smells. "But, go bathe," he said to me. "Wash yourself when you get home."]

(p. 10)

No sé qué es más horrible, si la furia de los mosquitos o ese olor a petróleo. [I don't know what's more horrible, the fury of the mosquitos or the smell of oil.]

(p. 14)

"Huelo a cojón de oso. [Smells like a bear's testicle.]

(p. 9)

Sangre

Y luego le pasé el dedo por el filo—cómo—cortaba. [And then I passed my finger over the blade as if I were cutting myself.]

(p. 19)

El agua cae sobre mi cabeza, rueda por mi cuerpo, llega al suelo completamente enrojecida por el polvo. [The water falls over my head, surrounds my body, and falls to the floor completely red and covered in dust.]

(p. 22)

Likewise, the protagonist clearly feels engulfed by his mother and grandmother. In fact, in the short story **"Bestial entre las flores"** (also in the volume *Con los Ojos Cerrados*), Arenas's protagonist actually contemplates the double assassination of his mother and grandmother. Arenas is less explicit in **"Comienza el Desfile"**; however, the protagonist's hatred for his mother and grandmother, symbolized by their rural existence, is evident:

Y la vieja: "Ay, que nos morimos de hambre." Y el viejo: "Comemierdas, piensan ganar la guerra con banderitas." Y mi madre: "Qué destino, qué destino." Y Lourdes: "Me quieres o no me quieres? Dilo de una vez". Y estas cucarachas, y estos mosquitos inmortales. [And the old lady: "Ay, that we die of hunger." And the old man: "Shiteaters, do they think they are going to win the war with a bunch of bandits." And my mother: "What a fate, what a fate." And Lourdes, "Do you love me or don't you love me? Tell me one more time." And those cockroaches and immortal mosquitos. For those reasons, and because of the damned heat (the roof was made of fiberglass), and because of that hot town, without anything, not even porches, almost without trees. This and that and who knows how many more things.]

(Arenas, 1972, p. 13)

Through his depiction of exfluence such as tears, blood, and sweat along with the abject flows of dust, water, and odors, Arenas acknowledges the anxious masculine relationship to the male body. He is able to examine the visibility of that body, the traverse of its boundaries, the representability of its products, the corporeal conditions of male subjectivity, and the unavoidable materiality of the signifying process itself (Thomas, 1996, p. 15). The subject/object relationship is formed by the exclusion of abject substances (1996, p. 15). Since masculinity does not exist outside representation, it risks losing itself in the process of self-representation (abjection) depicted by Arenas; that is, the subject is capable of changing itself, slipping out through its own fissures and cracks.

Arenas therefore creates a geographical space in which fusion and abjection threaten established social order. However, Arenas firmly establishes his protagonist within a *larger familial order* that, while taking on a new form during the *desfile,* always remains present. The protagonist throughout the story is mesmerized by an unnamed figure to whom the story is addressed. It is as if the protagonist finally sees a possible alternative to the repressive, feminized atmosphere of his house—not in a mythical *papi* figure, but in the image of his own brother, a young man who "ni siquiera tiene barba" [doesn't even have a beard], like the protagonist himself, but who is surrounded in triumph by the entire *pueblo.* Arenas simultaneously sees and desires *himself* as his protagonist first responds to the sight of the young man with a simple "Te miro" [I see you]. The rest of the story continues to be addressed to this man. The protagonist both desires and identifies with the man, creating the possibility of a mutually recognized relationship in which both men triumph together. It is the possibility of "dos huérfanos completamente desamparados, en medio de un noche que bien podía no tener fin" [two completely helpless orphans in the midst of a night that could never end] (Oveido, 1983, p. 44). The protagonist is excited at the possibility of his *own savior.* Before Arenas wrote of destructive erotic adventures, he created a protagonist who hoped to survive on love alone. He desperately hoped this love could save him from the domestic hierarchy in which his female relatives determined good from bad, the permitted from the disallowed, and suffocated him under their oppressive authority (Oveido, 1983, p. 44).

THE EROTIC SUBJECT

Certainly Arenas's protagonist was not the only young Cuban to feel repressed in the conservative environment of rural Cuba. Many other Cubans joined the revolutionary bands roaming the country. Many other Cubans found friendship and affection among the other discontented *rebeldes*. What separates **"Comienza el Desfile"** from other works depicting the incipient Cuban revolution is the manner in which Arenas acknowledges a certain *erotic* attachment to the revolution and its adherents. There can be little doubt that the protagonist is sexually attracted to the young man. His descriptions rely on a corporeality that highlights both the man's body and their two bodies in conjunction. The other man almost emerges from the dust:

> [La] polvareda que se alza, que asciende, que nos envuelve, que nos cae de pronto como un gran mosquitero. Hasta que tú apareces de nuevo, con el uniforme desarrapado, con la escopeta que bamboleas, que te ajustas a la espalda, que enarbolas triunfante. [The dust that rises, that ascends, that surrounds us, that falls on us like a great mosquito net. Until you appear again, with your uniform almost off, shotgun swinging, adjusted on your back, which hoists itself up in triumph.]

> (Arenas, 1972, p. 10)

Arenas (1972) continues describing their union, which fluctuates between actual encounters and the fantasies of the protagonist:

> Entre ellos estás tú. Te llamo a voz en cuello. Tú, en cuanto me ves, dejas el grupo. Vienes corriendo hasta mí. Me tiras el brazo por la espalda. Y empiezas a hablarme. [You are in the middle of them. I call to you. You, as soon as you see me, leave the group. You come running toward me. You throw your hand on my back. And you begin to speak.]

> (p. 20)

> Otra botella de Paticruzado. "Bebe tú primero," me dices. "No, tú," digo; pero bebo yo. De nuevo enrojecemos. Qué calor, qué polvareda. Estamos pegajosos. Uno al lado del otro seguimos avanzando. [Another bottle of *Paticruzado.* "Drink first," you tell me. "No, you," I say, but I drink. Soon we are red again. What heat, what dust. We are sticky together. We continue together.]

> (p. 14)

> Lo palpo, con pena, pero no te lo enseño. Los dos juntos casi corremos. [I touch him, with embarrassment, but do not show it. We are together, practically running.]

> (p. 12)

> Y ya todos te rodean. Y las putas de la Chomba y de Pueblo Nuevo ya se te acercan. Y una te toca la cara. "Pero qué joven—es dice—: ni siquiera tienen barba." Y tú las miras y te echas a reír. [And now everyone surrounds you. The bitches of La Chomba and of Pueblo Nuevo surround you. And one of them touches your face. "But how young," she says, "not even a beard." And you look at them and begin to laugh.]

> (p. 20)

> Tú delante, volviéndote, mirándome. Para tí, los elogios: para ti, las miradas de las Pupos. Te ajustas la escopeta al hombro y sigues conversando. Los dos vamos empapados. [You behind, returning, looking at me. For you, praise: for you, the stares of the Pupos. You adjust the shotgun on your shoulder and continue talking. The two of us go, drenched together.]

> (p. 13)

And finally, the moment when the other man symbolically gives himself to the protagonist in the form of a large knife:

> Ya cuando estamos de pie te metes una mano dentro de la camisa. "Toma," me dices. Y me entregas un cuchillo con funda y todo. "Vete a Holgúin, raja un casquito, quítale el rifle. Y ven para acá." [And when we are almost standing you reach under your shirt. "Take it," you say to me. And you give me the knife with a cover and everything. "Go to Holgúin, kill a *casquito,* take his rifle. And then come back."]

> (Arenas, 1972, p. 16)

The protagonist is conflicted throughout the remainder of the narrative by his love of the knife and the consequences of its use:

> Y saco el cuchillo. Y entonces, por primera vez, lo desenfundo y lo contemplo, deslumbrado. . . . "Estás loco—dice abuela—crees que con catorce años eres ya un hombre. Déjate de faineras y entra en el cuarto." [And I took out the knife. And then, for the first time, I noticed, contemplated the dazzling thing. It was a sparkling knife; without marks. It had a formidable blade, like from a razor. My mother screamed and lost her balance. "Are you crazy," said my grandmother. "Do you think that at fourteen you are a man. Stop pretending and go in your room."]

> (Arenas, 1972, p. 17)

> El casquito, de pie, hace la guardia frente a la planta eléctrica. A veces se mueve. Camina de uno a otro extremo de la gran portería metálica. El rifle al hombro. El casquito silba. El casquito va y viene. Se queda quieto. Mira para todos los sitios. Yo me voy acercando. A veces, con disimulo, me palpo el cuchillo por encima de la camisa. [The *casquito* stands guard in front of the electric plant. At times he moves. He moves from one end of the thing to the other. The rifle on his shoulder. The *casquito* whistles. The *casquito* goes and comes. He stays quiet. He looks around. I approach him. A few times, I touch the knife under my shirt. . . . I continue approaching him. The *cosquito* is very young. I cross in front. I stop at the other corner. I look behind me. I think he sees me too. I continue walking. I stop. I return. Still, a little bit closer, I stop again. I stare at him. He also looks at me. We have been looking at each other for a little while. He stares at me and he motions. He probably thinks I'm a fag and I'm looking for some fun.]

> (Arenas, 1972, pp. 17-18)

Arenas thus contemplates the possible union of two groups of men in the symbolic gift of the knife: first, the union of the protagonist and his revolutionary hero, and second, the union of the protagonist and the *cosquito.* Indeed, the aborted attack on the *cosquito* reads more like a public sex pickup than a violent encounter. Because the knife is capable of symbolizing the male genitalia in one form or another, the protagonist is then left with the impossible dilemma of using the knife as a way of fulfilling heterosexual violence and conquest—indeed, as a way of assuming the revolutionary stance by killing the *casquito*—or simply holding onto the knife in hopes that it can be enjoyed not as instrument of *death,* but an instrument of *pleasure.* He chooses the latter. But in the end it would have made no difference if he had killed the *casquito* because the revolutionary fervor had already swept his (hoped for) lover away. The knife is revealed as more *phallus* than *penis,* promising power, not pleasure. Thus, in the end, the protagonist unceremoniously lays the knife down on the bathroom floor and bathes himself completely.

"Soy yo": Becoming the Constitutive Subject

In addition to the sensual language employed by Arenas and the symbolic usage of the knife, the fact that the story is written *to* the other man, addressing him as *tú* throughout the story, brings the two of them closer together. This closeness must be semantically maintained since the *desfile,* which first brought the two together, eventually threatens their union in the end. In fact, the protagonist's final address, meant for his "tú" counterpart goes unsaid:

> Tú hablas, siempre sonriendo; siempre mostrando la escopeta; pero si alguien trata de tocarla, tú no se lo permites. Yo te sigo observando. Todos te han rodeado. [They surround you and begin to ask you questions. You speak, always smiling, always showing the shotgun, but if anyone tries to touch it, you do not allow it. I continue to watch you. The people surround you more and more, they ask you questions, they praise you. I raise my hand, try to greet you, try to say to you: "I'll see you around." But I couldn't get near you. The mass has surrounded you.]

(Arenas, 1972, p. 21)

Here the protagonist realizes the futility of his efforts to unite with the young man. He is already captured by another, by the entire nation, it seems, so that the narrative now expands from that of the *family* to that of *history* as well (Estévez, 1994, p. 864). Not only do his mother and grandmother deny him a [homo]erotic experience, but the Cuban nation as well. Thus, although Arenas speaks both from and about the body, he does not fall into ahistorical formulations. His discourse of the body, indeed of bodily experience, can take place only inside history and historical constructs. Putting the body on the line is an unorthodox way of historicizing that discourse (Thomas, 1996, p. 39). As Gallop (1988) writes,

> Locating thinking in a desiring body is also, in another vocabulary, locating thinking in the subject of history. To read for and affirm confusion, contradiction is to insist on thinking in the body in history. Those confusions mark the sites where thinking is literally knotted to the subject's historical and material place.

(p. 132)

Whereas Arenas's later works depict Cuban men in different states of awareness and affiliation with their homoerotic desires, **"Comienza el Desfile"** is exactly that, a beginning. The *desfile* is not only an amalgam of bodies, passions, and pleasures in the midst of revolution, but also a preview of the protagonist's eventual fate: to be lost and confused, on the verge of union, then disoriented once again, confined to aborted opportunities and familial (dis)engagements, nearing something, but never quite there; no, always *here.* But in the middle of this chaos, Arenas offers something else. Embedded in the text is a coming out of sorts, somewhere lost in the dialogue, but fully discernable, where the protagonist engages the revolution as a necessary stage toward finding himself. As he runs off with the rebels, he leaves his family a note, warning, "No le digan nada a nadie" [don't tell anyone anything] (1972, p. 11). Again, after receiving the knife, he says "No te digo nada" [I say nothing to you] (1972, p. 16). However, he shouldn't worry, as his mother refuses to even fry eggs, fearing that "el ruido puede traer sospechas" [the noise could bring suspicion] (1972, p. 18). Finally, however, the protagonist makes his triumphant return, proclaiming "Soy yo,—digo. Soy yo" [It's me, it's me] (1972, p. 16). He is thus proclaiming not only that he is *here,* but that he *is.* He has become the subject "I," through his mutual desire *for* and identification *with* the rebels.

Becoming his own subject, however, requires an almost Herculean effort, and in the end he offers a laconic "Estoy cansado," in response to the enthusiastic greeting offered him by his congratulatory family. "Debes estar muriéndote de hambre," says his grandmother. "Quieres que te prepare algo?" [You ought to be dying of hunger. Do you want me to prepare something for you?] (Arenas, 1972, p. 21). Instead, he must bathe. He has become himself through the revolution, but the revolution does not become him. He is left yearning to reveal his own body, to be free of the dust, the blood, the tears, urine, saliva, and shit; Soy yo. [I am what I am.] He is himself. And in the end, Arenas confirms the impossible—the acknowledgment of homosexuality as "a finally accepted and validated part of national life" (Sánchez-Eppler, 1994, p. 9). In the end, it is his family that utters the final affirmation: "Te estamos esperando" [We're waiting for you] (Arenas, 1972, p. 22).

A Carnivalesque Critique

Both "El Matadero" and **"Comienza el Desfile"** are uniquely suited for a *carnivalesque* analysis. A number of writers, including Bakhtin (1968), Burke (1978), Ladurie (1979), and Green (1999), have interpreted the "*carnalvalesque* tradition" through its essential opposition to the world of daily life, as a kind of opposition or rebellion to the mundane structure of everyday existence (Turner, 1969). It has been understood as a celebration of the flesh in which the prohibitions of normal life give away to simple pleasure (Bakhtin, 1968). Referring to Brazilian *carnaval,* one of Parker's informants, Joâo, confirms Bakhtin's analysis:

> It's like in that song from the film Black Orpheus: *Tristeza nao tem fim, felicidade sim* (Sadness has no end, but happiness ends). Leaving sadness, the struggle of day-to-day life, forgotten inside an imaginary drawer, the people allow themselves to be carried away by the reality of fantasy *(uma fantasia real)* in the three days of carnaval. They are three days of merrymaking, sweat, and beer, but everything comes to an end on Shrove Tuesday.
>
> (Parker, 1991, p. 141)

Carnaval thus becomes a separate space outside of time, a "utopic illusion" of sorts, which offers an alternative vision of life as it might be rather than it is (Parker, 1991, p. 161). In order to maintain this fantasy, Brazilian *carnaval* is characterized by a chaotic mixing of bodies, reminiscent of Echeverría's and Arenas's short stories:

> The sexual rhythm of the year gets faster during the summer, principally with the arrival of carnaval. With the heat of the summer, people have more energy for everything. . . . Libertine *sacanagem* becomes especially active during this period of the year. Everyone tries to find the sun, and the beaches become super-full with sweaty and golden bodies. Clothes become a key for the exhibitionism and display of the body, of the gifts of nature. Everything is very semi-nude, especially in cities where there are beaches. The nights are exhilarating and there is no place where there aren't people. They are hot nights, propitious for love, sex, freedom of the body. In the summer, nothing is a sin *(nada é pecado),* principally with the arrival of carnaval mixing with the summer and tropicalism of this country. (Antônio)
>
> (Parker, 1991, p. 147)

Brazilian *carnaval* therefore exemplifies Thomas's suggestion that the male body must be examined, put into full view, in order to expose the anxieties of masculinity and heterosexuality. Likewise, *carnaval* is immersed in its own *abjection,* oozing out exfluence at every available moment, and out of every available orifice:

> Within a society full of ups and downs, the permissiveness of the carnaval is not interrupted by anything, and bodies, souls, and semen are left at their will, giving to everyone the freedom to do what they really desire. It is a good period for prostitution and the buyers of pleasure. Everything is sold, everything is bought, everything is given, everything is received with a lewd and inviting smile on the face. Beaches, corners, bars, bathrooms, parks, buses, trains, and other places are stages for sensuality and sex. The streets become completely given over to the beat of samba and the frenzy of sweaty bodies having sex. (Joâo)
>
> (Parker, 1991, p. 148)

Although the explicit sexual imagery represented in Brazilian *carnaval* is not present in "El Matadero" or **"Comienza el Desfile,"** the two stories share the *carni-valesque* mingling of bodies and bodily fluids as the participants struggle to maintain themselves in a chaotic, yet temporary, suspension of morality. All three scenes share a spatial arrangement in which bodies are continuously uniting and drifting, leaving traces here and there—splattered excrement, purple-hued blood, tears flowing into rivers, testicular odors, semen dripping from the pricks of sodomites, even flying shit. It is not so much that "sin ceases to exist," as Parker claims, but that the power to define sin is altered. The mass now becomes master as man loses control of his own body and merges with the bodies of others. Parker (1991) claims, "The *povo* (people) in turn is offered a new and different awareness of its sensuality, its material unity and community" (p. 144). In much the same way as occurs during *carnaval,* the characters in "El Matadero" and those in **"Comienza el Desfile"** are subject to new forms of organization. Their desires are not only fulfilled in this new setting, but also have the capacity to transform themselves, even creating new desires.

It should be noted, however, that *carnaval*'s sexual imagery and licentiousness is not simply a transgressive reversal of gender and sexual norms. Likewise, the sodomy depicted in "El Matadero" is not a transgression against the prevailing sexual order but an *enactment* of that sexual order. Similarly, Arenas's inability to consummate his relationship with the revolutionary youth is not in any way opposed to the somatic and emotional fervor of the Castro revolution. The Brazilian *carnaval*—like the two short stories depicted in this chapter—acts as both an inversion and intensification of gender and sexual ideologies. In reference to the cross-dressing images that predominate during *carnaval,* Green (1999) maintains that "while the satorical inversion [of gender] implies reversal of the status quo, it also works to reinforce pervasive standards of the feminine, and therefore, the masculine" (p. 204). Parker agrees, using a discussion of *samba* to illustrate how *carnaval* can also serve to maintain, even intensify, dominant gender and sexual constructs:

> If much of the sexual symbolism of carnaval seems to undercut the certainty of established classifications, relativizing and destroying them through grotesque combinations of elaborate transvestisms, then in a strange way this world of samba that has been integrated into the structure of Brazilian carnaval seems to display them in an intensified or exaggerated form. Samba itself, at least in its most popular manifestations, is created within a fundamentally male space: the popular male bars where the predominantly male composures spend their free time, and where women who wish to avoid being labeled as putas or piranhas are unlikely to venture. Even the language, the poetry, of samba, is a kind of male discourse, which often focuses on the suffering and injustice imposed, it is claimed, upon men by women. These distinctions are even more obvious in the movements and gestures of

samba dancers, with their strikingly sexual choreography, their pelvic thrusts, their grinding hips, their elaborately simulated transactions. If the transvestite seems to terrorize the normal distinctions of gender and sexuality, then the *mulandro* (rogue, scoundrel) and the *mulata* loudly proclaim them.

(Parker, 1991, p. 154)

Both "El Matadero" and **"Comienza el Desfile"** also take place in decidedly male spaces. When females are present, they are either degraded negros ("El Matadero") or annoying relatives (**"Comienza el Desfile"**). They are either covered in shit ("El Matadero") or speaking shit (**"Comienza el Desfile"**). While the *carnaval,* the slaughterhouse, and the revolutionary parade, may be accurately described as a search for liberty and freedom, that search still takes place within a given set of gender and sexual heteronormative assumptions. Likewise, the seemingly chaotic parades, movements, and flows in are guided by the understandings of gender and sexuality that existed at particular historical moments.

I introduce the Brazilian *carnaval* partly because most readers can conceptualize the energy, vitality, and sensuousness of the well-known event. The image of escaping to Brazil and enjoying a few days of debauchery provides a welcome relief from the more mundane realities of our daily lives. But *carnaval* should not be thought of merely as an escape from everyday life. Instead, perhaps the Brazilian *carnaval* reflects the *carnavalesque* mixing of bodies already present in Brazil rather than the need to create a space for sexual transgression. The mixing of bodies already present in the overcrowded urban areas of Brazil, much like the amalgam of bodies in "El Materdero" and **"Comieza el Desfile,"** creates the urge to simultaneously fulfill sexual desires while discovering new desires. If this notion can be sustained, then perhaps both Echeverría and Arenas were trying to develop a space where new desires could be appropriated, elucidated, and, eventually, fulfilled. As in Brazilian *carnaval,* the fusion of bodies both intensifies and inverts dominant gender and sexual images. They are reinscribed as they are contested.

There is something compelling about Echeverría's ethnographic eroticism. It complements what those of us who regularly sleep with Latin American men already know: that even in the supposedly neutral bedroom, historical accounts of the power relations embedded in the active/passive dichotomy are still very real. "El Matadero," in some sense, justifies the conclusions of the active/passive theorists: hegemonic, machismo masculinity—by perpetuating active/passive, male/female dualities—allows men to sleep with other men. Although I agree with the conclusion that hegemonic masculinity is more likely to sustain, rather than curtail, [homo]sexual liaisons, I do not wish to perpetuate active/passive constructions of Latin male sexuality. In the case of nineteenth-century Argentina, however, these active/passive constructs, apparently, were still firmly embedded in the consciousness of individual men. This does not imply, nevertheless, that one can rely exclusively on this construct. By engaging in a creative, multifaceted critique of the "depth semantics" underlying Echeverría's text, I have hopefully broadened the inquiry beyond simple active/passive formulations. In doing so, I discovered, first, that the unitarian was actually getting sodomized, and second, that this sodomization has significance beyond mere power structures. By using vague allusions to sodomy, Echeverría offers—to those readers able to fully *inhabit* the work—a window through which to observe *what is also going on;* that is, what actually feels good, better, and best, and is capable of romanticizing or stabilizing gang rape into a positive expression of male-male intimacy. The next step, I suppose, is an examination of other Argentinean nineteenth-century texts in search of these intimate relationships that certainly did exist. It does not promise to be an easy task, but the rewards are substantial. Perhaps this can be the first step toward recovering the historical roots of a deeply personal, sexually intimate, loving relationship sustained by symmetry and balance which contemporary and former commentaries alike would have us believe does not exist between men in Latin America. I know better than that.

Whereas Echeverría created a space where same-sex male desire could be fulfilled, Arenas's protagonist inhabits a space, *un desfile,* in which the fulfillment of desire is subordinate to the creation of desire. Through the Cuban revolution and its material manifestation in *el desfile,* the protagonist is exposed to the male world. He stands next to male bodies, sharing rum, sweat, rivers, tears, and triumphs. *El desfile* provides the setting in which multiple forms of desire converge. First, the protagonist's Freudian sense of lack is evident throughout the text, as he mourns his lack of food, water, trees, and most certainly a life of his own. Likewise, as Parker suggests, the need to unite with one's opposite drives the sexually transgressive atmosphere of the Brazilian carnaval and acts as a fulfillment of lack or an acknowledgment of loss. Nevertheless, **"Comienza el Desfile"** does not solely rely on a fusion of opposites to produce desires; instead, a type of *identificatory* desire exists in which the possibility of a mutually recognized love is acknowledged.

The mentality of the masses offers the rare opportunity for mutually identified individuals to recognize one another. As Parker suggests, sexuality is intimately linked to the social, and it is not surprising that Arenas's protagonist must inhabit a social space in order to develop and contemplate his own desires. His burgeoning sexuality will forever be linked to revolutionary fervor. The revolution thus provides him with a sexual identity, as does the *carnaval* for Brazilians. "With all of its chaos and confusion, its contradictions and its juxtapositions, its exaggerated sexuality and its transgressive laughter," writes Parker (1991), "the *carnaval* stands as an ironic answer to the search for a sense of identity that has troubled Brazilian thinking for more than a century" (p. 163). The same can be said for Cubans—for the protagonist in **"Comienza el Desfile"** and for Arenas himself. Identity is formed within the performance of the *desfile,* the enacting of the revolution. Likewise, it is the *superdesfile* of the samba schools and the bloody slaughterhouse of the Argentine Civil War.

I have struggled throughout this book with this notion of identity. On one hand, I resist the impulse to bestow upon macho men any so-called "gay" identity. However, this is not to say they do not have *any* discernable identity. For example, by exposing his sexual exploits with another man, Junior is articulating a particular sexual identity. This identity may allow him (or has already allowed him) an ongoing sexual relationship with other men, more than he acknowledged in our talk together. I cannot look Junior in the eyes—listening to his sincere speech—and in good conscience say, as does Judith Butler, that identity is mere fabrication. If he is not real, than neither is my love for him.

Macho men like Junior can represent themselves in many ways, and the identity exposed through that representational practice—either in speech, act, or literary work—is most certainly *real*. The problem, however, is getting them to talk about it. Junior is the exception. In general, masculine-identified Hispanic men are reticent to talk about their sexual relationships with other men. The macho man survives partly through his own silence, but this is not to say that he has no discernible identity. Furthermore, many Hispanic men *do* have a very public, highly articulated [homo]sexual identity. The following chapter introduces some of these men and uses their own words as a way of questioning the very propositions that animate this book.

Notes

1. The term *carnivalesque* refers to Bakhtin's sense of the carnivalesque: "the playful, sexual and scatological language" (Limón, 1989, p. 473) used to mock authority.

2. Due to legal issues involving the estate of Reinaldo Arenas, I have been unable to obtain permission to use longer excerpts from his work. I have, therefore, included smaller extracts of his original Spanish in "Comienza el Desfile," while retaining the longer passage in my English translation. I apologize for any difficulty or confusion this might cause the reader.

Bibliography

Arenas, Reinaldo (1972). Comienza el Desfile. In Arenas, Reinaldo, *Con Los Ojos Cerrados* (pp. 1-14). Montevideo: Editorial S.R.L. Montevideo.

———. (1990). *Viaje a La Habana.* Miami: Universal.

———. (1993). *Before Night Falls.* Translated by Dolores M. Koch. New York: Penguin.

Bakhtin, Mikhail (1968). *Rabelais and His World.* Cambridge, MA: MIT Press.

———. (1984). *Rabelais and His World.* Translated by Hélène Iswolsky. Boomington: Indiana University Press.

Bondi, Liz (1990). Feminism, Postmodernism and Geography: Space for Women? *Antipode* 22: 156-167.

Burke, Peter (1978). *Popular Culture in Early Modern Europe.* New York: Harper and Row.

Echeverría, Esteban (1871). El Matadero. *Revista del Rio de la Plata* (Buenos Aires) 1(2): 576-588.

Estévez, Abilio (1994). Between Nightfall and Vengeance: Remembering Reinaldo Arenas. *Michigan Quarterly Review* 33(4): 859-867.

Gallop, Jane (1988). *Thinking Through the Body.* New York: Columbia University Press.

Green, James (1999). *Beyond Carnival: Male Homosexuality in Twentieth-Century Brazil.* Chicago: The University of Chicago Press.

Ladurie, Emmanuel Le Roy (1979). *Carnival in Romans.* New York: Braziller.

Limón, José (1989). Carne, Carnales and the Carnivalesque: Bakhtinian Batos, Disorder and Narrative Discourse. *American Ethnologist* 16: 471-486.

Oviedo, José Miguel (1983). Termina el Desfile. *Vuelta.* 71(711): 43-46.

Parker, Richard G. (1991). *Bodies, Pleasures, and Passions.* Boston: Beacon Press.

———. (1999). *Beneath the Equator.* New York: Routledge.

Sánchez-Eppler, Benigno (1994). Call My Son Ismael: Exiled Paternity and Father/Son Eroticism in Reinaldo Arenas and Jose Marti. *Differences: A Journal of Feminist Cultural Studies* 6(1): 69-129. Electronic Transmission: 1-18.

Thomas, Calvin (1996). *Male Matters: Masculinity, Anxiety, and the Male Body on the Line.* Urbana: University of Illinois Press.

Turner, Victor (1969). *The Ritual Process: Structure and Anti-Structure.* Chicago: University of Chicago Press.

Laurie Vickroy (essay date winter 2005)

SOURCE: Vickroy, Laurie. "The Traumas of Unbelonging: Reinaldo Arenas's Recuperations of Cuba." *MELUS* 30, no. 4 (winter 2005): 109-28.

[*In the following essay, Vickroy focuses on the "traumatic" events in Arenas's life—his oppression, dislocation, and eventual exile from his Cuban homeland—and analyzes how "his imagination and art, especially through the lenses of gender and sexuality, become the means to express and, to some extent, overcome trauma."*]

Comparatists have recognized in recent decades a shift away from exclusively national literatures and notions of place-bound culture. Increasingly we are dealing with what Bruce Robbins calls "different modalities of situatedness-in-displacement" (250) as globalization, migration, and forced exile have separated people from places and made conceptions of ethnicity less static and more mobile, fluid, and hybrid as they are subject to a greater variety of cultural influences.[1] However, these conditions also raise the question of the relationship between culture and self, and feeling bound to a place remains an imperative for some, particularly if the separation from homeland is traumatic. While situations of displacement often foster survival through cultural adaptability, in the context of traumatic exile a lost home can remain not only psychically embedded as a place of origin and identity but also of an anguished dissolution of self. The case of contemporary Cuba and in particular the work of exiled Cuban writer Reinaldo Arenas (1943-1990) is exemplary, specifically in how the traumas of revolution, oppression, and dislocation produce a fragmented, isolated, and dissociated identity and an aesthetic sensibility compelled to both critique and reconnect to homeland.

Arenas's estrangements from authorities and other Cubans both before and after he flees Cuba fuel his imagination, provoking recreations of Cuba through which he can revisit in some way his losses and hopes for his country and himself. His own displacement also mirrors other Cubans' fragmented political, cultural, and psychological life. Writing most of his work in exile in the US,[2] he chronicles his own persecution for being homosexual and uncompromisingly observes how in Cuban society a powerful, masculinized cultural order attempts to suppress other influences, more specifically, the nexus of art, gender, and sexuality that he associates with the feminine. Like many trauma writers, Arenas adopts a testimonial approach to bear witness for a suppressed past (Vickroy 5). His writing carries the imprint of overwhelming, psychologically disruptive events, and he attempts to reshape cultural memory of these events in his focus on artists' authenticity and survival, and in imaginatively revisiting emotionally over-determined contexts symptomatic of traumas. Art provides mediated structures by which he withstands attempts to obliterate his person and his work. This study will establish the traumatic contexts of Arenas's life and then will analyze how his imagination and art, especially through the lenses of gender and sexuality, become the means to express and, to some extent, overcome trauma.

Trauma narratives, I contend, are personalized responses to this century's emerging awareness of the catastrophic effects of wars, poverty, colonization, and oppression on the individual psyche. They are often concerned with human-made traumatic situations and are implicit critiques of the ways social, economic, and political structures can create and perpetuate trauma (Vickroy 4). They highlight postcolonial concerns with rearticulating the lives and voices of marginal people, and reveal trauma as an indicator of social injustice or oppression, as the ultimate cost of destructive sociocultural institutions (Vickroy x). Many of these narratives have characteristics of testimonio or testimonial narrative that seeks to create a feeling of lived experience and expresses a "problematic collective social situation" through a representative individual (Beverley 94-95). Testifying to the past has been an urgent task for many fiction writers in recent decades as they attempt to preserve personal and collective memories from assimilation, repression, or misrepresentations (Vickroy 1).

Arenas exemplifies this approach in his recounting of the effects of Castro's regime, describing aspects of Cuban culture lying outside of official versions, and revealing the follies of Cuban life and history as he sees them. Arenas shares trauma victims' feelings of helplessness under persecution, a sense of being tainted, and lacking social support that would aid healing (Van der Kolk and Van der Hart 446; Herman 47; Langer 84-96). Exile then compounds his sense of fragmented identity, which he finds profoundly disturbing, and, like many traumatized, he will go to great lengths to create or maintain a sense of agency and order. Thus Arenas engages in repetitive rewriting in order to act and feel a greater sense of wholeness, to overcome helplessness and fear, to resist oppression, and to reveal truths. Like other trauma narrativists, he testifies to his pain and calls upon readers to be the witnesses unavailable to him in Cuba. Fellow exiled writer Octavio Armand describes how exiles engage in "A permanent construction and reconstruction of what has been lost. . . . Because of the . . . pressing need to overcome or sublimate helplessness" (21). Similarly, Arenas is guided by an obsession with the past, which can be gauged by how only 32 out of 317 pages of his autobiography cover the final 10 years of his life, indicating a more powerful relation to his Cuban past than his present or future.

The trauma of exile, both within and outside the island, pervades Arenas's considerations of Cuba. The Cuban situation of trauma and exile is a unique one. Mark Falcoff observes, "While all the revolutions of modern history have produced sizable exile communities, in no other case has the diaspora been so proportionately large, so well organized, so geographically concentrated and so physically proximate to its country of origin. The result is a cultural hybrid—a community that is functionally American, but dwells spiritually in a cloud of imminence" (4). Imminence refers here to many Cubans' sense that return will eventually be possible. Louis

Perez describes the traumatic changes wrought by the revolution, particularly on prosperous Cubans who looked to the US as a model and protector, expecting that the US would remove Castro. Though this was never realized, they maintained their need to return and yet recreate Cuba elsewhere in the interim (498-500). This recreation has occurred in Miami, albeit nostalgically. David Rieff's psychologically revealing book analyzes the lingering wounds of Cuban exiles, which produce a fixation on the past, extreme anti-Castro politics, and fantasy structures of return and triumph. Their identities are exclusively bound up in culture and place, though these obsessions have begun to wane with subsequent generations of Cuban Americans thirty to forty years later. Ibis Gómez-Vega notes how many Cubans left "at a time when the country need[ed] them most" and that many became "victims to the public and private chaos created by the socialists' need to control every moment of people's lives, every thought in their heads. . . . The Cubans who have fled . . . have left behind not only their homeland but their families . . . and this is part of the pain which most Cubans cannot shed . . . easily" (233-34). Cristina Garcia describes the feelings of Cuban exiles as

> a form of banishment. It is a severing from one's homeland, a rift between here and there, a longing unsoothed, the terrible sense of unbelonging. . . . For Cubans today, both on and off the island, a profound sense of exile and alienation persists. One doesn't ever feel fully at home in Havana or Miami, Madrid or Mexico City. New lexicons have evolved inside and outside Cuba that reflect starkly different realities. Invariably, something or someone is missing from the picture.
>
> (176-77)

Though Arenas did not identify with most Cuban exiles,[3] many of the potentially traumatic features of their exile are reflected in Arenas's own life and works. These features include suffering the loss of homeland, a fragmented or diminished sense of self, a sense of homelessness and dislocation, isolation, and alienation. Much of this is replayed in the loss of Arenas's manuscripts through confiscation and the importance of their recreation in order to retain his identity as a writer, a man, and a Cuban. His response to these traumas is manifest in his obsessive textual recreations of what has been lost. Repetition is an attempt to master traumas, Freud and others have observed, but can also indicate emotional stasis and possession by the past. His work indicates that Cuba is a formative and continuing influence, and he attempts to recreate it as part of a process of testifying to injustice and redressing wrongs. To understand his imperatives in this regard, Arenas's traumas both within and outside Cuba must be elaborated.

Arenas received a state-mandated education, something he never would have received as a peasant before the revolution, and, employed as a librarian, achieves a life and identity as a writer because of the Cuban revolution. Though he embraces its idealism initially, he is ever aware of the proscriptions against homosexuality in his society. After a brief period of publishing in Cuba in the late 1960s, he runs afoul of the political and economic vagaries that transform the state's cultural policies into hard-line Soviet style demands for literature that serves and supports the revolution. Arenas's work, which always extols freedom, and which he begins to publish abroad without state sanction, makes him increasingly marginal and eventually the state brands him a criminal figure.[4]

He is eventually persecuted, imprisoned, and censored for being homosexual, but mostly for refusing to write state-approved works. Arenas's humiliations of false arrest, escape attempts, suicide attempts, torture, and imprisonment are chronicled in his autobiography *Before Night Falls* (157-207). Mehuron describes the trauma of these experiences as an "ethical humiliation" (43) that is also described by Arenas:

> They wanted me to make a confession stating that I was a counter-revolutionary, that I regretted the ideological weakness I had shown in my published writings, and that the Revolution had been extraordinarily fair with me. . . . I did not want to recant anything, I did not think that I had to recant anything; but after three months at State Security, I signed the confession. Needless to say, this only proves my cowardice, my weakness, the certainty that I am not the stuff of which heroes are made, and that fear, in my case, had won over moral principles.
>
> (*Before* 204)

A significant effect of trauma is that victims feel helpless, diminished, and tainted, all apparent from Arenas's account. Because of this forced renunciation of his work, Arenas must reclaim and reconstruct his ethical self through his writing. He must also break the traumatic silence of those oppressed or denied by the state because they criticize its excesses.

Arenas's work "performs the work of cultural memory, retrieving much that has been effaced by authoritarian deployments of power through terror" (Mehuron 47).[5] Arenas illustrates the consequences of this power over individuals through his own life experiences recounted in *Before Night Falls* and the novel *The Color of Summer,* and in an unrelenting ridicule of Castro through irreverent portrayal that undermines his authority. With humor that is both distancing and perhaps therapeutic, Arenas makes fun of his own painful retraction in *The Color of Summer,* but also depicts writing again: "'Everything I have written before this day . . . is garbage, and should be consigned to the garbage heap. From this day forward I shall be a man, and shall become a worthy child of this marvelous Revolution.' . . . As soon as he could he traded all the cigarettes he had left for blank paper, and once more began the story of his novel" (332-33).

The fact that others were publishing who did not provoke the regime must have made Arenas feel more marginal and rejected.[6] After Arenas emerges from two years of forced labor (state rehabilitation for his homosexuality) and then prison (for an unsubstantiated morals charge), he suffers more punishments: poverty (he loses his job), his manuscripts continue to be confiscated (abetted by the betrayals of his aunt and others), and because of the state's disapproval he is treated as a pariah, a non-person denied out of fear by those who know him (Santí 227). These denials and negations of himself again necessitate his obsessive returns to writing to assert himself and his view of the world.

Arenas's experience as an exile in the US is both similar to and different from other exiles. He wanted to leave Cuba so he could be free of persecution and regain his artistic voice. His wish was fulfilled in the Mariel boatlifts of 1980, where, like other undesirables (criminals, gays, etc.), he was allowed by Castro to leave. Once outside Cuba, Arenas can write what he wants; he can rail about his life and criticize Castro and his regime. "I screamed; it was my treasure, it was all I had" (*Before* 288). However, like many exiles, he feels alienated, too disconnected from his culture, friends, and even himself in the US, where, like other Cuban exiles, his writing is "stifled by lack of communication, rootlessness, solitude, implacable materialism, and above all, envy" (*Color* [*The Color of Summer*] 253). He likens his situation to the histories of other exiled Cuban writers: "on our island we have been condemned to silence, to ostracism, censorship, and prison; in exile, despised and forsaken by our fellow exiles" (*Before* 291).

Exile involves another loss of self for Arenas because he is now disconnected from the place that had formed his life view and imagination. "I ceased to exist when I went into exile; I started to run away from myself" (293). He likens the exile to a person looking for a loved one's face and not finding it (293). Though he finds a more amenable life in New York City, where he partakes enthusiastically of the city's gay and cultural scenes, he contracts AIDS. Nevertheless, Cuba remains his focus and passion in the majority of his work in his post-Cuba years.

In his last years he wrote many works including the novel *The Color of Summer* and the autobiography *Before Night Falls,* both finished just before his death in 1990 and published posthumously (Manrique 1). This free but ungrounded exile life is the context out of which he tells his life story in the autobiography and satirizes Cuban life and history in *The Color of Summer. Before Night Falls* straightforwardly chronicles his hardships, but *The Color of Summer,* despite the largely absurdist comic context, also repeats autobiographical details and switches to moods of rage, fear,

and sadness. The novel's traumatic markings are also revealed in comic distance and in emotionally overdetermined contexts. Like other Cuban exiles, he tries to recreate his beloved place of origin through his imagination. It is not a replica, but a product of memory that thoughtfully examines losses and miseries. Not only Cuba, but his exile from it, broadens his consciousness and fuels his imaginative ability for recreation. "Living in exile has brought me the world of nostalgia, it has offered me a series of things that I never would have experienced in Cuba. Perhaps my fortune has been the historical, social, and personal calamities I have suffered, which have given diversity to my creative experience" (Arenas, "Interview" 148).

Arenas attempts to recreate the diversity of Cuba through a multi-voiced narrative filtered through the writer's voice and dialogue and through a multitude of genres: drama, the picaresque, satire, letters, magic realism, historical analysis, and the chivalric quest, among others. This combination creates a simultaneously carnivalesque, grotesque, poetic, and tragic portrait of Cuba under its dictator, Fifo (obviously Castro) set in the future, 1999. These genres allow Arenas to amplify the passions, frustrations, absurdity, and pain of everyday living under an intrusive regime. His trauma narrative, like Toni Morrison's *Beloved,* combines testimonial elements with multiple subject positionings to create a dialogical conception of witnessing, where many voices, emotions, and experiences intermingle to produce individual and collective memory and to counteract silence and forgetting imposed by powerful interests (Vickroy 27).

Narrative fragmentation also conveys the complex multiplicity of culture, hybrid identity, and expression. Though the narrative consists largely of nonchronological short pieces, the fate of the island, geographical and political, underlies the plot. Andrew Hurley and Francisco Soto have noted Arenas's deft use of the carnivalesque, as Bakhtin describes it, the mixing of the sublime and the ridiculous in order to attack authority (Hurley 458-60; Soto *Pentagonia* 99). He unravels the traumatic effects of power by satirically exposing the excesses and unreasonable demands of a dictator: Fifo commands dead writers be brought back to life to commemorate his fiftieth (really fortieth) anniversary in power.

This carnivalesque approach is also evident in Arenas's depictions of the erotically charged carnival celebrating the dictator's rule. The "ass-wiggling" crowd is outwardly obedient to the regime, if inwardly resentful, and when swayed by music and moving bodies, devolves into an anarchic orgy. This metaphor of the nation of whores signals the oppression that makes people docile and hypocritical, but also suggests it has to be eased occasionally to attenuate frustration. Further, this state-sanctioned chaos reveals the culture's contradictory impulses toward order and freedom. Similarly irreverent are the "religious" ceremonies in honor of the atheistic Fifo: the universal worship of the "Holy Hammer," or phallus of a beautiful young man on a parade float, satirizing the extreme code of masculinity in Cuba, and the hypocrisy of denying homosexuality even while engaging in it.

Imagination and self-expression play critical roles in the narrative and ensure the survival of the traumatized self for Arenas, who articulates this struggle in the personalized form of letters. Letters in *The Color of Summer* recount Arenas's insights into past and present, an analysis of a life in exile, and the possibilities of writing from there. His letter writers are three personas or aspects of Arenas himself, illustrating the necessity of personal fragmentation for social survival (Soto, *Arenas* 58), and a traumatized splitting of the individual forced to hide his true life and thoughts: there is Gabriel, the good son who pretends to live a straight life for his mother; Reinaldo, his writer-self; and Skunk in a Funk, the authentic homosexual self he is with his friends. "Skunk" (who has escaped to the US) writes repeatedly to Reinaldo (still in Cuba) to reconnect with the writer who had hoped that when he left Cuba he could bring his writing and message to the world. He has lost much of that hope, however, as he lists his many disappointments: expatriate writers afraid to criticize Castro, his certain doom from AIDS, the materialism and shallowness of the US, and the sadism and sexual bartering among gay men in the US.

Through Skunk, Arenas articulates his own diminished sense of self that he links to his disconnection from Cuba: "Down there, I was at least real, even though what you might call painfully Real. Up here, I'm a shadow" (171); "I don't exist, yet I suffer from my existence" (294). This trauma of unbelonging dominates Arenas's life after he is made the state's enemy and has to leave. "How can I go on living . . . I am just a shell of myself, the old dried-out rind of myself. . . . If I live another hundred years here, I will still be a stranger, a foreigner, an alien" (296). Eventually his Cuban self writes back, reminding him of the abjection of living under tyranny, of not only having to accept oppression and humiliation but to "applaud [it] enthusiastically" (351). Certainly his imminent death from AIDS must have devastated Arenas, and his continued sense of unbelonging, which already existed in Cuba, is perhaps exacerbated by life in the US, but, more importantly, one senses that the freedom of exile also brings loneliness and a missing sense of self as connected to place. The community of artists he once knew in Cuba before the severe repression of dissident thought is fragmented by ideological differences in the larger world, where Arenas is faced with many defenders of Castro.[7]

For Arenas the situation and mission of the artist must be to resist appropriation and oppression; therefore, the authentic artist is a political rebel and social outcast. The silence and hopelessness that characterize trauma are indicators and consequences of power relations and must be resisted. Under repressive cultural policies the artist risks punishment by the state and often has to resort to secrecy and subterfuge to ensure his or her work will survive. The Cuban artists' community is devastated by state surveillance and suppression. Arenas portrays several actual Cuban artists, including himself, who are persecuted by the state, and whose creative lives are curtailed by poverty, forced labor, or imprisonment. Declaring his artistry and his homosexuality to be essential aspects of himself, Arenas challenges a homophobic and dogmatic state by his very existence. He refuses to submit his writing for approval by the state apparatus' cultural organization, UNEAC (Cuban National Union of Writers and Artists). His constant rewriting of his manuscript, continually lost through misadventures or betrayals (a running gag in *The Color of Summer,* but also a reality of Arenas's life),[8] symbolizes his struggle for authentic expression against a state which feels art should only be in its service. "Arenas'[s] militancy was in support of individual freedom. If one thing is constantly repeated throughout his work it is the challenging and undermining of all systems of power that attempt to establish themselves as absolute authority. . . . His rebelliousness and subversion were creative and directed toward positive and life-affirming actions: the right of individuals to express themselves freely" (Soto, *Arenas* 32). His writing is witness to the life he wants to live: in complete freedom to express any view and in any form.

The loss of art, and hence cultural expression, occurs frequently in the novel. The eminent poet Virgilio Pinera reads his poems in gatherings made secret to avoid party officials and immediately burns them in fear of regime spies. Art offends the state, Arenas suggests, because it takes people away from the realities of daily life into worlds of beauty and imagination, and by focusing on individual and collective suffering it resists the doctrine of revolutionary collective optimism that conveys a false sense of existence that denies suffering. Art's destruction represents a traumatic loss of self and voice, but also a terrible loss to Cuban cultural identity since artists are either deprived of their country, absorbed by the state, or silenced. The state becomes the culture instead of art. Telling examples of the interconnection of art, identity, and culture are articulated when 1) Arenas's three selves become united only in the library, where books open up the world, beauty, and ideas, and 2) when he says "All of my characters form a single mocking, despairing spirit, the spirit of my work, which is also, perhaps, the spirit of our country" (352).

Imaginatively he reinvokes committed exiled artists who also had to express their love of Cuba from a distance. He emphasizes women artists, historical and contemporary, as similarly marginalized as gays, and though he satirizes them, he also analogizes their lives and work to the difficulties of being a suppressed artist. Two historical portraits include the nineteenth-century writers Gertrudis Gomez de Avallaneda and La Condesa de Merlin. Avalleneda was a romantic poet and rebellious exile (Harter 51). Resurrected to celebrate Fifo's 50 years in power, she resists his appropriation of her work for the state by heading to the US in a boat (which eventually sinks). While escaping she meets writer and activist José Martí (who remains a Cuban cultural hero), also resurrected, returning to Cuba, despite death threats, to lead another revolution and to escape the materialism and superficiality of the US. Their dialogue articulates the dilemmas of many exiles and artists, including Arenas: she says if Cuba cannot be saved, then save yourself and find somewhere free to write, and Martí replies life has to have meaning even if one has to die for a cause (*Color* 51-60).

Arenas's inclusion of Maria de las Mercedes Santa Cruz y Montalvo, la Condesa de Merlin, suggests lost historical legacies and the need for art and beauty amid deprivations. Merlin, another exile, spent much of her lifetime in Europe and her depictions of Cuba were attacked because of male critical bias and because she lived abroad for so long (Rodenas, *Gender* 218). She was, however, a perfect example of the displaced artist. Having spent many years in France and Spain, she adapted to different cultures and was a patroness of the arts, with a celebrated salon. Her work does, however, reflect the loss of her homeland and the compulsion to recreate it within the imaginative space of her writing.

In Arenas's irreverent portrayal, Merlin's name and prodigious sexuality link her with the gay queens and their rivalries. Arenas himself used Merlin's name as a pseudonym in case his letters were intercepted by the police (231). Although he discredits her writing like many male critics, Arenas also uses Merlin as an alterego or a "projection for unresolved homosexual fantasies," and he even updates Merlin's work in his own *Voyage to Havana* (231). In *The Color of Summer* Merlin returns to Cuba from France to find that her ancestral home has been turned into a gigantic men's urinal by the state. This, and Merlin's singing, which moves and distracts the sexually engaged men in the urinal, indicate the degree of the regime's destruction of Cuba's cultural legacy and suggest the powerful beauty of art. For Arenas and other contemporary Cuban writers, Merlin symbolizes a lingering "gender and cultural marginality" and "elusive nationality" for Cubans (239-40).

Arenas's most affecting portrayal of a woman artist is his embellishment of the actual life and work of painter Blanca Romero. Forced into prostitution when her husband is jailed, she is reduced to stealing painting supplies from other artists who are supported by the state for their conformity. She cannot sell her works, which Arenas calls "extraordinary" (*Before* 250). In *The Color of Summer* she embodies artists' suffering under Castro while trying to maintain artistic authenticity, becoming the fictional Carla Mortera, whose works inspire Skunk in a Funk's meditations on the power of art. Suggesting the magical realist effects of her work, he says viewers experienced a visceral, bodily response to her imagery; they "had injured themselves on the leaves and flowers" (*Color* 370).

Looking at one of Carla's portraits, Skunk tries to explain the layers of meaning communicated through it, suggesting the power of art, through beauty, to reveal the pain underlying the surfaces of existence and the consolation of this truthfulness that is camouflaged by authorities and quotidian life.

> This painting, like all extraordinary things in this world, had the wondrous ability to hint at depths of mystery, at facet after facet of significance. . . . This lovely young poet was holding a book . . . she was looking outward at the spectator of the painting. To Skunk in a Funk this meant that all the terrible truth the book contained was useless, that there was something more terrible still that lay beneath the first discovery, and beneath that, things still more terrible. . . . That work was touched with an infinite grief, as terrible as the resignation that also filled it. . . . One could say that it was the sum of all misfortunes, all calamities, concentrated in one horrific, stoic act of wisdom. That woman, that painting, was not a painting; it was a spell, an awesome and irrepeatable force that could have been born only out of an ecstasy of genius and madness. It was enigma and consolation; it was faith in the belief that come what may, life does still have meaning; and was absolute despair.
>
> (370-71)

The sight of a room full of her paintings makes Skunk "entranced, and temporarily oblivious to all the world's horrors—especially the horror of being alive—[he] could not tear himself from the portrait" (371). For Skunk, the painting expresses the traumas of life that are often repressed and, in doing so, in shaping them artistically, fulfills a consolatory, even therapeutic function of art in provoking thought, engagement, and grief rather than silencing or suppressing human pain.

Like many Cuban artists, Carla creates without benefit of traveling outside Cuba to see other artists' works, and without institutional support. Despite poverty, surveillance, and cultural sterility, Carla's frenzy of creation, 300 paintings in a month, is Arenas's metaphor for the powerful need for self-expression, particularly when it is threatened. When she borrows the name of Skunk's manuscript for one of her paintings, he acknowledges their shared gender and artistic identification: Skunk "knew that Carla and she were a single person and that their works therefore complimented one another" (389). When she exhibits her works in the eighteenth-century convent (coincidentally, Merlin's school) that she and her friends have ransacked, it becomes for many viewers a magical experience. When Carla returns to view her paintings again, she discovers that they have been destroyed by Fifo's men. She then ends her life (and the block she lives on) in a self-immolation. This self-sacrifice demonstrates the compelling need for self-expression, becoming sometimes a matter of life and death, with resonance in Arenas's own life, finishing this manuscript as he was dying of AIDS. Through Blanca/Carla, Arenas explores the obstacles to artistic creation under a hostile regime, art's capacity to articulate human depth, and art's simultaneous necessity and fragility.

Arenas empowers the feminine in association with art, attributing rare artistic insight to women or gay men, from greats like Pinera and Lezama Lima to the less successful queens like Delphin Proust and the aspiring writers of bilious autobiographies he nicknames the Brontë sisters. This feminization challenges the hyper-masculine, logistical, heterosexual military structure of the regime that has almost destroyed him. Arenas depicts very few heterosexual male artists to make the point that Cuban society has marginalized such activity, deeming it effeminate. Arenas's own penchant for fantasies, words, and stories was considered pejoratively feminine and freakish by his own family, as he recounts in **Before Night Falls.** Further, his mother's disappointment at his failure to lead a conventional masculine, heterosexual life becomes a source of constant pain and anger for him. She is absorbed by homophobic cultural standards that prevent her accepting her son's identity as gay or as an artist. He cannot show her his frankly homosexual writing, which he considers a fundamental part of himself.

Artistic critiques of Cuba figure largely in Arenas's works, reshaping cultural memory through the portrayal of an array of unofficial Cuban lives, and using parodic metaphors for how a repressive society controls and wounds its members but also for how they survive. Creative manifestations of Cuban life abound in *The Color of Summer* as mocking refusals to conform, as critiques of repressive forces, and as examples of how art consoles the artist in its revelations. Arenas is trying to preserve ignored or broken aspects of Cuban life. He fills what he fears will be a void of silence in recreating the 1960s and 1970s.

> I feel an endless desolation, an inconsolable grief for all that evil [Cubans' history and bowing to repression], and yet a furious tenderness when I think of my past and present. That desolation and that love have in

some way compelled me to write this pentagony,[9] which in addition to being the history of my fury and my love is also a metaphor for my country.

(*Color* 255)

His imaginative approach transforms the desperate, violent, and sometimes joyous street life of gay men into literary culture, demonstrating their penchant for the creativity of everyday life in the face of deprivation. Arenas gives us picaresque episodes of their daily pleasures, dangers, and thwarted desires: Eachurbod's semi-chivalric quest to get laid in a men's latrine, super queen La Reine des Araignees's ("Queen of the Spiders") epic sexual cross-country adventures in a truck, among others. In **"New Thoughts of Pascal or Thoughts of Hell,"** he analyzes the intertwining of individual and social conflicts in Cuba: "Poverty makes us criminals; money makes us murderers"; "Friends are more dangerous than enemies because they can get closer to you" (187). Like many artists, Arenas plays out an integration of self and the world in his work (Rose 77). He documents this world and his own survival, as well as employing experimental, absurd, and nightmare techniques to convey the nature of this experience.

Some of Arenas's most effective and creative reconfigurations are in his hybrid and gendered uses of language and metaphor. Arenas's multigendering and transgendering of speech, as Hurley notes (463), is manifest in gay men being referred to as she, or sometimes as both genders in one sentence. The effects are gender confusion, in contrast to the insistent machismo of Cuban authorities and the "bull tops," men who only penetrate other men, and so believe they are not homosexual themselves. The nicknames of the queens connote power, aristocracy, and distinction. Their monikers include La Reine des Araignees, the duchess, Super-Satanic, etc. The recital of the "Seven Major Categories of Queenhood" at Fifo's ceremonies links male and female with universal attributes and professions, but which go against traditional gender categories. For example, the second category, Beauty, "produces great artists and impassioned suicides," citing the examples of Dostoevsky, Woolf, and Proust, all writers of ambiguous sexuality (78-79). With these gender reconfigurations, Arenas asks readers to rethink gender categories and dominant masculinization instituted by state control.

Arenas's metaphorical creations of animals and the natural environment reflect the natural beauties of his Caribbean home, but they also implicate humanity's animal-like nature and demonstrate the perversion of nature linked to the Castro regime. Arenas's nickname, Skunk in a Funk, humorously suggests the status of a sad outsider, and La Reine des Araignees the cruel side of Arenas's sometime friend, writer Delphin Proust. The novel's title refers to the glare of the sun. Once associated with the beautiful, sunny beaches Arenas and his friends formerly loved and frequented, then eventually denied to all except the elite and tourists, the sun has become the washed-out spotlight of state scrutiny and inhibitions. Fifo is depicted as trying to change the natural world for economic advantage; he wants to plant apple trees, though the Cuban climate and geography will not support them. The most extreme metaphor of power and nature is the Bloodthirsty Shark, Fifo's favorite henchman, trained to sadistically kill and rape dissidents, or the "rodents" who gnaw away at the island's base to escape the island prison. The shark evokes nature but also sometimes a cruelly devouring sexuality that has resonance for Arenas as his own sexual life has devoured him. Moreover, the image is effective in satirizing the brutalities of state terror. Even the shark eventually turns away from Fifo, as his sexual inclinations guide him into a very public acrobatic sexual encounter with the "queen" Mayoya, which Fifo regards as treason. The shark finds himself condemned to death by the jealous dictator and evades attempts on his life, leading other sea creatures to gnaw at the base of Cuba as well. All turn against Fifo once the island is gnawed away and his buried arsenal becomes inaccessible. The solipsistic and murderous leader ends up in the jaws of the shark.

In imagining lost or suppressed aspects of Cuba, Arenas helps situate exiles, but also explores the symbolic and narrative possibilities of a new world order. His explorations of how gender and sexuality inform imagination are linked to conflict and persecution and their resultant traumas, but also to a restorative art that provides a place of contemplation of, and possibilities for, greater freedom. The novel, as Bakhtin envisions it, and as Arenas practices it, illustrates culture as multifaceted, contradictory. If one particular viewpoint wins out, the others are driven underground and the complex reality becomes obscured: hence Arenas's critiques of systems, capitalist or totalitarian, which stifle human imagination. He demonstrates that artistic expression is crucial to articulating traumas: in his obsessive need to rewrite his lost works and the Cuban past, to witness for the oppressed, and to demonstrate the value of the creative imagination to express human experience and to reveal absurd and destructive patterns of behavior.

Arenas, who would probably agree with Derek Walcott's dictum of "history as a prison" (qtd. in Punter 49), notes this essential contradiction about Cuba:

> Two attitudes, two personalities, always seem to be in conflict throughout our history: on the one hand, the incurable rebels, lovers of freedom and therefore of creativity and experimentation; and on the other, the power-hungry opportunists and demagogues, and thus

purveyors of dogma, crime, and the basest of ambitions. These attitudes have recurred over time . . . always the drums of militarism stifling the rhythm of poetry and life.

(Before 90)

In his imaginary liberation of Cuba, the island floats aimlessly because the people cannot agree where to steer it. "Every single person wanted . . . to govern the island the way they wanted to, and to steer it in the direction they wanted to go in, no matter what the next person thought" (*Color* 455). Consequently, it ends up sinking. His own traumas, and Cuba's, still haunt Arenas's imagination. Though he ends his novel with the defeat of the despot, the people's self-destruction also indicates his fear that the old dialectical patterns of freedom and oppression will continue. Writing without hope for his own future, he hopes for his country to work through and break free of these repetitions but cannot imagine yet how this can happen.

Notes

1. The United Nations Refugee Agency currently places the number of people uprooted from their countries due to armed conflicts or economic needs at 20 million. This does not include people displaced within their own countries, estimated at another 20-25 million (UN 6). The number of Cuban exiles to the US and elsewhere is estimated at 700,000 since 1959 (Alvarez-Borland).

2. Of Arenas's 23 books, one was published in Cuba (1967), four in Latin America (1972-86), thirteen in Spain (1981-92), and five in the US (1986-91). These are first publications in Spanish and do not include the numerous translations of his work. Seven of these works were published posthumously (Soto, *Pentagonia* 177-78).

3. Arenas often has conflicted relations with other Cuban exiles and academics he meets who do not share his views of Castro or are not concerned with literature or gay life (*Before* 290; Obejas 2). He is particularly alienated by Miami, which he considers a "caricature" of Cuba, a "plastic world, lacking all mystery, where loneliness was often much more invasive" (*Before* 292-93).

4. As the revolution acquired an increasingly Communist bent, Castro adopted a Stalinesque criminal code toward gays and dissidents and a strict political and moral stance against homosexuality and art as non-essential activities that could destabilize Cuban society (Mehuron 49). Castro enforced "heterosexual familialism" as the social structure he believed was most invested in building a new society (Mehuron 42). Rodenas notes that "the years 1968-71 mark a turning point in Cuban culture toward greater state control and

ideological rigor demanded of the writer" ("Literature" 287), and Arango refers to the extreme dogmatism of the "Gray Five Years" (1971-76) (122). See articles by Sanchez-Eppler, Epps, and Mehuron for extended discussions of the treatment of gays in Cuba and Arenas's fictional responses. Such policies were devastating to many writers, wearing them down or forcing them to recant publicly or to go into exile (Santí 231). Herberto Padillo, a once defiant writer like Arenas, is forced to recant his work and inform on others after being beaten by police in prison. His confession is filmed and the other writers he names as similar offenders are told to also rise and confess, including Virgilio Pinera and Jose Lezama Lima (who refuses) (*Before* 136-37). Padillo's humiliation is savagely lampooned and at the same time expiated in *The Color of Summer.*

5. "[Arenas's] . . . peasant aesthetic dramatizes the raw hunger for food, the ferocious orality of need and freedom exercised by the basic irreverence of erotic conquest and poetic license. The experiential materials of this aesthetic, compounded by life under the dictatorships of Batista and Castro include the sterilization of the earth by one-crop economic policies; perpetual, gnawing hunger; dehumanized labor without end or reward by militarist labor recruitment policies; the absence (censorship) of literature; the death of private space by housing shortages and neighborhood surveillance mechanisms; the virtual shrinkage of future possibilities by imprisonment and torture in the Cuban State Security systems; and compulsory militarist masculinity exacted by the Castroist revolutionary legal and moral codes" (Mehuron 47).

6. The Unesco Statistical Yearbook and the Anuario Estadistico de Cuba report publication of literary texts between the years 1975 and 1985 averaged around 300 books annually (cited in Johnson 115). Though Arenas was published overseas during this time, he was not often compensated for it, compounding the frustration of not being read by his own people, those who would most fully understand his work.

7. Arenas had several conflicts with Castro sympathizers, who could not be convinced of the human rights abuses occurring in Cuba (*Before* 301-303).

8. Arenas's manuscript of *Farewell to the Sea* was confiscated and had to be rewritten three times (Soto, *Arenas,* Twayne 34). Sanchez-Eppler notes Arenas's "obsessive capacity for rewriting his life" occurring "both in the sense of revisiting the same scenes in different books . . . and recomposing

the same book, after successive losses, confiscations and complicated smuggling, and reunification with his manuscripts" (157).

9. The pentagony is five novels constituting a "secret history of Cuban society and a writer's autobiography," according to Arenas (Soto, "Documentary" 1). They include *Singing from the Well, The Palace of the White Skunks, Farewell to the Sea, The Color of Summer,* and *The Assault.*

Works Cited

Alvarez-Borland, Isabel. *Cuban American Literature of Exile.* Charlottesville: U of Virginia P, 1998.

Arango, Arturo. "To Write in Cuba, Today." *South Atlantic Quarterly* 96.1 (1997): 117-28.

Arenas, Reinaldo. *The Assault.* Trans. Andrew Hurley. New York: Penguin, 2001.

———. *Before Night Falls.* New York: Penguin, 1993.

———. *The Color of Summer.* New York: Penguin, 2000.

———. *Farewell to the Sea.* Trans. Andrew Hurley. New York: Viking Penguin, 1986.

———. Interview by Francisco Soto. *Reinaldo Arenas.* Twayne's World Author Series. New York: Twayne, 1998. 137-54.

———. *The Palace of the White Skunks.* Trans. Andrew Hurley. New York: Viking Penguin, 1990.

———. *Singing from the Well.* Trans. Andrew Hurley. New York: Viking Penguin, 1987.

Armand, Octavio. "Poetry as Eruv: On the Condition of Exile." Trans. Carol Maier. *Index on Censorship* 18.3 (1989): 19-21.

Beverley, John. "The Margin at the Center: On Testimonio (Testimonial Narrative)." *De/Colonizing the Subject: The Politics of Gender in Women's Autobiography.* Ed. Sidonie Smith and Julia Watson. Minneapolis: U of Minnesota P, 1992. 91-111.

Epps, Brad. "Proper Conduct: Reinaldo Arenas, Fidel Castro, and the Politics of Homosexuality." *Journal of the History of Sexuality* 6.21 (1995): 231-83.

Falcoff, Mark. "The Cuban Diaspora: Beyond the Stereotype." *Miami Herald.* 11 June 1995, C1+.

Garcia, Cristina. "Tenderhearts." *Cuba on the Verge.* Ed. Terry McCoy. Boston: Bullfinch, 2003. 176-77.

Gómez-Vega, Ibis. "Metaphors of Entrapment: Caribbean Women Writers Face the Wreckage of History." *Journal of Political and Military Sociology* 25.2 (1997): 231-47.

Harter, Hugh A. *Gertrudis Gomez de Avellaneda.* Twayne's World Author Series. Boston: Twayne, 1981.

Herman, Judith Lewis. *Trauma and Recovery.* New York: Basic, 1992.

Hurley, Andrew. "Afterword." Arenas. *The Color of Summer.* 456-65.

Johnson, Peter T. "Cuban Academic Publishing and Self-Perceptions." *Cuban Studies* 18. Ed. Carmelo Mesa-Lago. Pittsburgh PA: U of Pittsburgh P, 1988. 103-22.

Langer, Lawrence. *Holocaust Testimonies: The Ruins of Memory.* New Haven: Yale UP, 1991.

Manrique, Jaime. "Reinaldo Arenas (1943-1990)." *Bomb* 82.110 (2002-03): 1-2.

Mehuron, Kate. "Queer Territories in the Americas: Reinaldo Arenas' Prose." *Prose Studies* 17.1 (1994): 39-63.

Obejas, Achy. "'Before Night' Falls Short of Revealing Full Reinaldo Arenas Story." *Chicago Tribune.* 8 Feb. 2001: 5.

Perez, Louis A. *On Becoming Cuban: Identity, Nationality, and Culture.* New York: Harper Collins, 2002.

Punter, David. *Postcolonial Imaginings: Fictions of a New World Order.* Lanham MD: Rowman and Littlefield, 2000.

Rieff, David. *The Exile: Cuba in the Heart of Miami.* New York: Simon & Schuster, 1993.

Robbins, Bruce. "Comparative Cosmopolitanisms." *Cosmopolitics: Thinking and Feeling Beyond the Nation.* Ed. Pheng Cheah and Bruce Robbins. Minneapolis: U of Minnesota P, 1998. 246-64.

Rodenas, Adriana Mendez. *Gender and Nationalism in Colonial Cuba: The Travels of Santa Cruz y Montalvo, Condesa de Merlin.* Nashville TN: Vanderbilt UP, 1998.

———. "Literature and Politics in the Cuban Revolution." *A History of Literature in the Caribbean.* Vol 1. *Hispanic and Francophone Regions.* Ed. A. James Arnold. Amsterdam: John Benjamins, 1994. 283-94.

Rose, Gilbert J. *The Power of Form.* Madison: International Universities, 1992.

Sanchez-Eppler, Benigno. "Reinaldo Arenas, Re-writer Revenant, and the Repatriation of Cuban Homoerotic Desire." *Queer Diasporas.* Ed. Cindy Patton and Benigno Sanchez-Eppler. Durham NC: Duke UP, 2000. 154-82.

Santí, Enrico. "The Life and Times of Reinaldo Arenas." *Michigan Quarterly Review* 23.2 (1984): 227-36.

Soto, Francisco. "Reinaldo Arenas and the Cuban Documentary Novel." *Utah Foreign Language Review* 1.18 (1991-92): 1-18.

———. *Reinaldo Arenas: The Pentagonia.* Gainesville FL: UP of Florida, 1994.

———. *Reinaldo Arenas.* Twayne's World Author Series. New York: Twayne, 1998.

United Nations High Commissioner for Refugees. "The Changing Face of Protection." *Refugees* 3.132 (2003): 1-32.

Van der Kolk, Bessel and Onno Van der Hart. "The Intrusive Past: The Flexibility of Memory and the Engraving of Trauma." *American Imago* 48.4 (1991): 425-54.

Vickroy, Laurie. *Trauma and Survival in Contemporary Fiction.* Charlottesville: U of Virginia P, 2002.

Angela L. Willis (essay date winter 2005)

SOURCE: Willis, Angela L. "Revisiting the Circuitous Odyssey of the Baroque Picaresque Novel: Reinaldo Arenas's *El mundo alucinante.*" *Comparative Literature* 57, no. 1 (winter 2005): 61-83.

[*In the following essay, Willis investigates the relationship of* Hallucinations *to the sixteenth- and seventeenth-century picaresque novel tradition in Spain, attempting to explain why Arenas "would have intentionally chosen to frame his tale in a literary style that flourished four centuries earlier on the other side of the Atlantic."*]

> "Legendo simulque peragrando"
>
> —*Guzmán de Alfarache* 1.74

It is a critical commonplace that *Lazarillo de Tormes*'s appearance in 1554 engendered a literary tradition, usually referred to as the "picaresque" (be that the picaresque novel, genre, mode, frame, style, or strain), that played a dominant role in Hispanic letters during Spain's Renaissance (here, chiefly designating the sixteenth century) and the "historical baroque period" (mainly the late sixteenth and entire seventeenth centuries).[1] However, the picaresque has not remained restricted to the Peninsula during the peak of its empire. Rather, we shall find that the picaresque novel—specifically one written in a decidedly baroque fashion—has resurfaced as recently as 1969 in the Cuban author Reinaldo Arenas's *El mundo alucinante (Hallucinations).*[2] In this transtemporal, trans-Atlantic investigation, I first demonstrate that the baroque picaresque is a Hispanic literary constant or, at a minimum, that it cyclically reappears. I examine how *El mundo alucinante* engages in dialogues with two canonical baroque picaresque novels of sixteenth- and seventeenth-century Spain: Mateo Alemánn's *Guzmán de Alfarache* (1599/1604) and Francisco de Quevedo's *El buscón* (*The Scavenger,*

1626). I also briefly examine how Arenas employed his primary historical source, Fray Servando's *Memorias* (The Memoirs of Fray Servando Teresa de Mier). Ultimately, I attempt to explain why Arenas, a Cuban who reached maturity under Castro's rule, would have intentionally chosen to frame his tale in a literary style that flourished four centuries earlier on the other side of the Atlantic.

According to Reinaldo Arenas, **El mundo alucinante** was written in 1965 and awarded "First Honorable Mention" in UNEAC's (la Unión de Escritores y Artistas Cubanos [the Cuban Writers and Artists Union]) 1966 literary competition.[3] Suspiciously, though, no "winner" was declared. Thus, while Arenas's novel received the honor of "Primera Mención," in this political game **EMA** [*El mundo alucinante*] "won" without winning outright. Consequently, it was denied the possibility of publication in Cuba. The manuscript was later smuggled off the island by friends (the Camachos), who then had it translated into French and published in 1968 as **Le monde hallucinant.** Arenas did not know of its publication in France, or of the fact that it had won several prestigious awards in Europe, until he was arrested by the Cuban government. Indeed, his choice to publish **El mundo alucinante** without the consent of Castro's regime helped to ensure him a life of persecution and imprisonment. Although the Spanish text was finally published in 1969 in Mexico, to this day **EMA** remains mostly unseen by Cuba's readers. Apparently, Arenas's novelization of eighteenth-century Mexican Independence leader Fray Servando Teresa de Mier's *Memorias* is considered threatening to the goals of the Revolution.

Fray Servando Teresa de Mier y Noriega (1763-1827), generally referred to as Fray Servando or Fray Mier, was a colonial Mexican friar who spent most of his life in prison for attempting to delegitimize the Spanish presence in the New World by arguing that there had been a pre-Columbian Christian evangelization of America.[4] According to Mier, because Jesus had sent Saint Thomas the Apostle to America to spread the Gospel and Christianity to the autochthonous "Indians," the Spaniards lacked a legitimate reason to be in America (*la cause justa*), much less a justification to exploit its natural resources and people. Fray Servando's *Memorias* are comprised of the *Apología,* in which he defends his earth-shattering speech and theories, as well as the *Relación,* in which he recounts the stories of his travels, adventures, and incarcerations as he fled from one country and continent to the next.

One may easily imagine how the picaresque-like adventures of the *historical* Mier's *novelistic* life and death, as depicted in his autobiographical texts, caught the attention of fiction writer Reinaldo Arenas. In fact, Mier himself recognized the novelistic, improbable aspects of his adventures. In his *Memorias,* he anticipates his pub-

lic's response, telling his reader that when he related the story of his life to one of his many jailors, his captor reacted with incredulity: "Mi historia le pareció una novela, y seguramente fingida" (*Relación* 2.205; "My life story must have seemed to him like a novel, and surely a fictitious one"). Mier's *Apología* frequently approximates the picaresque narrative's structure and thematics, and it reveals a baroque style. Just as Lazarillo de Tormes defends his *caso* (although we are never told *why* he must do so), so Mier defends his actions, possibly to save his life. In vindicating his honor for posterity—"Es tiempo de instruir a la posteridad sobre la verdad . . . para que . . . [se] haga justicia a mi memoria, pues esta apología ya no puede servirme en esta vida" (*Apología* 4; "It's time to instruct posterity of the truth so that justice be done to my memory. This apology can no longer serve me in this life")—Mier's ostensible goal was formally to defend his theory regarding the pre-conquest evangelization of America. But there was a second—and perhaps more urgent—motive as well: to avenge himself against the deceased Archbishop Haro and his henchmen, who had indefatigably pursued him both in Spain and America.

Again like the author of *Lazarillo* and his fellow Golden Age pícaros, Fray Servando generally writes to an unspecified reader, whose textual presence helps to shape the narration. Like Guzmán, who regularly harasses his reader, Mier attacks a *tú* (an informal/friendly *you*), who most frequently appears to represent the Archbishop Haro. More commonly, though, Mier writes to the world at large, so that it may know of the wrongs he has suffered at the hands of the Spanish government, which he equates with the Spanish Inquisition. Like the Golden Age pícaros, Mier criticizes his society, including the government, the church, and the nobility. The *Apología*'s style is tangled, labyrinthine, complex, and virtually incomprehensible at times. In a word, it is baroque: neither concise nor to the point, and often difficult, if not impossible, to understand, given its contradictions, digressions, circuitous or even faulty logic, and erudite vocabulary. Mier's web of foreign and learned words, historical anecdotes, and parenthetical digressions may even encourage the reader to overlook the lack of rational development in his arguments.

While many critics readily point to Mier's *alucinaciones* and often mad deductions, we must remember that he was writing from prison to defend his status, nobility, honor, and even his very life. Consequently, a contradictory style—that is, one in which he must belie his own beliefs in order to try to save his life and nobility—was perhaps inevitable. Did he really believe all that he claimed, or was he merely astutely rallying support to end the legitimacy of the Spanish Empire in America? We shall never know. Regardless, he repeatedly declared that he had *not* "denied the tradition of the Virgin of Guadalupe," despite consistently denying—at the very least—the *way* in which her apparition was conventionally understood (that the Virgin revealed herself first to the Indian Juan Diego in 1531).[5] Acknowledging that his theories go well beyond common beliefs, he takes a critical stab at the Spaniards, tempering his seemingly outlandish hypotheses by reminding us that the proof he needs no longer exists thanks to the *hogueras* that consumed all of the indigenous texts (*Apología* 52-53).

Another baroque dimension in Fray Servando's thought involves nationality or ethnicity. Like the protagonists in *El buscón* and, especially, in *Guzmán de Alfarache,* Mier constructs an identity composed of diverse and even conflicting racial and/or national categories. For example, at times he is a Spaniard, at others a "native" Mexican, or simply an "American." More frequently, however, he is a *criollo,* or a person of Spanish ancestry whose ancestors fought alongside the original *conquistadores.* That Arenas, a perennial dissenter, would have been attracted to this conflicted, quintessential rebel, who seems to have written the *Memorias* in the tradition of Spain's Golden Age pícaros, should immediately be apparent.

Many theorists have chosen to restrict the picaresque and the baroque to specific time periods. For example, Alexander Parker's *Los pícaros en la literatura: La novel a picaresca en España y Europa* (1599-1753) limits the pícaro's literary existence to the period between *Guzmán*'s publication in 1599 and the appearance of Smollett's *Count Fathom* in 1753.[6] Moreover, as early as 1931, Marcel Bataillon went so far as to state that, "Le roman picaresque est bien mort, et il ne ressuscitera pas" (38; "The picaresque novel is quite dead, and it will never be resuscitated"). Jenaro Taléns, in contrast, argues that the pícaro is not manifested in only one specific epoch, but is a recurring "tipo humano genérico" (41; "generic human type"). Agreeing with Taléns, Jorge Manrique de Aragón maintains that the picaresque is "una constante de la vida española" (214; "a constant of Spanish life"). More importantly for this project, Manrique argues that the picaresque not only transcends the "classic" Golden Age in Spain (c. 1500-1700), but also the spatial boundaries of the Iberian Peninsula: "a lo largo de los siglos posteriores, el fenómeno picaresco se manifiesta patentemente casi como una constante de la vida española . . . *se adapta como camaleón a las circunstancias de los tiempos, también se amolda astutamente a las condiciones geográficas de los distintos países*" (349, my emphasis; "throughout the following centuries, the picaresque phenomenon is almost like a constant of Spanish life . . . *it adapts like a chameleon to the circumstances of the times; it also adapts itself astutely to the geographic conditions of different countries*"). Although Manrique

does not specify the "distintos países," one may logically infer that he refers—at least in part—to Spain's legacy in Spanish America.

Similarly, although numerous critics argue that the use of the term *baroque* should be restricted to seventeenth-century Europe, others argue that it designates various traits that reemerge cyclically. For example, in 1935 the Catalan philosopher and art critic Eugenio d'Ors suggested the plausibility of a baroque revival (*Du baroque*), identifying a "Constant Baroque," or a "Baroque Spirit" that he interpreted as "una constante histórica que atraviesa todas las épocas" (qtd, in Carilla 13). Likewise, Guillermo Díaz-Plaja's influential *El espíritu del barroco* examines not only the baroque's origins in Spain, but also its flourishing expansion in Spanish America. The Cuban novelist-philosopher-musicologist Alejo Carpentier generally agrees with d'Ors and Díaz-Plaja, while simultaneously granting America a "privileged position" in baroque aesthetics ("Lo barroco y lo real maravilloso"). Placing the baroque at the center of Latin America's beliefs and its artistic renderings of life, Carpentier maintains that, given Latin America's historical uniqueness, it has "been baroque" since its very beginnings: "Todo lo que se refiere a la cosmogonía americana . . . está dentro de lo barroco" (110-11). Additionally, scholars such as Roberto González Echevarría, Severo Sarduy, and Dolores Koch have pointed to a neobaroque movement in late twentieth-century literature, particularly in Cuban letters.[7]

We must ask, then, whether or not the baroque picaresque novel arises from certain historical/socio-political and/or literary circumstances. Specifically, we must determine why Cuban Reinaldo Arenas structures and stylizes his twentieth-century *El mundo alucinante* within the parameters of seventeenth-century Spanish narrative. This awareness of a tradition implies parody and intertextuality, and that is precisely what we find when Arenas rewrites Mier's *Memorias* in baroque picaresque fashion.[8]

Before proceeding further, however, we must first address some basic but essential questions regarding genre and period distinctions. First, does the classification of works of art in terms of artistic movements, periods, or genres benefit the reading public at large, or even the scholar? Second, if such categories are indeed beneficial, by applying the sixteenth- and seventeenth-century labels "picaresque" and" "baroque" to a Cuban novel published in 1969, do we dilute or misconstrue their original meaning? In what follows I attempt to heed Peter Dunn's call for the *cautious* usage of taxonomy as a means of "recognition":

> This need—to recognize things according to their kind or their categories in order to become receptive to them—is not an exclusively literary one. Indeed, our

encounters with all the products of culture require that we recognize initially the kind to which they belong, within broad or narrow limits . . . Genres are more than a system of classification employed by historians and critics, and their function has always been something more than the ascription of themes and subjects to forms and styles.

(*Fiction* 22)

The prudent study of genres—or, again, of movements or periods—advances the study of art. Generic patterns allow the reader/listener/viewer to discern a relationship between works which, at first glance, may appear entirely dissimilar. Eduardo Béjar discusses the fact that genres must be fairly wide in their scope, as each work, while imitating certain aspects of a genre, concurrently breaks the mold. He cites Tzvetan Todorov's famous explanation of genre: "que la obra 'desobedezca' a sugénero no lo hace inexistente; se está tentado a decir: al contrario . . . Primero parace que la trangresión, para existir como tal, tiene neccesidad de una ley—que será precisamente transgredida" (Béjar 183; "that the work 'disobeys' its genre does not make it [the genre] non-existent; one is tempted to say: on the contrary . . . First, it seems as if the transgression, for it to exist as such, must have a rule [law] that precisely will be transgressed"). Thus, each new imitator brings its own unique traits to the generic family.

Given that each work of a generic family incorporates innovations, it is of course impossible to provide an "absolute" list of characteristics. Thus, it should come as no surprise that, as Dunn points out, the Golden Age interpreters of the picaresque did not perceive it as having an overly rigorous form. Describing first Vicente Espinel's *Marcos de Obregón* and then the picaresque in general, Dunn states: "What it tells us about picaresque . . . is that writers did not necessarily regard it as a genre, whose integrity had to be preserved, but as a *bundle of possibilities,* which could be taken apart and exploited separately" (*Picaresque Novel* 94, my emphasis). Dunn also cites Ludwig Wittgenstein's interpretation of genre as one of "family resemblance[s]" to describe the picaresque (*Picaresque Fiction* 49).

The term *baroque* should likewise be approached as a set of possibilities or family resemblances that are most readily apparent during the seventeenth century, but which may have surfaced (or will surface) in other epochs and movements. A "densification" of these traits occurred during the historical Baroque period, as Heinrich Wölfflin pointed out when introducing the term in his late nineteenth-century studies of art and architecture.[9] Wölfflin writes: "The central idea of the Italian Renaissance is that of perfect proportion" (9), whereas in contrast:

The baroque uses the same system of forms, but in place of the perfect, the completed, gives the restless, the becoming, in place of the limited, the conceivable, gives the limitless, the colossal. The ideal of beautiful proportion vanishes, interest concentrates not on being, but on happening. The masses, heavy and thickset, come into movement.

(*Principles* 10)

For Wölfflin, the baroque's principal attributes are asymmetry, disproportion, movement, incompletion, proliferation, density, and the gargantuan. One should observe how these properties disallow transparency and favor obfuscation. To date, scholars frequently employ the traits that Wölfflin had first attributed to the baroque, and Wölfflin's theories readily pertain not only to the plastic arts, but also to literature. Indeed, his insights into the baroque plastic arts in *Principles* are central to my analysis of the baroque picaresque novel, particularly its structure, though I also stress the interaction of certain stylistic and thematic traits.[10]

In 1984 Reinaldo Arenas firmly established his own fascination with the picaresque in his little-known prologue (**"Presentación"**) to his equally obscure modernized version of *Lazarillo de Tormes* (written for English-speaking students of Spanish).[11] In it he contends:

La historia de un niño huérfano que no quiere morirse de hambre—aunque todo conspira para que así sea—es, aparentemente, el tema fundamental de esta obra del siglo XVI que marca el nacimiento de la novela contemporánea: el antecedente más ilustre de *El ingenioso hidalgo don Quijote de la Mancha,* de Miguel de Cervantes.

Lazarillo de Tormes se publica en 1554 en tres ediciones simultáneas- en Burgos y Alcalá, España, y en Amberes, que es hoy ciudad belga. Por la maestría con que el libro está escrito, es posible suponer que su autor era un hombre ilustrado, tal vez ilustre y hasta famoso en aquel tiempo. Pero las críticas que en el libro se hacen a la Iglesia Católica, así como a los representantes más destacados—curas, jueces, caballeros, arciprestes . . . de la sociedad española del siglo XVI, parecen haber determinado que el autor prefiriese permanecer en el anonimato. Así evitaba problemas con la Inquisición—entiéndase 'justicia'—, muy activa en ese tiempo.

La obra, además de crear un género literario—el de la novela picaresca, es un fresco de toda una sociedad y de todo un siglo; y es también un espejo de la condición humana. Lazarillo se asombra ante la falta de bondad de muchas personas que encuentra en su camino. A pesar de las vicisitudes y trabajos que sufre, de la picardía de que tiene que hacer uso para sobrevivir dentro de una sociedad en crisis, Lazarillo nunca se desprende de una ingenuidad y un candor naturales que lo salvan, mostrándose como un joven travieso y astuto, pero noble.

La estructura aparentemente sencilla de esta obra, sin embargo, es insólita en aquellos tiempos. La historia se cuenta a una segunda persona, con la cual supuestamente se conversa o se le rinde un informe. El lenguaje está desprovisto de toda retórica: ni sentencioso ni re-buscado, ni vulgar ni académico, ni pobre ni inflado. La ironía, el sarcasmo y hasta la exageración, trazan con mano maestra situaciones y personajes que se nos hacen inolvidables desde nuestra primera lectura.

Es fácil identificar en nuestros días los equivalentes a Lazarillo y a los demás personajes de la obra, tal es su universalidad. Encontremos también en ella lo que es patrimonio del genio: la recreación de un instante, de una vida, de un tiempo, de un mundo. Todo ello pudo haber quedado en la simple crónica o el trabajo so-ciológico, pero la ficción lo ha rescatado para siempre de un modo más vivo y permanente.

                                                        (xiv-xv)

In Spain, during the sixteenth century, a book told the life story of an orphan who refused to die of starvation, though everything seemed to conspire against him. It marks the birth of the contemporary novel and its most illustrious predecessor of *El ingenioso hidalgo don Quijote de la Mancha* by Miguel de Cervantes.

The book is written with such skill that it seems prob-able its author was a well-read man, perhaps well born or even celebrated during his time. Its kind of criticism against the Catholic Church, as well as against the no-table representatives of Spanish society during the six-teenth century—priests, judges, noblemen, religious dignitaries—seems to have determined that its author remain anonymous, thus avoiding problems with the Inquisition—that is, "the law"—so active during that time.

Besides creating a literary genre, the picaresque novel, the book is like a mural depicting a society and an era. It is also a mirror reflecting the human condition. Laz-arillo wonders at the lack of virtue he sees in most of the people he meets. In spite of all the troubles he goes through and all the crises he survives, Lazarillo never loses his natural candor, which is his saving grace. He behaves like a shrewd and mischievous youth, yet re-mains noble.

The structure of this work is deceivingly simple and, for its time, unusual. The story is addressed to a second person, to whom the narrator offers a report of the events which take place. The language is devoid of all rhetoric: it is neither terse nor artificial, neither vulgar nor academic, neither poor nor inflated. Irony, sarcasm, and even exaggeration skillfully delineate situations and characters that become unforgettable from our first reading.

It is easy to identify present-day counterparts to Laz-arillo and the rest of the characters throughout the book. This shows their universality. We also witness in this work what is only the prerogative of genius: the recre-ation of an instant, of a life, of an epoch, of a particular world. It all could have resulted in a simple chronicle or a sociological treatise, but fiction has rescued it for-ever in a more vibrant and personal way.

                                                        (xii-xiii)

Arenas argues that *Lazarillo* spurred "the birth of the contemporary novel," and he maintains that pícaro-types exist even today. In this prologue, Arenas also summarizes what he perceives to be the most important elements of *Lazarillo,* and, implicitly, of the picaresque novel itself:

> 1. The protagonist is a young, unlucky individual who relentlessly fights against all odds, but who never loses his hope or "candor."
>
> 2. Though he is mischievous, he remains "noble." His very survival justifies his behavior.
>
> 3. The picaresque novel criticizes institutions of social control, especially of the Church and the Inquisition in *Lazarillo*'s case. Thus, it functions like a panoramic "mural" of society.
>
> 4. Structurally, the tale is written as a missive or report and is addressed to a *destinataire.*
>
> 5. The novel's language is simple, yet replete with col-orful "irony, sarcasm, and even exaggeration."

Indeed, since the novel's initial appearance, critics have noted its picaresque and baroque elements, particularly those in the vein of Francisco de Quevedo's *El buscón.* Even the first review of the novel reveals an awareness of the Quevedian tendencies in Arenas's writing:

> L'art de Reinaldo Arenas . . . n'est pas dans l'humour rosse mais bien dans la satire féroce, dans la phrase au vitriol. A l'instar de son illustre prédécesseur Francisco de Quevedo, l'auteur du *Monde hallucinant* excelle à créer une ambiance fantastique, souvent cauche-mardesque, dans laquelle l'optimisme béat, l'hypocrisie et le mensonge sont fustigés sans appel.
>
>   (Couffon 3)

> The art of Reinaldo Arenas is not that of vicious humor but rather that of fierce satire, the language of vitriol. Following the example of his predecessor, Francisco de Quevedo, the author of *Monde hallucinant* excels at creating a fantastical ambiance, often nightmarish, in which blissful optimism, hypocrisy, and lies are fusti-gated irrevocably.

Couffon underscores Arenas's fierce satire, his creation of fantastical, nightmarish ambiances ("cauchemar-desque"), and his ruthless denunciation of naïve opti-mism, hypocrisy, and lies. Couffon compares all of these traits to Quevedo's thematics and style, even suggesting that Arenas followed directly in the master's footsteps ("A l'instar de son illustre prédécesseur").

Since Couffon's 1969 review, the majority of Arenas's critics have examined either the baroque or the picar-esque attributes of *EMA* without considering the inter-action between the two phenomena in the completed novel.[12] Addressing these important aspects concurrently while also specifying a Cuban neobaroque, Dolores Koch remarks that "casi todos se preocupan por la retórica y la filosofía barrocas" (141; "almost all con-temporary Cuban writers are concerned about the rheto-ric and philosophy of the baroque") and convincingly establishes the need for a study such as this one (137-38).[13]

Perhaps the most significant evidence regarding **EMA**'s picaresque status comes from Arenas himself. In the letter/brief essay "Fray Servando, víctima infatigable," dated July 13, 1980, that serves as an introduction to the Tusquets edition of **EMA,** Arenas stresses the picaresque qualities of his novelistic *fraile:* "En fray Servando, hombre de mil dimensiones, cándido, *pícaro,* aventurero, exaltado, ese desgarramiento por lo imposible (su patria) ocurre en el centro mismo de una de las más populosas ciudades europeas, entre el torbellino de anónimos rostros y el estruendo de innumerables ideas, generalmente contradictorias" (18, my emphasis; "In Fray Servando ['s text]—a man of a thousand dimensions, candid, picaro, adventurous, impassioned, that broken heart, for the impossible (his country)—all occurs precisely in the center of one of the most populated European cities, among the whirlwind of anonymous faces and the din of innumerable ideas, generally contradictory").[14] As Arenas read the *fraile*'s *Memorias,* he envisioned the Mexican Independence leader's seemingly *in*-credible life as picaresque and "contradictoria" (a relevant term when one considers Wölfflin's description of the baroque as "incomplete" and "asymmetrical"). Arenas puts aside any doubt regarding **EMA**'s relationship to the picaresque when he pens on the back cover of the Diógenes 1978 edition: "Esta es la vida de Fray Servando Teresa de Mier. Tal como fue, tal como pudo haber sido, *tal como a mí me hubiera gustado que hubiera sido . . . Alegre, desenfadada, picaresca*" (my emphasis). I propose that **EMA** represents Arenas's hallucinatory, *picaresque* interpretation of Mier's life—"as it could have been," and as he "would have liked for it to have been."[15]

As Reinaldo Arenas and fellow admirers of the canonical picaresque novel have observed, its most basic structural element is that of a fictitious autobiography addressed to a specified reader (or various readers). The customarily repentant, adult pícaro reminisces about his life's adventures and narrates his foibles. While doing so, he also points out those of his society. However, the stated beliefs of the first person picaresque narrator often contradict his actions, a situation which contributes to the numerous incongruities that fill the pages of the baroque picaresque novel. As Claudio Guillén has observed, the picaresque novel is quite often the confession of a liar, and Arenas's references to Fray Servando as "contradictorio" are reminiscent of that assessment. Since Francisco Rico and others have explained the need for Lázaro's *caso,* or his confession of acquiescing as his wife frolics with the local priest, we've learned that we must be skeptical of the pícaro's revelations. His text is one of numerous perspectives.

For example, prior to the first "Capítulo Primero" in Guzmán's "gargantuan" and highly "decorated" novel (that is, filled with constant digressions), Mateo Alemán erases any illusions that Guzmán's story was truly conceived by a pícaro when he reveals himself as the author, aiming two very disparate prologues at his reading publics. The first, "Al vulgo," is a virtual tirade in which Alemán defends his text from the anticipated attacks of a crude audience. His tone is extremely aggressive and confrontational: "No es nuevo para mí, aunque lo sea para ti, oh enemigo vulgo, los muchos malos amigos que tienes, lo poco que vales y sabes, cuán mordaz, envidioso y avariento eres . . . !" (1.82; "It is nothing new for me, even though it is for you, oh crude enemy, those many bad friends you have, the little that you appreciate things and that you know—how caustic, envious, and greedy you are!"). In the second prologue, titled "Del mismo al discreto lector," Alemán advises the prudent—and longed for—reader to take to heart the well-intentioned advice of his story. He claims that the text was written with this "discreto lector" in mind: "Y tu . . . a quien verdaderamente consideré cuando esta obra escribía . . . Haz como leas lo que leyeres y no te rías de la conseja y se te pase el consejo; recibe los que te doy . . . : no los eches como barreduras al muladar [la basura] del olvido" (1.86; "And you . . . whom I truly considered when I was writing this work . . . Do as you read that which you will read and don't laugh at the tale, ignoring its moral; receive the advice that I give you and don't throw it out like trash to the dumps of oblivion"). Alemán even ends this note to the judicious reader with a friendly, "*Vale, amice*" (1.87). Nonetheless, more often than not, Guzmán engages in a dialogue with the "vulgo" rather than the sought-after sagacious reader. Even in the introductory comments to the "discrete reader," one perceives a certain paranoia in Alemán's tone, as if he anticipates and fears that even *this* reader will not heed, and may even laugh at, his warnings, that his advice may be "thrown out like a piece of trash."

Frequently, Guzmán's and Alemán's voices intertwine, becoming indistinguishable. Alemán, of a *converso* family, spews hostility at a public that chastises the Jew and the convert. Moreover, in moments of apparent confusion between the author's voice and that of his protagonist, the question of exactly *which* Guzmán is speaking—the young pícaro or the contrite *former* pícaro—has also proved difficult to answer (see Rico and Reed). These contradictions in turn lead to confusion regarding the narrator's depiction of temporality, his *supposed* repentance, and his antagonistic, splintered identity.[16] It is also of interest to note that, despite the fact that Guzmán plays the role of a fictitious narrator and that he *does* direct his narration at a specified audience, he does *not* appear to have any particular purpose for his "alarde," or general confession, beyond the previously mentioned didactic ones. Unlike Lazarillo, who appears to be seeking some sort of pardon from "Vuestra Merced" (for his quiet acquiescence as a cuckold),

Guzmán's *purported* intention is simply to share the story of his life as a sinner who ultimately finds God's grace so that the reader not repeat his same mistakes.[17]

In *El buscón,* yet another fictitious autobiography, the first person narrator, Pablos, recounts the adventures, peccadilloes, and outright crimes of his well-traveled path. Evidencing Quevedo's adherence to the now established tradition of directing the picaresque text to a specified reader, Pablos initiates his story with "Yo, señora, soy de Segovia" ("I, Madame, am from Segovia"; or in some editions and manuscripts, "Yo señor" ["I, Sir"]). As in Lazarillo's story, Quevedo creates a scenario in which a socially superior individual, "Vuestra Merced," has requested that the pícaro recount his life. Like Guzmán, Pablos addresses various readers throughout the text: not only "Vuestra Merced," but also a "pío lector" (230) and almost immediately thereafter, and in direct contrast, a potential rogue ("por si fueres pícaro, letor," 231). Quevedo also reveals a lack of sympathy for his narrator, as if the aristocratic author apparently experienced difficulties in assuming the voice of the low-life rogue, and even mocks his purported protagonist at times. Hence, the perspective of the true author completely diverges from that of the fictitious narrator, causing the poetic illusion of a first person pícaro-narrator's tale to be broken. Linguistic acrobatics, known to the baroque scholar as *conceptos,* and erudite commentary on various types of literature also help the reader recognize when Quevedo is interfering in the pícaro's telling (see, for example, his description of the miserly school master Cabra).

Reinaldo Arenas's *EMA* recalls all of these fundamental underpinnings of the classical picaresque novel, with two important differences: first, Arenas's narrative is based—at least in part—on the life of an historical figure rather than an—*entirely*—fictional creation; second, unlike the authors of *Lazarillo, Guzmán,* and *El buscón,* who tried to *distinguish* their own voices from that of their respective pícaros, Arenas fully admits the *confluence* of his voice with that of the historical Mier. In the letter that serves as a prologue to the novel, Arenas confesses to the long-deceased Mier, "Lo más útil fue descubrir que tú y yo somos la misma persona" (9; "The most useful discovery of all was to learn that you and I are the same person"). The narrative voice is further problematized in baroque fashion, as it constantly vacillates—with no apparent pattern—between first, second, and third person perspectives, with the "personalities" of these distinct voices completely inconsistent. In fact, Arenas multiplies the three basic narrative voices into endless perspectives, as there are even dissenting first, second, and third person grammatical positions.[18]

In *EMA,* therefore, one encounters a baroque, everproliferating and multiplying text. Some chapters offer only one rendering of an escapade, while others present more than three. The narrators' hermetic, convoluted form and style impede clear communication, and most episodes are followed by accounts that completely contradict them. The first telling of an account may offer a first person narrator, the second, a third person narrator, and so on. For example, the first Chapter 1 begins: "Venimos del corojal. No venimos del corojal" (11; "We are coming back from the prickly palms. We are coming from the prickly palms"). This statement accurately sets the antagonistic tone of the entire narration. The second Chapter 1 begins "Ya vienes del corojal" (14), while the third offers a similar rendition, but with a third person narrator. The narrators relentlessly question their textual fellows as one version of a story challenges and even annihilates its counterparts. There is no clear message, no absolute truth. Neither, however, is there any discernible pattern to the voices. The three grammatical positions (I, you, he) exhibit great fluctuation in attitude and demeanor. Temporal differences are also pervasive throughout the text (for example, "vienes" versus "venimos del corojal" ["you come/are coming" versus "we come/are coming/came from the prickly palms"]), and nothing is readily understood in this hallucinatory world.

In his Borgesian reading of the *fraile*'s *Memorias,* Arenas actively relives Mier's tales; *EMA* is the final product of his interactive reading. Arenas imitates the classical picaresque trope of the fictitious first person pícaro narrator who composes his narrative for a "Vuestra Merced"; however, he also innovates, dedicating the novel to *Mier himself.* Arenas declares this by positioning the letter entitled "Querido Servando"—in which he poetically explains that he and Mier are the "same person"—before the body of the text. Consequently, Arenas, who had been the reader of the historical Mier's *Memorias,* now has inverted their roles: the deceased and fictionalized Mier becomes the desired hypothetical reader of Arenas's novel. Ironically, then, the Mexican *fraile* is the principal reader in the text and—simultaneously—the original author of the *Memorias,* while, for his part, Arenas is the implicit primary reader of the *Memorias* and its secondary author. Novelistically, Fray Servando, the *destinataire,* is now asked to relive his own adventures, "rereading" them in Arenas's fictionalized version. As Alemán knew, "Legendo simulque peragrando" (*Guzmán* 1.74).

EMA also structurally mirrors the picaresque novel in its picaresque epigraphs that summarize the adventures to ensue in the chapters, and as an adventure story that takes place in a knavish setting. Because the *trotamundos* perennially leaps from one low-life way of survival (often servitude) to the next, critics have historically referred to the pícaro as a *mozo de muchos amos* (boy of many masters). While attending to the needs of the various representatives of his community, the pícaro censures those who behave in uncharitable, hypocritical ways. Whereas the *Memorias* of the Mier *de carne y hueso* does *not* begin with childhood, but rather with the trials and tribulations that Mier suffered because of his pronouncement in favor of a pre-Conquest evangelization of America, Reinaldo Arenas's novelized version intentionally "picarizes" the Mexican monk's life story with a *fictionalized picaresque* "reality" for Mier's childhood and the desertion of his family, neither of which occur in the autobiographical texts. Like his picaresque kin, the novelized Fray Servando's family proves to be less than desirable and could be viewed as the catalyst in his decision to leave home. In addition, the experiences that the young Servando undergoes at home foreshadow those to come: persecution and more persecution. In the first scene of the novel, for example, Mier's schoolmaster, twin sisters, mother, the *zopilotes,* cacti—the world in general—all attack and harass him.

EMA's Chapter 2, which also consists of three "subchapters," depicts Servando's archetypically picaresque departure from Monterrey'. Like Lazarillo, Mier takes leave as his mother watches from the doorway (17). Mirroring Guzmán's fate, Arenas's protagonist advances on a mule (that appears to laugh) until he is attacked by "un ejército de arrieros" (17; "an army of mule skinners"). The uncharitable mule skinners—strikingly reminiscent of Guzmán's earliest "friend" on the road—steal his bestial companion. He then must continue his trek on foot. Servando complains of the vicissitudes he endures while traveling, including the treatment and food that he receives in an inn (*mesón*). The reader will recall that a famished Lazarillo must eat turnips (*nabos*), steal bread from a locked bread box—and sips of wine for the pain. For his part, while on the road, Guzmán is tricked into eating *huevos empollados,* or fertilized eggs, and mule meat; and, in classic Quevedian style, Pablos complains that he does not even *need* to defecate while in Cabra's house because of an absolute lack of sustenance. In the departure sequence of *EMA* similar misadventures plague the protagonist as he travels down a treacherous path that leads him to an interminable series of prisons. Hunger forces Fray Servando to eat "atole batido de leche de una india" (a maizebased drink mixed with an Indian's milk)—though it is reportedly "delicioso." Though *atole* is a common maize-based drink, here it is spiked with sand. Fray Servando grumbles:

> después de mucho andar por tierras calientes y heladas y por llanuras tan grandes que uno camina y cree que está siempre en el mismo lugar, . . . después de dormir en mesones (donde le robaban a uno hasta el cabello, dicen que para hacer colchones); después de eso y otras cosas (entre ellas el llevar la barriga reventando del atole de arena que nos vendieron en el mesón, por lo cual voy dejando el rastro por donde quiera que cruzo), parece que ya llego.
>
> (18)

after walking so much through hot and frozen lands and through plains so expansive that you walk and walk and still believe that you are in the same place, . . . after sleeping in inns (where they even steal your hair, they say to make mattresses); after that and other things (among them carrying around a stomach that is bursting with *atole* made of sand that they sold us in an inn, which I leave traces of wherever I go), it seems that I am [finally] arriving.

This passage in which the ailing pícaro reports to have "left traces" of his having passed through various locales displays a grotesque, eschatological humor similar to that of Quevedo—one that recurs throughout the text. In another episode, the protagonist discusses eating a soup that consists of the bones of a muleskinner's wife (Chapter 11). Further, as Mier sleeps in one of many dreadful *mesones,* the inn keeper robs Servando of his clothes (because he has no money to pay for his keep), a fate that similarly befell Guzmán.

Another structural characteristic of the picaresque novel is the education of the young rogue, which frequently coincides with his servitude. This instruction may or may not manifest itself in the form of a tangible school and teacher; life itself is shown to be a lesson. Thus, although Arenas's Mier travels to Mexico City to receive a formal education with the Dominicans, just as Pablos had gone with Don Dieguito to study in Alcalá de Henares, and Guzmán had studied to be a priest in Seville (who ironically succumbs to the temptation of a woman named Gracia), the pícaro's greater education occurs on the streets of life. Given all of the torment that Mier experiences at the hands of the Spanish Colonial government and the Inquisition—of course, the picaresque revels in criticism of the Church—he must learn to persevere in the most adverse of circumstances. Consequently, while serving various *amos,* like all pícaros, Mier perfects his arsenal of *artimañas* (tricks) and masters his ability to ingratiate himself with his superiors (as does Guzmán with the captains of the galley and Pablos with prison wardens). After having made a fantastical escape from the sea vessel *La Nueva Empresa,* only to land in the possibly worse distination of a slave ship, Fray Servando disguises himself as an African slave and serves the slave traders. Arenas's Mier proves to be a true heir of Pablos and Guzmán when he affirms: "Entonces yo, que conocía las miserias de toda esa calaña y sus puntos débiles, fingí gran devoción. Me incliné ante ellos y, con gran humildad, prometí eterna fidelidad y obediencia. Y, como conocía sus costumbres tan bien (por ser las mías), me ofrecí de criado" (51; "Then I, who knew the miseries of that type of people and all of their weak points, feigned great devotion. I bowed down before them, and, with great humility, promised eternal fidelity and obedience. And, as I was so familiar with their customs (for they were mine), I offered myself as a servant").

Like the protagonists in Alemán's and Quevedo's text, Arenas's pícaro also becomes an expert in *la jacarandina,* or the street slang of thugs, and even uses the term *capeadores,* or cape thieves, which hints at direct intertextuality among the works of Arenas, Alemán, and Quevedo. In *EMA*'s Chapter 11, upon Fray Servando's departure from the grotesque *mulero*'s home, the host offers a "muchacho trapero" to accompany the friar on his journey (70). The narrator reports that Mier and his "servant" arrived at Valladolid "siempre acompañados por los hombres de Chalflandín,[19] gente muy fina que les hicieron aprender *la jacarandina*" (71; "always accompanied by Chalflandín's men, very fine people who taught them the slang of the thugs"). This image of the pícaro's learning the language of *rufianes* evokes Guzmán's description of how his panhandler "brothers" tell him of the ridiculous "Ordenanzas mendicativas" by which he must abide. The scene more overtly resonates, however, with one from *El buscón* in which Quevedo's protagonist brags that, with the hit man Matorrales, "*Estudié la jacarandina* y en pocos días era rabí de los otros rufianes" (Quevedo 237, my emphasis; "I studied the slang and in just a few days I was a rabbi among the other ruffians"). Moreover, Arenas's sarcastic description of the gang of highway robbers led by Chalflandín as "gente muy fina" is suggestive of Pablos's depiction of his fellow prisonmates as "los buenos caballeros" and the like (Quevedo 185).[20] In Rabelaisian, carnivalesque fashion, Arenas enumerates a list of outlaws who reportedly escorted Mier during his journey towards Valladolid: "acompañado por guspateros,/alcatiferos,/cuatreros,/cicateros,/pededoreros,/ *capeadores,*/enjibadores/y gerifaltes de gran tomares y poco dares" (71, my emphasis; "in the company of hustlers, bustlers, rustlers, racketeers, pocketeers, crooks, rooks, and falcons who give less than they take" [trans. Brotherston 91]). The modern reader (as well, perhaps, as the noncriminal) would need a dictionary to decipher the meaning of these terms, all typical of the (at least literary) jargon of thieves and assassins of seventeenth-century Spain. These are not words that a twentieth-century Cuban writer could readily cite. The reference to *capeadores,* or cape thieves, and their fellows reveals intertextuality with *El buscón.* In Quevedo's novel, Pablos, now the self-proclaimed "Don Felipe Tristán," encounters his former master and, to a certain degree, childhood friend, Diego. Diego quickly recognizes the disguised Pablos and uncovers the charlatan's ploy to marry his (Diego's) wealthy cousin by deceiving her about his "wealth." Diego pretends not to recognize Pablos, and later, in retribution, switches his *capa* with that of Pablos so that his own enemies will mistakenly attack—the ironically attempting to be *mis*-taken as a noble—Pablos. When Pablos is ambushed, he confuses these "gents" with *capeadores* and yells for justice, "¡A los capeadores!" (211).

Yet another example of Fray Servando's apparently following in the path of his picaresque brethren occurs when he serves "el conde de Gijón," a rich *indiano* living in France. Of his experience with this moronic "superior" who literally throws money to the wind, Mier comments: "Iba yo de *lazarillo* del Conde de Gijón" (123, my emphasis). In order to procure his own financial survival, he tends to the needs of the rich *indiano,* working as his translator in Paris (the Count reportedly speaks neither French nor Spanish well). Analogous to his picaresque ancestors, the novelized Fray Servando thus acts as a *mozo de muchos amos,* and learns skills of deception, or perhaps survival techniques, from the unjust world that surrounds him. The preceding textual examples—complete with swindling inn keepers, muleteers, interminable hunger, servitude, thieves, an education through "hard knocks," and a cunning world in general—all replicate the typical *environs* of the picaresque. Although many of the *fraile*'s travels, adventures, and marvelous escapes are evident in his autobiographical *Memorias,* Arenas amplifies and exaggerates their picaresque elements.

Structurally, the pícaro's text traces the evolution of a naive boy, hoping for better days to come, into the cynical pícaro. Innocence is lost in the picaresque "school of life." As the pícaro physically travels, he emotionally and intellectually proceeds from innocence to disillusionment; *desengaño,* of course, is also a sentiment that permeates baroque texts. The pícaro runs from a world lying in wait, from his "tainted" blood, from his lowly genealogy, from his sexuality, from his past. He flees because he is persecuted, disenfranchised, and marginalized, or simply because he prefers the liberties afforded by *la picardía.* The rogue frequently rebels and praises freedom from authority, or as Guzmán says, "la gloriosa libertad" (1.131, 265). However, the retreating pícaro tends to find himself alone in his perennial quest for autonomy. The pícaro's journey is symbolized by his lonely confinement in the "watchtower," which allows him to observe humanity but prohibits his full participation in the world before him. Conscious of this, Mateo Alemán very aptly chose the subtitle *Atalaya de la vida humana,* or the "human watchtower," for the *Segunda Parte de Guzmán de Alfarache.*

The frenetic activities of the pícaro reveal his attempts to gain social status and/or freedom. Constant changes of identity accompany constant movement from place to place. However, the pícaro's movements are generally futile, as they carry him back to his initial point of departure. Thus, the journey of the pícaro is typically circular, and this circularity denotes a type of trap or labyrinth in direct opposition to freedom. As the pícaro appears to rise in social status, he simultaneously approaches his own demise. Though Guzmán treks throughout much of Spain and Italy, he ends his journey where it began: in Seville, the pícaro's preferred metropolis. In *El buscón,* a Sisyphean destiny awaits Pablos as well, though for different reasons. Whereas the more than likely *converso* Alemán could empathize with his *converso* pícaro, the aristocratic Quevedo could not permit upstarts with tainted blood, such as Pablos, to have access to his noble world—even within the realm of fiction. Pablos is *not* a romantic figure in search of individual liberties; Quevedo would not allow him such a luxury. Thus, although Pablos does not return to his native Segovia in the final pages of the novel, as does Guzmán to Seville, he uselessly repeats his self-destructive actions.

Like the traditional pícaro, Arenas's *fraile* must flee from his home, as his survival necessitates that he escape the abuse of his indifferent mother. Once freed from his family, the *fraile* is subsequently persecuted by fellow men of the cloth, female suitors—including the historical Lady Hamilton, Madame de Stäel, and the fictional "Orlando, rara mujer" (of Virigina Woolf's *Orlando*)—beggars, governments, churches, lions, rats, scorpions, vultures, dogs . . . Entities of every terrestrial and imaginary design forever pursue the fictional Fray Servando, just as they had his historical antecedent and his novelistic creator, Arenas. Fray Servando also must fight his social and cultural background, his ideals, and sexual temptation. The historical Mexican *criollo* likewise suffered because of a deep sense of national and continental identity. In his *Memoiras,* bemoaning the destiny to which his hybrid, burgeoning American consciousness had condemned him, he more often describes himself as a *criollo* and an *americano,* rather than as a Spaniard or a European. Caught between clashing cultures, the friar's uncertain identity recalls that of Alemán's *converso,* who is also isolated between two contradictory world views.

Like Guzmán and Pablos, *EMA*'s Fray Servando constantly finds himself alone in the *atalaya de la vida humana.* Unable to reconcile his ideals with reality, he is forced to escape into a hallucinatory interior world that the reader, presumably like the principal character, cannot easily distinguish from reality. Mier invites rats, mules, and imaginary *frailes*—doubles of himself—to be his interlocutors, and while Mier is constantly surrounded by others, their only design is to cage him. Thus, Mier must reside in a lonely watchtower. His own ideals of absolute freedom and total independence, however, prove to be a more formidable enemy than those who would drive him to hide his identity. His undying convictions land him in a world of perpetual solitude, in a string of prisons whose punishments transcend all of the torture that his many tormentors could possibly contrive. Fray Servando's ideal is that of uncompromising liberty—politically, personally, and even sexually. Thus, although in a scene in which his fellow novices and "el Padre Terencio" attempt to induct him

into a world of homosexuality, he resists (23-27); *EMA*'s narrators view this abstinence as a form of self-inflicted slavery. The *fraile*'s odyssey in search of liberation, along with his constant self-abnegation, both free and restrain him. That is why he never achieves happiness, even though his jailors are consistently destroyed by their own fears of his absolute ideals of personal (and national) independence.[21] As he suffers a life of isolation in a seemingly endless succession of incarcerations, he searches ceaselessly for an ever-elusive liberty. The goal of absolute independence has itself become a prison.

Once again, the circle is a manifestation of a labyrinthine jail. *EMA* has a circular structure, as do *El buscón* and *Guzmán de Alfarache.* In the last pages of the novel, the *fraile fantástico* returns to his exact point of departure, the *corojal.* Just as the novel begins with: "Venimos del corojal. No venimos del corojal" (11), it ends with the *tú* voice reporting: "Y luego volviste a Monterrey, pues ya eras un muchacho. Y emprendiste el regreso a la casa, desde el corojal" (222; "And later you returned to Monterrey, for you were already a boy. And you embarked upon your return back home, from the prickly palms"). Like Guzmán and Pablos, the *fraile trotamundos* is forced to retrace his steps, thus revealing the futility of his attempts to gain genuine liberty and to improve society. Perhaps the most noteworthy moment of *desengaño* in the novel occurs when Fray Servando is on the verge of death. The omniscient third person voice reveals Mier's desolation and disillusionment: "Y de golpe . . . presintió que durante toda su vida había sido estafado" (302; "And suddenly, he had the premonition that he had been tricked his entire life"). The narrator then discloses Mier's profound sense of having wasted his life:

> Y el fraile dudó. Y sintió miedo. Miedo de que al final de aquellos vastos recintos no hubiese nadie esperándolo. Miedo a quedarse flotando sobre un vacío infinito, girando por un tiempo despoblado, por una soledad inalterable donde ni siquiera existiría el consuelo de la fe. Miedo a quedar totalmente engañado.
>
> (216)

> And the friar doubted. And he felt afraid. Fear that at the end of those vast places there would be no one waiting for him. Fear that he would end up floating above an infinite emptiness, turning round and round through a deserted time, through an unalterable solitude where not even the consolation of faith would exist. Fear that he would end up being completely disillusioned.

In these last moments of his life, *el fraile* loses his faith and his ideals, the very essence of his being. A better example of *desengaño barroco* would be almost impossible to find. Indeed, this type of baroque disillusionment is one of the greatest, and saddest, ways in which Arenas and Mier were indeed "la misma persona."

To conclude, I wish to return to the question of why Arenas would have chosen the baroque picaresque for his fictionalized rendition of the life of Fray Servando Teresa de Mier. The picaresque format allows its writer to assume alternate identities, and thus to criticize more freely what (s)he perceives as the wrongs of society (even from an elitist perspective, as in Quevedo's case). While Alemán and Quevedo generally experience difficulties in their endeavors to differentiate their own views from those of the pícaro, Arenas revels in his convergence with his rogue. Although the pícaro and his author are not necessarily the same being, the pícaro is, at least intermittently, an embodiment of the ideology of his author. The picaresque novel necessarily then resonates with Bakhtinian carnivalesque voices: the author dons the pícaro's mask. From behind the safe distance of this disguise, the novelist may express sentiments that otherwise may not be uttered; hence, he may unmask, even ridicule, his fellows and enemies without restraint, or irreverently deconstruct the purported values of his society.

As José A. Maravall, Werner Weisbach, and Stephen Gilman, among others, have demonstrated, the baroque represents an interaction with power—be it the *dirigista* discourse of the ruling party, attempting to control its denizens, as in Quevedo's *El buscón,* or, as in Alemán's *Guzmán* and Arenas's *EMA,* a status quo that can only be reproached furtively. Typically, the baroque picaresque author expresses discontent against absolute rule, against the obligation of singing the praises of the state, against isolation, against being an outcast or a hybrid. Since the pícaro's fictitious autobiography in large part evinces a treatise on freedom—Guzmán's "la gloriosa libertad"—and its relationship to power, the baroque picaresque, with its proliferating perspectives and open structure, offers the disenchanted and the persecuted a means of rebellion and escape, a way of asserting individuality and personal liberty.

While Reinaldo Arenas did not have to endure the Spanish Inquisition, as a homosexual artist opposed to Fidel Castro's Revolution, did he not suffer a very similar fate? As the *converso* Alemán had done almost three hundred years earlier, Arenas wrote from the position of the ostracized "other." Were his artistic intentions not hampered and censored by the state, just as those of Alemán, Quevedo, and even Mier had been? In **Antes que anochezca,** Arenas claims that, as an adolescent, he initially supported Fidel Castro's Revolution against the dictatorship of Fulgencio Batista (1933-40, 1940-44, and 1954-58). On New Year's Day, 1959, many Cuban intellectuals stormed Havana, hoping to improve the *whole* of Cuba and, perhaps naively, committed to establishing a Utopia on the Island under Castro. Quickly, the artists' hopes were dashed, as artistic creativity that did not overtly support the Revolution and art that was not readily accessible to the masses were seen to di-

rectly threaten Marxist goals. In 1961, Castro's "Palabras a los intelectuales" ("Advice for the Intellectuals") erased any doubts about the socialist (and later communist) nature of the Revolution. Castro then reportedly delivered the now-famous warning to artists and intellectuals: "Dentro de la Revolución, todo; contra la Revolución, nada" (qtd. in Béjar 19; "For the Revolution, everything; against the Revolution, nothing"). In 1961, the UNEAC was formed, presided over by Nicolás Guillén, with the authority to determine the validity of art of the Revolution. Like Alemán and Quevedo under the watchful gaze of the Counter-Reformation, Arenas was expected to reflect the ideology of the ruling party in his writings. Indeed, according to an October, 1968, UNEAC declaration in the *Granma Weekly Review,* "'The writer must contribute to the Revolution through his work, and this involves conceiving of literature as a means of struggle, a weapon against weaknesses and problems that, directly or indirectly, could hinder this advance'" (qtd. in Menton 112). While composing *EMA* in 1965, Arenas was undoubtedly aware of just these "duties" and "obligations" as a soldier of the Revolution: the individual must sacrifice his/her own liberty and artistic freedom for the good of the whole.

In the lives of the authors of all of the narratives in this analysis, one finds the common thread of a despotic regime that attempts to control the behavior of its people, particularly that of the artist. In Spain's Golden Age, the Catholic Church and its *Santo Oficio* sought to curb the flow of converts to Protestantism, while more recently Fidel Castro has struggled to maintain enthusiasm for a failed revolution. The traditional picaresque frame, with its fictitious first person voice, offers its authors the opportunity to scrutinize society *ostensibly* from another's perspective—the pícaro's. In general terms, the oppression of both the Counter-Reformation and communism seek to lessen the importance of the individual, focusing instead on the importance of God, the Church, or the common good; the picaresque, in contrast, tends to stress the acceptance of plurality, of individuals among the masses.

The pícaro's constant movement symbolizes his desire for social improvement, or perhaps even for escape from an island-prison. In his narrative, Alemán—a *converso*—rages against the world's historical hatred of the Jew. In contrast, Quevedo avenges his social insecurities and losses precisely through the creation and destruction of his pícaro. In *EMA,* Reinaldo Arenas too aims his vindictive pen at many enemies. The historical Fray Servando had sought vengeance against the Spanish Inquisition and Colonial rule in his *Memorias;* Arenas in turn reflects Mier's vengeful nature in his novel. Beyond the historical Mier's rancor, though, Arenas simultaneously infuses his own outrage at Castro's government and society's prejudices against homosexuality, which Castro's henchmen attempted to obliterate in large part between 1963 and 1965. Not surprisingly, homoerotic innuendo pervades *EMA.*

Doubling as Mier, Arenas was able to express his personal disillusionment and discontent with the Cuba of his day. This kind of vengeful anger points to the *desengaño* ubiquitous in baroque letters. In Arenas's deconstruction of the utopian dream, only in hallucinations and fantasy may Paradise be created anew. Through sarcasm, ludic play, and multiple narrative voices, Arenas mocks Cuba's failed Utopia. Through *EMA*'s parody of this dream, through baroque excess, "unnecessary" textual ornamentation, and outrageous *desmesura,* Arenas predicted the reality of communism's totalitarianism: cruelty, relentless monotony, bare necessities, food shortages, ration cards, and endless lines. By drawing upon the baroque's enigmatic, hermetic discourse and the picaresque tradition of manifold and even contradictory accounts of the adventures of a perennially rebellious protagonist, Arenas novelistically destroys the goals of Marxist history: to provide a clear, uniform, teleologically optimistic message for the masses, and to promote the common good over personal liberties. By employing cacophonous and carnivalesque voices, the illusion of Paradise rediscovered is fustigated relentlessly. Both Mier and Arenas emphasized the critical importance of the independence of a society, which in turn should guarantee the individual rights of its constituents. In his novel, using Mexico and France as models derived from Mier's *Memorias,* Arenas illustrates that Utopia did not spring from the French or the Mexican Revolutions, and in doing so he implies that neither will it ever take root under Castro's regime.

The historical Mier wrote his account from within the Inquisition's prisons, and, consequently, he could not express himself unabashedly. Reassessing the archival records in *EMA,* Arenas rewrites Mier's life in his own fantasized, creative, hallucinatory, baroque picaresque fashion. While Arenas follows the basic outline of Mier's autobiography, he also deconstructs the official accounts by offering multiple perspectives and by reinventing the *fraile fantástico*'s journeys, situating them in a magical world with threatening rats who dance and talk, cavedwelling monsters, and a lion who at one point metamorphoses into a woman and symbolizes the endless persecution of Fray Servando. Arenas utilizes the extreme, the seemingly impossible, the strange, the grotesque and the erotic—in short, all that the Archive omits, or that never occurred outside of Arenas's own fantasy. Reflecting his own personal life, the Cuban novelist repeatedly insinuates that his pícaro was gay. In *EMA,* Arenas thus unapologetically merges the autobiography of the historical Fray Servando with his own: "tú y yo somos la misma persona." When Arenas made this statement he was in effect predicting his own fu-

ture: he had not yet become an official enemy of the state; he had not yet been forced to hide from his own version of the Spanish Inquisition, Cuba's Revolutionary government; he had not become a radical dissident; and he had not yet been forced to reside in the infamous Cuban prison El Morro—one of the many prisons in which the historical Fray Servando had been incarcerated two centuries prior.

The pícaro—like Cuba's revolutionaries—seeks freedom and a better life, but does not find it. His life is a prison, and a better future is merely an elusive dream. For a writer trapped in an island prison, what metaphor could be more apt than the circuitous, pointless, circular path of the pícaro?

Notes

1. Among its commonly cited sixteenth- and seventeenth-century Spanish *novelistic* imitators are the likewise anonymous *La segunda parte del Lazarillo* (The Second Part of Lazarillo, 1555), Mateo Alemán's *Guzmán de Alfarache* (1599/1604), Francisco López de Úbeda's *La pícara Justina* (1605), Vicente Espinel's *La vida de Marcos de Obregón* (The History of the Life of the Squire Marcos Obregón, 1618), another *La segunda parte del Lazarillo* (1620), by Juan de Luna, Francisco de Quevedo's *El buscón,* and Estebanillo González's *Estebanillo González* (1646). These represent only a few of *Lazarillo*'s many novelistic offspring; picaresque short stories, *entremeses,* and plays also were in vogue during Spain's Golden Age.

2. Throughout this work, Arenas's *El mundo alucinante* will frequently be abbreviated as *EMA.* Unless otherwise noted, all citations will be from the following edition: *El mundo alucinante* (México: Diógenes, 1978). All translations from the Spanish in the essay are mine unless otherwise noted.

3. Arenas records this in both his autobiography, *Antes que anochezca* (Before Night Falls, 101), and is 1980 foreword to the Tusquets edition of *EMA,* published in 1997 (21-22).

4. In "La curiosidad barroca" (*Expresión americana*), José Lezama Lima discusses the temerities committed by Fray Servando and Sor Juana Inés de la Cruz, among others, in their rebellion against the established colonial society. For Lezama, these temerities characterize artists of this period. Lezama views Mier as a figure embodying traits of both the Baroque and Romanticism.

5. Mier argues that all aspects of Juan Diego's vision could essentially be attributed to a Christian play, combined with Aztec beliefs. He writes that "la historia de Guadalupe es una comedia del indio

Valeriano, forjada sobre la mitología azteca tocante a la Tonantzin" (*Apología* 43). To further fortify his theory, he offers an extremely confounding—though fascinating—commentary about the types of *capas* and *telas* that the various echelons of Indians used. He suggests that, because Juan Diego was of a lower social class, he could not have been carrying the *lienzo* that popular belief claimed was his, and on which the Virgin and her white roses supposedly left their imprints (*Apología* 44-50). At a minimum, then, Fray Servando radically challenges the way in which her apparition was commonly believed to have occurred, while simultaneously undermining Guadalupe's primacy (along with Spain's mission to America).

6. I follow Parker and Dunn in employing the Spanish idiom "pícaro" without italics. The words typically used in English translation, "rogue," "picaroon," "knave," etc., do not have the same connotations as the Spanish "pícaro."

7. Although I do observe some of the subtle differences between the seventeenth-century baroque and what has been referred to as the twentieth-century neobaroque, I abstain for the most part from stressing the distinctions between them. In general, while seventeenth-century baroque authors find this world to be dismal, they at least have hope in the hereafter. For the majority of neobaroque writers, on the other hand—inheritors not only of the baroque but also of the more recent existentialist tradition—modernity lacks even that possibility. Stylistically, the neobaroque manifests itself as a natural continuation of the exaggerated style of the baroque and displays even more ludic self-consciousness on the part of the author. Furthermore, many Cuban neobaroque authors—Arenas, Severo Sarduy, and José Lezama Lima, among them—have explored erotic (frequently homoerotic) sexual taboos as part of their subversive, transgressive texts. Given that baroque narrative first took root in the New World during Imperial Spain's *Contrarreforma*, it is only logical that the inhabitants of America would eventually use this same artistic tradition as a weapon against colonial forces, transforming it into the "*Contraconquisia,*" as Lezama Lima would say. Although examining the "neobaroque" in relation to twentieth-century avant-garde and/or post-modernist texts might also prove fruitful, such a project falls well beyond the limitations of this study. See Brownlee and Béjar.

8. In *Ensayo de Contraconquista,* Gonzalo Celorio discusses this intentionality of baroque and, more specifically, neobaroque writing: "Quizá una diferencia entre los barrocos del siglo XVII y los neobarrocos de neustros días consista en que aquéllos no sabían que eran barrocos y éstos vaya que lo saben" (100; "Perhaps a difference between the baroque [writers] of the seventeenth century and the neobaroque of our day is that they [seventeenth-century writers] did not know they were baroque, and these [of today] absolutely do"). In line with Severo Sarduy, Celorio also underlines the importance of the neobaroque's intertextuality and parody.

As somewhat of an aside, we should note that in his rewrite of Fray Servando's *Memorias,* Arenas also participates in what Fernando Aínsa, Roberto González Echevarría, and Seymour Menton, among others, have called the "nueva novela histórica latinoamericana." Examples include Alejo Carpentier's *El reino de este mundo* (1949) and *El arpa y la sombra* (1979), Abel Posse's *Daimón* (1978), Fernando del Paso's *Noticias del imperio* (1994), Antonio Benítez Rojo's *El mar de las lentejas* (1979), Gabriel García Márquez's *El general en su laberinto* (1989), Mario Vargas Llosa's *La guerra del fin de mundo* (1981), and Augusto Roa Bastos's *Yo el supremo* (1974). In the "la nueva novela histórica latinoamericana" (abbreviated here as NNHLA), Latin American novelists challenge the *rôle* of the traditional historian by presenting a viewpoint of the past that differs from that of the Official Archive. By introducing multiple narrative voices, the NNHLA authors repeatedly deny the possibility of one objective "Truth." Since these authors often fictionalize historical accounts in autobiographical form—utilizing, for example, the first person voice, interior monologues, and/or a diary format—the reader is drawn into the intimate thoughts and feelings of the historical figure, eliminating historical distance and any hope for objectivity. With such techniques, as Aínsa affirms, these writers essay to "dar voz a lo que la historia ha negado" (6), finally offering "subalterns" and other minorities the opportunity to speak out. Furthermore, influenced by Jorge Luis Borges, NNHLA authors use anachronisms and experiment with time and space to offer non-occidental, frequently indigenous, understandings of the world and its events. The world of these novels, in short, exists outside of our European linear and "historical" perceptions of time and space.

9. In *El barroco literario hispánico,* Emilio Carilla echoes this argument: "De nuevo, no se trata de atribuir al Barroco lo que encontramos en todos los tiempos. Sin embargo, es indudable que en pocas épocas, o ninguna, encontramos una abundancia tal y tan notables ejemplos" (84-85). These formal characteristics are not by any means exclusive to the baroque; however, in a baroque *ouevre,*

one typically finds a "high concentration" of them in conjunction with certain ideological constraints.

10. Wölfflin's arguments sparked a debate that ensues to this day, as scholars have yet to agree on the precise interpretation of "baroque" and its descendants, such as "el barroco americano," "el barroco de las Indias," and "el neobarroco." Although most historians and philosophers commonly limit the baroque to the epoch of decline, excess, and decadence (in Spenglerian terms) that followed the Renaissance in Europe, I argue that styles and forms of belief can and do recur. Theories of a historical baroque period, as well as those of a *resurgence* of baroque ideology and stylistics, are thus both valid. Once again, it should be noted that the principal aim of this inquiry is not to look for distinctions between the classic baroque and the "neobarroco," but rather to uncover evidence of continuity and to thus legitimize usage of the terms *baroque* and *picaresque* in relation to twentieth-century narrative.

11. Arenas reworks the classic tale in modernized prose in order to reach contemporary readers, particularly the English-speaking student of Spanish (the edition even includes suggestions for teachers, footnotes, and a glossary). Arenas's introduction appears in both Spanish and English, although I have not been able to determine whether or not Arenas also wrote the English translation. The original manuscript of Arenas's *Lazarillo* is available at Princeton University's Firestone Collection of Rare Books and Manuscripts, along with his correspondence with Dolores Koch (one of the text's editors) and Regents Publishing. In a separate project, I examine *how* Arenas reconstructs his *Lazarillo*.

12. For instance, Liliane Hasson recognizes similarities between *EMA*'s and Quevedo's "sátira feroz" ("ferocious satire") (114). For his part, Carlos Rangel argues that: "Uno de los mayores placeres de la lectura es hallar en las palabras que estamos leyendo eco de otros textos" (1; "One of the greatest pleasures of reading is finding in the words that we are reading echoes of other texts"), and he notes parallels between scenes from Arenas's *EMA* (the *buscadores* section of the "Jardines del Rey" ["The King's Garden] scene) and Quevedo's "El sueño del infierno" ("The Dream about Hell"), but without offering either analysis or explanation. Soren Triff, too, confirms the appropriation of Quevedian stylistics in Arenas's *ouevre*, specifying that "El autor [Arenas] parece preferir lo conceptista antes que lo ornamental del barroco" (187; "the author seems to prefer conceits over the ornamental aspects of the baroque"). Félix Lugo Nazario also highlights the Quevedian elements in Arenas's dialogue, pointing out that in *EMA* Arenas continues in the Quevedian baroque tradition of *conceptismo* as well as that of *desengaño* (disillusionment) (52). Strangely, though, while his investigation focuses on intertextuality—he even notes how *EMA* at times mimics the "confessional format" so typical of the picaresque— Nazario never mentions the picaresque novel. René Jara likewise fails to note the picaresque elements, although he does mention characteristics fundamental to the picaresque, such as the protagonist's *soledad* (solitude), the hostility of the world represented by the narrative, the novel's "condición de testigo de los vicios de su época" (223; "condition of being a witness to the vices of his epoch"), and its intertextuality with the "novela de aventuras" or "novela bizantina" (231).

In contrast, Shaw uncovers picaresque traits in *EMA* as he traces Quevedo's influence (and that of other classic baroque writers). However, in the end he declares that Arenas's novel is not "picaresque" but rather, more vaguely, "antirealista." While noting the great "classical" baroque influence on Arenas, Shaw remarks: "A pesar de algunos episodios picarescos, *El mundo alucinante* no es propiamente una novela picaresca. Si bien se puede ver la influencia de Quevedo, más fuertes aún son las de Rabelais . . . y de Gracián. Como el de Andrenio en *El criticón*, el viaje de Fray Servando se convierte en una larga peregrinación en busca de lo quimérico; la libertad, la justicia, el triunfo de la razón" (180; "Despite a few picaresque episodes, *El mundo alucinante* is not exactly a picaresque novel. If one can easily recognize Quevedo's influence, Rabelais's . . . and Gracián's are even more evident. As is Andrenio's trip in *El criticón*, Fray Servando's journey becomes a long pilgrimage in search of the chimerical: freedom, justice, and the triumph of reason.") While I support almost all of Shaw's characterizations, his denying *EMA* picaresque status seems shortsighted. More on target, Oscar Rodríguez Ortiz underscores the novel's baroque and picaresque elements, suggesting that "el itinerario dentro del modelo básico apela asimismo a otras connotaciones al inscribirse en las formas de un discurso picaresco, de la aventura de viaje por regiones desconocidas y especialmente al gran discurso de la sátira y de la invectiva" (qtd. in Valero 228; "the itinerary's basic model also recalls other connotations as it falls within the parameters of the forms of picaresque discourse, of travel adventures through unknown regions, and especially of the discourse of satire and invective.")

13. Although Lourdes María Tomás seems at first glance to answer Koch's call to compare *EMA*

and the picaresque in depth, her often insightful analysis ultimately misses the mark regarding the novel's baroque picaresque genealogy. Indeed, her conclusion—"En el caso de la narrativa picaresca, sin embargo, no podemos referirnos a un conflicto, sino *a una franca no pertenencia de la obra a ese género*" (265, my emphasis; "with respect to picaresque narrative, however, we cannot talk about a conflict, but rather an absolute non-pertinence of this work to that genre.")—might have been quite different, if, while establishing her parameters of the picaresque, she had considered the baroque. Tomás bases her definition of the picaresque primarily on *Lazarillo,* which most critics regard as a Renaissance text; and while Tomás does refer to *Guzmán* and *La pícara Justina,* she discards *El buscón* almost altogether because it is not overtly didactic (303). From a critical standpoint, this is quite puzzling, given the numerous scholars who clearly identify the Quevedian influence in *EMA.* Furthermore, many critics, including Bataillon, who views *El buscón* as the apogee of the picaresque novel (24), would disagree with her contention that Quevedo's text is not really picaresque because it lacks didacticism.

14. The Tusquets edition of *EMA,* in which this letter is found, was not published until 1997. I am unaware of its general availability before then.

15. In a forthcoming study, I examine precisely how Arenas's novel interfaces with the historical *Memorias* as well as other "historical" texts about Mier.

16. Severo Sarduy, expanding upon Wölfflin's theories, envisions the baroque's multiplicity as elliptical in nature, as an art form in which any center is denied, in contrast with the quintessential, symmetrical circle of Renaissance art. Sarduy also points to Johannes Kepler's (1571-1630) discovery of Mar's elliptical rotation around the sun to help to explain the ensuing baroque movement.

17. Though I do not have ample space to delve into the issue here, I disagree with critics who find that Guzmán sincerely repents during the mutiny on board the galley; to the contrary, he simply proves himself to be a recidivist who takes advantage of a situation for his own survival. The narrator's false conversion does not justify the text's existence within the realm of fiction (as does "Vuestra Merced's" demand that Lazarillo explain his *caso*). Further, though the picaresque novel is a bildungsroman which presents the ever-changing, contradictory perspectives of the young pícaro versus that of the adult (perhaps) former pícaro, fundamental *moral change* is not an essential trait of the picaresque, as is demonstrated by *Lazarillo, El buscón,* and, in my view, *Guzmán de Alfarache.*

18. Arenas also repeatedly uses literary word-play, exaggeration, and *conceptismo.* Somewhat reminiscent of Quevedo's portrayal of Cabra's hungry facial features, Mier's body is similarly dehumanized as the individual parts are personified. The *padre alucinado* dreams that he jumps to escape from a prison window. Upon colliding with the ground, he is broken into pieces. Voracious rats are delighted at the prospects of such a meal: "Las ratas salieron triunfantes y empezaron a cargar con sus pedazos. Cada pedazo del fraile tenía sus propios gritos; de modo que por unos momentos en toda la celda se escuchó como una armonía de gritos: roncos, estridentes, desafinados y alucinantes. Pero el hambre hizo a los animales engullir aquella carne chillona, y sus estómagos se llenaron de resonancias. Yahora las ratas (gritando por dentro) salían" (62-63). Not only is Mier's body broken into a mosaic of screaming parts, but those parts are then incorporated into the rats' stomachs, which squeal with independent voices.

19. This evidently legendary figure appears in the *Memorias* as well. However, in the *Relación,* he and his bandits inspire fear. Mier writes: "Sería largo contar los trabajos que pasé descansando de día, caminando de noche, echándome fuera del camino a cada ruido que oía, debatiéndome con los perros que en batallones ocupan los pueblos, y temblando de los ladrones que, capitaneados por Chafaldin, desolaban a Castilla la Vieja . . . Compadecióse de mí un arriero que iba para esta villa, me puso sobre un borrico y me llevó a alojar a casa de un buen hombre, su bienhechor" (2.13; "It would be a long story to recount the difficulties that I endured resting by day, walking by night, getting off the road every time I heard a noise, fighting with the dogs that occupied the town in gangs, and trembling for [fear of] the thieves led by Chafaldin, as they laid waste to Castilla la Vieja. A mule skinner who was headed for that town felt sorry for me, and put me on a donkey, and took me to a house where I could stay with a good man, his benefactor"). Note that Arenas changed the highwayman's name from "Chafaldin" to "Chalflandín."

20. Cervantes also parodies this type of discourse in "Rinconete y Cortadillo." When Cervantes's young pícaros begin their careers as thieves in Seville, they are immediately met by a fellow rogue who initiates them into the world of *rufianes* and *"el germanesco o la germanía"* (207). They, too, are initially baffled by the language of the "brotherhood" of thieves and require the *mozo*'s translation when they enter Seville (206). Cervantes also underscores the disillusionment

common to the picaresque; the young boys set out with illusions of freedom only to find another form of oppression in Monipodio's "cofradía."

21. See, for example, Chapter 24, "De la prisión de Los Toribios. El encadenamiento del fraile," in which Fray Servando becomes a ball of chains. The weight of the interminable handcuffs, shackles, leg irons, and bonds forces the prison to sink. His escape is fantastical, cartoon-like, as he goes rolling through Spain, shattering all in his path, until he finally lands at sea (where he witnesses none other than the battle of Trafalgar).

Works Cited

Aínsa, Fernando. "La nueva novela histórica latinoamericana." *Plural* 240 (September 1991): 82-85.

Alemán, Mateo. *Guzmán de Alfarache.* Ed. Benito Brancaforte. Madrid: Cátedra, 1979.

Arenas, Reinaldo. *Antes que anochezca.* Barcelona: Tusquets Editores, 1992.

———. Foreword and Prologue ("Presentación"). *Lazarillo de Tormes.* Ed. and trans. José Olivio Jiménez. New York: Regents Publishing, 1984.

———. *Hallucinations.* Trans. Gordon Brotherston. New York: Harper and Row, 1971.

———. *El mundo alucinante.* México, D.F.: Editorial Diógenes, 1978.

———. *El mundo alucinante.* Barcelona: Tusquets Editores, 1997.

Bataillon, Marcel. *Le roman picaresque.* Paris: La Renaissance du Livre, 1931.

Béjar, Eduardo C. *La textualidad de Reinaldo Arenas (Juegos de la escritura posmoderna).* Madrid: Editorial Playor, 1987.

Brownlee, Marina. *The Cultural Labyrinth of María de Zayas.* Philadelphia: University of Pennsylvania Press, 2000.

Carilla, Emilio. *El barroco literario hispánico.* Buenos Aires: Editorial Nova, 1969.

Carpentier, Alejo. "Lo barroco y lo real maravilloso." *Tientos y diferencias.* Havana: UNEAC, 1974.

Celorio, Gonzalo. *Ensayo de contraconquista.* México, DF: Tusquets, 2001.

Cervantes, Miguel de. "Rinconete y Cortadillo." *Novelas ejemplares I.* 2 vols. Ed. Harry Sieber. Madrid: Cátedra, 1989.

Couffon, Claude. "Un contestaire cubain: Reinaldo Arenas." *Le monde des livres* 22 Mar. 1969, supplement: 6.

Díaz-Plaja, Guillermo. *El espíritu del barroco.* Barcelona: Editorial Crítica, 1983.

D'Ors, Eugenio. *Lo barroco.* Madrid: Águilar, 1964.

Dunn, Peter N. *Spanish Picaresque Fiction: A New Literary History.* Ithaca: Cornell University Press, 1993.

———. *The Spanish Picaresque Novel.* Boston: Twayne Publishers, 1979.

Gilman, Stephen. "An Introduction to the Ideology of the Baroque in Spain." *Symposium* 1 (1946): 82-107.

González Echevarría, Roberto. *Celestina's Brood: Continuities of the Baroque in Spanish and Latin American Literature.* Durham: Duke University Press, 1993.

———. *Myth and Archive: A Theory of Latin American Narrative.* New York: Cambridge University Press, 1990.

Guillén, Claudio. *The Anatomies of Roguery.* New York: Garland Publishing Co., 1987.

Hasson, Liliane. "Reinaldo Arenas, Francia y 'El libro de las flores.'" *Reinaldo Arenas: Recuerdo y presencia.* Ed. Reinaldo Sanchez. Miami: Ediciones Universal, 1994. 109-20.

Jara, René. "Aspectos de la intertextualidad en *El mundo alucinante.*" *Texto Crítico* 5.13 (1979): 219-35.

Koch, Dolores M. "Elementos barrocos en *El mundo alucinante.*" *Reinaldo Arenas: Alucinaciones, fantasía, y realidad.* Ed. Perla Rozencvaig and Julio Hernández Miyares. Glenview: Scott, Foresman/Montesinos. 136-46.

Lazarillo de Tormes. Introduction and ed. Francisco Rico. Madrid: Cátedra, 1988.

Lezama Lima, José. *La expresión americana y otros ensayos.* Montevideo: Arca, 1969.

Lugo Nazario, Félix. *La alucinación y los recursos literarios en las novelas de Reinaldo Arenas.* Miami: Ediciones Universal, 1995.

Manrique de Aragón, Jorge. *Peligrosidad social y picaresca.* San Antonio de Calogne (Gerona): Hijos de José Bosch, 1977.

Maravall, José Antonio. *La cultura del barroco.* Barcelona: Ariel, 1980.

Menton, Seymour. *Latin America's New Historical Novel.* Austin: University of Texas Press, 1993.

———. *Prose Fiction of the Cuban Revolution.* Austin: University of Texas Press, 1975.

Mier, Fray Servando Teresa de. *Memorias.* 1946. Ed. Antonio Castro Leal. 2 vols. México City: Editorial Porrúa, 1982.

Parker, Alexander A. *Los pícaros en la literatura: La novela picaresca en España y Europa (1599-1753).* Madrid: Editorial Gredos, 1971.

Quevedo, Francisco de. *El buscón.* Ed. Ignacio Arellano. Madrid: Colección Austral (Espasa-Calpe), 1993.

Reed, Helen H. *The Reader in the Picaresque Novel.* London: Tamesis Books Limited, 1984.

Rico, Francisco. *La novela picaresca y el punto de vista.* Barcelona: Editorial Seix Barral, 1969.

Shaw, Donald. *Nueva narrativa hispanoamericana.* Madrid: Cátedra, 1983.

Taléns, Jenaro. *Novela picaresca y práctica de la transgresión.* Gijón: Ediciones Júcar, 1975.

Tomás, Lourdes. *Géneros en "El mundo alucinante" de Reinaldo Arenas: La reescritura y su función.* Diss. New York University, 1991. Ann Arbor: UMI, 1991. 9134698.

Triff, Soren. "Los ensayos dispersos de Reinaldo Arenas." *Reinaldo Arenas: Recuerdo y presencia.* Ed. Reinaldo Sánchez. Miami: Ediciones Universal, 1994. 183-99.

Valero, Roberto. *El desamparado humor de Reinaldo Arenas.* North Miami: Hallmark Press, 1991.

Weisbach, Werner. *El barroco: arte de la contrarreforma.* Madrid: Espasa-Calpe, 1948.

Wölfflin, Heinrich. *Principles of Art History.* Trans. M.D. Hottinger. New York: Dover Publications, 1950.

———. *Renaissance and Baroque.* Trans. Kathrin Simon. London: Collins, 1964.

FURTHER READING

Biographies

Manrique, Jaime. "The Last Days of Reinaldo Arenas: A Sadness as Deep as the Sea." In *Eminent Maricones: Arenas, Lorca, Puig, and Me,* pp. 62-9. Madison: University of Wisconsin Press, 1999.

Personal reminiscence of Manrique's friendship with Arenas during the days before Arenas's suicide in 1990.

Ocasio, Rafael. *Cuba's Political and Sexual Outlaw: Reinaldo Arenas,* Gainesville: University Press of Florida, 2003, 212 p.

Book-length biocritical study of Arenas "as an indefatigable counterrevolutionary and as a sexual and political dissident."

Santí, Enrico Mario. "The Life and Times of Reinaldo Arenas." *Michigan Quarterly Review* 23, no. 2 (spring 1984): 226-36.

Brief biography of Arenas, focusing, in particular, on his difficult years in Cuba before he emigrated to the U.S.

Criticism

Ellis, Robert Richmond. "The Queer Birds of Juan Goytisolo and Reinaldo Arenas." *Romance Quarterly* 42, no. 1 (winter 1995): 47-60.

Analyzes how Juan Goytisolo, in his novel *Las virtudes del pájaro solitario,* and Arenas, in his novella *Arturo, la estrella más brillante,* "configure homoerotic desire" in order "to shed further light on the complexity of gay-male sexuality as a theme among Spanish-language writers."

Estevez, Abilio. "Between Nightfall and Vengence: Remembering Reinaldo Arenas." In *Bridges to Cuba/Puentes a Cuba,* edited by Ruth Behar, pp. 305-13. Ann Arbor: University of Michigan Press, 1995.

Comments on Arenas's skills as a writer and critiques, in particular, his autobiography, *Before Night Falls.*

Mac Adam, Alfred J. "The Novel of Persecution: From William Godwin to Reinaldo Arenas." In *Textual Confrontations: Comparative Readings in Latin American Literature,* pp. 89-116. Chicago: University of Chicago Press, 1987.

Compares William Godwin's late eighteenth-century novel *Things as They Are; or, The Adventures of Caleb Williams* and Arenas's *Hallucinations* in their respective treatments of the theme of the fugitive or prisoner artist and their use of "romance structures" as central devices in their narratives.

Pato, Hilda. "The Power of Abjection: Reinaldo Arenas in his *Palacio.*" *Revista Canadiense de Estudios Hispánicos* 23, no. 1 (fall 1998): 144-54.

Applies Julia Kristeva's theory of "abjection" to a reading of Arenas's *The Palace of the White Skunks,* noting "the chief textual manifestations" of the theme of abjection and the significance of its "apparent inescapability" in the novel.

Rodriguez-Monegal, Emir. "The Labyrinthine World of Reinaldo Arenas." *Latin American Literary Review* 8, no. 16 (spring-summer 1980): 126-31.

Critiques a number of Arenas's novels and short stories, asserting that his works are representations of a "single text," one based on the idea "that narrative does not progress but endlessly moves in all directions at the same time."

Sánchez-Eppler, Benigno. "Reinaldo Arenas, Re-writer Revenant, and the Re-patriation of Cuban Homoerotic Desire." In *Queer Diasporas,* edited by Cindy Patton and Benigno Sánchez-Eppler, pp. 154-82. Durham, N.C.: Duke University Press, 2000.

> Studies *Before Night Falls* to illustrate how the "vector" of Arenas's "displacement" out of Cuba and his past life "creates a corresponding vector of return in memory and narration, to both the places and the times left behind."

Soto, Francisco. "Reinaldo Arenas's *Persecución*: Extra- and Intertextual Links to Virgilio Piñera." *Latin American Theatre Review* 34, no. 2 (spring 2001): 39-54.

> Critiques Arenas's play *Persecución,* which he describes as "an audacious, critical, and experimental text . . . that explores more the possibilities of expression of fiction and the nuances of poetic verse than drama."

Vilaseca, David. "Writing 'AIDS': Identity, Metaphor and the Enjoyment of the *Sinthome* in Hervé Guibert and Reinaldo Arenas." In *Hindsight and the Real: Subjectivity in Gay Hispanic Autobiography,* pp. 71-110. Oxford: Peter Lang, 2003.

> Focuses on the ways in which Arenas and the French author and photographer Hervé Guibert, in their respective autobiographical writings, "construct their own identities" as individuals with AIDS, "and particularly on the fact that their constructions of self are unavoidably linked to figuration and to metaphorical uses of language."

Additional coverage of Arenas's life and career is contained in the following sources published by Thomson Gale: *Concise Major 21st-Century Writers,* Ed. 1; *Contemporary Authors,* Vols. 124, 128, 133; *Contemporary Authors New Revision Series,* Vols. 73, 106; *Contemporary Literary Criticism,* Vol. 41; *Dictionary of Literary Biography,* Vol. 145; *DISCovering Authors Modules: Multicultural Authors*; *Encyclopedia of World Literature in the 20th Century,* Ed. 3; *Gay & Lesbian Literature,* Ed.. 2; *Hispanic Literature Criticism,* Vol. 1; *Hispanic Writers,* Ed. 1; *Latin American Writers*; *Latin American Writers Supplement,* Ed. 1; *Literature Resource Center*; *Major 20th-Century Writers,* Ed. 2; *Major 21st-Century Writers*; *Reference Guide to Short Fiction,* Ed. 2; *Reference Guide to World Literature,* Ed. 3; and *World Literature and Its Times,* Ed. 1.

Carl Zuckmayer
1896-1977

German playwright, novelist, short story writer, poet, screenwriter, essayist, and autobiographer.

The following entry provides an overview of Zuckmayer's life and works. For additional information on his career, see *CLC,* Volume 18.

INTRODUCTION

Carl Zuckmayer is considered one of the most significant German playwrights of the twentieth century. He enjoyed popular success comparable to that of such contemporaries as Bertolt Brecht and Gerhart Hauptmann, and his plays *Der Hauptmann von Köpenick* (1931; *The Captain of Köpenick*) and *Des Teufels General* (1946; *The Devil's General*) were among the most frequently produced works on the West German stage after World War II. A sympathetic treatment of the common people and their concerns and a deep regard for nature are characteristic features of Zuckmayer's plays, and contributed to his appeal with audiences. His realistic dramas, such as *Der fröhliche Weinberg* (1925), are also credited with bringing an end to expressionism on the German stage. Zuckmayer maintained his stylistic techniques and humanistic outlook in his later plays, despite new tastes in the German theater, and his popularity and critical acclaim diminished as a result. His work remains, however, an important example of twentieth-century German drama.

BIOGRAPHICAL INFORMATION

Zuckmayer was born December 27, 1896, in the village of Nackenheim in the Rhineland. He was raised in a middle-class family by his father, a factory-owner also named Carl, and his mother, Amalie Friedericke Auguste Goldschmidt Zuckmayer. As a young boy he attended public schools, including the Gymnasium in Mainz. During World War I, Zuckmayer enlisted in the German army and rose to the rank of lieutenant before the war ended. Though initially patriotic and supportive of the war, he later became disillusioned and adopted pacifistic ideas, which he revealed in his first poems published in 1917 in the magazine *Die Aktion.* After the war, Zuckmayer attended the University of Frankfurt and the University of Heidelberg but gave up his studies to pursue a writing career. In 1920, he married his

childhood sweetheart, Annemarie Gans, but their marriage ended in less than a year. Also in 1920, Zuckmayer's first play, *Kreuzweg,* was produced in Berlin. It was written in an expressionist style and closed after only three performances.

Through a friend's influence, Zuckmayer was given a position as *Dramaturg,* or theatrical consultant, in Kiel in the fall of 1922. He was dismissed from the position in 1923 after the production of *Eunuch,* his adaptation of Terence's *Eunuchus,* which the city council considered obscene. He then became *Dramaturg* at the Schauspielhaus in Munich. His third play, *Pankraz erwacht,* influenced by the work of Bertolt Brecht, was also considered a failure after its premiere in 1925. In the same year, Zuckmayer met and married actress Alice von Herdan and soon after wrote his first successful play, *Der fröhliche Weinberg.* The drama was rejected by fifteen theaters in Berlin before critic Paul Fechter awarded it the prestigious Kleist Prize. Zuckmayer's next play, *Schinderhannes* (1927), was inspired by the language and folklore of the Hunsrück region of Rhineland. He continued writing plays, including *Katharina Knie* (1928), but began experimenting with other genres, as well. In 1926, he published a collection of poems titled *Der Baum,* and in 1930 he wrote the script for the film *Der blaue Engel* (*The Blue Angel*), which was based on a novel by Heinrich Mann and launched the acting career of Marlene Dietrich. One of Zuckmayer's most important plays, *The Captain of Köpenick,* premiered on March 5, 1931. After Adolf Hitler's rise to power in 1933, Zuckmayer's plays were banned. The Nazis opposed Zuckmayer's pacifistic views and, in particular, his public condemnation of Joseph Goebbels, the Nazi propaganda chief. Despite the ban on Zuckmayer's work, his next play, *Der Schelm von Bergen,* was staged in Vienna and published in Germany in 1934. As a result of the events leading up to World War II, Zuckmayer moved to Austria, then to Switzerland, and finally to the United States, where he wrote *The Devil's General.* In the late 1940s, the play was produced in German theaters, where it became wildly successful. Zuckmayer continued to write plays, including *Barbara Blomberg* (1949) and *Der Gesang im Feuerofen* (1950). At the request of Gerhart Hauptmann's widow, he also completed *Herbert Engelmann* (1952), a play left unfinished by Hauptmann at the time of his death. Zuckmayer's popularity waned in the 1950s, especially following the production of *Das kalte Licht* (*The Cold Light*) in 1955. As he grew older, Zuckmayer became more discursive and polemical in his writings, and his gift for character delineation, dialogue, and dramatic atmosphere waned. In 1958, Zuckmayer and his wife returned to Europe and settled in Saas-Fée, Switzerland. His final play, *Der Rattenfänger,* modeled after the Pied Piper tale, was produced in 1975. Zuckmayer died after a fall on January 18, 1977, in Visp, Switzerland.

MAJOR WORKS

Much of Zuckmayer's work is concerned with humanistic ideals. His plays and prose emphasize the interdependence of human beings, while asserting the need for a connection between humanity and the natural world. His work was greatly influenced by nature, folk traditions and culture, and the concerns and attitudes of the common people, and they tended to incorporate sentimental themes. As a result, his plays were often more popular with audiences than critics.

Zuckmayer's first play to receive critical recognition was *Der fröhliche Weinberg.* The play is a comedy that employs satire and parody, as well as humor, and takes place in the Zuckmayer's rural hometown of Nackenheim. The action centers on Jean Gunderloch, a vineyard owner who arranges the engagement of his illegitimate daughter to a foppish pedant. The girl, however, is already in love with a virile boatman. Humorous sequences, including a drunken brawl, ensue, but the play concludes with a happy ending. Zuckmayer relied on authentic regional dialect for the dialogue and incorporated several traditional Rhine-Hessian folk songs in the drama. Though the play's humor and earthy language offended several groups—from Jews to the military—*Der fröhliche Weinberg* was very popular with audiences in Berlin, achieving notoriety as a result of the extreme reaction it elicited from the public. It also established Zuckmayer's reputation and, almost single-handedly, brought an end to the dominance of expressionism on the German stage.

Many critics consider *The Captain of Köpenick* Zuckmayer's best play. It is based on an incident in 1906 that occurred in Wilhelmine Germany, in which a cobbler and ex-convict named Wilhelm Voigt obtained a uniform and posed as an army captain. Voigt then commandeered a troop of soldiers, arrested the city treasurer, and stole four thousand marks, which he redistributed to the soldiers for food and beer before he disappeared. The play balances its comedic elements with a more serious satirical commentary on military life. Before relating the actual events in the play, Zuckmayer follows the history of the uniform itself, and in so doing presents a critical portrait of military life. The uniform is first intended for a new captain, who is later forced to resign after breaking the law. Next, a newly appointed lieutenant, who is also the mayor of Köpenick, purchases the uniform in order to impress his

mother. But he returns it to a tailor when he gains weight and can no longer fit in it. The garment is then used as a costume and later abandoned at a used clothing shop, where Voigt purchases it. Scholars have interpreted the uniform's devolution as Zuckmayer's commentary on the fate of the military. Critics have also noted the disparity between the flawed actions of society, represented by the military, and the isolated individual who exposes its weaknesses.

The Devil's General, set in Berlin in 1941, is one of Zuckmayer's most popular plays. The main character, General Harras, is modeled after Zuckmayer's friend Ernst Udet, who was killed while testing a new airplane in 1941. In the play, Harras, in order to continue his profession flying airplanes, reluctantly aligns himself with the Nazi regime. His friend Oderbruch, however, participates in a conspiracy to sabotage the military aircrafts for which Harras is responsible. After Harras agrees to become the "devil's" general, he commits suicide by flying one of the airplanes he knows has been sabotaged. While the play satirizes the Nazi regime, it also condemns those members of German society who, like Harras, disapproved of Hitler but refused to speak or act against his policies. Yet contrary to Zuckmayer's intent, audiences sympathized with the likeable Harras, overlooking his guilt, and criticized instead the actions of Oderbruch, whom they perceived as self-righteous and rigidly pious. In addition to studying the psychological effects of a totalitarian regime on the individual, Zuckmayer presents a sober portrait of German society in the play through his depiction of various characters, such as Sigbert von Mohrungen, a self-interested member of the upper class; Colonel Eilers, a young war hero whose faith in his country blinds him to reality; and "Pützchen," a nefarious young woman who embraces the tenets of Nazi feminism.

CRITICAL RECEPTION

In Germany and surrounding countries, including Austria and Switzerland, Zuckmayer is widely regarded as one of the major playwrights of the twentieth century. During the height of his career, in the years before and after World War II, he was often ranked with some of the leading writers in German literature—with Brecht, Hauptmann, and Thomas Mann. His so-called German Trilogy—*The Captain of Köpenick, Der fröhliche Weinberg,* and *The Devil's General*—achieved epic stature for its penetrating dramatization of the three significant periods in German twentieth-century history: Wilhelmine Germany, the Weimar Republic, and the Third Reich, respectively. In these, his best works as a playwright, Zuckmayer has been praised for his powerful realism, his skill at delineating character and dramatic atmosphere, his concern for common people, and his commitment to individual life in the face of world events.

Critics generally acknowledge that after *The Devil's General* Zuckmayer's work declined in quality and relevance to the changing landscape of post-World War II Germany and Europe. His later plays, such as *The Cold Light, Die Uhr schlägt eins* (1961), and *Das Leben des Horace A. W. Tabor* (1964), lack the dramatic realism and subtle characterization of his earlier works, often relying on clichés, excessive plotting, and discursive argumentation to carry the action forward. As Siegfried Mews asserted, "the substance of his plays grew weaker while his persistently proclaimed moral convictions began to ring hollow." A new generation of critics, during the second half of the twentieth century, also discerned limitations in even the best of Zuckmayer's plays. They argued that his "epic" approach to drama tended to present plot for plot's sake and that his dramatic vision lacked a true ideological commitment, such as can be found in the works of Brecht. These scholars also lamented that Zuckmayer's individualistic and humanitarian world view, one that held humanity accountable in a universe controlled by God, was inadequate to convey the chaos of the modern world in the theater.

Despite the critical disagreement over Zuckmayer's place in world literature, he remains a popular figure in his home country, where his plays continue to be staged, his books published and widely read, and his works adapted for television and radio broadcasts. And though he wrote a considerable body of work in genres other than drama, including poetry, fiction, and a much praised autobiography, *Als wär's ein Stück von mir: Horen der Freundschaft* (1966; *A Part of Myself*), his reputation rests firmly on such masterworks as *The Captain of Köpenick* and *The Devil's General*. In these plays, Zuckmayer drew his inspiration from the themes of popular art, fairy tales, chronicles, and anecdotes. His ongoing appeal with popular audiences resides in the compassion for common people that these stories convey.

PRINCIPAL WORKS

Kreuzweg (play) 1920

Eunuch [adaptor; from *Eunuchus* by Terence] (play) 1923

Der fröhliche Weinberg (play) 1925

Pankraz erwacht (play) 1925

Der Baum (poetry) 1926

Ein Bauer aus dem Taunus und andere Geschichten (short stories) 1927

Schinderhannes (play) 1927

Katharina Knie (play) 1928

Rivalen [adaptor; from *What Price Glory?* by Maxwell Anderson and Laurence Stalling] (play) 1928

Schinderhannes [*The Prince of Rogues*] (screenplay) 1929

Der blaue Engel [*The Blue Angel*; with Karl Vollmoeller and Robert Liebmann] (screenplay) 1930

Kakadu-Kakada (play) 1930

Der Hauptmann von Köpenick [*The Captain of Köpenick*] (play) 1931

Kat [with Heinz Hilpert] (play) 1931

Die Affenhochzeit [*Monkey Wedding*] (novella) 1932

*Der Hauptmann von Köpenick [*The Captain of Köpenick*] (screenplay) 1932

Eine Liebesgeschichte (novella) 1934

Der Schelm von Bergen (play) 1934

Escape Me Never (screenplay) 1935

Salwàre oder Die Magdalena von Bozen [*The Moon in the South*] (novel) 1935

Rembrandt (screenplay) 1936

Ein Sommer in Österreich (novel) 1937

Bellman (play) 1938; revised as *Ulla Winblad,* 1953

Herr über Leben und Tod (novel) 1938

Pro Domo (autobiography) 1938

Second Wind (autobiography) 1940

Somewhere in France [with Fritz Kortner] (play) 1941

Der Seelenbräu (novella) 1945

Des Teufels General [*The Devil's General*] (play) 1946

Gesammelte Werke. 4 vols. (plays, novels, and novellas) 1947-52

Die Brüder Grimm: Ein deutscher Beitrag zur Humanität (essays) 1948

Barbara Blomberg (play) 1949

Der Gesang im Feuerofen (play) 1950

Herbert Engelmann [with Gerhart Hauptmann] (play) 1952

*Der fröhliche Weinberg [*The Grapes Are Ripe*; with Kurt J. Brown] (screenplay) 1953

Engele von Loewen (short stories) 1955

Das kalte Licht [*The Cold Light*] (play) 1955

Die Fastnachtsbeichte [*Carnival Confession*] (novella) 1959

Gedichte (poetry) 1960

Gesammelte Werke. 4 vols. (plays, novels, and novellas) 1960

Die Uhr schlägt eins (play) 1961

†Three Stories (short stories) 1963

Das Leben des Horace A. W. Tabor (play) 1964

Als wär's ein Stück von mir: Horen der Freundschaft [*A Part of Myself*] (autobiography) 1966

Kranichtanz (play) 1967

Der Rattenfänger (play) 1975

Werkausgabe in zehn Bänden, 1920-1975. 10 vols. (autobiography, poetry, novellas, short stories, and plays) 1976

Gedichte (poetry) 1977

Sitting Bull: Ein Indianer-Roman und einige Geschichten (unfinished novel) 1984

*These works are adapted from Zuckmayer's plays.

†This work comprises the stories "Die Geschichte eines Bauern aus dem Taunus," "Die Affenhochzeit," and "Die wandernden Hütten."

CRITICISM

Helmut Boeninger (essay date January 1952)

SOURCE: Boeninger, Helmut. "A Play and Two Authors: Zuckmayer's Version of Hauptmann's 'Herbert Engelmann.'" *Monatshefte* 44, no. 1 (January 1952): 341-48.

[*In the following essay, Boeninger highlights the ways in which Zuckmayer revised and improved Gerhart Hauptmann's play* Herbert Engelmann.]

Literary criticism concerns itself, generally, with the finished products of a poet, novelist, or dramatist. Sometimes the critic has an opportunity to gain insight into the genesis of poetic works when he finds, besides the finished version, earlier, unfinished or unmatured versions of a piece of literature. The comparative study of several versions of the same literary work reveals the poet's mind at work, so to speak; the creative process of literary endeavor appears in sharper relief.

While it is on the whole not a large part of published literature which can thus be studied with the help of other extant versions, it is indeed a rare occurrence when two authors have, successively, expended their efforts upon a single work. Such is the case with the drama **Herbert Engelmann.** Gerhart Hauptmann, the ranking dramatist of his generation, wrote it in 1924 and never published it. It was one of the many manuscripts found among his effects when he died. The executors of his literary will decided to submit the drama to Carl Zuckmayer, the outstanding dramatist of the next generation, with the suggestion that he give to it that form which in his estimation the subject matter and existing treatment merited.

The result is the unusual occurrence of the publication of one drama under the names of two dramatists. Our age has of course familiarized us with the practice of team-production, especially in the field of stage works. The literary critic would consider the usual results of such collaboration—film scripts, librettos for musical productions, or comedies of the more evanescent kind—rather beneath the dignity of his professional attention. But when the names are of the rank of Hauptmann and Zuckmayer, the matter deserves our attention.

The following observations summarize the results of a close scrutiny of the two versions, as published in one volume by C. H. Beck, Munich, 1952. In order to facilitate the understanding of these observations for those who may not be familiar with the play, a brief synopsis is given:

The locale of the first two acts is the pension run by Frau Kurnick in Berlin. The time is a few years after the first World War, that is, contemporaneous with the

writing of the play in its first version. The third and fourth acts play in a small dwelling in the outskirts of Berlin, about half a year later.

The characters assembled in the pension represent the heterogeneous and unstable composition of the German middle class of the time. They have all been physically and psychologically uprooted by the war and the subsequent social and economic changes. Frau Kurnick, a pastor's widow, has no liking for running the boarding house and harks back to better and calmer times in the parish. There are two former majors, who in the course of the play appear to have attached themselves to the police force, criminal division. They are representatives of the *old* Law and *old* Order. Adventurers and eccentrics, spiritists and stage flotsam constitute the background against which the main characters move. Herbert Engelmann, now returned from war and captivity in Siberia, had been a rather brilliant student at the beginning of the war; he enlisted and went through its hell, experiencing as complete an array of horrors as is possible to ascribe to one human's fate. He is a moral and physical wreck. Christa, daughter of the house, through her love (that is, pity) for him, tries to save him, finally marries him, and her endeavor for his salvation seems a success. Then (Act III) an event from Herbert's recent, post-war past catches up with him: he has committed murder and robbery, is tried, and freed for lack of evidence. The fourth act offers him an opportunity to start anew by going away to finish his interrupted studies. Christa cannot conceal any longer from him that she knew intuitively right along of the blot on his past. It is from the hell of his own conscience that she had wanted to save him, to offer him a new life, a future. Now that this future is in his grasp the realization of her sacrifice truly redeems him. He recognizes that the only future for him, "freed for lack of evidence," is in another world. He ends his life, at peace with himself, and Christa accepts this last sacrifice on her part: to be widowed in order to give him peace.

Zuckmayer himself gives us a number of do's and don'ts which he followed in his revision of Hauptmann's original. He attempted to preserve the general tone of language, which he calls that of an elevated matter-of-factness. That called for no more effort on his part than the kind of correction any manuscript receives upon second or third reading: an improving of grammar was necessary for instance. When Hauptmann says: "Das Zimmer ist schon . . . an einen Kriegsbeschädigten zugesagt," Zuckmayer has it: ". . . ei*nem* Kriegsbeschädigten zugesagt." [Gerhart Hauptmann and Carl Zuckmayer. **Herbert Engelmann.** München: C. H. Beck'sche Verlagsbuchhandlung. 1952.] Hauptmann's "Es geht mir besser wie andern Leuten" appears properly in Zuckmayer as ". . . besser als andern Leuten." Hauptmann's misuse of the conditional in expressions like: "Es würde mir lieber sein" is corrected into: "Es wäre mir lieber." The somewhat bookish simple past tense" . . . dem Fürsten gelang es nicht," becomes the more colloquial present perfect ". . . ist es nicht gelungen." Zuckmayer's penchant for grammatical niceties is evident when he changes "Sein Vater hatte einen Kramladen in dem Dorfe, wo dein Großvater Gutsbesitzer war" into: "Sein Vater hatte den Kramladen in dem Dorfe, in dem der meine Gutsbesitzer war."

Zuckmayer further changes Hauptmann's language and achieves what he calls *Verknappung* and *Verhärtung*. A stepping up of the tempo of expression is evident throughout the revision, either by omissions or by rearrangement to facilitate a more rapid flow of the words. Examples:

Hauptmann	*Zuckmayer*
Sie haben mir sogar eine kleine *Kühnheit* hie und da ungestraft hingehen lassen, so daß ich in meinem Glücksrausch vielleicht etwas zu übermütig geworden bin. Und so habe ich denn vielleicht einen *unerlaubten Schritt* getan, der aber schließlich als *eine Verfehlung aus Leidenschaft* zu betrachen ist.	. . . auch wenn ich eine unverzeihliche *Kühnheit* begangen, einen *unerlaubten Schritt* gewagt habe, so dürfte er doch, als eine *Verfehlung aus Leidenschaft,* Verzeihung finden.

Hauptmann	*Zuckmayer*
Christa, ich bin vollständig ohne Vorurteil. Und überdies eine Frau wie Sie, eine Erscheinung wie Sie darf sich überall sehen lassen. Ich wünsche mit Ihnen Furore zu machen, Sie sind nicht die erste und nicht die letzte Frau, die sich meine Kreise im Sturm erobert hat und erobern wird. Mit Bezug auf die Frauen ist man bei uns in gewissen Fällen weiterzig.	Ich bin, wie Sie wissen, ein Mann ohne jegliches Vorurteil. . . . Und eine Frau wie Sie, mit Ihrer Erscheinung, Ihrem Charme, Ihrem liebenswürdigen Geist, würde sich meine Kreise im Sturm erobern. Mit Ihnen könnte ich mich überall sehen lassen, ich würde mit Ihnen Furore machen. Gerade in dieser Beziehung ist man in meinen Kreisen recht weiterzig.

Space does not permit more examples. There is hardly a page where it could not be pointed out that Zuckmayer increased the tempo and heightened the accent of the verbal utterances.

To achieve this, he often inserts little new speeches, merely to interrupt the long flow of one person's talk. Thus the dialogue becomes alive and pulsating where it might have dragged. Such insertions also serve to tighten the logical sequence of utterances where gaps seemed to disturb the understanding.

Insertions are regular in Zuckmayer's stage directions. His sense of drama compels him to tie together the spoken word and the stage action, which he describes in considerable detail, often in so doing furnishing additional characterization. There is, for instance, in Hauptmann, a brief stage description of the doings leading to a "séance" or secret meeting of some of the fringe characters in the pension. Zuckmayer seizes upon this opportunity to deliver a perfectly hilarious sequence of stage business, which accentuates the eccentric character of the persons involved while furnishing some needed comic relief in the somber atmosphere.

This same zest for vivid, life-like representation on stage impels Zuckmayer to execute a scene which had been left in rudimentary form. Hauptmann has the guests of the pension arrive for dinner and then merely proceeds to enumerate in a long list of about two dozen items the topics of conversation. Zuckmayer follows this list, using approximately half of the items in the executed version of the dialogue. The crazy-quilt pattern of talk among these "off-center" characters is an ingenious characterization of these people, their time, and its thoroughly confused moral and intellectual climate. This scene serves to extend the uncertainty, lurking surprise, loss of clear delineation, and mixture of the good and the bad, the sound and the sick, which is the atmosphere in which the main character moves. Significantly, Zuckmayer lets Engelmann sit through this conversation hardly saying a word—increasing the mystery about him.

The most obvious addition in Zuckmayer's version is one new character: the widow of the murdered man. Zuckmayer felt that this addition was necessary to vivify the main theme of the play: the impact of murder upon the survivors, upon society. In a brief scene, this woman is introduced to the audience in conversation with Herbert's young wife, whose agony in talking to this poor victim of Herbert's act is all too apparent. Through this scene Zuckmayer increases in the spectator the impression that Herbert's wife knows and has known for some time the dark and evil something threatening from his past.

While the study of the details of Zuckmayer's changes in the textual form of the play could be carried into great detail with illuminating results, it must suffice here to summarize these aspects of his work. It may be said that the language was brought up to date by more modern or more appropriate idiom; it was cleaned up in its purely grammatical aspects. There is a great deal more accent upon the essential in the spoken word, an accent which at times seems to have shifted slightly to a new (Zuckmayer's) plane, and away from the existing (Hauptmann's) emphasis. There is much more precise indication of stage action, with considerable addition in this sphere. With sure touch the experienced dramatist of the contemporary stage improves the already dramatic version of his senior.

More important than these aspects of change are those alterations, additions, and shifts which reflect a change in attitude, interpretation, or philosophical approach.

In his own explanatory remarks concerning the revision, Zuckmayer states his belief that the work is essentially a historical play, but not a *Zeitstück*. Rather, he sees its action and theme laid "Between the times." Thus, his treatment reflects the idea that neither the time of the first writing of the play (1924) nor that of the second writing (1951) should be strictly determining. The human tragedy contained in the play should appear over and above the incidentals of the times.

This, if one pauses to reflect, is a difficult assignment. Hauptmann's version frankly places the action in the present, that is, the immediate post-war period. By references to events, names, and conditions, the reader or spectator is left little latitude in fixing this point in time. Zuckmayer altered enough of the references to the locale and the specific time to make the play live both in its original time and in ours. One significant change of this sort is the switch in Herbert's professional interests. Hauptmann's Herbert dabbles in medicine, has published a few short stories, and is at work on a novel which is laboriously being completed chapter by chapter. Zuckmayer's Herbert also works in his study, but his field is physics, modern atomic physics, perhaps not as advanced as the year 1952—or even the year 1945, which augured a new era—but certainly much more likely to make his absorption and fascination understandable to a contemporary audience than the writing of a novel would.

References to Freudian psychology are more matter-of-fact, more direct, and more informed. One of the characters in Hauptmann's play suggests to Herbert's future mother-in-law: "Weshalb also weiter darum herumreden? Wenn Sie wollen, stelle ich gern mal eine Generaluntersuchung mit ihm an. Wenn er selbst will, notabene. Denn bisher hat er jede Anregung dieser Art geflissentlich überhört." In Zuckmayer we find: "Warum also weiter drum herumreden? Ich halte es für einen Fall von manischer Depression mit schizophrenem Einschlag." This is the tone of present day drawing room conversation on the popular level.

A striking example of both accentuation and shift in attitude owing to the changed times appears in Act III when Herbert's friends, cabaret artists, come to congratulate him upon the success of one of his criminalistic sketches, the writing of which is a somewhat sinister and ominous hobby of his. But Herbert is irretrievably moody and has just expressed an extremely pessimistic, even nihilistic outlook. Whereupon Goldstein, his friend, launches upon the following attempt at rescue: "Mensch, hör endlich mit deinem verwünschten Schopenhauerschen Pessimismus auf. Es geht dir doch gut, was kohlst du denn! Der Krieg ist vorüber, allenthalben atmet man langsam auf." Zuckmayer adds zest, incidental characterization of Goldstein, and the much more cynical wisdom of a later time: 'Mensch, Meier, hör endlich auf zu klönen. Es geht dir doch prima. Du lebst hier wie Bolle auf'm Milchwagen. Was kohlst du denn? Der Krieg ist vorüber, in Locarno liegense sich in den Armen, die Sowjets mit den Lords von England Wang an Wang, da fließen die Tränen zusammen, der gerechte Briand und unser Stehauf-Stresemännchen schmatzen einander schon beim Frühstück ab, die Mark ist stabilisiert, es gibt wieder Schlagsahne, die Theater gehen, die Revolution ist wegen Mangels an Beteiligung abgesagt, der rote Hölz sitzt in Moabit, der braune Adolf in Landsberg, die Welt atmet auf. Was willst du mehr?"

The exploitation of the obvious and deplorable parallels of the time after World War I and World War II is carried to the limit of the historically supportable!

The central problem of the play could be stated thus: war as mass murder is approved by society; but murder as an individual crime is condemned by all standards of ethics. The attitude toward this problem in the two versions of the play gives not only a clue to the basic philosophies of the two writers; it reflects fundamental and subtle changes of interpretation and characterization. We find it both in omissions and additions. Zuckmayer, in his own explanation, suspects that Hauptmann himself, had he finished the play, would have made Herbert Engelmann a more struggling, searching character than he appears in the original version, where his troubles are fairly completely explained on the basis of his war experience, the demoralizing effect of killing the enemy "eye to eye" plus the disillusioning reception which the homecoming soldier receives. Many of the utterances in Hauptmann's version seem familiar indeed when compared with some of Hauptmann's earlier writings. Environment and heredity play a dominant role in shaping human fate. The individual is buffeted about by life's cruelty until he acts cruelly out of mere instinct for survival. Thus Hauptmann has Herbert indulge in endless recollections of his horrible war experiences, and the supporting characters likewise refer to those experiences as the real explanation for Herbert's strange behavior, his sudden fits of fear, his persecution complexes, and so on. We can almost see the traditional naturalistic writer saying: take a sensitive and brilliant child, rear him in the sheltered atmosphere of an upper bourgeois, intellectual home; have him study and excel in his work. Then thrust him into this cauldron called war while he is still pliable, young, impressionable, and unstable. The result will *inevitably* be that his mind will crack, his moral fiber be destroyed; his actions will respond to basic, animal instincts of survival and self-assertion. So runs the argument in Hauptmann's play. This *inevitability* of the course of action is the crucial point to watch, because with it left intact, no amount of changing can create a human tragedy out of a merely unfortunate occurrence.

Zuckmayer shapes this tragedy by toning down and partly omitting the frequent references to the formative influences in Herbert's life. First, however, he accentuates this immediate past by creating a tense dramatic incident which shows Herbert losing control of himself to the point of seizing a knife and wielding it while expounding his wild hatred for those who did not fight, those who merely sat in the rear, those who profited from war. Such a tendency to violence fits in with the accumulating references to the murder in his past.

Another significant and typical addition occurs in an utterance of Christa, shortly after this violent scene. A friend of the family inquires about Christa's and Herbert's marriage plans. Christa indicates certain hindrances, which the inquirer interprets as financial worries. Hauptmann has her then answer: "Des Verdienens wegen zögern wir schließlich auch nicht. Er steht nur immer noch auf dem Standpunkt, er könne als kranker Mensch nicht heiraten. Die Kriegsfolgen müßten erst überwunden sein." Zuckmayer adds, after using these words more or less unchanged, the following significant comments: "Es müßte erst alles—überwunden sein. Dabei gibt es doch Tausende, die auch an den Kriegsfolgen leiden, und sich allmählich wieder erholen, vielleicht gerade durch eine Ehe . . . durch ein richtiges Leben. . . . Manchmal—kann ich ihn gar nicht ganz verstehen." What has Zuckmayer done here to adapt the play's argument to his own conception? Instead of *Kriegsfolgen,* he merely says *alles,* leaving the argument open as to where the cause for Herbert's troubles lies. Then he singles Herbert out of the mass of others who also suffered from the war. He is different! Others get over it, normally, in the course of time. There is something personally, individually different about him—he is an individual, not a product of events like thousands of others. And Christa foreshadows for us the play's idea by her reference to the healing influence of marriage, that is, the germinal idea of her sacrifice is here indicated. And her admission that she does not really understand him brings out the uncertainty, the struggling state of his soul.

Three additional examples of shift in interpretation must suffice for a recognition of Zuckmayer's superior treatment.

First, at Herbert's arrest Hauptmann has him leave the stage with the words: "Also kommen Sie jetzt," and the stage direction says: "Im Abgehen beginnt bei ihm wieder das Schütteln." That is Hauptmann's reference to Herbert's "illness," nervous disorder, involuntary, inevitable reaction to excitement. Zuckmayer omits this stage direction, with the result that Herbert leaves not

as a man who is still, or again, merely the victim of circumstances, but a man fully awake to his situation, consciously acting in consistency with his earlier "battle" mood. Responsibility lies with him!

Secondly, in the final discussion between Herbert and Christa, Zuckmayer makes a pointed addition, which crystallizes his position. In Hauptmann's version, Herbert explains his deed: "Ich bin nicht allein gewesen, ich weiß es nicht. Sobald man begonnen hat, ist man wahnsinnig." Whereupon Christa exonerates him with the words, ". . . du hast vorher und nachher furchtbar gelitten und alles vor Gott und den Menschen abgebüßt." Zuckmayer however elaborates both positions as follows: ". . . sobald man begonnen hat, ist man im Wahn. Jetzt, erst in dieser Stunde ist der Wahn vergangen." And Christa: "Du warst allein. Du fühltest dich . . . verlassen. Du standest vor dem Abgrund, du wolltest dich wehren, dich retten . . . war es nicht so, Herbert?" Actually, she suggests, without believing, absolution in true Hauptmann fashion. Herbert's answer: ". . . Ich hatte das Leben, den Tod verachten gelernt. Was war mir ein Mensch—einer unter Millionen? Ja, ich dachte, was ich vernichte, was ich mir nehme, könne ich tausendfach zurückerstatten. Das war mein Wahn. Jetzt aber weiß ich: jedesmal, wenn ein Mensch stirbt, stirbt Gott. Denn das Leben ist heilig, Christa. Nur das Leben ist heilig. Jedes einzelne Leben auf der Welt. Wer das verletzt, ist gerichtet." There can be no doubt here that Zuckmayer intends to focus the argument upon absolutes, upon permanent values, away from the relativistic *tout comprendre—tout pardonner.*

Thus we have to understand the closing words of the drama in their respective forms. Christa, after Herbert's death: "Mutter, du meinst doch nicht, er ist tot?" Which brings her mother's, and thus Hauptmann's answer: "Ja! Und wo je einem Menschen, wird Gott ihm verzeihen, wenn er freiwillig aus dem Leben gegangen ist." Zuckmayer has the mother merely answer: "Er ist im Frieden." Thus he eliminates any "official" pronouncement of absolution wherein, so to speak, God's proxy officiates. Instead, he removes the judgment from the human sphere and suggests the certainty of forgiveness in the overtones of the two words "in peace": peace of mind, peace of soul, peace from men, peace from conscience.

Zuckmayer, the contemporary dramatist, who has given us in one of his latest dramas (**Der Gesang im Feuerofen**) his credo of Christian love, here revises a drama by Hauptmann in such a way, that it can have meaning in our time and stand under his, Zuckmayer's, name. The younger dramatist has brought to life the timebound, temporal drama of his senior.

Murray B. Peppard (essay date January 1952)

SOURCE: Peppard, Murray B. "Moment of Moral Decision: Carl Zuckmayer's Latest Plays." *Monatshefte* 44, no. 1 (January 1952): 349-56.

[*In the following essay, Peppard asserts that the theme of moral evasion is central to Zuckmayer's plays* The Devil's General *and* Der Gesang im Feuerofen.]

Since the war three new plays by Carl Zuckmayer have appeared on the German stage and enjoyed considerable success. The first and probably best-known, *Des Teufels General,* [*Des Teufels General.* Berlin; Suhrkamp Verlag Vorm S. Fischer, 1947], was begun in 1942 and completed in 1945. *Der Gesang im Feuerofen* [*Der Gesang im Feuerofen.* Frankfurt am Main: S. Fischer Verlag, 1950.] was inspired by a notice in a newspaper in 1948, although the play did not appear until 1950. Both of these dramas deal with the second World War, the first concerning itself with an internal German problem, the second with the problematical issue of the German occupation of France. *Barbara Blomberg,* [*Barbara Blomberg.* Frankfurt a. M., 1949.] which appeared in 1949, is both less serious than the previously mentioned plays and more remote from contemporary problems. All three plays represent a new development in Zuckmayer's technique and have in common an even greater emphasis on humanity than that which distinguishes his earlier works. What is new and common to all three plays, but especially the first two mentioned, is the focus upon moral problems. This concentration upon moral considerations has, especially in *Des Teufels General* and *Der Gesang im Feuerofen,* influenced the structure and dramatic technique to a striking degree. This is not to say that the plays are but moralizing sermons, nor should it be inferred that they are *Tendenzdramen* in the service of a particular creed or doctrine. There is in them, however, a new tone that distinguishes them from Zuckmayer's earlier works. Before his exile most of Zuckmayer's works are exuberant and full of the joy of life. The affirmation of life with all its attendant joys and sorrows is still the theme of the novel *Salwàre* (written 1936), in spite of its tragic conclusion. The characters in his post-war plays also have a zest for living, but this is now tempered by the critically evaluating moral basis of his writing. From *Pro Domo* (1938) through the brochures on Mierendorff (1944) and the Grimm brothers (1948) one can observe the emphasis on ethical and humane considerations becoming central in his writings.

This shift of emphasis in Zuckmayer can be demonstrated by an analysis of *Des Teufels General* and *Der Gesang im Feuerofen.* What is striking about both plays is the long exposition. The first act of *Des Teufels General* falls but little short of being half the play. In *Der Gesang im Feuerofen* the expository element is also large. In both plays the attention devoted to detailed and evocative description of the setting is significant. How much Zuckmayer was concerned with evoking a well-rounded picture of Nazi Germany can be observed in the care and detail with which the scenes of the first act of *Des Teufels General* are drawn. The conflicts that make up the plot are developed slowly and gradually at first, but as the plays progress the tempo increases and the tension mounts until the climax. Both are synthetic plays, but the classical pyramidal scheme set up by Gustav Freytag does not apply to either, since the action ascends in a straight line to a high point at the end. This is true even in *Der Gesang im Feuerofen,* for the scenes after the fire belong as a kind of epilogue to the framework of the play. Both plays culminate in a moment of moral decision, in *Des Teufels General* in Harras' decision to sign the inspection report and shield Oderbruch by his own death, in *Der Gesang im Feuerofen* in the decision of the Maquis to forgive their enemies. Even *Barbara Blomberg* depends on the decision of the heroine to be herself and to conquer or succumb as what she is without pretense or sham. Barbara Blomberg steers her way through a maze of intrigue, plot, and counterplot, and a complex political situation simply by following the dictates of her heart and her feminine intuition. The plot is a little improbable unless one accepts Zuckmayer's thesis that genuine humanity can triumph over intrigue.

This gradual development of the plot and the long and detailed expositions are dictated by the nature of the inner conflicts of the plays. The wealth of piquant scenes in *Des Teufels General,* for example, and the nature of the plots with their obvious political implications and complications should not blind one to the fact that both plays are essentially dramas of inner human conflict which are portraying eternal human conflicts of a significance which transcends their specific German or European setting. Fundamental to both plays is the conflict between loyalty to one's government and the demands of conscience and humane tolerance. The length of the exposition is determined by another factor. As we have mentioned, the plays culminate in a moral decision and are thus constructed with this end in view. But in addition, the action preliminary to the final resolution must be of sufficient length to permit the author to demonstrate both the failure to come to the right decision, that is, to do the humane and moral thing when it is required, and the attempts to evade the decision. Once the issue is joined one must take sides. Harras' failure to come to grips with the problem and to face the necessity of making a decision makes up a large part of the essential or inner action of *Des Teufels General.* In *Der Gesang im Feuerofen* the lines are drawn clearly at an earlier stage, but like *Des Teufels General* the play culminates in a carefully motivated sacrificial death which gives the ultimate meaning to the play. Since it starts with the results of the moral collapse of Louis Creveaux, the question of guilt and retribution is presented at the outset and the necessity of taking sides and making decisions is more insistent from the beginning.

General Harras, the devil's general, is presented at first as a man of robust good conscience, able to make fun of the Nazis, and feeling himself quite above politics. He has great contempt for the Party and claims to have seen through the Nazis from the first. While reproaching the industrialists for their support of Hitler, he is able to excuse himself by saying that he likes to fly and that flying is the whole content of his life. That this attitude amounts to a fatal inconsistency does not occur to him at first. Yet he is gaining privately and personally from something which his better judgment condemns. He blames his indolence for his continuing to drift along while avoiding facing the real issues. Until late in the play he continues to voice his faith in the basic goodness of life with an optimism little warranted by the circumstances. As his life and career become more and more endangered by the Gestapo—the main part of the outer action—we see him at his bravest and most gallant. The inner action of the play, however, consists in his gradual awakening to the seriousness of his moral position. This awakening takes place in four stages: after learning that Bergmann, a Jew whom he had tried to save, has committed suicide, he gives up his self-deception: "Jeder hat seinen Gewissensjuden, oder mehrere, damit er nachts schlafen kann. Aber damit kauft man sich nicht frei. Das ist Selbstbetrug. An dem, was den tausend anderen geschieht, die wir nicht kennen und denen wir nicht helfen, sind wir deshalb doch schuldig. Schuldig und verdammt, in alle Ewigkeit. Das Gemeine zulassen ist schlimmer, als es tun" (88 [*Des Teufels General*]). With these words the play has reached a turning point. But Harras has not yet come to a course of action, nor is he clear in his own mind that a course of action and not mere insight into the mess around him is necessary. The second stage in his awakening is his interview with Hartmann. In the face of the young man's sincerity and need for guidance Harras finds it difficult to comfort him with phrases and has to satisfy himself and Hartmann with the assurance that there is justice in the world: "Aber glauben Sie mir—es gibt ein Recht. Es gibt einen Ausgleich. Vielleicht nicht für den einzelnen. Vielleicht nicht an der Oberfläche des Lebens—jedoch im Kern. Die Welt nimmt ihren Lauf, das Bestimmte erfüllt sich. Es wird keine Schuld erlassen" (125). A minute before, Harras has paved the way for his own final dramatic act by assuring Hartmann: "Wo aber ein Mensch sich erneuert—da wird die Welt neu geschaffen." At the moment this is said largely just to reassure Hartmann, but the statement is also an assertion of Zuckmayer's own faith. This optimistic faith in the moral course of the world and the comfort that Harras derives from the thought are rudely shaken by the scene that follows immediately afterward.

This scene is the interview with Eilers' widow. Not until now does Harras come to realize his full responsibility. Her accusations he cannot answer, for she has put his guilt in its proper light: "Nichts haben Sie getan. Man tut nichts ohne Glauben. Sie haben nicht geglaubt, woran Eilers glaubte. Und dennoch haben Sie ihn dafür sterben lassen. Sinnlos sterben. Sie haben zugeschaut, und ihn nicht gerettet. Das ist die Schuld, für die es kein Verzeihen gibt" (127). Lashed by her probing he asks in his despair and in a last evasive attempt to exonerate himself: "Was weiß ein Mensch? Was kann ein Mensch denn wissen?" And: "Wer bin ich denn—daß ich es ändern sollte?" The final breakthrough comes in his conversation with Oderbruch, his closest and most trusted friend, who, he now finds out, is a leader of the resistance to Hitler and willing to sacrifice him in order to continue sabotaging the planes. In his revelation the highpoints of the inner and outer action coincide. For a moment, but a moment only, he is almost ready to betray Oderbruch in order to save himself from the Gestapo. But after Oderbruch has simply and forcefully stated his case Harras makes his decision to shield Oderbruch. At the moment when he asks Oderbruch to help him he has sealed his own doom, but his soul is saved. His life is all that he has left with which to pay his debt: "Wer auf Erden des Teufels General wurde und ihm die Bahn gebombt hat—der muß ihm auch Quartier in der Hölle machen" (136).

Hartmann, an idealistic young flier whose whole education has been shaped by the Nazis, has come through his experience at the front to see into the rottenness of the Nazi regime. One of Harras' last acts is to commend him to Oderbruch. Thus there is in addition to Harras a second character who finds the way to the right. But there remains the problem of Oderbruch, who has never doubted or wavered or gone through any development within the course of the play. From the first he has been sure of his path and secure in the faith that he is right. His certainty and the depth of his conviction guide Harras to his final decision. From what source does Oderbruch draw his certainty? When pressed by Harras to tell what it is that gives him the strength to struggle and suffer almost without hope, he answers: "Es ist das Ewige Recht. . . . Recht ist das unerbittlich waltende Gesetz—dem Geist, Natur und Leben unterworfen sind. Wenn es erfüllt wird—heißt es Freiheit" (135). This is on the surface a secular reply, but it implies a faith in a divine order of the world so constituted that the possibility of justice exists, and so it is understood by Harras, who had confessed his faith in God to Hartmann. Thus, while there is presented no evidence of any particular creed or religion, the atmosphere of the play in its final resolution is religious, and the stern idealism of Oderbruch, although stated in secular terms, is ultimately of a religious nature.

The development of Harras and Hartmann to the point where they can act is accompanied by the presentation of several moral failures. The first act ends with Detlev's excusing himself for his cooperation in spying on Harras. He has no pretty words to justify himself for doing that of which he feels deeply ashamed, but merely succumbs to the pressures brought to bear on him. "Glaubst du, ich mache das gern? Zum Kotzen is mir das. Aber—wat heißt hier Schweinehund. Hierzuland is jeder sich selbst der Nächste. Ich hab schon 1916 die Neese voll gehabt. Was willste machen, wenn einer daherkommt und hält dir 'ne Ansprache: 'Nun, hören Sie mal zu, Mann. Sie als Kellner haben eine besondere Gelegenheit, dem Staate zu dienen.'—Und schaut dir so eiskalt ins Ooge. Da kannste nicht nein sagen, Mensch. Außerdem hab ich Familie" (65). In a higher social class the manufacturer Mohrungen suffers more articulately and feels acutely the loss of his honor. But he is able to excuse himself in finer language, speaks of his duty, and claims that no one has free will any more but must do what he is forced to do. In both plays Zuckmayer presents all the lazy excuses and all the rationalizations that people are capable of imagining in order to avoid personal responsibility and the necessity of committing themselves.

In **Barbara Blomberg** also the theme of moral evasion is treated. Typical is Ferdinand, who retreats behind the excuse that he is acting under orders (161-2). Barbara Blomberg herself asks her daughter: "Glaubst du, es würde anders in diesem Land, wenn ich anders lebte? Glaubst du, es würde anders—auf der Welt? . . . Glaubst du denn, daß das Elend der Andren geringer wird, wenn du dich selber elend machst?" (143). This, of course, concerns just the message that Zuckmayer wishes to give in his plays, namely that it does matter what the individual does, that it is important for every individual to solve his problems and not shirk his moral duty. For one's life, and if need be one's death, will count and will be remembered. At the climax of **Der Gesang im Feuerofen** Francine asks: "Und was wird bleiben, von unsrer Liebe und unserm Tod? Wer wird Kunde geben, wer trägt unser Vermächtnis? Wer wird wissen, wie wir gestorben sind?" From Francis she receives the reply: "Die Steine werden es wissen, die nicht verbrennen können. Die Erde wird Kunde bewahren, die uns überlebt. Die Lüfte werden das Wort von unsren Lippen tragen" (143). "Groß ist die Macht der Toten" is the refrain of the personified elements of Nature in the scene following the burning of the castle.

The inner structure of **Der Gesang im Feuerofen** is similar to that outlined in the discussion above. Again it is a question of steadily rising tension and of an ascending line of action to a climax at the end. As in **Des Teufels General,** Zuckmayer explores the various possibilities of avoiding decision, of blinding oneself to the facts, and of yielding to external forces in spite of one's better judgment. The French gendarme Albert has a classic rationalization of the position of one who is just going along with the prevailing system. "Ich gebe es zu, es ist nicht ganz angenehm, für die Deutschen zu arbeiten. Aber man tut's ja auch für unser Land, das keine Wahl hat. Der Befehl kommt von unsrer Regierung, und wir haben ihn auszuführen, sonst nichts" (35). And again: "Das sind Gerüchte, man weiß nicht, was stimmt. Wir sind jedenfalls durch die Befehle unserer Regierung gedeckt." He sums up aptly the attitude of those who have morally resigned in the words: "Ich sage, der Zufall regiert die Welt, und einen Gott gibt es keinen. Jeder muß schaun, wie er durchkommt" (85). Earlier we have seen the German Peter agree to spy on Major Mühlstein in a scene reminiscent of the first act of **Des Teufels General.** In the end he deserts and is killed by the Maquis, but such a death, motivated only by the desire to save his own skin, is futile and meaningless. Even Major Mühlstein, in some of his traits reminiscent of General Harras, is an ineffective person in spite of his sympathetic qualities. He too is caught in the system and does not have the courage to break out. He prides himself on being an officer of the old school and a Christian, but although he disapproves of what is going on he does nothing effective to stop it. "Ja, was tun wir dagegen? Wir sind Befehlsempfänger, mein Herr. Allesamt. Eine Welt von Befehlsempfängern" (93). The pathetic figure of Neyroud is typical of the moral confusion that may result from a conflict of loyalties. His son is a leader of the Maquis, yet Neyroud feels that he cannot revolt against the government from which he receives his orders. Thus he acts against the dictates of his conscience until at last he has to face the fact that he has been instrumental in bringing about his son's death. In the midst of this confusion people react either nobly or ignobly, there is no middle ground. Even a mother's sacrifice for her son may not be a noble thing. Just how clearly Zuckmayer is emphasizing the need for the larger humanitarian values to precede even some of the basic ties and loyalties of family is illustrated in the capture of the fugitives attempting to escape over the border. The mother still has brandy and money, although she had sworn she had not when the uncle was in need of them. Her reward for this is that her son turns away from her with revulsion even though she had lied just to save him.

As in **Des Teufels General** there are, however, also positive reactions to the moral dilemmas in which the characters are enmeshed. Sylvester's decision to warn the Maquis is treachery to his own nation, but this underlines again the fact that the interests of humanity take precedence over national loyalty. Like Hartmann of **Des Teufels General,** his experiences at the front have provided him with an understanding of the evils of the Nazi regime. Early in the play he answers the statements of Albert quoted above by saying there is no chance in what happens and that the Germans know what they are doing. Martin too chooses death as the only way out for a German in his position. Yet his death is meaningful, for it is a sacrificial death. Marcel, whose position in the play's inner action corresponds most nearly to the development of General Harras, must also struggle through to the necessary clarity in moral judgments. A fervent patriot, he is on what he considers to be the right side from the beginning. A man of action, his motives are clear and his goals understood and approved by all from the outset. But in the conversations with Francis it becomes evident that the wish to rid France of the Germans does not justify acts which conflict with the demands of humanity. Marcel is outspokenly irreligious. "Himmel und Hölle sind mir unbekannt. Für mich sind die guten und die bösen Mächte durchaus von dieser Welt, und wenn wir die bösen bekämpfen wollen, brauchen wir klare, direkte Ziele, wie auf dem Schießplatz" (112). Marcel goes on to justify his struggle and his attitude in terms of life on this earth and of tangible goals to be reached this side of heaven. His certainty and conviction and the single-mindedness with which he pursues his aims remind one of Oderbruch. He has not yet learned that love is stronger than hate and that the salvation of the soul is at least as important as the attainment of any worldly ends. Much of his failure to see this stems from the fact that he views the struggle purely as a national one and thinks in terms of French and German rather than in terms of humanity. Francis, in answer to the above quotation, says in part:

> Es geht um eine Entscheidung, die schneidet mitten durch alle Völker und alle Menschen hindurch. . . . Wir haben die Wahl zu treffen, hier und heute, ob wir das Leben erniedrigen wollen zu einer blinden Funktion—oder ob wir es lieben können, als Gottes Geschenk, in jedem seiner Geschöpfe, noch im Feind, noch in Tod und Vernichtung. Es muß eine Liebe sein, die stärker brennt als der Haß. . . . Wir haften für dieses Leben mit unsrer Seele, die ein Teil ist vom Wunderbaren, von der geheimen Schönheit und Ordnung, der sie entstammt. Wir sind noch für den Zufall verantwortlich, wenn er mit Steinen wirft—denn es kommt nicht darauf an, was uns trifft,—nur wie wir es bestehn, und was wir uns daraus machen. Das ist die Freiheit, Marcel—die einzige, die allen gemeinsam ist.

Not until later, in face of a death that seems about to render futile all his striving, does Marcel come to an understanding of Francis' point of view and achieve insight into the higher perspective of Francis. Then comes his moment of moral decision as he embraces Sylvester and with this gesture forgives his enemies in the spirit that Francis has desired.

The above analysis overemphasizes the moralizing tendency of the plays in order to illustrate their structure and the course of the inner action. It would not be fair to Zuckmayer's dramatic talent to overlook the fact that both plays abound in exciting, stageworthy action. Good

entertainment has been skillfully combined with a serious message. Real, whole people are presented in his plays, not just ideological phantoms. Neither of the plays discussed consists of a conflict of angels with devils, but of men with men, for Zuckmayer's sense of humor and his love of mankind have prevented him from painting in black and white. Although Sprenger in *Der Gesang im Feuerofen* works for the forces of evil, he is not portrayed as a villain but as a man of great personal courage endowed with some admirable traits. There are no villains in these plays, but only people who are weak or who have chosen the wrong side. It is not party, nor nation, nor religion, nor the cause that makes the ends or means right, but only doing the human, the humane thing that is always right. What Zuckmayer is showing are the fates of men caught up in a system that is so powerful and compelling that one must look deep within one's own conscience to find again the source of humanity and humaneness which can help one to find one's way. Man is not the victim of fate nor of the power of circumstance, but has free will and is responsible for his actions. Under the pressure of a ruthless totalitarian regime some men make the wrong choice, some fail to see that a choice must be made to preserve their integrity and human decency, and some see the evil but are too weak to stand up for the right. Zuckmayer refuses to sit in judgment on these people, for, as he wrote in the pamphlet on Mierendorff: "Deutschland ist schuldig geworden vor der Welt. Wir aber, die wir es nicht verhindern konnten, gehören in diesem großen Weltprozeß nicht unter seine Richter" (39). The same refusal to pass judgment is an essential element of *Der Gesang im Feuerofen.*

The question of right and wrong is not a simple one. But one does have certain criteria. In *Pro Domo* Zuckmayer expresses the belief that one may find the right way by discovering within oneself certain basic and eternal values (86-90, et passim). In *Der Gesang im Feuerofen,* a religiously oriented play, the need for God and His help is more explicit. God's will with men may at times be inscrutable. But some things are known, namely what God does not want. When asked who knows God's will, Barbara Blomberg answers: "Man kennt seinen Willen nicht. Aber es kommt in jedem Leben der Augenblick, in dem man ahnt, was er nicht von uns will" (181). There is no morally justifiable excuse for not knowing at least what is not right. The issues may seem obscure, but it is still possible to find clarity and certainty. Zuckmayer's recent plays are intended as a contribution to this clarity. This is the purpose of drama in our day, for, as he wrote in *Pro Domo*:

> Es handelt sich hier um die tiefste Notwendigkeit des dramatischen Schaffens überhaupt: um die nachformende Bannung des Lebens, der Schöpfung, ihrer Zwiespälte und ihrer heimlich bindenden und lösenden Gewalt, um die Darstellung unserer metaphysischen Bestimmtheit, ihres Grauens und ihrer Gnade—um die

produktive Überwindung des Chaos, der Zerspaltenheit, der Moira, der Ananke, der dunklen Sphynx-Sprüche unseres Schicksals.

(76)

Murray B. Peppard (essay date December 1957)

SOURCE: Peppard, Murray B. "Carl Zuckmayer: Cold Light in a Divided World." *Monatshefte* 49, no. 7 (December 1957): 121-29.

[*In the following essay, Peppard discerns patterns and similarities between Zuckmayer's play* Das kalte Licht *and his other major post-war dramas, including* The Devil's General, Der Gesang im Feuerofen, *and* Herbert Engelmann.]

After the lyric intermezzo *Ulla Winblad* Zuckmayer has turned again to a topical and political play with *Das Kalte Licht.* The premiere in Hamburg, September 3, 1955, under the direction of Gustaf Gründgens, was greeted with great enthusiasm. During the winter season of 1955-56 the play appeared on the program of more than thirty West German theaters. The stage version involved several cuts of the original text in order to make it more stage-worthy. Nevertheless the Gründgens stage version quite correctly made the ideational content of the play the focus of the action. In this first version the emphasis was all on stark realism and contemporary stage settings with a minimum of illusion. The topical nature of the play is evident from its historical basis, which is the case of the atomic physicist and spy Klaus Fuchs and his famous trial in England. Although Zuckmayer in his afterword makes clear that the Klaus Fuchs case serves only as the starting point and general framework for the play, the parallels are too close and the memory of Fuchs' betrayal too alive to prevent the public from being reminded of recent history.

With this drama Zuckmayer resumes the succession of his serious plays from *Des Teufels General* through *Herbert Engelmann.* Since the war there seems to be in Zuckmayer's production a fairly regular alternation between plays dealing with serious subject matter and those lighter plays which are drawn from history or legend. Just as in earlier years *Der Schelm von Bergen* followed *Der Hauptmann von Köpenick,* so after the war *Barbara Blomberg* followed *Des Teufels General* and *Herbert Engelmann* preceded the operatic *Ulla Winblad.* The more serious plays, the only ones with which we shall be concerned, tend to be based on a factual framework and to deal with the problematics of our times. None of them is called a tragedy; they are entitled simply "Drama." The latest of these serious plays has much in common with its predecessors. The central theme is again that of an essentially good man going

astray, awakening to his error, and making atonement. In accepting the basic plot of *Herbert Engelmann* as given by Hauptmann, Zuckmayer treats the criminal after his crime. In the remaining plays under consideration the protagonist is shown in the process of going astray. All the plays end on a conciliatory note, whether it be the sacrificial death of General Harras, the release by suicide of Herbert Engelmann, or the voluntary surrender of Kristof Wolters. Even the satirical comedy *Der Hauptmann von Köpenick* ends in a burst of releasing and redeeming laughter—the satire and the course of the action culminating at the moment when the cobbler sees himself in the mirror and is able to join in the laughter.

In the two plays most closely related, *Des Teufels General* and *Das Kalte Licht,* Zuckmayer is dealing with one of the most important problems of man today, namely the maintenance of individual freedom and conscience in a confused and divided world. In both plays the central character loses his way in life, becomes burdened with guilt in his normal confusion, which he tries to cover up by boisterous cynicism (the devil's general), or by appeals to an impersonal science (Wolters), and finally achieves or regains his moral stability in an attempt to atone for what he has done. Both protagonists sell their souls to the devil: Harras serves Hitler through his devotion to flying, Wolters betrays atomic secrets to Russia through his dedication to an ideal of science. Both stumble more or less blindly into their errors, and both come to the full realization of the situation only late in the play. In both plays a long exposition and a slowly rising dramatic action explore the possibilities for error and for evasion of the decisions that must be made, while the situation of the central character in the world of his time is being sharply delineated. The plays culminate in the correction of the inner confusion of the protagonists, in a moment "in which everything is transformed" (*Das Kalte Licht,* [Frankfurt am Main, 1955] 150). It is this moment of inner transformation, of suddenly awakened inner clarity, toward which Zuckmayer's serious plays all move.

In *Des Teufels General* and in *Der Gesang im Feuerofen* Zuckmayer had dramatized the conflicts arising from the clash between the demands of national loyalty and those of conscience. In both plays he found a solution by emphasizing the priority of humanity over national or military loyalty. Common to both plays also is the fact that the central character awakes from his moral slumber through the confrontation with a person who has remained "intact": Harras and Oderbruch, Sylvester and Sylvaine in *Der Gesang im Feuerofen.* Like this latter play *Das Kalte Licht* has an international cast of characters with the possibilities of conflict and tension that might naturally arise. But the conflict is not determined by national ties, and nationalism is not an issue except in the person of the English scientist Ketterick, who represents an old-fashioned type of nationalism and blind service to one's country. Part of the appeal of communism for Wolters is its alleged international nature. It is possible for him to believe that in giving secrets to Russia he is in an indirect way giving them to all mankind. Early in the play he asserts that the benefits of science belong to the whole world ([*Das Kalte Licht*] p. 60). Buschmann, the Russian contact agent, appeals to this flocculent feeling of cosmopolitanism in Wolters when he describes the war (before the entry of Russia) as an outmoded imperialistic war. The remoteness of the powers to whom Wolters sells himself, the missionary nature of the Russian propaganda, the incalculability of the consequences of his acts, the imponderability of the nature of his disclosures, the aura of awe and mystery surrounding the discoveries achieved by an abstract and coldly calculating rationalism, the concept of knowledge as international property—all this combines to obscure the real nature of what he does and to prevent him from seeing his acts in their true light. Buschmann quite properly accuses Wolters of a "Flucht in die Abstraktion" (p. 13). The choices that the hero must make in this play are more subtle than in the previous plays, in fact, there seems at first to be no choice, no problem of conscience nor any decision of an ethical nature. The progress of the play consists in Wolter's awakening to the fact that there is a problem.

This process of gradual awakening constitutes what may be called the inner action of the play, which takes place in the soul of Wolters. The structure of the play is that which we have come to expect from Zuckmayer: colorful scenes that contribute indirectly to the advancement of the plot, episodic by-play with robust humor, and lyric interludes. The sense of time in a Zuckmayer play of this type is always important, for the elapsed time by the calendar and the felt time of an audience are usually different—yet somehow also coincident. There is an epic element in the plays of Zuckmayer which does not result from narrative or from a recounting of the past, but from the time indicated in the stage directions. This time lapse is necessary for the growth and change of the central character. Perhaps the most striking example is the lapse of ten years in *Der Hauptmann von Köpenick.* Again in *Das Kalte Licht* an eleven-year time span is indicated. As seen in the struggles and conflicts within Wolters the time element is compressed and unified and divorced from the calendar in so far as it is psychological development in a single person. The swift march of events in a world at war are mirrored both in the responses of the individuals in the dramatic scenes which unroll before us and in the topical allusions. Ketterick is a constant and reminds us by his unchanging attitudes that intellectual positions may be more permanent than changing world conditions. The frequent changes of scene, from England to America and back, also contribute to the sense that the audience has of a pattern or mosaic of episodes which only in their sum give an impression of a total dramatic structure. Zuckmayer has never really given up his Expressionistic beginnings, as one can see from the fact that his plays can be viewed as giving successive "stations" in the life of the central figure quite in the Expressionistic manner. The episodic by-play contains some of the best and most convincing scenes, as for example the shipboard scene with Friedländer, who reminds one of Werfel's Jakobowsky.

The time span of the play as representing historical events is from 1939 to 1950. But time in our present world has a way of out-speeding what seem to be constants. The betrayal of atomic secrets to Russia is estimated to have speeded up their program by eighteen months. At the time of composition of the drama, the gain of eighteen months had long since ceased to be a factor in world politics. The rapid march of modern events has made the exciting happening of six years ago a thing of the relatively remote past. What the play is conjuring up in its dialogue and action is then not the historical past, nor a series of moments that changed the course of world events, but on the contrary it is bringing alive to the audience the motives for Wolters' betrayal. What is being reconstructed in dramatic form is not a turning-point in world history, but the dilemma of conscience of modern man. In *Des Teufels General* and in *Der Gesang im Feuerofen* the dramatic action showed the central characters groping their way through various possibilities of avoiding decision or of making the wrong one; in *Herbert Engelmann* the crime was already given; what remained to be motivated were its causes, its nature, and the effect on the persons involved, namely the shattering of the natural unit of trust and confidence, the family. In *Das Kalte Licht* on the other hand it is a problem of defining the mistake itself and of finding out what is right or wrong in an uncharted region. The only guide is, as in all Zuckmayer's plays, the principle of human decency. Wolters' only criterion is the nature of his relation to those who are bound to him in trust. On the political level Zuckmayer has not tried to answer all the questions he has raised, but rather he demonstrates the effect of a "wrong" choice on the conscience of the individual concerned, and even more by the effect that the steps taken have on those who trust and love the person concerned. The final "right" choice may lead to the destruction of the hero: Engelmann, Harras, the German deserters in *Der Gesang im Feuerofen,* and Wolters. The self-destruction of the hero through moral awakening is the basis of the tragic element in Zuckmayer's post-war plays.

The lack of a clear-cut right or wrong course of action in the non-personal sphere is dramatized in part in the early conversations between Buschmann and Wolters, in part in the person of the flutter-brained Fillebrown. In the group around Ketterick Zuckmayer has brought to the stage the various responses to the moral and political confusion resulting from the impact of atomic science on traditional values that were already unsettled. In addition he has succeeded in recapturing the sense of rush and pressure of the war period and the excitement of the race for technological supremacy. Fillebrown, a type once known as a "parlor pink," illustrates in a light vein the dissociation of thinking in the fields of science and politics. He is a humorously drawn caricature of the scientist who dabbles in politics in an amateurish, bumbling way. In spite of Buschmann's reproaches, Wolters would like to be unpolitical and divorce his activities as a scientist from politics. The exposition of the play is largely concerned with his failure to live a completely cerebral life, a life which suppresses or hides his emotions and evades the responsibilities of his personal ties. None of the characters shown in the play is a whole man, except perhaps Ketterick, who is consistent at the price of being narrow and brutal. Wolters would like to be nothing but a scientist, but he fails in his attempt to divide his life into separate compartments, and he fails on two levels, the personal, and the political. Half-hearted idealism that does not involve the whole man leads Wolters to sell his soul to communism. It is ironic that the era that freed the individual and saw the great growth of individual independence should also have created greater masses or mobs evoked by the herd instinct, collectives that are more fanatic and intense than that of any age since that which burned heretics and witches. The atomization of the individual has led many to find themselves again by submerging themselves in a collective. All this Wolters can see in Buschmann, who combines resigned cynicism with a kind of despairing devotion, and is not seduced by it. But what other choices does he have? There is an emotional vacuum in Wolters, an affective void not filled adequately by formulas and mathematical concepts. In part he is isolated by his fate—he has just fled from Nazi Germany—in part by his scientific work, but mainly by his own underdeveloped emotional life. Yet every step he takes as an important scientist means necessarily a commitment. In an ideal society it might perhaps be possible to claim that knowledge is for all, but given the rift in the world which actually exists, sides must be taken, and the refusal to see this is evasion of moral responsibility and wilful self-delusion.

It is apparently impossible for man to live merely by facts and formulas. In the premiere Gründgens was careful to provide illusionless scenery, perhaps too coldly realistic in such scenes as the tennis court scene, and to create an atmosphere of hard, cold facts consonant with the factual, non-sentimental attitudes of secularized scientists. All the more striking is the scene in Las Mesas when the atom bomb is successful, for here a new mysticism and a new irrationality seem necessarily to spring from the logical extension of cold reason. The hopes and fears of those scientists who realize the implications of the tremendous new power that has been released are as real as those of the uninformed layman. The audience is prepared for this by the scene on shipboard in which Friedländer wins the chess game from the mathematical genius Wolters.

It is typical of all Zuckmayer's plays that the mainsprings of man's life are shown to be in his personal and emotional life. Where intimate personal relationships are destroyed, confusion in other areas results. This is the basis of Zuckmayer's version of *Herbert Engelmann.* The failure in personal relations, most notably the impossibility of maintaining his marriage, is what drives Engelmann to his final drastic way out. Engelmann is not motivated by abstract considerations of justice or morality, but rather by the inability to be honest with the persons to whom he is bound by ties of love. The same idea is dramatized in the different atmosphere of *Des Teufels General.* When Harras is awakened in the depths of his being by his love for Diddo, he breaks out of the self-centeredness that had permitted him to play the game of war. And it is the respect and affection for Anne Eilers and Oderbruch that make it possible for him to see himself clearly at last as the devil's general. In this play it is a subordinate who betrays his superior for the sake of a higher principle than that of personal loyalty. In *Das Kalte Licht* it is again the subordinate Wolters who betrays his superior Ketterick and breaks the community of trust that might have guided him on the right path. But the important difference from the earlier play is that this time the betrayal results from confusion and not from dedication to an ideal.

In the afterword to *Herbert Engelmann* Zuckmayer mentions the attempt of Engelmann to find an escape in love. In that play it is clearly shown that the successful trial, which satisfies society and the public, does not solve the inner problem of Engelmann, whose life is still poisoned by his guilt. His relation to his own conscience and to his loving and trusting wife is not cleared by the trial. Similarly Wolters does not find himself absolved even in his own eyes after his break with the Russian agents. Only an act of repentance can put him at peace with himself and Hjördis, the one person whose trust and faith in him he wishes to restore. In *Herbert Engelmann* Zuckmayer changed Hauptmann's "God will pardon" at the end of the play to "He has found peace." This play, perhaps more than any other by Zuckmayer, is based on the thesis that if one is not at peace with himself one is necessarily at war with society. *Das Kalte Licht* is also focussed on the man-woman relationship. Wolters, although confused, is not clearly at war with himself at the beginning of the play. It is only after the tennis court scene that he realizes that his relationship to Hjördis is being destroyed by his actions in other fields. And at the end the discovery that Hjördis had not sent Ketterick with the note about the rendezvous in Santa Fe is the signal for his decision to confess. The play ends with the suggestion that she will wait for Wolters.

Equally important is the temptation of power. Toward the end of Wolters' first meeting with the old Bolshevist Buschmann a small child bounces a ball into Wolters' hands. Twice he throws it back to the child. As he holds the ball in his hand he says: "Die Macht auf Erden, die ist in ein paar Formeln komprimiert. Und wer die weiß—der könnte den Erdball so in der Hand halten—und wägen—und wegwerfen, wenn er ihn nicht mehr liebt" (p. 16). This scene is echoed at the conclusion of the play, where this time Northon throws the ball back to the child. The last words of the play are: "Hier—Fang!" Power may be such a little thing, easily thrown away or to another person. A few formulas or a few symbols which can be written on a scrap of paper represent power in this play. The lure of power over destiny motivates Buschmann also, and is an important part of his disillusioned devotion to a cause that he knows will destroy him. He is able to present this power to Wolters as a power to do good, and from this derives much of the tempting force of his arguments. Power is not really a child's ball that can be held in the hand or thrown back to a person standing offstage, but it is true that the consequences of the "few formulas" are unpredictable, remote, impersonal and beyond the purview of an individual. Wolters does not at first feel any responsibility for his acts, which are but intermediate acts in a game which he cannot oversee. The use and consequences of his information he surrenders into the hands of a remote and unknown force.

Like Buschmann then he has surrendered to the collective and has given up his own conscience to that of a cause. In doing so he betrays the community of trust of which he should be a part. He does not feel himself to be a member of the team around Ketterick, does not even feel the loyalty that the parlor pink Fillebrown shows, and until late in the play seems unaware that the other atomic scientists are held together by a team spirit as well as their sense of service to a scientific goal. Personal loyalty to Ketterick is made more difficult by Ketterick's personality and narrow nationalism. Early in the play it is made clear that Wolters is homeless in both a physical and a spiritual sense. As a displaced German and temporary internee by the British it is easy to see how national loyalties might lose meaning for him. It seems as if Wolters were adrift from all the normal ties of church, family, fatherland and friends. We know that the deportation from England left a mark on Wolters' prototype, Klaus Fuchs. The English security police found under his bed after the war a satchel containing a jacket with the prisoner of war number still sewed on it. In this part of the play Zuckmayer has remained close to his sources, even giving the same date for the trip to Canada in the transport ship. The histori-

cal Klaus Fuchs twice signed a pledge of secrecy, in England in 1941, in America in 1943. Zuckmayer has made an impressive scene out of the first signing by making it at the same time the first meeting between Wolters and Ketterick. In this first interview Ketterick is concisely and superbly characterized. He states his position frankly and tersely as that of a British patriot totally dedicated to his cause. The dialogue brings out strikingly the narrowness, firmness, and devotion of Ketterick, and at the same time reveals to the audience the doubts, hesitation, and reservations of Wolters. When he mentions the fact that an oath has for him no religious significance, Ketterick asks for his hand in a gesture of man-to-man faith. When Wolters accepts, he has pledged his loyalty to a man, a team, and a cause. There is no place here for excuses to the effect that he is not yet a British subject, or that England had once wronged him. The whole scene, including the surprise reunion with Hjördis, is based a note of loyal personal relations. Ketterick expressly casts out considerations of national loyalty, emphasizes his lack of interest in Wolters' political past (he had been a communist in Germany), and asks only for a gentleman's word.

The turning point of the play and the end of the exposition come in the seventh and eighth scenes. The scene on the tennis court ends with Wolters admitting that he has forfeited Hjördis' trust and confidence. She does not even know that he has passed on important secrets; it is enough for her that he has somehow practiced deceit. Following this first rupture of personal relations comes the scene where the principal authors of the atomic bomb begin to face the moral issues involved in its use. Into the mouth of the feather-brained Fillebrown is put the key statement: "Unser Problem hat weniger mit Politik zu schaffen, mehr mit Menschlichkeit" (p. 103). The test pilot, Löwenschild, and Merminod reach a kind of agreement to the principle that none of them can take upon himself the responsibility of sharing or disseminating the dangerous knowledge that they possess, since they cannot be responsible for nor oversee the effects of their acts. The word "Judas," which recurs thematically in this discourse, is dramatic irony for the audience. For Wolters, when it is first used, it names precisely for the first time the nature of his acts. Fillebrown, who is a loyal member of the team in spite of his muddle-headed enthusiasm for Russia, asks the final question: "Aber darf man denn Vertrauen haben—in eine Welt, die sich vor lauter Gegensätzen selbst nicht kennt." From Löwenschild, the director of the atomic research project, Wolters hears the answer: "Es gibt etwas, woran wir glauben, worauf wir vertrauen dürfen—auch in unserer Welt der erschütterten Fundamente—das ist die Lauterkeit eines Menschen" (pp. 106-7). This statement sums up succinctly the philosophy not only of this play but of all Zuckmayer's plays. Trust in the essential goodness of man is always his highest criterion of action. Later in the play Northon, in the process of winning over Wolters, echoes the above in his own words. "In einer gespaltenen Welt müssen wir beides [Gut und Böse] dort suchen, wo es am nächsten liegt. Das ist: in uns selbst" (p. 147).

From this point on until Hjördis' final words of faith in Wolters are spoken to Northon in the final scene the problem whose solution is being dramatized is the attempt to restore Wolters to the community of trust in which he belongs. When this is achieved Wolters confesses. In **Das Kalte Licht** there is no thought of atonement through death or self-sacrifice as in the previous serious plays. There is no purpose in Wolters' committing suicide, for example. The impact of what he has done, the very nature of the betrayal itself, is not clear. His death would be a personal act in expiation of a deed of a highly impersonal, imponderable nature. This leaves room for no response other than the given one of a personal repentance and soul-searching. Perhaps no punishment is adequate and no atonement apposite for what happened. When one recalls the moral indignation and confused excitement in many parts of the world at the execution of the Rosenbergs and the conflicting voices anent the Oppenheimer case, one can see that justice in such cases moves along nearly unexplored paths. Nowhere does Zuckmayer belittle the seriousness of betraying military secrets in war time. But what he does make plausible in our play is that a man may come to make such a betrayal without a positively criminal nature. He dramatizes the way in which a fundamentally good man may go astray in the modern world for a while and then find himself when confronted with an "intakt Gebliebenen." Wolters never does come to experience deeply the international consequences of his betrayal, but rather comes to see that he has failed in his personal obligations. Just being human in the best sense of the word has been violated, and this is the realization to which Northon ultimately brings Wolters. His last act in the play is to assure Hjördis through Northon that he had never lied to her. With her acceptance of this assurance the community of faith is restored and the play is over.

From the beginning in moral confusion to the conclusion in reconciliation one can see close parallels to the other serious plays of Zuckmayer. There emerges a general pattern for the plays of this type: a long exposition which explores the possibilities, sets the scene, the milieu, and the moral climate, includes lyric or comic interludes and episodes; a turning-point where the protagonist is forced into a decision; a moment of moral awakening followed by the decisive act of the protagonist in atoning for his error, and a conciliatory conclusion. Within this dramatic structure the emphasis remains in all the plays on the essential goodness of man and on his capacity to do right by listening to his own conscience and being human in the fullest and finest sense of the word.

Henry Glade (essay date December 1960)

SOURCE: Glade, Henry. "Carl Zuckmayer's Theory of Aesthetics." *Monatshefte* 52, no. 7 (December 1960): 163-70.

[*In the following essay, Glade proposes that Zuckmayer's lesser known theoretical essays, such as* Die Brüder Grimm, Pro Domo, *and* Die langen, Wege, *reflect the author's "deep-souled attunement with the forces of nature."*]

Carl Zuckmayer, recognized as one of the foremost German dramatists today, has yet other accomplishments to his credit.[1] Among these, of course, are his poetry and fiction; but it is not often realized that he has created a considerable body of theory. His major publications in this area include **Pro Domo, Die Brüder Grimm,** and **Die Langen Wege.**[2] It is to them and to his two articles **"Jugend und Theater"** and **"Notizen zur Situation des Dramas"**[3] that this investigation will give particular attention.

At the outset, it is well to realize that Zuckmayer has not provided a particularly orderly formulation of his ideas in a familiar didactic pattern, as an author with a more philosophic turn of mind might have done. Indeed, an effective grasp of his conceptions presupposes a knowledge of his reactions to the changing pattern of his life together with the first, more implicit statement of these reactions in his dramas. The subsequent generalizations in his theory are always descriptive of the conflicts and possible reconciliations in everyday living; they can hardly be called the analytical insights of a reflective mind.

Thus, the evolving core of Zuckmayer's aesthetics is revealed in the particular spirit of his dramatic works in each successive phase of his literary creativity. Consequently, his aesthetic formulations at any given stage provide an analysis of the dramas he wrote in that period—if due allowance is made for discrepancies between obvious intent and actual execution. If his aesthetics is assessed on its intrinsic merits, as is the primary purpose of this study, it can be designated, in briefest fashion, as a pantheistic credo in which the eros force plays the key role. Significantly enough, the emphasis on critical speculations is the result of his postwar literary self-consciousness along with his genuine concern for the moral welfare of men. The effusiveness of his expositions tends, however, to vitiate the message. Certainly in his theorizing he is no match for his great antipodal contemporary, the late Brecht, who evolved a disciplined and cogent aesthetics.

Any individual's aesthetics is necessarily grounded in his *Weltanschauung*, which, in turn, is conditioned to a considerable extent by the interactions of his personality with the developing environmental opportunities and pressures. Zuckmayer's world-view has its roots in the man-and-animal-loving world of the Rhine-Hessian, and it can be characterized further as a robust and joyful affirmation of life and a feeling of innate oneness with nature. His mode of thinking is instinctive, imaginative, and impulsively spontaneous. Hence his philosophizing tends to take form through intuitive and imaginative concepts. He is apt to cast these into the mold of poetic images, taken primarily from nature and the animal world.

The propelling force of Zuckmayer's creativity has been an intense dramatic instinct that became manifest at a very early age and has continued ever since (***Pro Domo,*** p. 68). Thus the discussion in ***Die langen Wege,*** as a convenient example, is punctuated continuously by fresh incidents and dramatic interludes.

As might be expected then, Zuckmayer tends to disparage intellectual approaches and clever analyses, and he especially dislikes the over-intellectualized dissections that lead to no humanitarian solution.[4] In place of intellect, which is almost a bad word in Zuckmayer's book of values, he extols the virtues of man's imaginative powers, based upon a nature-life synthesis. Zuckmayer encounters nature-life on his long walks which are undertaken without any definite goals (***Die langen Wege,*** p. 29). Whether or not he is rationalizing a deep-seated love for extensive exercise of this sort, the attendant process of "Geh-Denken" (p. 13) has, in point of fact, become with him a necessity for creative productivity.

This "Geh-Denken" process based on the nature-life equation, is, epistemologically, an experience of nature as life in its totality. For, to Zuckmayer, there is no such thing as a simple contemplation ("keine 'reine' Anschauung") but rather a "persönliche, leidenschaftliche Teilnahme, ein gegenseitiges Verhältnis des Besitzens und Besessenseins" (p. 52). Displayed here is Zuckmayer's ever-present striving for a recognition, in the panerotic and mystical sense, of an ultimate reality which exists primarily in the symbiotic relationship of man with nature, its process of growth and its animal world.[5] The perennial dualism of intellect and nature is thus reduced to a monistic reconciliation, and, in the final analysis, this is achieved through the power of the natural eros. This eros or the instinctive drive for unitary experience of the life-force *per se* constitutes the very core of Zuckmayer's philosophy of nature. He perceives this nature as free of any exotic or impressionistic ornament. His is a rustic, biologically realistic, quasi-mystic, and dramatically gripping view of nature. In his own words: "Es kam . . . nicht . . . auf das 'Schöne,' im Sinn einer ästhetischen Auswahl, an, sondern auf die tiefere, heftigere, nacktere Schönheit des gesamten Lebensvorgangs, einschließlich seiner Gewalttätigkeit, seines Zerfalls und seines Grauens."[6]

Thus it may be said that Zuckmayer's thought has its primary source in his deep-souled attunement with the forces of nature—his *Urerlebnis.* Consequently, his view of life is characterized by a continuing attempt to make his conceptualization of nature-love central to his theory. Zuckmayer's aesthetics becomes most explicit during his latest period of creative effort, as he seeks to justify his life and destiny through his efforts to bring more effective meaning to the contemporary situation.

As stated earlier, Zuckmayer consistently tends to deduce his aesthetics from the prevalent tenor of his works. Therefore, it is best analyzed in line with the unfolding pattern of his creative development. As seen by Zuckmayer himself, there are two major periods of literary creativity. The first or spontaneous period, extending from 1925-1932 (or from ***Der fröhliche Weinberg*** to ***Der Hauptmann von Köpenick***), can be classified as realistic-folklore. Logically, this period yields no theoretical treatises. The second, or deliberate, period from 1933 to the present can be subdivided into an initial phase from 1933-1939 (or from ***Der Schelm von Bergen*** to ***Herr über Leben und Tod***) which is characterized by the interpretation of realistic and metaphysical elements, and a later phase, 1940 to the present (or from ***Des Teufels General*** to ***Das kalte Licht***) in which the vexing socio-political problems of the present day are drawn upon for subject matter and in which Zuckmayer tends toward a more complex orientation involving realistic, metaphysical and symbolical elements.

The essay ***Pro Domo*** (1938), the only theoretical work from the 1933-39 phase, presents among other things Zuckmayer's first exposition of aesthetic theory. The fusion of realistic and metaphysical elements that has already been mentioned as a distinguishing literary characteristic of this phase is reflected in the major premise of his aesthetics, that is, the espousal of a metaphysical theater which is deeply anchored in the vital forces of all life: "Die Schaubühne ist eine metaphysische Anstalt, mehr noch als eine moralische, und um das zu sein und zu bleiben, muß sie bis in alle Fasern von vitaler Wirklichkeit, vom leibhaften Eros, von allen Essenzen des Menschenlebens, durchtränkt werden." (pp. 78-79)

The essence of this credo is derived from Zuckmayer's pantheistic outlook, or more specifically from the drive to conceptualize an innate and deeply ingrained eros that becomes evident during this phase. It is revealed here in its nature-art parallelisms, or the superimposition, whether witting or unwitting, of the nature philosophy on his aesthetics. Here Zuckmayer's presumed belief in nature as protean and incommensurable leads him to establish a rationale of character delineation in which logical motivation constitutes the least important factor.[7] His philosophy thus grounded in an equation of nature and human nature,[8] Zuckmayer argues that all human actions have their source in the subconscious recesses, "den Quellen der tieferen Wirklichkeit" (p. 82).

The depiction of this "deeper reality" *per se* constitutes the most important aspect of Zuckmayer's theory of aesthetics at this time. It is a reality which remains as inscrutable and inexorable as life or nature itself, and this very fact, to Zuckmayer, gives an intimation of the true essence of life. This, in turn, provides a link with the divine which is symbolized by beauty in the non-aesthetic sense in which the term was previously defined:

> So tut sich im Wandelbaren und Motivlosen der menschlichen Natur, im Sprunghaften und Antilogischen ihrer Handlungen, im blindlings Getriebenen, Unkorrekten, bewußtlos Wallenden und Strömenden, kurz: im Lebendigen,—in der Stärke, Gewalt und Unerbittlichkeit des Lebens,—jener Wahrsinn dar, den wir aus Ahnungs- und Traumgründen her als den göttlichen,—jene Schönheit, die wir als heimliches Maß aller Dinge, als die himmlische und urewige, in uns tragen—und die wir im gottversuchenden, im luziferischen Drange des künstlerischen Schöpferwillens, auf die Erde herabzwingen.

(p. 84)

Thus the task of a writer becomes just this wresting of "the secret measure of all things" from life by overcoming the basic dualism productively through a recreating or exorcising of life. In this, Zuckmayer's powerful eros drive is ever striving for a unitary realization of all existence.

> . . . es handelt sich um . . . die nachformende Bannung des Lebens, der Schöpfung, ihrer Zwiespälte und ihrer heimlich bindenden und lösenden Gewalt, um die Darstellung unserer metaphysischen Bestimmtheit, ihres Grauens und ihrer Gnade,—um die produktive Überwindung des Chaos, der Zerspaltenheit, der Moira, der Ananke, der dunklen Sphynx-Sprüche unseres Schicksals.

(p. 76)

To recapitulate, Zuckmayer's theory of aesthetics at this time resolves itself into a very definite proposition. The artist's highest task is to make of art a reflection of nature-life through a creative reconciliation of the destructive dualisms inherent in all existence. More specifically, this reconciliation is achieved through beauty or eros in nature. Art in those terms is pressed into the service of eros, mirroring man's essential grounding in the laws of nature, while nature itself symbolizes the incommensurable and ultimately the divine essence: "Kunst wird in diesem Sinne zum ewigen Gleichnis der Natur—des Unsterblichen also im Spiegel der Vergänglichkeit—und Natur zum Gleichnis der heimlich wirkenden Gottheit." (p. 63)

Zuckmayer's theorizing during the next major phase of literary creativity (1940 to the present) provides a more rounded and detailed aesthetics. As in the preceding phase, the main lineaments of his aesthetics are evolved from the dominant tenor of his dramatic works and therefore reflect changes in his basic view and presentation. The most significant of these is a predominant concern for a realization of his ideal of *Humanität,* which comprises both ethics and a transcendental or eros force.

Zuckmayer, the man of action, realizes apparently with some regret the extremely limited influence that his own craft can exert on the actual course of history.[9] All the greater, however, and indeed without limitations, is his belief in the influence the dramatist can wield in the creation of a moral climate for our generation and succeeding ones. Zuckmayer's specific program for a moral regeneration remains somewhat vague in its phrasing, since he has recourse in general to the catch-all terminology of love. The propagation of love or the creation of a positive "Stromkreis der Liebe" within the context of his **"Jugend und Theater"** seems specifically directed against overcoming its opposite, hatred (pp. 9-10).

Here, typically, the theorist merely confirms the dramatic craftsman. Zuckmayer's great concern over ethical and humanitarian considerations has become an integral part of his post-war dramas and often has led him to sacrifice the attractive and dramatic solutions of which he is a past master.[10]

What subject matter is a dramatist of our day to choose if he is imbued with such humanitarian love? Zuckmayer's answer is that he is to mirror our time. Here Zuckmayer makes a distinction between topical (*aktuell*) and present-day (*gegenwärtig*). In his definition of the terms, the topical identifies a type of drama dealing merely with contemporary socio-political affairs or with current fads, such as the existentialism of Jean-Paul Sartre. As conceived by Zuckmayer, the present-day type of drama is characterized by the fact that, while it draws on momentary conditions and problems for actual content-matter, it does so in such a way as to transcend the merely topical and relate itself to the eternal verities.

Zuckmayer's treatment of Hauptmann's *Herbert Engelmann* fragment furnishes us with a particularly lucid example of his demands for combining contemporary pertinency with ideology or ethos. As the comparative study of Boeninger shows, the most essential inner modification that the play underwent was the fact that Zuckmayer recreated Hauptmann's "timebound, temporal drama" in such a way as "to focus the argument upon absolutes, upon permanent values."[11]

And yet, the ethical grounding is to be just one desideratum in the creation of a theater whose themes are to be drawn from the contemporary ideologies. Most important to Zuckmayer, as his eros drive asserts its supremacy again, is the added dimension which lends eternal qualities to the present-day subject matter. This is achieved through a sense of awe, "das große Staunen vor der Erscheinung des Menschen, der Welt, der Schöpfung" (**"Jugend und Theater,"** p. 11).

To create such a sense of "magic realism," the dramatist is to delve deeply into the vital elements of his epoch in addition to its mental, ethical, and spiritual ones. This brings the consideration back to the nature-life equation, or more specifically to Zuckmayer's "Geh-Denken" process. Substituting life for walking and poetry for thinking, he suggests an intimate interrelationship of life and poetry: ". . . . Dichten und Leben sind nicht wie Traum und Wirklichkeit verschieden oder verschwistert . . . sondern sie stehen in einem viel engeren, fast untrennbaren und kaum darstellbaren Verhältnis der Kongruenz und der Doppelgestalt." (*Die langen Wege,* p. 77)

Here again Zuckmayer's constant endeavor is to resolve all dualisms into a monism through the agency of eros. This emphasizes one of the main tenets of his previous aesthetic period, in which he proclaimed that the function of the dramatist is to exorcise life or fate. Actually, this is *still* his belief. In **"Jugend und Theater"** he uses the dance, as one of the original forms of all theatrical expressions, to give a detailed picture of the dualism inherent throughout all manifestations of nature. In the dance of primitive people there were the gruesome and barbaric instincts as well as the tender and humane ones, and this conflict is still implicit in all art form.[12] It is this dualistic factor which is to be exorcised—"Der Dämon muß gebannt werden, indem man ihn darstellt, in eine Mitte zwingt, einkreist und absorbiert" (p. 13).

If the situation is applied to the relationship between actors and audience, the same proposition holds true. A cruel instinct of the audience projects itself mercilessly upon the actors, who represent the more tender instincts and who, through this process, are rescued from their isolation to become a part of the whole. But the cathartic effect as it extends to the audience is Zuckmayer's special concern; to him this is one of the most important functions of the drama. The dramatist, through his gift of synthesis, conjures up the healing forces of wholeness. Through creative participation in the spectacle of the drama man catches a glimpse of the underlying harmony which is of God, and by such an embrace of the whole, he secures the cathartic effect or gains in some measure a realization of the soundness to be found in the ultimate total. It is dramatic creation of this wholeness that Zuckmayer sees as the supreme task of the dramatist.

Thus, the dramatist becomes a healer giving men through eros an awareness of their potential wholeness. More specifically, he brings about a catharsis by giving

an intimation of the incommensurable unitary force in which all dualisms and all chaos are resolved and which reveals divine essence. Again, as in the previous period, beauty, as an outer manifestation of eros, is the closest man can get to an actual perception of the fundamental unity. Beauty becomes the primary linking concept between macrocosm and microcosm. The search for beauty in nature equates itself with a search for unity through the agency of the eros drive, and this search is visualized or symbolized through beauty (**Grimm,** p. 42). This type of beauty constitutes the pivotal concept in what, it is hoped, has emerged as an aesthetics, grounded in a strikingly pantheistic *Weltanschauung*.

Zuckmayer's own words may stand here as a summarizing statement for his aesthetic objectives:

> Es ist . . . die Aufgabe des Dramas, die Sendung der Tragödie: Heil zu künden. Hier scheint mir die höchste Forderung an die Tragödie zu liegen: daß sie uns heil entläßt—nicht versehrt, verletzt, vermindert. Heil: im Sinne des sokratischen Eros, der ein Welt-Heiland ist. Die Katharsis aller großen Dramen ist von einem Widerschein durchfunkelt, der die Hoffnung schürt auf das Bestehen eines größeren, ewigen Lichtes unbekannter Substanz—darin der mächtige Ursprung, das geheime Ziel aller Seelen lebt, und in dem sich unser Gut und Böse, Gerecht und Ungerecht auf einer göttlichen Waage ausgleicht.

("Notizen zur Situation des Dramas")

The type of drama that results from such a view Zuckmayer designates as poetic theatre,[13] characterized by its complex substance and by its subservience to the demands of a true *Humanität*. This *Humanität* is to be created by the transcendental or eros force which binds all elements of existence into a deep and meaningful whole.

> Eine neue Menschlichkeit, auf die allein es ankommt, wird nur aus einer neuen Schau und Erkenntnis wachsen können, die das Spirituelle, das Magische, das Über-Rationale, die Wirksamkeit eines höheren *Daimonions* und einer tieferen Bestimmtheit unserer Existenz, in das Ringen um die irdischen Umstände und ihre Sinngebung aktiv einbezieht.

("Jugend und Theater," p. 7)

Notes

1. This paper was read, in a shorter form, at the twelfth annual University of Kentucky Foreign Language Conference at Lexington, Kentucky, in April, 1959.

2. *Pro Domo,* in *Schriftenreihe "Ausblicke"* (Stockholm: Bermann-Fischer, 1938); *Die Brüder Grimm, Ein deutscher Beitrag zur Humanität* (Frankfurt a/M: Suhrkamp, 1948); *Die langen Wege, Ein Stück Rechenschaft* (Frankfurt a/M: Fischer, 1952).

3. "Jugend und Theater," *Der Monat,* III (April, 1951), 3-14; "Notizen zur Situation des Dramas," *Frankfurter Allgemeine Zeitung,* September 23, 1953, p. 7.

4. Most striking, in this connection, is his diatribe against existentialism of the Sartre variety. Cf. "Notizen zur Situation des Dramas."

5. This tendency is particularly noticeable in *Die langen Wege.* There his landscapes are simply thought images and symbolic reflections of the walker.

6. *Die langen Wege,* p. 55. Cf. Luise Rinser's inspired words: "Zuckmayer liebt die Natur . . . [Die] Natur lieben heißt sie 'erkennen,' beinahe im biblischen Sinn. Weitab von naturwissenschaftlichem Erforschen, Experimentieren, Analysieren. Erkennen heißt: das Wesen eines jeden Geschaffenen mit allen Sinnen erfassen . . . in einer Art erotisch-mystischer Vereinigung mit einer Kreatur das Geheimnis ihres Seins, ihrer Schönheit, ihrer Wachstumsgesetze, kurz ihre Wesenheit auf unmittelbare Weise erfahren." ("Porträtskizze," in *Fülle der Zeit, Carl Zuckmayer und sein Werk,* Frankfurt a/M: 1956, p. 15.)

7. "Logik, Kausalität, oder, in menschlichem Bezug, 'Motivierung,' scheint mir das nebensächlichste und unmaßgeblichste aller ihrer [dramaturgischen] konstruktiven Elemente zu sein." (*Pro Domo,* p. 81.)

8. Cf. the following statement: "Denn ist nicht das Wunderbare und wahrhaft Verewigungswürdige der menschlichen Natur, wie aller Natur überhaupt: Daß sie—über einem fürs zeitliche Auge nicht zu umfassenden Grundriß geheimster Planung,—in freiem ungebundenem Kräftespiel, ohne sichtbare Ziele oder Zwecke, ja ohne Andeutung von einem begrifflich wägbaren Sinn—sich unermeßlich entfaltet . . . immer wieder im Wandel unzählbarer Verlarvungen ihr Wesen verbergend . . ." (Ibid., pp. 81-82).

9. Cf. Luise Rinser's observations: "Zuck . . . hat ein heimliches Ideal, einen Knabentraum von sich selber: er sieht sich als Mann der Tat. Nicht umsonst gilt seine Liebe Karl May . . . und nicht von ungefähr bewundert er Udet und Mierendorff, die aktive Männer des öffentlichen Lebens waren . . . und es geschah auch nicht nur aus politisch-humanitärer Absicht und nicht nur um der Aktualität willen, daß er zum Helden des 'Kalten Lichts' einen Atomspion wählte, einen Mann der Tat also und einen, der sich in ein gefährliches Abenteuer einläßt" ("Porträtskizze," in *Fülle der Zeit,* pp. 21-22).

10. Cf. *Der Gesang,* whose unattractive and undramatic metaphysical and ethical core reflects not only Zuckmayer's sense of responsibility but also his self-sacrificial qualities and his courage. It should be noted, in this connection, that Zuckmayer has made significant changes in some of his plays merely for the sake of creating an aura of love (see the change of characterization of Oderbruch in the film version of *Des Teufels General*). Cf. Weber's remarks: "Die Besorgnis, vielleicht Mißverständnisse, Bitterkeiten und Ressentiments auszulösen und so die Wirkung abzuschwächen oder gar in falsche Bahnen geleitet zu sehen, veranlaßt ihn zu Korrekturen, die er früher wahrscheinlich rundweg abgelehnt hätte . . . Er will ja nicht aufputschen, skandalisieren oder radikalisieren, sondern Umdenken, Umkehr und Zustimmung durch die Überzeugungskraft von Vernunft und Gefühl erreichen." (Paul Friedrich Weber: "Im Gespräch," in *Fülle der Zeit,* p. 73.)

11. Helmut Boeninger, "A Play and Two Authors, Zuckmayer's Version of Hauptmann's *Herbert Engelmann,*" *Monatshefte,* XLIV (November 1952), 348. Cf. Zuckmayer's own remarks: "Es ist, obwohl auf eine ganz bestimmte, scharf abgegrenzte Epoche fixiert, kein 'Zeitstück'—es ist eine menschliche Tragödie, von der man eher sagen könnte, daß sie 'zwischen den Zeiten' stattfindet, und deren Probleme und Charaktere nicht unter einem aktuellen Aspekt anzuschauen sind." (Gerhart Hauptmann-Carl Zuckmayer, *Herbert Engelmann,* München: C. H. Beck, 1952, p. 274).

12. The fuller statement reads as follows: "Alles vitale Theater . . . kommt vom tänzerischen Antrieb . . . Und wie bei den tänzerischen Beschwörungen der Fruchtbarkeit und des Todes primitiver Naturvölker, umschließt es die wilden, grausamen, barbarischen Instinkte, die Nachtschatten, die in der menschlichen Natur, im menschlichen Eros angelegt sind, ebenso wie die zarten und gütigen, die brüderlichen und mütterlichen Erstrahlungen." ("Jugend und Theater," pp. 12-13).

13. Ibid., p. 13. It may be noted in this connection that Happ in his analysis of the entire dramatic output uses that very designation. A. Happ, *Dichterisches Theater,* in *Fülle der Zeit,* p. 31-33.

Siegfried H. Muller (essay date January 1962)

SOURCE: Muller, Siegfried H. "Another Note on 'Herbert Engelmann.'" *Monatshefte* 54, no. 1 (January 1962): 291-96.

[In the following essay, Muller assesses Zuckmayer's reworking of Gerhart Hauptmann's Herbert Engelmann, *emphasizing Zuckmayer's changes to the language and plot of the play.]*

On the occasion of the one hundredth anniversary of Gerhart Hauptmann's birth the first four of ten projected volumes of the Centenary Edition of his works, an estimated total of twelve thousand pages, will be published under the competent editorship of Professor Hans Egon Hass, assisted by his staff of collaborators. To the delight of Hauptmann researchers and enthusiasts, almost one third of this set will constitute a part of hitherto unpublished material which remained in the poet's literary legacy in various stages of completion. To be sure, a few items from this tremendous reservoir, some finished, some as fragments, have appeared in print since the end of the War.

Among these, two arouse especial interest for being completed or executed by another author—the only works of Hauptmann's published in such a manner. However, the matter of treatment is different. The novel *Winckelmann. Das Verhängnis* is a fusion of two versions with some additions by Frank Thiess,[1] and until more of Hauptmann's manuscripts become available, it will be impossible to unravel the extent of the original and of the contribution of the editor who produced the published version.[2] The four-act tragedy **Herbert Engelmann** contains in one volume an allegedly uncompleted "Urfassung" together with another version executed by Carl Zuckmayer.[3]

The drama in the Zuckmayer version had its world première in Vienna in the *Akademietheater* on March 8, 1952; it was produced for the first time in Germany four weeks later in the *Theater der Berliner Freien Volksbühne*,[4] to be followed by productions in Mannheim, Mainz, and other German cities. The unique presentation of the two texts invites intriguing studies in a quest for the answers to a host of questions, e. g.: To what extent was Hauptmann's version unfinished? What is the nature of Zuckmayer's changes in language, structure, plot, characterization, and impact on the stage? What were the reasons for his changes? To what extent could he or any author of his standing penetrate into the work of the forerunner? Could he be expected to restrain his individuality sufficiently to conform to the spirit of the manuscript? What was the effectiveness of the drama in the stage production, the real touchstone, and how much of it could be attributed to the ultimate rounding out? Finally, should it have been changed at all, or is the allegedly uncompleted version a great piece of craftsmanship in its own right? By further extension, one might inquire if the same criteria for "finishing" apply to literature as to other arts. Nobody would propose to complete Gaudí's *Sagrada Famiglia,* Berlioz' *Damnation of Faust,* or the missing arms of the *Venus de Milo*!

Scholarship has merely begun to scrutinize some of these many aspects, and four writings are noteworthy. Before the appearance of the book, Peter Suhrkamp in an article entitled "Herbert Engelmann. Der Streit um Gerhart Hauptmanns Nachlaßwerk"[5] describes the state of Hauptmann's 1941 manuscript and points out its unfinished nature. C. F. W. Behl is one of the first to criticize the book texts in his essay "Zuckmayers Hauptmann-Drama."[6] He also explains the reason why Hauptmann changed the hero's profession from that of a free-lance writer to a bacteriologist, which he did not carry through consistently: Hauptmann had been approached repeatedly by Paul Rose in the early 1940's for a possible stage production, but it became painfully manifest that in the political climate of the time, the figure of a pacifist novelist would be unthinkable. Possibly unaware of the reason for Hauptmann's change or disregarding it, Zuckmayer makes Engelmann an atomic physicist who, to be sure, speculates only on the beneficial use of nuclear radiation in its application to medical therapy. The nature and merits of many of Zuckmayer's changes and additions are submitted to careful examination in Helmut Boeninger's essay "A Play and Two Authors. Zuckmayer's version of Hauptmann's 'Herbert Engelmann',"[7] while Blake Lee Spahr in "A Note on 'Herbert Engelmann'"[8] takes issue with Boeninger for not having included all the important changes and purports to fill *these* gaps. In addition, we have a number of criticisms of the various productions. While the reactions of theater critics usually do not reflect intensive study of the printed text as well, they nevertheless reveal the impressions of an intellectual viewer whose senses react to the immediacy of the stage action before him. To this extent, the critics' judgments demand attention, and it may be said that except for the dubious ending, the production was generally hailed as a successful enrichment of the contemporary German stage repertoire.

A thorough analysis of the purely linguistic changes made by Zuckmayer in Hauptmann's text and a criticism of each writer's stylistic idiosyncrasies thus revealed, would easily reach book proportions. Boeninger thus limits himself to general statements. In a *Nachwort* to the two versions, Zuckmayer defends his *verknappen und härten* of Hauptmann's rhetoric, yet it remains enigmatic why he felt it necessary to make many very minute changes such as putting *am* instead of *an dem,* (pp. 10, 128) just to mention one of many examples. It seems more reasonable to reduce Kohlrausch's monthly board from three hundred to two hundred dollars, (pp. 13, 131) and to increase Herbert's fellowship from 100 to 150 gold marks (pp. 109, 261), but why does Hauptmann's Herbert drink wine (p. 109) and jokingly speak of selling matches in the Budapester Straße, (p. 25) while Zuckmayer's drinks champagne (p. 260) and sells matches on Wittenbergplatz (p. 159)? Boeninger claims that Zuckmayer made "necessary" improvements in Hauptmann's grammar. This is generally true, but it may be argued that Hauptmann did not intend having his persons always speak correctly; possibly their faulty or careless diction was supposed to reflect the results of the turmoil of the war experiences and the subsequent conditions of moral decadence. A change from "Von wem sprecht ihr?" (p. 86) to "Von was sprecht ihr?" (p. 237) is a questionable improvement. The change from "Braucht sich Herbert verstecken?" (p. 91) to "Braucht sich Herbert zu verstecken?" (p. 243) is a grammatical correction, but again the omission of the preposition may have been intentional with Hauptmann.[9]

As regards the plot of the play, the motivation of Herbert's suicide after his acquittal for lack of evidence has been the subject of controversial elucidation and quests for justification.[10] Spahr makes a subtle case for an argument that Herbert actually expects a trial in his certainty that he will be caught. This theory does not seem thoroughly convincing, especially in view of Herbert's attempt at escape, though there is a remote plausibility. Two factors, which curiously enough are not drawn upon to buttress this interpretation, are that Herbert merely rented and did not buy his house, perhaps anticipating only a brief stay before a possible judicial conviction, and that he selected as his residence the very same locality in which the slain man's widow lives. Zuckmayer significantly calls attention to it by adding a line for Christa: "Er hatte sich nun mal diesen Ort in den Kopf gesetzt" (p. 231). Or is his moving there in part an indication of a murderer's morbid compulsion to revisit the locale of his crime, transferred in this case to the victim's widow?

One significant improvement which seems to have escaped general notice so far is that Zuckmayer brought order into the chronology of events which in Hauptmann's version is partly inconsistent. Since this facet has not been treated before by any other researcher, it may be dealt with here in some detail.

The time of action is specified by Hauptmann as "etwa um 1923 (Höhepunkt der Inflationszeit)" (p. 7), and this indication is taken over literally by Zuckmayer (p. 125). The murder is supposed to have been committed soon after Herbert's return from the war "around 1920" (p. 78), which is in keeping with the high value of the 2500 marks involved in the robbery. But in Act III, which plays in October and can at the earliest be in 1923—because six months later the *Goldmark* is mentioned—there is a statement that the widow of the murdered man was again questioned "after a year and a half" (p. 79). Assuming that this space of time is to be reckoned from the first inquest, we arrive at the beginning of 1922 as the date of the murder or a time at which 2500 marks were no longer a substantial amount. Moreover, this date would be only six months before the play opens, or later than "soon after" Herbert's return from the war. His and Christa's relations, however, indicate that he had been living in her mother's boarding house for some time. In the third act we hear Frau

Kurnick say that Kohlrausch discussed the affair with Riedel in the boarding house "over a year ago" (p. 85), so that the interval between the first and third acts would have to be at least this span of time. Act I, however, plays "not far from Christmas" (p. 32), while the third act plays in the middle of October (p. 88). Furthermore, the decided change of relations between Herbert and Christa points to the fact that some time must have elapsed between the first and second acts. Whereas at first he did not want to marry her for reasons of health, his attitude has now become the direct opposite. One might conceivably argue that his mental unbalance does not let him always act logically.

Zuckmayer, on the other hand, adds several references to contemporary events bearing out his statement that the drama is "auf eine ganz bestimmte, scharf abgegrenzte Epoche fixiert" (p. 274). These additions enable us to assign exact dates to each act. Fixation of the epoch in general is heightened by reference to Briand, Hindenburg, Stresemann, Schacht, Dietrich Eckart, Rabindranath Tagore, and Elisabeth Bergner. He thus follows the intent which Hauptmann expressed in 1941 of wanting to strengthen the historical aspect.[11] His third act plays at a time when the *Rentenmark* (p. 214) (introduced November 16, 1923) is legal tender, a reference to the sex fiend Haarmann is added (p. 218) (confession on July 9, 1924), the song hit "Oh Katharina" is heard (p. 228) (copyrighted March, 1924), and at the same period Hitler serves time in Landsberg (p. 219) (where he was prisoner from April to December, 1924). Unfortunately, Zuckmayer went too far in his eagerness and introduced three anachronisms. First, he mentioned the Locarno Conference as being held at the same time (p. 219), whereas it did not take place until October of the following year. Incidentally, the Soviets did not participate, as erroneously stated (p. 219). Secondly, in 1924 Hölz was no longer in the Moabit prison (p. 219) but in Breslau, and thirdly, Professor Bergius (p. 261), who in 1925 is said to endorse Engelmann for a fellowship in Heidelberg, had been dead since 1921.

Thus, with the aid of the stage direction (p. 215), the third act may be pinpointed as playing in October, 1924. Accordingly, Zuckmayer changes the date of the crime to "a few years ago" (p. 223), which corresponds better to the worth of the 2500 marks. He also changes the time of the conversation between the two detectives to "almost a year ago" (p. 236), and besides, this need not have occurred immediately after Kohlrausch's moving into the boarding house. In Act I, a price of "one and a half million" is mentioned for a packet of narcotics (p. 154), so that the action must be some time before the currency revaluation, i. e., before November 16, 1923. That the second act follows some time later is apparent from the changed relations between the lovers and the reference to Kohlrausch's going out in the evening "once again" (pp. 57, 200). Moreover, his attitude has caused or threatened the departure of two other guests (pp. 59, 202). As the stage instructions indicate that the act takes place on a winter afternoon, it can only be the winter of 1923. Act III then plays, as shown above, in October 1924, and the last act six months later (pp. 97, 249), i. e., in the spring of 1925. One wonders why Zuckmayer, who made so many changes, did not give the precise dates for each act in the beginning of the play but retained literally Hauptmann's notation "etwa um 1923 (Höhepunkt der Inflationszeit)."

Whether in a reworking, Hauptmann would have corrected the factual errors is idle speculation.[12] Inconsistencies in the time element need not detract materially from the stage effectiveness of this drama any more than they disturb the spectator of *Rose Bernd* or Goethe's *Faust.* For the theater presentation, a stage manager competent enough to produce, e. g., a Kafka play on the basis of his fragmentary novels, could be expected to furnish the missing dialogue in the dinner scene in Act I, which was merely sketched by Hauptmann, but eloquently carried out by Zuckmayer.[13] If Hauptmann's drama was considered needy of completion, no more competent writer than Zuckmayer could have been chosen.[14] Yet even without his finishing touches, Hauptmann's work may lay claim to high regard in the vivid description of the motley collection of scurrilous types as a thematic counterpart to *Die Ratten,* which he considered it to be,[15] or as the psychological and compassionate study of a tortured soul like *Dorothea Angermann,* which belongs to the author's same work period.[16]

Notes

1. Published 1954 by C. Bertelsmann, Gütersloh.

2. For a cursory evaluation cf. C. F. W. Behl's article "Amalgam," *Deutsche Rundschau,* March 3, 1955, 266-270.

3. Published 1952 by C. H. Beck, Munich. Behl claims that the Hauptmann version contains inaccuracies. ("Das Vermächtnis Gerhart Hauptmanns und seine Schicksale," *Schlesien,* 1961/2, p. 3.)

4. It has been proposed to rename this theater *Gerhart-Hauptmann-Theater.*

5. Published September 22, 1949, in *Neue Zeit.*

6. *Deutsche Rundschau,* LXXVIII (June, 1952), 609-611.

7. *Monatshefte,* XLIV (November, 1952), 341-348. Understandably, such comparisons are all too easily exposed to the possibility of overstressing, and to the lurking danger of reading subtle reasons into passages where less complex ones may suffice. Thus, Zuckmayer's omission of divine forgiveness at the end, on which Boeninger elabo-

rates, may be explained simply by the author's religious convictions and his endeavor not to offend Catholic sensitivities by condoning self-destruction.

8. *Monatshefte,* XLVI (November, 1954), 339-345.

9. Hauptmann's writings abound with both constructions mostly depending on the speaker, but also occurring in his autobiographical writings. In this connection it is to be noted that in discussing the textual version of the Centenary Edition during the Gerhart Hauptmann Conference in Berlin, March 5 to 7, 1962, Professor Hass declared that the *zu,* where missing after *brauchen,* will not be added.

10. From Vienna critiques: "inkonsequente psychologische Gestaltung des Titelhelden . . . billigbanale Lösung" (Bienek); "freiwilliges Opfer . . . erschüttert, aber nicht überzeugt" (Hrastnik); "Tod, der nicht erschüttert" (Mühlbauer); "müßte sich Herbert der Gerechtigkeit dennoch stellen" (Schreyvogel). From Berlin critiques: "Sein Freitod ein neuer Verstoß gegen die Heiligkeit des Lebens" (Haemmerling); "Schluß völlig unglaubhaft" (Lorsch); "Schluß empört . . . der Tod kommt als Widersinn" (Wandel). The following statement by C. F. W. Behl in an earlier article "Ein Gerhart Hauptmann-Drama—unvollendet," in *Die Minute,* August, 1949, has probably escaped general notice. In it he reports that "Hauptmann im Oktober 1941 einen neuen Schluß diktiert hat, bei dem—wenn ich mich recht entsinne— Engelmann schließlich doch ins Leben zurückfindet."

11. C. F. W. Behl, *Zwiesprache mit Gerhart Hauptmann.* Munich: Kurt Desch, 1949, p. 75.

12. Cf. Behl's statement in *Die Minute,* op. cit.: "Wie seine endgültige Entscheidung gefallen wäre, läßt sich nicht sagen. Es ist durchaus möglich, daß er den 'Herbert Engelmann' schließlich doch in der vorliegenden Fassung für abgeschlossen erklärt und den Bühnen übergeben haben würde."

13. Gerhart Wandel writes in *Westdeutsche Rundschau,* April 16, 1952: "Hauptmann verstand es meisterhaft, Menschen am Rande zu zeichnen. Zuckmayers Charaktere beeindrucken nicht; was makabre Stimmung ergeben soll, wird zur Karikatur."

14. Hauptmann is quoted by Rudolph K. Goldschmit-Jentner in "Weiterdichten, wo ein anderer aufhörte," *Die Neue Zeitung,* August 24, 1951, as saying almost prophetically: "Ich sehe viel von mir in seinen Werken weiterwachsen."

15. *Zwiesprache mit Gerhart Hauptmann,* op. cit., p. 67, and Behl's article in *Die Minute,* op. cit.

16. The semblance of names is remarkable, the more so as an earlier title of a conception that merged into *Dorothea Angermann* was *Peter Hollmann.*

Henry Glade (essay date 1963)

SOURCE: Glade, Henry. "The Motif of Encounter in Zuckmayer's Dramas." *Kentucky Foreign Language Quarterly* 10, no. 4 (1963): 183-90.

[*In the following essay, Glade stresses that the treatment of encounters, which are present in many of Zuckmayer's dramas, reveals the author's monistic and naturalistic philosophical beliefs.*]

Although the significance of the phenomenon of "encounter" (*Begegnung*) in Zuckmayer's works has not escaped the attention of perceptive critics,[1] a concentrated exposition has yet to be undertaken. It is the purpose of this study to explore fully the pivotal position of this phenomenon in Zuckmayer's dramas,[2] where it is important in both a structural and a symbolical sense.

Encounter, to Zuckmayer, is more than mere accidental contact or clash of characters leading to conflict of a physical or even psychological sort. It is both a catalysis and a challenge to adjustment or readjustment. It must be realized, of course, that an author's fundamental motif is necessarily grounded in his *Weltanschauung*.[3] Consequently, it may be well to set down, in brief fashion, the bases of Zuckmayer's world view.

It can be stated axiomatically that any analysis of Zuckmayer has to be predicated on his thoroughly monistic and naturalistic philosophy; for Zuckmayer's primal experience (*Urerlebnis*) is nature seen framed within the special Rhenish-Hessian perspective. It is from this nature-life equation that his concept of life and its ethos is derived. To state matters most simply, the law of the natural is enthroned here.[4] The early plays (from *Der fröhliche Weinberg* to *Der Hauptmann von Köpenick,* 1925-1932) are a superb demonstration of this law. This is particularly true of the first play. Here nature as the ultimate criterion of human integration furnishes the fundamental dichotomy of the play in terms of the natural vs. the unnatural which is embodied in the grouping of Gunderloch-Annemarie-Klärchen-Jochen vs. Knuzius.[5]

From *Der Schelm von Bergen* (1934) on, the plays show a marked development of a more reflective perspective. This change in orientation is Zuckmayer's conscious attempt to formulate the rationale of life in transcendental and ethical terms. More specifically, the new approach includes both the macrocosmic and microcosmic poles of life and their manifestation through

fate and freedom. The emerging ideal may be described as a "love of destiny," which, in essence, is but the psychological and transcendental factor of the primary nature-life equation. Zuckmayer's fundamental outlook of necessity remains monistic. The fate-freedom polarity consequently has a monistic resolution through a conscious wholeness of selfhood in the sense of a synthesis of the self's potentials. This synthesis, in Zuckmayer's words, is "to restore the natural relationship of man to organic life" or is the perception of man's relationship to the universe, that is to say, the divine.[6] It is important to note the degree to which synthesis is derived from Zuckmayer's pantheism, or, more specifically, from his powerful eros drive. Indeed, the very core of Zuckmayer's philosophy is recognition of this eros or the instinctive drive for unitary experience of the life-force per se.

The practical question is what specifically operates to create or further this synthesis. Zuckmayer, who neither by temperament nor background is a philosopher, does not attempt to state the matter analytically, but rather proceeds to illustrate the actual process of synthesis by dramatizing the struggle to achieve wholeness in the individual case. What Zuckmayer sees as a prime instrumentation of the synthesis is the motif in his creative work. The operation of the encounter motif is most commonly found in the union of two persons. However temporary this union may be, it inevitably leads to the recognition of a higher mode of existence. Thus, the friction of character is not the essence of the drama, as already pointed out, but the special catalysis of the impact. Also, encounter may be centered in an event, or it can be the tangible realization of the naturalistic or naïve eros in self-transcendence and the consequent demonstration of man's link with the divine.[7]

In the dramas of Zuckmayer's early period (1925-1932), the phenomenon of encounter is presented obliquely and there is no self-consciousness in its operation. In *Schinderhannes* the high point of the drama is the hero's encounter with his beloved Julchen when she points out to him his reckless defiance of the law of nature and the senselessness of his plan of attacking the French army with his small band of robbers ("Du hebst aus der falsche Schulter").[8] In *Katherina Knie* there is a first indication of the later and more explicitly stated view of an unescapable event which links man to the larger unitary pattern, comprising all existence (metaphorically expressed here in terms of "the great secret umbilical cord").[9] Finally, in *Der Hauptmann von Köpenick* Voigt's encounter with the tubercular seamstress on the threshold of death provides the turning in this drama. For it is only through this encounter in purest humanity that Voigt subsequently is receptive to the discovery of divine authority through his inner voice[10]—an encounter which leads to the recognition of the ultimate law of life as man's responsibility to God in terms of fullest self-realization.

The encounter-phenomenon assumes explicit significance in the first phase of Zuckmayer's more reflective period of creativity (1933-1940). In fact, in *Der Schelm von Bergen* (1934) which initiates this new phase, the encounter-phenomenon provides the play's leitmotif. The empress and Vincent, the executioner's son, who are pivotal figures in the plot development, embody the expanded concept of encounter.

The empress is an unfulfilled woman, consumed like a *"fruchtlos Bäumelein nach der Hoffnung."*[11] Goaded by her sister's eulogies of the executioner's magic powers, she, too, ventures forth to consult him. It is thus, in the role of a wise counselor, that the executioner is portrayed. He has the gift of intuitive perception which enables him to recognize the fated line between the microcosm and the macrocosm—between man and his destiny. This is shown in his statement to the empress:

SCHARFRICHTER:

. . . Ihr könnt des Segens gewiss sein, in der rechten Stund. Euch fehlet nichts, als die Begegnung.

KAISERIN:

Die Begegnung?

SCHARFRICHTER:

Es ist ein Wort aus der Sterndeutersprache. Jed Gestirn has seine Begegnung mit einer andren, wegkreuzenden Welt . . . Solch Begegnung aber kann keiner nit machen, keiner erzwingen, und lässt sich keinem dazu verhelfen. Sie kommt von selbst, oder gar nit.[12]

Within the medieval context of this play, the deterministic aspect of encounter, appropriately enough, is seen as the inexorable and predestined movement of the planets toward their conjunction and the effect on the life and destiny of the empress. As defined in *Die langen Wege,* encounter is a transitory phenomenon. Its essence is viewed as awareness of one another and its goal is recognition—"Ihr [der Begegnung] Ziel ist der Schritt vom Gewahren zum Erkennen."[13] The recognition that emerges as the purpose of encounter is to be understood in its Biblical or pan-erotic sense:

Das "Erkennen" bedeutet in Luthers Bibelsprache die Vereinigung der beiden, die einander und ihres verschiedenen Geschlechts, ihres Dranges nacheinander, gewahr geworden sind. . . . Er ging hinein, heisst es im biblischen Bericht, und scherzte mit ihr. Der Scherz, das Spiel (gleich dem Liebes-Spielen in der Natur) wird zur *Form* der leiblichen Begegnung. . . .[14]

This recognition, resulting from the encounter-phenomenon, is not permanent, but rather "ein dauernd wiederkehrender, mächtiger Vorgang im Lebensvollzug, ein Element und zugleich ein Symbol des Lebens überhaupt."[15]

Not long after the executioner's prediction, the inevitable encounter materializes in the empress' meeting with Vincent, the executioner's son. There is no feeling of guilt involved in their relationship. As set forth in the rationale of the empress' prayer and in Zuckmayer's reflections, their love affirms the law of self-realization. For, as first noted by Jacobius, the phenomenon of encounter is linked to that of self-realization: ". . . Erfüllung des Ichs im Du, in Vollendung einer neuen höheren Einheit, ist Sinn und Ziel der Begegnung."[16]

Furthermore, through their encounter they are linked to the transcendental and divinely ordained pattern. This is evidenced in Bishop Scheitspalter's statement: "Wenn Er den Gipfel wollte . . . hätt Er die Welt . . . nicht so erfüllt mit unvollkommener Schönheit."[17] The "imperfect beauty" of Scheitspalter identifies the outer sign of manifestation of the microcosmic-macrocosmic link and its mediating force of eros or beauty as being ultimately of divine essence. It becomes the secret measure of all existence, and a glimpse of this is caught by Vincent in his encounter with the empress:

In diesem Schreiten, deinem Schritt vermählt—fühl ich das Mass, das tief geheime Wort—das alle Weltgestalt erweckt—und das wir meinen, wenn wir Schönheit sagen—du bist schön.[18]

Critics generally agree that Zuckmayer enters a new creative phase of his work in or around 1940. The most significant change during this period is Zuckmayer's primary interest in subject matter of present-day import. The other dominant aspect setting this period off from the preceding one is that the emphasis on ethical values becomes central in his dramas. This emphasis is reflected in the further development of the phenomenon of encounter. In place of the former pan-erotic foundation for the recognition of wholeness, it now predominantly assumes the form of moral integrity based on friendship and trust, or a "Liebesbedürfnis, im Sinn des gegenseitigen Vertrauens, des Schenkens und Erweckens von Vertrauen und Zuneigung."[19]

This new direction becomes strikingly evident in *Des Teufels General* (1945), which ushers in the new creative cycle. Midway in the drama the hero, Harras, inches away gradually from his hedonism and vital mode of living toward an ethically motivated life filled with religious overtones. Harras' gravest sin is his swerving from the path of the natural law that attains ethical significance in this play. Consequently, his recognition of his guilt is brought about through the new ethical aspect of the phenomenon of encounter.

As first observed by Peppard, there are four major stages in Harras' "gradual awakening to the seriousness of his moral position."[20] Each stage builds its action within the framework of the encounter-phenomenon. In the first place, there is the indirect impact of Bergmann and its transcendental challenge. Through Bergmann's suicide Harras is jolted into realizing his criminal complicity by default of any action on behalf of the thousands of Jews being massacred every day.[21]

The catalysis in the encounter with Hartmann results in the recognition of religious guilt; for it is through this earnest young man's search for reorientation that Harras' sense of responsibility is aroused. At the close of this dialogue Harras is compelled to face the full measure of religious guilt, as is evidenced in his answer to Hartmann's question about his belief in God:

> . . . die grösste Findung aller Zeiten habe ich nicht erkannt. Sie heisst Gott. In vielerlei Gestalten—immer Gott. . . . Ich kenne ihn nicht. Aber ich kenne den Teufel. Den hab ich gesehen—Aug in Auge. Drum weiss ich, dass es Gott geben muss. Mir hat er sein Angesicht verhüllt. Dir wird er begegnen.[22]

The encounter-phenomenon with Anne Eilers leads in turn to Harras' recognition of moral guilt. He acknowledges her accusations by accepting the ultimate responsibility for her husband's death. The fourth encounter, the dialogue with Oderbruch, brings about Harras' recognition of the eternal laws of justice. Justice, to Oderbruch, is a natural eros-type of inexorable law in all creation, and its ultimate manifestation is man's fulfillment of the natural impulses which are here imbued with moral significance. Thus, to do the natural thing would mean to do the morally right and decent thing.

In **Barbara Blomberg** (1949) the heroine evolves from an embittered, revengeful woman in ruthless pursuit of her maternal prerogatives into a person who is able to transcend herself through the phenomenon of encounter. Anthony Ratcliff seems to be brought into the plot primarily for the purpose of Barbara's elevation through the catalysis of contact. Barbara's love for him does in fact have a mellowing and ennobling effect on her. Under the impact of her involvement with Ratcliff, she retreats gradually from her former intransigent position.

As a result of her relationship with Don Juan Barbara comes to recognize the ethical ideal of love as self-sacrifice. When it becomes apparent that Don Juan's intervention on her behalf would compromise his precarious position at the Spanish court, Barbara does not press her demands. Instead, she renounces her own plans of future happiness in favor of a future for her son and Ratcliff. Her renunciation constitutes the high point of the drama. She has attained the highest form of love—a selfless love. She has transmuted "das Leid, das uns das Leben zufügt . . . in eine grössere Liebe. In eine Liebe—die nicht mehr besitzen will."[23]

In **Der Gesang im Feuerofen** (1950) the motif is expressed most convincingly through the Sylvester-Sylvaine encounter in love, since through it they discover the meaning of life in terms of a sense of wholeness and the unity of all creation, including even life and death. More importantly, the phenomenon of encounter is poignantly focused on an ineluctable fate in the face of which the resistance fighters learn to recognize the validity of Francis' gospel. It is a gospel that states man's transcendental responsibility to become positively reconciled to fate through love. Love as the synthesis of Zuckmayer's freedom-fate polarity here entails a Tolstoyan negation of mere human volition.

In **Ulla Winblad oder Musik und Leben des Carl Michael Bellman** (1953) Bellman's explanation for drinking provides a significant new aspect of encounter. Here the range of the phenomenon is extended through the almost mystical experience with the ultimate unity of all existence. It is Bellman's belief that man frees himself from outer bondage through intoxication, in a way not unlike dreaming, and thus gains a real sense of the secret order of essential oneness ("Im Traum und im Rausch sind wir verknüpft ins Schweben der Gestirne, und atmen ein und aus im Takte der heimlichen Ordnung, die keinen Zwang mehr weiss").[24]

In **Das kalte Licht** (1955) the psychological catharsis of the hero Wolters is brought about (according to Zuckmayer's formula in the epilogue) through the confrontation with persons who have remained intact. Through the impact of the clash in standards with Löwenschild, Wolters gains the inchoate recognition of the guilt of breach of confidence. But it is primarily through the catalyst Northon that he recognizes his moral and religious guilt. To cure Wolters' psyche and to make him realize the measure of his guilt, Northon depends upon trust, fairness, and the power of conscience which is equated with the Quaker philosophy of the "inner light." The ultimate guide and final arbiter in Northon's metaphysics is conscience, and his definition of conscience points clearly to the eros as its point of reference.[25]

To sum up, what this study has sought to demonstrate is that the motif of encounter is of signal importance because of its role as a dramatic device for the instrumentation of the basic tenets of Zuckmayer's **Weltanschauung.** The analysis of the underlying motif in the individual dramas has brought into focus the dominant pattern of the two phases of Zuckmayer's more reflective period (1933-). This was seen as a shift primarily from encounter leading to a recognition of an ultimate reality in the pan-erotic and mystical sense to recognition of love in an ethical sense.

Intrinsic to the nature of the motif, as interpreted by Kayser,[26] is the employment of the double aspect of concreteness and symbolism. In these terms, the concrete characteristic of the motif is shown in the encounter per se (whether that be intra-personal, transcendental, or self-transcendental) and in the resulting recognition. Dramaturgically, logically enough, encounter here has an important structural function through its employment at the focal or turning point of a given drama in either the inner action or outer action or both. Symbolically, the motif precipitates the dramatic goal which the hero or heroine tends to reach at the very end of the dramas: a symbolical recognition through the encounter-phenomenon of the life-force per se. This dramatic outcome reflects Zuckmayer's deepest conviction of the healing effects arising from man's embrace of either the microcosmic or macrocosmic whole or of both:

> . . . wir sind auf der Welt nicht allein. Vom Lebendigen allezeit umgeben, von der Erdnatur umschlungen und durchtränkt, in kosmische und astrale Relationen bewusstlos einbezogen, der menschlichen Gesellschaft bewusst und immerfort verantwortlich, weist jeder, auch der einsamste Einzel-Weg, auf die Begegnung hin. . . . Und nur darauf kommt es an. Nur daraus erwächst uns eine Gewissheit auf unseren ungesicherten, unbekannten Wegen. Es gibt die liebende Begegnung auf dieser Welt. Es gibt die Freude. Es gibt die Freundschaft. Es gibt das Vertrauen.[27]

Finally, it should be pointed out that there is little doubt that in his latest dramas Zuckmayer's high sense of responsibility for creating a new moral climate for our time is developed at the expense of poetic and dramatic values. But even in this esthetically unattractive form, Zuckmayer may perhaps be making a real contribution to the solution of modern man's predicament. The haunting question of modern man's separateness and loneliness is resolved by Zuckmayer through the encounter-phenomenon reflecting the natural eros drive. Man is never alone, since the contents of the universe are in him and envelop him in a "vieltönige, orchestrale Koordinatensystem des Irdischen und des Ausserirdischen, Geschöpflichen und Schöpferischen, Göttlichen und Menschlichen."[28] It is through the catalysis of the encounter-phenomenon, then, that the individual's potentials are quickened to an attainment of a sense of belonging, a trust-in-life and a metaphysical knowledge of wholeness. The attainment of these realities in life does not require acceptance of Zuckmayer's pantheism or any particular philosophy or religion. For, in a somewhat oversimplified form, Zuckmayer's message is this: In experience together, when men react sincerely from their natural depths they are actually one, or at least they perceive how they can be at-one.

Notes

1. See Arnold J. Jacobius, "Das Schauspiel Carl Zuckmayers: Wesen, Gehalt und Beziehung zu dem Gesamtwerk," m. Bibliographie 1920-1954 (diss. New York University, 1955).

   Murray B. Peppard, "Moments of Moral Decision: Carl Zuckmayer's Latest Plays," *Monatshefte,* XLIV (November, 1952), 349-356; "Carl Zuckmayer: Cold Light in a Divided World," *Monatshefte,* XLIX (March, 1957), 121-129.

   Ingeborg Engelsing-Malek, *"Amor Fati" in Zuckmayers Dramen* (Konstanz: Rosgarten Verlag, 1960).

2. This analysis is based on the dramatic *oeuvre,* since it is Zuckmayer's most congenial and chief creative vehicle. It should be noted, however, that the phenomenon of encounter also plays a significant role in Zuckmayer's prose fiction.

3. Cf. Wolfgang Kayser, *Das sprachliche Kunstwerk* (Bern: Francke Verlag, 1948), p. 70.

4. For a more detailed exposition of Zuckmayer's *Weltanschauung* see my "Carl Zuckmayer's Theory of Aesthetics," *Monatshefte,* LII (April-May, 1960), 163-170.

5. Cf. Johannes Urzidil, "Zuckmayer und die Natur," *Fülle der Zeit, Carl Zuckmayer und sein Werk* (Frankfurt a/M: Fischer, 1956), p. 114.

6. Carl Zuckmayer, *Second Wind* (London: Harrap, 1941), p. 239; *Die Brüder Grimm, ein deutscher Beitrag zur Humanität* (Frankfurt a/M: Suhrkamp, 1948), p. 19.

7. Zuckmayer, *Die langen Wege, ein Stück Rechenschaft* (Frankfurt a/M: Fischer, 1952), pp. 45-50.

8. Zuckmayer, "Schinderhannes," *Die deutschen Dramen* (Frankfurt a/M: Fischer, 1951), p. 59.

9. Zuckmayer, "Katherina Knie," *Komödie und Volksstück* (Frankfurt a/M: Fischer, 1950), p. 168.

10. I am indebted to Mrs. Engelsing for this view. Op. cit., p. 63.

11. Zuckmayer, "Der Schelm von Bergen," *Komödie un Volksstück,* p. 193.

12. *Der Schelm von Bergen,* p. 214.

13. *Die langen Wege,* p. 49.

14. Idem.

15. Idem.

16. Ibid., p. 121.

17. *Der Schelm von Bergen,* p. 245.

18. Ibid., p. 254.

19. *Die langen Wege,* p. 51.

20. Peppard, *Moments of Moral Decision,* p. 351.

21. I am indebted to Jaspers for the concept of transcendental guilt. Karl Jaspers, *Die Schuldfrage. Ein Beitrag zur deutschen Frage* (Zürich: Artemis, 1946), p. 10.

22. Zuckmayer, "Des Teufels General," *Die deutschen Dramen,* pp. 377-378.

23. Zuckmayer, *Barbara Blomberg* (Amsterdam: Bermann-Fischer, 1948), p. 217.

24. Zuckmayer, *Ulla Winblad oder Musik und Leben des Carl Michael* Bellman (Frankfurt a/M: Fischer, 1953), p. 37. Zuckmayer himself, through the ecstasy induced by intoxicants, reaches out toward the transcendental unifying eros force which provides an intuition of divine essence for him.

25. Zuckmayer, *Das kalte Licht,* (Frankfurt a/M: Fischer, 1955), p. 138.

26. Kayser, p. 63.

27. *Die langen Wege,* pp. 46, 51.

28. Ibid., p. 45.

Siegfried Mews (essay date fall 1972)

SOURCE: Mews, Siegfried. "From Karl May to Horace A. W. Tabor: Carl Zuckmayer's View of America." *Mosaic* 6, no. 1 (fall 1972): 125-42.

[*In the following essay, Mews observes Zuckmayer's allusions to American culture and society in such dramas as* Das Leben des Horace A. W. Tabor *and* Das kalte Licht, *as well as in his essay "Amerika ist anders."*]

> "Er hatte die Fehler seines Volkes und die Tugenden eines Menschen."
>
> ("He shared the faults of his people and possessed the virtues of a man.")

With this rhetorical flourish Carl Zuckmayer ended his address, entitled **"Amerika ist anders,"**[1] in which he set out to interpret the phenomenon of the American to his German-speaking audience. Interestingly, the tribute Zuckmayer pays to the American people whom he had come to know fairly well during his years of exile in the U.S. is taken from the epitaph of the Indian Chingachgook in the last chapter of James Fenimore Cooper's Leatherstocking Tale *The Pioneers* (1823).[2]

At first glance, it may come as somewhat of a surprise to see an Indian elevated to the position of the prototypal American; an Indian, moreover, whose entirely fictional character would seem to make him ill-suited to serve as a model for modern American man. Yet, on closer inspection of Carl Zuckmayer's *oeuvre* it becomes quite obvious that his view and concept of America is, to a large extent, determined by his fascination with the frontier world of the American Indian. To be more explicit: it is not so much the Indian as encountered in historical, anthropological, folkloristic accounts or other scholarly works, but rather the Indian of prose fiction.

It was James Fenimore Cooper with his Leatherstocking Tales who helped shape and influence Zuckmayer's image of America—a debt which was indirectly acknowledged by the writer himself.[3] However, far more influential with regard to Zuckmayer's concept of the New World was the redoubtable Karl May—without doubt the young Zuckmayer's main source of information on matters American. True, Zuckmayer was in good company in his admiration for Karl May, but few writers of stature so wholeheartedly embraced and even emulated the most popular promulgator of fictional lore about the Wild West as did Zuckmayer.[4]

Almost five years after the young writer's first and unsuccessful attempt to conquer the Berlin stage with his drama *Kreuzweg* (10 December 1920, Staatstheater), the budding dramatist repeated his venture with *Pankraz erwacht.*[5] Although Zuckmayer claims: "Brecht fand es [the drama *Pankraz erwacht*] gut—es war mein einziges, das unter seinem Einfluss entstanden ist" [*A Part of Myself*][6]—one may, upon reading the play in question, attribute at least some validity to the ironic interjection of one discerning spectator at the premiere of *Pankraz erwacht.* The anonymous spectator shouted: "Hoch lebe Karl May."[7]

It can hardly be denied that the setting of the play which is subtitled **"Ein Stück aus dem Fernen Westen"** and takes place "in einem balladesken Pionier-Amerika"[8] exhibits a close affinity to the fictional Wild West as encountered in the novels of Karl May. It is the atmosphere of exotic escape literature which pervades *Pankraz erwacht.* Apart from the milieu, traces of Karl May's influence may also be discovered in the anti-Yankee, pro-Indian and pro-Negro sentiments expressed in the play, in the implicit condemnation of the lust for gold, in the strong representation of the German element among the *dramatis personae,* and in the friendship between the old scout Florymont and the Sioux Teton Osage—who is endowed with traits of the noble savage. Without doubt, this friendship between two males of differing races is derived from the literary models of both Cooper's Natty Bumppo and Chingachgook and Karl May's Old Shatterhand and Winnetou. Even Zuckmayer's highly idiosyncratic use of English words and phrases—the most flagrant example of which is perhaps the use of "Good by" [sic] in addressing arriving rather than departing guests[9]—can be traced to Karl May.

It should not be overlooked, however, that one would do great injustice to Zuckmayer's play were one to declare it to be nothing but a dramatic adaptation of themes and motifs to be found in Karl May's fictional world. In at least one respect Carl Zuckmayer departs radically from his revered model: in his explicit treatment of sex, including incest and miscegenation. This topic was deliberately shunned by both Cooper and Karl May who wanted to preserve their heroes' pristine innocence.

Precisely the pervasiveness of sex and violence in *Pankraz erwacht* offers a clue to Zuckmayer's somewhat enigmatic remark, quoted above, as to Brecht's influence on his play. Brecht's early plays *Trommeln in der Nacht, Baal,* and *Im Dickicht* [*der Städte*] with which Zuckmayer was familiar, were interpreted by him to possess less a social and revolutionary impetus ("sozialrevolutionäres Element") than "anarchischen Vitalismus" and even a "heidnisch-religiösen, naturmythischen Zug" ("a religious note of pagan nature myth").[10] Pankraz, the hero of the play, exhibits exactly the traits Zuckmayer attributes to Brecht's early plays in general: overwhelming vitality as the source of pronounced sexuality and a close affinity to nature, a mystical bond between man and nature.

Yet, the analogies between *Pankraz erwacht* and, for example, *Im Dickicht* which also takes place in an American milieu, are not entirely compelling. Brecht's very choice of the "Riesenstadt Chicago" with its alienation caused by social factors is in stark contrast to Zuckmayer's backwoods in which man communicates with nature. As Herbert Ihering perceptively remarked, there remains a fundamental difference:

> Wenn Brecht im 'Dickicht' selten der Exotik als romantischer Ausflucht verfällt, wenn seine Sprache die Situation der Personen aufreisst, so gibt Zuckmayer [in *Pankraz erwacht*] keine Auseinandersetzung mit der Welt, sondern Weltflucht. Und je wilder es zugeht, desto schwächer und dünner wird die dichterische Persönlichkeit.[11]

Zuckmayer's strengths tended to become weaknesses, Ihering claimed: "seine Derbheit, seine Drastik, seine Leidenschaft [grenzt] oft an Kraftmeierei."[12] Indeed, there is a sufficient display of unabashed machismo to justify Ihering's claim: witness for example the following stanza of the "nordamerikanisches Holzfällerlied." In its defiant glorification of forthright virility it smacks of the "billige Sexualität" which Brecht was to castigate later in his "Anmerkungen zum Volksstück," and it lacks the redeeming virtue of social concern which can be discerned even in Brecht's early plays:

> Horch, wir stampfen auf den Flössen,
> Durch den Fluss mit starken Stössen
> Wie man auch die Weiber stösst,
> Wenn sie sich auf unsern Schössen
> Ihre weisse Brust entblössen
> und ihr Haar sich löst.[13]

In retrospect, Carl Zuckmayer judged his play, which he did not deem worthy to be included in his *Gesammelte Werke* "ein ungegorenes, ungleichmässiges Stück,

mit skizzenhafter Fabel, ohne Proportion und Mass."[14] The critics were hardly more charitable in their pronouncements on Carl Zuckmayer's first dramatic effort in which he sought to come to terms with the phenomenon America; the famous Alfred Kerr summed up his verdict in the terse phrase: "Stück und Autor können wir getrost vergessen."[15]

Alfred Kerr was only partially right, however. To be sure, *Pankraz erwacht* fell into almost total oblivion, but the spectacular rise of the dramatist Zuckmayer who, as a consequence of the disaster he experienced with *Pankraz erwacht,* had decided to follow less extravagant, exotic and more natural, realistic dramatic goals,[16] was to begin less than a year later with the hugely successful Berlin premiere of *Der fröhliche Weinberg* on 22 December 1925.

But before he embarked on a course that was to produce the major plays of the late twenties and early thirties, culminating in *Der Hauptmann von Köpenick* (1931), and bid a temporary farewell to the artistic treatment of the New World, Carl Zuckmayer once more indulged in his predilection for the American Indian. This predilection went so far that his daughter was given the name of Winnetou in 1926—ample testimony of Carl Zuckmayer's infatuation with Karl May.

In *Sitting Bull. Ein Indianer-Roman,* which originated somewhat later than *Pankraz erwacht,*[17] elements of the *Entwicklungsroman,* the adventure story à la Karl May, and *littérature engagée* are mingled. The novel is fragmentary; in all likelihood it was not completed because Carl Zuckmayer had felt the need to deal with subject matter and themes that, corresponding to the dramatist's newly-found artistic creed, were more firmly rooted in the German reality as he had experienced it.[18] On the whole, the incomplete novel is a more mature work than *Pankraz erwacht*; the sensational aspects such as incest, miscegenation, and blatant displays of masculinity are either absent or appear muted. In short, the very fact that Zuckmayer chose a historical figure as the hero of his narrative, and the planned inclusion of such historical events as Custer's last stand in 1876, seem to point in the direction of a stronger emphasis on facts rather than fiction in Zuckmayer's artistic presentation of America. According to the outline of the novel, it was intended to depict the development of Sitting Bull from "Jugend, Mannbarkeit, Wachstum . . . im Wechsel von Witterung und Landschaft" to his death in the "Einsamkeit winterlicher Hochgebirge."[19] The novel was also designed to deal with the larger issues of the Indian's struggle against the white man. Sitting Bull is sympathetically drawn and he clearly emerges as the defender of the Indian's just cause, as the champion of the Indian's fight against his exploitation, expropriation, and extinction by the white man who, for the most part, is depicted as cruel, greedy, and filled with race prejudice. To be sure, the positive portrayal of the Indian had a well-established tradition in European literature; yet in endowing a historical figure with the traditional traits of the noble savage and presenting the white men as villains (again borrowing from literary tradition)[20] Carl Zuckmayer inadvertently became a precursor of a kind of semi-documentary fiction such as Dee Brown's *Bury my Heart at Wounded Knee* which only now, almost a century after the West was won, seeks to dispel the myths which the conquest of Indian territory had generated.

It is not very likely that Carl Zuckmayer consciously used historical accounts written from the Indian's point of view; the fact remains that a writer who had never set foot on American soil anticipated in his partisanship for the lost cause of the original American, who also appears as a better human being because of his ecological concern,[21] recent trends to establish a historically accurate picture of the westward expansion, a picture which is less biased in favor of the white man.

Carl Zuckmayer's role as friend and champion of the red man should not be exaggerated, however. As has been mentioned before, the writer is primarily indebted to fiction for his concept of the American West. This can be most clearly seen in the figure of the scout Florymont who makes his appearance in both *Pankraz erwacht* and *Sitting Bull.* Old Florymont distinctly resembles Cooper's Natty Bumppo, the hunter and scout who is friend of the Indians, shuns "civilized" regions with their despoiled nature and longs for the freedom of the wilderness. Even individual incidents such as the prairie fire are patterned after Cooper.[22]

Indeed, the American West of James Fenimore Cooper and Karl May continued to occupy the dramatist who had, since the performance of *Der fröhliche Weinberg,* became one of the foremost dramatists of the Golden Twenties by producing plays which were far removed from the world of the trapper and the Indian.

In 1929 the self-styled "Halb-Indianer und Karl-May-Philologe"[23] Carl Zuckmayer enthusiastically professed his great admiration for Karl May's achievements in the realm of fiction and specifically rejected "die Frage nach der Wahrscheinlichkeit"[24] as irrelevant in the face of Karl May's creation of "eine Welt . . . , deren geheime, innere Wahrheit über die greifbare und sichtbare Wirklichkeit triumphiert."[25] This world, Carl Zuckmayer asserted, had assumed the dimensions of a myth comparable to or even surpassing that created by Homer. Although Carl Zuckmayer's unequivocal endorsement should be taken with a grain of salt, because it was directed at a youthful and somewhat uncritical reading public, his approval and admiration must be taken as genuine and sincere expressions of long-held views. The two articles in which he expounded those views are merely theoretical formulations of the author's sentiments as they are to be encountered in both *Pankraz erwacht* and *Sitting Bull.* In particular, one might single out the narrative technique of the "Ich-Form . . . seiner [Karl Mays] Erzählungen,"[26] which encouraged the complete identification of reader and hero, and the theme of "Kampf für den Indianer, sein [Karl Mays] Gefühl für diese prachtvolle, noble und wehrlos zu Boden getretene Menschenrasse."[27] Clearly, a mode of presentation—whether in prose narrative or drama—which allowed for close identification of spectator/reader and hero would strike a most responsive chord in a dramatist who never was to adhere to detached objectivity, scientific analysis or Brecht's theory of "Verfremdung." If we are to believe Carl Zuckmayer's account, his own responses as a spectator on the occasion of the dramatized *Winnetou's* performance were highly emotional and totally lacked critical detachment.[28] As to the pro-Indian sentiments, we have seen in the case of *Sitting Bull* that Carl Zuckmayer wholeheartedly adopted Karl May's view of the Indian.

Once more, if only in passing, did Carl Zuckmayer pay tribute to Karl May. The short story *Die Affenhochzeit,* written and first published in 1932,[29] provides an interesting adaptation of his admired model to the conditions of contemporary Berlin. The parvenu ostentation, crass materialism, and unenlightened self-interest of the Berlin bourgeoisie are effectively contrasted with the natural, unaffected, humane behavior of the artist Georg Rottenbach and his friends. Significantly, Georg Rottenbach has a *nom de guerre* derived from the "Welt des kindlichen Abenteuers."[30] Both "Fährtensucher," the very word with which the story begins, and its English equivalent, pathfinder, evoke associations of trappers and Indians. Moreover, Georg's friends, whose "Kriegsnamen" are taken from the novels of Karl May—his name is explicitly mentioned—congregate around a symbolic "Lagerfeuer" and swap stories which are not intended for delicate female ears. Not surprisingly, at a social gala affair the camp fire companions begin, inspired by having imbibed immeasurable quantities of alcohol, a "Revolution des guten Geschmacks, des Geistes und Herzens, des menschlichen Taktgefühls"[31] against the supercilious, shallow parody of true learning perpetrated by one of the guests.

The employment of fictional characters who have preserved their essentially Mayan traits—such as youthful enthusiasm, sincerity, and defiance of social convention—amidst a sophisticated and complex urban environment indicates that, although Carl Zuckmayer had lost none of his infatuation with Karl May, he did, in accordance with his general development, "domesticate" his characters by transferring them to a recognizable contemporary setting.

It can be said then that during the first phase of the writer's creativity (from approximately 1920 to 1933)

Karl May remained virtually unchallenged as the main source for Carl Zuckmayer's notions concerning the New World. The almost exclusive reliance on Karl May was only abated by the fact that, in the late twenties and early thirties, the writer enlarged his vision by becoming an active intermediary in the service of "Weltliteratur" through his adaptations of Anderson's and Stalling's *What Price Glory* in 1929[32] and Hemingway's *A Farewell to Arms*[33] in 1931. Pauline Steiner and Horst Frenz[34] have advanced convincing arguments in support of their opinion that Carl Zuckmayer did not merely translate but actually adapted *What Price Glory* by altering "characters, language, and structure of the original"[35] in order to reinforce its latent anti-war and anti-military tendencies. As Carl Zuckmayer himself includes his adaptation among the "Handwerksarbeiten, Fingerübungen, Etüden"[36] preparatory to his masterpiece, *Der Hauptmann von Köpenick,* one may safely conclude that it was the play's inherent anti-war tendency rather than its "Americanness" which motivated him to undertake his adaptation. After all, since Erich-Maria Remarque's *Im Westen nichts Neues* (1929), novels and plays critical of the military establishment were in vogue and *Der Hauptmann von Köpenick* itself with its satire directed against the military and bureaucratic order may be seen in this light. Similarly, despite Carl Zuckmayer's retrospective assertion that he and Heinz Hilpert made "eine Dramatisierung des Romans 'In einem anderen Land' (A Farewell to Arms) von Ernest Hemingway, hauptsächlich weil Käthe Dorsch die Gestalt der 'Kat' verkörpern wollte,"[37] it probably comes closer to the truth that the dramatist saw in Hemingway's novel the expression of views and convictions which he himself held at a time when his *Hauptmann von Köpenick* conquered the stages of Berlin and Germany.[38] At any rate, in 1931 Carl Zuckmayer had professed his admiration for the "so schnell berühmt gewordenen Roman"[39] and its creator and had minimized his own role by distinguishing between his "deutsche Nachdichtung" of *What Price Glory,* and the less creative task of "eine rein dramaturgische Arbeit"[40] in the case of Hemingway.

While the close acquaintance with and active mediation of contemporary American literature undoubtedly broadened Carl Zuckmayer's perspective vis-à-vis the phenomenon America, it should be borne in mind that the two works in question, because of their European settings, convey genuine, indigenous American experiences to only a limited extent. Further, the process of adaptation *per se* resulted in a loss of "Americanness"; apart from Zuckmayer's difficulties with authentic American English in *What Price Glory,*[41] the dramatist endowed his adaptation with "die naiv-animalische Feier muskelstarker und gedankenarmer Männlichkeit . . . Freude am herzhaft Muskulären"[42]—traits which are a Zuckmayer hallmark as has been noted by many critics.[43]

Carl Zuckmayer's purely theoretical knowledge about the New World was eventually to be replaced by a thorough first-hand acquaintance. After having been exiled from Germany proper and having been forced to flee his last domicile in Austria, the banished writer ultimately found himself in the country which had occupied such a prominent place in his imagination. Ironically, Zuckmayer professes not to have felt any desire to embark on the voyage to the New World. As a dyed-in-the-wool European he shared in all the current prejudices about the land that was first to become his sanctuary and eventually his new home. In 1938, from the comparatively safe haven of a Zürich tavern, America appeared to be

> Ein Land ohne Tradition, ohne Kultur, ohne Drang nach Schönheit oder Form, ohne Metaphysik und ohne Weinstuben, ein Land des Kunstdüngers und der Büchsenöffner, ohne Grazie und ohne Misthaufen, ohne Klassik und ohne Schlamperei, ohne Melos, ohne Apoll, ohne Dionysos.[44]

The dictum **"Amerika ist anders"**[45] proved true in a twofold sense: not only was America different from Europe but it also did not correspond to the preconceived notions of the newly arrived émigré Zuckmayer who, shortly before setting foot on American soil, had directed part of his creative efforts towards the mythical American past in the "Filmnovelle 'Pocahontas.'"[46] The New World still seemed to be a "wild continent" full of adventures, and the frontier spirit was far from extinct. Thus it looks as if Carl Zuckmayer's youthful notions of America as a land full of unexpected adventures and surprising happenings had been confirmed and his more recently acquired ideas of an overly civilized, antiseptic and mechanistic society had been proved false. Paradoxically, it was the dramatist's confrontation with the dangerous and sensational metropolis New York rather than his encounter with the Wild West which provided the impetus for the formulation of his initial reaction. After all, the once proud and fierce Indians of the West whom Zuckmayer saw had been completely domesticated and were performing war dances for the tourists. The fleeting vision of genuine cowboys provided but a poor substitute for the regret Zuckmayer must have felt at the sight of the degenerate state in which the heroes of his youth lived.[47]

There is no need to retell the trials and tribulations the author underwent upon arrival in America as the autobiography *Als wär's ein Stück von mir* offers a vivid account of these years. Suffice it to state that the writer's attempts to become established on the American literary scene, including his dismal experience in Hollywood, failed.[48] In contrast to many of his fellow exiled writers, who were similarly unsuccessful in making a living by means of their pen,[49] Carl Zuckmayer had the courage to temporarily abandon his literary career and start all over again as a farmer. This radical new departure, which Zuckmayer considered a typically American trait was, without doubt, in the spirit of the enterprising and undaunted pioneers.[50] The only difference between the old pioneers and the new one was that in Zuckmayer's case the Western plains were replaced by the Eastern hills of Vermont and that the tame goat had to serve as a substitute for the wild, roaming buffalo.

The hard existence as a Vermont farmer was not very conducive to literary effort. As Carl Zuckmayer remarked sardonically: "Die Kombination 'Dichter und Bauer' [gehört] unabänderlich der Opernwelt [an]."[51] Yet during this time he managed to create one of the greatest successes of post-World-War II German theatre—*Des Teufels General.* Many critics marveled at how faithfully the exiled writer had recaptured the atmosphere prevailing in a segment of German society at the beginning of World War II.[52] The hugely positive reception the play received can be attributed to the fact that it is eminently a "German" play which depicts the predicament of many Germans in a crucial period of their history in a sympathetic, non-accusatory way. It is safe to say then that the only major work to originate in Carl Zuckmayer's years of exile reflects his preoccupation with the fate of Germany rather than with that of America. Nevertheless, there are distinct indications that the dramatist's extended exposure to America had left its mark. In the minor figure of the American journalist Buddy Lawrence, who appears in the second act of the play, the dramatist has for the first time drawn a genuine contemporary American. His main function is to provide a wholesome contrast to the perverted mentality of many Germans on which Nazism thrived and which Zuckmayer had branded as an extremely dangerous state of mind before.[53] As Harras, who exhibits many character traits of Zuckmayer himself,[54] says:

> Ach, Buddy'wie man sich manchmal sehnt—nach einem simplen Volk ohne Wahn- und Aberwitz. Nach Fussballern, Monteuren, Gummikauern, Kindsköpfen. Wie man es über hat, die Wichtigkeit, die Bedeutung, den Todesrausch, das gespaltene Innenleben, den faustischen Geldbriefträger, den dämonischen Blockwart. Die Halbbildung hat uns den Unterleib mit Metaphysik erfüllt und den Kopf mit Darmgasen. Das Unverdauliche zieht uns hinab.[55]

Without doubt, Carl Zuckmayer simplified matters by contrasting in prototypal fashion the unsophisticated American people to the philosophically inclined Germans. Further, he betrays his wishful thinking by repeatedly having the American journalist express his unrequited love for Germany. The comparatively minor role of Buddy Lawrence and his function as the author's mouthpiece offer a clear indication of Zuckmayer's real concern during the years of World War II. Not the desire to formulate his new experiences on American soil but rather grave concern for Germany provided the most powerful stimulus for the writer.

This preoccupation with German affairs could also take the form of nostalgia. In the tale *Der Seelenbräu,* written at the beginning of 1945, Carl Zuckmayer evoked "das verlorene Paradies Henndorf [near Salzburg]."[56] Any evocation of the past would be incomplete without mentioning "playing Indians" which, similarly to its function in *Die Affenhochzeit,* signifies in *Der Seelenbräu* revolt against established tradition and authority.[57] One is faced with the curious phenomenon that the exiled writer reminisces, if only in passing, in the land of the real Indians about the fictional Indians of his youth. Even in the profoundly serious *Des Teufels General* there are allusions to them.[58]

While Zuckmayer's major creative efforts in the war years were primarily directed towards a (future) German reading public, one should not totally overlook his endeavors to acquaint the American public with German affairs and, in particular, to draw attention to the existence of the "other Germany."[59] Zuckmayer's services as an intermediary in America were necessarily limited. As has been noted before, the lack of leisure, the absence of a sound economic basis for writing, linguistic difficulties and other factors prevented Zuckmayer from becoming established either in the American theater or on the book market. More favorable circumstances prevailed upon the dramatist's return to war-ravaged Germany in 1946. As a civilian employee of the U.S. War Department he had occasion to study whatever was left of intellectual and cultural life in postwar Germany. *Des Teufels General* itself, once the Allied Authorities permitted it to be performed in Germany proper after its Zürich world premiere in December 1946, constituted one of the most incisive and significant contributions to the new German theatre.

Apart from the writing of original plays and prose works,[60] Carl Zuckmayer continued his activities as a literary intermediary. In 1947, Carl Zuckmayer's adaptation of John van Druten's Broadway success *I Remember Mama* was performed in the "Zürcher Schauspielhaus" under the title *Die Unvergessliche.*[61] The American version of the play was in turn based on Kathryn Forbes' [Kathryn McLean's] novel *Mama's Bank Account* (1943). Its appeal can be explained in terms of "the common human experience," i.e., the extolling of the virtues of family life and the depiction of the "basic things in human life."[62] Certainly, the "recognized ingredients for a popular success" such as "sex, . . . love interest, . . . suspense"[63] were lacking in this portrayal of a Norwegian immigrant family in San Francisco around 1910. The play presents a curious contrast to the profoundly moving drama *Des Teufels General* because, as the critic of the *Neue Zürcher Zeitung* correctly noted, there was a notable lack of "Erschütterung, Verstrickung" in the play which was chiefly concerned with "Harmlosigkeiten."[64] Although John van Druten acknowledged his indebtedness to Thornton

Wilder with regard to the use of a narrator,[65] the employment of an innovative "epic" technique is not counterbalanced by, for example, a commensurate social awareness. It is idle to speculate why Carl Zuckmayer decided to adapt for the German stage a popular sentimental comedy rather than more incisive fare such as Thornton Wilder's plays which the American theatre had to offer; as the impressum of the printed German version suggests, it may have been a commission which the dramatist had to carry out for the U.S. government.[66] At any rate, the lot of the immigrants and the warmth, compassion, integrity, and resourcefulness of the mother may have struck a responsive chord in Carl Zuckmayer; the fact remains that the presentation of idyllic family life at the beginning of the century which is not even noticeably disturbed by upheavals in the socio-economic realm[67] was hardly designed to acquaint the German theater audience either with contemporary America or to afford it an objective view of its past. The merciful silence that prevails in Carl Zuckmayer's autobiography offers telling evidence concerning the adaptor's opinion of his work.

Far more consequential, because of the emotions it stirred up in Germany, was the film *Decision before Dawn* (1950) for which Carl Zuckmayer wrote the German screen play. The film, which in its German version was called *Entscheidung vor Morgengrauen* (1951),[68] treated the fate of a young German prisoner-of-war in 1945 who decided to engage in espionage for the Americans. This decision to work for the enemy and the subsequent acts of espionage of the young German are reminiscent of the actions of Oderbruch in *Des Teufels General.* In both cases the characters concerned accepted the stigma of traitor and the possibly fatal consequences in order to follow a moral imperative which bade them defy traditional concepts of loyalty and duty. In both cases Carl Zuckmayer defended the treason of the protagonists—stressing, however, "überparteiliche Wahrheitsliebe und Ehrlichkeit"[69] of the film. One may safely assume that it was not so much the "Americanness" which aroused Carl Zuckmayer's interest in the film but rather the complex problem of active resistance against an immoral authority, a problem which is also predominant in *Des Teufels General.* Other, though less significant, efforts to introduce American films to Germany in the early fifties were the German film scenarios Carl Zuckmayer produced for *The Moon is Blue* (*Die Jungfrau auf dem Dach,* 1952) and *The Man with the Golden Arm* (*Der Mann mit dem goldenen Arm,* 1955). The non-availability of texts makes it too difficult to comment on Carl Zuckmayer's achievement as a transmitter of U.S. movies; it should be recognized that these film scenarios, even if they do not constitute major creative efforts, testify to the fact of the dramatist's constant preoccupation with the American cultural scene.

In the early fifties Carl Zuckmayer's essay **"Amerika ist anders"** appeared.[70] It is the writer's most cohesive and extended treatment of America and seeks to dispel European prejudices by providing a balanced picture based on an intimate, first-hand knowledge. As has been noted before, Carl Zuckmayer did not escape the danger of romanticizing the New World through the employment of one James Fenimore Cooper's fictional characters as his spokesman. Yet the romantic view was supplemented by a more realistic vision as is evidenced by the project of an uncompleted comedy, *Mein neuer Vetter,* which was to deal with the fortunes of a German immigrant to the U.S. and the difficulties of his getting used to a totally different life style.[71] Only in 1955, almost ten years after *Des Teufels General,* do representatives of the New World reappear in a major work. The drama *Das kalte Licht* is on the surface a play about an exiled German scientist's betrayal of atomic secrets to the Soviet Union during World War II but actually about "die Krise des Vertrauens, . . . die Denk- und Vertrauenskrise der Gegenwart"[72] on an almost global scale. In keeping with his tendency to utilize actual happenings (the case of the atomic spy, Dr. Klaus Fuchs, comes readily to mind) for a dramatic presentation of far-reaching moral problems, Carl Zuckmayer employs a broadly developed realistic milieu which serves as the background for Kristof Wolters' treason and atonement. Part of this milieu is formed by the scenes taking place in the U.S. In II, 5 a species of American belonging to the lower strata of society is introduced: a bum in Central Park, New York City. To be sure, this bum has his counterparts in the German plays, e.g., in some of the down-and-out characters populating the **"Herberge zur Heimat"** in I, 6 of *Der Hauptmann von Köpenick.* Still, he is a man *sui generis* who, in contrast to his German counterparts, exhibits the spirit of independence peculiar to the citizen of a free country. Interestingly, Carl Zuckmayer composed the Bum scene originally in English, perhaps in the hopes of ultimately having the play translated and produced in the U.S.[73]

In the scenes taking place in Las Mesas (II, 6-8), the thinly disguised atomic research center Los Alamos, the group of international scientists, their staff, and families counts a sufficient number of naturalized or native American citizens among its members so that one can speak of a microcosm of American society, which exists in strictly enforced isolation. Needless to say, most of the *dramatis personae* are, because of their limited role, not fully rounded characters. They are, however, of interest to us because of the ideas and attitudes they represent. There is, first of all, the cultured and humanitarian director of the research center, Nikolas Löwenschild, a naturalized American of both German and Russian descent. Although he and his team were instrumental in producing the atom bomb, he fears the consequences of its use and hopes that it will never be employed. Another male character, the test pilot Roy, reiterates with conviction the thesis of civilian and legislative control over all warlike actions. Thus, by implication, one of the fundamental constitutional principles is praised. But the most telling opinion about America is offered by a representative of an ethnic minority, a "Halb- oder Viertelneger"[74] with the paradoxical (and unlikely) name Frederick Schiller Lee. The Negro's name is said to be derived from both the herald of freedom, Friedrich von Schiller, and the well-known general of the anti-abolitionist Confederacy, Robert E. Lee. Thus the bearer of this name is, in somewhat heavy-handed allusion, supposed to symbolize in his existence the inner contradictions of America itself. Noteworthy is Frederick Schiller Lee's belief in the redeeming and regenerative virtues of his country despite many personal disappointments: "Denn wir glauben an das Paradox Amerika, wir lieben es, und wir haben das Vertrauen, dass aus dem freien Spiel der Gegensätze das Schöne und Fruchtbare geboren wird in dieser Welt."[75] It is safe to assume that these words also express the author's belief in the fundamental vigor and adaptability of American society which would enable it to overcome all internal stresses.

The female characters round out the picture. Miss Fitch is the efficient secretary who is thoroughly at home in a world dominated by bureaucratic military regulations to such an extent that infants are automatically rotated through the playground facilities. Pretty, coquettish and naive, Precious does not much deviate in her brief appearances from the stereotype of a millionaire's spoiled daughter in Hollywood films. Only the Pueblo Indian Tsebaya, "die freundliche Ureinwohnerin"[76] as she is addressed by Löwenschild, is endowed with positive traits. Like previous Indians Zuckmayer created, she possesses the mystical-magical closeness to nature, her world is populated by the spirits of a naive and unspoiled imagination which sustains her. Her harmonious, balanced existence is in obvious contrast to that of the people around her whose tranquility is shattered when they reflect upon the consequences of their research activities.

In *Das kalte Licht* Carl Zuckmayer had considerably extended and deepened his depiction of contemporary American society—though it must not be overlooked that this depiction is only peripherally related to the central issues of the play. Nevertheless, there seems to be implicit praise for the American socio-political system which guarantees its members freedom of choice in contrast to the practice of the Soviet Union where the individual is totally subordinated to the collective.

An additional minor facet was added in *Die Uhr schlägt eins* (1961). In the highly improbable "historisches Drama aus der Gegenwart," as the play is subtitled, Zuckmayer sought to compress a dramatic presentation of all the moral and spiritual problems, including those related to the "unbewältigte Vergangenheit," which be-

set the materially affluent German "economic miracle" society of the early fifties. The U.S. Army is not shown here in its most favorable light. Its only member to appear briefly in the play (and, for that matter, the only American) is the not quite appropriately named Negro sergeant Sloppy, who is also a boxer. Unlike the refined and unblemished Frederick Schiller Lee in *Das kalte Licht,* Sloppy is the corrupt protector of Turo von Heydenkamp and his gang to whom he sells arms and ammunition. The severity of Carl Zuckmayer's indictment of criminal practices in the U.S. Army is lessened by extenuating circumstances for Sloppy: with his dishonest gains he wants to settle in Paris. Understandably, "Von Alabama hat er genug."[77]

The foregoing observations have shown that, beginning with *Des Teufels General,* Carl Zuckmayer paid increasing attention to problems of topical interest. In such plays as *Der Gesang im Feuerofen, Das kalte Licht, Die Uhr schlägt eins,* there either are no representatives of the New World to be found or they do not play a major role. Only after having reestablished his permanent residence in Europe did Carl Zuckmayer write a work which reflects the dramatist's American experience. The one-act-play *Kranichtanz,* published in 1961[78] but not performed until 1967, was generally praised as a realistic, well-motivated play.[79] The New England scene and the rural characters which inhabit it are reminiscent of Carl Zuckmayer's days as a farmer in Vermont. The play provides a lot of local color, particularly through the frequent use of not fully integrated English words.[80] But in a sense the generation conflict between Loren King and his son Dave, as well as the tragic triangular situation Rhoda Atwood finds herself in, transcend the geographical and chronological limitations imposed upon it and lend it a more universal validity.

It is a different matter with *Das Leben des Horace A. W. Tabor* (1964). Here the dramatist seized upon a uniquely and genuinely American subject matter: the hero's authentic, swift rise from rags to riches (and his downfall). Little wonder that this topic was recommended to the newly-arrived immigrant as one that would insure his success on the American stage. Carl Zuckmayer's preoccupation with the fate of Germany during his stay in the U.S. during World War II prevented him from dealing with indigenous material. The wheel had almost come full circle; the dramatist returned to his early love, the fascinating "Buntheit und Abenteuerlichkeit" of the West in the frontier and post-frontier days. But the writer was careful to disclaim any elements of "Wildwest-Romantik"[81] in his play. Rather than indulging in unbridled exoticism as in *Pankraz erwacht,* Carl Zuckmayer endeavored to depict realistically the Colorado milieu in the seventies and eighties of the nineteenth century—the milieu in which Horace A. W. Tabor rose to economic power and political prominence, only to be forced to return to his humble beginnings. At the same time, however, the dramatist insisted on making the reality on stage transparent by transcending the naturalistically specific times and places of the action and transforming them into "die Zeit der grossen Improvisationen" and "die Welt der unerhörten Glücksfälle, der enormen Verluste."[82] As the subtitle of the play, "a play from the days of the last kings," indicates, it is the atmosphere of the fairy tale, in which riches and power are magically bestowed upon the pure in heart, that pervades the drama.

In the last analysis, neither the employment of elements of the realistic-naturalistic theater in which "man pokert, säuft, schlingt Essen hinunter"[83] nor the fairy tale characteristics satisfied the critics. As Petra Kipphoff observed, the objections raised against Zuckmayer's play are both of a formal-structural and a thematic nature.[84] One could not, such astute critics as Friedrich Luft implied, continue writing naively realistic plays as if there had never been a Brecht, Beckett, or Ionesco.[85] Further, the evasion of contemporary issues and the flight into both a seemingly uncomplicated and exotic past in which men like Tabor were not basically affected by either personal disaster or far-reaching social changes, aroused many critics' ire. *Der Spiegel,* not known for putting things too delicately, recommended the drama to the "Children's Hour"[86] of the German broadcasting companies. Marianne Kesting deplored the almost total lack "einer politischen, sozialen oder psychologischen Analyse" and accused Carl Zuckmayer of formulating "einen Stoff, wie er in der amerikanischen Filmindustrie heute zum Aufbau des amerikanischen Mythos benutzt wird."[87] It is true, the dramatist fails singularly to come to grips with the social dimension determining the life-styles and behaviors of the characters in the play. His tentative attempts to replace the world of Karl May in **Pankraz erwacht** by that of Karl Marx in **Tabor** are often inadequate and unintentionally comical. It is rather strange, to say the very least, to encounter the Marxist "Bonanzamillionär" Stratton who indulges in such upper-class diversions as playing poker for extremely high stakes with the very rich "um das Verhalten der Ausbeuter zu studieren."[88] In addition, Stratton offers to bail out Tabor financially as a kind of reward for Tabor's "class-conscious" behavior during his days as a capitalist exploiter when he had bloodily suppressed a justified strike with his private army.[89]

As the foregoing discussion has shown, Carl Zuckmayer does not convey to his German readers and theater public an image of America that would strike one as particularly modern or "relevant." The frequently reiterated predilection for the pre-industrialized, non-urban, somewhat primitive and exotic America of the Pioneer and the Indian pervades the writer's entire work.[90] Not surprisingly, there is little room for the problems besetting a complex, urban society. If such questions as racial discrimination, social injustice, misuse of political, economic, or military power are raised at all, they are usually answered only perfunctorily. One may find the picture Zuckmayer presents of America and its inhabitants deficient and, perhaps, even a bit simplistic. But then, unlike his contemporary and erstwhile friend Bert Brecht, Carl Zuckmayer never professed to be a socially or politically engagé writer. Rather, he considered it his main task to promote by dramatic and theatrical means

> die Wiederherstellung der menschlichen Gestalt in ihrer Ganzheit, in ihrer Bezogenheit aufs Weltganze, in ihrem kreatürlichen und kosmischen Zusammenhang, nicht analytisch zerlegt, nicht von den Parolen und Forderungen des Tages einseitig verzerrt, sondern in Verhängnis und Gnade. . . .[91]

Whether one agrees with Carl Zuckmayer's views or not, one owes respect to a writer who, in the face of quickly changing dramatic fads has remained faithful to both his fundamental concern and his essential mode of artistic expression—a writer who in his portrayal of the New World deeply believed in the fundamental strength of American society which would enable it to return to the virtues of the past and eventually to overcome all ills besetting it.

Notes

1. "Ein Vortrag gehalten am 10. November 1948 im Auditorium Maximum der Züricher Universität." First published in *Neue Schweizer Rundschau,* N.F. 16/8 (December 1948), 451-474, and repeatedly thereafter. The concluding words quoted above are missing in *Neue Schweizer Rundschau*; they appear in the subsequent editions I was able to check. In the following, this edition will be quoted: *Interview mit Amerika,* ed. Alfred Gong (München, 1962), pp. 381-412.

2. James Fenimore Cooper, *The Pioneers.* Afterword by Robert E. Spiller (New York: Signet Books, 1964), p. 431: ". . . and it may be said of him [Chingachgook] that his faults were those of an Indian and his virtues those of a man." Zuckmayer is in error in his assumption that "Lederstrumpf" [Natty Bumppo] had these words inscribed on the Indian's tombstone. Most likely he quoted from memory on the basis of a German translation or adaptation of Cooper's novel he had read in his youth.

3. Cf. "Palaver über Karl May," *Vossische Zeitung* (14 April 1929).

4. In the essay, "Karl der Deutsche," *Der Spiegel,* 16/37 (12 September 1962), 56, Karl Liebknecht, Albert Einstein, Adolf Hitler, Albert Schweitzer, Hermann Hesse, Thomas Mann, Ernst Bloch, among others, are listed as readers of Karl May.

5. The first and only performance took place "in einer Matinee der 'Jungen Bühne' im 'Deutschen Theater'" on 15 February 1925 according to Carl Zuckmayer, *Als wär's ein Stück von mir* (Frankfurt am Main und Hamburg, 1969), p. 333. In its published ("Bühnenmanuskript") version the play is called *Kiktalian oder die Hinterwäldler* (Potsdam, 1925). After an extensive search I was able to ascertain only two locations of the typescript: The Zuckmayer archive in Saas-Fee and the "Sonderarchiv" of the "Bibliothek des Deutschen Literaturarchivs" in Marbach. The latter institution provided a Xerox copy of the play.

6. *Als wär's ein Stück von mir*, p. 327. ("Brecht liked the drama—it is the only one of my plays which he influenced.") Zuckmayer's autobiography is also available in an abbreviated English version: *A Part of Myself*, trans. Richard and Clara Winston (New York, 1970). In part, the translations of the English version will be used.

7. ("Long live Karl May.") As reported by both Monty Jacobs, *Vossische Zeitung* (17 February 1925), and Herbert Ihering, *Von Reinhardt bis Brecht*, vol. II (Berlin, 1959), 98, in their respective reviews of the play.

8. ("A drama from the Far West," "in a romanticized pioneer America.") *Als wär's ein Stück von mir*, p. 327.

9. *Kiktahan*, p. 14. Also pointed out by Monty Jacobs in his review (cf. n. 7). For Karl May's use of English, see Richard H. Cracroft, "The American West of Karl May," *American Quarterly*, 19 (1967), 254.

10. *Als wär's ein Stück von mir*, pp. 321-22.

11. ("Whereas Brecht in *In the Jungle* rarely indulges in exoticism as a form of romantic escape, whereas he demonstrates the circumstances in which his characters are caught through his language, Zuckmayer does not engage in confronting the world but in escaping from it. The wilder the happenings, the greater the loss of poetic substance in the play.") Herbert Ihering, *Von Reinhardt bis Brecht*, p. 97. It should be noted that the "giant city Chicago" figures more prominently in the second version of *In the Jungle* (1927) than in the first version which Zuckmayer knew well.

12. ("His roughness, his drastic expressions, his passion often border on he-manship.") *Ibid.*, p. 96.

13. The "Song of the North American Lumberjacks" smacks of "cheap sexuality" which Brecht castigated in his "Notes on the Popular Play." In rough translation: "Hark, we are beating [on] our rafts with strong thrusts through the river. These thrusts are similar to those used in trysts with women when they bare their white breasts on our laps and their hair becomes undone." *Kiktahan*, p. 25.

14. ("Uneven and murky, sketchy in plot, badly organized.") *Als wär's ein Stück von mir*, p. 334. Cf. *Gesammelte Werke*, 4 vols. (Frankfurt am Main, 1960).

15. ("No need to be further concerned with either play or author.") As quoted in *Als wär's ein Stück von mir*, p. 335.

16. ("I wanted to reach out to nature, life, the truth without divorcing myself from the demands of the hour, the burning questions of my own time.") "Ich wollte an die Natur heran, ans Leben und an die Wahrheit, ohne mich von den Forderungen des Tages, vom brennenden Stoff meiner Zeit zu entfernen." *Als wär's ein Stück von mir*, p. 335.

17. *Pankraz erwacht* [*Kiktahan*] originated in the fall of 1923 (*Als wär's ein Stück von mir*, p. 327), *Sitting Bull* 1924-1925 (*Gesammelte Werke*, vol. I, 151.)

18. Two of the dramas from this period, *Schinderhannes* and *Der Hauptmann von Köpenick* (together with the later *Des Teufels General*) were subsequently included in the volume *Die deutschen Dramen* (Stockholm, 1947). Zuckmayer's preoccupation with the fate of Germany was supplemented by turning to its people. This fact is indicated by *Komödie und Volksstück* (Frankfurt am Main, 1950)—the title given the volume which comprises *Der fröhliche Weinberg*, *Katharina Knie* (1928), and *Der Schelm von Bergen* (1934).

19. (From "youth, manhood, growing up . . . in the change of weather and landscape" to the "loneliness of wintery high mountains.") *Gesammelte Werke*, vol. I, 153, 154. Zuckmayer's portrayal of Sitting Bull is not factually correct in all respects.

20. The appropriately named Bloody Sam is a particularly obvious example of an arch villain.

21. In contrast to the Indians' preservation of natural resources and animal life, the U.S. cavalry is depicted as a ruthless destroyer of life. Cf. the chapter "Der Büffelmord" in *Gesammelte Werke*, vol. I, 190-92.

22. There are some differences, however. The chapter "Präriebrand" in *Gesammelte Werke*, vol. I, 192-95 seems to be a composite of the experiences of both the trapper's party and those of Hard-Heart in chapters 23 and 24 of *The Prairie*.

23. "Winnetou auf der Bühne," *Vossische Zeitung* (6 December 1929).

24. ("The question of probability.") "Palaver über Karl May," *Vossische Zeitung* (14 April 1929).

25. ("A world whose secret, inner truth surpasses reality which can be visualized and grasped.") *Ibid.*

26. ("Karl May's tales written in the first person.") *Ibid.*

27. ("Fight for the Indian, his sentiments for this magnificent, noble, and defenselessly violated race.") *Ibid.*

28. "Winnetou auf der Bühne." As he states in this article, Carl Zuckmayer himself had planned to write a drama on the subject of Winnetou.

29. (*The Monkey Wedding.*) Arnold John Jacobius, *Carl Zuckmayer. Eine Bibliographie 1917-1971.* Ab 1955 fortgeführt und auf den jüngsten Stand gebracht von Harro Kieser (Frankfurt am Main, 1971), p. 24.

30. ("World of youthful adventure.") *Gesammelte Werke,* vol. I, 251.

31. ("A revolution of good taste, of the spirit and heart, of tact.") *Ibid.,* p. 282.

32. Under the German title *Rivalen. Ein Stück in drei Akten. Nach dem amerikanischen Schauspiel von Maxwell Anderson und Laurence Stallings, frei bearbeitet von Carl Zuckmayer* (Berlin, 1929).

33. Under the German title "Kat." According to Jacobius, *Bibliographie,* p. 70, (see n. 29), the adaptation was never published. The only copy of the MS. I know of is in Saas-Fee. Regrettably, Frau Heuberger, Carl Zuckmayer's secretary, informed me on 4 March 1972 that she would not be able to send me a Xerox copy of the MS. Presumably, Carl Zuckmayer used the German translation *In einem andern Land* (A Farewell to Arms). Deutsche Übertragung von Annemarie Horschitz (Berlin, 1930) for his adaptation.

34. "Anderson and Stalling's *What Price Glory?* and Carl Zuckmayer's *Rivalen,*" *The German Quarterly,* 20 (1947), 239-251.

35. *Ibid.,* p. 240.

36. ("Pieces of craftsmanship, finger exercises, études.") *Als wär's ein Stück von mir,* p. 371.

37. ("A dramatization of the novel *A Farewell to Arms* by Ernest Hemingway mainly because Käthe Dorsch wanted to play the part of 'Kat' [Catherine].") *Ibid.,* p. 379.

38. See *ibid.,* pp. 375 ff.

39. ("The novel that had become famous so quickly.") "In einem andern Land," *Vossische Zeitung* (25 August 1931).

40. *Ibid.*

41. See H. Frenz and P. Steiner, "Anderson and Stalling's *What Price Glory?*" 248.

42. ("The naive, animalistic glorification of masculinity which relies on its muscles rather than its brains . . . delight in the unabashedly muscular.") Albert Schulze-Vellinghausen, "Rivalen," *Theaterkritik 1952-1960* (Velber, 1961), p. 135.

43. Cf., e.g., n. 11.

44. ("A country without tradition, without culture, without the desire for beauty or form, without metaphysics and without wine taverns, a country of chemical fertilizers and of can openers but without grace and dung heaps, without classicism and slovenliness, without Melos, Apollo, Dionysus.") "Amerika ist anders," pp. 384-85.

45. ("America is different.") Title of Carl Zuckmayer's essay referred to in n. 1 and n. 44.

46. Unpublished according to Jacobius, *Bibliographie,* p. 335. Not available from Saas-Fee (letter from Frau Heuberger, see n. 33).

47. *Als wär's ein Stück von mir,* pp. 391 ff.

48. Apart from the autobiographical *Second Wind,* with an Introduction by Dorothy Thompson, translated by Elizabeth Reynolds Hapgood (New York, 1940), only a very few articles and stories—none of them too important—appeared in American magazines.

49. For the difficulties many exiled writers encountered in their profession, see Robert E. Cazden, *German Exile Literature in America 1933-1950. A History of the Free German Press and Book Trade* (Chicago, 1970).

50. "Amerika ist anders," p. 403: ". . . ich musste ungefähr so primitiv beginnen wie ein Ansiedler in den Zeiten des alten Lederstrumpf." ("I had to begin about as primitively as a settler during the time of old Leatherstocking.")

51. ("The symbiosis of poet and farmer belongs irrevocably to the world of opera.") *Ibid.,* p. 401.

52. Cf., e.g., Erich Müller-Gangloff, "Faust als Fliegergeneral," *Berliner Hefte für geistiges Leben,* 4 (1949), 90: ". . . erstaunlich . . . , dass ein Emigrant ein derart bis in die feinsten Nuancen realistisches Bild des Hitlerregimes zeichnen konnte. . . ." ("[It is] astonishing that an emigrant could draw such a picture of the Hitler regime—a picture which was faithful even in the subtlest nuances.")

53. Cf. *Pro Domo* (Stockholm, 1938), pp. 41-42.

54. As far as I can see, Luise Rinser, "Porträtskizze," *Fülle der Zeit. Carl Zuckmayer und sein Werk* (Frankfurt am Main, 1956), pp. 21 ff., was the

first to point out the autobiographical traits in Harras. Cf. also Henry Glade, "Carl Zuckmayer's *The Devil's General* as Autobiography," *Modern Drama*, 9 (1966-1967), 54-61.

55. *Gesammelte Werke,* vol. III, 587. There is also a not entirely commendable English translation of *The Devil's General* by Ingrid G. and William F. Gilbert in *Masters of Modern Drama,* ed. H. M. Block and R. G. Shedd (New York, 1962), pp. 911-958. "Oh, Buddy, how I long sometimes for a simple nation without conceit and absurdity. How I long for football players, mechanics, gum chewers, childlike persons. How sick I am of pretentious importance, significance, the intoxication with death, the two souls, the Faustian letter carrier, the demonic Block Warden. Our half-culture has filled our bellies with metaphysics and our heads with intestinal gases. The indigestible pulls us on down."

56. *Als wär's ein Stück von mir,* p. 454.

57. The newly arrived "Junglehrer" who "auf die albernste und würdeloseste Weise mit ihnen [den Schulkindern] Indianer gespielt [hat]" questions the long-established authority of the "Dechant" in musical matters (*Gesammelte Werke,* vol. II, 259). (The "young teacher" who played cowboys and Indians with the pupils in the silliest and most undignified manner.") It comes hardly as a surprise that the "Junglehrer" is an outsider who is even (wrongly) suspected of Communist leanings.

58. Hitler is parodistically referred to as "Manitu" and "The Great Spirit." *Gesammelte Werke,* vol. III, 517, 519. According to Zuckmayer, Karl May fulfilled his role as guide and mentor also in the "anteroom to hell" Hollywood. Cf. *Die langen Wege* (Frankfurt am Main, 1952), pp. 28-29.

59. Cf. Arnold John Jacobius, *Motive und Dramaturgie im Schauspiel Carl Zuckmayers* (Frankfurt am Main, 1971), pp. 39 ff.

60. Cf. the chronological table, *ibid.,* p. 130.

61. Jacobius, *Bibliographie,* p. 70, lists the title as follows: *Die Unvergessliche* ('I remember Mama'); ein Stück in zwei Akten, von John van Druten; deutsche Bearbeitung von Carl Zuckmayer. (Als Sonderdruck veröffentlicht: 'Property of the Director of Information Control, Theater and Music Branch, APO 742, U.S. Army.') 1947. Inquiries addressed to Mr. Jacobius, Frau Heuberger, the U.S. Army, and the Library of Congress remained without result as to the availability of a copy of the book.

62. John van Druten, "We all 'Remember Mama,'" *New York Times Magazine* (14 October 1945), 24-25.

63. *Ibid.*

64. ("Moving experiences," "harmless trifles.") "John van Druten: 'Die Unvergessliche,'" *Neue Zürcher Zeitung* (20 September 1947), 6.

65. John van Druten, "We all 'Remember Mama,'" 24-25.

66. See n. 61.

67. Cf., e.g., the casual references to a strike lasting for weeks. John van Druten, *I Remember Mama* (New York, 1944), pp. 114, 129.

68. "'Entscheidung vor Morgengrauen.' Diskussion um einen politischen Film," *Der Monat,* 5 (January 1953), 418-432.

69. ("Totally unbiased desire for truth and honesty.") Carl Zuckmayer, "War es Verrat?" *Der Monat,* 5 (January 1953), 421.

70. Cf. n. 1.

71. Jacobius, *Motive und Dramaturgie,* pp. 61-62, n. 8.

72. ("The lack of confidence and trust, the intellectual crisis of the present.") Carl Zuckmayer, "Nachwort," *Das kalte Licht* (Frankfurt am Main, 1956), p. 162.

73. It is hardly surprising that Zuckmayer's English is not entirely flawless. Cf., e.g., "After a cautious look at the Bum *for making it sure . . .*" [my italics]. "Anhang," *Das kalte Licht,* p. 153. The German version of II, 5 is not an exact translation of the English original. Cf., e.g., the omission of "kike" in the German for obvious reasons.

74. *Das kalte Licht,* p. 96.

75. ("We believe in the paradox which is America, we love it and we are confident that the unrestricted interaction of opposing forces will bring forth everything that is beautiful and fertile.") *Ibid.,* p. 106.

76. ("The friendly native.") *Ibid.,* p. 97.

77. ("He had his fill of Alabama.") Carl Zuckmayer, *Die Uhr schlägt eins* (Frankfurt am Main, 1961), p. 20.

78. *Die Neue Rundschau,* 72 (1961), 794-811.

79. Cf., e.g., Elisabeth Brock-Sulzer in *Theater heute,* 8 (February 1967), 30-31; Urs Widmer in *Die Welt* (17 January 1967).

80. E.g., "Front-Porch, Locust-Pond, Deerland-County, Greyhound, Lumberjack," etc. Names such as Jolly Atwood and Booby Campbell betray Zuckmayer's inclination to employ the unusual.

81. Carl Zuckmayer, "Nachwort," *Das Leben des Horace A. W. Tabor* (Frankfurt am Main, 1964), p. 150.

82. ("The time of the great improvisations," "the world of the unheard-of strokes of fortune and enormous losses.") *Ibid.*, p. 5.

83. ("One plays poker, drinks and eats heartily.") Petra Kipphoff, "Nicht angepasst," *Die Zeit* (27 November 1964), p. 24.

84. *Ibid.*

85. Friedrich Luft, "Zurück zur dramatischen Unschuld," *Die Welt* (20 November 1964).

86. "Zuckmayer-Premiere," *Der Spiegel*, 18/48 (25 November 1964), 142.

87. ("[Lack] of political, social or psychological analysis," "subject matter which is today used by the American film industry to produce the American myth.") Marianne Kesting, "Carl Zuckmayer. Zwischen Volksstück und Kolportage," *Panorama des zeitgenössischen Theaters*, rev. und erw. Neuausg. (München, 1969), p. 283.

88. ("In order to be able to study the behavior of the capitalist exploiters.") Carl Zuckmayer, *Des Leben des Horace A. W. Tabor*, p. 127.

89. *Ibid.*, p. 128.

90. In his review of *Western Saga. Klassische Wildwestgeschichten*, ed. Herbert Frenzel (Köln, Berlin, 1964) [an anthology of prose narratives ranging from Chateaubriand to Steinbeck], "Der Pionier als Leitbild," *Der Spiegel*, 18/45 (4 November 1964), 138, 141, Carl Zuckmayer once again evoked the world of the pioneer and Indian.

91. ("The restoration of the human gestalt in its totality, in its interrelationship to the world as a whole, in its both creatural and cosmic context—the restoration of the human gestalt not analytically scrutinized, not distorted by the slogans of the day, but in its dependence on fate and grace.") Carl Zuckmayer, "Jugend und Theater," *Der Monat*, 3 (April 1951), 6.

Roy C. Cowen (essay date winter 1976)

SOURCE: Cowen, Roy C. "Type-Casting in Carl Zuckmayer's *The Devil's General*." *University of Dayton Review* 13, no. 1 (winter 1976): 81-94.

[*In the following essay, Cowen argues that Zuckmayer created "factually accurate" character-types in his play* The Devil's General.]

In his autobiography **A Part of Myself**, Carl Zuckmayer records the reactions to the first performance of **The Devil's General**.[1] On the day after the premiere on 14 December 1946 in Zürich, Zuckmayer met Carl Jakob Burckhardt, about whose judgment he writes: "He was the first to tell me what I afterwards heard from countless Germans: that was what it was like—the way I had presented it in this play; that I had captured the truth which cannot be found in documents, only in literature, and which cannot be delineated with hatred, but only with love" (400/558f.). And about the first performance in Germany eleven months later Zuckmayer says:

> The Germans saw themselves in the mirror of their own times. Many of those present had been in concentration camps, in penal battalions, in the Resistance, or simply in the army. They could not understand how this play could have been written by a man who had been living abroad, who had not been on the scene during those years, who had not personally shared their experiences. The play corresponded to the reality as they had known it, down to the smallest detail.
>
> (402/560)

We recognize that Zuckmayer felt particular pride in having been able to capture the different levels and diverse motivations of the characters—while writing in a foreign country.[2]

Obviously, it was Zuckmayer's intention to encompass, as far as possible, the complete spectrum of German life under Hitler and his system. In turn, he projects on this panoramic background the story of a personal friend and adventurous individualist whose fate gave rise to the play. In his autobiography Zuckmayer recounts the circumstances surrounding the genesis of **The Devil's General**:

> In December 1941 . . . the American newspapers had carried a brief item: Ernst Udet, Chief of the Air Force Supply Service of the German Army, had suffered a fatal accident in trying out a new weapon and had been honored with a state funeral. That was all. There were no commentaries, no surmises about his death. Fatal accident; state funeral.
>
> I kept thinking about it all the time. Again and again I saw him as I had seen him in 1936, during my last reckless visit to Berlin. . . .
>
> He was in civilian dress, but he was already a high-ranking officer in the Luftwaffe. "Shake the dust of this country from your shoes," he said to me. "Clear out of here and don't come back. There is no more decency here."
>
> "And what about you?" I asked.
>
> "I'm completely sold on flying," he said lightly, almost casually. "I can't disentangle any more. But one of these days the devil will fetch us all."

* * *

Now, on that late fall evening in 1942, a year after Udet's death, I was trudging back to the farm with my carrying basket. . . . Suddenly I paused. "State funeral," I said aloud.

The last word of the tragedy.

I did not know what had happened in reality, and did not care.

The whole story was there in my mind—without a gap.

(381f./534f.)

In other words, Zuckmayer wanted to reveal how a situation had come into being and was sufficiently characterized by the phrase "state funeral." Yet this situation is itself the tragedy of an entire people. Zuckmayer concedes that he did not know the real events leading up to Udet's death; nor did he care. Everything he needed to know lies in "state funeral" as an ironic comment on one man and on an entire people. For not only was this state funeral the hypocritical "funeral" by the "state" for one of its victims but also the funeral of the state itself, both militarily and morally.

In order to carry out his intentions, however, Zuckmayer, because he was living in exile in America, had to deduce the situation as well as the events preceding the ironic "state funeral." In turn, he was forced to apply types that represented each in its own way, the logically inferable aspects of the situation.[3] Moreover, the characters had to represent a quantitatively complete protrait of the state of affairs. For we sense from the very beginning that Zuckmayer is not interested in creating but portraying, not trying to interpret but to reproduce.

Bertolt Brecht had already tried to dramatize the rise of Naziism according to its latent social cause, but we have to admit that his dramas on *Arturo Ui* and on *The Roundheads and the Peakheads,* by their simplification of the issues, do not provide a convincing picture of Nazi Germany. Reduction to one interpretative idea, be it based on Marxism or any other view, could not encompass the situation's social complexity. How unconvincing his other dramas remain is nowhere revealed more clearly than in Brecht's own powerful work on the *Fear and Misery of the Third Reich* with its naturalistic technique and scenic breadth, for in it the very diversity of reactions to, and effects of, Naziism become evident.

For his own part, Zuckmayer seems to turn to an almost naturalistic technique to portray the events in 1941.[4] Naturalism is, of course, based on a largely quantitative concept of truth: the more you know about the characters, situations and actions, that is to say, the more data you can accumulate, the closer you come to the truth. Since, however, all aspects of characters, situations or actions can never be ascertained, the complete truth, the avowed goal of historical Naturalism, can only be approached, never attained.[5] Whether we can ever establish the one, absolute truth regarding the causes of human actions in general must remain a moot point. Certainly, however, anyone writing in 1942-1946, indeed even today, still seems to be standing too close to Nazi Germany to be able to find the one, all-embracing truth. Instead, he must—and even this seems far from easy—content himself with many smaller truths, that is, with simple facts. In turn, we see how Zuckmayer's account of Berlin and Naziism in 1941, regardless of its revealed truths or insights, proved convincing to audiences in 1946/47, not in the least because they all saw themselves in one or more of the characters. Consequently, the popularity and general acceptance of *The Devil's General* substantiates, if nothing else, the quantitative success of the play in amassing factually accurate character-types, in being "convincing."

First of all, almost every geographical area of Germany is represented in *The Devil's General.* For example, we hear that Pfundtmayer is "a Bavarian powerhouse," that Hastenteuffel is Westphalian and Writzky a "sharp boy" from Berlin (916/508). Northern Germany is also exemplified by Hansen (= Lüttjohann) from the *Waterkant* (= North Sea coast, 929/542). The wealthy and less so in the *Rheinland* can be seen in Mohrungen and Hartmann. Harras calls Baron Pflungk "ole Saxon" (919/517), and he tells Eilers that Oderbruch stems from Silesian Catholics (923/526). Indeed, we even have a transplanted Frenchman in François and an American newsman Buddy Lawrence, who represents the naive foreign enthusiasm for things German, if not for Hitler. With every major area of Germany, a conquered country and a neutral one represented, we are convinced that we are in fact viewing war-time Germany as a totality.

Moreover, certain areas carry specific historical associations according to the role they played in the rise of Hitler and his minions. We need think only of Bavaria, where Hitler first found his support. The historical aspects of this geographical area provide the basis for the character of Pfundtmayer, who indignantly berates Harras:

Genurrull! Genurrull! You made it Harry! But if ya really think about it—I was al'ays in the party—right from the Bloody March in '23—marched right behind the Fuehrer too—a little ta the left. . . . And now, in uniform, what am I now? A poor ole Captain—me, with my low party number and all. And you—you're the Genurrull! Ya call that justice?

(917/511 f.)

The geographical and historical facts one would associate with Bavaria are all present in a character as typical as he is unpleasant.

Just as the greatest possible horizontal breadth is achieved, so is the greatest possible vertical range. For example, the first time we see von Mohrungen, Eilers,

Pflungk, Schmidt-Lausitz and Hansen (= Lüttjohann), they are crowded about on the threshold, where they apply the extremes of courtesy toward higher ranks. Consequently, the audience is immediately apprised of the hierarchy they embody. Moreover, the stage directions virtually call for typified characterization (913/500f.). Mohrungen must look like what he is, "a good-looking man of about fifty with grey temples, representative of the old upper class of heavy industry," and "his junker-like conservative outlook is subdued by a southern German naturalness." Pflungk appears to have no character, and he will prove to have none, but he must also display the looks of an "elegant grey-hound," a dog associated with the nobility and its "smooth manners." Schmidt-Lausitz' appearance likewise corresponds totally to the type of party-fanatic he represents. Even Eilers looks like what he is: "Durchschnitt," average, and here we must understand the average as the common denominator. His death will incite Harras to action, whereby we can recognize that not his exceptional qualities but his very lack of them will imbue Harras' reaction with more sweeping implications. No less characteristic are the women: Olivia Geiss, the diva, has a "full bust of the professional singer" (917/512) and, in her own way as an artist, presents a feminine counterpart to Harras: just as he can separate flying from the political system that allows him to fulfill his goals as a flier, so Olivia, who feels disgust for the Nazis and sympathy for their enemies, nevertheless accepts Goering's presence at the performance of *Die lustige Witwe* and even wishes that Hitler, whose coming would have been an even greater compliment to her as an artist, had been there. Diddo, the *ingenue,* looks like "a school-girl who is going to her first ball." And Lyra, who will appeal to Pfundtmayer and, in the German text is called the "Tankstelle" (filling-station), suggests decadence by her monocle and excessive cosmetics. In other words, Zuckmayer achieves type-casting effects by avoiding any discrepancy between a character's appearance and what he represents. Similar observations could be made regarding the figures around Harras like Korrianke, his chauffeur. In no case could the audience remark: he doesn't look like a . . . , or sound like a . . . , or act like a . . . ,

No less synchronized or typified is the march of different age groups across the stage: we have the pre-Hitler and Hitler-generations and perhaps even the post-Hitler survivor, if Pflungk proves successful in his attempts to hedge his bets (he is already thinking about his own chances if Hitler loses the war). In turn, the two important generations can be sub-divided along predictable lines into the supporters and opponents of the regime. Among the younger members of the group there are the indoctrinated and the not indoctrinated. Indeed, the indoctrinated are sub-divided again into the type that has learned only the idealistic and the type that has learned

only the cynical. Pootsie (= Pützchen) outlines the contrast succinctly in an early dialogue with Harras. Regarding herself she says:

> We modern girls have nothing against marriage if it's the right man. But just stop and think for a minute all the rigmarole we have to go through; the proofs of Aryan blood, all the way down to your great-grandfather's big toe. Health certificate, proof of fertility, semen count, and so forth. Yes, it's all necessary on account of race—but who wants to wait around for all that? With your normal drives—you can grow old and rancid in the process.

> (914/504)

But she describes Hartmann, another example of Nazi education: "He's a sharp boy—three sports prizes, twelve planes shot down and tip-top ideology. But something's missing—I don't know what—real dash. He doesn't dance, imagine!" (914/504). Hartmann has become what the Nazi leadership wanted him to become, and Pootsie what the leadership itself is.[6] Consequently, when the marriage between Hartmann and Pootsie, which seems to have been made in Nazi heaven, does not take place because he lacks papers on his grandmother, he accepts the rational of the process, and she dismisses it with cynical indifference. Hartmann, who is ready to sacrifice himself for the Nazi cause, will later be converted to self-sacrifice for the anti-Nazi cause. Through Hartmann Zuckmayer expresses a belief, if not directly in a new German humanity, then at least in the limits of the Nazi indoctrination. Only where exposure to the Nazis has destroyed the moral fiber does the effect seem permanent, as with Pootsie, who is loyal to neither persons or principles. After discovering the letter from Bergmann she would join forces with Harras, an "enemy of the state," but ultimately denounces him because he, as a person, has rejected her.

Logically speaking, we would have to distinguish yet another possibility among the members of the Hitler-generation: the person remaining uncorrupted by the ideals or the persons of Naziism. Here Diddo appears. In Act II she says to Harras:

> Look . . . I . . . often I don't know where I'm at anymore. I was only twelve in 1933. . . . If you come right down to it, you see only what crosses your path. I only know one thing. I would like to get out, out! Why, I couldn't even explain. But sometimes I think if I were my age and were Jewish and had to emigrate—maybe it wouldn't be so bad. Maybe it would even be better. To see the world—my God! New York . . . And the ocean—and the harbours—maybe China—or Rio de Janeiro. Me, I wouldn't care. I could do anything: wash dishes, wipe children, factory work—only to be free—outside! Sometimes I envy the Jews madly.

> I mean the ones outside.

> (938/565f.)

Her view of emigration is, of course, quite naive. Nevertheless, she does point up that not everyone has been misled or morally destroyed. She also reveals the serious flaw of a Hartmann, who cannot dance, i.e. be light-hearted, or, for that matter, of a supposedly devil-may-care Pootsie, who is really cynical and ambitious beyond her years: their seriousness. In most of Zuckmayer's works, to laugh is to be human, but both of these people have lost their youth and ability to be happy. Harras underlines this aspect by his commentary to Diddo: "Maybe they'll throw us out at the right time because we're so illegally happy" (938/566). How little the Hitler-generation understands about being young and happy is also revealed by the everyman Eilers, who is described as unusually serious (913/501).

Among the members of the older generation, all possible motives for their participation are likewise systematically explored. The active contributors to Hitler's rise to, and retention of, power reveal their reasons, one by one. Pfundtmayer, the crude bully, wanted to raise himself from his obviously humble station, but only to enjoy the wine, women and song that would then become available to him. Schmidt-Lausitz, who is vaguely reminiscent of Goebbels, not in the least because he implies frustration as an author through his hatred of Remarque and Ullstein (927/536), promised himself more intangible rewards. Von Mohrungen represents all too patently the responsibility of his class and even repeats the slogans of the 20's and 30's with which the industrialists were won over by the Nazis. Ironically, he expresses in conclusion the slogan that links him with Pootsie and Hartmann: "We don't live just to be happy, after all. After all, we do have to make sacrifices" (954/584). Once again, we hear how life has become such an inhumanly serious business for the Nazis and their supporters.

Yet Mohrungen represents only the successful *Mitläufer* ("fellow-traveller"). Aware of the other side of the coin, Zuckmayer doen not ignore the unsuccessful type of *Mitläufer* like Schlick, the Expressionist painter. Believing that a German could paint only in Germany, Schlick after 1933 divorced his Jewish wife, who with their children disappeared; but he is still considered "degenerate" (944/581f.). As a calculated, logically inferable contrast and alternative to Schlick, the wife of Bergmann, the Jewish physician, albeit unseen, plays her role. Unlike the painter, she does not abandon her Jewish spouse but rather chooses suicide with him. Like the active Nazis Pfundtmayer and Schmidt-Lausitz, the *Mitläufer* also represent all logically and historically deducible motives. There remains, however, yet another reason to be a *Mitläufer*: survival. Such is the case with Eilers and his wife. When poor average Eilers questions how Germany can combine such terror and beauty, his far more perceptive wife answers:

> Don't question, darling. Believe. Believe. Remember what you wrote to me—when you left the first time? I know it by heart. I say it to myself over and over. "Let nothing confuse you—Let nothing make you waver. Believe with every fiber of your being in Germany—in yourself—in us—in our mission—Whoever believes will survive. Believe!"
>
> (923/527)

Here we find an almost existentialist, forced belief, possible only with the believer's eyes closed to the truth. In Eilers, Zuckmayer has answered the question of why so many German men fought so well, and why their women let them, why Hitler apparently received so much support, yet achieved and held power without an active majority.

All of these types have a common trait: they reveal the impact of social change on man's behavior. There is no suggestion of the demonic, dionysian in Germans and German culture, as for example, in Mann's *Doktor Faustus*.[7] No Satanic overtones appear in the ardent Nazis, as in Hochhuth's *Deputy*.[8] Likewise, the uncanny, grotesque yet humorous Oskar Mazarath with his tin drum finds no counterpart. As a matter of fact, through Harras that very tendency among Germans toward the metaphysical, the Faustian and demonic is ridiculed:

> How sick I am of Significance, the Intoxication of Death, the demonic Block Warden, the split inner life, the Faustian Mail Carrier. Our half-culture has filled our bellies with metaphysics and our heads with intestinal gas. "The indigestible pulls us on down." We have become a nation of constipated public school teachers who exchanged the rod for the riding whip in order to disfigure the human face. Cloud-chasers and slaves of death. A miserable nation.
>
> (946/587)[9]

The problem lies not in the fact that the Germans are demonic but in their seeing themselves as such. Like Brecht, Zuckmayer considers the social causes, but unlike the *Stückeschreiber,* he eschews a single, facile interpretation. The only unifying factor is the Germans' tendency to take themselves too seriously and their resultant misery. Yet Zuckmayer, by his almost too "slick" use of geographical and social types, attempts a quantitatively complete presentation of all conceivable reactions—economic, artistic, moral and otherwise—to Nazi rule and war. The main danger of such type-casting lies in the very fact that each character personifies attributes so thoroughly, so purely, that he comes close to becoming a mere abstraction of historical forces.

Against this panoramic background he portrays a man who is supposedly least interested in social pressures or values.[10] If the secondary figures appear as almost too "slick" type-casting, then General Harras borders dangerously on a Hollywood-type hero.[11] When we first see him, for example, he is still holding his empty glass in his hand, and a cigarette is hanging from the corner of his mouth. Moreover, Harras' single-minded indifference to political and social changes seems to produce a too striking contrast to the secondary characters. Following faithfully Udet's remarks cited above, Zuckmayer lets his protagonist explain his motives: he could have made a career of stunt and daredevil flying in America (Udet did exhibition flying there), but he would have been only a "sort of flying clown." He could have made movies, but "those boys have no imagination, and that was precisely the positive factor in this whole business here for me, at least" (921/522). He continues:

> Nowhere else in the world but here would I have been given these possibilities, these unlimited means—this power. These five years, making the Luftwaffe airborne—I don't regret them. . . . Spain, of course, was slightly sickening. But the first two years, when it really started up, we had something to offer, there was some style to it then. The best, most exact, most effective machinery that ever existed in the history of war.
>
> (921/522)

Yet Harras seems like an anachronism, like the last knight of the air, for he still lives the life of a flier in World War I. Nowhere does this emerge with greater clarity than in his story about how he received the old watch from the first pilot he had shot down (939/568f.). And later in the act another symbol appears: the picture of his best enemy in the previous war. It had been sent by the mother, whom Harras later visited. Pootsie, whose attitude so resembles that of the leadership in 1941, scornfully comments: "The famous chivalric gesture. Good for the historic reputation but antiquated" (943/579). Despite his obvious technical expertise and ability, Harras is basically still living in the past, and consequently he has never succumbed to, nor undertaken active opposition against, nor fled from, the Nazi regime. Far from being merely a technician, he still loves the age of individual "style." Yet, as glamourous as he appears to all—not in the least as a representative, as Detlev says in the beginning, of "die alte Schule"—he has virtually become a relique. As the play progresses, it becomes increasingly evident that this living monument to a past age and out-dated standards will not be allowed to stand much longer.

With his emphasis on types, however, Zuckmayer has also suggested a model for Harras himself. Seen as an anachronism, Harras' situation resembles not so much that of some trite, banal Hollywood hero but rather that of Georg Büchner's Danton, who, in his *Weltschmerz*, is very German indeed.[12] We recall, for example, Lacroix's words in Act I of *Danton's Death*: "Danton, you are a dead saint, but the Revolution knows no reliques. It has thrown the bones of all kings into the street and all columns out of the churches. Do you believe they would let you stand as a monument?" (25). Harras has become just such a relique.[13] And the more Harras leans

toward several other themes from *Danton's Death*, the more the very obvious type-casting of the secondary characters is brought into a new perspective.

Admittedly, several German authors and works are alluded to: Kleist's *Prince Frederick of Homburg* (919/516), Matthias Claudius (923/527) and Goethe (930/545; 946/587).[14] But no allusion is as pointed and lengthy as Diddo's speech in Act II:

> I've always wanted to play a madwoman. I don't know why. Perhaps to get rid of something that's trapped inside me, that might not come out otherwise. But maybe that has no place on the stage. Do you know *Danton's Death* by Buechner? (Harras *nods*) Sometimes when I'm walking down the street, I'm Lucille—They've murdered my lover—The hangman of the revolution stalks through the night—And suddenly I must step out of the darkness and call: "Long Live the King!" That's how I would like to die. Is that mad?
>
> (946/586)

And if this is not enough, one need only note how often Harras steps to the window, for each time he expresses thoughts similar to Danton's in his famous window scene in II, 5 of *Danton's Death*.

One of the most important scenes in *Danton's Death* deals with Danton's confrontation with Robespierre in Act I. As soon becomes apparent, not two political principles but rather two ways of life underly their conflict. Thus we hear from Danton:

> There are only epicureans and only crude ones or refined ones at that. Christ was the most subtle; that is the only difference that I can make out between men. Each one acts according to his nature, that is, he does what gives him pleasure. It's cruel, isn't it, "Incorruptible," to knock the props out from under you like this?
>
> (27)

Indeed, the political philosophy of the Dantonists stems from this view, as we hear in Herault's statement:

> Every man must be able to assert himself and behave according to his own nature. He might be reasonable or unreasonable, educated or uneducated, good or bad— that is no concern of the state. We are all fools, and none of us has the right to impose his own particular foolishness on another. Every man must be able to enjoy life in his own way, but only in a way that no one may have his pleasure at the cost of another or disturb him in his form of pleasure.
>
> (11)

Such a philosophy and the politics it spawns assume the individual as the greatest unit. Danton has lost faith in all principles, all attempts to communicate beyond his own person, and, as a result, he feels buried alive in the world of his body, knowing only what his senses can communicate. In short, Danton, the hedonist, represents the ultimate stage of individualism.

For his part, Harras also advocates by word and deed extreme hedonism, a fact not ignored by his friends and enemies. For example, Olivia Geiss calls Harras a *GenuBmensch* (hedonist) and says to him that the Nazis are after him for that very reason (940/572). We remember that Danton liked to flirt with death (39), and we now find the same flirtation driving Harras. Even Schmidt-Lausitz recognizes Harras' nature as a gambler: "It might appeal to you," he says to Harras, "to challenge the devil to a round of poker in hope of outbluffing him" (953/603). For the absolute hedonist, who believes in nothing beyond his own person, there can be no greater stake than his own life. Gambling with his life provides the ultimate titillation.

Like Danton, Harras personifies individualism in its most extreme form, not in the least because, like Danton, he stresses throughout the play that the attacks on him are personal. And like the French revolutionary, he depends on the strength of his personality to repulse the attacks on him. But the day of reckoning finally catches up with Harras. His deadliest enemy is Schmidt-Lausitz, who, in giving him 10 days to expose the saboteur, says: "In me you see a mortal enemy. You are quite correct. There isn't room enough under the sun for us both" (935/559). We note, however, that the tone is less political than existential, that Schmidt-Lausitz' relationship to Harras resembles Robespierre's to Danton.[15] Robespierre, the Incorruptible, hates his opposite because of his vices, particularly the sexual ones, for Danton "wants to hitch the horses of the Revolution to a brothel" (28).[16] The parallel between Danton's and Harras' situation is in fact summarized by Olivia, who expresses her own hedonism through sex, when she says:

> And besides, you had too much success with women. That's the worst of it. With our Nazis everything is really jealousy, bed-jealousy above all. But on that point they're way below zero—always wanting to go to war and make out like great men—it's all a fake. . . . First great sounds—then it's all over before it really began and off they run, back to duty.
>
> (940f./572f.)

And throughout the play, Harras, like Danton, continues to make jokes in the face of his all too serious opponents, serious because they have sublimated personal pleasures in the attempt to realize an abstract ideal.

Danton, as the hedonistic cynic, as the individualist, cannot accept the fact that his opponents persist in their actions, in their continued belief in such vague, abstract principles as they mouth. He therefore sees them as helpless actors, playing roles in which they have themselves come to believe. Consequently, Danton challenges Robespierre:

> Robespierre, you are disgustingly righteous. I would be ashamed to run around between heaven and earth with such a moral expression on my face, just for the miser-

able pleasure of finding others worse than myself. Isn't there anything in you that doesn't sometimes quite softly, secretly say: you're lying, you're lying!
>
> (26)

At the same time, Danton realizes that just as the Revolution has formed them, not vice versa (32), so the roles they have played have taken them over. Lacroix reports: "And Collot screamed like mad that they should tear off their masks" (24). And Danton answers: "Then their faces will come off with them." Throughout *Danton's Death* the image of role-playing and theater appears correspondingly often as a symbol of the effect of the Revolution even on its supposed "leaders." In turn, a similar image-pattern recurs with no less impact in *The Devil's General.*

Harras' cynicism finds almost its equal in Pootsie's, and it is she who says to him: "I am not that stupid, Harry. We all put on a little act. You do too. We have a habit of over-playing in public and forget ourselves that we are doing it. Harry, things can't go on like this with you" (947/590). She even repeats this image a short time later (948/592). Harras himself shows a similar insight in his dialogue with Oderbruch, who says a beard would be too much a mask, when he retorts: "Yes—it's better to hide yourself behind a naked face" (950/596). Indeed, Harras' Danton-like fatigue, his approaching the end, reveals itself when he can no longer carry out his theatrical banter with Korrianke (vid. 950/598). Even to the end, however, Harras tries to remain true to his role. He rejects the suicide suggested by Schmidt-Lausitz' leaving him a pistol; instead, he plays the gambler to the last and entrusts his fate to a "Gottesurteil" (divine judgement) (957/616). It would be a serious mistake—admittedly it has been made frequently[17]—to continue seeing Harras' death as a suicide pure and simple. He cannot know for sure that the ME41-1303 is defective. When he calls his flight a "divine judgment," he means the chance element. Danton could have killed himself, but instead he stands trial and closes his speech with a monumental testament to his belief in the individual: "Now you know Danton; in a few hours he will be sleeping in the arms of fame" (54). If Danton had, by any slim chance, won his plea, he would have saved his life; even while losing his life, however, he assures himself of fame. If Harras' flight succeeds, he will land in Switzerland; if it fails, he will have a "state funeral."

Thus we see that Zuckmayer has not idealized Harras out of all proportion. His guilt, like Danton's, still weighs too heavily, even in death. Ann is right in her criticism of Harras:

> Do you believe this war is just? You know that it is unjust. Then why do you let it happen? Why don't you acknowledge it? Do you believe our leadership is good? You know it is ruinous. Why do you watch it? You put on a great show of courage with your sarcasm and

lukewarm doubt. What good is that to anybody? You are a part of the rottenness. You are guilty of every murder committed in the name of Germany. You stink of death!

(955/609)

Harras can only take refuge in the argument:

That is madness. Don't you see what is happening in the world? The nations are in turmoil. Do I know where they will end? Can I stop them? Change their direction? . . . Who am I anyway? Am I more than a man? Can I know more—do more—suffer more—than a man? I'm no God.

(955/609)

These sentiments echo clearly Danton's abhorrence of the "Must" *(MuB)* (41) and the corresponding biblical passage, cited by Büchner in a letter (II, 426): "Woe unto the world because of offences! for it must needs be that offences come; but woe to that man by whom the offence cometh!" (Matthew 18, 7). Like Danton, Harras has played a role to the death. Like Danton, he has also come to realize that he has been playing a role, that he could ultimately do nothing to eliminate evil, but for that very reason he admits: "Permitting viciousness is worse than doing it" (940/571).

We now return to our problem of type-casting. As naturalistic as this play seems to be, such types, not by their nature, but by their convenient convergence at one time in one place, seem to flaunt pure realism. Back during the heyday of Naturalism, Alfred Kerr pointed out one unresolvable paradox of realistic drama: it must limit itself to a short span of time yet contain all of the important information regarding what is happening, who is doing it, and why it has come to be. It is, however, in real life never the case that all information about the situation and characters is naturally brought up by the participants in an action.[18] Similarly, we could say that Zuckmayer tests our credulity by the "coincidental" appearance of all main *types* in the Third Reich at the same time in the same place.

Our insight into the role-playing by all of them, on the other hand, reveals the essentially theatrical nature of that world. How far it has all come is brought home by the dialogue between Harras and Buddy Lawrence, once again with Bücherian undertones. To Lawrence's profession of love for the Germans, Harras answers: "Me too. To the point of hate. Just like an actor who loves and hates the character he plays, the role to which he has been sentenced—love and hate" (946/587). Harras continues: "We all act. We are hidden in roles and don't know their end. We don't even know their character. How much evil is in yourself? Ask the author. Is he crazy? Or a swindler? Should he be worshipped—or nailed to the cross?" And when Diddo asks whether they are playing grand opera, comedy or tragedy, Har-

ras answers with a smile: "Everything together." In order to emphasize this very fact that so many wanted to, or were forced to, play a role—one can also include Detlev, the spy for the Gestapo—Zuckmayer pushes his type-casting to an extreme—just as the times themselves did. Thus the play will end with the irony of a "state funeral," the most farcical piece of theatrics, but also, as we have seen in Zuckmayer's description of his inspiration for the play, the phrase that characterizes the situation as a whole.

In turn, Harras must be viewed in a new light. During the later 60's a serious attempt was made to revive ***The Devil's General*** throughout Germany, but the public reception of the play fell far short of the enthusiasm shown right after the war.[19] Above all, the role of Harras was criticized, despite the fact that Zuckmayer had felt obligated to expand the conversation between the general and the saboteur Oderbruch. But his changes, on the one hand to make Oderbruch more human through a sense of guilt about Eilers, on the other to give Harras a concrete plan of action by letting him suggest that Hitler, not the average Germans, must be killed—such changes did not save the play from a negative reception. Above all, Harras is roundly condemned and the play for glorifying him.

By 1967, of course, the political climate had changed. One might say that the public now felt itself far enough removed from the events of the Third Reich to want them interpreted, indeed that the public believed it had already interpreted them correctly. But Zuckmayer sought only even more balance through his changes, for, as we already noted, he wanted from the beginning to portray the times, not reduce them to one idea. Whether or not we like Harras or even agree with him remains as inconsequential as whether we like Danton or any other literary figure. After all, Büchner had himself said about his portrayal of the French Revolutionaries that he was not a teacher of morality but only a writer of history who wanted to show them as they had been, not as they should have been.[20] In other words, Büchner is, in effect, making a plea for understanding, particularly in the face of human weakness.

In his drama about Harras, Zuckmayer also hits the heart of the human problem. Harras always thinks in terms of the individual. But Oderbruch represents the shame of a German who has gone beyond his person as such. Consequently, Oderbruch proves just as "serious," albeit in the opposite direction, as Schmidt-Lausitz.[21] Indeed, as a reaction against the very type of personal charisma shown by Harras as well as against ambition or self-salvation, Oderbruch's group remains virtually nameless. What we see in Harras, therefore, is not the man completely above and beyond the events, the self-indulgent hero, nor the person thoroughly enmeshed in them, but rather the man who instinctively rejects a prescribed role. Yet, by playing out his own personal role, he reveals how human the others are. If Zuckmayer made Harras personality attractive, then he did him no real service, for he did so only to make his guilt and weakness even more obvious. And regardless of our feelings toward Harras and the rest, we have to concede one thing: for many, that was what it was like. What, however, could be more important for a dramatist who said that he wanted to portray life and the burning questions of his time, not solve them?[22] In conclusion, we must hear Zuckmayer as well as Harras when the latter says: "Ich bin kein Denker, und kein Prophet. Ich bin ein Zeitgenosse" (547) (I am no thinker and no prophet; I am a contemporary).

Notes

1. Carl Zuckmayer, *A Part of Myself,* Translated by Richard and Clara Winston, (New York: Harcourt Brace Jovanovich, 1970) is a translation of the author's *Als wär's ein Stück von mir,* (Vienna: S. Fischer, 1966). Translated by Ingrid G. and William F. Gilbert, *The Devil's General* appears in *Masters of Modern Drama,* ed. by Haskell M. Block and Robert G. Shedd (New York: Random House, 1962), pp. 911-958. This translation is, however, of the original version. The second, definitive version appears in Carl Zuckmayer, *Gesammelte Werke,* vol. III (Berlin/Frankfurt: S. Fischer, 1960), pp. 495-618. Page references for all quotations will be given first to the translation, secondly to the German text.

2. Murray B. Peppard, "Moment of Moral Decision: Carl Zuckmayer's Latest Plays," *Monatshefte,* 44 (1952), 349-356, calls attention to the unusually long exposition in *The Devil's General* and "how much Zuckmayer was concerned with evoking a well-rounded picture of Nazi Germany" (p. 349).

3. Ingeborg Engelsing-Malek, *"Amor Fati" in Zuckmayers Dramen* (Konstanz: Rosgarten, 1960), p. 88, divides the characters into four groups: 1) the young people (Ann and Friedrich Eilers, Hartmann, Diddo); 2) the Nazis (Schmidt-Lausitz, Pfundtmayer. Pützchen); 3) those who have learned to bow to the power at the moment (Detlev, Mohrungen, Pflungk); 4) those who serve a hated system and yet try to remain true to their character (Harras, Lüttjohann, Korrianke, Olivia Geiss). These groupings, however, reveal nothing about Zuckmayer's analytical approach, nor do they allow for any subtle or logical differences between characters within a given group.

4. Most critics call this drama "naturalistic," e.g., Volker Wehdeking, "Mythologisches Ungewitter. Carl Zuckmayers problematisches Exildrama 'Des Teufels General'," *Die deutsche Exilliteratur 1933-1945,* ed. Manfred Durzak (Stuttgart: Reclam, 1973), pp. 509-519. Wehdeking, who calls Act I a combination of the best *Sekundenstil* of the Naturalists Holz, schlaf and Hauptmann with the virtues of the "New Objectivity" (p. 510) and in its dialogue and structure a masterful achievement of the naturalist tradition (p. 517), admittedly sees Expressionist elements in Act II and Schiller's pathos in Act III. Be that as it may, the theme of our study draws mainly on the exposition in Act I, not on the personal development of Harras in II and III. Zuckmayer's debt to Naturalism in almost all of his works is, however, brought out in the excellent study by Wolfgang Paulsen, "Carl Zuckmayer," *Deutsche Literatur im 20. Jahrhundert,* ed. by Hermann Friedmann and Otto Mann, Vol II: *Gestalten,* 4th edition (Heidelberg: Rothe, 1961), pp. 302-322.

5. Thus Theodor Fontane in his famous review of Ibsen's *Ghosts,* as performed on the *Freie Bühne* in 1889, could correctly surmise that the naturalistic approach results in "conviction" *(Überseugung),* not truth, which, for him, was something quite different. *Vid.* my *Naturalismus: Kommentar zu einer Epoche* (Munich: Winkler, 1973), pp. 48-50.

6. The comparison of Pootsie (= Pützchen) to "the eternal Lillith—the personification of evil in woman," made by Henry Glade, "Carl Zuckmayer's *The Devil's General* as Autobiography," *Modern Drama,* 9 (1966-67), seems quite strained; Glade cites Schlick's description of her, but the distraught and guilt-ridden painter can scarcely be considered a reliable judge.

7. Erich Müller-Gangloff, "Faust als Fliegergeneral," *Berliner Hefte für geistiges Leben,* 4 (1949), 90-93, asserts "demonic" qualities for Pützchen and Schmidt-Lausitz, but he offers no substantial proof. Likewise, Wilfried Adling, "Des Teufels General," *Die Entwicklung des Dramatikers Carl Zuckmayer,* Schriften zur Theaterwissenschaft, ed. by the Theaterhochschule Leipzig, Vol. 1 (Berlin: Henschel, 1959), pp. 177-217, who speaks for the Marxist critics, sees a "demonization" of fascism by Zuckmayer and condemns him for such a "limited" view.

8. Thus Murray Peppard, *op. cit.,* asserts: "There are no villains . . . but only people who are weak or who have chosen the wrong side" (p. 356). This view, however, overlooks the fact that there can be villains without metaphysical implications.

9. Nevertheless, many critics still stress the supposed "Faustian" aspects of Harras' mania for flying and his presumed "pact" with the devil, e.g., Henry Glade, *op. cit.,* p. 58. If his problem is indeed "Faustian," then Harras himself seems unaware of it.

10. There are, of course, patently autobiographical elements in Zuckmayer's portrait of Harras (= Udet). See, for example, Luise Rinser, "Porträtskizze," *Fülle der Zeit: Carl Zuckmayer und sein Werk* (Frankfurt am Main: S. Fischer), pp. 13-30. On the problems arising from the autobiographical intrusions, see Henry Glade, *op. cit.*

11. To be sure, Arnold Bauer, *Carl Zuckmayer,* Köpfe des XX. Jahrhunderts, Vol. 62 (Berlin: Colloquium, 1970). p. 73, cites Elisabeth Langgässer's comment at a performance in 1947: "Das ist ein antiker Held." See also Rudolf Lange, *Carl Zuckmayer,* Friedrichs Dramatiker des Welttheaters, Vol. 33 (Velber: Friedrich, 1973), p. 72. Nevertheless, and despite the classical aspects of the protagonist's progress toward his tragic decision, Zuckmayer's experience in the film industry does seem to make itself felt; of course, we recall that Zuckmayer did write most of the dialogue for, among others, *Der Blaue Engel.* Also the influence of Hemingway could be suggested; see, for example, Wayne Kvam, "Zuckmayer, Hilpert, and Hemingway," *PMLA,* 91 (1976), 194-205, on Zuckmayer's adaptation of *A Farewell to Arms,* though Kvam emphasizes Hemingway's influence on earlier works. Moreover, Hemingway's works belong to the most frequently filmed, and Zuckmayer's *Hauptmann von Köpenick* and *Devil's General* did become vehicles for two of the postwar "super-stars" of Germany: Heinz Rühmann and Curd Jürgens.

12. Zuckmayer has, of course, documented amply his interest in Büchner in his autobiography (unfortunately several instances are omitted in the translation). All page references to Büchner's works are to: *Georg Büchner, Sämtliche Werke und Briefe* (Hamburger Ausgabe), ed. by Werner R. Lehmann (Hamburg: Wegner, 1967 ff.). When no volume number is given. Volume I is understood. Translations are my own.

13. John Jacobius, *Motive und Dramaturgie im Schauspiel Carl Zuckmayers,* Schriften zur Literatur, Vol. 19 (Frankfurt am Main: Athenäum, 1971), calls attention to several passages that echo Büchnerian chords; unfortunately, however, he does not delve deeper into any parallels.

14. Obviously, Harras' name also represents an allusion to Rudolf der Harras, Gessler's riding-master in Schiller's *Wilhelm Tell* and himself in a "Devil's General" of sorts.

15. Engelsing-Malek, *op. cit.,* p. 83, sees a similar structure in *Der fröhliche Weinberg* and Knuzius as a less intelligent and less dangerous predecessor of Schmidt-Lausitz, but the latter comparison seems, at best, strained.

16. Maurice B. Benn, *The Drama of Revolt: A Critical Study of Georg Büchner,* Anglica Germanica Series 2 (London et al.: Cambridge U. Press, 1976), p. 146, writes: "The envy which causes the downfall of Danton is to a great extent sexual envy." On Danton's hedonism see also my article "Grabbe's *Don Juan und Faust* and Büchner's *Dantons Tod*: Epicureanism and *Weltschmerz,*" *PMLA,* 82 (1967), 342-351.

17. A laudible exception is Henry Glade, *op. cit.,* p. 60.

18. See Alfred Kerr, "Technik des realistischen Dramas," *Gesammelte Schriften in Zwei Reihen, Erste Reihe: Die Welt im Drama, 1. Band: Das neue Drama* (Berlin S. Fischer, 1917), pp. 425-445.

19. For selected reviews of the original version and the later performances, see *Zuckmayer: Des Teufels General,* bearbeitet von Siegfried Mews, Grundlagen und Gedanken zum Verständnis des Dramas (Frankfurt am Main: Diesterweg, 1973). Mews also offers an excellent orientation in the research on the play and a bibliography as well as detailed notes on the text.

20. See Büchner's letter of 28 July 1835 to his family (II, 443f.).

21. Oderbruch has proved to be one of the most controversial characters in the play, not in the least because he, no less than Schmidt-Lausitz, believes that the "ends justify the means." See, for example, Hanns Braun, "Glosse zu 'Des Teufels General'," *Hochland,* 40 (1947-48), 498-500.

22. See *A Part of Myself,* 279f. (396).

Arnold Bauer (essay date 1976)

SOURCE: Bauer, Arnold. "German Legend—German Truth." In *Carl Zuckmayer,* translated by Edith Simmons, pp. 41-64. New York: Frederick Ungar Publishing Co., 1976.

[*In the following essay, Bauer outlines the genesis of Zuckmayer's drama* The Captain of Köpenick.]

Not surprisingly, Carl Zuckmayer, encouraged by the success of **The Merry Vineyard,** which was almost unheard-of in recent theater history, again chose a local theme for his next play. While still in Kiel, he had prepared a ballad version of the **Mainzer Moritat vom Schinderhannes** (**Mainz Thriller about Schinderhannes**) for a matinee and occasionally recited the poem himself. The playwright now recognized that his use of ordinary people and simple emotions as legitimate theatrical devices had set him on a course bound to lead to wide audience approval but was also a dangerous track because some rather provincial guardians of tradition on the German right felt he had trespassed into their territory.

His depiction of Schinderhannes, the "noble robber," may have contributed to the misunderstandings of his purpose. If the tradition is to be believed, the historical Johann Bückler (Schinderhannes) roamed the forests of the Hunsrück with his band of robbers, and as a hardened highwayman, shrank from no brutality. He was, in short, an unscrupulous law-breaker and disturber of the peace. His sad career, begun as an executioner's assistant, came to an abrupt end in 1803, when he died on the gallows, convicted of several murders. That this notorious Schinderhannes should have been a friend of the poor and a patriot during the skirmishes with the French occupation troops seems highly questionable and may well be pure legend. However, it was precisely the legend—popular in a variety of forms ever since Robin Hood—that attracted Zuckmayer. He was interested not so much in creating another "outlaw because of honor lost" (after Schiller's Karl Moor) and torn by inner conflicts, but rather a poetically transfigured fighter for social justice and national freedom. Despite these romantic overtones, Zuckmayer turned the character of Johann Bückler into a vigorous robber hero, full of humor and generous spirit—in short, a "capital fellow," a man after the author's own heart. He is such a loving person that he even manages to arouse the passionate devotion of an innocent country girl. Julchen (Julie), who displays great emotional strength, became one of the most famous heroines of the German stage, a figure that moved audiences not so much with words as simply by her presence. The animated performance of the great actress Käthe Dorsch—it was one of her best roles—helped to make the character powerfully convincing. The play opened in 1927 in Berlin. The audience applauded it, but there was still much well-intentioned criticism. What distinguished Zuckmayer from his contemporaries and helped him to be continuously successful was his remarkable ability to strike a balance between the tragic and the brighter side of life. This was particularly true in regard to his rustic scenes and his skillfully drawn characterizations of simple people and their earthy humor. Carl Zuckmayer had truly been "reading the lips" of his people, as Luther had once counseled.

Zuckmayer's skill at enlivening the action with colorful images and scenes added to his popularity. Perfectly chosen local accents sustained the atmosphere of tension in the plot. During the love scenes between Johann Bückler and his Julchen, the language turned soft and plain, almost like a folksong. Without sentimentality, many scenes attain the melodious tone of pure poetry. Zuckmayer's folk romance—as *Schinderhannes* [*Mainzer Moritat vom Schinderhannes*] might best be

called—once again gave to the theater what was typical of the theater: moments of emotion, at times lyrical and at others dramatically tense. The scene where Hannes tricks the French who have a warrant for his arrest, by pretending to be a forest ranger and luring them into a trap, is remarkably tense. But there are tender moments also, as when the foolhardy and outnumbered rebel refuses to flee because he is searching for his Julchen.

Even Zuckmayer's descriptions and stage directions have poetic strength. None other than Max Liebermann, the grand old impressionist artist, designed the stage setting for the Berlin opening. Zuckmayer's directions for the third act call for "an undulating wheat field, ready for harvest; above it the sky floats in a saturated, golden-brown evening glow. A small field path. To the side, shrubbery and willows, hiding the river. An embankment separates the path from the wheat field, so that the ears of the grain are far above eye level. Some peasants, among them farmer Raab, weary and slow, straggle home from work, their scythes on their shoulders." Although one might call such art folk based, (like the paintings of Millet) the scene, especially the performance of Käthe Dorsch, moved even the inexorably critical Alfred Kerr. Of course, even the genius of Dorsch might have availed nothing if the scene itself had not contained so much artistry.

In the fourth and last act, before the execution of Johann Bückler and his accomplices, the playwright brilliantly demonstrated his special gift for creating group scenes. He captured the voices of the agitated populace in pure and natural idioms. Here is his description of the scene: "Before the gates of Mainz, first light of dawn. In the background, against the morning sky, the steeples and rooftops of the city. An enormous crowd of people presses toward the scaffold, seen on a hill behind a temporary wooden partition. In the foreground the path leading to the spectators' stand. At the entries to the stands, policemen and ticket collectors hold back those who cannot afford to pay. Some groups come and go, others have ensconced themselves on projections from the walls, on benches, on sheds, and in tree branches, for a better view. Pamphlet vendors, pretzel sellers, and begging street urchins fill the air with a high-pitched, monotonous clamor. Uninterrupted, sometimes from afar, sometimes near, the Schinderhannes' tune is heard above the shrieks of a barrel organ and the thin whimper of children. The human noise bubbles with a rhythmic buzz."

Every word from the mob characterizes people caught up in mass hysteria. Each robust colloquialism had once been overheard by the playwright himself, in just that tone of voice, although the circumstances may have been different. The mob is like a dramatic chorus presaging the outbreak of a revolution or the beginning of a war. There are those who do not care and those who are simply curious, lusting for sensation; then there are the fanatics, the sadistically uninhibited, eager to lynch the delinquent. A young, skeptical spectator is denigrated as a "Jew boy." The street gangs, vagabonds, and beggars roaming about the stage are nothing more than "hoods." As soon as one compares this name-calling and boastfully strong language with Zuckmayer's memoirs of childhood (going back almost seven decades), it is obvious where the vocabulary originated. The child had never forgotten the language of the Mainz street gangs, the jargon of laborers, craftsmen, policemen, and soldiers. Zuckmayer's later plays and stories lead one to marvel again and again at the fidelity of his aural memory.

Zuckmayer's subsidiary characters, especially figures in the mob, are often more true to life than some of his overdrawn or idealized heroes and heroines. However, Schinderhannes and his Julchen maintain their proper folk tone until the final curtain. That tone, now familiar on the stage, was the voice of the people. In his review Alfred Kerr admitted that "Zuckmayer's strength lies in his original freshness. (But even freshness, my son of the present, has its limits.) Zuckmayer's strength: local human nature [*das Volkstum*], Zuckmayer's weakness: folksiness [*das Volkstümliche*]."

Kerr's distinction between *Volkstum* and *volkstümlich,* which at first seems nothing more than a play on words, becomes meaningful when Zuckmayer's third play, *Katharina Knie,* is compared with the earlier work. In *The Merry Vineyard* and in *Schinderhannes, Volkstum* was, aside from the colorful milieu and the picturesque language, primarily the people's actual character, with its strong traits and its romantic longings. *Volkstümlich* was—and Kerr probably meant it that way—that which the people liked, even if it was not quite true to life, such as the sentimental and the affectedly touching. Zuckmayer's "high-wire act" (the subtitle of *Katharina Knie*) again deals with characters and scenes from his native region, although the dialect is closer to that of the Rhine-Pfalz. But this prettily colored circus poster is presented through the naively ecstatic eyes of the boy who had once marveled at the world of gypsies and vagabonds. Zuckmayer tries to make his audience believe that the glitter of a poverty-stricken traveling circus could so possess a human being that she would sacrifice personal happiness to her career. Katharina's passion for the ring and her loyalty beyond the grave to her father, the old circus director Knie, are stronger than the sincere love of the farmer Rothacker, to whom she is engaged and in whose house she had once worked as a servant.

The image of Papa Knie, who will not admit that the glory of the traveling circus had passed forever, is sentimental. On top of the economic situation, the competition of films has made the circus a losing business. The clowns have every reason to feel the proverbial sadness behind their grotesque masks. The daring trapeze artists and the strong tumblers are hardly prepared to face the inevitable. The bailiff's sad part becomes almost comic as he tries to collect debts. But Katharina's optimistic charm and her unswerving confidence triumph in the end, drawing the others along. The bailiff settles for the golden engagement ring, and Katharina's last command, "Order the horses!" means that the show will go on. The spirit of the circus has triumphed once more.

The setting and the loving attention Zuckmayer paid to detail are again genuine. Clearly he had been charmed by the magic of the circus and the fairgrounds in his youth. Out of the comedies and tragedies of his circus folk, he fashioned a childishly simple elegy, although the social background and the shading of the inflationary period are quite authentic. The Berlin critics—including Herbert Ihering, who was well disposed toward Zuckmayer—unanimously rejected the play; and the reviews have remained negative to this day.

Kerr alone, having apparently succumbed to a weakness for his "Zuckzuckmayer" ("Tic-tic-mayer"), noted that the brilliant part for a great actor such as Basserman did not write itself. The kinds of exhibitionist tricks Albert Basserman used to overcome traps of his role were recorded by Walther Kiaulehn in his book on Berlin: "Old Knie has an interminable monologue during the first act. Basserman avoided the dangers inherent in this tirade by busying his hands, while talking, with actions typical for a circus man: he braided a whip, held the end between his teeth, worked nimbly with his fingers, chewed his speech around the whip end, fastened the new string onto the handle, continued to talk, found something further to do with the whip, and talked some more. Finally, whip and monologue were finished, and Basserman cracked it with the last word." Unfortunately, the chronicler did not report whether the procedure employed by the great mime had been his own idea or the director's. It may be assumed that Zuckmayer participated in the staging, as he always did in the rehearsals of his plays, but he does not mention the incident in his memoirs. The only reference to *Katharina Knie* is an anecdote about a lawsuit brought against him by a real circus family named Knie, in Switzerland. The suit was finally settled to everyone's satisfaction. Like the brothers Knie, most theatergoers were deeply touched by the play, and this public reaction has also proved to be permanent.

In 1927, the year he had completed *Schinderhannes* in Berlin, Zuckmayer also wrote a collection of short stories, *Der Bauer aus dem Taunus und andere Geschichten* (*The Peasant from Taunus and Other Stories*). The title novella describes the curious fate of a soldier on furlough during the First World War. The peasant, no longer a young man, has obtained permission in

1918 to go home and till his land. The war is drawing to a close, and suddenly a restlessness comes over him. He leaves his wife and native village to return to the Eastern front. As his buddies are preparing to return to Germany during the collapse of the front, he continues on his way in the opposite direction. He is not motivated by a desire to die heroically but, rather, by the wish to preserve a human life: that of a child that had been born to him of a beloved woman in the faraway land. To find the woman and child seems all but impossible in view of the confusion caused by the retreating armies of the Austrians and Germans. But he finally locates them behind the enemy lines. Despite dangers and obstacles, he succeeds in beating his way back to Germany with the child (the mother has died in the meantime). The child now becomes part of his family, accepted even by his wife.

Zuckmayer fashioned this moving human story with the clarity and simplicity of an old woodcut. The indictment against the war was less important to him than the monument to the peaceful sentiment and pure feelings of genuine people who stolidly pursue their way, moving straight ahead through the muddle and gloom.

Despite the divided response to his "high-wire act," Zuckmayer's reputation as a playwright and forceful storyteller had become so solid that the honors and commissions kept coming one after another. A little over thirty, he was a famous man. In 1929 he received the Georg Büchner Prize, given by the city of Darmstadt, and during the same year he shared with Renée Schickele and Max Mell the "Dramatists Prize of the Heidelberg Festival." The film industry also made use of his scenarios. Barely a year after the enormous success of *The Merry Vineyard,* his first play was made into a movie. Zuckmayer also made significant contributions to the script of *Der blaue Engel* (*The Blue Angel*), the film by Josef von Sternberg based on the novel *Professor Unrat* by Heinrich Mann. A year earlier he had adapted the American play about the First World War, *What Price Glory,* by Maxwell Anderson and Laurence Stallings, known in Germany as *Rivalen* (*Rivals*).

Still in the year of his fabulous success as a dramatist, his sudden wealth allowed him to buy a country home near Salzburg, the Wiesmühl in Henndorf; but he continued to maintain his apartment in Berlin. He and his wife, Alice Herdan-Zuckmayer, gathered around them a large circle of old and new friends including war buddies such as the air force officer Ernst Udet (the prototype for General Harras in *The Devil's General*), Erich Maria Remarque, the author of the successful war novel, *Im Westen nichts Neues* (*All Quiet on the Western Front*), Max Krell, the editor of the Ullstein publishing house, and numerous others from the theater, press, and film.

For a long time Zuckmayer contemplated the idea of a play on the theme of Till Eulenspiegel. The character of the Low German roguish jester and popular hero had always captivated him, and he intended to place the figure in a situation of contemporary relevance. But his ideas never crystallized into a clear concept. Perhaps he was also held back by the fact that Gerhart Hauptmann had written an epic on the same topic some years earlier, in which the famous vagabond had become a stylized tragic symbol of German destiny. But Hauptmann's *Till Eulenspiegel* turned out to be a failure, perhaps at least in part because of the exorbitant price of the collectors' edition in which it was published. Zuckmayer has not explained the reasons for abandoning the material that had attracted him for so long, but we may assume that he no longer felt convinced that anything flowing from his pen would automatically gain success.

It was the actor Fritz Kortner, who had played the leading part in *Rivalen,* who suggested a dramatization of the story of the Captain of Köpenick. Zuckmayer was immediately taken with the idea of a satire on Prussian militarism. The proverbial "Köpenickiad" was still fresh in the memory of his contemporaries, and the crafty swindles of the poor cobbler and recidivist convict had truly Eulenspiegel-like traits. At least one characteristic was shared by the false captain and the medieval thief: both used the weapon of the underdog cunning, to pull the mighty by the nose, thereby preserving the appearance of innocence. Who would possibly suspect that such a creature—the most wretched of wretches—was anything but a poor devil and slow-witted dolt?

Eulenspiegel had been the clever rebel among despised and oppressed peasants. The cobbler Voigt—the alleged captain—belonged to the poorest of the poor, "the fifth estate," to whom the state and the authorities refused even the right to live and work. The social implications of the popular rascal of legend were probably of secondary importance to Zuckmayer. He, like many others, saw first of all a situation in which the apparent prestige of the military caste and authoritarian state could be unmasked and ridiculed.

Zuckmayer subtitled his new play, which turned out to be his best, *A German Fairytale in Four Acts.* Like other such stories, it could produce tears and laughter at the same time. The fate of the homeless, haunted man was tragic, but everything cheered up when the tables were turned, as if by magic. And Zuckmayer's fairy tale actually included a magic charm: the uniform. It was a long shot, but he used it masterfully. While adapting the rather undramatic anecdote to the stage, he found in the uniform (a necessary item of the plot) a secondary, magical meaning. It became the counterpart of the small, insignificant man. Zuckmayer himself reported how fascinated he had been by the idea.

> Suddenly I saw it: *this* was my "Eulenspiegel," poor devil, made wise by want, who exemplified the truth to

an era and a people. For though the story was more than twenty years old, at this moment—in 1930, when the National Socialists were taking their place in the Reichstag as the second-strongest party and were once again throwing the country into a new fever of uniforms—it was once again a reflection, an Eulenspiegel image [owl's mirror image] of the mischief and the dangers growing in Germany. But it also reflected the hope of overcoming these perils, by the same means as the footloose shoemaker, using his native wit and human insight.

Once I had made up my mind to write the play, I rejected all offers of collaboration. Joint and collective work were never my style. I was also certain that I could master the material only in my own way, not by "cracking the whip," but by conjuring up the image of man. I retained the fairy-tale aspect of the original Eulenspiegel concept. It seemed to me that telling a story like a fairy tale, even while using a comic tone, was the way to extend it beyond the immediate case and imbue it with a timeless sense of truth.

Like some other masterpieces in epic and dramatic literature—those of Kleist, Gottfried Keller, and Gerhart Hauptmann come to mind—Zuckmayer's tragicomedy was based on a newspaper article. Dated 1906, it read: "Yesterday, a man impersonating a military captain led a detachment of soldiers from the Tegel rifle range to the Köpenick town hall, arrested the mayor, robbed the treasury, and drove off in a carriage."

At this time, this clever prank had caused quite a sensation; it clearly showed the people how power was obtained in a monarchy that called itself "constitutional." An officer's uniform, even one as shabby as that of cobbler Voigt, gave one enough "identification" to engage in acts of violence, not only in this but in other situations as well. For example, a few years later, in Zabern, Alsace, another military officer (a real one this time) arbitrarily arrested anyone he chose and locked his victims into a cellar. Blind faith in the authority invested in a uniform and uncritical acceptance of orders and regulations from above were considered to be virtues in the state's subjects. Their intelligence should be restricted, as a Prussian district president once said. A liberal Berlin newspaper hit the nail on the head when it wrote: "His trump card was the officer's uniform."

Yet Wilhelm Voigt should not be seen as an incorrigible swindler. Carl Zuckmayer presents him as certainly a cunning but basically an upright little man who respects the power of the state, a victim of a merciless class system and a petty, rigid, order-loving bureaucracy which has taken away the ex-convict's right to work and settle down, thereby depriving him of the right to live. As a seventeen-year-old shoemaker's apprentice Voigt, in desperate need, had forged some money orders, thereby robbing the German mails of about three hundred talers all told. Yet he had been sentenced to prison for fifteen years. After his release, no community, not even his hometown, wanted him. His attempt to obtain his papers by taking matters into his own hands and breaking into a police station resulted in another prison term. Zuckmayer incorporated the horrors of such a judicial system in his scenario. He saw the ex-convict, who had spent thirty years behind bars, as a poor devil indeed, and rightfully so. Voigt was a man whom society had wronged far more than he had sinned against it.

Not with the teasing probes of the bitter satirist, but with the sympathy of a compassionate though bemused observer, the playwright fused his images into a realistic whole. The "burlesque" of the discarded uniform ran parallel to the shoemaker's thorny road. It was a superb comic device to allow these lines to intersect (in contrast to the laws of mathematics, where parallels only meet in infinity). Zuckmayer, however, was not a metaphysician speculating about mathematical concepts; in this work at least he was a determinist. His Prussian "Satyricon" developed by necessity along a chain of social connections. The uniform migrated from the best tailor shop in Potsdam to the officer of the guard, Captain von Schlettow, and when he has worn it out, to the mayor of Köpenick, Obermüller, who uses it for military exercises in the hope of obtaining a commission as a reserve officer. Having finally outlasted its usefulness, it winds up at a secondhand shop in Berlin. Meanwhile, Wilhelm Voigt has received "military" training, thanks to the patriotic prison director. Voigt knows the Prussian code by heart; in fact, without knowing it, he has prepared himself for his big role in life.

Although Zuckmayer lacked the biting wit of the true satirist, the character of this frustrated strategist, who becomes the unwitting cause of the comedy about the uniform, has all the earmarks of satire. In the first part of the play (during which, Kerr wrote, he died laughing, only to discover, in the second act, that he was still alive), he created a masterpiece of social parody. It might even have been interpreted as a model for the theater of the absurd, with its "troop movements" in the prison chapel. But as a realist, Zuckmayer never allowed his audience to forget that he was presenting, not the product of a ludicrous imagination, but an apparent historical reality in all its grotesque contradictions.

As the play progresses, comic and tragic elements coalesce more and more, until they finally merge. This is particularly true in the crucial reversal of tragicomic fate during the scene where the shoemaker's plan takes on full form. Voigt is reading the story of the town musicians of Bremen to a young girl on her deathbed. Many critics felt that this scene was more sentimental than poetic. But the scene is dramatically motivated because it leads to the decisive cue, pronounced by the rooster in the fairy tale: "Come along . . . we can always find something better than death." This motto for a human comedy might have served as a more appropriate epigraph for the entire play than even the line the author chose from *Rumpelstiltskin*—"No," said the dwarf, "let us talk about man."

At the end of **The Captain of Köpenick** there is another almost surrealist comic scene. After being questioned at headquarters, Voigt wants to look at himself in a mirror. The police officers, in a good mood, grant him his wish; after all, the man has become a worldwide sensation, and even His Majesty the Emperor has been most personally amused by him and the "magic power" of the uniform. "Impossible," declares the shoemaker upon seeing himself for the first time as a captain. Zuckmayer left out the happy ending. In the case of Voigt the shoemaker, life had written it. As reported in the chronicles, Wilhelm Voigt, after having served another sentence, traveled all over Germany, appearing in nightclubs and carnivals. As a child, Carl Zuckmayer had himself seen Voigt perform in Mainz. For Zuckmayer, "all's well" indeed when it "ends well." Only the German fetishism for uniforms was destined to a bad end. When Zuckmayer's German fairy tale was performed at the Deutsches Theater in 1931, the brown battalions of Adolf Hitler were already preparing for another, more terrible uniform craze.

Critics and public—the nationalists excepted—received the play most enthusiastically. Herbert Ihering, already one of Zuckmayer's great champions, hailed **The Captain of Köpenick** as his best play. Ihering recognized its importance as a historical picture "of civil, military, and imperial Germany." A long run was predicted, especially since the play contained seventy-three speaking parts.

During the twelve years of Hitler's Reich, **The Captain of Köpenick** was banned, along with other plays, from all German theaters. Shortly after the end of the war Zuckmayer's masterpiece was presented again in a number of German theaters. The play was seen as a suitable medium for the so-called reeducation of the German people that the Allies were striving for. (**The Devil's General,** a piece less suitable for such purposes, was presented for the first time in Germany in 1947, in Frankfurt.)

A personal memory seems pertinent here. In the fall of 1946, shortly after Carl Zuckmayer had returned to Germany as a United States cultural officer, he attended a performance of **The Captain of Köpenick** at the Heidelberg municipal theater. The final applause was marred by catcalls from the balcony. Students, young veterans, took personally Zuckmayer's scorn of the uniform craze and heckled the author when he took a bow. Zuckmayer reacted spontaneously and invited the young people to join him for a drink and talk. The students ac-

cepted, and the former First World War officer found just the right conversational tone to reach an understanding with these misguided young veterans frustrated by defeat.

In **The Captain of Köpenick** Carl Zuckmayer unequivocally confirmed the humanistic creed of his youth. With this play he clearly rejected the powers responsible for the German catastrophe. Two years before Hitler's rise to power he had decided that there was no turning back for him. "Inner emigration" was impossible without compromising his love for his country and its language. Perhaps the decision to leave Germany was somewhat easier for him than for his like-minded friends because he already had a second home, a house he could fill with friends and guests, in Austria. On the estate in Henndorf, near Salzburg, there was a constant coming and going of people, especially during the festival season.

Although the storm clouds were now gathering over Austria—the German National Socialists threatened from without, and there were domestic troubles as well—Zuckmayer enjoyed a time of contemplative creativity in his country hideaway from 1933 to 1938. His literary efforts of that period, especially the prose pieces inspired by the landscape, as well as poetry and plays, reveal that he was anxious to avoid direct involvement in politics. It might be called an escape into nature, or at least a covert withdrawal and contemplation of his true impulses and inclinations. Away from the politics of the day and all the heated discussions surrounding him, he focused on the elemental forces governing his temperament. Inspired by Eros and Bacchus, he did not avoid the problems of his time but transposed them into events and figures that became timeless mirrors of the dissonances in the world.

For a short time Zuckmayer's plays continued to be performed in German theaters, even after the National Socialists had come to power. The magazine *Berliner Illustrierte,* having stopped a serialized version of one of Zuckmayer's stories, courageously resumed it after the author had voiced his personal objection to the suppression. **"Eine Liebesgeschichte"** ("A Love Story") deals with a genuine, profound conflict. The hero, an imperial Prussian officer, ostracized for flouting convention, sacrifices his career, and ultimately his life, for the woman he loves, a singer and a commoner.

During the years of his secluded life in Henndorf Zuckmayer often worked for the movies. Of the scripts he wrote for the London producer Alexander Korda, the best-known and most important was for the life of Rembrandt starring Charles Laughton. The premiere of his next play, however, did not take place in the Reich; **Der Schelm von Bergen** (**The Knave of Bergen**) opened in 1934 at Vienna's Burgtheater. It was characteristic of his political restraint during those crucial early stages of the Hitler era that he shifted the action into the remote past and placed a personal conflict at the center play, thus leaving it in the sphere of the purely human. A legendary German empress secretly secures advice and assistance from an executioner, who is to provide her with a remedy for her barrenness. (During the Middle Ages, executioners often dabbled in the healing arts as a sideline, especially since they had jurisdiction over the blood of the condemned, which according to superstition, could cure all sorts of afflictions.) While traveling to her secret consultations, the empress meets and falls in love with a young man, little realizing that he is the son of the executioner. Nor does the man know the identity of his lady love. After the sudden death of his father, he is to assume the duties of the executioner, as the law demanded. He fears the implications of this horrible office, but he is mercifully spared when an imperial pardon abolishes the death penalty—as a result of the emperor's joy over a newborn son. The emperor even pardons the youth, who is knighted in the end.

Zuckmayer's anecdotal plot was not intended to condemn the conditions at an imaginary imperial court. The playwright was much more concerned with man's right to the fulfillment of his personal goals and desires. (What is done for love cannot be a sin, "for it is a fragment torn from the heart of God, and it burns like the heart of God that never turns to ashes.") Reactions to the play were mixed. The author was accused of escaping into the past. The authenticity of his stage setting was recognized, but he was criticized for the pseudo-medieval language his characters used.

Most of Zuckmayer's time during the years he lived in Henndorf was devoted to his stories. *Ulla Winblad,* a play completed in 1937, could not be performed in Austria. It opened in 1938 at the Schauspielhaus in Zurich. Among the prose works written between 1934 and 1938 were **"Ein Sommer in Österreich"** (**"A Summer in Austria"**), *Herr über Leben und Tod* (*Master over Life and Death*), and the novel *Salwàre oder Die Magdalena von Bozen* (*Salwàre, or Magdalene of Bozen*). The novella *Der Seelenbräu* (*The Life Brew*), in which Zuckmayer paid homage to the Austrian way of life, was written in 1945, in nostalgic remembrance, after the author had already come to America.

Salwàre, with its romantic subtitle, was the result of a journey through the southern Tyrol in 1935. This novel, the longest work Zuckmayer ever wrote, and one not mentioned in his memoirs (perhaps he did not consider it worth mentioning, strikingly uncovers the strengths and weaknesses of his narrative craft. Using the first person, he describes the experiences and encounters of a visitor to a castle of a nobleman who is his friend. The lord of this castle is a successful writer himself, a man of the world who nevertheless appreciates aristo-

cratic seclusion and prefers to arrange his personal life along aesthetic lines rather than cope with the problems of the society outside his closed circle. His esoteric tendencies are so strong that he lives like a stranger even within his own family—his wife, his children, and his aging mother. Only with his sister, an equally aristocratic personality of unusual beauty, does he form a close relationship. She is his confidante and coworker. The theme of incestuous love between the siblings is gently suggested.

At the castle, amid the magnificent scenery of the forest and high mountains, there is much entertaining on a grand scale, although the lord of the manor generally stays aloof. The narrator, as chronicler of the family conflicts and dramatic confusion of feelings, is drawn into the whirl, reluctantly but with a strange sense of fascination. The company, increased during the social season by guests from the international set, the theater, and the literary world, represents something like a "magic mountain" in miniature: a self-contained society in "splendid isolation." Drawn deeper and deeper into the conflict, the chronicler becomes a shocked witness to the dramatic self-destruction of the aristocratic sister and brother.

As an epic creator, always cognizant of the fullness of life, Zuckmayer was apparently not satisfied with the tragic theme of this novel. He invented a series of subsidiary plots: a love story which, in contrast to the aristocratic atmosphere in the Alpine castle, takes place in the humble surroundings of a country inn, and additional secondary incidents that form a sort of detective story. Such intertwining, suspenseful plot elements are characteristic of the traditional novel. Zuckmayer's main characters appear somewhat romantically overdrawn; the tragic pathos of their behavior is stretched to the very limits of the probable. As usual, the secondary characters seem more realistic and closer to life. But the author is most successful in his visually impressive description of the colorful South-Tyrolean landscape. Despite the quality of these literally "picturesque" scenic descriptions, the reader is asked to breathe rather more mountain air than is good for him.

The delightful story of *Der Seelenbräu* proved how fresh and vivid the happy years in Austria remained in Carl Zuckmayer's memory. He began to write it in an effort to share his anxieties about the fate of his beloved Salzburg and its people. The characterizations of the old, coarse, but upright village parson and his counterpart, the patronizingly generous owner of the brewery of the "life brew," reveal a heretofore hidden inclination toward the baroque. It becomes a sort of musical main theme, reuniting the two opposing characters. The vehicle for this rapprochement is the budding romance between the new teacher (and composer) and an upperclass young woman.

The pastoral tone of such an undemanding story allowed the author to wallow in local color. As he admitted himself, a "searing nostalgia" had prompted him to conjure up the "paradise lost" of Henndorf. He took particular pleasure in dwelling on the extravagant portrayal of a rural carnival. That carnival becomes the focus for the development of various conflicts that are eventually resolved in good cheer and harmony.

Zuckmayer's idyllic retreat at Henndorf came to an abrupt end when the German troups marched into Austria in March 1938. Now he could no longer be spared the fate of emigration; he had to accept it. His escape across the border into Switzerland succeeded at literally the very last minute. Following the example of his Captain of Köpenick, he did not identify himself to the SS border patrols as a writer but nonchalantly played the part of a traveling German officer, a veteran of the First World War. That earned him the necessary respect.

The first stop on the road of exile was Zurich, where his play *Bellman* opened in the same year, 1938. In its revised version the play has been produced under the title *Ulla Winblad,* but the subtitle continued to be *The Music and Life of Carl Michael Bellman.* Bellman, known in the history of literature as the "Villon of the Swedish rococo," was a man with whom Zuckmayer could identify. While still a student at Heidelberg, he had taken great spontaneous delight in reciting the songs and scenes from the life of the Nordic poet, accompanying himself on the guitar. But the final version of the play was not completed until 1953. It was the first of Zuckmayer's plays to use a ballad-like epic style, a sequence of tableaux rather than a dramatic progression of scenes. Typical of this style were the interludes, in which characters of Bellman's imagination appeared to offer commentary, as well as the insertions of original songs by the Swedish poet into the scenes. Quotations and notes supported the action on the stage, a procedure not entirely unlike that used by Bertolt Brecht.

Like many other dramatizers of actual events, Carl Zuckmayer contented himself with a few selected approximations to historical facts. He alludes to the plot against the tolerant and art-loving King Gustav III, who was assassinated at a masked ball during a palace revolt in 1792. But all this remained background material. In the foreground—at times played on a forestage—were the antics of Bellman, a man addicted to wine, women, and song. His sweetheart, Ulla Winblad, also a historical figure, was freely transformed. The only verified fact was that Ulla Winblad, sweetheart and later wife of a chamberlain and mistress of the king, did live at the Swedish court. The complex conflict with Bellman, who purportedly pursued her with his jealousy, is probably a poetic invention. With the death of Gustav III, Bellman lost his benefactor. The new aristocrats accused him of traitorous intrigues and locked him up in a dungeon. In Zuckmayer's version Ulla Winblad attempts to rescue her former lover, for whom she still harbors some sentiment. She plans to take Bellman abroad, but the sick and shattered balladeer no longer has the strength to flee and dies in her arms—a melodramatic ending, totally in keeping with the play. Just before giving up the ghost, the dying poet softly and tenderly sings a melancholy love song to his lute: "Skoal to you and me!" His last words sound enthusiastic: "To have loved the unperfectible remains our last victory. Now I perceive your smile in the skies. A smile remains—when all is ended." Bellman dies, glass in hand, on his lips a drinking song to life and the sun. His deeper view of life was also Zuckmayer's, to whom existence without love was empty indeed.

The play, performed in November, 1938, in its first version, also made a few political allusions. They were typical of Zuckmayer's personal understanding of a refugee's fate. There were phrases praising "every homeland in the world" and celebrating life and the earth, which for Zuckmayer was the "mother of us all," just as heaven was the "father of us all." With this tone, the poet achieved an almost unpolitical view of international politics. According to his ideal conception, the meaning of art was "the blending of utmost freedom with utmost discipline." Love was to complement reason. When Zuckmayer's king and other characters express such gems of wisdom as that the state, as a work of art, should mean more than an ant hill, they are no doubt revealing the author's political beliefs. Yet the true poetry of the play rests less on its pseudo-political pronouncements than on the inventive creation of imaginary characters taken from the "epistles" of Bellman, with old singing and drinking buddies coming along for the ride.

Although many passages of *Bellman* mirror the fate of a man without a country, that fate is always romantically transformed. Zuckmayer's residence in Chardonne on Lake Geneva in Switzerland was still an idyl, a dream exile, where he could celebrate family festivities, joined by his brother, a musician who had emigrated to Turkey, and his parents, who came to visit.

Bibliography

Works by Carl Zuckmayer Available in English

The Captain of Kopenick. Translated by Elizabeth Montague. Microfilm of typewritten copy. New York, Columbia University, 1959.

Siegfried Mews (essay date 1981)

SOURCE: Mews, Siegfried. "The Last Plays." In *Carl Zuckmayer,* pp. 120-34. Boston: Twayne Publishers, 1981.

[In the following essay, Mews offers interpretations of Zuckmayer's last plays, including Die Uhr schlägt eins, Kranichtanz, Das Leben des Horace A. W. Tabor, *and* Der Rattenfänger.*]*

I THE CLOCK STRIKES ONE

After the production of **Cold Light** in 1955 there was an uncharacteristic lapse of six years before another Zuckmayer premiere—still an event that demanded the critics' attention—took place. The drama **The Clock Strikes One** is, in many respects, a continuation of themes and problems dramatized in the preceding plays. In Zuckmayer's own view the play deals with that "tragic guilt that all men incur more or less 'innocently' in times of dishonor—unless they are martyrs or saints."[1] Unlike **The Devil's General, The Song of the Fiery Furnace,** and **Cold Light, The Clock Strikes One** was not based on an actual occurrence, or so the playwright claimed.[2] Further, whereas the former plays tended toward fairly lengthy discussions at the cost of dramatic action, the present drama almost achieved the opposite effect by presenting too much action in a comparatively brief drama.[3]

The drama that premiered on 14 October 1961 at the Vienna Burgtheater has the slightly paradoxical subtitle **A Historical Drama of the Present.** The striking of the clock referred to in the title denotes that it is past midnight and a new day is beginning; at the same time, the subtitle suggests that the problems of the past continue to haunt the present—a present, however, that by the time of the play's writing had become almost historical.[4]

The play is, then, an attempt to come to terms with Germany's Nazi past, a contribution to the so-called *Vergangenheitsbewältigung*—although in a distinctly Zuckmayerian mode. The action takes place in 1953 and 1954, that is, during a period when Germany's economic recovery often referred to as economic miracle (*Wirtschaftswunder*) set in. The material prosperity of Jörg Holtermann, a successful industrialist, belies the shadows of the past that beset his family. It is ultimately the aura of guilt intuitively sensed by Gerhard, the youngest of the Holtermanns' two children, that impels him to reject his parents' life style and strike out on his own. Curiously, however, he joins a gang of criminals whose leader, Turo von Heydenkamp, he adopts as a model. Gerhard's mother Gudula, next to him the main character in the play and the one perhaps most likely to arouse the spectators' sympathy and pity, has never been able to overcome her past and continues incessantly to probe her guilt. Gerhard's going astray exacerbates her problem; whereas her daughter from a previous marriage serves as a constant reminder of her culpability, Gerhard held the promise for a brighter future—a promise that now will not be fulfilled. As she confesses to Turo, whom she had asked to release his hold on her son, she was previously married to a successful Jewish musician who, when the Nazis came to power, was beaten and tortured so severely that he asked his wife to end his suffering by giving him poison—a request to which she acceded. In order to save herself and her daughter she had to swear that her daughter was the offspring of an adulterous union with her present husband, Holtermann, who, in 1933, had come to her aid. Turo, chief of a gang of men who have become criminals as a consequence of their having been uprooted and emotionally scarred by their experiences in World War II, has a past that even surpasses Gudula's in its gruesome and not entirely unsensational aspects.

As a young child Turo witnessed how his father, a Latvian estate owner, was carried off and his mother raped and then killed by a mob. Later in life Turo joined the German army and became officer of a unit at the Russian front in World War II. In memory of his mother, a beautiful Tartar princess, he called his outfit "The Golden Horde"—the same name he has given his gang—and waged his private war against the Soviet Union not for ideological reasons but to punish the presumable murderers of his parents.

Unlike Gudula, Turo has accepted his guilt by adopting a nihilistic and stoic stance—he reads Seneca. He does not provide any particular justification for his recent activities except the need to go underground after the war in order to escape punishment. Curiously, the previous victims do not seem to be better off than their oppressors; one of the members of Turo's gang is a fatalistic Jew who survived the concentration camps but is shot by police during an unsuccessful hijacking attempt.

The third character whose guilt is most obvious but who, as a man completely without conscience, almost totally ignores it, is Dr. Flühvogel, a university lecturer and Gerhard's tutor. There is bitter irony in the fact that Flühvogel asks for the hand in marriage of Gudula's daughter—who could have been one of his potential victims. For Flühvogel is a former concentration camp doctor who had been charged with selecting those who in the Nazis' view were "superfluous eaters." Gudula, who has gone insane after learning that Turo and Gerhard have left the country as a result of the abortive hijacking at which a policeman was killed, instinctively recoils from Flühvogel. The enormity of his crimes becomes apparent in Gudula's use of Christ's words to the devil, "Get thee hence" (**WA [Werkausgabe in zehn Bänden]**, 10:65). But there is no accounting for Flühvogel's further fate, no attempt at poetic justice, and no effort to elucidate the function of ex-Nazis in post—World War II German society.

With the eighth scene the place of action shifts to Hanoi, then in French Indochina, where Turo and Gerhard, soldiers in the French Foreign Legion, spend their off-duty hours in an establishment of doubtful reputation. Zuckmayer, intimately familiar with a soldierly milieu, provides some colorful touches for this scene. But his tendency to rely on exaggerated effects and stereotyped characters is also in evidence here. Just as Flühvogel corresponds perhaps too closely to the cliché of the brutal, inhuman doctor of a concentration camp, so the girl, with whom Gerhard flees, turns out to be a Communist agent. Gerhard, however, does not become a deserter because of qualms about his role in the Indochina War but as a consequence of his having killed his corporal out of jealousy.

The last scene takes place in the hospital of a French garrison. Gerhard has been caught but, in view of a rare tropical disease he has contracted, been given a brief reprieve before being shot as a deserter. His father comes to see him; his last act of mercy is to empty the hypodermic needle that was intended to make Gerhard fit for the execution. In the end, in a departure from realism, the attending nurse assumes the features of Gerhard's dead mother—she had been killed in a car accident after Gerhard's flight—and, reconciled with his fate, Gerhard dies.

In the dialogue of the final scene questions such as the responsibility of the individual for his actions, human guilt, and God's mercy are voiced once more. But one wonders whether Gerhard's recognition that he failed his mission in life is convincingly presented; unlike the tale **Carnival Confession,** in which the carnival atmosphere provides a perfect foil for the exploration of the main characters' guilt, the thrilling events in **The Clock Strikes One** tend to obscure the inner action, that is, Gerhard's spiritual purification. One wonders further whether a drama that is ostensibly concerned with coming to terms with the political past should entirely dispense with the ideological dimension. True, "Zuckmayer places all his hope and faith for the future in the individual, because . . . the individual alone is capable of insight, spiritual growth, and the conscious shaping of his life."[5] Yet even a rudimentary degree of political awareness on the part of the main characters might have added to their depth.

Some reviewers of the Viennese premiere guardedly applauded the drama or rather the performance—and especially that of Paula Wessely in the role of the mother[6]—although they did not fail to point out that the play relied on thrilling effects. Other critics were less charitable. The weekly news magazine *Der Spiegel,* renowned for its caustic style, seized upon the opportunity for a pun provided by Zuckmayer's title. Instead of **Die Uhr schlägt eins,** *Der Spiegel* headlined its review "Schlägt dreizehn" (*es schlägt dreizehn,* / "that's the limit") and termed the action of the play "monstrous."[7]

For good reasons, the drama is rarely performed and seldom mentioned in the secondary literature.

II DANCE OF THE HERONS AND THE LIFE OF HORACE A. W. TABOR

Although published in 1961,[8] the drama **Dance of the Herons** was not performed until 1967 when the Zurich Schauspielhaus honored the playwright, a Swiss resident for more than a decade, on the occasion of his seventieth birthday. The gap between the publication of the play and its premiere—unprecedented in Zuckmayer's career—can be explained by the fact that **Dance of the Herons** is a one-act play requiring only approximately thirty minutes for its performance. Hence a suitable opportunity had to present itself before the play could be staged.

Curiously, whereas Zuckmayer professes to have conceived the idea for **The Clock Strikes One** in the American jungle,[9] his first drama that has an entirely realistic American setting seems to have originated after the playwright's permanent return to Europe. Like **The Clock Strikes One,** the play takes place in the present; however, in **Dance of the Herons** Zuckmayer confines himself to the domestic sphere and develops the dramatic conflicts from there instead of attempting to deal with a host of problems within the confines of a play. By limiting himself to the domestic sphere and a correspondingly small number of characters, Zuckmayer achieved a degree of density, economy, and concentration that induced many critics to compare **Dance of the Herons** to the last act of a tragedy in which pent-up emotions explode in a sudden outburst of violence.[10]

The play takes place in the living room of an old farm house in New England during the morning hours of a spring day. The preservation of the classical unities of time and place in combination with the limited number of characters—five, in all—sustains the forceful unified action. Loren King, manager of the Atwoods' farm, sees his dream of again acquiring a farm owned and operated by his own family shattered when his son Dave marries a model who poses for underwear ads and whom he therefore considers to be disreputable. The conflict between father and son results from an irreconcilable difference in outlook; whereas the father plans and builds for the future, the son belongs to a generation that is content to live day by day and enjoy instant gratification.

The day of reckoning has also come for Rhoda, an extraordinarily strong-willed woman, and her husband Jolly Atwood, the owners of the farm. When Jolly, a weakling and alcohol-addicted playboy, returns from a hunt, he imitates the mating dance of the male heron. Rhoda, transformed into the hunter, shoots her husband whom she both despises and pities. She rejects the suggestion by Loren, presumably her lover, to declare the shooting an accident and accepts full responsibility for the murder. In a final evocation of Greek tragedy, the stage direction at the end of the play states that she looks upon the corpse with the glance of both "priestess and victim" (**WA,** 10:104).

Although Zuckmayer could hardly have written the play without having spent a number of years as a farmer in Vermont, its merits do not primarily derive from its "Americanness." To be sure, the playwright provides local color by, for example, liberally sprinkling his text with slightly Germanized Americanisms such as "Front-Porch, Locust-Pond, Deerland-Country, Greyhound, Lumberjack." Ultimately, however, the tragic resolution of the conflict tends to transcend the geographical and chronological limitations of the setting. Conversely, it was precisely Zuckmayer's realism that induced one critic to observe Zuckmayer had demonstrated that naturalist theater continued to be a legitimate theatrical mode of expression in the sixties.[11]

Dance of the Herons had signaled Zuckmayer's adopting a somewhat different direction in his choice of topics to be dramatized. In his second-to-last drama, *The Life of Horace A. W. Tabor*—written after *Dance of the Herons* but first performed on 18 November 1964, approximately three years before the one-act play—Zuckmayer again drew on his experiences as an American resident and seized upon a genuinely and uniquely American subject: an authentic hero's rise from rags to riches and, in a significant deviation from the pattern of the success story, his sudden downfall. It is hardly surprising that, in 1939, the story of the erstwhile "silver king" Tabor and his wife Baby Doe was recommended to the newly arrived immigrant as a project with the potential of a surefire Broadway success.[12] Only a few years before Zuckmayer had set foot on American soil, in 1936, newspapers had reported Baby Doe's demise; she had been found frozen to death in her dilapidated shack in Leadville, Colorado. Until the very last she believed—contrary to the opinion of the experts—that the silver mine "The Matchless" she had inherited from Tabor would yield new treasures.

But at that time the dramatist lacked sufficient familiarity with his host country to tackle indigenous material that Douglas Moore, composer of the opera *The Ballad of Baby Doe* (1956), considered a "great American story."[13] In addition, Zuckmayer was too preoccupied with the fate of Europe in general and Germany in particular—as both the unsuccessful *Somewhere in France*[14] and the hugely successful *The Devil's General*[15] demonstrate to varying degrees. As a consequence, we are faced with the somewhat paradoxical fact that, despite its authentic American subject, the play was not written during Zuckmayer's stay in the United States but rather after the playwright's return to Europe. It

was also in Europe, at the Zurich Schauspielhaus, that the play premiered some twenty-five years after Zuckmayer had first heard of Tabor and Baby Doe.[16] Needless to say, the expectations of the German-speaking public differed considerably from those of American theatergoers; they may well have influenced Zuckmayer's dramatic concept.

Despite Zuckmayer's insistence that he had not intended any evocation of the Wild West, it is fair to say that he did not entirely escape the danger of making concessions to popular European preconceptions about the United States. Many critics, at any rate, made explicit references to the Wild West in the headlines of their reviews.[17] A closer look at the text reveals, however, that *The Life of Horace A. W. Tabor* is not, by any means, simply an improved version of the early drama *Pankraz Awakens*.[18] On the contrary, although the first act begins in the run-down golddigger town of Leadville in 1879, the playwright endeavors to de-emphasize the adventuresome and exotic elements by referring to phenomena of the modern industrial world such as environmental pollution and social problems. Only as part of the exposition, presented by means of reports, dialogue, and as a play within a play, does the colorful past of the pioneer and the fight against the Indians play a role. Other conflicts, that is, primarily those between workers and their employers, dominate the present.

Tabor himself—he and his wife Augusta run a post office and general store in Leadville—has renounced the false romanticism of golddigging and succumbed to a pessimistic attitude that is quite uncharacteristic of an inhabitant of the New World. But by a stroke of luck he is able to acquire cheaply two thirds of a silver vein from two German immigrants that proves to be almost inexhaustible. Only two years later—the second act takes place in 1881—Tabor, now a wealthy man, fully subscribes to the idea of progress that for him is almost synonymous with prosperity and profit. Hence he considers a strike by his workers a criminal act; if necessary, he is prepared to use his private army in order to preserve law and order.

The third act takes place one year later and shows Tabor at the height of his power; his economic rise from rags to riches is reflected in his newly gained political prominence. He has been elected governor of Colorado; somewhat later he will become senator. In addition, Tabor's fabulous wealth has excited the people's imagination; his extraordinary good fortune provides the stuff for popular lore and legends. When Tabor first sets eyes on Baby Doe, she appropriately sings the song of silver king Tabor. The song emphasizes Tabor's foremost characteristic—his luck. According to the playwright, Tabor lived in the "time of great improvisations . . . in the world of unheard-of strokes of luck and enormous losses" (**WA,** 10:107). As the subtitle of the play, *A*

Drama from the Days of the Last Kings, suggests, Zuckmayer conceived of Tabor's wealth as being of magical origin.

Tabor's ostentatious display of wealth and his illicit relationship with Baby Doe have alienated him from his wife Augusta who, motivated by social compassion, tends to the needs of the exploited miners. Although she grants him a divorce so that he is free to marry Baby Doe, it is precisely at the moment when his fortune seems to have reached a new peak, at the lavish and spectacular wedding feast, that his empire begins to crumble as a consequence of unfavorable developments in the stock market. In only a little more than three years—the wedding scene in act 4, scene 3 takes place in Washington in 1883, the following first scene of act 5 in Denver, Christmas 1886—Tabor has lost his entire fortune and is reduced to poverty again. Miraculously, however, Augusta returns to Tabor, and Baby Doe remains faithful to him. In the last scene of the play Tabor dies a poor but happy man in a play that in almost Brechtian "epic" fashion spans twenty years of his life[19]—from 1879 to 1899—yet essentially concentrates on the seven years—from 1879 to 1886—of Tabor's rise and fall.

In the view of a number of critics Zuckmayer's play lacked relevance in the middle sixties, at a time when the documentary drama had begun to assert itself. Both Zuckmayer's choice of subject matter—usually decried as a Western or golddigger story—and the artistic means chosen to present this subject—essentially realism—these critics argued, lacked modern appeal and were an insufficient attempt at historical analysis. In fact, one critic went so far as to charge that Zuckmayer had dramatized material that was also used by Hollywood for "the creation of the American myth."[20] To be sure, Zuckmayer delights in the creation of a milieu that is populated by colorful characters whose very names hint at the unusual. Thus we encounter John Savage, a former medicine man of the Cheyenne Indians, Buckskin Joe, an old golddigger, "Chicken-Bill" Lovell, a prospector, and Harvey "Vulture" Doe, the former husband of Baby Doe. Particularly the last named appears as the prototypal Chicago gangster when, during his brief presence on stage, he successfully blackmails Tabor. At the same time, however, in accordance with his avowed intention of minimizing the ingredients to be found in Westerns, Zuckmayer stressed the "documentary" character of his drama by appending a list of works he consulted (*WA,* 10:261-62)—a procedure far more familiar from, for example, Rolf Hochhuth's documentary drama *The Deputy* (1963) than from Zuckmayer.

At any rate, in the final analysis it was not the playwright's aim to explore the social dimensions of an important phase of American history; rather, Zuckmayer was fascinated by the figure of Tabor whose rapid rise and fall—despite its peculiarly American traits—seems to transcend the specific time and place of the action. That Tabor's fate is not primarily determined by socio-economic factors and that he refuses to be cast in a mold is evident, for example, from the apt characterization of one of his fellow bonanza millionaires who calls him a "mystic, . . . not an entrepreneur, . . . not a modern man" (*WA,* 10:235). On the one hand, Tabor is not a true capitalist in the fashion of Pierpont Mauler in Brecht's *Saint Joan of the Stockyards;* on the other, as an avowed individualist he neither fully grasps nor sympathizes with the ideas of social reform that are advocated in the play by the character Stratton. Stratton, incidentally a historical figure, is presented by Zuckmayer as a Marxist millionaire—the seeming contradiction notwithstanding.

Tabor's existence is, in the last analysis, little affected by the laws of economics. The repeated references to his fortune, the subtitle, and initial stage directions of the play suggest—quite apart from Zuckmayer's additional comments—that the atmosphere of the fairy tale, in which riches and power are bestowed upon the pure in heart, pervades the drama. There is, indeed, a popular play (*Volksstück*) by the nineteenth-century Viennese playwright Ferdinand Raimund, entitled *The Farmer as Millionaire,* that bears a remarkable structural-thematic resemblance to Zuckmayer's drama. Raimund presents, although within the confines of the *Romantic, Original, Magic Fairy Tale* (thus his subtitle), the rise and fall of a humble man, his temporary delusion, and ultimate happiness that is preceded by the recognition of the errors of his ways. Zuckmayer's drama lacks Raimund's didactic application; however, like Raimund Zuckmayer is primarily interested in the "purely human" devoid of its social and political implications.[21] *Der Spiegel,* hardly noted for subtle understatement, was quick to seize upon the fairy-tale aspects of Zuckmayer's drama and recommended it to the children's hour of the German broadcasting companies.[22] Other critics expressed more balanced but not entirely positive views. The astute Friedrich Luft, for example, asseverated in his review that one could no longer write naively realistic plays as if Brecht, Beckett, or Ionesco had never existed.

The objections raised against Zuckmayer's play concerning the choice of subject matter, the lack of social relevance, the realistic means of presentation, and the creation of a fairy-tale atmosphere have their common denominator in the implicit or explicit assumption that Zuckmayer is no longer "modern" by virtue of the fact that he adhered to both his dramatic creed and his essential means of expression. Lack of modernity, in turn, almost automatically denotes a dramatist of less consequence, many critics seem to infer. Yet such views have not remained unchallenged. One perceptive reviewer observed correctly that critics form only part of the theatrical establishment.[23] Some directors, many actors—

for whom Zuckmayer wrote highly rewarding roles—and large segments of the theatergoing public constitute Zuckmayer's following. To be sure, these followers tend to be less vociferous and articulate than the critics. Nevertheless, their loyalty to Zuckmayer provides an indication that the playwright continued to be a viable force in the theater—even if, as in the case of *The Life of Horace A. W. Tabor,* he shunned the message play and made an only partially successful transition from the exoticism, inspired by Karl May, of *Pankraz Awakens* to a play in which the social dimensions, represented by the ideas of Karl Marx as interpreted by Stratton, come clearer into focus.

III *The Pied Piper*

Literary history in general and theater history in particular do not abound with writers and dramatists who achieved a ripe old age of undiminished creativity. Goethe, George Bernard Shaw, and Gerhart Hauptmann come readily to mind as examples of productive longevity. If we leave the complex question of artistic stature aside, Zuckmayer can easily be added to this list of creative grand old men of letters. What to many might have appeared to be the sum of his life and literary output, the autobiography *A Part of Myself* (1966), should prove not to be Zuckmayer's last work. A few weeks after the playwright had celebrated his seventy-eighth birthday, his last drama, *The Pied Piper,* premiered at the Zurich Schauspielhaus on 22 February 1975. The Swiss theater thereby continued a tradition of first performances of Zuckmayer's plays that reached as far back as the premiere of *Bellman* in 1938 and included such notable events as the first performance of *The Devil's General* in 1946 as well as the premieres of the third-to-last and second-to-last dramas *Dance of the Herons* and *The Life of Horace A. W. Tabor,* respectively.

Curiously, *The Pied Piper* appears to be less a work inspired, in the Goethean sense, by the wisdom, maturity, and contemplative attitude of old age than a play that exhibits youthful impetuosity and partisan overtones. Zuckmayer achieved this effect by reinterpreting the ancient legend of the Pied Piper of Hamelin, a subject to which a prominent citizen of Hamelin had drawn his attention approximately ten years before the play was actually completed. In fact, my English rendering of Zuckmayer's original title *Der Rattenfänger*[24] as *The Pied Piper* has been prompted by Robert Browning's beloved "Child's Story" in verse, entitled *The Pied Piper of Hamelin* (1842), rather than by the attempt to provide a literal translation.[25] Precisely the fact that there is only one document relating the event of 26 June 1284, an inscription on the so-called Pied Piper's house in Hamelin, which briefly reports the abduction of one hundred thirty children, enabled Zuckmayer to give his own interpretation of the legend. Apart from Brown-

ing's humorous verse narrative with its gentle moral, there are other literary reworkings. Suffice it to mention Goethe's playful "Rattenfängerlied" [Song of the Pied Piper, 1804] and Achim von Arnim and Clemens Brentano's inclusion of the orally extant "The Pied Piper of Hamelin" in the first part of their famed collection of folk songs, *The Boy's Magic Horn* (1806). The freedom from the restraints of historical accuracy induced the nineteenth-century novelist Wilhelm Raabe to offer his own version of the events in his prose narrative *The Children of Hamelin* (1863). Raabe dispensed with a vital ingredient of the legend, the invasion of Hamelin by the rats, altogether. Instead of having the Pied Piper rid the city of the rats and then, when he is refused his promised reward, disappear with the children in a small mountain near the city, he has the socially rejected Pied Piper lead the city's male youths into an ambush where they are slain by their enemies.

We may infer from Zuckmayer's afterword to his dramatization that he studied the historical literature on the subject rather than the literary interpretations of the legend. The dramatist retained all important elements of the legend such as the rat plague, the city's deliverance from the rats by the Pied Piper, the withholding of his just reward, and his disappearance with the city's children. However, from the very beginning it is clear that Zuckmayer's reinterpretation differs from those of his predecessors by virtue of the fact that the social tensions existing in medieval Hamelin assume utmost importance. Actually, the *dramatis personae* are grouped according to their social status, and the inhabitants are rigidly divided into the patricians of the city proper and those lesser citizens who live outside the city walls. Before the play begins, a narrator draws the spectators' attention to the rigidly enforced class distinction that separates the city.

The rat plague that besets Hamelin turns out to be a monstrous scheme on the part of the ruling class in general and of the city's regent in particular. The rats are allowed to multiply—in the quarter of the poor outside the city walls it is even prohibited to kill them—because they devour everything and thus keep the price of flour at an artificially high level. The city regent's greed and desire to reap windfall profits, however, threaten to destroy the entire city, owing to the fact that the rats can no longer be contained outside the city walls. Social unrest among the poorer populace is rampant; in addition, the children of the well-to-do have turned away from their morally corrupt parents and established an anachronistic hippie counterculture replete with drug or rather herb sniffing.

Bunting, so called on account of his colorful dress (*bunt,* "colorful"), arrives at Hamelin during this politically volatile situation. He has fled the Eastern territories where he had been educated by the Teutonic Knights but where, as a Slav, he was destined to spend his life in servitude. Bunting finds employment as the assistant to the executioner with jurisdiction over the poor. His curious power over rats by means of playing his pipe—construed by the superstitious to be magic but explained by Bunting to be a natural phenomenon—does not remain unnoticed for long. An agreement is reached between Gruelhot, the city regent, and Bunting. Rather than money Bunting demands a parcel of land and all rights of a free citizen if he should succeed in leading the rats out of the city to the Weser river where they will drown. Despite Bunting's success in ridding the city of the rats, he is denied his recompense. Instead, the authorities make a counterproposal to the effect that Bunting will be handsomely rewarded if he leads the undesirable poorer citizens into virtual slavery by inducing them to become colonists in the Eastern territories. Bunting refuses to have any part in such a devilish scheme and demands both political rights and economic fair play for the poor citizens. But the planned uprising of the underprivileged is prevented by the arrival of the duke of Brunswick's soldiers. They, unlike their predecessors in previous Zuckmayer plays, have no redeeming qualities whatsoever and are depicted with severity. Thus Rikke, the executioner's daughter with whom Bunting is in love, commits suicide in a particularly grisly fashion to avoid being ravished by the soldiers. Meanwhile Bunting, who had escaped the authorities, is recaptured again and sentenced to death for inciting a riot. At the last moment, Gruelhot is presented with an ultimatum. His two children are being held hostage by the other children of the city and will die unless Bunting is released unharmed. The voluntary departure of the children with Bunting in search of a better and freer land concludes the play proper.

In a sense, *The Pied Piper* represents the sum of Zuckmayer's dramatic efforts, owing to the fact that he displays a considerable range of techniques and devices.[26] It sports, for example, a narrator who, however, is less evident in the text than he was at the Zurich premiere.[27] Further, songs interrupt the action, and vivid scenes taking place among the people interchange with highly stylized scenes in the milieu of the upper classes. The entire play is structured loosely into twenty-one scenes, of which eighteen were performed in Zurich, in two "sequences," and thus exhibits an "epic" tendency slightly reminiscent of Brecht's theater.

In fact, it is not entirely unjustified to see Brecht's influence at work.[28] Apart from the aforementioned narrator and the songs (such as Zuckmayer had used before, however), the rigid division of the characters into rulers and ruled, into exploiters and exploited, and the absence of a middle class corresponds somewhat to the Brechtian scheme of things in which the tendency toward social polarization is quite pronounced. Further,

the use of the profit motif, that is, that the rats are being permitted to eat wheat in order to keep prices high, results in a scathing indictment of an unjust social order that rivals Brecht's condemnation of a society split into antagonistic classes.

At the same time, these points of comparison should not obscure the fact that the play is essentially Zuckmayerian in spirit. For example, it does not end with a clearly stated moral or with an appeal to the spectators to change that which is rotten in Hamelin and, by inference, elsewhere; rather, the promised land to which Bunting leads the children appears dimly on the horizon. It is a hope-inspiring vision, not necessarily a concrete goal that can be achieved by means of concerted action. In contrast to such plays as *Cold Light* and *The Clock Strikes One,* however, Zuckmayer places his hope and trust not solely on the individual but on an entire generation of disenchanted children and youths who, to be sure, are dependent on Bunting's leadership.

The process of regeneration is aided by the fact that poetic justice prevails in the case of the chief perpetrator of evil, Gruelhot, and his informer, a baker of consecrated wafers. Gruelhot commits suicide by hanging himself after his wife's death and his children's turning against him; the baker, ironically, meets his end when he is on the point of claiming his reward for the betrayal of Bunting. But Zuckmayer only condemns the worst offenders. The old and humble Bishop Ludger, who significantly speaks the last words of the play, will, together with a crippled youth left behind in the exodus, endeavor to heal the wounds in the bereft and leaderless city. Ludger thus clearly emerges as the moral victor over his opponent, the proud and power-wielding prior.

Zuckmayer's concept of Bunting, the central figure of the drama, does not correspond to the character of the medieval legend. To be sure, like the traditional Pied Piper Bunting has power over animals and men; however, he uses his power not to entice but to advance progressive social ideas. Yet even Bunting succumbs briefly to the lust for power, although in the end he assumes the role of the children's leader to the promised land.

Whereas Zuckmayer retains the medieval setting and alludes both to such ingredients of the legend as the disappearance of the children in the Koppen, a modest hill near Hamelin, and their resurfacing in Transylvania, there are aspects of the play that clearly relate it to the present. Thus Bunting appears as a man of reason in a world of medieval superstition. This superstition is manipulated by Gruelhot to a certain extent when he proposes to charge Bunting with the use of black magic. Gruelhot, at any rate, occasionally uses the modern bureaucrat's phraseology and avails himself of the services of an informer to assess the mood of the populace. The entire power structure functions in modern fashion; it is replete with such types as the executioner who willingly carries out orders without ever asking for their justification until he realizes that he contributed to upholding social injustice. Further, there are allusions to racial persecution; Bunting himself suffered at the hands of the Teutonic Knights precisely because he was a member of an "inferior" race. The baker of consecrated wafers incites a riot against the Jews of the city—an event indicative both of medieval pogroms and modern-day oppression of racial minorities. Finally, there are the youths of the city who, in rejecting the world of their parents, have adopted the life-style of the Hippies.

Several critics, although they were not necessarily persuaded by the virtues of the play, noted that **The Pied Piper** represented a convincing demonstration of Zuckmayer's essential humanity, such as he had retained throughout his life. In the final analysis, one critic remarked, it was beside the point to charge Zuckmayer with the failure of providing new directions either in the theater, in the underlying philosophy of his plays or their social implications.[29] In fact, Bunting's "Psalm of the Murdered Souls" (*WA,* 10:360-61) uses the motifs of drowning and decay that are familiar from the brief cooperation in the twenties between the pre-Marxist Brecht and Zuckmayer.[30] But whereas there is no room for God in Brecht's universe, in Zuckmayer's play God is not totally absent even in the face of intense suffering. Thus Bunting asks after the death of his beloved Rikke: "Is there Someone who permits all this to happen and is yet merciful?" (*WA,* 10:360). Exactly the problem of human suffering had been declared the "bedrock of atheism" by one of the characters in *Danton's Death* by Georg Büchner,[31] that eminent precursor of the moderns, approximately one hundred sixty years before. As is evident from the conclusion of his play, Zuckmayer viewed man's existential situation less bleakly than either Büchner or Brecht. Such guarded optimism may, perhaps, be unjustified; still, one cannot but respect the tenacity with which Zuckmayer continued to present his vision of man.

Notes

1. Letter of Carl Zuckmayer to Paula Wessely, dated Corpus Christi 1961, in *Blätter der Carl-Zuckmayer-Gesellschaft* 4, no. 4 (1 November 1978): 124. See also Horst Bienek, *Werkstattgespräche mit Schriftstellern* (Munich, 1962), p. 171.

2. See Carl Zuckmayer and Heinz Rosenthal, "Gespräch über das Stück," in *Carl Zuckmayer. Das Bühnenwerk in Spiegel der Kritik,* ed. Barbara Glauert (Frankfurt, 1977), p. 345.

3. See Rudolf Lange, *Carl Zuckmayer* (Velber, 1969), p. 84.

4. See Zuckmayer and Rosenthal, "Gespräch," p. 346.

5. Helen Swediuk-Cheyne, Intro., *Die Uhr schlägt eins. Ein historisches Drama aus der Gegenwart,* by Carl Zuckmayer (Berne, Peter Lang, 1977), p. 17.

6. See the reviews by Otto F. Beer, Oskar Maurus Fontana, and Piero Rismondo in *Carl Zuckmayer,* ed. Glauert, pp. 348-57.

7. Anon., "Zuckmayer: Schlägt dreizehn," *Der Spiegel,* 25 October 1961, pp. 86, 88-89.

8. Carl Zuckmayer, "Kranichtanz," *Die Neue Rundschau* 72, no. 4 (1961): 794-811.

9. See the interview with Zuckmayer, in *Carl Zuckmayer,* ed. Glauert, p. 346. See also Zuckmayer's letter to Günther Fleckenstein of 29 April 1976, in *Blätter der Carl-Zuckmayer-Gesellschaft* 3, no. 1 (1 March 1977): 20.

10. See the review of W. v. O., in *Carl Zuckmayer,* ed. Glauert, p. 380.

11. See the review by Thomas Terry; quoted by Lange, *Carl Zuckmayer,* p. 122.

12. See Carl Zuckmayer, "Epilog for the Reader," *WA,* 10:259.

13. See the jacket of the opera recording, MCM Academy Series, n.p., n.d.

14. See chapter 3, section 4, pp. 77-79.

15. See chapter 4, section 1, pp. 83-90.

16. It should be noted that it is characteristic of Zuckmayer to gain "productive distance" from his subject matter. See Wolfgang Paulsen, "Carl Zuckmayer," in *Deutsche Literatur im 20. Jahrhundert: Strukturen und Gestalten.* 5th rev. ed., ed. Otto Mann and Wolfgang Rothe (Berne, 1967), 2:355.

17. See the reviews listed in Arnold John Jacobius, *Carl Zuckmayer: Eine Bibliographie 1917-1971* (Frankfurt, 1971), pp. 267-77. For a more detailed interpretation of the play, see Siegfried Mews, "Von Karl May zu Karl Marx: Zuckmayers Bonanza-Millionär Tabor," in *Die USA und Deutschland. Wechselseitige Spiegelungen in der Literatur der Gegenwart,* ed. Wolfgang Paulsen (Berne, 1976), pp. 84-91.

18. See chapter 1, section 4, pp. 27-29.

19. Carl Zuckmayer, "Anmerkungen zu einem Theaterstück," in *Carl Zuckmayer,* ed. Glauert, p. 361, draws attention to the "epic" tendency of his drama. At the same time, however, he disclaims the use of Brechtian "epic theater" devices.

20. Marianne Kesting, "Carl Zuckmayer—Zwischen Volksstück und Kolportage," in *Panorama des zeitgenössischen Theaters.* Rev. and enl. ed. (Munich, 1969), p. 283.

21. See Urs Helmensdorfer, Intro., *Das Mädchen aus der Feenwelt oder Der Bauer als Millionär. Romantisches Original-Zaubermärchen mit Gesang in drei Aufzügen,* by Ferdinand Raimund (Berlin: de Gruyter, 1966), p. 92.

22. Anon., "Zuckmayer-Premiere," *Der Spiegel,* 25 November 1964, p. 142.

23. See the review by Petra Kipphoff, in *Carl Zuckmayer,* ed. Glauert, pp. 369-73.

24. Carl Zuckmayer, *Der Rattenfänger: Eine Fabel* (Frankfurt, 1975).

25. *Rattenfänger* simply means "rat catcher."

26. See the review by I. V., *Neue Zürcher Zeitung,* 24 February 1975.

27. See Carl Zuckmayer, "Stoff und Quellen," in *Carl Zuckmayer,* ed. Glauert, pp. 386-87.

28. See the review by Georg Hensel, in *Carl Zuckmayer,* ed. Glauert, pp. 390-94.

29. See the review by Kurt Heinz, in *Carl Zuckmayer,* ed. Glauert, p. 388.

30. See chapter 1, section 4, pp. 27-29.

31. Georg Büchner, *Complete Plays and Prose,* trans. Carl Richard Mueller (New York: Hill and Wang, 1963), p. 44.

Selected Bibliography

PRIMARY SOURCES

1. GERMAN EDITIONS

a. Most complete editions

Gesammelte Werke. 4 vols. Frankfurt: S. Fischer, 1960.

Werkausgabe in zehn Bänden 1920-1975. 10 vols. Frankfurt: Fischer Taschenbuch Verlag, 1976.

c. Works (adaptations, dramas, prose narratives) not included in either GW or WA

"*Pankraz erwacht.* Stück aus dem fernen Westen in drei Akten." Edited by Barbara Glauert. In *Carl Zuckmayer '78. Ein Jahrbuch.* Frankfurt: S. Fischer, 1978. Pp. 47-163.

d. Essays, short pieces, and anthologies

Carl Zuckmayer. Das Bühnenwerk im Spiegel der Kritik. Edited by Barbara Glauert. Frankfurt: S. Fischer, 1977. Includes the following shorter pieces by Zuck-

mayer: "Ein Brief [*Kat*]" (1931); "Ein deutsches Märchen" (1931); "Gespräch über das Stück [*Die Uhr schlägt eins*]" (1961); "Der Kaiser im 'Schelm von Bergen'" (1934); "Das Leben des Horace A. W. Tabor. Anmerkungen zu einem Theaterstück" (1965); "Persönliche Notizen zu meinem Stück 'Des Teufels General'" (1948); "Meine 'Rivalen-Bearbeitung'" (n.d.); "Der Schinderhannes" (1927); "Stoff und Quellen [Der Rattenfänger]" (1975); "Wie 'Ulla Winblad' entstand" (1965).

2. ENGLISH EDITIONS

"The Devil's General." Translated by Ingrid G. and William F. Gilbert. In *Masters of Modern Drama,* edited by H. M. Block and R. G. Shedd. New York: Random House, 1962. Pp. 911-58.

Carnival Confession. Translated by John and Necke Mander. London: Methuen, 1961.

A Part of Myself: Portrait of an Epoch. Translated by Richard and Clara Winston. New York: Harcourt Brace Jovanovich, 1970.

SECONDARY SOURCES

1. BIBLIOGRAPHIES AND REVIEW ESSAYS

BIENEK, HORST. "Carl Zuckmayer." In *Werkstattgespräche mit Schriftstellern.* Munich: Hanser, 1962. Pp. 164-78, 224.

GLAUERT, BARBARA, ed. *Carl Zuckmayer: Das Bühnenwerk im Spiegel der Kritik.* Frankfurt: S. Fischer, 1977.

JACOBIUS, ARNOLD JOHN. *Motive und Dramaturgie im Schauspiel Carl Zuckmayers.* Frankfurt: Athenäum, 1971.

KESTING, MARIANNE. "Carl Zuckmayer—Zwischen Volksstück und Kolportage." *Panorama des zeitgenössischen Theaters.* Rev. and enl. ed. Munich: Piper, 1969. Pp. 278-83.

LANGE, RUDOLF. *Carl Zuckmayer.* Velber: Friedrich, 1969.

MEWS, SIEGFRIED. "Von Karl May zu Karl Marx: Zuckmayers Bonanza-Millionär Tabor." In *Die USA und Deutschland. Wechselseitige Spiegelungen in der Literatur der Gegenwart,* edited by Wolfgang Paulsen. Berne: Francke, 1976, pp. 84-91.

PAULSEN, WOLFGANG. "Carl Zuckmayer." In *Deutsche Literatur im 20. Jahrhundert: Strukturen und Gestalten.* 5th rev. ed. Edited by Otto Mann and Wolfgang Rothe. Berne: Francke, 1967. 2: 332-61, 441-42.

3. CRITICAL WORKS IN ENGLISH

SWEDIUK-CHEYNE, HELEN. Introduction to *Die Uhr schlägt eins: Ein historisches Drama aus der Gegenwart,* by Carl Zuckmayer. Berne: Lang, 1977.

Charles W. Hoffman (essay date 1983)

SOURCE: Hoffman, Charles W. "Zuckmayer's *Hauptmann von Köpenick*: Of Laughter, Uniforms, and the Basement." *Philological Papers* 29 (1983): 46-52.

[*In the following essay, Hoffman investigates the balance between the serious message and comic devices of Zuckmayer's play* The Captain of Köpenick.]

It has been over fifty years since Carl Zuckmayer's ***Hauptmann von Köpenick*** had its first performance in 1931 in Berlin's Deutsches Theater, but critical interest in the play is still strong. Or, better, is once again strong, since scholars were comparatively silent on Zuckmayer in the late fifties and early sixties. In recent years, however, there have been monographs on the playwright with separate chapters devoted to this, his major work, not one but two anthologies of background material on the play, and articles in the journals.[1] Such interest is perhaps a bit surprising, for the ***Hauptmann von Köpenick*** is rarely produced nowadays: few companies can afford to stage a work that needs actors and actresses for some seventy speaking parts, the realistic costuming for so many characters, and twenty changes of set if done without cuts. More to the point, the play is hardly deathless theater nor—because it is so thoroughly realistic—is it difficult to comprehend. So why the increased scholarly attention? One reason is no doubt that Zuckmayer turned eighty in December 1976, and died less than a month later. Both events triggered publications on the author, his oeuvre, and his major writings.[2] Certainly as important, however, as far as the ***Hauptmann*** is concerned, has been the lively current interest in the late Weimar years and the search there for the roots of fascism. Recent critics (e.g., Mews, Koester, and Engelsing-Malek[3]) have recognized more clearly than their predecessors could or at least did that, although the historical incident on which the play is based took place in 1906, Zuckmayer was writing just as much about pre-Hitler Germany as he was about Wilhelminian Germany. The Berlin of the drama may be the Berlin of 1906, but it is also very much the Berlin of 1930 and 1931. With this recognition has come ideological controversy, as room for conflicting interpretation has been discovered in the text.[4] But it is likely that the main reason for the ongoing critical attention still lies in something that has been there and seen all along: the play's humor. Germanists eager to write on comedy which can also qualify as significant literature do not have a great many choices, and of the few the ***Hauptmann von Köpenick*** is among the most relevant and the most accessible. If this assumption is correct, it can be of use to identify, and review somewhat more systematically than has been done thus far, the sources of humor in the play and to look again at its balance between comedy and serious import.

It is interesting to note that the ***Hauptmann*** has long been favorite classroom reading, not only in this country with students advanced enough to manage the dialect but in Germany as well.[5] This is surely due in part to the warning Zuckmayer intended his play to be.[6] But one suspects that it is also due in good measure to the fact that from the work an entire compendium of the devices of traditional comedy, from the simplest to the most sophisticated, can be developed. There is no pie-in-the-face; there are no pratfalls; and the one occurrence of physical mishap (the arrest of the deserter in the flophouse in Scene vi) is decidedly not there for laughs.[7] But on the level of primitive device there are occasional slapstick, out-and-out farce (the best example being Mayor Obermüller's frantic attempts in Scene x to squeeze a fatter body into the old uniform), and what must surely be the most explicit instance of bathroom humor in all dramatic literature. It is in the bathroom of the Schlesischer Bahnhof that the hero changes into the Captain's uniform which he has just bought in the rummage store and gets his first chance to test its effectiveness in Scene xvii. A trainman, more and more impatient to get into the restroom, snaps to attention when "the Captain" emerges, acknowledging not just the power of clothes to command respect despite the man inside them but also the greater right of those in authority to use the facilities.

Higher on the scale of comic sophistication, the drama is filled with individual comic incidents: misunderstandings, double entendres, gag situations, and the like. Often these are important in their own right, contributing only very casually to the overall plot development and getting our laughter because we know from the historical event of 1906 how the play is going to end—as the characters (for a long time including Voigt himself) do not. This wealth of peripheral incidents has been seen as a weakness. Writing of the premiere in 1931, Herbert Ihering called the ***Hauptmann von Köpenick*** simply "eine amüsante Anekdotensammlung";[8] in 1947 Paul Rilla complained that there is too much of the cabaret in this "behagliches, preussisches Anekdotengeplänkel" for the play to be palatable after the Third Reich;[9] and the word "Bilderbogen" is hardly ever missing from any discussion of the work. But before one agrees with this accusation, he would do well to look at the very unusual structure of the play. Critics are fond of citing its obvious episodic nature and pointing out that it has not one but two "heroes." In the first two of the three acts scenes showing the decline of the resplendent uniform alternate with scenes in which Voigt grows as a positive if ever more hopeless human being in our eyes. But what is sometimes overlooked is that the real action and basic plot of the play—Voigt's commandeering the soldiers, taking over the town hall in Köpenick, and the final deal that will get him his passport once the new prison sentence is served—does not occur until the last four scenes some three hours into the work's total running time of more than four. Everything up to now, including a ten-year break between the action of the first act and that of the last two, is motivation: for telling the audience, on the one hand, why the bluff is going to work and, on the other, why Voigt—locked more and more tightly by the bureaucracy into a situation without escape—has no further alternative but to try it. The reason for such an unbalanced and rambling structure is that Zuckmayer's very serious message is developed more in these two lengthy but preliminary strands than in the main action itself. But such a structure is narrative and epic rather than dramatic and means that the author—to say nothing of the director of a stage production and the actors—has the difficult task of holding the playgoer's attention for three-fourths of the evening. The steady stream of isolated comic incidents is there in large part to do that job.

Before we look at the bluff in Köpenick in greater detail, a few words about another sophisticated source of the play's humor are in order: its language. On the obvious level there are the constant puns, the gags ("Bis hierher hat uns Gott geführt/In seiner grossen Güte," the prisoners sing as Scene viii in the penitentiary chapel opens), the pompous and completely meaningless rhetoric of Capt. von Schleinitz' speech at the officers' ball (Scene xiii), Voigt's rejoinders to the officials and bureaucrats which the latter understand literally but behind which we see a double meaning. But more important and deeply woven into the total fabric is the use throughout the play of dialect, particularly *contrast* of dialect, for comic effect. Wormser's conversations with von Schlettow or with the mayor cause laughter in part because the tailor so clearly knows how to manipulate his upperclass customers with servility and appeal to their pride, but in large part as well because of the clash between their stuffy bureaucratese and the lively Yiddish-tinged Berlin *Platt* spoken by Wormser.

The play's most striking instance of such dialect clash comes not in a conversation between two characters, of course, but in the flophouse in Scene vi, where one bum speaks Bavarian, another Saxon, a third Swabian, another Hamburg, Voigt and others thick Berlin *Platt.* For the reader, and especially for the listener, the result is a veritable Tower of Babel—or, better, a flophouse of Babel.

As always in the *Hauptmann von Köpenick,* there is of course serious method here along with the surface madness. For one thing, Zuckmayer uses language and dialogue as the Naturalists did: to characterize, to individualize, to reproduce auditory reality as accurately as possible. The warning of the play is real and if it is to be understood as such, the society represented on the stage and the characters have to be taken as real too. (Parenthetically, though this does not strike us today as

unusual, it is well to remember that the play—*Neue Sachlichkeit* par excellence—is only six or seven years away from Expressionism, which used language in exactly the opposite way: to typify characters according to function, not to individualize them.) More importantly, the two worlds of this play—the "little man" on the one hand and on the other the petty officials of the business world and the government who are his real antagonists—play by different rules. And it is in good measure through Zuckmayer's skillful handling of language and dialogue that the audience is made to see the split. Hoprecht, the convinced but sympathetic champion of law and order, and Voigt mean something emotionally quite different when they talk together of justice and "Heimat" in the drama's crucial, central Scene xiv; the police and the passport bureaucrats do not hear Voigt's double meanings because they simply do not speak or understand his language.

There are other comic devices in the play—the repetition of situation, for example, and especially of police station setting: Potsdam, Rixdorf, Alexanderplatz, and Köpenick—Voigt plays a part in all of them! But the point just made about Zuckmayer's use of dialogue to distinguish Voigt from the other characters has led to the main event, to the bluff in Köpenick. One reason it succeeds and one source of the comedy is, of course, that by now the "little man" has learned to understand and, above all, to speak the language of his antagonists. Laughter comes now from the fact that Voigt plays by the rules of the system and beats the authorities at their own game. It stems too from the constant dramatic irony, though now of course this excludes Voigt. Finally, and most importantly, the comic effect of the principal action stems from incongruity, *not* (as is so often the case in high comedy) from inconsistency. Voigt is consistent to the end when he surrenders in exchange for another prison term plus the guarantee of a passport on his release, and those who follow his orders are consistent too. But incongruity—between character and action, between appearance and substance ("Schale" and "Kern," as Voigt puts it in the earlier Scene v in the Café National to his friend Kalle)—is at the comic heart of the matter when an utter down-and-out can don a Captain's uniform, tattered, ill-fitting, full of champagne spots, as shabby as its wearer, and command the obedience that Voigt does at Köpenick and the admiration he gets later at the police headquarters. It is of course this incongruity that causes Voigt to stammer out the play's final word—"Unmöglich!" or in John Mortimer's fine English translation "ri-ri-ridiculous"[10]—when he stands before the mirror and sees himself, finally, as "the Captain of Köpenick."

This final moment of the action is the crowning moment in the drama; but at the same time it caps and makes explicit the serious warning Zuckmayer intended his work to give to a Germany in which the Nazis had become the second most popular and important political party, a Germany with more than five million people unemployed and listening with growing desperation to ideological extremes that promised direction, purpose, stability. It is impossible (Zuckmayer wanted to suggest in 1931) to imagine the knee-jerk obedience to authority and the militaristic thinking that the play shows as anything but the stuff of comedy—"ri-ri-ridiculous," Zuckmayer hoped, to think that it might become real life. And the mirror—an ever-present motif in the literature and films of the late twenties and early thirties (think of *Steppenwolf* and *Kleiner Mann, was nun?*, think of *Berlin Alexanderplatz* and Kästner and *M*)—, aimed out (according to the final stage directions) at the audience, was to be the last thing the playgoer of 1931 saw as the curtain fell.

The last sentence indicates where one must look for the serious message of the **Hauptmann von Köpenick,** but some further words are in order. Study of the secondary literature suggests that commentators not infrequently see the uniform as the main butt of Zuckmayer's satire and a few the military as the enemy. Rilla, for example, speaks of a triumph of the uniform (p. 8) and calls the play a "Theaterstück, womit Zuckmayer dem preussischen Militarismus eine Narrenkappe aufsetzte, die eine Tarnkappe war" (p. 10), by which he means that the playwright trivializes with his humor and his "Illuminierung jenes preussischen Idylls" (p. 8) what he should have been castigating more severely. Many (though not all) of those who wrote about the play when it first opened in 1931—e.g., Ihering and Diebold[11]—tended to present it primarily as a "Militärschwank" or "eine militärische Satire"; and Ludwig Marcuse was apparently the first to speak of the "Fetisch Uniform," a slogan which has reappeared in the literature ever since, as the author's target.[12] Marcuse criticizes Zuckmayer for writing "ein historisches Stück, das er nicht auf die Kämpfe unserer Zeit bezieht" and for molding "ein Thema, welches schärfste Gesellschaftskritik fordert, zu einem harmlosen Witzblatt" (p. 171)—that is, for treating Prussian militarism with the conciliatory weapon of satire and for failing to address the need for a change in the class structure of late Weimar Germany. Finally, of course, what led the Nazis to condemn the play so vehemently and to ban it immediately in January 1933, was the same thing that led to their hatred of Remarque's *Im Westen nichts Neues*: its presumed degradation of the German uniform and its mockery of the military tradition.

While it is obviously true that Zuckmayer pokes fun at the uniform, identifying it simply as the symbol for militarism is too facile and seeing in it the primary target of the play's attack puts the accents wrong.[13] At *no* point in the drama is Voigt's antagonist of the moment a member of the military; only briefly and rarely are he and members of the military even on the stage at the

same time. The people who frustrate his attempts to lead a normal, everyday life are, rather, personnel managers, shopkeepers, and above all the subaltern officials of government and society—the clerks and magistrates who issue passports and work permits and residence papers. These people may act like officers but they are all civilians, and that is just the point. It is not the von Schlettows and the von Schleinitzes who worry Zuckmayer. What frightens him is the recognition that a military mentality—passing the buck, using a caste system of rank and privilege, loving the giving of orders and showing one's authority to those of lesser position, instinctively obeying anything that comes down from above - has completely permeated the thinking and the behavior of the subaltern civilian bureaucracy. In a large, modern, centralized state, where this bureaucracy conrols both the social and private lives of the everyday citizen, such a situation is the end of freedom. And Zuckmayer wrote the play to urge—via laughter and satire—a change before the fait accompli of his historical comedy should (again!) become real life. In vain of course, as it turned out, for it was precisely this lower middle class, these frustrated subaltern officials who wore the brown shirts and provided Hitler with the broad base of his popular support.

When one's focus is adjusted to this historical perspective, it becomes very clear how precarious the play's balance between comedy and serious warning—and perhaps for that very reason how remarkable an achievement the **Hauptmann von Köpenick** is. The comic devices are all there, and our laughter at seeing the little man triumph over blindness and arrogance and conformity is hearty laughter. But at the same time we are constantly reminded that it would not take much for things to come out differently from the way they do in this "German fairy tale" (as the satiric subtitle of the drama calls it) and that they would almost certainly do so in real life. The little man's human essence is very nearly destroyed by authority and red tape; and his predicament fills us with that sense of frightful uncertainty so characteristic of late Weimar, the realization that there is something very nasty down there in the basement and that Zuckmayer is afraid lest it win out over his mirror.

Notes

1. The two anthologies both contain extensive bibliographies: Siegfried Mews, ed., *Carl Zuckmayer*: Der Hauptmann von Köpenick, Grundlagen und Gedanken zum Verständnis des Drama, No. 6363 (Frankfurt am Main/Berlin/München: Moritz Diesterweg, 1972) and Hartmut Scheible, ed., *Carl Zuckmayer*: Der Hauptmann von Köpenick: *Erläuterungen und Dokumente,* Universal-Bibliothek, No. 8138 (Stuttgart: Reclam, 1977). For further information on the secondary literature see also

Mews's two *Forschungsberichte*: "Die Zuckmay-erforschung der sechziger Jahre," *MLN* 87 (1972): 465-93, and "Special Report: Carl Zuckmayer (27 December 1896-18 January 1977)," *GQ* [*The German Quarterly*] 50 (1977): 298-308.

2. The death prompted, among other publications, a memorial volume of essays, tributes, reviews, and bibliographical data, *Carl Zuckmayer '78: Ein Jahrbuch* (Frankfurt am Main: Suhrkamp, 1978). And the principal publication marking the birthday was a *Festschrift für Carl Zuckmayer,* edited by the Landes Hauptstadt Mainz and the Carl-Zuckmayer-Gesellschaft (Mainz: Krach, 1976).

3. Mews, "Special Report," p. 301 and his *Carl Zuckmayer,* passim; Rudolf Koester, "The Ascent of the Criminal in German Comedy," *GQ* 43 (1970): 384; and Ingeborg Engelsing-Malek, *"Amor fati" in Zuckmayers Dramen* (Konstanz: Rosgarten, 1960), esp. p. 48 and p. 64.

4. Jürgen Hein's essay "Zuckmayer: *Der Hauptmann von Köpenick,*" in *Die deutsche Komödie,* ed. Walter Hinck (Düsseldorf: August Bagel, 1977), pp. 269-86, summarizes and contrasts the ideological stances of the drama's commentators from the premiere in 1931 to the seventies.

5. A fair amount of the recent interest in the play has an explicit pedagogical focus. The only separate postwar edition of the text is in the series "Schulausgaben moderner Autoren" (Frankfurt am Main: S. Fischer, 1956). Mews' anthology is in a series "Für den Schulgebrauch zusammengestellt." And Paul Riegel's "Carl Zuckmayer: *Der Hauptmann von Köpenick,*" in *Europäische Dramen von Ibsen bis Zuckmayer,* ed. Ludwig Büttner (Frankfurt am Main/Berlin/Bonn: Moritz Diesterweg, 1961), pp. 195-208, is written by a classroom teacher for classroom teachers. Riegel praises the *Hauptmann* as "one of the few modern dramas" which has appeal for student and teacher alike and which is suitable for classroom use (p. 197).

6. Zuckmayer, *Als wär's ein Stück von mir* (Frankfurt am Main: S. Fischer, 1966), p. 444. See also his description of the drama as a conscious "Warnung (oder Exempel)" to Sibylle Werner, cited in her *"Der Hauptmann von Köpenick*: Wirklichkeit und Dichtung am Beispiel des Dramas von Carl Zuckmayer," M.A. thesis, Univ. of Maryland 1954, p. 103.

7. Textual references in this paper are to Zuckmayer, *Die deutschen Dramen* (Frankfurt am Main/Berlin: S. Fischer, 1951). Though the play is divided into three acts, the scenes are numbered consecutively without regard for act division.

8. In the *Berliner Börsen-Courier,* 6 March 1931, as quoted by Scheible, p. 38.

9. "Zuckmayer und die Uniform," in *Literatur: Kritik und Polemik* (Berlin: Henschelverlag, 1953), p. 9.

10. John Mortimer, The Captain of Köpenick: *An Adaptation for the National Theatre Company* (London: Methuen, 1971). A good way of testing the earlier claim that the play's structure is epic rather than dramatic, by the way, is to compare the original text to this adaptation. Mortimer eliminates nearly an hour from the running time of the play, deleting three scenes entirely and shortening many others. Some scenes are combined and staged on the same set. And eliminating one of the two intermissions by cutting from three acts to two works to lessen the theatergoer's impression of diffuseness and drag. The result is a version tighter in dramatic structure, less epic, and better suited to modern theater staging than the original, as Zuckmayer himself argues in his "Author's Preface" (n. pag.) in the Mortimer volume.

11. Bernhard Diebold in the *Frankfurter Zeitung,* 8 March 1931, as quoted by Scheible, pp. 30-35.

12. "Ein deutsches Märchen," in *Frankfurter Generalanzeiger,* 7 March 1931, as quoted in *Carl Zuckmayer: Das Bühnenwerk im Spiegel der Kritik,* ed. Barbara Glauert (Frankfurt am Main: S. Fischer, 1977), 170-72.

13. Postwar critics, at least those not hampered by the ideological blinders of a Rilla, by and large agree that the issue is "eine Militarisierung des gesamten Lebens" (Mews, *Carl Zuckmayer,* p. 51), not militarism as such.

Anthony Waine (essay date July 1993)

SOURCE: Waine, Anthony. "Carl Zuckmayer's *Des Teufels General* as a Critique of the Cult of Masculinity." *Forum for Modern Language Studies* 29, no. 3 (July 1993): 257-70.

[*In the following essay, Waine analyses the character, personality, and masculine ego of General Harras, the protagonist of Zuckmayer's drama* The Devil's General.]

On 29 January 1933, in the final hours of the demise of the Weimar Republic, Carl Zuckmayer attended the Berlin Press Ball, accompanied by his wife and his mother. There he met a number of old friends including the World War I fighter pilot ace, Ernst Udet. The two men not only shared the same year of birth, 1896, but also a similar disposition, as the following detail from his memoirs, *Als wär's ein Stück von mir,* reveals: "Udet und ich, die sich zwischendurch Kognak geben ließen, waren bald in dem Zustand, in dem man kein Blatt mehr vor den Mund nimmt."[1] Their outspokenness had been provoked by the way in which many of the guests were openly displaying their military medals, something which had never been the case at previous balls. There was, however, an element of self-contradiction in Udet's attitude for he too was wearing, as was his custom, the Pour le Mérite decoration, albeit under his necktie, but he did remove it and put it away in his pocket. The two men considered other, more primitive and outrageous forms of behaviour: "Weißt du was", schlug er mir vor, "jetzt lassen wir beide uns die Hosen runter und hängen unsere nackten Hintern über die Logenbrüstung."[2] Though they never actually carried out their threat, it indicated their sense of personal estrangement from the changing political mood as well as a male adolescent way of expressing their feelings. Other aspects of Udet's character and lifestyle which come to light in Zuckmayer's description of the evening were his passion for fast cars, his charm towards females and his life as an adventurer.

What emerges from Zuckmayer's portrait of Udet is both the sense of his being larger than life and of the peculiarly male camaraderie which existed between two men whose identities had been forged by their experience of the First World War. Luise Rinser in her penetrating character study of Zuckmayer has highlighted the significance of this particular experience for him (and millions of other men of his generation):

> Daß ein Mann, der solcherart unlösbar verwurzelt ist mit seiner Heimat, ein "Patriot" ist, das ist nicht verwunderlich, zudem er einer Generation angehört, für die es zur Lebensordnung und zu den ebenso selbstverständlichen wie hohen Tugenden eines Mannes zählte, fürs Vaterland zu kämpfen. Knaben fast noch, lernten sie töten. Das war in Ordnung für sie, und der Krieg war ihr frühes und großes Abenteuer, er war ihre erste Begegnung mit dem Leben in seiner nacktesten Form, er war ihre Art der pathetischen Rebellion, die erste Prüfung ihrer Männlichkeit, und für viele Anstoß und Durchbruch der schöpferischen Kräfte, wie die Kriegsliteratur und die Literatur überhaupt nach dem ersten Weltkrieg beweist.[3]

It was of course during the First World War that Udet's passion for flying, to which he was to become fatally addicted, was first triggered. At their last meeting in 1936, by which time Zuckmayer was already in exile, Udet confessed to his friend why he had chosen not only to continue to live in Germany but also to serve the Nazis as the Chief of the Airforce Supply Service: "Ich [. . .] bin der Luftfahrt verfallen. Ich kann da nicht mehr raus. Aber eines Tages wird uns alle der Teufel holen."[4] When, therefore, the news of Udet's death in December 1941 reached him on his farm in Vermont in the United States one can imagine Zuckmayer's profound sense of shock at losing a friend whose life story and personality structure were in many

respects so similar to his own. The news then appears to have been effectively repressed for a whole year until it resurfaced creatively and cathartically in the form of a plot for a tragedy which would explore how an individual who had few illusions about the kind of state in which he was living nevertheless chose to stay and indeed to assume a position of strategic military responsibility. The drama thus born was *Des Teufels General,* a title which alludes to Udet's own words cited above. Yet whilst it is evident that Udet's life (and death) gave Zuckmayer a painfully tangible external stimulus to create the drama, other equally tangible yet internal factors were also at work. In other words the biographical portrayal of Udet is used with and enriched by the personal experiences and fantasies of the author himself.

Zuckmayer's tendency to project himself into his characters has been observed by several critics. Wolfgang Paulsen wrote of his dramatic characters in general: "Und der Dichter selbst ist einer unter ihnen, denn sie alle sind Spiegelungen seines Ich, wodurch sich ihre offensichtliche Familienähnlichkeit und das ständige Wiederkehren bestimmter Typen erklärt",[5] whilst Henry Glade writing specifically about *Des Teufels General* claims: "In his superb portrayal of Harras Zuckmayer draws largely on congenial elements of his own soul."[6] But it is Luise Rinser who spells out more explicitly than anyone else just how far the author identifies with the central figure of his play:

> Nicht jedermann weiß es, aber viele wissen, daß Zuckmayer in diesem Harras den von ihm bewunderten Flieger Udet und sein Schicksal unter Hitlers Regime dargestellt hat. Wer aber weiß, daß Zuck in Harras sich selber darstellt? Ich meine damit nicht, was allerdings auch stimmt, daß er seinem Helden viele Eigenschaften zulegte, die seine eigenen sind: das Saufen, die Freundestreue, das rasche Entflammtsein von jungen Mädchen, die Verführer-Allüren, die absolute Respektlosigkeit vor sogenannten Respektspersonen, der Leichtsinn, die souveräne Verachtung der Gefahr, die "Schnauze", die behutsame Hand für junge Menschen, und andres: Gutes, Indifferentes, Törichtes, Großartiges und Liebenswertes. Ich meine etwas anderes: Zuck, der bei aller Männlichkeit doch schließlich ein Literat geworden ist, hat ein heimliches Ideal, einen Knabentraum von sich selber: er sieht sich als Mann der Tat.[7]

Rinser's thumbnail sketch of the author emphasises more than anything else the strong sense of masculine identity exuded by him and of course shared by General Harras. Few critics have failed to mention this characteristic of the General but some have been particularly savage in their indictment of the author's seemingly unquestioning championing of the macho ethos embodied not only by the central figure but by other subsidiary figures too. For example Marianne Kesting accuses Zuckmayer of having created "die Legende von den großen Zeiten, von den echten Kerlen und zünftigen Soldaten, die leider nur unter der falschen Flagge versammelt waren" and of having glorified "eine Figur, die, genau betrachtet, sich durch eine gute Portion Naivität und mangelnde Denkkraft auszeichnet."[8] The Marxist critic Paul Rilla was even more scathing:

> "Kein niedriger Zug trübt diese Gestalt", hieß es in einer Kritik. Das ist sicher richtig, soweit es die Absicht des Autors betrifft, denn die Charakterausstattung des Generals Harras umfaßt alles, was der Dichter Zuckmayer seit je für lobund preiswürdig hält. Also was ist der General Harras? Eben: ein Kerl. Was aber ist ein Zuckmayerscher Kerl? Ein Viechskerl. Gewoben aus Rauf- Sauf- und Sexualromantik.[9]

There is admittedly an element of truth in the claims made by Kesting and Rilla. Even in her much more non-judgmental analysis, already referred to, Luise Rinser also stresses the disparate ingredients which add up to an almost Hemingwayesque "he-man" type of male. But it would be very one-sided to see Zuckmayer as an uncritical purveyor of male stereotypes, especially in a drama which seeks, successfully, to expose the moral bankruptcy of a political ideology (National Socialism) which so ruthlessly promulgated the myth of the German male's power and supremacy. The deconstruction of Harras' male ego goes hand in hand with the unmasking of a society which is destructive and self-destructive. Therefore Rinser's contention that Harras was a "Wunschbild"[10] of Zuckmayer cannot be accepted. It is my view that, far from being an ideal or model, Zuckmayer has looked at himself and his fellow men such as Ernst Udet critically, and, under the guise of an apparently heroic, non-conformist figure, has in fact produced an anthropologically tinted study of a male who is the product not only of his immediate historical and ideological circumstances but also of traditional, gender-specific ways of thinking and behaviour which reach back to medieval times. No wonder that the word "Ritterzeit" and the epithet "ritterlich" are used on at least two occasions in the play to describe male behaviour.

What has also been overlooked by critics so far in their discussions of Zuckmayer's approach to his central character is the fact that Harras is approximately 45 years of age, which links him not only biographically with Udet but of course with Zuckmayer himself. It is in fact possible to see Harras as an individual at the crossroads of his existence whose manly values and qualities have been the sustaining basis for his existence but who now gradually comes to the realisation that what has been good for him personally as a man has not been beneficial to himself or to others as a human. My analysis will therefore dwell on three interrelated aspects of masculinity as they are manifest in the historical context of German society in the first half of this century, against whose backdrop *Des Teufels General* takes place. Firstly I shall examine the five principal personae of Harras' masculine make-up: the warrior, the technocrat, the nonconforming individualist, the philanderer, and the hedonist. Secondly I shall demonstrate not only how Harras personifies a specific cult of masculinity but how other members of society, in particular the women, passively conspire to erect and buttress this cult. Thirdly I shall try to prove, by looking not only at Harras' metamorphosis from "Mann" to "Mensch" but especially at the evolution of the personality of the symbolically named Hartmann, how Zuckmayer is pointing beyond the cult of masculinity to a community based upon humanity.

Harras' foremost role is that of a warrior. His bellicosity is extended right through into the very physical contours of his private existence. The second act of the play is set in Harras' bachelor apartment in Berlin. The stage directions are most revealing. His apartment is described as a kind of temple to the male art of aggression, predation and survival. Harras is identified with the universal manifestations of this particular art: "Da und dort die wilde Fratze einer afrikanischen Tanzmaske. In einer Ecke Beduinenlanzen, orientalische Flinten und Handwaffen, Bogen und Pfeile, ein arabischer Sattel, eine Negertrommel" ([*Des Teufels General*. Berlin: Suhrkamp Verlag Vorm S. Fischer, 1947.] p. 74). Harras' tribal celebrations, for which his flat has become famous throughout Berlin ("die berüchtigte Räuberhöhle", as Pützchen calls it), are enacted in an adjoining room "als Bar eingerichtet, deren Rahmen aus angesplitterten Propellern und allen möglichen Bruchstücken zerschossener oder abgestürzter Flugzeuge besteht. Sie ist auch innen mit phantastischem Gerümpel, Kriegs- und Reisetrophäen, Photographien von Fliegern, Mädchen und wilden Tieren vollgestopft" (p. 74). Zuckmayer is indulging in more than mere naturalistic milieu evocation here. When Harras comes to realise in the course of this act that he has become a prisoner in his own home we, the spectators, only feel partial sympathy for him. For the images visually conveyed by the aforementioned trappings of his den make us realise all too clearly that Harras has become a victim of his own deep-rooted passion for fighting and adventure.

Harras' often metaphorically flavoured language also provides glimpses into his warrior mentality. Justifying why he had agreed to serve the Nazis by helping to build up the Luftwaffe he says: "Und wenn ein alter Wolf mal wieder Blut geleckt hat, dann rennt er mit'm Rudel, auf Deubel komm raus—ob einem nun die Betriebsleitung paßt oder nicht" (p. 39). The animal imagery reinforces the picture of a man driven by primitive, predatory urges. The mythology of the Wild West provides another source of self-delineation when Harras speculates on whether the Gestapo might be intriguing against him: "Sie meinen, die könnten meinen Skalp billiger haben?" (p. 43). Images culled from the arena of modern sporting combat also pepper his speech. For example, when in the course of the action Harras feels increasingly threatened by his Nazi masters and his fighting and survival instincts are aroused, he threatens retaliation: "Ich werd ihnen noch eins vor den Latz knallen, und wenn's in der zwölften Runde ist" (p. 99).

Harras' fairly untrammelled belligerence is, however, most clearly and unequivocally articulated in his allegiance to the credo of militarism. Here no metaphors or sundry figures of speech conceal his real meaning. When a comrade from the days of the First World War arrives he immediately performs a ritual with him dating back to that especially gory and barbaric conflict and proudly announces: "So haben wir uns nämlich jeden Abend in der Fliegermesse begrüßt—damals, bei Cambrai und vor Verdun. *Das war noch 'n Krieg*" (p. 23—my italics). He is effusive in his welcoming of the four pilots from Eilers' squadron who have just been decorated for their bravery. He proudly assures them: "Ihr seid in Ordnung, Jungens" (p. 24). Indeed, the evening celebrations, which last the entire first act, have been arranged by Harras in honour of the military successes of squadron leader Eilers: "ich trinke auf Friedrich Eilers, auf seinen fünfzigsten Luftsieg, den wir heute feiern, auf seinen hundertsten, und auf seine gesunde Heimkehr" (p. 16). Harras acknowledges and admires the warrior (especially the victorious one) in other men, and he in turn is identified first and foremost as just such a man. Thus even though Harras is not a member of the Nazi party, unlike Eilers, the latter assures him of their fundamental common vocation and identity: "Aber wo's darauf ankommt, da gibt's keinen Unterschied. Soldat ist Soldat" (p. 20).

When at the very end of the first act Harras engages the young, idealistic but sensitive officer Hartmann in conversation, he does so not as one human being to another but as a soldier and as a man: "Schau—ich bin doch selbst ein alter Soldat. Ich verstehe doch was von dem Geschäft" (p. 68). Nevertheless for the first time in the entire act Harras reflects in a mellow, self-aware and rational way about the connections between warfare, destruction and masculinity:

> Ich rede von dir, mein Junge. Von dir, und von mir. Von uns Männern sozusagen. Männer sind eine komische Tiergattung. Von Zeit zu Zeit packt sie der große Koller, und sie müssen ihn austoben. Wir verpassen ungern eine Gelegenheit, um übern Strang zu hauen. Der Krieg—ist eine unserer ältesten Ausreden dafür. Männer sind natürlich nie ganz normal. Bei uns ist immer eine Schraube los - oder was verdreht im inneren Mechanismus [. . .] Wir bauen die Oberfläche der Welt nach eigenem Entwurf, und dann zerstören wir sie, bis zum Souterrain [. . .]
>
> (p. 70.)

Harras appears to be positing an anthropological view of the male species in which a man appears to be predetermined to behave in a particular way. Though we as spectators find Harras' (self-)insights and the confessional tone with which they are conveyed positive, we cannot fail to regard them as an apologia. For Harras cannot define himself in any categories other than those which for all his adult life have been satisfying and binding: "Ich bin kein Denker, und kein Prophet. Ich bin ein Zeitgenosse. Ein Techniker, ein Soldat" (p. 69).

It is symptomatic of his self-definition as a contemporary male that he should reject the abstract, word-centred moral vocations of thinker and philosopher in preference for the masculine, deed-centred activities of technocrat and soldier. War and technology indeed go hand in hand for Harras, whose very task it is to harness the fruits of technology in order to maximise the destructive potential of the Luftwaffe. The fighter jet is the very symbol of the fusion of the two worlds and of Harras' two principal roles in life: "Mein Lebensinhalt—das war immer die Fliegerei. Das hab ich gemacht von der Pike auf—schon als Freiwilliger im Jahre 14—, und nu kann ich's nicht mehr bleiben lassen" (p. 20). Whilst a short while later, and more inebriated, the General publicly declares: "General oder Zirkusclown. Ich bin Flieger, sonst nix" (p. 27). And finally he sums up the contents and achievements of his life with a mixture of bravado and self-satisfaction: "Ich riskiere mein Leben seit 'nem Vierteljahrhundert—jeden zweiten Tag, mindestens. Und—es war sehr schön, alles in allem. Genug Mädchen, genug zu trinken—ziemlich viel Fliegerei—und—'n paar bessere Augenblicke. Was will man mehr" (p. 37).

Thus the inveterate fighter pilot and technocrat Harras has come to worship technology as an ersatz religion glorifying the male's creative powers. In the long dialogue with Hartmann, already quoted from, Harras praises the beauty of the literally man-made world: "Der ursprüngliche Entwurf aber—nach dem es uns immer zieht—der ist schön [. . .] Und was wir selber machen, voll Bosheit und Hintertücke—es hilft nichts—wenn es gelingt, ist es schön. Ein Panzerkreuzer ist schön. Und ein schwerer Bomber. Und eine Jagdmaschine—so schön wie ein Pferd im Sprung. Und eine Stahlbrücke über einen Fluß" (p. 70). Harras' fetishisation of man-made objects, especially those which are deployed in the sphere of human aggression, has already been alluded to in the critical survey of the decorations adorning his apartment ("Beduinenlanzen, orientalische Flinten und Handwaffen [. . .] phantastisch(es) Gerümpel, Kriegs- und Reisetrophäen"). This fetishistic obsession with technology, primitive and advanced, blinds him to his responsibility to people rather than things, to peace rather than war. Of his achievement in creating a modern German airforce he is in no doubt: "Die fünf Jahre, in denen wir die Luftwaffe flügge gemacht haben—die waren nicht verloren [. . .] als es richtig losging, die ersten zwei Jahre—da hatten wir was zu bieten, da war immerhin Stil drin. Die beste, exakteste, wirksamste Maschinerie, die es in der Kriegs-geschichte gegeben hat" (p. 39).

Harras has derived pleasure from playing the role of a warrior, and as the last two paragraphs charting his relationship to technology have illustrated, he has derived equal amounts of pleasure from his role as a technocrat. In fact the guiding principle in the General's life seems to be the pursuit and the experience of pleasure, and this brings me to examine the third manifestation of his maleness. The opera singer Olivia who has known Harras, by all accounts intimately, for many years says to him: "Du bist ein Genußmensch. Du willst nichts auslassen" (p. 100). Almost the entire first act bears testimony to this accurate character assessment. It is set in a high-class restaurant, one of the few to be granted a special licence to remain open at such a late hour in the middle of war. Whilst rations have already been imposed on the great mass of the German people, the privileged guests at Otto's restaurant can enjoy a fairly sumptuous buffet meal and seemingly endless quantities of alcohol, of which Harras is easily the most conspicuous consumer. His very first entrance is that of the Epicurean: "Das geleerte Glas hält er noch in der Hand, eine Zigarette hängt im Mundwinkel" (p. 11). Furthermore, as Siegfried Mews has pointed out, "Harras [. . .] empfindet durchaus keine Gewissensbisse, die hier wörtlich aufzufassenden "Früchte" der anfänglichen Siege des durch die Nazis angezettelten Zweiten Weltkrieges zu genießen."[11] Harras' hedonism, though superficially attractive and amusing, is revealed by Zuckmayer to be a serious impediment to grasping rationally and morally the fundamental truths of one's existence. Furthermore hedonism can border dangerously close on narcissism, and when Oderbruch, the resistance fighter, explains in the crucial closing stages of the action why he and others are risking their lives opposing the evil regime, he is surely implicitly censuring his friend and superior when he declares: "Aber alle [. . .] sind gekommen, weil sie etwas mehr lieben als sich selbst" (p. 151).

Harras' narcissistic tendencies and his undigsuised hedonistic proclivities are both intrinsically linked to his bachelor status. They are quite possibly the reason for it and most certainly one consequence of it. This also applies to his activities, displayed and referred to on many occasions in the course of the play, as a philanderer, and this constitutes the fourth outlet for his male drives. Unwilling and unable to commit himself to any one woman because of his aforementioned passion for fighting, adventure and technology, Harras leads the life of an old-fashioned "Hollywood-type hero".[12] Once again we recall that amidst the very male ambience of his flat the bar is "mit [. . .] Photographien von [. . .] Mädchen [. . .] vollgestopft". They form part of the myth of the virile, charismatic, swashbuckling male. Women are fascinated as much by the mythology as by the real-ity. His most recent conquest, the naive nineteen-year-old Diddo, confesses: "Und daß du ein Schwerverbrecher bist, was die Frauen anlangt, das braucht mir keiner zu erzählen. Das ist mir auch gleich. Oder nein, ich mag es sogar" (p. 90). Even the much more cynical, self-assured Pützchen is captivated by Harras' nimbus and offers herself up for the sybaritic rites regularly enacted in "seiner berühmten Propellerbar. Da soll's zugehen! Also Geschichten hab ich gehört [. . .] Ist es wahr, daß die Serviermädels nur Feigenblätter tragen bei euren Festivitäten? Ich komm als Serviermädel, sag ich Ihnen" (p. 25).

Finally, one can also see Harras' hedonism and his womanising as attributes of an individualistic personality which traditionally (and most certainly in Germany in the first half of this century) men had been able to develop and project more easily than women. His individualism[13] is expressed in an ostentatious and even aggressive non-conformism which is, arguably, his most endearing quality. He is, in every sense, his own man, in contrast to the types surrounding him, whose opinions have been imbibed from other sources and whose own individuality has been repressed. He, on the other hand, constantly takes risks with what he says and with what he does, and does not think of the consequences. Thus when Olivia informs him of the predicament of a Jewish couple, the Bergmanns, Harras organises a secret plan to help to fly them to safety. His home is a refuge for *personae non gratae* in Nazi Germany. For example, the American journalist Buddy Lawrence, who has already been ordered to leave the country and is under surveillance, turns up at Harras' flat and is given shelter. Similarly the banned, so-called decadent painter Schlick also drops by and, despite his provocative statements in front of the other guests which could have been a dangerous embarrassment to Harras, he is given hospitality.

Despite such acts of personal courage and defiance and despite his public reputation as cynical debunker of Nazi authority, Harras' individualistic style and machismo philosophy prevent him from allying himself with any other persons or groups (as Oderbruch does) to actively resist the system. Harras is a lone wolf,[14] temperamentally unable to translate his natural aggressions into constructive and collective counter-action. Instead he uses his gargantuan energies to satisfy the dictates of his male ego. But the playwright is at pains to stress, particularly in the first two acts of the drama, that whilst Harras' overcharged male ego may be due to some freak of nature or even to some fundamental flaw in his makeup it is also the result of conditioning processes which reach back into his childhood. Women, in particular, are shown to be agents of his masculinisation and his subsequent mythologisation, from which Harras seeks in vain to escape when, by the third act, he is finally confronted with his ethical self and his inescapable responsibility. I am certainly not implying that women are wittingly the accomplices of Harras' misdeeds. They too are the products of a conditioning process, stretching back at least as far as the foundations of the Prussian state, whereby the German male was stereotyped as an invincible, heroic warrior and the German woman's duty was to bear, rear and revere this superior being. The apotheosis of the man was enshrined most fervently in the ideology of National Socialism. I shall now indicate how I believe the female figures in *Des Teufels General* have also helped to construct the cult of masculinity of which Harras is at once high priest and slave.

In this "psychologische Studie in drei Akten"[15] Zuckmayer inserts a number of private dialogues which enable his protagonist to explain his motives. One such self-analytical exchange takes place early in the first act when Harras is ostensibly discussing political and industrial questions with Sigbert von Mohrungen. He tells the latter how he has been mindful throughout his career of pleasing his proud mother. His military achievements and honours, whilst meaning little to him, have brought the mother great joy: "Wenn ich Erfolg hatte— dann war—ganz ehrlich—mein erster Gedanke immer: das Telegramm an die Mutter—" (p. 40). Harras acknowledges this wish to please (and no doubt gain approval) from a doting mother as a powerful motivating force: "Vermutlich hat jeder Mann irgendeine Frau, wegen der er tut, was er tut. Sonst würden wir uns weniger abschuften, glauben Sie mir. Für mich hat sich nie eine bessere gefunden" (p. 40). It is noticeable that Harras resorts to the basic, generic categories of "Mann" and "Frau" to define his relationship to his mother and thereby to highlight the sense of masculinity derived from this source. He even appears to intimate that his love of his mother has never been matched by his love of another woman.

If adulation from the opposite sex and the concomitant heightening of gender awareness (and prowess!) are already so firmly entrenched in Harras' psyche then his subsequent adult life, right up to the point at which the play opens, has seen the process continued (with the idolisation also added to of course by his male comrades). Thus Anne Eilers, the wife of the squadron leader, who has never met Harras before, confesses within minutes of their first encounter: "Wenn Sie gehört hätten, wie er mir immer von Ihnen erzählt hat. Eifersüchtig hätte man werden können. Harras ist der Erste—nach dem Führer natürlich—und dann kommt lange nichts" (p. 20). The tribute is both ironic, in so far as Harras already has deep misgivings about Hitler, and yet symptomatic of Harras' status as a near mythical folk hero. This status is buttressed still further a short while later with the entrance of Olivia and her nineteen-year-old niece (with whom Harras falls in love). In introducing Harras she says: "Komm her, Did-

doche, da kannste en Held kennelerne, aus der gute alte Zeit" (p. 28). Not surprisingly Diddo falls head over heels in love with the General, though it is impossible to tell whether it is real love she feels or simply a form of late adolescent hero worship.

Olivia's massaging of the male ego continues unabated into the second act. She reduces the escalating conflict between the Nazi hierarchy and Harras to the most basic level imaginable, namely that of male virility and the envy caused in those who feel inadequate: "Du hast zuviel Erfolg bei Frauen gehabt. Das ist das Schlimmste. Bei denen ist doch alles Neid. Bettneid, vor allen Dingen. Denn in dem Punkt sind sie tief unter Minus [. . .]" (p. 100). Whether or not Olivia is correct in her hypothesis is not important; what is of consequence though is the impact it will have on Harras' already bloated self-esteem, especially when she then implicitly eulogises his sexual potency to the detriment of all the other Nazi bigwigs whose manliness in this area she appears to have tested—and found wanting: "Da, wo ein Mann herzeigen muß, was er wirklich wert ist, da hilft kein gestählter Körper. Und keine eiserne Energie. Das hat einer von Natur—oder gar nicht. Die Brüder kennt man doch. Erst große Töne, dann fertig, eh's angefangen hat, und nur rasch wieder 'zum Dienst'" (p. 100). All the female figures in the play (at least in the first two acts) indirectly share the responsibility for Harras' ultimate tragedy, which evolves essentially from his enslavement to the cult of masculinity, thereby ensuring his fatal entanglement in an ideology (fascism) which itself reveres and promotes the intrinsic values of this cult—fame, pleasure and power.

It is therefore psychologically consistent that it should be a woman who—inadvertently—confronts him with the naked truth about himself.[16] Pützchen represents in a sense the female counterpart to Harras. She is cynical, aggressive and self-confident, so self-confident in fact that she offers herself to Harras as the person who can propel him to become Hitler's right-hand man: "In einem Jahr können Sie der Größte sein—die Macht hinterm Führer—und jeden abkrageln, der Ihnen nicht gefällt. Macht ist Leben. Macht ist Genuß. Mensch— wenn Sie zugreifen—ich mache Sie ganz groß!!" (p. 123). Despite holding diametrically opposed political views to Harras—she is a fanatical member of the *Bund deutscher Mädel*—she too is infatuated with his aura of manliness: "Es gibt nicht so viele Männer auf der Welt. Richtige Männer. Sie sind ein Mann [. . .] Ich stell mir einen Mann vor, der's schafft, der das Rennen macht—an der Spitze der Nation. Sie könnten es schaffen, Harry, Sie müssen es schaffen" (p. 122). Her words echo those of Olivia just a few scenes earlier, but they are much more brutally honest about what Harras really is—not a human, not even a man, but "ein Raubtier, Sie haben Habichtsaugen, und Reißzähne wie ein Wolf" (p. 123). The diction may be hyperbolic, the tone fanatical but the message is unmistakeable. Harras, significantly, does not contradict her but merely asks her to leave. He has almost certainly recognised at last his true identity in the picture she has painted, a picture which, incidentally, is reflected in the grotesque decor of his apartment (or "Schauerkabinett" as he himself calls it) where the conversation takes place. The acute attack of fear which he experiences on her leaving is not the result of her subsequent threatening revelation that she has read the letter from the Bergmanns, thanking him for his readiness to help to smuggle them out of Germany, but the consequence of being confronted with the inhuman myth he has allowed himself to become. Harras' tragically belated moral regeneration can now commence.

This process has been recognised and well documented by most commentators on this play. What has not, however, been noted in the discussions of especially the third and final act ("Verdammnis") is how Harras' verbal self-presentation and self-projection have changed. In the first act, in particular, Harras was orally dominant. After the initial scene involving the restaurant staff his was the first voice to be heard offstage and from then on he proceeded to initiate conversations, interlink the conversing groups, and comment on the statements of others. He was a consummate oratorical performer, whose powers of expression were countered only by Schmidt-Lausitz and Pützchen. His speeches revealed him to be the high priest of an essentially male ritual and his pronouncements were liberally sprinkled with words such as "Herren", "Männer" and particularly "Jungens".[17] By the third act, however, Harras' monopolistic verbal claims have been broken by other characters (male and female) whose own personalities are developing. Lieutenant Hartmann, Anne Eilers and Oderbruch all assert themselves against a much more contrite, self-doubting and defensive Harras. Not only is his tone different but his register too. The words "Mensch" and "menschlich" replace the male-centred jargon of the first and second acts as the humanisation of Harras gathers pace. With Anne Eilers in particular he identifies himself as a human being as opposed to a man: "Was weiß ein Mensch? Was kann ein Mensch denn wissen?" he pleads with her. And speaking almost as if the metamorphosis he is undergoing has engendered an identity crisis he cries: "Wer bin ich denn—?! Bin ich denn mehr als ein Mensch? Kann ich mehr wissen—mehr tun—mehr leiden als ein Mensch? Ich bin doch—ich bin doch kein Gott!!" (p. 144-5). Hitherto Harras would have had no problem in answering this rhetorical question for he was certain of his fundamentally male identity. Now that the cult which he has helped to foster, and which has also been constructed by his acolytes, is disintegrating he is no longer certain of his sense of self, other than to reiterate the word "Mensch" in all its myriad manifestations ("Menschheit", "Menschenalter", "Menschenseele",

"Menschenleben" etc.) in the vain hope that he can atone for his crime of having served the devil, that is, Hitler. Increasingly, however, in the course of this act Harras realises that his old identity can never be truly shed. Unlike Hartmann, his age and the magnitude of his complicity are against him.

Hartmann's name is revealing, both in respect of his relationship to Harras and in the context of the discussion of masculinity. The two men share the same three letters in the prefix of their surnames. It is a device which unites the two and forces us therefore to regard their fates as being inextricably intertwined. In the first act Harras senses instinctively and accurately that something is eating away at the brave young airman's soul: "Sonderbarer Kerl. Kaum über zwanzig—und redet die ganze Nacht kein Wort" (p. 62). Their long conversation, in which Harras' monologues predominate, marks the culmination of the first act. Harras appears almost as a father figure to the young officer who has been jilted by his fiancée, the formidable Pützchen, on account of an adulterated Aryan pedigree. Harras enlightens him especially on the subject of sacrificing oneself on the battlefield, for Harras does not share the Nazis' glorification of death in battle and he returns suitably sobered to the front. However, in the final act the roles are reversed as Hartmann returns from having witnessed appalling crimes against defenceless civilians committed in the name of the German people, and now educates Harras about the sordid truth of the ideal in whose cause they have both been enlisted. Furthermore Hartmann invites his former mentor to examine himself in relation to God, whom he is now discovering, and thereby compels Harras to shift his *Weltanschauung* from a man-centred one, as expounded in Act One— "Ich rede von dir, mein Junge. Von dir und von mir. Von uns Männern sozusagen"—to a God-oriented one: "Aber die größte Findung aller Zeiten habe ich nicht erkannt. Sie heißt Gott. In vielerlei Gestalten—immer Gott" (p. 141). Harras is taking leave of the allegiance to cult and turning to true Christian worship. When finally Harras places Hartmann in the service of the resistance fighter Oderbruch we should see this action dialectically and metaphysically. The spirit of the ageing, cynical and condemned Har-ras is transplanted to that of the young Christian convert Hart-mann.[18]

But Hartmann's name carries other overtones besides those associated with Harras. The two parts of his surname literally signify "hard man" yet also phonetically the prefix sounds like the English word "heart", a fact which would not have escaped the author's notice since he wrote the play whilst living in exile in the United States of America. The transformation which Hartmann in fact undergoes is one from a male warrior, fearless in battle (or "geradezu tollkühn", to quote his squadron leader) to a human being whose heart now begins to rule his head—a head which had been filled with National Socialist propaganda ever since he can remember: "Ich hatte nie ein Zuhause, Herr General, bis— [. . .]—ich zur Hitler-Jugend kam. Meine Heimat war das Schulungslager. Die Ordensburg. Und dann—die Truppe" (p. 68-9). Indeed Harras, his father-confessor, was the catalyst in his discovery of his real feelings, for at the end of their therapeutic conversation in Act One the stage direction informs us: "HARTMANN hebt sein Glas zu den Lippen, ohne zu trinken. Er sitzt unbewegt, und es laufen Tränen über sein Gesicht" (p. 70). One could see this outpouring of repressed emotion as the beginning of his liberation from "gender" and the discovery of his own human sensitivity and vulnerability—thus foreshadowing that of Harras one act later who also breaks down: "Herrgott im Himmel. Ich habe Angst. Ich habe Angst. Ich habe Angst—*Verstummt*" (p. 124).

These two men's painful discovery of their human and spiritual emotions, and ultimately, of their true selves as fallible human beings, once they are able to see beyond the walls which their gender and their society have constructed around them, reveals Zuckmayer to be an iconoclastic social analyst. Far from having glorified the male, as some critics have maintained, Zuckmayer has demythologised him without at the same time debasing him, or elevating the female as his cultural or emotional superior. Indeed, the women in the play are drawn as realistically as the men, in so far as they are as much the prisoners of ideological and cultural conditioning as the men and cannot therefore help but reinforce the values inherent in their society. The predominant value, according to this play, in this specific society which existed in Germany between 1933 and 1945, but whose origin, certainly for Harras, was the fateful experience of the First World War, was that of militarism. It is ingrained not just in one but in several generations. Zuckmayer reveals this value to be especially virulent in a whole cross-section of German society and by so doing exposes one of the wellsprings of German fascism. But he also highlights how one particular individual, in whose overmasculinised make-up this particular trait was especially deeply embedded, could allow his "besseres Ich", as he once terms it in a conversation with his youthful "Doppelgänger" Hartmann, to be so deceived about the diabolical compromises it was making that he became *Des Teufels General.* On the one hand, therefore, we must see this *Zeitstück* as an acute and provocative investigation into the modern German male psyche. But as the last section of my article has made clear, the drama also reveals the male's potentiality to construct a self which embodies human and ethical qualities. Harras glimpses this self in Act Three but is too burdened with guilt to rebuild his existence anew. Oderbruch and his new ally Hartmann will, however, continue consciously to work together not only to resist the "Teufel", Hitler, but unconsciously to destroy the senescent patriarchy which seeks to perpetuate male values and myths. Their service is by definition to humankind. Therefore Zuckmayer, writing in exile between 1942 and 1945, is not just an iconoclast, as already stated, but also an idealist with a potent vision of a humane society.

Notes

1. Carl Zuckmayer, *Als wär's ein Stück von mir* (Frankfurt am Main, 1969), p. 385.

2. *Als wär's ein Stück von mir*, p. 385.

3. Luise Rinser, "Carl Zuckmayer", in: *Der Schwerpunkt* (Frankfurt am Main, 1960), p. 60.

4. *Als wär's ein Stück von mir*, p. 451.

5. Wolfgang Paulsen, "Carl Zuckmayer", in: *Deutsche Literatur im zwanzigsten Jahrhundert*, ed. Herbert Friedmann and Otto Mann, vol. II (Heidelberg, 1961), p. 310.

6. Henry Glade, "Carl Zuckmayer's *The Devil's General* as Autobiography", in *Modern Drama* 9, Spring 1966, p. 54.

7. Luise Rinser, p. 58.

8. Marianne Kesting, "Carl Zuckmayer", in: *Panorama des zeitgenössischen Theaters* (Munich, 1969), p. 280.

9. Paul Rilla, "Carl Zuckmayer. *Des Teufels General*" in: *Das deutsche Drama vom Expressionismus bis zur Gegenwart,* ed. Manfred Brauneck (Bamberg, 1970), p. 104.

10. Luise Rinser, p. 58.

11. Siegfried Mews, *Carl Zuckmayer. Des Teufels General* (Frankfurt am Main, 1979), p. 28.

12. Roy C. Cowen, "Type-Casting in Carl Zuckmayer's *The Devil's General*", in: *University of Dayton Review* 13 (1976), p. 87 and note 12, pp. 93-4.

13. Cowen draws some interesting parallels with Büchner's characterisation of Danton, p. 89.

14. In certain respects he reminds one of the "Steppenwolf" Harry Haller in Hermann Hesse's famous novel of 1927. Perhaps his name Harry Harras is more than coincidental in view of the fact that both men, despite their very differing backgrounds, are facing crises determined in part by their age, temperament and socio-historical conditions.

15. Friedrich Luft, "Zwiespältiges Stück", in S. Mews, p. 71.

16. It is surprising that Henry Glade, in an otherwise perceptive analysis of the importance of encounters in Zuckmayer's works, should overlook the

exchange between Harras and Pützchen: Henry Glade, "Das Begegnungsmotiv in Carl Zuckmayers Dramen", in: *Blätter der Carl Zuckmayer Gesellschaft* 4 (November, 1978), 153-60.

17. See Thomas Ayck: "8General Harras ficht mit Wortspielereien, Frivolitäten und Spott um seine Identität. Aber diese Identität hat er bereits durch seine Entscheidung zum Mitmachen an der Nazi-Herrschaft verspielt. Er täuscht sich vor, daß er diese Entscheidung nie getroffen habe. Die Sprache, *der närrische Männlichkeitston* (my italics—AEW), ist das Blendwerk, mit dem er sich und seine Umwelt verwirrt." *Zuckmayer* (Reinbek, 1977), pp. 118-9.

18. See Siegfried Mews: "In contrast to both Harras and Oderbruch, young Lieutenant Hartmann, who becomes disillusioned with National Socialism and turns towards the resistance movement at the end of the play, is an essentially positive figure in that he seems to point the way towards a better future." *Carl Zuckmayer* (Boston, 1981), p. 89.

Mariatte C. Denman (essay date fall 2003)

SOURCE: Denman, Mariatte C. "Nostalgia for a Better Germany: Carl Zuckmayer's *Des Teufels General.*" *The German Quarterly* 76, no. 4 (fall 2003): 369-80.

[*In the following essay, Denman discusses the cultural subtext of Zuckmayer's play* The Devil's General.]

The challenge the *Volksbühne* in Berlin faced in 1996 was to offer a new, pertinent view of Carl Zuckmayer's classic, *Des Teufels General.* Criticizing National Socialism for its abuse of Germany's name and German ideals, this staple of German postwar drama focuses on the question of national identity. Director Frank Castorf staged a provocative re-interpretation of the play by assigning the role of Harras, a German Luftwaffe general, to an actress in the first half of the play and to an actor in the remaining half.[1] Despite the unconventional gendering of the protagonist, the contemporary performance nevertheless fell prey to the traditional conceptions of Germanness inherent in the play. The slippery road to sentimentality began in the second part of the performance. One critic noted that, while the female actor—as the queer general—transformed Harras into a figure that is "kahlköpfig, glitzernd, gefährlich, fern aller treudeutschen Biederkeit," the male actor evoked a "grelles Portrait eines nun plötzlich geduckten, verschwitzten Jammerdeutschen—*des Teufels General* als armer Teufel und geprügelter Hund" (Heinrichs 15). Harras, driven by his personal ambition of flying, collaborates with the Nazis, "ein deutscher Mann, ein deutscher Held, eine deutsche Eiche" (Heinrichs 15). In 1996, when the quest

for national identity was making headlines, Castorf's performance was seen as an attempt to re-assess the parameters of West German national identity. The ambivalence in this production reveals that the deeply ingrained postwar myth of the Wehrmacht soldier can be broken only temporarily through travesty and grotesque moments.

The following historical and textual examination elucidates the dramatic strategies that construct Harras as the figure with whom the audience identified most. Harras can be read on several textual and cultural layers that the audience of the forties easily superimposed on each other. In addition to offering an interpretation of German history, the play proposes a nostalgic notion of soldierly virtues through a discourse of masculinity. *Des Teufels General* does not just criticize the National Socialist cult of heroism in order to proffer a new definition of humanism (Wayne 258-70). Rather, in the final scene Zuckmayer conjoins particular notions of masculinity with a narrative of self-sacrifice and atonement. The positive reviews of the play indicate that two years after the defeat of the German army and a few months after the Nuremberg trials in 1946, the interplay of historical and cultural references offered postwar German audiences a sense of conciliation and national identity.

In *Des Teufels General,* Zuckmayer draws on his personal memories of Ernst Udet (1896-1941), his friend and a Luftwaffe general, and on his own WWI experiences. As a result, Harras is molded into a "reizvolles Amalgam aus Humanismus und penetranter Männlichkeit" (Wehdeking 87), an "echter deutscher Held," and a man in conflict with his conscience (Ott 411).[2] This conflict becomes life-threatening when Harras, whose unabashed criticism of the Nazis is no secret, is held responsible for the sabotage of airplanes in which German pilots are killed. Following his arrest, the Nazis offer him an ultimatum. In return for his release, he has to find those responsible for the sabotage within ten days. Unexpectedly, Oderbruch, a serious and reliable engineer who worked closely with him for years, confesses to being a member of the resistance. Rather than betray his friend and the resistance movement, Harras commits suicide in one of the defective airplanes. The play concludes with the SS officer ordering a state funeral for him.

Des Teufels General premiered in Zurich in December 1946 and in Hamburg in November 1947, despite the Allies' skepticism regarding its depiction of German militarism. Between 1947 and 1950 the play was performed 3,238 times in the American and British sectors, making it one of the most successful and most discussed plays in the immediate postwar years (Pfäfflin 331). During the 1963 Auschwitz trials Zuckmayer withdrew his play from the stage because he believed it could be misconstrued. Three years later, after having revised it, he allowed it to be performed again. These revisions revolve around the final dialogue between Harras and the resistance fighter Oderbruch and have no bearing on the catalytic ending that conveys Harras's suicide as a conciliatory heroic act. I shall argue that this is one reason the play contributed to a revisionist understanding of National Socialism despite Zuckmayer's intent.

Des Teufels General was so popular that Zuckmayer considered making it into a film in 1949. This move from literature to film was not unusual for Zuckmayer, who was one of the few German playwrights to write film scripts, as for instance the 1929 film adaptation of Heinrich Mann's novel *Der blaue Engel,* directed by Sternberg and starring Marlene Dietrich.[3] Between 1949 and 1960, Zuckmayer left influential marks on postwar German popular culture by contributing to eleven films and two TV movies, most of them adaptations of his own literary works. Propagating a sense of *Bodenständigkeit* and family values, these films underscored restorative tendencies in West Germany. In 1954, five years after Zuckmayer's first notes on the film, Helmut Käutner produced and directed *Des Teufels General.*

Käutner was advised by Allied military experts on how to make the film more "realistic" by omitting controversial political issues mentioned in the play, such as philo-Semitic notions, references to communism, and the pogroms at the eastern front (Käutner 411).[4] For instance changes in Oderbruch's dialogue indicating that he was not responsible for the airplane crashes reflect the parameters of German Cold War cultural politics in the wake of Germany's rearmament (Becker 79-94). As a result Harras appears as a "less reckless, more sensible man, more in keeping with the ideal of the responsible citizen-soldier envisioned for the Bundeswehr" (Plater 258). While the first version of the play clearly referred to the National Socialist past by retaining Ernst Udet as a model for Harras and addressing political issues related to National Socialism, the cinematic adaptation of the film in the fifties is more concerned with a new West German definition of soldiering unscathed by the National Socialist legacy of war crimes. The film rehabilitated the German resistance in that Oderbruch sabotages the planes but does not cause the death of his own comrades. By disassociating Harras from the volatile issues of Germany's past, the film clearly reverberates with views popular in Germany of the early fifties. Opinion polls taken in 1951 and 1953 indicate that "a majority of Germans rejected the notion of German war crimes, and 55 percent felt that German soldiers in World War II had nothing to reproach themselves for in their behavior regarding the countries they had occupied" (Plater 263).

While *Des Teufels General* was a success on stage, it drew considerable criticism from theater critics and was followed by Zuckmayer's open letters and his participation in public forums to defend his play. Why was the play so popular and what were the pivotal issues that stirred the controversy? With which issues did reviewers who praised the play identify most? Given the cultural context of the play it comes as no surprise that many reviews lauded Zuckmayer's *Zeitstück* for its authentic representation of the army and National Socialism.[5] As one critic noted, this play is the most accurate and human representation of the dark years of Germany under National Socialism (Govet, in Ott 334). Other critics maintained that, rather than offer a simple dualistic interpretation of Germany's national socialist legacy in black-and-white terms, Zuckmayer depicts the ambiguity and conflict of one person who was drawn into working for the Nazis because of his own personal ambitions and his passion for flying. As they argued, the play convincingly demonstrates the complex process of how characters, despite their good intentions, find themselves misguided by "falsche Ideale" (*Theater der Zeit* [1947] 33). Harras's late realization of his personal entanglement in guilt is another aspect that was praised. But this "späte[r] Sohn" of a "preussische Junkerkultur" (Bab 240), the collaborator who was not a member of the party, but who heroically atones for his guilt with his life, was seen mostly in positive terms. Another reviewer was convinced that audiences could identify with the realistic depiction of the apolitical and carefree Harras and with his sense of duty. Only through identification and not through a moralistic lesson could viewers begin to reflect on the past, he argued (M.G. 229). A survey among students attests that they viewed Harras as a decent German who not only served the fatherland without joining the party and getting involved with the Nazis, but also helped "rassisch" persecuted friends—the word "Jewish" still being taboo for many in the late 1940s—against the orders of the state.[6]

In 1947 the cultural journal *Der Ruf* argued in a similar vein, praising the play for being refreshing, written by a German author who is not ashamed of his love for Germany (Schirrmacher 13). In this narrative the figure of the general and the author Zuckmayer converge, as is most apparent in the description of Harras as the "Jew honoris causa" (*Des Teufels General* 348). Finally, in the view of another critic, as the expression of a sense of patriotism (Roth 270) and not just Harras's atonement, the play attests to the "Unzerstörbarkeit des Guten" in both the world and Germany (Halperin 255). Not only those in support of the play conflated the facts of National Socialism with Zuckmayer's fiction. Those who opposed it also feared its potential to evoke a sense of reality that would entice people to identify with the main character. They wondered whether German audiences were mature enough to understand the message of the play correctly. What impact would it have on young people? Would it trigger a second stab-in-the-back legend?[7] Most critical reviews were concerned with Harras's depiction as a hero for the wrong cause who is cast as a harmless, apolitical petit bourgeois when in fact he was infatuated with power, contributing to and causing the destruction of others.

The most detailed and lengthy critique was written by Paul Rilla, a well known critic living in East Berlin who was most disturbed by the role the uniform and the Wehrmacht play in the drama: "Zuckmayers Abscheu gilt dem Kerl in SS-Uniform. Trägt der Kerl die Uniform des Fliegergenerals, dann ist das natürlich ganz etwas anderes" (259). What is Zuckmayer's "Kerl" other than a mix of "Rauf-, Sauf- und Sexualromantik?" he asked—someone who is fascinated by the aesthetization of war, the "beauty" of flying but who in the end escapes responsibility?

> Hier haben wir ihn ganz, den Mythos in Wehrmachtsuniform, den Mythos jenes Widerstandes, der in der befriedigten Konstatierung besteht, daß die fünf Jahre Hitlerscher Aufrüstung keine verlorenen waren, indem wir doch, als es richtig losging, der Welt was zu bieten hatten, nämlich die wirksamste Kriegsmaschinerie der Geschichte.
>
> (Rilla 263)

While one reviewer praised the well depicted opposition between the Wehrmacht and the Nazis, most critics faulted the play for obfuscating the army's role in the crimes of the National Socialist regime. As they argued, the play never questions officers of the Wehrmacht for not only serving, but also guiding National Socialist leaders during the war. Despite Harras's sense of personal guilt, others argued, the play thus suggests the rehabilitation of Wehrmacht officers while projecting a romantic notion of the past.[8] Herbert Ihering, the famous theater critic who had disapproved of Zuckmayer's play *Der Hauptmann von Köpenick* for proffering an ambivalent view on militarism, claimed it took courage for contemporary theaters *not* to perform *Des Teufels General.* Moreover the positive depiction of a member of the Wehrmacht would invite an interpretation of the play that supported notions of the "wackeren Haudegen" and "treudeutschen Draufgänger" (Ihering 342).

Zuckmayer considered this fear that the play would contribute to the spread of extreme nationalistic, militaristic, and apologetic tendencies unfounded and responded in an open letter to Ihering, published in the weekly paper *Sonntag* in 1948. Militarist circles, he insisted, viewed Harras as unpatriotic and Oderbruch as a criminal. The broad public, however, which was undecided and had sensed there was something wrong with National Socialism, viewed the play as an inspiration. Even before Ihering's review Zuckmayer felt the need to justify and explain his play in a statement printed in *Die Wandlung,* a cultural journal edited by Dolf Sternberger, Carl Jaspers, Marie Luise Kaschnitz, and others

(Ott 332). Emphasizing that the play was not supposed to document, but rather to symbolize the tragedy of resistance without offering final answers, Zuckmayer defended Oderbruch. He admitted he had trouble with this character himself since he could not identify at all with him; and yet he needed to portray Oderbruch's actions in drastic ways to clearly illuminate the core of the conflict. Zuckmayer also assigned Harras the role of a redeemer who sacrifices his life to reestablish mercy in the world. A glimpse of hope, he maintained, is evoked in the play through the figure of the young officer Hartmann, whose recognition of the National Socialist war crimes against civilians and Jews and his transformation in the course of the plot corresponds to the current mind-set of the younger generation in Germany.

This overview of the debate surrounding the reception of *Des Teufels General* illustrates the degree of audience identification with Harras, who was seen by both sides as epitomizing either the decent common German or the despicable Wehrmacht. Both sides agreed that Oderbruch did not accurately represent the resistance, although this was the underlying theme of the play. Zuckmayer initially dedicated the play to "dem Unbekannten Kämpfer" and later to his friends in the Wehrmacht who died in the aftermath of 20 July 1944. In contrast to this dedication the action focuses on Harras, the collaborator, rather than Oderbruch.

Besides drawing on genre-related codes to convey their messages, theater plays are embedded in a cultural context which becomes as much part of the interpretation as the text of the drama itself. This is particularly apparent in the many historical references to the importance of the post-WWI aviation era in *Des Teufels General.* Harras thus serves not just as a symbol for an individual struggle in the face of a dictatorship supported by the masses. As a cultural icon, with a sense of self-reliance, individuality, and courage he clearly embodies ideals popularly associated with German national character.

Zuckmayer conceived of the play when he read the notice of Ernst Udet's death in an American newspaper in 1941. The article claimed that Udet "sei beim Ausprobieren einer neuen Waffe tödlich verunglückt und mit Staatsbegräbnis beerdigt worden," as Zuckmayer recalls the press note in his memoirs (*Als wär's ein Stück von mir* 601). In 1936, during their last encounter, Udet encouraged Zuckmayer to leave Germany. When asked what would happen to him, he responded that he was "der Luftwaffe verfallen. Ich kann da nicht mehr raus. Aber eines Tages wird uns alle der Teufel holen" (*Als wär's ein Stück von mir* 601).

Obviously Zuckmayer's memories of Udet served as a matrix for *Des Teufels General.* Critics referring to Ernst Udet in the 1940s did not need to explain that he was one of the WWI ace pilots adorned with the Iron Cross and buried with the highest state honors in 1941. By the end of WWI, at the age of twenty-two, Udet was honored for having shot down the second highest number of enemy planes. In the Weimar years and in the early 1930s, he became a popular sport pilot who played the clownish "fliegender Professor," dressed in old uniforms, performing audacious aerial acrobatics in front of enthusiastic Berlin crowds. He also participated in films (e.g., *Mein Fliegerleben* and co-starred with Leni Riefenstahl in *Die Hölle von Piz Palü*). In his 1935 autobiography he stressed his fascination for flying and technology. In many ways Udet's autobiography resembles texts by some members of the Freikorps and Ernst Jünger, promoting war and revealing a fascination for war technology as the basis of male identity. Ending his autobiography with the statement that after having lived in an alienated world that had disregarded the virtues of soldiering, Udet praises Hitler for providing him and his comrades with a new sense of belonging (Udet 182).[9] The same year his old flying comrade Göring made him a colonel and later an aircraft ordnance general. Blamed by Göring and Hitler for the unsuccessful air battle over England, he allegedly committed suicide by shooting himself with a pistol.[10] Soon after the Nazis propagated the story that he had died while trying out a new machine and commemorated him as a war hero. After 1945 Udet remained a well known flying hero among veterans.[11]

It wasn't just the Nazis who were aware of Udet's popularity and thus reluctant to reveal the real reason for his death for fear of upsetting the Wehrmacht. Zuckmayer was also acutely aware of this danger. Because of Udet's fame and because of the role flying aces played in German society Zuckmayer could count on getting his ideological message across effectively. Aside from Zuckmayer's personal reasons for choosing Udet as a model for Harras the fact that the flying ace represents much more than the fate of an individual Luftwaffe pilot under Nazism played a significant role in this decision. Like other famous German aviation heroes Udet played a specific role in the post-WWI collective German memory, allowing Zuckmayer's contemporaries to recognize immediately the cultural clues operative in the play's subtext.

In *A Nation of Flyers* Peter Fritzsche argues that aviation was a formative element of the German popular imagination during WWI and the Weimar period. WWI was not only the era of mass mobilization but also of technological progress. Aviation played a major role in the battle for imperialistic dominance and the project of national self-fashioning during the two world wars. Beginning in 1915 war aces were treated like popular celebrities glorified for their self-discipline, self-reliance, courage, and technological skills. As such they were also immediately co-opted by the government's war propaganda machine and used for instance in the effort to sell war bonds to support research into new aviation technology. In contrast to the common soldier in the trenches, the celebrated aces became symbols of national superiority and imperialism. Even though these ideological concepts were soon overshadowed by the atrocities of war, the myth of the war ace remained an integral part of the collective WWI memory.

In compliance with the Versailles Treaty Germany's air force remained dismantled until 1926. Nevertheless, flying sustained national importance in the form of gliding clubs, and zeppelin and air shows, such as those in Berlin in which Udet participated. These extremely popular events provided the nation with a sense of civic unity and national accomplishment. Aviation also symbolized a new era and a new definition of mankind. As many post-WWI texts attest, visions of technology fused with new models of man that also transcended gender boundaries. As never before many women became aviators, among them the famous Hanna Reitsch.

During National Socialism the focus on the self-reliant individual pilot shifted toward the notion of an individual willing to submit himself to a collective. Therefore it is not by chance that Göring, and not Udet, became the minister of aviation, as Fritzsche points out (92). Although the former had fewer victories to show for, he was a better team-player than Udet, who revered "more aristocratic and irreverent notions of flying" (Fritzsche 92). National Socialist school curricula even implemented "lessons of airmindedness" to "make Germany a nation of fliers."[12] As Fritzsche notes:

> Teachers of biology, chemistry, mathematics, and physics were expected to examine the natural history of flight, while their counterparts in history, geography, and literature were directed to teach aviation as an allegory for Germany's national revival and a critical variable in its geopolitical future.
>
> (200)

Contrasted with those characters affiliated with National Socialism and those in Oderbruch's sphere, and praised by any number of women for his heroic and virile manliness, Harras conveys a nostalgic image of soldierly masculinity. As close readings of several exemplary scenes evince, one could in fact interpret the entire play as seeking to negotiate heroism since this issue emerges several times in the course of the plot. The backdrop of the first act is the celebration of those officers who received medals for their achievements. The theme of heroism is at the core of several dialogues, as for instance when Anne, Friedrich Eiler's wife, expresses her admiration for Harras. Olivia, Harras's former lover and friend of many years, introduces him to her adopted daughter Diddo as a hero from the good old times when social hierarchies were still in place:

Komm her Diddoche, da kannste en Held kennelerne, aus der guten alten Zeit, wo die Prominente noch vorne gestande hawwe und die Statiste hinne, beim Applaus. Heutzutage sin ja alles Helde. Hinne, vorne, un in der Mitte.

(268)

In her view the Nazis are pursuing Harras because they suffer from sexual envy and impotence. Her comment is underscored by the caricaturesque representation of several Nazis in the play such as Harras's former WWI comrade, Pfrundmayer, a simple-minded anti-Semitic disciple of Hitler. The cultural minister Dr. Schmidt-Lausitz reminded critics more of a stiff, petty school teacher than a ferocious Nazi.

National Socialist ideology turns into a charade when Pützchen, a young Nazi woman dressed in a sexy BDM uniform, proudly discloses her notions of women's role in the *Volksgemeinschaft.* But even the power hungry Pützchen admits adoring Harras's masculinity and claims that good men like him are hard to find. Called a witch of the NS Blocksberg by Harras's painter friend, Pützchen pokes fun at men who are not manly in her eyes, particularly those who collaborate with the Nazis out of fear. She is the only character in the play who does not believe Harras joined the army for love of flying but to gain power and fame. When Harras refuses to accept her offer of salvation, she threatens to betray him for trying to rescue a Jewish friend who eventually commits suicide. And Jews had been a subject of their previous conversation. When Pützchen told Harras he sounded like a Jew, he calls himself a Jew of "honoris causa" (348). In the end Harras is so furious that he threatens her with a heavy African whip (366). Undaunted, she leaves the scene, calling him a traitor. She clearly wins the verbal stand-off, leaving Harras defeated in his own home, replete with such masculinist symbols as military trophies, airplane parts, collector's items such as African arrows and spears, and photographs of women. Subsequently Harras collapses, holding his throat as if suffocating, and fearfully calls out to God. This scene concludes the otherwise rather naturalistic second act in an Expressionist mode, with five light beams in the background resembling an outstretched hand and Harras's voice emerging from the darkness, as the stage directions indicate.

Pützchen, rather than the other Nazi, is cast as the devil who tempts Harras with the power and hope of saving his reputation. The woman in uniform clearly indicates the transgression of cultural boundaries and values. Dressed in a tight, exaggerated BDM uniform as specified in the stage directions, she represents National Socialism as a travesty of heroism and humanism since she assertively challenges Harras's male power as well as his sense of freedom. Seeing freedom as a struggle for power, despising nature, and having no sense of inner strength, Pützchen appears as a "dehumanized product of an inhumane ideology"—which is diametrically opposed to those values Zuckmayer cherishes (Balinka 97).

Besides Pützchen and Schmidt-Lausitz there are sympathetic exceptions among the National Socialists depicted in the play, such as the young officers Friedrich Eilers and Hartmann. Harras praises the young duty-conscious Eilers for his reliable service and his air victories. In a moment of privacy with his wife Anne Eilers quotes poems by Matthias Claudius, thus expressing his fears about the military escalation. Only when Anne reminds him of the higher goals of the *Volksgemeinschaft* does he regain his courage. This conversation reveals Eilers's vulnerability, even though he is described as a model soldier and a blind follower of National Socialist ideology. In the third act Eilers's death caused by a sabotaged airplane prompts Harras's decision to commit suicide. The sense of soldierly achievement beyond politics is also the reason Harras never criticizes Eiler for his support of National Socialism. In fact, Eiler's death upsets him because it involves a random act of violence against one's comrades and therefore does not follow what Harras considers the rules of traditional warfare and military honor.

In another even more important scene Harras and the young Hartmann, also a recipient of a medal of honor who eventually abandons National Socialist ideology and joins the resistance, discuss concepts of heroism and masculinity. Heartbroken because Pützchen has refused to marry him due to an "Unklarheit" in his family register (306), Hartmann tells Harras that he finds solace in imagining an honorable death on the battlefield—a wish induced by National Socialist propaganda (308). Feeling homeless and fatherless since his father died in WWI, he explains that he experienced a sense of belonging in the Hitler youth and the army. Irritated by the young man's obsession with death, Harras sets out to convince him that happiness and beauty, not death, are worth living for. Yet, while rejecting the National Socialist myth of heroic sacrifice for the *Volksgemeinschaft,* Harras's values and ideals are nevertheless intertwined with soldiering. Invoking a nostalgic view of the decent warrior as well as an aesthetics of warfare and technology, his ideals of masculinity resemble Ernst Jünger's notions of soldiering in his works on WWI.

In his conversation with Hartmann, Harras characterizes men as a strange "Tiergattung," equally capable of creating a beauty equal to nature and destroying the world; epitomizing this duality are the aesthetics of *Panzerkreuzer* and bombers (311). The scene with Hartmann complements other scenes in the first act in which Harras justifies his decision to join the air force because of his personal infatuation with flying. He calls himself a technician and soldier who is proud of having built the strongest air force in the world even though he knew "ein kleiner Weltkrieg" would emerge (279). During the course of the play, however, Harras realizes that the aesthetics of warfare can no longer justify the ongoing war being conducted by the Nazis.

In sum, the two young officers who believe in National Socialist ideology are depicted as naïve and vulnerable human beings misled by others. Eilers is eventually killed when his sabotaged airplane crashes, a sacrifice to the goals of the resistance. His death prevents Harras from joining the resistance, as he considers Eilers not the enemy but an innocent man. Harras thereby differentiates between a soldierly sense of duty and performance and the abuse of the army by the Nazis, even though his own experience does not legitimize such a schism. He will perpetuate the notion that in the Second World War the distinction between intention and result could be sustained. The encounter with Hartmann and the way Harras cares for him point toward another issue that is related to the notion of masculinity prevailing throughout the play. As long as a man fulfills his soldierly duties, Harras respects him. Thus the war experience and male bonding account for Harras's sense of Germanness. The cultural subtext of the play focuses on an uncontested, autonomous individual whose fate happens to be entangled with that of German history. Furthermore, it suggests that WWII was conducted according to warfare traditions that honored the individual soldier, regardless of his ideological convictions. Harras's notion of heroism also points to a time prior to National Socialism, before ideals of warfare intersected with racism and the mass murder of civilians. In *Des Teufels General* the depiction of Harras purports an ideal of soldiering based on chivalry, fairness, and courage, an ideal prevalent among WWI aces. Women are clearly not part of the male public sphere of soldiering, as they merely serve to confirm Harras's masculine virility. The only exception is Pützchen, the assertive National Socialist *femme fatale*—a configuration that anticipates later interpretations of fascism as bearing feminine attributes.

Pützchen's encounter with Harras points to another conflict in the play. For Harras *Heimat* consists of memories of WWI and his achievements as a general in the Luftwaffe in the late 1930s. Yet the scene with Pützchen highlights the fact that traditional values of soldiering and Germanness are no longer respected and validated. This particular nexus of masculinity and Germanness is the main reason why not only National Socialists but also Oderbruch are constructed in such a way that postwar audiences could not identify with them. In comparison to the two young officers, National Socialists—Schmidt-Lausitz, Pützchen, and later Mohrungen—appear in a rather exaggerated and distorted form that evokes the inversion of the values that Harras represents. Yet, in the eyes of Zuckmayer and many critics he functions both as a universal example of a man caught in a moral conflict and as a symbol of freedom. The strategies of identification are established not only through what Harras says about himself and how he is depicted, but also through the constellation of figures around him.

Zuckmayer dedicated the play to the German resistance within the army, yet critics and audience objected to Oderbruch's actions. When Zuckmayer read the newspaper notice about Udet's death he probably did not know that this message was a cover-up for Udet's suicide. But somehow word must have gotten through to him, for why else did he have Harras choose suicide? Zuckmayer never wrote about the play's conclusion. Yet we can speculate about his reasons for retaining the original ending, as the entire play deals with a protagonist who epitomizes a particular conception of heroic masculinity fused with notions of Germanness. Although many critics agreed that Harras went too far in his military ambitions, they nevertheless accepted his suicide as an atonement for his guilt. Why is it that this act is rarely seen as an escape from responsibility? Not only Oderbruch's words and his sabotage of German warplanes make him appear a traitor—like the National Socialist figure in the play, Zuckmayer also casts him as Harras's opposite.

The first time Oderbruch appears on stage is after Harras feels he has lost the battle, at the height of his anxieties in the second act. Before his appearance Oderbruch is mentioned in several conversations as being a reliable expert in his field, who has worked his way up from modest beginnings. Yet the stage directions describe him as an inconspicuous, discreet, and slightly limping forty-year-old wearing a gray work uniform without medals. In addition his speech is brief, hesitating, and controlled. Already in terms of the visual representation of Oderbruch we can see that he is not an equal partner to the virile, bold and outspoken Harras. Neither does he represent a notion of heroism according to pre-National Socialist concepts of manliness based on individualism and self-reliance as evoked throughout the drama. Instead, as the plot unfolds, we learn that Oderbruch is part of a larger movement of anonymous members willing to sacrifice their own lives and the lives of their people to higher ideals. As he explains, he joined the resistance because he was ashamed of being German. At the core of the resistance as Zuckmayer represents it is thus the question of what it means to be German under National Socialism.

The first impression of Oderbruch's physical appearance is further underscored by the arguments he presents supporting the goals of the resistance in his attempt to convince Harras in the final scene. The 1946 abbreviated version of the final dialogue between Harras and Oderbruch begins with Harras's question, why the resistance hits "uns—aus dem Dunkel, aus dem Hinterhalt?—Warum trefft ihr uns—anstatt des Feindes?" (390) Implied in this question is also Eiler's death in a sabotaged warplane. Moreover, Harras sets up a schism between the Wehrmacht and the Nazis that Oderbruch's arguments cannot overcome. Responding to Harras's version of a stab-in-the-back myth, Oderbruch believes that ". . . wenn Deutschland in diesem Krieg siegt—dann ist Deutschland verloren. Dann ist die Welt verloren" (390). Harras, again thinking in military terms, cannot imagine a defeat without foreign occupation and "Unterjochung" (391). Consequently, while he does not betray the resistance, he also cannot join it. In the last scene Oderbruch encourages Harras to escape to another country in order to support the resistance from abroad. Instead Harras refuses by saying:

> Zu spät mein Freund. Für so was—bin ich nicht mehr gut. Wer auf Erden des Teufels General wurde und ihm die Bahn gebomt hat—der muß ihm auch Quartier in der Hölle machen. . . . Der Weg ist mir immer noch offen—falls er mir einfällt. Aber—Begnadigung? Nee. Kann ich nicht verwenden.

(395)

Instead he commits suicide by taking off in a defective airplane. The play concludes with Oderbruch and Hartmann reciting the Lord's Prayer. Harras's final air stunt is reminiscent of those heroic acts performed in WWI with a sense of pride, self-reliance, and independence.

Evoking a nostalgic sense of Germanness and heroic masculinity, the play (and the 1955 film) criticizes not only National Socialism for its abuse of German ideals and national identity; it also questions the legitimacy of the resistance. Harras's apotheosis as *Opfer,* implying the double meaning of a victim of National Socialism and a sacrifice for a better Germany, conflates universal ideals of individualism and freedom with ideals of soldiering and national identity. In fact, *Des Teufels General* invokes the myth of the victimized member of the Wehrmacht who heroically sacrificed his life for the fatherland—in this case the better Germany—but was not involved with the National Socialist geopolitics of extermination.

As an allegorical reading of National Socialism the play establishes a sense of Germanness and resolves historical tensions for the postwar audience on two levels: the strained relationship among Germans as represented in the resistance movement and the Wehrmacht soldier, and the relationship between Germans and the occupying forces. Undermining the notion of loyalty, the staple of military masculinity, the resistance movement was not rehabilitated in the eyes of the West German public.

In the immediate postwar period deserters and members of the resistance were still viewed as traitors.[13] A deserting Harras would certainly not have offered a potential for identification to the audience.

The epitome of an autonomous subject, Harras embodies a belated resistance not only to the Nazis but to any system that undermines individual autonomy. Moreover, the notion of resistance propagated in the play strongly reverberated with the audience's resentment of the Allies, not just because they had initially refused to grant permission for the performance of *Des Teufels General.* Harras's view that the defeat of the German army would lead to enslavement reflected the sentiments of the audience toward the Allies in 1947. Beginning in 1946, the relationship between Germans and members of the occupying nations began to deteriorate. Difficult food distribution, housing shortages, growing administrative obstacles, and the disparities between the British, French, American, and Soviet zones generated resentment in Germany. Germans attributed the misery of the postwar years almost exclusively to the inability of the Allies to be as efficient and organized as the Germans. In particular the Allies' plans for dismantling German factories (many of them arms factories) in 1947 triggered stiff resistance from German politicians. This dismantling was a matter of life and death, according to Adenauer, who had declared in the same year that Germans would have to come to grips with the fact that they would remain under Allied control for some time to come (Forschepoth 82).

Deep-seated resentments also stemmed from the ways in which the Allies rebuilt Germany. Expecting the Allies to be liberators who would help Germany become an autonomous, democratic nation as soon as possible, many intellectuals increasingly expressed disappointment about Allied attempts to democratize Germany through a process of denazification and reeducation. Like many politicians and the general populace they considered themselves superior to the Allies and failed to acknowledge their moral and political responsibility for the past. As historian Joseph Forschepoth has argued, blaming the Allies for the difficult economic and social conditions allowed them to circumvent a confrontation with the causes of the war and National Socialism. Moreover, the "consistently intensifying criticism [. . .] aimed at creating self-confidence or, better yet, reviving and validating an old German sense of self-assurance that had been battered by defeat and occupation" (Forschepoth 88). This observation is significant given the success of *Des Teufels General* that at the core revitalizes a notion of autonomous subjectivity rooted in familiar values with which the audience could identify. For the audience between 1947 and 1949 Harras's figure and his resistance against the Nazis was thus coded in several ways: the staging of Nazi Germany, even, or perhaps because of its distorted form, allowed viewers depending on their experience with National Socialism to remember the glories of the time, to mourn the loss of these values, to yearn for a nostalgic sense of Germanness, and to find confirmation of their personal disapproval of the Nazi regime and the Allies.

Notes

1. All roles are assigned to the opposite sex in the first part and are then reassigned following the second act. See Günther Rühle, "Was sagen Sie, Herr General?" *Theater Heute* 11 (1996): 12-13, for a precise description of the cabaret-like figures.

2. As Zuckmayer writes to his biographer Emanuel Ludwig Reindl: "Wie wäre Dein eigenes Verhalten, Dein eigenes Los, mit Deinem Naturell, Temperament, Leichtsinn usw. hättest Du nicht das Glück einer 'nicht-arischen' Großmutter und stündest mitten drin?" (Ott 332) Notable is that Zuckmayer did not call his mother Jewish, nor did he see himself as being Jewish when he applied for American citizenship.

3. In the previous year Zuckmayer had cooperated with Kurt Bernhard who directed the silent film *Schinderhannes* based on the drama with the same title (1923). Zuckmayer wrote the scripts for *Katharina Knie* (1929), the first film version of *Der Hauptmann von Köpenick* (1931), *Escape me never* (1935), and *Rembrandt* (1936). Additional examples of Zuckmayer's theater plays that were adapted in films include *Der Fröhliche Weinberg* (1952), *Herr über Leben und Tod* (1954), *Des Teufels General* (1954), *Der Hauptmann von Köpenick* (1956), for which Zuckmayer, together with Käutner, wrote the script, a second script version of *Schinderhannes* (1958), and *Die Fasnachtsbeichte* (1960). See Ott for commentaries on each of these adaptations, 403-25. The most successful film adaptation of Zuckmayer's plays, however, was Käutner's 1956 *Der Hauptmann von Köpenick*. This film opened the Venice Biennial as the second postwar German film, won several prizes, and five months after its opening had been seen by 10 million people. Set in a specific historical context, both Zuckmayer's plays and film adaptations negotiate a particular kind of masculinity related to militarism. Yet they use the uniform as a semiotic sign of soldiering in different ways. While the Weimar play uses the uniform as masquerade to critically point out the reminiscences of Prussian militarism in the wake of Germany's emerging National Socialism, *Des Teufels General* sets up a scheme that justifies militarism but rejects National Socialism. On the discrepancy between Zuckmayer's drama *Der Hauptmann von Köpenick* and the film, see Russell Berman.

4. As Käutner notes: "Ich habe versucht, *Des Teufels General* so zu machen, wie es wirklich hätte sein können" (Ott 411).

5. For theater reviews on *Des Teufels General,* see Josef Halperin's notes (Glauert 253) and several reviews assembled in *Theater der Zeit* 12 (1947): 32-33.

6. For an overview see Frank Stern. *The Whitewashing of the Yellow Badge: Antisemitism and Philosemitism in Postwar Germany.* Oxford: Pergamon Press, 1992.

7. See summary of the debate *Theater der Zeit* 12 (1947): 33.

8. "Deutsche Diskussion um Zuckmayer." *Tagesanzeiger* 14 February 1948 (cited in Glauert 236); Rolfkurt Gebeschus "Kritik vor der Premiere." *Weltbühne* 29 June 1948 (cited in Glauert 250). It was because of such concerns addressed by Paul Rilla and others that the play was not allowed to be performed in the eastern sectors. In 1950, as a response to *Des Teufels General,* Hedda Zinner wrote *General Landt,* a play based on Martha Dodd's depiction of Udet in her novel *Die den Wind säen.* In contrast to Zuckmayer Zinner shows the consequences of the general's opportunism and collaboration with the Nazis. He not only betrays his Jewish friend but is also responsible for the death of members of the resistance and Russian partisans. Set between 1933 and 1960, the play suggests the continuation of militarism in West German society that hails Landt for his war heroism.

9. The editor of the English translation of Udet's autobiography, *Mein Fliegerleben* (1935), claims that the last pages of the book in praise of Hitler may have been added by the Nazis. This argument, however, might have been used by the editor to exonerate Udet from his involvement in National Socialism. In 1935 Udet joined the army; tensions between Göring and Udet began only after the invasion of Russia and the war on Britain.

10. See also "Ernst Udet," *The Encyclopedia of the Third Reich* 975.

11. See for instance the note in the veteran's magazine, *Der Frontsoldat erzählt* 11 (1952): 305: "Aus dem ersten Weltkrieg, als einer der kühnsten Jagdflieger und Sieger in 62 Luftkämpfen bekannt, hatte Ernst Udet die neue deutsche Luftwaffe als Generalluftzeugmeister aktionsfähig gemacht." Interesting in this account is the fact that Udet is praised for the success of the *Luftwaffe* in the early years of WW II. In 1952, discussions on Germany's rearmament were well underway and, as this note suggests, the war fought by the German army seemed to offer a reason to be proud again.

12. Flying as a metaphor for superiority and community is reiterated in the opening scenes showing Hitler descending from the clouds in Leni Riefenstahl's propaganda film *Triumph des Willens.*

13. For a discussion of the German resistance under the Third Reich in postwar Germany, see for instance Bill Niven as well as Michael Geyer and Jon W. Boyer.

Works Cited

Bab, Julius. "Carl Zuckmayers Drama "Des Teufels General." *Carl Zuckmayer. Das Bühnenwerk im Spiegel der Kritik.* Ed. Barbara Glauert. 239.

Balinka, Ansuma. *The Central Women Figures in Carl Zuckmayer's Dramas.* Bern: Peter Lang, 1978.

Becker, Wolfgang, and Norbert Schöll, eds. *In Jenen Tagen . . . Wie der deutsche Nachkriegsfilm die Vergangenheit bewältigte.* Opladen: Leske und Budrich, 1995.

Berman, Russell. "A Return to Arms: Käutner's *The Captain of Köpenick* (1956)." *German Film and Literature Adaptations and Transformations.* Ed. Eric Rentschler. New York: Mesunen, 1986. 161-75.

Echternkamp, Jörg. "Arbeit am Mythos. Soldatengenerationen der Wehrmacht im Urteil der west- und ostdeutschen Nachkriegsgesellschaft." *Nachkrieg in Deutschland.* Ed. Klaus Naumann. Hamburg: Hamburger Edition, 2001. 421-43.

Forschepoth, Josef. "German Reaction to Defeat and Occupation." *West Germany under Construction.* Ed. Robert Moeller. Ann Arbor: U of Michigan, P, 1997. 73-89.

Fritzsche, Peter. *A Nation of Fliers. German Aviation and the Popular Imagination.* Cambridge: Harvard UP, 1992.

Geyer, Michael. "Der Kalte Krieg, die Deutschen und die Angst. Die westdeutsche Opposition gegen Wiederbewaffnung und Kernwaffen." *Nachkrieg in Deutschland.* Ed. Klaus Naumann. Hamburg: Hamburger Edition, 2001. 267-318.

Geyer, Michael, and John W. Boyer, eds. *Resistance against the Third Reich, 1933-1990.* Chicago: U Chicago P, 1994.

Glauert, Barbara, ed. *Carl Zuckmayer. Das Bühnenwerk im Spiegel der Kritik.* Frankfurt a.M.: Fischer, 1977.

Govet, Henry. *Carl Zuckmayer 1896-1977.* Ott and Pfäfflin 334.

Halperin, Joseph. "Für Carl Zuckmayer." *Carl Zuckmayer. Das Bühnenwerk im Spiegel der Kritik.* Glauert 252.

Heinrichs, Benjamin. "Des Teufels und der liebe Zuck," *Die Zeit* 44 (1996): 15.

Ihering, Herbert. Letter 12 August 1948. *Carl Zuckmayer 1896-1977.* Ott and Pfäfflin 342-44.

M.G. "'Des Teufels General'." Ein Drama von Carl Zuckmayer. Erstaufführung an den Frankfurter Städtischen Bühnen. (1947). *Carl Zuckmayer. Das Bühnenwerk im Spiegel der Kritik.* Glauert 229-34.

Niven, Bill. *Facing the Nazi Past. United Germany and the Legacy of the Third Reich.* London: Routledge, 2002.

Ott, Ulrich, and Friedrich Pfäfflin, eds. *Carl Zuckmayer 1896-1977. 'Ich wollte nur Theater machen.'* Stuttgart: Deutsche Schillergesellschaft, 1996.

Plater, Edward M. V. "Helmut Käutner's Film Adaptation of *Des Teufels General.*" *Literature Film Quarterly* 22.4 (1994): 253-64.

Rilla, Paul. "Zuckmayer und die Uniform" (1952). *Carl Zuckmayer. Das Bühnenwerk im Spiegel der Kritik.* Glauert 255-69.

Roth, Dieter. "Über Zuckmayers 'Des Teufels General.'" *Carl Zuckmayer. Das Bühnenwerk im Spiegel der Kritik.* Glauert 269-70.

Schirrmacher, Carl. Review of *Des Teufels General. Der Ruf* 22 (1947): 13.

Theater der Zeit 12 (1947): 33.

Udet, Ernst. *Mein Fliegerleben.* Berlin: Ullstein, 1935.

Wayne, Anthony. "Carl Zuckmayer's *Des Teufels General* as a Critique of the Cult of Masculinity." *Forum for Modern Language Studies* 14. 3 (1996): 258-70.

Wehdeking, Volker. "Mythologisches Ungewitter. Carl Zuckmayer's problematisches Exildrama 'Des Teufels General,'" 1973. *Carl Zuckmayer. Materialien zu Leben und Werk.* Ed. Harro Kieser. Frankfurt a.M.: Fischer, 1986. 86-102.

Zentner, Christian, and Friedemann Bedürftig, eds. *The Encyclopedia of the Third Reich.* Trans. Amy Hackett. 2 vols. New York: Macmillan, 1991.

Zuckmayer, Carl. "Persönliche Notiz zu meinem Stück 'Des Teufels General.'" *Die Wandlung* 3 (1948): 332-33.

———. *Des Teufels General. Gesammelte Werke. Vol. 1.* Stockholm: Bermann-Fischer, 1947.

———. *Als wär's ein Stück von mir.* Frankfurt a. M.: Fischer, 1966.

FURTHER READING

Biography

Loram, Ian C. "Carl Zuckmayer: An Introduction." *The German Quarterly* 27, no. 3 (May 1954): 137-49.

Offers a brief but intimate portrait of Carl Zuckmayer, emphasizing his sense of humor, his philosophy of life, and his success as a playwright, novelist, essayist, and poet.

Criticism

Balinkin, Ausma. *The Central Women Figures in Carl Zuckmayer's Dramas,* Bern, Switzerland: Peter Lang, 1978, 115 p.

Analyzes the female characters in Zuckmayer's plays, noting the manner in which they "evolve and vary from his early dramas to the present ones" and highlighting their "recurrent characteristics, traits, and attitudes" which make them "the vibrant, full-bloodied feminine stage personalities so rare in contemporary literature."

Glade, Henry. "Carl Zuckmayer's *The Devil's General* as Autobiography." *Modern Drama* 9, no. 1 (May 1966): 54-61.

Interprets the first half of Zuckmayer's drama *The Devil's General* as an autobiographical character study.

Guder, G. "Carl Zuckmayer's Post-War Dramas." *Modern Languages* 35, no. 2 (March 1954): 54-6.

Discusses the significance of the protagonist's inner voice in Zuckmayer's post-war dramas, including *The Captain of Köpenick, The Devil's General, Barbara Blomberg,* and *Der Gesang im Feuerofen.*

Loram, Ian C. "Carl Zuckmayer: German Playwright in America." *Educational Theatre Journal* 9, no. 1 (March 1957): 177-83.

Traces Zuckmayer's journey to literary notoriety, beginning with the failure of his first play, *Kreuzweg,* to the enormous success of such later works as *Der fröhliche Weinberg, The Devil's General,* and *Herbert Engelmann.*

Mews, Siegfried. "Carl Zuckmayer (27 December 1896-18 January 1977)." *The German Quarterly* 50, no. 3 (May 1977): 298-308.

Reviews several posthumously published compendiums of Zuckmayer's work, including *Work Edition,* which includes several of his major dramas, and *Reader,* which contains both dramas and prose narratives.

———. "The Fall of France on Stage: Zuckmayer's *Somewhere in France* and Brecht's *The Visions of Simone Machard.*" In *Modern War on Stage and Screen/ Der Moderne Krieg Auf Der Bühne,* edited by Wolfgang Görtschacher and Holger Klein, pp. 101-15. Lewiston, N.Y.: The Edwin Mellen Press, 1997.

Compares Zuckmayer's play *Somewhere in France* to Bertolt Brecht's *The Visions of Simone Machard,* noting that both plays seek to illustrate the impact of modern warfare on French society.

Mews, Siegfried and Raymond English. "The *Jungle* Transcended: Brecht and Zuckmayer." In *Essays on Brecht: Theater and Politics,* edited by Siegfried Mews and Herbert Knust, pp. 79-98. Chapel Hill: The University of North Carolina Press, 1974.

Establishes a link between Bertolt Brecht and Carl Zuckmayer by exploring parallels in the structures, themes, and imagery of their work.

Patterson, Michael. "'Bewältigung der Vergangenheit' or 'Überwältigung der Befangenheit': Nazism and the War in Post-War German Theatre." *Modern Drama* 33, no. 1 (March 1990): 120-28.

Highlights post-World War II German dramas, such as Zuckmayer's *The Devil's General* and Wolfgang Borchert's *The Man Outside,* that "attempt to come to terms with the German past."

Speidel, E. "The Stage as Metaphysical Institution: Zuckmayer's Dramas 'Schinderhannes' and 'Der Hauptmann von Köpenick.'" *The Modern Language Review* 63 (1968): 425-36.

Examines the relationship between the individual and society in Zuckmayer's *The Captain of Köpenick* and *Schinderhannes.*

Steiner, Pauline and Horst Frenz. "Anderson and Stalling's *What Price Glory?* and Carl Zuckmayer's *Rivalen.*" *The German Quarterly* 20, no. 4 (November 1947): 239-51.

Asserts that Zuckmayer's German adaptation of the Maxwell Anderson play *What Price Glory?*—which debuted under the title *Rivalen*—provided Zuckmayer with a vehicle for dissent against militarism.

Wagener, Hans. *Carl Zuckmayer Criticism: Tracing Endangered Fame,* Columbia, S.C.: Camden House, 1995, 185 p.

Book-length survey of Zuckmayer's dramas that includes a detailed record of scholarly criticism on his major plays, poetry, prose, and film collections.

Additional coverage of Zuckmayer's life and career is contained in the following sources published by Thomson Gale: *Contemporary Authors,* **Vols. 69-72;** *Contempor ary Literary Criticism,* **Vol. 18;** *Dictionary of Literary Biography,* **Vols. 56, 124;** *Encyclopedia of World Literature in the 20th Century,* **Ed. 3;** *Literature Resource Center***; and** *Reference Guide to World Literature,* **Eds. 2, 3.**

How to Use This Index

The main references

Calvino, Italo
1923-1985 .... CLC **5, 8, 11, 22, 33, 39,**
73; SSC 3, 48

list all author entries in the following Thomson Gale Literary Criticism series:

AAL = *Asian American Literature*
BG = *The Beat Generation: A Gale Critical Companion*
BLC = *Black Literature Criticism*
BLCS = *Black Literature Criticism Supplement*
CLC = *Contemporary Literary Criticism*
CLR = *Children's Literature Review*
CMLC = *Classical and Medieval Literature Criticism*
DC = *Drama Criticism*
FL = *Feminism in Literature: A Gale Critical Companion*
GL = *Gothic Literature: A Gale Critical Companion*
HLC = *Hispanic Literature Criticism*
HLCS = *Hispanic Literature Criticism Supplement*
HR = *Harlem Renaissance: A Gale Critical Companion*
LC = *Literature Criticism from 1400 to 1800*
NCLC = *Nineteenth-Century Literature Criticism*
NNAL = *Native North American Literature*
PC = *Poetry Criticism*
SSC = *Short Story Criticism*
TCLC = *Twentieth-Century Literary Criticism*
WLC = *World Literature Criticism, 1500 to the Present*
WLCS = *World Literature Criticism Supplement*

The cross-references

See also CA 85-88, 116; CANR 23, 61;
DAM NOV; DLB 196; EW 13; MTCW 1, 2;
RGSF 2; RGWL 2; SFW 4; SSFS 12

list all author entries in the following Thomson Gale biographical and literary sources:

AAYA = *Authors & Artists for Young Adults*
AFAW = *African American Writers*
AFW = *African Writers*
AITN = *Authors in the News*
AMW = *American Writers*
AMWR = *American Writers Retrospective Supplement*
AMWS = *American Writers Supplement*
ANW = *American Nature Writers*
AW = *Ancient Writers*
BEST = *Bestsellers*
BPFB = *Beacham's Encyclopedia of Popular Fiction: Biography and Resources*
BRW = *British Writers*
BRWS = *British Writers Supplement*
BW = *Black Writers*
BYA = *Beacham's Guide to Literature for Young Adults*
CA = *Contemporary Authors*
CAAS = *Contemporary Authors Autobiography Series*
CABS = *Contemporary Authors Bibliographical Series*
CAD = *Contemporary American Dramatists*
CANR = *Contemporary Authors New Revision Series*
CAP = *Contemporary Authors Permanent Series*
CBD = *Contemporary British Dramatists*
CCA = *Contemporary Canadian Authors*
CD = *Contemporary Dramatists*
CDALB = *Concise Dictionary of American Literary Biography*

CDALBS = *Concise Dictionary of American Literary Biography Supplement*
CDBLB = *Concise Dictionary of British Literary Biography*
CMW = *St. James Guide to Crime & Mystery Writers*
CN = *Contemporary Novelists*
CP = *Contemporary Poets*
CPW = *Contemporary Popular Writers*
CSW = *Contemporary Southern Writers*
CWD = *Contemporary Women Dramatists*
CWP = *Contemporary Women Poets*
CWRI = *St. James Guide to Children's Writers*
CWW = *Contemporary World Writers*
DA = *DISCovering Authors*
DA3 = *DISCovering Authors 3.0*
DAB = *DISCovering Authors: British Edition*
DAC = *DISCovering Authors: Canadian Edition*
DAM = *DISCovering Authors: Modules*
   DRAM: *Dramatists Module;* **MST:** *Most-studied Authors Module;*
   MULT: *Multicultural Authors Module;* **NOV:** *Novelists Module;*
   POET: *Poets Module;* **POP:** *Popular Fiction and Genre Authors Module*
DFS = *Drama for Students*
DLB = *Dictionary of Literary Biography*
DLBD = *Dictionary of Literary Biography Documentary Series*
DLBY = *Dictionary of Literary Biography Yearbook*
DNFS = *Literature of Developing Nations for Students*
EFS = *Epics for Students*
EXPN = *Exploring Novels*
EXPP = *Exploring Poetry*
EXPS = *Exploring Short Stories*
EW = *European Writers*
FANT = *St. James Guide to Fantasy Writers*
FW = *Feminist Writers*
GFL = *Guide to French Literature,* Beginnings to 1789, 1798 to the Present
GLL = *Gay and Lesbian Literature*
HGG = *St. James Guide to Horror, Ghost & Gothic Writers*
HW = *Hispanic Writers*
IDFW = *International Dictionary of Films and Filmmakers: Writers and Production Artists*
IDTP = *International Dictionary of Theatre: Playwrights*
LAIT = *Literature and Its Times*
LAW = *Latin American Writers*
JRDA = *Junior DISCovering Authors*
MAICYA = *Major Authors and Illustrators for Children and Young Adults*
MAICYAS = *Major Authors and Illustrators for Children and Young Adults Supplement*
MAWW = *Modern American Women Writers*
MJW = *Modern Japanese Writers*
MTCW = *Major 20th-Century Writers*
NCFS = *Nonfiction Classics for Students*
NFS = *Novels for Students*
PAB = *Poets: American and British*
PFS = *Poetry for Students*
RGAL = *Reference Guide to American Literature*
RGEL = *Reference Guide to English Literature*
RGSF = *Reference Guide to Short Fiction*
RGWL = *Reference Guide to World Literature*
RHW = *Twentieth-Century Romance and Historical Writers*
SAAS = *Something about the Author Autobiography Series*
SATA = *Something about the Author*
SFW = *St. James Guide to Science Fiction Writers*
SSFS = *Short Stories for Students*
TCWW = *Twentieth-Century Western Writers*
WLIT = *World Literature and Its Times*
WP = *World Poets*
YABC = *Yesterday's Authors of Books for Children*
YAW = *St. James Guide to Young Adult Writers*

Literary Criticism Series
Cumulative Author Index

Aragon, Louis 1897-1982 .... **CLC 3, 22; TCLC 123**
See also CA 69-72; CAAS 108; CANR 28, 71; DAM NOV, POET; DLB 72, 258; EW 11; EWL 3; GFL 1789 to the Present; GLL 2; LMFS 2; MTCW 1, 2; RGWL 2, 3

Arany, Janos 1817-1882 .... **NCLC 34**

Aranyos, Kakay 1847-1910
See Mikszath, Kalman

Aratus of Soli c. 315B.C.-c. 240B.C. .... **CMLC 64**
See also DLB 176

Arbuthnot, John 1667-1735 .... **LC 1**
See also DLB 101

Archer, Herbert Winslow
See Mencken, H(enry) L(ouis)

Archer, Jeffrey 1940- .... **CLC 28**
See also AAYA 16; BEST 89:3; BPFB 1; CA 77-80; CANR 22, 52, 95, 136; CPW; DA3; DAM POP; INT CANR-22; MTFW 2005

Archer, Jeffrey Howard
See Archer, Jeffrey

Archer, Jules 1915- .... **CLC 12**
See also CA 9-12R; CANR 6, 69; SAAS 5; SATA 4, 85

Archer, Lee
See Ellison, Harlan

Archilochus c. 7th cent. B.C.- .... **CMLC 44**
See also DLB 176

Arden, John 1930- .... **CLC 6, 13, 15**
See also BRWS 2; CA 13-16R; 4; CANR 31, 65, 67, 124; CBD; CD 5, 6; DAM DRAM; DFS 9; DLB 13, 245; EWL 3; MTCW 1

Arenas, Reinaldo 1943-1990 .. **CLC 41; HLC 1; TCLC 191**
See also CA 128; CAAE 124; CAAS 133; CANR 73, 106; DAM MULT; DLB 145; EWL 3; GLL 2; HW 1; LAW; LAWS 1; MTCW 2; MTFW 2005; RGSF 2; RGWL 3; WLIT 1

Arendt, Hannah 1906-1975 .... **CLC 66, 98**
See also CA 17-20R; CAAS 61-64; CANR 26, 60; DLB 242; MTCW 1, 2

Aretino, Pietro 1492-1556 .... **LC 12**
See also RGWL 2, 3

Arghezi, Tudor .... **CLC 80**
See Theodorescu, Ion N.
See also CA 167; CDWLB 4; DLB 220; EWL 3

Arguedas, Jose Maria 1911-1969 .... **CLC 10, 18; HLCS 1; TCLC 147**
See also CA 89-92; CANR 73; DLB 113; EWL 3; HW 1; LAW; RGWL 2, 3; WLIT 1

Argueta, Manlio 1936- .... **CLC 31**
See also CA 131; CANR 73; CWW 2; DLB 145; EWL 3; HW 1; RGWL 3

Arias, Ron 1941- .... **HLC 1**
See also CA 131; CANR 81, 136; DAM MULT; DLB 82; HW 1, 2; MTCW 2; MTFW 2005

Ariosto, Lodovico
See Ariosto, Ludovico
See also WLIT 7

Ariosto, Ludovico 1474-1533 ... **LC 6, 87; PC 42**
See Ariosto, Lodovico
See also EW 2; RGWL 2, 3

Aristides
See Epstein, Joseph

Aristophanes 450B.C.-385B.C. .... **CMLC 4, 51; DC 2; WLCS**
See also AW 1; CDWLB 1; DA; DA3; DAB; DAC; DAM DRAM, MST; DFS 10; DLB 176; LMFS 1; RGWL 2, 3; TWA; WLIT 8

Aristotle 384B.C.-322B.C. .... **CMLC 31; WLCS**
See also AW 1; CDWLB 1; DA; DA3; DAB; DAC; DAM MST; DLB 176; RGWL 2, 3; TWA; WLIT 8

Arlt, Roberto (Godofredo Christophersen) 1900-1942 .... **HLC 1; TCLC 29**
See also CA 131; CAAE 123; CANR 67; DAM MULT; DLB 305; EWL 3; HW 1, 2; IDTP; LAW

Armah, Ayi Kwei 1939- . **BLC 1; CLC 5, 33, 136**
See also AFW; BRWS 10; BW 1; CA 61-64; CANR 21, 64; CDWLB 3; CN 1, 2, 3, 4, 5, 6, 7; DAM MULT, POET; DLB 117; EWL 3; MTCW 1; WLIT 2

Armatrading, Joan 1950- .... **CLC 17**
See also CA 186; CAAE 114

Armin, Robert 1568(?)-1615(?) .... **LC 120**

Armitage, Frank
See Carpenter, John (Howard)

Armstrong, Jeannette (C.) 1948- .... **NNAL**
See also CA 149; CCA 1; CN 6, 7; DAC; DLB 334; SATA 102

Arnette, Robert
See Silverberg, Robert

Arnim, Achim von (Ludwig Joachim von Arnim) 1781-1831 .. **NCLC 5, 159; SSC 29**
See also DLB 90

Arnim, Bettina von 1785-1859 ...... **NCLC 38, 123**
See also DLB 90; RGWL 2, 3

Arnold, Matthew 1822-1888 ..... **NCLC 6, 29, 89, 126; PC 5; WLC 1**
See also BRW 5; CDBLB 1832-1890; DA; DAB; DAC; DAM MST, POET; DLB 32, 57; EXPP; PAB; PFS 2; TEA; WP

Arnold, Thomas 1795-1842 .... **NCLC 18**
See also DLB 55

Arnow, Harriette (Louisa) Simpson 1908-1986 .... **CLC 2, 7, 18**
See also BPFB 1; CA 9-12R; CAAS 118; CANR 14; CN 2, 3, 4; DLB 6; FW; MTCW 1, 2; RHW; SATA 42; SATA-Obit 47

Arouet, Francois-Marie
See Voltaire

Arp, Hans
See Arp, Jean

Arp, Jean 1887-1966 .... **CLC 5; TCLC 115**
See also CA 81-84; CAAS 25-28R; CANR 42, 77; EW 10

Arrabal
See Arrabal, Fernando

Arrabal (Teran), Fernando
See Arrabal, Fernando
See also CWW 2

Arrabal, Fernando 1932- ... **CLC 2, 9, 18, 58**
See Arrabal (Teran), Fernando
See also CA 9-12R; CANR 15; DLB 321; EWL 3; LMFS 2

Arreola, Juan Jose 1918-2001 .... **CLC 147; HLC 1; SSC 38**
See also CA 131; CAAE 113; CAAS 200; CANR 81; CWW 2; DAM MULT; DLB 113; DNFS 2; EWL 3; HW 1, 2; LAW; RGSF 2

Arrian c. 89(?)-c. 155(?) .... **CMLC 43**
See also DLB 176

Arrick, Fran .... **CLC 30**
See Gaberman, Judie Angell
See also BYA 6

Arrley, Richmond
See Delany, Samuel R., Jr.

Artaud, Antonin (Marie Joseph) 1896-1948 .... **DC 14; TCLC 3, 36**
See also CA 149; CAAE 104; DA3; DAM DRAM; DFS 22; DLB 258, 321; EW 11; EWL 3; GFL 1789 to the Present; MTCW 2; MTFW 2005; RGWL 2, 3

Arthur, Ruth M(abel) 1905-1979 ..... **CLC 12**
See also CA 9-12R; CAAS 85-88; CANR 4; CWRI 5; SATA 7, 26

Artsybashev, Mikhail (Petrovich) 1878-1927 .... **TCLC 31**
See also CA 170; DLB 295

Arundel, Honor (Morfydd) 1919-1973 .... **CLC 17**
See also CA 21-22; CAAS 41-44R; CAP 2; CLR 35; CWRI 5; SATA 4; SATA-Obit 24

Arzner, Dorothy 1900-1979 .... **CLC 98**

Asch, Sholem 1880-1957 .... **TCLC 3**
See also CAAE 105; DLB 333; EWL 3; GLL 2; RGHL

Ascham, Roger 1516(?)-1568 .... **LC 101**
See also DLB 236

Ash, Shalom
See Asch, Sholem

Ashbery, John 1927- ... **CLC 2, 3, 4, 6, 9, 13, 15, 25, 41, 77, 125, 221; PC 26**
See Berry, Jonas
See also AMWS 3; CA 5-8R; CANR 9, 37, 66, 102, 132; CP 1, 2, 3, 4, 5, 6, 7; DA3; DAM POET; DLB 5, 165; DLBY 1981; EWL 3; INT CANR-9; MAL 5; MTCW 1, 2; MTFW 2005; PAB; PFS 11; RGAL 4; TCLE 1:1; WP

Ashdown, Clifford
See Freeman, R(ichard) Austin

Ashe, Gordon
See Creasey, John

Ashton-Warner, Sylvia (Constance) 1908-1984 .... **CLC 19**
See also CA 69-72; CAAS 112; CANR 29; CN 1, 2, 3; MTCW 1, 2

Asimov, Isaac 1920-1992 ..... **CLC 1, 3, 9, 19, 26, 76, 92**
See also AAYA 13; BEST 90:2; BPFB 1; BYA 4, 6, 7, 9; CA 1-4R; CAAS 137; CANR 2, 19, 36, 60, 125; CLR 12, 79; CMW 4; CN 1, 2, 3, 4, 5; CPW; DA3; DAM POP; DLB 8; DLBY 1992; INT CANR-19; JRDA; LAIT 5; LMFS 2; MAICYA 1, 2; MAL 5; MTCW 1, 2; MTFW 2005; RGAL 4; SATA 1, 26, 74; SCFW 1, 2; SFW 4; SSFS 17; TUS; YAW

Askew, Anne 1521(?)-1546 .... **LC 81**
See also DLB 136

Assis, Joaquim Maria Machado de
See Machado de Assis, Joaquim Maria

Astell, Mary 1666-1731 .... **LC 68**
See also DLB 252, 336; FW

Astley, Thea (Beatrice May) 1925-2004 .... **CLC 41**
See also CA 65-68; CAAS 229; CANR 11, 43, 78; CN 1, 2, 3, 4, 5, 6, 7; DLB 289; EWL 3

Astley, William 1855-1911
See Warung, Price

Aston, James
See White, T(erence) H(anbury)

Asturias, Miguel Angel 1899-1974 .... **CLC 3, 8, 13; HLC 1; TCLC 184**
See also CA 25-28; CAAS 49-52; CANR 32; CAP 2; CDWLB 3; DA3; DAM MULT, NOV; DLB 113, 290, 329; EWL 3; HW 1; LAW; LMFS 2; MTCW 1, 2; RGWL 2, 3; WLIT 1

Atares, Carlos Saura
See Saura (Atares), Carlos

Athanasius c. 295-c. 373 .... **CMLC 48**

Atheling, William
  See Pound, Ezra (Weston Loomis)

Atheling, William, Jr.
  See Blish, James (Benjamin)

Atherton, Gertrude (Franklin Horn)
  1857-1948 .... **TCLC 2**
  See also CA 155; CAAE 104; DLB 9, 78,
  186; HGG; RGAL 4; SUFW 1; TCWW 1,
  2

Atherton, Lucius
  See Masters, Edgar Lee

Atkins, Jack
  See Harris, Mark

Atkinson, Kate 1951- .... **CLC 99**
  See also CA 166; CANR 101, 153; DLB
  267

Attaway, William (Alexander)
  1911-1986 .... **BLC 1; CLC 92**
  See also BW 2, 3; CA 143; CANR 82;
  DAM MULT; DLB 76; MAL 5

Atticus
  See Fleming, Ian; Wilson, (Thomas) Woodrow

Atwood, Margaret 1939- . **CLC 2, 3, 4, 8, 13,
  15, 25, 44, 84, 135, 232, 239; PC 8;
  SSC 2, 46; WLC 1**
  See also AAYA 12, 47; AMWS 13; BEST
  89:2; BPFB 1; CA 49-52; CANR 3, 24,
  33, 59, 95, 133; CN 2, 3, 4, 5, 6, 7; CP 1,
  2, 3, 4, 5, 6, 7; CPW; CWP; DA; DA3;
  DAB; DAC; DAM MST, NOV, POET;
  DLB 53, 251, 326; EWL 3; EXPN; FL
  1:5; FW; GL 2; INT CANR-24; LAIT 5;
  MTCW 1, 2; MTFW 2005; NFS 4, 12,
  13, 14, 19; PFS 7; RGSF 2; SATA 50,
  170; SSFS 3, 13; TCLE 1:1; TWA; WWE
  1; YAW

Atwood, Margaret Eleanor
  See Atwood, Margaret

Aubigny, Pierre d'
  See Mencken, H(enry) L(ouis)

Aubin, Penelope 1685-1731(?) .... **LC 9**
  See also DLB 39

Auchincloss, Louis 1917- ..... **CLC 4, 6, 9, 18,
  45; SSC 22**
  See also AMWS 4; CA 1-4R; CANR 6, 29,
  55, 87, 130; CN 1, 2, 3, 4, 5, 6, 7; DAM
  NOV; DLB 2, 244; DLBY 1980; EWL 3;
  INT CANR-29; MAL 5; MTCW 1; RGAL
  4

Auchincloss, Louis Stanton
  See Auchincloss, Louis

Auden, W(ystan) H(ugh) 1907-1973 . **CLC 1,
  2, 3, 4, 6, 9, 11, 14, 43, 123; PC 1;
  WLC 1**
  See also AAYA 18; AMWS 2; BRW 7;
  BRWR 1; CA 9-12R; CAAS 45-48;
  CANR 5, 61, 105; CDBLB 1914-1945;
  CP 1, 2; DA; DA3; DAB; DAC; DAM
  DRAM, MST, POET; DLB 10, 20; EWL
  3; EXPP; MAL 5; MTCW 1, 2; MTFW
  2005; PAB; PFS 1, 3, 4, 10; TUS; WP

Audiberti, Jacques 1899-1965 .... **CLC 38**
  See also CA 252; CAAS 25-28R; DAM
  DRAM; DLB 321; EWL 3

Audubon, John James 1785-1851 . **NCLC 47**
  See also AMWS 16; ANW; DLB 248

Auel, Jean M(arie) 1936- .... **CLC 31, 107**
  See also AAYA 7, 51; BEST 90:4; BPFB 1;
  CA 103; CANR 21, 64, 115; CPW; DA3;
  DAM POP; INT CANR-21; NFS 11;
  RHW; SATA 91

Auerbach, Berthold 1812-1882 .... **NCLC 171**
  See also DLB 133

Auerbach, Erich 1892-1957 .... **TCLC 43**
  See also CA 155; CAAE 118; EWL 3

Augier, Emile 1820-1889 .... **NCLC 31**
  See also DLB 192; GFL 1789 to the Present

August, John
  See De Voto, Bernard (Augustine)

Augustine, St. 354-430 .... **CMLC 6; WLCS**
  See also DA; DA3; DAB; DAC; DAM
  MST; DLB 115; EW 1; RGWL 2, 3;
  WLIT 8

Aunt Belinda
  See Braddon, Mary Elizabeth

Aunt Weedy
  See Alcott, Louisa May

Aurelius
  See Bourne, Randolph S(illiman)

Aurelius, Marcus 121-180 .... **CMLC 45**
  See Marcus Aurelius
  See also RGWL 2, 3

Aurobindo, Sri
  See Ghose, Aurabinda

Aurobindo Ghose
  See Ghose, Aurabinda

Ausonius, Decimus Magnus c. 310-c.
  394 .... **CMLC 88**
  See also RGWL 2, 3

Austen, Jane 1775-1817 ...... **NCLC 1, 13, 19,
  33, 51, 81, 95, 119, 150; WLC 1**
  See also AAYA 19; BRW 4; BRWC 1;
  BRWR 2; BYA 3; CDBLB 1789-1832;
  DA; DA3; DAB; DAC; DAM MST, NOV;
  DLB 116; EXPN; FL 1:2; GL 2; LAIT 2;
  LATS 1:1; LMFS 1; NFS 1, 14, 18, 20,
  21; TEA; WLIT 3; WYAS 1

Auster, Paul 1947- .... **CLC 47, 131, 227**
  See also AMWS 12; CA 69-72; CANR 23,
  52, 75, 129; CMW 4; CN 5, 6, 7; DA3;
  DLB 227; MAL 5; MTCW 2; MTFW
  2005; SUFW 2; TCLE 1:1

Austin, Frank
  See Faust, Frederick (Schiller)

Austin, Mary (Hunter) 1868-1934 . **TCLC 25**
  See also ANW; CA 178; CAAE 109; DLB
  9, 78, 206, 221, 275; FW; TCWW 1, 2

Averroes 1126-1198 .... **CMLC 7**
  See also DLB 115

Avicenna 980-1037 .... **CMLC 16**
  See also DLB 115

Avison, Margaret (Kirkland) 1918- .. **CLC 2,
  4, 97**
  See also CA 17-20R; CANR 134; CP 1, 2,
  3, 4, 5, 6, 7; DAC; DAM POET; DLB 53;
  MTCW 1

Axton, David
  See Koontz, Dean R.

Ayckbourn, Alan 1939- ...... **CLC 5, 8, 18, 33,
  74; DC 13**
  See also BRWS 5; CA 21-24R; CANR 31,
  59, 118; CBD; CD 5, 6; DAB; DAM
  DRAM; DFS 7; DLB 13, 245; EWL 3;
  MTCW 1, 2; MTFW 2005

Aydy, Catherine
  See Tennant, Emma (Christina)

Ayme, Marcel (Andre) 1902-1967 ... **CLC 11;
  SSC 41**
  See also CA 89-92; CANR 67, 137; CLR
  25; DLB 72; EW 12; EWL 3; GFL 1789
  to the Present; RGSF 2; RGWL 2, 3;
  SATA 91

Ayrton, Michael 1921-1975 .... **CLC 7**
  See also CA 5-8R; CAAS 61-64; CANR 9,
  21

Aytmatov, Chingiz
  See Aitmatov, Chingiz (Torekulovich)
  See also EWL 3

Azorin .... **CLC 11**
  See Martinez Ruiz, Jose
  See also DLB 322; EW 9; EWL 3

Azuela, Mariano 1873-1952 .. **HLC 1; TCLC
  3, 145**
  See also CA 131; CAAE 104; CANR 81;
  DAM MULT; EWL 3; HW 1, 2; LAW;
  MTCW 1, 2; MTFW 2005

Ba, Mariama 1929-1981 .... **BLCS**
  See also AFW; BW 2; CA 141; CANR 87;
  DNFS 2; WLIT 2

Baastad, Babbis Friis
  See Friis-Baastad, Babbis Ellinor

Bab
  See Gilbert, W(illiam) S(chwenck)

Babbis, Eleanor
  See Friis-Baastad, Babbis Ellinor

Babel, Isaac
  See Babel, Isaak (Emmanuilovich)
  See also EW 11; SSFS 10

Babel, Isaak (Emmanuilovich)
  1894-1941(?) . **SSC 16, 78; TCLC 2, 13,
  171**
  See Babel, Isaac
  See also CA 155; CAAE 104; CANR 113;
  DLB 272; EWL 3; MTCW 2; MTFW
  2005; RGSF 2; RGWL 2, 3; TWA

Babits, Mihaly 1883-1941 .... **TCLC 14**
  See also CAAE 114; CDWLB 4; DLB 215;
  EWL 3

Babur 1483-1530 .... **LC 18**

Babylas 1898-1962
  See Ghelderode, Michel de

Baca, Jimmy Santiago 1952- . **HLC 1; PC 41**
  See also CA 131; CANR 81, 90, 146; CP 6,
  7; DAM MULT; DLB 122; HW 1, 2;
  LLW; MAL 5

Baca, Jose Santiago
  See Baca, Jimmy Santiago

Bacchelli, Riccardo 1891-1985 .... **CLC 19**
  See also CA 29-32R; CAAS 117; DLB 264;
  EWL 3

Bach, Richard 1936- .... **CLC 14**
  See also AITN 1; BEST 89:2; BPFB 1; BYA
  5; CA 9-12R; CANR 18, 93, 151; CPW;
  DAM NOV, POP; FANT; MTCW 1;
  SATA 13

Bach, Richard David
  See Bach, Richard

Bache, Benjamin Franklin
  1769-1798 .... **LC 74**
  See also DLB 43

Bachelard, Gaston 1884-1962 ...... **TCLC 128**
  See also CA 97-100; CAAS 89-92; DLB
  296; GFL 1789 to the Present

Bachman, Richard
  See King, Stephen

Bachmann, Ingeborg 1926-1973 .... **CLC 69**
  See also CA 93-96; CAAS 45-48; CANR
  69; DLB 85; EWL 3; RGHL; RGWL 2, 3

Bacon, Francis 1561-1626 ..... **LC 18, 32, 131**
  See also BRW 1; CDBLB Before 1660;
  DLB 151, 236, 252; RGEL 2; TEA

Bacon, Roger 1214(?)-1294 .... **CMLC 14**
  See also DLB 115

Bacovia, George 1881-1957 .... **TCLC 24**
  See Vasiliu, Gheorghe
  See also CDWLB 4; DLB 220; EWL 3

Badanes, Jerome 1937-1995 .... **CLC 59**
  See also CA 234

Bage, Robert 1728-1801 .... **NCLC 182**
  See also DLB 39; RGEL 2

Bagehot, Walter 1826-1877 .... **NCLC 10**
  See also DLB 55

Bagnold, Enid 1889-1981 .... **CLC 25**
  See also AAYA 75; BYA 2; CA 5-8R;
  CAAS 103; CANR 5, 40; CBD; CN 2;
  CWD; CWRI 5; DAM DRAM; DLB 13,
  160, 191, 245; FW; MAICYA 1, 2; RGEL
  2; SATA 1, 25

Bagritsky, Eduard .... **TCLC 60**
  See Dzyubin, Eduard Georgievich

Bagrjana, Elisaveta
  See Belcheva, Elisaveta Lyubomirova

Bagryana, Elisaveta .... **CLC 10**
See Belcheva, Elisaveta Lyubomirova
See also CA 178; CDWLB 4; DLB 147;
EWL 3

Bailey, Paul 1937- .... **CLC 45**
See also CA 21-24R; CANR 16, 62, 124;
CN 1, 2, 3, 4, 5, 6, 7; DLB 14, 271; GLL
2

Baillie, Joanna 1762-1851 ...... **NCLC 71, 151**
See also DLB 93; GL 2; RGEL 2

Bainbridge, Beryl 1934- ...... **CLC 4, 5, 8, 10,
14, 18, 22, 62, 130**
See also BRWS 6; CA 21-24R; CANR 24,
55, 75, 88, 128; CN 2, 3, 4, 5, 6, 7; DAM
NOV; DLB 14, 231; EWL 3; MTCW 1,
2; MTFW 2005

Baker, Carlos (Heard)
1909-1987 .... **TCLC 119**
See also CA 5-8R; CAAS 122; CANR 3,
63; DLB 103

Baker, Elliott 1922-2007 .... **CLC 8**
See also CA 45-48; CAAS 257; CANR 2,
63; CN 1, 2, 3, 4, 5, 6, 7

Baker, Elliott Joseph
See Baker, Elliott

Baker, Jean H. .... **TCLC 3, 10**
See Russell, George William

Baker, Nicholson 1957- .... **CLC 61, 165**
See also AMWS 13; CA 135; CANR 63,
120, 138; CN 6; CPW; DA3; DAM POP;
DLB 227; MTFW 2005

Baker, Ray Stannard 1870-1946 .... **TCLC 47**
See also CAAE 118

Baker, Russell 1925- .... **CLC 31**
See also BEST 89:4; CA 57-60; CANR 11,
41, 59, 137; MTCW 1, 2; MTFW 2005

Bakhtin, M.
See Bakhtin, Mikhail Mikhailovich

Bakhtin, M. M.
See Bakhtin, Mikhail Mikhailovich

Bakhtin, Mikhail
See Bakhtin, Mikhail Mikhailovich

Bakhtin, Mikhail Mikhailovich
1895-1975 .... **CLC 83; TCLC 160**
See also CA 128; CAAS 113; DLB 242;
EWL 3

Bakshi, Ralph 1938(?)- .... **CLC 26**
See also CA 138; CAAE 112; IDFW 3

Bakunin, Mikhail (Alexandrovich)
1814-1876 .... **NCLC 25, 58**
See also DLB 277

Baldwin, James 1924-1987 ... **BLC 1; CLC 1,
2, 3, 4, 5, 8, 13, 15, 17, 42, 50, 67, 90,
127; DC 1; SSC 10, 33, 98; WLC 1**
See also AAYA 4, 34; AFAW 1, 2; AMWR
2; AMWS 1; BPFB 1; BW 1; CA 1-4R;
CAAS 124; CABS 1; CAD; CANR 3, 24;
CDALB 1941-1968; CN 1, 2, 3, 4; CPW;
DA; DA3; DAB; DAC; DAM MST,
MULT, NOV, POP; DFS 11, 15; DLB 2,
7, 33, 249, 278; DLBY 1987; EWL 3;
EXPS; LAIT 5; MAL 5; MTCW 1, 2;
MTFW 2005; NCFS 4; NFS 4; RGAL 4;
RGSF 2; SATA 9; SATA-Obit 54; SSFS
2, 18; TUS

Baldwin, William c. 1515-1563 .... **LC 113**
See also DLB 132

Bale, John 1495-1563 .... **LC 62**
See also DLB 132; RGEL 2; TEA

Ball, Hugo 1886-1927 .... **TCLC 104**

Ballard, J.G. 1930- .... **CLC 3, 6, 14, 36, 137;
SSC 1, 53**
See also AAYA 3, 52; BRWS 5; CA 5-8R;
CANR 15, 39, 65, 107, 133; CN 1, 2, 3,
4, 5, 6, 7; DA3; DAM NOV, POP; DLB
14, 207, 261, 319; EWL 3; HGG; MTCW
1, 2; MTFW 2005; NFS 8; RGEL 2;
RGSF 2; SATA 93; SCFW 1, 2; SFW 4

Balmont, Konstantin (Dmitriyevich)
1867-1943 .... **TCLC 11**
See also CA 155; CAAE 109; DLB 295;
EWL 3

Baltausis, Vincas 1847-1910
See Mikszath, Kalman

Balzac, Honore de 1799-1850 ... **NCLC 5, 35,
53, 153; SSC 5, 59, 102; WLC 1**
See also DA; DA3; DAB; DAC; DAM
MST, NOV; DLB 119; EW 5; GFL 1789
to the Present; LMFS 1; RGSF 2; RGWL
2, 3; SSFS 10; SUFW; TWA

Bambara, Toni Cade 1939-1995 .... **BLC 1;
CLC 19, 88; SSC 35; TCLC 116;
WLCS**
See also AAYA 5, 49; AFAW 2; AMWS 11;
BW 2, 3; BYA 12, 14; CA 29-32R; CAAS
150; CANR 24, 49, 81; CDALBS; DA;
DA3; DAC; DAM MST, MULT; DLB 38,
218; EXPS; MAL 5; MTCW 1, 2; MTFW
2005; RGAL 4; RGSF 2; SATA 112; SSFS
4, 7, 12, 21

Bamdad, A.
See Shamlu, Ahmad

Bamdad, Alef
See Shamlu, Ahmad

Banat, D. R.
See Bradbury, Ray

Bancroft, Laura
See Baum, L(yman) Frank

Banim, John 1798-1842 .... **NCLC 13**
See also DLB 116, 158, 159; RGEL 2

Banim, Michael 1796-1874 .... **NCLC 13**
See also DLB 158, 159

Banjo, The
See Paterson, A(ndrew) B(arton)

Banks, Iain
See Banks, Iain M.
See also BRWS 11

Banks, Iain M. 1954- .... **CLC 34**
See Banks, Iain
See also CA 128; CAAE 123; CANR 61,
106; DLB 194, 261; EWL 3; HGG; INT
CA-128; MTFW 2005; SFW 4

Banks, Iain Menzies
See Banks, Iain M.

Banks, Lynne Reid .... **CLC 23**
See Reid Banks, Lynne
See also AAYA 6; BYA 7; CLR 86; CN 4,
5, 6

Banks, Russell 1940- . **CLC 37, 72, 187; SSC
42**
See also AAYA 45; AMWS 5; CA 65-68;
15; CANR 19, 52, 73, 118; CN 4, 5, 6, 7;
DLB 130, 278; EWL 3; MAL 5; MTCW
2; MTFW 2005; NFS 13

Banville, John 1945- .... **CLC 46, 118, 224**
See also CA 128; CAAE 117; CANR 104,
150; CN 4, 5, 6, 7; DLB 14, 271, 326;
INT CA-128

Banville, Theodore (Faullain) de
1832-1891 .... **NCLC 9**
See also DLB 217; GFL 1789 to the Present

Baraka, Amiri 1934- .... **BLC 1; CLC 1, 2, 3,
5, 10, 14, 33, 115, 213; DC 6; PC 4;
WLCS**
See Jones, LeRoi
See also AAYA 63; AFAW 1, 2; AMWS 2;
BW 2, 3; CA 21-24R; CABS 3; CAD;
CANR 27, 38, 61, 133; CD 3, 5, 6;
CDALB 1941-1968; CP 4, 5, 6, 7; CPW;
DA; DA3; DAC; DAM MST, MULT,
POET, POP; DFS 3, 11, 16; DLB 5, 7,
16, 38; DLBD 8; EWL 3; MAL 5; MTCW
1, 2; MTFW 2005; PFS 9; RGAL 4;
TCLE 1:1; TUS; WP

Baratynsky, Evgenii Abramovich
1800-1844 .... **NCLC 103**
See also DLB 205

Barbauld, Anna Laetitia
1743-1825 .... **NCLC 50, 185**
See also DLB 107, 109, 142, 158, 336;
RGEL 2

Barbellion, W. N. P. .... **TCLC 24**
See Cummings, Bruce F(rederick)

Barber, Benjamin R. 1939- .... **CLC 141**
See also CA 29-32R; CANR 12, 32, 64, 119

Barbera, Jack (Vincent) 1945- .... **CLC 44**
See also CA 110; CANR 45

Barbey d'Aurevilly, Jules-Amedee
1808-1889 .... **NCLC 1; SSC 17**
See also DLB 119; GFL 1789 to the Present

Barbour, John c. 1316-1395 .... **CMLC 33**
See also DLB 146

Barbusse, Henri 1873-1935 .... **TCLC 5**
See also CA 154; CAAE 105; DLB 65;
EWL 3; RGWL 2, 3

Barclay, Alexander c. 1475-1552 .... **LC 109**
See also DLB 132

Barclay, Bill
See Moorcock, Michael

Barclay, William Ewert
See Moorcock, Michael

Barea, Arturo 1897-1957 .... **TCLC 14**
See also CA 201; CAAE 111

Barfoot, Joan 1946- .... **CLC 18**
See also CA 105; CANR 141

Barham, Richard Harris
1788-1845 .... **NCLC 77**
See also DLB 159

Baring, Maurice 1874-1945 .... **TCLC 8**
See also CA 168; CAAE 105; DLB 34;
HGG

Baring-Gould, Sabine 1834-1924 ... **TCLC 88**
See also DLB 156, 190

Barker, Clive 1952- .... **CLC 52, 205; SSC 53**
See also AAYA 10, 54; BEST 90:3; BPFB
1; CA 129; CAAE 121; CANR 71, 111,
133; CPW; DA3; DAM POP; DLB 261;
HGG; INT CA-129; MTCW 1, 2; MTFW
2005; SUFW 2

Barker, George Granville
1913-1991 .... **CLC 8, 48; PC 77**
See also CA 9-12R; CAAS 135; CANR 7,
38; CP 1, 2, 3, 4, 5; DAM POET; DLB
20; EWL 3; MTCW 1

Barker, Harley Granville
See Granville-Barker, Harley
See also DLB 10

Barker, Howard 1946- .... **CLC 37**
See also CA 102; CBD; CD 5, 6; DLB 13,
233

Barker, Jane 1652-1732 .... **LC 42, 82**
See also DLB 39, 131

Barker, Pat 1943- .... **CLC 32, 94, 146**
See also BRWS 4; CA 122; CAAE 117;
CANR 50, 101, 148; CN 6, 7; DLB 271,
326; INT CA-122

Barker, Patricia
See Barker, Pat

Barlach, Ernst (Heinrich)
1870-1938 .... **TCLC 84**
See also CA 178; DLB 56, 118; EWL 3

Barlow, Joel 1754-1812 .... **NCLC 23**
See also AMWS 2; DLB 37; RGAL 4

Barnard, Mary (Ethel) 1909- .... **CLC 48**
See also CA 21-22; CAP 2; CP 1

Barnes, Djuna 1892-1982 .... **CLC 3, 4, 8, 11,
29, 127; SSC 3**
See Steptoe, Lydia
See also AMWS 3; CA 9-12R; CAAS 107;
CAD; CANR 16, 55; CN 1, 2, 3; CWD;
DLB 4, 9, 45; EWL 3; GLL 1; MAL 5;
MTCW 1, 2; MTFW 2005; RGAL 4;
TCLE 1:1; TUS

Barnes, Jim 1933- .... **NNAL**
See also CA 175; 108, 175; 28; DLB 175

Becker, Jurek 1937-1997 .... **CLC 7, 19**
   See also CA 85-88; CAAS 157; CANR 60,
   117; CWW 2; DLB 75, 299; EWL 3;
   RGHL

Becker, Walter 1950- .... **CLC 26**

Becket, Thomas a 1118(?)-1170 .... **CMLC 83**

Beckett, Samuel 1906-1989 ... **CLC 1, 2, 3, 4,**
   6, 9, 10, 11, 14, 18, 29, 57, 59, 83; DC
   22; SSC 16, 74; TCLC 145; WLC 1
   See also BRWC 2; BRWR 1; BRWS 1; CA
   5-8R; CAAS 130; CANR 33, 61; CBD;
   CDBLB 1945-1960; CN 1, 2, 3, 4; CP 1,
   2, 3, 4; DA; DA3; DAB; DAC; DAM
   DRAM, MST, NOV; DFS 2, 7, 18; DLB
   13, 15, 233, 319, 321, 329; DLBY 1990;
   EWL 3; GFL 1789 to the Present; LATS
   1:2; LMFS 2; MTCW 1, 2; MTFW 2005;
   RGSF 2; RGWL 2, 3; SSFS 15; TEA;
   WLIT 4

Beckford, William 1760-1844 .... **NCLC 16**
   See also BRW 3; DLB 39, 213; GL 2; HGG;
   LMFS 1; SUFW

Beckham, Barry (Earl) 1944- .... **BLC 1**
   See also BW 1; CA 29-32R; CANR 26, 62;
   CN 1, 2, 3, 4, 5, 6; DAM MULT; DLB 33

Beckman, Gunnel 1910- .... **CLC 26**
   See also CA 33-36R; CANR 15, 114; CLR
   25; MAICYA 1, 2; SAAS 9; SATA 6

Becque, Henri 1837-1899 .... **DC 21; NCLC 3**
   See also DLB 192; GFL 1789 to the Present

Becquer, Gustavo Adolfo
   1836-1870 .... **HLCS 1; NCLC 106**
   See also DAM MULT

Beddoes, Thomas Lovell 1803-1849 .. **DC 15;**
   NCLC 3, 154
   See also BRWS 11; DLB 96

Bede c. 673-735 .... **CMLC 20**
   See also DLB 146; TEA

Bedford, Denton R. 1907-(?) .... **NNAL**

Bedford, Donald F.
   See Fearing, Kenneth (Flexner)

Beecher, Catharine Esther
   1800-1878 .... **NCLC 30**
   See also DLB 1, 243

Beecher, John 1904-1980 .... **CLC 6**
   See also AITN 1; CA 5-8R; CAAS 105;
   CANR 8; CP 1, 2, 3

Beer, Johann 1655-1700 .... **LC 5**
   See also DLB 168

Beer, Patricia 1924- .... **CLC 58**
   See also CA 61-64; CAAS 183; CANR 13,
   46; CP 1, 2, 3, 4, 5, 6; CWP; DLB 40;
   FW

Beerbohm, Max
   See Beerbohm, (Henry) Max(imilian)

Beerbohm, (Henry) Max(imilian)
   1872-1956 .... **TCLC 1, 24**
   See also BRWS 2; CA 154; CAAE 104;
   CANR 79; DLB 34, 100; FANT; MTCW
   2

Beer-Hofmann, Richard
   1866-1945 .... **TCLC 60**
   See also CA 160; DLB 81

Beg, Shemus
   See Stephens, James

Begiebing, Robert J(ohn) 1946- .... **CLC 70**
   See also CA 122; CANR 40, 88

Begley, Louis 1933- .... **CLC 197**
   See also CA 140; CANR 98; DLB 299;
   RGHL; TCLE 1:1

Behan, Brendan (Francis)
   1923-1964 .... **CLC 1, 8, 11, 15, 79**
   See also BRWS 2; CA 73-76; CANR 33,
   121; CBD; CDBLB 1945-1960; DAM
   DRAM; DFS 7; DLB 13, 233; EWL 3;
   MTCW 1, 2

Behn, Aphra 1640(?)-1689 .. **DC 4; LC 1, 30,**
   42, 135; PC 13; WLC 1
   See also BRWS 3; DA; DA3; DAB; DAC;
   DAM DRAM, MST, NOV, POET; DFS
   16, 24; DLB 39, 80, 131; FW; TEA;
   WLIT 3

Behrman, S(amuel) N(athaniel)
   1893-1973 .... **CLC 40**
   See also CA 13-16; CAAS 45-48; CAD;
   CAP 1; DLB 7, 44; IDFW 3; MAL 5;
   RGAL 4

Bekederemo, J. P. Clark
   See Clark Bekederemo, J.P.
   See also CD 6

Belasco, David 1853-1931 .... **TCLC 3**
   See also CA 168; CAAE 104; DLB 7; MAL
   5; RGAL 4

Belcheva, Elisaveta Lyubomirova
   1893-1991 .... **CLC 10**
   See Bagryana, Elisaveta

Beldone, Phil ''Cheech''
   See Ellison, Harlan

Beleno
   See Azuela, Mariano

Belinski, Vissarion Grigoryevich
   1811-1848 .... **NCLC 5**
   See also DLB 198

Belitt, Ben 1911- .... **CLC 22**
   See also CA 13-16R; 4; CANR 7, 77; CP 1,
   2, 3, 4, 5, 6; DLB 5

Belknap, Jeremy 1744-1798 .... **LC 115**
   See also DLB 30, 37

Bell, Gertrude (Margaret Lowthian)
   1868-1926 .... **TCLC 67**
   See also CA 167; CANR 110; DLB 174

Bell, J. Freeman
   See Zangwill, Israel

Bell, James Madison 1826-1902 .... **BLC 1;**
   TCLC 43
   See also BW 1; CA 124; CAAE 122; DAM
   MULT; DLB 50

Bell, Madison Smartt 1957- ..... **CLC 41, 102,**
   223
   See also AMWS 10; BPFB 1; CA 183; 111,
   183; CANR 28, 54, 73, 134; CN 5, 6, 7;
   CSW; DLB 218, 278; MTCW 2; MTFW
   2005

Bell, Marvin (Hartley) 1937- .... **CLC 8, 31**
   See also CA 21-24R; 14; CANR 59, 102;
   CP 1, 2, 3, 4, 5, 6, 7; DAM POET; DLB
   5; MAL 5; MTCW 1; PFS 25

Bell, W. L. D.
   See Mencken, H(enry) L(ouis)

Bellamy, Atwood C.
   See Mencken, H(enry) L(ouis)

Bellamy, Edward 1850-1898 ..... **NCLC 4, 86,**
   147
   See also DLB 12; NFS 15; RGAL 4; SFW
   4

Belli, Gioconda 1948- .... **HLCS 1**
   See also CA 152; CANR 143; CWW 2;
   DLB 290; EWL 3; RGWL 3

Bellin, Edward J.
   See Kuttner, Henry

Bello, Andres 1781-1865 .... **NCLC 131**
   See also LAW

Belloc, (Joseph) Hilaire (Pierre Sebastien
   Rene Swanton) 1870-1953 .... **PC 24;**
   TCLC 7, 18
   See also CA 152; CAAE 106; CLR 102;
   CWRI 5; DAM POET; DLB 19, 100, 141,
   174; EWL 3; MTCW 2; MTFW 2005;
   SATA 112; WCH; YABC 1

Belloc, Joseph Peter Rene Hilaire
   See Belloc, (Joseph) Hilaire (Pierre Sebastien Rene Swanton)

Belloc, Joseph Pierre Hilaire
   See Belloc, (Joseph) Hilaire (Pierre Sebastien Rene Swanton)

Belloc, M. A.
   See Lowndes, Marie Adelaide (Belloc)

Belloc-Lowndes, Mrs.
   See Lowndes, Marie Adelaide (Belloc)

Bellow, Saul 1915-2005 ...... **CLC 1, 2, 3, 6, 8,**
   10, 13, 15, 25, 33, 34, 63, 79, 190, 200;
   SSC 14, 101; WLC 1
   See also AITN 2; AMW; AMWC 2; AMWR
   2; BEST 89:3; BPFB 1; CA 5-8R; CAAS
   238; CABS 1; CANR 29, 53, 95, 132;
   CDALB 1941-1968; CN 1, 2, 3, 4, 5, 6,
   7; DA; DA3; DAB; DAC; DAM MST,
   NOV, POP; DLB 2, 28, 299, 329; DLBD
   3; DLBY 1982; EWL 3; MAL 5; MTCW
   1, 2; MTFW 2005; NFS 4, 14; RGAL 4;
   RGHL; RGSF 2; SSFS 12, 22; TUS

Belser, Reimond Karel Maria de 1929-
   See Ruyslinck, Ward
   See also CA 152

Bely, Andrey .... **PC 11; TCLC 7**
   See Bugayev, Boris Nikolayevich
   See also DLB 295; EW 9; EWL 3

Belyi, Andrei
   See Bugayev, Boris Nikolayevich
   See also RGWL 2, 3

Bembo, Pietro 1470-1547 .... **LC 79**
   See also RGWL 2, 3

Benary, Margot
   See Benary-Isbert, Margot

Benary-Isbert, Margot 1889-1979 .... **CLC 12**
   See also CA 5-8R; CAAS 89-92; CANR 4,
   72; CLR 12; MAICYA 1, 2; SATA 2;
   SATA-Obit 21

Benavente (y Martinez), Jacinto
   1866-1954 .... **DC 26; HLCS 1; TCLC 3**
   See also CA 131; CAAE 106; CANR 81;
   DAM DRAM, MULT; DLB 329; EWL 3;
   GLL 2; HW 1, 2; MTCW 1, 2

Benchley, Peter 1940-2006 .... **CLC 4, 8**
   See also AAYA 14; AITN 2; BPFB 1; CA
   17-20R; CAAS 248; CANR 12, 35, 66,
   115; CPW; DAM NOV, POP; HGG;
   MTCW 1, 2; MTFW 2005; SATA 3, 89,
   164

Benchley, Peter Bradford
   See Benchley, Peter

Benchley, Robert (Charles)
   1889-1945 .... **TCLC 1, 55**
   See also CA 153; CAAE 105; DLB 11;
   MAL 5; RGAL 4

Benda, Julien 1867-1956 .... **TCLC 60**
   See also CA 154; CAAE 120; GFL 1789 to
   the Present

Benedict, Ruth 1887-1948 .... **TCLC 60**
   See also CA 158; CANR 146; DLB 246

Benedict, Ruth Fulton
   See Benedict, Ruth

Benedikt, Michael 1935- .... **CLC 4, 14**
   See also CA 13-16R; CANR 7; CP 1, 2, 3,
   4, 5, 6, 7; DLB 5

Benet, Juan 1927-1993 .... **CLC 28**
   See also CA 143; EWL 3

Benet, Stephen Vincent 1898-1943 ..... **PC 64;**
   SSC 10, 86; TCLC 7
   See also AMWS 11; CA 152; CAAE 104;
   DA3; DAM POET; DLB 4, 48, 102, 249,
   284; DLBY 1997; EWL 3; HGG; MAL 5;
   MTCW 2; MTFW 2005; RGAL 4; RGSF
   2; SSFS 22; SUFW; WP; YABC 1

Benet, William Rose 1886-1950 ..... **TCLC 28**
   See also CA 152; CAAE 118; DAM POET;
   DLB 45; RGAL 4

Benford, Gregory 1941- .... **CLC 52**
   See also BPFB 1; CA 175; 69-72, 175; 27;
   CANR 12, 24, 49, 95, 134; CN 7; CSW;
   DLBY 1982; MTFW 2005; SCFW 2;
   SFW 4

Benford, Gregory Albert
   See Benford, Gregory

Cumulative Author Index

Bourjaily, Vance (Nye) 1922- .... **CLC 8, 62**
See also CA 1-4R; 1; CANR 2, 72; CN 1, 2, 3, 4, 5, 6, 7; DLB 2, 143; MAL 5
Bourne, Randolph S(illiman)
1886-1918 .... **TCLC 16**
See also AMW; CA 155; CAAE 117; DLB 63; MAL 5
Bova, Ben 1932- .... **CLC 45**
See also AAYA 16; CA 5-8R; 18; CANR 11, 56, 94, 111, 157; CLR 3, 96; DLBY 1981; INT CANR-11; MAICYA 1, 2; MTCW 1; SATA 6, 68, 133; SFW 4
Bova, Benjamin William
See Bova, Ben
Bowen, Elizabeth (Dorothea Cole)
1899-1973 . **CLC 1, 3, 6, 11, 15, 22, 118; SSC 3, 28, 66; TCLC 148**
See also BRWS 2; CA 17-18; CAAS 41-44R; CANR 35, 105; CAP 2; CDBLB 1945-1960; CN 1; DA3; DAM NOV; DLB 15, 162; EWL 3; EXPS; FW; HGG; MTCW 1, 2; MTFW 2005; NFS 13; RGSF 2; SSFS 5, 22; SUFW 1; TEA; WLIT 4
Bowering, George 1935- .... **CLC 15, 47**
See also CA 21-24R; 16; CANR 10; CN 7; CP 1, 2, 3, 4, 5, 6, 7; DLB 53
Bowering, Marilyn R(uthe) 1949- .... **CLC 32**
See also CA 101; CANR 49; CP 4, 5, 6, 7; CWP; DLB 334
Bowers, Edgar 1924-2000 .... **CLC 9**
See also CA 5-8R; CAAS 188; CANR 24; CP 1, 2, 3, 4, 5, 6, 7; CSW; DLB 5
Bowers, Mrs. J. Milton 1842-1914
See Bierce, Ambrose (Gwinett)
Bowie, David .... **CLC 17**
See Jones, David Robert
Bowles, Jane (Sydney) 1917-1973 ..... **CLC 3, 68**
See Bowles, Jane Auer
See also CA 19-20; CAAS 41-44R; CAP 2; CN 1; MAL 5
Bowles, Jane Auer
See Bowles, Jane (Sydney)
See also EWL 3
Bowles, Paul 1910-1999 ..... **CLC 1, 2, 19, 53; SSC 3, 98**
See also AMWS 4; CA 1-4R; 1; CAAS 186; CANR 1, 19, 50, 75; CN 1, 2, 3, 4, 5, 6; DA3; DLB 5, 6, 218; EWL 3; MAL 5; MTCW 1, 2; MTFW 2005; RGAL 4; SSFS 17
Bowles, William Lisle 1762-1850 . **NCLC 103**
See also DLB 93
Box, Edgar
See Vidal, Gore
See also GLL 1
Boyd, James 1888-1944 .... **TCLC 115**
See also CA 186; DLB 9; DLBD 16; RGAL 4; RHW
Boyd, Nancy
See Millay, Edna St. Vincent
See also GLL 1
Boyd, Thomas (Alexander)
1898-1935 .... **TCLC 111**
See also CA 183; CAAE 111; DLB 9; DLBD 16, 316
Boyd, William (Andrew Murray)
1952- .... **CLC 28, 53, 70**
See also CA 120; CAAE 114; CANR 51, 71, 131; CN 4, 5, 6, 7; DLB 231
Boyesen, Hjalmar Hjorth
1848-1895 .... **NCLC 135**
See also DLB 12, 71; DLBD 13; RGAL 4
Boyle, Kay 1902-1992 .... **CLC 1, 5, 19, 58, 121; SSC 5, 102**
See also CA 13-16R; 1; CAAS 140; CANR 29, 61, 110; CN 1, 2, 3, 4, 5; CP 1, 2, 3, 4, 5; DLB 4, 9, 48, 86; DLBY 1993; EWL 3; MAL 5; MTCW 1, 2; MTFW 2005; RGAL 4; RGSF 2; SSFS 10, 13, 14

Boyle, Mark
See Kienzle, William X.
Boyle, Patrick 1905-1982 .... **CLC 19**
See also CA 127
Boyle, T. C.
See Boyle, T. Coraghessan
See also AMWS 8
Boyle, T. Coraghessan 1948- ..... **CLC 36, 55, 90; SSC 16**
See Boyle, T. C.
See also AAYA 47; BEST 90:4; BPFB 1; CA 120; CANR 44, 76, 89, 132; CN 6, 7; CPW; DA3; DAM POP; DLB 218, 278; DLBY 1986; EWL 3; MAL 5; MTCW 2; MTFW 2005; SSFS 13, 19
Boz
See Dickens, Charles (John Huffam)
Brackenridge, Hugh Henry
1748-1816 .... **NCLC 7**
See also DLB 11, 37; RGAL 4
Bradbury, Edward P.
See Moorcock, Michael
See also MTCW 2
Bradbury, Malcolm (Stanley)
1932-2000 .... **CLC 32, 61**
See also CA 1-4R; CANR 1, 33, 91, 98, 137; CN 1, 2, 3, 4, 5, 6, 7; CP 1; DA3; DAM NOV; DLB 14, 207; EWL 3; MTCW 1, 2; MTFW 2005
Bradbury, Ray 1920- ... **CLC 1, 3, 10, 15, 42, 98, 235; SSC 29, 53; WLC 1**
See also AAYA 15; AITN 1, 2; AMWS 4; BPFB 1; BYA 4, 5, 11; CA 1-4R; CANR 2, 30, 75, 125; CDALB 1968-1988; CN 1, 2, 3, 4, 5, 6, 7; CPW; DA; DA3; DAB; DAC; DAM MST, NOV, POP; DLB 2, 8; EXPN; EXPS; HGG; LAIT 3, 5; LATS 1:2; LMFS 2; MAL 5; MTCW 1, 2; MTFW 2005; NFS 1, 22; RGAL 4; RGSF 2; SATA 11, 64, 123; SCFW 1, 2; SFW 4; SSFS 1, 20; SUFW 1, 2; TUS; YAW
Braddon, Mary Elizabeth
1837-1915 .... **TCLC 111**
See also BRWS 8; CA 179; CAAE 108; CMW 4; DLB 18, 70, 156; HGG
Bradfield, Scott 1955- .... **SSC 65**
See also CA 147; CANR 90; HGG; SUFW 2
Bradfield, Scott Michael
See Bradfield, Scott
Bradford, Gamaliel 1863-1932 .... **TCLC 36**
See also CA 160; DLB 17
Bradford, William 1590-1657 .... **LC 64**
See also DLB 24, 30; RGAL 4
Bradley, David (Henry), Jr. 1950- .... **BLC 1; CLC 23, 118**
See also BW 1, 3; CA 104; CANR 26, 81; CN 4, 5, 6, 7; DAM MULT; DLB 33
Bradley, John Ed 1958- .... **CLC 55**
See also CA 139; CANR 99; CN 6, 7; CSW
Bradley, John Edmund, Jr.
See Bradley, John Ed
Bradley, Marion Zimmer
1930-1999 .... **CLC 30**
See Chapman, Lee; Dexter, John; Gardner, Miriam; Ives, Morgan; Rivers, Elfrida
See also AAYA 40; BPFB 1; CA 57-60; 10; CAAS 185; CANR 7, 31, 51, 75, 107; CPW; DA3; DAM POP; DLB 8; FANT; FW; MTCW 1, 2; MTFW 2005; SATA 90, 139; SATA-Obit 116; SFW 4; SUFW 2; YAW
Bradshaw, John 1933- .... **CLC 70**
See also CA 138; CANR 61
Bradstreet, Anne 1612(?)-1672 .... **LC 4, 30, 130; PC 10**
See also AMWS 1; CDALB 1640-1865; DA; DA3; DAC; DAM MST, POET; DLB 24; EXPP; FW; PFS 6; RGAL 4; TUS; WP

Brady, Joan 1939- .... **CLC 86**
See also CA 141
Bragg, Melvyn 1939- .... **CLC 10**
See also BEST 89:3; CA 57-60; CANR 10, 48, 89, 158; CN 1, 2, 3, 4, 5, 6, 7; DLB 14, 271; RHW
Brahe, Tycho 1546-1601 .... **LC 45**
See also DLB 300
Braine, John (Gerard) 1922-1986 . **CLC 1, 3, 41**
See also CA 1-4R; CAAS 120; CANR 1, 33; CDBLB 1945-1960; CN 1, 2, 3, 4; DLB 15; DLBY 1986; EWL 3; MTCW 1
Braithwaite, William Stanley (Beaumont)
1878-1962 .... **BLC 1; HR 1:2; PC 52**
See also BW 1; CA 125; DAM MULT; DLB 50, 54; MAL 5
Bramah, Ernest 1868-1942 .... **TCLC 72**
See also CA 156; CMW 4; DLB 70; FANT
Brammer, Billy Lee
See Brammer, William
Brammer, William 1929-1978 .... **CLC 31**
See also CA 235; CAAS 77-80
Brancati, Vitaliano 1907-1954 .... **TCLC 12**
See also CAAE 109; DLB 264; EWL 3
Brancato, Robin F(idler) 1936- .... **CLC 35**
See also AAYA 9, 68; BYA 6; CA 69-72; CANR 11, 45; CLR 32; JRDA; MAICYA 2; MAICYAS 1; SAAS 9; SATA 97; WYA; YAW
Brand, Dionne 1953- .... **CLC 192**
See also BW 2; CA 143; CANR 143; CWP; DLB 334
Brand, Max
See Faust, Frederick (Schiller)
See also BPFB 1; TCWW 1, 2
Brand, Millen 1906-1980 .... **CLC 7**
See also CA 21-24R; CAAS 97-100; CANR 72
Branden, Barbara .... **CLC 44**
See also CA 148
Brandes, Georg (Morris Cohen)
1842-1927 .... **TCLC 10**
See also CA 189; CAAE 105; DLB 300
Brandys, Kazimierz 1916-2000 .... **CLC 62**
See also CA 239; EWL 3
Branley, Franklyn M(ansfield)
1915-2002 .... **CLC 21**
See also CA 33-36R; CAAS 207; CANR 14, 39; CLR 13; MAICYA 1, 2; SAAS 16; SATA 4, 68, 136
Brant, Beth (E.) 1941- .... **NNAL**
See also CA 144; FW
Brant, Sebastian 1457-1521 .... **LC 112**
See also DLB 179; RGWL 2, 3
Brathwaite, Edward Kamau
1930- .... **BLCS; CLC 11; PC 56**
See also BRWS 12; BW 2, 3; CA 25-28R; CANR 11, 26, 47, 107; CDWLB 3; CP 1, 2, 3, 4, 5, 6, 7; DAM POET; DLB 125; EWL 3
Brathwaite, Kamau
See Brathwaite, Edward Kamau
Brautigan, Richard (Gary)
1935-1984 .... **CLC 1, 3, 5, 9, 12, 34, 42; TCLC 133**
See also BPFB 1; CA 53-56; CAAS 113; CANR 34; CN 1, 2, 3; CP 1, 2, 3, 4; DA3; DAM NOV; DLB 2, 5, 206; DLBY 1980, 1984; FANT; MAL 5; MTCW 1; RGAL 4; SATA 56
Brave Bird, Mary .... **NNAL**
See Crow Dog, Mary
Braverman, Kate 1950- .... **CLC 67**
See also CA 89-92; CANR 141; DLB 335

Brecht, (Eugen) Bertolt (Friedrich)
1898-1956 ..... **DC 3; TCLC 1, 6, 13, 35,
169; WLC 1**
See also CA 133; CAAE 104; CANR 62;
CDWLB 2; DA; DA3; DAB; DAC; DAM
DRAM, MST; DFS 4, 5, 9; DLB 56, 124;
EW 11; EWL 3; IDTP; MTCW 1, 2;
MTFW 2005; RGHL; RGWL 2, 3; TWA
Brecht, Eugen Berthold Friedrich
See Brecht, (Eugen) Bertolt (Friedrich)
Bremer, Fredrika 1801-1865 .... **NCLC 11**
See also DLB 254
Brennan, Christopher John
1870-1932 .... **TCLC 17**
See also CA 188; CAAE 117; DLB 230;
EWL 3
Brennan, Maeve 1917-1993 ... **CLC 5; TCLC
124**
See also CA 81-84; CANR 72, 100
Brenner, Jozef 1887-1919
See Csath, Geza
See also CA 240
Brent, Linda
See Jacobs, Harriet A(nn)
Brentano, Clemens (Maria)
1778-1842 .... **NCLC 1**
See also DLB 90; RGWL 2, 3
Brent of Bin Bin
See Franklin, (Stella Maria Sarah) Miles
(Lampe)
Brenton, Howard 1942- .... **CLC 31**
See also CA 69-72; CANR 33, 67; CBD;
CD 5, 6; DLB 13; MTCW 1
Breslin, James 1930-
See Breslin, Jimmy
See also CA 73-76; CANR 31, 75, 139;
DAM NOV; MTCW 1, 2; MTFW 2005
Breslin, Jimmy .... **CLC 4, 43**
See Breslin, James
See also AITN 1; DLB 185; MTCW 2
Bresson, Robert 1901(?)-1999 .... **CLC 16**
See also CA 110; CAAS 187; CANR 49
Breton, Andre 1896-1966 .. **CLC 2, 9, 15, 54;
PC 15**
See also CA 19-20; CAAS 25-28R; CANR
40, 60; CAP 2; DLB 65, 258; EW 11;
EWL 3; GFL 1789 to the Present; LMFS
2; MTCW 1, 2; MTFW 2005; RGWL 2,
3; TWA; WP
Breton, Nicholas c. 1554-c. 1626 .... **LC 133**
See also DLB 136
Breytenbach, Breyten 1939(?)- .. **CLC 23, 37,
126**
See also CA 129; CAAE 113; CANR 61,
122; CWW 2; DAM POET; DLB 225;
EWL 3
Bridgers, Sue Ellen 1942- .... **CLC 26**
See also AAYA 8, 49; BYA 7, 8; CA 65-68;
CANR 11, 36; CLR 18; DLB 52; JRDA;
MAICYA 1, 2; SAAS 1; SATA 22, 90;
SATA-Essay 109; WYA; YAW
Bridges, Robert (Seymour)
1844-1930 .... **PC 28; TCLC 1**
See also BRW 6; CA 152; CAAE 104; CD-
BLB 1890-1914; DAM POET; DLB 19,
98
Bridie, James .... **TCLC 3**
See Mavor, Osborne Henry
See also DLB 10; EWL 3
Brin, David 1950- .... **CLC 34**
See also AAYA 21; CA 102; CANR 24, 70,
125, 127; INT CANR-24; SATA 65;
SCFW 2; SFW 4
Brink, Andre 1935- .... **CLC 18, 36, 106**
See also AFW; BRWS 6; CA 104; CANR
39, 62, 109, 133; CN 4, 5, 6, 7; DLB 225;
EWL 3; INT CA-103; LATS 1:2; MTCW
1, 2; MTFW 2005; WLIT 2

Brinsmead, H. F.
See Brinsmead, H(esba) F(ay)
Brinsmead, H. F(ay)
See Brinsmead, H(esba) F(ay)
Brinsmead, H(esba) F(ay) 1922- ...... **CLC 21**
See also CA 21-24R; CANR 10; CLR 47;
CWRI 5; MAICYA 1, 2; SAAS 5; SATA
18, 78
Brittain, Vera (Mary) 1893(?)-1970 . **CLC 23**
See also BRWS 10; CA 13-16; CAAS 25-
28R; CANR 58; CAP 1; DLB 191; FW;
MTCW 1, 2
Broch, Hermann 1886-1951 .... **TCLC 20**
See also CA 211; CAAE 117; CDWLB 2;
DLB 85, 124; EW 10; EWL 3; RGWL 2,
3
Brock, Rose
See Hansen, Joseph
See also GLL 1
Brod, Max 1884-1968 .... **TCLC 115**
See also CA 5-8R; CAAS 25-28R; CANR
7; DLB 81; EWL 3
Brodkey, Harold (Roy) 1930-1996 .. **CLC 56;
TCLC 123**
See also CA 111; CAAS 151; CANR 71;
CN 4, 5, 6; DLB 130
Brodsky, Iosif Alexandrovich 1940-1996
See Brodsky, Joseph
See also AITN 1; CA 41-44R; CAAS 151;
CANR 37, 106; DA3; DAM POET;
MTCW 1, 2; MTFW 2005; RGWL 2, 3
Brodsky, Joseph . **CLC 4, 6, 13, 36, 100; PC
9**
See Brodsky, Iosif Alexandrovich
See also AAYA 71; AMWS 8; CWW 2;
DLB 285, 329; EWL 3; MTCW 1
Brodsky, Michael 1948- .... **CLC 19**
See also CA 102; CANR 18, 41, 58, 147;
DLB 244
Brodsky, Michael Mark
See Brodsky, Michael
Brodzki, Bella .... **CLC 65**
Brome, Richard 1590(?)-1652 .... **LC 61**
See also BRWS 10; DLB 58
Bromell, Henry 1947- .... **CLC 5**
See also CA 53-56; CANR 9, 115, 116
Bromfield, Louis (Brucker)
1896-1956 .... **TCLC 11**
See also CA 155; CAAE 107; DLB 4, 9,
86; RGAL 4; RHW
Broner, E(sther) M(asserman)
1930- .... **CLC 19**
See also CA 17-20R; CANR 8, 25, 72; CN
4, 5, 6; DLB 28
Bronk, William (M.) 1918-1999 .... **CLC 10**
See also CA 89-92; CAAS 177; CANR 23;
CP 3, 4, 5, 6, 7; DLB 165
Bronstein, Lev Davidovich
See Trotsky, Leon
Bronte, Anne
See Bronte, Anne
Bronte, Anne 1820-1849 ..... **NCLC 4, 71, 102**
See also BRW 5; BRWR 1; DA3; DLB 21,
199; TEA
Bronte, (Patrick) Branwell
1817-1848 .... **NCLC 109**
Bronte, Charlotte
See Bronte, Charlotte
Bronte, Charlotte 1816-1855 ...... **NCLC 3, 8,
33, 58, 105, 155; WLC 1**
See also AAYA 17; BRW 5; BRWC 2;
BRWR 1; BYA 2; CDBLB 1832-1890;
DA; DA3; DAB; DAC; DAM MST, NOV;
DLB 21, 159, 199; EXPN; FL 1:2; GL 2;
LAIT 2; NFS 4; TEA; WLIT 4
Bronte, Emily
See Bronte, Emily (Jane)

Bronte, Emily (Jane) 1818-1848 ... **NCLC 16,
35, 165; PC 8; WLC 1**
See also AAYA 17; BPFB 1; BRW 5;
BRWC 1; BRWR 1; BYA 3; CDBLB
1832-1890; DA; DA3; DAB; DAC; DAM
MST, NOV, POET; DLB 21, 32, 199;
EXPN; FL 1:2; GL 2; LAIT 1; TEA;
WLIT 3
Brontes
See Bronte, Anne; Bronte, Charlotte; Bronte,
Emily (Jane)
Brooke, Frances 1724-1789 .... **LC 6, 48**
See also DLB 39, 99
Brooke, Henry 1703(?)-1783 .... **LC 1**
See also DLB 39
Brooke, Rupert (Chawner)
1887-1915 .. **PC 24; TCLC 2, 7; WLC 1**
See also BRWS 3; CA 132; CAAE 104;
CANR 61; CDBLB 1914-1945; DA;
DAB; DAC; DAM MST, POET; DLB 19,
216; EXPP; GLL 2; MTCW 1, 2; MTFW
2005; PFS 7; TEA
Brooke-Haven, P.
See Wodehouse, P(elham) G(renville)
Brooke-Rose, Christine 1926(?)- ..... **CLC 40,
184**
See also BRWS 4; CA 13-16R; CANR 58,
118; CN 1, 2, 3, 4, 5, 6, 7; DLB 14, 231;
EWL 3; SFW 4
Brookner, Anita 1928- . **CLC 32, 34, 51, 136,
237**
See also BRWS 4; CA 120; CAAE 114;
CANR 37, 56, 87, 130; CN 4, 5, 6, 7;
CPW; DA3; DAB; DAM POP; DLB 194,
326; DLBY 1987; EWL 3; MTCW 1, 2;
MTFW 2005; NFS 23; TEA
Brooks, Cleanth 1906-1994 . **CLC 24, 86, 110**
See also AMWS 14; CA 17-20R; CAAS
145; CANR 33, 35; CSW; DLB 63; DLBY
1994; EWL 3; INT CANR-35; MAL 5;
MTCW 1, 2; MTFW 2005
Brooks, George
See Baum, L(yman) Frank
Brooks, Gwendolyn 1917-2000 .... **BLC 1;
CLC 1, 2, 4, 5, 15, 49, 125; PC 7;
WLC 1**
See also AAYA 20; AFAW 1, 2; AITN 1;
AMWS 3; BW 2, 3; CA 1-4R; CAAS 190;
CANR 1, 27, 52, 75, 132; CDALB 1941-
1968; CLR 27; CP 1, 2, 3, 4, 5, 6, 7;
CWP; DA; DA3; DAC; DAM MST,
MULT, POET; DLB 5, 76, 165; EWL 3;
EXPP; FL 1:5; MAL 5; MBL; MTCW 1,
2; MTFW 2005; PFS 1, 2, 4, 6; RGAL 4;
SATA 6; SATA-Obit 123; TUS; WP
Brooks, Mel 1926-
See Kaminsky, Melvin
See also CA 65-68; CANR 16; DFS 21
Brooks, Peter (Preston) 1938- .... **CLC 34**
See also CA 45-48; CANR 1, 107
Brooks, Van Wyck 1886-1963 .... **CLC 29**
See also AMW; CA 1-4R; CANR 6; DLB
45, 63, 103; MAL 5; TUS
Brophy, Brigid (Antonia)
1929-1995 .... **CLC 6, 11, 29, 105**
See also CA 5-8R; 4; CAAS 149; CANR
25, 53; CBD; CN 1, 2, 3, 4, 5, 6; CWD;
DA3; DLB 14, 271; EWL 3; MTCW 1, 2
Brosman, Catharine Savage 1934- ..... **CLC 9**
See also CA 61-64; CANR 21, 46, 149
Brossard, Nicole 1943- .... **CLC 115, 169**
See also CA 122; 16; CANR 140; CCA 1;
CWP; CWW 2; DLB 53; EWL 3; FW;
GLL 2; RGWL 3
Brother Antoninus
See Everson, William (Oliver)
Brothers Grimm
See Grimm, Jacob Ludwig Karl; Grimm,
Wilhelm Karl

Cabral de Melo Neto, Joao
1920-1999 .... **CLC 76**
See Melo Neto, Joao Cabral de
See also CA 151; DAM MULT; DLB 307;
LAW; LAWS 1

Cabrera Infante, G. 1929-2005 ... **CLC 5, 25,
45, 120; HLC 1; SSC 39**
See also CA 85-88; CAAS 236; CANR 29,
65, 110; CDWLB 3; CWW 2; DA3; DAM
MULT; DLB 113; EWL 3; HW 1, 2;
LAW; LAWS 1; MTCW 1, 2; MTFW
2005; RGSF 2; WLIT 1

Cabrera Infante, Guillermo
See Cabrera Infante, G.

Cade, Toni
See Bambara, Toni Cade

Cadmus and Harmonia
See Buchan, John

Caedmon fl. 658-680 .... **CMLC 7**
See also DLB 146

Caeiro, Alberto
See Pessoa, Fernando (Antonio Nogueira)

Caesar, Julius .... **CMLC 47**
See Julius Caesar
See also AW 1; RGWL 2, 3; WLIT 8

Cage, John (Milton), (Jr.)
1912-1992 .... **CLC 41; PC 58**
See also CA 13-16R; CAAS 169; CANR 9,
78; DLB 193; INT CANR-9; TCLE 1:1

Cahan, Abraham 1860-1951 .... **TCLC 71**
See also CA 154; CAAE 108; DLB 9, 25,
28; MAL 5; RGAL 4

Cain, G.
See Cabrera Infante, G.

Cain, Guillermo
See Cabrera Infante, G.

Cain, James M(allahan) 1892-1977 .. **CLC 3,
11, 28**
See also AITN 1; BPFB 1; CA 17-20R;
CAAS 73-76; CANR 8, 34, 61; CMW 4;
CN 1, 2; DLB 226; EWL 3; MAL 5;
MSW; MTCW 1; RGAL 4

Caine, Hall 1853-1931 .... **TCLC 97**
See also RHW

Caine, Mark
See Raphael, Frederic (Michael)

Calasso, Roberto 1941- .... **CLC 81**
See also CA 143; CANR 89

Calderon de la Barca, Pedro
1600-1681 . **DC 3; HLCS 1; LC 23, 136**
See also DFS 23; EW 2; RGWL 2, 3; TWA

Caldwell, Erskine 1903-1987 ... **CLC 1, 8, 14,
50, 60; SSC 19; TCLC 117**
See also AITN 1; AMW; BPFB 1; CA 1-4R;
1; CAAS 121; CANR 2, 33; CN 1, 2, 3,
4; DA3; DAM NOV; DLB 9, 86; EWL 3;
MAL 5; MTCW 1, 2; MTFW 2005;
RGAL 4; RGSF 2; TUS

Caldwell, (Janet Miriam) Taylor (Holland)
1900-1985 .... **CLC 2, 28, 39**
See also BPFB 1; CA 5-8R; CAAS 116;
CANR 5; DA3; DAM NOV, POP; DLBD
17; MTCW 2; RHW

Calhoun, John Caldwell
1782-1850 .... **NCLC 15**
See also DLB 3, 248

Calisher, Hortense 1911- ..... **CLC 2, 4, 8, 38,
134; SSC 15**
See also CA 1-4R; CANR 1, 22, 117; CN
1, 2, 3, 4, 5, 6, 7; DA3; DAM NOV; DLB
2, 218; INT CANR-22; MAL 5; MTCW
1, 2; MTFW 2005; RGAL 4; RGSF 2

Callaghan, Morley Edward
1903-1990 ..... **CLC 3, 14, 41, 65; TCLC
145**
See also CA 9-12R; CAAS 132; CANR 33,
73; CN 1, 2, 3, 4; DAC; DAM MST; DLB
68; EWL 3; MTCW 1, 2; MTFW 2005;
RGEL 2; RGSF 2; SSFS 19

Callimachus c. 305B.C.-c.
240B.C. .... **CMLC 18**
See also AW 1; DLB 176; RGWL 2, 3

Calvin, Jean
See Calvin, John
See also DLB 327; GFL Beginnings to 1789

Calvin, John 1509-1564 .... **LC 37**
See Calvin, Jean

Calvino, Italo 1923-1985 .... **CLC 5, 8, 11, 22,
33, 39, 73; SSC 3, 48; TCLC 183**
See also AAYA 58; CA 85-88; CAAS 116;
CANR 23, 61; DAM NOV; DLB
196; EW 13; EWL 3; MTCW 1, 2; MTFW
2005; RGHL; RGSF 2; RGWL 2, 3; SFW
4; SSFS 12; WLIT 7

Camara Laye
See Laye, Camara
See also EWL 3

Camden, William 1551-1623 .... **LC 77**
See also DLB 172

Cameron, Carey 1952- .... **CLC 59**
See also CA 135

Cameron, Peter 1959- .... **CLC 44**
See also AMWS 12; CA 125; CANR 50,
117; DLB 234; GLL 2

Camoens, Luis Vaz de 1524(?)-1580
See Camoes, Luis de
See also EW 2

Camoes, Luis de 1524(?)-1580 . **HLCS 1; LC
62; PC 31**
See Camoens, Luis Vaz de
See also DLB 287; RGWL 2, 3

Campana, Dino 1885-1932 .... **TCLC 20**
See also CA 246; CAAE 117; DLB 114;
EWL 3

Campanella, Tommaso 1568-1639 .... **LC 32**
See also RGWL 2, 3

Campbell, John W(ood, Jr.)
1910-1971 .... **CLC 32**
See also CA 21-22; CAAS 29-32R; CANR
34; CAP 2; DLB 8; MTCW 1; SCFW 1,
2; SFW 4

Campbell, Joseph 1904-1987 .... **CLC 69;
TCLC 140**
See also AAYA 3, 66; BEST 89:2; CA 1-4R;
CAAS 124; CANR 3, 28, 61, 107; DA3;
MTCW 1, 2

Campbell, Maria 1940- .... **CLC 85; NNAL**
See also CA 102; CANR 54; CCA 1; DAC

Campbell, (John) Ramsey 1946- ..... **CLC 42;
SSC 19**
See also AAYA 51; CA 228; 57-60, 228;
CANR 7, 102; DLB 261; HGG; INT
CANR-7; SUFW 1, 2

Campbell, (Ignatius) Roy (Dunnachie)
1901-1957 .... **TCLC 5**
See also AFW; CA 155; CAAE 104; DLB
20, 225; EWL 3; MTCW 2; RGEL 2

Campbell, Thomas 1777-1844 .... **NCLC 19**
See also DLB 93, 144; RGEL 2

Campbell, Wilfred .... **TCLC 9**
See Campbell, William

Campbell, William 1858(?)-1918
See Campbell, Wilfred
See also CAAE 106; DLB 92

Campbell, William Edward March
1893-1954
See March, William
See also CAAE 108

Campion, Jane 1954- .... **CLC 95, 229**
See also AAYA 33; CA 138; CANR 87

Campion, Thomas 1567-1620 .... **LC 78**
See also CDBLB Before 1660; DAM POET;
DLB 58, 172; RGEL 2

Camus, Albert 1913-1960 ...... **CLC 1, 2, 4, 9,
11, 14, 32, 63, 69, 124; DC 2; SSC 9,
76; WLC 1**
See also AAYA 36; AFW; BPFB 1; CA 89-
92; CANR 131; DA; DA3; DAB; DAC;
DAM DRAM, MST, NOV; DLB 72, 321,
329; EW 13; EWL 3; EXPN; EXPS; GFL
1789 to the Present; LATS 1:2; LMFS 2;
MTCW 1, 2; MTFW 2005; NFS 6, 16;
RGHL; RGSF 2; RGWL 2, 3; SSFS 4;
TWA

Canby, Vincent 1924-2000 .... **CLC 13**
See also CA 81-84; CAAS 191

Cancale
See Desnos, Robert

Canetti, Elias 1905-1994 .. **CLC 3, 14, 25, 75,
86; TCLC 157**
See also CA 21-24R; CAAS 146; CANR
23, 61, 79; CDWLB 2; CWW 2; DA3;
DLB 85, 124, 329; EW 12; EWL 3;
MTCW 1, 2; MTFW 2005; RGWL 2, 3;
TWA

Canfield, Dorothea F.
See Fisher, Dorothy (Frances) Canfield

Canfield, Dorothea Frances
See Fisher, Dorothy (Frances) Canfield

Canfield, Dorothy
See Fisher, Dorothy (Frances) Canfield

Canin, Ethan 1960- .... **CLC 55; SSC 70**
See also CA 135; CAAE 131; DLB 335;
MAL 5

Cankar, Ivan 1876-1918 .... **TCLC 105**
See also CDWLB 4; DLB 147; EWL 3

Cannon, Curt
See Hunter, Evan

Cao, Lan 1961- .... **CLC 109**
See also CA 165

Cape, Judith
See Page, P(atricia) K(athleen)
See also CCA 1

Capek, Karel 1890-1938 .... **DC 1; SSC 36;
TCLC 6, 37; WLC 1**
See also CA 140; CAAE 104; CDWLB 4;
DA; DA3; DAB; DAC; DAM DRAM,
MST, NOV; DFS 7, 11; DLB 215; EW
10; EWL 3; MTCW 2; MTFW 2005;
RGSF 2; RGWL 2, 3; SCFW 1, 2; SFW 4

Capella, Martianus fl. 4th cent. - .. **CMLC 84**

Capote, Truman 1924-1984 . **CLC 1, 3, 8, 13,
19, 34, 38, 58; SSC 2, 47, 93; TCLC
164; WLC 1**
See also AAYA 61; AMWS 3; BPFB 1; CA
5-8R; CAAS 113; CANR 18, 62; CDALB
1941-1968; CN 1, 2, 3; CPW; DA; DA3;
DAB; DAC; DAM MST, NOV, POP;
DLB 2, 185, 227; DLBY 1980, 1984;
EWL 3; EXPS; GLL 1; LAIT 3; MAL 5;
MTCW 1, 2; MTFW 2005; NCFS 2;
RGAL 4; RGSF 2; SATA 91; SSFS 2;
TUS

Capra, Frank 1897-1991 .... **CLC 16**
See also AAYA 52; CA 61-64; CAAS 135

Caputo, Philip 1941- .... **CLC 32**
See also AAYA 60; CA 73-76; CANR 40,
135; YAW

Caragiale, Ion Luca 1852-1912 ...... **TCLC 76**
See also CA 157

Card, Orson Scott 1951- .... **CLC 44, 47, 50**
See also AAYA 11, 42; BPFB 1; BYA 5, 8;
CA 102; CANR 27, 47, 73, 102, 106, 133;
CLR 116; CPW; DA3; DAM POP; FANT;
INT CANR-27; MTCW 1, 2; MTFW
2005; NFS 5; SATA 83, 127; SCFW 2;
SFW 4; SUFW 2; YAW

Cardenal, Ernesto 1925- .... **CLC 31, 161;
HLC 1; PC 22**
See also CA 49-52; CANR 2, 32, 66, 138;
CWW 2; DAM MULT, POET; DLB 290;
EWL 3; HW 1, 2; LAWS 1; MTCW 1, 2;
MTFW 2005; RGWL 2, 3

Cather, Willa (Sibert) 1873-1947 . **SSC 2, 50;
TCLC 1, 11, 31, 99, 132, 152; WLC 1**
See also AAYA 24; AMW; AMWC 1;
AMWR 1; BPFB 1; CA 128; CAAE 104;
CDALB 1865-1917; CLR 98; DA; DA3;
DAB; DAC; DAM MST, NOV; DLB 9,
54, 78, 256; DLBD 1; EWL 3; EXPN;
EXPS; FL 1:5; LAIT 3; LATS 1:1; MAL
5; MBL; MTCW 1, 2; MTFW 2005; NFS
2, 19; RGAL 4; RGSF 2; RHW; SATA
30; SSFS 2, 7, 16; TCWW 1, 2; TUS

Catherine II
See Catherine the Great
See also DLB 150

Catherine the Great 1729-1796 .... **LC 69**
See Catherine II

Cato, Marcus Porcius
234B.C.-149B.C. .... **CMLC 21**
See Cato the Elder

Cato, Marcus Porcius, the Elder
See Cato, Marcus Porcius

Cato the Elder
See Cato, Marcus Porcius
See also DLB 211

Catton, (Charles) Bruce 1899-1978 . **CLC 35**
See also AITN 1; CA 5-8R; CAAS 81-84;
CANR 7, 74; DLB 17; MTCW 2; MTFW
2005; SATA 2; SATA-Obit 24

Catullus c. 84B.C.-54B.C. .... **CMLC 18**
See also AW 2; CDWLB 1; DLB 211;
RGWL 2, 3; WLIT 8

Cauldwell, Frank
See King, Francis (Henry)

Caunitz, William J. 1933-1996 .... **CLC 34**
See also BEST 89:3; CA 130; CAAE 125;
CAAS 152; CANR 73; INT CA-130

Causley, Charles (Stanley)
1917-2003 .... **CLC 7**
See also CA 9-12R; CAAS 223; CANR 5,
35, 94; CLR 30; CP 1, 2, 3, 4, 5; CWRI
5; DLB 27; MTCW 1; SATA 3, 66; SATA-
Obit 149

Caute, (John) David 1936- .... **CLC 29**
See also CA 1-4R; 4; CANR 1, 33, 64, 120;
CBD; CD 5, 6; CN 1, 2, 3, 4, 5, 6, 7;
DAM NOV; DLB 14, 231

Cavafy, C(onstantine) P(eter) .... **PC 36;
TCLC 2, 7**
See Kavafis, Konstantinos Petrou
See also CA 148; DA3; DAM POET; EW
8; EWL 3; MTCW 2; PFS 19; RGWL 2,
3; WP

Cavalcanti, Guido c. 1250-c.
1300 .... **CMLC 54**
See also RGWL 2, 3; WLIT 7

Cavallo, Evelyn
See Spark, Muriel

Cavanna, Betty .... **CLC 12**
See Harrison, Elizabeth (Allen) Cavanna
See also JRDA; MAICYA 1; SAAS 4;
SATA 1, 30

Cavendish, Margaret Lucas
1623-1673 .... **LC 30, 132**
See also DLB 131, 252, 281; RGEL 2

Caxton, William 1421(?)-1491(?) .... **LC 17**
See also DLB 170

Cayer, D. M.
See Duffy, Maureen (Patricia)

Cayrol, Jean 1911-2005 .... **CLC 11**
See also CA 89-92; CAAS 236; DLB 83;
EWL 3

Cela (y Trulock), Camilo Jose
See Cela, Camilo Jose
See also CWW 2

Cela, Camilo Jose 1916-2002 .... **CLC 4, 13,
59, 122; HLC 1; SSC 71**
See Cela (y Trulock), Camilo Jose
See also BEST 90:2; CA 21-24R; 10; CAAS
206; CANR 21, 32, 76, 139; DAM MULT;

DLB 322; DLBY 1989; EW 13; EWL 3;
HW 1; MTCW 1, 2; MTFW 2005; RGSF
2; RGWL 2, 3

Celan, Paul .... **CLC 10, 19, 53, 82; PC 10**
See Antschel, Paul
See also CDWLB 2; DLB 69; EWL 3;
RGHL; RGWL 2, 3

Celine, Louis-Ferdinand .. **CLC 1, 3, 4, 7, 9,
15, 47, 124**
See Destouches, Louis-Ferdinand
See also DLB 72; EW 11; EWL 3; GFL
1789 to the Present; RGWL 2, 3

Cellini, Benvenuto 1500-1571 .... **LC 7**
See also WLIT 7

Cendrars, Blaise .... **CLC 18, 106**
See Sauser-Hall, Frederic
See also DLB 258; EWL 3; GFL 1789 to
the Present; RGWL 2, 3; WP

Centlivre, Susanna 1669(?)-1723 .... **DC 25;
LC 65**
See also DLB 84; RGEL 2

Cernuda (y Bidon), Luis
1902-1963 .... **CLC 54; PC 62**
See also CA 131; CAAS 89-92; DAM
POET; DLB 134; EWL 3; GLL 1; HW 1;
RGWL 2, 3

Cervantes, Lorna Dee 1954- ..... **HLCS 1; PC
35**
See also CA 131; CANR 80; CP 7; CWP;
DLB 82; EXPP; HW 1; LLW

Cervantes (Saavedra), Miguel de
1547-1616 .... **HLCS; LC 6, 23, 93; SSC
12; WLC 1**
See also AAYA 56; BYA 1, 14; DA; DAB;
DAC; DAM MST, NOV; EW 2; LAIT 1;
LATS 1:1; LMFS 1; NFS 8; RGSF 2;
RGWL 2, 3; TWA

Cesaire, Aime 1913- ..... **BLC 1; CLC 19, 32,
112; DC 22; PC 25**
See also BW 2, 3; CA 65-68; CANR 24,
43, 81; CWW 2; DA3; DAM MULT,
POET; DLB 321; EWL 3; GFL 1789 to
the Present; MTCW 1, 2; MTFW 2005;
WP

Chabon, Michael 1963- ... **CLC 55, 149; SSC
59**
See also AAYA 45; AMWS 11; CA 139;
CANR 57, 96, 127, 138; DLB 278; MAL
5; MTFW 2005; NFS 25; SATA 145

Chabrol, Claude 1930- .... **CLC 16**
See also CA 110

Chairil Anwar
See Anwar, Chairil
See also EWL 3

Challans, Mary 1905-1983
See Renault, Mary
See also CA 81-84; CAAS 111; CANR 74;
DA3; MTCW 2; MTFW 2005; SATA 23;
SATA-Obit 36; TEA

Challis, George
See Faust, Frederick (Schiller)

Chambers, Aidan 1934- .... **CLC 35**
See also AAYA 27; CA 25-28R; CANR 12,
31, 58, 116; JRDA; MAICYA 1, 2; SAAS
12; SATA 1, 69, 108, 171; WYA; YAW

Chambers, James 1948-
See Cliff, Jimmy
See also CAAE 124

Chambers, Jessie
See Lawrence, D(avid) H(erbert Richards)
See also GLL 1

Chambers, Robert W(illiam)
1865-1933 .... **SSC 92; TCLC 41**
See also CA 165; DLB 202; HGG; SATA
107; SUFW 1

Chambers, (David) Whittaker
1901-1961 .... **TCLC 129**
See also CAAS 89-92; DLB 303

Chamisso, Adelbert von
1781-1838 .... **NCLC 82**
See also DLB 90; RGWL 2, 3; SUFW 1

Chance, James T.
See Carpenter, John (Howard)

Chance, John T.
See Carpenter, John (Howard)

Chandler, Raymond (Thornton)
1888-1959 .... **SSC 23; TCLC 1, 7, 179**
See also AAYA 25; AMWC 2; AMWS 4;
BPFB 1; CA 129; CAAE 104; CANR 60,
107; CDALB 1929-1941; CMW 4; DA3;
DLB 226, 253; DLBD 6; EWL 3; MAL
5; MSW; MTCW 1, 2; MTFW 2005; NFS
17; RGAL 4; TUS

Chang, Diana 1934- .... **AAL**
See also CA 228; CWP; DLB 312; EXPP

Chang, Eileen 1921-1995 .... **AAL; SSC 28;
TCLC 184**
See Chang Ai-Ling; Zhang Ailing
See also CA 166

Chang, Jung 1952- .... **CLC 71**
See also CA 142

Chang Ai-Ling
See Chang, Eileen
See also EWL 3

Channing, William Ellery
1780-1842 .... **NCLC 17**
See also DLB 1, 59, 235; RGAL 4

Chao, Patricia 1955- .... **CLC 119**
See also CA 163; CANR 155

Chaplin, Charles Spencer
1889-1977 .... **CLC 16**
See Chaplin, Charlie
See also CA 81-84; CAAS 73-76

Chaplin, Charlie
See Chaplin, Charles Spencer
See also AAYA 61; DLB 44

Chapman, George 1559(?)-1634 . **DC 19; LC
22, 116**
See also BRW 1; DAM DRAM; DLB 62,
121; LMFS 1; RGEL 2

Chapman, Graham 1941-1989 .... **CLC 21**
See Monty Python
See also CA 116; CAAS 129; CANR 35, 95

Chapman, John Jay 1862-1933 .... **TCLC 7**
See also AMWS 14; CA 191; CAAE 104

Chapman, Lee
See Bradley, Marion Zimmer
See also GLL 1

Chapman, Walker
See Silverberg, Robert

Chappell, Fred (Davis) 1936- .... **CLC 40, 78,
162**
See also CA 198; 5-8R, 198; 4; CANR 8,
33, 67, 110; CN 6; CP 6, 7; CSW; DLB
6, 105; HGG

Char, Rene(-Emile) 1907-1988 .... **CLC 9, 11,
14, 55; PC 56**
See also CA 13-16R; CAAS 124; CANR
32; DAM POET; DLB 258; EWL 3; GFL
1789 to the Present; MTCW 1, 2; RGWL
2, 3

Charby, Jay
See Ellison, Harlan

Chardin, Pierre Teilhard de
See Teilhard de Chardin, (Marie Joseph)
Pierre

Chariton fl. 1st cent. (?)- .... **CMLC 49**

Charlemagne 742-814 .... **CMLC 37**

Charles I 1600-1649 .... **LC 13**

Charriere, Isabelle de 1740-1805 .. **NCLC 66**
See also DLB 313

Chartier, Alain c. 1392-1430 .... **LC 94**
See also DLB 208

Chartier, Emile-Auguste
See Alain

Charyn, Jerome 1937- .... **CLC 5, 8, 18**
See also CA 5-8R; 1; CANR 7, 61, 101, 158; CMW 4; CN 1, 2, 3, 4, 5, 6, 7; DLBY 1983; MTCW 1
Chase, Adam
See Marlowe, Stephen
Chase, Mary (Coyle) 1907-1981 .... **DC 1**
See also CA 77-80; CAAS 105; CAD; CWD; DFS 11; DLB 228; SATA 17; SATA-Obit 29
Chase, Mary Ellen 1887-1973 .... **CLC 2; TCLC 124**
See also CA 13-16; CAAS 41-44R; CAP 1; SATA 10
Chase, Nicholas
See Hyde, Anthony
See also CCA 1
Chateaubriand, Francois Rene de
1768-1848 .... **NCLC 3, 134**
See also DLB 119; EW 5; GFL 1789 to the Present; RGWL 2, 3; TWA
Chatelet, Gabrielle-Emilie Du
See du Chatelet, Emilie
See also DLB 313
Chatterje, Sarat Chandra 1876-1936(?)
See Chatterji, Saratchandra
See also CAAE 109
Chatterji, Bankim Chandra
1838-1894 .... **NCLC 19**
Chatterji, Saratchandra .... **TCLC 13**
See Chatterje, Sarat Chandra
See also CA 186; EWL 3
Chatterton, Thomas 1752-1770 .... **LC 3, 54**
See also DAM POET; DLB 109; RGEL 2
Chatwin, (Charles) Bruce
1940-1989 .... **CLC 28, 57, 59**
See also AAYA 4; BEST 90:1; BRWS 4; CA 85-88; CAAS 127; CPW; DAM POP; DLB 194, 204; EWL 3; MTFW 2005
Chaucer, Daniel
See Ford, Ford Madox
See also RHW
Chaucer, Geoffrey 1340(?)-1400 .. **LC 17, 56; PC 19, 58; WLCS**
See also BRW 1; BRWC 1; BRWR 2; CD-BLB Before 1660; DA; DA3; DAB; DAC; DAM MST, POET; DLB 146; LAIT 1; PAB; PFS 14; RGEL 2; TEA; WLIT 3; WP
Chavez, Denise 1948- .... **HLC 1**
See also CA 131; CANR 56, 81, 137; DAM MULT; DLB 122; FW; HW 1, 2; LLW; MAL 5; MTCW 2; MTFW 2005
Chaviaras, Strates 1935-
See Haviaras, Stratis
See also CA 105
Chayefsky, Paddy .... **CLC 23**
See Chayefsky, Sidney
See also CAD; DLB 7, 44; DLBY 1981; RGAL 4
Chayefsky, Sidney 1923-1981
See Chayefsky, Paddy
See also CA 9-12R; CAAS 104; CANR 18; DAM DRAM
Chedid, Andree 1920- .... **CLC 47**
See also CA 145; CANR 95; EWL 3
Cheever, John 1912-1982 ..... **CLC 3, 7, 8, 11, 15, 25, 64; SSC 1, 38, 57; WLC 2**
See also AAYA 65; AMWS 1; BPFB 1; CA 5-8R; CAAS 106; CABS 1; CANR 5, 27, 76; CDALB 1941-1968; CN 1, 2, 3; CPW; DA; DA3; DAB; DAC; DAM MST, NOV, POP; DLB 2, 102, 227; DLBY 1980, 1982; EWL 3; EXPS; INT CANR-5; MAL 5; MTCW 1, 2; MTFW 2005; RGAL 4; RGSF 2; SSFS 2, 14; TUS
Cheever, Susan 1943- .... **CLC 18, 48**
See also CA 103; CANR 27, 51, 92, 157; DLBY 1982; INT CANR-27

Chekhonte, Antosha
See Chekhov, Anton (Pavlovich)
Chekhov, Anton (Pavlovich)
1860-1904 .... **DC 9; SSC 2, 28, 41, 51, 85, 102; TCLC 3, 10, 31, 55, 96, 163; WLC 2**
See also AAYA 68; BYA 14; CA 124; CAAE 104; DA; DA3; DAB; DAC; DAM DRAM, MST; DFS 1, 5, 10, 12; DLB 277; EW 7; EWL 3; EXPS; LAIT 3; LATS 1:1; RGSF 2; RGWL 2, 3; SATA 90; SSFS 5, 13, 14; TWA
Cheney, Lynne V. 1941- .... **CLC 70**
See also CA 89-92; CANR 58, 117; SATA 152
Chernyshevsky, Nikolai Gavrilovich
See Chernyshevsky, Nikolay Gavrilovich
See also DLB 238
Chernyshevsky, Nikolay Gavrilovich
1828-1889 .... **NCLC 1**
See Chernyshevsky, Nikolai Gavrilovich
Cherry, Carolyn Janice .... **CLC 35**
See Cherryh, C.J.
See also AAYA 24; BPFB 1; DLBY 1980; FANT; SATA 93; SCFW 2; SFW 4; YAW
Cherryh, C.J. 1942-
See Cherry, Carolyn Janice
See also CA 65-68; CANR 10, 147; SATA 172
Chesnutt, Charles W(addell)
1858-1932 .... **BLC 1; SSC 7, 54; TCLC 5, 39**
See also AFAW 1, 2; AMWS 14; BW 1, 3; CA 125; CAAE 106; CANR 76; DAM MULT; DLB 12, 50, 78; EWL 3; MAL 5; MTCW 1, 2; MTFW 2005; RGAL 4; RGSF 2; SSFS 11
Chester, Alfred 1929(?)-1971 .... **CLC 49**
See also CA 196; CAAS 33-36R; DLB 130; MAL 5
Chesterton, G(ilbert) K(eith)
1874-1936 . **PC 28; SSC 1, 46; TCLC 1, 6, 64**
See also AAYA 57; BRW 6; CA 132; CAAE 104; CANR 73, 131; CDBLB 1914-1945; CMW 4; DAM NOV, POET; DLB 10, 19, 34, 70, 98, 149, 178; EWL 3; FANT; MSW; MTCW 1, 2; MTFW 2005; RGEL 2; RGSF 2; SATA 27; SUFW 1
Chettle, Henry 1560-1607(?) .... **LC 112**
See also DLB 136; RGEL 2
Chiang, Pin-chin 1904-1986
See Ding Ling
See also CAAS 118
Chief Joseph 1840-1904 .... **NNAL**
See also CA 152; DA3; DAM MULT
Chief Seattle 1786(?)-1866 .... **NNAL**
See also DA3; DAM MULT
Ch'ien, Chung-shu 1910-1998 .... **CLC 22**
See Qian Zhongshu
See also CA 130; CANR 73; MTCW 1, 2
Chikamatsu Monzaemon 1653-1724 ... **LC 66**
See also RGWL 2, 3
Child, Francis James 1825-1896 . **NCLC 173**
See also DLB 1, 64, 235
Child, L. Maria
See Child, Lydia Maria
Child, Lydia Maria 1802-1880 .. **NCLC 6, 73**
See also DLB 1, 74, 243; RGAL 4; SATA 67
Child, Mrs.
See Child, Lydia Maria
Child, Philip 1898-1978 .... **CLC 19, 68**
See also CA 13-14; CAP 1; CP 1; DLB 68; RHW; SATA 47
Childers, (Robert) Erskine
1870-1922 .... **TCLC 65**
See also CA 153; CAAE 113; DLB 70

Childress, Alice 1920-1994 . **BLC 1; CLC 12, 15, 86, 96; DC 4; TCLC 116**
See also AAYA 8; BW 2, 3; BYA 2; CA 45-48; CAAS 146; CAD; CANR 3, 27, 50, 74; CLR 14; CWD; DA3; DAM DRAM, MULT, NOV; DFS 2, 8, 14; DLB 7, 38, 249; JRDA; LAIT 5; MAICYA 1, 2; MAI-CYAS 1; MAL 5; MTCW 1, 2; MTFW 2005; RGAL 4; SATA 7, 48, 81; TUS; WYA; YAW
Chin, Frank (Chew, Jr.) 1940- .... **AAL; CLC 135; DC 7**
See also CA 33-36R; CAD; CANR 71; CD 5, 6; DAM MULT; DLB 206, 312; LAIT 5; RGAL 4
Chin, Marilyn (Mei Ling) 1955- .... **PC 40**
See also CA 129; CANR 70, 113; CWP; DLB 312
Chislett, (Margaret) Anne 1943- ...... **CLC 34**
See also CA 151
Chitty, Thomas Willes 1926- .... **CLC 11**
See Hinde, Thomas
See also CA 5-8R; CN 7
Chivers, Thomas Holley
1809-1858 .... **NCLC 49**
See also DLB 3, 248; RGAL 4
Choi, Susan 1969- .... **CLC 119**
See also CA 223
Chomette, Rene Lucien 1898-1981
See Clair, Rene
See also CAAS 103
Chomsky, Avram Noam
See Chomsky, Noam
Chomsky, Noam 1928- .... **CLC 132**
See also CA 17-20R; CANR 28, 62, 110, 132; DA3; DLB 246; MTCW 1, 2; MTFW 2005
Chona, Maria 1845(?)-1936 .... **NNAL**
See also CA 144
Chopin, Kate .... **SSC 8, 68; TCLC 127; WLCS**
See Chopin, Katherine
See also AAYA 33; AMWR 2; AMWS 1; BYA 11, 15; CDALB 1865-1917; DA; DAB; DLB 12, 78; EXPN; EXPS; FL 1:3; FW; LAIT 3; MAL 5; MBL; NFS 3; RGAL 4; RGSF 2; SSFS 2, 13, 17; TUS
Chopin, Katherine 1851-1904
See Chopin, Kate
See also CA 122; CAAE 104; DA3; DAC; DAM MST, NOV
Chretien de Troyes c. 12th cent. - . **CMLC 10**
See also DLB 208; EW 1; RGWL 2, 3; TWA
Christie
See Ichikawa, Kon
Christie, Agatha (Mary Clarissa)
1890-1976 .. **CLC 1, 6, 8, 12, 39, 48, 110**
See also AAYA 9; AITN 1, 2; BPFB 1; BRWS 2; CA 17-20R; CAAS 61-64; CANR 10, 37, 108; CBD; CDBLB 1914-1945; CMW 4; CN 1, 2; CPW; CWD; DA3; DAB; DAC; DAM NOV; DFS 2; DLB 13, 77, 245; MSW; MTCW 1, 2; MTFW 2005; NFS 8; RGEL 2; RHW; SATA 36; TEA; YAW
Christie, Philippa .... **CLC 21**
See Pearce, Philippa
See also BYA 5; CANR 109; CLR 9; DLB 161; MAICYA 1; SATA 1, 67, 129
Christine de Pisan
See Christine de Pizan
See also FW
Christine de Pizan 1365(?)-1431(?) ...... **LC 9, 130; PC 68**
See Christine de Pisan; de Pizan, Christine
See also DLB 208; FL 1:1; RGWL 2, 3

DAM MST, NOV, POP; DLB 68; EWL 3;
HGG; INT CANR-17; MTCW 1, 2;
MTFW 2005; RGEL 2; TWA

Davies, Sir John 1569-1626 .... **LC 85**
See also DLB 172

Davies, Walter C.
See Kornbluth, C(yril) M.

Davies, William Henry 1871-1940 ... **TCLC 5**
See also BRWS 11; CA 179; CAAE 104;
DLB 19, 174; EWL 3; RGEL 2

Davies, William Robertson
See Davies, Robertson

Da Vinci, Leonardo 1452-1519 ..... **LC 12, 57, 60**
See also AAYA 40

Davis, Angela (Yvonne) 1944- .... **CLC 77**
See also BW 2, 3; CA 57-60; CANR 10,
81; CSW; DA3; DAM MULT; FW

Davis, B. Lynch
See Bioy Casares, Adolfo; Borges, Jorge
Luis

Davis, Frank Marshall 1905-1987 ...... **BLC 1**
See also BW 2, 3; CA 125; CAAS 123;
CANR 42, 80; DAM MULT; DLB 51

Davis, Gordon
See Hunt, E. Howard

Davis, H(arold) L(enoir) 1896-1960 . **CLC 49**
See also ANW; CA 178; CAAS 89-92; DLB
9, 206; SATA 114; TCWW 1, 2

Davis, Hart
See Poniatowska, Elena

Davis, Natalie Zemon 1928- .... **CLC 204**
See also CA 53-56; CANR 58, 100

Davis, Rebecca (Blaine) Harding
1831-1910 .... **SSC 38; TCLC 6**
See also AMWS 16; CA 179; CAAE 104;
DLB 74, 239; FW; NFS 14; RGAL 4;
TUS

Davis, Richard Harding
1864-1916 .... **TCLC 24**
See also CA 179; CAAE 114; DLB 12, 23,
78, 79, 189; DLBD 13; RGAL 4

Davison, Frank Dalby 1893-1970 ..... **CLC 15**
See also CA 217; CAAS 116; DLB 260

Davison, Lawrence H.
See Lawrence, D(avid) H(erbert Richards)

Davison, Peter (Hubert) 1928-2004 . **CLC 28**
See also CA 9-12R; 4; CAAS 234; CANR
3, 43, 84; CP 1, 2, 3, 4, 5, 6, 7; DLB 5

Davys, Mary 1674-1732 .... **LC 1, 46**
See also DLB 39

Dawson, (Guy) Fielding (Lewis)
1930-2002 .... **CLC 6**
See also CA 85-88; CAAS 202; CANR 108;
DLB 130; DLBY 2002

Dawson, Peter
See Faust, Frederick (Schiller)
See also TCWW 1, 2

Day, Clarence (Shepard, Jr.)
1874-1935 .... **TCLC 25**
See also CA 199; CAAE 108; DLB 11

Day, John 1574(?)-1640(?) .... **LC 70**
See also DLB 62, 170; RGEL 2

Day, Thomas 1748-1789 .... **LC 1**
See also DLB 39; YABC 1

Day Lewis, C(ecil) 1904-1972 . **CLC 1, 6, 10; PC 11**
See Blake, Nicholas; Lewis, C. Day
See also BRWS 3; CA 13-16; CAAS 33-
36R; CANR 34; CAP 1; CP 1; CWRI 5;
DAM POET; DLB 15, 20; EWL 3;
MTCW 1, 2; RGEL 2

Dazai Osamu .... **SSC 41; TCLC 11**
See Tsushima, Shuji
See also CA 164; DLB 182; EWL 3; MJW;
RGSF 2; RGWL 2, 3; TWA

de Andrade, Carlos Drummond
See Drummond de Andrade, Carlos

de Andrade, Mario 1892(?)-1945
See Andrade, Mario de
See also CA 178; HW 2

Deane, Norman
See Creasey, John

Deane, Seamus (Francis) 1940- ...... **CLC 122**
See also CA 118; CANR 42

de Beauvoir, Simone
See Beauvoir, Simone de

de Beer, P.
See Bosman, Herman Charles

De Botton, Alain 1969- .... **CLC 203**
See also CA 159; CANR 96

de Brissac, Malcolm
See Dickinson, Peter (Malcolm de Brissac)

de Campos, Alvaro
See Pessoa, Fernando (Antonio Nogueira)

de Chardin, Pierre Teilhard
See Teilhard de Chardin, (Marie Joseph)
Pierre

de Crenne, Helisenne c. 1510-c.
1560 .... **LC 113**

Dee, John 1527-1608 .... **LC 20**
See also DLB 136, 213

Deer, Sandra 1940- .... **CLC 45**
See also CA 186

De Ferrari, Gabriella 1941- .... **CLC 65**
See also CA 146

de Filippo, Eduardo 1900-1984 ... **TCLC 127**
See also CA 132; CAAS 114; EWL 3;
MTCW 1; RGWL 2, 3

Defoe, Daniel 1660(?)-1731 .... **LC 1, 42, 108; WLC 2**
See also AAYA 27; BRW 3; BRWR 1; BYA
4; CDBLB 1660-1789; CLR 61; DA;
DA3; DAB; DAC; DAM MST, NOV;
DLB 39, 95, 101, 336; JRDA; LAIT 1;
LMFS 1; MAICYA 1, 2; NFS 9, 13;
RGEL 2; SATA 22; TEA; WCH; WLIT 3

de Gouges, Olympe
See de Gouges, Olympe

de Gouges, Olympe 1748-1793 .... **LC 127**
See also DLB 313

de Gourmont, Remy(-Marie-Charles)
See Gourmont, Remy(-Marie-Charles) de

de Gournay, Marie le Jars
1566-1645 .... **LC 98**
See also DLB 327; FW

de Hartog, Jan 1914-2002 .... **CLC 19**
See also CA 1-4R; CAAS 210; CANR 1;
DFS 12

de Hostos, E. M.
See Hostos (y Bonilla), Eugenio Maria de

de Hostos, Eugenio M.
See Hostos (y Bonilla), Eugenio Maria de

Deighton, Len .... **CLC 4, 7, 22, 46**
See Deighton, Leonard Cyril
See also AAYA 6; BEST 89:2; BPFB 1; CD-
BLB 1960 to Present; CMW 4; CN 1, 2,
3, 4, 5, 6, 7; CPW; DLB 87

Deighton, Leonard Cyril 1929-
See Deighton, Len
See also AAYA 57; CA 9-12R; CANR 19,
33, 68; DA3; DAM NOV, POP; MTCW
1, 2; MTFW 2005

Dekker, Thomas 1572(?)-1632 ..... **DC 12; LC 22**
See also CDBLB Before 1660; DAM
DRAM; DLB 62, 172; LMFS 1; RGEL 2

de Laclos, Pierre Ambroise Franois
See Laclos, Pierre-Ambroise Francois

Delacroix, (Ferdinand-Victor-)Eugene
1798-1863 .... **NCLC 133**
See also EW 5

Delafield, E. M. .... **TCLC 61**
See Dashwood, Edmee Elizabeth Monica
de la Pasture
See also DLB 34; RHW

de la Mare, Walter (John)
1873-1956 ..... **PC 77; SSC 14; TCLC 4, 53; WLC 2**
See also CA 163; CDBLB 1914-1945; CLR
23; CWRI 5; DA3; DAB; DAC; DAM
MST, POET; DLB 19, 153, 162, 255, 284;
EWL 3; EXPP; HGG; MAICYA 1, 2;
MTCW 2; MTFW 2005; RGEL 2; RGSF
2; SATA 16; SUFW 1; TEA; WCH

de Lamartine, Alphonse (Marie Louis Prat)
See Lamartine, Alphonse (Marie Louis Prat)
de

Delaney, Franey
See O'Hara, John (Henry)

Delaney, Shelagh 1939- .... **CLC 29**
See also CA 17-20R; CANR 30, 67; CBD;
CD 5, 6; CDBLB 1960 to Present; CWD;
DAM DRAM; DFS 7; DLB 13; MTCW 1

Delany, Martin Robison
1812-1885 .... **NCLC 93**
See also DLB 50; RGAL 4

Delany, Mary (Granville Pendarves)
1700-1788 .... **LC 12**

Delany, Samuel R., Jr. 1942- ... **BLC 1; CLC 8, 14, 38, 141**
See also AAYA 24; AFAW 2; BPFB 1; BW
2, 3; CA 81-84; CANR 27, 43, 116; CN
2, 3, 4, 5, 6, 7; DAM MULT; DLB 8, 33;
FANT; MAL 5; MTCW 1, 2; RGAL 4;
SATA 92; SCFW 1, 2; SFW 4; SUFW 1

de la Parra, (Ana) Teresa (Sonojo)
1890(?)-1936 .... **TCLC 185**
See Parra Sanojo, Ana Teresa de la
See also CA 178; HW 2

De La Ramee, Marie Louise 1839-1908
See Ouida
See also CA 204; SATA 20

de la Roche, Mazo 1879-1961 .... **CLC 14**
See also CA 85-88; CANR 30; DLB 68;
RGEL 2; RHW; SATA 64

De La Salle, Innocent
See Hartmann, Sadakichi

de Laureamont, Comte
See Lautreamont

Delbanco, Nicholas 1942- ..... **CLC 6, 13, 167**
See also CA 189; 17-20R, 189; 2; CANR
29, 55, 116, 150; CN 7; DLB 6, 234

Delbanco, Nicholas Franklin
See Delbanco, Nicholas

del Castillo, Michel 1933- .... **CLC 38**
See also CA 109; CANR 77

Deledda, Grazia (Cosima)
1875(?)-1936 .... **TCLC 23**
See also CA 205; CAAE 123; DLB 264,
329; EWL 3; RGWL 2, 3; WLIT 7

Deleuze, Gilles 1925-1995 .... **TCLC 116**
See also DLB 296

Delgado, Abelardo (Lalo) B(arrientos)
1930-2004 .... **HLC 1**
See also CA 131; 15; CAAS 230; CANR
90; DAM MST, MULT; DLB 82; HW 1,
2

Delibes, Miguel .... **CLC 8, 18**
See Delibes Setien, Miguel
See also DLB 322; EWL 3

Delibes Setien, Miguel 1920-
See Delibes, Miguel
See also CA 45-48; CANR 1, 32; CWW 2;
HW 1; MTCW 1

DeLillo, Don 1936- ..... **CLC 8, 10, 13, 27, 39, 54, 76, 143, 210, 213**
See also AMWC 2; AMWS 6; BEST 89:1;
BPFB 1; CA 81-84; CANR 21, 76, 92,
133; CN 3, 4, 5, 6, 7; CPW; DA3; DAM
NOV, POP; DLB 6, 173; EWL 3; MAL 5;
MTCW 1, 2; MTFW 2005; RGAL 4; TUS

de Lisser, H. G.
See De Lisser, H(erbert) G(eorge)
See also DLB 117

Dorset
See Sackville, Thomas
Dos Passos, John (Roderigo)
1896-1970 ... **CLC 1, 4, 8, 11, 15, 25, 34, 82; WLC 2**
See also AMW; BPFB 1; CA 1-4R; CAAS 29-32R; CANR 3; CDALB 1929-1941; DA; DA3; DAB; DAC; DAM MST, NOV; DLB 4, 9, 274, 316; DLBD 1, 15; DLBY 1996; EWL 3; MAL 5; MTCW 1, 2; MTFW 2005; NFS 14; RGAL 4; TUS
Dossage, Jean
See Simenon, Georges (Jacques Christian)
Dostoevsky, Fedor Mikhailovich
1821-1881 .. **NCLC 2, 7, 21, 33, 43, 119, 167; SSC 2, 33, 44; WLC 2**
See Dostoevsky, Fyodor
See also AAYA 40; DA; DA3; DAB; DAC; DAM MST, NOV; EW 7; EXPN; NFS 3, 8; RGSF 2; RGWL 2, 3; SSFS 8; TWA
Dostoevsky, Fyodor
See Dostoevsky, Fedor Mikhailovich
See also DLB 238; LATS 1:1; LMFS 1, 2
Doty, M. R.
See Doty, Mark
Doty, Mark 1953(?)- .... **CLC 176; PC 53**
See also AMWS 11; CA 183; 161, 183; CANR 110; CP 7
Doty, Mark A.
See Doty, Mark
Doty, Mark Alan
See Doty, Mark
Doughty, Charles M(ontagu)
1843-1926 .... **TCLC 27**
See also CA 178; CAAE 115; DLB 19, 57, 174
Douglas, Ellen .... **CLC 73**
See Haxton, Josephine Ayres; Williamson, Ellen Douglas
See also CN 5, 6, 7; CSW; DLB 292
Douglas, Gavin 1475(?)-1522 .... **LC 20**
See also DLB 132; RGEL 2
Douglas, George
See Brown, George Douglas
See also RGEL 2
Douglas, Keith (Castellain)
1920-1944 .... **TCLC 40**
See also BRW 7; CA 160; DLB 27; EWL 3; PAB; RGEL 2
Douglas, Leonard
See Bradbury, Ray
Douglas, Michael
See Crichton, Michael
Douglas, (George) Norman
1868-1952 .... **TCLC 68**
See also BRW 6; CA 157; CAAE 119; DLB 34, 195; RGEL 2
Douglas, William
See Brown, George Douglas
Douglass, Frederick 1817(?)-1895 ..... **BLC 1; NCLC 7, 55, 141; WLC 2**
See also AAYA 48; AFAW 1, 2; AMWC 1; AMWS 3; CDALB 1640-1865; DA; DA3; DAC; DAM MST, MULT; DLB 1, 43, 50, 79, 243; FW; LAIT 2; NCFS 2; RGAL 4; SATA 29
Dourado, (Waldomiro Freitas) Autran
1926- .... **CLC 23, 60**
See also CA 25-28R, 179; CANR 34, 81; DLB 145, 307; HW 2
Dourado, Waldomiro Freitas Autran
See Dourado, (Waldomiro Freitas) Autran
Dove, Rita 1952- .. **BLCS; CLC 50, 81; PC 6**
See also AAYA 46; AMWS 4; BW 2; CA 109; 19; CANR 27, 42, 68, 76, 97, 132; CDALBS; CP 5, 6, 7; CSW; CWP; DA3; DAM MULT, POET; DLB 120; EWL 3; EXPP; MAL 5; MTCW 2; MTFW 2005; PFS 1, 15; RGAL 4

Dove, Rita Frances
See Dove, Rita
Doveglion
See Villa, Jose Garcia
Dowell, Coleman 1925-1985 .... **CLC 60**
See also CA 25-28R; CAAS 117; CANR 10; DLB 130; GLL 2
Dowson, Ernest (Christopher)
1867-1900 .... **TCLC 4**
See also CA 150; CAAE 105; DLB 19, 135; RGEL 2
Doyle, A. Conan
See Doyle, Sir Arthur Conan
Doyle, Sir Arthur Conan
1859-1930 ..... **SSC 12, 83, 95; TCLC 7; WLC 2**
See Conan Doyle, Arthur
See also AAYA 14; BRWS 2; CA 122; CAAE 104; CANR 131; CDBLB 1890-1914; CLR 106; CMW 4; DA; DA3; DAB; DAC; DAM MST, NOV; DLB 18, 70, 156, 178; EXPS; HGG; LAIT 2; MSW; MTCW 1, 2; MTFW 2005; RGEL 2; RGSF 2; RHW; SATA 24; SCFW 1, 2; SFW 4; SSFS 2; TEA; WCH; WLIT 4; WYA; YAW
Doyle, Conan
See Doyle, Sir Arthur Conan
Doyle, John
See Graves, Robert
Doyle, Roddy 1958- .... **CLC 81, 178**
See also AAYA 14; BRWS 5; CA 143; CANR 73, 128; CN 6, 7; DA3; DLB 194, 326; MTCW 2; MTFW 2005
Doyle, Sir A. Conan
See Doyle, Sir Arthur Conan
Dr. A
See Asimov, Isaac; Silverstein, Alvin; Silverstein, Virginia B(arbara Opshelor)
Drabble, Margaret 1939- ...... **CLC 2, 3, 5, 8, 10, 22, 53, 129**
See also BRWS 4; CA 13-16R; CANR 18, 35, 63, 112, 131; CDBLB 1960 to Present; CN 1, 2, 3, 4, 5, 6, 7; CPW; DA3; DAB; DAC; DAM MST, NOV, POP; DLB 14, 155, 231; EWL 3; FW; MTCW 1, 2; MTFW 2005; RGEL 2; SATA 48; TEA
Drakulic, Slavenka 1949- .... **CLC 173**
See also CA 144; CANR 92
Drakulic-Ilic, Slavenka
See Drakulic, Slavenka
Drapier, M. B.
See Swift, Jonathan
Drayham, James
See Mencken, H(enry) L(ouis)
Drayton, Michael 1563-1631 .... **LC 8**
See also DAM POET; DLB 121; RGEL 2
Dreadstone, Carl
See Campbell, (John) Ramsey
Dreiser, Theodore 1871-1945 .... **SSC 30; TCLC 10, 18, 35, 83; WLC 2**
See also AMW; AMWC 2; AMWR 2; BYA 15, 16; CA 132; CAAE 106; CDALB 1865-1917; DA; DA3; DAC; DAM MST, NOV; DLB 9, 12, 102, 137; DLBD 1; EWL 3; LAIT 2; LMFS 2; MAL 5; MTCW 1, 2; MTFW 2005; NFS 8, 17; RGAL 4; TUS
Dreiser, Theodore Herman Albert
See Dreiser, Theodore
Drexler, Rosalyn 1926- .... **CLC 2, 6**
See also CA 81-84; CAD; CANR 68, 124; CD 5, 6; CWD; MAL 5
Dreyer, Carl Theodor 1889-1968 ...... **CLC 16**
See also CAAS 116
Drieu la Rochelle, Pierre
1893-1945 .... **TCLC 21**
See also CA 250; CAAE 117; DLB 72; EWL 3; GFL 1789 to the Present

Drieu la Rochelle, Pierre-Eugene 1893-1945
See Drieu la Rochelle, Pierre
Drinkwater, John 1882-1937 .... **TCLC 57**
See also CA 149; CAAE 109; DLB 10, 19, 149; RGEL 2
Drop Shot
See Cable, George Washington
Droste-Hulshoff, Annette Freiin von
1797-1848 .... **NCLC 3, 133**
See also CDWLB 2; DLB 133; RGSF 2; RGWL 2, 3
Drummond, Walter
See Silverberg, Robert
Drummond, William Henry
1854-1907 .... **TCLC 25**
See also CA 160; DLB 92
Drummond de Andrade, Carlos
1902-1987 .... **CLC 18; TCLC 139**
See Andrade, Carlos Drummond de
See also CA 132; CAAS 123; DLB 307; LAW
Drummond of Hawthornden, William
1585-1649 .... **LC 83**
See also DLB 121, 213; RGEL 2
Drury, Allen (Stuart) 1918-1998 .... **CLC 37**
See also CA 57-60; CAAS 170; CANR 18, 52; CN 1, 2, 3, 4, 5, 6; INT CANR-18
Druse, Eleanor
See King, Stephen
Dryden, John 1631-1700 ..... **DC 3; LC 3, 21, 115; PC 25; WLC 2**
See also BRW 2; CDBLB 1660-1789; DA; DAB; DAC; DAM DRAM, MST, POET; DLB 80, 101, 131; EXPP; IDTP; LMFS 1; RGEL 2; TEA; WLIT 3
du Bellay, Joachim 1524-1560 .... **LC 92**
See also DLB 327; GFL Beginnings to 1789; RGWL 2, 3
Duberman, Martin 1930- .... **CLC 8**
See also CA 1-4R; CAD; CANR 2, 63, 137; CD 5, 6
Dubie, Norman (Evans) 1945- .... **CLC 36**
See also CA 69-72; CANR 12, 115; CP 3, 4, 5, 6, 7; DLB 120; PFS 12
Du Bois, W(illiam) E(dward) B(urghardt)
1868-1963 ...... **BLC 1; CLC 1, 2, 13, 64, 96; HR 1:2; TCLC 169; WLC 2**
See also AAYA 40; AFAW 1, 2; AMWC 1; AMWS 2; BW 1, 3; CA 85-88; CANR 34, 82, 132; CDALB 1865-1917; DA; DA3; DAC; DAM MST, MULT, NOV; DLB 47, 50, 91, 246, 284; EWL 3; EXPP; LAIT 2; LMFS 2; MAL 5; MTCW 1, 2; MTFW 2005; NCFS 1; PFS 13; RGAL 4; SATA 42
Dubus, Andre 1936-1999 ..... **CLC 13, 36, 97; SSC 15**
See also AMWS 7; CA 21-24R; CAAS 177; CANR 17; CN 5, 6; CSW; DLB 130; INT CANR-17; RGAL 4; SSFS 10; TCLE 1:1
Duca Minimo
See D'Annunzio, Gabriele
Ducharme, Rejean 1941- .... **CLC 74**
See also CAAS 165; DLB 60
du Chatelet, Emilie 1706-1749 .... **LC 96**
See Chatelet, Gabrielle-Emilie Du
Duchen, Claire .... **CLC 65**
Duclos, Charles Pinot- 1704-1772 .... **LC 1**
See also GFL Beginnings to 1789
Ducornet, Erica 1943-
See Ducornet, Rikki
See also CA 37-40R; CANR 14, 34, 54, 82; SATA 7
Ducornet, Rikki .... **CLC 232**
See Ducornet, Erica
Dudek, Louis 1918-2001 .... **CLC 11, 19**
See also CA 45-48; 14; CAAS 215; CANR 1; CP 1, 2, 3, 4, 5, 6, 7; DLB 88

Duerrenmatt, Friedrich 1921-1990 ... **CLC 1, 4, 8, 11, 15, 43, 102**
See Durrenmatt, Friedrich
See also CA 17-20R; CANR 33; CMW 4; DAM DRAM; DLB 69, 124; MTCW 1, 2

Duffy, Bruce 1953(?)- .... **CLC 50**
See also CA 172

Duffy, Maureen (Patricia) 1933- ...... **CLC 37**
See also CA 25-28R; CANR 33, 68; CBD; CN 1, 2, 3, 4, 5, 6, 7; CP 5, 6, 7; CWD; CWP; DFS 15; DLB 14, 310; FW; MTCW 1

Du Fu
See Tu Fu
See also RGWL 2, 3

Dugan, Alan 1923-2003 .... **CLC 2, 6**
See also CA 81-84; CAAS 220; CANR 119; CP 1, 2, 3, 4, 5, 6, 7; DLB 5; MAL 5; PFS 10

du Gard, Roger Martin
See Martin du Gard, Roger

Duhamel, Georges 1884-1966 .... **CLC 8**
See also CA 81-84; CAAS 25-28R; CANR 35; DLB 65; EWL 3; GFL 1789 to the Present; MTCW 1

Dujardin, Edouard (Emile Louis) 1861-1949 .... **TCLC 13**
See also CAAE 109; DLB 123

Duke, Raoul
See Thompson, Hunter S.

Dulles, John Foster 1888-1959 .... **TCLC 72**
See also CA 149; CAAE 115

Dumas, Alexandre (pere) 1802-1870 .... **NCLC 11, 71; WLC 2**
See also AAYA 22; BYA 3; DA; DA3; DAB; DAC; DAM MST, NOV; DLB 119, 192; EW 6; GFL 1789 to the Present; LAIT 1, 2; NFS 14, 19; RGWL 2, 3; SATA 18; TWA; WCH

Dumas, Alexandre (fils) 1824-1895 ...... **DC 1; NCLC 9**
See also DLB 192; GFL 1789 to the Present; RGWL 2, 3

Dumas, Claudine
See Malzberg, Barry N(athaniel)

Dumas, Henry L. 1934-1968 .... **CLC 6, 62**
See also BW 1; CA 85-88; DLB 41; RGAL 4

du Maurier, Daphne 1907-1989 .. **CLC 6, 11, 59; SSC 18**
See also AAYA 37; BPFB 1; BRWS 3; CA 5-8R; CAAS 128; CANR 6, 55; CMW 4; CN 1, 2, 3, 4; CPW; DA3; DAB; DAC; DAM MST, POP; DLB 191; GL 2; HGG; LAIT 3; MSW; MTCW 1, 2; NFS 12; RGEL 2; RGSF 2; RHW; SATA 27; SATA-Obit 60; SSFS 14, 16; TEA

Du Maurier, George 1834-1896 ..... **NCLC 86**
See also DLB 153, 178; RGEL 2

Dunbar, Paul Laurence 1872-1906 ... **BLC 1; PC 5; SSC 8; TCLC 2, 12; WLC 2**
See also AAYA 75; AFAW 1, 2; AMWS 2; BW 1, 3; CA 124; CAAE 104; CANR 79; CDALB 1865-1917; DA; DA3; DAC; DAM MST, MULT, POET; DLB 50, 54, 78; EXPP; MAL 5; RGAL 4; SATA 34

Dunbar, William 1460(?)-1520(?) .... **LC 20; PC 67**
See also BRWS 8; DLB 132, 146; RGEL 2

Dunbar-Nelson, Alice .... **HR 1:2**
See Nelson, Alice Ruth Moore Dunbar

Duncan, Dora Angela
See Duncan, Isadora

Duncan, Isadora 1877(?)-1927 .... **TCLC 68**
See also CA 149; CAAE 118

Duncan, Lois 1934- .... **CLC 26**
See also AAYA 4, 34; BYA 6, 8; CA 1-4R; CANR 2, 23, 36, 111; CLR 29; JRDA; MAICYA 1, 2; MAICYAS 1; MTFW 2005; SAAS 2; SATA 1, 36, 75, 133, 141; SATA-Essay 141; WYA; YAW

Duncan, Robert 1919-1988 ... **CLC 1, 2, 4, 7, 15, 41, 55; PC 2, 75**
See also BG 1:2; CA 9-12R; CAAS 124; CANR 28, 62; CP 1, 2, 3, 4; DAM POET; DLB 5, 16, 193; EWL 3; MAL 5; MTCW 1, 2; MTFW 2005; PFS 13; RGAL 4; WP

Duncan, Sara Jeannette 1861-1922 .... **TCLC 60**
See also CA 157; DLB 92

Dunlap, William 1766-1839 .... **NCLC 2**
See also DLB 30, 37, 59; RGAL 4

Dunn, Douglas (Eaglesham) 1942- .... **CLC 6, 40**
See also BRWS 10; CA 45-48; CANR 2, 33, 126; CP 1, 2, 3, 4, 5, 6, 7; DLB 40; MTCW 1

Dunn, Katherine 1945- .... **CLC 71**
See also CA 33-36R; CANR 72; HGG; MTCW 2; MTFW 2005

Dunn, Stephen 1939- .... **CLC 36, 206**
See also AMWS 11; CA 33-36R; CANR 12, 48, 53, 105; CP 3, 4, 5, 6, 7; DLB 105; PFS 21

Dunn, Stephen Elliott
See Dunn, Stephen

Dunne, Finley Peter 1867-1936 ...... **TCLC 28**
See also CA 178; CAAE 108; DLB 11, 23; RGAL 4

Dunne, John Gregory 1932-2003 ..... **CLC 28**
See also CA 25-28R; CAAS 222; CANR 14, 50; CN 5, 6, 7; DLBY 1980

Dunsany, Lord .... **TCLC 2, 59**
See Dunsany, Edward John Moreton Drax Plunkett
See also DLB 77, 153, 156, 255; FANT; IDTP; RGEL 2; SFW 4; SUFW 1

Dunsany, Edward John Moreton Drax Plunkett 1878-1957
See Dunsany, Lord
See also CA 148; CAAE 104; DLB 10; MTCW 2

Duns Scotus, John 1266(?)-1308 ... **CMLC 59**
See also DLB 115

du Perry, Jean
See Simenon, Georges (Jacques Christian)

Durang, Christopher 1949- .... **CLC 27, 38**
See also CA 105; CAD; CANR 50, 76, 130; CD 5, 6; MTCW 2; MTFW 2005

Durang, Christopher Ferdinand
See Durang, Christopher

Duras, Claire de 1777-1832 .... **NCLC 154**

Duras, Marguerite 1914-1996 . **CLC 3, 6, 11, 20, 34, 40, 68, 100; SSC 40**
See also BPFB 1; CA 25-28R; CAAS 151; CANR 50; CWW 2; DFS 21; DLB 83, 321; FL 1:5; GFL 1789 to the Present; IDFW 4; MTCW 1, 2; RGWL 2, 3; TWA

Durban, (Rosa) Pam 1947- .... **CLC 39**
See also CA 123; CANR 98; CSW

Durcan, Paul 1944- .... **CLC 43, 70**
See also CA 134; CANR 123; CP 1, 5, 6, 7; DAM POET; EWL 3

d'Urfe, Honore
See Urfe, Honore d'

Durfey, Thomas 1653-1723 .... **LC 94**
See also DLB 80; RGEL 2

Durkheim, Emile 1858-1917 .... **TCLC 55**
See also CA 249

Durrell, Lawrence (George) 1912-1990 ..... **CLC 1, 4, 6, 8, 13, 27, 41**
See also BPFB 1; BRWS 1; CA 9-12R; CAAS 132; CANR 40, 77; CDBLB 1945-1960; CN 1, 2, 3, 4; CP 1, 2, 3, 4, 5; DAM NOV; DLB 15, 27, 204; DLBY 1990; EWL 3; MTCW 1, 2; RGEL 2; SFW 4; TEA

Durrenmatt, Friedrich
See Duerrenmatt, Friedrich
See also CDWLB 2; EW 13; EWL 3; RGHL; RGWL 2, 3

Dutt, Michael Madhusudan 1824-1873 .... **NCLC 118**

Dutt, Toru 1856-1877 .... **NCLC 29**
See also DLB 240

Dwight, Timothy 1752-1817 .... **NCLC 13**
See also DLB 37; RGAL 4

Dworkin, Andrea 1946-2005 ..... **CLC 43, 123**
See also CA 77-80; 21; CAAS 238; CANR 16, 39, 76, 96; FL 1:5; FW; GLL 1; INT CANR-16; MTCW 1, 2; MTFW 2005

Dwyer, Deanna
See Koontz, Dean R.

Dwyer, K. R.
See Koontz, Dean R.

Dybek, Stuart 1942- .... **CLC 114; SSC 55**
See also CA 97-100; CANR 39; DLB 130; SSFS 23

Dye, Richard
See De Voto, Bernard (Augustine)

Dyer, Geoff 1958- .... **CLC 149**
See also CA 125; CANR 88

Dyer, George 1755-1841 .... **NCLC 129**
See also DLB 93

Dylan, Bob 1941- ..... **CLC 3, 4, 6, 12, 77; PC 37**
See also CA 41-44R; CANR 108; CP 1, 2, 3, 4, 5, 6, 7; DLB 16

Dyson, John 1943- .... **CLC 70**
See also CA 144

Dzyubin, Eduard Georgievich 1895-1934
See Bagritsky, Eduard
See also CA 170

E. V. L.
See Lucas, E(dward) V(errall)

Eagleton, Terence (Francis) 1943- .. **CLC 63, 132**
See also CA 57-60; CANR 7, 23, 68, 115; DLB 242; LMFS 2; MTCW 1, 2; MTFW 2005

Eagleton, Terry
See Eagleton, Terence (Francis)

Early, Jack
See Scoppettone, Sandra
See also GLL 1

East, Michael
See West, Morris L(anglo)

Eastaway, Edward
See Thomas, (Philip) Edward

Eastlake, William (Derry) 1917-1997 .... **CLC 8**
See also CA 5-8R; 1; CAAS 158; CANR 5, 63; CN 1, 2, 3, 4, 5, 6; DLB 6, 206; INT CANR-5; MAL 5; TCWW 1, 2

Eastman, Charles A(lexander) 1858-1939 .... **NNAL; TCLC 55**
See also CA 179; CANR 91; DAM MULT; DLB 175; YABC 1

Eaton, Edith Maude 1865-1914 .... **AAL**
See Far, Sui Sin
See also CA 154; DLB 221, 312; FW

Eaton, (Lillie) Winnifred 1875-1954 .... **AAL**
See also CA 217; DLB 221, 312; RGAL 4

Eberhart, Richard 1904-2005 ...... **CLC 3, 11, 19, 56; PC 76**
See also AMW; CA 1-4R; CAAS 240; CANR 2, 125; CDALB 1941-1968; CP 1, 2, 3, 4, 5, 6, 7; DAM POET; DLB 48; MAL 5; MTCW 1; RGAL 4

Eberhart, Richard Ghormley
See Eberhart, Richard

Eberstadt, Fernanda 1960- .... **CLC 39**
See also CA 136; CANR 69, 128

Echegaray (y Eizaguirre), Jose (Maria Waldo) 1832-1916 .... **HLCS 1; TCLC 4**
See also CAAE 104; CANR 32; DLB 329; EWL 3; HW 1; MTCW 1

Echeverria, (Jose) Esteban (Antonino) 1805-1851 .... **NCLC 18**
See also LAW

Echo
See Proust, (Valentin-Louis-George-Eugene) Marcel

Eckert, Allan W. 1931- .... **CLC 17**
See also AAYA 18; BYA 2; CA 13-16R; CANR 14, 45; INT CANR-14; MAICYA 2; MAICYAS 1; SAAS 21; SATA 29, 91; SATA-Brief 27

Eckhart, Meister 1260(?)-1327(?) .. **CMLC 9, 80**
See also DLB 115; LMFS 1

Eckmar, F. R.
See de Hartog, Jan

Eco, Umberto 1932- .... **CLC 28, 60, 142**
See also BEST 90:1; BPFB 1; CA 77-80; CANR 12, 33, 55, 110, 131; CPW; CWW 2; DA3; DAM NOV, POP; DLB 196, 242; EWL 3; MSW; MTCW 1, 2; MTFW 2005; NFS 22; RGWL 3; WLIT 7

Eddison, E(ric) R(ucker) 1882-1945 .... **TCLC 15**
See also CA 156; CAAE 109; DLB 255; FANT; SFW 4; SUFW 1

Eddy, Mary (Ann Morse) Baker 1821-1910 .... **TCLC 71**
See also CA 174; CAAE 113

Edel, (Joseph) Leon 1907-1997 .. **CLC 29, 34**
See also CA 1-4R; CAAS 161; CANR 1, 22, 112; DLB 103; INT CANR-22

Eden, Emily 1797-1869 .... **NCLC 10**

Edgar, David 1948- .... **CLC 42**
See also CA 57-60; CANR 12, 61, 112; CBD; CD 5, 6; DAM DRAM; DFS 15; DLB 13, 233; MTCW 1

Edgerton, Clyde (Carlyle) 1944- ...... **CLC 39**
See also AAYA 17; CA 134; CAAE 118; CANR 64, 125; CN 7; CSW; DLB 278; INT CA-134; TCLE 1:1; YAW

Edgeworth, Maria 1768-1849 ... **NCLC 1, 51, 158; SSC 86**
See also BRWS 3; DLB 116, 159, 163; FL 1:3; FW; RGEL 2; SATA 21; TEA; WLIT 3

Edmonds, Paul
See Kuttner, Henry

Edmonds, Walter D(umaux) 1903-1998 .... **CLC 35**
See also BYA 2; CA 5-8R; CANR 2; CWRI 5; DLB 9; LAIT 1; MAICYA 1, 2; MAL 5; RHW; SAAS 4; SATA 1, 27; SATA-Obit 99

Edmondson, Wallace
See Ellison, Harlan

Edson, Margaret 1961- ...... **CLC 199; DC 24**
See also CA 190; DFS 13; DLB 266

Edson, Russell 1935- .... **CLC 13**
See also CA 33-36R; CANR 115; CP 2, 3, 4, 5, 6, 7; DLB 244; WP

Edwards, Bronwen Elizabeth
See Rose, Wendy

Edwards, G(erald) B(asil) 1899-1976 .... **CLC 25**
See also CA 201; CAAS 110

Edwards, Gus 1939- .... **CLC 43**
See also CA 108; INT CA-108

Edwards, Jonathan 1703-1758 .... **LC 7, 54**
See also AMW; DA; DAC; DAM MST; DLB 24, 270; RGAL 4; TUS

Edwards, Sarah Pierpont 1710-1758 .. **LC 87**
See also DLB 200

Efron, Marina Ivanovna Tsvetaeva
See Tsvetaeva (Efron), Marina (Ivanovna)

Egeria fl. 4th cent. - .... **CMLC 70**

Egoyan, Atom 1960- .... **CLC 151**
See also AAYA 63; CA 157; CANR 151

Ehle, John (Marsden, Jr.) 1925- ...... **CLC 27**
See also CA 9-12R; CSW

Ehrenbourg, Ilya (Grigoryevich)
See Ehrenburg, Ilya (Grigoryevich)

Ehrenburg, Ilya (Grigoryevich) 1891-1967 .... **CLC 18, 34, 62**
See Erenburg, Il'ia Grigor'evich
See also CA 102; CAAS 25-28R; EWL 3

Ehrenburg, Ilyo (Grigoryevich)
See Ehrenburg, Ilya (Grigoryevich)

Ehrenreich, Barbara 1941- .... **CLC 110**
See also BEST 90:4; CA 73-76; CANR 16, 37, 62, 117; DLB 246; FW; MTCW 1, 2; MTFW 2005

Eich, Gunter
See Eich, Gunter
See also RGWL 2, 3

Eich, Gunter 1907-1972 .... **CLC 15**
See Eich, Gunter
See also CA 111; CAAS 93-96; DLB 69, 124; EWL 3

Eichendorff, Joseph 1788-1857 .... **NCLC 8**
See also DLB 90; RGWL 2, 3

Eigner, Larry .... **CLC 9**
See Eigner, Laurence (Joel)
See also CA 23; CP 1, 2, 3, 4, 5, 6; DLB 5; WP

Eigner, Laurence (Joel) 1927-1996
See Eigner, Larry
See also CA 9-12R; CAAS 151; CANR 6, 84; CP 7; DLB 193

Eilhart von Oberge c. 1140-c. 1195 .... **CMLC 67**
See also DLB 148

Einhard c. 770-840 .... **CMLC 50**
See also DLB 148

Einstein, Albert 1879-1955 .... **TCLC 65**
See also CA 133; CAAE 121; MTCW 1, 2

Eiseley, Loren
See Eiseley, Loren Corey
See also DLB 275

Eiseley, Loren Corey 1907-1977 ...... **CLC 7**
See Eiseley, Loren
See also AAYA 5; ANW; CA 1-4R; CAAS 73-76; CANR 6; DLBD 17

Eisenstadt, Jill 1963- .... **CLC 50**
See also CA 140

Eisenstein, Sergei (Mikhailovich) 1898-1948 .... **TCLC 57**
See also CA 149; CAAE 114

Eisner, Simon
See Kornbluth, C(yril) M.

Eisner, Will 1917-2005 .... **CLC 237**
See also AAYA 52; CA 108; CAAS 235; CANR 114, 140; MTFW 2005; SATA 31, 165

Eisner, William Erwin
See Eisner, Will

Ekeloef, (Bengt) Gunnar 1907-1968 .... **CLC 27; PC 23**
See Ekelof, (Bengt) Gunnar
See also CA 123; CAAS 25-28R; DAM POET

Ekelof, (Bengt) Gunnar 1907-1968
See Ekeloef, (Bengt) Gunnar
See also DLB 259; EW 12; EWL 3

Ekelund, Vilhelm 1880-1949 .... **TCLC 75**
See also CA 189; EWL 3

Ekwensi, C. O. D.
See Ekwensi, Cyprian (Odiatu Duaka)

Ekwensi, Cyprian (Odiatu Duaka) 1921- .... **BLC 1; CLC 4**
See also AFW; BW 2, 3; CA 29-32R; CANR 18, 42, 74, 125; CDWLB 3; CN 1, 2, 3, 4, 5, 6; CWRI 5; DAM MULT; DLB 117; EWL 3; MTCW 1, 2; RGEL 2; SATA 66; WLIT 2

Elaine .... **TCLC 18**
See Leverson, Ada Esther

El Crummo
See Crumb, R.

Elder, Lonne III 1931-1996 ..... **BLC 1; DC 8**
See also BW 1, 3; CA 81-84; CAAS 152; CAD; CANR 25; DAM MULT; DLB 7, 38, 44; MAL 5

Eleanor of Aquitaine 1122-1204 ... **CMLC 39**

Elia
See Lamb, Charles

Eliade, Mircea 1907-1986 .... **CLC 19**
See also CA 65-68; CAAS 119; CANR 30, 62; CDWLB 4; DLB 220; EWL 3; MTCW 1; RGWL 3; SFW 4

Eliot, A. D.
See Jewett, (Theodora) Sarah Orne

Eliot, Alice
See Jewett, (Theodora) Sarah Orne

Eliot, Dan
See Silverberg, Robert

Eliot, George 1819-1880 ...... **NCLC 4, 13, 23, 41, 49, 89, 118, 183; PC 20; SSC 72; WLC 2**
See Evans, Mary Ann
See also BRW 5; BRWC 1, 2; BRWR 2; CDBLB 1832-1890; CN 7; CPW; DA; DA3; DAB; DAC; DAM MST, NOV; DLB 21, 35, 55; FL 1:3; LATS 1:1; LMFS 1; NFS 17, 20; RGEL 2; RGSF 2; SSFS 8; TEA; WLIT 3

Eliot, John 1604-1690 .... **LC 5**
See also DLB 24

Eliot, T(homas) S(tearns) 1888-1965 ...... **CLC 1, 2, 3, 6, 9, 10, 13, 15, 24, 34, 41, 55, 57, 113; PC 5, 31; WLC 2**
See also AAYA 28; AMW; AMWC 1; AMWR 1; BRW 7; BRWR 2; CA 5-8R; CAAS 25-28R; CANR 41; CBD; CDALB 1929-1941; DA; DA3; DAB; DAC; DAM DRAM, MST, POET; DFS 4, 13; DLB 7, 10, 45, 63, 245, 329; DLBY 1988; EWL 3; EXPP; LAIT 3; LATS 1:1; LMFS 2; MAL 5; MTCW 1, 2; MTFW 2005; NCFS 5; PAB; PFS 1, 7, 20; RGAL 4; RGEL 2; TUS; WLIT 4; WP

Elisabeth of Schonau c. 1129-1165 .... **CMLC 82**

Elizabeth 1866-1941 .... **TCLC 41**

Elizabeth I 1533-1603 .... **LC 118**
See also DLB 136

Elkin, Stanley L. 1930-1995 ...... **CLC 4, 6, 9, 14, 27, 51, 91; SSC 12**
See also AMWS 6; BPFB 1; CA 9-12R; CAAS 148; CANR 8, 46; CN 1, 2, 3, 4, 5, 6; CPW; DAM NOV, POP; DLB 2, 28, 218, 278; DLBY 1980; EWL 3; INT CANR-8; MAL 5; MTCW 1, 2; MTFW 2005; RGAL 4; TCLE 1:1

Elledge, Scott .... **CLC 34**

Eller, Scott
See Shepard, Jim

Elliott, Don
See Silverberg, Robert

Cumulative Author Index

Garcilaso de la Vega, El Inca
1539-1616 .... **HLCS 1; LC 127**
See also DLB 318; LAW

Gard, Janice
See Latham, Jean Lee

Gard, Roger Martin du
See Martin du Gard, Roger

Gardam, Jane (Mary) 1928- .... **CLC 43**
See also CA 49-52; CANR 2, 18, 33, 54,
106; CLR 12; DLB 14, 161, 231; MAI-
CYA 1, 2; MTCW 1; SAAS 9; SATA 39,
76, 130; SATA-Brief 28; YAW

Gardner, Herb(ert George)
1934-2003 .... **CLC 44**
See also CA 149; CAAS 220; CAD; CANR
119; CD 5, 6; DFS 18, 20

Gardner, John, Jr. 1933-1982 ... **CLC 2, 3, 5,
7, 8, 10, 18, 28, 34; SSC 7**
See also AAYA 45; AITN 1; AMWS 6;
BPFB 2; CA 65-68; CANR 33, 73; CDALBS; CN 2, 3; CPW; DA3;
DAM NOV, POP; DLB 2; DLBY 1982;
EWL 3; FANT; LATS 1:2; MAL 5;
MTCW 1, 2; MTFW 2005; NFS 3; RGAL
4; RGSF 2; SATA 40; SATA-Obit 31;
SSFS 8

Gardner, John (Edmund) 1926- ...... **CLC 30**
See also CA 103; CANR 15, 69, 127; CMW
4; CPW; DAM POP; MTCW 1

Gardner, Miriam
See Bradley, Marion Zimmer
See also GLL 1

Gardner, Noel
See Kuttner, Henry

Gardons, S. S.
See Snodgrass, W.D.

Garfield, Leon 1921-1996 .... **CLC 12**
See also AAYA 8, 69; BYA 1, 3; CA 17-
20R; CAAS 152; CANR 38, 41, 78; CLR
21; DLB 161; JRDA; MAICYA 1, 2;
MAICYAS 1; SATA 1, 32, 76; SATA-Obit
90; TEA; WYA; YAW

Garland, (Hannibal) Hamlin
1860-1940 .... **SSC 18; TCLC 3**
See also CAAE 104; DLB 12, 71, 78, 186;
MAL 5; RGAL 4; RGSF 2; TCWW 1, 2

Garneau, (Hector de) Saint-Denys
1912-1943 .... **TCLC 13**
See also CAAE 111; DLB 88

Garner, Alan 1934- .... **CLC 17**
See also AAYA 18; BYA 3, 5; CA 178; 73-
76, 178; CANR 15, 64, 134; CLR 20;
CPW; DAB; DAM POP; DLB 161, 261;
FANT; MAICYA 1, 2; MTCW 1, 2;
MTFW 2005; SATA 18, 69; SATA-Essay
108; SUFW 1, 2; YAW

Garner, Hugh 1913-1979 .... **CLC 13**
See Warwick, Jarvis
See also CA 69-72; CANR 31; CCA 1; CN
1, 2; DLB 68

Garnett, David 1892-1981 .... **CLC 3**
See also CA 5-8R; CAAS 103; CANR 17,
79; CN 1, 2; DLB 34; FANT; MTCW 2;
RGEL 2; SFW 4; SUFW 1

Garnier, Robert c. 1545-1590 .... **LC 119**
See also DLB 327; GFL Beginnings to 1789

Garrett, George (Palmer, Jr.) 1929- . **CLC 3,
11, 51; SSC 30**
See also AMWS 7; BPFB 2; CA 202; 1-4R,
202; 5; CANR 1, 42, 67, 109; CN 1, 2, 3,
4, 5, 6, 7; CP 1, 2, 3, 4, 5, 6, 7; CSW;
DLB 2, 5, 130, 152; DLBY 1983

Garrick, David 1717-1779 .... **LC 15**
See also DAM DRAM; DLB 84, 213;
RGEL 2

Garrigue, Jean 1914-1972 .... **CLC 2, 8**
See also CA 5-8R; CAAS 37-40R; CANR
20; CP 1; MAL 5

Garrison, Frederick
See Sinclair, Upton

Garrison, William Lloyd
1805-1879 .... **NCLC 149**
See also CDALB 1640-1865; DLB 1, 43,
235

Garro, Elena 1920(?)-1998 .. **HLCS 1; TCLC
153**
See also CA 131; CAAS 169; CWW 2;
DLB 145; EWL 3; HW 1; LAWS 1; WLIT
1

Garth, Will
See Hamilton, Edmond; Kuttner, Henry

Garvey, Marcus (Moziah, Jr.)
1887-1940 ... **BLC 2; HR 1:2; TCLC 41**
See also BW 1; CA 124; CAAE 120; CANR
79; DAM MULT

Gary, Romain .... **CLC 25**
See Kacew, Romain
See also DLB 83, 299; RGHL

Gascar, Pierre .... **CLC 11**
See Fournier, Pierre
See also EWL 3; RGHL

Gascoigne, George 1539-1577 .... **LC 108**
See also DLB 136; RGEL 2

Gascoyne, David (Emery)
1916-2001 .... **CLC 45**
See also CA 65-68; CAAS 200; CANR 10,
28, 54; CP 1, 2, 3, 4, 5, 6, 7; DLB 20;
MTCW 1; RGEL 2

Gaskell, Elizabeth Cleghorn
1810-1865 .... **NCLC 5, 70, 97, 137; SSC
25, 97**
See also BRW 5; CDBLB 1832-1890; DAB;
DAM MST; DLB 21, 144, 159; RGEL 2;
RGSF 2; TEA

Gass, William H. 1924- . **CLC 1, 2, 8, 11, 15,
39, 132; SSC 12**
See also AMWS 6; CA 17-20R; CANR 30,
71, 100; CN 1, 2, 3, 4, 5, 6, 7; DLB 2,
227; EWL 3; MAL 5; MTCW 1, 2;
MTFW 2005; RGAL 4

Gassendi, Pierre 1592-1655 .... **LC 54**
See also GFL Beginnings to 1789

Gasset, Jose Ortega y
See Ortega y Gasset, Jose

Gates, Henry Louis, Jr. 1950- ... **BLCS; CLC
65**
See also BW 2, 3; CA 109; CANR 25, 53,
75, 125; CSW; DA3; DAM MULT; DLB
67; EWL 3; MAL 5; MTCW 2; MTFW
2005; RGAL 4

Gatos, Stephanie
See Katz, Steve

Gautier, Theophile 1811-1872 .. **NCLC 1, 59;
PC 18; SSC 20**
See also DAM POET; DLB 119; EW 6;
GFL 1789 to the Present; RGWL 2, 3;
SUFW; TWA

Gay, John 1685-1732 .... **LC 49**
See also BRW 3; DAM DRAM; DLB 84,
95; RGEL 2; WLIT 3

Gay, Oliver
See Gogarty, Oliver St. John

Gay, Peter 1923- .... **CLC 158**
See also CA 13-16R; CANR 18, 41, 77,
147; INT CANR-18; RGHL

Gay, Peter Jack
See Gay, Peter

Gaye, Marvin (Pentz, Jr.)
1939-1984 .... **CLC 26**
See also CA 195; CAAS 112

Gebler, Carlo 1954- .... **CLC 39**
See also CA 133; CAAE 119; CANR 96;
DLB 271

Gee, Maggie 1948- .... **CLC 57**
See also CA 130; CANR 125; CN 4, 5, 6,
7; DLB 207; MTFW 2005

Gee, Maurice 1931- .... **CLC 29**
See also AAYA 42; CA 97-100; CANR 67,
123; CLR 56; CN 2, 3, 4, 5, 6, 7; CWRI
5; EWL 3; MAICYA 2; RGSF 2; SATA
46, 101

Gee, Maurice Gough
See Gee, Maurice

Geiogamah, Hanay 1945- .... **NNAL**
See also CA 153; DAM MULT; DLB 175

Gelbart, Larry
See Gelbart, Larry (Simon)
See also CAD; CD 5, 6

Gelbart, Larry (Simon) 1928- .... **CLC 21, 61**
See Gelbart, Larry
See also CA 73-76; CANR 45, 94

Gelber, Jack 1932-2003 ...... **CLC 1, 6, 14, 79**
See also CA 1-4R; CAAS 216; CAD;
CANR 2; DLB 7, 228; MAL 5

Gellhorn, Martha (Ellis)
1908-1998 .... **CLC 14, 60**
See also CA 77-80; CAAS 164; CANR 44;
CN 1, 2, 3, 4, 5, 6 7; DLBY 1982, 1998

Genet, Jean 1910-1986 .. **CLC 1, 2, 5, 10, 14,
44, 46; DC 25; TCLC 128**
See also CA 13-16R; CANR 18; DA3;
DAM DRAM; DFS 10; DLB 72, 321;
DLBY 1986; EW 13; EWL 3; GFL 1789
to the Present; GLL 1; LMFS 2; MTCW
1, 2; MTFW 2005; RGWL 2, 3; TWA

Genlis, Stephanie-Felicite Ducrest
1746-1830 .... **NCLC 166**
See also DLB 313

Gent, Peter 1942- .... **CLC 29**
See also AITN 1; CA 89-92; DLBY 1982

Gentile, Giovanni 1875-1944 .... **TCLC 96**
See also CAAE 119

Geoffrey of Monmouth c.
1100-1155 .... **CMLC 44**
See also DLB 146; TEA

George, Jean
See George, Jean Craighead

George, Jean Craighead 1919- .... **CLC 35**
See also AAYA 8, 69; BYA 2, 4; CA 5-8R;
CANR 25; CLR 1; 80; DLB 52; JRDA;
MAICYA 1, 2; SATA 2, 68, 124, 170;
WYA; YAW

George, Stefan (Anton) 1868-1933 . **TCLC 2,
14**
See also CA 193; CAAE 104; EW 8; EWL
3

Georges, Georges Martin
See Simenon, Georges (Jacques Christian)

Gerald of Wales c. 1146-c. 1223 ... **CMLC 60**

Gerhardi, William Alexander
See Gerhardie, William Alexander

Gerhardie, William Alexander
1895-1977 .... **CLC 5**
See also CA 25-28R; CAAS 73-76; CANR
18; CN 1, 2; DLB 36; RGEL 2

Gerson, Jean 1363-1429 .... **LC 77**
See also DLB 208

Gersonides 1288-1344 .... **CMLC 49**
See also DLB 115

Gerstler, Amy 1956- .... **CLC 70**
See also CA 146; CANR 99

Gertler, T. .... **CLC 34**
See also CA 121; CAAE 116

Gertsen, Aleksandr Ivanovich
See Herzen, Aleksandr Ivanovich

Ghalib .... **NCLC 39, 78**
See Ghalib, Asadullah Khan

Ghalib, Asadullah Khan 1797-1869
See Ghalib
See also DAM POET; RGWL 2, 3

Ghelderode, Michel de 1898-1962 ..... **CLC 6,
11; DC 15; TCLC 187**
See also CA 85-88; CANR 40, 77; DAM
DRAM; DLB 321; EW 11; EWL 3; TWA

Cumulative Author Index

Ghiselin, Brewster 1903-2001 .... **CLC 23**
See also CA 13-16R; 10; CANR 13; CP 1,
2, 3, 4, 5, 6, 7

Ghose, Aurabinda 1872-1950 .... **TCLC 63**
See Ghose, Aurobindo
See also CA 163

Ghose, Aurobindo
See Ghose, Aurabinda
See also EWL 3

Ghose, Zulfikar 1935- .... **CLC 42, 200**
See also CA 65-68; CANR 67; CN 1, 2, 3,
4, 5, 6, 7; CP 1, 2, 3, 4, 5, 6, 7; DLB 323;
EWL 3

Ghosh, Amitav 1956- .... **CLC 44, 153**
See also CA 147; CANR 80, 158; CN 6, 7;
DLB 323; WWE 1

Giacosa, Giuseppe 1847-1906 .... **TCLC 7**
See also CAAE 104

Gibb, Lee
See Waterhouse, Keith (Spencer)

Gibbon, Edward 1737-1794 .... **LC 97**
See also BRW 3; DLB 104, 336; RGEL 2

Gibbon, Lewis Grassic .... **TCLC 4**
See Mitchell, James Leslie
See also RGEL 2

Gibbons, Kaye 1960- .... **CLC 50, 88, 145**
See also AAYA 34; AMWS 10; CA 151;
CANR 75, 127; CN 7; CSW; DA3; DAM
POP; DLB 292; MTCW 2; MTFW 2005;
NFS 3; RGAL 4; SATA 117

Gibran, Kahlil 1883-1931 . **PC 9; TCLC 1, 9**
See also CAAE 104; DA3; DAM
POET, POP; EWL 3; MTCW 2; WLIT 6

Gibran, Khalil
See Gibran, Kahlil

Gibson, Mel 1956- .... **CLC 215**

Gibson, William 1914- .... **CLC 23**
See also CA 9-12R; CAD; CANR 9, 42, 75,
125; CD 5, 6; DA; DAB; DAC; DAM
DRAM, MST; DFS 2; DLB 7; LAIT 2;
MAL 5; MTCW 2; MTFW 2005; SATA
66; YAW

Gibson, William 1948- .... **CLC 39, 63, 186,
192; SSC 52**
See also AAYA 12, 59; AMWS 16; BPFB
2; CA 133; CAAE 126; CANR 52, 90,
106; CN 6, 7; CPW; DA3; DAM POP;
DLB 251; MTCW 2; MTFW 2005; SCFW
2; SFW 4

Gibson, William Ford
See Gibson, William

Gide, Andre (Paul Guillaume)
1869-1951 ...... **SSC 13; TCLC 5, 12, 36,
177; WLC 3**
See also CA 124; CAAE 104; DA; DA3;
DAB; DAC; DAM MST, NOV; DLB 65,
321, 330; EW 8; EWL 3; GFL 1789 to
the Present; MTCW 1, 2; MTFW 2005;
NFS 21; RGSF 2; RGWL 2, 3; TWA

Gifford, Barry (Colby) 1946- .... **CLC 34**
See also CA 65-68; CANR 9, 30, 40, 90

Gilbert, Frank
See De Voto, Bernard (Augustine)

Gilbert, W(illiam) S(chwenck)
1836-1911 .... **TCLC 3**
See also CA 173; CAAE 104; DAM DRAM,
POET; RGEL 2; SATA 36

Gilbert of Poitiers c. 1085-1154 .... **CMLC 85**

Gilbreth, Frank B(unker), Jr.
1911-2001 .... **CLC 17**
See also CA 9-12R; SATA 2

Gilchrist, Ellen (Louise) 1935- .. **CLC 34, 48,
143; SSC 14, 63**
See also BPFB 2; CA 116; CAAE 113;
CANR 41, 61, 104; CN 4, 5, 6, 7; CPW;
CSW; DAM POP; DLB 130; EWL 3;
EXPS; MTCW 1, 2; MTFW 2005; RGAL
4; RGSF 2; SSFS 9

Giles, Molly 1942- .... **CLC 39**
See also CA 126; CANR 98

Gill, Eric .... **TCLC 85**
See Gill, (Arthur) Eric (Rowton Peter
Joseph)

Gill, (Arthur) Eric (Rowton Peter Joseph)
1882-1940
See Gill, Eric
See also CAAE 120; DLB 98

Gill, Patrick
See Creasey, John

Gillette, Douglas .... **CLC 70**

Gilliam, Terry 1940- .... **CLC 21, 141**
See Monty Python
See also AAYA 19, 59; CA 113; CAAE 108;
CANR 35; INT CA-113

Gilliam, Terry Vance
See Gilliam, Terry

Gillian, Jerry
See Gilliam, Terry

Gilliatt, Penelope (Ann Douglass)
1932-1993 .... **CLC 2, 10, 13, 53**
See also AITN 2; CA 13-16R; CAAS 141;
CANR 49; CN 1, 2, 3, 4, 5; DLB 14

Gilligan, Carol 1936- .... **CLC 208**
See also CA 142; CANR 121; FW

Gilman, Charlotte (Anna) Perkins (Stetson)
1860-1935 ...... **SSC 13, 62; TCLC 9, 37,
117**
See also AAYA 75; AMWS 11; BYA 11;
CA 150; CAAE 106; DLB 221; EXPS;
FL 1:5; FW; HGG; LAIT 2; MBL; MTCW
2; MTFW 2005; RGAL 4; RGSF 2; SFW
4; SSFS 1, 18

Gilmour, David 1946- .... **CLC 35**

Gilpin, William 1724-1804 .... **NCLC 30**

Gilray, J. D.
See Mencken, H(enry) L(ouis)

Gilroy, Frank D(aniel) 1925- .... **CLC 2**
See also CA 81-84; CAD; CANR 32, 64,
86; CD 5, 6; DFS 17; DLB 7

Gilstrap, John 1957(?)- .... **CLC 99**
See also CA 160; CANR 101

Ginsberg, Allen 1926-1997 .... **CLC 1, 2, 3, 4,
6, 13, 36, 69, 109; PC 4, 47; TCLC
120; WLC 3**
See also AAYA 33; AITN 1; AMWC 1;
AMWS 2; BG 1:2; CA 1-4R; CAAS 157;
CANR 2, 41, 63, 95; CDALB 1941-1968;
CP 1, 2, 3, 4, 5, 6; DA; DA3; DAB; DAC;
DAM MST, POET; DLB 5, 16, 169, 237;
EWL 3; GLL 1; LMFS 2; MAL 5; MTCW
1, 2; MTFW 2005; PAB; PFS 5; RGAL 4;
TUS; WP

Ginzburg, Eugenia ....'...................... **CLC 59**
See Ginzburg, Evgeniia

Ginzburg, Evgeniia 1904-1977
See Ginzburg, Eugenia
See also DLB 302

Ginzburg, Natalia 1916-1991 .... **CLC 5, 11,
54, 70; SSC 65; TCLC 156**
See also CA 85-88; CAAS 135; CANR 33;
DFS 14; DLB 177; EW 13; EWL 3;
MTCW 1, 2; MTFW 2005; RGHL;
RGWL 2, 3

Giono, Jean 1895-1970 .... **CLC 4, 11; TCLC
124**
See also CA 45-48; CAAS 29-32R; CANR
2, 35; DLB 72, 321; EWL 3; GFL 1789
to the Present; MTCW 1; RGWL 2, 3

Giovanni, Nikki 1943- ...... **BLC 2; CLC 2, 4,
19, 64, 117; PC 19; WLCS**
See also AAYA 22; AITN 1; BW 2, 3; CA
29-32R; 6; CANR 18, 41, 60, 91, 130;
CDALBS; CLR 6, 73; CP 2, 3, 4, 5, 6, 7;
CSW; CWP; CWRI 5; DA; DA3; DAB;
DAC; DAM MST, MULT, POET; DLB 5,

41; EWL 3; EXPP; INT CANR-18; MAI-
CYA 1, 2; MAL 5; MTCW 1, 2; MTFW
2005; PFS 17; RGAL 4; SATA 24, 107;
TUS; YAW

Giovene, Andrea 1904-1998 .... **CLC 7**
See also CA 85-88

Gippius, Zinaida (Nikolaevna) 1869-1945
See Hippius, Zinaida (Nikolaevna)
See also CA 212; CAAE 106

Giraudoux, Jean(-Hippolyte)
1882-1944 .... **TCLC 2, 7**
See also CA 196; CAAE 104; DAM
DRAM; DLB 65, 321; EW 9; EWL 3;
GFL 1789 to the Present; RGWL 2, 3;
TWA

Gironella, Jose Maria (Pous)
1917-2003 .... **CLC 11**
See also CA 101; CAAS 212; EWL 3;
RGWL 2, 3

Gissing, George (Robert)
1857-1903 .... **SSC 37; TCLC 3, 24, 47**
See also BRW 5; CA 167; CAAE 105; DLB
18, 135, 184; RGEL 2; TEA

Gitlin, Todd 1943- .... **CLC 201**
See also CA 29-32R; CANR 25, 50, 88

Giurlani, Aldo
See Palazzeschi, Aldo

Gladkov, Fedor Vasil'evich
See Gladkov, Fyodor (Vasilyevich)
See also DLB 272

Gladkov, Fyodor (Vasilyevich)
1883-1958 .... **TCLC 27**
See Gladkov, Fedor Vasil'evich
See also CA 170; EWL 3

Glancy, Diane 1941- .... **CLC 210; NNAL**
See also CA 225; 136, 225; 24; CANR 87,
162; DLB 175

Glanville, Brian (Lester) 1931- .... **CLC 6**
See also CA 5-8R; 9; CANR 3, 70; CN 1,
2, 3, 4, 5, 6, 7; DLB 15, 139; SATA 42

Glasgow, Ellen (Anderson Gholson)
1873-1945 .... **SSC 34; TCLC 2, 7**
See also AMW; CA 164; CAAE 104; DLB
9, 12; MAL 5; MBL; MTCW 2; MTFW
2005; RGAL 4; RHW; SSFS 9; TUS

Glaspell, Susan 1882(?)-1948 ..... **DC 10; SSC
41; TCLC 55, 175**
See also AMWS 3; CA 154; CAAE 110;
DFS 8, 18, 24; DLB 7, 9, 78, 228; MBL;
RGAL 4; SSFS 3; TCWW 2; TUS; YABC
2

Glassco, John 1909-1981 .... **CLC 9**
See also CA 13-16R; CAAS 102; CANR
15; CN 1, 2; CP 1, 2, 3; DLB 68

Glasscock, Amnesia
See Steinbeck, John (Ernst)

Glasser, Ronald J. 1940(?)- .... **CLC 37**
See also CA 209

Glassman, Joyce
See Johnson, Joyce

Gleick, James (W.) 1954- .... **CLC 147**
See also CA 137; CAAE 131; CANR 97;
INT CA-137

Glendinning, Victoria 1937- .... **CLC 50**
See also CA 127; CAAE 120; CANR 59,
89; DLB 155

Glissant, Edouard (Mathieu)
1928- .... **CLC 10, 68**
See also CA 153; CANR 111; CWW 2;
DAM MULT; EWL 3; RGWL 3

Gloag, Julian 1930- .... **CLC 40**
See also AITN 1; CA 65-68; CANR 10, 70;
CN 1, 2, 3, 4, 5, 6

Glowacki, Aleksander
See Prus, Boleslaw

Greenberg, Richard 1959(?)- .... **CLC 57**
See also CA 138; CAD; CD 5, 6; DFS 24
Greenblatt, Stephen J(ay) 1943- ...... **CLC 70**
See also CA 49-52; CANR 115
Greene, Bette 1934- .... **CLC 30**
See also AAYA 7, 69; BYA 3; CA 53-56;
CANR 4, 146; CLR 2; CWRI 5; JRDA;
LAIT 4; MAICYA 1, 2; NFS 10; SAAS
16; SATA 8, 102, 161; WYA; YAW
Greene, Gael .... **CLC 8**
See also CA 13-16R; CANR 10
Greene, Graham 1904-1991 .. **CLC 1, 3, 6, 9,
14, 18, 27, 37, 70, 72, 125; SSC 29;
WLC 3**
See also AAYA 61; AITN 2; BPFB 2;
BRWR 2; BRWS 1; BYA 3; CA 13-16R;
CAAS 133; CANR 35, 61, 131; CBD;
CDBLB 1945-1960; CMW 4; CN 1, 2, 3,
4; DA; DA3; DAB; DAC; DAM MST,
NOV; DLB 13, 15, 77, 100, 162, 201,
204; DLBY 1991; EWL 3; MSW; MTCW
1, 2; MTFW 2005; NFS 16; RGEL 2;
SATA 20; SSFS 14; TEA; WLIT 4
Greene, Robert 1558-1592 .... **LC 41**
See also BRWS 8; DLB 62, 167; IDTP;
RGEL 2; TEA
Greer, Germaine 1939- .... **CLC 131**
See also AITN 1; CA 81-84; CANR 33, 70,
115, 133; FW; MTCW 1, 2; MTFW 2005
Greer, Richard
See Silverberg, Robert
Gregor, Arthur 1923- .... **CLC 9**
See also CA 25-28R; 10; CANR 11; CP 1,
2, 3, 4, 5, 6, 7; SATA 36
Gregor, Lee
See Pohl, Frederik
Gregory, Lady Isabella Augusta (Persse)
1852-1932 .... **TCLC 1, 176**
See also BRW 6; CA 184; CAAE 104; DLB
10; IDTP; RGEL 2
Gregory, J. Dennis
See Williams, John A(lfred)
Gregory of Nazianzus, St.
329-389 .... **CMLC 82**
Grekova, I. .... **CLC 59**
See Ventsel, Elena Sergeevna
See also CWW 2
Grendon, Stephen
See Derleth, August (William)
Grenville, Kate 1950- .... **CLC 61**
See also CA 118; CANR 53, 93, 156; CN
7; DLB 325
Grenville, Pelham
See Wodehouse, P(elham) G(renville)
Greve, Felix Paul (Berthold Friedrich)
1879-1948
See Grove, Frederick Philip
See also CA 141, 175; CAAE 104; CANR
79; DAC; DAM MST
Greville, Fulke 1554-1628 .... **LC 79**
See also BRWS 11; DLB 62, 172; RGEL 2
Grey, Lady Jane 1537-1554 .... **LC 93**
See also DLB 132
Grey, Zane 1872-1939 .... **TCLC 6**
See also BPFB 2; CA 132; CAAE 104;
DA3; DAM POP; DLB 9, 212; MTCW 1,
2; MTFW 2005; RGAL 4; TCWW 1, 2;
TUS
Griboedov, Aleksandr Sergeevich
1795(?)-1829 .... **NCLC 129**
See also DLB 205; RGWL 2, 3
Grieg, (Johan) Nordahl (Brun)
1902-1943 .... **TCLC 10**
See also CA 189; CAAE 107; EWL 3
Grieve, C(hristopher) M(urray)
1892-1978 .... **CLC 11, 19**
See MacDiarmid, Hugh; Pteleon
See also CA 5-8R; CAAS 85-88; CANR
33, 107; DAM POET; MTCW 1; RGEL 2

Griffin, Gerald 1803-1840 .... **NCLC 7**
See also DLB 159; RGEL 2
Griffin, John Howard 1920-1980 ..... **CLC 68**
See also AITN 1; CA 1-4R; CAAS 101;
CANR 2
Griffin, Peter 1942- .... **CLC 39**
See also CA 136
Griffith, D(avid Lewelyn) W(ark)
1875(?)-1948 .... **TCLC 68**
See also CA 150; CAAE 119; CANR 80
Griffith, Lawrence
See Griffith, D(avid Lewelyn) W(ark)
Griffiths, Trevor 1935- .... **CLC 13, 52**
See also CA 97-100; CANR 45; CBD; CD
5, 6; DLB 13, 245
Griggs, Sutton (Elbert)
1872-1930 .... **TCLC 77**
See also CA 186; CAAE 123; DLB 50
Grigson, Geoffrey (Edward Harvey)
1905-1985 .... **CLC 7, 39**
See also CA 25-28R; CAAS 118; CANR
20, 33; CP 1, 2, 3, 4; DLB 27; MTCW 1,
2
Grile, Dod
See Bierce, Ambrose (Gwinett)
Grillparzer, Franz 1791-1872 .... **DC 14;
NCLC 1, 102; SSC 37**
See also CDWLB 2; DLB 133; EW 5;
RGWL 2, 3; TWA
Grimble, Reverend Charles James
See Eliot, T(homas) S(tearns)
Grimke, Angelina (Emily) Weld
1880-1958 .... **HR 1:2**
See Weld, Angelina (Emily) Grimke
See also BW 1; CA 124; DAM POET; DLB
50, 54
Grimke, Charlotte L(ottie) Forten
1837(?)-1914
See Forten, Charlotte L.
See also BW 1; CA 124; CAAE 117; DAM
MULT, POET
Grimm, Jacob Ludwig Karl
1785-1863 .... **NCLC 3, 77; SSC 36**
See Grimm Brothers
See also CLR 112; DLB 90; MAICYA 1, 2;
RGSF 2; RGWL 2, 3; SATA 22; WCH
Grimm, Wilhelm Karl 1786-1859 .. **NCLC 3,
77; SSC 36**
See Grimm Brothers
See also CDWLB 2; CLR 112; DLB 90;
MAICYA 1, 2; RGSF 2; RGWL 2, 3;
SATA 22; WCH
Grimm and Grim
See Grimm, Jacob Ludwig Karl; Grimm,
Wilhelm Karl
Grimm Brothers .... **SSC 88**
See Grimm, Jacob Ludwig Karl; Grimm,
Wilhelm Karl
See also CLR 112
Grimmelshausen, Hans Jakob Christoffel
von
See Grimmelshausen, Johann Jakob Christ-
offel von
See also RGWL 2, 3
Grimmelshausen, Johann Jakob Christoffel
von 1621-1676 .... **LC 6**
See Grimmelshausen, Hans Jakob Christof-
fel von
See also CDWLB 2; DLB 168
Grindel, Eugene 1895-1952
See Eluard, Paul
See also CA 193; CAAE 104; LMFS 2
Grisham, John 1955- .... **CLC 84**
See also AAYA 14, 47; BPFB 2; CA 138;
CANR 47, 69, 114, 133; CMW 4; CN 6,
7; CPW; CSW; DA3; DAM POP; MSW;
MTCW 2; MTFW 2005
Grosseteste, Robert 1175(?)-1253 . **CMLC 62**
See also DLB 115

Grossman, David 1954- .... **CLC 67, 231**
See also CA 138; CANR 114; CWW 2;
DLB 299; EWL 3; RGHL; WLIT 6
Grossman, Vasilii Semenovich
See Grossman, Vasily (Semenovich)
See also DLB 272
Grossman, Vasily (Semenovich)
1905-1964 .... **CLC 41**
See Grossman, Vasilii Semenovich
See also CA 130; CAAE 124; MTCW 1;
RGHL
Grove, Frederick Philip .... **TCLC 4**
See Greve, Felix Paul (Berthold Friedrich)
See also DLB 92; RGEL 2; TCWW 1, 2
Grubb
See Crumb, R.
Grumbach, Doris 1918- .... **CLC 13, 22, 64**
See also CA 5-8R; 2; CANR 9, 42, 70, 127;
CN 6, 7; INT CANR-9; MTCW 2; MTFW
2005
Grundtvig, Nikolai Frederik Severin
1783-1872 .... **NCLC 1, 158**
See also DLB 300
Grunge
See Crumb, R.
Grunwald, Lisa 1959- .... **CLC 44**
See also CA 120; CANR 148
Gryphius, Andreas 1616-1664 .... **LC 89**
See also CDWLB 2; DLB 164; RGWL 2, 3
Guare, John 1938- .... **CLC 8, 14, 29, 67; DC
20**
See also CA 73-76; CAD; CANR 21, 69,
118; CD 5, 6; DAM DRAM; DFS 8, 13;
DLB 7, 249; EWL 3; MAL 5; MTCW 1,
2; RGAL 4
Guarini, Battista 1537-1612 .... **LC 102**
Gubar, Susan (David) 1944- .... **CLC 145**
See also CA 108; CANR 45, 70, 139; FW;
MTCW 1; RGAL 4
Gudjonsson, Halldor Kiljan 1902-1998
See Halldor Laxness
See also CA 103; CAAS 164
Guenter, Erich
See Eich, Gunter
Guest, Barbara 1920-2006 ... **CLC 34; PC 55**
See also BG 1:2; CA 25-28R; CAAS 248;
CANR 11, 44, 84; CP 1, 2, 3, 4, 5, 6, 7;
CWP; DLB 5, 193
Guest, Edgar A(lbert) 1881-1959 ... **TCLC 95**
See also CA 168; CAAE 112
Guest, Judith 1936- .... **CLC 8, 30**
See also AAYA 7, 66; CA 77-80; CANR
15, 75, 138; DA3; DAM NOV, POP;
EXPN; INT CANR-15; LAIT 5; MTCW
1, 2; MTFW 2005; NFS 1
Guevara, Che .... **CLC 87; HLC 1**
See Guevara (Serna), Ernesto
Guevara (Serna), Ernesto
1928-1967 .... **CLC 87; HLC 1**
See Guevara, Che
See also CA 127; CAAS 111; CANR 56;
DAM MULT; HW 1
Guicciardini, Francesco 1483-1540 ..... **LC 49**
Guido delle Colonne c. 1215-c.
1290 .... **CMLC 90**
Guild, Nicholas M. 1944- .... **CLC 33**
See also CA 93-96
Guillemin, Jacques
See Sartre, Jean-Paul
Guillen, Jorge 1893-1984 . **CLC 11; HLCS 1;
PC 35**
See also CA 89-92; CAAS 112; DAM
MULT, POET; DLB 108; EWL 3; HW 1;
RGWL 2, 3

Guillen, Nicolas (Cristobal)
1902-1989 .... **BLC 2; CLC 48, 79; HLC 1; PC 23**
See also BW 2; CA 125; CAAE 116; CAAS 129; CANR 84; DAM MST, MULT, POET; DLB 283; EWL 3; HW 1; LAW; RGWL 2, 3; WP

Guillen y Alvarez, Jorge
See Guillen, Jorge

Guillevic, (Eugene) 1907-1997 .... **CLC 33**
See also CA 93-96; CWW 2

Guillois
See Desnos, Robert

Guillois, Valentin
See Desnos, Robert

Guimaraes Rosa, Joao 1908-1967 .... **HLCS 2**
See Rosa, Joao Guimaraes
See also CA 175; LAW; RGSF 2; RGWL 2, 3

Guiney, Louise Imogen
1861-1920 .... **TCLC 41**
See also CA 160; DLB 54; RGAL 4

Guinizelli, Guido c. 1230-1276 ...... **CMLC 49**
See Guinizzelli, Guido

Guinizzelli, Guido
See Guinizelli, Guido
See also WLIT 7

Guiraldes, Ricardo (Guillermo)
1886-1927 .... **TCLC 39**
See also CA 131; EWL 3; HW 1; LAW; MTCW 1

Gumilev, Nikolai (Stepanovich)
1886-1921 .... **TCLC 60**
See Gumilyov, Nikolay Stepanovich
See also CA 165; DLB 295

Gumilyov, Nikolay Stepanovich
See Gumilev, Nikolai (Stepanovich)
See also EWL 3

Gump, P. Q.
See Card, Orson Scott

Gunesekera, Romesh 1954- .... **CLC 91**
See also BRWS 10; CA 159; CANR 140; CN 6, 7; DLB 267, 323

Gunn, Bill .... **CLC 5**
See Gunn, William Harrison
See also DLB 38

Gunn, Thom(son William)
1929-2004 . **CLC 3, 6, 18, 32, 81; PC 26**
See also BRWS 4; CA 17-20R; CAAS 227; CANR 9, 33, 116; CDBLB 1960 to Present; CP 1, 2, 3, 4, 5, 6, 7; DAM POET; DLB 27; INT CANR-33; MTCW 1; PFS 9; RGEL 2

Gunn, William Harrison 1934(?)-1989
See Gunn, Bill
See also AITN 1; BW 1, 3; CA 13-16R; CAAS 128; CANR 12, 25, 76

Gunn Allen, Paula
See Allen, Paula Gunn

Gunnars, Kristjana 1948- .... **CLC 69**
See also CA 113; CCA 1; CP 6, 7; CWP; DLB 60

Gunter, Erich
See Eich, Gunter

Gurdjieff, G(eorgei) I(vanovich)
1877(?)-1949 .... **TCLC 71**
See also CA 157

Gurganus, Allan 1947- .... **CLC 70**
See also BEST 90:1; CA 135; CANR 114; CN 6, 7; CPW; CSW; DAM POP; GLL 1

Gurney, A. R.
See Gurney, A(lbert) R(amsdell), Jr.
See also DLB 266

Gurney, A(lbert) R(amsdell), Jr.
1930- .... **CLC 32, 50, 54**
See Gurney, A. R.
See also AMWS 5; CA 77-80; CAD; CANR 32, 64, 121; CD 5, 6; DAM DRAM; EWL 3

Gurney, Ivor (Bertie) 1890-1937 ... **TCLC 33**
See also BRW 6; CA 167; DLBY 2002; PAB; RGEL 2

Gurney, Peter
See Gurney, A(lbert) R(amsdell), Jr.

Guro, Elena (Genrikhovna)
1877-1913 .... **TCLC 56**
See also DLB 295

Gustafson, James M(oody) 1925- ... **CLC 100**
See also CA 25-28R; CANR 37

Gustafson, Ralph (Barker)
1909-1995 .... **CLC 36**
See also CA 21-24R; CANR 8, 45, 84; CP 1, 2, 3, 4, 5, 6; DLB 88; RGEL 2

Gut, Gom
See Simenon, Georges (Jacques Christian)

Guterson, David 1956- .... **CLC 91**
See also CA 132; CANR 73, 126; CN 7; DLB 292; MTCW 2; MTFW 2005; NFS 13

Guthrie, A(lfred) B(ertram), Jr.
1901-1991 .... **CLC 23**
See also CA 57-60; CAAS 134; CANR 24; CN 1, 2, 3; DLB 6, 212; MAL 5; SATA 62; SATA-Obit 67; TCWW 1, 2

Guthrie, Isobel
See Grieve, C(hristopher) M(urray)

Guthrie, Woodrow Wilson 1912-1967
See Guthrie, Woody
See also CA 113; CAAS 93-96

Guthrie, Woody .... **CLC 35**
See Guthrie, Woodrow Wilson
See also DLB 303; LAIT 3

Gutierrez Najera, Manuel
1859-1895 .... **HLCS 2; NCLC 133**
See also DLB 290; LAW

Guy, Rosa (Cuthbert) 1925- .... **CLC 26**
See also AAYA 4, 37; BW 2; CA 17-20R; CANR 14, 34, 83; CLR 13; DLB 33; DNFS 1; JRDA; MAICYA 1, 2; SATA 14, 62, 122; YAW

Gwendolyn
See Bennett, (Enoch) Arnold

H. D. .... **CLC 3, 8, 14, 31, 34, 73; PC 5**
See Doolittle, Hilda
See also FL 1:5

H. de V.
See Buchan, John

Haavikko, Paavo Juhani 1931- .. **CLC 18, 34**
See also CA 106; CWW 2; EWL 3

Habbema, Koos
See Heijermans, Herman

Habermas, Juergen 1929- .... **CLC 104**
See also CA 109; CANR 85, 162; DLB 242

Habermas, Jurgen
See Habermas, Juergen

Hacker, Marilyn 1942- ...... **CLC 5, 9, 23, 72, 91; PC 47**
See also CA 77-80; CANR 68, 129; CP 3, 4, 5, 6, 7; CWP; DAM POET; DLB 120, 282; FW; GLL 2; MAL 5; PFS 19

Hadewijch of Antwerp fl. 1250- ... **CMLC 61**
See also RGWL 3

Hadrian 76-138 .... **CMLC 52**

Haeckel, Ernst Heinrich (Philipp August)
1834-1919 .... **TCLC 83**
See also CA 157

Hafiz c. 1326-1389(?) .... **CMLC 34**
See also RGWL 2, 3; WLIT 6

Hagedorn, Jessica T(arahata)
1949- .... **CLC 185**
See also CA 139; CANR 69; CWP; DLB 312; RGAL 4

Haggard, H(enry) Rider
1856-1925 .... **TCLC 11**
See also BRWS 3; BYA 4, 5; CA 148; CAAE 108; CANR 112; DLB 70, 156, 174, 178; FANT; LMFS 1; MTCW 2; RGEL 2; RHW; SATA 16; SCFW 1, 2; SFW 4; SUFW 1; WLIT 4

Hagiosy, L.
See Larbaud, Valery (Nicolas)

Hagiwara, Sakutaro 1886-1942 .... **PC 18; TCLC 60**
See Hagiwara Sakutaro
See also CA 154; RGWL 3

Hagiwara Sakutaro
See Hagiwara, Sakutaro
See also EWL 3

Haig, Fenil
See Ford, Ford Madox

Haig-Brown, Roderick (Langmere)
1908-1976 .... **CLC 21**
See also CA 5-8R; CAAS 69-72; CANR 4, 38, 83; CLR 31; CWRI 5; DLB 88; MAICYA 1, 2; SATA 12; TCWW 2

Haight, Rip
See Carpenter, John (Howard)

Haij, Vera
See Jansson, Tove (Marika)

Hailey, Arthur 1920-2004 .... **CLC 5**
See also AITN 2; BEST 90:3; BPFB 2; CA 1-4R; CAAS 233; CANR 2, 36, 75; CCA 1; CN 1, 2, 3, 4, 5, 6, 7; CPW; DAM NOV, POP; DLB 88; DLBY 1982; MTCW 1, 2; MTFW 2005

Hailey, Elizabeth Forsythe 1938- ..... **CLC 40**
See also CA 188; 93-96, 188; 1; CANR 15, 48; INT CANR-15

Haines, John (Meade) 1924- .... **CLC 58**
See also AMWS 12; CA 17-20R; CANR 13, 34; CP 1, 2, 3, 4, 5; CSW; DLB 5, 212; TCLE 1:1

Ha Jin 1956- .... **CLC 109**
See Jin, Xuefei
See also CA 152; CANR 91, 130; DLB 244, 292; MTFW 2005; NFS 25; SSFS 17

Hakluyt, Richard 1552-1616 .... **LC 31**
See also DLB 136; RGEL 2

Haldeman, Joe 1943- .... **CLC 61**
See Graham, Robert
See also AAYA 38; CA 179; 53-56, 179; 25; CANR 6, 70, 72, 130; DLB 8; INT CANR-6; SCFW 2; SFW 4

Haldeman, Joe William
See Haldeman, Joe

Hale, Janet Campbell 1947- .... **NNAL**
See also CA 49-52; CANR 45, 75; DAM MULT; DLB 175; MTCW 2; MTFW 2005

Hale, Sarah Josepha (Buell)
1788-1879 .... **NCLC 75**
See also DLB 1, 42, 73, 243

Halevy, Elie 1870-1937 .... **TCLC 104**

Haley, Alex(ander Murray Palmer)
1921-1992 .... **BLC 2; CLC 8, 12, 76; TCLC 147**
See also AAYA 26; BPFB 2; BW 2, 3; CA 77-80; CAAS 136; CANR 61; CDALBS; CPW; CSW; DA; DA3; DAB; DAC; DAM MST, MULT, POP; DLB 38; LAIT 5; MTCW 1, 2; NFS 9

Haliburton, Thomas Chandler
1796-1865 .... **NCLC 15, 149**
See also DLB 11, 99; RGEL 2; RGSF 2

Hall, Donald 1928- ... **CLC 1, 13, 37, 59, 151, 240; PC 70**
See also AAYA 63; CA 5-8R; 7; CANR 2, 44, 64, 106, 133; CP 1, 2, 3, 4, 5, 6, 7; DAM POET; DLB 5; MAL 5; MTCW 2; MTFW 2005; RGAL 4; SATA 23, 97

Hall, Donald Andrew, Jr.
See Hall, Donald

Hall, Frederic Sauser
See Sauser-Hall, Frederic

Hall, James
See Kuttner, Henry

Hall, James Norman 1887-1951 ..... **TCLC 23**
See also CA 173; CAAE 123; LAIT 1;
RHW 1; SATA 21

Hall, Joseph 1574-1656 .... **LC 91**
See also DLB 121, 151; RGEL 2

Hall, Marguerite Radclyffe
See Hall, Radclyffe

Hall, Radclyffe 1880-1943 .... **TCLC 12**
See also BRWS 6; CA 150; CAAE 110;
CANR 83; DLB 191; MTCW 2; MTFW
2005; RGEL 2; RHW

Hall, Rodney 1935- .... **CLC 51**
See also CA 109; CANR 69; CN 6, 7; CP
1, 2, 3, 4, 5, 6, 7; DLB 289

Hallam, Arthur Henry
1811-1833 .... **NCLC 110**
See also DLB 32

Halldor Laxness .... **CLC 25**
See Gudjonsson, Halldor Kiljan
See also DLB 293; EW 12; EWL 3; RGWL
2, 3

Halleck, Fitz-Greene 1790-1867 .... **NCLC 47**
See also DLB 3, 250; RGAL 4

Halliday, Michael
See Creasey, John

Halpern, Daniel 1945- .... **CLC 14**
See also CA 33-36R; CANR 93; CP 3, 4, 5,
6, 7

Hamburger, Michael 1924-2007 ... **CLC 5, 14**
See also CA 196; 5-8R, 196; 4; CANR 2,
47; CP 1, 2, 3, 4, 5, 6, 7; DLB 27

Hamburger, Michael Peter Leopold
See Hamburger, Michael

Hamill, Pete 1935- .... **CLC 10**
See also CA 25-28R; CANR 18, 71, 127

Hamilton, Alexander
1755(?)-1804 .... **NCLC 49**
See also DLB 37

Hamilton, Clive
See Lewis, C.S.

Hamilton, Edmond 1904-1977 .... **CLC 1**
See also CA 1-4R; CANR 3, 84; DLB 8;
SATA 118; SFW 4

Hamilton, Elizabeth 1758-1816 ... **NCLC 153**
See also DLB 116, 158

Hamilton, Eugene (Jacob) Lee
See Lee-Hamilton, Eugene (Jacob)

Hamilton, Franklin
See Silverberg, Robert

Hamilton, Gail
See Corcoran, Barbara (Asenath)

Hamilton, (Robert) Ian 1938-2001 . **CLC 191**
See also CA 106; CAAS 203; CANR 41,
67; CP 1, 2, 3, 4, 5, 6, 7; DLB 40, 155

Hamilton, Jane 1957- .... **CLC 179**
See also CA 147; CANR 85, 128; CN 7;
MTFW 2005

Hamilton, Mollie
See Kaye, M.M.

Hamilton, (Anthony Walter) Patrick
1904-1962 .... **CLC 51**
See also CA 176; CAAS 113; DLB 10, 191

Hamilton, Virginia 1936-2002 .... **CLC 26**
See also AAYA 2, 21; BW 2, 3; BYA 1, 2,
8; CA 25-28R; CAAS 206; CANR 20, 37,
73, 126; CLR 1, 11, 40; DAM MULT;
DLB 33, 52; DLBY 2001; INT CANR-
20; JRDA; LAIT 5; MAICYA 1, 2; MAI-
CYAS 1; MTCW 1, 2; MTFW 2005;
SATA 4, 56, 79, 123; SATA-Obit 132;
WYA; YAW

Hammett, (Samuel) Dashiell
1894-1961 .... **CLC 3, 5, 10, 19, 47; SSC
17; TCLC 187**
See also AAYA 59; AITN 1; AMWS 4;
BPFB 2; CA 81-84; CANR 42; CDALB
1929-1941; CMW 4; DA3; DLB 226, 280;
DLBD 6; DLBY 1996; EWL 3; LAIT 3;
MAL 5; MSW; MTCW 1, 2; MTFW
2005; NFS 21; RGAL 4; RGSF 2; TUS

Hammon, Jupiter 1720(?)-1800(?) .... **BLC 2;
NCLC 5; PC 16**
See also DAM MULT, POET; DLB 31, 50

Hammond, Keith
See Kuttner, Henry

Hamner, Earl (Henry), Jr. 1923- ...... **CLC 12**
See also AITN 2; CA 73-76; DLB 6

Hampton, Christopher 1946- .... **CLC 4**
See also CA 25-28R; CD 5, 6; DLB 13;
MTCW 1

Hampton, Christopher James
See Hampton, Christopher

Hamsun, Knut .... **TCLC 2, 14, 49, 151**
See Pedersen, Knut
See also DLB 297, 330; EW 8; EWL 3;
RGWL 2, 3

Handke, Peter 1942- .... **CLC 5, 8, 10, 15, 38,
134; DC 17**
See also CA 77-80; CANR 33, 75, 104, 133;
CWW 2; DAM DRAM, NOV; DLB 85,
124; EWL 3; MTCW 1, 2; MTFW 2005;
TWA

Handy, W(illiam) C(hristopher)
1873-1958 .... **TCLC 97**
See also BW 3; CA 167; CAAE 121

Hanley, James 1901-1985 ..... **CLC 3, 5, 8, 13**
See also CA 73-76; CAAS 117; CANR 36;
CBD; CN 1, 2, 3; DLB 191; EWL 3;
MTCW 1; RGEL 2

Hannah, Barry 1942- .. **CLC 23, 38, 90; SSC
94**
See also BPFB 2; CA 110; CAAE 108;
CANR 43, 68, 113; CN 4, 5, 6, 7; CSW;
DLB 6, 234; INT CA-110; MTCW 1;
RGSF 2

Hannon, Ezra
See Hunter, Evan

Hansberry, Lorraine (Vivian)
1930-1965 ... **BLC 2; CLC 17, 62; DC 2**
See also AAYA 25; AFAW 1, 2; AMWS 4;
BW 1, 3; CA 109; CAAS 25-28R; CABS
3; CAD; CANR 58; CDALB 1941-1968;
CWD; DA; DA3; DAB; DAC; DAM
DRAM, MST, MULT; DFS 2; DLB 7, 38;
EWL 3; FL 1:6; FW; LAIT 4; MAL 5;
MTCW 1, 2; MTFW 2005; RGAL 4; TUS

Hansen, Joseph 1923-2004 .... **CLC 38**
See Brock, Rose; Colton, James
See also BPFB 2; CA 29-32R; 17; CAAS
233; CANR 16, 44, 66, 125; CMW 4;
DLB 226; GLL 1; INT CANR-16

Hansen, Karen V. 1955- .... **CLC 65**
See also CA 149; CANR 102

Hansen, Martin A(lfred)
1909-1955 .... **TCLC 32**
See also CA 167; DLB 214; EWL 3

Hanson, Kenneth O(stlin) 1922- .... **CLC 13**
See also CA 53-56; CANR 7; CP 1, 2, 3, 4,
5

Hardwick, Elizabeth 1916- .... **CLC 13**
See also AMWS 3; CA 5-8R; CANR 3, 32,
70, 100, 139; CN 4, 5, 6; CSW; DA3;
DAM NOV; DLB 6; MBL; MTCW 1, 2;
MTFW 2005; TCLE 1:1

Hardy, Thomas 1840-1928 .... **PC 8; SSC 2,
60; TCLC 4, 10, 18, 32, 48, 53, 72, 143,
153; WLC 3**
See also AAYA 69; BRW 6; BRWC 1, 2;
BRWR 1; CA 123; CAAE 104; CDBLB
1890-1914; DA; DA3; DAB; DAC; DAM
MST, NOV, POET; DLB 18, 19, 135, 284;

EWL 3; EXPN; EXPP; LAIT 2; MTCW
1, 2; MTFW 2005; NFS 3, 11, 15, 19; PFS
3, 4, 18; RGEL 2; RGSF 2; TEA; WLIT
4

Hare, David 1947- . **CLC 29, 58, 136; DC 26**
See also BRWS 4; CA 97-100; CANR 39,
91; CBD; CD 5, 6; DFS 4, 7, 16; DLB
13, 310; MTCW 1; TEA

Harewood, John
See Van Druten, John (William)

Harford, Henry
See Hudson, W(illiam) H(enry)

Hargrave, Leonie
See Disch, Thomas M.

**Hariri, Al- al-Qasim ibn 'Ali Abu
Muhammad al-Basri**
See al-Hariri, al-Qasim ibn 'Ali Abu Mu-
hammad al-Basri

Harjo, Joy 1951- ..... **CLC 83; NNAL; PC 27**
See also AMWS 12; CA 114; CANR 35,
67, 91, 129; CP 6, 7; CWP; DAM MULT;
DLB 120, 175; EWL 3; MTCW 2; MTFW
2005; PFS 15; RGAL 4

Harlan, Louis R(udolph) 1922- .... **CLC 34**
See also CA 21-24R; CANR 25, 55, 80

Harling, Robert 1951(?)- .... **CLC 53**
See also CA 147

Harmon, William (Ruth) 1938- .... **CLC 38**
See also CA 33-36R; CANR 14, 32, 35;
SATA 65

Harper, F. E. W.
See Harper, Frances Ellen Watkins

Harper, Frances E. W.
See Harper, Frances Ellen Watkins

Harper, Frances E. Watkins
See Harper, Frances Ellen Watkins

Harper, Frances Ellen
See Harper, Frances Ellen Watkins

Harper, Frances Ellen Watkins
1825-1911 ..... **BLC 2; PC 21; TCLC 14**
See also AFAW 1, 2; BW 1, 3; CA 125;
CAAE 111; CANR 79; DAM MULT,
POET; DLB 50, 221; MBL; RGAL 4

Harper, Michael S(teven) 1938- ... **CLC 7, 22**
See also AFAW 2; BW 1; CA 224; 33-36R,
224; CANR 24, 108; CP 2, 3, 4, 5, 6, 7;
DLB 41; RGAL 4; TCLE 1:1

Harper, Mrs. F. E. W.
See Harper, Frances Ellen Watkins

Harpur, Charles 1813-1868 .... **NCLC 114**
See also DLB 230; RGEL 2

Harris, Christie
See Harris, Christie (Lucy) Irwin

Harris, Christie (Lucy) Irwin
1907-2002 .... **CLC 12**
See also CA 5-8R; CANR 6, 83; CLR 47;
DLB 88; JRDA; MAICYA 1, 2; SAAS 10;
SATA 6, 74; SATA-Essay 116

Harris, Frank 1856-1931 .... **TCLC 24**
See also CA 150; CAAE 109; CANR 80;
DLB 156, 197; RGEL 2

Harris, George Washington
1814-1869 .... **NCLC 23, 165**
See also DLB 3, 11, 248; RGAL 4

Harris, Joel Chandler 1848-1908 ..... **SSC 19;
TCLC 2**
See also CA 137; CAAE 104; CANR 80;
CLR 49; DLB 11, 23, 42, 78, 91; LAIT 2;
MAICYA 1, 2; RGSF 2; SATA 100; WCH;
YABC 1

**Harris, John (Wyndham Parkes Lucas)
Beynon** 1903-1969
See Wyndham, John
See also CA 102; CAAS 89-92; CANR 84;
SATA 118; SFW 4

Harris, MacDonald .... **CLC 9**
See Heiney, Donald (William)

Harris, Mark 1922-2007 .... **CLC 19**
See also CA 5-8R; 3; CANR 2, 55, 83; CN
1, 2, 3, 4, 5, 6, 7; DLB 2; DLBY 1980
Harris, Norman .... **CLC 65**
Harris, (Theodore) Wilson 1921- .... **CLC 25,**
159
See also BRWS 5; BW 2, 3; CA 65-68; 16;
CANR 11, 27, 69, 114; CDWLB 3; CN 1,
2, 3, 4, 5, 6, 7; CP 1, 2, 3, 4, 5, 6, 7; DLB
117; EWL 3; MTCW 1; RGEL 2
Harrison, Barbara Grizzuti
1934-2002 .... **CLC 144**
See also CA 77-80; CAAS 205; CANR 15,
48; INT CANR-15
Harrison, Elizabeth (Allen) Cavanna
1909-2001
See Cavanna, Betty
See also CA 9-12R; CAAS 200; CANR 6,
27, 85, 104, 121; MAICYA 2; SATA 142;
YAW
Harrison, Harry (Max) 1925- .... **CLC 42**
See also CA 1-4R; CANR 5, 21, 84; DLB
8; SATA 4; SCFW 2; SFW 4
Harrison, James
See Harrison, Jim
Harrison, James Thomas
See Harrison, Jim
Harrison, Jim 1937- .... **CLC 6, 14, 33, 66,**
143; SSC 19
See also AMWS 8; CA 13-16R; CANR 8,
51, 79, 142; CN 5, 6; CP 1, 2, 3, 4, 5, 6;
DLBY 1982; INT CANR-8; RGAL 4;
TCWW 2; TUS
Harrison, Kathryn 1961- .... **CLC 70, 151**
See also CA 144; CANR 68, 122
Harrison, Tony 1937- .... **CLC 43, 129**
See also BRWS 5; CA 65-68; CANR 44,
98; CBD; CD 5, 6; CP 2, 3, 4, 5, 6, 7;
DLB 40, 245; MTCW 1; RGEL 2
Harriss, Will(ard Irvin) 1922- .... **CLC 34**
See also CA 111
Hart, Ellis
See Ellison, Harlan
Hart, Josephine 1942(?)- .... **CLC 70**
See also CA 138; CANR 70, 149; CPW;
DAM POP
Hart, Moss 1904-1961 .... **CLC 66**
See also CA 109; CAAS 89-92; CANR 84;
DAM DRAM; DFS 1; DLB 7, 266; RGAL
4
Harte, (Francis) Bret(t)
1836(?)-1902 ... **SSC 8, 59; TCLC 1, 25;**
WLC 3
See also AMWS 2; CA 140; CAAE 104;
CANR 80; CDALB 1865-1917; DA;
DA3; DAC; DAM MST; DLB 12, 64, 74,
79, 186; EXPS; LAIT 2; RGAL 4; RGSF
2; SATA 26; SSFS 3; TUS
Hartley, L(eslie) P(oles) 1895-1972 ... **CLC 2,**
22
See also BRWS 7; CA 45-48; CAAS 37-
40R; CANR 33; CN 1; DLB 15, 139;
EWL 3; HGG; MTCW 1, 2; MTFW 2005;
RGEL 2; RGSF 2; SUFW 1
Hartman, Geoffrey H. 1929- .... **CLC 27**
See also CA 125; CAAE 117; CANR 79;
DLB 67
Hartmann, Sadakichi 1869-1944 ... **TCLC 73**
See also CA 157; DLB 54
Hartmann von Aue c. 1170-c.
1210 .... **CMLC 15**
See also CDWLB 2; DLB 138; RGWL 2, 3
Hartog, Jan de
See de Hartog, Jan
Haruf, Kent 1943- .... **CLC 34**
See also AAYA 44; CA 149; CANR 91, 131
Harvey, Caroline
See Trollope, Joanna

Harvey, Gabriel 1550(?)-1631 .... **LC 88**
See also DLB 167, 213, 281
Harwood, Ronald 1934- .... **CLC 32**
See also CA 1-4R; CANR 4, 55, 150; CBD;
CD 5, 6; DAM DRAM; MST; DLB 13
Hasegawa Tatsunosuke
See Futabatei, Shimei
Hasek, Jaroslav (Matej Frantisek)
1883-1923 .... **SSC 69; TCLC 4**
See also CA 129; CAAE 104; CDWLB 4;
DLB 215; EW 9; EWL 3; MTCW 1, 2;
RGSF 2; RGWL 2, 3
Hass, Robert 1941- ... **CLC 18, 39, 99; PC 16**
See also AMWS 6; CA 111; CANR 30, 50,
71; CP 3, 4, 5, 6, 7; DLB 105, 206; EWL
3; MAL 5; MTFW 2005; RGAL 4; SATA
94; TCLE 1:1
Hastings, Hudson
See Kuttner, Henry
Hastings, Selina .... **CLC 44**
See also CA 257
Hastings, Selina Shirley
See Hastings, Selina
Hathorne, John 1641-1717 .... **LC 38**
Hatteras, Amelia
See Mencken, H(enry) L(ouis)
Hatteras, Owen .... **TCLC 18**
See Mencken, H(enry) L(ouis); Nathan,
George Jean
Hauff, Wilhelm 1802-1827 .... **NCLC 185**
See also DLB 90; SUFW 1
Hauptmann, Gerhart (Johann Robert)
1862-1946 .... **SSC 37; TCLC 4**
See also CA 153; CAAE 104; CDWLB 2;
DAM DRAM; DLB 66, 118, 330; EW 8;
EWL 3; RGSF 2; RGWL 2, 3; TWA
Havel, Vaclav 1936- ..... **CLC 25, 58, 65, 123;**
DC 6
See also CA 104; CANR 36, 63, 124; CD-
WLB 4; CWW 2; DA3; DAM DRAM;
DFS 10; DLB 232; EWL 3; LMFS 2;
MTCW 1, 2; MTFW 2005; RGWL 3
Haviaras, Stratis .... **CLC 33**
See Chaviaras, Strates
Hawes, Stephen 1475(?)-1529(?) .... **LC 17**
See also DLB 132; RGEL 2
Hawkes, John 1925-1998 ... **CLC 1, 2, 3, 4, 7,**
9, 14, 15, 27, 49
See also BPFB 2; CA 1-4R; CAAS 167;
CANR 2, 47, 64; CN 1, 2, 3, 4, 5, 6; DLB
2, 7, 227; DLBY 1980, 1998; EWL 3;
MAL 5; MTCW 1, 2; MTFW 2005;
RGAL 4
Hawking, S. W.
See Hawking, Stephen W.
Hawking, Stephen W. 1942- ..... **CLC 63, 105**
See also AAYA 13; BEST 89:1; CA 129;
CAAE 126; CANR 48, 115; CPW; DA3;
MTCW 2; MTFW 2005
Hawkins, Anthony Hope
See Hope, Anthony
Hawthorne, Julian 1846-1934 .... **TCLC 25**
See also CA 165; HGG
Hawthorne, Nathaniel 1804-1864 ... **NCLC 2,**
10, 17, 23, 39, 79, 95, 158, 171; SSC 3,
29, 39, 89; WLC 3
See also AAYA 18; AMW; AMWC 1;
AMWR 1; BPFB 2; BYA 3; CDALB
1640-1865; CLR 103; DA; DA3; DAB;
DAC; DAM MST, NOV; DLB 1, 74, 183,
223, 269; EXPN; EXPS; GL 2; HGG;
LAIT 1; NFS 1, 20; RGAL 4; RGSF 2;
SSFS 1, 7, 11, 15; SUFW 1; TUS; WCH;
YABC 2
Hawthorne, Sophia Peabody
1809-1871 .... **NCLC 150**
See also DLB 183, 239

Haxton, Josephine Ayres 1921-
See Douglas, Ellen
See also CA 115; CANR 41, 83
Hayaseca y Eizaguirre, Jorge
See Echegaray (y Eizaguirre), Jose (Maria
Waldo)
Hayashi, Fumiko 1904-1951 .... **TCLC 27**
See Hayashi Fumiko
See also CA 161
Hayashi Fumiko
See Hayashi, Fumiko
See also DLB 180; EWL 3
Haycraft, Anna 1932-2005
See Ellis, Alice Thomas
See also CA 122; CAAS 237; CANR 90,
141; MTCW 2; MTFW 2005
Hayden, Robert E(arl) 1913-1980 ..... **BLC 2;**
CLC 5, 9, 14, 37; PC 6
See also AFAW 1, 2; AMWS 2; BW 1, 3;
CA 69-72; CAAS 97-100; CABS 2;
CANR 24, 75, 82; CDALB 1941-1968;
CP 1, 2, 3; DA; DAC; DAM MST, MULT,
POET; DLB 5, 76; EWL 3; EXPP; MAL
5; MTCW 1, 2; PFS 1; RGAL 4; SATA
19; SATA-Obit 26; WP
Haydon, Benjamin Robert
1786-1846 .... **NCLC 146**
See also DLB 110
Hayek, F(riedrich) A(ugust von)
1899-1992 .... **TCLC 109**
See also CA 93-96; CAAS 137; CANR 20;
MTCW 1, 2
Hayford, J(oseph) E(phraim) Casely
See Casely-Hayford, J(oseph) E(phraim)
Hayman, Ronald 1932- .... **CLC 44**
See also CA 25-28R; CANR 18, 50, 88; CD
5, 6; DLB 155
Hayne, Paul Hamilton 1830-1886 . **NCLC 94**
See also DLB 3, 64, 79, 248; RGAL 4
Hays, Mary 1760-1843 .... **NCLC 114**
See also DLB 142, 158; RGEL 2
Haywood, Eliza (Fowler)
1693(?)-1756 .... **LC 1, 44**
See also BRWS 12; DLB 39; RGEL 2
Hazlitt, William 1778-1830 ...... **NCLC 29, 82**
See also BRW 4; DLB 110, 158; RGEL 2;
TEA
Hazzard, Shirley 1931- .... **CLC 18, 218**
See also CA 9-12R; CANR 4, 70, 127; CN
1, 2, 3, 4, 5, 6, 7; DLB 289; DLBY 1982;
MTCW 1
Head, Bessie 1937-1986 ...... **BLC 2; CLC 25,**
67; SSC 52
See also AFW; BW 2, 3; CA 29-32R; CAAS
119; CANR 25, 82; CDWLB 3; CN 1, 2,
3, 4; DA3; DAM MULT; DLB 117, 225;
EWL 3; EXPS; FL 1:6; FW; MTCW 1, 2;
MTFW 2005; RGSF 2; SSFS 5, 13; WLIT
2; WWE 1
Headon, (Nicky) Topper 1956(?)- ..... **CLC 30**
Heaney, Seamus 1939- . **CLC 5, 7, 14, 25, 37,**
74, 91, 171, 225; PC 18; WLCS
See also AAYA 61; BRWR 1; BRWS 2; CA
85-88; CANR 25, 48, 75, 91, 128; CD-
BLB 1960 to Present; CP 1, 2, 3, 4, 5, 6,
7; DA3; DAB; DAM POET; DLB 40,
330; DLBY 1995; EWL 3; EXPP; MTCW
1, 2; MTFW 2005; PAB; PFS 2, 5, 8, 17;
RGEL 2; TEA; WLIT 4
Hearn, (Patricio) Lafcadio (Tessima Carlos)
1850-1904 .... **TCLC 9**
See also CA 166; CAAE 105; DLB 12, 78,
189; HGG; MAL 5; RGAL 4
Hearne, Samuel 1745-1792 .... **LC 95**
See also DLB 99
Hearne, Vicki 1946-2001 .... **CLC 56**
See also CA 139; CAAS 201

Cumulative Author Index

Ionesco, Eugene 1912-1994 ... **CLC 1, 4, 6, 9, 11, 15, 41, 86; DC 12; WLC 3**
See also CA 9-12R; CAAS 144; CANR 55, 132; CWW 2; DA; DA3; DAB; DAC; DAM DRAM, MST; DFS 4, 9; DLB 321; EW 13; EWL 3; GFL 1789 to the Present; LMFS 2; MTCW 1, 2; MTFW 2005; RGWL 2, 3; SATA 7; SATA-Obit 79; TWA

Iqbal, Muhammad 1877-1938 .... **TCLC 28**
See also CA 215; EWL 3

Ireland, Patrick
See O'Doherty, Brian

Irenaeus St. 130- .... **CMLC 42**

Irigaray, Luce 1930- .... **CLC 164**
See also CA 154; CANR 121; FW

Iron, Ralph
See Schreiner, Olive (Emilie Albertina)

Irving, John 1942- . **CLC 13, 23, 38, 112, 175**
See also AAYA 8, 62; AMWS 6; BEST 89:3; BPFB 2; CA 25-28R; CANR 28, 73, 112, 133; CN 3, 4, 5, 6, 7; CPW; DA3; DAM NOV, POP; DLB 6, 278; DLBY 1982; EWL 3; MAL 5; MTCW 1, 2; MTFW 2005; NFS 12, 14; RGAL 4; TUS

Irving, John Winslow
See Irving, John

Irving, Washington 1783-1859 . **NCLC 2, 19, 95; SSC 2, 37; WLC 3**
See also AAYA 56; AMW; CDALB 1640-1865; CLR 97; DA; DA3; DAB; DAC; DAM MST; DLB 3, 11, 30, 59, 73, 74, 183, 186, 250, 254; EXPS; GL 2; LAIT 1; RGAL 4; RGSF 2; SSFS 1, 8, 16; SUFW 1; TUS; WCH; YABC 2

Irwin, P. K.
See Page, P(atricia) K(athleen)

Isaacs, Jorge Ricardo 1837-1895 ... **NCLC 70**
See also LAW

Isaacs, Susan 1943- .... **CLC 32**
See also BEST 89:1; BPFB 2; CA 89-92; CANR 20, 41, 65, 112, 134; CPW; DA3; DAM POP; INT CANR-20; MTCW 1, 2; MTFW 2005

Isherwood, Christopher 1904-1986 ... **CLC 1, 9, 11, 14, 44; SSC 56**
See also AMWS 14; BRW 7; CA 13-16R; CAAS 117; CANR 35, 97, 133; CN 1, 2, 3; DA3; DAM DRAM, NOV; DLB 15, 195; DLBY 1986; EWL 3; IDTP; MTCW 1, 2; MTFW 2005; RGAL 4; RGEL 2; TUS; WLIT 4

Ishiguro, Kazuo 1954- . **CLC 27, 56, 59, 110, 119**
See also AAYA 58; BEST 90:2; BPFB 2; BRWS 4; CA 120; CANR 49, 95, 133; CN 5, 6, 7; DA3; DAM NOV; DLB 194, 326; EWL 3; MTCW 1, 2; MTFW 2005; NFS 13; WLIT 4; WWE 1

Ishikawa, Hakuhin
See Ishikawa, Takuboku

Ishikawa, Takuboku 1886(?)-1912 ..... **PC 10; TCLC 15**
See Ishikawa Takuboku
See also CA 153; CAAE 113; DAM POET

Iskander, Fazil (Abdulovich) 1929- .. **CLC 47**
See Iskander, Fazil' Abdulevich
See also CA 102; EWL 3

Iskander, Fazil' Abdulevich
See Iskander, Fazil (Abdulovich)
See also DLB 302

Isler, Alan (David) 1934- .... **CLC 91**
See also CA 156; CANR 105

Ivan IV 1530-1584 .... **LC 17**

Ivanov, V.I.
See Ivanov, Vyacheslav

Ivanov, Vyacheslav 1866-1949 .... **TCLC 33**
See also CAAE 122; EWL 3

Ivanov, Vyacheslav Ivanovich
See Ivanov, Vyacheslav

Ivask, Ivar Vidrik 1927-1992 .... **CLC 14**
See also CA 37-40R; CAAS 139; CANR 24

Ives, Morgan
See Bradley, Marion Zimmer
See also GLL 1

Izumi Shikibu c. 973-c. 1034 .... **CMLC 33**

J. R. S.
See Gogarty, Oliver St. John

Jabran, Kahlil
See Gibran, Kahlil

Jabran, Khalil
See Gibran, Kahlil

Jackson, Daniel
See Wingrove, David

Jackson, Helen Hunt 1830-1885 .... **NCLC 90**
See also DLB 42, 47, 186, 189; RGAL 4

Jackson, Jesse 1908-1983 .... **CLC 12**
See also BW 1; CA 25-28R; CAAS 109; CANR 27; CLR 28; CWRI 5; MAICYA 1, 2; SATA 2, 29; SATA-Obit 48

Jackson, Laura (Riding) 1901-1991 .... **PC 44**
See Riding, Laura
See also CA 65-68; CAAS 135; CANR 28, 89; DLB 48

Jackson, Sam
See Trumbo, Dalton

Jackson, Sara
See Wingrove, David

Jackson, Shirley 1919-1965 . **CLC 11, 60, 87; SSC 9, 39; TCLC 187; WLC 3**
See also AAYA 9; AMWS 9; BPFB 2; CA 1-4R; CAAS 25-28R; CANR 4, 52; CDALB 1941-1968; DA; DA3; DAC; DAM MST; DLB 6, 234; EXPS; HGG; LAIT 4; MAL 5; MTCW 2; MTFW 2005; RGAL 4; RGSF 2; SATA 2; SSFS 1; SUFW 1, 2

Jacob, (Cyprien-)Max 1876-1944 .... **TCLC 6**
See also CA 193; CAAE 104; DLB 258; EWL 3; GFL 1789 to the Present; GLL 2; RGWL 2, 3

Jacobs, Harriet A(nn) 1813(?)-1897 .... **NCLC 67, 162**
See also AFAW 1, 2; DLB 239; FL 1:3; FW; LAIT 2; RGAL 4

Jacobs, Jim 1942- .... **CLC 12**
See also CA 97-100; INT CA-97-100

Jacobs, W(illiam) W(ymark) 1863-1943 .... **SSC 73; TCLC 22**
See also CA 167; CAAE 121; DLB 135; EXPS; HGG; RGEL 2; RGSF 2; SSFS 2; SUFW 1

Jacobsen, Jens Peter 1847-1885 .... **NCLC 34**

Jacobsen, Josephine (Winder) 1908-2003 .... **CLC 48, 102; PC 62**
See also CA 33-36R; 18; CAAS 218; CANR 23, 48; CCA 1; CP 2, 3, 4, 5, 6, 7; DLB 244; PFS 23; TCLE 1:1

Jacobson, Dan 1929- ...... **CLC 4, 14; SSC 91**
See also AFW; CA 1-4R; CANR 2, 25, 66; CN 1, 2, 3, 4, 5, 6, 7; DLB 14, 207, 225, 319; EWL 3; MTCW 1; RGSF 2

Jacqueline
See Carpentier (y Valmont), Alejo

Jacques de Vitry c. 1160-1240 ...... **CMLC 63**
See also DLB 208

Jagger, Michael Philip
See Jagger, Mick

Jagger, Mick 1943- .... **CLC 17**
See also CA 239

Jahiz, al- c. 780-c. 869 .... **CMLC 25**
See also DLB 311

Jakes, John 1932- .... **CLC 29**
See also AAYA 32; BEST 89:4; BPFB 2; CA 214; 57-60, 214; CANR 10, 43, 66, 111, 142; CPW; CSW; DA3; DAM NOV,

POP; DLB 278; DLBY 1983; FANT; INT CANR-10; MTCW 1, 2; MTFW 2005; RHW; SATA 62; SFW 4; TCWW 1, 2

James I 1394-1437 .... **LC 20**
See also RGEL 2

James, Andrew
See Kirkup, James

James, C(yril) L(ionel) R(obert) 1901-1989 .... **BLCS; CLC 33**
See also BW 2; CA 125; CAAE 117; CAAS 128; CANR 62; CN 1, 2, 3, 4; DLB 125; MTCW 1

James, Daniel (Lewis) 1911-1988
See Santiago, Danny
See also CA 174; CAAS 125

James, Dynely
See Mayne, William (James Carter)

James, Henry Sr. 1811-1882 .... **NCLC 53**

James, Henry 1843-1916 .... **SSC 8, 32, 47; TCLC 2, 11, 24, 40, 47, 64, 171; WLC 3**
See also AMW; AMWC 1; AMWR 1; BPFB 2; BRW 6; CA 132; CAAE 104; CDALB 1865-1917; DA; DA3; DAB; DAC; DAM MST, NOV; DLB 12, 71, 74, 189; DLBD 13; EWL 3; EXPS; GL 2; HGG; LAIT 2; MAL 5; MTCW 1, 2; MTFW 2005; NFS 12, 16, 19; RGAL 4; RGEL 2; RGSF 2; SSFS 9; SUFW 1; TUS

James, M. R. .... **SSC 93**
See James, Montague (Rhodes)
See also DLB 156, 201

James, Montague (Rhodes) 1862-1936 .... **SSC 16; TCLC 6**
See James, M. R.
See also CA 203; CAAE 104; HGG; RGEL 2; RGSF 2; SUFW 1

James, P. D. .... **CLC 18, 46, 122, 226**
See White, Phyllis Dorothy James
See also BEST 90:2; BPFB 2; BRWS 4; CDBLB 1960 to Present; CN 4, 5, 6; DLB 87, 276; DLBD 17; MSW

James, Philip
See Moorcock, Michael

James, Samuel
See Stephens, James

James, Seumas
See Stephens, James

James, Stephen
See Stephens, James

James, William 1842-1910 .... **TCLC 15, 32**
See also AMW; CA 193; CAAE 109; DLB 270, 284; MAL 5; NCFS 5; RGAL 4

Jameson, Anna 1794-1860 .... **NCLC 43**
See also DLB 99, 166

Jameson, Fredric (R.) 1934- .... **CLC 142**
See also CA 196; DLB 67; LMFS 2

James VI of Scotland 1566-1625 .... **LC 109**
See also DLB 151, 172

Jami, Nur al-Din 'Abd al-Rahman 1414-1492 .... **LC 9**

Jammes, Francis 1868-1938 .... **TCLC 75**
See also CA 198; EWL 3; GFL 1789 to the Present

Jandl, Ernst 1925-2000 .... **CLC 34**
See also CA 200; EWL 3

Janowitz, Tama 1957- .... **CLC 43, 145**
See also CA 106; CANR 52, 89, 129; CN 5, 6, 7; CPW; DAM POP; DLB 292; MTFW 2005

Jansson, Tove (Marika) 1914-2001 ... **SSC 96**
See also CA 17-20R; CAAS 196; CANR 38, 118; CLR 2; CWW 2; DLB 257; EWL 3; MAICYA 1, 2; RGSF 2; SATA 3, 41

Japrisot, Sebastien 1931- .... **CLC 90**
See Rossi, Jean-Baptiste
See also CMW 4; NFS 18

Keneally, Thomas 1935- .... **CLC 5, 8, 10, 14, 19, 27, 43, 117**
See also BRWS 4; CA 85-88; CANR 10, 50, 74, 130; CN 1, 2, 3, 4, 5, 6, 7; CPW; DA3; DAM NOV; DLB 289, 299, 326; EWL 3; MTCW 1, 2; MTFW 2005; NFS 17; RGEL 2; RGHL; RHW

Kennedy, A(lison) L(ouise) 1965- ... **CLC 188**
See also CA 213; 168, 213; CANR 108; CD 5, 6; CN 6, 7; DLB 271; RGSF 2

Kennedy, Adrienne (Lita) 1931- .... **BLC 2; CLC 66; DC 5**
See also AFAW 2; BW 2, 3; CA 103; 20; CABS 3; CAD; CANR 26, 53, 82; CD 5, 6; DAM MULT; DFS 9; DLB 38; FW; MAL 5

Kennedy, John Pendleton
1795-1870 .... **NCLC 2**
See also DLB 3, 248, 254; RGAL 4

Kennedy, Joseph Charles 1929-
See Kennedy, X. J.
See also CA 201; 1-4R, 201; CANR 4, 30, 40; CWRI 5; MAICYA 2; MAICYAS 1; SATA 14, 86, 130; SATA-Essay 130

Kennedy, William 1928- .. **CLC 6, 28, 34, 53, 239**
See also AAYA 1, 73; AMWS 7; BPFB 2; CA 85-88; CANR 14, 31, 76, 134; CN 4, 5, 6, 7; DA3; DAM NOV; DLB 143; DLBY 1985; EWL 3; INT CANR-31; MAL 5; MTCW 1, 2; MTFW 2005; SATA 57

Kennedy, X. J. .... **CLC 8, 42**
See Kennedy, Joseph Charles
See also AMWS 15; CA 9; CLR 27; CP 1, 2, 3, 4, 5, 6, 7; DLB 5; SAAS 22

Kenny, Maurice (Francis) 1929- ..... **CLC 87; NNAL**
See also CA 144; 22; CANR 143; DAM MULT; DLB 175

Kent, Kelvin
See Kuttner, Henry

Kenton, Maxwell
See Southern, Terry

Kenyon, Jane 1947-1995 .... **PC 57**
See also AAYA 63; AMWS 7; CA 118; CAAS 148; CANR 44, 69; CP 6, 7; CWP; DLB 120; PFS 9, 17; RGAL 4

Kenyon, Robert O.
See Kuttner, Henry

Kepler, Johannes 1571-1630 .... **LC 45**

Ker, Jill
See Conway, Jill K(er)

Kerkow, H. C.
See Lewton, Val

Kerouac, Jack 1922-1969 ...... **CLC 1, 2, 3, 5, 14, 29, 61; TCLC 117; WLC**
See Kerouac, Jean-Louis Lebris de
See also AAYA 25; AMWC 1; AMWS 3; BG 3; BPFB 2; CDALB 1941-1968; CP 1; CPW; DLB 2, 16, 237; DLBD 3; DLBY 1995; EWL 3; GLL 1; LATS 1:2; LMFS 2; MAL 5; NFS 8; RGAL 4; TUS; WP

Kerouac, Jean-Louis Lebris de 1922-1969
See Kerouac, Jack
See also AITN 1; CA 5-8R; CAAS 25-28R; CANR 26, 54, 95; DA; DA3; DAB; DAC; DAM MST, NOV, POET, POP; MTCW 1, 2; MTFW 2005

Kerr, (Bridget) Jean (Collins)
1923(?)-2003 .... **CLC 22**
See also CA 5-8R; CAAS 212; CANR 7; INT CANR-7

Kerr, M. E. .... **CLC 12, 35**
See Meaker, Marijane
See also AAYA 2, 23; BYA 1, 7, 8; CLR 29; SAAS 1; WYA

Kerr, Robert .... **CLC 55**

Kerrigan, (Thomas) Anthony 1918- .. **CLC 4, 6**
See also CA 49-52; 11; CANR 4

Kerry, Lois
See Duncan, Lois

Kesey, Ken 1935-2001 .... **CLC 1, 3, 6, 11, 46, 64, 184; WLC 3**
See also AAYA 25; BG 1:3; BPFB 2; CA 1-4R; CAAS 204; CANR 22, 38, 66, 124; CDALB 1968-1988; CN 1, 2, 3, 4, 5, 6, 7; CPW; DA; DA3; DAB; DAC; DAM MST, NOV, POP; DLB 2, 16, 206; EWL 3; EXPN; LAIT 4; MAL 5; MTCW 1, 2; MTFW 2005; NFS 2; RGAL 4; SATA 66; SATA-Obit 131; TUS; YAW

Kesselring, Joseph (Otto)
1902-1967 .... **CLC 45**
See also CA 150; DAM DRAM, MST; DFS 20

Kessler, Jascha (Frederick) 1929- ...... **CLC 4**
See also CA 17-20R; CANR 8, 48, 111; CP 1

Kettelkamp, Larry (Dale) 1933- .... **CLC 12**
See also CA 29-32R; CANR 16; SAAS 3; SATA 2

Key, Ellen (Karolina Sofia)
1849-1926 .... **TCLC 65**
See also DLB 259

Keyber, Conny
See Fielding, Henry

Keyes, Daniel 1927- .... **CLC 80**
See also AAYA 23; BYA 11; CA 181; 17-20R, 181; CANR 10, 26, 54, 74; DA; DA3; DAC; DAM MST, NOV; EXPN; LAIT 4; MTCW 2; MTFW 2005; NFS 2; SATA 37; SFW 4

Keynes, John Maynard
1883-1946 .... **TCLC 64**
See also CA 162, 163; CAAE 114; DLBD 10; MTCW 2; MTFW 2005

Khanshendel, Chiron
See Rose, Wendy

Khayyam, Omar 1048-1131 ... **CMLC 11; PC 8**
See Omar Khayyam
See also DA3; DAM POET; WLIT 6

Kherdian, David 1931- .... **CLC 6, 9**
See also AAYA 42; CA 192; 21-24R, 192; 2; CANR 39, 78; CLR 24; JRDA; LAIT 3; MAICYA 1, 2; SATA 16, 74; SATA-Essay 125

Khlebnikov, Velimir .... **TCLC 20**
See Khlebnikov, Viktor Vladimirovich
See also DLB 295; EW 10; EWL 3; RGWL 2, 3

Khlebnikov, Viktor Vladimirovich 1885-1922
See Khlebnikov, Velimir
See also CA 217; CAAE 117

Khodasevich, V.F.
See Khodasevich, Vladislav

Khodasevich, Vladislav
1886-1939 .... **TCLC 15**
See also CAAE 115; DLB 317; EWL 3

Khodasevich, Vladislav Felitsianovich
See Khodasevich, Vladislav

Kielland, Alexander Lange
1849-1906 .... **TCLC 5**
See also CAAE 104

Kiely, Benedict 1919-2007 . **CLC 23, 43; SSC 58**
See also CA 1-4R; CAAS 257; CANR 2, 84; CN 1, 2, 3, 4, 5, 6, 7; DLB 15, 319; TCLE 1:1

Kienzle, William X. 1928-2001 .... **CLC 25**
See also CA 93-96; 1; CAAS 203; CANR 9, 31, 59, 111; CMW 4; DA3; DAM POP; INT CANR-31; MSW; MTCW 1, 2; MTFW 2005

Kierkegaard, Soren 1813-1855 ..... **NCLC 34, 78, 125**
See also DLB 300; EW 6; LMFS 2; RGWL 3; TWA

Kieslowski, Krzysztof 1941-1996 .... **CLC 120**
See also CA 147; CAAS 151

Killens, John Oliver 1916-1987 .... **CLC 10**
See also BW 2; CA 77-80; 2; CAAS 123; CANR 26; CN 1, 2, 3, 4; DLB 33; EWL 3

Killigrew, Anne 1660-1685 .... **LC 4, 73**
See also DLB 131

Killigrew, Thomas 1612-1683 .... **LC 57**
See also DLB 58; RGEL 2

Kim
See Simenon, Georges (Jacques Christian)

Kincaid, Jamaica 1949- ...... **BLC 2; CLC 43, 68, 137, 234; SSC 72**
See also AAYA 13, 56; AFAW 2; AMWS 7; BRWS 7; BW 2, 3; CA 125; CANR 47, 59, 95, 133; CDALBS; CDWLB 3; CLR 63; CN 4, 5, 6, 7; DA3; DAM MULT, NOV; DLB 157, 227; DNFS 1; EWL 3; EXPS; FW; LATS 1:2; LMFS 2; MAL 5; MTCW 2; MTFW 2005; NCFS 1; NFS 3; SSFS 5, 7; TUS; WWE 1; YAW

King, Francis (Henry) 1923- .... **CLC 8, 53, 145**
See also CA 1-4R; CANR 1, 33, 86; CN 1, 2, 3, 4, 5, 6, 7; DAM NOV; DLB 15, 139; MTCW 1

King, Kennedy
See Brown, George Douglas

King, Martin Luther, Jr. 1929-1968 . **BLC 2; CLC 83; WLCS**
See also BW 2, 3; CA 25-28; CANR 27, 44; CAP 2; DA; DA3; DAB; DAC; DAM MST, MULT; LAIT 5; LATS 1:2; MTCW 1, 2; MTFW 2005; SATA 14

King, Stephen 1947- .... **CLC 12, 26, 37, 61, 113, 228; SSC 17, 55**
See also AAYA 1, 17; AMWS 5; BEST 90:1; BPFB 2; CA 61-64; CANR 1, 30, 52, 76, 119, 134; CN 7; CPW; DA3; DAM NOV, POP; DLB 143; DLBY 1980; HGG; JRDA; LAIT 5; MTCW 1, 2; MTFW 2005; RGAL 4; SATA 9, 55, 161; SUFW 1, 2; WYAS 1; YAW

King, Stephen Edwin
See King, Stephen

King, Steve
See King, Stephen

King, Thomas 1943- .... **CLC 89, 171; NNAL**
See also CA 144; CANR 95; CCA 1; CN 6, 7; DAC; DAM MULT; DLB 175, 334; SATA 96

Kingman, Lee .... **CLC 17**
See Natti, (Mary) Lee
See also CWRI 5; SAAS 3; SATA 1, 67

Kingsley, Charles 1819-1875 .... **NCLC 35**
See also CLR 77; DLB 21, 32, 163, 178, 190; FANT; MAICYA 2; MAICYAS 1; RGEL 2; WCH; YABC 2

Kingsley, Henry 1830-1876 .... **NCLC 107**
See also DLB 21, 230; RGEL 2

Kingsley, Sidney 1906-1995 .... **CLC 44**
See also CA 85-88; CAAS 147; CAD; DFS 14, 19; DLB 7; MAL 5; RGAL 4

Kingsolver, Barbara 1955- .... **CLC 55, 81, 130, 216**
See also AAYA 15; AMWS 7; CA 134; CAAE 129; CANR 60, 96, 133; CDALBS; CN 7; CPW; CSW; DA3; DAM POP; DLB 206; INT CA-134; LAIT 5; MTCW 2; MTFW 2005; NFS 5, 10, 12, 24; RGAL 4; TCLE 1:1

Cumulative Author Index

Korolenko, V.G.
See Korolenko, Vladimir G.
Korolenko, Vladimir
See Korolenko, Vladimir G.
Korolenko, Vladimir G.
1853-1921 .... **TCLC 22**
See also CAAE 121; DLB 277
Korolenko, Vladimir Galaktionovich
See Korolenko, Vladimir G.
Korzybski, Alfred (Habdank Skarbek)
1879-1950 .... **TCLC 61**
See also CA 160; CAAE 123
Kosinski, Jerzy 1933-1991 ..... **CLC 1, 2, 3, 6,
10, 15, 53, 70**
See also AMWS 7; BPFB 2; CA 17-20R;
CAAS 134; CANR 9, 46; CN 1, 2, 3, 4;
DA3; DAM NOV; DLB 2, 299; DLBY
1982; EWL 3; HGG; MAL 5; MTCW 1,
2; MTFW 2005; NFS 12; RGAL 4;
RGHL; TUS
Kostelanetz, Richard (Cory) 1940- .. **CLC 28**
See also CA 13-16R; 8; CANR 38, 77; CN
4, 5, 6; CP 2, 3, 4, 5, 6, 7
Kostrowitzki, Wilhelm Apollinaris de
1880-1918
See Apollinaire, Guillaume
See also CAAE 104
Kotlowitz, Robert 1924- .... **CLC 4**
See also CA 33-36R; CANR 36
Kotzebue, August (Friedrich Ferdinand) von
1761-1819 .... **NCLC 25**
See also DLB 94
Kotzwinkle, William 1938- ..... **CLC 5, 14, 35**
See also BPFB 2; CA 45-48; CANR 3, 44,
84, 129; CLR 6; CN 7; DLB 173; FANT;
MAICYA 1, 2; SATA 24, 70, 146; SFW
4; SUFW 2; YAW
Kowna, Stancy
See Szymborska, Wislawa
Kozol, Jonathan 1936- .... **CLC 17**
See also AAYA 46; CA 61-64; CANR 16,
45, 96; MTFW 2005
Kozoll, Michael 1940(?)- .... **CLC 35**
Kramer, Kathryn 19(?)- .... **CLC 34**
Kramer, Larry 1935- .... **CLC 42; DC 8**
See also CA 126; CAAE 124; CANR 60,
132; DAM POP; DLB 249; GLL 1
Krasicki, Ignacy 1735-1801 .... **NCLC 8**
Krasinski, Zygmunt 1812-1859 .... **NCLC 4**
See also RGWL 2, 3
Kraus, Karl 1874-1936 .... **TCLC 5**
See also CA 216; CAAE 104; DLB 118;
EWL 3
Kreve (Mickevicius), Vincas
1882-1954 .... **TCLC 27**
See also CA 170; DLB 220; EWL 3
Kristeva, Julia 1941- .... **CLC 77, 140**
See also CA 154; CANR 99; DLB 242;
EWL 3; FW; LMFS 2
Kristofferson, Kris 1936- .... **CLC 26**
See also CA 104
Krizanc, John 1956- .... **CLC 57**
See also CA 187
Krleza, Miroslav 1893-1981 .... **CLC 8, 114**
See also CA 97-100; CAAS 105; CANR
50; CDWLB 4; DLB 147; EW 11; RGWL
2, 3
Kroetsch, Robert (Paul) 1927- .... **CLC 5, 23,
57, 132**
See also CA 17-20R; CANR 8, 38; CCA 1;
CN 2, 3, 4, 5, 6, 7; CP 6, 7; DAC; DAM
POET; DLB 53; MTCW 1
Kroetz, Franz
See Kroetz, Franz Xaver
Kroetz, Franz Xaver 1946- .... **CLC 41**
See also CA 130; CANR 142; CWW 2;
EWL 3
Kroker, Arthur (W.) 1945- .... **CLC 77**
See also CA 161

Kroniuk, Lisa
See Berton, Pierre (Francis de Marigny)
Kropotkin, Peter (Aleksieevich)
1842-1921 .... **TCLC 36**
See Kropotkin, Petr Alekseevich
See also CA 219; CAAE 119
Kropotkin, Petr Alekseevich
See Kropotkin, Peter (Aleksieevich)
See also DLB 277
Krotkov, Yuri 1917-1981 .... **CLC 19**
See also CA 102
Krumb
See Crumb, R.
Krumgold, Joseph (Quincy)
1908-1980 .... **CLC 12**
See also BYA 1, 2; CA 9-12R; CAAS 101;
CANR 7; MAICYA 1, 2; SATA 1, 48;
SATA-Obit 23; YAW
Krumwitz
See Crumb, R.
Krutch, Joseph Wood 1893-1970 ..... **CLC 24**
See also ANW; CA 1-4R; CAAS 25-28R;
CANR 4; DLB 63, 206, 275
Krutzch, Gus
See Eliot, T(homas) S(tearns)
Krylov, Ivan Andreevich
1768(?)-1844 .... **NCLC 1**
See also DLB 150
Kubin, Alfred (Leopold Isidor)
1877-1959 .... **TCLC 23**
See also CA 149; CAAE 112; CANR 104;
DLB 81
Kubrick, Stanley 1928-1999 .... **CLC 16;
TCLC 112**
See also AAYA 30; CA 81-84; CAAS 177;
CANR 33; DLB 26
Kumin, Maxine 1925- .... **CLC 5, 13, 28, 164;
PC 15**
See also AITN 2; AMWS 4; ANW; CA
1-4R; 8; CANR 1, 21, 69, 115, 140; CP 2,
3, 4, 5, 6, 7; CWP; DA3; DAM POET;
DLB 5; EWL 3; EXPP; MTCW 1, 2;
MTFW 2005; PAB; PFS 18; SATA 12
Kundera, Milan 1929- . **CLC 4, 9, 19, 32, 68,
115, 135, 234; SSC 24**
See also AAYA 2, 62; BPFB 2; CA 85-88;
CANR 19, 52, 74, 144; CDWLB 4; CWW
2; DA3; DAM NOV; DLB 232; EW 13;
EWL 3; MTCW 1, 2; MTFW 2005; NFS
18; RGSF 2; RGWL 3; SSFS 10
Kunene, Mazisi 1930-2006 .... **CLC 85**
See also BW 1, 3; CA 125; CAAS 252;
CANR 81; CP 1, 6, 7; DLB 117
Kunene, Mazisi Raymond
See Kunene, Mazisi
Kunene, Mazisi Raymond Fakazi Mngoni
See Kunene, Mazisi
Kung, Hans .... **CLC 130**
See Kung, Hans
Kung, Hans 1928-
See Kung, Hans
See also CA 53-56; CANR 66, 134; MTCW
1, 2; MTFW 2005
Kunikida Doppo 1869(?)-1908
See Doppo, Kunikida
See also DLB 180; EWL 3
Kunitz, Stanley 1905-2006 ..... **CLC 6, 11, 14,
148; PC 19**
See also AMWS 3; CA 41-44R; CAAS 250;
CANR 26, 57, 98; CP 1, 2, 3, 4, 5, 6, 7;
DA3; DLB 48; INT CANR-26; MAL 5;
MTCW 1, 2; MTFW 2005; PFS 11;
RGAL 4
Kunitz, Stanley Jasspon
See Kunitz, Stanley
Kunze, Reiner 1933- .... **CLC 10**
See also CA 93-96; CWW 2; DLB 75; EWL
3

Kuprin, Aleksander Ivanovich
1870-1938 .... **TCLC 5**
See Kuprin, Aleksandr Ivanovich; Kuprin,
Alexandr Ivanovich
See also CA 182; CAAE 104
Kuprin, Aleksandr Ivanovich
See Kuprin, Aleksander Ivanovich
See also DLB 295
Kuprin, Alexandr Ivanovich
See Kuprin, Aleksander Ivanovich
See also EWL 3
Kureishi, Hanif 1954- .. **CLC 64, 135; DC 26**
See also BRWS 11; CA 139; CANR 113;
CBD; CD 5, 6; CN 6, 7; DLB 194, 245;
GLL 2; IDFW 4; WLIT 4; WWE 1
Kurosawa, Akira 1910-1998 ..... **CLC 16, 119**
See also AAYA 11, 64; CA 101; CAAS 170;
CANR 46; DAM MULT
Kushner, Tony 1956- .... **CLC 81, 203; DC 10**
See also AAYA 61; AMWS 9; CA 144;
CAD; CANR 74, 130; CD 5, 6; DA3;
DAM DRAM; DFS 5; DLB 228; EWL 3;
GLL 1; LAIT 5; MAL 5; MTCW 2;
MTFW 2005; RGAL 4; RGHL; SATA 160
Kuttner, Henry 1915-1958 .... **TCLC 10**
See also CA 157; CAAE 107; DLB 8;
FANT; SCFW 1, 2; SFW 4
Kutty, Madhavi
See Das, Kamala
Kuzma, Greg 1944- .... **CLC 7**
See also CA 33-36R; CANR 70
Kuzmin, Mikhail (Alekseevich)
1872(?)-1936 .... **TCLC 40**
See also CA 170; DLB 295; EWL 3
Kyd, Thomas 1558-1594 .. **DC 3; LC 22, 125**
See also BRW 1; DAM DRAM; DFS 21;
DLB 62; IDTP; LMFS 1; RGEL 2; TEA;
WLIT 3
Kyprianos, Iossif
See Samarakis, Antonis
L. S.
See Stephen, Sir Leslie
Labe, Louise 1521-1566 .... **LC 120**
See also DLB 327
Labrunie, Gerard
See Nerval, Gerard de
La Bruyere, Jean de 1645-1696 .... **LC 17**
See also DLB 268; EW 3; GFL Beginnings
to 1789
LaBute, Neil 1963- .... **CLC 225**
See also CA 240
Lacan, Jacques (Marie Emile)
1901-1981 .... **CLC 75**
See also CA 121; CAAS 104; DLB 296;
EWL 3; TWA
Laclos, Pierre-Ambroise Francois
1741-1803 .... **NCLC 4, 87**
See also DLB 313; EW 4; GFL Beginnings
to 1789; RGWL 2, 3
Lacolere, Francois
See Aragon, Louis
La Colere, Francois
See Aragon, Louis
La Deshabilleuse
See Simenon, Georges (Jacques Christian)
Lady Gregory
See Gregory, Lady Isabella Augusta (Persse)
Lady of Quality, A
See Bagnold, Enid
**La Fayette, Marie-(Madelaine Pioche de la
Vergne)** 1634-1693 .... **LC 2**
See Lafayette, Marie-Madeleine
See also GFL Beginnings to 1789; RGWL
2, 3
Lafayette, Marie-Madeleine
See La Fayette, Marie-(Madelaine Pioche
de la Vergne)
See also DLB 268

Cumulative Author Index

Milne, A. A. 1882-1956 .... **TCLC 6, 88**
See also BRWS 5; CA 133; CAAE 104; CLR 1, 26, 108; CMW 4; CWRI 5; DA3; DAB; DAC; DAM MST; DLB 10, 77, 100, 160; FANT; MAICYA 1, 2; MTCW 1, 2; MTFW 2005; RGEL 2; SATA 100; WCH; YABC 1

Milne, Alan Alexander
See Milne, A. A.

Milner, Ron(ald) 1938-2004 ..... **BLC 3; CLC 56**
See also AITN 1; BW 1; CA 73-76; CAAS 230; CAD; CANR 24, 81; CD 5, 6; DAM MULT; DLB 38; MAL 5; MTCW 1

Milnes, Richard Monckton
1809-1885 .... **NCLC 61**
See also DLB 32, 184

Milosz, Czeslaw 1911-2004 .... **CLC 5, 11, 22, 31, 56, 82; PC 8; WLCS**
See also AAYA 62; CA 81-84; CAAS 230; CANR 23, 51, 91, 126; CDWLB 4; CWW 2; DA3; DAM MST, POET; DLB 215, 331; EW 13; EWL 3; MTCW 1, 2; MTFW 2005; PFS 16; RGHL; RGWL 2, 3

Milton, John 1608-1674 ..... **LC 9, 43, 92; PC 19, 29; WLC 4**
See also AAYA 65; BRW 2; BRWR 2; CD-BLB 1660-1789; DA; DA3; DAB; DAC; DAM MST, POET; DLB 131, 151, 281; EFS 1; EXPP; LAIT 1; PAB; PFS 3, 17; RGEL 2; TEA; WLIT 3; WP

Min, Anchee 1957- .... **CLC 86**
See also CA 146; CANR 94, 137; MTFW 2005

Minehaha, Cornelius
See Wedekind, Frank

Miner, Valerie 1947- .... **CLC 40**
See also CA 97-100; CANR 59; FW; GLL 2

Minimo, Duca
See D'Annunzio, Gabriele

Minot, Susan (Anderson) 1956- ...... **CLC 44, 159**
See also AMWS 6; CA 134; CANR 118; CN 6, 7

Minus, Ed 1938- .... **CLC 39**
See also CA 185

Mirabai 1498(?)-1550(?) .... **PC 48**
See also PFS 24

Miranda, Javier
See Bioy Casares, Adolfo
See also CWW 2

Mirbeau, Octave 1848-1917 .... **TCLC 55**
See also CA 216; DLB 123, 192; GFL 1789 to the Present

Mirikitani, Janice 1942- .... **AAL**
See also CA 211; DLB 312; RGAL 4

Mirk, John (?)-c. 1414 .... **LC 105**
See also DLB 146

Miro (Ferrer), Gabriel (Francisco Victor)
1879-1930 .... **TCLC 5**
See also CA 185; CAAE 104; DLB 322; EWL 3

Misharin, Alexandr .... **CLC 59**

Mishima, Yukio ... **CLC 2, 4, 6, 9, 27; DC 1; SSC 4; TCLC 161; WLC 4**
See Hiraoka, Kimitake
See also AAYA 50; BPFB 2; GLL 1; MJW; RGSF 2; RGWL 2, 3; SSFS 5, 12

Mistral, Frederic 1830-1914 .... **TCLC 51**
See also CA 213; CAAE 122; DLB 331; GFL 1789 to the Present

Mistral, Gabriela
See Godoy Alcayaga, Lucila
See also DLB 283, 331; DNFS 1; EWL 3; LAW; RGWL 2, 3; WP

Mistry, Rohinton 1952- ... **CLC 71, 196; SSC 73**
See also BRWS 10; CA 141; CANR 86, 114; CCA 1; CN 6, 7; DAC; DLB 334; SSFS 6

Mitchell, Clyde
See Ellison, Harlan

Mitchell, Emerson Blackhorse Barney
1945- .... **NNAL**
See also CA 45-48

Mitchell, James Leslie 1901-1935
See Gibbon, Lewis Grassic
See also CA 188; CAAE 104; DLB 15

Mitchell, Joni 1943- .... **CLC 12**
See also CA 112; CCA 1

Mitchell, Joseph (Quincy)
1908-1996 .... **CLC 98**
See also CA 77-80; CAAS 152; CANR 69; CN 1, 2, 3, 4, 5, 6; CSW; DLB 185; DLBY 1996

Mitchell, Margaret (Munnerlyn)
1900-1949 .... **TCLC 11, 170**
See also AAYA 23; BPFB 2; BYA 1; CA 125; CAAE 109; CANR 55, 94; CDALBS; DA3; DAM NOV, POP; DLB 9; LAIT 2; MAL 5; MTCW 1, 2; MTFW 2005; NFS 9; RGAL 4; RHW; TUS; WYAS 1; YAW

Mitchell, Peggy
See Mitchell, Margaret (Munnerlyn)

Mitchell, S(ilas) Weir 1829-1914 .... **TCLC 36**
See also CA 165; DLB 202; RGAL 4

Mitchell, W(illiam) O(rmond)
1914-1998 .... **CLC 25**
See also CA 77-80; CAAS 165; CANR 15, 43; CN 1, 2, 3, 4, 5, 6; DAC; DAM MST; DLB 88; TCLE 1:2

Mitchell, William (Lendrum)
1879-1936 .... **TCLC 81**
See also CA 213

Mitford, Mary Russell 1787-1855 ... **NCLC 4**
See also DLB 110, 116; RGEL 2

Mitford, Nancy 1904-1973 .... **CLC 44**
See also BRWS 10; CA 9-12R; CN 1; DLB 191; RGEL 2

Miyamoto, (Chujo) Yuriko
1899-1951 .... **TCLC 37**
See Miyamoto Yuriko
See also CA 170, 174

Miyamoto Yuriko
See Miyamoto, (Chujo) Yuriko
See also DLB 180

Miyazawa, Kenji 1896-1933 .... **TCLC 76**
See Miyazawa Kenji
See also CA 157; RGWL 3

Miyazawa Kenji
See Miyazawa, Kenji
See also EWL 3

Mizoguchi, Kenji 1898-1956 .... **TCLC 72**
See also CA 167

Mo, Timothy (Peter) 1950- .... **CLC 46, 134**
See also CA 117; CANR 128; CN 5, 6, 7; DLB 194; MTCW 1; WLIT 4; WWE 1

Modarressi, Taghi (M.) 1931-1997 ... **CLC 44**
See also CA 134; CAAE 121; INT CA-134

Modiano, Patrick (Jean) 1945- .... **CLC 18, 218**
See also CA 85-88; CANR 17, 40, 115; CWW 2; DLB 83, 299; EWL 3; RGHL

Mofolo, Thomas (Mokopu)
1875(?)-1948 .... **BLC 3; TCLC 22**
See also AFW; CA 153; CAAE 121; CANR 83; DAM MULT; DLB 225; EWL 3; MTCW 2; MTFW 2005; WLIT 2

Mohr, Nicholasa 1938- .... **CLC 12; HLC 2**
See also AAYA 8, 46; CA 49-52; CANR 1, 32, 64; CLR 22; DAM MULT; DLB 145; HW 1, 2; JRDA; LAIT 5; LLW; MAICYA 2; MAICYAS 1; RGAL 4; SAAS 8; SATA 8, 97; SATA-Essay 113; WYA; YAW

Moi, Toril 1953- .... **CLC 172**
See also CA 154; CANR 102; FW

Mojtabai, A(nn) G(race) 1938- ..... **CLC 5, 9, 15, 29**
See also CA 85-88; CANR 88

Moliere 1622-1673 ..... **DC 13; LC 10, 28, 64, 125, 127; WLC 4**
See also DA; DA3; DAB; DAC; DAM DRAM, MST; DFS 13, 18, 20; DLB 268; EW 3; GFL Beginnings to 1789; LATS 1:1; RGWL 2, 3; TWA

Molin, Charles
See Mayne, William (James Carter)

Molnar, Ferenc 1878-1952 .... **TCLC 20**
See also CA 153; CAAE 109; CANR 83; CDWLB 4; DAM DRAM; DLB 215; EWL 3; RGWL 2, 3

Momaday, N. Scott 1934- ...... **CLC 2, 19, 85, 95, 160; NNAL; PC 25; WLCS**
See also AAYA 11, 64; AMWS 4; ANW; BPFB 2; BYA 12; CA 25-28R; CANR 14, 34, 68, 134; CDALBS; CN 2, 3, 4, 5, 6, 7; CPW; DA; DA3; DAB; DAC; DAM MST, MULT, NOV, POP; DLB 143, 175, 256; EWL 3; EXPP; INT CANR-14; LAIT 4; LATS 1:2; MAL 5; MTCW 1, 2; MTFW 2005; NFS 10; PFS 2, 11; RGAL 4; SATA 48; SATA-Brief 30; TCWW 1, 2; WP; YAW

Monette, Paul 1945-1995 .... **CLC 82**
See also AMWS 10; CA 139; CAAS 147; CN 6; GLL 1

Monroe, Harriet 1860-1936 .... **TCLC 12**
See also CA 204; CAAE 109; DLB 54, 91

Monroe, Lyle
See Heinlein, Robert A.

Montagu, Elizabeth 1720-1800 .... **NCLC 7, 117**
See also FW

Montagu, Mary (Pierrepont) Wortley
1689-1762 .... **LC 9, 57; PC 16**
See also DLB 95, 101; FL 1:1; RGEL 2

Montagu, W. H.
See Coleridge, Samuel Taylor

Montague, John (Patrick) 1929- ..... **CLC 13, 46**
See also CA 9-12R; CANR 9, 69, 121; CP 1, 2, 3, 4, 5, 6, 7; DLB 40; EWL 3; MTCW 1; PFS 12; RGEL 2; TCLE 1:2

Montaigne, Michel (Eyquem) de
1533-1592 .... **LC 8, 105; WLC 4**
See also DA; DAB; DAC; DAM MST; DLB 327; EW 2; GFL Beginnings to 1789; LMFS 1; RGWL 2, 3; TWA

Montale, Eugenio 1896-1981 ... **CLC 7, 9, 18; PC 13**
See also CA 17-20R; CAAS 104; CANR 30; DLB 114, 331; EW 11; EWL 3; MTCW 1; PFS 22; RGWL 2, 3; TWA; WLIT 7

Montesquieu, Charles-Louis de Secondat
1689-1755 .... **LC 7, 69**
See also DLB 314; EW 3; GFL Beginnings to 1789; TWA

Montessori, Maria 1870-1952 ...... **TCLC 103**
See also CA 147; CAAE 115

Montgomery, (Robert) Bruce 1921(?)-1978
See Crispin, Edmund
See also CA 179; CAAS 104; CMW 4

Montgomery, L(ucy) M(aud)
1874-1942 .... **TCLC 51, 140**
See also AAYA 12; BYA 1; CA 137; CAAE 108; CLR 8, 91; DA3; DAC; DAM MST; DLB 92; DLBD 14; JRDA; MAICYA 1,

2; MTCW 2; MTFW 2005; RGEL 2;
SATA 100; TWA; WCH; WYA; YABC 1

Montgomery, Marion, Jr. 1925- .... **CLC 7**
See also AITN 1; CA 1-4R; CANR 3, 48,
162; CSW; DLB 6

Montgomery, Marion H. 1925-
See Montgomery, Marion, Jr.

Montgomery, Max
See Davenport, Guy (Mattison, Jr.)

Montherlant, Henry (Milon) de
1896-1972 .... **CLC 8, 19**
See also CA 85-88; CAAS 37-40R; DAM
DRAM; DLB 72, 321; EW 11; EWL 3;
GFL 1789 to the Present; MTCW 1

Monty Python
See Chapman, Graham; Cleese, John
(Marwood); Gilliam, Terry; Idle, Eric;
Jones, Terence Graham Parry; Palin,
Michael (Edward)
See also AAYA 7

Moodie, Susanna (Strickland)
1803-1885 .... **NCLC 14, 113**
See also DLB 99

Moody, Hiram 1961-
See Moody, Rick
See also CA 138; CANR 64, 112; MTFW
2005

Moody, Minerva
See Alcott, Louisa May

Moody, Rick .... **CLC 147**
See Moody, Hiram

Moody, William Vaughan
1869-1910 .... **TCLC 105**
See also CA 178; CAAE 110; DLB 7, 54;
MAL 5; RGAL 4

Mooney, Edward 1951-
See Mooney, Ted
See also CA 130

Mooney, Ted .... **CLC 25**
See Mooney, Edward

Moorcock, Michael 1939- ...... **CLC 5, 27, 58,
236**
See Bradbury, Edward P.
See also AAYA 26; CA 45-48; 5; CANR 2,
17, 38, 64, 122; CN 5, 6, 7; DLB 14, 231,
261, 319; FANT; MTCW 1, 2; MTFW
2005; SATA 93, 166; SCFW 1, 2; SFW 4;
SUFW 1, 2

Moorcock, Michael John
See Moorcock, Michael

Moore, Alan 1953- .... **CLC 230**
See also AAYA 51; CA 204; CANR 138;
DLB 261; MTFW 2005; SFW 4

Moore, Brian 1921-1999 ... **CLC 1, 3, 5, 7, 8,
19, 32, 90**
See Bryan, Michael
See also BRWS 9; CA 1-4R; CAAS 174;
CANR 1, 25, 42, 63; CCA 1; CN 1, 2, 3,
4, 5, 6; DAB; DAC; DAM MST; DLB
251; EWL 3; FANT; MTCW 1, 2; MTFW
2005; RGEL 2

Moore, Edward
See Muir, Edwin
See also RGEL 2

Moore, G. E. 1873-1958 .... **TCLC 89**
See also DLB 262

Moore, George Augustus
1852-1933 .... **SSC 19; TCLC 7**
See also BRW 6; CA 177; CAAE 104; DLB
10, 18, 57, 135; EWL 3; RGEL 2; RGSF
2

Moore, Lorrie .... **CLC 39, 45, 68**
See Moore, Marie Lorena
See also AMWS 10; CN 5, 6, 7; DLB 234;
SSFS 19

Moore, Marianne (Craig)
1887-1972 .... **CLC 1, 2, 4, 8, 10, 13, 19,
47; PC 4, 49; WLCS**
See also AMW; CA 1-4R; CAAS 33-36R;
CANR 3, 61; CDALB 1929-1941; CP 1;
DA; DA3; DAB; DAC; DAM MST,
POET; DLB 45; DLBD 7; EWL 3; EXPP;
FL 1:6; MAL 5; MBL; MTCW 1, 2;
MTFW 2005; PAB; PFS 14, 17; RGAL 4;
SATA 20; TUS; WP

Moore, Marie Lorena 1957- .... **CLC 165**
See Moore, Lorrie
See also CA 116; CANR 39, 83, 139; DLB
234; MTFW 2005

Moore, Michael 1954- .... **CLC 218**
See also AAYA 53; CA 166; CANR 150

Moore, Thomas 1779-1852 .... **NCLC 6, 110**
See also DLB 96, 144; RGEL 2

Moorhouse, Frank 1938- .... **SSC 40**
See also CA 118; CANR 92; CN 3, 4, 5, 6,
7; DLB 289; RGSF 2

Mora, Pat 1942- .... **HLC 2**
See also AMWS 13; CA 129; CANR 57,
81, 112; CLR 58; DAM MULT; DLB 209;
HW 1, 2; LLW; MAICYA 2; MTFW
2005; SATA 92, 134

Moraga, Cherríe 1952- ...... **CLC 126; DC 22**
See also CA 131; CANR 66, 154; DAM
MULT; DLB 82, 249; FW; GLL 1; HW 1,
2; LLW

Morand, Paul 1888-1976 .... **CLC 41; SSC 22**
See also CA 184; CAAS 69-72; DLB 65;
EWL 3

Morante, Elsa 1918-1985 .... **CLC 8, 47**
See also CA 85-88; CAAS 117; CANR 35;
DLB 177; EWL 3; MTCW 1, 2; MTFW
2005; RGHL; RGWL 2, 3; WLIT 7

Moravia, Alberto .... **CLC 2, 7, 11, 27, 46;
SSC 26**
See Pincherle, Alberto
See also DLB 177; EW 12; EWL 3; MTCW
2; RGSF 2; RGWL 2, 3; WLIT 7

More, Hannah 1745-1833 ...... **NCLC 27, 141**
See also DLB 107, 109, 116, 158; RGEL 2

More, Henry 1614-1687 .... **LC 9**
See also DLB 126, 252

More, Sir Thomas 1478(?)-1535 ... **LC 10, 32,
140**
See also BRWC 1; BRWS 7; DLB 136, 281;
LMFS 1; RGEL 2; TEA

Moreas, Jean .... **TCLC 18**
See Papadiamantopoulos, Johannes
See also GFL 1789 to the Present

Moreton, Andrew Esq.
See Defoe, Daniel

Morgan, Berry 1919-2002 .... **CLC 6**
See also CA 49-52; CAAS 208; DLB 6

Morgan, Claire
See Highsmith, Patricia
See also GLL 1

Morgan, Edwin (George) 1920- .... **CLC 31**
See also BRWS 9; CA 5-8R; CANR 3, 43,
90; CP 1, 2, 3, 4, 5, 6, 7; DLB 27

Morgan, (George) Frederick
1922-2004 .... **CLC 23**
See also CA 17-20R; CAAS 224; CANR
21, 144; CP 2, 3, 4, 5, 6, 7

Morgan, Harriet
See Mencken, H(enry) L(ouis)

Morgan, Jane
See Cooper, James Fenimore

Morgan, Janet 1945- .... **CLC 39**
See also CA 65-68

Morgan, Lady 1776(?)-1859 .... **NCLC 29**
See also DLB 116, 158; RGEL 2

Morgan, Robin (Evonne) 1941- .... **CLC 2**
See also CA 69-72; CANR 29, 68; FW;
GLL 2; MTCW 1; SATA 80

Morgan, Scott
See Kuttner, Henry

Morgan, Seth 1949(?)-1990 .... **CLC 65**
See also CA 185; CAAS 132

**Morgenstern, Christian (Otto Josef
Wolfgang)** 1871-1914 .... **TCLC 8**
See also CA 191; CAAE 105; EWL 3

Morgenstern, S.
See Goldman, William

Mori, Rintaro
See Mori Ogai
See also CAAE 110

Mori, Toshio 1910-1980 .... **AAL; SSC 83**
See also CA 244; CAAE 116; DLB 312;
RGSF 2

Moricz, Zsigmond 1879-1942 .... **TCLC 33**
See also CA 165; DLB 215; EWL 3

Morike, Eduard (Friedrich)
1804-1875 .... **NCLC 10**
See also DLB 133; RGWL 2, 3

Mori Ogai 1862-1922 .... **TCLC 14**
See Ogai
See also CA 164; DLB 180; EWL 3; RGWL
3; TWA

Moritz, Karl Philipp 1756-1793 .... **LC 2**
See also DLB 94

Morland, Peter Henry
See Faust, Frederick (Schiller)

Morley, Christopher (Darlington)
1890-1957 .... **TCLC 87**
See also CA 213; CAAE 112; DLB 9; MAL
5; RGAL 4

Morren, Theophil
See Hofmannsthal, Hugo von

Morris, Bill 1952- .... **CLC 76**
See also CA 225

Morris, Julian
See West, Morris L(anglo)

Morris, Steveland Judkins (?)-
See Wonder, Stevie

Morris, William 1834-1896 . **NCLC 4; PC 55**
See also BRW 5; CDBLB 1832-1890; DLB
18, 35, 57, 156, 178, 184; FANT; RGEL
2; SFW 4; SUFW

Morris, Wright (Marion) 1910-1998 . **CLC 1,
3, 7, 18, 37; TCLC 107**
See also AMW; CA 9-12R; CAAS 167;
CANR 21, 81; CN 1, 2, 3, 4, 5, 6; DLB
2, 206, 218; DLBY 1981; EWL 3; MAL
5; MTCW 1, 2; MTFW 2005; RGAL 4;
TCWW 1, 2

Morrison, Arthur 1863-1945 .... **SSC 40;
TCLC 72**
See also CA 157; CAAE 120; CMW 4;
DLB 70, 135, 197; RGEL 2

Morrison, Chloe Anthony Wofford
See Morrison, Toni

Morrison, James Douglas 1943-1971
See Morrison, Jim
See also CA 73-76; CANR 40

Morrison, Jim .... **CLC 17**
See Morrison, James Douglas

Morrison, John Gordon 1904-1998 ... **SSC 93**
See also CA 103; CANR 92; DLB 260

Morrison, Toni 1931- ..... **BLC 3; CLC 4, 10,
22, 55, 81, 87, 173, 194; WLC 4**
See also AAYA 1, 22, 61; AFAW 1, 2;
AMWC 1; AMWS 3; BPFB 1; BW 2, 3;
CA 29-32R; CANR 27, 42, 67, 113, 124;
CDALB 1968-1988; CLR 99; CN 3, 4, 5,
6, 7; CPW; DA; DA3; DAB; DAC; DAM
MST, MULT, NOV, POP; DLB 6, 33, 143,
331; DLBY 1981; EWL 3; EXPN; FL 1:6;
FW; GL 3; LAIT 2, 4; LATS 1:2; LMFS
2; MAL 5; MBL; MTCW 1, 2; MTFW
2005; NFS 1, 6, 8, 14; RGAL 4; RHW;
SATA 57, 144; SSFS 5; TCLE 1:2; TUS;
YAW

Paine, Thomas 1737-1809 .... **NCLC 62**
See also AMWS 1; CDALB 1640-1865;
DLB 31, 43, 73, 158; LAIT 1; RGAL 4;
RGEL 2; TUS

Pakenham, Antonia
See Fraser, Antonia

Palamas, Costis
See Palamas, Kostes

Palamas, Kostes 1859-1943 .... **TCLC 5**
See Palamas, Kostis
See also CA 190; CAAE 105; RGWL 2, 3

Palamas, Kostis
See Palamas, Kostes
See also EWL 3

Palazzeschi, Aldo 1885-1974 .... **CLC 11**
See also CA 89-92; CAAS 53-56; DLB 114,
264; EWL 3

Pales Matos, Luis 1898-1959 .... **HLCS 2**
See Pales Matos, Luis
See also DLB 290; HW 1; LAW

Paley, Grace 1922- .. **CLC 4, 6, 37, 140; SSC
8**
See also AMWS 6; CA 25-28R; CANR 13,
46, 74, 118; CN 2, 3, 4, 5, 6, 7; CPW;
DA3; DAM POP; DLB 28, 218; EWL 3;
EXPS; FW; INT CANR-13; MAL 5;
MBL; MTCW 1, 2; MTFW 2005; RGAL
4; RGSF 2; SSFS 3, 20

Palin, Michael (Edward) 1943- .... **CLC 21**
See Monty Python
See also CA 107; CANR 35, 109; SATA 67

Palliser, Charles 1947- .... **CLC 65**
See also CA 136; CANR 76; CN 5, 6, 7

Palma, Ricardo 1833-1919 .... **TCLC 29**
See also CA 168; LAW

Pamuk, Orhan 1952- .... **CLC 185**
See also CA 142; CANR 75, 127; CWW 2;
WLIT 6

Pancake, Breece Dexter 1952-1979
See Pancake, Breece D'J
See also CA 123; CAAS 109

Pancake, Breece D'J .... **CLC 29; SSC 61**
See Pancake, Breece Dexter
See also DLB 130

Panchenko, Nikolai .... **CLC 59**

Pankhurst, Emmeline (Goulden)
1858-1928 .... **TCLC 100**
See also CAAE 116; FW

Panko, Rudy
See Gogol, Nikolai (Vasilyevich)

Papadiamantis, Alexandros
1851-1911 .... **TCLC 29**
See also CA 168; EWL 3

Papadiamantopoulos, Johannes 1856-1910
See Moreas, Jean
See also CA 242; CAAE 117

Papini, Giovanni 1881-1956 .... **TCLC 22**
See also CA 180; CAAE 121; DLB 264

Paracelsus 1493-1541 .... **LC 14**
See also DLB 179

Parasol, Peter
See Stevens, Wallace

Pardo Bazan, Emilia 1851-1921 .... **SSC 30;
TCLC 189**
See also EWL 3; FW; RGSF 2; RGWL 2, 3

Pareto, Vilfredo 1848-1923 .... **TCLC 69**
See also CA 175

Paretsky, Sara 1947- .... **CLC 135**
See also AAYA 30; BEST 90:3; CA 129;
CAAE 125; CANR 59, 95; CMW 4;
CPW; DA3; DAM POP; DLB 306; INT
CA-129; MSW; RGAL 4

Parfenie, Maria
See Codrescu, Andrei

Parini, Jay (Lee) 1948- .... **CLC 54, 133**
See also CA 229; 97-100, 229; 16; CANR
32, 87

Park, Jordan
See Kornbluth, C(yril) M.; Pohl, Frederik

Park, Robert E(zra) 1864-1944 ..... **TCLC 73**
See also CA 165; CAAE 122

Parker, Bert
See Ellison, Harlan

Parker, Dorothy (Rothschild)
1893-1967 . **CLC 15, 68; PC 28; SSC 2,
101; TCLC 143**
See also AMWS 9; CA 19-20; CAAS 25-
28R; CAP 2; DA3; DAM POET; DLB 11,
45, 86; EXPP; FW; MAL 5; MBL;
MTCW 1, 2; MTFW 2005; PFS 18;
RGAL 4; RGSF 2; TUS

Parker, Robert B. 1932- .... **CLC 27**
See also AAYA 28; BEST 89:4; BPFB 3;
CA 49-52; CANR 1, 26, 52, 89, 128;
CMW 4; CPW; DAM NOV, POP; DLB
306; INT CANR-26; MSW; MTCW 1;
MTFW 2005

Parker, Robert Brown
See Parker, Robert B.

Parker, Theodore 1810-1860 .... **NCLC 186**
See also DLB 1, 235

Parkin, Frank 1940- .... **CLC 43**
See also CA 147

Parkman, Francis, Jr. 1823-1893 .. **NCLC 12**
See also AMWS 2; DLB 1, 30, 183, 186,
235; RGAL 4

Parks, Gordon 1912-2006 .... **BLC 3; CLC 1,
16**
See also AAYA 36; AITN 2; BW 2, 3; CA
41-44R; CAAS 249; CANR 26, 66, 145;
DA3; DAM MULT; DLB 33; MTCW 2;
MTFW 2005; SATA 8, 108; SATA-Obit
175

Parks, Suzan-Lori 1964(?)- .... **DC 23**
See also AAYA 55; CA 201; CAD; CD 5,
6; CWD; DFS 22; RGAL 4

Parks, Tim(othy Harold) 1954- ...... **CLC 147**
See also CA 131; CAAE 126; CANR 77,
144; CN 7; DLB 231; INT CA-131

Parmenides c. 515B.C.-c.
450B.C. .... **CMLC 22**
See also DLB 176

Parnell, Thomas 1679-1718 .... **LC 3**
See also DLB 95; RGEL 2

Parr, Catherine c. 1513(?)-1548 .... **LC 86**
See also DLB 136

Parra, Nicanor 1914- ... **CLC 2, 102; HLC 2;
PC 39**
See also CA 85-88; CANR 32; CWW 2;
DAM MULT; DLB 283; EWL 3; HW 1;
LAW; MTCW 1

Parra Sanojo, Ana Teresa de la
1890-1936 .... **HLCS 2**
See de la Parra, (Ana) Teresa (Sonojo)
See also LAW

Parrish, Mary Frances
See Fisher, M(ary) F(rances) K(ennedy)

Parshchikov, Aleksei 1954- .... **CLC 59**
See Parshchikov, Aleksei Maksimovich

Parshchikov, Aleksei Maksimovich
See Parshchikov, Aleksei
See also DLB 285

Parson, Professor
See Coleridge, Samuel Taylor

Parson Lot
See Kingsley, Charles

Parton, Sara Payson Willis
1811-1872 .... **NCLC 86**
See also DLB 43, 74, 239

Partridge, Anthony
See Oppenheim, E(dward) Phillips

Pascal, Blaise 1623-1662 .... **LC 35**
See also DLB 268; EW 3; GFL Beginnings
to 1789; RGWL 2, 3; TWA

Pascoli, Giovanni 1855-1912 .... **TCLC 45**
See also CA 170; EW 7; EWL 3

Pasolini, Pier Paolo 1922-1975 .. **CLC 20, 37,
106; PC 17**
See also CA 93-96; CAAS 61-64; CANR
63; DLB 128, 177; EWL 3; MTCW 1;
RGWL 2, 3

Pasquini
See Silone, Ignazio

Pastan, Linda (Olenik) 1932- .... **CLC 27**
See also CA 61-64; CANR 18, 40, 61, 113;
CP 3, 4, 5, 6, 7; CSW; CWP; DAM
POET; DLB 5; PFS 8, 25

Pasternak, Boris 1890-1960 ... **CLC 7, 10, 18,
63; PC 6; SSC 31; TCLC 188; WLC 4**
See also BPFB 3; CA 127; CAAS 116; DA;
DA3; DAB; DAC; DAM MST, NOV,
POET; DLB 302, 331; EW 10; MTCW 1,
2; MTFW 2005; RGSF 2; RGWL 2, 3;
TWA; WP

Patchen, Kenneth 1911-1972 .... **CLC 1, 2, 18**
See also BG 1:3; CA 1-4R; CAAS 33-36R;
CANR 3, 35; CN 1; CP 1; DAM POET;
DLB 16, 48; EWL 3; MAL 5; MTCW 1;
RGAL 4

Pater, Walter (Horatio) 1839-1894 . **NCLC 7,
90, 159**
See also BRW 5; CDBLB 1832-1890; DLB
57, 156; RGEL 2; TEA

Paterson, A(ndrew) B(arton)
1864-1941 .... **TCLC 32**
See also CA 155; DLB 230; RGEL 2; SATA
97

Paterson, Banjo
See Paterson, A(ndrew) B(arton)

Paterson, Katherine 1932- .... **CLC 12, 30**
See also AAYA 1, 31; BYA 1, 2, 7; CA 21-
24R; CANR 28, 59, 111; CLR 7, 50;
CWRI 5; DLB 52; JRDA; LAIT 4; MAI-
CYA 1, 2; MAICYAS 1; MTCW 1; SATA
13, 53, 92, 133; WYA; YAW

Paterson, Katherine Womeldorf
See Paterson, Katherine

Patmore, Coventry Kersey Dighton
1823-1896 .... **NCLC 9; PC 59**
See also DLB 35, 98; RGEL 2; TEA

Paton, Alan 1903-1988 ..... **CLC 4, 10, 25, 55,
106; TCLC 165; WLC 4**
See also AAYA 26; AFW; BPFB 3; BRWS
2; BYA 1; CA 13-16; CAAS 125; CANR
22; CAP 1; CN 1, 2, 3, 4; DA; DA3;
DAB; DAC; DAM MST, NOV; DLB 225;
DLBD 17; EWL 3; EXPN; LAIT 4;
MTCW 1, 2; MTFW 2005; NFS 3, 12;
RGEL 2; SATA 11; SATA-Obit 56; TWA;
WLIT 2; WWE 1

Paton Walsh, Gillian
See Paton Walsh, Jill
See also AAYA 47; BYA 1, 8

Paton Walsh, Jill 1937- .... **CLC 35**
See Paton Walsh, Gillian; Walsh, Jill Paton
See also AAYA 11; CANR 38, 83, 158; CLR
2, 65; DLB 161; JRDA; MAICYA 1, 2;
SAAS 3; SATA 4, 72, 109; YAW

Patsauq, Markoosie 1942- .... **NNAL**
See also CA 101; CLR 23; CWRI 5; DAM
MULT

Patterson, (Horace) Orlando (Lloyd)
1940- .... **BLCS**
See also BW 1; CA 65-68; CANR 27, 84;
CN 1, 2, 3, 4, 5, 6

Patton, George S(mith), Jr.
1885-1945 .... **TCLC 79**
See also CA 189

Paulding, James Kirke 1778-1860 ... **NCLC 2**
See also DLB 3, 59, 74, 250; RGAL 4

Paulin, Thomas Neilson
See Paulin, Tom

Paulin, Tom 1949- .... **CLC 37, 177**
See also CA 128; CAAE 123; CANR 98;
CP 3, 4, 5, 6, 7; DLB 40

Petrakis, Harry Mark 1923- .... **CLC 3**
    See also CA 9-12R; CANR 4, 30, 85, 155;
    CN 1, 2, 3, 4, 5, 6, 7
Petrarch 1304-1374 .... **CMLC 20; PC 8**
    See also DA3; DAM POET; EW 2; LMFS
    1; RGWL 2, 3; WLIT 7
Petronius c. 20-66 .... **CMLC 34**
    See also AW 2; CDWLB 1; DLB 211;
    RGWL 2, 3; WLIT 8
Petrov, Evgeny .... **TCLC 21**
    See Kataev, Evgeny Petrovich
Petry, Ann (Lane) 1908-1997 .. **CLC 1, 7, 18;**
    TCLC 112
    See also AFAW 1, 2; BPFB 3; BW 1, 3;
    BYA 2; CA 5-8R; 6; CAAS 157; CANR
    4, 46; CLR 12; CN 1, 2, 3, 4, 5, 6; DLB
    76; EWL 3; JRDA; LAIT 1; MAICYA 1,
    2; MAICYAS 1; MTCW 1; RGAL 4;
    SATA 5; SATA-Obit 94; TUS
Petursson, Halligrimur 1614-1674 .... **LC 8**
Peychinovich
    See Vazov, Ivan (Minchov)
Phaedrus c. 15B.C.-c. 50 .... **CMLC 25**
    See also DLB 211
Phelps (Ward), Elizabeth Stuart
    See Phelps, Elizabeth Stuart
    See also FW
Phelps, Elizabeth Stuart
    1844-1911 .... **TCLC 113**
    See Phelps (Ward), Elizabeth Stuart
    See also CA 242; DLB 74
Philips, Katherine 1632-1664 . **LC 30; PC 40**
    See also DLB 131; RGEL 2
Philipson, Ilene J. 1950- .... **CLC 65**
    See also CA 219
Philipson, Morris H. 1926- .... **CLC 53**
    See also CA 1-4R; CANR 4
Phillips, Caryl 1958- ..... **BLCS; CLC 96, 224**
    See also BRWS 5; BW 2; CA 141; CANR
    63, 104, 140; CBD; CD 5, 6; CN 5, 6, 7;
    DA3; DAM MULT; DLB 157; EWL 3;
    MTCW 2; MTFW 2005; WLIT 4; WWE
    1
Phillips, David Graham
    1867-1911 .... **TCLC 44**
    See also CA 176; CAAE 108; DLB 9, 12,
    303; RGAL 4
Phillips, Jack
    See Sandburg, Carl (August)
Phillips, Jayne Anne 1952- .... **CLC 15, 33,**
    139; SSC 16
    See also AAYA 57; BPFB 3; CA 101;
    CANR 24, 50, 96; CN 4, 5, 6, 7; CSW;
    DLBY 1980; INT CANR-24; MTCW 1,
    2; MTFW 2005; RGAL 4; RGSF 2; SSFS
    4
Phillips, Richard
    See Dick, Philip K.
Phillips, Robert (Schaeffer) 1938- .... **CLC 28**
    See also CA 17-20R; 13; CANR 8; DLB
    105
Phillips, Ward
    See Lovecraft, H. P.
Philostratus, Flavius c. 179-c.
    244 .... **CMLC 62**
Piccolo, Lucio 1901-1969 .... **CLC 13**
    See also CA 97-100; DLB 114; EWL 3
Pickthall, Marjorie L(owry) C(hristie)
    1883-1922 .... **TCLC 21**
    See also CAAE 107; DLB 92
Pico della Mirandola, Giovanni
    1463-1494 .... **LC 15**
    See also LMFS 1
Piercy, Marge 1936- .... **CLC 3, 6, 14, 18, 27,**
    62, 128; PC 29
    See also BPFB 3; CA 187; 21-24R, 187; 1;
    CANR 13, 43, 66, 111; CN 3, 4, 5, 6, 7;
    CP 1, 2, 3, 4, 5, 6, 7; CWP; DLB 120,
    227; EXPP; FW; MAL 5; MTCW 1, 2;
    MTFW 2005; PFS 9, 22; SFW 4

Piers, Robert
    See Anthony, Piers
Pieyre de Mandiargues, Andre 1909-1991
    See Mandiargues, Andre Pieyre de
    See also CA 103; CAAS 136; CANR 22,
    82; EWL 3; GFL 1789 to the Present
Pilnyak, Boris 1894-1938 . **SSC 48; TCLC 23**
    See Vogau, Boris Andreyevich
    See also EWL 3
Pinchback, Eugene
    See Toomer, Jean
Pincherle, Alberto 1907-1990 ...... **CLC 11, 18**
    See Moravia, Alberto
    See also CA 25-28R; CAAS 132; CANR
    33, 63, 142; DAM NOV; MTCW 1;
    MTFW 2005
Pinckney, Darryl 1953- .... **CLC 76**
    See also BW 2, 3; CA 143; CANR 79
Pindar 518(?)B.C.-438(?)B.C. .... **CMLC 12;**
    PC 19
    See also AW 1; CDWLB 1; DLB 176;
    RGWL 2
Pineda, Cecile 1942- .... **CLC 39**
    See also CA 118; DLB 209
Pinero, Arthur Wing 1855-1934 .... **TCLC 32**
    See also CA 153; CAAE 110; DAM DRAM;
    DLB 10; RGEL 2
Pinero, Miguel (Antonio Gomez)
    1946-1988 .... **CLC 4, 55**
    See also CA 61-64; CAAS 125; CAD;
    CANR 29, 90; DLB 266; HW 1; LLW
Pinget, Robert 1919-1997 .... **CLC 7, 13, 37**
    See also CA 85-88; CAAS 160; CWW 2;
    DLB 83; EWL 3; GFL 1789 to the Present
Pink Floyd
    See Barrett, (Roger) Syd; Gilmour, David;
    Mason, Nick; Waters, Roger; Wright, Rick
Pinkney, Edward 1802-1828 .... **NCLC 31**
    See also DLB 248
Pinkwater, D. Manus
    See Pinkwater, Daniel Manus
Pinkwater, Daniel
    See Pinkwater, Daniel Manus
Pinkwater, Daniel M.
    See Pinkwater, Daniel Manus
Pinkwater, Daniel Manus 1941- .... **CLC 35**
    See also AAYA 1, 46; BYA 9; CA 29-32R;
    CANR 12, 38, 89, 143; CLR 4; CSW;
    FANT; JRDA; MAICYA 1, 2; SAAS 3;
    SATA 8, 46, 76, 114, 158; SFW 4; YAW
Pinkwater, Manus
    See Pinkwater, Daniel Manus
Pinsky, Robert 1940- .... **CLC 9, 19, 38, 94,**
    121, 216; PC 27
    See also AMWS 6; CA 29-32R; 4; CANR
    58, 97, 138; CP 3, 4, 5, 6, 7; DA3; DAM
    POET; DLBY 1982, 1998; MAL 5;
    MTCW 2; MTFW 2005; PFS 18; RGAL
    4; TCLE 1:2
Pinta, Harold
    See Pinter, Harold
Pinter, Harold 1930- .. **CLC 1, 3, 6, 9, 11, 15,**
    27, 58, 73, 199; DC 15; WLC 4
    See also BRWR 1; BRWS 1; CA 5-8R;
    CANR 33, 65, 112, 145; CBD; CD 5, 6;
    CDBLB 1960 to Present; CP 1; DA; DA3;
    DAB; DAC; DAM DRAM, MST; DFS 4,
    5, 7, 14; DLB 13, 310, 331; EWL 3;
    IDFW 3, 4; LMFS 2; MTCW 1, 2; MTFW
    2005; RGEL 2; RGHL; TEA
Piozzi, Hester Lynch (Thrale)
    1741-1821 .... **NCLC 57**
    See also DLB 104, 142
Pirandello, Luigi 1867-1936 .. **DC 5; SSC 22;**
    TCLC 4, 29, 172; WLC 4
    See also CA 153; CAAE 104; CANR 103;
    DA; DA3; DAB; DAC; DAM DRAM,
    MST; DFS 4, 9; DLB 264, 331; EW 8;
    EWL 3; MTCW 2; MTFW 2005; RGSF
    2; RGWL 2, 3; WLIT 7

Pirsig, Robert M(aynard) 1928- ... **CLC 4, 6,**
    73
    See also CA 53-56; CANR 42, 74; CPW 1;
    DA3; DAM POP; MTCW 1, 2; MTFW
    2005; SATA 39
Pisan, Christine de
    See Christine de Pizan
Pisarev, Dmitrii Ivanovich
    See Pisarev, Dmitry Ivanovich
    See also DLB 277
Pisarev, Dmitry Ivanovich
    1840-1868 .... **NCLC 25**
    See Pisarev, Dmitrii Ivanovich
Pix, Mary (Griffith) 1666-1709 .... **LC 8**
    See also DLB 80
Pixerecourt, (Rene Charles) Guilbert de
    1773-1844 .... **NCLC 39**
    See also DLB 192; GFL 1789 to the Present
Plaatje, Sol(omon) T(shekisho)
    1878-1932 .... **BLCS; TCLC 73**
    See also BW 2, 3; CA 141; CANR 79; DLB
    125, 225
Plaidy, Jean
    See Hibbert, Eleanor Alice Burford
Planche, James Robinson
    1796-1880 .... **NCLC 42**
    See also RGEL 2
Plant, Robert 1948- .... **CLC 12**
Plante, David 1940- .... **CLC 7, 23, 38**
    See also CA 37-40R; CANR 12, 36, 58, 82,
    152; CN 2, 3, 4, 5, 6, 7; DAM NOV;
    DLBY 1983; INT CANR-12; MTCW 1
Plante, David Robert
    See Plante, David
Plath, Sylvia 1932-1963 ..... **CLC 1, 2, 3, 5, 9,**
    11, 14, 17, 50, 51, 62, 111; PC 1, 37;
    WLC 4
    See also AAYA 13; AMWR 2; AMWS 1;
    BPFB 3; CA 19-20; CANR 34, 101; CAP
    2; CDALB 1941-1968; DA; DA3; DAB;
    DAC; DAM MST, POET; DLB 5, 6, 152;
    EWL 3; EXPN; EXPP; FL 1:6; FW; LAIT
    4; MAL 5; MBL; MTCW 1, 2; MTFW
    2005; NFS 1; PAB; PFS 1, 15; RGAL 4;
    SATA 96; TUS; WP; YAW
Plato c. 428B.C.-347B.C. .... **CMLC 8, 75;**
    WLCS
    See also AW 1; CDWLB 1; DA; DA3;
    DAB; DAC; DAM MST; DLB 176; LAIT
    1; LATS 1:1; RGWL 2, 3; WLIT 8
Platonov, Andrei
    See Klimentov, Andrei Platonovich
Platonov, Andrei Platonovich
    See Klimentov, Andrei Platonovich
    See also DLB 272
Platonov, Andrey Platonovich
    See Klimentov, Andrei Platonovich
    See also EWL 3
Platt, Kin 1911- .... **CLC 26**
    See also AAYA 11; CA 17-20R; CANR 11;
    JRDA; SAAS 17; SATA 21, 86; WYA
Plautus c. 254B.C.-c. 184B.C. .... **CMLC 24,**
    92; DC 6
    See also AW 1; CDWLB 1; DLB 211;
    RGWL 2, 3; WLIT 8
Plick et Plock
    See Simenon, Georges (Jacques Christian)
Plieksans, Janis
    See Rainis, Janis
Plimpton, George 1927-2003 .... **CLC 36**
    See also AITN 1; AMWS 16; CA 21-24R;
    CAAS 224; CANR 32, 70, 103, 133; DLB
    185, 241; MTCW 1, 2; MTFW 2005;
    SATA 10; SATA-Obit 150
Pliny the Elder c. 23-79 .... **CMLC 23**
    See also DLB 211
Pliny the Younger c. 61-c. 112 ...... **CMLC 62**
    See also AW 2; DLB 211

Powys, John Cowper 1872-1963 ... **CLC 7, 9, 15, 46, 125**
See also CA 85-88; CANR 106; DLB 15, 255; EWL 3; FANT; MTCW 1, 2; MTFW 2005; RGEL 2; SUFW

Powys, T(heodore) F(rancis) 1875-1953 .... **TCLC 9**
See also BRWS 8; CA 189; CAAE 106; DLB 36, 162; EWL 3; FANT; RGEL 2; SUFW

Pozzo, Modesta
See Fonte, Moderata

Prado (Calvo), Pedro 1886-1952 ... **TCLC 75**
See also CA 131; DLB 283; HW 1; LAW

Prager, Emily 1952- .... **CLC 56**
See also CA 204

Pratchett, Terry 1948- .... **CLC 197**
See also AAYA 19, 54; BPFB 3; CA 143; CANR 87, 126; CLR 64; CN 6, 7; CPW; CWRI 5; FANT; MTFW 2005; SATA 82, 139; SFW 4; SUFW 2

Pratolini, Vasco 1913-1991 .... **TCLC 124**
See also CA 211; DLB 177; EWL 3; RGWL 2, 3

Pratt, E(dwin) J(ohn) 1883(?)-1964 . **CLC 19**
See also CA 141; CAAS 93-96; CANR 77; DAC; DAM POET; DLB 92; EWL 3; RGEL 2; TWA

Premchand .... **TCLC 21**
See Srivastava, Dhanpat Rai
See also EWL 3

Prescott, William Hickling 1796-1859 .... **NCLC 163**
See also DLB 1, 30, 59, 235

Preseren, France 1800-1849 .... **NCLC 127**
See also CDWLB 4; DLB 147

Preussler, Otfried 1923- .... **CLC 17**
See also CA 77-80; SATA 24

Prevert, Jacques (Henri Marie) 1900-1977 .... **CLC 15**
See also CA 77-80; CAAS 69-72; CANR 29, 61; DLB 258; EWL 3; GFL 1789 to the Present; IDFW 3, 4; MTCW 1; RGWL 2, 3; SATA-Obit 30

Prevost, (Antoine Francois) 1697-1763 .... **LC 1**
See also DLB 314; EW 4; GFL Beginnings to 1789; RGWL 2, 3

Price, Reynolds 1933- .. **CLC 3, 6, 13, 43, 50, 63, 212; SSC 22**
See also AMWS 6; CA 1-4R; CANR 1, 37, 57, 87, 128; CN 1, 2, 3, 4, 5, 6, 7; CSW; DAM NOV; DLB 2, 218, 278; EWL 3; INT CANR-37; MAL 5; MTFW 2005; NFS 18

Price, Richard 1949- .... **CLC 6, 12**
See also CA 49-52; CANR 3, 147; CN 7; DLBY 1981

Prichard, Katharine Susannah 1883-1969 .... **CLC 46**
See also CA 11-12; CANR 33; CAP 1; DLB 260; MTCW 1; RGEL 2; RGSF 2; SATA 66

Priestley, J(ohn) B(oynton) 1894-1984 .... **CLC 2, 5, 9, 34**
See also BRW 7; CA 9-12R; CAAS 113; CANR 33; CDBLB 1914-1945; CN 1, 2, 3; DA3; DAM DRAM, NOV; DLB 10, 34, 77, 100, 139; DLBY 1984; EWL 3; MTCW 1, 2; MTFW 2005; RGEL 2; SFW 4

Prince 1958- .... **CLC 35**
See also CA 213

Prince, F(rank) T(empleton) 1912-2003 .... **CLC 22**
See also CA 101; CAAS 219; CANR 43, 79; CP 1, 2, 3, 4, 5, 6, 7; DLB 20

Prince Kropotkin
See Kropotkin, Peter (Aleksieevich)

Prior, Matthew 1664-1721 .... **LC 4**
See also DLB 95; RGEL 2

Prishvin, Mikhail 1873-1954 .... **TCLC 75**
See Prishvin, Mikhail Mikhailovich

Prishvin, Mikhail Mikhailovich
See Prishvin, Mikhail
See also DLB 272; EWL 3

Pritchard, William H(arrison) 1932- .... **CLC 34**
See also CA 65-68; CANR 23, 95; DLB 111

Pritchett, V(ictor) S(awdon) 1900-1997 ... **CLC 5, 13, 15, 41; SSC 14**
See also BPFB 3; BRWS 3; CA 61-64; CAAS 157; CANR 31, 63; CN 1, 2, 3, 4, 5, 6; DA3; DAM NOV; DLB 15, 139; EWL 3; MTCW 1, 2; MTFW 2005; RGEL 2; RGSF 2; TEA

Private 19022
See Manning, Frederic

Probst, Mark 1925- .... **CLC 59**
See also CA 130

Procaccino, Michael
See Cristofer, Michael

Proclus c. 412-c. 485 .... **CMLC 81**

Prokosch, Frederic 1908-1989 ...... **CLC 4, 48**
See also CA 73-76; CAAS 128; CANR 82; CN 1, 2, 3, 4; CP 1, 2, 3, 4; DLB 48; MTCW 2

Propertius, Sextus c. 50B.C.-c. 16B.C. .... **CMLC 32**
See also AW 2; CDWLB 1; DLB 211; RGWL 2, 3; WLIT 8

Prophet, The
See Dreiser, Theodore

Prose, Francine 1947- .... **CLC 45, 231**
See also AMWS 16; CA 112; CAAE 109; CANR 46, 95, 132; DLB 234; MTFW 2005; SATA 101, 149

Protagoras c. 490B.C.-420B.C. ...... **CMLC 85**
See also DLB 176

Proudhon
See Cunha, Euclides (Rodrigues Pimenta) da

Proulx, Annie
See Proulx, E. Annie

Proulx, E. Annie 1935- .... **CLC 81, 158**
See also AMWS 7; BPFB 3; CA 145; CANR 65, 110; CN 6, 7; CPW 1; DA3; DAM POP; DLB 335; MAL 5; MTCW 2; MTFW 2005; SSFS 18, 23

Proulx, Edna Annie
See Proulx, E. Annie

Proust, (Valentin-Louis-George-Eugene) Marcel 1871-1922 ..... **SSC 75; TCLC 7, 13, 33; WLC 5**
See also AAYA 58; BPFB 3; CA 120; CAAE 104; CANR 110; DA; DA3; DAB; DAC; DAM MST, NOV; DLB 65; EW 8; EWL 3; GFL 1789 to the Present; MTCW 1, 2; MTFW 2005; RGWL 2, 3; TWA

Prowler, Harley
See Masters, Edgar Lee

Prudentius, Aurelius Clemens 348-c. 405 .... **CMLC 78**
See also EW 1; RGWL 2, 3

Prudhomme, Rene Francois Armand 1839-1907
See Sully Prudhomme, Rene-Francois-Armand
See also CA 170

Prus, Boleslaw 1845-1912 .... **TCLC 48**
See also RGWL 2, 3

Pryor, Aaron Richard
See Pryor, Richard

Pryor, Richard 1940-2005 .... **CLC 26**
See also CA 152; CAAE 122; CAAS 246

Pryor, Richard Franklin Lenox Thomas
See Pryor, Richard

Przybyszewski, Stanislaw 1868-1927 .... **TCLC 36**
See also CA 160; DLB 66; EWL 3

Pseudo-Dionysius the Areopagite fl. c. 5th cent. - .... **CMLC 89**
See also DLB 115

Pteleon
See Grieve, C(hristopher) M(urray)
See also DAM POET

Puckett, Lute
See Masters, Edgar Lee

Puig, Manuel 1932-1990 .... **CLC 3, 5, 10, 28, 65, 133; HLC 2**
See also BPFB 3; CA 45-48; CANR 2, 32, 63; CDWLB 3; DA3; DAM MULT; DLB 113; DNFS 1; EWL 3; GLL 1; HW 1, 2; LAW; MTCW 1, 2; MTFW 2005; RGWL 2, 3; TWA; WLIT 1

Pulitzer, Joseph 1847-1911 .... **TCLC 76**
See also CAAE 114; DLB 23

Purchas, Samuel 1577(?)-1626 .... **LC 70**
See also DLB 151

Purdy, A(lfred) W(ellington) 1918-2000 .... **CLC 3, 6, 14, 50**
See also CA 81-84; 17; CAAS 189; CANR 42, 66; CP 1, 2, 3, 4, 5, 6, 7; DAC; DAM MST, POET; DLB 88; PFS 5; RGEL 2

Purdy, James (Amos) 1923- .... **CLC 2, 4, 10, 28, 52**
See also AMWS 7; CA 33-36R; 1; CANR 19, 51, 132; CN 1, 2, 3, 4, 5, 6, 7; DLB 2, 218; EWL 3; INT CANR-19; MAL 5; MTCW 1; RGAL 4

Pure, Simon
See Swinnerton, Frank Arthur

Pushkin, Aleksandr Sergeevich
See Pushkin, Alexander (Sergeyevich)
See also DLB 205

Pushkin, Alexander (Sergeyevich) 1799-1837 .... **NCLC 3, 27, 83; PC 10; SSC 27, 55, 99; WLC 5**
See Pushkin, Aleksandr Sergeevich
See also DA; DA3; DAB; DAC; DAM DRAM, MST, POET; EW 5; EXPS; RGSF 2; RGWL 2, 3; SATA 61; SSFS 9; TWA

P'u Sung-ling 1640-1715 .... **LC 49; SSC 31**

Putnam, Arthur Lee
See Alger, Horatio, Jr.

Puttenham, George 1529(?)-1590 ...... **LC 116**
See also DLB 281

Puzo, Mario 1920-1999 .... **CLC 1, 2, 6, 36, 107**
See also BPFB 3; CA 65-68; CAAS 185; CANR 4, 42, 65, 99, 131; CN 1, 2, 3, 4, 5, 6; CPW; DA3; DAM NOV, POP; DLB 6; MTCW 1, 2; MTFW 2005; NFS 16; RGAL 4

Pygge, Edward
See Barnes, Julian

Pyle, Ernest Taylor 1900-1945
See Pyle, Ernie
See also CA 160; CAAE 115

Pyle, Ernie .... **TCLC 75**
See Pyle, Ernest Taylor
See also DLB 29; MTCW 2

Pyle, Howard 1853-1911 .... **TCLC 81**
See also AAYA 57; BYA 2, 4; CA 137; CAAE 109; CLR 22, 117; DLB 42, 188; DLBD 13; LAIT 1; MAICYA 1, 2; SATA 16, 100; WCH; YAW

Pym, Barbara (Mary Crampton) 1913-1980 .... **CLC 13, 19, 37, 111**
See also BPFB 3; BRWS 2; CA 13-14; CAAS 97-100; CANR 13, 34; CAP 1; DLB 14, 207; DLBY 1987; EWL 3; MTCW 1, 2; MTFW 2005; RGEL 2; TEA

Robinson, Edwin Arlington
1869-1935 .... **PC 1, 35; TCLC 5, 101**
See also AAYA 72; AMW; CA 133; CAAE
104; CDALB 1865-1917; DA; DAC;
DAM MST, POET; DLB 54; EWL 3;
EXPP; MAL 5; MTCW 1, 2; MTFW
2005; PAB; PFS 4; RGAL 4; WP

Robinson, Henry Crabb
1775-1867 .... **NCLC 15**
See also DLB 107

Robinson, Jill 1936- .... **CLC 10**
See also CA 102; CANR 120; INT CA-102

Robinson, Kim Stanley 1952- .... **CLC 34**
See also AAYA 26; CA 126; CANR 113,
139; CN 6, 7; MTFW 2005; SATA 109;
SCFW 2; SFW 4

Robinson, Lloyd
See Silverberg, Robert

Robinson, Marilynne 1944- ...... **CLC 25, 180**
See also AAYA 69; CA 116; CANR 80, 140;
CN 4, 5, 6, 7; DLB 206; MTFW 2005;
NFS 24

Robinson, Mary 1758-1800 .... **NCLC 142**
See also DLB 158; FW

Robinson, Smokey .... **CLC 21**
See Robinson, William, Jr.

Robinson, William, Jr. 1940-
See Robinson, Smokey
See also CAAE 116

Robison, Mary 1949- .... **CLC 42, 98**
See also CA 116; CAAE 113; CANR 87;
CN 4, 5, 6, 7; DLB 130; INT CA-116;
RGSF 2

Roches, Catherine des 1542-1587 ...... **LC 117**
See also DLB 327

Rochester
See Wilmot, John
See also RGEL 2

Rod, Edouard 1857-1910 .... **TCLC 52**

Roddenberry, Eugene Wesley 1921-1991
See Roddenberry, Gene
See also CA 110; CAAS 135; CANR 37;
SATA 45; SATA-Obit 69

Roddenberry, Gene .... **CLC 17**
See Roddenberry, Eugene Wesley
See also AAYA 5; SATA-Obit 69

Rodgers, Mary 1931- .... **CLC 12**
See also BYA 5; CA 49-52; CANR 8, 55,
90; CLR 20; CWRI 5; INT CANR-8;
JRDA; MAICYA 1, 2; SATA 8, 130

Rodgers, W(illiam) R(obert)
1909-1969 .... **CLC 7**
See also CA 85-88; DLB 20; RGEL 2

Rodman, Eric
See Silverberg, Robert

Rodman, Howard 1920(?)-1985 .... **CLC 65**
See also CAAS 118

Rodman, Maia
See Wojciechowska, Maia (Teresa)

Rodo, Jose Enrique 1871(?)-1917 .... **HLCS 2**
See also CA 178; EWL 3; HW 2; LAW

Rodolph, Utto
See Ouologuem, Yambo

Rodriguez, Claudio 1934-1999 .... **CLC 10**
See also CA 188; DLB 134

Rodriguez, Richard 1944- .... **CLC 155; HLC 2**
See also AMWS 14; CA 110; CANR 66,
116; DAM MULT; DLB 82, 256; HW 1,
2; LAIT 5; LLW; MTFW 2005; NCFS 3;
WLIT 1

Roelvaag, O(le) E(dvart) 1876-1931
See Rolvaag, O(le) E(dvart)
See also AAYA 75; CA 171; CAAE 117

Roethke, Theodore (Huebner)
1908-1963 .... **CLC 1, 3, 8, 11, 19, 46,
101; PC 15**
See also AMW; CA 81-84; CABS 2;
CDALB 1941-1968; DA3; DAM POET;
DLB 5, 206; EWL 3; EXPP; MAL 5;
MTCW 1, 2; PAB; PFS 3; RGAL 4; WP

Rogers, Carl R(ansom)
1902-1987 .... **TCLC 125**
See also CA 1-4R; CAAS 121; CANR 1,
18; MTCW 1

Rogers, Samuel 1763-1855 .... **NCLC 69**
See also DLB 93; RGEL 2

Rogers, Thomas Hunton 1927-2007 . **CLC 57**
See also CA 89-92; CANR 163; INT CA-
89-92

Rogers, Will(iam Penn Adair)
1879-1935 .... **NNAL; TCLC 8, 71**
See also CA 144; CAAE 105; DA3; DAM
MULT; DLB 11; MTCW 2

Rogin, Gilbert 1929- .... **CLC 18**
See also CA 65-68; CANR 15

Rohan, Koda
See Koda Shigeyuki

Rohlfs, Anna Katharine Green
See Green, Anna Katharine

Rohmer, Eric .... **CLC 16**
See Scherer, Jean-Marie Maurice

Rohmer, Sax .... **TCLC 28**
See Ward, Arthur Henry Sarsfield
See also DLB 70; MSW; SUFW

Roiphe, Anne 1935- .... **CLC 3, 9**
See also CA 89-92; CANR 45, 73, 138;
DLBY 1980; INT CA-89-92

Roiphe, Anne Richardson
See Roiphe, Anne

Rojas, Fernando de 1475-1541 ... **HLCS 1, 2;
LC 23**
See also DLB 286; RGWL 2, 3

Rojas, Gonzalo 1917- .... **HLCS 2**
See also CA 178; HW 2; LAWS 1

Roland (de la Platiere), Marie-Jeanne
1754-1793 .... **LC 98**
See also DLB 314

**Rolfe, Frederick (William Serafino Austin
Lewis Mary)** 1860-1913 .... **TCLC 12**
See Al Siddik
See also CA 210; CAAE 107; DLB 34, 156;
RGEL 2

Rolland, Romain 1866-1944 .... **TCLC 23**
See also CA 197; CAAE 118; DLB 65, 284,
332; EWL 3; GFL 1789 to the Present;
RGWL 2

Rolle, Richard c. 1300-c. 1349 ...... **CMLC 21**
See also DLB 146; LMFS 1; RGEL 2

Rolvaag, O(le) E(dvart) .... **TCLC 17**
See Roelvaag, O(le) E(dvart)
See also DLB 9, 212; MAL 5; NFS 5;
RGAL 4

Romain Arnaud, Saint
See Aragon, Louis

Romains, Jules 1885-1972 .... **CLC 7**
See also CA 85-88; CANR 34; DLB 65,
321; EWL 3; GFL 1789 to the Present;
MTCW 1

Romero, Jose Ruben 1890-1952 .... **TCLC 14**
See also CA 131; CAAE 114; EWL 3; HW
1; LAW

Ronsard, Pierre de 1524-1585 . **LC 6, 54; PC
11**
See also DLB 327; EW 2; GFL Beginnings
to 1789; RGWL 2, 3; TWA

Rooke, Leon 1934- .... **CLC 25, 34**
See also CA 25-28R; CANR 23, 53; CCA
1; CPW; DAM POP

Roosevelt, Franklin Delano
1882-1945 .... **TCLC 93**
See also CA 173; CAAE 116; LAIT 3

Roosevelt, Theodore 1858-1919 ..... **TCLC 69**
See also CA 170; CAAE 115; DLB 47, 186,
275

Roper, William 1498-1578 .... **LC 10**

Roquelaure, A. N.
See Rice, Anne

Rosa, Joao Guimaraes 1908-1967 ... **CLC 23;
HLCS 1**
See Guimaraes Rosa, Joao
See also CAAS 89-92; DLB 113, 307; EWL
3; WLIT 1

Rose, Wendy 1948- . **CLC 85; NNAL; PC 13**
See also CA 53-56; CANR 5, 51; CWP;
DAM MULT; DLB 175; PFS 13; RGAL
4; SATA 12

Rosen, R. D.
See Rosen, Richard (Dean)

Rosen, Richard (Dean) 1949- .... **CLC 39**
See also CA 77-80; CANR 62, 120; CMW
4; INT CANR-30

Rosenberg, Isaac 1890-1918 .... **TCLC 12**
See also BRW 6; CA 188; CAAE 107; DLB
20, 216; EWL 3; PAB; RGEL 2

Rosenblatt, Joe .... **CLC 15**
See Rosenblatt, Joseph
See also CP 3, 4, 5, 6, 7

Rosenblatt, Joseph 1933-
See Rosenblatt, Joe
See also CA 89-92; CP 1, 2; INT CA-89-92

Rosenfeld, Samuel
See Tzara, Tristan

Rosenstock, Sami
See Tzara, Tristan

Rosenstock, Samuel
See Tzara, Tristan

Rosenthal, M(acha) L(ouis)
1917-1996 .... **CLC 28**
See also CA 1-4R; 6; CAAS 152; CANR 4,
51; CP 1, 2, 3, 4, 5, 6; DLB 5; SATA 59

Ross, Barnaby
See Dannay, Frederic; Lee, Manfred B.

Ross, Bernard L.
See Follett, Ken

Ross, J. H.
See Lawrence, T(homas) E(dward)

Ross, John Hume
See Lawrence, T(homas) E(dward)

Ross, Martin 1862-1915
See Martin, Violet Florence
See also DLB 135; GLL 2; RGEL 2; RGSF
2

Ross, (James) Sinclair 1908-1996 ... **CLC 13;
SSC 24**
See also CA 73-76; CANR 81; CN 1, 2, 3,
4, 5, 6; DAC; DAM MST; DLB 88;
RGEL 2; RGSF 2; TCWW 1, 2

Rossetti, Christina 1830-1894 ... **NCLC 2, 50,
66, 186; PC 7; WLC 5**
See also AAYA 51; BRW 5; BYA 4; CLR
115; DA; DA3; DAB; DAC; DAM MST,
POET; DLB 35, 163, 240; EXPP; FL 1:3;
LATS 1:1; MAICYA 1, 2; PFS 10, 14;
RGEL 2; SATA 20; TEA; WCH

Rossetti, Christina Georgina
See Rossetti, Christina

Rossetti, Dante Gabriel 1828-1882 . **NCLC 4,
77; PC 44; WLC 5**
See also AAYA 51; BRW 5; CDBLB 1832-
1890; DA; DAB; DAC; DAM MST,
POET; DLB 35; EXPP; RGEL 2; TEA

Rossi, Cristina Peri
See Peri Rossi, Cristina

Rossi, Jean-Baptiste 1931-2003
See Japrisot, Sebastien
See also CA 201; CAAS 215

Saba, Umberto 1883-1957 .... **TCLC 33**
See also CA 144; CANR 79; DLB 114;
EWL 3; RGWL 2, 3

Sabatini, Rafael 1875-1950 .... **TCLC 47**
See also BPFB 3; CA 162; RHW

Sabato, Ernesto 1911- ... **CLC 10, 23; HLC 2**
See also CA 97-100; CANR 32, 65; CD-
WLB 3; CWW 2; DAM MULT; DLB 145;
EWL 3; HW 1, 2; LAW; MTCW 1, 2;
MTFW 2005

Sa-Carneiro, Mario de 1890-1916 . **TCLC 83**
See also DLB 287; EWL 3

Sacastru, Martin
See Bioy Casares, Adolfo
See also CWW 2

Sacher-Masoch, Leopold von
1836(?)-1895 .... **NCLC 31**

Sachs, Hans 1494-1576 .... **LC 95**
See also CDWLB 2; DLB 179; RGWL 2, 3

Sachs, Marilyn 1927- .... **CLC 35**
See also AAYA 2; BYA 6; CA 17-20R;
CANR 13, 47, 150; CLR 2; JRDA; MAI-
CYA 1, 2; SAAS 2; SATA 3, 68, 164;
SATA-Essay 110; WYA; YAW

Sachs, Marilyn Stickle
See Sachs, Marilyn

Sachs, Nelly 1891-1970 .. **CLC 14, 98; PC 78**
See also CA 17-18; CAAS 25-28R; CANR
87; CAP 2; DLB 332; EWL 3; MTCW 2;
MTFW 2005; PFS 20; RGHL; RGWL 2,
3

Sackler, Howard (Oliver)
1929-1982 .... **CLC 14**
See also CA 61-64; CAAS 108; CAD;
CANR 30; DFS 15; DLB 7

Sacks, Oliver 1933- .... **CLC 67, 202**
See also CA 53-56; CANR 28, 50, 76, 146;
CPW; DA3; INT CANR-28; MTCW 1, 2;
MTFW 2005

Sacks, Oliver Wolf
See Sacks, Oliver

Sackville, Thomas 1536-1608 .... **LC 98**
See also DAM DRAM; DLB 62, 132;
RGEL 2

Sadakichi
See Hartmann, Sadakichi

Sa'dawi, Nawal al-
See El Saadawi, Nawal
See also CWW 2

Sade, Donatien Alphonse Francois
1740-1814 .... **NCLC 3, 47**
See also DLB 314; EW 4; GFL Beginnings
to 1789; RGWL 2, 3

Sade, Marquis de
See Sade, Donatien Alphonse Francois

Sadoff, Ira 1945- .... **CLC 9**
See also CA 53-56; CANR 5, 21, 109; DLB
120

Saetone
See Camus, Albert

Safire, William 1929- .... **CLC 10**
See also CA 17-20R; CANR 31, 54, 91, 148

Sagan, Carl 1934-1996 .... **CLC 30, 112**
See also AAYA 2, 62; CA 25-28R; CAAS
155; CANR 11, 36, 74; CPW; DA3;
MTCW 1, 2; MTFW 2005; SATA 58;
SATA-Obit 94

Sagan, Francoise .... **CLC 3, 6, 9, 17, 36**
See Quoirez, Francoise
See also CWW 2; DLB 83; EWL 3; GFL
1789 to the Present; MTCW 2

Sahgal, Nayantara (Pandit) 1927- .... **CLC 41**
See also CA 9-12R; CANR 11, 88; CN 1,
2, 3, 4, 5, 6, 7; DLB 323

Said, Edward W. 1935-2003 .... **CLC 123**
See also CA 21-24R; CAAS 220; CANR
45, 74, 107, 131; DLB 67; MTCW 2;
MTFW 2005

Saint, H(arry) F. 1941- .... **CLC 50**
See also CA 127

St. Aubin de Teran, Lisa 1953-
See Teran, Lisa St. Aubin de
See also CA 126; CAAE 118; CN 6, 7; INT
CA-126

Saint Birgitta of Sweden c.
1303-1373 .... **CMLC 24**

Sainte-Beuve, Charles Augustin
1804-1869 .... **NCLC 5**
See also DLB 217; EW 6; GFL 1789 to the
Present

Saint-Exupery, Antoine de
1900-1944 .... **TCLC 2, 56, 169; WLC**
See also AAYA 63; BPFB 3; BYA 3; CA
132; CAAE 108; CLR 10; DA3; DAM
NOV; DLB 72; EW 12; EWL 3; GFL
1789 to the Present; LAIT 3; MAICYA 1,
2; MTCW 1, 2; MTFW 2005; RGWL 2,
3; SATA 20; TWA

**Saint-Exupery, Antoine Jean Baptiste Marie
Roger de**
See Saint-Exupery, Antoine de

St. John, David
See Hunt, E. Howard

St. John, J. Hector
See Crevecoeur, Michel Guillaume Jean de

Saint-John Perse
See Leger, (Marie-Rene Auguste) Alexis
Saint-Leger
See also EW 10; EWL 3; GFL 1789 to the
Present; RGWL 2

Saintsbury, George (Edward Bateman)
1845-1933 .... **TCLC 31**
See also CA 160; DLB 57, 149

Sait Faik .... **TCLC 23**
See Abasiyanik, Sait Faik

Saki .... **SSC 12; TCLC 3; WLC 5**
See Munro, H(ector) H(ugh)
See also BRWS 6; BYA 11; LAIT 2; RGEL
2; SSFS 1; SUFW

Sala, George Augustus 1828-1895 . **NCLC 46**

Saladin 1138-1193 .... **CMLC 38**

Salama, Hannu 1936- .... **CLC 18**
See also CA 244; EWL 3

Salamanca, J(ack) R(ichard) 1922- .. **CLC 4,
15**
See also CA 193; 25-28R, 193

Salas, Floyd Francis 1931- .... **HLC 2**
See also CA 119; 27; CANR 44, 75, 93;
DAM MULT; DLB 82; HW 1, 2; MTCW
2; MTFW 2005

Sale, J. Kirkpatrick
See Sale, Kirkpatrick

Sale, John Kirkpatrick
See Sale, Kirkpatrick

Sale, Kirkpatrick 1937- .... **CLC 68**
See also CA 13-16R; CANR 10, 147

Salinas, Luis Omar 1937- ... **CLC 90; HLC 2**
See also AMWS 13; CA 131; CANR 81,
153; DAM MULT; DLB 82; HW 1, 2

Salinas (y Serrano), Pedro
1891(?)-1951 .... **TCLC 17**
See also CAAE 117; DLB 134; EWL 3

Salinger, J.D. 1919- . **CLC 1, 3, 8, 12, 55, 56,
138; SSC 2, 28, 65; WLC 5**
See also AAYA 2, 36; AMW; AMWC 1;
BPFB 3; CA 5-8R; CANR 39, 129;
CDALB 1941-1968; CLR 18; CN 1, 2, 3,
4, 5, 6, 7; CPW 1; DA; DA3; DAB; DAC;
DAM MST, NOV, POP; DLB 2, 102, 173;
EWL 3; EXPN; LAIT 4; MAICYA 1, 2;
MAL 5; MTCW 1, 2; MTFW 2005; NFS
1; RGAL 4; RGSF 2; SATA 67; SSFS 17;
TUS; WYA; YAW

Salisbury, John
See Caute, (John) David

Sallust c. 86B.C.-35B.C. .... **CMLC 68**
See also AW 2; CDWLB 1; DLB 211;
RGWL 2, 3

Salter, James 1925- .. **CLC 7, 52, 59; SSC 58**
See also AMWS 9; CA 73-76; CANR 107,
160; DLB 130

Saltus, Edgar (Everton) 1855-1921 . **TCLC 8**
See also CAAE 105; DLB 202; RGAL 4

Saltykov, Mikhail Evgrafovich
1826-1889 .... **NCLC 16**
See also DLB 238:

Saltykov-Shchedrin, N.
See Saltykov, Mikhail Evgrafovich

Samarakis, Andonis
See Samarakis, Antonis
See also EWL 3

Samarakis, Antonis 1919-2003 .... **CLC 5**
See Samarakis, Andonis
See also CA 25-28R; 16; CAAS 224; CANR
36

Sanchez, Florencio 1875-1910 .... **TCLC 37**
See also CA 153; DLB 305; EWL 3; HW 1;
LAW

Sanchez, Luis Rafael 1936- .... **CLC 23**
See also CA 128; DLB 305; EWL 3; HW 1;
WLIT 1

Sanchez, Sonia 1934- .... **BLC 3; CLC 5, 116,
215; PC 9**
See also BW 2, 3; CA 33-36R; CANR 24,
49, 74, 115; CLR 18; CP 2, 3, 4, 5, 6, 7;
CSW; CWP; DA3; DAM MULT; DLB 41;
DLBD 8; EWL 3; MAICYA 1, 2; MAL 5;
MTCW 1, 2; MTFW 2005; SATA 22, 136;
WP

Sancho, Ignatius 1729-1780 .... **LC 84**

Sand, George 1804-1876 ..... **NCLC 2, 42, 57,
174; WLC 5**
See also DA; DA3; DAB; DAC; DAM
MST, NOV; DLB 119, 192; EW 6; FL 1:3;
FW; GFL 1789 to the Present; RGWL 2,
3; TWA

Sandburg, Carl (August) 1878-1967 . **CLC 1,
4, 10, 15, 35; PC 2, 41; WLC 5**
See also AAYA 24; AMW; BYA 1, 3; CA
5-8R; CAAS 25-28R; CANR 35; CDALB
1865-1917; CLR 67; DA; DA3; DAB;
DAC; DAM MST, POET; DLB 17, 54,
284; EWL 3; EXPP; LAIT 2; MAICYA 1,
2; MAL 5; MTCW 1, 2; MTFW 2005;
PAB; PFS 3, 6, 12; RGAL 4; SATA 8;
TUS; WCH; WP; WYA

Sandburg, Charles
See Sandburg, Carl (August)

Sandburg, Charles A.
See Sandburg, Carl (August)

Sanders, (James) Ed(ward) 1939- .... **CLC 53**
See Sanders, Edward
See also BG 1:3; CA 13-16R; 21; CANR
13, 44, 78; CP 1, 2, 3, 4, 5, 6, 7; DAM
POET; DLB 16, 244

Sanders, Edward
See Sanders, (James) Ed(ward)
See also DLB 244

Sanders, Lawrence 1920-1998 .... **CLC 41**
See also BEST 89:4; BPFB 3; CA 81-84;
CAAS 165; CANR 33, 62; CMW 4;
CPW; DA3; DAM POP; MTCW 1

Sanders, Noah
See Blount, Roy (Alton), Jr.

Sanders, Winston P.
See Anderson, Poul

Sandoz, Mari(e Susette) 1900-1966 .. **CLC 28**
See also CA 1-4R; CAAS 25-28R; CANR
17, 64; DLB 9, 212; LAIT 2; MTCW 1,
2; SATA 5; TCWW 1, 2

Sandys, George 1578-1644 .... **LC 80**
See also DLB 24, 121

Saner, Reg(inald Anthony) 1931- .... **CLC 9**
See also CA 65-68; CP 3, 4, 5, 6, 7

Schnitzler, Arthur 1862-1931 ..... **DC 17; SSC 15, 61; TCLC 4**
See also CAAE 104; CDWLB 2; DLB 81, 118; EW 8; EWL 3; RGSF 2; RGWL 2, 3

Schoenberg, Arnold Franz Walter 1874-1951 .... **TCLC 75**
See also CA 188; CAAE 109

Schonberg, Arnold
See Schoenberg, Arnold Franz Walter

Schopenhauer, Arthur 1788-1860 . **NCLC 51, 157**
See also DLB 90; EW 5

Schor, Sandra (M.) 1932(?)-1990 ..... **CLC 65**
See also CAAS 132

Schorer, Mark 1908-1977 .... **CLC 9**
See also CA 5-8R; CAAS 73-76; CANR 7; CN 1, 2; DLB 103

Schrader, Paul (Joseph) 1946- . **CLC 26, 212**
See also CA 37-40R; CANR 41; DLB 44

Schreber, Daniel 1842-1911 .... **TCLC 123**

Schreiner, Olive (Emilie Albertina) 1855-1920 .... **TCLC 9**
See also AFW; BRWS 2; CA 154; CAAE 105; DLB 18, 156, 190, 225; EWL 3; FW; RGEL 2; TWA; WLIT 2; WWE 1

Schulberg, Budd (Wilson) 1914- .. **CLC 7, 48**
See also BPFB 3; CA 25-28R; CANR 19, 87; CN 1, 2, 3, 4, 5, 6, 7; DLB 6, 26, 28; DLBY 1981, 2001; MAL 5

Schulman, Arnold
See Trumbo, Dalton

Schulz, Bruno 1892-1942 .. **SSC 13; TCLC 5, 51**
See also CA 123; CAAE 115; CANR 86; CDWLB 4; DLB 215; EWL 3; MTCW 2; MTFW 2005; RGSF 2; RGWL 2, 3

Schulz, Charles M. 1922-2000 .... **CLC 12**
See also AAYA 39; CA 9-12R; CAAS 187; CANR 6, 132; INT CANR-6; MTFW 2005; SATA 10; SATA-Obit 118

Schulz, Charles Monroe
See Schulz, Charles M.

Schumacher, E(rnst) F(riedrich) 1911-1977 .... **CLC 80**
See also CA 81-84; CAAS 73-76; CANR 34, 85

Schumann, Robert 1810-1856 ...... **NCLC 143**

Schuyler, George Samuel 1895-1977 . **HR 1:3**
See also BW 2; CA 81-84; CAAS 73-76; CANR 42; DLB 29, 51

Schuyler, James Marcus 1923-1991 .. **CLC 5, 23**
See also CA 101; CAAS 134; CP 1, 2, 3, 4, 5; DAM POET; DLB 5, 169; EWL 3; INT CA-101; MAL 5; WP

Schwartz, Delmore (David) 1913-1966 ... **CLC 2, 4, 10, 45, 87; PC 8**
See also AMWS 2; CA 17-18; CAAS 25-28R; CANR 35; CAP 2; DLB 28, 48; EWL 3; MAL 5; MTCW 1, 2; MTFW 2005; PAB; RGAL 4; TUS

Schwartz, Ernst
See Ozu, Yasujiro

Schwartz, John Burnham 1965- .... **CLC 59**
See also CA 132; CANR 116

Schwartz, Lynne Sharon 1939- .... **CLC 31**
See also CA 103; CANR 44, 89, 160; DLB 218; MTCW 2; MTFW 2005

Schwartz, Muriel A.
See Eliot, T(homas) S(tearns)

Schwarz-Bart, Andre 1928-2006 .... **CLC 2, 4**
See also CA 89-92; CAAS 253; CANR 109; DLB 299; RGHL

Schwarz-Bart, Simone 1938- . **BLCS; CLC 7**
See also BW 2; CA 97-100; CANR 117; EWL 3

Schwerner, Armand 1927-1999 .... **PC 42**
See also CA 9-12R; CAAS 179; CANR 50, 85; CP 2, 3, 4, 5, 6; DLB 165

Schwitters, Kurt (Hermann Edward Karl Julius) 1887-1948 .... **TCLC 95**
See also CA 158

Schwob, Marcel (Mayer Andre) 1867-1905 .... **TCLC 20**
See also CA 168; CAAE 117; DLB 123; GFL 1789 to the Present

Sciascia, Leonardo 1921-1989 .. **CLC 8, 9, 41**
See also CA 85-88; CAAS 130; CANR 35; DLB 177; EWL 3; MTCW 1; RGWL 2, 3

Scoppettone, Sandra 1936- .... **CLC 26**
See Early, Jack
See also AAYA 11, 65; BYA 8; CA 5-8R; CANR 41, 73, 157; GLL 1; MAICYA 2; MAICYAS 1; SATA 9, 92; WYA; YAW

Scorsese, Martin 1942- .... **CLC 20, 89, 207**
See also AAYA 38; CA 114; CAAE 110; CANR 46, 85

Scotland, Jay
See Jakes, John

Scott, Duncan Campbell 1862-1947 .... **TCLC 6**
See also CA 153; CAAE 104; DAC; DLB 92; RGEL 2

Scott, Evelyn 1893-1963 .... **CLC 43**
See also CA 104; CAAS 112; CANR 64; DLB 9, 48; RHW

Scott, F(rancis) R(eginald) 1899-1985 .... **CLC 22**
See also CA 101; CAAS 114; CANR 87; CP 1, 2, 3, 4; DLB 88; INT CA-101; RGEL 2

Scott, Frank
See Scott, F(rancis) R(eginald)

Scott, Joan .... **CLC 65**

Scott, Joanna 1960- .... **CLC 50**
See also CA 126; CANR 53, 92

Scott, Paul (Mark) 1920-1978 ...... **CLC 9, 60**
See also BRWS 1; CA 81-84; CAAS 77-80; CANR 33; CN 1, 2; DLB 14, 207, 326; EWL 3; MTCW 1; RGEL 2; RHW; WWE 1

Scott, Ridley 1937- .... **CLC 183**
See also AAYA 13, 43

Scott, Sarah 1723-1795 .... **LC 44**
See also DLB 39

Scott, Sir Walter 1771-1832 .... **NCLC 15, 69, 110; PC 13; SSC 32; WLC 5**
See also AAYA 22; BRW 4; BYA 2; CD-BLB 1789-1832; DA; DAB; DAC; DAM MST, NOV, POET; DLB 93, 107, 116, 144, 159; GL 3; HGG; LAIT 1; RGEL 2; RGSF 2; SSFS 10; SUFW 1; TEA; WLIT 3; YABC 2

Scribe, (Augustin) Eugene 1791-1861 . **DC 5; NCLC 16**
See also DAM DRAM; DLB 192; GFL 1789 to the Present; RGWL 2, 3

Scrum, R.
See Crumb, R.

Scudery, Georges de 1601-1667 .... **LC 75**
See also GFL Beginnings to 1789

Scudery, Madeleine de 1607-1701 .. **LC 2, 58**
See also DLB 268; GFL Beginnings to 1789

Scum
See Crumb, R.

Scumbag, Little Bobby
See Crumb, R.

Seabrook, John
See Hubbard, L. Ron

Seacole, Mary Jane Grant 1805-1881 .... **NCLC 147**
See also DLB 166

Sealy, I(rwin) Allan 1951- .... **CLC 55**
See also CA 136; CN 6, 7

Search, Alexander
See Pessoa, Fernando (Antonio Nogueira)

Sebald, W(infried) G(eorg) 1944-2001 .... **CLC 194**
See also BRWS 8; CA 159; CAAS 202; CANR 98; MTFW 2005; RGHL

Sebastian, Lee
See Silverberg, Robert

Sebastian Owl
See Thompson, Hunter S.

Sebestyen, Igen
See Sebestyen, Ouida

Sebestyen, Ouida 1924- .... **CLC 30**
See also AAYA 8; BYA 7; CA 107; CANR 40, 114; CLR 17; JRDA; MAICYA 1, 2; SAAS 10; SATA 39, 140; WYA; YAW

Sebold, Alice 1963(?)- .... **CLC 193**
See also AAYA 56; CA 203; MTFW 2005

Second Duke of Buckingham
See Villiers, George

Secundus, H. Scriblerus
See Fielding, Henry

Sedges, John
See Buck, Pearl S(ydenstricker)

Sedgwick, Catharine Maria 1789-1867 .... **NCLC 19, 98**
See also DLB 1, 74, 183, 239, 243, 254; FL 1:3; RGAL 4

Sedulius Scottus 9th cent. -c. 874 .. **CMLC 86**

Seelye, John (Douglas) 1931- .... **CLC 7**
See also CA 97-100; CANR 70; INT CA-97-100; TCWW 1, 2

Seferiades, Giorgos Stylianou 1900-1971
See Seferis, George
See also CA 5-8R; CAAS 33-36R; CANR 5, 36; MTCW 1

Seferis, George .... **CLC 5, 11; PC 66**
See Seferiades, Giorgos Stylianou
See also DLB 332; EW 12; EWL 3; RGWL 2, 3

Segal, Erich (Wolf) 1937- .... **CLC 3, 10**
See also BEST 89:1; BPFB 3; CA 25-28R; CANR 20, 36, 65, 113; CPW; DAM POP; DLBY 1986; INT CANR-20; MTCW 1

Seger, Bob 1945- .... **CLC 35**

Seghers, Anna .... **CLC 7**
See Radvanyi, Netty
See also CDWLB 2; DLB 69; EWL 3

Seidel, Frederick (Lewis) 1936- .... **CLC 18**
See also CA 13-16R; CANR 8, 99; CP 1, 2, 3, 4, 5, 6, 7; DLBY 1984

Seifert, Jaroslav 1901-1986 . **CLC 34, 44, 93; PC 47**
See also CA 127; CDWLB 4; DLB 215, 332; EWL 3; MTCW 1, 2

Sei Shonagon c. 966-1017(?) ..... **CMLC 6, 89**

Sejour, Victor 1817-1874 .... **DC 10**
See also DLB 50

Sejour Marcou et Ferrand, Juan Victor
See Sejour, Victor

Selby, Hubert, Jr. 1928-2004 ..... **CLC 1, 2, 4, 8; SSC 20**
See also CA 13-16R; CAAS 226; CANR 33, 85; CN 1, 2, 3, 4, 5, 6, 7; DLB 2, 227; MAL 5

Selzer, Richard 1928- .... **CLC 74**
See also CA 65-68; CANR 14, 106

Sembene, Ousmane
See Ousmane, Sembene
See also AFW; EWL 3; WLIT 2

Senancour, Etienne Pivert de 1770-1846 .... **NCLC 16**
See also DLB 119; GFL 1789 to the Present

Sender, Ramon (Jose) 1902-1982 ...... **CLC 8; HLC 2; TCLC 136**
See also CA 5-8R; CAAS 105; CANR 8; DAM MULT; DLB 322; EWL 3; HW 1; MTCW 1; RGWL 2, 3

Silverstein, Shel 1932-1999 .... **PC 49**
See also AAYA 40; BW 3; CA 107; CAAS 179; CANR 47, 74, 81; CLR 5, 96; CWRI 5; JRDA; MAICYA 1, 2; MTCW 2; MTFW 2005; SATA 33, 92; SATA-Brief 27; SATA-Obit 116

Silverstein, Virginia B(arbara Opshelor) 1937- .... **CLC 17**
See also CA 49-52; CANR 2; CLR 25; JRDA; MAICYA 1, 2; SATA 8, 69, 124

Sim, Georges
See Simenon, Georges (Jacques Christian)

Simak, Clifford D(onald) 1904-1988 . **CLC 1, 55**
See also CA 1-4R; CAAS 125; CANR 1, 35; DLB 8; MTCW 1; SATA-Obit 56; SCFW 1, 2; SFW 4

Simenon, Georges (Jacques Christian) 1903-1989 .... **CLC 1, 2, 3, 8, 18, 47**
See also BPFB 3; CA 85-88; CAAS 129; CANR 35; CMW 4; DA3; DAM POP; DLB 72; DLBY 1989; EW 12; EWL 3; GFL 1789 to the Present; MSW; MTCW 1, 2; MTFW 2005; RGWL 2, 3

Simic, Charles 1938- .... **CLC 6, 9, 22, 49, 68, 130; PC 69**
See also AMWS 8; CA 29-32R; 4; CANR 12, 33, 52, 61, 96, 140; CP 2, 3, 4, 5, 6, 7; DA3; DAM POET; DLB 105; MAL 5; MTCW 2; MTFW 2005; PFS 7; RGAL 4; WP

Simmel, Georg 1858-1918 .... **TCLC 64**
See also CA 157; DLB 296

Simmons, Charles (Paul) 1924- .... **CLC 57**
See also CA 89-92; INT CA-89-92

Simmons, Dan 1948- .... **CLC 44**
See also AAYA 16, 54; CA 138; CANR 53, 81, 126; CPW; DAM POP; HGG; SUFW 2

Simmons, James (Stewart Alexander) 1933- .... **CLC 43**
See also CA 105; 21; CP 1, 2, 3, 4, 5, 6, 7; DLB 40

Simms, William Gilmore 1806-1870 .... **NCLC 3**
See also DLB 3, 30, 59, 73, 248, 254; RGAL 4

Simon, Carly 1945- .... **CLC 26**
See also CA 105

Simon, Claude 1913-2005 ... **CLC 4, 9, 15, 39**
See also CA 89-92; CAAS 241; CANR 33, 117; CWW 2; DAM NOV; DLB 83, 332; EW 13; EWL 3; GFL 1789 to the Present; MTCW 1

Simon, Claude Eugene Henri
See Simon, Claude

Simon, Claude Henri Eugene
See Simon, Claude

Simon, Marvin Neil
See Simon, Neil

Simon, Myles
See Follett, Ken

Simon, Neil 1927- .... **CLC 6, 11, 31, 39, 70, 233; DC 14**
See also AAYA 32; AITN 1; AMWS 4; CA 21-24R; CAD; CANR 26, 54, 87, 126; CD 5, 6; DA3; DAM DRAM; DFS 2, 6, 12, 18., 24; DLB 7, 266; LAIT 4; MAL 5; MTCW 1, 2; MTFW 2005; RGAL 4; TUS

Simon, Paul 1941(?)- .... **CLC 17**
See also CA 153; CAAE 116; CANR 152

Simon, Paul Frederick
See Simon, Paul

Simonon, Paul 1956(?)- .... **CLC 30**

Simonson, Rick .... **CLC 70**

Simpson, Harriette
See Arnow, Harriette (Louisa) Simpson

Simpson, Louis 1923- ... **CLC 4, 7, 9, 32, 149**
See also AMWS 9; CA 1-4R; 4; CANR 1, 61, 140; CP 1, 2, 3, 4, 5, 6, 7; DAM POET; DLB 5; MAL 5; MTCW 1, 2; MTFW 2005; PFS 7, 11, 14; RGAL 4

Simpson, Mona 1957- .... **CLC 44, 146**
See also CA 135; CAAE 122; CANR 68, 103; CN 6, 7; EWL 3

Simpson, Mona Elizabeth
See Simpson, Mona

Simpson, N(orman) F(rederick) 1919- .... **CLC 29**
See also CA 13-16R; CBD; DLB 13; RGEL 2

Sinclair, Andrew (Annandale) 1935- . **CLC 2, 14**
See also CA 9-12R; 5; CANR 14, 38, 91; CN 1, 2, 3, 4, 5, 6, 7; DLB 14; FANT; MTCW 1

Sinclair, Emil
See Hesse, Hermann

Sinclair, Iain 1943- .... **CLC 76**
See also CA 132; CANR 81, 157; CP 5, 6, 7; HGG

Sinclair, Iain MacGregor
See Sinclair, Iain

Sinclair, Irene
See Griffith, D(avid Lewelyn) W(ark)

Sinclair, Julian
See Sinclair, May

Sinclair, Mary Amelia St. Clair (?)-
See Sinclair, May

Sinclair, May 1865-1946 .... **TCLC 3, 11**
See also CA 166; CAAE 104; DLB 36, 135; EWL 3; HGG; RGEL 2; RHW; SUFW

Sinclair, Roy
See Griffith, D(avid Lewelyn) W(ark)

Sinclair, Upton 1878-1968 ...... **CLC 1, 11, 15, 63; TCLC 160; WLC 5**
See also AAYA 63; AMWS 5; BPFB 3; BYA 2; CA 5-8R; CAAS 25-28R; CANR 7; CDALB 1929-1941; DA; DA3; DAB; DAC; DAM MST, NOV; DLB 9; EWL 3; INT CANR-7; LAIT 3; MAL 5; MTCW 1, 2; MTFW 2005; NFS 6; RGAL 4; SATA 9; TUS; YAW

Sinclair, Upton Beall
See Sinclair, Upton

Singe, (Edmund) J(ohn) M(illington) 1871-1909 .... **WLC**

Singer, Isaac
See Singer, Isaac Bashevis

Singer, Isaac Bashevis 1904-1991 .. **CLC 1, 3, 6, 9, 11, 15, 23, 38, 69, 111; SSC 3, 53, 80; WLC 5**
See also AAYA 32; AITN 1, 2; AMW; AMWR 2; BPFB 3; BYA 1, 4; CA 1-4R; CAAS 134; CANR 1, 39, 106; CDALB 1941-1968; CLR 1; CN 1, 2, 3, 4; CWRI 5; DA; DA3; DAB; DAC; DAM MST, NOV; DLB 6, 28, 52, 278, 332, 333; DLBY 1991; EWL 3; EXPS; HGG; JRDA; LAIT 3; MAICYA 1, 2; MAL 5; MTCW 1, 2; MTFW 2005; RGAL 4; RGHL; RGSF 2; SATA 3, 27; SATA-Obit 68; SSFS 2, 12, 16; TUS; TWA

Singer, Israel Joshua 1893-1944 .... **TCLC 33**
See Zinger, Yisroel-Yehoyshue
See also CA 169; DLB 333; EWL 3

Singh, Khushwant 1915- .... **CLC 11**
See also CA 9-12R; 9; CANR 6, 84; CN 1, 2, 3, 4, 5, 6, 7; DLB 323; EWL 3; RGEL 2

Singleton, Ann
See Benedict, Ruth

Singleton, John 1968(?)- .... **CLC 156**
See also AAYA 50; BW 2, 3; CA 138; CANR 67, 82; DAM MULT

Siniavskii, Andrei
See Sinyavsky, Andrei (Donatevich)
See also CWW 2

Sinjohn, John
See Galsworthy, John

Sinyavsky, Andrei (Donatevich) 1925-1997 .... **CLC 8**
See Siniavskii, Andrei; Sinyavsky, Andrey Donatovich; Tertz, Abram
See also CA 85-88; CAAS 159

Sinyavsky, Andrey Donatovich
See Sinyavsky, Andrei (Donatevich)
See also EWL 3

Sirin, V.
See Nabokov, Vladimir (Vladimirovich)

Sissman, L(ouis) E(dward) 1928-1976 .... **CLC 9, 18**
See also CA 21-24R; CAAS 65-68; CANR 13; CP 2; DLB 5

Sisson, C(harles) H(ubert) 1914-2003 .... **CLC 8**
See also BRWS 11; CA 1-4R; 3; CAAS 220; CANR 3, 48, 84; CP 1, 2, 3, 4, 5, 6, 7; DLB 27

Sitting Bull 1831(?)-1890 .... **NNAL**
See also DA3; DAM MULT

Sitwell, Dame Edith 1887-1964 ..... **CLC 2, 9, 67; PC 3**
See also BRW 7; CA 9-12R; CANR 35; CDBLB 1945-1960; DAM POET; DLB 20; EWL 3; MTCW 1, 2; MTFW 2005; RGEL 2; TEA

Siwaarmill, H. P.
See Sharp, William

Sjoewall, Maj 1935- .... **CLC 7**
See Sjowall, Maj
See also CA 65-68; CANR 73

Sjowall, Maj
See Sjoewall, Maj
See also BPFB 3; CMW 4; MSW

Skelton, John 1460(?)-1529 ..... **LC 71; PC 25**
See also BRW 1; DLB 136; RGEL 2

Skelton, Robin 1925-1997 .... **CLC 13**
See Zuk, Georges
See also AITN 2; CA 5-8R; 5; CAAS 160; CANR 28, 89; CCA 1; CP 1, 2, 3, 4, 5, 6; DLB 27, 53

Skolimowski, Jerzy 1938- .... **CLC 20**
See also CA 128

Skram, Amalie (Bertha) 1847-1905 .... **TCLC 25**
See also CA 165

Skvorecky, Josef 1924- . **CLC 15, 39, 69, 152**
See also CA 61-64; 1; CANR 10, 34, 63, 108; CDWLB 4; CWW 2; DA3; DAC; DAM NOV; DLB 232; EWL 3; MTCW 1, 2; MTFW 2005

Slade, Bernard 1930- .... **CLC 11, 46**
See Newbound, Bernard Slade
See also CA 9; CCA 1; CD 6; DLB 53

Slaughter, Carolyn 1946- .... **CLC 56**
See also CA 85-88; CANR 85; CN 5, 6, 7

Slaughter, Frank G(ill) 1908-2001 ... **CLC 29**
See also AITN 2; CA 5-8R; CAAS 197; CANR 5, 85; INT CANR-5; RHW

Slavitt, David R(ytman) 1935- ..... **CLC 5, 14**
See also CA 21-24R; 3; CANR 41, 83; CN 1, 2; CP 1, 2, 3, 4, 5, 6, 7; DLB 5, 6

Slesinger, Tess 1905-1945 .... **TCLC 10**
See also CA 199; CAAE 107; DLB 102

Slessor, Kenneth 1901-1971 .... **CLC 14**
See also CA 102; CAAS 89-92; DLB 260; RGEL 2

Slowacki, Juliusz 1809-1849 .... **NCLC 15**
See also RGWL 3

Smart, Christopher 1722-1771 .... **LC 3, 134; PC 13**
See also DAM POET; DLB 109; RGEL 2

Smart, Elizabeth 1913-1986 .... **CLC 54**
   See also CA 81-84; CAAS 118; CN 4; DLB
   88
Smiley, Jane 1949- ...... **CLC 53, 76, 144, 236**
   See also AAYA 66; AMWS 6; BPFB 3; CA
   104; CANR 30, 50, 74, 96, 158; CN 6, 7;
   CPW 1; DA3; DAM POP; DLB 227, 234;
   EWL 3; INT CANR-30; MAL 5; MTFW
   2005; SSFS 19
Smiley, Jane Graves
   See Smiley, Jane
Smith, A(rthur) J(ames) M(arshall)
   1902-1980 .... **CLC 15**
   See also CA 1-4R; CAAS 102; CANR 4;
   CP 1, 2, 3; DAC; DLB 88; RGEL 2
Smith, Adam 1723(?)-1790 .... **LC 36**
   See also DLB 104, 252, 336; RGEL 2
Smith, Alexander 1829-1867 .... **NCLC 59**
   See also DLB 32, 55
Smith, Anna Deavere 1950- .... **CLC 86**
   See also CA 133; CANR 103; CD 5, 6; DFS
   2, 22
Smith, Betty (Wehner) 1904-1972 .... **CLC 19**
   See also AAYA 72; BPFB 3; BYA 3; CA
   5-8R; CAAS 33-36R; DLBY 1982; LAIT
   3; RGAL 4; SATA 6
Smith, Charlotte (Turner)
   1749-1806 .... **NCLC 23, 115**
   See also DLB 39, 109; RGEL 2; TEA
Smith, Clark Ashton 1893-1961 .... **CLC 43**
   See also CA 143; CANR 81; FANT; HGG;
   MTCW 2; SCFW 1, 2; SFW 4; SUFW
Smith, Dave .... **CLC 22, 42**
   See Smith, David (Jeddie)
   See also CP 3, 4, 5, 6, 7; DLB 5
Smith, David (Jeddie) 1942-
   See Smith, Dave
   See also CA 49-52; CANR 1, 59, 120;
   CSW; DAM POET
Smith, Iain Crichton 1928-1998 .... **CLC 64**
   See also BRWS 9; CA 21-24R; CAAS 171;
   CN 1, 2, 3, 4, 5, 6; CP 1, 2, 3, 4, 5, 6;
   DLB 40, 139, 319; RGSF 2
Smith, John 1580(?)-1631 .... **LC 9**
   See also DLB 24, 30; TUS
Smith, Johnston
   See Crane, Stephen (Townley)
Smith, Joseph, Jr. 1805-1844 .... **NCLC 53**
Smith, Kevin 1970- .... **CLC 223**
   See also AAYA 37; CA 166; CANR 131
Smith, Lee 1944- .... **CLC 25, 73**
   See also CA 119; CAAE 114; CANR 46,
   118; CN 7; CSW; DLB 143; DLBY 1983;
   EWL 3; INT CA-119; RGAL 4
Smith, Martin
   See Smith, Martin Cruz
Smith, Martin Cruz 1942- .. **CLC 25; NNAL**
   See also BEST 89:4; BPFB 3; CA 85-88;
   CANR 6, 23, 43, 65, 119; CMW 4; CPW;
   DAM MULT, POP; HGG; INT CANR-
   23; MTCW 2; MTFW 2005; RGAL 4
Smith, Patti 1946- .... **CLC 12**
   See also CA 93-96; CANR 63
Smith, Pauline (Urmson)
   1882-1959 .... **TCLC 25**
   See also DLB 225; EWL 3
Smith, Rosamond
   See Oates, Joyce Carol
Smith, Sheila Kaye
   See Kaye-Smith, Sheila
Smith, Stevie 1902-1971 .... **CLC 3, 8, 25, 44;**
   PC 12
   See also BRWS 2; CA 17-18; CAAS 29-
   32R; CANR 35; CAP 2; CP 1; DAM
   POET; DLB 20; EWL 3; MTCW 1, 2;
   PAB; PFS 3; RGEL 2; TEA
Smith, Wilbur 1933- .... **CLC 33**
   See also CA 13-16R; CANR 7, 46, 66, 134;
   CPW; MTCW 1, 2; MTFW 2005

Smith, William Jay 1918- .... **CLC 6**
   See also AMWS 13; CA 5-8R; CANR 44,
   106; CP 1, 2, 3, 4, 5, 6, 7; CSW; CWRI
   5; DLB 5; MAICYA 1, 2; SAAS 22;
   SATA 2, 68, 154; SATA-Essay 154; TCLE
   1:2
Smith, Woodrow Wilson
   See Kuttner, Henry
Smith, Zadie 1975- .... **CLC 158**
   See also AAYA 50; CA 193; MTFW 2005
Smolenskin, Peretz 1842-1885 .... **NCLC 30**
Smollett, Tobias (George) 1721-1771 ... **LC 2,**
   46
   See also BRW 3; CDBLB 1660-1789; DLB
   39, 104; RGEL 2; TEA
Snodgrass, W.D. 1926- .... **CLC 2, 6, 10, 18,**
   68; PC 74
   See also AMWS 6; CA 1-4R; CANR 6, 36,
   65, 85; CP 1, 2, 3, 4, 5, 6, 7; DAM POET;
   DLB 5; MAL 5; MTCW 1, 2; MTFW
   2005; RGAL 4; TCLE 1:2
Snorri Sturluson 1179-1241 .... **CMLC 56**
   See also RGWL 2, 3
Snow, C(harles) P(ercy) 1905-1980 ... **CLC 1,**
   4, 6, 9, 13, 19
   See also BRW 7; CA 5-8R; CAAS 101;
   CANR 28; CDBLB 1945-1960; CN 1, 2;
   DAM NOV; DLB 15, 77; DLBD 17;
   EWL 3; MTCW 1, 2; MTFW 2005; RGEL
   2; TEA
Snow, Frances Compton
   See Adams, Henry (Brooks)
Snyder, Gary 1930- . **CLC 1, 2, 5, 9, 32, 120;**
   PC 21
   See also AAYA 72; AMWS 8; ANW; BG
   1:3; CA 17-20R; CANR 30, 60, 125; CP
   1, 2, 3, 4, 5, 6, 7; DA3; DAM POET; DLB
   5, 16, 165, 212, 237, 275; EWL 3; MAL
   5; MTCW 2; MTFW 2005; PFS 9, 19;
   RGAL 4; WP
Snyder, Zilpha Keatley 1927- .... **CLC 17**
   See also AAYA 15; BYA 1; CA 252; 9-12R,
   252; CANR 38; CLR 31, 121; JRDA;
   MAICYA 1, 2; SAAS 2; SATA 1, 28, 75,
   110, 163; SATA-Essay 112, 163; YAW
Soares, Bernardo
   See Pessoa, Fernando (Antonio Nogueira)
Sobh, A.
   See Shamlu, Ahmad
Sobh, Alef
   See Shamlu, Ahmad
Sobol, Joshua 1939- .... **CLC 60**
   See Sobol, Yehoshua
   See also CA 200; RGHL
Sobol, Yehoshua 1939-
   See Sobol, Joshua
   See also CWW 2
Socrates 470B.C.-399B.C. .... **CMLC 27**
Soderberg, Hjalmar 1869-1941 ...... **TCLC 39**
   See also DLB 259; EWL 3; RGSF 2
Soderbergh, Steven 1963- .... **CLC 154**
   See also AAYA 43; CA 243
Soderbergh, Steven Andrew
   See Soderbergh, Steven
Sodergran, Edith (Irene) 1892-1923
   See Soedergran, Edith (Irene)
   See also CA 202; DLB 259; EW 11; EWL
   3; RGWL 2, 3
Soedergran, Edith (Irene)
   1892-1923 .... **TCLC 31**
   See Sodergran, Edith (Irene)
Softly, Edgar
   See Lovecraft, H. P.
Softly, Edward
   See Lovecraft, H. P.
Sokolov, Alexander V(sevolodovich) 1943-
   See Sokolov, Sasha
   See also CA 73-76

Sokolov, Raymond 1941- .... **CLC 7**
   See also CA 85-88
Sokolov, Sasha .... **CLC 59**
   See Sokolov, Alexander V(sevolodovich)
   See also CWW 2; DLB 285; EWL 3; RGWL
   2, 3
Solo, Jay
   See Ellison, Harlan
Sologub, Fyodor .... **TCLC 9**
   See Teternikov, Fyodor Kuzmich
   See also EWL 3
Solomons, Ikey Esquir
   See Thackeray, William Makepeace
Solomos, Dionysios 1798-1857 .... **NCLC 15**
Solwoska, Mara
   See French, Marilyn
Solzhenitsyn, Aleksandr I. 1918- .. **CLC 1, 2,**
   4, 7, 9, 10, 18, 26, 34, 78, 134, 235; SSC
   32; WLC 5
   See Solzhenitsyn, Aleksandr Isayevich
   See also AAYA 49; AITN 1; BPFB 3; CA
   69-72; CANR 40, 65, 116; DA; DA3;
   DAB; DAC; DAM MST, NOV; DLB 302,
   332; EW 13; EXPS; LAIT 4; MTCW 1,
   2; MTFW 2005; NFS 6; RGSF 2; RGWL
   2, 3; SSFS 9; TWA
Solzhenitsyn, Aleksandr Isayevich
   See Solzhenitsyn, Aleksandr I.
   See also CWW 2; EWL 3
Somers, Jane
   See Lessing, Doris
Somerville, Edith Oenone
   1858-1949 .... **SSC 56; TCLC 51**
   See also CA 196; DLB 135; RGEL 2; RGSF
   2
Somerville & Ross
   See Martin, Violet Florence; Somerville,
   Edith Oenone
Sommer, Scott 1951- .... **CLC 25**
   See also CA 106
Sommers, Christina Hoff 1950- ...... **CLC 197**
   See also CA 153; CANR 95
Sondheim, Stephen (Joshua) 1930- . **CLC 30,**
   39, 147; DC 22
   See also AAYA 11, 66; CA 103; CANR 47,
   67, 125; DAM DRAM; LAIT 4
Sone, Monica 1919- .... **AAL**
   See also DLB 312
Song, Cathy 1955- .... **AAL; PC 21**
   See also CA 154; CANR 118; CWP; DLB
   169, 312; EXPP; FW; PFS 5
Sontag, Susan 1933-2004 ... **CLC 1, 2, 10, 13,**
   31, 105, 195
   See also AMWS 3; CA 17-20R; CAAS 234;
   CANR 25, 51, 74, 97; CN 1, 2, 3, 4, 5, 6,
   7; CPW; DA3; DAM POP; DLB 2, 67;
   EWL 3; MAL 5; MBL; MTCW 1, 2;
   MTFW 2005; RGAL 4; RHW; SSFS 10
Sophocles 496(?)B.C.-406(?)B.C. .... **CMLC 2,**
   47, 51, 86; DC 1; WLCS
   See also AW 1; CDWLB 1; DA; DA3;
   DAB; DAC; DAM DRAM, MST; DFS 1,
   4, 8, 24; DLB 176; LAIT 1; LATS 1:1;
   LMFS 1; RGWL 2, 3; TWA; WLIT 8
Sordello 1189-1269 .... **CMLC 15**
Sorel, Georges 1847-1922 .... **TCLC 91**
   See also CA 188; CAAE 118
Sorel, Julia
   See Drexler, Rosalyn
Sorokin, Vladimir .... **CLC 59**
   See Sorokin, Vladimir Georgievich
   See also CA 258
Sorokin, Vladimir Georgievich
   See Sorokin, Vladimir
   See also DLB 285

Sorrentino, Gilbert 1929-2006 .... **CLC 3, 7, 14, 22, 40**
  See also CA 77-80; CAAS 250; CANR 14, 33, 115, 157; CN 3, 4, 5, 6, 7; CP 1, 2, 3, 4, 5, 6, 7; DLB 5, 173; DLBY 1980; INT CANR-14

Soseki
  See Natsume, Soseki
  See also MJW

Soto, Gary 1952- ... **CLC 32, 80; HLC 2; PC 28**
  See also AAYA 10, 37; BYA 11; CA 125; CAAE 119; CANR 50, 74, 107, 157; CLR 38; CP 4, 5, 6, 7; DAM MULT; DLB 82; EWL 3; EXPP; HW 1, 2; INT CA-125; JRDA; LLW; MAICYA 2; MAICYAS 1; MAL 5; MTCW 2; MTFW 2005; PFS 7; RGAL 4; SATA 80, 120, 174; WYA; YAW

Soupault, Philippe 1897-1990 .... **CLC 68**
  See also CA 147; CAAE 116; CAAS 131; EWL 3; GFL 1789 to the Present; LMFS 2

Souster, (Holmes) Raymond 1921- .... **CLC 5, 14**
  See also CA 13-16R; 14; CANR 13, 29, 53; CP 1, 2, 3, 4, 5, 6, 7; DA3; DAC; DAM POET; DLB 88; RGEL 2; SATA 63

Southern, Terry 1924(?)-1995 .... **CLC 7**
  See also AMWS 11; BPFB 3; CA 1-4R; CAAS 150; CANR 1, 55, 107; CN 1, 2, 3, 4, 5, 6; DLB 2; IDFW 3, 4

Southerne, Thomas 1660-1746 .... **LC 99**
  See also DLB 80; RGEL 2

Southey, Robert 1774-1843 .... **NCLC 8, 97**
  See also BRW 4; DLB 93, 107, 142; RGEL 2; SATA 54

Southwell, Robert 1561(?)-1595 .... **LC 108**
  See also DLB 167; RGEL 2; TEA

Southworth, Emma Dorothy Eliza Nevitte 1819-1899 .... **NCLC 26**
  See also DLB 239

Souza, Ernest
  See Scott, Evelyn

Soyinka, Wole 1934- .. **BLC 3; CLC 3, 5, 14, 36, 44, 179; DC 2; WLC 5**
  See also AFW; BW 2, 3; CA 13-16R; CANR 27, 39, 82, 136; CD 5, 6; CDWLB 3; CN 6, 7; CP 1, 2, 3, 4, 5, 6, 7; DA; DA3; DAB; DAC; DAM DRAM, MST, MULT; DFS 10; DLB 125, 332; EWL 3; MTCW 1, 2; MTFW 2005; RGEL 2; TWA; WLIT 2; WWE 1

Spackman, W(illiam) M(ode) 1905-1990 .... **CLC 46**
  See also CA 81-84; CAAS 132

Spacks, Barry (Bernard) 1931- .... **CLC 14**
  See also CA 154; CANR 33, 109; CP 3, 4, 5, 6, 7; DLB 105

Spanidou, Irini 1946- .... **CLC 44**
  See also CA 185

Spark, Muriel 1918-2006 .... **CLC 2, 3, 5, 8, 13, 18, 40, 94; PC 72; SSC 10**
  See also BRWS 1; CA 5-8R; CAAS 251; CANR 12, 36, 76, 89, 131; CDBLB 1945-1960; CN 1, 2, 3, 4, 5, 6, 7; CP 1, 2, 3, 4, 5, 6, 7; DA3; DAB; DAC; DAM MST, NOV; DLB 15, 139; EWL 3; FW; INT CANR-12; LAIT 4; MTCW 1, 2; MTFW 2005; NFS 22; RGEL 2; TEA; WLIT 4; YAW

Spark, Muriel Sarah
  See Spark, Muriel

Spaulding, Douglas
  See Bradbury, Ray

Spaulding, Leonard
  See Bradbury, Ray

Speght, Rachel 1597-c. 1630 .... **LC 97**
  See also DLB 126

Spence, J. A. D.
  See Eliot, T(homas) S(tearns)

Spencer, Anne 1882-1975 ...... **HR 1:3; PC 77**
  See also BW 2; CA 161; DLB 51, 54

Spencer, Elizabeth 1921- .... **CLC 22; SSC 57**
  See also CA 13-16R; CANR 32, 65, 87; CN 1, 2, 3, 4, 5, 6, 7; CSW; DLB 6, 218; EWL 3; MTCW 1; RGAL 4; SATA 14

Spencer, Leonard G.
  See Silverberg, Robert

Spencer, Scott 1945- .... **CLC 30**
  See also CA 113; CANR 51, 148; DLBY 1986

Spender, Stephen 1909-1995 ..... **CLC 1, 2, 5, 10, 41, 91; PC 71**
  See also BRWS 2; CA 9-12R; CAAS 149; CANR 31, 54; CDBLB 1945-1960; CP 1, 2, 3, 4, 5, 6; DA3; DAM POET; DLB 20; EWL 3; MTCW 1, 2; MTFW 2005; PAB; PFS 23; RGEL 2; TEA

Spengler, Oswald (Arnold Gottfried) 1880-1936 .... **TCLC 25**
  See also CA 189; CAAE 118

Spenser, Edmund 1552(?)-1599 ...... **LC 5, 39, 117; PC 8, 42; WLC 5**
  See also AAYA 60; BRW 1; CDBLB Before 1660; DA; DA3; DAB; DAC; DAM MST, POET; DLB 167; EFS 2; EXPP; PAB; RGEL 2; TEA; WLIT 3; WP

Spicer, Jack 1925-1965 .... **CLC 8, 18, 72**
  See also BG 1:3; CA 85-88; DAM POET; DLB 5, 16, 193; GLL 1; WP

Spiegelman, Art 1948- .... **CLC 76, 178**
  See also AAYA 10, 46; CA 125; CANR 41, 55, 74, 124; DLB 299; MTCW 2; MTFW 2005; RGHL; SATA 109, 158; YAW

Spielberg, Peter 1929- .... **CLC 6**
  See also CA 5-8R; CANR 4, 48; DLBY 1981

Spielberg, Steven 1947- .... **CLC 20, 188**
  See also AAYA 8, 24; CA 77-80; CANR 32; SATA 32

Spillane, Frank Morrison .... **CLC 3, 13**
  See Spillane, Mickey
  See also BPFB 3; CMW 4; DLB 226; MSW

Spillane, Mickey 1918-2006
  See Spillane, Frank Morrison
  See also CA 25-28R; CAAS 252; CANR 28, 63, 125; DA3; MTCW 1, 2; MTFW 2005; SATA 66; SATA-Obit 176

Spinoza, Benedictus de 1632-1677 ... **LC 9, 58**

Spinrad, Norman (Richard) 1940- ... **CLC 46**
  See also BPFB 3; CA 233; 37-40R, 233; 19; CANR 20, 91; DLB 8; INT CANR-20; SFW 4

Spitteler, Carl 1845-1924 .... **TCLC 12**
  See also CAAE 109; DLB 129, 332; EWL 3

Spitteler, Karl Friedrich Georg
  See Spitteler, Carl

Spivack, Kathleen (Romola Drucker) 1938- .... **CLC 6**
  See also CA 49-52

Spivak, Gayatri Chakravorty 1942- .... **CLC 233**
  See also CA 154; CAAE 110; CANR 91; FW; LMFS 2

Spofford, Harriet (Elizabeth) Prescott 1835-1921 .... **SSC 87**
  See also CA 201; DLB 74, 221

Spoto, Donald 1941- .... **CLC 39**
  See also CA 65-68; CANR 11, 57, 93

Springsteen, Bruce 1949- .... **CLC 17**
  See also CA 111

Springsteen, Bruce F.
  See Springsteen, Bruce

Spurling, Hilary 1940- .... **CLC 34**
  See also CA 104; CANR 25, 52, 94, 157

Spurling, Susan Hilary
  See Spurling, Hilary

Spyker, John Howland
  See Elman, Richard (Martin)

Squared, A.
  See Abbott, Edwin A.

Squires, (James) Radcliffe 1917-1993 .... **CLC 51**
  See also CA 1-4R; CAAS 140; CANR 6, 21; CP 1, 2, 3, 4, 5

Srivastava, Dhanpat Rai 1880(?)-1936
  See Premchand
  See also CA 197; CAAE 118

Stacy, Donald
  See Pohl, Frederik

Stael
  See Stael-Holstein, Anne Louise Germaine Necker
  See also EW 5; RGWL 2, 3

Stael, Germaine de
  See Stael-Holstein, Anne Louise Germaine Necker
  See also DLB 119, 192; FL 1:3; FW; GFL 1789 to the Present; TWA

Stael-Holstein, Anne Louise Germaine Necker 1766-1817 .... **NCLC 3, 91**
  See Stael; Stael, Germaine de

Stafford, Jean 1915-1979 .. **CLC 4, 7, 19, 68; SSC 26, 86**
  See also CA 1-4R; CAAS 85-88; CANR 3, 65; CN 1, 2; DLB 2, 173; MAL 5; MTCW 1, 2; MTFW 2005; RGAL 4; RGSF 2; SATA-Obit 22; SSFS 21; TCWW 1, 2; TUS

Stafford, William (Edgar) 1914-1993 .... **CLC 4, 7, 29; PC 71**
  See also AMWS 11; CA 5-8R; 3; CAAS 142; CANR 5, 22; CP 1, 2, 3, 4, 5; DAM POET; DLB 5, 206; EXPP; INT CANR-22; MAL 5; PFS 2, 8, 16; RGAL 4; WP

Stagnelius, Eric Johan 1793-1823 . **NCLC 61**

Staines, Trevor
  See Brunner, John (Kilian Houston)

Stairs, Gordon
  See Austin, Mary (Hunter)

Stalin, Joseph 1879-1953 .... **TCLC 92**

Stampa, Gaspara c. 1524-1554 .. **LC 114; PC 43**
  See also RGWL 2, 3; WLIT 7

Stampflinger, K. A.
  See Benjamin, Walter

Stancykowna
  See Szymborska, Wislawa

Standing Bear, Luther 1868(?)-1939(?) .... **NNAL**
  See also CA 144; CAAE 113; DAM MULT

Stanislavsky, Constantin 1863(?)-1938 .... **TCLC 167**
  See also CAAE 118

Stanislavsky, Konstantin
  See Stanislavsky, Constantin

Stanislavsky, Konstantin Sergeievich
  See Stanislavsky, Constantin

Stanislavsky, Konstantin Sergeivich
  See Stanislavsky, Constantin

Stanislavsky, Konstantin Sergeyevich
  See Stanislavsky, Constantin

Stannard, Martin 1947- .... **CLC 44**
  See also CA 142; DLB 155

Stanton, Elizabeth Cady 1815-1902 .... **TCLC 73**
  See also CA 171; DLB 79; FL 1:3; FW

Stanton, Maura 1946- .... **CLC 9**
  See also CA 89-92; CANR 15, 123; DLB 120

Stanton, Schuyler
  See Baum, L(yman) Frank

Stapledon, (William) Olaf 1886-1950 .... **TCLC 22**
  See also CA 162; CAAE 111; DLB 15, 255; SCFW 1, 2; SFW 4

Turgenev, Ivan (Sergeevich)
1818-1883 ..... **DC 7; NCLC 21, 37, 122;
SSC 7, 57; WLC 6**
See also AAYA 58; DA; DAB; DAC; DAM
MST, NOV; DFS 6; DLB 238, 284; EW
6; LATS 1:1; NFS 16; RGSF 2; RGWL 2,
3; TWA

Turgot, Anne-Robert-Jacques
1727-1781 .... **LC 26**
See also DLB 314

Turner, Frederick 1943- .... **CLC 48**
See also CA 227; 73-76, 227; 10; CANR
12, 30, 56; DLB 40, 282

Turton, James
See Crace, Jim

Tutu, Desmond M(pilo) 1931- .. **BLC 3; CLC
80**
See also BW 1, 3; CA 125; CANR 67, 81;
DAM MULT

Tutuola, Amos 1920-1997 ..... **BLC 3; CLC 5,
14, 29; TCLC 188**
See also AFW; BW 2, 3; CA 9-12R; CAAS
159; CANR 27, 66; CDWLB 3; CN 1, 2,
3, 4, 5, 6; DA3; DAM MULT; DLB 125;
DNFS 2; EWL 3; MTCW 1, 2; MTFW
2005; RGEL 2; WLIT 2

Twain, Mark .... **SSC 6, 26, 34, 87; TCLC 6,
12, 19, 36, 48, 59, 161, 185; WLC 6**
See Clemens, Samuel Langhorne
See also AAYA 20; AMW; AMWC 1; BPFB
3; BYA 2, 3, 11, 14; CLR 58, 60, 66; DLB
11; EXPN; EXPS; FANT; LAIT 2; MAL
5; NCFS 4; NFS 1, 6; RGAL 4; RGSF 2;
SFW 4; SSFS 1, 7, 16, 21; SUFW; TUS;
WCH; WYA; YAW

Tyler, Anne 1941- . **CLC 7, 11, 18, 28, 44, 59,
103, 205**
See also AAYA 18, 60; AMWS 4; BEST
89:1; BPFB 3; BYA 12; CA 9-12R; CANR
11, 33, 53, 109, 132; CDALBS; CN 1, 2,
3, 4, 5, 6, 7; CPW; CSW; DAM NOV,
POP; DLB 6, 143; DLBY 1982; EWL 3;
EXPN; LATS 1:2; MAL 5; MBL; MTCW
1, 2; MTFW 2005; NFS 2, 7, 10; RGAL
4; SATA 7, 90, 173; SSFS 17; TCLE 1:2;
TUS; YAW

Tyler, Royall 1757-1826 .... **NCLC 3**
See also DLB 37; RGAL 4

Tynan, Katharine 1861-1931 .... **TCLC 3**
See also CA 167; CAAE 104; DLB 153,
240; FW

Tyndale, William c. 1484-1536 .... **LC 103**
See also DLB 132

Tyutchev, Fyodor 1803-1873 .... **NCLC 34**

Tzara, Tristan 1896-1963 .... **CLC 47; PC 27;
TCLC 168**
See also CA 153; CAAS 89-92; DAM
POET; EWL 3; MTCW 2

Uchida, Yoshiko 1921-1992 .... **AAL**
See also AAYA 16; BYA 2, 3; CA 13-16R;
CAAS 139; CANR 6, 22, 47, 61;
CDALBS; CLR 6, 56; CWRI 5; DLB 312;
JRDA; MAICYA 1, 2; MTCW 1, 2;
MTFW 2005; SAAS 1; SATA 1, 53;
SATA-Obit 72

Udall, Nicholas 1504-1556 .... **LC 84**
See also DLB 62; RGEL 2

Ueda Akinari 1734-1809 .... **NCLC 131**

Uhry, Alfred 1936- .... **CLC 55**
See also CA 133; CAAE 127; CAD; CANR
112; CD 5, 6; CSW; DA3; DAM DRAM,
POP; DFS 11, 15; INT CA-133; MTFW
2005

Ulf, Haerved
See Strindberg, (Johan) August

Ulf, Harved
See Strindberg, (Johan) August

Ulibarri, Sabine R(eyes)
1919-2003 .... **CLC 83; HLCS 2**
See also CA 131; CAAS 214; CANR 81;
DAM MULT; DLB 82; HW 1, 2; RGSF 2

Unamuno (y Jugo), Miguel de
1864-1936 .. **HLC 2; SSC 11, 69; TCLC
2, 9, 148**
See also CA 131; CAAE 104; CANR 81;
DAM MULT, NOV; DLB 108, 322; EW
8; EWL 3; HW 1, 2; MTCW 1, 2; MTFW
2005; RGSF 2; RGWL 2, 3; SSFS 20;
TWA

Uncle Shelby
See Silverstein, Shel

Undercliffe, Errol
See Campbell, (John) Ramsey

Underwood, Miles
See Glassco, John

Undset, Sigrid 1882-1949 .. **TCLC 3; WLC 6**
See also CA 129; CAAE 104; DA; DA3;
DAB; DAC; DAM MST, NOV; DLB 293,
332; EW 9; EWL 3; FW; MTCW 1, 2;
MTFW 2005; RGWL 2, 3

Ungaretti, Giuseppe 1888-1970 ... **CLC 7, 11,
15; PC 57**
See also CA 19-20; CAAS 25-28R; CAP 2;
DLB 114; EW 10; EWL 3; PFS 20;
RGWL 2, 3; WLIT 7

Unger, Douglas 1952- .... **CLC 34**
See also CA 130; CANR 94, 155

Unsworth, Barry (Forster) 1930- .... **CLC 76,
127**
See also BRWS 7; CA 25-28R; CANR 30,
54, 125; CN 6, 7; DLB 194, 326

Updike, John 1932- . **CLC 1, 2, 3, 5, 7, 9, 13,
15, 23, 34, 43, 70, 139, 214; SSC 13, 27;
WLC 6**
See also AAYA 36; AMW; AMWC 1;
AMWR 1; BPFB 3; BYA 12; CA 1-4R;
CABS 1; CANR 4, 33, 51, 94, 133;
CDALB 1968-1988; CN 1, 2, 3, 4, 5, 6,
7; CP 1, 2, 3, 4, 5, 6, 7; CPW 1; DA;
DA3; DAB; DAC; DAM MST, NOV,
POET, POP; DLB 2, 5, 143, 218, 227;
DLBD 3; DLBY 1980, 1982, 1997; EWL
3; EXPP; HGG; MAL 5; MTCW 1, 2;
MTFW 2005; NFS 12, 24; RGAL 4;
RGSF 2; SSFS 3, 19; TUS

Updike, John Hoyer
See Updike, John

Upshaw, Margaret Mitchell
See Mitchell, Margaret (Munnerlyn)

Upton, Mark
See Sanders, Lawrence

Upward, Allen 1863-1926 .... **TCLC 85**
See also CA 187; CAAE 117; DLB 36

Urdang, Constance (Henriette)
1922-1996 .... **CLC 47**
See also CA 21-24R; CANR 9, 24; CP 1, 2,
3, 4, 5, 6; CWP

Urfe, Honore d' 1567(?)-1625 .... **LC 132**
See also DLB 268; GFL Beginnings to
1789; RGWL 2, 3

Uriel, Henry
See Faust, Frederick (Schiller)

Uris, Leon 1924-2003 .... **CLC 7, 32**
See also AITN 1, 2; BEST 89:2; BPFB 3;
CA 1-4R; CAAS 217; CANR 1, 40, 65,
123; CN 1, 2, 3, 4, 5, 6; CPW 1; DA3;
DAM NOV, POP; MTCW 1, 2; MTFW
2005; RGHL; SATA 49; SATA-Obit 146

Urista (Heredia), Alberto (Baltazar)
1947- .... **HLCS 1**
See Alurista
See also CA 182; CANR 2, 32; HW 1

Urmuz
See Codrescu, Andrei

Urquhart, Guy
See McAlmon, Robert (Menzies)

Urquhart, Jane 1949- .... **CLC 90**
See also CA 113; CANR 32, 68, 116, 157;
CCA 1; DAC; DLB 334

Usigli, Rodolfo 1905-1979 .... **HLCS 1**
See also CA 131; DLB 305; EWL 3; HW 1;
LAW

Usk, Thomas (?)-1388 .... **CMLC 76**
See also DLB 146

Ustinov, Peter (Alexander)
1921-2004 .... **CLC 1**
See also AITN 1; CA 13-16R; CAAS 225;
CANR 25, 51; CBD; CD 5, 6; DLB 13;
MTCW 2

U Tam'si, Gerald Felix Tchicaya
See Tchicaya, Gerald Felix

U Tam'si, Tchicaya
See Tchicaya, Gerald Felix

Vachss, Andrew 1942- .... **CLC 106**
See also CA 214; 118, 214; CANR 44, 95,
153; CMW 4

Vachss, Andrew H.
See Vachss, Andrew

Vachss, Andrew Henry
See Vachss, Andrew

Vaculik, Ludvik 1926- .... **CLC 7**
See also CA 53-56; CANR 72; CWW 2;
DLB 232; EWL 3

Vaihinger, Hans 1852-1933 .... **TCLC 71**
See also CA 166; CAAE 116

Valdez, Luis (Miguel) 1940- ..... **CLC 84; DC
10; HLC 2**
See also CA 101; CAD; CANR 32, 81; CD
5, 6; DAM MULT; DFS 5; DLB 122;
EWL 3; HW 1; LAIT 4; LLW

Valenzuela, Luisa 1938- .... **CLC 31, 104;
HLCS 2; SSC 14, 82**
See also CA 101; CANR 32, 65, 123; CD-
WLB 3; CWW 2; DAM MULT; DLB 113;
EWL 3; FW; HW 1, 2; LAW; RGSF 2;
RGWL 3

Valera y Alcala-Galiano, Juan
1824-1905 .... **TCLC 10**
See also CAAE 106

Valerius Maximus fl. 20- .... **CMLC 64**
See also DLB 211

Valery, (Ambroise) Paul (Toussaint Jules)
1871-1945 .... **PC 9; TCLC 4, 15**
See also CA 122; CAAE 104; DA3; DAM
POET; DLB 258; EW 8; EWL 3; GFL
1789 to the Present; MTCW 1, 2; MTFW
2005; RGWL 2, 3; TWA

Valle-Inclan, Ramon (Maria) del
1866-1936 .... **HLC 2; TCLC 5**
See del Valle-Inclan, Ramon (Maria)
See also CA 153; CAAE 106; CANR 80;
DAM MULT; DLB 134; EW 8; EWL 3;
HW 2; RGSF 2; RGWL 2, 3

Vallejo, Antonio Buero
See Buero Vallejo, Antonio

Vallejo, Cesar (Abraham)
1892-1938 .... **HLC 2; TCLC 3, 56**
See also CA 153; CAAE 105; DAM MULT;
DLB 290; EWL 3; HW 1; LAW; RGWL
2, 3

Valles, Jules 1832-1885 .... **NCLC 71**
See also DLB 123; GFL 1789 to the Present

Vallette, Marguerite Eymery
1860-1953 .... **TCLC 67**
See Rachilde
See also CA 182; DLB 123, 192

Valle Y Pena, Ramon del
See Valle-Inclan, Ramon (Maria) del

Van Ash, Cay 1918-1994 .... **CLC 34**
See also CA 220

Vanbrugh, Sir John 1664-1726 .... **LC 21**
See also BRW 2; DAM DRAM; DLB 80;
IDTP; RGEL 2

Van Campen, Karl
See Campbell, John W(ood, Jr.)

Villehardouin, Geoffroi de
1150(?)-1218(?) .... **CMLC 38**

Villiers, George 1628-1687 .... **LC 107**
See also DLB 80; RGEL 2

Villiers de l'Isle Adam, Jean Marie Mathias Philippe Auguste 1838-1889 ... **NCLC 3; SSC 14**
See also DLB 123, 192; GFL 1789 to the Present; RGSF 2

Villon, Francois 1431-1463(?) . **LC 62; PC 13**
See also DLB 208; EW 2; RGWL 2, 3; TWA

Vine, Barbara .... **CLC 50**
See Rendell, Ruth
See also BEST 90:4

Vinge, Joan (Carol) D(ennison)
1948- .... **CLC 30; SSC 24**
See also AAYA 32; BPFB 3; CA 93-96; CANR 72; SATA 36, 113; SFW 4; YAW

Viola, Herman J(oseph) 1938- .... **CLC 70**
See also CA 61-64; CANR 8, 23, 48, 91; SATA 126

Violis, G.
See Simenon, Georges (Jacques Christian)

Viramontes, Helena Maria 1954- .... **HLCS 2**
See also CA 159; DLB 122; HW 2; LLW

Virgil
See Vergil
See also CDWLB 1; DLB 211; LAIT 1; RGWL 2, 3; WLIT 8; WP

Visconti, Luchino 1906-1976 .... **CLC 16**
See also CA 81-84; CAAS 65-68; CANR 39

Vitry, Jacques de
See Jacques de Vitry

Vittorini, Elio 1908-1966 .... **CLC 6, 9, 14**
See also CA 133; CAAS 25-28R; DLB 264; EW 12; EWL 3; RGWL 2, 3

Vivekananda, Swami 1863-1902 .... **TCLC 88**

Vizenor, Gerald Robert 1934- .... **CLC 103; NNAL**
See also CA 205; 13-16R, 205; 22; CANR 5, 21, 44, 67; DAM MULT; DLB 175, 227; MTCW 2; MTFW 2005; TCWW 2

Vizinczey, Stephen 1933- .... **CLC 40**
See also CA 128; CCA 1; INT CA-128

Vliet, R(ussell) G(ordon)
1929-1984 .... **CLC 22**
See also CA 37-40R; CAAS 112; CANR 18; CP 2, 3

Vogau, Boris Andreyevich 1894-1938
See Pilnyak, Boris
See also CA 218; CAAE 123

Vogel, Paula A. 1951- .... **CLC 76; DC 19**
See also CA 108; CAD; CANR 119, 140; CD 5, 6; CWD; DFS 14; MTFW 2005; RGAL 4

Voigt, Cynthia 1942- .... **CLC 30**
See also AAYA 3, 30; BYA 1, 3, 6, 7, 8; CA 106; CANR 18, 37, 40, 94, 145; CLR 13, 48; INT CANR-18; JRDA; LAIT 5; MAICYA 1, 2; MAICYAS 1; MTFW 2005; SATA 48, 79, 116, 160; SATA-Brief 33; WYA; YAW

Voigt, Ellen Bryant 1943- .... **CLC 54**
See also CA 69-72; CANR 11, 29, 55, 115; CP 5, 6, 7; CSW; CWP; DLB 120; PFS 23

Voinovich, Vladimir 1932- .. **CLC 10, 49, 147**
See also CA 81-84; 12; CANR 33, 67, 150; CWW 2; DLB 302; MTCW 1

Voinovich, Vladimir Nikolaevich
See Voinovich, Vladimir

Vollmann, William T. 1959- ...... **CLC 89, 227**
See also CA 134; CANR 67, 116; CN 7; CPW; DA3; DAM NOV, POP; MTCW 2; MTFW 2005

Voloshinov, V. N.
See Bakhtin, Mikhail Mikhailovich

Voltaire 1694-1778 . **LC 14, 79, 110; SSC 12; WLC 6**
See also BYA 13; DA; DA3; DAB; DAC; DAM DRAM, MST; DLB 314; EW 4; GFL Beginnings to 1789; LATS 1:1; LMFS 1; NFS 7; RGWL 2, 3; TWA

von Aschendrof, Baron Ignatz
See Ford, Ford Madox

von Chamisso, Adelbert
See Chamisso, Adelbert von

von Daeniken, Erich 1935- .... **CLC 30**
See also AITN 1; CA 37-40R; CANR 17, 44

von Daniken, Erich
See von Daeniken, Erich

von Eschenbach, Wolfram c. 1170-c. 1220 .... **CMLC 5**
See Eschenbach, Wolfram von
See also CDWLB 2; DLB 138; EW 1; RGWL 2

von Hartmann, Eduard
1842-1906 .... **TCLC 96**

von Hayek, Friedrich August
See Hayek, F(riedrich) A(ugust von)

von Heidenstam, (Carl Gustaf) Verner
See Heidenstam, (Carl Gustaf) Verner von

von Heyse, Paul (Johann Ludwig)
See Heyse, Paul (Johann Ludwig von)

von Hofmannsthal, Hugo
See Hofmannsthal, Hugo von

von Horvath, Odon
See von Horvath, Odon

von Horvath, Odon
See von Horvath, Odon

von Horvath, Odon 1901-1938 .... **TCLC 45**
See von Horvath, Oedoen
See also CA 194; CAAE 118; DLB 85, 124; RGWL 2, 3

von Horvath, Oedoen
See von Horvath, Odon
See also CA 184

von Kleist, Heinrich
See Kleist, Heinrich von

Vonnegut, Kurt, Jr.
See Vonnegut, Kurt

Vonnegut, Kurt 1922-2007 .... **CLC 1, 2, 3, 4, 5, 8, 12, 22, 40, 60, 111, 212; SSC 8; WLC 6**
See also AAYA 6, 44; AITN 1; AMWS 2; BEST 90:4; BPFB 3; BYA 3, 14; CA 1-4R; CANR 1, 25, 49, 75, 92; CDALB 1968-1988; CN 1, 2, 3, 4, 5, 6, 7; CPW 1; DA; DA3; DAB; DAC; DAM MST, NOV, POP; DLB 2, 8, 152; DLBD 3; DLBY 1980; EWL 3; EXPN; EXPS; LAIT 4; LMFS 2; MAL 5; MTCW 1, 2; MTFW 2005; NFS 3; RGAL 4; SCFW; SFW 4; SSFS 5; TUS; YAW

Von Rachen, Kurt
See Hubbard, L. Ron

von Sternberg, Josef
See Sternberg, Josef von

Vorster, Gordon 1924- .... **CLC 34**
See also CA 133

Vosce, Trudie
See Ozick, Cynthia

Voznesensky, Andrei (Andreievich)
1933- .... **CLC 1, 15, 57**
See Voznesensky, Andrey
See also CA 89-92; CANR 37; CWW 2; DAM POET; MTCW 1

Voznesensky, Andrey
See Voznesensky, Andrei (Andreievich)
See also EWL 3

Wace, Robert c. 1100-c. 1175 .... **CMLC 55**
See also DLB 146

Waddington, Miriam 1917-2004 .... **CLC 28**
See also CA 21-24R; CAAS 225; CANR 12, 30; CCA 1; CP 1, 2, 3, 4, 5, 6, 7; DLB 68

Wagman, Fredrica 1937- .... **CLC 7**
See also CA 97-100; INT CA-97-100

Wagner, Linda W.
See Wagner-Martin, Linda (C.)

Wagner, Linda Welshimer
See Wagner-Martin, Linda (C.)

Wagner, Richard 1813-1883 ..... **NCLC 9, 119**
See also DLB 129; EW 6

Wagner-Martin, Linda (C.) 1936- .... **CLC 50**
See also CA 159; CANR 135

Wagoner, David (Russell) 1926- .... **CLC 3, 5, 15; PC 33**
See also AMWS 9; CA 1-4R; 3; CANR 2, 71; CN 1, 2, 3, 4, 5, 6, 7; CP 1, 2, 3, 4, 5, 6, 7; DLB 5, 256; SATA 14; TCWW 1, 2

Wah, Fred(erick James) 1939- .... **CLC 44**
See also CA 141; CAAE 107; CP 1, 6, 7; DLB 60

Wahloo, Per 1926-1975 .... **CLC 7**
See also BPFB 3; CA 61-64; CANR 73; CMW 4; MSW

Wahloo, Peter
See Wahloo, Per

Wain, John (Barrington) 1925-1994 . **CLC 2, 11, 15, 46**
See also CA 5-8R; 4; CAAS 145; CANR 23, 54; CDBLB 1960 to Present; CN 1, 2, 3, 4, 5; CP 1, 2, 3, 4, 5; DLB 15, 27, 139, 155; EWL 3; MTCW 1, 2; MTFW 2005

Wajda, Andrzej 1926- .... **CLC 16, 219**
See also CA 102

Wakefield, Dan 1932- .... **CLC 7**
See also CA 211; 21-24R, 211; 7; CN 4, 5, 6, 7

Wakefield, Herbert Russell
1888-1965 .... **TCLC 120**
See also CA 5-8R; CANR 77; HGG; SUFW

Wakoski, Diane 1937- ...... **CLC 2, 4, 7, 9, 11, 40; PC 15**
See also CA 216; 13-16R, 216; 1; CANR 9, 60, 106; CP 1, 2, 3, 4, 5, 6, 7; CWP; DAM POET; DLB 5; INT CANR-9; MAL 5; MTCW 2; MTFW 2005

Wakoski-Sherbell, Diane
See Wakoski, Diane

Walcott, Derek 1930- ... **BLC 3; CLC 2, 4, 9, 14, 25, 42, 67, 76, 160; DC 7; PC 46**
See also BW 2; CA 89-92; CANR 26, 47, 75, 80, 130; CBD; CD 5, 6; CDWLB 3; CP 1, 2, 3, 4, 5, 6, 7; DA3; DAB; DAC; DAM MST, MULT, POET; DLB 117, 332; DLBY 1981; DNFS 1; EFS 1; EWL 3; LMFS 2; MTCW 1, 2; MTFW 2005; PFS 6; RGEL 2; TWA; WWE 1

Waldman, Anne (Lesley) 1945- .... **CLC 7**
See also BG 1:3; CA 37-40R; 17; CANR 34, 69, 116; CP 1, 2, 3, 4, 5, 6, 7; CWP; DLB 16

Waldo, E. Hunter
See Sturgeon, Theodore (Hamilton)

Waldo, Edward Hamilton
See Sturgeon, Theodore (Hamilton)

Walker, Alice 1944- ...... **BLC 3; CLC 5, 6, 9, 19, 27, 46, 58, 103, 167; PC 30; SSC 5; WLCS**
See also AAYA 3, 33; AFAW 1, 2; AMWS 3; BEST 89:4; BPFB 3; BW 2, 3; CA 37-40R; CANR 9, 27, 49, 66, 82, 131; CDALB 1968-1988; CN 4, 5, 6, 7; CPW; CSW; DA; DA3; DAB; DAC; DAM MST, MULT, NOV, POET, POP; DLB 6, 33, 143; EWL 3; EXPN; EXPS; FL 1:6; FW; INT CANR-27; LAIT 3; MAL 5; MBL; MTCW 1, 2; MTFW 2005; NFS 5; RGAL 4; RGSF 2; SATA 31; SSFS 2, 11; TUS; YAW

Waugh, Evelyn (Arthur St. John)
1903-1966 .. **CLC 1, 3, 8, 13, 19, 27, 44, 107; SSC 41; WLC 6**
See also BPFB 3; BRW 7; CA 85-88; CAAS 25-28R; CANR 22; CDBLB 1914-1945; DA; DA3; DAB; DAC; DAM MST, NOV, POP; DLB 15, 162, 195; EWL 3; MTCW 1, 2; MTFW 2005; NFS 13, 17; RGEL 2; RGSF 2; TEA; WLIT 4

Waugh, Harriet 1944- .... **CLC 6**
See also CA 85-88; CANR 22

Ways, C. R.
See Blount, Roy (Alton), Jr.

Waystaff, Simon
See Swift, Jonathan

Webb, Beatrice (Martha Potter)
1858-1943 .... **TCLC 22**
See also CA 162; CAAE 117; DLB 190; FW

Webb, Charles (Richard) 1939- .... **CLC 7**
See also CA 25-28R; CANR 114

Webb, Frank J. .... **NCLC 143**
See also DLB 50

Webb, James, Jr.
See Webb, James

Webb, James 1946- .... **CLC 22**
See also CA 81-84; CANR 156

Webb, James H.
See Webb, James

Webb, James Henry
See Webb, James

Webb, Mary Gladys (Meredith)
1881-1927 .... **TCLC 24**
See also CA 182; CAAS 123; DLB 34; FW; RGEL 2

Webb, Mrs. Sidney
See Webb, Beatrice (Martha Potter)

Webb, Phyllis 1927- .... **CLC 18**
See also CA 104; CANR 23; CCA 1; CP 1, 2, 3, 4, 5, 6, 7; CWP; DLB 53

Webb, Sidney (James) 1859-1947 .. **TCLC 22**
See also CA 163; CAAE 117; DLB 190

Webber, Andrew Lloyd .... **CLC 21**
See Lloyd Webber, Andrew
See also DFS 7

Weber, Lenora Mattingly
1895-1971 .... **CLC 12**
See also CA 19-20; CAAS 29-32R; CAP 1; SATA 2; SATA-Obit 26

Weber, Max 1864-1920 .... **TCLC 69**
See also CA 189; CAAE 109; DLB 296

Webster, John 1580(?)-1634(?) ...... **DC 2; LC 33, 84, 124; WLC 6**
See also BRW 2; CDBLB Before 1660; DA; DAB; DAC; DAM DRAM, MST; DFS 17, 19; DLB 58; IDTP; RGEL 2; WLIT 3

Webster, Noah 1758-1843 .... **NCLC 30**
See also DLB 1, 37, 42, 43, 73, 243

Wedekind, Benjamin Franklin
See Wedekind, Frank

Wedekind, Frank 1864-1918 .... **TCLC 7**
See also CA 153; CAAE 104; CANR 121, 122; CDWLB 2; DAM DRAM; DLB 118; EW 8; EWL 3; LMFS 2; RGWL 2, 3

Wehr, Demaris .... **CLC 65**

Weidman, Jerome 1913-1998 .... **CLC 7**
See also AITN 2; CA 1-4R; CAAS 171; CAD; CANR 1; CD 1, 2, 3, 4, 5; DLB 28

Weil, Simone (Adolphine)
1909-1943 .... **TCLC 23**
See also CA 159; CAAE 117; EW 12; EWL 3; FW; GFL 1789 to the Present; MTCW 2

Weininger, Otto 1880-1903 .... **TCLC 84**

Weinstein, Nathan
See West, Nathanael

Weinstein, Nathan von Wallenstein
See West, Nathanael

Weir, Peter (Lindsay) 1944- .... **CLC 20**
See also CA 123; CAAE 113

Weiss, Peter (Ulrich) 1916-1982 .. **CLC 3, 15, 51; TCLC 152**
See also CA 45-48; CAAS 106; CANR 3; DAM DRAM; DFS 3; DLB 69, 124; EWL 3; RGHL; RGWL 2, 3

Weiss, Theodore (Russell)
1916-2003 .... **CLC 3, 8, 14**
See also CA 189; 9-12R, 189; 2; CAAS 216; CANR 46, 94; CP 1, 2, 3, 4, 5, 6, 7; DLB 5; TCLE 1:2

Welch, (Maurice) Denton
1915-1948 .... **TCLC 22**
See also BRWS 8, 9; CA 148; CAAE 121; RGEL 2

Welch, James (Phillip) 1940-2003 ..... **CLC 6, 14, 52; NNAL; PC 62**
See also CA 85-88; CAAS 219; CANR 42, 66, 107; CN 5, 6, 7; CP 2, 3, 4, 5, 6, 7; CPW; DAM MULT, POP; DLB 175, 256; LATS 1:1; NFS 23; RGAL 4; TCWW 1, 2

Weldon, Fay 1931- . **CLC 6, 9, 11, 19, 36, 59, 122**
See also BRWS 4; CA 21-24R; CANR 16, 46, 63, 97, 137; CDBLB 1960 to Present; CN 3, 4, 5, 6, 7; CPW; DAM POP; DLB 14, 194, 319; EWL 3; FW; HGG; INT CANR-16; MTCW 1, 2; MTFW 2005; RGEL 2; RGSF 2

Wellek, Rene 1903-1995 .... **CLC 28**
See also CA 5-8R; 7; CAAS 150; CANR 8; DLB 63; EWL 3; INT CANR-8

Weller, Michael 1942- .... **CLC 10, 53**
See also CA 85-88; CAD; CD 5, 6

Weller, Paul 1958- .... **CLC 26**

Wellershoff, Dieter 1925- .... **CLC 46**
See also CA 89-92; CANR 16, 37

Welles, (George) Orson 1915-1985 .. **CLC 20, 80**
See also AAYA 40; CA 93-96; CAAS 117

Wellman, John McDowell 1945-
See Wellman, Mac
See also CA 166; CD 5

Wellman, Mac .... **CLC 65**
See Wellman, John McDowell; Wellman, John McDowell
See also CAD; CD 6; RGAL 4

Wellman, Manly Wade 1903-1986 ... **CLC 49**
See also CA 1-4R; CAAS 118; CANR 6, 16, 44; FANT; SATA 6; SATA-Obit 47; SFW 4; SUFW

Wells, Carolyn 1869(?)-1942 .... **TCLC 35**
See also CA 185; CAAE 113; CMW 4; DLB 11

Wells, H(erbert) G(eorge) 1866-1946 . **SSC 6, 70; TCLC 6, 12, 19, 133; WLC 6**
See also AAYA 18; BPFB 3; BRW 6; CA 121; CAAE 110; CDBLB 1914-1945; CLR 64; DA; DA3; DAB; DAC; DAM MST, NOV; DLB 34, 70, 156, 178; EWL 3; EXPS; HGG; LAIT 3; LMFS 2; MTCW 1, 2; MTFW 2005; NFS 17, 20; RGEL 2; RGSF 2; SATA 20; SCFW 1, 2; SFW 4; SSFS 3; SUFW; TEA; WCH; WLIT 4; YAW

Wells, Rosemary 1943- .... **CLC 12**
See also AAYA 13; BYA 7, 8; CA 85-88; CANR 48, 120; CLR 16, 69; CWRI 5; MAICYA 1, 2; SAAS 1; SATA 18, 69, 114, 156; YAW

Wells-Barnett, Ida B(ell)
1862-1931 .... **TCLC 125**
See also CA 182; DLB 23, 221

Welsh, Irvine 1958- .... **CLC 144**
See also CA 173; CANR 146; CN 7; DLB 271

Welty, Eudora 1909-2001 .... **CLC 1, 2, 5, 14, 22, 33, 105, 220; SSC 1, 27, 51; WLC 6**
See also AAYA 48; AMW; AMWR 1; BPFB 3; CA 9-12R; CAAS 199; CABS 1; CANR 32, 65, 128; CDALB 1941-1968; CN 1, 2, 3, 4, 5, 6, 7; CSW; DA; DA3; DAB; DAC; DAM MST, NOV; DLB 2, 102, 143; DLBD 12; DLBY 1987, 2001; EWL 3; EXPS; HGG; LAIT 3; MAL 5; MBL; MTCW 1, 2; MTFW 2005; NFS 13, 15; RGAL 4; RGSF 2; RHW; SSFS 2, 10; TUS

Welty, Eudora Alice
See Welty, Eudora

Wen I-to 1899-1946 .... **TCLC 28**
See also EWL 3

Wentworth, Robert
See Hamilton, Edmond

Werfel, Franz (Viktor) 1890-1945 ... **TCLC 8**
See also CA 161; CAAE 104; DLB 81, 124; EWL 3; RGWL 2, 3

Wergeland, Henrik Arnold
1808-1845 .... **NCLC 5**

Wersba, Barbara 1932- .... **CLC 30**
See also AAYA 2, 30; BYA 6, 12, 13; CA 182; 29-32R, 182; CANR 16, 38; CLR 3, 78; DLB 52; JRDA; MAICYA 1, 2; SAAS 2; SATA 1, 58; SATA-Essay 103; WYA; YAW

Wertmueller, Lina 1928- .... **CLC 16**
See also CA 97-100; CANR 39, 78

Wescott, Glenway 1901-1987 .. **CLC 13; SSC 35**
See also CA 13-16R; CAAS 121; CANR 23, 70; CN 1, 2, 3, 4; DLB 4, 9, 102; MAL 5; RGAL 4

Wesker, Arnold 1932- .... **CLC 3, 5, 42**
See also CA 1-4R; 7; CANR 1, 33; CBD; CD 5, 6; CDBLB 1960 to Present; DAB; DAM DRAM; DLB 13, 310, 319; EWL 3; MTCW 1; RGEL 2; TEA

Wesley, Charles 1707-1788 .... **LC 128**
See also DLB 95; RGEL 2

Wesley, John 1703-1791 .... **LC 88**
See also DLB 104

Wesley, Richard (Errol) 1945- .... **CLC 7**
See also BW 1; CA 57-60; CAD; CANR 27; CD 5, 6; DLB 38

Wessel, Johan Herman 1742-1785 .... **LC 7**
See also DLB 300

West, Anthony (Panther)
1914-1987 .... **CLC 50**
See also CA 45-48; CAAS 124; CANR 3, 19; CN 1, 2, 3, 4; DLB 15

West, C. P.
See Wodehouse, P(elham) G(renville)

West, Cornel 1953- .... **BLCS; CLC 134**
See also CA 144; CANR 91, 159; DLB 246

West, Cornel Ronald
See West, Cornel

West, Delno C(loyde), Jr. 1936- .... **CLC 70**
See also CA 57-60

West, Dorothy 1907-1998 ...... **HR 1:3; TCLC 108**
See also BW 2; CA 143; CAAS 169; DLB 76

West, (Mary) Jessamyn 1902-1984 ... **CLC 7, 17**
See also CA 9-12R; CAAS 112; CANR 27; CN 1, 2, 3; DLB 6; DLBY 1984; MTCW 1, 2; RGAL 4; RHW; SATA-Obit 37; TCWW 2; TUS; YAW

West, Morris L(anglo) 1916-1999 ..... **CLC 6, 33**
See also BPFB 3; CA 5-8R; CAAS 187; CANR 24, 49, 64; CN 1, 2, 3, 4, 5, 6; CPW; DLB 289; MTCW 1, 2; MTFW 2005

Wouk, Herman 1915- .... **CLC 1, 9, 38**
See also BPFB 2, 3; CA 5-8R; CANR 6, 33, 67, 146; CDALBS; CN 1, 2, 3, 4, 5, 6; CPW; DA3; DAM NOV, POP; DLBY 1982; INT CANR-6; LAIT 4; MAL 5; MTCW 1, 2; MTFW 2005; NFS 7; TUS

Wright, Charles 1935- ... **CLC 6, 13, 28, 119, 146**
See also AMWS 5; CA 29-32R; 7; CANR 23, 36, 62, 88, 135; CP 3, 4, 5, 6, 7; DLB 165; DLBY 1982; EWL 3; MTCW 1, 2; MTFW 2005; PFS 10

Wright, Charles Stevenson 1932- ..... **BLC 3; CLC 49**
See also BW 1; CA 9-12R; CANR 26; CN 1, 2, 3, 4, 5, 6, 7; DAM MULT, POET; DLB 33

Wright, Frances 1795-1852 .... **NCLC 74**
See also DLB 73

Wright, Frank Lloyd 1867-1959 .... **TCLC 95**
See also AAYA 33; CA 174

Wright, Harold Bell 1872-1944 .... **TCLC 183**
See also BPFB 3; CAAE 110; DLB 9; TCWW 2

Wright, Jack R.
See Harris, Mark

Wright, James (Arlington) 1927-1980 .... **CLC 3, 5, 10, 28; PC 36**
See also AITN 2; AMWS 3; CA 49-52; CAAS 97-100; CANR 4, 34, 64; CDALBS; CP 1, 2; DAM POET; DLB 5, 169; EWL 3; EXPP; MAL 5; MTCW 1, 2; MTFW 2005; PFS 7, 8; RGAL 4; TUS; WP

Wright, Judith 1915-2000 ... **CLC 11, 53; PC 14**
See also CA 13-16R; CAAS 188; CANR 31, 76, 93; CP 1, 2, 3, 4, 5, 6, 7; CWP; DLB 260; EWL 3; MTCW 1, 2; MTFW 2005; PFS 8; RGEL 2; SATA 14; SATA-Obit 121

Wright, L(aurali) R. 1939- .... **CLC 44**
See also CA 138; CMW 4

Wright, Richard (Nathaniel) 1908-1960 ... **BLC 3; CLC 1, 3, 4, 9, 14, 21, 48, 74; SSC 2; TCLC 136, 180; WLC 6**
See also AAYA 5, 42; AFAW 1, 2; AMW; BPFB 3; BW 1; BYA 2; CA 108; CANR 64; CDALB 1929-1941; DA; DA3; DAB; DAC; DAM MST, MULT, NOV; DLB 76, 102; DLBD 2; EWL 3; EXPN; LAIT 3, 4; MAL 5; MTCW 1, 2; MTFW 2005; NCFS 1; NFS 1, 7; RGAL 4; RGSF 2; SSFS 3, 9, 15, 20; TUS; YAW

Wright, Richard B(ruce) 1937- .... **CLC 6**
See also CA 85-88; CANR 120; DLB 53

Wright, Rick 1945- .... **CLC 35**

Wright, Rowland
See Wells, Carolyn

Wright, Stephen 1946- .... **CLC 33**
See also CA 237

Wright, Willard Huntington 1888-1939
See Van Dine, S. S.
See also CA 189; CAAE 115; CMW 4; DLBD 16

Wright, William 1930- .... **CLC 44**
See also CA 53-56; CANR 7, 23, 154

Wroth, Lady Mary 1587-1653(?) .... **LC 30, 139; PC 38**
See also DLB 121

Wu Ch'eng-en 1500(?)-1582(?) .... **LC 7**

Wu Ching-tzu 1701-1754 .... **LC 2**

Wulfstan c. 10th cent. -1023 .... **CMLC 59**

Wurlitzer, Rudolph 1938(?)- .... **CLC 2, 4, 15**
See also CA 85-88; CN 4, 5, 6, 7; DLB 173

Wyatt, Sir Thomas c. 1503-1542 . **LC 70; PC 27**
See also BRW 1; DLB 132; EXPP; PFS 25; RGEL 2; TEA

Wycherley, William 1640-1716 .... **LC 8, 21, 102, 136**
See also BRW 2; CDBLB 1660-1789; DAM DRAM; DLB 80; RGEL 2

Wyclif, John c. 1330-1384 .... **CMLC 70**
See also DLB 146

Wylie, Elinor (Morton Hoyt) 1885-1928 .... **PC 23; TCLC 8**
See also AMWS 1; CA 162; CAAE 105; DLB 9, 45; EXPP; MAL 5; RGAL 4

Wylie, Philip (Gordon) 1902-1971 ... **CLC 43**
See also CA 21-22; CAAS 33-36R; CAP 2; CN 1; DLB 9; SFW 4

Wyndham, John .... **CLC 19**
See Harris, John (Wyndham Parkes Lucas) Beynon
See also DLB 255; SCFW 1, 2

Wyss, Johann David Von 1743-1818 .... **NCLC 10**
See also CLR 92; JRDA; MAICYA 1, 2; SATA 29; SATA-Brief 27

Xenophon c. 430B.C.-c. 354B.C. ... **CMLC 17**
See also AW 1; DLB 176; RGWL 2, 3; WLIT 8

Xingjian, Gao 1940-
See Gao Xingjian
See also CA 193; DFS 21; DLB 330; RGWL 3

Yakamochi 718-785 .... **CMLC 45; PC 48**

Yakumo Koizumi
See Hearn, (Patricio) Lafcadio (Tessima Carlos)

Yamada, Mitsuye (May) 1923- .... **PC 44**
See also CA 77-80

Yamamoto, Hisaye 1921- .... **AAL; SSC 34**
See also CA 214; DAM MULT; DLB 312; LAIT 4; SSFS 14

Yamauchi, Wakako 1924- .... **AAL**
See also CA 214; DLB 312

Yanez, Jose Donoso
See Donoso (Yanez), Jose

Yanovsky, Basile S.
See Yanovsky, V(assily) S(emenovich)

Yanovsky, V(assily) S(emenovich) 1906-1989 .... **CLC 2, 18**
See also CA 97-100; CAAS 129

Yates, Richard 1926-1992 .... **CLC 7, 8, 23**
See also AMWS 11; CA 5-8R; CAAS 139; CANR 10, 43; CN 1, 2, 3, 4, 5; DLB 2, 234; DLBY 1981, 1992; INT CANR-10; SSFS 24

Yau, John 1950- .... **PC 61**
See also CA 154; CANR 89; CP 4, 5, 6, 7; DLB 234, 312

Yearsley, Ann 1753-1806 .... **NCLC 174**
See also DLB 109

Yeats, W. B.
See Yeats, William Butler

Yeats, William Butler 1865-1939 . **PC 20, 51; TCLC 1, 11, 18, 31, 93, 116; WLC 6**
See also AAYA 48; BRW 6; BRWR 1; CA 127; CAAE 104; CANR 45; CDBLB 1890-1914; DA; DA3; DAB; DAC; DAM DRAM, MST, POET; DLB 10, 19, 98, 156, 332; EWL 3; EXPP; MTCW 1, 2; MTFW 2005; NCFS 3; PAB; PFS 1, 2, 5, 7, 13, 15; RGEL 2; TEA; WLIT 4; WP

Yehoshua, A.B. 1936- .... **CLC 13, 31**
See also CA 33-36R; CANR 43, 90, 145; CWW 2; EWL 3; RGHL; RGSF 2; RGWL 3; WLIT 6

Yehoshua, Abraham B.
See Yehoshua, A.B.

Yellow Bird
See Ridge, John Rollin

Yep, Laurence 1948- .... **CLC 35**
See also AAYA 5, 31; BYA 7; CA 49-52; CANR 1, 46, 92, 161; CLR 3, 17, 54; DLB 52, 312; FANT; JRDA; MAICYA 1, 2; MAICYAS 1; SATA 7, 69, 123, 176; WYA; YAW

Yep, Laurence Michael
See Yep, Laurence

Yerby, Frank G(arvin) 1916-1991 ..... **BLC 3; CLC 1, 7, 22**
See also BPFB 3; BW 1, 3; CA 9-12R; CAAS 136; CANR 16, 52; CN 1, 2, 3, 4, 5; DAM MULT; DLB 76; INT CANR-16; MTCW 1; RGAL 4; RHW

Yesenin, Sergei Aleksandrovich
See Esenin, Sergei

Yevtushenko, Yevgeny (Alexandrovich) 1933- ...... **CLC 1, 3, 13, 26, 51, 126; PC 40**
See Evtushenko, Evgenii Aleksandrovich
See also CA 81-84; CANR 33, 54; DAM POET; EWL 3; MTCW 1; RGHL

Yezierska, Anzia 1885(?)-1970 .... **CLC 46**
See also CA 126; CAAS 89-92; DLB 28, 221; FW; MTCW 1; RGAL 4; SSFS 15

Yglesias, Helen 1915- .... **CLC 7, 22**
See also CA 37-40R; 20; CANR 15, 65, 95; CN 4, 5, 6, 7; INT CANR-15; MTCW 1

Yokomitsu, Riichi 1898-1947 .... **TCLC 47**
See also CA 170; EWL 3

Yonge, Charlotte (Mary) 1823-1901 .... **TCLC 48**
See also CA 163; CAAE 109; DLB 18, 163; RGEL 2; SATA 17; WCH

York, Jeremy
See Creasey, John

York, Simon
See Heinlein, Robert A.

Yorke, Henry Vincent 1905-1974 ..... **CLC 13**
See Green, Henry
See also CA 85-88; CAAS 49-52

Yosano, Akiko 1878-1942 ... **PC 11; TCLC 59**
See also CA 161; EWL 3; RGWL 3

Yoshimoto, Banana .... **CLC 84**
See Yoshimoto, Mahoko
See also AAYA 50; NFS 7

Yoshimoto, Mahoko 1964-
See Yoshimoto, Banana
See also CA 144; CANR 98, 160; SSFS 16

Young, Al(bert James) 1939- ... **BLC 3; CLC 19**
See also BW 2, 3; CA 29-32R; CANR 26, 65, 109; CN 2, 3, 4, 5, 6, 7; CP 1, 2, 3, 4, 5, 6, 7; DAM MULT; DLB 33

Young, Andrew (John) 1885-1971 ...... **CLC 5**
See also CA 5-8R; CANR 7, 29; CP 1; RGEL 2

Young, Collier
See Bloch, Robert (Albert)

Young, Edward 1683-1765 .... **LC 3, 40**
See also DLB 95; RGEL 2

Young, Marguerite (Vivian) 1909-1995 .... **CLC 82**
See also CA 13-16; CAAS 150; CAP 1; CN 1, 2, 3, 4, 5, 6

Young, Neil 1945- .... **CLC 17**
See also CA 110; CCA 1

Young Bear, Ray A. 1950- ... **CLC 94; NNAL**
See also CA 146; DAM MULT; DLB 175; MAL 5

Yourcenar, Marguerite 1903-1987 ... **CLC 19, 38, 50, 87**
See also BPFB 3; CA 69-72; CANR 23, 60, 93; DAM NOV; DLB 72; DLBY 1988; EW 12; EWL 3; GFL 1789 to the Present; GLL 1; MTCW 1, 2; MTFW 2005; RGWL 2, 3

Literary Criticism Series
Cumulative Topic Index

This index lists all topic entries in Thomson Gale's *Children's Literature Review* (CLR), *Classical and Medieval Literature Criticism* (CMLC), *Contemporary Literary Criticism* (CLC), *Drama Criticism* (DC), *Literature Criticism from 1400 to 1800* (LC), *Nineteenth-Century Literature Criticism* (NCLC), *Short Story Criticism* (SSC), and *Twentieth-Century Literary Criticism* (TCLC). The index also lists topic entries in the Gale Critical Companion Collection, which includes the following publications: *The Beat Generation* (BG), *Feminism in Literature* (FL), *Gothic Literature* (GL), and *Harlem Renaissance* (HR).

Topic Index

Topic Index

TCLC Cumulative Nationality Index

Saba, Umberto **33**
Tozzi, Federigo **31**
Verga, Giovanni (Carmelo) **3**

JAMAICAN

De Lisser, H(erbert) G(eorge) **12**
Garvey, Marcus (Moziah Jr.) **41**
Mais, Roger **8**
Redcam, Tom **25**

JAPANESE

Abé, Kōbō **131**
Akutagawa Ryunosuke **16**
Dazai Osamu **11**
Endō, Shūsaku **152**
Futabatei, Shimei **44**
Hagiwara, Sakutaro **60**
Hayashi, Fumiko **27**
Ishikawa, Takuboku **15**
Kunikida, Doppo **99**
Masaoka, Shiki **18**
Mishima, Yukio **161**
Miyamoto, (Chujo) Yuriko **37**
Miyazawa, Kenji **76**
Mizoguchi, Kenji **72**
Mori Ogai **14**
Nagai, Kafu **51**
Nishida, Kitaro **83**
Noguchi, Yone **80**
Santoka, Taneda **72**
Shiga, Naoya **172**
Shimazaki Toson **5**
Suzuki, Daisetz Teitaro **109**
Yokomitsu, Riichi **47**
Yosano Akiko **59**

LATVIAN

Berlin, Isaiah **105**
Rainis, Jānis **29**

LEBANESE

Gibran, Kahlil **1, 9**

LESOTHAN

Mofolo, Thomas (Mokopu) **22**

LITHUANIAN

Kreve (Mickevicius), Vincas **27**

MARTINIQUE

Fanon, Frantz **188**

MEXICAN

Azuela, Mariano **3**
Gamboa, Federico **36**
Garro, Elena **153**
Gonzalez Martinez, Enrique **72**
Ibargüengoitia, Jorge **148**
Nervo, (Jose) Amado (Ruiz de) **11**
Reyes, Alfonso **33**
Romero, José Rubén **14**
Villaurrutia, Xavier **80**

NEPALI

Devkota, Laxmiprasad **23**

NEW ZEALANDER

Mander, (Mary) Jane **31**
Mansfield, Katherine **2, 8, 39, 164**

NICARAGUAN

Darío, Rubén **4**

NIGERIAN

Okigbo, Christopher **171**
Tutuola, Amos **188**

NORWEGIAN

Bjoernson, Bjoernstjerne (Martinius) **7, 37**
Bojer, Johan **64**
Grieg, (Johan) Nordahl (Brun) **10**
Hamsun, Knut **151**
Ibsen, Henrik (Johan) **2, 8, 16, 37, 52**
Kielland, Alexander Lange **5**
Lie, Jonas (Lauritz Idemil) **5**
Obstfelder, Sigbjoern **23**
Skram, Amalie (Bertha) **25**
Undset, Sigrid **3**

PAKISTANI

Iqbal, Muhammad **28**

PERUVIAN

Arguedas, José María **147**
Palma, Ricardo **29**
Vallejo, César (Abraham) **3, 56**

POLISH

Asch, Sholem **3**
Borowski, Tadeusz **9**
Conrad, Joseph **1, 6, 13, 25, 43, 57**
Herbert, Zbigniew **168**
Peretz, Isaac Loeb **16**
Prus, Boleslaw **48**
Przybyszewski, Stanislaw **36**
Reymont, Wladyslaw (Stanislaw) **5**
Schulz, Bruno **5, 51**
Sienkiewicz, Henryk (Adam Alexander Pius) **3**
Singer, Israel Joshua **33**
Witkiewicz, Stanislaw Ignacy **8**

PORTUGUESE

Pessoa, Fernando (António Nogueira) **27**
Sa-Carniero, Mario de **83**

PUERTO RICAN

Hostos (y Bonilla), Eugenio Maria de **24**

ROMANIAN

Bacovia, George **24**
Caragiale, Ion Luca **76**
Rebreanu, Liviu **28**

RUSSIAN

Adamov, Arthur **189**
Aldanov, Mark (Alexandrovich) **23**
Andreyev, Leonid (Nikolaevich) **3**
Annensky, Innokenty (Fyodorovich) **14**
Artsybashev, Mikhail (Petrovich) **31**
Babel, Isaak (Emmanuilovich) **2, 13, 171**
Bagritsky, Eduard **60**
Bakhtin, Mikhail **160**
Balmont, Konstantin (Dmitriyevich) **11**
Bely, Andrey **7**
Berdyaev, Nikolai (Aleksandrovich) **67**
Bergelson, David **81**
Blok, Alexander (Alexandrovich) **5**
Bryusov, Valery Yakovlevich **10**
Bulgakov, Mikhail (Afanas'evich) **2, 16, 159**
Bulgya, Alexander Alexandrovich **53**
Bunin, Ivan Alexeyevich **6**
Chekhov, Anton (Pavlovich) **3, 10, 31, 55, 96, 163**
Der Nister **56**
Eisenstein, Sergei (Mikhailovich) **57**
Esenin, Sergei (Alexandrovich) **4**
Fadeyev, Alexander **53**
Gladkov, Fyodor (Vasilyevich) **27**
Gumilev, Nikolai (Stepanovich) **60**
Gurdjieff, G(eorgei) I(vanovich) **71**
Guro, Elena **56**
Hippius, Zinaida **9**
Ilf, Ilya **21**
Ivanov, Vyacheslav Ivanovich **33**
Kandinsky, Wassily **92**

Khlebnikov, Velimir **20**
Khodasevich, Vladislav (Felitsianovich) **15**
Klimentov, Andrei Platonovich **14**
Korolenko, Vladimir Galaktionovich **22**
Kropotkin, Peter (Alekseevich) **36**
Kuprin, Aleksander Ivanovich **5**
Kuzmin, Mikhail **40**
Lenin, V. I. **67**
Mandelstam, Osip (Emilievich) **2, 6**
Mayakovski, Vladimir (Vladimirovich) **4, 18**
Merezhkovsky, Dmitry Sergeyevich **29**
Nabokov, Vladimir (Vladimirovich) **108, 189**
Olesha, Yuri **136**
Pasternak, Boris **188**
Pavlov, Ivan Petrovich **91**
Petrov, Evgeny **21**
Pilnyak, Boris **23**
Prishvin, Mikhail **75**
Remizov, Aleksei (Mikhailovich) **27**
Rozanov, Vassili **104**
Shestov, Lev **56**
Sologub, Fyodor **9**
Stalin, Joseph **92**
Stanislavsky, Konstantin **167**
Tolstoy, Alexey Nikolaevich **18**
Tolstoy, Leo (Nikolaevich) **4, 11, 17, 28, 44, 79, 173**
Trotsky, Leon **22**
Tsvetaeva (Efron), Marina (Ivanovna) **7, 35**
Zabolotsky, Nikolai Alekseevich **52**
Zamyatin, Evgeny Ivanovich **8, 37**
Zhdanov, Andrei Alexandrovich **18**
Zoshchenko, Mikhail (Mikhailovich) **15**

SCOTTISH

Barrie, J(ames) M(atthew) **2, 164**
Brown, George Douglas **28**
Buchan, John **41**
Cunninghame Graham, Robert (Gallnigad) Bontine **19**
Davidson, John **24**
Doyle, Arthur Conan **7**
Frazer, J(ames) G(eorge) **32**
Lang, Andrew **16**
MacDonald, George **9, 113**
Muir, Edwin **2, 87**
Murray, James Augustus Henry **117**
Sharp, William **39**
Tey, Josephine **14**

SLOVENIAN

Cankar, Ivan **105**

SOUTH AFRICAN

Bosman, Herman Charles **49**
Campbell, (Ignatius) Roy (Dunnachie) **5**
La Guma, Alex **140**
Mqhayi, S(amuel) E(dward) K(rune Loliwe) **25**
Paton, Alan **165**
Plaatje, Sol(omon) T(shekisho) **73**
Schreiner, Olive (Emilie Albertina) **9**
Smith, Pauline (Urmson) **25**
Vilakazi, Benedict Wallet **37**

SPANISH

Alas (y Urena), Leopoldo (Enrique Garcia) **29**
Aleixandre, Vicente **113**
Barea, Arturo **14**
Baroja (y Nessi), Pio **8**
Benavente (y Martinez), Jacinto **3**
Blasco Ibáñez, Vicente **12**
Echegaray (y Eizaguirre), Jose (Maria Waldo) **4**
García Lorca, Federico **1, 7, 49, 181**
Jiménez (Mantecón), Juan Ramón **4, 183**
Machado (y Ruiz), Antonio **3**
Martinez Sierra, Gregorio **6**
Martinez Sierra, Maria (de la O'LeJarraga) **6**
Miro (Ferrer), Gabriel (Francisco Victor) **5**

TCLC-191 Title Index

ISBN-13: 978-0-7876-9966-6
ISBN-10: 0-7876-9966-7

9 780787 699666

COMSEWOGUE PUBLIC LIBRARY

3 0620 00301 6242

For Reference

Not to be taken from this room